Place-of-Service Codes for Professional Claims

Listed below are place-of-service codes and descriptions. These codes should be used on professional claims to specify the entity where service(s) were rendered. Check with individual payers (eg, Medicare, Medicaid, other private insurance) for reimbursement policies regarding these codes. If you would like to comment on a code(s) or description(s), please send your request to posinfo@cms.hhs.gov.

Place of Service Code(s)	Place of Service Name	Place of Service Description
01	Pharmacy	A facility or location where drugs and other medically related items and services are sold, dispensed, or otherwise provided directly to patients. (effective 10/1/05)
02	Unassigned	N/A
03	School	A facility whose primary purpose is education.
04	Homeless shelter	A facility or location whose primary purpose is to provide temporary housing to homeless individuals (eg, emergency shelters, individual, or family shelters).
05	Indian Health Service freestanding facility	A facility or location, owned and operated by the Indian Health Service, that provides diagnostic, therapeutic (surgical and nonsurgical), and rehabilitation services to American Indians and Alaska Natives who do not require hospitalization.
06	Indian Health Service provider-based facility	A facility or location, owned and operated by the Indian Health Service, that provides diagnostic, therapeutic (surgical and nonsurgical), and rehabilitation services rendered by, or under the supervision of, physicians to American Indians and Alaska Natives admitted as inpatients or outpatients.
07	Tribal 638 freestanding facility	A facility or location, owned and operated by a federally recognized American Indian or Alaska Native tribe or tribal organization under a 638 agreement, that provides diagnostic, therapeutic (surgical and nonsurgical), and rehabilitation services to tribal members who do not require hospitalization.
08	Tribal 638 provider-based facility	A facility or location, owned and operated by a federally recognized American Indian or Alaska Native tribe or tribal organization under a 638 agreement, that provides diagnostic, therapeutic (surgical and nonsurgical), and rehabilitation services to tribal members admitted as inpatients or outpatients.
09	Prison-correctional facility	A prison, jail, reformatory, work farm, detention center, or any other similar facility maintained by federal, state, or local authorities for the purpose of confinement or rehabilitation of adult or juvenile criminal offenders. (effective 7/1/06)
10	Unassigned	N/A
11	Office	Location, other than a hospital, skilled nursing facility, military treatment facility, community health center, state or local public health clinic, or intermediate care facility, where the health professional routinely provides health examinations, diagnosis, and treatment of illness or injury on an ambulatory basis.
12	Home	Location, other than a hospital or other facility, where the patient receives care in a private residence.
13	Assisted living facility	Congregate residential facility with self-contained living units providing assessment of each resident's needs and on-site support 24 hours a day, seven days a week, with the capacity to deliver or arrange for services including some health care and other services. (effective 10/1/03)
14	Group home	A residence, with shared living areas, where clients receive supervision and other services such as social and/or behavioral services, custodial service, and minimal services (eg, medication administration) (effective 4/1/04)
15	Mobile unit	A facility or unit that moves from place to place and is equipped to provide preventive, screening, diagnostic, and/or treatment services.
16-19	Unassigned	N/A
20	Urgent care facility	Location, distinct from a hospital emergency department, an office, or a clinic, whose purpose is to diagnose and treat illness or injury for unscheduled, ambulatory patients seeking immediate medical attention.
21	Inpatient hospital	A facility, other than psychiatric, that primarily provides diagnostic, therapeutic (both surgical and nonsurgical), and rehabilitation services by, or under, the supervision of physicians to patients admitted for a variety of medical conditions.
22	Outpatient hospital	A portion of a hospital that provides diagnostic, therapeutic (both surgical and nonsurgical), and rehabilitation services to sick or injured persons who do not require hospitalization or institutionalization.
23	Emergency room—hospital	A portion of a hospital where emergency diagnosis and treatment of illness or injury is provided.
24	Ambulatory surgical center	A freestanding facility, other than a physician's office, where surgical and diagnostic services are provided on an ambulatory basis.
25	Birthing center	A facility, other than a hospital's maternity facilities or a physician's office, that provides a setting for labor, delivery, and immediate postpartum care as well as immediate care of newborn infants.
26	Military treatment facility	A medical facility operated by one or more of the uniformed services. Military treatment facility also refers to certain former US Public Health Service facilities now designated as uniformed service treatment facilities.
27-30	Unassigned	N/A
31	Skilled nursing facility	A facility that primarily provides inpatient skilled nursing care and related services to patients who require medical, nursing, or rehabilitative services but does not provide the level of care or treatment available in a hospital.

32	Nursing facility	A facility that primarily provides to residents skilled nursing care and related services for the rehabilitation of injured, disabled, or sick persons, or, on a regular basis, health-related care services above the level of custodial care to other than mentally retarded individuals.
33	Custodial care facility	A facility that provides room, board, and other personal assistance services, generally on a long-term basis, and does not include a medical component.
34	Hospice	A facility, other than a patient's home, in which palliative and supportive care for terminally ill patients and their families are provided.
35-40	Unassigned	N/A
41	Ambulance—land	A land vehicle specifically designed, equipped, and staffed for lifesaving and transporting the sick or injured.
42	Ambulance—air or water	An air or water vehicle specifically designed, equipped, and staffed for lifesaving and transporting the sick or injured.
43-48	Unassigned	N/A
49	Independent clinic	A location, not part of a hospital and not described by any other place-of-service code, that is organized and operated to provide preventive, diagnostic, therapeutic, rehabilitative, or palliative services to outpatients only. (effective 10/1/03)
50	Federally qualified health center	A facility located in a medically underserved area that provides Medicare beneficiaries preventive primary medical care under the general direction of a physician.
51	Inpatient psychiatric facility	A facility that provides inpatient psychiatric services for the diagnosis and treatment of mental illness on a 24-hour basis, by or under the supervision of a physician.
52	Psychiatric facility— partial hospitalization	A facility for the diagnosis and treatment of mental illness that provides a planned therapeutic program for patients who do not require full-time hospitalization but who need broader programs than are possible from outpatient visits to a hospital-based or hospital-affiliated facility.
53	Community mental health center	A facility that provides the following services: outpatient services, including specialized outpatient services for children, the elderly, individuals who are chronically ill, and residents of the community mental health center's mental health services area who have been discharged from inpatient treatment at a mental health facility; 24-hour-a-day emergency care services; day treatment, other partial hospitalization services, or psychosocial rehabilitation services; screening for patients being considered for admission to state mental health facilities to determine the appropriateness of such admission; and consultation and education services.
54	Intermediate care facility/mentally retarded	A facility that primarily provides health-related care and services above the level of custodial care to mentally retarded individuals but does not provide the level of care or treatment available in a hospital or skilled nursing facility.
55	Residential substance abuse treatment facility	A facility that provides treatment for substance (alcohol and drug) abuse to live-in residents who do not require acute medical care. Services include individual and group therapy and counseling, family counseling, laboratory tests, drugs and supplies, psychological testing, and room and board.
56	Psychiatric residential treatment center	A facility or distinct part of a facility for psychiatric care that provides a total 24-hour therapeutically planned and professionally staffed group living and learning environment.
57	Nonresidential substance abuse treatment facility	A location that provides treatment for substance (alcohol and drug) abuse on an ambulatory basis. Services include individual and group therapy and counseling, family counseling, laboratory tests, drugs and supplies, and psychological testing. (effective 10/1/03)
58-59	Unassigned	N/A
60	Mass immunization center	A location where providers administer pneumococcal pneumonia and influenza virus vaccinations and submit these services as electronic media claims or paper claims or by using the roster billing method. This generally takes place in a mass immunization setting, such as a public health center, pharmacy, or mall but may include a physician office setting.
61	Comprehensive inpatient rehabilitation facility	A facility that provides comprehensive rehabilitation services under the supervision of a physician to inpatients with physical disabilities. Services include physical therapy, occupational therapy, speech pathology, social or psychological services, and orthotics and prosthetics services.
62	Comprehensive outpatient rehabilitation facility	A facility that provides comprehensive rehabilitation services under the supervision of a physician to outpatients with physical disabilities. Services include physical therapy, occupational therapy, and speech pathology services.
63-64	Unassigned	N/A
65	End-stage renal disease treatment facility	A facility, other than a hospital, that provides dialysis treatment, maintenance, and/or training to patients or caregivers on an ambulatory or home-care basis.
66-70	Unassigned	N/A
71	Public health clinic	A facility maintained by either state or local health departments that provides ambulatory primary medical care under the general direction of a physician. (effective 10/1/03)
72	Rural health clinic	A certified facility located in a rural, medically underserved area that provides ambulatory primary medical care under the general direction of a physician.
73-80	Unassigned	N/A
81	Independent laboratory	A laboratory certified to perform diagnostic and/or clinical tests independent of an institution or a physician's office.
82-98	Unassigned	N/A
99	Other place of service	Other place of service not identified above.

Stay on top of critical CPT code changes

As the AMA's official communication tool for circulating accurate information and guidance on CPT codes and issues, this insightful monthly newsletter should be part of every compliance program. Each issue features articles used for answering day-to-day coding questions, appealing insurance denials and validating coding to auditors.

Enhance your coding proficiency—Case studies and clinical examples offer insight into confusing coding situations

Direct link to AMA coding experts— Coding consultation section features a "question and answer" format drawn from the CPT Information Services helpline

Keep informed on critical code changes—Get timely, up-to-date information on code changes and correct code assignment

E-mail *amy.burgess@ama-assn.org* to request a free sample issue, and an issue will be e-mailed to you promptly.

New Edition
CPT® Assistant Archives 1990-2006

Enjoy convenient access to 17 years of *CPT® Assistant* newsletter articles on your computer desktop. Search past and present issues of the AMA's authoritative coding newsletter by keyword, phrase, CPT code number, newsletter issue, article index or codebook table of contents. Includes a cumulative index of article titles and a complete historical CPT code list that references when a code was added, deleted and/or revised.

CD-ROM, Shipping included
Order #: OP516907CCW (single user license fee)
Price: $320.00 **AMA member price: $240.00**

Subscribe today!

You'll receive 12 or 24 monthly issues, special report bulletins, the frequently asked questions/answers bonus issue and the ability to earn CEU credits toward AAPC and AHIMA certification. Call (800) 621-8335 to order or go online to *www.amabookstore.com*.

Order #: CA500900CCW
Price: $199.00/one year; $299.00/two year
AMA member price: $149.00/one year; $205.00/two years

AMA
AMERICAN MEDICAL ASSOCIATION

current procedural terminology

cpt®
2007

Standard Edition

Michael Beebe
Joyce A. Dalton
Martha Espronceda, AAS
Desiree D. Evans, AAS
Rejina L. Glenn
Gloria Green, BA
DeHandro Hayden, BS

Anita Majerowicz, MS, RHIA
Janette Meggs, RHIA
Marie L. Mindeman, BA, RHIT
Karen E. O'Hara, BS, CCS-P
Mary R. O'Heron, RHIA, CCS-P
Danielle Pavloski, BS, RHIT, CCS-P
Desiree Rozell, MPA

Lianne Stancik, RHIT
Peggy Thompson, MS, RHIA, CCS
Susan Tracy, BA, RHIT
Jennifer Trajkovski, BS, RHIT
Ada Walker, CCA

AMA
AMERICAN
MEDICAL
ASSOCIATION

Executive Vice President, Chief Executive Officer: Michael D. Maves, MD, MBA
Chief Operating Officer: Bernard L. Hengesbaugh
Senior Vice President, Publishing and Business Services: Robert A. Musacchio, PhD
Vice President, Business Products: Anthony J. Frankos
Director, Editorial and Operations: Mary Lou White
Director, CPT Product Development: Dan Reyes
Senior Acquisition Editor: Elise Schumacher
Director of Marketing, Business Marketing and Communication: Pam Palmersheim
Director of Sales, Business Products: J.D. Kinney
Director, Production and Manufacturing: Jean Roberts
Manager, Marketing and Strategic Planning: Erin Kalitowski
Developmental Editor: Carol Brockman
Senior Production Coordinator: Rosalyn Carlton
Senior Production Coordinator: Boon Ai Tan
Senior Print Coordinator: Ronnie Summers
Marketing Manager: Leigh Bottiger

Standard ISBN: 1-57947-790-9
Standard ISBN: 978-1-57947-790-5
ISSN: 0276-8283

1st Edition printed 1966
2nd Edition printed 1970
3rd Edition printed 1973
4th Edition printed 1977
Revised: 1978, 1979, 1980, 1981, 1982, 1984, 1985,
1986, 1987, 1988, 1989, 1990, 1991, 1992, 1993, 1994,
1995, 1996, 1997, 1998, 1999, 2000, 2001, 2002, 2003, 2004, 2005, 2006

To purchase additional CPT products, contact the American Medical Association Customer Service
at 800 621-8335.

To request a license for distribution of products containing or reprinting CPT codes and/or guidelines,
please see our Web site at *www.ama-assn.org/go/cpt* or contact the American Medical Association CPT
Intellectual Property Services, 515 N. State Street, Chicago, Illinois 60610, 312 464-5022.

AC35:OP054107:10/06

Foreword

Current Procedural Terminology (CPT®), Fourth Edition, is a listing of descriptive terms and identifying codes for reporting medical services and procedures performed by physicians. The purpose of the terminology is to provide a uniform language that will accurately describe medical, surgical, and diagnostic services, and will thereby provide an effective means for reliable nationwide communication among physicians, patients, and third parties. *CPT 2007* is the most recent revision of a work that first appeared in 1966.

CPT descriptive terms and identifying codes currently serve a wide variety of important functions in the field of medical nomenclature. The CPT codebook is useful for administrative management purposes such as claims processing and for the development of guidelines for medical care review. The uniform language is also applicable to medical education and outcomes, health services and quality research by providing a useful basis for local, regional, and national utilization comparisons. The CPT codebook is the most widely accepted nomenclature for the reporting of physician procedures and services under government and private health insurance programs. In 2000, the CPT code set was designated by the Department of Health and Human Services as the national coding standard for physician and other health care professional services and procedures under the Health Insurance Portability and Accountability Act (HIPAA). This means that for all financial and administrative health care transactions sent electronically, the CPT code set will need to be used.

The changes that appear in this revision have been prepared by the CPT Editorial Panel with the assistance of physicians representing all specialties of medicine, and with important contributions from many third-party payers and governmental agencies.

The American Medical Association trusts that this revision will continue the usefulness of its predecessors in identifying, describing, and coding medical, surgical, and diagnostic services.

Michael D. Maves, MD, MBA
Executive Vice President, CEO

Acknowledgments

Publication of the annual CPT codebook represents many challenges and opportunities. From reconciling the many differences of opinion about the best way to describe a procedure, to the last details on placement of a semicolon, many individuals and organizations devote their energies and expertise to the preparation of this revision.

The editorial staff wishes to express sincere thanks to the many national medical specialty societies, health insurance organizations and agencies, and individual physicians and other health professionals who have made contributions.

Thanks are due to Robert A. Musacchio, PhD, Sr VP, American Medical Association; Claudia Bonnell, Blue Cross and Blue Shield Association; Nelly Leon-Chisen, American Hospital Association; Tom Wilder, America's Health Insurance Plans; and Sue Bowman, RHIA, American Health Information Management Association, for their invaluable assistance in enhancing the CPT code set.

For their assistance in development of the CPT Category II codes:

Ronald A. Gabel, MD,
Darryl T Gray, MD, ScD
Trent T. Haywood, MD, JD
Peter A. Hollmann, MD
Susan M. Nedza, MD
Gregory Pawlson, MD, MPH
Sylvia Publ, RHIA, MBA
Phil Renner, MBA
Sam J. W. Romeo, MD, MBA
Paul M. Schyve, MD
Sharon Sprenger, RHIA, PHQ, MPA
Sally Turbyville, MA

We recognize the following people for efforts in working with the Physician Consortium for Performance Improvement and other quality measurement organizations:

Karen S. Kmetick, PhD
Heidi Bossley, MSN, MBA
Kendra Hanley, MS, CHE

Dedication

We dedicate *CPT 2007* to Karen Borman, MD. Her years of leadership as a Panel member and Vice-Chair of the CPT Editorial Panel were dedicated to setting high standards and improving the CPT code set. Her selfless and remarkable endeavors on behalf of the CPT process were critical to the movement of the CPT code set into the new millennium.

Dr Borman served as a CPT Advisor from 1995 to 2000, on the CPT Editorial Panel from 1997 to 2005, and as Vice-Chair from 2000 to 2005. She will have more time now to mentor her residents while continuing to pursue her interests in health policy.

AMA CPT Editorial Panel

Chair
Tracy R. Gordy, MD*
Vice-Chair
Karen R. Borman, MD*
William T. Thorwarth, Jr, MD* (10/05)
James S. Adamson, Jr, MD*
Joel F. Bradley, Jr, MD
Patrick J. Cafferty, MPAS, PA-C
Simon Philip Cohn, MD
Helene M. Fearon, PT*
Samuel Hassenbusch III, MD, PhD
M. Bradford Henley, MD, MBA† (10/05)
Lee Harold Hilborne, MD, MPH
Peter A. Hollmann, MD
Glenn D. Littenberg, MD
Andrea H. McGuire, MD
Bernard M. Rosof, MD, MACP† (4/06)
Kenneth B. Simon, MD, MBA
Stanley W. Stead, MD, MBA*
J. Martin Tucker, MD
Richard W. Waguespack, MD

Secretary
Michael Beebe
*Member of the CPT Executive Committee
†New Panel Member October 2005, April and June 2006
‡New Advisors

AMA CPT Advisory Committee

American Academy of Allergy, Asthma and Immunology
Donald W. Aaronson, MD
American Academy of Child & Adolescent Psychiatry
David I. Berland, MD
American Academy of Dermatology Association
Dirk M. Elston, MD
American Academy of Facial Plastic and Reconstructive Surgery
Mark V. Connelly, MD
American Academy of Family Physicians
David A. Ellington, MD
American Academy of Neurology
Marc Nuwer, MD, PhD
American Academy of Ophthalmology
Michael X. Repka, MD
American Academy of Orthopaedic Surgeons
M. Bradford Henley, MD
American Academy of Otolaryngic Allergy
Harold R. Wright, Jr, MD
American Academy of Otolaryngology-Head and Neck Surgery
Joseph E. Leonard, MD‡
American Academy of Pain Medicine
Eduardo M. Fraifeld, MD
American Academy of Pediatrics
Richard A. Molteni, MD
American Academy of Physical Medicine and Rehabilitation
Francis P. Lagattuta, MD
American Academy of Sleep Medicine
Samuel A. Fleishman, MD
American Association for Thoracic Surgery
James M. Levett, MD
Kirk R. Kanter, MD‡
American Association of Clinical Endocrinologists
Satti Sethu-Kumar Reddy, MD
Eric A. Orzek, MD, FACE, CDE‡
American Association of Electrodiagnostic Medicine
Kyle W. Ruffling, MD

American Association of Gynecologic Laparoscopists
Jodi Kaigh, MD
American Association of Neurological Surgeons
Jeffrey Cozzens, MD
American Association of Public Health Physicians
Arvind K. Goyal, MD, MPH
American Clinical Neurophysiology Society
Marc Nuwer, MD, PhD
American College of Allergy, Asthma and Immunology
Gary N. Gross, MD
American College of Cardiology
Diane E. Wallis, MD, FACC
American College of Chest Physicians
Steve G. Peters, MD
American College of Emergency Physicians
Peter L. Sawchuk, MD
Kenneth L. DeHart, MD, FACEP‡
American College of Gastroenterology
Robert B. Cameron, MD
American College of Medical Genetics
David B. Flannery, MD
American College of Medical Quality
Joel Grossman, MD
American College of Nuclear Physicians
Gary L. Dillehay, MD
American College of Obstetricians and Gynecologists
J. Craig Strafford, MD
Jordan G. Pritzker, MD, MBA, FACOG‡
American College of Occupational and Environmental Medicine
Elizabeth Genovese, MD, MBA
American College of Physicians
H. Christopher Alexander III, MD, MACR, FACP
American College of Preventive Medicine
Fred T. Nobrega, MD
American College of Radiation Oncology
Thomas J. Weatherall, Jr, MD
American College of Radiology
Richard Duszak, Jr, MD
American College of Rheumatology
Robert J. Lloyd, MD
American College of Surgeons
Albert E. Bothe, Jr, MD, FACS
American Dental Association
Charles A. Crago, MD, DMD
American Gastroenterological Association
Joel V. Brill, MD
American Geriatric Society
Robert A. Zorowitz, MD, MBA
American Institute of Ultrasound in Medicine
Harvey L. Nisenbaum, MD
American Medical Directors Association
Dennis L. Stone, MD, MBA
American Medical Group Association
Susan K. Turney, MD
David E. Hooper, MD‡
American Orthopaedic Association
Blair C. Filler, MD
American Orthopaedic Foot and Ankle Society
Walter J. Pedowitz, MD
American Osteopathic Association
Boyd R. Buser, DO
American Pediatric Surgical Association
John P. Crow, MD
American Psychiatric Association
Chester W. Schmidt, Jr, MD

American Roentgen Ray Society
Geraldine B. McGinty, MD, MBA
American Society for Aesthetic Plastic Surgery, Inc.
Paul R. Weiss, MD
American Society for Clinical Pathology
Mark S. Synovec, MD
American Society for Dermatologic Surgery
Pamela K. Phillips, MD
American Society for Gastrointestinal Endoscopy
Robert B. Cameron, MD‡
American Society for Reproductive Medicine
John T. Queenan, Jr, MD
American Society for Surgery of the Hand
Daniel J. Nagle, MD
American Society for Therapeutic Radiology and Oncology
Michael L. Steinberg, MD
American Society of Abdominal Surgeons
Louis F. Alfano, Jr, MD
American Society of Anesthesiologists
H. J. Przybylo, Jr, MD
American Society of Bariatric Physicians
Mary C. Vernon, MD
American Society of Cataract and Refractive Surgery
Stephen S. Lane, MD
American Society of Clinical Oncology
William C. Penley, MD
American Society of Colon and Rectal Surgeons
David A. Margolin, MD
Guy R. Orangio, MD, FACS, FASCRS‡
American Society of Cytopathology
Patricia A. Gregg, MD
American Society of General Surgeons
Charles Drueck III, MD, FACS
American Society of Hematology
Samuel M. Silver, MD, PhD
American Society of Neuroimaging
Mircea A. Morariu, Jr, MD
American Society of Neuroradiology
Robert A. Murray, MD
American Society of Ophthalmic Plastic and Reconstructive Surgery
L. Neal Freeman, MD, MBA, CCS-P, FACS
American Society of Plastic Surgeons
Raymond V. Janevicius, MD
American Thoracic Society
Stephen P. Hoffmann, MD
American Urological Association
Jeffrey A. Dann, MD
Association of University Radiologists
Bob W. Gayler, MD
College of American Pathologists
Stephen N. Bauer, MD
James P. Almas, MD, FCAP‡
Congress of Neurological Surgeons
R. Patrick Jacob, MD
Contact Lens Association of Ophthalmologists
Charles B. Slonim, MD, FACS
Infectious Disease Society of America
Lawrence P. Martinelli, MD
International Spinal Injection Society
Claire Tibiletti, MD
National Association of Medical Examiners
Paul A. Raslavicus, MD
North American Spine Society
William Mitchell, MD
Radiological Society of North America
Richard E. Fulton, MD

Renal Physicians Association
Richard J. Hamburger, MD
Society for Investigative Dermatology
Stephen P. Stone, MD
Society for Vascular Surgery
Anton N. Sidawy, MD
Society of American Gastrointestinal Endoscopic Surgeons
Paresh C. Shah, MD
Society of Critical Care Medicine
George A. Sample, MD
Society of Interventional Radiology
Katharine L. Krol, MD
Society of Nuclear Medicine
Kenneth A. McKusick, MD
Society of Radiologists in Ultrasound
Robert L. Bree, MD
Society of Thoracic Surgeons
Keith S. Naunheim, MD
Cameron D. Wright, MD‡
The Academy of Pharamaceutical Physicians and Investigators
Grant Bagley, MD
The Endocrine Society
Richard A. Guthrie, MD‡
The Triological Society
James H. Kelly, MD
United States and Canadian Academy of Pathology
David S. Wilkinson, MD, PhD

AMA Health Care Professionals Advisory Committee (HCPAC)

Tracy R. Gordy, MD, Co-Chair
AMA CPT Editorial Panel
Helene Fearon, PT, Co-Chair
AMA CPT Editorial Panel
American Academy of Physician Assistants
Terry E. Carlisle, PA-C, MPAS‡
American Association of Naturopathatic Physicians
Wendell B. Milliman, ND
American Association for Respiratory Care
Susan Rinaldo-Gallo, Med, RRT
American Chiropractic Association
Craig S. Little, DC
American Dietetic Association
Keith Thomas-Ayoob, EdD, RD, FADA, CSP
American Massage Therapy Association
Whitney W. Lowe
American Nurses Association
David Keepnews, PhD, JD, RN
American Occupational Therapy Association
Leslie F. Davison, MS, Ed, OTR/L
American Optometric Association
Douglas C. Morrow, OD
American Physical Therapy Association
Paul A. Rockar, Jr, PT, MS
American Podiatric Medical Association
Michael J. King, DPM
American Psychological Association
Antonio E. Puente, PhD
American Speech-Language Hearing Association
R. Wayne Holland, EdD
National Association of Social Workers
Nelda Spyres, ACSW, LCSW
National Society of Genetic Counselors
Debra L. Doyle, MS, CGC
Pharmacist Services Technical Advisory Coalition
Daniel E. Buffington, PharmD, MBA

Contents

Contents

Introduction

Current Procedural Terminology (*CPT*®), Fourth Edition, is a set of codes, descriptions, and guidelines intended to describe procedures and services performed by physicians and other health care providers. Each procedure or service is identified with a five-digit code. The use of CPT codes simplifies the reporting of services.

Inclusion of a descriptor and its associated five-digit code number in the CPT codebook is based on whether the procedure is consistent with contemporary medical practice and is performed by many practitioners in clinical practice in multiple locations. Inclusion in the CPT codebook does not represent endorsement by the American Medical Association (AMA) of any particular diagnostic or therapeutic procedure. Inclusion or exclusion of a procedure does not imply any health insurance coverage or reimbursement policy.

The CPT code set is published annually in the late summer or early fall as both electronic data files and books. The release of CPT data files on the Internet typically precedes the book by several weeks. In any case, January 1 is the effective date for use of the update of the CPT code set. The interval between the release of the update and the effective date is considered the implementation period and is intended to allow physicians and other providers, payers, and vendors to incorporate CPT changes into their systems. The exception to this schedule of release and effective dates are CPT Category III and vaccine product codes, which are released twice a year on January 1 or July 1 with effective dates for use six months later. The CPT Category II codes are released three times yearly with effective dates for use three months later.

The main body of the Category I material is listed in six sections. Each section is divided into subsections with anatomic, procedural, condition, or descriptor subheadings. The procedures and services with their identifying codes are presented in numeric order with one exception—the entire **Evaluation and Management** section (99201-99499) appears at the beginning of the listed procedures. These items are used by most physicians in reporting a significant portion of their services.

Section Numbers and Their Sequences

Category I
Evaluation and Management99201-99499
Anesthesiology00100-01999, 99100-99140
Surgery .10021-69990
Radiology (Including Nuclear Medicine and Diagnostic
 Ultrasound) .70010-79999
Pathology and Laboratory80048-89356
Medicine
 (except Anesthesiology) . . 90281-99199, 99500-99602

Category II .0001F-6005F
Category III .0016T-0170T

The first and last code numbers and the subsection name of the items appear at the top margin of most pages (eg, "11010-11306 Surgery/Integumentary System"). The continuous pagination of the CPT codebook is found on the lower margin of each page along with explanation of any code symbols that are found on that page.

Instructions for Use of the CPT Codebook

Select the name of the procedure or service that accurately identifies the service performed. Do not select a CPT code that merely approximates the service provided. If no such procedure or service exists, then report the service using the appropriate unlisted procedure or service code. In surgery, it may be an operation; in medicine, a diagnostic or therapeutic procedure; in radiology, a radiograph. Other additional procedures performed or pertinent special services are also listed. When necessary, any modifying or extenuating circumstances are added. Any service or procedure should be adequately documented in the medical record.

It is important to recognize that the listing of a service or procedure and its code number in a specific section of this book does not restrict its use to a specific specialty group. Any procedure or service in any section of this book may be used to designate the services rendered by any qualified physician or other qualified health care professional.

Instructions, typically included as parenthetical notes, with selected codes indicate that a code should not be reported with another code or codes. These instructions are intended to prevent errors of significant probability and are not all inclusive. For example, the code with such instructions may be a component of another code and therefore it would be incorrect to report both codes even when the component service is performed. These instructions are not intended as a listing of all possible code combinations that should not be reported, nor to indicate all possible code combinations that are appropriately reported. When reporting codes for services provided, it is important to ensure the accuracy and quality of coding through verification of the intent of the code by use of the related guidelines, parenthetical instructions, and coding resources, including *CPT Assistant* and other publications resulting from collaborative efforts of the American Medical Association with the medical specialty societies (eg, *Clinical Examples in Radiology*).

Format of the Terminology

The CPT code set has been developed as stand-alone descriptions of medical procedures. However, some of the procedures in the CPT codebook are not printed in their entirety but refer back to a common portion of the procedure listed in a preceding entry. This is evident when an entry is followed by one or more indentations. This is done in an effort to conserve space.

Example

25100	Arthrotomy, wrist joint; with biopsy
25105	with synovectomy

Note that the common part of code 25100 (the part before the semicolon) should be considered part of code 25105. Therefore, the full procedure represented by code 25105 should read:

25105	Arthrotomy, wrist joint; with synovectomy

Requests to Update the CPT Nomenclature

The effectiveness of the CPT nomenclature depends on constant updating to reflect changes in medical practice. This can only be accomplished through the interest and timely suggestions of practicing physicians, medical specialty societies, state medical associations, and other organizations and agencies. Accordingly, the AMA welcomes correspondence, inquiries, and suggestions concerning old and new procedures, as well as other matters such as codes and indices.

To submit a suggestion to add, delete, or revise procedures contained in the CPT codebook, please contact:
CPT Editorial Research & Development
American Medical Association
515 North State Street
Chicago, Illinois 60610

Coding change request forms are available at the AMA's CPT Web site: www.ama-assn.org/ama/pub/category/3866.html.

All proposed changes of the CPT codebook will be considered by the CPT Editorial Panel with consultation of appropriate medical specialty societies.

Guidelines

Specific guidelines are presented at the beginning of each of the six sections. These guidelines define items that are necessary to appropriately interpret and report the procedures and services contained in that section. For example, in the **Medicine** section, specific instructions are provided for handling unlisted services or procedures, special reports, and supplies and materials provided. Guidelines also provide explanations regarding terms that apply only to a particular section. For instance, **Radiology Guidelines** provide a definition of the unique term, "radiological supervision and interpretation." While in **Anesthesia**, a discussion of reporting time is included.

Add-on Codes

Some of the listed procedures are commonly carried out in addition to the primary procedure performed. These additional or supplemental procedures are designated as add-on codes with the "**+**" symbol and they are listed in **Appendix D** of the CPT codebook. Add-on codes in *CPT 2007* can be readily identified by specific descriptor nomenclature that includes phrases such as "each additional" or "(List separately in addition to primary procedure)."

The add-on code concept in *CPT 2007* applies only to add-on procedures or services performed by the same physician. Add-on codes describe additional intra-service work associated with the primary procedure, eg, additional digit(s), lesion(s), neurorrhaphy(s), vertebral segment(s), tendon(s), joint(s).

Add-on codes are always performed in addition to the primary service or procedure and must never be reported as a stand-alone code. All add-on codes found in the CPT codebook are exempt from the multiple procedure concept (see the modifier 51 definition in **Appendix A**).

Modifiers

A modifier provides the means by which the reporting physician can indicate that a service or procedure that has been performed has been altered by some specific circumstance but not changed in its definition or code. The judicious application of modifiers obviates the necessity for separate procedure listings that may describe the modifying circumstance. Modifiers may be used to indicate to the recipient of a report that:

- A service or procedure had both a professional and technical component.

- A service or procedure was performed by more than one physician and/or in more than one location.

- A service or procedure was increased or reduced.

- Only part of a service was performed.

- An adjunctive service was performed.

- A bilateral procedure was performed.

- A service or procedure was provided more than once.

- Unusual events occurred.

Example

A physician providing diagnostic or therapeutic radiology services, ultrasound, or nuclear medicine services in a hospital would add modifier 26 to report the professional component.

73090 with modifier 26 = Professional component only for an X ray of the forearm

Example

Two surgeons may be required to manage a specific surgical problem. When two surgeons work together as primary surgeons performing distinct part(s) of a procedure, each surgeon should report his/her distinct operative

work by adding modifier 62 to the procedure code and any associated code(s) for that procedure as long as both surgeons continue to work together as primary surgeons. Each surgeon should report the co-surgery once using the same procedure code. Modifier 62 would be applicable. For instance, a neurological surgeon and an otolaryngologist are working as co-surgeons in performing transsphenoidal excision of a pituitary neoplasm.

The first surgeon would report:

61548 with modifier 62 = Hypophysectomy or excision of pituitary tumor, transnasal or transseptal approach, nonstereotactic + two surgeons modifier

AND the second surgeon would report:

61548 with modifier 62 = Hypophysectomy or excision of pituitary tumor, transnasal or transseptal approach, nonstereotactic + two surgeons modifier

If additional procedure(s) (including add-on procedure[s]) are performed during the same surgical session, separate code(s) may also be reported with modifier 62 added. It should be noted that if a co-surgeon acts as an assistant in the performance of additional procedure(s) during the same surgical session, those services may be reported using separate procedure code(s) with modifier 80 or modifier 82 added, as appropriate. A complete listing of modifiers is found in **Appendix A**.

Unlisted Procedure or Service

It is recognized that there may be services or procedures performed by physicians that are not found in the CPT codebook. Therefore, a number of specific code numbers have been designated for reporting unlisted procedures. When an unlisted procedure number is used, the service or procedure should be described. Each of these unlisted procedural code numbers (with the appropriate accompanying topical entry) relates to a specific section of the book and is presented in the guidelines of that section.

Special Report

A service that is rarely provided, unusual, variable, or new may require a special report in determining medical appropriateness of the service. Pertinent information should include an adequate definition or description of the nature, extent, and need for the procedure and the time, effort, and equipment necessary to provide the service. Additional items may include complexity of symptoms, final diagnosis, pertinent physical findings, diagnostic and therapeutic procedures, concurrent problems, and follow-up care.

Code Symbols

A summary listing of additions, deletions, and revisions applicable to the CPT codebook is found in **Appendix B**. New procedure numbers added to the CPT codebook are identified throughout the text with the symbol ● placed before the code number. In instances where a code revision has resulted in a substantially altered procedure descriptor, the symbol ▲ is placed before the code number. The symbols ► ◄ are used to indicate new and revised text other than the procedure descriptors. These symbols indicate CPT Editorial Panel actions. The AMA reserves the right to correct typographical error and make stylistic improvements. CPT add-on codes are annotated by the symbol ✚ and are listed in **Appendix D**. The symbol ⊘ is used to identify codes that are exempt from the use of modifier 51 but have not been designated as CPT add-on procedures or services. A list of codes exempt from modifier 51 usage is included in **Appendix E**. The symbol ⊙ is used to identify codes that include moderate sedation (see **Appendix G**). The symbol ∕ is used to identify codes for vaccines that are pending FDA approval (see **Appendix K**).

Alphabetical Reference Index

This codebook features an expanded alphabetical index that includes listings by procedure and anatomic site. Procedures and services commonly known by their eponyms or other designations are also included.

CPT 2007 in Electronic Formats

CPT 2007 procedure codes and descriptions are available on CD-ROM as data files and electronic software. Data files are available in ASCII and EBCDIC formats and can be imported into any billing and claims reporting software that accepts a text (TXT) file format. *CPT 2007 Electronic Professional* software, now with *Netter's Atlas of Human Anatomy for CPT Coding*, provides access to the entire *CPT 2007 Professional Edition* codebook on your desktop. Easy-to-use and fully searchable, this invaluable software contains all of the favorite *CPT Professional* features plus quick linking access between CPT codes, guidelines, modifiers, appendixes, index, and more. For more information call 800 621-8335 or visit www.amabookstore.com.

Additional CPT Resources

The AMA publishes additional CPT coding books and software to ensure your practice has current, complete, and compliant coding resources.

CPT® Assistant Newsletter

As the AMA's official communication tool for circulating accurate information and guidance on CPT codes and issues, this insightful monthly newsletter should be part of every compliance program. Each issue features articles used for answering day-to-day coding questions, appealing insurance denials, and validating coding to auditors. *CPT Assistant* keeps you informed on critical code changes, enhances your coding proficiency through case studies and clinical examples, and provides a coding consultation section featuring questions and answers drawn from the *CPT® Information Services*.

E-mail amy.burgess@ama-assn.org to request a free sample issue.

Subscriptions to *CPT® Assistant* can be purchased by calling the AMA's Unified Services Center at 800 621-8335. Individual back issues are available for purchase and immediate download at www.amabookstore.com.

CPT® Assistant Archives 1990–2006 (Available February 2007)

Enjoy convenient access to 17 years of *CPT® Assistant* newsletter articles on your computer desktop. Search past issues of the AMA's authoritative coding newsletter by keyword, phrase, CPT code number, newsletter issue, article index, or codebook table of contents. The new edition of this product offers simple search capabilities, menu screens, a cumulative index of article titles, and a complete historical CPT code list from 1990-2006 that references when a code was added, deleted, and/or revised. Call 800 621-8335 or visit www.amabookstore.com for more information.

Clinical Examples in Radiology Newsletter

Understand the correct application of radiology CPT codes with this authoritative guide from the AMA and the American College of Radiology (ACR). A quarterly newsletter, it provides expert advice and guidance of especially high value to the day-to-day needs of radiology coding professionals. Each issue features clinical examples, radiology coding FAQs, a documentation challenge, and a radiology test case. Special report bulletins are also mailed throughout the year covering important news and issues related to radiology coding. Email amy.burgess@ ama-assn.org to request a free sample issue.

CPT® Changes 2007: An Insider's View

An indispensable guide for CPT codebook users. This book provides the official AMA interpretations and rationales for every new, revised, and deleted CPT code and guideline change. This valuable resource provides useful clinical examples and procedural descriptions to help explain the practical application for each new CPT code, and an "at-a-glance" tabular review of 2007 changes helps you easily determine the level to which your particular field has been affected by the changes. Call 800 621-8335 or visit www.amabookstore.com for more information.

CPT® Changes Archives 2000–2007

Access current and historical CPT code and guideline changes on your computer desktop. An invaluable electronic library, use it to search the AMA's best-selling *CPT® Changes: An Insider's View* by keyword, phrase, CPT code number, edition, and CPT codebook table of contents. This product offers simple, intuitive search capabilities and a complete historical CPT code list from 1990-2007 that references when a code was added, deleted, and/or revised. Call 800 621-8335 or visit www.amabookstore.com for more information.

More AMA Coding Resources

Check out these additional AMA coding resources at www.amabookstore.com:

- New—*CPT® Reference of Clinical Examples: Official Coding Scenarios for Correct Coding*
- New—*Netter's Atlas of Anatomy for CPT® and ICD-9-CM Coding: Musculoskeletal*
- *CPT® for Outpatient Services*
- *Practical E/M: Documentation and Coding Solutions for Quality Patient Care*
- *Coding with Modifiers: A Guide to Correct CPT® and HCPCS Level II Modifier Usage*
- *Principles of CPT® Coding*
- *Netter's Atlas of Human Anatomy for CPT® Coding*
- *CPT® Coding Workbook: Coding Challenges and Exercises for Instructors and Students*
- *CPT® Specialty Resources*
- *CodeManager®* software

Additional References

For best coding results, you will need to use other reference materials in addition to your coding books. These references include a medical dictionary and one or more anatomy books that can be purchased from the American Medical Association by calling 800 621-8335.

Medical Dictionaries

Merriam-Webster's Medical Desk Dictionary.
Springfield, Mass: Merriam Webster.
OP941493

Stedman's Medical Dictionary, 27th ed.
Baltimore, Md: Williams & Wilkins; 2000.
OP982900

Anatomy References

Kirschner, CG. *Netter's Atlas of Anatomy for CPT® and ICD-9-CM Coding Series: Musculoskeletal*.
Chicago, Ill: American Medical Association; *Coming Soon*.
OP492206

Kirschner, CG. *Netter's Atlas of Human Anatomy for CPT® Coding*.
Chicago, Ill: American Medical Association; 2005.
OP490605

Netter, FH. *Atlas of Human Anatomy*. 3rd ed.
East Hanover, NJ: Novartis; 2003.
OP936798

Evaluation and Management (E/M) Services Guidelines

In addition to the information presented in the Introduction, several other items unique to this section are defined or identified here.

Classification of Evaluation and Management (E/M) Services

The E/M section is divided into broad categories such as office visits, hospital visits, and consultations. Most of the categories are further divided into two or more subcategories of E/M services. For example, there are two subcategories of office visits (new patient and established patient) and there are two subcategories of hospital visits (initial and subsequent). The subcategories of E/M services are further classified into levels of E/M services that are identified by specific codes. This classification is important because the nature of physician work varies by type of service, place of service, and the patient's status.

The basic format of the levels of E/M services is the same for most categories. First, a unique code number is listed. Second, the place and/or type of service is specified, eg, office consultation. Third, the content of the service is defined, eg, comprehensive history and comprehensive examination. (See "Levels of E/M Services," page 3, for details on the content of E/M services.) Fourth, the nature of the presenting problem(s) usually associated with a given level is described. Fifth, the time typically required to provide the service is specified. (A detailed discussion of time is provided on page 4.)

Definitions of Commonly Used Terms

Certain key words and phrases are used throughout the E/M section. The following definitions are intended to reduce the potential for differing interpretations and to increase the consistency of reporting by physicians in differing specialties.

New and Established Patient

Solely for the purposes of distinguishing between new and established patients, **professional services** are those face-to-face services rendered by a physician and reported by a specific CPT code(s). A new patient is one who has not received any professional services from the physician or another physician of the same specialty who belongs to the same group practice, within the past three years.

An established patient is one who has received professional services from the physician or another physician of the same specialty who belongs to the same group practice, within the past three years.

In the instance where a physician is on call for or covering for another physician, the patient's encounter will be classified as it would have been by the physician who is not available.

No distinction is made between new and established patients in the emergency department. E/M services in the emergency department category may be reported for any new or established patient who presents for treatment in the emergency department.

►The decision tree on page 2 is provided to aid in determining whether to report the E/M service provided as a new or an established patient encounter.◄

Chief Complaint

A chief complaint is a concise statement describing the symptom, problem, condition, diagnosis, or other factor that is the reason for the encounter, usually stated in the patient's words.

Concurrent Care

Concurrent care is the provision of similar services, eg, hospital visits, to the same patient by more than one physician on the same day. When concurrent care is provided, no special reporting is required. Modifier 75 has been deleted.

Counseling

Counseling is a discussion with a patient and/or family concerning one or more of the following areas:

- Diagnostic results, impressions, and/or recommended diagnostic studies
- Prognosis
- Risks and benefits of management (treatment) options
- Instructions for management (treatment) and/or follow-up
- Importance of compliance with chosen management (treatment) options
- Risk factor reduction
- Patient and family education

(For psychotherapy, see 90804-90857)

Evaluation and Management Guidelines

Decision Tree for New vs Established Patients

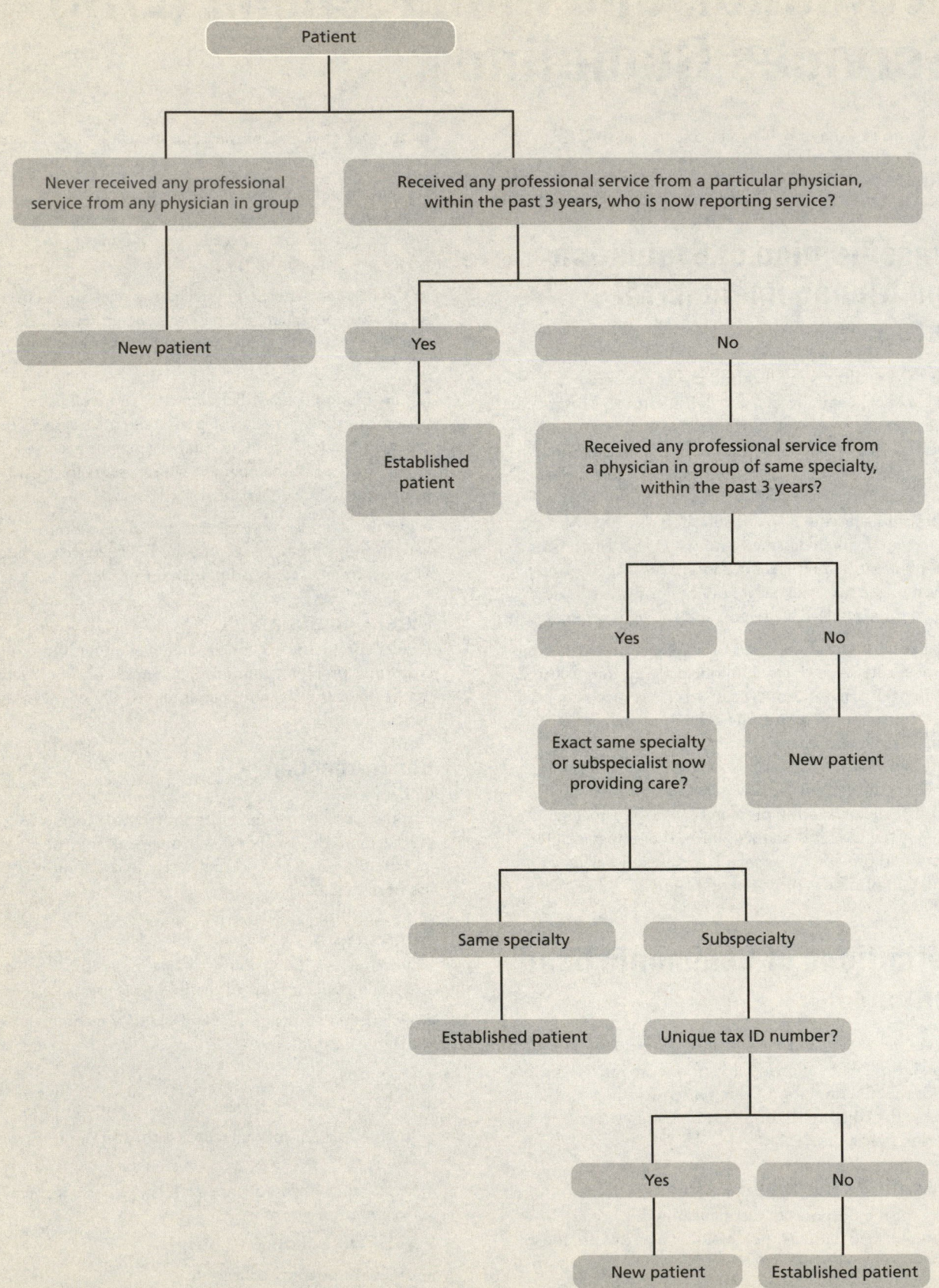

⊙ =Moderate sedation ✚ =Add-on code ⟋ =FDA approval pending

Family History

A review of medical events in the patient's family that includes significant information about:

- The health status or cause of death of parents, siblings, and children

- Specific diseases related to problems identified in the Chief Complaint or History of the Present Illness, and/or System Review

- Diseases of family members that may be hereditary or place the patient at risk

History of Present Illness

A chronological description of the development of the patient's present illness from the first sign and/or symptom to the present. This includes a description of location, quality, severity, timing, context, modifying factors, and associated signs and symptoms significantly related to the presenting problem(s).

Levels of E/M Services

Within each category or subcategory of E/M service, there are three to five levels of E/M services available for reporting purposes. Levels of E/M services are **not** interchangeable among the different categories or subcategories of service. For example, the first level of E/M services in the subcategory of office visit, new patient, does not have the same definition as the first level of E/M services in the subcategory of office visit, established patient.

The levels of E/M services include examinations, evaluations, treatments, conferences with or concerning patients, preventive pediatric and adult health supervision, and similar medical services, such as the determination of the need and/or location for appropriate care. Medical screening includes the history, examination, and medical decision-making required to determine the need and/or location for appropriate care and treatment of the patient (eg, office and other outpatient setting, emergency department, nursing facility). The levels of E/M services encompass the wide variations in skill, effort, time, responsibility, and medical knowledge required for the prevention or diagnosis and treatment of illness or injury and the promotion of optimal health. Each level of E/M services may be used by all physicians.

The descriptors for the levels of E/M services recognize seven components, six of which are used in defining the levels of E/M services. These components are:

- History
- Examination
- Medical decision making
- Counseling
- Coordination of care
- Nature of presenting problem
- Time

The first three of these components (history, examination, and medical decision making) are considered the **key** components in selecting a level of E/M services. (See "Determine the Extent of History Obtained," page 6.)

The next three components (counseling, coordination of care, and the nature of the presenting problem) are considered **contributory** factors in the majority of encounters. Although the first two of these contributory factors are important E/M services, it is not required that these services be provided at every patient encounter.

Coordination of care with other providers or agencies without a patient encounter on that day is reported using the case management codes.

The final component, time, is discussed in detail (see page 4).

Any specifically identifiable procedure (ie, identified with a specific CPT code) performed on or subsequent to the date of initial or subsequent E/M services should be reported separately.

The actual performance and/or interpretation of diagnostic tests/studies ordered during a patient encounter are not included in the levels of E/M services. Physician performance of diagnostic tests/studies for which specific CPT codes are available may be reported separately, in addition to the appropriate E/M code. The physician's interpretation of the results of diagnostic tests/studies (ie, professional component) with preparation of a separate distinctly identifiable signed written report may also be reported separately, using the appropriate CPT code with modifier 26 appended.

The physician may need to indicate that on the day a procedure or service identified by a CPT code was performed, the patient's condition required a significant separately identifiable E/M service above and beyond other services provided or beyond the usual preservice and postservice care associated with the procedure that was performed. The E/M service may be caused or prompted by the symptoms or condition for which the procedure and/or service was provided. This circumstance may be reported by adding modifier 25 to the appropriate level of E/M service. As such, different diagnoses are not required for reporting of the procedure and the E/M services on the same date.

Nature of Presenting Problem

A presenting problem is a disease, condition, illness, injury, symptom, sign, finding, complaint, or other reason for encounter, with or without a diagnosis being established at the time of the encounter. The E/M codes recognize five types of presenting problems that are defined as follows:

Minimal: A problem that may not require the presence of the physician, but service is provided under the physician's supervision.

Evaluation and Management Guidelines *(sidebar)*

Self-limited or minor: A problem that runs a definite and prescribed course, is transient in nature, and is not likely to permanently alter health status OR has a good prognosis with management/compliance.

Low severity: A problem where the risk of morbidity without treatment is low; there is little to no risk of mortality without treatment; full recovery without functional impairment is expected.

Moderate severity: A problem where the risk of morbidity without treatment is moderate; there is moderate risk of mortality without treatment; uncertain prognosis OR increased probability of prolonged functional impairment.

High severity: A problem where the risk of morbidity without treatment is high to extreme; there is a moderate to high risk of mortality without treatment OR high probability of severe, prolonged functional impairment.

Past History

A review of the patient's past experiences with illnesses, injuries, and treatments that includes significant information about:

- Prior major illnesses and injuries
- Prior operations
- Prior hospitalizations
- Current medications
- Allergies (eg, drug, food)
- Age appropriate immunization status
- Age appropriate feeding/dietary status

Social History

An age appropriate review of past and current activities that includes significant information about:

- Marital status and/or living arrangements
- Current employment
- Occupational history
- Use of drugs, alcohol, and tobacco
- Level of education
- Sexual history
- Other relevant social factors

System Review (Review of Systems)

An inventory of body systems obtained through a series of questions seeking to identify signs and/or symptoms that the patient may be experiencing or has experienced. For the purposes of the CPT codebook the following elements of a system review have been identified:

- Constitutional symptoms (fever, weight loss, etc)
- Eyes
- Ears, nose, mouth, throat
- Cardiovascular
- Respiratory
- Gastrointestinal
- Genitourinary
- Musculoskeletal
- Integumentary (skin and/or breast)
- Neurological
- Psychiatric
- Endocrine
- Hematologic/lymphatic
- Allergic/immunologic

The review of systems helps define the problem, clarify the differential diagnosis, identify needed testing, or serves as baseline data on other systems that might be affected by any possible management options.

Time

The inclusion of time in the definitions of levels of E/M services has been implicit in prior editions of the CPT codebook. The inclusion of time as an explicit factor beginning in *CPT 1992* is done to assist physicians in selecting the most appropriate level of E/M services. It should be recognized that the specific times expressed in the visit code descriptors are averages and, therefore, represent a range of times that may be higher or lower depending on actual clinical circumstances.

Time is **not** a descriptive component for the emergency department levels of E/M services because emergency department services are typically provided on a variable intensity basis, often involving multiple encounters with several patients over an extended period of time. Therefore, it is often difficult for physicians to provide accurate estimates of the time spent face-to-face with the patient.

Studies to establish levels of E/M services employed surveys of practicing physicians to obtain data on the amount of time and work associated with typical E/M services. Since "work" is not easily quantifiable, the codes must rely on other objective, verifiable measures that correlate with physicians' estimates of their "work." It has been demonstrated that physicians' estimations of **intraservice** time (as explained on the next page), both within and across specialties, is a variable that is predictive of the "work" of E/M services. This same research has shown there is a strong relationship between intraservice time and total time for E/M services. Intraservice time, rather than total time, was chosen for inclusion with the codes because of its relative ease of measurement and because of its direct correlation with measurements of the total amount of time and work associated with typical E/M services.

Intraservice times are defined as **face-to-face** time for office and other outpatient visits and as **unit/floor** time for hospital and other inpatient visits. This distinction is necessary because most of the work of typical office visits takes place during the face-to-face time with the patient, while most of the work of typical hospital visits takes place during the time spent on the patient's floor or unit.

Face-to-face time (office and other outpatient visits and office consultations): For coding purposes, face-to-face time for these services is defined as only that time that the physician spends face-to-face with the patient and/or family. This includes the time in which the physician performs such tasks as obtaining a history, performing an examination, and counseling the patient.

Physicians also spend time doing work before or after the face-to-face time with the patient, performing such tasks as reviewing records and tests, arranging for further services, and communicating further with other professionals and the patient through written reports and telephone contact.

This **non-face-to-face** time for office services—also called pre- and postencounter time—is not included in the time component described in the E/M codes. However, the pre- and post-face-to-face work associated with an encounter was included in calculating the total work of typical services in physician surveys.

Thus, the face-to-face time associated with the services described by any E/M code is a valid proxy for the total work done before, during, and after the visit.

Unit/floor time (hospital observation services, inpatient hospital care, initial and follow-up hospital consultations, nursing facility): For reporting purposes, intraservice time for these services is defined as unit/floor time, which includes the time that the physician is present on the patient's hospital unit and at the bedside rendering services for that patient. This includes the time in which the physician establishes and/or reviews the patient's chart, examines the patient, writes notes, and communicates with other professionals and the patient's family.

In the hospital, pre- and post-time includes time spent off the patient's floor performing such tasks as reviewing pathology and radiology findings in another part of the hospital.

This pre- and postvisit time is not included in the time component described in these codes. However, the pre- and postwork performed during the time spent off the floor or unit was included in calculating the total work of typical services in physician surveys.

Thus, the unit/floor time associated with the services described by any code is a valid proxy for the total work done before, during, and after the visit.

Unlisted Service

An E/M service may be provided that is not listed in this section of the CPT codebook. When reporting such a service, the appropriate "Unlisted" code may be used to indicate the service, identifying it by "Special Report," as discussed in the following paragraph. The "Unlisted Services" and accompanying codes for the E/M section are as follows:

99429 **Unlisted preventive** medicine service

99499 **Unlisted evaluation and management** service

►Results/Testing/Reports◄

►Results are the technical component of a service. Testing leads to results; results lead to interpretation. Reports are the work product of the interpretation of numerous test results.◄

Special Report

An unlisted service or one that is unusual, variable, or new may require a special report demonstrating the medical appropriateness of the service. Pertinent information should include an adequate definition or description of the nature, extent, and need for the procedure and the time, effort, and equipment necessary to provide the service. Additional items that may be included are complexity of symptoms, final diagnosis, pertinent physical findings, diagnostic and therapeutic procedures, concurrent problems, and follow-up care.

Clinical Examples

Clinical examples of the codes for E/M services are provided to assist physicians in understanding the meaning of the descriptors and selecting the correct code. The clinical examples are listed in Appendix C. Each example was developed by physicians in the specialties shown.

The same problem, when seen by physicians in different specialties, may involve different amounts of work. Therefore, the appropriate level of encounter should be reported using the descriptors rather than the examples.

The examples have been tested for validity and approved by the CPT Editorial Panel. Physicians were given the examples and asked to assign a code or assess the amount of time and work involved. Only examples that were rated consistently have been included in Appendix C.

Table 1
Categories and Subcategories of Service

Category/Subcategory	Code Numbers	Category/Subcategory	Code Numbers
Office or Other Outpatient Services		Domiciliary, Rest Home or	
New Patient	99201-99205	Custodial Care Services	
Established Patient	99211-99215	New Patient	99324-99328
Hospital Observation Services		Established Patient	99334-99337
Hospital Observation Discharge Services	99217	Domiciliary, Rest Home (eg, Assisted	
Initial Hospital Observation Services	99218-99220	Living Facility), or Home Care Plan	
Hospital Observation or Inpatient Care		Oversight Services	99339-99340
Services (Including Admission and		Home Services	
Discharge Services)	99234-99236	New Patient	99341-99345
Hospital Inpatient Services		Established Patient	99347-99350
Initial Hospital Care	99221-99223	Prolonged Services	
Subsequent Hospital Care	99231-99233	With Direct Patient Contact	99354-99357
Hospital Discharge Services	99238-99239	Without Direct Patient Contact	99358-99359
Consultations		Standby Services	99360
Office Consultations	99241-99245	Case Management Services	
Initial Inpatient Consultations	99251-99255	Team Conferences	99361-99362
Emergency Department Services	99281-99288	Telephone Calls	99371-99373
Pediatric Patient Transport	99289-99290	Care Plan Oversight Services	99374-99380
Critical Care Services		Preventive Medicine Services	
Adult (over 24 months of age)	99291-99292	New Patient	99381-99387
Pediatric	99293-99294	Established Patient	99391-99397
Neonatal	99295-99296	Individual Counseling	99401-99404
Continuing Intensive Care Services	99298-99300	Group Counseling	99411-99412
Nursing Facility Services		Other	99420-99429
Initial Nursing Facility Care	99304-99306	Newborn Care	99431-99440
Subsequent Nursing Facility Care	99307-99310	Special E/M Services	99450-99456
Nursing Facility Discharge Services	99315-99316	Other E/M Services	99499
Other Nursing Facility Services	99318		

Instructions for Selecting a Level of E/M Service

Identify the Category and Subcategory of Service

The categories and subcategories of codes available for reporting E/M services are shown in Table 1.

Review the Reporting Instructions for the Selected Category or Subcategory

Most of the categories and many of the subcategories of service have special guidelines or instructions unique to that category or subcategory. Where these are indicated, eg, "Inpatient Hospital Care," special instructions will be presented preceding the levels of E/M services.

Review the Level of E/M Service Descriptors and Examples in the Selected Category or Subcategory

The descriptors for the levels of E/M services recognize seven components, six of which are used in defining the levels of E/M services. These components are:

- History
- Examination
- Medical decision making
- Counseling
- Coordination of care
- Nature of presenting problem
- Time

The first three of these components (ie, history, examination, and medical decision making) should be considered the **key** components in selecting the level of E/M services. An exception to this rule is in the case of visits that consist predominantly of counseling or coordination of care (see numbered paragraph 3, page 8).

The nature of the presenting problem and time are provided in some levels to assist the physician in determining the appropriate level of E/M service.

Determine the Extent of History Obtained

The extent of the history is dependent upon clinical judgment and on the nature of the presenting problems(s). The levels of E/M services recognize four types of history that are defined as follows:

Problem focused: Chief complaint; brief history of present illness or problem.

Expanded problem focused: Chief complaint; brief history of present illness; problem pertinent system review.

Detailed: Chief complaint; extended history of present illness; problem pertinent system review extended to include a review of a limited number of additional systems; **pertinent** past, family, and/or social history **directly related to the patient's problems.**

Comprehensive: Chief complaint; extended history of present illness; review of systems that is directly related to the problem(s) identified in the history of the present illness plus a review of all additional body systems; **complete** past, family, and social history.

The comprehensive history obtained as part of the preventive medicine E/M service is not problem-oriented and does not involve a chief complaint or present illness. It does, however, include a comprehensive system review and comprehensive or interval past, family, and social history as well as a comprehensive assessment/history of pertinent risk factors.

Determine the Extent of Examination Performed

The extent of the examination performed is dependent on clinical judgment and on the nature of the presenting problem(s). The levels of E/M services recognize four types of examination that are defined as follows:

Problem focused: A limited examination of the affected body area or organ system.

Expanded problem focused: A limited examination of the affected body area or organ system and other symptomatic or related organ system(s).

Detailed: An extended examination of the affected body area(s) and other symptomatic or related organ system(s).

Comprehensive: A general multisystem examination or a complete examination of a single organ system. **Note:** The comprehensive examination performed as part of the preventive medicine E/M service is multisystem, but its extent is based on age and risk factors identified.

For the purposes of these CPT definitions, the following body areas are recognized:

- Head, including the face
- Neck
- Chest, including breasts and axilla
- Abdomen
- Genitalia, groin, buttocks
- Back
- Each extremity

For the purposes of these CPT definitions, the following organ systems are recognized:

- Eyes
- Ears, nose, mouth, and throat
- Cardiovascular
- Respiratory
- Gastrointestinal
- Genitourinary
- Musculoskeletal
- Skin
- Neurologic
- Psychiatric
- Hematologic/lymphatic/immunologic

Determine the Complexity of Medical Decision Making

Medical decision making refers to the complexity of establishing a diagnosis and/or selecting a management option as measured by:

- The number of possible diagnoses and/or the number of management options that must be considered
- The amount and/or complexity of medical records, diagnostic tests, and/or other information that must be obtained, reviewed, and analyzed
- The risk of significant complications, morbidity, and/or mortality, as well as comorbidities, associated with the patient's presenting problems(s), the diagnostic procedure(s), and/or the possible management options

Four types of medical decision making are recognized: straightforward, low complexity, moderate complexity, and high complexity. To qualify for a given type of decision making, two of the three elements in Table 2 must be met or exceeded.

Comorbidities/underlying diseases, in and of themselves, are not considered in selecting a level of E/M services *unless* their presence significantly increases the complexity of the medical decision making.

Select the Appropriate Level of E/M Services Based on the Following

1. For the following categories/subcategories, **all of the key components,** ie, history, examination, and medical decision making, must meet or exceed the stated requirements to qualify for a particular level of E/M service: office, new patient; hospital observation services; initial hospital care; office consultations; initial inpatient consultations; emergency department services; initial nursing facility care; domiciliary care, new patient; and home, new patient.

Evaluation and Management Guidelines

Table 2
Complexity of Medical Decision Making

Number of Diagnoses or Management Options	Amount and/or Complexity of Data to be Reviewed	Risk of Complications and/or Morbidity or Mortality	Type of Decision Making
minimal	minimal or none	minimal	**straightforward**
limited	limited	low	**low complexity**
multiple	moderate	moderate	**moderate complexity**
extensive	extensive	high	**high complexity**

2. For the following categories/subcategories, **two of the three key components** (ie, history, examination, and medical decision making) must meet or exceed the stated requirements to qualify for a particular level of E/M services: office, established patient; subsequent hospital care; subsequent nursing facility care; domiciliary care, established patient; and home, established patient.

3. When counseling and/or coordination of care dominates (more than 50%) the physician/patient and/or family encounter (face-to-face time in the office or other outpatient setting or floor/unit time in the hospital or nursing facility), then **time** may be considered the key or controlling factor to qualify for a particular level of E/M services. This includes time spent with parties who have assumed responsibility for the care of the patient or decision making whether or not they are family members (eg, foster parents, person acting in locum parentis, legal guardian). The extent of counseling and/or coordination of care must be documented in the medical record.

Evaluation and Management

Office or Other Outpatient Services

The following codes are used to report evaluation and management services provided in the physician's office or in an outpatient or other ambulatory facility. A patient is considered an outpatient until inpatient admission to a health care facility occurs.

To report services provided to a patient who is admitted to a hospital or nursing facility in the course of an encounter in the office or other ambulatory facility, see the notes for initial hospital inpatient care (page 11) or initial nursing facility care (page 21).

For services provided by physicians in the emergency department, see 99281-99285.

For observation care, see 99217-99220.

For observation or inpatient care services (including admission and discharge services), see 99234-99236.

New Patient

99201 **Office or other outpatient visit** for the evaluation and management of a new patient, which requires these three key components:

- **A problem focused history;**

- **A problem focused examination;**

- **Straightforward medical decision making.**

Counseling and/or coordination of care with other providers or agencies are provided consistent with the nature of the problem(s) and the patient's and/or family's needs.

Usually, the presenting problem(s) are self limited or minor. Physicians typically spend 10 minutes face-to-face with the patient and/or family.

99202 **Office or other outpatient visit** for the evaluation and management of a new patient, which requires these three key components:

- **An expanded problem focused history;**

- **An expanded problem focused examination;**

- **Straightforward medical decision making.**

Counseling and/or coordination of care with other providers or agencies are provided consistent with the nature of the problem(s) and the patient's and/or family's needs.

Usually, the presenting problem(s) are of low to moderate severity. Physicians typically spend 20 minutes face-to-face with the patient and/or family.

99203 **Office or other outpatient visit** for the evaluation and management of a new patient, which requires these three key components:

- **A detailed history;**

- **A detailed examination;**

- **Medical decision making of low complexity.**

Counseling and/or coordination of care with other providers or agencies are provided consistent with the nature of the problem(s) and the patient's and/or family's needs.

Usually, the presenting problem(s) are of moderate severity. Physicians typically spend 30 minutes face-to-face with the patient and/or family.

99204 **Office or other outpatient visit** for the evaluation and management of a new patient, which requires these three key components:

- **A comprehensive history;**

- **A comprehensive examination;**

- **Medical decision making of moderate complexity.**

Counseling and/or coordination of care with other providers or agencies are provided consistent with the nature of the problem(s) and the patient's and/or family's needs.

Usually, the presenting problem(s) are of moderate to high severity. Physicians typically spend 45 minutes face-to-face with the patient and/or family.

99205 **Office or other outpatient visit** for the evaluation and management of a new patient, which requires these three key components:

- **A comprehensive history;**

- **A comprehensive examination;**

- **Medical decision making of high complexity.**

Counseling and/or coordination of care with other providers or agencies are provided consistent with the nature of the problem(s) and the patient's and/or family's needs.

Usually, the presenting problem(s) are of moderate to high severity. Physicians typically spend 60 minutes face-to-face with the patient and/or family.

Established Patient

99211 **Office or other outpatient visit** for the evaluation and management of an established patient, that may not require the presence of a physician. Usually, the presenting problem(s) are minimal. Typically, 5 minutes are spent performing or supervising these services.

99212 **Office or other outpatient visit** for the evaluation and management of an established patient, which requires at least two of these three key components:

- **A problem focused history;**
- **A problem focused examination;**
- **Straightforward medical decision making.**

Counseling and/or coordination of care with other providers or agencies are provided consistent with the nature of the problem(s) and the patient's and/or family's needs.

Usually, the presenting problem(s) are self limited or minor. Physicians typically spend 10 minutes face-to-face with the patient and/or family.

99213 **Office or other outpatient visit** for the evaluation and management of an established patient, which requires at least two of these three key components:

- **An expanded problem focused history;**
- **An expanded problem focused examination;**
- **Medical decision making of low complexity.**

Counseling and coordination of care with other providers or agencies are provided consistent with the nature of the problem(s) and the patient's and/or family's needs.

Usually, the presenting problem(s) are of low to moderate severity. Physicians typically spend 15 minutes face-to-face with the patient and/or family.

99214 **Office or other outpatient visit** for the evaluation and management of an established patient, which requires at least two of these three key components:

- **A detailed history;**
- **A detailed examination;**
- **Medical decision making of moderate complexity.**

Counseling and/or coordination of care with other providers or agencies are provided consistent with the nature of the problem(s) and the patient's and/or family's needs.

Usually, the presenting problem(s) are of moderate to high severity. Physicians typically spend 25 minutes face-to-face with the patient and/or family.

99215 **Office or other outpatient visit** for the evaluation and management of an established patient, which requires at least two of these three key components:

- **A comprehensive history;**
- **A comprehensive examination;**
- **Medical decision making of high complexity.**

Counseling and/or coordination of care with other providers or agencies are provided consistent with the nature of the problem(s) and the patient's and/or family's needs.

Usually, the presenting problem(s) are of moderate to high severity. Physicians typically spend 40 minutes face-to-face with the patient and/or family.

Hospital Observation Services

The following codes are used to report evaluation and management services provided to patients designated/admitted as "observation status" in a hospital. It is not necessary that the patient be located in an observation area designated by the hospital.

If such an area does exist in a hospital (as a separate unit in the hospital, in the emergency department, etc), these codes are to be utilized if the patient is placed in such an area.

For definitions of key components and commonly used terms, please see **Evaluation and Management Services Guidelines.**

Typical times have not yet been established for this category of services.

Observation Care Discharge Services

Observation care discharge of a patient from "observation status" includes final examination of the patient, discussion of the hospital stay, instructions for continuing care, and preparation of discharge records. For observation or inpatient hospital care including the admission and discharge of the patient on the same date, see codes 99234-99236 as appropriate.

99217 **Observation care discharge** day management (This code is to be utilized by the physician to report all services provided to a patient on discharge from "observation status" if the discharge is on other than the initial date of "observation status." To report services to a patient designated as "observation status" or "inpatient status" and discharged on the same date, use the codes for Observation or Inpatient Care Services [including Admission and Discharge Services, 99234-99236 as appropriate.])

Initial Observation Care

New or Established Patient

The following codes are used to report the encounter(s) by the supervising physician with the patient when designated as "observation status." This refers to the initiation of observation status, supervision of the care plan for observation and performance of periodic reassessments. For observation encounters by other physicians, see Office or Other Outpatient Consultation codes (99241-99245).

To report services provided to a patient who is admitted to the hospital after receiving hospital observation care services on the same date, see the notes for initial hospital inpatient care (page 12). For a patient admitted to the hospital on a date subsequent to the date of observation status, the hospital admission would be reported with the appropriate Initial Hospital Care code (99221-99223). For a patient admitted and discharged from observation or inpatient status on the same date, the services should be reported with codes 99234-99236 as appropriate. Do not report observation discharge (99217) in conjunction with a hospital admission.

When "observation status" is initiated in the course of an encounter in another site of service (eg, hospital emergency department, physician's office, nursing facility) all evaluation and management services provided by the supervising physician in conjunction with initiating "observation status" are considered part of the initial observation care when performed on the same date. The observation care level of service reported by the supervising physician should include the services related to initiating "observation status" provided in the other sites of service as well as in the observation setting.

Evaluation and management services on the same date provided in sites that are related to initiating "observation status" should NOT be reported separately.

These codes may not be utilized for post-operative recovery if the procedure is considered part of the surgical "package." These codes apply to all evaluation and management services that are provided on the same date of initiating "observation status."

99218 **Initial observation care,** per day, for the evaluation and management of a patient which requires these three key components:

- **A detailed or comprehensive history;**

- **A detailed or comprehensive examination; and**

- **Medical decision making that is straightforward or of low complexity.**

Counseling and/or coordination of care with other providers or agencies are provided consistent with the nature of the problem(s) and the patient's and/or family's needs.

Usually, the problem(s) requiring admission to "observation status" are of low severity.

99219 **Initial observation care,** per day, for the evaluation and management of a patient, which requires these three key components:

- **A comprehensive history;**

- **A comprehensive examination; and**

- **Medical decision making of moderate complexity.**

Counseling and/or coordination of care with other providers or agencies are provided consistent with the nature of the problem(s) and the patient's and/or family's needs.

Usually, the problem(s) requiring admission to "observation status" are of moderate severity.

99220 **Initial observation care,** per day, for the evaluation and management of a patient, which requires these three key components:

- **A comprehensive history;**

- **A comprehensive examination; and**

- **Medical decision making of high complexity.**

Counseling and/or coordination of care with other providers or agencies are provided consistent with the nature of the problem(s) and the patient's and/or family's needs.

Usually, the problem(s) requiring admission to "observation status" are of high severity.

Hospital Inpatient Services

The following codes are used to report evaluation and management services provided to hospital inpatients. Hospital inpatient services include those services provided to patients in a "partial hospital" setting. These codes are to be used to report these partial hospitalization services. See also psychiatry notes in the full text of CPT codebook.

For definitions of key components and commonly used terms, please see **Evaluation and Management Services Guidelines.** For Hospital Observation Services, see 99218-99220. For a patient admitted and discharged from observation or inpatient status on the same date, the services should be reported with codes 99234-99236 as appropriate.

Initial Hospital Care

New or Established Patient

The following codes are used to report the first hospital inpatient encounter with the patient by the admitting physician.

For initial inpatient encounters by physicians other than the admitting physician, see initial inpatient consultation codes (99251-99255) or subsequent hospital care codes (99231-99233) as appropriate.

When the patient is admitted to the hospital as an inpatient in the course of an encounter in another site of service (eg, hospital emergency department, observation status in a hospital, physician's office, nursing facility) all evaluation and management services provided by that physician in conjunction with that admission are considered part of the initial hospital care when performed on the same date as the admission. The inpatient care level of service reported by the admitting physician should include the services related to the admission he/she provided in the other sites of service as well as in the inpatient setting.

Evaluation and management services on the same date provided in sites that are related to the admission "observation status" should NOT be reported separately. For a patient admitted and discharged from observation or inpatient status on the same date, the services should be reported with codes 99234-99236 as appropriate.

99221 **Initial hospital care,** per day, for the evaluation and management of a patient, which requires these three key components:

- **A detailed or comprehensive history;**

- **A detailed or comprehensive examination; and**

- **Medical decision making that is straightforward or of low complexity.**

Counseling and/or coordination of care with other providers or agencies are provided consistent with the nature of the problem(s) and the patient's and/or family's needs.

Usually, the problem(s) requiring admission are of low severity. Physicians typically spend 30 minutes at the bedside and on the patient's hospital floor or unit.

99222 **Initial hospital care,** per day, for the evaluation and management of a patient, which requires these three key components:

- **A comprehensive history;**

- **A comprehensive examination; and**

- **Medical decision making of moderate complexity.**

Counseling and/or coordination of care with other providers or agencies are provided consistent with the nature of the problem(s) and the patient's and/or family's needs.

Usually, the problem(s) requiring admission are of moderate severity. Physicians typically spend 50 minutes at the bedside and on the patient's hospital floor or unit.

99223 **Initial hospital care,** per day, for the evaluation and management of a patient, which requires these three key components:

- **A comprehensive history;**

- **A comprehensive examination; and**

- **Medical decision making of high complexity.**

Counseling and/or coordination of care with other providers or agencies are provided consistent with the nature of the problem(s) and the patient's and/or family's needs.

Usually, the problem(s) requiring admission are of high severity. Physicians typically spend 70 minutes at the bedside and on the patient's hospital floor or unit.

Subsequent Hospital Care

All levels of subsequent hospital care include reviewing the medical record and reviewing the results of diagnostic studies and changes in the patient's status (ie, changes in history, physical condition and response to management) since the last assessment by the physician.

99231 **Subsequent hospital care,** per day, for the evaluation and management of a patient, which requires at least two of these three key components:

- **A problem focused interval history;**

- **A problem focused examination;**

- **Medical decision making that is straightforward or of low complexity.**

Counseling and/or coordination of care with other providers or agencies are provided consistent with the nature of the problem(s) and the patient's and/or family's needs.

Usually, the patient is stable, recovering or improving. Physicians typically spend 15 minutes at the bedside and on the patient's hospital floor or unit.

99232 **Subsequent hospital care,** per day, for the evaluation and management of a patient, which requires at least two of these three key components:

- **An expanded problem focused interval history;**

- **An expanded problem focused examination;**

- **Medical decision making of moderate complexity.**

Counseling and/or coordination of care with other providers or agencies are provided consistent with the nature of the problem(s) and the patient's and/or family's needs.

Usually, the patient is responding inadequately to therapy or has developed a minor complication. Physicians typically spend 25 minutes at the bedside and on the patient's hospital floor or unit.

99233　**Subsequent hospital care,** per day, for the evaluation and management of a patient, which requires at least two of these three key components:

- **A detailed interval history;**

- **A detailed examination;**

- **Medical decision making of high complexity.**

Counseling and/or coordination of care with other providers or agencies are provided consistent with the nature of the problem(s) and the patient's and/or family's needs.

Usually, the patient is unstable or has developed a significant complication or a significant new problem. Physicians typically spend 35 minutes at the bedside and on the patient's hospital floor or unit.

Observation or Inpatient Care Services (Including Admission and Discharge Services)

The following codes are used to report observation or inpatient hospital care services provided to patients admitted and discharged on the same date of service. When a patient is admitted to the hospital from observation status on the same date, the physician should report only the initial hospital care code. The initial hospital care code reported by the admitting physician should include the services related to the observation status services he/she provided on the same date of inpatient admission.

When "observation status" is initiated in the course of an encounter in another site of service (eg, hospital emergency department, physician's office, nursing facility) all evaluation and management services provided by the supervising physician in conjunction with initiating "observation status" are considered part of the initial observation care when performed on the same date. The observation care level of service should include the services related to initiating "observation status" provided in the other sites of service as well as in the observation setting when provided by the same physician.

For patients admitted to observation or inpatient care and discharged on a different date, see codes 99218-99220 and 99217, or 99221-99223 and 99238, 99239.

99234　**Observation or inpatient hospital care,** for the evaluation and management of a patient including admission and discharge on the same date which requires these three key components:

- **A detailed or comprehensive history;**

- **A detailed or comprehensive examination; and**

- **Medical decision making that is straightforward or of low complexity.**

Counseling and/or coordination of care with other providers or agencies are provided consistent with the nature of the problem(s) and the patient's and/or family's needs.

Usually the presenting problem(s) requiring admission are of low severity.

99235　**Observation or inpatient hospital care,** for the evaluation and management of a patient including admission and discharge on the same date which requires these three key components:

- **A comprehensive history;**

- **A comprehensive examination; and**

- **Medical decision making of moderate complexity.**

Counseling and/or coordination of care with other providers or agencies are provided consistent with the nature of the problem(s) and the patient's and/or family's needs.

Usually the presenting problem(s) requiring admission are of moderate severity.

99236　**Observation or inpatient hospital care,** for the evaluation and management of a patient including admission and discharge on the same date which requires these three key components:

- **A comprehensive history;**

- **A comprehensive examination; and**

- **Medical decision making of high complexity.**

Counseling and/or coordination of care with other providers or agencies are provided consistent with the nature of the problem(s) and the patient's and/or family's needs.

Usually the presenting problem(s) requiring admission are of high severity.

Evaluation and Management

Hospital Discharge Services

The hospital discharge day management codes are to be used to report the total duration of time spent by a physician for final hospital discharge of a patient. The codes include, as appropriate, final examination of the patient, discussion of the hospital stay, even if the time spent by the physician on that date is not continuous, instructions for continuing care to all relevant caregivers, and preparation of discharge records, prescriptions and referral forms. For a patient admitted and discharged from observation or inpatient status on the same date, the services should be reported with codes 99234-99236 as appropriate.

99238 **Hospital discharge day management;** 30 minutes or less

99239 more than 30 minutes

> (These codes are to be utilized by the physician to report all services provided to a patient on the date of discharge, if other than the initial date of inpatient status. To report services to a patient who is admitted as an inpatient, and discharged on the same date, see codes 99234-99236 for observation or inpatient hospital care including the admission and discharge of the patient on the same date. To report concurrent care services provided by a physician(s) other than the attending physician, use subsequent hospital care codes (99231-99233) on the day of discharge.)

> (For Observation Care Discharge, use 99217)

> (For observation or inpatient hospital care including the admission and discharge of the patient on the same date, see 99234-99236)

> (For Nursing Facility Care Discharge, see 99315, 99316)

> (For discharge services provided to newborns admitted and discharged on the same date, use 99435)

Consultations

A consultation is a type of service provided by a physician whose opinion or advice regarding evaluation and/or management of a specific problem is requested by another physician or other appropriate source.

A physician consultant may initiate diagnostic and/or therapeutic services at the same or subsequent visit.

The written or verbal request for a consult may be made by a physician or other appropriate source and documented in the patient's medical record. The consultant's opinion and any services that were ordered or performed must also be documented in the patient's medical record and communicated by written report to the requesting physician or other appropriate source.

▶A "consultation" initiated by a patient and/or family, and not requested by a physician or other appropriate source (eg, physician assistant, nurse practitioner, doctor of chiropractic, physical therapist, occupational therapist, speech-language pathologist, psychologist, social worker, lawyer, or insurance company), is not reported using the consultation codes but may be reported using the office visit, home service, or domiciliary/rest home care codes.◀

If a consultation is mandated, eg, by a third-party payer, modifier 32 should also be reported.

Any specifically identifiable procedure (ie, identified with a specific CPT code) performed on or subsequent to the date of the initial consultation should be reported separately.

▶If subsequent to the completion of a consultation the consultant assumes responsibility for management of a portion or all of the patient's condition(s), the appropriate **Evaluation and Management** services code for the site of service should be reported. In the hospital or nursing facility setting, the consulting physician should use the appropriate inpatient consultation code for the initial encounter and then subsequent hospital or nursing facility care codes. In the office setting, the physician should use the appropriate office or other outpatient consultation codes and then the established patient office or other outpatient services codes.◀

For definitions of key components and commonly used terms, please see **Evaluation and Management Services Guidelines.**

Office or Other Outpatient Consultations

New or Established Patient

▶The following codes are used to report consultations provided in the physician's office or in an outpatient or other ambulatory facility, including hospital observation services, home services, domiciliary, rest home, or emergency department (see the preceding consultation definition above). Follow-up visits in the consultant's office or other outpatient facility that are initiated by the physician consultant or patient are reported using the appropriate codes for established patients, office visits (99211-99215), domiciliary, rest home (99334-99337), or home (99347-99350). If an additional request for an opinion or advice regarding the same or a new problem is received from another physician or other appropriate source and documented in the medical record, the office consultation codes may be used again.◀

99241 **Office consultation** for a new or established patient, which requires these three key components:

- **A problem focused history;**
- **A problem focused examination; and**
- **Straightforward medical decision making.**

Counseling and/or coordination of care with other providers or agencies are provided consistent with the nature of the problem(s) and the patient's and/or family's needs.

Usually, the presenting problem(s) are self limited or minor. Physicians typically spend 15 minutes face-to-face with the patient and/or family.

99242 **Office consultation** for a new or established patient, which requires these three key components:

- **An expanded problem focused history;**
- **An expanded problem focused examination; and**
- **Straightforward medical decision making.**

Counseling and/or coordination of care with other providers or agencies are provided consistent with the nature of the problem(s) and the patient's and/or family's needs.

Usually, the presenting problem(s) are of low severity. Physicians typically spend 30 minutes face-to-face with the patient and/or family.

99243 **Office consultation** for a new or established patient, which requires these three key components:

- **A detailed history;**
- **A detailed examination; and**
- **Medical decision making of low complexity.**

Counseling and/or coordination of care with other providers or agencies are provided consistent with the nature of the problem(s) and the patient's and/or family's needs.

Usually, the presenting problem(s) are of moderate severity. Physicians typically spend 40 minutes face-to-face with the patient and/or family.

99244 **Office consultation** for a new or established patient, which requires these three key components:

- **A comprehensive history;**
- **A comprehensive examination; and**
- **Medical decision making of moderate complexity.**

Counseling and/or coordination of care with other providers or agencies are provided consistent with the nature of the problem(s) and the patient's and/or family's needs.

Usually, the presenting problem(s) are of moderate to high severity. Physicians typically spend 60 minutes face-to-face with the patient and/or family.

99245 **Office consultation** for a new or established patient, which requires these three key components:

- **A comprehensive history;**
- **A comprehensive examination; and**
- **Medical decision making of high complexity.**

Counseling and/or coordination of care with other providers or agencies are provided consistent with the nature of the problem(s) and the patient's and/or family's needs.

Usually, the presenting problem(s) are of moderate to high severity. Physicians typically spend 80 minutes face-to-face with the patient and/or family.

▶Inpatient Consultations◀

New or Established Patient

▶The following codes are used to report physician consultations provided to hospital inpatients, residents of nursing facilities, or patients in a partial hospital setting. Only one consultation should be reported by a consultant per admission. Subsequent services during the same admission are reported using Subsequent Hospital Care codes (99231-99233) or Subsequent Nursing Facility Care codes (99307-99310), including services to complete the initial consultation, monitor progress, revise recommendations, or address a new problem.◀

▲ **99251** **Inpatient consultation** for a new or established patient, which requires these three key components:

- **A problem focused history;**
- **A problem focused examination; and**
- **Straightforward medical decision making.**

Counseling and/or coordination of care with other providers or agencies are provided consistent with the nature of the problem(s) and the patient's and/or family's needs.

Usually, the presenting problem(s) are self limited or minor. Physicians typically spend 20 minutes at the bedside and on the patient's hospital floor or unit.

▲ **99252** **Inpatient consultation** for a new or established patient, which requires these three key components:

- **An expanded problem focused history;**
- **An expanded problem focused examination; and**
- **Straightforward medical decision making.**

Counseling and/or coordination of care with other providers or agencies are provided consistent with the nature of the problem(s) and the patient's and/or family's needs.

Usually, the presenting problem(s) are of low severity. Physicians typically spend 40 minutes at the bedside and on the patient's hospital floor or unit.

Evaluation and Management

▲ **99253** **Inpatient consultation** for a new or established patient, which requires these three key components:

- **A detailed history;**
- **A detailed examination; and**
- **Medical decision making of low complexity.**

Counseling and/or coordination of care with other providers or agencies are provided consistent with the nature of the problem(s) and the patient's and/or family's needs.

Usually, the presenting problem(s) are of moderate severity. Physicians typically spend 55 minutes at the bedside and on the patient's hospital floor or unit.

▲ **99254** **Inpatient consultation** for a new or established patient, which requires these three key components:

- **A comprehensive history;**
- **A comprehensive examination; and**
- **Medical decision making of moderate complexity.**

Counseling and/or coordination of care with other providers or agencies are provided consistent with the nature of the problem(s) and the patient's and/or family's needs.

Usually, the presenting problem(s) are of moderate to high severity. Physicians typically spend 80 minutes at the bedside and on the patient's hospital floor or unit.

▲ **99255** **Inpatient consultation** for a new or established patient, which requires these three key components:

- **A comprehensive history;**
- **A comprehensive examination; and**
- **Medical decision making of high complexity.**

Counseling and/or coordination of care with other providers or agencies are provided consistent with the nature of the problem(s) and the patient's and/or family's needs.

Usually, the presenting problem(s) are of moderate to high severity. Physicians typically spend 110 minutes at the bedside and on the patient's hospital floor or unit.

Emergency Department Services

New or Established Patient

The following codes are used to report evaluation and management services provided in the emergency department. No distinction is made between new and established patients in the emergency department.

An emergency department is defined as an organized hospital-based facility for the provision of unscheduled episodic services to patients who present for immediate medical attention. The facility must be available 24 hours a day.

For critical care services provided in the emergency department, see Critical Care notes and 99291, 99292.

For evaluation and management services provided to a patient in an observation area of a hospital, see 99217-99220.

For observation or inpatient care services (including admission and discharge services), see 99234-99236.

99281 **Emergency department visit** for the evaluation and management of a patient, which requires these three key components:

- **A problem focused history;**
- **A problem focused examination; and**
- **Straightforward medical decision making.**

Counseling and/or coordination of care with other providers or agencies are provided consistent with the nature of the problem(s) and the patient's and/or family's needs.

Usually, the presenting problem(s) are self limited or minor.

99282 **Emergency department visit** for the evaluation and management of a patient, which requires these three key components:

- **An expanded problem focused history;**
- **An expanded problem focused examination; and**
- **Medical decision making of low complexity.**

Counseling and/or coordination of care with other providers or agencies are provided consistent with the nature of the problem(s) and the patient's and/or family's needs.

Usually, the presenting problem(s) are of low to moderate severity.

99283 **Emergency department visit** for the evaluation and management of a patient, which requires these three key components:

- **An expanded problem focused history;**
- **An expanded problem focused examination; and**
- **Medical decision making of moderate complexity.**

Counseling and/or coordination of care with other providers or agencies are provided consistent with the nature of the problem(s) and the patient's and/or family's needs.

Usually, the presenting problem(s) are of moderate severity.

99284 **Emergency department visit** for the evaluation and management of a patient, which requires these three key components:

- **A detailed history;**
- **A detailed examination; and**
- **Medical decision making of moderate complexity.**

Counseling and/or coordination of care with other providers or agencies are provided consistent with the nature of the problem(s) and the patient's and/or family's needs.

Usually, the presenting problem(s) are of high severity, and require urgent evaluation by the physician but do not pose an immediate significant threat to life or physiologic function.

99285 **Emergency department visit** for the evaluation and management of a patient, which requires these three key components within the constraints imposed by the urgency of the patient's clinical condition and/or mental status:

- **A comprehensive history;**
- **A comprehensive examination; and**
- **Medical decision making of high complexity.**

Counseling and/or coordination of care with other providers or agencies are provided consistent with the nature of the problem(s) and the patient's and/or family's needs.

Usually, the presenting problem(s) are of high severity and pose an immediate significant threat to life or physiologic function.

Other Emergency Services

In physician directed emergency care, advanced life support, the physician is located in a hospital emergency or critical care department, and is in two-way voice communication with ambulance or rescue personnel outside the hospital. The physician directs the performance of necessary medical procedures, including but not limited to: telemetry of cardiac rhythm; cardiac and/or pulmonary resuscitation; endotracheal or esophageal obturator airway intubation; administration of intravenous fluids and/or administration of intramuscular, intratracheal or subcutaneous drugs; and/or electrical conversion of arrhythmia.

99288 **Physician direction of** emergency medical systems (EMS) emergency care, advanced life support

Pediatric Critical Care Patient Transport

The following codes 99289 and 99290 are used to report the physical attendance and direct face-to-face care by a physician during the interfacility transport of a critically ill or critically injured pediatric patient. For the purpose of reporting codes 99289 and 99290, face-to-face care begins when the physician assumes primary responsibility of the pediatric patient at the referring hospital/facility, and ends when the receiving hospital/facility accepts responsibility for the pediatric patient's care. Only the time the physician spends in direct face-to-face contact with the patient during the transport should be reported. Pediatric patient transport services involving less than 30 minutes of face-to-face physician care should not be reported using codes 99289, 99290. Procedure(s) or service(s) performed by other members of the transporting team may not be reported by the supervising physician.

▶The following services are included when performed during the pediatric patient transport by the physician providing critical care and may not be reported separately: routine monitoring evaluations (eg, heart rate, respiratory rate, blood pressure, and pulse oximetry), the interpretation of cardiac output measurements (93561, 93562), chest x-rays (71010, 71015, 71020), pulse oximetry (94760, 94761, 94762), blood gases and information data stored in computers (eg, ECGs, blood pressures, hematologic data) (99090), gastric intubation (43752, 91105), temporary transcutaneous pacing (92953), ventilatory management (94002-94004, 94660, 94662) and vascular access procedures (36000, 36400, 36405, 36406, 36410, 36415, 36540, 36600). Any services performed which are not listed above should be reported separately.◀

Critical care is the direct delivery by a physician(s) of medical care for a critically ill or critically injured patient. A critical illness or injury acutely impairs one or more vital organ systems such that there is a high probability of imminent or life threatening deterioration in the patient's condition. Critical care involves high complexity decision making to assess, manipulate, and support vital system function(s) to treat single or multiple vital organ system failure and/or to prevent further life threatening deterioration of the patient's condition. Examples of vital organ system failure include, but are not limited to: central nervous system failure, circulatory failure, shock, renal, hepatic, metabolic, and/or respiratory failure.

Providing medical care to a critically ill, injured, or postoperative patient qualifies as a critical care service only if both the illness or injury and the treatment being provided meet the above requirements.

Evaluation and Management

The direction of emergency care to transporting staff by a physician located in a hospital or other facility by two-way communication is not considered direct face-to-face care and should not be reported with codes 99289, 99290. Physician directed emergency care through outside voice communication to transporting staff personnel is reported with code 99288.

The emergency department services codes (99281-99285), initial hospital care codes (99221-99223), hourly critical care codes (99291, 99292), or initial date neonatal intensive care code (99295) are only reported after the patient has been admitted to the emergency department, the inpatient floor or the critical care unit of the receiving facility.

Code 99289 is used to report the first 30-74 minutes of direct face-to-face time with the transport pediatric patient and should be reported only once on a given date. Code 99290 is used to report each additional 30 minutes provided on a given date. Face-to-face services less than 30 minutes should not be reported with these codes.

99289 Critical care services delivered by a physician, face-to-face, during an interfacility transport of critically ill or critically injured pediatric patient, 24 months of age or less; first 30-74 minutes of hands on care during transport

+ 99290 each additional 30 minutes (List separately in addition to code for primary service)

(Use 99290 in conjunction with 99289)

(Critical care of less than 30 minutes total duration should be reported with the appropriate E/M code)

Critical Care Services

Critical care is the direct delivery by a physician(s) of medical care for a critically ill or critically injured patient. A critical illness or injury acutely impairs one or more vital organ systems such that there is a high probability of imminent or life threatening deterioration in the patient's condition. Critical care involves high complexity decision making to assess, manipulate, and support vital system function(s) to treat single or multiple vital organ system failure and/or to prevent further life threatening deterioration of the patient's condition. Examples of vital organ system failure include, but are not limited to: central nervous system failure, circulatory failure, shock, renal, hepatic, metabolic, and/or respiratory failure. Although critical care typically requires interpretation of multiple physiologic parameters and/or application of advanced technology(s), critical care may be provided in life threatening situations when these elements are not present. Critical care may be provided on multiple days, even if no changes are made in the treatment rendered to the patient, provided that the patient's condition continues to require the level of physician attention described above.

Providing medical care to a critically ill, injured, or post-operative patient qualifies as a critical care service only if both the illness or injury and the treatment being provided meet the above requirements. Critical care is usually, but not always, given in a critical care area, such as the coronary care unit, intensive care unit, pediatric intensive care unit, respiratory care unit, or the emergency care facility.

Inpatient critical care services provided to infants 29 days through 24 months of age are reported with pediatric critical care codes 99293 and 99294. The pediatric critical care codes are reported as long as the infant/young child qualifies for critical care services during the hospital stay through 24 months of age. Inpatient critical care services provided to neonates (28 days of age or less) are reported with the neonatal critical care codes 99295 and 99296. The neonatal critical care codes are reported as long as the neonate qualifies for critical care services during the hospital stay through the 28th postnatal day. The reporting of the pediatric and neonatal critical care services is not based on time or the type of unit (eg, pediatric or neonatal critical care unit) and it is not dependent upon the type of provider delivering the care. To report critical care services provided in the outpatient setting (eg, emergency department or office), for neonates and pediatric patients up through 24 months of age, see the hourly Critical Care codes 99291, 99292. If the same physician provides critical care services for a neonatal or pediatric patient in both the outpatient and inpatient settings on the same day, report only the appropriate Neonatal or Pediatric Critical Care code (99293-99296) for all critical care services provided on that day. For additional instructions on reporting these services, see the Neonatal and Pediatric Critical Care section and codes 99293-99296.

Services for a patient who is not critically ill but happens to be in a critical care unit are reported using other appropriate E/M codes.

Critical care and other E/M services may be provided to the same patient on the same date by the same physician.

▶The following services are included in reporting critical care when performed during the critical period by the physician(s) providing critical care: the interpretation of cardiac output measurements (93561, 93562), chest x-rays (71010, 71015, 71020), pulse oximetry (94760, 94761, 94762), blood gases, and information data stored in computers (eg, ECGs, blood pressures, hematologic data (99090)); gastric intubation (43752, 91105); temporary transcutaneous pacing (92953); ventilatory management (94002-94004, 94660, 94662); and vascular access procedures (36000, 36410, 36415, 36540, 36600). Any services performed which are not listed above should be reported separately.◀

Codes 99291, 99292 should be reported for the physician's attendance during the transport of critically ill or critically injured patients over 24 months of age to or from a facility or hospital. For physician transport services of critically ill or critically injured pediatric patients 24 months of age or less see 99289, 99290.

The critical care codes 99291 and 99292 are used to report the total duration of time spent by a physician providing critical care services to a critically ill or critically injured patient, even if the time spent by the physician on that date is not continuous. For any given period of time spent providing critical care services, the physician must devote his or her full attention to the patient and, therefore, cannot provide services to any other patient during the same period of time.

Time spent with the individual patient should be recorded in the patient's record. The time that can be reported as critical care is the time spent engaged in work directly related to the individual patient's care whether that time was spent at the immediate bedside or elsewhere on the floor or unit. For example, time spent on the unit or at the nursing station on the floor reviewing test results or imaging studies, discussing the critically ill patient's care with other medical staff or documenting critical care services in the medical record would be reported as critical care, even though it does not occur at the bedside. Also, when the patient is unable or clinically incompetent to participate in discussions, time spent on the floor or unit with family members or surrogate decision makers obtaining a medical history, reviewing the patient's condition or prognosis, or discussing treatment or limitation(s) of treatment may be reported as critical care, provided that the conversation bears directly on the management of the patient.

Time spent in activities that occur outside of the unit or off the floor (eg, telephone calls, whether taken at home, in the office, or elsewhere in the hospital) may not be reported as critical care since the physician is not immediately available to the patient. Time spent in activities that do not directly contribute to the treatment of the patient may not be reported as critical care, even if they are performed in the critical care unit (eg, participation in administrative meetings or telephone calls to discuss other patients). Time spent performing separately reportable procedures or services should not be included in the time reported as critical care time.

Code 99291 is used to report the first 30-74 minutes of critical care on a given date. It should be used only once per date even if the time spent by the physician is not continuous on that date. Critical care of less than 30 minutes total duration on a given date should be reported with the appropriate E/M code.

Code 99292 is used to report additional block(s) of time, of up to 30 minutes each beyond the first 74 minutes. (See table below.)

The following examples illustrate the correct reporting of critical care services:

Total Duration of Critical Care	Codes
less than 30 minutes (less than 30 minutes)	appropriate E/M codes
30-74 minutes (30 minutes - 1 hr. 14 min.)	99291 X 1
75-104 minutes (1 hr. 15 min. - 1 hr. 44 min.)	99291 X 1 AND 99292 X 1
105-134 minutes (1 hr. 45 min. - 2 hr. 14 min.)	99291 X 1 AND 99292 X 2
135 - 164 minutes (2 hr. 15 min. - 2 hr. 44 min.)	99291 X 1 AND 99292 X 3
165 - 194 minutes (2 hr. 45 min. - 3 hr. 14 min.)	99291 X 1 AND 99292 X 4
194 minutes or longer (3 hr. 14 min. - etc.)	99291 and 99292 as appropriate (see illustrated reporting examples above)

99291 **Critical care, evaluation and management** of the critically ill or critically injured patient; first 30-74 minutes

+ 99292 each additional 30 minutes (List separately in addition to code for primary service)

(Use 99292 in conjunction with 99291)

Inpatient Neonatal and Pediatric Critical Care Services

The following codes (99293-99296) are used to report services provided by a physician directing the inpatient care of a critically ill neonate/infant. The same definitions for critical care services apply for the adult, child, and neonate.

The initial day neonatal critical care code (99295) can be used in addition to codes 99360, 99436 or 99440 as appropriate, when the physician is present for the delivery (99360 or 99436) and newborn resuscitation (99440) is required. Other procedures performed as a necessary part of the resuscitation (eg, endotracheal intubation (31500)) are also reported separately when performed as part of the pre-admission delivery room care. In order to report these procedures separately, they must be performed as a necessary component of the resuscitation and not simply as a convenience before admission to the neonatal intensive care unit.

Codes 99295, 99296 are used to report services provided by a physician directing the inpatient care of a critically ill neonate through the first 28 days of life. They represent care starting with the date of admission (99295) and subsequent day(s) (99296) and may be reported only once per day, per patient.

Codes 99293, 99294 are used to report services provided by a physician directing the inpatient care of a critically ill infant or young child from 29 days of postnatal age through 24 months of age. They represent care starting with the date of admission (99293) and subsequent day(s) (99294) and may be reported by a single physician only once per day, per patient in a given setting. The critically ill or critically injured child older than 24 months of age would be reported with hourly critical care service codes (99291, 99292).

When a neonate or infant is not critically ill, but requires intensive observation, frequent interventions and other intensive care services, the Continuing Intensive Care Services codes (99298, 99299, 99300) should be used to report services for those neonates/infants with present body weight of 5000 grams or less. When the present body weight of those neonates/infants exceeds 5000 grams, the Subsequent Hospital Care Services codes (99231-99233) should be used.

To report critical care services provided in the outpatient setting (eg, emergency department or office) for neonates and pediatric patients up through 24 months of age, see the hourly Critical Care codes 99291, 99292. If the same physician provides critical care services for a neonatal or pediatric patient in both the outpatient and inpatient settings on the same day, report only the appropriate Neonatal or Pediatric Critical Care code (99293-99296) for all critical care services provided on that day.

Care rendered under 99293-99296 includes management, monitoring, and treatment of the patient including respiratory, pharmacologic control of the circulatory system, enteral and parenteral nutrition, metabolic and hematologic maintenance, parent/family counseling, case management services, and personal direct supervision of the health care team in the performance of cognitive and procedural activities.

▶The pediatric and neonatal critical care codes include those procedures listed above for the hourly critical care codes (99291, 99292). In addition, the following procedures are also included in the bundled (global) pediatric and neonatal critical care service codes (99293-99296): umbilical venous (36510) and umbilical arterial catheters (36660), other arterial catheters (36140, 36620), central (36555) or peripheral vessel catheterization (36000), vascular access procedures (36400, 36405, 36406), vascular punctures (36420, 36600), oral or nasogastric tube placement (43752), endotracheal intubation (31500), lumbar puncture (62270), suprapubic bladder aspiration (51000), bladder catheterization (51701, 51702), ventilatory management

(94002-94004), continuous positive airway pressure (CPAP) (94660), surfactant administration (94610), intravascular fluid administration (90760-90761), transfusion of blood components (36430, 36440), invasive or non-invasive electronic monitoring of vital signs, bedside pulmonary function testing (94375), and/or monitoring or interpretation of blood gases or oxygen saturation (94760-94762). Any services performed which are not listed above should be reported separately.◀

For additional instructions, see descriptions listed for 99293-99296

Inpatient Pediatric Critical Care

99293 **Initial inpatient pediatric critical care,** per day, for the evaluation and management of a critically ill infant or young child, 29 days through 24 months of age

99294 **Subsequent inpatient pediatric critical care,** per day, for the evaluation and management of a critically ill infant or young child, 29 days through 24 months of age

Inpatient Neonatal Critical Care

99295 **Initial inpatient neonatal critical care,** per day, for the evaluation and management of a critically ill neonate, 28 days of age or less

This code is reserved for the date of admission for neonates who are critically ill. Critically ill neonates require cardiac and/or respiratory support (including ventilator or nasal CPAP when indicated), continuous or frequent vital sign monitoring, laboratory and blood gas interpretations, follow-up physician reevaluations, and constant observation by the health care team under direct physician supervision. Immediate preoperative evaluation and stabilization of neonates with life threatening surgical or cardiac conditions are included under this code. Neonates with life threatening surgical or cardiac conditions are included under this code.

Care for neonates who require an intensive care setting but who are not critically ill is reported using the initial hospital care codes (99221-99223).

99296 **Subsequent inpatient neonatal critical care,** per day, for the evaluation and management of a critically ill neonate, 28 days of age or less

A critically ill neonate will require cardiac and/or respiratory support (including ventilator or nasal CPAP when indicated), continuous or frequent vital sign monitoring, laboratory and blood gas interpretations, follow-up physician re-evaluations throughout a 24-hour period, and constant observation by the health care team under direct physician supervision.

(Subsequent care for neonates who require an intensive setting but who are not critically ill is reported using either the intensive low birth weight services codes (99298, 99299) or the subsequent hospital care codes (99231-99233))

Continuing Intensive Care Services

Codes 99298, 99299, 99300 are used to report services subsequent to the day of admission provided by a physician directing the continuing intensive care of the low birth weight (LBW, 1500-2500 grams present body weight) infant, very low birth weight (VLBW, less than 1500 grams present body weight) infant, or normal weight (2501-5000 grams present body weight) newborn who do not meet the definition of critically ill but continue to require intensive observation, frequent interventions, and other intensive services. Codes 99298, 99299, 99300 represent subsequent day(s) of care and may be reported only once per calendar day, per patient and are global codes with the same services bundled as outlined under codes 99293-99296.

For additional instructions, see descriptions listed for 99298, 99299, 99300.

99298 **Subsequent intensive care,** per day, for the evaluation and management of the recovering very low birth weight infant (present body weight less than 1500 g)

Infants with present body weight less than 1500 grams who are not critically ill but continue to require intensive cardiac and respiratory monitoring, continuous and/or frequent vital sign monitoring, heat maintenance, enteral and/or parenteral nutritional adjustments, laboratory and oxygen monitoring and constant observation by the health care team under direct physician supervision.

99299 **Subsequent intensive care,** per day, for the evaluation and management of the recovering low birth weight infant (present body weight of 1500-2500 g)

Infants with present body weight of 1500-2500 grams who are not critically ill but continue to require intensive cardiac and respiratory monitoring, continuous and/or frequent vital sign monitoring, heat maintenance, enteral and/or parenteral nutritional adjustments, laboratory and oxygen monitoring, and constant observation by the health care team under direct physician supervision.

99300 Subsequent intensive care, per day, for the evaluation and management of the recovering infant (present body weight of 2501-5000 g)

Infants with present body weight of 2501-5000 grams who are not critically ill but continue to require intensive cardiac and respiratory monitoring, continuous and/or frequent vital sign monitoring, heat maintenance, enteral and/or parenteral nutritional adjustments, laboratory and oxygen monitoring, and constant observation by the health care team under direct physician supervision.

Nursing Facility Services

The following codes are used to report evaluation and management services to patients in Nursing Facilities (formerly called Skilled Nursing Facilities (SNFs), Intermediate Care Facilities (ICFs), or Long-Term Care Facilities (LTCFs)).

These codes should also be used to report evaluation and management services provided to a patient in a psychiatric residential treatment center (a facility or a distinct part of a facility for psychiatric care, which provides a 24-hour therapeutically planned and professionally staffed group living and learning environment). If procedures such as medical psychotherapy are provided in addition to evaluation and management services, these should be reported in addition to the evaluation and management services provided.

Nursing facilities that provide convalescent, rehabilitative, or long term care are required to conduct comprehensive, accurate, standardized, and reproducible assessments of each resident's functional capacity using a Resident Assessment Instrument (RAI). All RAIs include the Minimum Data Set (MDS), Resident Assessment Protocols (RAPs) and utilization guidelines. The MDS is the primary screening and assessment tool; the RAPs trigger the identification of potential problems and provide guidelines for follow-up assessments.

Physicians have a central role in assuring that all residents receive thorough assessments and that medical plans of care are instituted or revised to enhance or maintain the residents' physical and psychosocial functioning. This role includes providing input in the development of the MDS and a multi-disciplinary plan of care, as required by regulations pertaining to the care of nursing facility residents.

Two major subcategories of nursing facility services are recognized: Initial Nursing Facility Care and Subsequent Nursing Facility Care. Both subcategories apply to new or established patients.

For definitions of key components and commonly used terms, please see **Evaluation and Management Services Guidelines.**

(For care plan oversight services provided to nursing facility residents, see 99379-99380)

Initial Nursing Facility Care

New or Established Patient

When the patient is admitted to the nursing facility in the course of an encounter in another site of service (eg, hospital emergency department, physician's office), all evaluation and management services provided by that physician in conjunction with that admission are considered part of the initial nursing facility care when

Evaluation and Management

performed on the same date as the admission or readmission. The nursing facility care level of service reported by the admitting physician should include the services related to the admission he/she provided in the other sites of service as well as in the nursing facility setting.

Hospital discharge or observation discharge services performed on the same date of nursing facility admission or readmission may be reported separately. For a patient discharged from inpatient status on the same date of nursing facility admission or readmission, the hospital discharge services should be reported with codes 99238, 99239 as appropriate. For a patient discharged from observation status on the same date of nursing facility admission or readmission, the observation care discharge services should be reported with code 99217. For a patient admitted and discharged from observation or inpatient status on the same date, see codes 99234-99236.

(For nursing facility care discharge, see 99315, 99316)

Typical unit times have not been established for 99304-99306.

(99301-99303 have been deleted)

99304 Initial nursing facility care, per day, for the evaluation and management of a patient which requires these three key components:

- **A detailed or comprehensive history;**

- **A detailed or comprehensive examination; and**

- **Medical decision making that is straightforward or of low complexity.**

Counseling and/or coordination of care with other providers or agencies are provided consistent with the nature of the problem(s) and the patient's and/or family's needs.

Usually, the problem(s) requiring admission are of low severity.

99305 Initial nursing facility care, per day, for the evaluation and management of a patient which requires these three key components:

- **A comprehensive history;**

- **A comprehensive examination; and**

- **Medical decision making of moderate complexity.**

Counseling and/or coordination of care with other providers or agencies are provided consistent with the nature of the problem(s) and the patient's and/or family's needs.

Usually, the problem(s) requiring admission are of moderate severity.

99306 Initial nursing facility care, per day, for the evaluation and management of a patient, which requires these three key components:

- **A comprehensive history;**

- **A comprehensive examination; and**

- **Medical decision making of high complexity.**

Counseling and/or coordination of care with other providers or agencies are provided consistent with the nature of the problem(s) and the patient's and/or family's needs.

Usually, the problem(s) requiring admission are of high severity.

Subsequent Nursing Facility Care

All levels of subsequent nursing facility care include reviewing the medical record and reviewing the results of diagnostic studies and changes in the patient's status (ie, changes in history, physical condition, and response to management) since the last assessment by the physician.

99307 Subsequent nursing facility care, per day, for the evaluation and management of a patient, which requires at least two of these three key components:

- **A problem focused interval history;**

- **A problem focused examination;**

- **Straightforward medical decision making.**

Counseling and/or coordination of care with other providers or agencies are provided consistent with the nature of the problem(s) and the patient's and/or family's needs.

Usually, the patient is stable, recovering, or improving.

99308 Subsequent nursing facility care, per day, for the evaluation and management of a patient, which requires at least two of these three key components:

- **An expanded problem focused interval history;**

- **An expanded problem focused examination;**

- **Medical decision making of low complexity.**

Counseling and/or coordination of care with other providers or agencies are provided consistent with the nature of the problem(s) and the patient's and/or family's needs.

Usually, the patient is responding inadequately to therapy or has developed a minor complication.

99309 Subsequent nursing facility care, per day, for the evaluation and management of a patient, which requires at least two of these three key components:

- **A detailed interval history;**

- **A detailed examination;**

- **Medical decision making of moderate complexity.**

Counseling and/or coordination of care with other providers or agencies are provided consistent with the nature of the problem(s) and the patient's and/or family's needs.

Usually, the patient has developed a significant complication or a significant new problem.

99310 Subsequent nursing facility care, per day, for the evaluation and management of a patient, which requires at least two of these three key components:

- **A comprehensive interval history;**
- **A comprehensive examination;**
- **Medical decision making of high complexity.**

Counseling and/or coordination of care with other providers or agencies are provided consistent with the nature of the problem(s) and the patient's and/or family's needs.

The patient may be unstable or may have developed a significant new problem requiring immediate physician attention.

(99311-99313 have been deleted)

Nursing Facility Discharge Services

The nursing facility discharge day management codes are to be used to report the total duration of time spent by a physician for the final nursing facility discharge of a patient. The codes include, as appropriate, final examination of the patient, discussion of the nursing facility stay, even if the time spent by the physician on that date is not continuous. Instructions are given for continuing care to all relevant caregivers, and preparation of discharge records, prescriptions and referral forms.

99315 Nursing facility discharge day management; 30 minutes or less

99316 more than 30 minutes

Other Nursing Facility Services

99318 Evaluation and management of a patient involving an annual nursing facility assessment, which requires these three key components:

- **A detailed interval history;**
- **A comprehensive examination; and**
- **Medical decision making that is of low to moderate complexity.**

Counseling and/or coordination of care with other providers or agencies are provided consistent with the nature of the problem(s) and the patient's and/or family's needs.

Usually, the patient is stable, recovering, or improving.

(Do not report 99318 on the same date of service as nursing facility services codes 99304-99316)

Domiciliary, Rest Home (eg, Boarding Home), or Custodial Care Services

The following codes are used to report evaluation and management services in a facility which provides room, board and other personal assistance services, generally on a long-term basis. They also are used to report evaluation and management services in an assisted living facility.

The facility's services do not include a medical component.

For definitions of key components and commonly used terms, please see **Evaluation and Management Services Guidelines.**

(For care plan oversight services provided to a patient in a domiciliary facility under the care of a home health agency, see 99374-99375)

(For care plan oversight services provided to a patient in a domiciliary facility under the individual supervision of a physician, see 99339, 99340)

New Patient

(99321-99323 have been deleted)

99324 Domiciliary or rest home visit for the evaluation and management of a new patient, which requires these three key components:

- **A problem focused history;**
- **A problem focused examination; and**
- **Straightforward medical decision making.**

Counseling and/or coordination of care with other providers or agencies are provided consistent with the nature of the problem(s) and the patient's and/or family's needs.

Usually, the presenting problem(s) are of low severity. Physicians typically spend 20 minutes with the patient and/or family or caregiver.

99325 Domiciliary or rest home visit for the evaluation and management of a new patient, which requires these three key components:

- **An expanded problem focused history;**
- **An expanded problem focused examination; and**
- **Medical decision making of low complexity.**

Counseling and/or coordination of care with other providers or agencies are provided consistent with the nature of the problem(s) and the patient's and/or family's needs.

Usually, the presenting problem(s) are of moderate severity. Physicians typically spend 30 minutes with the patient and/or family or caregiver.

Evaluation and Management

99326 Domiciliary or rest home visit for the evaluation and management of a new patient, which requires these three key components:

- **A detailed history;**

- **A detailed examination; and**

- **Medical decision making of moderate complexity.**

Counseling and/or coordination of care with other providers or agencies are provided consistent with the nature of the problem(s) and the patient's and/or family's needs.

Usually, the presenting problem(s) are of moderate to high severity. Physicians typically spend 45 minutes with the patient and/or family or caregiver.

99327 Domiciliary or rest home visit for the evaluation and management of a new patient, which requires these three key components:

- **A comprehensive history;**

- **A comprehensive examination; and**

- **Medical decision making of moderate complexity.**

Counseling and/or coordination of care with other providers or agencies are provided consistent with the nature of the problem(s) and the patient's and/or family's needs.

Usually, the presenting problem(s) are of high severity. Physicians typically spend 60 minutes with the patient and/or family or caregiver.

99328 Domiciliary or rest home visit for the evaluation and management of a new patient, which requires these three key components:

- **A comprehensive history;**

- **A comprehensive examination; and**

- **Medical decision making of high complexity.**

Counseling and/or coordination of care with other providers or agencies are provided consistent with the nature of the problem(s) and the patient's and/or family's needs.

Usually, the patient is unstable or has developed a significant new problem requiring immediate physician attention. Physicians typically spend 75 minutes with the patient and/or family or caregiver.

Established Patient

(99331-99333 have been deleted)

99334 Domiciliary or rest home visit for the evaluation and management of an established patient, which requires at least two of these three key components:

- **A problem focused interval history;**

- **A problem focused examination;**

- **Straightforward medical decision making.**

Counseling and/or coordination of care with other providers or agencies are provided consistent with the nature of the problem(s) and the patient's and/or family's needs.

Usually, the presenting problem(s) are self-limited or minor. Physicians typically spend 15 minutes with the patient and/or family or caregiver.

99335 Domiciliary or rest home visit for the evaluation and management of an established patient, which requires at least two of these three key components:

- **An expanded problem focused interval history;**

- **An expanded problem focused examination;**

- **Medical decision making of low complexity.**

Counseling and/or coordination of care with other providers or agencies are provided consistent with the nature of the problem(s) and the patient's and/or family's needs.

Usually, the presenting problem(s) are of low to moderate severity. Physicians typically spend 25 minutes with the patient and/or family or caregiver.

99336 Domiciliary or rest home visit for the evaluation and management of an established patient, which requires at least two of these three key components:

- **A detailed interval history;**

- **A detailed examination;**

- **Medical decision making of moderate complexity.**

Counseling and/or coordination of care with other providers or agencies are provided consistent with the nature of the problem(s) and the patient's and/or family's needs.

Usually, the presenting problem(s) are of moderate to high severity. Physicians typically spend 40 minutes with the patient and/or family or caregiver.

99337 Domiciliary or rest home visit for the evaluation and management of an established patient, which requires at least two of these three key components:

- **A comprehensive interval history;**

- **A comprehensive examination;**

- **Medical decision making of moderate to high complexity.**

Counseling and/or coordination of care with other providers or agencies are provided consistent with the nature of the problem(s) and the patient's and/or family's needs.

Usually, the presenting problem(s) are of moderate to high severity. The patient may be unstable or may have developed a significant new problem requiring immediate physician attention. Physicians typically spend 60 minutes with the patient and/or family or caregiver.

Domiciliary, Rest Home (eg, Assisted Living Facility), or Home Care Plan Oversight Services

(For instructions on the use of 99339, 99340, see introductory notes for 99374-99380)

(For care plan oversight services for patients under the care of a home health agency, hospice, or nursing facility, see 99374-99380)

99339 Individual physician supervision of a patient (patient not present) in home, domiciliary or rest home (eg, assisted living facility) requiring complex and multidisciplinary care modalities involving regular physician development and/or revision of care plans, review of subsequent reports of patient status, review of related laboratory and other studies, communication (including telephone calls) for purposes of assessment or care decisions with health care professional(s), family member(s), surrogate decision maker(s) (eg, legal guardian) and/or key caregiver(s) involved in patient's care, integration of new information into the medical treatment plan and/or adjustment of medical therapy, within a calendar month; 15-29 minutes

99340 30 minutes or more

(Do not report 99339, 99340 for patients under the care of a home health agency, enrolled in a hospice program, or for nursing facility residents)

Home Services

The following codes are used to report evaluation and management services provided in a private residence.

For definitions of key components and commonly used terms, please see **Evaluation and Management Services Guidelines.**

(For care plan oversight services provided to a patient in the home under the care of a home health agency, see 99374-99375)

(For care plan oversight services provided to a patient in the home under the individual supervision of a physician, see 99339, 99340)

New Patient

99341 **Home visit** for the evaluation and management of a new patient, which requires these three key components:

- **A problem focused history;**
- **A problem focused examination; and**
- **Straightforward medical decision making.**

Counseling and/or coordination of care with other providers or agencies are provided consistent with the nature of the problem(s) and the patient's and/or family's needs.

Usually, the presenting problem(s) are of low severity. Physicians typically spend 20 minutes face-to-face with the patient and/or family.

99342 **Home visit** for the evaluation and management of a new patient, which requires these three key components:

- **An expanded problem focused history;**
- **An expanded problem focused examination; and**
- **Medical decision making of low complexity.**

Counseling and/or coordination of care with other providers or agencies are provided consistent with the nature of the problem(s) and the patient's and/or family's needs.

Usually, the presenting problem(s) are of moderate severity. Physicians typically spend 30 minutes face-to-face with the patient and/or family.

99343 **Home visit** for the evaluation and management of a new patient, which requires these three key components:

- **A detailed history;**
- **A detailed examination; and**
- **Medical decision making of moderate complexity.**

Counseling and/or coordination of care with other providers or agencies are provided consistent with the nature of the problem(s) and the patient's and/or family's needs.

Usually, the presenting problem(s) are of moderate to high severity. Physicians typically spend 45 minutes face-to-face with the patient and/or family.

99344 **Home visit** for the evaluation and management of a new patient, which requires these three components:

- **A comprehensive history;**
- **A comprehensive examination; and**
- **Medical decision making of moderate complexity.**

Counseling and/or coordination of care with other providers or agencies are provided consistent with the nature of the problem(s) and the patient's and/or family's needs.

Usually, the presenting problem(s) are of high severity. Physicians typically spend 60 minutes face-to-face with the patient and/or family.

99345 **Home visit** for the evaluation and management of a new patient, which requires these three key components:

- **A comprehensive history;**

- **A comprehensive examination; and**

- **Medical decision making of high complexity.**

Counseling and/or coordination of care with other providers or agencies are provided consistent with the nature of the problem(s) and the patient's and/or family's needs.

Usually, the patient is unstable or has developed a significant new problem requiring immediate physician attention. Physicians typically spend 75 minutes face-to-face with the patient and/or family.

Established Patient

99347 **Home visit** for the evaluation and management of an established patient, which requires at least two of these three key components:

- **A problem focused interval history;**

- **A problem focused examination;**

- **Straightforward medical decision making.**

Counseling and/or coordination of care with other providers or agencies are provided consistent with the nature of the problem(s) and the patient's and/or family's needs.

Usually, the presenting problem(s) are self limited or minor. Physicians typically spend 15 minutes face-to-face with the patient and/or family.

99348 **Home visit** for the evaluation and management of an established patient, which requires at least two of these three key components:

- **An expanded problem focused interval history;**

- **An expanded problem focused examination;**

- **Medical decision making of low complexity.**

Counseling and/or coordination of care with other providers or agencies are provided consistent with the nature of the problem(s) and the patient's and/or family's needs.

Usually, the presenting problem(s) are of low to moderate severity. Physicians typically spend 25 minutes face-to-face with the patient and/or family.

99349 **Home visit** for the evaluation and management of an established patient, which requires at least two of these three key components:

- **A detailed interval history;**

- **A detailed examination;**

- **Medical decision making of moderate complexity.**

Counseling and/or coordination of care with other providers or agencies are provided consistent with the nature of the problem(s) and the patient's and/or family's needs.

Usually, the presenting problem(s) are moderate to high severity. Physicians typically spend 40 minutes face-to-face with the patient and/or family.

99350 **Home visit** for the evaluation and management of an established patient, which requires at least two of these three key components:

- **A comprehensive interval history;**

- **A comprehensive examination;**

- **Medical decision making of moderate to high complexity.**

Counseling and/or coordination of care with other providers or agencies are provided consistent with the nature of the problem(s) and the patient's and/or family's needs.

Usually, the presenting problem(s) are of moderate to high severity. The patient may be unstable or may have developed a significant new problem requiring immediate physician attention. Physicians typically spend 60 minutes face-to-face with the patient and/or family.

Prolonged Services

Prolonged Physician Service With Direct (Face-To-Face) Patient Contact

Codes 99354-99357 are used when a physician provides prolonged service involving direct (face-to-face) patient contact that is beyond the usual service in either the inpatient or outpatient setting. This service is reported in addition to other physician services, including evaluation and management services at any level. Appropriate codes should be selected for supplies provided or procedures performed in the care of the patient during this period.

Codes 99354-99357 are used to report the total duration of face-to-face time spent by a physician on a given date providing prolonged service, even if the time spent by the physician on that date is not continuous.

Code 99354 or 99356 is used to report the first hour of prolonged service on a given date, depending on the place of service.

Either code also may be used to report a total duration of prolonged service of 30-60 minutes on a given date. Either code should be used only once per date, even if the time spent by the physician is not continuous on that date. Prolonged service of less than 30 minutes total duration on a given date is not separately reported because the work involved is included in the total work of the evaluation and management codes.

Code 99355 or 99357 is used to report each additional 30 minutes beyond the first hour, depending on the place of service. Either code may also be used to report the final 15-30 minutes of prolonged service on a given date. Prolonged service of less than 15 minutes beyond the first hour or less than 15 minutes beyond the final 30 minutes is not reported separately.

The following examples illustrate the correct reporting of prolonged physician service with direct patient contact in the office setting:

Total Duration of Prolonged Services	Code(s)
less than 30 minutes (less than 30 minutes)	Not reported separately
30-74 minutes (30 minutes - 1 hr. 14 min.)	99354 X 1
75-104 minutes (1 hr. 15 min. - 1 hr. 44 min.)	99354 X 1 AND 99355 X 1
105-134 minutes (1 hr. 45 min. - 2 hr. 14 min.)	99354 X 1 AND 99355 X 2
135-164 minutes (2 hr. 15 min. - 2 hr. 44 min.)	99354 X 1 AND 99355 X 3
165-194 minutes (2 hr. 45 min. - 3 hr. 14 min.)	99354 X 1 AND 99355 X 4

+ **99354** Prolonged physician service in the office or other outpatient setting requiring direct (face-to-face) patient contact beyond the usual service (eg, prolonged care and treatment of an acute asthmatic patient in an outpatient setting); first hour (List separately in addition to code for office or other outpatient **Evaluation and Management** service)

(Use 99354 in conjunction with 99201-99215, 99241-99245, 99304-99350)

+ **99355** each additional 30 minutes (List separately in addition to code for prolonged physician service)

(Use 99355 in conjunction with 99354)

+ **99356** Prolonged physician service in the inpatient setting, requiring direct (face-to-face) patient contact beyond the usual service (eg, maternal fetal monitoring for high risk delivery or other physiological monitoring, prolonged care of an acutely ill inpatient); first hour (List separately in addition to code for inpatient Evaluation and Management service)

(Use 99356 in conjunction with 99221-99233, 99251-99255)

+ **99357** each additional 30 minutes (List separately in addition to code for prolonged physician service)

(Use 99357 in conjunction with 99356)

Prolonged Physician Service Without Direct (Face-To-Face) Patient Contact

Codes 99358 and 99359 are used when a physician provides prolonged service not involving direct (face-to-face) care that is beyond the usual service in either the inpatient or outpatient setting.

This service is to be reported in addition to other physician service, including evaluation and management services at any level.

Codes 99358 and 99359 are used to report the total duration of non-face-to-face time spent by a physician on a given date providing prolonged service, even if the time spent by the physician on that date is not continuous. Code 99358 is used to report the first hour of prolonged service on a given date regardless of the place of service.

It may also be used to report a total duration of prolonged service of 30-60 minutes on a given date. It should be used only once per date even if the time spent by the physician is not continuous on that date.

Prolonged service of less than 30 minutes total duration on a given date is not separately reported.

Code 99359 is used to report each additional 30 minutes beyond the first hour regardless of the place of service. It may also be used to report the final 15-30 minutes of prolonged service on a given date.

Prolonged service of less than 15 minutes beyond the first hour or less than 15 minutes beyond the final 30 minutes is not reported separately.

+ **99358** **Prolonged evaluation and management service** before and/or after direct (face-to-face) patient care (eg, review of extensive records and tests, communication with other professionals and/or the patient/family); first hour (List separately in addition to code(s) for other physician service(s) and/or inpatient or outpatient Evaluation and Management service)

+ **99359** each additional 30 minutes (List separately in addition to code for prolonged physician service)

(Use 99359 in conjunction with 99358)

(To report telephone calls, see 99371-99373)

Physician Standby Services

Code 99360 is used to report physician standby service that is requested by another physician and that involves prolonged physician attendance without direct (face-to-face) patient contact. The physician may not be providing care or services to other patients during this period. This code is not used to report time spent proctoring another physician. It is also not used if the period of standby ends with the performance of a procedure subject to a "surgical" package by the physician who was on standby.

Code 99360 is used to report the total duration of time spent by a physician on a given date on standby. Standby service of less than 30 minutes total duration on a given date is not reported separately.

Second and subsequent periods of standby beyond the first 30 minutes may be reported only if a full 30 minutes of standby was provided for each unit of service reported.

99360 **Physician standby service,** requiring prolonged physician attendance, each 30 minutes (eg, operative standby, standby for frozen section, for cesarean/high risk delivery, for monitoring EEG)

(For hospital mandated on call services, see 99026, 99027)

(99360 may be reported in addition to 99431, 99440 as appropriate)

(Do not report 99360 in conjunction with 99436)

Case Management Services

Physician case management is a process in which a physician is responsible for direct care of a patient, and for coordinating and controlling access to or initiating and/or supervising other health care services needed by the patient.

Team Conferences

99361 **Medical conference** by a physician with interdisciplinary team of health professionals or representatives of community agencies to coordinate activities of patient care (patient not present); approximately 30 minutes

99362 approximately 60 minutes

►Anticoagulant Management◄

►Anticoagulant services are intended to describe the outpatient management of warfarin therapy, including ordering, review, and interpretation of International Normalized Ratio (INR) testing, communication with patient, and dosage adjustments as appropriate.

When reporting these services, the work of anticoagulant management may not be used as a basis for reporting an Evaluation and Management service or Care Plan Oversight time during the reporting period. Do not report these services with 99371-99373, 0074T when telephone or on-line services address anticoagulation with warfarin management. If a significant, separately identifiable E/M service is performed, report the appropriate E/M service code using modifier 25.

These services are outpatient services only. When anticoagulation therapy is initiated or continued in the inpatient or observation setting, a new period begins after discharge and is reported with 99364. Do not report 99363-99364 with 99217-99239, 99291-99300, 99304-99318 or other code(s) for physician review, interpretation, and patient management of home INR testing for a patient with mechanical heart valve(s).

Any period less than 60 continuous outpatient days is not reported. If less than the specified minimum number of services per period are performed, do not report the anticoagulant management services (99363-99364).◄

● **99363** Anticoagulant management for an outpatient taking warfarin, physician review and interpretation of International Normalized Ratio (INR) testing, patient instructions, dosage adjustment (as needed), and ordering of additional tests; initial 90 days of therapy (must include a minimum of 8 INR measurements)

● **99364** each subsequent 90 days of therapy (must include a minimum of 3 INR measurements)

Telephone Calls

99371 **Telephone call** by a physician to patient or for consultation or medical management or for coordinating medical management with other health care professionals (eg, nurses, therapists, social workers, nutritionists, physicians, pharmacists); simple or brief (eg, to report on tests and/or laboratory results, to clarify or alter previous instructions, to integrate new information from other health professionals into the medical treatment plan, or to adjust therapy)

99372 intermediate (eg, to provide advice to an established patient on a new problem, to initiate therapy that can be handled by telephone, to discuss test results in detail, to coordinate medical management of a new problem in an established patient, to discuss and evaluate new information and details, or to initiate new plan of care)

99373 complex or lengthy (eg, lengthy counseling session with anxious or distraught patient, detailed or prolonged discussion with family members regarding seriously ill patient, lengthy communication necessary to coordinate complex services of several different health professionals working on different aspects of the total patient care plan)

Care Plan Oversight Services

Care Plan Oversight Services are reported separately from codes for office/outpatient, hospital, home, nursing facility or domiciliary services. The complexity and approximate physician time of the care plan oversight services provided within a 30-day period determine code selection. Only one physician may report services for a given period of time, to reflect that physician's sole or predominant supervisory role with a particular patient. These codes should not be reported for supervision of patients in nursing facilities or under the care of home health agencies unless they require recurrent supervision of therapy.

The work involved in providing very low intensity or infrequent supervision services is included in the pre- and post-encounter work for home, office/outpatient and nursing facility or domiciliary visit codes.

> (For care plan oversight services of patients in the home, domiciliary, or rest home (eg, assisted living facility) under the individual supervision of a physician, see 99339, 99340)

99374 **Physician supervision** of a patient under care of home health agency (patient not present) in home, domiciliary or equivalent environment (eg, Alzheimer's facility) requiring complex and multidisciplinary care modalities involving regular physician development and/or revision of care plans, review of subsequent reports of patient status, review of related laboratory and other studies, communication (including telephone calls) for purposes of assessment or care decisions with health care professional(s), family member(s), surrogate decision maker(s) (eg, legal guardian) and/or key caregiver(s) involved in patient's care, integration of new information into the medical treatment plan and/or adjustment of medical therapy, within a calendar month; 15-29 minutes

99375 30 minutes or more

99377 **Physician supervision** of a hospice patient (patient not present) requiring complex and multidisciplinary care modalities involving regular physician development and/or revision of care plans, review of subsequent reports of patient status, review of related laboratory and other studies, communication (including telephone calls) for purposes of assessment or care decisions with health care professional(s), family member(s), surrogate decision maker(s) (eg, legal guardian) and/or key caregiver(s) involved in patient's care, integration of new information into the medical treatment plan and/or adjustment of medical therapy, within a calendar month; 15-29 minutes

99378 30 minutes or more

99379 **Physician supervision** of a nursing facility patient (patient not present) requiring complex and multidisciplinary care modalities involving regular physician development and/or revision of care plans, review of subsequent reports of patient status, review of related laboratory and other studies, communication (including telephone calls) for purposes of assessment or care decisions with health care professional(s), family member(s), surrogate decision maker(s) (eg, legal guardian) and/or key caregiver(s) involved in patient's care, integration of new information into the medical treatment plan and/or adjustment of medical therapy, within a calendar month; 15-29 minutes

99380 30 minutes or more

Preventive Medicine Services

The following codes are used to report the preventive medicine evaluation and management of infants, children, adolescents and adults.

The extent and focus of the services will largely depend on the age of the patient.

If an abnormality/ies is encountered or a preexisting problem is addressed in the process of performing this preventive medicine evaluation and management service, and if the problem/abnormality is significant enough to require additional work to perform the key components of a problem-oriented E/M service, then the appropriate Office/Outpatient code 99201-99215 should also be reported. Modifier 25 should be added to the Office/Outpatient code to indicate that a significant, separately identifiable Evaluation and Management service was provided by the same physician on the same day as the preventive medicine service. The appropriate preventive medicine service is additionally reported.

An insignificant or trivial problem/abnormality that is encountered in the process of performing the preventive medicine evaluation and management service and which does not require additional work and the performance of the key components of a problem-oriented E/M service should not be reported.

The "comprehensive" nature of the Preventive Medicine Services codes 99381-99397 reflects an age and gender appropriate history/exam and is NOT synonymous with the "comprehensive" examination required in Evaluation and Management codes 99201-99350.

Codes 99381-99397 include counseling/anticipatory guidance/risk factor reduction interventions which are provided at the time of the initial or periodic comprehensive preventive medicine examination. (Refer to codes 99401-99412 for reporting those counseling/anticipatory guidance/risk factor reduction interventions that are provided at an encounter separate from the preventive medicine examination.)

Immunizations and ancillary studies involving laboratory, radiology, other procedures, or screening tests identified with a specific CPT code are reported separately. For immunizations, see 90465-90474 and 90476-90749.

New Patient

99381 **Initial comprehensive preventive medicine** evaluation and management of an individual including an age and gender appropriate history, examination, counseling/anticipatory guidance/risk factor reduction interventions, and the ordering of appropriate immunization(s), laboratory/diagnostic procedures, new patient; infant (age younger than 1 year)

99382 early childhood (age 1 through 4 years)

99383 late childhood (age 5 through 11 years)

99384 adolescent (age 12 through 17 years)

99385 18-39 years

99386 40-64 years

99387 65 years and older

Established Patient

99391 **Periodic comprehensive preventive medicine** reevaluation and management of an individual including an age and gender appropriate history, examination, counseling/anticipatory guidance/risk factor reduction interventions, and the ordering of appropriate immunization(s), laboratory/diagnostic procedures, established patient; infant (age younger than 1 year)

99392 early childhood (age 1 through 4 years)

99393 late childhood (age 5 through 11 years)

99394 adolescent (age 12 through 17 years)

99395 18-39 years

99396 40-64 years

99397 65 years and older

Counseling and/or Risk Factor Reduction Intervention

New or Established Patient

These codes are used to report services provided to individuals at a separate encounter for the purpose of promoting health and preventing illness or injury.

Preventive medicine counseling and risk factor reduction interventions provided as a separate encounter will vary with age and should address such issues as family problems, diet and exercise, substance abuse, sexual practices, injury prevention, dental health, and diagnostic and laboratory test results available at the time of the encounter.

These codes are not to be used to report counseling and risk factor reduction interventions provided to patients with symptoms or established illness. For counseling individual patients with symptoms or established illness, use the appropriate office, hospital or consultation or other evaluation and management codes. For counseling groups of patients with symptoms or established illness, use 99078.

Preventive Medicine, Individual Counseling

99401 **Preventive medicine counseling** and/or risk factor reduction intervention(s) provided to an individual (separate procedure); approximately 15 minutes

99402 approximately 30 minutes

99403 approximately 45 minutes

99404 approximately 60 minutes

Preventive Medicine, Group Counseling

99411 **Preventive medicine counseling** and/or risk factor reduction intervention(s) provided to individuals in a group setting (separate procedure); approximately 30 minutes

99412 approximately 60 minutes

Other Preventive Medicine Services

99420 **Administration and interpretation** of health risk assessment instrument (eg, health hazard appraisal)

99429 **Unlisted preventive** medicine service

Newborn Care

The following codes are used to report the services provided to newborns in several different settings.

For newborn hospital discharge services provided on a date subsequent to the admission date of the newborn, use 99238.

For discharge services provided to newborns admitted and discharged on the same date, use 99435.

99431 **History and examination** of the normal newborn infant, initiation of diagnostic and treatment programs and preparation of hospital records. (This code should also be used for birthing room deliveries.)

99432 **Normal newborn care** in other than hospital or birthing room setting, including physical examination of baby and conference(s) with parent(s)

99433 **Subsequent hospital care,** for the evaluation and management of a normal newborn, per day

Evaluation and Management

99435 **History and examination** of the normal newborn infant, including the preparation of medical records. (This code should only be used for newborns assessed and discharged from the hospital or birthing room on the same date.)

99436 **Attendance** at delivery (when requested by delivering physician) and initial stabilization of newborn

(99436 may be reported in addition to 99431)

(Do not report 99436 in conjunction with 99440)

99440 **Newborn resuscitation**: provision of positive pressure ventilation and/or chest compressions in the presence of acute inadequate ventilation and/or cardiac output

Special Evaluation and Management Services

The following codes are used to report evaluations performed to establish baseline information prior to life or disability insurance certificates being issued. This service is performed in the office or other setting, and applies to both new and established patients. When using these codes, no active management of the problem(s) is undertaken during the encounter.

If other evaluation and management services and/or procedures are performed on the same date, the appropriate E/M or procedure code(s) should be reported in addition to these codes.

Basic Life and/or Disability Evaluation Services

99450 **Basic life** and/or disability examination that includes:

- **Measurement of height, weight and blood pressure;**

- **Completion of a medical history following a life insurance pro forma;**

- **Collection of blood sample and/or urinalysis complying with "chain of custody" protocols; and**

- **Completion of necessary documentation/certificates.**

Work Related or Medical Disability Evaluation Services

99455 **Work related** or medical disability examination by the treating physician that includes:

- **Completion of a medical history commensurate with the patient's condition;**

- **Performance of an examination commensurate with the patient's condition;**

- **Formulation of a diagnosis, assessment of capabilities and stability, and calculation of impairment;**

- **Development of future medical treatment plan; and**

- **Completion of necessary documentation/certificates and report.**

99456 **Work related** or medical disability examination by other than the treating physician that includes:

- **Completion of a medical history commensurate with the patient's condition;**

- **Performance of an examination commensurate with the patient's condition;**

- **Formulation of a diagnosis, assessment of capabilities and stability, and calculation of impairment;**

- **Development of future medical treatment plan; and**

- **Completion of necessary documentation/certificates and report.**

(Do not report 99455, 99456 in conjunction with 99080 for the completion of Workman's Compensation forms)

Other Evaluation and Management Services

99499 **Unlisted evaluation and management** service

Evaluation and Management

Notes

Anesthesia Guidelines

Services involving administration of anesthesia are reported by the use of the anesthesia five-digit procedure code (00100-01999) plus modifier codes (defined under "Anesthesia Modifiers" later in these Guidelines).

The reporting of anesthesia services is appropriate by or under the responsible supervision of a physician. These services may include but are not limited to general, regional, supplementation of local anesthesia, or other supportive services in order to afford the patient the anesthesia care deemed optimal by the anesthesiologist during any procedure. These services include the usual preoperative and postoperative visits, the anesthesia care during the procedure, the administration of fluids and/or blood and the usual monitoring services (eg, ECG, temperature, blood pressure, oximetry, capnography, and mass spectrometry). Unusual forms of monitoring (eg, intra-arterial, central venous, and Swan-Ganz) are not included.

Items used by all physicians in reporting their services are presented in the **Introduction.** Some of the commonalities are repeated in this section for the convenience of those physicians referring to this section on **Anesthesia.** Other definitions and items unique to anesthesia are also listed.

To report moderate (conscious) sedation provided by a physician also performing the service for which conscious sedation is being provided, see codes 99143-99145.

For the procedures listed in Appendix G, when a second physician other than the health care professional performing the diagnostic or therapeutic services provides moderate (conscious) sedation in the facility setting (eg, hospital, outpatient hospital/ambulatory surgery center, skilled nursing facility), the second physician reports the associated moderate sedation procedure/service 99148-99150; when these services are performed by the second physician in the nonfacility setting (eg, physician office, freestanding imaging center), codes 99148-99150 would not be reported. Moderate sedation does not include minimal sedation (anxiolysis), deep sedation, or monitored anesthesia care (00100-01999).

To report regional or general anesthesia provided by a physician also performing the services for which the anesthesia is being provided, see modifier 47 in Appendix A.

Time Reporting

Time for anesthesia procedures may be reported as is customary in the local area. Anesthesia time begins when the anesthesiologist begins to prepare the patient for the induction of anesthesia in the operating room or in an equivalent area and ends when the anesthesiologist is no longer in personal attendance, that is, when the patient may be safely placed under postoperative supervision.

Physician's Services

Physician's services rendered in the office, home, or hospital; consultation; and other medical services are listed in the section titled **Evaluation and Management Services** (99201-99499 series) found on page 1. "Special Services and Reporting" (99000-99091 series) are listed in the **Medicine** section.

Materials Supplied by Physician

Supplies and materials provided by the physician (eg, sterile trays, drugs) over and above those usually included with the office visit or other services rendered may be listed separately. Drugs, tray supplies, and materials provided should be listed and identified with 99070 or the appropriate supply code.

Separate or Multiple Procedures

When multiple surgical procedures are performed during a single anesthetic administration, the anesthesia code representing the most complex procedure is reported. The time reported is the combined total for all procedures.

►Results/Testing/Reports◄

►Results are the technical component of a service. Testing leads to results; results lead to interpretation. Reports are the work product of the interpretation of numerous test results.◄

Special Report

A service that is rarely provided, unusual, variable, or new may require a special report in determining medical appropriateness of the service. Pertinent information should include an adequate definition or description of the nature, extent, and need for the procedure and the time, effort, and equipment necessary to provide the service. Additional items may include:

- Complexity of symptoms
- Final diagnosis
- Pertinent physical findings
- Diagnostic and therapeutic procedures
- Concurrent problems
- Follow-up care

Anesthesia Modifiers

All anesthesia services are reported by use of the anesthesia five-digit procedure code (00100-01999) plus the addition of a physical status modifier. The use of other optional modifiers may be appropriate.

Physical Status Modifiers

Physical Status modifiers are represented by the initial letter 'P' followed by a single digit from 1 to 6 as defined in the following list.

P1: A normal healthy patient

P2: A patient with mild systemic disease

P3: A patient with severe systemic disease

P4: A patient with severe systemic disease that is a constant threat to life

P5: A moribund patient who is not expected to survive without the operation

P6: A declared brain-dead patient whose organs are being removed for donor purposes

These six levels are consistent with the American Society of Anesthesiologists (ASA) ranking of patient physical status. Physical status is included in the CPT codebook to distinguish among various levels of complexity of the anesthesia service provided.

Example: 00100-P1

Qualifying Circumstances

More than one qualifying circumstance may be selected.

Many anesthesia services are provided under particularly difficult circumstances, depending on factors such as extraordinary condition of patient, notable operative conditions, and/or unusual risk factors. This section includes a list of important qualifying circumstances that significantly affect the character of the anesthesia service provided. These procedures would not be reported alone but would be reported as additional procedure numbers qualifying an anesthesia procedure or service.

+ 99100 Anesthesia for patient of extreme age, younger than 1 year and older than 70 (List separately in addition to code for primary anesthesia procedure)

(For procedure performed on infants younger than 1 year of age at time of surgery, see 00326, 00561, 00834, 00836)

+ 99116 Anesthesia complicated by utilization of total body hypothermia (List separately in addition to code for primary anesthesia procedure)

+ 99135 Anesthesia complicated by utilization of controlled hypotension (List separately in addition to code for primary anesthesia procedure)

+ 99140 Anesthesia complicated by emergency conditions (specify) (List separately in addition to code for primary anesthesia procedure)

(An emergency is defined as existing when delay in treatment of the patient would lead to a significant increase in the threat to life or body part.)

Anesthesia

Head

00100 Anesthesia for procedures on salivary glands, including biopsy

00102 Anesthesia for procedures involving plastic repair of cleft lip

00103 Anesthesia for reconstructive procedures of eyelid (eg, blepharoplasty, ptosis surgery)

00104 Anesthesia for electroconvulsive therapy

00120 Anesthesia for procedures on external, middle, and inner ear including biopsy; not otherwise specified

00124 otoscopy

00126 tympanotomy

00140 Anesthesia for procedures on eye; not otherwise specified

00142 lens surgery

00144 corneal transplant

00145 vitreoretinal surgery

00147 iridectomy

00148 ophthalmoscopy

00160 Anesthesia for procedures on nose and accessory sinuses; not otherwise specified

00162 radical surgery

00164 biopsy, soft tissue

00170 Anesthesia for intraoral procedures, including biopsy; not otherwise specified

00172 repair of cleft palate

00174 excision of retropharyngeal tumor

00176 radical surgery

00190 Anesthesia for procedures on facial bones or skull; not otherwise specified

00192 radical surgery (including prognathism)

00210 Anesthesia for intracranial procedures; not otherwise specified

00212 subdural taps

00214 burr holes, including ventriculography

00215 cranioplasty or elevation of depressed skull fracture, extradural (simple or compound)

00216 vascular procedures

00218 procedures in sitting position

00220 cerebrospinal fluid shunting procedures

00222 electrocoagulation of intracranial nerve

Neck

00300 Anesthesia for all procedures on the integumentary system, muscles and nerves of head, neck, and posterior trunk, not otherwise specified

00320 Anesthesia for all procedures on esophagus, thyroid, larynx, trachea and lymphatic system of neck; not otherwise specified, age 1 year or older

00322 needle biopsy of thyroid

 (For procedures on cervical spine and cord, see 00600, 00604, 00670)

00326 Anesthesia for all procedures on the larynx and trachea in children younger than 1 year of age

 (Do not report 00326 in conjunction with 99100)

00350 Anesthesia for procedures on major vessels of neck; not otherwise specified

00352 simple ligation

 (For arteriography, use 01916)

Thorax (Chest Wall and Shoulder Girdle)

00400 Anesthesia for procedures on the integumentary system on the extremities, anterior trunk and perineum; not otherwise specified

00402 reconstructive procedures on breast (eg, reduction or augmentation mammoplasty, muscle flaps)

00404 radical or modified radical procedures on breast

00406 radical or modified radical procedures on breast with internal mammary node dissection

00410 electrical conversion of arrhythmias

00450 Anesthesia for procedures on clavicle and scapula; not otherwise specified

00452 radical surgery

00454 biopsy of clavicle

00470 Anesthesia for partial rib resection; not otherwise specified

00472 thoracoplasty (any type)

00474 radical procedures (eg, pectus excavatum)

Anesthesia

Anesthesia

Intrathoracic

00500 Anesthesia for all procedures on esophagus

00520 Anesthesia for closed chest procedures; (including bronchoscopy) not otherwise specified

00522 needle biopsy of pleura

00524 pneumocentesis

00528 mediastinoscopy and diagnostic thoracoscopy not utilizing one lung ventilation

 (For tracheobronchial reconstruction, use 00539)

00529 mediastinoscopy and diagnostic thoracoscopy utilizing one lung ventilation

00530 Anesthesia for permanent transvenous pacemaker insertion

00532 Anesthesia for access to central venous circulation

00534 Anesthesia for transvenous insertion or replacement of pacing cardioverter-defibrillator

 (For transthoracic approach, use 00560)

00537 Anesthesia for cardiac electrophysiologic procedures including radiofrequency ablation

00539 Anesthesia for tracheobronchial reconstruction

00540 Anesthesia for thoracotomy procedures involving lungs, pleura, diaphragm, and mediastinum (including surgical thoracoscopy); not otherwise specified

00541 utilizing one lung ventilation

 ▶(For thoracic spine and cord anesthesia procedures via an anterior transthoracic approach, see 00625-00626)◀

00542 decortication

00546 pulmonary resection with thoracoplasty

00548 intrathoracic procedures on the trachea and bronchi

00550 Anesthesia for sternal debridement

00560 Anesthesia for procedures on heart, pericardial sac, and great vessels of chest; without pump oxygenator

00561 with pump oxygenator, younger than one year of age

 (Do not report 00561 in conjunction with 99100, 99116, and 99135)

00562 with pump oxygenator

00563 with pump oxygenator with hypothermic circulatory arrest

00566 Anesthesia for direct coronary artery bypass grafting without pump oxygenator

00580 Anesthesia for heart transplant or heart/lung transplant

Spine and Spinal Cord

00600 Anesthesia for procedures on cervical spine and cord; not otherwise specified

 (For myelography and discography, see radiological procedures 01905)

00604 procedures with patient in the sitting position

00620 Anesthesia for procedures on thoracic spine and cord; not otherwise specified

00622 thoracolumbar sympathectomy

● **00625** Anesthesia for procedures on the thoracic spine and cord, via an anterior transthoracic approach; not utilizing one lung ventilation

● **00626** utilizing one lung ventilation

 ▶(For anesthesia for thoracotomy procedures other than spinal, see 00540-00541)◀

00630 Anesthesia for procedures in lumbar region; not otherwise specified

00632 lumbar sympathectomy

00634 chemonucleolysis

00635 diagnostic or therapeutic lumbar puncture

00640 Anesthesia for manipulation of the spine or for closed procedures on the cervical, thoracic or lumbar spine

00670 Anesthesia for extensive spine and spinal cord procedures (eg, spinal instrumentation or vascular procedures)

Upper Abdomen

00700 Anesthesia for procedures on upper anterior abdominal wall; not otherwise specified

00702 percutaneous liver biopsy

00730 Anesthesia for procedures on upper posterior abdominal wall

00740 Anesthesia for upper gastrointestinal endoscopic procedures, endoscope introduced proximal to duodenum

00750 Anesthesia for hernia repairs in upper abdomen; not otherwise specified

00752 lumbar and ventral (incisional) hernias and/or wound dehiscence

00754 omphalocele

00756 transabdominal repair of diaphragmatic hernia

00770 Anesthesia for all procedures on major abdominal blood vessels

00790 Anesthesia for intraperitoneal procedures in upper abdomen including laparoscopy; not otherwise specified

00792 partial hepatectomy or management of liver hemorrhage (excluding liver biopsy)

00794 pancreatectomy, partial or total (eg, Whipple procedure)

00796 liver transplant (recipient)

 (For harvesting of liver, use 01990)

00797 gastric restrictive procedure for morbid obesity

Lower Abdomen

00800 Anesthesia for procedures on lower anterior abdominal wall; not otherwise specified

00802 panniculectomy

00810 Anesthesia for lower intestinal endoscopic procedures, endoscope introduced distal to duodenum

00820 Anesthesia for procedures on lower posterior abdominal wall

00830 Anesthesia for hernia repairs in lower abdomen; not otherwise specified

00832 ventral and incisional hernias

 (For hernia repairs in the infant 1 year of age or younger, see 00834, 00836)

00834 Anesthesia for hernia repairs in the lower abdomen not otherwise specified, younger than 1 year of age

 (Do not report 00834 in conjunction with 99100)

00836 Anesthesia for hernia repairs in the lower abdomen not otherwise specified, infants younger than 37 weeks gestational age at birth and younger than 50 weeks gestational age at time of surgery

 (Do not report 00836 in conjunction with 99100)

00840 Anesthesia for intraperitoneal procedures in lower abdomen including laparoscopy; not otherwise specified

00842 amniocentesis

00844 abdominoperineal resection

00846 radical hysterectomy

00848 pelvic exenteration

00851 tubal ligation/transection

00860 Anesthesia for extraperitoneal procedures in lower abdomen, including urinary tract; not otherwise specified

00862 renal procedures, including upper one-third of ureter, or donor nephrectomy

00864 total cystectomy

00865 radical prostatectomy (suprapubic, retropubic)

00866 adrenalectomy

00868 renal transplant (recipient)

 (For donor nephrectomy, use 00862)

 (For harvesting kidney from brain-dead patient, use 01990)

00870 cystolithotomy

00872 Anesthesia for lithotripsy, extracorporeal shock wave; with water bath

00873 without water bath

00880 Anesthesia for procedures on major lower abdominal vessels; not otherwise specified

00882 inferior vena cava ligation

Perineum

 (For perineal procedures on integumentary system, muscles and nerves, see 00300, 00400)

00902 Anesthesia for; anorectal procedure

00904 radical perineal procedure

00906 vulvectomy

00908 perineal prostatectomy

00910 Anesthesia for transurethral procedures (including urethrocystoscopy); not otherwise specified

00912 transurethral resection of bladder tumor(s)

00914 transurethral resection of prostate

00916 post-transurethral resection bleeding

00918 with fragmentation, manipulation and/or removal of ureteral calculus

00920 Anesthesia for procedures on male genitalia (including open urethral procedures); not otherwise specified

00921 vasectomy, unilateral or bilateral

00922 seminal vesicles

00924 undescended testis, unilateral or bilateral

00926 radical orchiectomy, inguinal

00928 radical orchiectomy, abdominal

00930 orchiopexy, unilateral or bilateral

00932 complete amputation of penis

00934 radical amputation of penis with bilateral inguinal lymphadenectomy

00936 radical amputation of penis with bilateral inguinal and iliac lymphadenectomy

00938 insertion of penile prosthesis (perineal approach)

00940 Anesthesia for vaginal procedures (including biopsy of labia, vagina, cervix or endometrium); not otherwise specified

00942 colpotomy, vaginectomy, colporrhaphy, and open urethral procedures

00944 vaginal hysterectomy

00948 cervical cerclage

00950 culdoscopy

00952 hysteroscopy and/or hysterosalpingography

Anesthesia

Anesthesia

Pelvis (Except Hip)

01112 Anesthesia for bone marrow aspiration and/or biopsy, anterior or posterior iliac crest

01120 Anesthesia for procedures on bony pelvis

01130 Anesthesia for body cast application or revision

01140 Anesthesia for interpelviabdominal (hindquarter) amputation

01150 Anesthesia for radical procedures for tumor of pelvis, except hindquarter amputation

01160 Anesthesia for closed procedures involving symphysis pubis or sacroiliac joint

01170 Anesthesia for open procedures involving symphysis pubis or sacroiliac joint

01173 Anesthesia for open repair of fracture disruption of pelvis or column fracture involving acetabulum

01180 Anesthesia for obturator neurectomy; extrapelvic

01190 intrapelvic

Upper Leg (Except Knee)

01200 Anesthesia for all closed procedures involving hip joint

01202 Anesthesia for arthroscopic procedures of hip joint

01210 Anesthesia for open procedures involving hip joint; not otherwise specified

01212 hip disarticulation

01214 total hip arthroplasty

01215 revision of total hip arthroplasty

01220 Anesthesia for all closed procedures involving upper two-thirds of femur

01230 Anesthesia for open procedures involving upper two-thirds of femur; not otherwise specified

01232 amputation

01234 radical resection

01250 Anesthesia for all procedures on nerves, muscles, tendons, fascia, and bursae of upper leg

01260 Anesthesia for all procedures involving veins of upper leg, including exploration

01270 Anesthesia for procedures involving arteries of upper leg, including bypass graft; not otherwise specified

01272 femoral artery ligation

01274 femoral artery embolectomy

Knee and Popliteal Area

01320 Anesthesia for all procedures on nerves, muscles, tendons, fascia, and bursae of knee and/or popliteal area

01340 Anesthesia for all closed procedures on lower one-third of femur

01360 Anesthesia for all open procedures on lower one-third of femur

01380 Anesthesia for all closed procedures on knee joint

01382 Anesthesia for diagnostic arthroscopic procedures of knee joint

01390 Anesthesia for all closed procedures on upper ends of tibia, fibula, and/or patella

01392 Anesthesia for all open procedures on upper ends of tibia, fibula, and/or patella

01400 Anesthesia for open or surgical arthroscopic procedures on knee joint; not otherwise specified

01402 total knee arthroplasty

01404 disarticulation at knee

01420 Anesthesia for all cast applications, removal, or repair involving knee joint

01430 Anesthesia for procedures on veins of knee and popliteal area; not otherwise specified

01432 arteriovenous fistula

01440 Anesthesia for procedures on arteries of knee and popliteal area; not otherwise specified

01442 popliteal thromboendarterectomy, with or without patch graft

01444 popliteal excision and graft or repair for occlusion or aneurysm

Lower Leg (Below Knee, Includes Ankle and Foot)

01462 Anesthesia for all closed procedures on lower leg, ankle, and foot

01464 Anesthesia for arthroscopic procedures of ankle and/or foot

01470 Anesthesia for procedures on nerves, muscles, tendons, and fascia of lower leg, ankle, and foot; not otherwise specified

01472 repair of ruptured Achilles tendon, with or without graft

01474 gastrocnemius recession (eg, Strayer procedure)

01480 Anesthesia for open procedures on bones of lower leg, ankle, and foot; not otherwise specified

01482 radical resection (including below knee amputation)

01484 osteotomy or osteoplasty of tibia and/or fibula

01486 total ankle replacement

01490 Anesthesia for lower leg cast application, removal, or repair

01500 Anesthesia for procedures on arteries of lower leg, including bypass graft; not otherwise specified

01502 embolectomy, direct or with catheter

01520 Anesthesia for procedures on veins of lower leg; not otherwise specified

01522 venous thrombectomy, direct or with catheter

Shoulder and Axilla

Includes humeral head and neck, sternoclavicular joint, acromioclavicular joint, and shoulder joint.

01610 Anesthesia for all procedures on nerves, muscles, tendons, fascia, and bursae of shoulder and axilla

01620 Anesthesia for all closed procedures on humeral head and neck, sternoclavicular joint, acromioclavicular joint, and shoulder joint

01622 Anesthesia for diagnostic arthroscopic procedures of shoulder joint

01630 Anesthesia for open or surgical arthroscopic procedures on humeral head and neck, sternoclavicular joint, acromioclavicular joint, and shoulder joint; not otherwise specified

01632 radical resection

01634 shoulder disarticulation

01636 interthoracoscapular (forequarter) amputation

01638 total shoulder replacement

01650 Anesthesia for procedures on arteries of shoulder and axilla; not otherwise specified

01652 axillary-brachial aneurysm

01654 bypass graft

01656 axillary-femoral bypass graft

01670 Anesthesia for all procedures on veins of shoulder and axilla

01680 Anesthesia for shoulder cast application, removal or repair; not otherwise specified

01682 shoulder spica

Upper Arm and Elbow

01710 Anesthesia for procedures on nerves, muscles, tendons, fascia, and bursae of upper arm and elbow; not otherwise specified

01712 tenotomy, elbow to shoulder, open

01714 tenoplasty, elbow to shoulder

01716 tenodesis, rupture of long tendon of biceps

01730 Anesthesia for all closed procedures on humerus and elbow

01732 Anesthesia for diagnostic arthroscopic procedures of elbow joint

01740 Anesthesia for open or surgical arthroscopic procedures of the elbow; not otherwise specified

01742 osteotomy of humerus

01744 repair of nonunion or malunion of humerus

01756 radical procedures

01758 excision of cyst or tumor of humerus

01760 total elbow replacement

01770 Anesthesia for procedures on arteries of upper arm and elbow; not otherwise specified

01772 embolectomy

01780 Anesthesia for procedures on veins of upper arm and elbow; not otherwise specified

01782 phleborrhaphy

Forearm, Wrist, and Hand

01810 Anesthesia for all procedures on nerves, muscles, tendons, fascia, and bursae of forearm, wrist, and hand

01820 Anesthesia for all closed procedures on radius, ulna, wrist, or hand bones

01829 Anesthesia for diagnostic arthroscopic procedures on the wrist

01830 Anesthesia for open or surgical arthroscopic/endoscopic procedures on distal radius, distal ulna, wrist, or hand joints; not otherwise specified

01832 total wrist replacement

01840 Anesthesia for procedures on arteries of forearm, wrist, and hand; not otherwise specified

01842 embolectomy

01844 Anesthesia for vascular shunt, or shunt revision, any type (eg, dialysis)

01850 Anesthesia for procedures on veins of forearm, wrist, and hand; not otherwise specified

01852 phleborrhaphy

01860 Anesthesia for forearm, wrist, or hand cast application, removal, or repair

Anesthesia

Radiological Procedures

01905 Anesthesia for myelography, discography, vertebroplasty

01916 Anesthesia for diagnostic arteriography/venography

(Do not report 01916 in conjunction with therapeutic codes 01924-01926, 01930-01933)

01920 Anesthesia for cardiac catheterization including coronary angiography and ventriculography (not to include Swan-Ganz catheter)

01922 Anesthesia for non-invasive imaging or radiation therapy

01924 Anesthesia for therapeutic interventional radiologic procedures involving the arterial system; not otherwise specified

01925 carotid or coronary

01926 intracranial, intracardiac, or aortic

01930 Anesthesia for therapeutic interventional radiologic procedures involving the venous/lymphatic system (not to include access to the central circulation); not otherwise specified

01931 intrahepatic or portal circulation (eg, transcutaneous porto-caval shunt (TIPS))

01932 intrathoracic or jugular

01933 intracranial

Burn Excisions or Debridement

01951 Anesthesia for second and third degree burn excision or debridement with or without skin grafting, any site, for total body surface area (TBSA) treated during anesthesia and surgery; less than four percent total body surface area

01952 between four and nine percent of total body surface area

+ 01953 each additional nine percent total body surface area or part thereof (List separately in addition to code for primary procedure)

(Use 01953 in conjunction with 01952)

Obstetric

01958 Anesthesia for external cephalic version procedure

01960 Anesthesia for vaginal delivery only

01961 Anesthesia for cesarean delivery only

01962 Anesthesia for urgent hysterectomy following delivery

01963 Anesthesia for cesarean hysterectomy without any labor analgesia/anesthesia care

(01964 has been deleted. To report, see 01965, 01966)

01965 Anesthesia for incomplete or missed abortion procedures

01966 Anesthesia for induced abortion procedures

01967 Neuraxial labor analgesia/anesthesia for planned vaginal delivery (this includes any repeat subarachnoid needle placement and drug injection and/or any necessary replacement of an epidural catheter during labor)

+ 01968 Anesthesia for cesarean delivery following neuraxial labor analgesia/anesthesia (List separately in addition to code for primary procedure performed)

(Use 01968 in conjunction with 01967)

+ 01969 Anesthesia for cesarean hysterectomy following neuraxial labor analgesia/anesthesia (List separately in addition to code for primary procedure performed)

(Use 01969 in conjunction with 01967)

Other Procedures

01990 Physiological support for harvesting of organ(s) from brain-dead patient

01991 Anesthesia for diagnostic or therapeutic nerve blocks and injections (when block or injection is performed by a different provider); other than the prone position

01992 prone position

(Do not report 01991 or 01992 in conjunction with 99143-99150)

▶(When regional intravenous administration of local anesthetic agent or other medication in the upper or lower extremity is used as the anesthetic for a surgical procedure, report the appropriate anesthesia code. To report a Bier block for pain management, use 64999. For intra-arterial or intravenous injections, see 90773, 90774)◀

▶(For intra-arterial or intravenous therapy for pain management, see 90773, 90774)◀

▶(01995 has been deleted)◀

01996 Daily hospital management of epidural or subarachnoid continuous drug administration

(Report code 01996 for daily hospital management of continuous epidural or subarachnoid drug administration performed after insertion of an epidural or subarachnoid catheter)

01999 Unlisted anesthesia procedure(s)

Surgery Guidelines

Items used by all physicians in reporting their services are presented in the **Introduction.** Some of the commonalities are repeated here for the convenience of those physicians referring to this section on **Surgery.** Other definitions and items unique to Surgery are also listed.

Physicians' Services

Physicians' services rendered in the office, home, or hospital, consultations, and other medical services are listed in the section entitled **Evaluation and Management Services** (99201-99499) found in the front of the book, beginning on page 9. "Special Services and Reports" (99000 series) is presented in the **Medicine** section.

CPT Surgical Package Definition

The services provided by the physician to any patient by their very nature are variable. The CPT codes that represent a readily identifiable surgical procedure thereby include, on a procedure-by-procedure basis, a variety of services. In defining the specific services "included" in a given CPT surgical code, the following services are always included in addition to the operation per se:

- Local infiltration, metacarpal/metatarsal/digital block or topical anesthesia
- Subsequent to the decision for surgery, one related E/M encounter on the date immediately prior to or on the date of procedure (including history and physical)
- Immediate postoperative care, including dictating operative notes, talking with the family and other physicians
- Writing orders
- Evaluating the patient in the postanesthesia recovery area
- Typical postoperative follow-up care

Follow-Up Care for Diagnostic Procedures

Follow-up care for diagnostic procedures (eg, endoscopy, arthroscopy, injection procedures for radiography) includes only that care related to recovery from the diagnostic procedure itself. Care of the condition for which the diagnostic procedure was performed or of other concomitant conditions is not included and may be listed separately.

Follow-Up Care for Therapeutic Surgical Procedures

Follow-up care for therapeutic surgical procedures includes only that care which is usually a part of the surgical service. Complications, exacerbations, recurrence, or the presence of other diseases or injuries requiring additional services should be separately reported.

Materials Supplied by Physician

Supplies and materials provided by the physician (eg, sterile trays/drugs), over and above those usually included with the procedure(s) rendered are reported separately. List drugs, trays, supplies, and materials provided. Identify as 99070 or specific supply code.

Reporting More Than One Procedure/Service

When a physician performs more than one procedure/service on the same date, same session or during a post-operative period (subject to the "surgical package" concept), several CPT modifiers may apply (see Appendix A for definition).

27 Multiple Outpatient Hospital E/M Encounters on the Same Date

For hospital outpatient reporting purposes, utilization of hospital resources related to separate and distinct E/M encounters performed in multiple outpatient hospital settings on the same date may be reported by adding modifier 27 to each appropriate level outpatient and/or emergency department E/M code(s). This modifier provides a means of reporting circumstances involving evaluation and management services provided by physician(s) in more than one (multiple) outpatient

hospital setting(s) (eg, hospital emergency department, clinic). **Note:** This modifier is not to be used for physician reporting of multiple E/M services performed by the same physician on the same date. For physician reporting of all outpatient evaluation and management services provided by the same physician on the same date and performed in multiple outpatient setting(s) (eg, hospital emergency department, clinic), see **Evaluation and Management, Emergency Department,** or **Preventive Medicine Services** codes.

51 Multiple Procedures

When multiple procedures/services (other than evaluation and management) are performed at the same session, report the most significant procedure first, with all other procedures listed with modifier 51 appended. For a list of procedures exempt from the use of modifier 51, see Appendices D and E.

58 Staged or Related Procedure or Service by the Same Physician During the Postoperative Period

When a procedure(s) is prospectively planned as a staged procedure, or when the secondary and subsequent procedure(s) is more extensive, or to indicate therapy following a diagnostic surgical procedure, use modifier 58 with the staged procedure(s).

59 Distinct Procedural Service

For procedure(s)/service(s) not ordinarily performed or encountered on the same day by the same physician, but appropriate under certain circumstances (eg, different site or organ system, separate excision or lesion), use modifier 59.

76 Repeat Procedure by Same Physician

When a procedure or service is repeated by the same physician subsequent to the original service, use modifier 76.

77 Repeat Procedure by Another Physician

When a procedure is repeated by another physician subsequent to the original service, use modifier 77.

78 Return to the Operating Room for a Related Procedure During the Postoperative Period

When a procedure, related to the initial procedure, requires a return to the operating room during the postoperative period of that initial procedure, use modifier 78.

79 Unrelated Procedure or Service by the Same Physician During the Postoperative Period

When a procedure, unrelated to the initial procedure, is performed by the same physician during the post-operative period of the initial procedure, use modifier 79.

91 Repeat Clinical Diagnostic Laboratory Test

In the course of treatment of the patient, it may be necessary to repeat the same laboratory test on the same day to obtain subsequent (multiple) test results. Under these circumstances, the laboratory test performed can be identified by its usual procedure number and the addition of modifier 91. **Note:** This modifier may not be used when tests are rerun to confirm initial results; due to testing problems with specimens or equipment; or for any other reason when a normal, one-time, reportable result is all that is required. This modifier may not be used when other code(s) describe a series of test results (eg, glucose tolerance tests, evocative/suppression testing). This modifier may only be used for laboratory test(s) performed more than once on the same day on the same patient.

Separate Procedure

Some of the procedures or services listed in the CPT codebook that are commonly carried out as an integral component of a total service or procedure have been identified by the inclusion of the term "separate procedure." The codes designated as "separate procedure" should not be reported in addition to the code for the total procedure or service of which it is considered an integral component.

However, when a procedure or service that is designated as a "separate procedure" is carried out independently or considered to be unrelated or distinct from other procedures/services provided at that time, it may be reported by itself, or in addition to other procedures/services by appending modifier 59 to the specific "separate procedure" code to indicate that the procedure is not considered to be a component of another procedure, but is a distinct, independent procedure. This may represent a different session or patient encounter, different procedure or surgery, different site or organ system, separate incision/excision, separate lesion, or separate injury (or area of injury in extensive injuries).

Subsection Information

Several of the subheadings or subsections have special needs or instructions unique to that section. Where these are indicated (eg, "Maternity Care and Delivery"), special **"Notes"** will be presented preceding those procedural terminology listings, referring to that subsection specifically. If there is an "Unlisted Procedure" code number (see below) for the individual subsection, it will also be shown. Those subsections within the **Surgery** section that have **"Notes"** are as follows:

Biopsy . 11100-11101

Removal of Skin Tags. 11200-11201

Shaving of Lesions. 11300-11313

Excision—Benign Lesions 11400-11471

Excision—Malignant Lesions 11600-11646

Repair (Closure) 12001-13160

Adjacent Tissue Transfer or
Rearrangement 14000-14350

▶Skin Replacement Surgery and
Skin Substitutes 15002-15431◀

 Allograft and Tissue Cultured Allogeneic Skin
 Substitutes 15300-15366

 Xenograft. 15400-15431

Flaps (Skin and/or Deep Tissue) 15570-15999

Burns, Local Treatment 16000-16036

Destruction 17000-17286

▶Mohs Micrographic Surgery 17311-17315◀

Breast—Excision 19100-19272

Musculoskeletal. 20000-29999

Wound Exploration—Trauma 20100-20103

Grafts (or Implants). 20900-20999

Introduction or Removal. 21076-21116

Spine: (Vertebral Column). 22100-22855

Spine: Excision 22100-22116

Spine: Osteotomy 22210-22226

Spine: Fracture/Dislocation. 22305-22328

Spine: Arthrodesis 22548-22812

Spine: Exploration 22830

Spinal Instrumentation 22840-22855

Casting and Strapping. 29000-29750

Musculoskeletal:
Endoscopy/Arthroscopy 29800-29999

Respiratory: Endoscopy 31231-31294, 31505-
 31579, 31615-31656, 32601-32665

Cardiovascular System. 33010-37799

Pacing Cardioverter-Pacemaker
or Defibrillator 33202-33249

▶Electrophysiologic Procedures 33250-33266◀

Venous—CABG. 33510-33516

Arteries and Veins 34001-35907

Endovascular Repair of Abdominal
Aortic Aneurysm 34800-34826

Endovascular Repair of
Illiac Aneurysm 34900

Transluminal Angioplasty 35450-35476

Transluminal Atherectomy 35480-35495

Bypass Graft 35500-35572

Composite Grafts. 35681-35683

Adjuvant Techniques 35685-35686

Vascular Injection Procedures:
Intravenous 36000-36015

Central Venous Access Procedures . . . 36555-36597

Transcatheter Procedures:
Intravenous 37195-37216

Intravascular Ultrasound. 37250-37251

Bone Marrow or Stem Cell
Services/Procedures 38204-38242

Hemic and Lymphatic Systems:
Laparoscopy 38570-38589

Digestive:
Endoscopy/Laparoscopy. 43200-43272,
 43280-43289, 43651-43659, 43770-43774,
 44180-44238, 44360-44397, 44970-44979,
 45300-45387, 45395-45397, 45400-45402,
 46600-46615, 47370-47379, 47550-47556,
 47560-47562, 49320-49329, 49650-49659

Pancreas Transplantation. 48550-48556

Herniotomy. 49491-49611

Renal Transplantation 50300-50380

Urodynamics 51725-51798

Endoscopy/Laparoscopy

 Urinary. 50541-50545, 50945-50980,
 51990-52648

 Male Genital 54690-54699, 55550-55559, 55866

 Female Genital 58545-58579, 58660-58679

 Endocrine 60650-60659

Maternity Care and Delivery 59000-59899

Nervous System:
Surgery of Skull Base. 61580-61619

Neurostimulators (Intracranial) 61850-61888,
 62160-62319

Neurostimulators (Spinal) 63650-63688

Neurostimulators (Peripheral Nerve). 64553-64595

Secondary Implants(s) 65125-65175

Removal Cataract. 66830-66999

Prophylaxis 67141-67145

Excision . 67800-67820

Reconstruction 67930-67999

Operating Microscope 69990

Unlisted Service or Procedure

A service or procedure may be provided that is not listed in this edition of the CPT codebook. When reporting such a service, the appropriate "Unlisted Procedure" code may be used to indicate the service, identifying it by "Special Report" as discussed in the section below. The "Unlisted Procedures" and accompanying codes for **Surgery** are as follows:

15999	Unlisted procedure, excision pressure ulcer
17999	Unlisted procedure, skin, mucous membrane and subcutaneous tissue
19499	Unlisted procedure, breast
20999	Unlisted procedure, musculoskeletal system, general
21089	Unlisted maxillofacial prosthetic procedure
21299	Unlisted craniofacial and maxillofacial procedure
21499	Unlisted musculoskeletal procedure, head
21899	Unlisted procedure, neck or thorax
22899	Unlisted procedure, spine
22999	Unlisted procedure, abdomen, musculoskeletal system
23929	Unlisted procedure, shoulder
24999	Unlisted procedure, humerus or elbow
25999	Unlisted procedure, forearm or wrist
26989	Unlisted procedure, hands or fingers
27299	Unlisted procedure, pelvis or hip joint
27599	Unlisted procedure, femur or knee
27899	Unlisted procedure, leg or ankle
28899	Unlisted procedure, foot or toes
29799	Unlisted procedure, casting or strapping
29999	Unlisted procedure, arthroscopy
30999	Unlisted procedure, nose
31299	Unlisted procedure, accessory sinuses
31599	Unlisted procedure, larynx
31899	Unlisted procedure, trachea, bronchi
32999	Unlisted procedure, lungs and pleura
33999	Unlisted procedure, cardiac surgery

36299	Unlisted procedure, vascular injection
37501	Unlisted vascular endoscopy procedure
37799	Unlisted procedure, vascular surgery
38129	Unlisted laparoscopy procedure, spleen
38589	Unlisted laparoscopy procedure, lymphatic system
38999	Unlisted procedure, hemic or lymphatic system
39499	Unlisted procedure, mediastinum
39599	Unlisted procedure, diaphragm
40799	Unlisted procedure, lips
40899	Unlisted procedure, vestibule of mouth
41599	Unlisted procedure, tongue, floor of mouth
41899	Unlisted procedure, dentoalveolar structures
42299	Unlisted procedure, palate, uvula
42699	Unlisted procedure, salivary glands or ducts
42999	Unlisted procedure, pharynx, adenoids, or tonsils
43289	Unlisted laparoscopy procedure, esophagus
43499	Unlisted procedure, esophagus
43659	Unlisted laparoscopy procedure, stomach
43999	Unlisted procedure, stomach
44238	Unlisted laparoscopy procedure, intestine (except rectum)
44799	Unlisted procedure, intestine
44899	Unlisted procedure, Meckel's diverticulum and the mesentery
44979	Unlisted laparoscopy procedure, appendix
45499	Unlisted laparoscopy procedure, rectum
45999	Unlisted procedure, rectum
46999	Unlisted procedure, anus
47379	Unlisted laparoscopic procedure, liver
47399	Unlisted procedure, liver
47579	Unlisted laparoscopy procedure, biliary tract
47999	Unlisted procedure, biliary tract
48999	Unlisted procedure, pancreas
49329	Unlisted laparoscopy procedure, abdomen, peritoneum and omentum
49659	Unlisted laparoscopy procedure, hernioplasty, herniorrhaphy, herniotomy
49999	Unlisted procedure, abdomen, peritoneum and omentum
50549	Unlisted laparoscopy procedure, renal
50949	Unlisted laparoscopy procedure, ureter
51999	Unlisted laparoscopy procedure, bladder
53899	Unlisted procedure, urinary system
54699	Unlisted laparoscopy procedure, testis

55559	Unlisted laparoscopy procedure, spermatic cord
55899	Unlisted procedure, male genital system
58578	Unlisted laparoscopy procedure, uterus
58579	Unlisted hysteroscopy procedure, uterus
58679	Unlisted laparoscopy procedure, oviduct, ovary
58999	Unlisted procedure, female genital system (nonobstetrical)
59897	Unlisted fetal invasive procedure, including ultrasound guidance
59898	Unlisted laparoscopy procedure, maternity care and delivery
59899	Unlisted procedure, maternity care and delivery
60659	Unlisted laparoscopy procedure, endocrine system
60699	Unlisted procedure, endocrine system
64999	Unlisted procedure, nervous system
66999	Unlisted procedure, anterior segment of eye
67299	Unlisted procedure, posterior segment
67399	Unlisted procedure, ocular muscle
67599	Unlisted procedure, orbit
67999	Unlisted procedure, eyelids
68399	Unlisted procedure, conjunctiva
68899	Unlisted procedure, lacrimal system
69399	Unlisted procedure, external ear
69799	Unlisted procedure, middle ear
69949	Unlisted procedure, inner ear
69979	Unlisted procedure, temporal bone, middle fossa approach

▶Results/Testing/Reports◀

▶Results are the technical component of a service. Testing leads to results; results lead to interpretation. Reports are the work product of the interpretation of numerous test results.◀

Special Report

A service that is rarely provided, unusual, variable, or new may require a special report in determining medical appropriateness of the service. Pertinent information should include an adequate definition or description of the nature, extent, and need for the procedure, and the time, effort, and equipment necessary to provide the service. Additional items which may be included are:

- Complexity of symptoms
- Final diagnosis
- Pertinent physical findings (such as size, locations, and number of lesion(s), if appropriate)
- Diagnostic and therapeutic procedures (including major and supplementary surgical procedures, if appropriate)
- Concurrent problems
- Follow-up care

Surgical Destruction

Surgical destruction is a part of a surgical procedure and different methods of destruction are not ordinarily listed separately unless the technique substantially alters the standard management of a problem or condition. Exceptions under special circumstances are provided for by separate code numbers.

Surgery Guidelines

Notes

⊙=Moderate sedation ✛=Add-on code ⟋=FDA approval pending

Surgery

General

10021 Fine needle aspiration; without imaging guidance

10022 with imaging guidance

►(For radiological supervision and interpretation, see 76942, 77002, 77012, 77021)◄

(For percutaneous needle biopsy other than fine needle aspiration, see 20206 for muscle, 32400 for pleura, 32405 for lung or mediastinum, 42400 for salivary gland, 47000, 47001 for liver, 48102 for pancreas, 49180 for abdominal or retroperitoneal mass, 60100 for thyroid, 62269 for spinal cord)

(For evaluation of fine needle aspirate, see 88172, 88173)

Integumentary System

Skin, Subcutaneous and Accessory Structures

Incision and Drainage

(For excision, see 11400, et seq)

10040 Acne surgery (eg, marsupialization, opening or removal of multiple milia, comedones, cysts, pustules)

10060 Incision and drainage of abscess (eg, carbuncle, suppurative hidradenitis, cutaneous or subcutaneous abscess, cyst, furuncle, or paronychia); simple or single

10061 complicated or multiple

10080 Incision and drainage of pilonidal cyst; simple

10081 complicated

(For excision of pilonidal cyst, see 11770-11772)

10120 Incision and removal of foreign body, subcutaneous tissues; simple

10121 complicated

(To report wound exploration due to penetrating trauma without laparotomy or thoracotomy, see 20100-20103, as appropriate)

(To report debridement associated with open fracture(s) and/or dislocation(s), use 11010-11012, as appropriate)

10140 Incision and drainage of hematoma, seroma or fluid collection

►(If imaging guidance is performed, see 76942, 77012, 77021)◄

10160 Puncture aspiration of abscess, hematoma, bulla, or cyst

►(If imaging guidance is performed, see 76942, 77012, 77021)◄

10180 Incision and drainage, complex, postoperative wound infection

(For secondary closure of surgical wound, see 12020, 12021, 13160)

Excision—Debridement

(For dermabrasions, see 15780-15783)

(For nail debridement, see 11720-11721)

(For burn(s), see 16000-16035)

11000 Debridement of extensive eczematous or infected skin; up to 10% of body surface

(For abdominal wall or genitalia debridement for necrotizing soft tissue infection, see 11004-11006)

+ **11001** each additional 10% of the body surface (List separately in addition to code for primary procedure)

(Use 11001 in conjunction with 11000)

11004 Debridement of skin, subcutaneous tissue, muscle and fascia for necrotizing soft tissue infection; external genitalia and perineum

11005 abdominal wall, with or without fascial closure

11006 external genitalia, perineum and abdominal wall, with or without fascial closure

+ **11008** Removal of prosthetic material or mesh, abdominal wall for necrotizing soft tissue infection (List separately in addition to code for primary procedure)

(Use 11008 in conjunction with 11004-11006)

(Do not report 11008 in conjunction with 11000-11001, 11010-11044)

(Report skin grafts or flaps separately when performed for closure at the same session as 11004-11008)

(When insertion of mesh is used for closure, use 49568)

(If orchiectomy is performed, use 54520)

(If testicular transplantation is performed, use 54680)

11010 Debridement including removal of foreign material associated with open fracture(s) and/or dislocation(s); skin and subcutaneous tissues

11011 skin, subcutaneous tissue, muscle fascia, and muscle

11012 skin, subcutaneous tissue, muscle fascia, muscle, and bone

11040 Debridement; skin, partial thickness

11041 skin, full thickness

11042	skin, and subcutaneous tissue
11043	skin, subcutaneous tissue, and muscle
11044	skin, subcutaneous tissue, muscle, and bone

(Do not report 11040-11044 in conjunction with 97597-97602)

Paring or Cutting

(To report destruction, see 17000-17004)

11055	Paring or cutting of benign hyperkeratotic lesion (eg, corn or callus); single lesion
11056	two to four lesions
11057	more than four lesions

Biopsy

During certain surgical procedures in the integumentary system, such as excision, destruction, or shave removals, the removed tissue is often submitted for pathologic examination. The obtaining of tissue for pathology during the course of these procedures is a routine component of such procedures. This obtaining of tissue is not considered a separate biopsy procedure and is not separately reported. The use of a biopsy procedure code (eg, 11100, 11101) indicates that the procedure to obtain tissue for pathologic examination was performed independently, or was unrelated or distinct from other procedures/services provided at that time. Such biopsies are not considered components of other procedures when performed on different lesions or different sites on the same date, and are to be reported separately.

(For biopsy of conjunctiva, use 68100; eyelid, use 67810)

11100	Biopsy of skin, subcutaneous tissue and/or mucous membrane (including simple closure), unless otherwise listed; single lesion
+ 11101	each separate/additional lesion (List separately in addition to code for primary procedure)

(Use 11101 in conjunction with 11100)

Removal of Skin Tags

Removal by scissoring or any sharp method, ligature strangulation, electrosurgical destruction or combination of treatment modalities including chemical or electrocauterization of wound, with or without local anesthesia.

11200	Removal of skin tags, multiple fibrocutaneous tags, any area; up to and including 15 lesions
+ 11201	each additional ten lesions (List separately in addition to code for primary procedure)

(Use 11201 in conjunction with 11200)

Shaving of Epidermal or Dermal Lesions

Shaving is the sharp removal by transverse incision or horizontal slicing to remove epidermal and dermal lesions without a full-thickness dermal excision. This includes local anesthesia, chemical or electrocauterization of the wound. The wound does not require suture closure.

11300	Shaving of epidermal or dermal lesion, single lesion, trunk, arms or legs; lesion diameter 0.5 cm or less
11301	lesion diameter 0.6 to 1.0 cm
11302	lesion diameter 1.1 to 2.0 cm
11303	lesion diameter over 2.0 cm
11305	Shaving of epidermal or dermal lesion, single lesion, scalp, neck, hands, feet, genitalia; lesion diameter 0.5 cm or less
11306	lesion diameter 0.6 to 1.0 cm
11307	lesion diameter 1.1 to 2.0 cm
11308	lesion diameter over 2.0 cm
11310	Shaving of epidermal or dermal lesion, single lesion, face, ears, eyelids, nose, lips, mucous membrane; lesion diameter 0.5 cm or less
11311	lesion diameter 0.6 to 1.0 cm
11312	lesion diameter 1.1 to 2.0 cm
11313	lesion diameter over 2.0 cm

Excision—Benign Lesions

Excision (including simple closure) of benign lesions of skin (eg, neoplasm, cicatricial, fibrous, inflammatory, congenital, cystic lesions), includes local anesthesia. See appropriate size and area below. For shave removal, see 11300 et seq., and for electrosurgical and other methods see 17000 et seq.

Excision is defined as full-thickness (through the dermis) removal of a lesion, including margins, and includes simple (non-layered) closure when performed. Report separately each benign lesion excised. Code selection is determined by measuring the greatest clinical diameter of the apparent lesion plus that margin required for complete excision (lesion diameter plus the most narrow margins required equals the excised diameter). The margins refer to the most narrow margin required to adequately excise the lesion, based on the physician's judgment. The measurement of lesion plus margin is made prior to excision. The excised diameter is the same whether the surgical defect is repaired in a linear fashion, or reconstructed (eg, with a skin graft).

The closure of defects created by incision, excision, or trauma may require intermediate or complex closure. Repair by intermediate or complex closure should be reported separately. For excision of benign lesions requiring more than simple closure, ie, requiring intermediate or complex closure, report 11400-11446 in addition to appropriate intermediate (12031-12057) or

complex closure (13100-13153) codes. For reconstructive closure, see 14000-14300, 15002-15261, 15570-15770. See page 51 for definition of intermediate or complex closure.

11400 Excision, benign lesion including margins, except skin tag (unless listed elsewhere), trunk, arms or legs; excised diameter 0.5 cm or less

11401 excised diameter 0.6 to 1.0 cm

11402 excised diameter 1.1 to 2.0 cm

11403 excised diameter 2.1 to 3.0 cm

11404 excised diameter 3.1 to 4.0 cm

11406 excised diameter over 4.0 cm

 (For unusual or complicated excision, add modifier 22)

11420 Excision, benign lesion including margins, except skin tag (unless listed elsewhere), scalp, neck, hands, feet, genitalia; excised diameter 0.5 cm or less

11421 excised diameter 0.6 to 1.0 cm

11422 excised diameter 1.1 to 2.0 cm

11423 excised diameter 2.1 to 3.0 cm

11424 excised diameter 3.1 to 4.0 cm

11426 excised diameter over 4.0 cm

 (For unusual or complicated excision, add modifier 22)

11440 Excision, other benign lesion including margins, except skin tag (unless listed elsewhere), face, ears, eyelids, nose, lips, mucous membrane; excised diameter 0.5 cm or less

11441 excised diameter 0.6 to 1.0 cm

11442 excised diameter 1.1 to 2.0 cm

11443 excised diameter 2.1 to 3.0 cm

11444 excised diameter 3.1 to 4.0 cm

11446 excised diameter over 4.0 cm

 (For unusual or complicated excision, add modifier 22)

 (For eyelids involving more than skin, see also 67800 et seq)

11450 Excision of skin and subcutaneous tissue for hidradenitis, axillary; with simple or intermediate repair

11451 with complex repair

11462 Excision of skin and subcutaneous tissue for hidradenitis, inguinal; with simple or intermediate repair

11463 with complex repair

11470 Excision of skin and subcutaneous tissue for hidradenitis, perianal, perineal, or umbilical; with simple or intermediate repair

11471 with complex repair

 (When skin graft or flap is used for closure, use appropriate procedure code in addition)

 (For bilateral procedure, add modifier 50)

Excision—Malignant Lesions

Excision (including simple closure) of malignant lesions of skin (eg, basal cell carcinoma, squamous cell carcinoma, melanoma) includes local anesthesia. (See appropriate size and body area below.) For destruction of malignant lesions of skin, see destruction codes 17260-17286.

Excision is defined as full-thickness (through the dermis) removal of a lesion including margins, and includes simple (non-layered) closure when performed. Report separately each malignant lesion excised. Code selection is determined by measuring the greatest clinical diameter of the apparent lesion plus that margin required for complete excision (lesion diameter plus the most narrow margins required equals the excised diameter). The margins refer to the most narrow margin required to adequately excise the lesion, based on the physician's judgment. The measurement of lesion plus margin is made prior to excision. The excised diameter is the same whether the surgical defect is repaired in a linear fashion, or reconstructed (eg, with a skin graft).

The closure of defects created by incision, excision, or trauma may require intermediate or complex closure. Repair by intermediate or complex closure should be reported separately. For excision of malignant lesions requiring more than simple closure, ie, requiring intermediate or complex closure, report 11600-11646 in addition to appropriate intermediate (12031-12057) or complex closure (13100-13153) codes. For reconstructive closure, see 14000-14300, 15002-15261, 15570-15770. See page 51 for definition of intermediate or complex closure.

When frozen section pathology shows the margins of excision were not adequate, an additional excision may be necessary for complete tumor removal. Use only one code to report the additional excision and re-excision(s) based on the final widest excised diameter required for complete tumor removal at the same operative session. To report a re-excision procedure performed to widen margins at a subsequent operative session, see codes 11600-11646, as appropriate. Append modifier 58 if the re-excision procedure is performed during the postoperative period of the primary excision procedure.

11600 Excision, malignant lesion including margins, trunk, arms, or legs; excised diameter 0.5 cm or less

11601 excised diameter 0.6 to 1.0 cm

11602 excised diameter 1.1 to 2.0 cm

11603 excised diameter 2.1 to 3.0 cm

11604 excised diameter 3.1 to 4.0 cm

11606 excised diameter over 4.0 cm

11620 Excision, malignant lesion including margins, scalp, neck, hands, feet, genitalia; excised diameter 0.5 cm or less

11621 excised diameter 0.6 to 1.0 cm

11622 excised diameter 1.1 to 2.0 cm

11623 excised diameter 2.1 to 3.0 cm

11624 excised diameter 3.1 to 4.0 cm

11626 excised diameter over 4.0 cm

11640 Excision, malignant lesion including margins, face, ears, eyelids, nose, lips; excised diameter 0.5 cm or less

11641 excised diameter 0.6 to 1.0 cm

11642 excised diameter 1.1 to 2.0 cm

11643 excised diameter 2.1 to 3.0 cm

11644 excised diameter 3.1 to 4.0 cm

11646 excised diameter over 4.0 cm

(For eyelids involving more than skin, see also 67800 et seq)

Nails

(For drainage of paronychia or onychia, see 10060, 10061)

11719 Trimming of nondystrophic nails, any number

11720 Debridement of nail(s) by any method(s); one to five

11721 six or more

11730 Avulsion of nail plate, partial or complete, simple; single

+ 11732 each additional nail plate (List separately in addition to code for primary procedure)

(Use 11732 in conjunction with 11730)

11740 Evacuation of subungual hematoma

11750 Excision of nail and nail matrix, partial or complete, (eg, ingrown or deformed nail) for permanent removal;

11752 with amputation of tuft of distal phalanx

(For skin graft, if used, use 15050)

11755 Biopsy of nail unit (eg, plate, bed, matrix, hyponychium, proximal and lateral nail folds) (separate procedure)

11760 Repair of nail bed

11762 Reconstruction of nail bed with graft

11765 Wedge excision of skin of nail fold (eg, for ingrown toenail)

Pilonidal Cyst

11770 Excision of pilonidal cyst or sinus; simple

11771 extensive

11772 complicated

(For incision of pilonidal cyst, see 10080, 10081)

Introduction

11900 Injection, intralesional; up to and including seven lesions

11901 more than seven lesions

(11900, 11901 are not to be used for preoperative local anesthetic injection)

(For veins, see 36470, 36471)

(For intralesional chemotherapy administration, see 96405, 96406)

11920 Tattooing, intradermal introduction of insoluble opaque pigments to correct color defects of skin, including micropigmentation; 6.0 sq cm or less

11921 6.1 to 20.0 sq cm

+ 11922 each additional 20.0 sq cm (List separately in addition to code for primary procedure)

(Use 11922 in conjunction with 11921)

11950 Subcutaneous injection of filling material (eg, collagen); 1 cc or less

11951 1.1 to 5.0 cc

11952 5.1 to 10.0 cc

11954 over 10.0 cc

11960 Insertion of tissue expander(s) for other than breast, including subsequent expansion

(For breast reconstruction with tissue expander(s), use 19357)

11970 Replacement of tissue expander with permanent prosthesis

11971 Removal of tissue expander(s) without insertion of prosthesis

11975 Insertion, implantable contraceptive capsules

11976 Removal, implantable contraceptive capsules

11977 Removal with reinsertion, implantable contraceptive capsules

11980 Subcutaneous hormone pellet implantation (implantation of estradiol and/or testosterone pellets beneath the skin)

11981 Insertion, non-biodegradable drug delivery implant

11982 Removal, non-biodegradable drug delivery implant

11983 Removal with reinsertion, non-biodegradable drug delivery implant

Repair (Closure)

Use the codes in this section to designate wound closure utilizing sutures, staples, or tissue adhesives (eg, 2-cyanoacrylate), either singly or in combination with each other, or in combination with adhesive strips. Wound closure utilizing adhesive strips as the sole repair material should be coded using the appropriate E/M code.

Definitions

The repair of wounds may be classified as Simple, Intermediate, or Complex.

Simple repair is used when the wound is superficial; eg, involving primarily epidermis or dermis, or subcutaneous tissues without significant involvement of deeper structures, and requires simple one layer closure. This includes local anesthesia and chemical or electrocauterization of wounds not closed.

Intermediate repair includes the repair of wounds that, in addition to the above, require layered closure of one or more of the deeper layers of subcutaneous tissue and superficial (non-muscle) fascia, in addition to the skin (epidermal and dermal) closure. Single-layer closure of heavily contaminated wounds that have required extensive cleaning or removal of particulate matter also constitutes intermediate repair.

Complex repair includes the repair of wounds requiring more than layered closure, viz., scar revision, debridement (eg, traumatic lacerations or avulsions), extensive undermining, stents or retention sutures. Necessary preparation includes creation of a defect for repairs (eg, excision of a scar requiring a complex repair) or the debridement of complicated lacerations or avulsions. Complex repair does not include excision of benign (11400-11446) or malignant (11600-11646) lesions.

Instructions for listing services at time of wound repair:

1. The repaired wound(s) should be measured and recorded in centimeters, whether curved, angular, or stellate.

2. When multiple wounds are repaired, add together the lengths of those in the same classification (see above) and from all anatomic sites that are grouped together into the same code descriptor. For example, add together the lengths of intermediate repairs to the trunk and extremities. Do not add lengths of repairs from different groupings of anatomic sites (eg, face and extremities). Also, do not add together lengths of different classifications (eg, intermediate and complex repairs).

When more than one classification of wounds is repaired, list the more complicated as the primary procedure and the less complicated as the secondary procedure, using modifier 51.

3. Decontamination and/or debridement: Debridement is considered a separate procedure only when gross contamination requires prolonged cleansing, when appreciable amounts of devitalized or contaminated tissue are removed, or when debridement is carried out separately without immediate primary closure. (For extensive debridement of soft tissue and/or bone, see 11040-11044.)

(For extensive debridement of soft tissue and/or bone, not associated with open fracture(s) and/or dislocation(s) resulting from penetrating and/or blunt trauma, see 11040-11044.)

(For extensive debridement of subcutaneous tissue, muscle fascia, muscle, and/or bone associated with open fracture(s) and/or dislocation(s), see 11010-11012.)

4. Involvement of nerves, blood vessels and tendons: Report under appropriate system (Nervous, Cardiovascular, Musculoskeletal) for repair of these structures. The repair of these associated wounds is included in the primary procedure unless it qualifies as a complex wound, in which case modifier 51 applies.

Simple ligation of vessels in an open wound is considered as part of any wound closure.

Simple "exploration" of nerves, blood vessels or tendons exposed in an open wound is also considered part of the essential treatment of the wound and is not a separate procedure unless appreciable dissection is required. If the wound requires enlargement, extension of dissection (to determine penetration), debridement, removal of foreign body(s), ligation or coagulation of minor subcutaneous and/or muscular blood vessel(s) of the subcutaneous tissue, muscle fascia, and/or muscle, not requiring thoracotomy or laparotomy, use codes 20100-20103, as appropriate.

Repair—Simple

Sum of lengths of repairs for each group of anatomic sites.

12001	Simple repair of superficial wounds of scalp, neck, axillae, external genitalia, trunk and/or extremities (including hands and feet); 2.5 cm or less
12002	2.6 cm to 7.5 cm
12004	7.6 cm to 12.5 cm
12005	12.6 cm to 20.0 cm
12006	20.1 cm to 30.0 cm
12007	over 30.0 cm
12011	Simple repair of superficial wounds of face, ears, eyelids, nose, lips and/or mucous membranes; 2.5 cm or less
12013	2.6 cm to 5.0 cm
12014	5.1 cm to 7.5 cm
12015	7.6 cm to 12.5 cm
12016	12.6 cm to 20.0 cm
12017	20.1 cm to 30.0 cm
12018	over 30.0 cm

12020 Treatment of superficial wound dehiscence; simple closure

12021 with packing

(For extensive or complicated secondary wound closure, use 13160)

Repair—Intermediate

Sum of lengths of repairs for each group of anatomic sites.

12031 Layer closure of wounds of scalp, axillae, trunk and/or extremities (excluding hands and feet); 2.5 cm or less

12032 2.6 cm to 7.5 cm

12034 7.6 cm to 12.5 cm

12035 12.6 cm to 20.0 cm

12036 20.1 cm to 30.0 cm

12037 over 30.0 cm

12041 Layer closure of wounds of neck, hands, feet and/or external genitalia; 2.5 cm or less

12042 2.6 cm to 7.5 cm

12044 7.6 cm to 12.5 cm

12045 12.6 cm to 20.0 cm

12046 20.1 cm to 30.0 cm

12047 over 30.0 cm

12051 Layer closure of wounds of face, ears, eyelids, nose, lips and/or mucous membranes; 2.5 cm or less

12052 2.6 cm to 5.0 cm

12053 5.1 cm to 7.5 cm

12054 7.6 cm to 12.5 cm

12055 12.6 cm to 20.0 cm

12056 20.1 cm to 30.0 cm

12057 over 30.0 cm

Repair—Complex

Reconstructive procedures, complicated wound closure.

Sum of lengths of repairs for each group of anatomic sites.

(For full thickness repair of lip or eyelid, see respective anatomical subsections)

13100 Repair, complex, trunk; 1.1 cm to 2.5 cm

(For 1.0 cm or less, see simple or intermediate repairs)

13101 2.6 cm to 7.5 cm

+ 13102 each additional 5 cm or less (List separately in addition to code for primary procedure)

(Use 13102 in conjunction with 13101)

13120 Repair, complex, scalp, arms, and/or legs; 1.1 cm to 2.5 cm

(For 1.0 cm or less, see simple or intermediate repairs)

13121 2.6 cm to 7.5 cm

+ 13122 each additional 5 cm or less (List separately in addition to code for primary procedure)

(Use 13122 in conjunction with 13121)

13131 Repair, complex, forehead, cheeks, chin, mouth, neck, axillae, genitalia, hands and/or feet; 1.1 cm to 2.5 cm

(For 1.0 cm or less, see simple or intermediate repairs)

13132 2.6 cm to 7.5 cm

+ 13133 each additional 5 cm or less (List separately in addition to code for primary procedure)

(Use 13133 in conjunction with 13132)

13150 Repair, complex, eyelids, nose, ears and/or lips; 1.0 cm or less

(See also 40650-40654, 67961-67975)

13151 1.1 cm to 2.5 cm

13152 2.6 cm to 7.5 cm

+ 13153 each additional 5 cm or less (List separately in addition to code for primary procedure)

(Use 13153 in conjunction with 13152)

13160 Secondary closure of surgical wound or dehiscence, extensive or complicated

(For packing or simple secondary wound closure, see 12020, 12021)

Adjacent Tissue Transfer or Rearrangement

For full thickness repair of lip or eyelid, see respective anatomical subsections.

Excision (including lesion) and/or repair by adjacent tissue transfer or rearrangement (eg, Z-plasty, W-plasty, V-Y plasty, rotation flap, advancement flap, double pedicle flap). When applied in repairing lacerations, the procedures listed must be developed by the surgeon to accomplish the repair. They do not apply when direct closure or rearrangement of traumatic wounds incidentally result in these configurations.

Skin graft necessary to close secondary defect is considered an additional procedure. For purposes of code selection, the term "defect" includes the primary and secondary defects. The primary defect resulting from the excision and the secondary defect resulting from flap design to perform the reconstruction are measured together to determine the code.

14000 Adjacent tissue transfer or rearrangement, trunk; defect 10 sq cm or less

14001 defect 10.1 sq cm to 30.0 sq cm

14020 Adjacent tissue transfer or rearrangement, scalp, arms and/or legs; defect 10 sq cm or less

14021 defect 10.1 sq cm to 30.0 sq cm

14040 Adjacent tissue transfer or rearrangement, forehead, cheeks, chin, mouth, neck, axillae, genitalia, hands and/or feet; defect 10 sq cm or less

14041 defect 10.1 sq cm to 30.0 sq cm

14060 Adjacent tissue transfer or rearrangement, eyelids, nose, ears and/or lips; defect 10 sq cm or less

14061 defect 10.1 sq cm to 30.0 sq cm

 (For eyelid, full thickness, see 67961 et seq)

14300 Adjacent tissue transfer or rearrangement, more than 30 sq cm, unusual or complicated, any area

14350 Filleted finger or toe flap, including preparation of recipient site

Skin Replacement Surgery and Skin Substitutes

Identify by size and location of the defect (recipient area) and the type of graft or skin substitute; includes simple debridement of granulation tissue or recent avulsion.

When a primary procedure such as orbitectomy, radical mastectomy, or deep tumor removal requires skin graft for definitive closure, see appropriate anatomical subsection for primary procedure and this section for skin graft or skin substitute.

►Use 15002-15005 for initial wound recipient site preparation.◄

Use 15100-15261 for autologous skin grafts. For autologous tissue-cultured epidermal grafts, use 15150-15157. For harvesting of autologous keratinocytes and dermal tissue for tissue-cultured skin grafts, use 15040. Procedures are coded by recipient site. Use 15170-15176 for acellular dermal replacement. Use modifier 58 for staged application procedure(s).

Repair of donor site requiring skin graft or local flaps is to be added as an additional procedure.

►Codes 15002-15005 describe burn and wound preparation or incisional or excisional release of scar contracture resulting in an open wound requiring a skin graft. Codes 15100-15431 describe the application of skin replacements and skin substitutes. The following definition should be applied to those codes that reference "100 sq cm or 1% of body area of infants and children" when determining the involvement of body size: The measurement of 100 sq cm is applicable to adults and children age 10 and older; percentages of body surface area apply to infants and children younger than the age of 10.

These codes are not intended to be reported for simple graft application alone or application stabilized with dressings (eg, by simple gauze wrap). The skin substitute/graft is anchored using the surgeon's choice of fixation. When services are performed in the office, the supply of the skin substitute/graft should be reported separately. Routine dressing supplies are not reported separately.◄

(For microvascular flaps, see 15756-15758)

Surgical Preparation

►(15000, 15001 have been deleted. To report, see 15002-15005)◄

● **15002** Surgical preparation or creation of recipient site by excision of open wounds, burn eschar, or scar (including subcutaneous tissues), or incisional release of scar contracture, trunk, arms, legs; first 100 sq cm or 1% of body area of infants and children

+● **15003** each additional 100 sq cm or each additional 1% of body area of infants and children (List separately in addition to code for primary procedure)

►(Use 15003 in conjunction with 15002)◄

● **15004** Surgical preparation or creation of recipient site by excision of open wounds, burn eschar, or scar (including subcutaneous tissues), or incisional release of scar contracture, face, scalp, eyelids, mouth, neck, ears, orbits, genitalia, hands, feet and/or multiple digits; first 100 sq cm or 1% of body area of infants and children

+● **15005** each additional 100 sq cm or each additional 1% of body area of infants and children (List separately in addition to code for primary procedure)

►(Use 15005 in conjunction with 15004)◄

►(Report 15002-15005 in conjunction with code for appropriate skin grafts or replacements [15050-15261, 15330-15336]. List the graft or replacement separately by its procedure number when the graft, immediate or delayed, is applied)◄

►(For excision of benign lesions, see 11400-11471)◄

►(For excision of malignant lesions, see 11600-11646)◄

►(For excision to prepare or create recipient site with dressings or materials not listed in 15040-15431, use 15002-15005 only)◄

►(For excision with immediate skin grafting, use 15002-15005 in conjunction with 15050-15261)◄

►(For excision with immediate allograft skin placement, use 15002-15005 in conjunction with 15300-15336 and 15360-15366)◄

►(For excision with immediate xenogeneic dermis placement, use 15002-15005 in conjunction with 15400-15421)◄

Surgery: Integumentary System

Grafts

Autograft/Tissue Cultured Autograft

15040 Harvest of skin for tissue cultured skin autograft, 100 sq cm or less

15050 Pinch graft, single or multiple, to cover small ulcer, tip of digit, or other minimal open area (except on face), up to defect size 2 cm diameter

15100 Split-thickness autograft, trunk, arms, legs; first 100 sq cm or less, or 1% of body area of infants and children (except 15050)

+ 15101 each additional 100 sq cm, or each additional 1% of body area of infants and children, or part thereof (List separately in addition to code for primary procedure)

(Use 15101 in conjunction with 15100)

15110 Epidermal autograft, trunk, arms, legs; first 100 sq cm or less, or 1% of body area of infants and children

+ 15111 each additional 100 sq cm, or each additional 1% of body area of infants and children, or part thereof (List separately in addition to code for primary procedure)

(Use 15111 in conjunction with 15110)

15115 Epidermal autograft, face, scalp, eyelids, mouth, neck, ears, orbits, genitalia, hands, feet, and/or multiple digits; first 100 sq cm or less, or 1% of body area of infants and children

+ 15116 each additional 100 sq cm, or each additional 1% of body area of infants and children, or part thereof (List separately in addition to code for primary procedure)

(Use 15116 in conjunction with 15115)

15120 Split-thickness autograft, face, scalp, eyelids, mouth, neck, ears, orbits, genitalia, hands, feet, and/or multiple digits; first 100 sq cm or less, or 1% of body area of infants and children (except 15050)

+ 15121 each additional 100 sq cm, or each additional 1% of body area of infants and children, or part thereof (List separately in addition to code for primary procedure)

(Use 15121 in conjunction with 15120)

(For eyelids, see also 67961 et seq)

15130 Dermal autograft, trunk, arms, legs; first 100 sq cm or less, or 1% of body area of infants and children

+ 15131 each additional 100 sq cm, or each additional 1% of body area of infants and children, or part thereof (List separately in addition to code for primary procedure)

(Use 15131 in conjunction with 15130)

15135 Dermal autograft, face, scalp, eyelids, mouth, neck, ears, orbits, genitalia, hands, feet, and/or multiple digits; first 100 sq cm or less, or 1% of body area of infants and children

+ 15136 each additional 100 sq cm, or each additional 1% of body area of infants and children, or part thereof (List separately in addition to code for primary procedure)

(Use 15136 in conjunction with 15135)

15150 Tissue cultured epidermal autograft, trunk, arms, legs; first 25 sq cm or less

+ 15151 additional 1 sq cm to 75 sq cm (List separately in addition to code for primary procedure)

(Do not report 15151 more than once per session)

(Use 15151 in conjunction with 15150)

+ 15152 each additional 100 sq cm, or each additional 1% of body area of infants and children, or part thereof (List separately in addition to code for primary procedure)

(Use 15152 in conjunction with 15151)

15155 Tissue cultured epidermal autograft, face, scalp, eyelids, mouth, neck, ears, orbits, genitalia, hands, feet, and/or multiple digits; first 25 sq cm or less

+ 15156 additional 1 sq cm to 75 sq cm (List separately in addition to code for primary procedure)

(Do not report 15156 more than once per session)

(Use 15156 in conjunction with 15155)

+ 15157 each additional 100 sq cm, or each additional 1% of body area of infants and children, or part thereof (List separately in addition to code for primary procedure)

(Use 15157 in conjunction with 15156)

Acellular Dermal Replacement

15170 Acellular dermal replacement, trunk, arms, legs; first 100 sq cm or less, or 1% of body area of infants and children

+ 15171 each additional 100 sq cm, or each additional 1% of body area of infants and children, or part thereof (List separately in addition to code for primary procedure)

(Use 15171 in conjunction with 15170)

15175 Acellular dermal replacement, face, scalp, eyelids, mouth, neck, ears, orbits, genitalia, hands, feet, and/or multiple digits; first 100 sq cm or less, or 1% of body area of infants and children

+ 15176 each additional 100 sq cm, or each additional 1% of body area of infants and children, or part thereof (List separately in addition to code for primary procedure)

(Use 15176 in conjunction with 15175)

15200 Full thickness graft, free, including direct closure of donor site, trunk; 20 sq cm or less

+ 15201 each additional 20 sq cm (List separately in addition to code for primary procedure)

(Use 15201 in conjunction with 15200)

15220 Full thickness graft, free, including direct closure of donor site, scalp, arms, and/or legs; 20 sq cm or less

+ 15221 each additional 20 sq cm (List separately in addition to code for primary procedure)

(Use 15221 in conjunction with 15220)

15240 Full thickness graft, free, including direct closure of donor site, forehead, cheeks, chin, mouth, neck, axillae, genitalia, hands, and/or feet; 20 sq cm or less

(For finger tip graft, use 15050)

(For repair of syndactyly, fingers, see 26560-26562)

+ 15241 each additional 20 sq cm (List separately in addition to code for primary procedure)

(Use 15241 in conjunction with 15240)

15260 Full thickness graft, free, including direct closure of donor site, nose, ears, eyelids, and/or lips; 20 sq cm or less

+ 15261 each additional 20 sq cm (List separately in addition to code for primary procedure)

(Use 15261 in conjunction with 15260)

(For eyelids, see also 67961 et seq)

(Repair of donor site requiring skin graft or local flaps, to be added as additional separate procedure)

Allograft/Tissue Cultured Allogeneic Skin Substitute

Application of a non-autologous human skin graft (ie, homograft) from a donor to a part of the recipient's body to resurface an area damaged by burns, traumatic injury, soft tissue infection and/or tissue necrosis or surgery.

15300 Allograft skin for temporary wound closure, trunk, arms, legs; first 100 sq cm or less, or 1% of body area of infants and children

+ 15301 each additional 100 sq cm, or each additional 1% of body area of infants and children, or part thereof (List separately in addition to code for primary procedure)

(Use 15301 in conjunction with 15300)

15320 Allograft skin for temporary wound closure, face, scalp, eyelids, mouth, neck, ears, orbits, genitalia, hands, feet, and/or multiple digits; first 100 sq cm or less, or 1% of body area of infants and children

+ 15321 each additional 100 sq cm, or each additional 1% of body area of infants and children, or part thereof (List separately in addition to code for primary procedure)

(Use 15321 in conjunction with 15320)

15330 Acellular dermal allograft, trunk, arms, legs; first 100 sq cm or less, or 1% of body area of infants and children

+ 15331 each additional 100 sq cm, or each additional 1% of body area of infants and children, or part thereof (List separately in addition to code for primary procedure)

(Use 15331 in conjunction with 15330)

15335 Acellular dermal allograft, face, scalp, eyelids, mouth, neck, ears, orbits, genitalia, hands, feet, and/or multiple digits; first 100 sq cm or less, or 1% of body area of infants and children

+ 15336 each additional 100 sq cm, or each additional 1% of body area of infants and children, or part thereof (List separately in addition to code for primary procedure)

(Use 15336 in conjunction with 15335)

15340 Tissue cultured allogeneic skin substitute; first 25 sq cm or less

+ 15341 each additional 25 sq cm

(Use 15341 in conjunction with 15340)

►(Do not report 15340, 15341 in conjunction with 11040-11042, 15002-15005)◄

(15342 has been deleted. To report, see 15170, 15175, 15340, 15360, 15365)

(15343 has been deleted. To report, see 15171, 15176, 15341, 15361, 15366)

(15350 has been deleted. To report, see 15300, 15320, 15330, 15335)

(15351 has been deleted. To report, see 15301, 15321, 15331, 15336)

15360 Tissue cultured allogeneic dermal substitute, trunk, arms, legs; first 100 sq cm or less, or 1% of body area of infants and children

+ 15361 each additional 100 sq cm, or each additional 1% of body area of infants and children, or part thereof (List separately in addition to code for primary procedure)

(Use 15361 in conjunction with 15360)

15365 Tissue cultured allogeneic dermal substitute, face, scalp, eyelids, mouth, neck, ears, orbits, genitalia, hands, feet, and/or multiple digits; first 100 sq cm or less, or 1% of body area of infants and children

+ 15366 each additional 100 sq cm, or each additional 1% of body area of infants and children, or part thereof (List separately in addition to code for primary procedure)

(Use 15366 in conjunction with 15365)

Surgery: Integumentary System

Surgery: Integumentary System

Xenograft

Application of a non-human skin graft or biologic wound dressing (eg, porcine tissue or pigskin) to a part of the recipient's body following debridement of the burn wound or area of traumatic injury, soft tissue infection and/or tissue necrosis, or surgery.

15400 Xenograft, skin (dermal), for temporary wound closure, trunk, arms, legs; first 100 sq cm or less, or 1% of body area of infants and children

+ **15401** each additional 100 sq cm, or each additional 1% of body area of infants and children, or part thereof (List separately in addition to code for primary procedure)

(Use 15401 in conjunction with 15400)

15420 Xenograft skin (dermal), for temporary wound closure, face, scalp, eyelids, mouth, neck, ears, orbits, genitalia, hands, feet, and/or multiple digits; first 100 sq cm or less, or 1% of body area of infants and children

+ **15421** each additional 100 sq cm, or each additional 1% of body area of infants and children, or part thereof (List separately in addition to code for primary procedure)

(Use 15421 in conjunction with 15420)

15430 Acellular xenograft implant; first 100 sq cm or less, or 1% of body area of infants and children

+ **15431** each additional 100 sq cm, or each additional 1% of body area of infants and children, or part thereof (List separately in addition to code for primary procedure)

(Use 15431 in conjunction with 15430)

▶(Do not report 15430, 15431 in conjunction with 11040-11042, 15002-15005, 0170T)◀

Flaps (Skin and/or Deep Tissues)

Regions listed refer to recipient area (not donor site) when flap is being attached in transfer or to final site.

Regions listed refer to donor site when tube is formed for later or when "delay" of flap is prior to transfer.

Procedures 15570-15738 do not include extensive immobilization (eg, large plaster casts and other immobilizing devices are considered additional separate procedures).

Repair of donor site requiring skin graft or local flaps is considered an additional separate procedure.

(For microvascular flaps, see 15756-15758)

▶(For flaps without inclusion of a vascular pedicle, see 15570-15576)◀

▶(For adjacent tissue transfer flaps, see 14000-14300)◀

15570 Formation of direct or tubed pedicle, with or without transfer; trunk

15572 scalp, arms, or legs

15574 forehead, cheeks, chin, mouth, neck, axillae, genitalia, hands or feet

15576 eyelids, nose, ears, lips, or intraoral

15600 Delay of flap or sectioning of flap (division and inset); at trunk

15610 at scalp, arms, or legs

15620 at forehead, cheeks, chin, neck, axillae, genitalia, hands, or feet

15630 at eyelids, nose, ears, or lips

15650 Transfer, intermediate, of any pedicle flap (eg, abdomen to wrist, Walking tube), any location

(For eyelids, nose, ears, or lips, see also anatomical area)

(For revision, defatting or rearranging of transferred pedicle flap or skin graft, see 13100-14300)

(Procedures 15732-15738 are described by donor site of the muscle, myocutaneous, or fasciocutaneous flap)

● **15731** Forehead flap with preservation of vascular pedicle (eg, axial pattern flap, paramedian forehead flap)

▶(For muscle, myocutaneous, or fasciocutaneous flap of the head or neck, use 15732)◀

15732 Muscle, myocutaneous, or fasciocutaneous flap; head and neck (eg, temporalis, masseter muscle, sternocleidomastoid, levator scapulae)

▶(For forehead flap with preservation of vascular pedicle, use 15731)◀

15734 trunk

15736 upper extremity

15738 lower extremity

Other Flaps and Grafts

Repair of donor site requiring skin graft or local flaps should be reported as an additional procedure.

15740 Flap; island pedicle

15750 neurovascular pedicle

15756 Free muscle or myocutaneous flap with microvascular anastomosis

(Do not report code 69990 in addition to code 15756)

15757 Free skin flap with microvascular anastomosis

(Do not report code 69990 in addition to code 15757)

15758 Free fascial flap with microvascular anastomosis

(Do not report code 69990 in addition to code 15758)

15760 Graft; composite (eg, full thickness of external ear or nasal ala), including primary closure, donor area

15770 derma-fat-fascia

15775 Punch graft for hair transplant; 1 to 15 punch grafts

15776 more than 15 punch grafts

 (For strip transplant, use 15220)

Other Procedures

15780 Dermabrasion; total face (eg, for acne scarring, fine wrinkling, rhytids, general keratosis)

15781 segmental, face

15782 regional, other than face

15783 superficial, any site, (eg, tattoo removal)

15786 Abrasion; single lesion (eg, keratosis, scar)

+ **15787** each additional four lesions or less (List separately in addition to code for primary procedure)

 (Use 15787 in conjunction with 15786)

15788 Chemical peel, facial; epidermal

15789 dermal

15792 Chemical peel, nonfacial; epidermal

15793 dermal

 (15810, 15811 have been deleted)

15819 Cervicoplasty

15820 Blepharoplasty, lower eyelid;

15821 with extensive herniated fat pad

15822 Blepharoplasty, upper eyelid;

15823 with excessive skin weighting down lid

 (For bilateral blepharoplasty, add modifier 50)

15824 Rhytidectomy; forehead

 (For repair of brow ptosis, use 67900)

15825 neck with platysmal tightening (platysmal flap, P-flap)

15826 glabellar frown lines

15828 cheek, chin, and neck

15829 superficial musculoaponeurotic system (SMAS) flap

 (For bilateral rhytidectomy, add modifier 50)

● **15830** Excision, excessive skin and subcutaneous tissue (includes lipectomy); abdomen, infraumbilical panniculectomy

 ►(Do not report 15830 in conjunction with 12031, 12032, 12034, 12035, 12036, 12037, 13100, 13101, 13102, 14000-14001, 14300)◄

 ►(15831 has been deleted. To report abdominoplasty with panniculectomy, use 15830 in conjunction with 15847. To report other abdominoplasty, use 17999)◄

15832 thigh

15833 leg

15834 hip

15835 buttock

15836 arm

15837 forearm or hand

15838 submental fat pad

15839 other area

 (For bilateral procedure, add modifier 50)

15840 Graft for facial nerve paralysis; free fascia graft (including obtaining fascia)

 (For bilateral procedure, add modifier 50)

15841 free muscle graft (including obtaining graft)

15842 free muscle flap by microsurgical technique

 (Do not report code 69990 in addition to code 15842)

15845 regional muscle transfer

 (For intravenous fluorescein examination of blood flow in graft or flap, use 15860)

 (For nerve transfers, decompression, or repair, see 64831-64876, 64905, 64907, 69720, 69725, 69740, 69745, 69955)

+● **15847** Excision, excessive skin and subcutaneous tissue (includes lipectomy), abdomen (eg, abdominoplasty) (includes umbilical transposition and fascial plication) (List separately in addition to code for primary procedure)

 ►(Use 15847 in conjunction with 15830)◄

 ►(For abdominal wall hernia repair, see 49491-49587)◄

 ►(To report other abdominoplasty, use 17999)◄

15850 Removal of sutures under anesthesia (other than local), same surgeon

15851 Removal of sutures under anesthesia (other than local), other surgeon

15852 Dressing change (for other than burns) under anesthesia (other than local)

15860 Intravenous injection of agent (eg, fluorescein) to test vascular flow in flap or graft

15876 Suction assisted lipectomy; head and neck

15877 trunk

15878 upper extremity

15879 lower extremity

Pressure Ulcers (Decubitus Ulcers)

15920 Excision, coccygeal pressure ulcer, with coccygectomy; with primary suture

15922 with flap closure

15931 Excision, sacral pressure ulcer, with primary suture;

15933 with ostectomy

Surgery: Integumentary System

Surgery: Integumentary System

15934 Excision, sacral pressure ulcer, with skin flap closure;

15935 with ostectomy

15936 Excision, sacral pressure ulcer, in preparation for muscle or myocutaneous flap or skin graft closure;

15937 with ostectomy

(For repair of defect using muscle or myocutaneous flap, use code(s) 15734 and/or 15738 in addition to 15936, 15937. For repair of defect using split skin graft, use codes 15100 and/or 15101 in addition to 15936, 15937)

15940 Excision, ischial pressure ulcer, with primary suture;

15941 with ostectomy (ischiectomy)

15944 Excision, ischial pressure ulcer, with skin flap closure;

15945 with ostectomy

15946 Excision, ischial pressure ulcer, with ostectomy, in preparation for muscle or myocutaneous flap or skin graft closure

(For repair of defect using muscle or myocutaneous flap, use code(s) 15734 and/or 15738 in addition to 15946. For repair of defect using split skin graft, use codes 15100 and/or 15101 in addition to 15946)

15950 Excision, trochanteric pressure ulcer, with primary suture;

15951 with ostectomy

15952 Excision, trochanteric pressure ulcer, with skin flap closure;

15953 with ostectomy

15956 Excision, trochanteric pressure ulcer, in preparation for muscle or myocutaneous flap or skin graft closure;

15958 with ostectomy

(For repair of defect using muscle or myocutaneous flap, use code(s) 15734 and/or 15738 in addition to 15956, 15958. For repair of defect using split skin graft, use codes 15100 and/or 15101 in addition to 15956, 15958)

15999 Unlisted procedure, excision pressure ulcer

▶(For free skin graft to close ulcer or donor site, see 15002 et seq)◀

Burns, Local Treatment

Procedures 16000-16036 refer to local treatment of burned surface only. Codes 16020-16030 include the application of materials (eg, dressings) not described in 15100-15431.

List percentage of body surface involved and depth of burn.

For necessary related medical services (eg, hospital visits, detention) in management of burned patients, see appropriate services in **Evaluation and Management** and **Medicine** sections.

For the application of skin grafts or skin substitutes, see 15100-15650.

16000 Initial treatment, first degree burn, when no more than local treatment is required

(16010, 16015 have been deleted. To report, see 16020-16030)

16020 Dressings and/or debridement of partial-thickness burns, initial or subsequent; small (less than 5% total body surface area)

16025 medium (eg, whole face or whole extremity, or 5% to 10% total body surface area)

16030 large (eg, more than one extremity, or greater than 10% total body surface area)

16035 Escharotomy; initial incision

+ 16036 each additional incision (List separately in addition to code for primary procedure)

(Use 16036 in conjunction with 16035)

(For debridement, curettement of burn wound, see 16020-16030)

Destruction

Destruction means the ablation of benign, premalignant or malignant tissues by any method, with or without curettement, including local anesthesia, and not usually requiring closure.

Any method includes electrosurgery, cryosurgery, laser and chemical treatment. Lesions include condylomata, papillomata, molluscum contagiosum, herpetic lesions, warts (ie, common, plantar, flat), milia, or other benign, premalignant (eg, actinic keratoses), or malignant lesions.

(For destruction of lesion(s) in specific anatomic sites, see 40820, 46900-46917, 46924, 54050-54057, 54065, 56501, 56515, 57061, 57065, 67850, 68135)

(For paring or cutting of benign hyperkeratotic lesions (eg, corns or calluses), see 11055-11057)

(For sharp removal or electrosurgical destruction of skin tags and fibrocutaneous tags, see 11200, 11201)

(For cryotherapy of acne, use 17340)

(For initiation or follow-up care of topical chemotherapy (eg, 5-FU or similar agents), see appropriate office visits)

(For shaving of epidermal or dermal lesions, see 11300-11313)

Destruction, Benign or Premalignant Lesions

▲ **17000** Destruction (eg, laser surgery, electrosurgery, cryosurgery, chemosurgery, surgical curettement), premalignant lesions (eg, actinic keratoses); first lesion

+ 17003 second through 14 lesions, each (List separately in addition to code for first lesion)

(Use 17003 in conjunction with 17000)

▶(For destruction of common or plantar warts, see 17110, 17111)◀

⊘▲ **17004** Destruction (eg, laser surgery, electrosurgery, cryosurgery, chemosurgery, surgical curettement), premalignant lesions (eg, actinic keratoses), 15 or more lesions

(Do not report 17004 in conjunction with 17000-17003)

17106 Destruction of cutaneous vascular proliferative lesions (eg, laser technique); less than 10 sq cm

17107 10.0 to 50.0 sq cm

17108 over 50.0 sq cm

▲ **17110** Destruction (eg, laser surgery, electrosurgery, cryosurgery, chemosurgery, surgical curettement), of benign lesions other than skin tags or cutaneous vascular lesions; up to 14 lesions

17111 15 or more lesions

17250 Chemical cauterization of granulation tissue (proud flesh, sinus or fistula)

(17250 is not to be used with removal or excision codes for the same lesion)

Destruction, Malignant Lesions, Any Method

17260 Destruction, malignant lesion (eg, laser surgery, electrosurgery, cryosurgery, chemosurgery, surgical curettement), trunk, arms or legs; lesion diameter 0.5 cm or less

17261 lesion diameter 0.6 to 1.0 cm

17262 lesion diameter 1.1 to 2.0 cm

17263 lesion diameter 2.1 to 3.0 cm

17264 lesion diameter 3.1 to 4.0 cm

17266 lesion diameter over 4.0 cm

17270 Destruction, malignant lesion (eg, laser surgery, electrosurgery, cryosurgery, chemosurgery, surgical curettement), scalp, neck, hands, feet, genitalia; lesion diameter 0.5 cm or less

17271 lesion diameter 0.6 to 1.0 cm

17272 lesion diameter 1.1 to 2.0 cm

17273 lesion diameter 2.1 to 3.0 cm

17274 lesion diameter 3.1 to 4.0 cm

17276 lesion diameter over 4.0 cm

17280 Destruction, malignant lesion (eg, laser surgery, electrosurgery, cryosurgery, chemosurgery, surgical curettement), face, ears, eyelids, nose, lips, mucous membrane; lesion diameter 0.5 cm or less

17281 lesion diameter 0.6 to 1.0 cm

17282 lesion diameter 1.1 to 2.0 cm

17283 lesion diameter 2.1 to 3.0 cm

17284 lesion diameter 3.1 to 4.0 cm

17286 lesion diameter over 4.0 cm

Mohs Micrographic Surgery

►Mohs micrographic surgery is a technique for the removal of complex or ill-defined skin cancer with histologic examination of 100% of the surgical margins. It requires a single physician to act in two integrated but separate and distinct capacities: surgeon and pathologist. If either of these responsibilities is delegated to another physician who reports the services separately, these codes should not be reported. The Mohs surgeon removes the tumor tissue and maps and divides the tumor specimen into pieces, and each piece is embedded into an individual tissue block for histopathologic examination. Thus a tissue block in Mohs surgery is defined as an individual tissue piece embedded in a mounting medium for sectioning.◄

If repair is performed, use separate repair, flap, or graft codes. If a biopsy of a suspected skin cancer is performed on the same day as Mohs surgery because there was no prior pathology confirmation of a diagnosis, then report diagnostic skin biopsy (11100, 11101) and frozen section pathology (88331) with modifier 59 to distinguish from the subsequent definitive surgical procedure of Mohs surgery.

►(17304-17310 have been deleted. To report, see 17311-17315)◄

(If additional special pathology procedures, stains or immunostains are required, use 88311-88314, 88342)

►(Do not report 88314 in conjunction with 17311-17315 for routine frozen section stain (eg, hematoxylin and eosin, toluidine blue) performed during Mohs surgery. When a nonroutine histochemical stain on frozen tissue is utilized, report 88314 with modifier 59)◄

►(Do not report 88302-88309 on the same specimen as part of the Mohs surgery)◄

● **17311** Mohs micrographic technique, including removal of all gross tumor, surgical excision of tissue specimens, mapping, color coding of specimens, microscopic examination of specimens by the surgeon, and histopathologic preparation including routine stain(s) (eg, hematoxylin and eosin, toluidine blue), head, neck, hands, feet, genitalia, or any location with surgery directly involving muscle, cartilage, bone, tendon, major nerves, or vessels; first stage, up to 5 tissue blocks

+● **17312** each additional stage after the first stage, up to 5 tissue blocks (List separately in addition to code for primary procedure)

►(Use 17312 in conjunction with 17311)◄

Surgery: Integumentary System

● **17313** Mohs micrographic technique, including removal of all gross tumor, surgical excision of tissue specimens, mapping, color coding of specimens, microscopic examination of specimens by the surgeon, and histopathologic preparation including routine stain(s) (eg, hematoxylin and eosin, toluidine blue), of the trunk, arms, or legs; first stage, up to 5 tissue blocks

+● **17314** each additional stage after the first stage, up to 5 tissue blocks (List separately in addition to code for primary procedure)

▶(Use 17314 in conjunction with 17313)◀

+● **17315** Mohs micrographic technique, including removal of all gross tumor, surgical excision of tissue specimens, mapping, color coding of specimens, microscopic examination of specimens by the surgeon, and histopathologic preparation including routine stain(s) (eg, hematoxylin and eosin, toluidine blue), each additional block after the first 5 tissue blocks, any stage (List separately in addition to code for primary procedure)

▶(Use 17315 in conjunction with 17311-17314)◀

Other Procedures

17340 Cryotherapy (CO_2 slush, liquid N_2) for acne

17360 Chemical exfoliation for acne (eg, acne paste, acid)

17380 Electrolysis epilation, each 30 minutes

(For actinotherapy, use 96900)

17999 Unlisted procedure, skin, mucous membrane and subcutaneous tissue

Breast

Incision

19000 Puncture aspiration of cyst of breast;

+ **19001** each additional cyst (List separately in addition to code for primary procedure)

(Use 19001 in conjunction with 19000)

▶(If imaging guidance is performed, see 76942, 77021, 77031, 77032)◀

19020 Mastotomy with exploration or drainage of abscess, deep

19030 Injection procedure only for mammary ductogram or galactogram

▶(For radiological supervision and interpretation, see 77053, 77054)◀

(For catheter lavage of mammary ducts for collection of cytology specimens, use Category III codes 0046T, 0047T)

Excision

(To report bilateral procedures, report modifier 50 with the procedure code)

Excisional breast surgery includes certain biopsy procedures, the removal of cysts or other benign or malignant tumors or lesions, and the surgical treatment of breast and chest wall malignancies. Biopsy procedures may be percutaneous or open, and they involve the removal of differing amounts of tissue for diagnosis.

Breast biopsies are reported using codes 19100-19103. The open excision of breast lesions (eg, lesions of the breast ducts, cysts, benign or malignant tumors), without specific attention to adequate surgical margins, with or without the preoperative placement of radiological markers, is reported using codes 19110-19126. Partial mastectomy procedures (eg, lumpectomy, tylectomy, quadrantectomy, or segmentectomy) describe open excisions of breast tissue with specific attention to adequate surgical margins.

Partial mastectomy procedures are reported using codes 19301 or 19302 as appropriate. Documentation for partial mastectomy procedures includes attention to the removal of adequate surgical margins surrounding the breast mass or lesion.

Total mastectomy procedures include simple mastectomy, complete mastectomy, subcutaneous mastectomy, modified radical mastectomy, radical mastectomy, and more extended procedures (eg, Urban type operation). Total mastectomy procedures are reported using codes 19303-19307 as appropriate.

Excisions or resections of chest wall tumors including ribs, with or without reconstruction, with or without mediastinal lymphadenectomy, are reported using codes 19260, 19271, or 19272. Codes 19260-19272 are not restricted to breast tumors and are used to report resections of chest wall tumors originating from any chest wall component. (For excision of lung or pleura, see 32310 et seq.)

19100 Biopsy of breast; percutaneous, needle core, not using imaging guidance (separate procedure)

(For fine needle aspiration, use 10021)

(For image guided breast biopsy, see 19102, 19103, 10022)

19101 open, incisional

19102 percutaneous, needle core, using imaging guidance

(For placement of percutaneous localization clip, use 19295)

19103 percutaneous, automated vacuum assisted or rotating biopsy device, using imaging guidance

▶(For imaging guidance performed in conjunction with 19102, 19103, see 76942, 77012, 77021, 77031, 77032)◀

(For placement of percutaneous localization clip, use 19295)

● **19105** Ablation, cryosurgical, of fibroadenoma, including ultrasound guidance, each fibroadenoma

►(Do not report 19105 in conjunction with 76940, 76942)◄

►(For adjacent lesions treated with one cryoprobe insertion, report once)◄

19110 Nipple exploration, with or without excision of a solitary lactiferous duct or a papilloma lactiferous duct

19112 Excision of lactiferous duct fistula

▲ **19120** Excision of cyst, fibroadenoma, or other benign or malignant tumor, aberrant breast tissue, duct lesion, nipple or areolar lesion (except 19300), open, male or female, one or more lesions

19125 Excision of breast lesion identified by preoperative placement of radiological marker, open; single lesion

+ **19126** each additional lesion separately identified by a preoperative radiological marker (List separately in addition to code for primary procedure)

(Use 19126 in conjunction with 19125)

►(19140-19240 have been deleted. To report, see 19300-19307)◄

19260 Excision of chest wall tumor including ribs

19271 Excision of chest wall tumor involving ribs, with plastic reconstruction; without mediastinal lymphadenectomy

19272 with mediastinal lymphadenectomy

(Do not report 19260, 19271, 19272 in conjunction with 32002, 32020, 32100, 32503, 32504)

Introduction

19290 Preoperative placement of needle localization wire, breast;

+ **19291** each additional lesion (List separately in addition to code for primary procedure)

(Use 19291 in conjunction with 19290)

►(For radiological supervision and interpretation, see 76942, 77031, 77032)◄

+ **19295** Image guided placement, metallic localization clip, percutaneous, during breast biopsy (List separately in addition to code for primary procedure)

(Use 19295 in conjunction with 19102, 19103)

19296 Placement of radiotherapy afterloading balloon catheter into the breast for interstitial radioelement application following partial mastectomy, includes imaging guidance; on date separate from partial mastectomy

+ **19297** concurrent with partial mastectomy (List separately in addition to code for primary procedure)

(Use 19297 in conjunction with 19301 or 19302)

⊙ **19298** Placement of radiotherapy afterloading brachytherapy catheters (multiple tube and button type) into the breast for interstitial radioelement application following (at the time of or subsequent to) partial mastectomy, includes imaging guidance

►Mastectomy Procedures◄

● **19300** Mastectomy for gynecomastia

● **19301** Mastectomy, partial (eg, lumpectomy, tylectomy, quadrantectomy, segmentectomy);

● **19302** with axillary lymphadenectomy

►(For placement of radiotherapy afterloading balloon/brachytherapy catheters, see 19296-19298)◄

● **19303** Mastectomy, simple, complete

►(For immediate or delayed insertion of implant, see 19340, 19342)◄

►(For gynecomastia, use 19300)◄

● **19304** Mastectomy, subcutaneous

►(For immediate or delayed insertion of implant, see 19340, 19342)◄

● **19305** Mastectomy, radical, including pectoral muscles, axillary lymph nodes

►(For immediate or delayed insertion of implant, see 19340, 19342)◄

● **19306** Mastectomy, radical, including pectoral muscles, axillary and internal mammary lymph nodes (Urban type operation)

►(For immediate or delayed insertion of implant, see 19340, 19342)◄

● **19307** Mastectomy, modified radical, including axillary lymph nodes, with or without pectoralis minor muscle, but excluding pectoralis major muscle

►(For immediate or delayed insertion of implant, see 19340, 19342)◄

Repair and/or Reconstruction

(To report bilateral procedures, report modifier 50 with the procedure code)

19316 Mastopexy

19318 Reduction mammaplasty

19324 Mammaplasty, augmentation; without prosthetic implant

19325 with prosthetic implant

(For flap or graft, use also appropriate number)

19328	Removal of intact mammary implant
19330	Removal of mammary implant material
19340	Immediate insertion of breast prosthesis following mastopexy, mastectomy or in reconstruction
19342	Delayed insertion of breast prosthesis following mastopexy, mastectomy or in reconstruction

(For supply of implant, use 99070)

(For preparation of custom breast implant, use 19396)

19350	Nipple/areola reconstruction
19355	Correction of inverted nipples
19357	Breast reconstruction, immediate or delayed, with tissue expander, including subsequent expansion
▲ **19361**	Breast reconstruction with latissimus dorsi flap, without prosthetic implant

▶(For insertion of prosthesis, use also 19340)◀

19364	Breast reconstruction with free flap

(Do not report code 69990 in addition to code 19364)

(19364 includes harvesting of the flap, microvascular transfer, closure of the donor site, and inset shaping the flap into a breast)

19366	Breast reconstruction with other technique

(For operating microscope, use 69990)

(For insertion of prosthesis, use also 19340 or 19342)

19367	Breast reconstruction with transverse rectus abdominis myocutaneous flap (TRAM), single pedicle, including closure of donor site;
19368	with microvascular anastomosis (supercharging)

(Do not report code 69990 in addition to code 19368)

19369	Breast reconstruction with transverse rectus abdominis myocutaneous flap (TRAM), double pedicle, including closure of donor site
19370	Open periprosthetic capsulotomy, breast
19371	Periprosthetic capsulectomy, breast
19380	Revision of reconstructed breast
19396	Preparation of moulage for custom breast implant

Other Procedures

(For microwave thermotherapy of the breast, use Category III code 0061T)

19499	Unlisted procedure, breast

Musculoskeletal System

Cast and strapping procedures appear at the end of this section.

The services listed below include the application and removal of the first cast or traction device only. Subsequent replacement of cast and/or traction device may require an additional listing.

Definitions

The terms "closed treatment," "open treatment," and "percutaneous skeletal fixation" have been carefully chosen to accurately reflect current orthopaedic procedural treatments.

Closed treatment specifically means that the fracture site is not surgically opened (exposed to the external environment and directly visualized). This terminology is used to describe procedures that treat fractures by three methods: 1) without manipulation; 2) with manipulation; or 3) with or without traction.

Open treatment is used when the fractured bone is either: 1) surgically opened (exposed to the external environment) and the fracture (bone ends) visualized and internal fixation may be used; or 2) the fractured bone is opened remote from the fracture site in order to insert an intramedullary nail across the fracture site (the fracture site is not opened and visualized).

Percutaneous skeletal fixation describes fracture treatment which is neither open nor closed. In this procedure, the fracture fragments are not visualized, but fixation (eg, pins) is placed across the fracture site, usually under X-ray imaging.

The type of fracture (eg, open, compound, closed) does not have any coding correlation with the type of treatment (eg, closed, open, or percutaneous) provided.

The codes for treatment of fractures and joint injuries (dislocations) are categorized by the type of manipulation (reduction) and stabilization (fixation or immobilization). These codes can apply to either open (compound) or closed fractures or joint injuries.

Skeletal traction is the application of a force (distracting or traction force) to a limb segment through a wire, pin, screw, or clamp that is attached (eg, penetrates) to bone.

Skin traction is the application of a force (longitudinal) to a limb using felt or strapping applied directly to skin only.

External fixation is the usage of skeletal pins plus an attaching mechanism/device used for temporary or definitive treatment of acute or chronic bony deformity.

Codes for obtaining autogenous bone grafts, cartilage, tendon, fascia lata grafts or other tissues through separate incisions are to be used only when the graft is not already listed as part of the basic procedure.

Re-reduction of a fracture and/or dislocation performed by the primary physician may be identified by the addition of the modifier 76 to the usual procedure number to indicate "Repeat Procedure by Same Physician." (See guidelines.)

Codes for external fixation are to be used only when external fixation is not already listed as part of the basic procedure.

All codes for suction irrigation have been deleted. To report, list only the primary surgical procedure performed (eg, sequestrectomy, deep incision).

Manipulation is used throughout the musculoskeletal fracture and dislocation subsections to specifically mean the attempted reduction or restoration of a fracture or joint dislocation to its normal anatomic alignment by the application of manually applied forces.

(For computer-assisted musculoskeletal surgical navigational orthopedic procedures, report 0054T-0056T)

General

Incision

20000	Incision of soft tissue abscess (eg, secondary to osteomyelitis); superficial
20005	deep or complicated

Wound Exploration—Trauma (eg, Penetrating Gunshot, Stab Wound)

20100-20103 relate to wound(s) resulting from penetrating trauma. These codes describe surgical exploration and enlargement of the wound, extension of dissection (to determine penetration), debridement, removal of foreign body(s), ligation or coagulation of minor subcutaneous and/or muscular blood vessel(s), of the subcutaneous tissue, muscle fascia, and/or muscle, not requiring thoracotomy or laparotomy. If a repair is done to major structure(s) or major blood vessel(s) requiring thoracotomy or laparotomy, then those specific code(s) would supersede the use of codes 20100-20103. To report Simple, Intermediate, or Complex repair of wound(s) that do not require enlargement of the wound, extension of dissection, etc., as stated above, use specific Repair code(s) in the **Integumentary System** section.

20100	Exploration of penetrating wound (separate procedure); neck
20101	chest
20102	abdomen/flank/back
20103	extremity

Excision

20150 Excision of epiphyseal bar, with or without autogenous soft tissue graft obtained through same fascial incision

(For aspiration of bone marrow, use 38220)

20200 Biopsy, muscle; superficial

20205 deep

20206 Biopsy, muscle, percutaneous needle

►(If imaging guidance is performed, see 76942, 77012, 77021)◄

(For fine needle aspiration, use 10021 or 10022)

(For evaulation of fine needle aspirate, see 88172-88173)

(For excision of muscle tumor, deep, see specific anatomic section)

20220 Biopsy, bone, trocar, or needle; superficial (eg, ilium, sternum, spinous process, ribs)

20225 deep (eg, vertebral body, femur)

(For bone marrow biopsy, use 38221)

►(For radiologic supervision and interpretation, see 77002, 77012, 77021)◄

20240 Biopsy, bone, open; superficial (eg, ilium, sternum, spinous process, ribs, trochanter of femur)

20245 deep (eg, humerus, ischium, femur)

20250 Biopsy, vertebral body, open; thoracic

20251 lumbar or cervical

(For sequestrectomy, osteomyelitis or drainage of bone abscess, see anatomical area)

Introduction or Removal

(For injection procedure for arthrography, see anatomical area)

20500 Injection of sinus tract; therapeutic (separate procedure)

20501 diagnostic (sinogram)

(For radiological supervision and interpretation, use 76080)

20520 Removal of foreign body in muscle or tendon sheath; simple

20525 deep or complicated

20526 Injection, therapeutic (eg, local anesthetic, corticosteroid), carpal tunnel

20550 Injection(s); single tendon sheath, or ligament, aponeurosis (eg, plantar "fascia")

20551 single tendon origin/insertion

20552 Injection(s); single or multiple trigger point(s), one or two muscle(s)

20553 single or multiple trigger point(s), three or more muscle(s)

►(If imaging guidance is performed, see 76942, 77002, 77021)◄

20600 Arthrocentesis, aspiration and/or injection; small joint or bursa (eg, fingers, toes)

20605 intermediate joint or bursa (eg, temporomandibular, acromioclavicular, wrist, elbow or ankle, olecranon bursa)

20610 major joint or bursa (eg, shoulder, hip, knee joint, subacromial bursa)

►(If imaging guidance is performed, see 76942, 77002, 77012, 77021)◄

20612 Aspiration and/or injection of ganglion cyst(s) any location

(To report multiple ganglion cyst aspirations/injections, use 20612 and append modifier 59)

20615 Aspiration and injection for treatment of bone cyst

20650 Insertion of wire or pin with application of skeletal traction, including removal (separate procedure)

⊘ **20660** Application of cranial tongs, caliper, or stereotactic frame, including removal (separate procedure)

20661 Application of halo, including removal; cranial

20662 pelvic

20663 femoral

20664 Application of halo, including removal, cranial, 6 or more pins placed, for thin skull osteology (eg, pediatric patients, hydrocephalus, osteogenesis imperfecta), requiring general anesthesia

20665 Removal of tongs or halo applied by another physician

20670 Removal of implant; superficial, (eg, buried wire, pin or rod) (separate procedure)

20680 deep (eg, buried wire, pin, screw, metal band, nail, rod or plate)

⊘ **20690** Application of a uniplane (pins or wires in one plane), unilateral, external fixation system

⊘ **20692** Application of a multiplane (pins or wires in more than one plane), unilateral, external fixation system (eg, Ilizarov, Monticelli type)

20693 Adjustment or revision of external fixation system requiring anesthesia (eg, new pin(s) or wire(s) and/or new ring(s) or bar(s))

20694 Removal, under anesthesia, of external fixation system

⊙=Moderate sedation ✚=Add-on code ✒=FDA approval pending

Replantation

20802 Replantation, arm (includes surgical neck of humerus through elbow joint), complete amputation

(To report replantation of incomplete arm amputation, see specific code(s) for repair of bone(s), ligament(s), tendon(s), nerve(s), or blood vessel(s) with modifier 52)

20805 Replantation, forearm (includes radius and ulna to radial carpal joint), complete amputation

(To report replantation of incomplete forearm amputation, see specific code(s) for repair of bone(s), ligament(s), tendon(s), nerve(s), or blood vessel(s) with modifier 52)

20808 Replantation, hand (includes hand through metacarpophalangeal joints), complete amputation

(To report replantation of incomplete hand amputation, see specific code(s) for repair of bone(s), ligament(s), tendon(s), nerve(s), or blood vessel(s) with modifier 52)

20816 Replantation, digit, excluding thumb (includes metacarpophalangeal joint to insertion of flexor sublimis tendon), complete amputation

(To report replantation of incomplete digit amputation, excluding thumb, see specific code(s) for repair of bone(s), ligament(s), tendon(s), nerve(s), or blood vessel(s) with modifier 52)

20822 Replantation, digit, excluding thumb (includes distal tip to sublimis tendon insertion), complete amputation

(To report replantation of incomplete digit amputation, excluding thumb, see specific code(s) for repair of bone(s), ligament(s), tendon(s), nerve(s), or blood vessel(s) with modifier 52)

20824 Replantation, thumb (includes carpometacarpal joint to MP joint), complete amputation

(To report replantation of incomplete thumb amputation, see specific code(s) for repair of bone(s), ligament(s), tendon(s), nerve(s), or blood vessel(s) with modifier 52)

20827 Replantation, thumb (includes distal tip to MP joint), complete amputation

(To report replantation of incomplete thumb amputation, see specific code(s) for repair of bone(s), ligament(s), tendon(s), nerve(s), or blood vessel(s) with modifier 52)

(To report replantation of complete leg amputation, see specific code(s) for repair of bone(s), ligament(s), tendon(s), nerve(s), or blood vessel(s) with modifier 52)

(To report replantation of incomplete leg amputation, see specific code(s) for repair of bone(s), ligament(s), tendon(s), nerve(s), or blood vessel(s) with modifier 52)

20838 Replantation, foot, complete amputation

(To report replantation of incomplete foot amputation, see specific code(s) for repair of bone(s), ligament(s), tendon(s), nerve(s), or blood vessel(s) with modifier 52)

Grafts (or Implants)

Codes for obtaining autogenous bone, cartilage, tendon, fascia lata grafts, or other tissues through separate skin/fascial incisions should be reported separately unless the code descriptor references the harvesting of the graft or implant (eg, includes obtaining graft).

Do not append modifier 62 to bone graft codes 20900-20938.

(For spinal surgery bone graft(s) see codes 20930-20938)

⊘ **20900** Bone graft, any donor area; minor or small (eg, dowel or button)

⊘ **20902** major or large

⊘ **20910** Cartilage graft; costochondral

⊘ **20912** nasal septum

(For ear cartilage, use 21235)

⊘ **20920** Fascia lata graft; by stripper

⊘ **20922** by incision and area exposure, complex or sheet

⊘ **20924** Tendon graft, from a distance (eg, palmaris, toe extensor, plantaris)

⊘ **20926** Tissue grafts, other (eg, paratenon, fat, dermis)

(Codes 20930-20938 are reported in addition to codes for the definitive procedure(s) without modifier 51)

⊘ **20930** Allograft for spine surgery only; morselized

⊘ **20931** structural

⊘ **20936** Autograft for spine surgery only (includes harvesting the graft); local (eg, ribs, spinous process, or laminar fragments) obtained from same incision

⊘ **20937** morselized (through separate skin or fascial incision)

⊘ **20938** structural, bicortical or tricortical (through separate skin or fascial incision)

(For needle aspiration of bone marrow for the purpose of bone grafting, use 38220)

Other Procedures

20950 Monitoring of interstitial fluid pressure (includes insertion of device, eg, wick catheter technique, needle manometer technique) in detection of muscle compartment syndrome

20955 Bone graft with microvascular anastomosis; fibula

20956 iliac crest

20957 metatarsal

20962 other than fibula, iliac crest, or metatarsal

(Do not report code 69990 in addition to codes 20955-20962)

20969 Free osteocutaneous flap with microvascular anastomosis; other than iliac crest, metatarsal, or great toe

20970 iliac crest

20972 metatarsal

20973 great toe with web space

(Do not report code 69990 in addition to codes 20969-20973)

(For great toe, wrap-around procedure, use 26551)

⊘ **20974** Electrical stimulation to aid bone healing; noninvasive (nonoperative)

⊘ **20975** invasive (operative)

20979 Low intensity ultrasound stimulation to aid bone healing, noninvasive (nonoperative)

⊙ **20982** Ablation, bone tumor(s) (eg, osteoid osteoma, metastasis) radiofrequency, percutaneous, including computed tomographic guidance

▶(Do not report 20982 in conjunction with 77013)◀

20999 Unlisted procedure, musculoskeletal system, general

Head

Skull, facial bones, and temporomandibular joint.

Incision

(For drainage of superficial abscess and hematoma, use 20000)

(For removal of embedded foreign body from dentoalveolar structure, see 41805, 41806)

21010 Arthrotomy, temporomandibular joint

(To report bilateral procedures, report 21010 with modifier 50)

Excision

21015 Radical resection of tumor (eg, malignant neoplasm), soft tissue of face or scalp

(To report excision of skull tumor for osteomyelitis, use 61501)

21025 Excision of bone (eg, for osteomyelitis or bone abscess); mandible

21026 facial bone(s)

21029 Removal by contouring of benign tumor of facial bone (eg, fibrous dysplasia)

21030 Excision of benign tumor or cyst of maxilla or zygoma by enucleation and curettage

21031 Excision of torus mandibularis

21032 Excision of maxillary torus palatinus

21034 Excision of malignant tumor of maxilla or zygoma

21040 Excision of benign tumor or cyst of mandible, by enucleation and/or curettage

(For enucleation and/or curettage of benign cysts or tumors of mandible not requiring osteotomy, use 21040)

(For excision of benign tumor or cyst of mandible requiring osteotomy, see 21046-21047)

21044 Excision of malignant tumor of mandible;

21045 radical resection

(For bone graft, use 21215)

21046 Excision of benign tumor or cyst of mandible; requiring intra-oral osteotomy (eg, locally aggressive or destructive lesion(s))

21047 requiring extra-oral osteotomy and partial mandibulectomy (eg, locally aggressive or destructive lesion(s))

21048 Excision of benign tumor or cyst of maxilla; requiring intra-oral osteotomy (eg, locally aggressive or destructive lesion(s))

21049 requiring extra-oral osteotomy and partial maxillectomy (eg, locally aggressive or destructive lesion(s))

21050 Condylectomy, temporomandibular joint (separate procedure)

(For bilateral procedures, report 21050 with modifier 50)

21060 Meniscectomy, partial or complete, temporomandibular joint (separate procedure)

(For bilateral procedures, report 21060 with modifier 50)

21070 Coronoidectomy (separate procedure)

(For bilateral procedures, report 21070 with modifier 50)

▶Head Prosthesis◀

(For application or removal of caliper or tongs, see 20660, 20665.) Codes 21076-21089 describe professional services for the rehabilitation of patients with oral, facial or other anatomical deficiencies by means of prostheses such as an artificial eye, ear, or nose or intraoral obturator to close a cleft. Codes 21076-21089 should only be used when the physician actually designs and prepares the prosthesis (ie, not prepared by an outside laboratory).

21076 Impression and custom preparation; surgical obturator prosthesis

21077 orbital prosthesis

21079 interim obturator prosthesis

21080 definitive obturator prosthesis

21081 mandibular resection prosthesis

21082 palatal augmentation prosthesis

21083 palatal lift prosthesis

21084 speech aid prosthesis

21085 oral surgical splint

21086 auricular prosthesis

21087 nasal prosthesis

21088 facial prosthesis

►Other Procedures◄

21089 Unlisted maxillofacial prosthetic procedure

►Introduction or Removal◄

21100 Application of halo type appliance for maxillofacial fixation, includes removal (separate procedure)

21110 Application of interdental fixation device for conditions other than fracture or dislocation, includes removal

(For removal of interdental fixation by another physician, see 20670-20680)

21116 Injection procedure for temporomandibular joint arthrography

►(For radiological supervision and interpretation, use 70332. Do not report 77002 in conjunction with 70332)◄

Repair, Revision, and/or Reconstruction

(For cranioplasty, see 21179, 21180 and 62116, 62120, 62140-62147)

21120 Genioplasty; augmentation (autograft, allograft, prosthetic material)

21121 sliding osteotomy, single piece

21122 sliding osteotomies, two or more osteotomies (eg, wedge excision or bone wedge reversal for asymmetrical chin)

21123 sliding, augmentation with interpositional bone grafts (includes obtaining autografts)

21125 Augmentation, mandibular body or angle; prosthetic material

21127 with bone graft, onlay or interpositional (includes obtaining autograft)

21137 Reduction forehead; contouring only

21138 contouring and application of prosthetic material or bone graft (includes obtaining autograft)

21139 contouring and setback of anterior frontal sinus wall

21141 Reconstruction midface, LeFort I; single piece, segment movement in any direction (eg, for Long Face Syndrome), without bone graft

21142 two pieces, segment movement in any direction, without bone graft

21143 three or more pieces, segment movement in any direction, without bone graft

21145 single piece, segment movement in any direction, requiring bone grafts (includes obtaining autografts)

21146 two pieces, segment movement in any direction, requiring bone grafts (includes obtaining autografts) (eg, ungrafted unilateral alveolar cleft)

21147 three or more pieces, segment movement in any direction, requiring bone grafts (includes obtaining autografts) (eg, ungrafted bilateral alveolar cleft or multiple osteotomies)

21150 Reconstruction midface, LeFort II; anterior intrusion (eg, Treacher-Collins Syndrome)

21151 any direction, requiring bone grafts (includes obtaining autografts)

21154 Reconstruction midface, LeFort III (extracranial), any type, requiring bone grafts (includes obtaining autografts); without LeFort I

21155 with LeFort I

21159 Reconstruction midface, LeFort III (extra and intracranial) with forehead advancement (eg, mono bloc), requiring bone grafts (includes obtaining autografts); without LeFort I

21160 with LeFort I

21172 Reconstruction superior-lateral orbital rim and lower forehead, advancement or alteration, with or without grafts (includes obtaining autografts)

(For frontal or parietal craniotomy performed for craniosynostosis, use 61556)

21175 Reconstruction, bifrontal, superior-lateral orbital rims and lower forehead, advancement or alteration (eg, plagiocephaly, trigonocephaly, brachycephaly), with or without grafts (includes obtaining autografts)

(For bifrontal craniotomy performed for craniosynostosis, use 61557)

21179 Reconstruction, entire or majority of forehead and/or supraorbital rims; with grafts (allograft or prosthetic material)

21180 with autograft (includes obtaining grafts)

(For extensive craniectomy for multiple suture craniosynostosis, use only 61558 or 61559)

21181 Reconstruction by contouring of benign tumor of cranial bones (eg, fibrous dysplasia), extracranial

21182 Reconstruction of orbital walls, rims, forehead, nasoethmoid complex following intra- and extracranial excision of benign tumor of cranial bone (eg, fibrous dysplasia), with multiple autografts (includes obtaining grafts); total area of bone grafting less than 40 sq cm

21183 total area of bone grafting greater than 40 sq cm but less than 80 sq cm

21184 total area of bone grafting greater than 80 sq cm

(For excision of benign tumor of cranial bones, see 61563, 61564)

Surgery: Musculoskeletal System

21188 Reconstruction midface, osteotomies (other than LeFort type) and bone grafts (includes obtaining autografts)

21193 Reconstruction of mandibular rami, horizontal, vertical, C, or L osteotomy; without bone graft

21194 with bone graft (includes obtaining graft)

21195 Reconstruction of mandibular rami and/or body, sagittal split; without internal rigid fixation

21196 with internal rigid fixation

21198 Osteotomy, mandible, segmental;

21199 with genioglossus advancement

(To report total osteotomy of the maxilla, see 21141-21160)

21206 Osteotomy, maxilla, segmental (eg, Wassmund or Schuchard)

21208 Osteoplasty, facial bones; augmentation (autograft, allograft, or prosthetic implant)

21209 reduction

21210 Graft, bone; nasal, maxillary or malar areas (includes obtaining graft)

(For cleft palate repair, see 42200-42225)

21215 mandible (includes obtaining graft)

21230 Graft; rib cartilage, autogenous, to face, chin, nose or ear (includes obtaining graft)

21235 ear cartilage, autogenous, to nose or ear (includes obtaining graft)

(To report graft augmentation of facial bones, use 21208)

21240 Arthroplasty, temporomandibular joint, with or without autograft (includes obtaining graft)

21242 Arthroplasty, temporomandibular joint, with allograft

21243 Arthroplasty, temporomandibular joint, with prosthetic joint replacement

21244 Reconstruction of mandible, extraoral, with transosteal bone plate (eg, mandibular staple bone plate)

21245 Reconstruction of mandible or maxilla, subperiosteal implant; partial

21246 complete

21247 Reconstruction of mandibular condyle with bone and cartilage autografts (includes obtaining grafts) (eg, for hemifacial microsomia)

21248 Reconstruction of mandible or maxilla, endosteal implant (eg, blade, cylinder); partial

21249 complete

(To report midface reconstruction, see 21141-21160)

21255 Reconstruction of zygomatic arch and glenoid fossa with bone and cartilage (includes obtaining autografts)

21256 Reconstruction of orbit with osteotomies (extracranial) and with bone grafts (includes obtaining autografts) (eg, micro-ophthalmia)

21260 Periorbital osteotomies for orbital hypertelorism, with bone grafts; extracranial approach

21261 combined intra- and extracranial approach

21263 with forehead advancement

21267 Orbital repositioning, periorbital osteotomies, unilateral, with bone grafts; extracranial approach

21268 combined intra- and extracranial approach

21270 Malar augmentation, prosthetic material

(For malar augmentation with bone graft, use 21210)

21275 Secondary revision of orbitocraniofacial reconstruction

21280 Medial canthopexy (separate procedure)

(For medial canthoplasty, use 67950)

21282 Lateral canthopexy

21295 Reduction of masseter muscle and bone (eg, for treatment of benign masseteric hypertrophy); extraoral approach

21296 intraoral approach

Other Procedures

21299 Unlisted craniofacial and maxillofacial procedure

Fracture and/or Dislocation

►(For operative repair of skull fracture, see 62000-62010)◄

►(21300 has been deleted)◄

►(To report closed treatment of skull fracture, use the appropriate Evaluation and Management code)◄

21310 Closed treatment of nasal bone fracture without manipulation

21315 Closed treatment of nasal bone fracture; without stabilization

21320 with stabilization

21325 Open treatment of nasal fracture; uncomplicated

21330 complicated, with internal and/or external skeletal fixation

21335 with concomitant open treatment of fractured septum

21336 Open treatment of nasal septal fracture, with or without stabilization

21337 Closed treatment of nasal septal fracture, with or without stabilization

21338 Open treatment of nasoethmoid fracture; without external fixation

21339 with external fixation

21340 Percutaneous treatment of nasoethmoid complex fracture, with splint, wire or headcap fixation, including repair of canthal ligaments and/or the nasolacrimal apparatus

21343 Open treatment of depressed frontal sinus fracture

21344 Open treatment of complicated (eg, comminuted or involving posterior wall) frontal sinus fracture, via coronal or multiple approaches

21345 Closed treatment of nasomaxillary complex fracture (LeFort II type), with interdental wire fixation or fixation of denture or splint

21346 Open treatment of nasomaxillary complex fracture (LeFort II type); with wiring and/or local fixation

21347 requiring multiple open approaches

21348 with bone grafting (includes obtaining graft)

21355 Percutaneous treatment of fracture of malar area, including zygomatic arch and malar tripod, with manipulation

21356 Open treatment of depressed zygomatic arch fracture (eg, Gillies approach)

21360 Open treatment of depressed malar fracture, including zygomatic arch and malar tripod

21365 Open treatment of complicated (eg, comminuted or involving cranial nerve foramina) fracture(s) of malar area, including zygomatic arch and malar tripod; with internal fixation and multiple surgical approaches

21366 with bone grafting (includes obtaining graft)

21385 Open treatment of orbital floor blowout fracture; transantral approach (Caldwell-Luc type operation)

21386 periorbital approach

21387 combined approach

21390 periorbital approach, with alloplastic or other implant

21395 periorbital approach with bone graft (includes obtaining graft)

21400 Closed treatment of fracture of orbit, except blowout; without manipulation

21401 with manipulation

21406 Open treatment of fracture of orbit, except blowout; without implant

21407 with implant

21408 with bone grafting (includes obtaining graft)

21421 Closed treatment of palatal or maxillary fracture (LeFort I type), with interdental wire fixation or fixation of denture or splint

21422 Open treatment of palatal or maxillary fracture (LeFort I type);

21423 complicated (comminuted or involving cranial nerve foramina), multiple approaches

21431 Closed treatment of craniofacial separation (LeFort III type) using interdental wire fixation of denture or splint

21432 Open treatment of craniofacial separation (LeFort III type); with wiring and/or internal fixation

21433 complicated (eg, comminuted or involving cranial nerve foramina), multiple surgical approaches

21435 complicated, utilizing internal and/or external fixation techniques (eg, head cap, halo device, and/or intermaxillary fixation)

(For removal of internal or external fixation device, use 20670)

21436 complicated, multiple surgical approaches, internal fixation, with bone grafting (includes obtaining graft)

21440 Closed treatment of mandibular or maxillary alveolar ridge fracture (separate procedure)

21445 Open treatment of mandibular or maxillary alveolar ridge fracture (separate procedure)

21450 Closed treatment of mandibular fracture; without manipulation

21451 with manipulation

21452 Percutaneous treatment of mandibular fracture, with external fixation

21453 Closed treatment of mandibular fracture with interdental fixation

21454 Open treatment of mandibular fracture with external fixation

21461 Open treatment of mandibular fracture; without interdental fixation

21462 with interdental fixation

21465 Open treatment of mandibular condylar fracture

21470 Open treatment of complicated mandibular fracture by multiple surgical approaches including internal fixation, interdental fixation, and/or wiring of dentures or splints

21480 Closed treatment of temporomandibular dislocation; initial or subsequent

21485 complicated (eg, recurrent requiring intermaxillary fixation or splinting), initial or subsequent

21490 Open treatment of temporomandibular dislocation

(For interdental wire fixation, use 21497)

(21493 and 21494 have been deleted. To report, use the applicable Evaluation and Management codes)

21495 Open treatment of hyoid fracture

(For laryngoplasty with open reduction of fracture, use 31584)

(To report treatment of closed fracture of larynx, use the applicable Evaluation and Management codes)

21497 Interdental wiring, for condition other than fracture

Other Procedures

21499 Unlisted musculoskeletal procedure, head

(For unlisted craniofacial or maxillofacial procedure, use 21299)

Neck (Soft Tissues) and Thorax

(For cervical spine and back, see 21920 et seq)

(For injection of fracture site or trigger point, use 20550)

Incision

(For incision and drainage of abscess or hematoma, superficial, see 10060, 10140)

21501 Incision and drainage, deep abscess or hematoma, soft tissues of neck or thorax;

(For posterior spine subfascial incision and drainage, see 22010-22015)

21502 with partial rib ostectomy

21510 Incision, deep, with opening of bone cortex (eg, for osteomyelitis or bone abscess), thorax

Excision

(For bone biopsy, see 20220-20251)

21550 Biopsy, soft tissue of neck or thorax

(For needle biopsy of soft tissue, use 20206)

21555 Excision tumor, soft tissue of neck or thorax; subcutaneous

21556 deep, subfascial, intramuscular

21557 Radical resection of tumor (eg, malignant neoplasm), soft tissue of neck or thorax

21600 Excision of rib, partial

(For radical resection of chest wall and rib cage for tumor, use 19260)

(For radical debridement of chest wall and rib cage for injury, see 11040-11044)

21610 Costotransversectomy (separate procedure)

21615 Excision first and/or cervical rib;

21616 with sympathectomy

21620 Ostectomy of sternum, partial

21627 Sternal debridement

(For debridement and closure, use 21750)

21630 Radical resection of sternum;

21632 with mediastinal lymphadenectomy

Repair, Revision, and/or Reconstruction

(For superficial wound, see **Integumentary System** section under Repair—Simple)

21685 Hyoid myotomy and suspension

21700 Division of scalenus anticus; without resection of cervical rib

21705 with resection of cervical rib

21720 Division of sternocleidomastoid for torticollis, open operation; without cast application

(For transection of spinal accessory and cervical nerves, see 63191, 64722)

21725 with cast application

21740 Reconstructive repair of pectus excavatum or carinatum; open

21742 minimally invasive approach (Nuss procedure), without thoracoscopy

21743 minimally invasive approach (Nuss procedure), with thoracoscopy

21750 Closure of median sternotomy separation with or without debridement (separate procedure)

Fracture and/or Dislocation

21800 Closed treatment of rib fracture, uncomplicated, each

21805 Open treatment of rib fracture without fixation, each

21810 Treatment of rib fracture requiring external fixation (flail chest)

21820 Closed treatment of sternum fracture

21825 Open treatment of sternum fracture with or without skeletal fixation

(For sternoclavicular dislocation, see 23520-23532)

Other Procedures

21899 Unlisted procedure, neck or thorax

Back and Flank

Excision

21920 Biopsy, soft tissue of back or flank; superficial

21925 deep

(For needle biopsy of soft tissue, use 20206)

21930 Excision, tumor, soft tissue of back or flank

21935 Radical resection of tumor (eg, malignant neoplasm), soft tissue of back or flank

Spine (Vertebral Column)

Cervical, thoracic, and lumbar spine.

Within the SPINE section, bone grafting procedures are reported separately and in addition to arthrodesis. For bone grafts in other Musculoskeletal sections, see specific code(s) descriptor(s) and/or accompanying guidelines.

To report bone grafts performed after arthrodesis, see codes 20930-20938. Bone graft codes are reported without modifier 51 (multiple procedure). Do not append modifier 62 to bone graft codes 20900-20938.

Example:

Posterior arthrodesis of L5-S1 for degenerative disc disease utilizing morselized autogenous iliac bone graft harvested through a separate fascial incision.

Report as 22612 and 20937.

Within the SPINE section, instrumentation is reported separately and in addition to arthrodesis. To report instrumentation procedures performed with definitive vertebral procedure(s), see codes 22840-22855. Instrumentation procedure codes 22840-22848 and 22851 are reported in addition to the definitive procedure(s) without modifier 51. Modifier 62 may not be appended to the definitive or add-on spinal instrumentation procedure code(s) 22840-22848 and 22850-22852.

Example:

Posterior arthrodesis of L4-S1, utilizing morselized autogenous iliac bone graft harvested through separate fascial incision, and pedicle screw fixation.

Report as 22612, 22614, 22842, and 20937.

Vertebral procedures are sometimes followed by arthrodesis and in addition may include bone grafts and instrumentation.

When arthrodesis is performed in addition to another procedure, the arthrodesis should be reported in addition to the original procedure with modifier 51 (multiple procedures). Examples are after osteotomy, fracture care, vertebral corpectomy and laminectomy. Since bone grafts and instrumentation are never performed without arthrodesis, modifier 51 (multiple procedures) is not used.

Arthrodesis, however, may be performed in the absence of other procedures and therefore when it is combined with another definitive procedure, modifier 51 (multiple procedure) is appropriate.

Example:

Treatment of a burst fracture of L2 by corpectomy followed by arthrodesis of L1-L3, utilizing anterior instrumentation L1-L3 and structural allograft.

Report as 63090, 22558-51, 22585, 22845, and 20931.

When two surgeons work together as primary surgeons performing distinct part(s) of a single reportable procedure, each surgeon should report his/her distinct operative work by appending modifier 62 to the single definitive procedure code. If additional procedure(s) (including add-on procedure(s)) are performed during the same surgical session, separate code(s) may be reported by each co-surgeon, with modifier 62 appended (see Appendix A).

Example:

A 42-year-old male with a history of posttraumatic degenerative disc disease at L3-4 and L4-5 (internal disc disruption) underwent surgical repair. Surgeon A performed an anterior exposure of the spine with mobilization of the great vessels. Surgeon B performed anterior (minimal) discectomy and fusion at L3-4 and L4-5 using anterior interbody technique.

Report surgeon A: 22558 append modifier 62, 22585 append modifier 62
Report surgeon B: 22558 append modifier 62, 22585 append modifier 62, 20931

(Do not append modifier 62 to bone graft code 20931)

(For injection procedure for myelography, use 62284)

(For injection procedure for discography, see 62290, 62291)

(For injection procedure, chemonucleolysis, single or multiple levels, use 62292)

(For injection procedure for facet joints, see 64470-64476, 64622-64627)

(For needle or trocar biopsy, see 20220-20225)

Incision

22010 Incision and drainage, open, of deep abscess (subfascial), posterior spine; cervical, thoracic, or cervicothoracic

22015 lumbar, sacral, or lumbosacral

(Do not report 22015 in conjunction with 22010)

(Do not report 22015 in conjunction with instrumentation removal, 10180, 22850, 22852)

(For incision and drainage of abscess or hematoma, superficial, see 10060, 10140)

Surgery: Musculoskeletal System

Excision

For the following codes, when two surgeons work together as primary surgeons performing distinct part(s) of partial vertebral body excision, each surgeon should report his/her distinct operative work by appending modifier 62 to the procedure code. In this situation, modifier 62 may be appended to the procedure code(s) 22100-22102, 22110-22114 and, as appropriate, to the associated additional vertebral segment add-on code(s) 22103, 22116 as long as both surgeons continue to work together as primary surgeons.

(For bone biopsy, see 20220-20251)

(To report soft tissue biopsy of back or flank, see 21920-21925)

(For needle biopsy of soft tissue, use 20206)

(To report excision of soft tissue tumor of back or flank, use 21930)

22100 Partial excision of posterior vertebral component (eg, spinous process, lamina or facet) for intrinsic bony lesion, single vertebral segment; cervical

22101 thoracic

22102 lumbar

+ 22103 each additional segment (List separately in addition to code for primary procedure)

(Use 22103 in conjunction with 22100, 22101, 22102)

22110 Partial excision of vertebral body, for intrinsic bony lesion, without decompression of spinal cord or nerve root(s), single vertebral segment; cervical

22112 thoracic

22114 lumbar

+ 22116 each additional vertebral segment (List separately in addition to code for primary procedure)

(Use 22116 in conjunction with 22110, 22112, 22114)

(For complete or near complete resection of vertebral body, see vertebral corpectomy, 63081-63091)

(For spinal reconstruction with bone graft (autograft, allograft) and/or methylmethacrylate of cervical vertebral body, use 63081 and 22554 and 20931 or 20938)

(For spinal reconstruction with bone graft (autograft, allograft) and/or methylmethacrylate of thoracic vertebral body, use 63085 or 63087 and 22556 and 20931 or 20938)

(For spinal reconstruction with bone graft (autograft, allograft) and/or methylmethacrylate of lumbar vertebral body, use 63087 or 63090 and 22558 and 20931 or 20938)

(For spinal reconstruction following vertebral body resection, use 63082 or 63086 or 63088 or 63091, and 22585)

(For harvest of bone autograft for vertebral reconstruction, see 20931 or 20938)

(For cervical spinal reconstruction with prosthetic replacement of resected vertebral bodies, see codes 63081 and 22554 and 20931 or 20938 and 22851)

(For thoracic spinal reconstruction with prosthetic replacement of resected vertebral bodies, see codes 63085 or 63087 and 22556 and 20931 or 20938 and 22851)

(For lumbar spinal reconstruction with prosthetic replacement of resected vertebral bodies, see codes 63087 or 63090 and 22558, and 20931 or 20938 and 22851)

(For osteotomy of spine, see 22210-22226)

Osteotomy

To report arthrodesis, see codes 22590-22632. (Report in addition to code(s) for the definitive procedure with modifier 51.)

To report instrumentation procedures, see codes 22840-22855. (Report in addition to code(s) for the definitive procedure(s) without modifier 51.) Do not append modifier 62 to spinal instrumentation codes 22840-22848 and 22850-22852.

To report bone graft procedures, see codes 20930-20938. (Report in addition to code(s) for the definitive procedure(s) without modifier 51.) Do not append modifier 62 to bone graft codes 20900-20938.

For the following codes, when two surgeons work together as primary surgeons performing distinct part(s) of an anterior spine osteotomy, each surgeon should report his/her distinct operative work by appending modifier 62 to the procedure code. In this situation, modifier 62 may be appended to the procedure code(s) 22210-22214, 22220-22224 and, as appropriate, to associated additional segment add-on code(s) 22216, 22226 as long as both surgeons continue to work together as primary surgeons.

22210 Osteotomy of spine, posterior or posterolateral approach, one vertebral segment; cervical

22212 thoracic

22214 lumbar

+ 22216 each additional vertebral segment (List separately in addition to primary procedure)

(Use 22216 in conjunction with 22210, 22212, 22214)

22220 Osteotomy of spine, including discectomy, anterior approach, single vertebral segment; cervical

22222 thoracic

22224 lumbar

+ 22226 each additional vertebral segment (List separately in addition to code for primary procedure)

(Use 22226 in conjunction with 22220, 22222, 22224)

(For vertebral corpectomy, see 63081-63091)

Fracture and/or Dislocation

To report arthrodesis, see codes 22590-22632. (Report in addition to code(s) for the definitive procedure with modifier 51.)

To report instrumentation procedures, see codes 22840-22855. (Report in addition to code(s) for the definitive procedure(s) without modifier 51.) Do not append modifier 62 to spinal instrumentation codes 22840-22848 and 22850-22852.

To report bone graft procedures, see codes 20930-20938. (Report in addition to code(s) for the definitive procedure(s) without modifier 51.) Do not append modifier 62 to bone graft codes 20900-20938.

For the following codes, when two surgeons work together as primary surgeons performing distinct part(s) of open fracture and/or dislocation procedure(s), each surgeon should report his/her distinct operative work by appending modifier 62 to the procedure code. In this situation, modifier 62 may be appended to the procedure code(s) 22318-22327 and, as appropriate, the associated additional fracture vertebrae or dislocated segment add-on code 22328 as long as both surgeons continue to work together as primary surgeons.

22305 Closed treatment of vertebral process fracture(s)

22310 Closed treatment of vertebral body fracture(s), without manipulation, requiring and including casting or bracing

22315 Closed treatment of vertebral fracture(s) and/or dislocation(s) requiring casting or bracing, with and including casting and/or bracing, with or without anesthesia, by manipulation or traction

(For spinal subluxation, use 97140)

22318 Open treatment and/or reduction of odontoid fracture(s) and or dislocation(s) (including os odontoideum), anterior approach, including placement of internal fixation; without grafting

22319 with grafting

22325 Open treatment and/or reduction of vertebral fracture(s) and/or dislocation(s), posterior approach, one fractured vertebrae or dislocated segment; lumbar

22326 cervical

22327 thoracic

+ 22328 each additional fractured vertebrae or dislocated segment (List separately in addition to code for primary procedure)

(Use 22328 in conjunction with 22325, 22326, 22327)

(For treatment of vertebral fracture by the anterior approach, see corpectomy 63081-63091, and appropriate arthrodesis, bone graft and instrument codes)

(For decompression of spine following fracture, see 63001-63091; for arthrodesis of spine following fracture, see 22548-22632)

Manipulation

(For spinal manipulation without anesthesia, use 97140)

22505 Manipulation of spine requiring anesthesia, any region

Vertebral Body, Embolization or Injection

22520 Percutaneous vertebroplasty, one vertebral body, unilateral or bilateral injection; thoracic

22521 lumbar

+ 22522 each additional thoracic or lumbar vertebral body (List separately in addition to code for primary procedure)

(Use 22522 in conjunction with 22520, 22521 as appropriate)

►(For radiological supervision and interpretation, see 72291, 72292)◄

22523 Percutaneous vertebral augmentation, including cavity creation (fracture reduction and bone biopsy included when performed) using mechanical device, one vertebral body, unilateral or bilateral cannulation (eg, kyphoplasty); thoracic

22524 lumbar

+ 22525 each additional thoracic or lumbar vertebral body (List separately in addition to code for primary procedure)

(Do not report 22525 in conjunction with 20225 when performed at the same level as 22523-22525)

(Use 22525 in conjunction with 22523, 22524)

►(For radiological supervision and interpretation, see 72291, 72292)◄

⊙● 22526 Percutaneous intradiscal electrothermal annuloplasty, unilateral or bilateral including fluoroscopic guidance; single level

⊙+● 22527 one or more additional levels (List separately in addition to code for primary procedure)

►(Do not report codes 22526, 22527 in conjunction with 77002, 77003)◄

►(For percutaneous intradiscal annuloplasty using method other than electrothermal, see 0062T, 0063T)◄

Arthrodesis

Arthrodesis may be performed in the absence of other procedures and therefore when it is combined with another definitive procedure (eg, osteotomy, fracture care, vertebral corpectomy or laminectomy), modifier 51 is appropriate. However, arthrodesis codes 22585, 22614, and 22632 are considered add-on procedure codes and should not be used with modifier 51.

To report instrumentation procedures, see 22840-22855. (Codes 22840-22848, 22851 are reported in conjunction with code(s) for the definitive procedure(s) without modifier 51. When instrumentation reinsertion or

removal is reported in conjunction with other definitive procedures including arthrodesis, decompression, and exploration of fusion, append modifier 51 to 22849, 22850, 22852, and 22855.) To report exploration of fusion, use 22830. (When exploration is reported in conjunction with other definitive procedures, including arthrodesis and decompression, append modifier 51 to 22830.) Do not append modifier 62 to spinal instrumentation codes 22840-22848 and 22850-22852.

To report bone graft procedures, see codes 20930-20938. (Report in addition to code(s) for the definitive procedure(s) without modifier 51.) Do not append modifier 62 to bone graft codes 20900-20938.

Lateral Extracavitary Approach Technique

22532 Arthrodesis, lateral extracavitary technique, including minimal discectomy to prepare interspace (other than for decompression); thoracic

22533 lumbar

+ 22534 thoracic or lumbar, each additional vertebral segment (List separately in addition to code for primary procedure)

(Use 22534 in conjunction with 22532 and 22533)

Anterior or Anterolateral Approach Technique

Procedure codes 22554-22558 are for SINGLE interspace; for additional interspaces, use 22585. A vertebral interspace is the non-bony compartment between two adjacent vertebral bodies, which contains the intervertebral disc, and includes the nucleus pulposus, annulus fibrosus, and two cartilagenous endplates.

For the following codes, when two surgeons work together as primary surgeons performing distinct part(s) of an anterior interbody arthrodesis, each surgeon should report his/her distinct operative work by appending modifier 62 to the procedure code. In this situation, modifier 62 may be appended to the procedure code(s) 22548-22558 and, as appropriate, to the associated additional interspace add-on code 22585 as long as both surgeons continue to work together as primary surgeons.

22548 Arthrodesis, anterior transoral or extraoral technique, clivus-C1-C2 (atlas-axis), with or without excision of odontoid process

(For intervertebral disc excision by laminotomy or laminectomy, see 63020-63042)

22554 Arthrodesis, anterior interbody technique, including minimal discectomy to prepare interspace (other than for decompression); cervical below C2

22556 thoracic

22558 lumbar

+ 22585 each additional interspace (List separately in addition to code for primary procedure)

(Use 22585 in conjunction with 22554, 22556, 22558)

Posterior, Posterolateral or Lateral Transverse Process Technique

To report instrumentation procedures, see codes 22840-22855. (Report in addition to code(s) for the definitive procedure(s) without modifier 51.) Do not append modifier 62 to spinal instrumentation codes 22840-22848 and 22850-22852.

To report bone graft procedures, see codes 20930-20938. (Report in addition to code(s) for the definitive procedure(s) without modifier 51.) Do not append modifier 62 to bone graft codes 20900-20938.

A vertebral segment describes the basic constituent part into which the spine may be divided. It represents a single complete vertebral bone with its associated articular processes and laminae. A vertebral interspace is the non-bony compartment between two adjacent vertebral bodies which contains the intervertebral disc, and includes the nucleus pulposus, annulus fibrosus, and two cartilagenous endplates.

22590 Arthrodesis, posterior technique, craniocervical (occiput-C2)

22595 Arthrodesis, posterior technique, atlas-axis (C1-C2)

22600 Arthrodesis, posterior or posterolateral technique, single level; cervical below C2 segment

22610 thoracic (with or without lateral transverse technique)

22612 lumbar (with or without lateral transverse technique)

+ 22614 each additional vertebral segment (List separately in addition to code for primary procedure)

(Use 22614 in conjunction with 22600, 22610, 22612)

22630 Arthrodesis, posterior interbody technique, including laminectomy and/or discectomy to prepare interspace (other than for decompression), single interspace; lumbar

+ 22632 each additional interspace (List separately in addition to code for primary procedure)

(Use 22632 in conjunction with 22630)

Spine Deformity (eg, Scoliosis, Kyphosis)

To report instrumentation procedures, see codes 22840-22855. (Report in addition to code(s) for the definitive procedure(s) without modifier 51.) Do not append modifier 62 to spinal instrumentation codes 22840-22848 and 22850-22852.

To report bone graft procedures, see codes 20930-20938. (Report in addition to code(s) for the definitive procedure(s) without modifier 51.) Do not append modifier 62 to bone graft codes 20900-20938.

A vertebral segment describes the basic constituent part into which the spine may be divided. It represents a single complete vertebral bone with its associated articular processes and laminae.

For the following codes, when two surgeons work together as primary surgeons performing distinct part(s) of an arthrodesis for spinal deformity, each surgeon should report his/her distinct operative work by appending modifier 62 to the procedure code. In this situation, modifier 62 may be appended to procedure code(s) 22800-22819 as long as both surgeons continue to work together as primary surgeons.

22800 Arthrodesis, posterior, for spinal deformity, with or without cast; up to 6 vertebral segments

22802 7 to 12 vertebral segments

22804 13 or more vertebral segments

22808 Arthrodesis, anterior, for spinal deformity, with or without cast; 2 to 3 vertebral segments

22810 4 to 7 vertebral segments

22812 8 or more vertebral segments

22818 Kyphectomy, circumferential exposure of spine and resection of vertebral segment(s) (including body and posterior elements); single or 2 segments

22819 3 or more segments

(To report arthrodesis, see 22800-22804 and add modifier 51)

Exploration

To report instrumentation procedures, see 22840-22855. (Codes 22840-22848, 22851 are reported in conjunction with code(s) for the definitive procedure(s) without modifier 51. When instrumentation reinsertion or removal is reported in conjunction with other definitive procedures including arthrodesis, decompression, and exploration of fusion, append modifier 51 to 22849, 22850, 22852 and 22855.) To report exploration of fusion, see 22830. (When exploration is reported in conjunction with other definitive procedures, including arthrodesis and decompression, append modifier 51 to 22830.)

(To report bone graft procedures, see 20930-20938)

22830 Exploration of spinal fusion

Spinal Instrumentation

Segmental instrumentation is defined as fixation at each end of the construct and at least one additional interposed bony attachment.

Non-segmental instrumentation is defined as fixation at each end of the construct and may span several vertebral segments without attachment to the intervening segments.

Insertion of spinal instrumentation is reported separately and in addition to arthrodesis. Instrumentation procedure codes 22840-22848, 22851 are reported in addition to the definitive procedure(s) without modifier 51. Do not append modifier 62 to spinal instrumentation codes 22840-22848 and 22850-22852.

To report bone graft procedures, see codes 20930-20938. (Report in addition to code(s) for definitive procedure(s) without modifier 51.) Do not append modifier 62 to bone graft codes 20900-20938.

A vertebral segment describes the basic constituent part into which the spine may be divided. It represents a single complete vertebral bone with its associated articular processes and laminae. A vertebral interspace is the non-bony compartment between two adjacent vertebral bodies, which contains the intervertebral disc, and includes the nucleus pulposus, annulus fibrosus, and two cartilagenous endplates.

►List 22840-22855 separately, in conjunction with code(s) for fracture, dislocation, arthrodesis or exploration of fusion of the spine 22325-22328, 22532-22534, 22548-22812, and 22830. Codes 22840-22848, 22851 are reported in conjunction with code(s) for the definitive procedure(s) without modifier 51. Codes 22849, 22850, 22852, and 22855 are subject to modifier 51 if reported with other definitive procedure(s), including arthrodesis, decompression, and exploration of fusion. Code 22849 should not be reported with 22850, 22852, and 22855 at the same spinal levels.◄

⊘ **22840** Posterior non-segmental instrumentation (eg, Harrington rod technique, pedicle fixation across one interspace, atlantoaxial transarticular screw fixation, sublaminar wiring at C1, facet screw fixation)

⊘ **22841** Internal spinal fixation by wiring of spinous processes

⊘ **22842** Posterior segmental instrumentation (eg, pedicle fixation, dual rods with multiple hooks and sublaminar wires); 3 to 6 vertebral segments

⊘ **22843** 7 to 12 vertebral segments

⊘ **22844** 13 or more vertebral segments

⊘ **22845** Anterior instrumentation; 2 to 3 vertebral segments

⊘ **22846** 4 to 7 vertebral segments

⊘ **22847** 8 or more vertebral segments

⊘ **22848** Pelvic fixation (attachment of caudal end of instrumentation to pelvic bony structures) other than sacrum

22849 Reinsertion of spinal fixation device

22850 Removal of posterior nonsegmental instrumentation (eg, Harrington rod)

⊘ **22851** Application of intervertebral biomechanical device(s) (eg, synthetic cage(s), threaded bone dowel(s), methylmethacrylate) to vertebral defect or interspace

22852 Removal of posterior segmental instrumentation

22855 Removal of anterior instrumentation

● **22857** Total disc arthroplasty (artificial disc), anterior approach, including discectomy to prepare interspace (other than for decompression), lumbar, single interspace

▶(Do not report 22857 in conjunction with 22558, 22845, 22851, 49010 when performed at the same level)◀

▶(For additional interspace, use Category III code 0163T)◀

● **22862** Revision including replacement of total disc arthroplasty (artificial disc) anterior approach, lumbar, single interspace

▶(Do not report 22862 in conjunction with 22558, 22845, 22851, 22865, 49010 when performed at the same level)◀

▶(For additional interspace, use Category III code 0165T)◀

● **22865** Removal of total disc arthroplasty (artificial disc), anterior approach, lumbar, single interspace

▶(Do not report 22865 in conjunction with 49010)◀

▶(For additional interspace, see Category III code 0164T)◀

▶(22857-22865 include fluoroscopy when performed)◀

▶(For decompression, see 63001-63048)◀

Other Procedures

22899 Unlisted procedure, spine

Abdomen

Excision

22900 Excision, abdominal wall tumor, subfascial (eg, desmoid)

Other Procedures

22999 Unlisted procedure, abdomen, musculoskeletal system

Shoulder

Clavicle, scapula, humerus head and neck, sterno-clavicular joint, acromioclavicular joint and shoulder joint.

Incision

23000 Removal of subdeltoid calcareous deposits, open

(For arthroscopic removal of bursal deposits, use 29999)

23020 Capsular contracture release (eg, Sever type procedure)

(For incision and drainage procedures, superficial, see 10040-10160)

23030 Incision and drainage, shoulder area; deep abscess or hematoma

23031 infected bursa

23035 Incision, bone cortex (eg, osteomyelitis or bone abscess), shoulder area

23040 Arthrotomy, glenohumeral joint, including exploration, drainage, or removal of foreign body

23044 Arthrotomy, acromioclavicular, sternoclavicular joint, including exploration, drainage, or removal of foreign body

Excision

23065 Biopsy, soft tissue of shoulder area; superficial

23066 deep

(For needle biopsy of soft tissue, use 20206)

23075 Excision, soft tissue tumor, shoulder area; subcutaneous

23076 deep, subfascial, or intramuscular

23077 Radical resection of tumor (eg, malignant neoplasm), soft tissue of shoulder area

23100 Arthrotomy, glenohumeral joint, including biopsy

23101 Arthrotomy, acromioclavicular joint or sternoclavicular joint, including biopsy and/or excision of torn cartilage

23105 Arthrotomy; glenohumeral joint, with synovectomy, with or without biopsy

23106 sternoclavicular joint, with synovectomy, with or without biopsy

23107 Arthrotomy, glenohumeral joint, with joint exploration, with or without removal of loose or foreign body

23120 Claviculectomy; partial

(For arthroscopic procedure, use 29824)

23125 total

23130 Acromioplasty or acromionectomy, partial, with or without coracoacromial ligament release

23140 Excision or curettage of bone cyst or benign tumor of clavicle or scapula;

23145 with autograft (includes obtaining graft)

23146 with allograft

23150 Excision or curettage of bone cyst or benign tumor of proximal humerus;

23155 with autograft (includes obtaining graft)

23156 with allograft

23170 Sequestrectomy (eg, for osteomyelitis or bone abscess), clavicle

23172 Sequestrectomy (eg, for osteomyelitis or bone abscess), scapula

23174 Sequestrectomy (eg, for osteomyelitis or bone abscess), humeral head to surgical neck

23180 Partial excision (craterization, saucerization, or diaphysectomy) bone (eg, osteomyelitis), clavicle

23182 Partial excision (craterization, saucerization, or diaphysectomy) bone (eg, osteomyelitis), scapula

23184 Partial excision (craterization, saucerization, or diaphysectomy) bone (eg, osteomyelitis), proximal humerus

23190 Ostectomy of scapula, partial (eg, superior medial angle)

23195 Resection, humeral head

(For replacement with implant, use 23470)

23200 Radical resection for tumor; clavicle

23210 scapula

23220 Radical resection of bone tumor, proximal humerus;

23221 with autograft (includes obtaining graft)

23222 with prosthetic replacement

Introduction or Removal

(For arthrocentesis or needling of bursa, use 20610)

(For K-wire or pin insertion or removal, see 20650, 20670, 20680)

23330 Removal of foreign body, shoulder; subcutaneous

23331 deep (eg, Neer hemiarthroplasty removal)

23332 complicated (eg, total shoulder)

23350 Injection procedure for shoulder arthrography or enhanced CT/MRI shoulder arthrography

►(For radiographic arthrography, radiological supervision and interpretation, use 73040. Fluoroscopy [77002] is inclusive of radiographic arthrography)◄

►(When fluoroscopic guided injection is performed for enhanced CT arthrography, use 23350, 77002, and 73201 or 73202)◄

►(When fluoroscopic guided injection is performed for enhanced MR arthrography, use 23350, 77002, and 73222 or 73223)◄

►(For enhanced CT or enhanced MRI arthrography, use 77002 and either 73201, 73202, 73222, or 73223)◄

(To report biopsy of the shoulder and joint, see 29805-29826)

Repair, Revision, and/or Reconstruction

23395 Muscle transfer, any type, shoulder or upper arm; single

23397 multiple

23400 Scapulopexy (eg, Sprengels deformity or for paralysis)

23405 Tenotomy, shoulder area; single tendon

23406 multiple tendons through same incision

23410 Repair of ruptured musculotendinous cuff (eg, rotator cuff) open; acute

23412 chronic

(For arthroscopic procedure, use 29827)

23415 Coracoacromial ligament release, with or without acromioplasty

(For arthroscopic procedure, use 29826)

23420 Reconstruction of complete shoulder (rotator) cuff avulsion, chronic (includes acromioplasty)

23430 Tenodesis of long tendon of biceps

23440 Resection or transplantation of long tendon of biceps

23450 Capsulorrhaphy, anterior; Putti-Platt procedure or Magnuson type operation

(To report arthroscopic thermal capsulorrhaphy, use 29999)

23455 with labral repair (eg, Bankart procedure)

(For arthroscopic procedure, use 29806)

23460 Capsulorrhaphy, anterior, any type; with bone block

23462 with coracoid process transfer

(To report open thermal capsulorrhaphy, use 23929)

23465 Capsulorrhaphy, glenohumeral joint, posterior, with or without bone block

(For sternoclavicular and acromioclavicular reconstruction, see 23530, 23550)

23466 Capsulorrhaphy, glenohumeral joint, any type multi-directional instability

23470 Arthroplasty, glenohumeral joint; hemiarthroplasty

23472 total shoulder (glenoid and proximal humeral replacement (eg, total shoulder))

(For removal of total shoulder implants, see 23331, 23332)

(For osteotomy, proximal humerus, use 24400)

23480 Osteotomy, clavicle, with or without internal fixation;

23485 with bone graft for nonunion or malunion (includes obtaining graft and/or necessary fixation)

23490 Prophylactic treatment (nailing, pinning, plating or wiring) with or without methylmethacrylate; clavicle

23491 proximal humerus

Fracture and/or Dislocation

23500 Closed treatment of clavicular fracture; without manipulation

23505 with manipulation

23515 Open treatment of clavicular fracture, with or without internal or external fixation

Surgery: Musculoskeletal System

Surgery: Musculoskeletal System

23520 Closed treatment of sternoclavicular dislocation; without manipulation

23525 with manipulation

23530 Open treatment of sternoclavicular dislocation, acute or chronic;

23532 with fascial graft (includes obtaining graft)

23540 Closed treatment of acromioclavicular dislocation; without manipulation

23545 with manipulation

23550 Open treatment of acromioclavicular dislocation, acute or chronic;

23552 with fascial graft (includes obtaining graft)

23570 Closed treatment of scapular fracture; without manipulation

23575 with manipulation, with or without skeletal traction (with or without shoulder joint involvement)

23585 Open treatment of scapular fracture (body, glenoid or acromion) with or without internal fixation

23600 Closed treatment of proximal humeral (surgical or anatomical neck) fracture; without manipulation

23605 with manipulation, with or without skeletal traction

23615 Open treatment of proximal humeral (surgical or anatomical neck) fracture, with or without internal or external fixation, with or without repair of tuberosity(s);

23616 with proximal humeral prosthetic replacement

23620 Closed treatment of greater humeral tuberosity fracture; without manipulation

23625 with manipulation

23630 Open treatment of greater humeral tuberosity fracture, with or without internal or external fixation

23650 Closed treatment of shoulder dislocation, with manipulation; without anesthesia

23655 requiring anesthesia

23660 Open treatment of acute shoulder dislocation

(Repairs for recurrent dislocations, see 23450-23466)

23665 Closed treatment of shoulder dislocation, with fracture of greater humeral tuberosity, with manipulation

23670 Open treatment of shoulder dislocation, with fracture of greater humeral tuberosity, with or without internal or external fixation

23675 Closed treatment of shoulder dislocation, with surgical or anatomical neck fracture, with manipulation

23680 Open treatment of shoulder dislocation, with surgical or anatomical neck fracture, with or without internal or external fixation

Manipulation

23700 Manipulation under anesthesia, shoulder joint, including application of fixation apparatus (dislocation excluded)

Arthrodesis

23800 Arthrodesis, glenohumeral joint;

23802 with autogenous graft (includes obtaining graft)

Amputation

23900 Interthoracoscapular amputation (forequarter)

23920 Disarticulation of shoulder;

23921 secondary closure or scar revision

Other Procedures

23929 Unlisted procedure, shoulder

Humerus (Upper Arm) and Elbow

Elbow area includes head and neck of radius and olecranon process.

Incision

(For incision and drainage procedures, superficial, see 10040-10160)

23930 Incision and drainage, upper arm or elbow area; deep abscess or hematoma

23931 bursa

23935 Incision, deep, with opening of bone cortex (eg, for osteomyelitis or bone abscess), humerus or elbow

24000 Arthrotomy, elbow, including exploration, drainage, or removal of foreign body

24006 Arthrotomy of the elbow, with capsular excision for capsular release (separate procedure)

Excision

24065 Biopsy, soft tissue of upper arm or elbow area; superficial

24066 deep (subfascial or intramuscular)

(For needle biopsy of soft tissue, use 20206)

24075 Excision, tumor, soft tissue of upper arm or elbow area; subcutaneous

24076 deep (subfascial or intramuscular)

24077 Radical resection of tumor (eg, malignant neoplasm), soft tissue of upper arm or elbow area

24100 Arthrotomy, elbow; with synovial biopsy only

24101 with joint exploration, with or without biopsy, with or without removal of loose or foreign body

24102 with synovectomy

24105 Excision, olecranon bursa

24110 Excision or curettage of bone cyst or benign tumor, humerus;

24115 with autograft (includes obtaining graft)

24116 with allograft

24120 Excision or curettage of bone cyst or benign tumor of head or neck of radius or olecranon process;

24125 with autograft (includes obtaining graft)

24126 with allograft

24130 Excision, radial head

 (For replacement with implant, use 24366)

24134 Sequestrectomy (eg, for osteomyelitis or bone abscess), shaft or distal humerus

24136 Sequestrectomy (eg, for osteomyelitis or bone abscess), radial head or neck

24138 Sequestrectomy (eg, for osteomyelitis or bone abscess), olecranon process

24140 Partial excision (craterization, saucerization, or diaphysectomy) bone (eg, osteomyelitis), humerus

24145 Partial excision (craterization, saucerization, or diaphysectomy) bone (eg, osteomyelitis), radial head or neck

24147 Partial excision (craterization, saucerization, or diaphysectomy) bone (eg, osteomyelitis), olecranon process

24149 Radical resection of capsule, soft tissue, and heterotopic bone, elbow, with contracture release (separate procedure)

 (For capsular and soft tissue release only, use 24006)

24150 Radical resection for tumor, shaft or distal humerus;

24151 with autograft (includes obtaining graft)

24152 Radical resection for tumor, radial head or neck;

24153 with autograft (includes obtaining graft)

24155 Resection of elbow joint (arthrectomy)

Introduction or Removal

 (For K-wire or pin insertion or removal, see 20650, 20670, 20680)

 (For arthrocentesis or needling of bursa or joint, use 20605)

24160 Implant removal; elbow joint

24164 radial head

24200 Removal of foreign body, upper arm or elbow area; subcutaneous

24201 deep (subfascial or intramuscular)

24220 Injection procedure for elbow arthrography

 ▶(For radiological supervision and interpretation, use 73085. Do not report 77002 in conjunction with 73085)◀

 (For injection for tennis elbow, use 20550)

Repair, Revision, and/or Reconstruction

24300 Manipulation, elbow, under anesthesia

 (For application of external fixation, see 20690 or 20692)

24301 Muscle or tendon transfer, any type, upper arm or elbow, single (excluding 24320-24331)

24305 Tendon lengthening, upper arm or elbow, each tendon

24310 Tenotomy, open, elbow to shoulder, each tendon

24320 Tenoplasty, with muscle transfer, with or without free graft, elbow to shoulder, single (Seddon-Brookes type procedure)

24330 Flexor-plasty, elbow (eg, Steindler type advancement);

24331 with extensor advancement

24332 Tenolysis, triceps

24340 Tenodesis of biceps tendon at elbow (separate procedure)

24341 Repair, tendon or muscle, upper arm or elbow, each tendon or muscle, primary or secondary (excludes rotator cuff)

24342 Reinsertion of ruptured biceps or triceps tendon, distal, with or without tendon graft

24343 Repair lateral collateral ligament, elbow, with local tissue

24344 Reconstruction lateral collateral ligament, elbow, with tendon graft (includes harvesting of graft)

24345 Repair medial collateral ligament, elbow, with local tissue

24346 Reconstruction medial collateral ligament, elbow, with tendon graft (includes harvesting of graft)

24350 Fasciotomy, lateral or medial (eg, tennis elbow or epicondylitis);

24351 with extensor origin detachment

24352 with annular ligament resection

24354 with stripping

24356 with partial ostectomy

24360 Arthroplasty, elbow; with membrane (eg, fascial)

24361 with distal humeral prosthetic replacement

24362 with implant and fascia lata ligament reconstruction

24363 with distal humerus and proximal ulnar prosthetic replacement (eg, total elbow)

Surgery: Musculoskeletal System

24365 Arthroplasty, radial head;

24366 with implant

24400 Osteotomy, humerus, with or without internal fixation

24410 Multiple osteotomies with realignment on intramedullary rod, humeral shaft (Sofield type procedure)

24420 Osteoplasty, humerus (eg, shortening or lengthening) (excluding 64876)

24430 Repair of nonunion or malunion, humerus; without graft (eg, compression technique)

24435 with iliac or other autograft (includes obtaining graft)

(For proximal radius and/or ulna, see 25400-25420)

24470 Hemiepiphyseal arrest (eg, cubitus varus or valgus, distal humerus)

24495 Decompression fasciotomy, forearm, with brachial artery exploration

24498 Prophylactic treatment (nailing, pinning, plating or wiring), with or without methylmethacrylate, humeral shaft

Fracture and/or Dislocation

24500 Closed treatment of humeral shaft fracture; without manipulation

24505 with manipulation, with or without skeletal traction

24515 Open treatment of humeral shaft fracture with plate/screws, with or without cerclage

24516 Treatment of humeral shaft fracture, with insertion of intramedullary implant, with or without cerclage and/or locking screws

24530 Closed treatment of supracondylar or transcondylar humeral fracture, with or without intercondylar extension; without manipulation

24535 with manipulation, with or without skin or skeletal traction

24538 Percutaneous skeletal fixation of supracondylar or transcondylar humeral fracture, with or without intercondylar extension

24545 Open treatment of humeral supracondylar or transcondylar fracture, with or without internal or external fixation; without intercondylar extension

24546 with intercondylar extension

24560 Closed treatment of humeral epicondylar fracture, medial or lateral; without manipulation

24565 with manipulation

24566 Percutaneous skeletal fixation of humeral epicondylar fracture, medial or lateral, with manipulation

24575 Open treatment of humeral epicondylar fracture, medial or lateral, with or without internal or external fixation

24576 Closed treatment of humeral condylar fracture, medial or lateral; without manipulation

24577 with manipulation

24579 Open treatment of humeral condylar fracture, medial or lateral, with or without internal or external fixation

(To report closed treatment of fractures without manipulation, see 24530, 24560, 24576, 24650, 24670)

(To report closed treatment of fractures with manipulation, see 24535, 24565, 24577, 24675)

24582 Percutaneous skeletal fixation of humeral condylar fracture, medial or lateral, with manipulation

24586 Open treatment of periarticular fracture and/or dislocation of the elbow (fracture distal humerus and proximal ulna and/or proximal radius);

24587 with implant arthroplasty

(See also 24361)

24600 Treatment of closed elbow dislocation; without anesthesia

24605 requiring anesthesia

24615 Open treatment of acute or chronic elbow dislocation

24620 Closed treatment of Monteggia type of fracture dislocation at elbow (fracture proximal end of ulna with dislocation of radial head), with manipulation

24635 Open treatment of Monteggia type of fracture dislocation at elbow (fracture proximal end of ulna with dislocation of radial head), with or without internal or external fixation

24640 Closed treatment of radial head subluxation in child, nursemaid elbow, with manipulation

24650 Closed treatment of radial head or neck fracture; without manipulation

24655 with manipulation

24665 Open treatment of radial head or neck fracture, with or without internal fixation or radial head excision;

24666 with radial head prosthetic replacement

24670 Closed treatment of ulnar fracture, proximal end (olecranon process); without manipulation

24675 with manipulation

24685 Open treatment of ulnar fracture proximal end (olecranon process), with or without internal or external fixation

Arthrodesis

24800 Arthrodesis, elbow joint; local

24802 with autogenous graft (includes obtaining graft)

Amputation

24900 Amputation, arm through humerus; with primary closure

24920 open, circular (guillotine)

24925 secondary closure or scar revision

24930 re-amputation

24931 with implant

24935 Stump elongation, upper extremity

24940 Cineplasty, upper extremity, complete procedure

Other Procedures

24999 Unlisted procedure, humerus or elbow

Forearm and Wrist

Radius, ulna, carpal bones, and joints.

Incision

25000 Incision, extensor tendon sheath, wrist (eg, deQuervains disease)

(For decompression median nerve or for carpal tunnel syndrome, use 64721)

25001 Incision, flexor tendon sheath, wrist (eg, flexor carpi radialis)

25020 Decompression fasciotomy, forearm and/or wrist, flexor OR extensor compartment; without debridement of nonviable muscle and/or nerve

25023 with debridement of nonviable muscle and/or nerve

(For decompression fasciotomy with brachial artery exploration, use 24495)

(For incision and drainage procedures, superficial, see 10060-10160)

(For debridement, see also 11000-11044)

25024 Decompression fasciotomy, forearm and/or wrist, flexor AND extensor compartment; without debridement of nonviable muscle and/or nerve

25025 with debridement of nonviable muscle and/or nerve

25028 Incision and drainage, forearm and/or wrist; deep abscess or hematoma

25031 bursa

25035 Incision, deep, bone cortex, forearm and/or wrist (eg, osteomyelitis or bone abscess)

25040 Arthrotomy, radiocarpal or midcarpal joint, with exploration, drainage, or removal of foreign body

Excision

25065 Biopsy, soft tissue of forearm and/or wrist; superficial

25066 deep (subfascial or intramuscular)

(For needle biopsy of soft tissue, use 20206)

25075 Excision, tumor, soft tissue of forearm and/or wrist area; subcutaneous

25076 deep (subfascial or intramuscular)

25077 Radical resection of tumor (eg, malignant neoplasm), soft tissue of forearm and/or wrist area

25085 Capsulotomy, wrist (eg, contracture)

25100 Arthrotomy, wrist joint; with biopsy

25101 with joint exploration, with or without biopsy, with or without removal of loose or foreign body

25105 with synovectomy

25107 Arthrotomy, distal radioulnar joint including repair of triangular cartilage, complex

● **25109** Excision of tendon, forearm and/or wrist, flexor or extensor, each

25110 Excision, lesion of tendon sheath, forearm and/or wrist

25111 Excision of ganglion, wrist (dorsal or volar); primary

25112 recurrent

(For hand or finger, use 26160)

25115 Radical excision of bursa, synovia of wrist, or forearm tendon sheaths (eg, tenosynovitis, fungus, Tbc, or other granulomas, rheumatoid arthritis); flexors

25116 extensors, with or without transposition of dorsal retinaculum

(For finger synovectomies, use 26145)

25118 Synovectomy, extensor tendon sheath, wrist, single compartment;

25119 with resection of distal ulna

25120 Excision or curettage of bone cyst or benign tumor of radius or ulna (excluding head or neck of radius and olecranon process);

(For head or neck of radius or olecranon process, see 24120-24126)

25125 with autograft (includes obtaining graft)

25126 with allograft

25130 Excision or curettage of bone cyst or benign tumor of carpal bones;

25135 with autograft (includes obtaining graft)

25136 with allograft

25145 Sequestrectomy (eg, for osteomyelitis or bone abscess), forearm and/or wrist

Surgery: Musculoskeletal System

25150 Partial excision (craterization, saucerization, or diaphysectomy) of bone (eg, for osteomyelitis); ulna

25151 radius

(For head or neck of radius or olecranon process, see 24145, 24147)

25170 Radical resection for tumor, radius or ulna

25210 Carpectomy; one bone

(For carpectomy with implant, see 25441-25445)

25215 all bones of proximal row

25230 Radial styloidectomy (separate procedure)

25240 Excision distal ulna partial or complete (eg, Darrach type or matched resection)

(For implant replacement, distal ulna, use 25442)

(For obtaining fascia for interposition, see 20920, 20922)

Introduction or Removal

(For K-wire, pin or rod insertion or removal, see 20650, 20670, 20680)

25246 Injection procedure for wrist arthrography

▶(For radiological supervision and interpretation, use 73115. Do not report 77002 in conjunction with 73115)◀

(For foreign body removal, superficial use 20520)

25248 Exploration with removal of deep foreign body, forearm or wrist

25250 Removal of wrist prosthesis; (separate procedure)

25251 complicated, including total wrist

25259 Manipulation, wrist, under anesthesia

(For application of external fixation, see 20690 or 20692)

Repair, Revision, and/or Reconstruction

25260 Repair, tendon or muscle, flexor, forearm and/or wrist; primary, single, each tendon or muscle

25263 secondary, single, each tendon or muscle

25265 secondary, with free graft (includes obtaining graft), each tendon or muscle

25270 Repair, tendon or muscle, extensor, forearm and/or wrist; primary, single, each tendon or muscle

25272 secondary, single, each tendon or muscle

25274 secondary, with free graft (includes obtaining graft), each tendon or muscle

25275 Repair, tendon sheath, extensor, forearm and/or wrist, with free graft (includes obtaining graft) (eg, for extensor carpi ulnaris subluxation)

25280 Lengthening or shortening of flexor or extensor tendon, forearm and/or wrist, single, each tendon

25290 Tenotomy, open, flexor or extensor tendon, forearm and/or wrist, single, each tendon

25295 Tenolysis, flexor or extensor tendon, forearm and/or wrist, single, each tendon

25300 Tenodesis at wrist; flexors of fingers

25301 extensors of fingers

25310 Tendon transplantation or transfer, flexor or extensor, forearm and/or wrist, single; each tendon

25312 with tendon graft(s) (includes obtaining graft), each tendon

25315 Flexor origin slide (eg, for cerebral palsy, Volkmann contracture), forearm and/or wrist;

25316 with tendon(s) transfer

25320 Capsulorrhaphy or reconstruction, wrist, open (eg, capsulodesis, ligament repair, tendon transfer or graft) (includes synovectomy, capsulotomy and open reduction) for carpal instability

25332 Arthroplasty, wrist, with or without interposition, with or without external or internal fixation

(For obtaining fascia for interposition, see 20920, 20922)

(For prosthetic replacement arthroplasty, see 25441-25446)

25335 Centralization of wrist on ulna (eg, radial club hand)

25337 Reconstruction for stabilization of unstable distal ulna or distal radioulnar joint, secondary by soft tissue stabilization (eg, tendon transfer, tendon graft or weave, or tenodesis) with or without open reduction of distal radioulnar joint

(For harvesting of fascia lata graft, see 20920, 20922)

25350 Osteotomy, radius; distal third

25355 middle or proximal third

25360 Osteotomy; ulna

25365 radius AND ulna

25370 Multiple osteotomies, with realignment on intramedullary rod (Sofield type procedure); radius OR ulna

25375 radius AND ulna

25390 Osteoplasty, radius OR ulna; shortening

25391 lengthening with autograft

25392 Osteoplasty, radius AND ulna; shortening (excluding 64876)

25393 lengthening with autograft

25394 Osteoplasty, carpal bone, shortening

Surgery: Musculoskeletal System

25400	Repair of nonunion or malunion, radius OR ulna; without graft (eg, compression technique)
25405	with autograft (includes obtaining graft)
25415	Repair of nonunion or malunion, radius AND ulna; without graft (eg, compression technique)
25420	with autograft (includes obtaining graft)
25425	Repair of defect with autograft; radius OR ulna
25426	radius AND ulna
25430	Insertion of vascular pedicle into carpal bone (eg, Hori procedure)
25431	Repair of nonunion of carpal bone (excluding carpal scaphoid (navicular)) (includes obtaining graft and necessary fixation), each bone
25440	Repair of nonunion, scaphoid carpal (navicular) bone, with or without radial styloidectomy (includes obtaining graft and necessary fixation)
25441	Arthroplasty with prosthetic replacement; distal radius
25442	distal ulna
25443	scaphoid carpal (navicular)
25444	lunate
25445	trapezium
25446	distal radius and partial or entire carpus (total wrist)
25447	Arthroplasty, interposition, intercarpal or carpometacarpal joints
	(For wrist arthroplasty, use 25332)
25449	Revision of arthroplasty, including removal of implant, wrist joint
25450	Epiphyseal arrest by epiphysiodesis or stapling; distal radius OR ulna
25455	distal radius AND ulna
25490	Prophylactic treatment (nailing, pinning, plating or wiring) with or without methylmethacrylate; radius
25491	ulna
25492	radius AND ulna

Fracture and/or Dislocation

►(For application of external fixation in addition to internal fixation, use 20690 and the appropriate internal fixation code)◄

25500	Closed treatment of radial shaft fracture; without manipulation
25505	with manipulation
25515	Open treatment of radial shaft fracture, with or without internal or external fixation

25520	Closed treatment of radial shaft fracture and closed treatment of dislocation of distal radioulnar joint (Galeazzi fracture/dislocation)
25525	Open treatment of radial shaft fracture, with internal and/or external fixation and closed treatment of dislocation of distal radioulnar joint (Galeazzi fracture/dislocation), with or without percutaneous skeletal fixation
25526	Open treatment of radial shaft fracture, with internal and/or external fixation and open treatment, with or without internal or external fixation of distal radioulnar joint (Galeazzi fracture/dislocation), includes repair of triangular fibrocartilage complex
25530	Closed treatment of ulnar shaft fracture; without manipulation
25535	with manipulation
25545	Open treatment of ulnar shaft fracture, with or without internal or external fixation
25560	Closed treatment of radial and ulnar shaft fractures; without manipulation
25565	with manipulation
25574	Open treatment of radial AND ulnar shaft fractures, with internal or external fixation; of radius OR ulna
25575	of radius AND ulna
▲ **25600**	Closed treatment of distal radial fracture (eg, Colles or Smith type) or epiphyseal separation, includes closed treatment of fracture of ulnar styloid, when performed; without manipulation
25605	with manipulation
	►(Do not report 25600, 25605 in conjunction with 25650)◄
● **25606**	Percutaneous skeletal fixation of distal radial fracture or epiphyseal separation
	►(Do not report 25606 in conjunction with 25650)◄
	►(For percutaneous treatment of ulnar styloid fracture, use 25651)◄
	►(For open treatment of ulnar styloid fracture, use 25652)◄
● **25607**	Open treatment of distal radial extra-articular fracture or epiphyseal separation, with internal fixation
	►(Do not report 25607 in conjunction with 25650)◄
	►(For percutaneous treatment of ulnar styloid fracture, use 25651)◄
	►(For open treatment of ulnar styloid fracture, use 25652)◄

● **25608** Open treatment of distal radial intra-articular fracture or epiphyseal separation; with internal fixation of 2 fragments

►(Do not report 25608 in conjunction with 25609)◄

● **25609** with internal fixation of 3 or more fragments

►(Do not report 25608, 25609 in conjunction with 25650)◄

►(For percutaneous treatment of ulnar styloid fracture, use 25651)◄

►(For open treatment of ulnar styloid fracture, use 25652)◄

►(25611 has been deleted. To report, use 25606)◄

►(25620 has been deleted. To report, see 25607-25609)◄

25622 Closed treatment of carpal scaphoid (navicular) fracture; without manipulation

25624 with manipulation

25628 Open treatment of carpal scaphoid (navicular) fracture, with or without internal or external fixation

25630 Closed treatment of carpal bone fracture (excluding carpal scaphoid (navicular)); without manipulation, each bone

25635 with manipulation, each bone

25645 Open treatment of carpal bone fracture (other than carpal scaphoid (navicular)), each bone

25650 Closed treatment of ulnar styloid fracture

►(Do not report 25650 in conjunction with 25600, 25605, 25607-25609)◄

25651 Percutaneous skeletal fixation of ulnar styloid fracture

25652 Open treatment of ulnar styloid fracture

25660 Closed treatment of radiocarpal or intercarpal dislocation, one or more bones, with manipulation

25670 Open treatment of radiocarpal or intercarpal dislocation, one or more bones

25671 Percutaneous skeletal fixation of distal radioulnar dislocation

25675 Closed treatment of distal radioulnar dislocation with manipulation

25676 Open treatment of distal radioulnar dislocation, acute or chronic

25680 Closed treatment of trans-scaphoperilunar type of fracture dislocation, with manipulation

25685 Open treatment of trans-scaphoperilunar type of fracture dislocation

25690 Closed treatment of lunate dislocation, with manipulation

25695 Open treatment of lunate dislocation

Arthrodesis

25800 Arthrodesis, wrist; complete, without bone graft (includes radiocarpal and/or intercarpal and/or carpometacarpal joints)

25805 with sliding graft

25810 with iliac or other autograft (includes obtaining graft)

25820 Arthrodesis, wrist; limited, without bone graft (eg, intercarpal or radiocarpal)

25825 with autograft (includes obtaining graft)

25830 Arthrodesis, distal radioulnar joint with segmental resection of ulna, with or without bone graft (eg, Sauve-Kapandji procedure)

Amputation

25900 Amputation, forearm, through radius and ulna;

25905 open, circular (guillotine)

25907 secondary closure or scar revision

25909 re-amputation

25915 Krukenberg procedure

25920 Disarticulation through wrist;

25922 secondary closure or scar revision

25924 re-amputation

25927 Transmetacarpal amputation;

25929 secondary closure or scar revision

25931 re-amputation

Other Procedures

25999 Unlisted procedure, forearm or wrist

Hand and Fingers

Incision

26010 Drainage of finger abscess; simple

26011 complicated (eg, felon)

26020 Drainage of tendon sheath, digit and/or palm, each

26025 Drainage of palmar bursa; single, bursa

26030 multiple bursa

26034 Incision, bone cortex, hand or finger (eg, osteomyelitis or bone abscess)

26035 Decompression fingers and/or hand, injection injury (eg, grease gun)

26037 Decompressive fasciotomy, hand (excludes 26035)

(For injury injury, use 26035)

26040 Fasciotomy, palmar (eg, Dupuytren's contracture); percutaneous

26045 open, partial

 (For fasciectomy, see 26121-26125)

26055 Tendon sheath incision (eg, for trigger finger)

26060 Tenotomy, percutaneous, single, each digit

26070 Arthrotomy, with exploration, drainage, or removal of loose or foreign body; carpometacarpal joint

26075 metacarpophalangeal joint, each

26080 interphalangeal joint, each

Excision

26100 Arthrotomy with biopsy; carpometacarpal joint, each

26105 metacarpophalangeal joint, each

26110 interphalangeal joint, each

26115 Excision, tumor or vascular malformation, soft tissue of hand or finger; subcutaneous

26116 deep (subfascial or intramuscular)

26117 Radical resection of tumor (eg, malignant neoplasm), soft tissue of hand or finger

26121 Fasciectomy, palm only, with or without Z-plasty, other local tissue rearrangement, or skin grafting (includes obtaining graft)

26123 Fasciectomy, partial palmar with release of single digit including proximal interphalangeal joint, with or without Z-plasty, other local tissue rearrangement, or skin grafting (includes obtaining graft);

+ 26125 each additional digit (List separately in addition to code for primary procedure)

 (Use 26125 in conjunction with 26123)

 (For fasciotomy, see 26040, 26045)

26130 Synovectomy, carpometacarpal joint

26135 Synovectomy, metacarpophalangeal joint including intrinsic release and extensor hood reconstruction, each digit

26140 Synovectomy, proximal interphalangeal joint, including extensor reconstruction, each interphalangeal joint

26145 Synovectomy, tendon sheath, radical (tenosynovectomy), flexor tendon, palm and/or finger, each tendon

 (For tendon sheath synovectomies at wrist, see 25115, 25116)

26160 Excision of lesion of tendon sheath or joint capsule (eg, cyst, mucous cyst, or ganglion), hand or finger

 (For wrist ganglion, see 25111, 25112)

 (For trigger digit, use 26055)

▲ **26170** Excision of tendon, palm, flexor or extensor, single, each tendon

 ►(Do not report 26170 in conjunction with 26390, 26415)◄

▲ **26180** Excision of tendon, finger, flexor or extensor, each tendon

 ►(Do not report 26180 in conjunction with 26390, 26415)◄

26185 Sesamoidectomy, thumb or finger (separate procedure)

26200 Excision or curettage of bone cyst or benign tumor of metacarpal;

26205 with autograft (includes obtaining graft)

26210 Excision or curettage of bone cyst or benign tumor of proximal, middle, or distal phalanx of finger;

26215 with autograft (includes obtaining graft)

26230 Partial excision (craterization, saucerization, or diaphysectomy) bone (eg, osteomyelitis); metacarpal

26235 proximal or middle phalanx of finger

26236 distal phalanx of finger

26250 Radical resection, metacarpal (eg, tumor);

26255 with autograft (includes obtaining graft)

26260 Radical resection, proximal or middle phalanx of finger (eg, tumor);

26261 with autograft (includes obtaining graft)

26262 Radical resection, distal phalanx of finger (eg, tumor)

Introduction or Removal

26320 Removal of implant from finger or hand

 (For removal of foreign body in hand or finger, see 20520, 20525)

Repair, Revision, and/or Reconstruction

26340 Manipulation, finger joint, under anesthesia, each joint

 (For application of external fixation, see 20690 or 20692)

26350 Repair or advancement, flexor tendon, not in zone 2 digital flexor tendon sheath (eg, no man's land); primary or secondary without free graft, each tendon

26352 secondary with free graft (includes obtaining graft), each tendon

26356 Repair or advancement, flexor tendon, in zone 2 digital flexor tendon sheath (eg, no man's land); primary, without free graft, each tendon

26357 secondary, without free graft, each tendon

26358 secondary, with free graft (includes obtaining graft), each tendon

26370 Repair or advancement of profundus tendon, with intact superficialis tendon; primary, each tendon

26372 secondary with free graft (includes obtaining graft), each tendon

26373 secondary without free graft, each tendon

26390 Excision flexor tendon, with implantation of synthetic rod for delayed tendon graft, hand or finger, each rod

26392 Removal of synthetic rod and insertion of flexor tendon graft, hand or finger (includes obtaining graft), each rod

26410 Repair, extensor tendon, hand, primary or secondary; without free graft, each tendon

26412 with free graft (includes obtaining graft), each tendon

26415 Excision of extensor tendon, with implantation of synthetic rod for delayed tendon graft, hand or finger, each rod

26416 Removal of synthetic rod and insertion of extensor tendon graft (includes obtaining graft), hand or finger, each rod

26418 Repair, extensor tendon, finger, primary or secondary; without free graft, each tendon

26420 with free graft (includes obtaining graft) each tendon

26426 Repair of extensor tendon, central slip, secondary (eg, boutonniere deformity); using local tissue(s), including lateral band(s), each finger

26428 with free graft (includes obtaining graft), each finger

26432 Closed treatment of distal extensor tendon insertion, with or without percutaneous pinning (eg, mallet finger)

26433 Repair of extensor tendon, distal insertion, primary or secondary; without graft (eg, mallet finger)

26434 with free graft (includes obtaining graft)

(For tenovaginotomy for trigger finger, use 26055)

26437 Realignment of extensor tendon, hand, each tendon

26440 Tenolysis, flexor tendon; palm OR finger, each tendon

26442 palm AND finger, each tendon

26445 Tenolysis, extensor tendon, hand OR finger, each tendon

26449 Tenolysis, complex, extensor tendon, finger, including forearm, each tendon

26450 Tenotomy, flexor, palm, open, each tendon

26455 Tenotomy, flexor, finger, open, each tendon

26460 Tenotomy, extensor, hand or finger, open, each tendon

26471 Tenodesis; of proximal interphalangeal joint, each joint

26474 of distal joint, each joint

26476 Lengthening of tendon, extensor, hand or finger, each tendon

26477 Shortening of tendon, extensor, hand or finger, each tendon

26478 Lengthening of tendon, flexor, hand or finger, each tendon

26479 Shortening of tendon, flexor, hand or finger, each tendon

26480 Transfer or transplant of tendon, carpometacarpal area or dorsum of hand; without free graft, each tendon

26483 with free tendon graft (includes obtaining graft), each tendon

26485 Transfer or transplant of tendon, palmar; without free tendon graft, each tendon

26489 with free tendon graft (includes obtaining graft), each tendon

26490 Opponensplasty; superficialis tendon transfer type, each tendon

26492 tendon transfer with graft (includes obtaining graft), each tendon

26494 hypothenar muscle transfer

26496 other methods

(For thumb fusion in opposition, use 26820)

26497 Transfer of tendon to restore intrinsic function; ring and small finger

26498 all four fingers

26499 Correction claw finger, other methods

26500 Reconstruction of tendon pulley, each tendon; with local tissues (separate procedure)

26502 with tendon or fascial graft (includes obtaining graft) (separate procedure)

▶(26504 has been deleted. To report, use 26390)◀

26508 Release of thenar muscle(s) (eg, thumb contracture)

26510 Cross intrinsic transfer, each tendon

26516 Capsulodesis, metacarpophalangeal joint; single digit

26517 two digits

26518 three or four digits

26520 Capsulectomy or capsulotomy; metacarpophalangeal joint, each joint

26525 interphalangeal joint, each joint

(To report carpometacarpal joint arthroplasty, use 25447)

26530 Arthroplasty, metacarpophalangeal joint; each joint

26531 with prosthetic implant, each joint

26535 Arthroplasty, interphalangeal joint; each joint

26536 with prosthetic implant, each joint

26540 Repair of collateral ligament, metacarpophalangeal or interphalangeal joint

26541 Reconstruction, collateral ligament, metacarpophalangeal joint, single; with tendon or fascial graft (includes obtaining graft)

26542 with local tissue (eg, adductor advancement)

26545 Reconstruction, collateral ligament, interphalangeal joint, single, including graft, each joint

26546 Repair non-union, metacarpal or phalanx, (includes obtaining bone graft with or without external or internal fixation)

26548 Repair and reconstruction, finger, volar plate, interphalangeal joint

26550 Pollicization of a digit

26551 Transfer, toe-to-hand with microvascular anastomosis; great toe wrap-around with bone graft

(For great toe with web space, use 20973)

26553 other than great toe, single

26554 other than great toe, double

(Do not report code 69990 in addition to codes 26551-26554)

26555 Transfer, finger to another position without microvascular anastomosis

26556 Transfer, free toe joint, with microvascular anastomosis

(Do not report code 69990 in addition to code 26556)

(To report great toe-to-hand transfer, use 20973)

26560 Repair of syndactyly (web finger) each web space; with skin flaps

26561 with skin flaps and grafts

26562 complex (eg, involving bone, nails)

26565 Osteotomy; metacarpal, each

26567 phalanx of finger, each

26568 Osteoplasty, lengthening, metacarpal or phalanx

26580 Repair cleft hand

26587 Reconstruction of polydactylous digit, soft tissue and bone

(For excision of polydactylous digit, soft tissue only, use 11200)

26590 Repair macrodactylia, each digit

26591 Repair, intrinsic muscles of hand, each muscle

26593 Release, intrinsic muscles of hand, each muscle

26596 Excision of constricting ring of finger, with multiple Z-plasties

(To report release of scar contracture or graft repairs see 11041-11042, 14040-14041, or 15120, 15240)

Fracture and/or Dislocation

26600 Closed treatment of metacarpal fracture, single; without manipulation, each bone

26605 with manipulation, each bone

26607 Closed treatment of metacarpal fracture, with manipulation, with external fixation, each bone

26608 Percutaneous skeletal fixation of metacarpal fracture, each bone

26615 Open treatment of metacarpal fracture, single, with or without internal or external fixation, each bone

26641 Closed treatment of carpometacarpal dislocation, thumb, with manipulation

26645 Closed treatment of carpometacarpal fracture dislocation, thumb (Bennett fracture), with manipulation

26650 Percutaneous skeletal fixation of carpometacarpal fracture dislocation, thumb (Bennett fracture), with manipulation, with or without external fixation

26665 Open treatment of carpometacarpal fracture dislocation, thumb (Bennett fracture), with or without internal or external fixation

26670 Closed treatment of carpometacarpal dislocation, other than thumb, with manipulation, each joint; without anesthesia

26675 requiring anesthesia

26676 Percutaneous skeletal fixation of carpometacarpal dislocation, other than thumb, with manipulation, each joint

26685 Open treatment of carpometacarpal dislocation, other than thumb; with or without internal or external fixation, each joint

26686 complex, multiple or delayed reduction

26700 Closed treatment of metacarpophalangeal dislocation, single, with manipulation; without anesthesia

26705 requiring anesthesia

26706 Percutaneous skeletal fixation of metacarpophalangeal dislocation, single, with manipulation

26715 Open treatment of metacarpophalangeal dislocation, single, with or without internal or external fixation

26720 Closed treatment of phalangeal shaft fracture, proximal or middle phalanx, finger or thumb; without manipulation, each

26725 with manipulation, with or without skin or skeletal traction, each

26727 Percutaneous skeletal fixation of unstable phalangeal shaft fracture, proximal or middle phalanx, finger or thumb, with manipulation, each

26735 Open treatment of phalangeal shaft fracture, proximal or middle phalanx, finger or thumb, with or without internal or external fixation, each

26740 Closed treatment of articular fracture, involving metacarpophalangeal or interphalangeal joint; without manipulation, each

26742 with manipulation, each

26746 Open treatment of articular fracture, involving metacarpophalangeal or interphalangeal joint, with or without internal or external fixation, each

26750 Closed treatment of distal phalangeal fracture, finger or thumb; without manipulation, each

26755 with manipulation, each

26756 Percutaneous skeletal fixation of distal phalangeal fracture, finger or thumb, each

26765 Open treatment of distal phalangeal fracture, finger or thumb, with or without internal or external fixation, each

26770 Closed treatment of interphalangeal joint dislocation, single, with manipulation; without anesthesia

26775 requiring anesthesia

26776 Percutaneous skeletal fixation of interphalangeal joint dislocation, single, with manipulation

26785 Open treatment of interphalangeal joint dislocation, with or without internal or external fixation, single

Arthrodesis

26820 Fusion in opposition, thumb, with autogenous graft (includes obtaining graft)

26841 Arthrodesis, carpometacarpal joint, thumb, with or without internal fixation;

26842 with autograft (includes obtaining graft)

26843 Arthrodesis, carpometacarpal joint, digit, other than thumb, each;

26844 with autograft (includes obtaining graft)

26850 Arthrodesis, metacarpophalangeal joint, with or without internal fixation;

26852 with autograft (includes obtaining graft)

26860 Arthrodesis, interphalangeal joint, with or without internal fixation;

+ 26861 each additional interphalangeal joint (List separately in addition to code for primary procedure)

(Use 26861 in conjunction with 26860)

26862 with autograft (includes obtaining graft)

+ 26863 with autograft (includes obtaining graft), each additional joint (List separately in addition to code for primary procedure)

(Use 26863 in conjunction with 26862)

Amputation

(For hand through metacarpal bones, use 25927)

26910 Amputation, metacarpal, with finger or thumb (ray amputation), single, with or without interosseous transfer

(For repositioning, see 26550, 26555)

26951 Amputation, finger or thumb, primary or secondary, any joint or phalanx, single, including neurectomies; with direct closure

26952 with local advancement flaps (V-Y, hood)

(For repair of soft tissue defect requiring split or full thickness graft or other pedicle flaps, see 15050-15758)

Other Procedures

26989 Unlisted procedure, hands or fingers

Pelvis and Hip Joint

Including head and neck of femur.

Incision

(For incision and drainage procedures, superficial, see 10040-10160)

26990 Incision and drainage, pelvis or hip joint area; deep abscess or hematoma

26991 infected bursa

26992 Incision, bone cortex, pelvis and/or hip joint (eg, osteomyelitis or bone abscess)

27000 Tenotomy, adductor of hip, percutaneous (separate procedure)

27001 Tenotomy, adductor of hip, open

(To report bilateral procedures, report 27001 with modifier 50)

27003 Tenotomy, adductor, subcutaneous, open, with obturator neurectomy

(To report bilateral procedures, report 27003 with modifier 50)

27005 Tenotomy, hip flexor(s), open (separate procedure)

27006 Tenotomy, abductors and/or extensor(s) of hip, open (separate procedure)

27025 Fasciotomy, hip or thigh, any type

(To report bilateral procedures, report 27025 with modifier 50)

27030 Arthrotomy, hip, with drainage (eg, infection)

27033 Arthrotomy, hip, including exploration or removal of loose or foreign body

27035 Denervation, hip joint, intrapelvic or extrapelvic intra-articular branches of sciatic, femoral, or obturator nerves

(For obturator neurectomy, see 64763, 64766)

27036 Capsulectomy or capsulotomy, hip, with or without excision of heterotopic bone, with release of hip flexor muscles (ie, gluteus medius, gluteus minimus, tensor fascia latae, rectus femoris, sartorius, iliopsoas)

Excision

27040 Biopsy, soft tissue of pelvis and hip area; superficial

27041 deep, subfascial or intramuscular

(For needle biopsy of soft tissue, use 20206)

27047 Excision, tumor, pelvis and hip area; subcutaneous tissue

27048 deep, subfascial, intramuscular

27049 Radical resection of tumor, soft tissue of pelvis and hip area (eg, malignant neoplasm)

27050 Arthrotomy, with biopsy; sacroiliac joint

27052 hip joint

27054 Arthrotomy with synovectomy, hip joint

27060 Excision; ischial bursa

27062 trochanteric bursa or calcification

(For arthrocentesis or needling of bursa, use 20610)

27065 Excision of bone cyst or benign tumor; superficial (wing of ilium, symphysis pubis, or greater trochanter of femur) with or without autograft

27066 deep, with or without autograft

27067 with autograft requiring separate incision

27070 Partial excision (craterization, saucerization) (eg, osteomyelitis or bone abscess); superficial (eg, wing of ilium, symphysis pubis, or greater trochanter of femur)

27071 deep (subfascial or intramuscular)

27075 Radical resection of tumor or infection; wing of ilium, one pubic or ischial ramus or symphysis pubis

27076 ilium, including acetabulum, both pubic rami, or ischium and acetabulum

27077 innominate bone, total

27078 ischial tuberosity and greater trochanter of femur

27079 ischial tuberosity and greater trochanter of femur, with skin flaps

27080 Coccygectomy, primary

(For pressure (decubitus) ulcer, see 15920, 15922 and 15931-15958)

Introduction or Removal

27086 Removal of foreign body, pelvis or hip; subcutaneous tissue

27087 deep (subfascial or intramuscular)

27090 Removal of hip prosthesis; (separate procedure)

27091 complicated, including total hip prosthesis, methylmethacrylate with or without insertion of spacer

27093 Injection procedure for hip arthrography; without anesthesia

▶(For radiological supervision and interpretation, use 73525. Do not report 77002 in conjunction with 73525)◀

27095 with anesthesia

▶(For radiological supervision and interpretation, use 73525. Do not report 77002 in conjunction with 73525)◀

27096 Injection procedure for sacroiliac joint, arthrography and/or anesthetic/steroid

(27096 is to be used only with imaging confirmation of intra-articular needle positioning)

(For radiological supervision and interpretation of sacroiliac joint arthrography, use 73542)

▶(For fluoroscopic guidance without formal arthrography, use 77003)◀

(Code 27096 is a unilateral procedure. For bilateral procedure, use modifier 50)

Repair, Revision, and/or Reconstruction

27097 Release or recession, hamstring, proximal

27098 Transfer, adductor to ischium

27100 Transfer external oblique muscle to greater trochanter including fascial or tendon extension (graft)

27105 Transfer paraspinal muscle to hip (includes fascial or tendon extension graft)

27110 Transfer iliopsoas; to greater trochanter of femur

27111 to femoral neck

27120 Acetabuloplasty; (eg, Whitman, Colonna, Haygroves, or cup type)

27122 resection, femoral head (eg, Girdlestone procedure)

27125 Hemiarthroplasty, hip, partial (eg, femoral stem prosthesis, bipolar arthroplasty)

(For prosthetic replacement following fracture of the hip, use 27236)

27130 Arthroplasty, acetabular and proximal femoral prosthetic replacement (total hip arthroplasty), with or without autograft or allograft

27132 Conversion of previous hip surgery to total hip arthroplasty, with or without autograft or allograft

Surgery: Musculoskeletal System

Surgery: Musculoskeletal System

27134 Revision of total hip arthroplasty; both components, with or without autograft or allograft

27137 acetabular component only, with or without autograft or allograft

27138 femoral component only, with or without allograft

27140 Osteotomy and transfer of greater trochanter of femur (separate procedure)

27146 Osteotomy, iliac, acetabular or innominate bone;

27147 with open reduction of hip

27151 with femoral osteotomy

27156 with femoral osteotomy and with open reduction of hip

27158 Osteotomy, pelvis, bilateral (eg, congenital malformation)

27161 Osteotomy, femoral neck (separate procedure)

27165 Osteotomy, intertrochanteric or subtrochanteric including internal or external fixation and/or cast

27170 Bone graft, femoral head, neck, intertrochanteric or subtrochanteric area (includes obtaining bone graft)

27175 Treatment of slipped femoral epiphysis; by traction, without reduction

27176 by single or multiple pinning, in situ

27177 Open treatment of slipped femoral epiphysis; single or multiple pinning or bone graft (includes obtaining graft)

27178 closed manipulation with single or multiple pinning

27179 osteoplasty of femoral neck (Heyman type procedure)

27181 osteotomy and internal fixation

27185 Epiphyseal arrest by epiphysiodesis or stapling, greater trochanter of femur

27187 Prophylactic treatment (nailing, pinning, plating or wiring) with or without methylmethacrylate, femoral neck and proximal femur

Fracture and/or Dislocation

27193 Closed treatment of pelvic ring fracture, dislocation, diastasis or subluxation; without manipulation

27194 with manipulation, requiring more than local anesthesia

27200 Closed treatment of coccygeal fracture

27202 Open treatment of coccygeal fracture

27215 Open treatment of iliac spine(s), tuberosity avulsion, or iliac wing fracture(s) (eg, pelvic fracture(s) which do not disrupt the pelvic ring), with internal fixation

27216 Percutaneous skeletal fixation of posterior pelvic ring fracture and/or dislocation (includes ilium, sacroiliac joint and/or sacrum)

27217 Open treatment of anterior ring fracture and/or dislocation with internal fixation (includes pubic symphysis and/or rami)

27218 Open treatment of posterior ring fracture and/or dislocation with internal fixation (includes ilium, sacroiliac joint and/or sacrum)

27220 Closed treatment of acetabulum (hip socket) fracture(s); without manipulation

27222 with manipulation, with or without skeletal traction

27226 Open treatment of posterior or anterior acetabular wall fracture, with internal fixation

27227 Open treatment of acetabular fracture(s) involving anterior or posterior (one) column, or a fracture running transversely across the acetabulum, with internal fixation

27228 Open treatment of acetabular fracture(s) involving anterior and posterior (two) columns, includes T-fracture and both column fracture with complete articular detachment, or single column or transverse fracture with associated acetabular wall fracture, with internal fixation

27230 Closed treatment of femoral fracture, proximal end, neck; without manipulation

27232 with manipulation, with or without skeletal traction

27235 Percutaneous skeletal fixation of femoral fracture, proximal end, neck

27236 Open treatment of femoral fracture, proximal end, neck, internal fixation or prosthetic replacement

27238 Closed treatment of intertrochanteric, peritrochanteric, or subtrochanteric femoral fracture; without manipulation

27240 with manipulation, with or without skin or skeletal traction

27244 Treatment of intertrochanteric, peritrochanteric, or subtrochanteric femoral fracture; with plate/screw type implant, with or without cerclage

27245 with intramedullary implant, with or without interlocking screws and/or cerclage

27246 Closed treatment of greater trochanteric fracture, without manipulation

27248 Open treatment of greater trochanteric fracture, with or without internal or external fixation

27250 Closed treatment of hip dislocation, traumatic; without anesthesia

27252 requiring anesthesia

27253 Open treatment of hip dislocation, traumatic, without internal fixation

27254 Open treatment of hip dislocation, traumatic, with acetabular wall and femoral head fracture, with or without internal or external fixation

(For treatment of acetabular fracture with fixation, see 27226, 27227)

27256 Treatment of spontaneous hip dislocation (developmental, including congenital or pathological), by abduction, splint or traction; without anesthesia, without manipulation

27257 with manipulation, requiring anesthesia

27258 Open treatment of spontaneous hip dislocation (developmental, including congenital or pathological), replacement of femoral head in acetabulum (including tenotomy, etc);

27259 with femoral shaft shortening

27265 Closed treatment of post hip arthroplasty dislocation; without anesthesia

27266 requiring regional or general anesthesia

Manipulation

27275 Manipulation, hip joint, requiring general anesthesia

Arthrodesis

27280 Arthrodesis, sacroiliac joint (including obtaining graft)

 (To report bilateral procedures, report 27280 with modifier 50)

27282 Arthrodesis, symphysis pubis (including obtaining graft)

27284 Arthrodesis, hip joint (including obtaining graft);

27286 with subtrochanteric osteotomy

Amputation

27290 Interpelviabdominal amputation (hindquarter amputation)

27295 Disarticulation of hip

Other Procedures

27299 Unlisted procedure, pelvis or hip joint

Femur (Thigh Region) and Knee Joint

Including tibial plateaus.

Incision

 (For incision and drainage of abscess or hematoma, superficial, see 10040-10160)

27301 Incision and drainage, deep abscess, bursa, or hematoma, thigh or knee region

27303 Incision, deep, with opening of bone cortex, femur or knee (eg, osteomyelitis or bone abscess)

27305 Fasciotomy, iliotibial (tenotomy), open

 (For combined Ober-Yount fasciotomy, use 27025)

27306 Tenotomy, percutaneous, adductor or hamstring; single tendon (separate procedure)

27307 multiple tendons

27310 Arthrotomy, knee, with exploration, drainage, or removal of foreign body (eg, infection)

 ▶(27315 has been deleted. To report, see 27325)◀

 ▶(27320 has been deleted. To report, see 27326)◀

Excision

27323 Biopsy, soft tissue of thigh or knee area; superficial

27324 deep (subfascial or intramuscular)

 (For needle biopsy of soft tissue, use 20206)

● **27325** Neurectomy, hamstring muscle

● **27326** Neurectomy, popliteal (gastrocnemius)

27327 Excision, tumor, thigh or knee area; subcutaneous

27328 deep, subfascial, or intramuscular

27329 Radical resection of tumor (eg, malignant neoplasm), soft tissue of thigh or knee area

27330 Arthrotomy, knee; with synovial biopsy only

27331 including joint exploration, biopsy, or removal of loose or foreign bodies

27332 Arthrotomy, with excision of semilunar cartilage (meniscectomy) knee; medial OR lateral

27333 medial AND lateral

27334 Arthrotomy, with synovectomy, knee; anterior OR posterior

27335 anterior AND posterior including popliteal area

27340 Excision, prepatellar bursa

27345 Excision of synovial cyst of popliteal space (eg, Baker's cyst)

27347 Excision of lesion of meniscus or capsule (eg, cyst, ganglion), knee

27350 Patellectomy or hemipatellectomy

27355 Excision or curettage of bone cyst or benign tumor of femur;

27356 with allograft

27357 with autograft (includes obtaining graft)

+ **27358** with internal fixation (List in addition to code for primary procedure)

 (Use 27358 in conjunction with 27355, 27356, or 27357)

27360 Partial excision (craterization, saucerization, or diaphysectomy) bone, femur, proximal tibia and/or fibula (eg, osteomyelitis or bone abscess)

27365 Radical resection of tumor, bone, femur or knee

 (For radical resection of tumor, soft tissue, use 27329)

Introduction or Removal

27370 Injection procedure for knee arthrography

▶(For radiological supervision and interpretation, use 73580. Do not report 77002 in conjunction with 73580)◀

27372 Removal of foreign body, deep, thigh region or knee area

(For removal of knee prosthesis including "total knee," use 27488)

(For surgical arthroscopic knee procedures, see 29870-29887)

Repair, Revision, and/or Reconstruction

27380 Suture of infrapatellar tendon; primary

27381 secondary reconstruction, including fascial or tendon graft

27385 Suture of quadriceps or hamstring muscle rupture; primary

27386 secondary reconstruction, including fascial or tendon graft

27390 Tenotomy, open, hamstring, knee to hip; single tendon

27391 multiple tendons, one leg

27392 multiple tendons, bilateral

27393 Lengthening of hamstring tendon; single tendon

27394 multiple tendons, one leg

27395 multiple tendons, bilateral

27396 Transplant, hamstring tendon to patella; single tendon

27397 multiple tendons

27400 Transfer, tendon or muscle, hamstrings to femur (eg, Egger's type procedure)

27403 Arthrotomy with meniscus repair, knee

(For arthroscopic repair, use 29882)

27405 Repair, primary, torn ligament and/or capsule, knee; collateral

27407 cruciate

(For cruciate ligament reconstruction, use 27427)

27409 collateral and cruciate ligaments

(For ligament reconstruction, see 27427-27429)

27412 Autologous chondrocyte implantation, knee

(Do not report 27412 in conjunction with 20926, 27331, 27570)

(For harvesting of chondrocytes, use 29870)

27415 Osteochondral allograft, knee, open

(For arthroscopic implant of osteochondral allograft, use 29867)

27418 Anterior tibial tubercleplasty (eg, Maquet type procedure)

27420 Reconstruction of dislocating patella; (eg, Hauser type procedure)

27422 with extensor realignment and/or muscle advancement or release (eg, Campbell, Goldwaite type procedure)

27424 with patellectomy

27425 Lateral retinacular release, open

(For arthroscopic lateral release, use 29873)

27427 Ligamentous reconstruction (augmentation), knee; extra-articular

27428 intra-articular (open)

27429 intra-articular (open) and extra-articular

(For primary repair of ligament(s) performed in conjunction with reconstruction, report 27405, 27407 or 27409 in conjunction with 27427, 27428 or 27429)

27430 Quadricepsplasty (eg, Bennett or Thompson type)

27435 Capsulotomy, posterior capsular release, knee

27437 Arthroplasty, patella; without prosthesis

27438 with prosthesis

27440 Arthroplasty, knee, tibial plateau;

27441 with debridement and partial synovectomy

27442 Arthroplasty, femoral condyles or tibial plateau(s), knee;

27443 with debridement and partial synovectomy

27445 Arthroplasty, knee, hinge prosthesis (eg, Walldius type)

27446 Arthroplasty, knee, condyle and plateau; medial OR lateral compartment

27447 medial AND lateral compartments with or without patella resurfacing (total knee arthroplasty)

(For revision of total knee arthroplasty, use 27487)

(For removal of total knee prosthesis, use 27488)

27448 Osteotomy, femur, shaft or supracondylar; without fixation

(To report bilateral procedures, report 27448 with modifier 50)

27450 with fixation

(To report bilateral procedures, report 27450 with modifier 50)

27454 Osteotomy, multiple, with realignment on intramedullary rod, femoral shaft (eg, Sofield type procedure)

27455 Osteotomy, proximal tibia, including fibular excision or osteotomy (includes correction of genu varus (bowleg) or genu valgus (knock-knee)); before epiphyseal closure

(To report bilateral procedures, report 27455 with modifier 50)

27457 after epiphyseal closure

(To report bilateral procedures, report 27457 with modifier 50)

Surgery: Musculoskeletal System

27465 Osteoplasty, femur; shortening (excluding 64876)

27466 lengthening

27468 combined, lengthening and shortening with femoral segment transfer

27470 Repair, nonunion or malunion, femur, distal to head and neck; without graft (eg, compression technique)

27472 with iliac or other autogenous bone graft (includes obtaining graft)

27475 Arrest, epiphyseal, any method (eg, epiphysiodesis); distal femur

27477 tibia and fibula, proximal

27479 combined distal femur, proximal tibia and fibula

27485 Arrest, hemiepiphyseal, distal femur or proximal tibia or fibula (eg, genu varus or valgus)

27486 Revision of total knee arthroplasty, with or without allograft; one component

27487 femoral and entire tibial component

27488 Removal of prosthesis, including total knee prosthesis, methylmethacrylate with or without insertion of spacer, knee

27495 Prophylactic treatment (nailing, pinning, plating or wiring) with or without methylmethacrylate, femur

27496 Decompression fasciotomy, thigh and/or knee, one compartment (flexor or extensor or adductor);

27497 with debridement of nonviable muscle and/or nerve

27498 Decompression fasciotomy, thigh and/or knee, multiple compartments;

27499 with debridement of nonviable muscle and/or nerve

Fracture and/or Dislocation

(For arthroscopic treatment of intercondylar spine(s) and tuberosity fracture(s) of the knee, see 29850, 29851)

(For arthroscopic treatment of tibial fracture, see 29855, 29856)

27500 Closed treatment of femoral shaft fracture, without manipulation

27501 Closed treatment of supracondylar or transcondylar femoral fracture with or without intercondylar extension, without manipulation

27502 Closed treatment of femoral shaft fracture, with manipulation, with or without skin or skeletal traction

27503 Closed treatment of supracondylar or transcondylar femoral fracture with or without intercondylar extension, with manipulation, with or without skin or skeletal traction

27506 Open treatment of femoral shaft fracture, with or without external fixation, with insertion of intramedullary implant, with or without cerclage and/or locking screws

27507 Open treatment of femoral shaft fracture with plate/screws, with or without cerclage

27508 Closed treatment of femoral fracture, distal end, medial or lateral condyle, without manipulation

27509 Percutaneous skeletal fixation of femoral fracture, distal end, medial or lateral condyle, or supracondylar or transcondylar, with or without intercondylar extension, or distal femoral epiphyseal separation

27510 Closed treatment of femoral fracture, distal end, medial or lateral condyle, with manipulation

27511 Open treatment of femoral supracondylar or transcondylar fracture without intercondylar extension, with or without internal or external fixation

27513 Open treatment of femoral supracondylar or transcondylar fracture with intercondylar extension, with or without internal or external fixation

27514 Open treatment of femoral fracture, distal end, medial or lateral condyle, with or without internal or external fixation

27516 Closed treatment of distal femoral epiphyseal separation; without manipulation

27517 with manipulation, with or without skin or skeletal traction

27519 Open treatment of distal femoral epiphyseal separation, with or without internal or external fixation

27520 Closed treatment of patellar fracture, without manipulation

27524 Open treatment of patellar fracture, with internal fixation and/or partial or complete patellectomy and soft tissue repair

27530 Closed treatment of tibial fracture, proximal (plateau); without manipulation

27532 with or without manipulation, with skeletal traction

(For arthroscopic treatment, see 29855, 29856)

27535 Open treatment of tibial fracture, proximal (plateau); unicondylar, with or without internal or external fixation

27536 bicondylar, with or without internal fixation

(For arthroscopic treatment, see 29855, 29856)

27538 Closed treatment of intercondylar spine(s) and/or tuberosity fracture(s) of knee, with or without manipulation

(For arthroscopic treatment, see 29850, 29851)

27540 Open treatment of intercondylar spine(s) and/or tuberosity fracture(s) of the knee, with or without internal or external fixation

27550 Closed treatment of knee dislocation; without anesthesia

27552 requiring anesthesia

27556 Open treatment of knee dislocation, with or without internal or external fixation; without primary ligamentous repair or augmentation/reconstruction

27557 with primary ligamentous repair

27558 with primary ligamentous repair, with augmentation/reconstruction

27560 Closed treatment of patellar dislocation; without anesthesia

(For recurrent dislocation, see 27420-27424)

27562 requiring anesthesia

27566 Open treatment of patellar dislocation, with or without partial or total patellectomy

Manipulation

27570 Manipulation of knee joint under general anesthesia (includes application of traction or other fixation devices)

Arthrodesis

27580 Arthrodesis, knee, any technique

Amputation

27590 Amputation, thigh, through femur, any level;

27591 immediate fitting technique including first cast

27592 open, circular (guillotine)

27594 secondary closure or scar revision

27596 re-amputation

27598 Disarticulation at knee

Other Procedures

27599 Unlisted procedure, femur or knee

Leg (Tibia and Fibula) and Ankle Joint

Incision

27600 Decompression fasciotomy, leg; anterior and/or lateral compartments only

27601 posterior compartment(s) only

27602 anterior and/or lateral, and posterior compartment(s)

(For incision and drainage procedures, superficial, see 10040-10160)

(For decompression fasciotomy with debridement, see 27892-27894)

27603 Incision and drainage, leg or ankle; deep abscess or hematoma

27604 infected bursa

27605 Tenotomy, percutaneous, Achilles tendon (separate procedure); local anesthesia

27606 general anesthesia

27607 Incision (eg, osteomyelitis or bone abscess), leg or ankle

27610 Arthrotomy, ankle, including exploration, drainage, or removal of foreign body

27612 Arthrotomy, posterior capsular release, ankle, with or without Achilles tendon lengthening

(See also 27685)

Excision

27613 Biopsy, soft tissue of leg or ankle area; superficial

27614 deep (subfascial or intramuscular)

(For needle biopsy of soft tissue, use 20206)

27615 Radical resection of tumor (eg, malignant neoplasm), soft tissue of leg or ankle area

27618 Excision, tumor, leg or ankle area; subcutaneous tissue

27619 deep (subfascial or intramuscular)

27620 Arthrotomy, ankle, with joint exploration, with or without biopsy, with or without removal of loose or foreign body

27625 Arthrotomy, with synovectomy, ankle;

27626 including tenosynovectomy

27630 Excision of lesion of tendon sheath or capsule (eg, cyst or ganglion), leg and/or ankle

27635 Excision or curettage of bone cyst or benign tumor, tibia or fibula;

27637 with autograft (includes obtaining graft)

27638 with allograft

27640 Partial excision (craterization, saucerization, or diaphysectomy) bone (eg, osteomyelitis or exostosis); tibia

27641 fibula

27645 Radical resection of tumor, bone; tibia

27646 fibula

27647 talus or calcaneus

Introduction or Removal

27648 Injection procedure for ankle arthrography

▶(For radiological supervision and interpretation, use 73615. Do not report 77002 in conjunction with 73615)◀

(For ankle arthroscopy, see 29894-29898)

Repair, Revision, and/or Reconstruction

27650 Repair, primary, open or percutaneous, ruptured Achilles tendon;

27652 with graft (includes obtaining graft)

27654 Repair, secondary, Achilles tendon, with or without graft

27656 Repair, fascial defect of leg

27658 Repair, flexor tendon, leg; primary, without graft, each tendon

27659 secondary, with or without graft, each tendon

27664 Repair, extensor tendon, leg; primary, without graft, each tendon

27665 secondary, with or without graft, each tendon

27675 Repair, dislocating peroneal tendons; without fibular osteotomy

27676 with fibular osteotomy

27680 Tenolysis, flexor or extensor tendon, leg and/or ankle; single, each tendon

27681 multiple tendons (through separate incision(s))

27685 Lengthening or shortening of tendon, leg or ankle; single tendon (separate procedure)

27686 multiple tendons (through same incision), each

27687 Gastrocnemius recession (eg, Strayer procedure)

(Toe extensors are considered as a group to be a single tendon when transplanted into midfoot)

27690 Transfer or transplant of single tendon (with muscle redirection or rerouting); superficial (eg, anterior tibial extensors into midfoot)

27691 deep (eg, anterior tibial or posterior tibial through interosseous space, flexor digitorum longus, flexor hallucis longus, or peroneal tendon to midfoot or hindfoot)

+ 27692 each additional tendon (List separately in addition to code for primary procedure)

(Use 27692 in conjunction with 27690, 27691)

27695 Repair, primary, disrupted ligament, ankle; collateral

27696 both collateral ligaments

27698 Repair, secondary, disrupted ligament, ankle, collateral (eg, Watson-Jones procedure)

27700 Arthroplasty, ankle;

27702 with implant (total ankle)

27703 revision, total ankle

27704 Removal of ankle implant

27705 Osteotomy; tibia

27707 fibula

27709 tibia and fibula

27712 multiple, with realignment on intramedullary rod (eg, Sofield type procedure)

(For osteotomy to correct genu varus (bowleg) or genu valgus (knock-knee), see 27455-27457)

27715 Osteoplasty, tibia and fibula, lengthening or shortening

27720 Repair of nonunion or malunion, tibia; without graft, (eg, compression technique)

27722 with sliding graft

27724 with iliac or other autograft (includes obtaining graft)

27725 by synostosis, with fibula, any method

27727 Repair of congenital pseudarthrosis, tibia

27730 Arrest, epiphyseal (epiphysiodesis), open; distal tibia

27732 distal fibula

27734 distal tibia and fibula

27740 Arrest, epiphyseal (epiphysiodesis), any method, combined, proximal and distal tibia and fibula;

27742 and distal femur

(For epiphyseal arrest of proximal tibia and fibula, use 27477)

27745 Prophylactic treatment (nailing, pinning, plating or wiring) with or without methylmethacrylate, tibia

Fracture and/or Dislocation

27750 Closed treatment of tibial shaft fracture (with or without fibular fracture); without manipulation

27752 with manipulation, with or without skeletal traction

27756 Percutaneous skeletal fixation of tibial shaft fracture (with or without fibular fracture) (eg, pins or screws)

27758 Open treatment of tibial shaft fracture, (with or without fibular fracture) with plate/screws, with or without cerclage

27759 Treatment of tibial shaft fracture (with or without fibular fracture) by intramedullary implant, with or without interlocking screws and/or cerclage

27760 Closed treatment of medial malleolus fracture; without manipulation

27762 with manipulation, with or without skin or skeletal traction

27766 Open treatment of medial malleolus fracture, with or without internal or external fixation

27780 Closed treatment of proximal fibula or shaft fracture; without manipulation

27781 with manipulation

27784 Open treatment of proximal fibula or shaft fracture, with or without internal or external fixation

27786 Closed treatment of distal fibular fracture (lateral malleolus); without manipulation

27788 with manipulation

27792 Open treatment of distal fibular fracture (lateral malleolus), with or without internal or external fixation

(For treatment of tibia and fibula shaft fractures, see 27750-27759)

27808 Closed treatment of bimalleolar ankle fracture, (including Potts); without manipulation

27810 with manipulation

27814 Open treatment of bimalleolar ankle fracture, with or without internal or external fixation

27816 Closed treatment of trimalleolar ankle fracture; without manipulation

27818 with manipulation

27822 Open treatment of trimalleolar ankle fracture, with or without internal or external fixation, medial and/or lateral malleolus; without fixation of posterior lip

27823 with fixation of posterior lip

27824 Closed treatment of fracture of weight bearing articular portion of distal tibia (eg, pilon or tibial plafond), with or without anesthesia; without manipulation

27825 with skeletal traction and/or requiring manipulation

27826 Open treatment of fracture of weight bearing articular surface/portion of distal tibia (eg, pilon or tibial plafond), with internal or external fixation; of fibula only

27827 of tibia only

27828 of both tibia and fibula

27829 Open treatment of distal tibiofibular joint (syndesmosis) disruption, with or without internal or external fixation

27830 Closed treatment of proximal tibiofibular joint dislocation; without anesthesia

27831 requiring anesthesia

27832 Open treatment of proximal tibiofibular joint dislocation, with or without internal or external fixation, or with excision of proximal fibula

27840 Closed treatment of ankle dislocation; without anesthesia

27842 requiring anesthesia, with or without percutaneous skeletal fixation

27846 Open treatment of ankle dislocation, with or without percutaneous skeletal fixation; without repair or internal fixation

27848 with repair or internal or external fixation

(For surgical or diagnostic arthroscopic procedures, see 29894-29898)

Manipulation

27860 Manipulation of ankle under general anesthesia (includes application of traction or other fixation apparatus)

Arthrodesis

27870 Arthrodesis, ankle, open

(For arthroscopic ankle arthrodesis, use 29899)

27871 Arthrodesis, tibiofibular joint, proximal or distal

Amputation

27880 Amputation, leg, through tibia and fibula;

27881 with immediate fitting technique including application of first cast

27882 open, circular (guillotine)

27884 secondary closure or scar revision

27886 re-amputation

27888 Amputation, ankle, through malleoli of tibia and fibula (eg, Syme, Pirogoff type procedures), with plastic closure and resection of nerves

27889 Ankle disarticulation

Other Procedures

27892 Decompression fasciotomy, leg; anterior and/or lateral compartments only, with debridement of nonviable muscle and/or nerve

(For decompression fasciotomy of the leg without debridement, use 27600)

27893 posterior compartment(s) only, with debridement of nonviable muscle and/or nerve

(For decompression fasciotomy of the leg without debridement, use 27601)

27894 anterior and/or lateral, and posterior compartment(s), with debridement of nonviable muscle and/or nerve

(For decompression fasciotomy of the leg without debridement, use 27602)

27899 Unlisted procedure, leg or ankle

Foot and Toes

Incision

(For incision and drainage procedures, superficial, see 10040-10160)

28001 Incision and drainage, bursa, foot

28002 Incision and drainage below fascia, with or without tendon sheath involvement, foot; single bursal space

28003 multiple areas

Surgery: Musculoskeletal System

28005　Incision, bone cortex (eg, osteomyelitis or bone abscess), foot

28008　Fasciotomy, foot and/or toe

　　　　(See also 28060, 28062, 28250)

28010　Tenotomy, percutaneous, toe; single tendon

28011　　　multiple tendons

　　　　(For open tenotomy, see 28230-28234)

28020　Arthrotomy, including exploration, drainage, or removal of loose or foreign body; intertarsal or tarsometatarsal joint

28022　　　metatarsophalangeal joint

28024　　　interphalangeal joint

　　　　▶(28030 has been deleted. To report, use 28055)◀

28035　Release, tarsal tunnel (posterior tibial nerve decompression)

　　　　(For other nerve entrapments, see 64704, 64722)

Excision

28043　Excision, tumor, foot; subcutaneous tissue

28045　　　deep, subfascial, intramuscular

28046　Radical resection of tumor (eg, malignant neoplasm), soft tissue of foot

28050　Arthrotomy with biopsy; intertarsal or tarsometatarsal joint

28052　　　metatarsophalangeal joint

28054　　　interphalangeal joint

● **28055**　Neurectomy, intrinsic musculature of foot

28060　Fasciectomy, plantar fascia; partial (separate procedure)

28062　　　radical (separate procedure)

　　　　(For plantar fasciotomy, see 28008, 28250)

28070　Synovectomy; intertarsal or tarsometatarsal joint, each

28072　　　metatarsophalangeal joint, each

28080　Excision, interdigital (Morton) neuroma, single, each

28086　Synovectomy, tendon sheath, foot; flexor

28088　　　extensor

28090　Excision of lesion, tendon, tendon sheath, or capsule (including synovectomy) (eg, cyst or ganglion); foot

28092　　　toe(s), each

28100　Excision or curettage of bone cyst or benign tumor, talus or calcaneus;

28102　　　with iliac or other autograft (includes obtaining graft)

28103　　　with allograft

28104　Excision or curettage of bone cyst or benign tumor, tarsal or metatarsal, except talus or calcaneus;

28106　　　with iliac or other autograft (includes obtaining graft)

28107　　　with allograft

28108　Excision or curettage of bone cyst or benign tumor, phalanges of foot

　　　　(For ostectomy, partial (eg, hallux valgus, Silver type procedure), use 28290)

28110　Ostectomy, partial excision, fifth metatarsal head (bunionette) (separate procedure)

28111　Ostectomy, complete excision; first metatarsal head

28112　　　other metatarsal head (second, third or fourth)

28113　　　fifth metatarsal head

28114　　　all metatarsal heads, with partial proximal phalangectomy, excluding first metatarsal (eg, Clayton type procedure)

28116　Ostectomy, excision of tarsal coalition

28118　Ostectomy, calcaneus;

28119　　　for spur, with or without plantar fascial release

28120　Partial excision (craterization, saucerization, sequestrectomy, or diaphysectomy) bone (eg, osteomyelitis or bossing); talus or calcaneus

28122　　　tarsal or metatarsal bone, except talus or calcaneus

　　　　(For partial excision of talus or calcaneus, use 28120)

　　　　(For cheilectomy for hallux rigidus, use 28289)

28124　　　phalanx of toe

28126　Resection, partial or complete, phalangeal base, each toe

28130　Talectomy (astragalectomy)

　　　　(For calcanectomy, use 28118)

28140　Metatarsectomy

28150　Phalangectomy, toe, each toe

28153　Resection, condyle(s), distal end of phalanx, each toe

28160　Hemiphalangectomy or interphalangeal joint excision, toe, proximal end of phalanx, each

28171　Radical resection of tumor, bone; tarsal (except talus or calcaneus)

28173　　　metatarsal

28175　　　phalanx of toe

　　　　(For talus or calcaneus, use 27647)

Introduction or Removal

28190　Removal of foreign body, foot; subcutaneous

28192　　　deep

28193　　　complicated

Repair, Revision, and/or Reconstruction

28200 Repair, tendon, flexor, foot; primary or secondary, without free graft, each tendon

28202 secondary with free graft, each tendon (includes obtaining graft)

28208 Repair, tendon, extensor, foot; primary or secondary, each tendon

28210 secondary with free graft, each tendon (includes obtaining graft)

28220 Tenolysis, flexor, foot; single tendon

28222 multiple tendons

28225 Tenolysis, extensor, foot; single tendon

28226 multiple tendons

28230 Tenotomy, open, tendon flexor; foot, single or multiple tendon(s) (separate procedure)

28232 toe, single tendon (separate procedure)

28234 Tenotomy, open, extensor, foot or toe, each tendon

(For tendon transfer to midfoot or hindfoot, see 27690, 27691)

28238 Reconstruction (advancement), posterior tibial tendon with excision of accessory tarsal navicular bone (eg, Kidner type procedure)

(For subcutaneous tenotomy, see 28010, 28011)

(For transfer or transplant of tendon with muscle redirection or rerouting, see 27690-27692)

(For extensor hallucis longus transfer with great toe IP fusion (Jones procedure), use 28760)

28240 Tenotomy, lengthening, or release, abductor hallucis muscle

28250 Division of plantar fascia and muscle (eg, Steindler stripping) (separate procedure)

28260 Capsulotomy, midfoot; medial release only (separate procedure)

28261 with tendon lengthening

28262 extensive, including posterior talotibial capsulotomy and tendon(s) lengthening (eg, resistant clubfoot deformity)

28264 Capsulotomy, midtarsal (eg, Heyman type procedure)

28270 Capsulotomy; metatarsophalangeal joint, with or without tenorrhaphy, each joint (separate procedure)

28272 interphalangeal joint, each joint (separate procedure)

28280 Syndactylization, toes (eg, webbing or Kelikian type procedure)

28285 Correction, hammertoe (eg, interphalangeal fusion, partial or total phalangectomy)

28286 Correction, cock-up fifth toe, with plastic skin closure (eg, Ruiz-Mora type procedure)

28288 Ostectomy, partial, exostectomy or condylectomy, metatarsal head, each metatarsal head

28289 Hallux rigidus correction with cheilectomy, debridement and capsular release of the first metatarsophalangeal joint

28290 Correction, hallux valgus (bunion), with or without sesamoidectomy; simple exostectomy (eg, Silver type procedure)

28292 Keller, McBride, or Mayo type procedure

28293 resection of joint with implant

28294 with tendon transplants (eg, Joplin type procedure)

28296 with metatarsal osteotomy (eg, Mitchell, Chevron, or concentric type procedures)

28297 Lapidus-type procedure

28298 by phalanx osteotomy

28299 by double osteotomy

28300 Osteotomy; calcaneus (eg, Dwyer or Chambers type procedure), with or without internal fixation

28302 talus

28304 Osteotomy, tarsal bones, other than calcaneus or talus;

28305 with autograft (includes obtaining graft) (eg, Fowler type)

28306 Osteotomy, with or without lengthening, shortening or angular correction, metatarsal; first metatarsal

28307 first metatarsal with autograft (other than first toe)

28308 other than first metatarsal, each

28309 multiple (eg, Swanson type cavus foot procedure)

28310 Osteotomy, shortening, angular or rotational correction; proximal phalanx, first toe (separate procedure)

28312 other phalanges, any toe

28313 Reconstruction, angular deformity of toe, soft tissue procedures only (eg, overlapping second toe, fifth toe, curly toes)

28315 Sesamoidectomy, first toe (separate procedure)

28320 Repair, nonunion or malunion; tarsal bones

28322 metatarsal, with or without bone graft (includes obtaining graft)

28340 Reconstruction, toe, macrodactyly; soft tissue resection

28341 requiring bone resection

28344 Reconstruction, toe(s); polydactyly

28345 syndactyly, with or without skin graft(s), each web

28360 Reconstruction, cleft foot

Fracture and/or Dislocation

28400 Closed treatment of calcaneal fracture; without manipulation

28405 with manipulation

28406 Percutaneous skeletal fixation of calcaneal fracture, with manipulation

28415 Open treatment of calcaneal fracture, with or without internal or external fixation;

28420 with primary iliac or other autogenous bone graft (includes obtaining graft)

28430 Closed treatment of talus fracture; without manipulation

28435 with manipulation

28436 Percutaneous skeletal fixation of talus fracture, with manipulation

28445 Open treatment of talus fracture, with or without internal or external fixation

28450 Treatment of tarsal bone fracture (except talus and calcaneus); without manipulation, each

28455 with manipulation, each

28456 Percutaneous skeletal fixation of tarsal bone fracture (except talus and calcaneus), with manipulation, each

28465 Open treatment of tarsal bone fracture (except talus and calcaneus), with or without internal or external fixation, each

28470 Closed treatment of metatarsal fracture; without manipulation, each

28475 with manipulation, each

28476 Percutaneous skeletal fixation of metatarsal fracture, with manipulation, each

28485 Open treatment of metatarsal fracture, with or without internal or external fixation, each

28490 Closed treatment of fracture great toe, phalanx or phalanges; without manipulation

28495 with manipulation

28496 Percutaneous skeletal fixation of fracture great toe, phalanx or phalanges, with manipulation

28505 Open treatment of fracture great toe, phalanx or phalanges, with or without internal or external fixation

28510 Closed treatment of fracture, phalanx or phalanges, other than great toe; without manipulation, each

28515 with manipulation, each

28525 Open treatment of fracture, phalanx or phalanges, other than great toe, with or without internal or external fixation, each

28530 Closed treatment of sesamoid fracture

28531 Open treatment of sesamoid fracture, with or without internal fixation

28540 Closed treatment of tarsal bone dislocation, other than talotarsal; without anesthesia

28545 requiring anesthesia

28546 Percutaneous skeletal fixation of tarsal bone dislocation, other than talotarsal, with manipulation

28555 Open treatment of tarsal bone dislocation, with or without internal or external fixation

28570 Closed treatment of talotarsal joint dislocation; without anesthesia

28575 requiring anesthesia

28576 Percutaneous skeletal fixation of talotarsal joint dislocation, with manipulation

28585 Open treatment of talotarsal joint dislocation, with or without internal or external fixation

28600 Closed treatment of tarsometatarsal joint dislocation; without anesthesia

28605 requiring anesthesia

28606 Percutaneous skeletal fixation of tarsometatarsal joint dislocation, with manipulation

28615 Open treatment of tarsometatarsal joint dislocation, with or without internal or external fixation

28630 Closed treatment of metatarsophalangeal joint dislocation; without anesthesia

28635 requiring anesthesia

28636 Percutaneous skeletal fixation of metatarsophalangeal joint dislocation, with manipulation

28645 Open treatment of metatarsophalangeal joint dislocation, with or without internal or external fixation

28660 Closed treatment of interphalangeal joint dislocation; without anesthesia

28665 requiring anesthesia

28666 Percutaneous skeletal fixation of interphalangeal joint dislocation, with manipulation

28675 Open treatment of interphalangeal joint dislocation, with or without internal or external fixation

Arthrodesis

28705 Arthrodesis; pantalar

28715 triple

28725 subtalar

28730 Arthrodesis, midtarsal or tarsometatarsal, multiple or transverse;

28735 with osteotomy (eg, flatfoot correction)

28737 Arthrodesis, with tendon lengthening and advancement, midtarsal, tarsal navicular-cuneiform (eg, Miller type procedure)

28740 Arthrodesis, midtarsal or tarsometatarsal, single joint

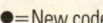

Surgery: Musculoskeletal System

28750 Arthrodesis, great toe; metatarsophalangeal joint

28755 interphalangeal joint

28760 Arthrodesis, with extensor hallucis longus transfer to first metatarsal neck, great toe, interphalangeal joint (eg, Jones type procedure)

(For hammertoe operation or interphalangeal fusion, use 28285)

Amputation

28800 Amputation, foot; midtarsal (eg, Chopart type procedure)

28805 transmetatarsal

28810 Amputation, metatarsal, with toe, single

28820 Amputation, toe; metatarsophalangeal joint

28825 interphalangeal joint

(For amputation of tuft of distal phalanx, use 11752)

Other Procedures

28890 Extracorporeal shock wave, high energy, performed by a physician, requiring anesthesia other than local, including ultrasound guidance, involving the plantar fascia

(For extracorporeal shock wave therapy involving musculoskeletal system not otherwise specified, see Category III codes 0019T, 0101T, 0102T)

28899 Unlisted procedure, foot or toes

Application of Casts and Strapping

The listed procedures apply when the cast application or strapping is a replacement procedure used during or after the period of follow-up care, or when the cast application or strapping is an initial service performed without a restorative treatment or procedure(s) to stabilize or protect a fracture, injury, or dislocation and/or to afford comfort to a patient. Restorative treatment or procedure(s) rendered by another physician following the application of the initial cast/splint/strap may be reported with a treatment of fracture and/or dislocation code.

A physician who applies the initial cast, strap or splint and also assumes all of the subsequent fracture, dislocation, or injury care cannot use the application of casts and strapping codes as an initial service, since the first cast/splint or strap application is included in the treatment of fracture and/or dislocation codes. (See notes under Musculoskeletal System, page 63.) A temporary cast/splint/strap is not considered to be part of the preoperative care, and the use of the modifier 56 is not applicable. Additional evaluation and management services are reportable only if significant identifiable further services are provided at the time of the cast application or strapping.

If cast application or strapping is provided as an initial service (eg, casting of a sprained ankle or knee) in which no other procedure or treatment (eg, surgical repair,

reduction of a fracture or joint dislocation) is performed or is expected to be performed by a physician rendering the initial care only, use the casting, strapping and/or supply code (99070) in addition to an evaluation and management code as appropriate.

Listed procedures include removal of cast or strapping.

(For orthotics management and training, see 97760-97762)

Body and Upper Extremity

Casts

29000 Application of halo type body cast (see 20661-20663 for insertion)

29010 Application of Risser jacket, localizer, body; only

29015 including head

29020 Application of turnbuckle jacket, body; only

29025 including head

29035 Application of body cast, shoulder to hips;

29040 including head, Minerva type

29044 including one thigh

29046 including both thighs

29049 Application, cast; figure-of-eight

29055 shoulder spica

29058 plaster Velpeau

29065 shoulder to hand (long arm)

29075 elbow to finger (short arm)

29085 hand and lower forearm (gauntlet)

29086 finger (eg, contracture)

Splints

29105 Application of long arm splint (shoulder to hand)

29125 Application of short arm splint (forearm to hand); static

29126 dynamic

29130 Application of finger splint; static

29131 dynamic

Strapping—Any Age

29200 Strapping; thorax

29220 low back

29240 shoulder (eg, Velpeau)

29260 elbow or wrist

29280 hand or finger

Lower Extremity

Casts

29305 Application of hip spica cast; one leg

29325 one and one-half spica or both legs

(For hip spica (body) cast, including thighs only, use 29046)

29345 Application of long leg cast (thigh to toes);

29355 walker or ambulatory type

29358 Application of long leg cast brace

29365 Application of cylinder cast (thigh to ankle)

29405 Application of short leg cast (below knee to toes);

29425 walking or ambulatory type

29435 Application of patellar tendon bearing (PTB) cast

29440 Adding walker to previously applied cast

29445 Application of rigid total contact leg cast

29450 Application of clubfoot cast with molding or manipulation, long or short leg

(To report bilateral procedure, use 29450 with modifier 50)

Splints

29505 Application of long leg splint (thigh to ankle or toes)

29515 Application of short leg splint (calf to foot)

Strapping—Any Age

29520 Strapping; hip

29530 knee

29540 ankle and/or foot

29550 toes

29580 Unna boot

29590 Denis-Browne splint strapping

Removal or Repair

Codes for cast removals should be employed only for casts applied by another physician.

29700 Removal or bivalving; gauntlet, boot or body cast

29705 full arm or full leg cast

29710 shoulder or hip spica, Minerva, or Risser jacket, etc.

29715 turnbuckle jacket

29720 Repair of spica, body cast or jacket

29730 Windowing of cast

29740 Wedging of cast (except clubfoot casts)

29750 Wedging of clubfoot cast

(To report bilateral procedure, use 29750 with modifier 50)

Other Procedures

29799 Unlisted procedure, casting or strapping

Endoscopy/Arthroscopy

Surgical endoscopy/arthroscopy always includes a diagnostic endoscopy/arthroscopy.

When arthroscopy is performed in conjunction with arthrotomy, add modifier 51.

29800 Arthroscopy, temporomandibular joint, diagnostic, with or without synovial biopsy (separate procedure)

29804 Arthroscopy, temporomandibular joint, surgical

(For open procedure, use 21010)

29805 Arthroscopy, shoulder, diagnostic, with or without synovial biopsy (separate procedure)

(For open procedure, see 23065-23066, 23100-23101)

29806 Arthroscopy, shoulder, surgical; capsulorrhaphy

(For open procedure, see 23450-23466)

(To report thermal capsulorrhaphy, use 29999)

29807 repair of SLAP lesion

29819 with removal of loose body or foreign body

(For open procedure, see 23040-23044, 23107)

29820 synovectomy, partial

(For open procedure, see 23105)

29821 synovectomy, complete

(For open procedure, see 23105)

29822 debridement, limited

(For open procedure, see specific open shoulder procedure performed)

29823 debridement, extensive

(For open procedure, see specific open shoulder procedure performed)

29824 distal claviculectomy including distal articular surface (Mumford procedure)

(For open procedure, use 23120)

29825 with lysis and resection of adhesions, with or without manipulation

(For open procedure, see specific open shoulder procedure performed)

Surgery: Musculoskeletal System

29826 decompression of subacromial space with partial acromioplasty, with or without coracoacromial release

(For open procedure, use 23130 or 23415)

29827 with rotator cuff repair

(For open or mini-open rotator cuff repair, use 23412)

(When arthroscopic subacromial decompression is performed at the same setting, use 29826 and append modifier 51)

(When arthroscopic distal clavicle resection is performed at the same setting, use 29824 and append modifier 51)

29830 Arthroscopy, elbow, diagnostic, with or without synovial biopsy (separate procedure)

29834 Arthroscopy, elbow, surgical; with removal of loose body or foreign body

29835 synovectomy, partial

29836 synovectomy, complete

29837 debridement, limited

29838 debridement, extensive

29840 Arthroscopy, wrist, diagnostic, with or without synovial biopsy (separate procedure)

29843 Arthroscopy, wrist, surgical; for infection, lavage and drainage

29844 synovectomy, partial

29845 synovectomy, complete

29846 excision and/or repair of triangular fibrocartilage and/or joint debridement

29847 internal fixation for fracture or instability

29848 Endoscopy, wrist, surgical, with release of transverse carpal ligament

(For open procedure, use 64721)

29850 Arthroscopically aided treatment of intercondylar spine(s) and/or tuberosity fracture(s) of the knee, with or without manipulation; without internal or external fixation (includes arthroscopy)

29851 with internal or external fixation (includes arthroscopy)

(For bone graft, use 20900, 20902)

29855 Arthroscopically aided treatment of tibial fracture, proximal (plateau); unicondylar, with or without internal or external fixation (includes arthroscopy)

29856 bicondylar, with or without internal or external fixation (includes arthroscopy)

(For bone graft, use 20900, 20902)

29860 Arthroscopy, hip, diagnostic with or without synovial biopsy (separate procedure)

29861 Arthroscopy, hip, surgical; with removal of loose body or foreign body

29862 with debridement/shaving of articular cartilage (chondroplasty), abrasion arthroplasty, and/or resection of labrum

29863 with synovectomy

29866 Arthroscopy, knee, surgical; osteochondral autograft(s) (eg, mosaicplasty) (includes harvesting of the autograft)

(Do not report 29866 in conjunction with 29870, 29871, 29875, 29884 when performed at the same session and/or 29874, 29877, 29879, 29885-29887 when performed in the same compartment)

29867 osteochondral allograft (eg, mosaicplasty)

(Do not report 29867 in conjunction with 27570, 29870, 29871, 29875, 29884 when performed at the same session and/or 29874, 29877, 29879, 29885-29887 when performed in the same compartment)

(Do not report 29867 in conjunction with 27415)

29868 meniscal transplantation (includes arthrotomy for meniscal insertion), medial or lateral

(Do not report 29868 in conjunction with 29870, 29871, 29875, 29880, 29883, 29884 when performed at the same session or 29874, 29877, 29881, 29882 when performed in the same compartment)

29870 Arthroscopy, knee, diagnostic, with or without synovial biopsy (separate procedure)

(For open autologous chondrocyte implantation of the knee, use 27412)

29871 Arthroscopy, knee, surgical; for infection, lavage and drainage

(For implantation of osteochondral graft for treatment of articular surface defect, see 27412, 27415, 29866, 29867)

29873 with lateral release

(For open lateral release, use 27425)

29874 for removal of loose body or foreign body (eg, osteochondritis dissecans fragmentation, chondral fragmentation)

29875 synovectomy, limited (eg, plica or shelf resection) (separate procedure)

29876 synovectomy, major, two or more compartments (eg, medial or lateral)

29877 debridement/shaving of articular cartilage (chondroplasty)

29879 abrasion arthroplasty (includes chondroplasty where necessary) or multiple drilling or microfracture

29880 with meniscectomy (medial AND lateral, including any meniscal shaving)

29881 with meniscectomy (medial OR lateral, including any meniscal shaving)

29882 with meniscus repair (medial OR lateral)

29883 with meniscus repair (medial AND lateral)

(For meniscal transplantation, medial or lateral, knee, use 29868)

29884 with lysis of adhesions, with or without manipulation (separate procedure)

29885 drilling for osteochondritis dissecans with bone grafting, with or without internal fixation (including debridement of base of lesion)

29886 drilling for intact osteochondritis dissecans lesion

29887 drilling for intact osteochondritis dissecans lesion with internal fixation

29888 Arthroscopically aided anterior cruciate ligament repair/augmentation or reconstruction

29889 Arthroscopically aided posterior cruciate ligament repair/augmentation or reconstruction

(Procedures 29888 and 29889 should not be used with reconstruction procedures 27427-27429)

29891 Arthroscopy, ankle, surgical, excision of osteochondral defect of talus and/or tibia, including drilling of the defect

29892 Arthroscopically aided repair of large osteochondritis dissecans lesion, talar dome fracture, or tibial plafond fracture, with or without internal fixation (includes arthroscopy)

29893 Endoscopic plantar fasciotomy

29894 Arthroscopy, ankle (tibiotalar and fibulotalar joints), surgical; with removal of loose body or foreign body

29895 synovectomy, partial

29897 debridement, limited

29898 debridement, extensive

29899 with ankle arthrodesis

(For open ankle arthrodesis, use 27870)

29900 Arthroscopy, metacarpophalangeal joint, diagnostic, includes synovial biopsy

(Do not report 29900 with 29901, 29902)

29901 Arthroscopy, metacarpophalangeal joint, surgical; with debridement

29902 with reduction of displaced ulnar collateral ligament (eg, Stenar lesion)

29999 Unlisted procedure, arthroscopy

Surgery: Musculoskeletal System

Notes

⊙=Moderate sedation ✚=Add-on code ✗=FDA approval pending

Respiratory System

Nose

Incision

30000 Drainage abscess or hematoma, nasal, internal approach

(For external approach, see 10060, 10140)

30020 Drainage abscess or hematoma, nasal septum

(For lateral rhinotomy, see specific application (eg, 30118, 30320))

Excision

30100 Biopsy, intranasal

(For biopsy skin of nose, see 11100, 11101)

30110 Excision, nasal polyp(s), simple

(30110 would normally be completed in an office setting)

(To report bilateral procedure, use 30110 with modifier 50)

30115 Excision, nasal polyp(s), extensive

(30115 would normally require the facilities available in a hospital setting)

(To report bilateral procedure, use 30115 with modifier 50)

30117 Excision or destruction (eg, laser), intranasal lesion; internal approach

30118 external approach (lateral rhinotomy)

30120 Excision or surgical planing of skin of nose for rhinophyma

30124 Excision dermoid cyst, nose; simple, skin, subcutaneous

30125 complex, under bone or cartilage

30130 Excision inferior turbinate, partial or complete, any method

(For excision of superior or middle turbinate, use 30999)

30140 Submucous resection inferior turbinate, partial or complete, any method

(Do not report 30130 or 30140 in conjunction with 30801, 30802, 30930)

(For submucous resection of superior or middle turbinate, use 30999)

(For endoscopic resection of concha bullosa of middle turbinate, use 31240)

(For submucous resection of nasal septum, use 30520)

(For reduction of turbinates, use 30140 with modifier 52)

30150 Rhinectomy; partial

30160 total

(For closure and/or reconstruction, primary or delayed, see **Integumentary System,** 13150-13160, 14060-14300, 15120, 15121, 15260, 15261, 15760, 20900-20912)

Introduction

30200 Injection into turbinate(s), therapeutic

30210 Displacement therapy (Proetz type)

30220 Insertion, nasal septal prosthesis (button)

Removal of Foreign Body

30300 Removal foreign body, intranasal; office type procedure

30310 requiring general anesthesia

30320 by lateral rhinotomy

Repair

(For obtaining tissues for graft, see 20900-20926, 21210)

30400 Rhinoplasty, primary; lateral and alar cartilages and/or elevation of nasal tip

(For columellar reconstruction, see 13150 et seq)

30410 complete, external parts including bony pyramid, lateral and alar cartilages, and/or elevation of nasal tip

30420 including major septal repair

30430 Rhinoplasty, secondary; minor revision (small amount of nasal tip work)

30435 intermediate revision (bony work with osteotomies)

30450 major revision (nasal tip work and osteotomies)

30460 Rhinoplasty for nasal deformity secondary to congenital cleft lip and/or palate, including columellar lengthening; tip only

30462 tip, septum, osteotomies

30465 Repair of nasal vestibular stenosis (eg, spreader grafting, lateral nasal wall reconstruction)

(30465 excludes obtaining graft. For graft procedure, see 20900-20926, 21210)

(30465 is used to report a bilateral procedure. For unilateral procedure, use modifier 52)

30520 Septoplasty or submucous resection, with or without cartilage scoring, contouring or replacement with graft

(For submucous resection of turbinates, use 30140)

Surgery: Respiratory System

Surgery: Respiratory System

30540 Repair choanal atresia; intranasal

30545 transpalatine

(Do not report modifier 63 in conjunction with 30540, 30545)

30560 Lysis intranasal synechia

30580 Repair fistula; oromaxillary (combine with 31030 if antrotomy is included)

30600 oronasal

30620 Septal or other intranasal dermatoplasty (does not include obtaining graft)

30630 Repair nasal septal perforations

Destruction

30801 Cautery and/or ablation, mucosa of inferior turbinates, unilateral or bilateral, any method; superficial

(For cautery and ablation of superior or middle turbinates, use 30999)

30802 intramural

(Do not report 30801, 30802, 30930 in conjunction with 30130 or 30140)

(For cautery performed for control of nasal hemorrhage, see 30901-30906)

Other Procedures

30901 Control nasal hemorrhage, anterior, simple (limited cautery and/or packing) any method

(To report bilateral procedure, use 30901 with modifier 50)

30903 Control nasal hemorrhage, anterior, complex (extensive cautery and/or packing) any method

(To report bilateral procedure, use 30903 with modifier 50)

30905 Control nasal hemorrhage, posterior, with posterior nasal packs and/or cautery, any method; initial

30906 subsequent

30915 Ligation arteries; ethmoidal

30920 internal maxillary artery, transantral

(For ligation external carotid artery, use 37600)

30930 Fracture nasal inferior turbinate(s), therapeutic

(Do not report 30801, 30802, 30930 in conjunction with 30130 or 30140)

(For fracture of superior or middle turbinate(s), use 30999)

30999 Unlisted procedure, nose

Accessory Sinuses

Incision

31000 Lavage by cannulation; maxillary sinus (antrum puncture or natural ostium)

(To report bilateral procedure, use 31000 with modifier 50)

31002 sphenoid sinus

31020 Sinusotomy, maxillary (antrotomy); intranasal

(To report bilateral procedure, use 31020 with modifier 50)

31030 radical (Caldwell-Luc) without removal of antrochoanal polyps

(To report bilateral procedure, use 31030 with modifier 50)

31032 radical (Caldwell-Luc) with removal of antrochoanal polyps

(To report bilateral procedure, use 31032 with modifier 50)

31040 Pterygomaxillary fossa surgery, any approach

(For transantral ligation of internal maxillary artery, use 30920)

31050 Sinusotomy, sphenoid, with or without biopsy;

31051 with mucosal stripping or removal of polyp(s)

31070 Sinusotomy frontal; external, simple (trephine operation)

(For frontal intranasal sinusotomy, use 31276)

31075 transorbital, unilateral (for mucocele or osteoma, Lynch type)

31080 obliterative without osteoplastic flap, brow incision (includes ablation)

31081 obliterative, without osteoplastic flap, coronal incision (includes ablation)

31084 obliterative, with osteoplastic flap, brow incision

31085 obliterative, with osteoplastic flap, coronal incision

31086 nonobliterative, with osteoplastic flap, brow incision

31087 nonobliterative, with osteoplastic flap, coronal incision

31090 Sinusotomy, unilateral, three or more paranasal sinuses (frontal, maxillary, ethmoid, sphenoid)

Excision

31200 Ethmoidectomy; intranasal, anterior

31201 intranasal, total

31205 extranasal, total

31225　Maxillectomy; without orbital exenteration

31230　　with orbital exenteration (en bloc)

　　(For orbital exenteration only, see 65110 et seq)

　　(For skin grafts, see 15120 et seq)

Endoscopy

A surgical sinus endoscopy includes a sinusotomy (when appropriate) and diagnostic endoscopy.

Codes 31231-31294 are used to report unilateral procedures unless otherwise specified.

The codes 31231-31235 for diagnostic evaluation refer to employing a nasal/sinus endoscope to inspect the interior of the nasal cavity and the middle and superior meatus, the turbinates, and the spheno-ethmoid recess. Any time a diagnostic evaluation is performed all these areas would be inspected and a separate code is not reported for each area.

31231　Nasal endoscopy, diagnostic, unilateral or bilateral (separate procedure)

31233　Nasal/sinus endoscopy, diagnostic with maxillary sinusoscopy (via inferior meatus or canine fossa puncture)

31235　Nasal/sinus endoscopy, diagnostic with sphenoid sinusoscopy (via puncture of sphenoidal face or cannulation of ostium)

31237　Nasal/sinus endoscopy, surgical; with biopsy, polypectomy or debridement (separate procedure)

31238　　with control of nasal hemorrhage

31239　　with dacryocystorhinostomy

31240　　with concha bullosa resection

　　(For endoscopic osteomeatal complex (OMC) resection with antrostomy and/or anterior ethmoidectomy, with or without removal of polyp(s), use 31254 and 31256)

　　(For endoscopic osteomeatal complex (OMC) resection with antrostomy, removal of antral mucosal disease, and/or anterior ethmoidectomy, with or without removal of polyp(s), use 31254 and 31267)

　　(For endoscopic frontal sinus exploration, osteomeatal complex (OMC) resection and/or anterior ethmoidectomy, with or without removal of polyp(s), use 31254 and 31276)

　　(For endoscopic frontal sinus exploration, osteomeatal complex (OMC) resection, antrostomy, and/or anterior ethmoidectomy, with or without removal of polyp(s), use 31254, 31256, and 31276)

　　(For endoscopic nasal diagnostic endoscopy, see 31231-31235)

　　(For endoscopic osteomeatal complex (OMC) resection, frontal sinus exploration, antrostomy, removal of antral mucosal disease, and/or anterior ethmoidectomy, with or without removal of polyp(s), use 31254, 31267, and 31276)

31254　Nasal/sinus endoscopy, surgical; with ethmoidectomy, partial (anterior)

31255　　with ethmoidectomy, total (anterior and posterior)

31256　Nasal/sinus endoscopy, surgical, with maxillary antrostomy;

　　(For endoscopic anterior and posterior ethmoidectomy (APE) and antrostomy, with or without removal of polyp(s), use 31255 and 31256)

　　(For endoscopic anterior and posterior ethmoidectomy (APE), antrostomy and removal of antral mucosal disease, with or without removal of polyp(s), use 31255 and 31267)

　　(For endoscopic anterior and posterior ethmoidectomy (APE), and frontal sinus exploration, with or without removal of polyp(s), use 31255 and 31276)

31267　　with removal of tissue from maxillary sinus

　　(For endoscopic anterior and posterior ethmoidectomy (APE), and frontal sinus exploration and antrostomy, with or without removal of polyp(s), use 31255, 31256, and 31276)

　　(For endoscopic anterior and posterior ethmoidectomy (APE), frontal sinus exploration, antrostomy, and removal of antral mucosal disease, with or without removal of polyp(s), use 31255, 31267, and 31276)

31276　Nasal/sinus endoscopy, surgical with frontal sinus exploration, with or without removal of tissue from frontal sinus

　　(For endoscopic anterior and posterior ethmoidectomy and sphenoidotomy (APS), with or without removal of polyp(s), use 31255, 31287 or 31288)

　　(For endoscopic anterior and posterior ethmoidectomy and sphenoidotomy (APS), and antrostomy, with or without removal of polyp(s), use 31255, 31256, and 31287 or 31288)

　　(For endoscopic anterior and posterior ethmoidectomy and sphenoidotomy (APS), antrostomy and removal of antral mucosal disease, with or without removal of polyp(s), use 31255, 31267, and 31287 or 31288)

　　(For endoscopic anterior and posterior ethmoidectomy and sphenoidotomy (APS), and frontal sinus exploration with or without removal of polyp(s), use 31255, 31287 or 31288, and 31276)

　　(For endoscopic anterior and posterior ethmoidectomy and sphenoidotomy (APS), with or without removal of polyp(s), with frontal sinus exploration and antrostomy, use 31255, 31256, 31287 or 31288, and 31276)

　　(For unilateral endoscopy of two or more sinuses, see 31231-31235)

　　(For endoscopic anterior and posterior ethmoidectomy and sphenoidotomy (APS), frontal sinus exploration, antrostomy and removal of antral mucosal disease, with or without removal of polyp(s), see 31255, 31267, 31287 or 31288 and 31276)

Surgery: Respiratory System

31287 Nasal/sinus endoscopy, surgical, with sphenoidotomy;

31288 with removal of tissue from the sphenoid sinus

31290 Nasal/sinus endoscopy, surgical, with repair of cerebrospinal fluid leak; ethmoid region

31291 sphenoid region

31292 Nasal/sinus endoscopy, surgical; with medial or inferior orbital wall decompression

31293 with medial orbital wall and inferior orbital wall decompression

31294 with optic nerve decompression

Other Procedures

(For hypophysectomy, transantral or transeptal approach, use 61548)

(For transcranial hypophysectomy, use 61546)

31299 Unlisted procedure, accessory sinuses

Larynx

Excision

31300 Laryngotomy (thyrotomy, laryngofissure); with removal of tumor or laryngocele, cordectomy

31320 diagnostic

31360 Laryngectomy; total, without radical neck dissection

31365 total, with radical neck dissection

31367 subtotal supraglottic, without radical neck dissection

31368 subtotal supraglottic, with radical neck dissection

31370 Partial laryngectomy (hemilaryngectomy); horizontal

31375 laterovertical

31380 anterovertical

31382 antero-latero-vertical

31390 Pharyngolaryngectomy, with radical neck dissection; without reconstruction

31395 with reconstruction

31400 Arytenoidectomy or arytenoidopexy, external approach

(For endoscopic arytenoidectomy, use 31560)

31420 Epiglottidectomy

Introduction

⊘ **31500** Intubation, endotracheal, emergency procedure

▶(For injection procedure for segmental bronchography, use 31656)◀

31502 Tracheotomy tube change prior to establishment of fistula tract

Endoscopy

For endoscopic procedures, code appropriate endoscopy of each anatomic site examined. If using operating microscope, telescope, or both, use the applicable code only once per operative session.

31505 Laryngoscopy, indirect; diagnostic (separate procedure)

31510 with biopsy

31511 with removal of foreign body

31512 with removal of lesion

31513 with vocal cord injection

31515 Laryngoscopy direct, with or without tracheoscopy; for aspiration

31520 diagnostic, newborn

(Do not report modifier 63 in conjunction with 31520)

31525 diagnostic, except newborn

31526 diagnostic, with operating microscope or telescope

(Do not report code 69990 in addition to code 31526)

31527 with insertion of obturator

31528 with dilation, initial

31529 with dilation, subsequent

31530 Laryngoscopy, direct, operative, with foreign body removal;

31531 with operating microscope or telescope

(Do not report code 69990 in addition to code 31531)

31535 Laryngoscopy, direct, operative, with biopsy;

31536 with operating microscope or telescope

(Do not report code 69990 in addition to code 31536)

31540 Laryngoscopy, direct, operative, with excision of tumor and/or stripping of vocal cords or epiglottis;

31541 with operating microscope or telescope

(Do not report code 69990 in addition to code 31541)

31545 Laryngoscopy, direct, operative, with operating microscope or telescope, with submucosal removal of non-neoplastic lesion(s) of vocal cord; reconstruction with local tissue flap(s)

31546 reconstruction with graft(s) (includes obtaining autograft)

(Do not report 31546 in addition to 20926 for graft harvest)

(For reconstruction of vocal cord with allograft, use 31599)

(Do not report 31545 or 31546 in conjunction with 31540, 31541, 69990)

31560 Laryngoscopy, direct, operative, with arytenoidectomy;

31561 with operating microscope or telescope

 (Do not report code 69990 in addition to code 31561)

31570 Laryngoscopy, direct, with injection into vocal cord(s), therapeutic;

31571 with operating microscope or telescope

 (Do not report code 69990 in addition to code 31571)

31575 Laryngoscopy, flexible fiberoptic; diagnostic

31576 with biopsy

31577 with removal of foreign body

31578 with removal of lesion

 (To report flexible fiberoptic endoscopic evaluation of swallowing, see 92612-92613)

 (To report flexible fiberoptic endoscopic evaluation with sensory testing, see 92614-92615)

 (To report flexible fiberoptic endoscopic evaluation of swallowing with sensory testing, see 92616-92617)

 (For flexible fiberoptic laryngoscopy as part of flexible fiberoptic endoscopic evaluation of swallowing and/or laryngeal sensory testing by cine or video recording, see 92612-92617)

31579 Laryngoscopy, flexible or rigid fiberoptic, with stroboscopy

Repair

31580 Laryngoplasty; for laryngeal web, two stage, with keel insertion and removal

31582 for laryngeal stenosis, with graft or core mold, including tracheotomy

31584 with open reduction of fracture

 (31585 and 31586 have been deleted. To report, use the appropriate Evaluation and Management codes)

31587 Laryngoplasty, cricoid split

31588 Laryngoplasty, not otherwise specified (eg, for burns, reconstruction after partial laryngectomy)

31590 Laryngeal reinnervation by neuromuscular pedicle

Destruction

31595 Section recurrent laryngeal nerve, therapeutic (separate procedure), unilateral

Other Procedures

31599 Unlisted procedure, larynx

Trachea and Bronchi

Incision

31600 Tracheostomy, planned (separate procedure);

31601 younger than two years

31603 Tracheostomy, emergency procedure; transtracheal

31605 cricothyroid membrane

31610 Tracheostomy, fenestration procedure with skin flaps

 (For endotracheal intubation, use 31500)

 (For tracheal aspiration under direct vision, use 31515)

31611 Construction of tracheoesophageal fistula and subsequent insertion of an alaryngeal speech prosthesis (eg, voice button, Blom-Singer prosthesis)

31612 Tracheal puncture, percutaneous with transtracheal aspiration and/or injection

31613 Tracheostoma revision; simple, without flap rotation

31614 complex, with flap rotation

Endoscopy

For endoscopy procedures, code appropriate endoscopy of each anatomic site examined. Surgical bronchoscopy always includes diagnostic bronchoscopy when performed by the same physician. Codes 31622-31646 include fluoroscopic guidance, when performed.

 (For tracheoscopy, see laryngoscopy codes 31515-31578)

⊙ **31615** Tracheobronchoscopy through established tracheostomy incision

⊙+ **31620** Endobronchial ultrasound (EBUS) during bronchoscopic diagnostic or therapeutic intervention(s) (List separately in addition to code for primary procedure(s))

 (Use 31620 in conjunction with 31622-31646)

⊙ **31622** Bronchoscopy, rigid or flexible, with or without fluoroscopic guidance; diagnostic, with or without cell washing (separate procedure)

⊙ **31623** with brushing or protected brushings

⊙ **31624** with bronchial alveolar lavage

⊙ **31625** with bronchial or endobronchial biopsy(s), single or multiple sites

⊙ **31628** with transbronchial lung biopsy(s), single lobe

 (31628 should be reported only once regardless of how many transbronchial lung biopsies are performed in a lobe)

 (To report transbronchial lung biopsies performed on additional lobe, use 31632)

Surgery: Respiratory System

⊙ **31629** with transbronchial needle aspiration biopsy(s), trachea, main stem and/or lobar bronchus(i)

(31629 should be reported only once for upper airway biopsies regardless of how many transbronchial needle aspiration biopsies are performed in the upper airway or in a lobe)

(To report transbronchial needle aspiration biopsies performed on additional lobe(s), use 31633)

31630 with tracheal/bronchial dilation or closed reduction of fracture

31631 with placement of tracheal stent(s) (includes tracheal/bronchial dilation as required)

(For placement of bronchial stent, see 31636, 31637)

(For revision of tracheal/bronchial stent, use 31638)

+ 31632 with transbronchial lung biopsy(s), each additional lobe (List separately in addition to code for primary procedure)

(Use 31632 in conjunction with 31628)

(31632 should be reported only once regardless of how many transbronchial lung biopsies are performed in a lobe)

+ 31633 with transbronchial needle aspiration biopsy(s), each additional lobe (List separately in addition to code for primary procedure)

(Use 31633 in conjunction with 31629)

(31633 should be reported only once regardless of how many transbronchial needle aspiration biopsies are performed in the trachea or the additional lobe)

⊙ **31635** with removal of foreign body

31636 with placement of bronchial stent(s) (includes tracheal/bronchial dilation as required), initial bronchus

+ 31637 each additional major bronchus stented (List separately in addition to code for primary procedure)

(Use 31637 in conjunction with 31636)

31638 with revision of tracheal or bronchial stent inserted at previous session (includes tracheal/bronchial dilation as required)

31640 with excision of tumor

31641 Bronchoscopy, (rigid or flexible); with destruction of tumor or relief of stenosis by any method other than excision (eg, laser therapy, cryotherapy)

(For bronchoscopic photodynamic therapy, report 31641 in addition to 96570, 96571 as appropriate)

31643 with placement of catheter(s) for intracavitary radioelement application

(For intracavitary radioelement application, see 77761-77763, 77781-77784)

⊙ **31645** with therapeutic aspiration of tracheobronchial tree, initial (eg, drainage of lung abscess)

⊙ **31646** with therapeutic aspiration of tracheobronchial tree, subsequent

(For catheter aspiration of tracheobronchial tree at bedside, use 31725)

⊙ **31656** with injection of contrast material for segmental bronchography (fiberscope only)

(For radiological supervision and interpretation, see 71040, 71060)

Introduction

(For endotracheal intubation, use 31500)

(For tracheal aspiration under direct vision, see 31515)

▶(31700, 31708, 31710 have been deleted)◀

31715 Transtracheal injection for bronchography

(For radiological supervision and interpretation, see 71040, 71060)

(For prolonged services, see 99354-99360)

31717 Catheterization with bronchial brush biopsy

31720 Catheter aspiration (separate procedure); nasotracheal

⊙ **31725** tracheobronchial with fiberscope, bedside

31730 Transtracheal (percutaneous) introduction of needle wire dilator/stent or indwelling tube for oxygen therapy

▶Excision, Repair◀

31750 Tracheoplasty; cervical

31755 tracheopharyngeal fistulization, each stage

31760 intrathoracic

31766 Carinal reconstruction

31770 Bronchoplasty; graft repair

31775 excision stenosis and anastomosis

(For lobectomy and bronchoplasty, use 32501)

31780 Excision tracheal stenosis and anastomosis; cervical

31781 cervicothoracic

31785 Excision of tracheal tumor or carcinoma; cervical

31786 thoracic

31800 Suture of tracheal wound or injury; cervical

31805 intrathoracic

31820 Surgical closure tracheostomy or fistula; without plastic repair

31825 with plastic repair

(For repair tracheoesophageal fistula, see 43305, 43312)

31830 Revision of tracheostomy scar

Other Procedures

31899 Unlisted procedure, trachea, bronchi

Lungs and Pleura

Incision

⊘ **32000** Thoracentesis, puncture of pleural cavity for aspiration, initial or subsequent

▶(If imaging guidance is performed, see 76942, 77002, 77012)◀

(For total lung lavage, use 32997)

⊘ **32002** Thoracentesis with insertion of tube with or without water seal (eg, for pneumothorax) (separate procedure)

(Do not report 32002 in conjunction with 19260, 19271, 19272, 32503, 32504)

▶(If imaging guidance is performed, see 76942, 77002, 77012)◀

32005 Chemical pleurodesis (eg, for recurrent or persistent pneumothorax)

⊙ **32019** Insertion of indwelling tunneled pleural catheter with cuff

(Do not report 32019 in conjunction with 32000-32005, 32020, 36000, 36410, 62318, 62319, 64450, 64470, 64475)

(If imaging guidance is performed, use 75989)

⊙⊘ **32020** Tube thoracostomy with or without water seal (eg, for abscess, hemothorax, empyema) (separate procedure)

(Do not report 32020 in conjunction with 19260, 19271, 19272, 32503, 32504)

(If imaging guidance is performed, use 75989)

32035 Thoracostomy; with rib resection for empyema

32036 with open flap drainage for empyema

32095 Thoracotomy, limited, for biopsy of lung or pleura

(To report wound exploration due to penetrating trauma without thoractomy, use 20102)

32100 Thoracotomy, major; with exploration and biopsy

(Do not report 32100 in conjunction with 19260, 19271, 19272, 32503, 32504)

32110 with control of traumatic hemorrhage and/or repair of lung tear

32120 for postoperative complications

32124 with open intrapleural pneumonolysis

32140 with cyst(s) removal, with or without a pleural procedure

32141 with excision-plication of bullae, with or without any pleural procedure

(For lung volume reduction, use 32491)

32150 with removal of intrapleural foreign body or fibrin deposit

32151 with removal of intrapulmonary foreign body

32160 with cardiac massage

(For segmental or other resections of lung, see 32480-32504)

32200 Pneumonostomy; with open drainage of abscess or cyst

⊙ **32201** with percutaneous drainage of abscess or cyst

(For radiological supervision and interpretation, use 75989)

32215 Pleural scarification for repeat pneumothorax

32220 Decortication, pulmonary (separate procedure); total

32225 partial

Excision

32310 Pleurectomy, parietal (separate procedure)

32320 Decortication and parietal pleurectomy

32400 Biopsy, pleura; percutaneous needle

▶(If imaging guidance is performed, see 76942, 77002, 77012, 77021)◀

(For fine needle aspiration, use 10021 or 10022)

(For evaluation of fine needle aspirate, see 88172, 88173)

32402 open

32405 Biopsy, lung or mediastinum, percutaneous needle

▶(For radiological supervision and interpretation, see 76942, 77002, 77012, 77021)◀

(For fine needle aspiration, use 10022)

(For evaluation of fine needle aspirate, see 88172, 88173)

▶Removal◀

32420 Pneumocentesis, puncture of lung for aspiration

32440 Removal of lung, total pneumonectomy;

32442 with resection of segment of trachea followed by broncho-tracheal anastomosis (sleeve pneumonectomy)

32445 extrapleural

(For extrapleural pneumonectomy, with empyemectomy, use 32445 and 32540)

(If lung resection is performed with chest wall tumor resection, report the appropriate chest wall tumor resection code, 19260-19272, in addition to lung resection code 32440-32445)

32480 Removal of lung, other than total pneumonectomy; single lobe (lobectomy)

32482 two lobes (bilobectomy)

32484 single segment (segmentectomy)

(For removal of lung with bronchoplasty, use 32501)

32486 with circumferential resection of segment of bronchus followed by broncho-bronchial anastomosis (sleeve lobectomy)

32488 all remaining lung following previous removal of a portion of lung (completion pneumonectomy)

(For total or segmental lobectomy, with concomitant decortication, use 32320 and the appropriate removal of lung code)

32491 excision-plication of emphysematous lung(s) (bullous or non-bullous) for lung volume reduction, sternal split or transthoracic approach, with or without any pleural procedure

32500 wedge resection, single or multiple

(If lung resection is performed with chest wall tumor resection, report the appropriate chest wall tumor resection code, 19260-19272, in addition to lung resection code 32480-32500)

+ 32501 Resection and repair of portion of bronchus (bronchoplasty) when performed at time of lobectomy or segmentectomy (List separately in addition to code for primary procedure)

(Use 32501 in conjunction with 32480, 32482, 32484)

(32501 is to be used when a portion of the bronchus to preserved lung is removed and requires plastic closure to preserve function of that preserved lung. It is not to be used for closure for the proximal end of a resected bronchus)

32503 Resection of apical lung tumor (eg, Pancoast tumor), including chest wall resection, rib(s) resection(s), neurovascular dissection, when performed; without chest wall reconstruction(s)

32504 with chest wall reconstruction

(Do not report 32503, 32504 in conjunction with 19260, 19271, 19272, 32002, 32020, 32100)

(32520, 32522, and 32525 have been deleted)

(For performance of lung resection in conjunction with chest wall resection, see 19260, 19271, 19272 and 32480-32500, 32503, 32504)

32540 Extrapleural enucleation of empyema (empyemectomy)

(For extrapleural enucleation of empyema (empyemectomy) with lobectomy, use 32540 and the appropriate removal of lung code)

Endoscopy

Surgical thoracoscopy always includes diagnostic thoracoscopy.

For endoscopic procedures, code appropriate endoscopy of each anatomic site examined.

32601 Thoracoscopy, diagnostic (separate procedure); lungs and pleural space, without biopsy

32602 lungs and pleural space, with biopsy

32603 pericardial sac, without biopsy

32604 pericardial sac, with biopsy

32605 mediastinal space, without biopsy

32606 mediastinal space, with biopsy

(Surgical thoracoscopy always includes diagnostic thoracoscopy)

32650 Thoracoscopy, surgical; with pleurodesis (eg, mechanical or chemical)

32651 with partial pulmonary decortication

32652 with total pulmonary decortication, including intrapleural pneumonolysis

32653 with removal of intrapleural foreign body or fibrin deposit

32654 with control of traumatic hemorrhage

32655 with excision-plication of bullae, including any pleural procedure

32656 with parietal pleurectomy

32657 with wedge resection of lung, single or multiple

32658 with removal of clot or foreign body from pericardial sac

32659 with creation of pericardial window or partial resection of pericardial sac for drainage

32660 with total pericardiectomy

32661 with excision of pericardial cyst, tumor, or mass

32662 with excision of mediastinal cyst, tumor, or mass

32663 with lobectomy, total or segmental

32664 with thoracic sympathectomy

32665 with esophagomyotomy (Heller type)

(For exploratory thoracoscopy, and exploratory thoracoscopy with biopsy, see 32601-32606)

Repair

32800 Repair lung hernia through chest wall

32810 Closure of chest wall following open flap drainage for empyema (Clagett type procedure)

32815 Open closure of major bronchial fistula

32820 Major reconstruction, chest wall (posttraumatic)

Lung Transplantation

Lung allotransplantation involves three distinct components of physician work:

1) *Cadaver donor pneumonectomy(s)*, which include(s) harvesting the allograft and cold preservation of the allograft (perfusing with cold preservation solution and cold maintenance) (use 32850).

2) *Backbench work*:

Preparation of a cadaver donor single lung allograft prior to transplantation, including dissection of the allograft from surrounding soft tissues to prepare the pulmonary venous/atrial cuff, pulmonary artery, and bronchus unilaterally (use 32855).

Preparation of a cadaver donor double lung allograft prior to transplantation, including dissection of the allograft from surrounding soft tissues to prepare the pulmonary venous/atrial cuff, pulmonary artery, and bronchus bilaterally (use 32856).

3) *Recipient lung allotransplantation*, which includes transplantation of a single or double lung allograft and care of the recipient (see 32851-32854).

32850 Donor pneumonectomy(s) (including cold preservation), from cadaver donor

32851 Lung transplant, single; without cardiopulmonary bypass

32852 with cardiopulmonary bypass

32853 Lung transplant, double (bilateral sequential or en bloc); without cardiopulmonary bypass

32854 with cardiopulmonary bypass

32855 Backbench standard preparation of cadaver donor lung allograft prior to transplantation, including dissection of allograft from surrounding soft tissues to prepare pulmonary venous/atrial cuff, pulmonary artery, and bronchus; unilateral

32856 bilateral

(For repair or resection procedures on the donor lung, see 32491, 32500, 35216, or 35276)

Surgical Collapse Therapy; Thoracoplasty

(See also 32503, 32504)

32900 Resection of ribs, extrapleural, all stages

32905 Thoracoplasty, Schede type or extrapleural (all stages);

32906 with closure of bronchopleural fistula

(For open closure of major bronchial fistula, use 32815)

(For resection of first rib for thoracic outlet compression, see 21615, 21616)

32940 Pneumonolysis, extraperiosteal, including filling or packing procedures

32960 Pneumothorax, therapeutic, intrapleural injection of air

Other Procedures

32997 Total lung lavage (unilateral)

(For bronchoscopic bronchial alveolar lavage, use 31624)

● **32998** Ablation therapy for reduction or eradication of one or more pulmonary tumor(s) including pleura or chest wall when involved by tumor extension, percutaneous, radiofrequency, unilateral

►(For imaging guidance and monitoring, see 76940, 77013, 77022)◄

32999 Unlisted procedure, lungs and pleura

Surgery: Respiratory System

Notes

Cardiovascular System

Selective vascular catheterizations should be coded to include introduction and all lesser order selective catheterizations used in the approach (eg, the description for a selective right middle cerebral artery catheterization includes the introduction and placement catheterization of the right common and internal carotid arteries).

Additional second and/or third order arterial catheterizations within the same family of arteries supplied by a single first order artery should be expressed by 36218 or 36248. Additional first order or higher catheterizations in vascular families supplied by a first order vessel different from a previously selected and coded family should be separately coded using the conventions described above.

> (For monitoring, operation of pump and other nonsurgical services, see 99190-99192, 99291, 99292, 99354-99360)

> (For other medical or laboratory related services, see appropriate section)

> (For radiological supervision and interpretation, see 75600-75978)

Heart and Pericardium

Pericardium

⊙ **33010** Pericardiocentesis; initial

> (For radiological supervision and interpretation, use 76930)

⊙ **33011** subsequent

> (For radiological supervision and interpretation, use 76930)

33015 Tube pericardiostomy

33020 Pericardiotomy for removal of clot or foreign body (primary procedure)

33025 Creation of pericardial window or partial resection for drainage

33030 Pericardiectomy, subtotal or complete; without cardiopulmonary bypass

33031 with cardiopulmonary bypass

33050 Excision of pericardial cyst or tumor

Cardiac Tumor

33120 Excision of intracardiac tumor, resection with cardiopulmonary bypass

33130 Resection of external cardiac tumor

Transmyocardial Revascularization

33140 Transmyocardial laser revascularization, by thoracotomy; (separate procedure)

+ 33141 performed at the time of other open cardiac procedure(s) (List separately in addition to code for primary procedure)

> (Use 33141 in conjunction with 33400-33496, 33510-33536, 33542)

Pacemaker or Pacing Cardioverter-Defibrillator

A pacemaker system includes a pulse generator containing electronics, a battery, and one or more electrodes (leads). Pulse generators are placed in a subcutaneous "pocket" created in either a subclavicular site or underneath the abdominal muscles just below the ribcage. Electrodes may be inserted through a vein (transvenous) or they may be placed on the surface of the heart (epicardial). The epicardial location of electrodes requires a thoracotomy for electrode insertion.

►A single chamber pacemaker system includes a pulse generator and one electrode inserted in either the atrium or ventricle. A dual chamber pacemaker system includes a pulse generator and one electrode inserted in the right atrium and one electrode inserted in the right ventricle. In certain circumstances, an additional electrode may be required to achieve pacing of the left ventricle (bi-ventricular pacing). In this event, transvenous (cardiac vein) placement of the electrode should be separately reported using code 33224 or 33225. Epicardial placement of the electrode should be separately reported using 33202-33203.◄

Like a pacemaker system, a pacing cardioverter-defibrillator system includes a pulse generator and electrodes, although pacing cardioverter-defibrillators may require multiple leads, even when only a single chamber is being paced. A pacing cardioverter-defibrillator system may be inserted in a single chamber (pacing in the ventricle) or in dual chambers (pacing in atrium and ventricle). These devices use a combination of antitachycardia pacing, low-energy cardioversion or defibrillating shocks to treat ventricular tachycardia or ventricular fibrillation.

Pacing cardioverter-defibrillator pulse generators may be implanted in a subcutaneous infraclavicular pocket or in an abdominal pocket. Removal of a pacing cardioverter-defibrillator pulse generator requires opening of the existing subcutaneous pocket and disconnection of the pulse generator from its electrode(s). A thoracotomy (or laparotomy in the case of abdominally placed pulse generators) is not required to remove the pulse generator.

Surgery: Cardiovascular System

►The electrodes (leads) of a pacing cardioverter-defibrillator system are positioned in the heart via the venous system (transvenously), in most circumstances. In certain circumstances, an additional electrode may be required to achieve pacing of the left ventricle (bi-ventricular pacing). In this event, transvenous (cardiac vein) placement of the electrode should be separately reported using code 33224 or 33225. Epicardial placement of the electrode should be separately reported using 33202-33203.

Electrode positioning on the epicardial surface of the heart requires thoracotomy, or thoracoscopic placement of the leads. Removal of electrode(s) may first be attempted by transvenous extraction (code 33244). However, if transvenous extraction is unsuccessful, a thoracotomy may be required to remove the electrodes (code 33243). Use codes 33212, 33213, 33240 as appropriate in addition to the thoracotomy or endoscopic epicardial lead placement codes to report the insertion of the generator if done by the same physician during the same session.◄

When the "battery" of a pacemaker or pacing cardioverter-defibrillator is changed, it is actually the pulse generator that is changed. Replacement of a pulse generator should be reported with a code for removal of the pulse generator and another code for insertion of a pulse generator.

Repositioning of a pacemaker electrode, pacing cardioverter-defibrillator electrode(s), or a left ventricular pacing electrode is reported using 33215 or 33226, as appropriate. Replacement of a pacemaker electrode, pacing cardioverter-defibrillator electrode(s), or a left ventricular pacing electrode is reported using 33206-33208, 33210-33213, or 33224, as appropriate.

(For electronic, telephonic analysis of internal pacemaker system, see 93731-93736)

(For radiological supervision and interpretation with insertion of pacemaker, use 71090)

►(33200, 33201 have been deleted)◄

● **33202** Insertion of epicardial electrode(s); open incision (eg, thoracotomy, median sternotomy, subxiphoid approach)

● **33203** endoscopic approach (eg, thoracoscopy, pericardioscopy)

►(When epicardial lead placement is performed by the same physician at the same session as insertion of the generator, report 33202, 33203 in conjunction with 33212, 33213, as appropriate)◄

⊙ **33206** Insertion or replacement of permanent pacemaker with transvenous electrode(s); atrial

⊙ **33207** ventricular

⊙ **33208** atrial and ventricular

(Codes 33206-33208 include subcutaneous insertion of the pulse generator and transvenous placement of electrode(s))

⊙ **33210** Insertion or replacement of temporary transvenous single chamber cardiac electrode or pacemaker catheter (separate procedure)

⊙ **33211** Insertion or replacement of temporary transvenous dual chamber pacing electrodes (separate procedure)

⊙ **33212** Insertion or replacement of pacemaker pulse generator only; single chamber, atrial or ventricular

⊙ **33213** dual chamber

►(Use 33212, 33213, as appropriate, in conjunction with the epicardial lead placement codes 33202, 33203 to report the insertion of the generator when done by the same physician during the same session)◄

⊙ **33214** Upgrade of implanted pacemaker system, conversion of single chamber system to dual chamber system (includes removal of previously placed pulse generator, testing of existing lead, insertion of new lead, insertion of new pulse generator)

►(When epicardial electrode placement is performed, report 33214 in conjunction with 33202, 33203)◄

33215 Repositioning of previously implanted transvenous pacemaker or pacing cardioverter-defibrillator (right atrial or right ventricular) electrode

⊙ **33216** Insertion of a transvenous electrode; single chamber (one electrode) permanent pacemaker or single chamber pacing cardioverter-defibrillator

⊙ **33217** dual chamber (two electrodes) permanent pacemaker or dual chamber pacing cardioverter-defibrillator

(Do not report 33216-33217 in conjunction with 33214)

⊙ **33218** Repair of single transvenous electrode for a single chamber, permanent pacemaker or single chamber pacing cardioverter-defibrillator

(For atrial or ventricular single chamber repair of pacemaker electrode(s) with replacement of pulse generator, see 33212 or 33213 and 33218 or 33220)

⊙ **33220** Repair of two transvenous electrodes for a dual chamber permanent pacemaker or dual chamber pacing cardioverter-defibrillator

⊙ **33222** Revision or relocation of skin pocket for pacemaker

⊙ **33223** Revision of skin pocket for single or dual chamber pacing cardioverter-defibrillator

33224 Insertion of pacing electrode, cardiac venous system, for left ventricular pacing, with attachment to previously placed pacemaker or pacing cardioverter-defibrillator pulse generator (including revision of pocket, removal, insertion, and/or replacement of generator)

►(When epicardial electrode placement is performed, report 33224 in conjunction with 33202, 33203)◄

+ 33225 Insertion of pacing electrode, cardiac venous system, for left ventricular pacing, at time of insertion of pacing cardioverter-defibrillator or pacemaker pulse generator (including upgrade to dual chamber system) (List separately in addition to code for primary procedure)

(Use 33225 in conjunction with 33206, 33207, 33208, 33212, 33213, 33214, 33216, 33217, 33222, 33233, 33234, 33235, 33240, 33249)

33226 Repositioning of previously implanted cardiac venous system (left ventricular) electrode (including removal, insertion and/or replacement of generator)

⊙ **33233** Removal of permanent pacemaker pulse generator

⊙ **33234** Removal of transvenous pacemaker electrode(s); single lead system, atrial or ventricular

⊙ **33235** dual lead system

33236 Removal of permanent epicardial pacemaker and electrodes by thoracotomy; single lead system, atrial or ventricular

33237 dual lead system

33238 Removal of permanent transvenous electrode(s) by thoracotomy

⊙ **33240** Insertion of single or dual chamber pacing cardioverter-defibrillator pulse generator

▶(Use 33240, as appropriate, in addition to the epicardial lead placement codes to report the insertion of the generator when done by the same physician during the same session)◀

⊙ **33241** Subcutaneous removal of single or dual chamber pacing cardioverter-defibrillator pulse generator

(For removal of electrode(s) by thoracotomy, use 33243 in conjunction with 33241)

(For removal of electrode(s) by transvenous extraction, use 33244 in conjunction with 33241)

(For removal and reinsertion of a pacing cardioverter-defibrillator system (pulse generator and electrodes), report 33241 and 33243 or 33244 and 33249)

(For repair of implantable cardioverter-defibrillator pulse generator and/or leads, see 33218, 33220)

33243 Removal of single or dual chamber pacing cardioverter-defibrillator electrode(s); by thoracotomy

⊙ **33244** by transvenous extraction

(For subcutaneous removal of the pulse generator, use 33241 in conjunction with 33243 or 33244)

▶(33245, 33246 have been deleted)◀

⊙ **33249** Insertion or repositioning of electrode lead(s) for single or dual chamber pacing cardioverter-defibrillator and insertion of pulse generator

(For removal and reinsertion of a pacing cardioverter-defibrillator system (pulse generator and electrodes), report 33241 and 33243 or 33244 and 33249)

(For insertion of implantable cardioverter-defibrillator lead(s), without thoracotomy, use 33216)

Electrophysiologic Operative Procedures

▶This family of codes describes the surgical treatment of supraventricular dysrhythmias. Tissue ablation, disruption and reconstruction can be accomplished by many methods including surgical incision or through the use of a variety of energy sources (eg, radiofrequency, cryotherapy, microwave, ultrasound, laser). If excision or isolation of the left atrial appendage by any method, including stapling, oversewing, ligation, or plication, is performed in conjunction with any of the atrial tissue ablation and reconstruction (maze) procedures (33254-33256, 33265-33266), it is considered part of the procedure. Codes 33254-33256 are only to be reported when there is no concurrently performed procedure that requires median sternotomy or cardiopulmonary bypass. When 33254-33256 are performed with a concurrent procedure that requires a median sternotomy or cardiopulmonary bypass, report the operative (nonthoracoscopic) electrophysiologic procedure with unlisted procedure code 33999.

Definitions

Limited operative ablation and reconstruction includes:

Surgical isolation of triggers of supraventricular dysrhythmias by operative ablation that isolates the pulmonary veins or other anatomically defined triggers in the left or right atrium.

Extensive operative ablation and reconstruction includes:

1. The services included in "*limited*"

2. Additional ablation of atrial tissue to eliminate sustained supraventricular dysrhythmias. This must include operative ablation that involves either the right atrium, the atrial septum, or left atrium in continuity with the atrioventricular annulus.◀

▶Incision◀

33250 Operative ablation of supraventricular arrhythmogenic focus or pathway (eg, Wolff-Parkinson-White, atrioventricular node re-entry), tract(s) and/or focus (foci); without cardiopulmonary bypass

33251 with cardiopulmonary bypass

▶(33253 has been deleted. To report, use 33254–33256)◀

Surgery: Cardiovascular System

● **33254** Operative tissue ablation and reconstruction of atria, limited (eg, modified maze procedure)

● **33255** Operative tissue ablation and reconstruction of atria, extensive (eg, maze procedure); without cardiopulmonary bypass

● **33256** with cardiopulmonary bypass

▶(Do not report 33254-33256 in conjunction with 32020, 32100, 33120, 33130, 33210, 33211, 33400-33507, 33510-33523, 33533-33548, 33600-33853, 33860-33863, 33910-33920)◀

33261 Operative ablation of ventricular arrhythmogenic focus with cardiopulmonary bypass

▶Endoscopy◀

● **33265** Endoscopy, surgical; operative tissue ablation and reconstruction of atria, limited (eg, modified maze procedure), without cardiopulmonary bypass

● **33266** operative tissue ablation and reconstruction of atria, extensive (eg, maze procedure), without cardiopulmonary bypass

▶(Do not report 33265-33266 in conjunction with 32020, 33210, 33211)◀

Patient-Activated Event Recorder

33282 Implantation of patient-activated cardiac event recorder

(Initial implantation includes programming. For subsequent electronic analysis and/or reprogramming, use 93727)

33284 Removal of an implantable, patient-activated cardiac event recorder

Wounds of the Heart and Great Vessels

33300 Repair of cardiac wound; without bypass

33305 with cardiopulmonary bypass

33310 Cardiotomy, exploratory (includes removal of foreign body, atrial or ventricular thrombus); without bypass

33315 with cardiopulmonary bypass

(Do not report removal of thrombus (33310-33315) in conjunction with other cardiac procedures unless a separate incision in the heart is required to remove the atrial or ventricular thrombus)

(If removal of thrombus with cardiopulmonary bypass (33315) is reported in conjunction with 33120, 33130, 33420-33430, 33460-33468, 33496, 33542, 33545, 33641-33647, 33670, 33681, 33975-33980 which requires a separate heart incision, report 33315 with modifier 59)

33320 Suture repair of aorta or great vessels; without shunt or cardiopulmonary bypass

33321 with shunt bypass

33322 with cardiopulmonary bypass

33330 Insertion of graft, aorta or great vessels; without shunt, or cardiopulmonary bypass

33332 with shunt bypass

33335 with cardiopulmonary bypass

Cardiac Valves

(For multiple valve procedures, see 33400-33478 and add modifier 51 to the secondary valve procedure code)

Aortic Valve

33400 Valvuloplasty, aortic valve; open, with cardiopulmonary bypass

33401 open, with inflow occlusion

33403 using transventricular dilation, with cardiopulmonary bypass

(Do not report modifier 63 in conjunction with 33401, 33403)

33404 Construction of apical-aortic conduit

33405 Replacement, aortic valve, with cardiopulmonary bypass; with prosthetic valve other than homograft or stentless valve

33406 with allograft valve (freehand)

(For aortic valve valvotomy, (commissurotomy) with inflow occlusion, use 33401)

(For aortic valve valvotomy, (commissurotomy) with cardiopulmonary bypass, use 33403)

33410 with stentless tissue valve

33411 Replacement, aortic valve; with aortic annulus enlargement, noncoronary cusp

33412 with transventricular aortic annulus enlargement (Konno procedure)

33413 by translocation of autologous pulmonary valve with allograft replacement of pulmonary valve (Ross procedure)

33414 Repair of left ventricular outflow tract obstruction by patch enlargement of the outflow tract

33415 Resection or incision of subvalvular tissue for discrete subvalvular aortic stenosis

33416 Ventriculomyotomy (-myectomy) for idiopathic hypertrophic subaortic stenosis (eg, asymmetric septal hypertrophy)

33417 Aortoplasty (gusset) for supravalvular stenosis

Mitral Valve

33420 Valvotomy, mitral valve; closed heart

33422 open heart, with cardiopulmonary bypass

33425 Valvuloplasty, mitral valve, with cardiopulmonary bypass;

33426 with prosthetic ring

33427 radical reconstruction, with or without ring

33430 Replacement, mitral valve, with cardiopulmonary bypass

Tricuspid Valve

33460 Valvectomy, tricuspid valve, with cardiopulmonary bypass

33463 Valvuloplasty, tricuspid valve; without ring insertion

33464 with ring insertion

33465 Replacement, tricuspid valve, with cardiopulmonary bypass

33468 Tricuspid valve repositioning and plication for Ebstein anomaly

Pulmonary Valve

33470 Valvotomy, pulmonary valve, closed heart; transventricular

(Do not report modifier 63 in conjunction with 33470)

33471 via pulmonary artery

(To report percutaneous valvuloplasty of pulmonary valve, use 92990)

33472 Valvotomy, pulmonary valve, open heart; with inflow occlusion

(Do not report modifier 63 in conjunction with 33472)

33474 with cardiopulmonary bypass

33475 Replacement, pulmonary valve

33476 Right ventricular resection for infundibular stenosis, with or without commissurotomy

33478 Outflow tract augmentation (gusset), with or without commissurotomy or infundibular resection

(Use 33478 in conjunction with 33768 when a cavopulmonary anastomosis to a second superior vena cava is performed)

Other Valvular Procedures

33496 Repair of non-structural prosthetic valve dysfunction with cardiopulmonary bypass (separate procedure)

(For reoperation, use 33530 in addition to 33496)

Coronary Artery Anomalies

Basic procedures include endarterectomy or angioplasty.

33500 Repair of coronary arteriovenous or arteriocardiac chamber fistula; with cardiopulmonary bypass

33501 without cardiopulmonary bypass

33502 Repair of anomalous coronary artery from pulmonary artery origin; by ligation

33503 by graft, without cardiopulmonary bypass

(Do not report modifier 63 in conjunction with 33502, 33503)

33504 by graft, with cardiopulmonary bypass

33505 with construction of intrapulmonary artery tunnel (Takeuchi procedure)

33506 by translocation from pulmonary artery to aorta

(Do not report modifier 63 in conjunction with 33505, 33506)

33507 Repair of anomalous (eg, intramural) aortic origin of coronary artery by unroofing or translocation

Endoscopy

Surgical vascular endoscopy always includes diagnostic endoscopy.

+ 33508 Endoscopy, surgical, including video-assisted harvest of vein(s) for coronary artery bypass procedure (List separately in addition to code for primary procedure)

(Use 33508 in conjunction with 33510-33523)

(For open harvest of upper extremity vein procedure, use 35500)

Venous Grafting Only for Coronary Artery Bypass

The following codes are used to report coronary artery bypass procedures using venous grafts only. These codes should NOT be used to report the performance of coronary artery bypass procedures using arterial grafts and venous grafts during the same procedure. See 33517-33523 and 33533-33536 for reporting combined arterial-venous grafts.

Procurement of the saphenous vein graft is included in the description of the work for 33510-33516 and should not be reported as a separate service or co-surgery. To report harvesting of an upper extremity vein, use 35500 in addition to the bypass procedure. To report harvesting of a femoropopliteal vein segment, report 35572 in addition to the bypass procedure. When surgical assistant performs graft procurement, add modifier 80 to 33510-33516.

33510 Coronary artery bypass, vein only; single coronary venous graft

33511 two coronary venous grafts

33512 three coronary venous grafts

33513 four coronary venous grafts

33514 five coronary venous grafts

33516 six or more coronary venous grafts

Combined Arterial-Venous Grafting for Coronary Bypass

The following codes are used to report coronary artery bypass procedures using venous grafts and arterial grafts during the same procedure. These codes may NOT be used alone.

To report combined arterial-venous grafts it is necessary to report two codes: 1) the appropriate combined arterial-venous graft code (33517-33523); and 2) the appropriate arterial graft code (33533-33536).

Procurement of the saphenous vein graft is included in the description of the work for 33517-33523 and should not be reported as a separate service or co-surgery. Procurement of the artery for grafting is included in the description of the work for 33533-33536 and should not be reported as a separate service or co-surgery, except when an upper extremity artery (eg, radial artery) is procured. To report harvesting of an upper extremity artery, use 35600 in addition to the bypass procedure. To report harvesting of an upper extremity vein, use 35500 in addition to the bypass procedure. To report harvesting of a femoropopliteal vein segment, report 35572 in addition to the bypass procedure. When surgical assistant performs arterial and/or venous graft procurement, add modifier 80 to 33517-33523, 33533-33536, as appropriate.

⊘ **33517** Coronary artery bypass, using venous graft(s) and arterial graft(s); single vein graft (List separately in addition to code for arterial graft)

⊘ **33518** two venous grafts (List separately in addition to code for arterial graft)

⊘ **33519** three venous grafts (List separately in addition to code for arterial graft)

⊘ **33521** four venous grafts (List separately in addition to code for arterial graft)

⊘ **33522** five venous grafts (List separately in addition to code for arterial graft)

⊘ **33523** six or more venous grafts (List separately in addition to code for arterial graft)

✚ **33530** Reoperation, coronary artery bypass procedure or valve procedure, more than one month after original operation (List separately in addition to code for primary procedure)

(Use 33530 in conjunction with 33400-33496; 33510-33536, 33863)

Arterial Grafting for Coronary Artery Bypass

The following codes are used to report coronary artery bypass procedures using either arterial grafts only or a combination of arterial-venous grafts. The codes include the use of the internal mammary artery, gastroepiploic artery, epigastric artery, radial artery, and arterial conduits procured from other sites.

To report combined arterial-venous grafts it is necessary to report two codes: 1) the appropriate arterial graft code (33533-33536); and 2) the appropriate combined arterial-venous graft code (33517-33523).

Procurement of the artery for grafting is included in the description of the work for 33533-33536 and should not be reported as a separate service or co-surgery, except when an upper extremity artery (eg, radial artery) is procured. To report harvesting of an upper extremity artery, use 35600 in addition to the bypass procedure. To report harvesting of an upper extremity vein, use 35500 in addition to the bypass procedure. To report harvesting of a femoropopliteal vein segment, report 35572 in addition to the bypass procedure. When surgical assistant performs arterial and/or venous graft procurement, add modifier 80 to 33517-33523, 33533-33536, as appropriate.

33533 Coronary artery bypass, using arterial graft(s); single arterial graft

33534 two coronary arterial grafts

33535 three coronary arterial grafts

33536 four or more coronary arterial grafts

33542 Myocardial resection (eg, ventricular aneurysmectomy)

33545 Repair of postinfarction ventricular septal defect, with or without myocardial resection

33548 Surgical ventricular restoration procedure, includes prosthetic patch, when performed (eg, ventricular remodeling, SVR, SAVER, DOR procedures)

(Do not report 33548 in conjunction with 32020, 33210, 33211, 33310, 33315)

(For Batista procedure or pachopexy, use 33999)

Coronary Endarterectomy

✚ **33572** Coronary endarterectomy, open, any method, of left anterior descending, circumflex, or right coronary artery performed in conjunction with coronary artery bypass graft procedure, each vessel (List separately in addition to primary procedure)

(Use 33572 in conjunction with 33510-33516, 33533-33536)

Surgery: Cardiovascular System

Single Ventricle and Other Complex Cardiac Anomalies

33600 Closure of atrioventricular valve (mitral or tricuspid) by suture or patch

33602 Closure of semilunar valve (aortic or pulmonary) by suture or patch

33606 Anastomosis of pulmonary artery to aorta (Damus-Kaye-Stansel procedure)

33608 Repair of complex cardiac anomaly other than pulmonary atresia with ventricular septal defect by construction or replacement of conduit from right or left ventricle to pulmonary artery

(For repair of pulmonary artery arborization anomalies by unifocalization, see 33925-33926)

33610 Repair of complex cardiac anomalies (eg, single ventricle with subaortic obstruction) by surgical enlargement of ventricular septal defect

(Do not report modifier 63 in conjunction with 33610)

33611 Repair of double outlet right ventricle with intraventricular tunnel repair;

(Do not report modifier 63 in conjunction with 33611)

33612 with repair of right ventricular outflow tract obstruction

33615 Repair of complex cardiac anomalies (eg, tricuspid atresia) by closure of atrial septal defect and anastomosis of atria or vena cava to pulmonary artery (simple Fontan procedure)

33617 Repair of complex cardiac anomalies (eg, single ventricle) by modified Fontan procedure

(Use 33617 in conjunction with 33768 when a cavopulmonary anastomosis to a second superior vena cava is performed)

33619 Repair of single ventricle with aortic outflow obstruction and aortic arch hypoplasia (hypoplastic left heart syndrome) (eg, Norwood procedure)

(Do not report modifier 63 in conjunction with 33619)

Septal Defect

33641 Repair atrial septal defect, secundum, with cardiopulmonary bypass, with or without patch

33645 Direct or patch closure, sinus venosus, with or without anomalous pulmonary venous drainage

▶(Do not report 33645 in conjunction with 33724, 33726)◀

33647 Repair of atrial septal defect and ventricular septal defect, with direct or patch closure

(Do not report modifier 63 in conjunction with 33647)

(For repair of tricuspid atresia (eg, Fontan, Gago procedures), use 33615)

33660 Repair of incomplete or partial atrioventricular canal (ostium primum atrial septal defect), with or without atrioventricular valve repair

33665 Repair of intermediate or transitional atrioventricular canal, with or without atrioventricular valve repair

33670 Repair of complete atrioventricular canal, with or without prosthetic valve

(Do not report modifier 63 in conjunction with 33670)

● **33675** Closure of multiple ventricular septal defects;

● **33676** with pulmonary valvotomy or infundibular resection (acyanotic)

● **33677** with removal of pulmonary artery band, with or without gusset

▶(Do not report 33675-33677 in conjunction with 32002, 32020, 32100, 33210, 33681, 33684, 33688)◀

▶(For transmyocardial closure, see Category III codes 0166T and 0167T)◀

▶(For percutaneous closure, use 93581)◀

▲ **33681** Closure of single ventricular septal defect, with or without patch;

33684 with pulmonary valvotomy or infundibular resection (acyanotic)

33688 with removal of pulmonary artery band, with or without gusset

▶(For pulmonary vein repair requiring creation of atrial septal defect, use 33724)◀

33690 Banding of pulmonary artery

(Do not report modifier 63 in conjunction with 33690)

33692 Complete repair tetralogy of Fallot without pulmonary atresia;

33694 with transannular patch

(Do not report modifier 63 in conjunction with 33694)

(For ligation and takedown of a systemic-to-pulmonary artery shunt, performed in conjunction with a congenital heart procedure; see 33924)

33697 Complete repair tetralogy of Fallot with pulmonary atresia including construction of conduit from right ventricle to pulmonary artery and closure of ventricular septal defect

(For ligation and takedown of a systemic-to-pulmonary artery shunt, performed in conjunction with a congenital heart procedure; see 33924)

Surgery: Cardiovascular System

Sinus of Valsalva

33702 Repair sinus of Valsalva fistula, with cardiopulmonary bypass;

33710 with repair of ventricular septal defect

33720 Repair sinus of Valsalva aneurysm, with cardiopulmonary bypass

33722 Closure of aortico-left ventricular tunnel

►Venous Anomalies◄

● **33724** Repair of isolated partial anomalous pulmonary venous return (eg, Scimitar Syndrome)

►(Do not report 33724 in conjunction with 32020, 33210, 33211)◄

● **33726** Repair of pulmonary venous stenosis

►(Do not report 33726 in conjunction with 32020, 33210, 33211)◄

33730 Complete repair of anomalous pulmonary venous return (supracardiac, intracardiac, or infracardiac types)

(Do not report modifier 63 in conjunction with 33730)

►(For partial anomalous pulmonary venous return, use 33724; for repair of pulmonary venous stenosis, use 33726)◄

33732 Repair of cor triatriatum or supravalvular mitral ring by resection of left atrial membrane

(Do not report modifier 63 in conjunction with 33732)

Shunting Procedures

33735 Atrial septectomy or septostomy; closed heart (Blalock-Hanlon type operation)

33736 open heart with cardiopulmonary bypass

(Do not report modifier 63 in conjunction with 33735, 33736)

33737 open heart, with inflow occlusion

(For transvenous method cardiac catheterization balloon atrial septectomy or septostomy (Rashkind type), use 92992)

(For blade method cardiac catheterization atrial septectomy or septostomy (Sang-Park septostomy), use 92993)

33750 Shunt; subclavian to pulmonary artery (Blalock-Taussig type operation)

33755 ascending aorta to pulmonary artery (Waterston type operation)

33762 descending aorta to pulmonary artery (Potts-Smith type operation)

(Do not report modifier 63 in conjunction with 33750, 33755, 33762)

33764 central, with prosthetic graft

33766 superior vena cava to pulmonary artery for flow to one lung (classical Glenn procedure)

33767 superior vena cava to pulmonary artery for flow to both lungs (bidirectional Glenn procedure)

+ **33768** Anastomosis, cavopulmonary, second superior vena cava (List separately in addition to primary procedure)

(Use 33768 in conjunction with 33478, 33617, 33767)

(Do not report 33768 in conjunction with 32020, 33210, 33211)

Transposition of the Great Vessels

33770 Repair of transposition of the great arteries with ventricular septal defect and subpulmonary stenosis; without surgical enlargement of ventricular septal defect

33771 with surgical enlargement of ventricular septal defect

33774 Repair of transposition of the great arteries, atrial baffle procedure (eg, Mustard or Senning type) with cardiopulmonary bypass;

33775 with removal of pulmonary band

33776 with closure of ventricular septal defect

33777 with repair of subpulmonic obstruction

33778 Repair of transposition of the great arteries, aortic pulmonary artery reconstruction (eg, Jatene type);

(Do not report modifier 63 in conjunction with 33778)

33779 with removal of pulmonary band

33780 with closure of ventricular septal defect

33781 with repair of subpulmonic obstruction

Truncus Arteriosus

33786 Total repair, truncus arteriosus (Rastelli type operation)

(Do not report modifier 63 in conjunction with 33786)

33788 Reimplantation of an anomalous pulmonary artery

(For pulmonary artery band, use 33690)

Aortic Anomalies

33800 Aortic suspension (aortopexy) for tracheal decompression (eg, for tracheomalacia) (separate procedure)

33802 Division of aberrant vessel (vascular ring);

33803 with reanastomosis

33813 Obliteration of aortopulmonary septal defect; without cardiopulmonary bypass

33814 with cardiopulmonary bypass

33820 Repair of patent ductus arteriosus; by ligation

33822 by division, younger than 18 years

33824 by division, 18 years and older

33840 Excision of coarctation of aorta, with or without associated patent ductus arteriosus; with direct anastomosis

33845 with graft

33851 repair using either left subclavian artery or prosthetic material as gusset for enlargement

33852 Repair of hypoplastic or interrupted aortic arch using autogenous or prosthetic material; without cardiopulmonary bypass

33853 with cardiopulmonary bypass

(For repair of hypoplastic left heart syndrome (eg, Norwood type), via excision of coarctation of aorta, use 33619)

Thoracic Aortic Aneurysm

33860 Ascending aorta graft, with cardiopulmonary bypass, with or without valve suspension;

33861 with coronary reconstruction

33863 with aortic root replacement using composite prosthesis and coronary reconstruction

(For graft of ascending aorta, with cardiopulmonary bypass and valve replacement, with or without coronary implant or valve suspension; use 33860 or 33861 and 33405 or 33406)

33870 Transverse arch graft, with cardiopulmonary bypass

33875 Descending thoracic aorta graft, with or without bypass

33877 Repair of thoracoabdominal aortic aneurysm with graft, with or without cardiopulmonary bypass

Endovascular Repair of Descending Thoracic Aorta

Codes 33880-33891 represent a family of procedures to report placement of an endovascular graft for repair of the descending thoracic aorta. These codes include all device introduction, manipulation, positioning, and deployment. All balloon angioplasty and/or stent deployment within the target treatment zone for the endoprosthesis, either before or after endograft deployment, are not separately reportable. Open arterial exposure and associated closure of the arteriotomy sites (eg, 34812, 34820, 34833, 34834), introduction of guidewires and catheters (eg, 36140, 36200-36218), and extensive repair or replacement of an artery (eg, 35226, 35286) should be additionally reported. Transposition of subclavian artery to carotid, and carotid-carotid bypass performed in conjunction with endovascular repair of the descending thoracic aorta (eg, 33889, 33891) should be separately reported. The primary codes, 33880 and 33881, include placement of all distal extensions, if required, in the distal thoracic aorta, while proximal extensions, if needed, are reported separately.

For fluoroscopic guidance in conjunction with endovascular repair of the thoracic aorta, see codes 75956-75959 as appropriate. Codes 75956 and 75957 include all angiography of the thoracic aorta and its branches for diagnostic imaging prior to deployment of the primary endovascular devices (including all routine components of modular devices), fluoroscopic guidance in the delivery of the endovascular components, and intraprocedural arterial angiography (eg, confirm position, detect endoleak, evaluate runoff). Code 75958 includes the analogous services for placement of each proximal thoracic endovascular extension. Code 75959 includes the analogous services for placement of a distal thoracic endovascular extension(s) placed during a procedure after the primary repair.

Other interventional procedures performed at the time of endovascular repair of the descending thoracic aorta should be additionally reported (eg, innominate, carotid, subclavian, visceral, or iliac artery transluminal angioplasty or stenting, arterial embolization, intravascular ultrasound) when performed before or after deployment of the aortic prostheses.

33880 Endovascular repair of descending thoracic aorta (eg, aneurysm, pseudoaneurysm, dissection, penetrating ulcer, intramural hematoma, or traumatic disruption); involving coverage of left subclavian artery origin, initial endoprosthesis plus descending thoracic aortic extension(s), if required, to level of celiac artery origin

(For radiological supervision and interpretation, use 75956 in conjunction with 33880)

33881 not involving coverage of left subclavian artery origin, initial endoprosthesis plus descending thoracic aortic extension(s), if required, to level of celiac artery origin

(For radiological supervision and interpretation, use 75957 in conjunction with 33881)

33883 Placement of proximal extension prosthesis for endovascular repair of descending thoracic aorta (eg, aneurysm, pseudoaneurysm, dissection, penetrating ulcer, intramural hematoma, or traumatic disruption); initial extension

(For radiological supervision and interpretation, use 75958 in conjunction with 33883)

(Do not report 33881, 33883 when extension placement converts repair to cover left subclavian origin. Use only 33880)

+ **33884** each additional proximal extension (List separately in addition to code for primary procedure)

(Use 33884 in conjunction with 33883)

(For radiological supervision and interpretation, use 75958 in conjunction with 33884)

Surgery: Cardiovascular System

33886 Placement of distal extension prosthesis(s) delayed after endovascular repair of descending thoracic aorta

(Do not report 33886 in conjunction with 33880, 33881)

(Report 33886 once, regardless of number of modules deployed)

(For radiological supervision and interpretation, use 75959 in conjunction with 33886)

33889 Open subclavian to carotid artery transposition performed in conjunction with endovascular repair of descending thoracic aorta, by neck incision, unilateral

(Do not report 33889 in conjunction with 35694)

33891 Bypass graft, with other than vein, transcervical retropharyngeal carotid-carotid, performed in conjunction with endovascular repair of descending thoracic aorta, by neck incision

(Do not report 33891 in conjunction with 35509, 35601)

Pulmonary Artery

33910 Pulmonary artery embolectomy; with cardiopulmonary bypass

33915 without cardiopulmonary bypass

33916 Pulmonary endarterectomy, with or without embolectomy, with cardiopulmonary bypass

33917 Repair of pulmonary artery stenosis by reconstruction with patch or graft

(33918, 33919 have been deleted. To report, see 33925, 33926)

33920 Repair of pulmonary atresia with ventricular septal defect, by construction or replacement of conduit from right or left ventricle to pulmonary artery

(For repair of other complex cardiac anomalies by construction or replacement of right or left ventricle to pulmonary artery conduit, use 33608)

33922 Transection of pulmonary artery with cardiopulmonary bypass

(Do not report modifier 63 in conjunction with 33922)

+ 33924 Ligation and takedown of a systemic-to-pulmonary artery shunt, performed in conjunction with a congenital heart procedure (List separately in addition to code for primary procedure)

(Use 33924 in conjunction with 33470-33475, 33600-33619, 33684-33688, 33692-33697, 33735-33767, 33770-33781, 33786, 33920-33922)

33925 Repair of pulmonary artery arborization anomalies by unifocalization; without cardiopulmonary bypass

33926 with cardiopulmonary bypass

Heart/Lung Transplantation

Heart with or without lung allotransplantation involves three distinct components of physician work:

1) *Cadaver donor cardiectomy with or without pneumonectomy*, which includes harvesting the allograft and cold preservation of the allograft (perfusing with cold preservation solution and cold maintenance) (see 33930, 33940).

2) *Backbench work*:

Preparation of a cadaver donor heart and lung allograft prior to transplantation, including dissection of the allograft from surrounding soft tissues to prepare the aorta, superior vena cava, inferior vena cava, and trachea for implantation (use 33933).

Preparation of a cadaver donor heart allograft prior to transplantation, including dissection of the allograft from surrounding soft tissues to prepare aorta, superior vena cava, inferior vena cava, pulmonary artery, and left atrium for implantation (use 33944).

3) *Recipient heart with or without lung allotransplantation*, which includes transplantation of allograft and care of the recipient (see 33935, 33945).

(For implantation of a total replacement heart system (artificial heart) with recipient cardiectomy or heart replacement system components, see Category III codes 0051T-0053T)

33930 Donor cardiectomy-pneumonectomy (including cold preservation)

33933 Backbench standard preparation of cadaver donor heart/lung allograft prior to transplantation, including dissection of allograft from surrounding soft tissues to prepare aorta, superior vena cava, inferior vena cava, and trachea for implantation

33935 Heart-lung transplant with recipient cardiectomy-pneumonectomy

33940 Donor cardiectomy (including cold preservation)

33944 Backbench standard preparation of cadaver donor heart allograft prior to transplantation, including dissection of allograft from surrounding soft tissues to prepare aorta, superior vena cava, inferior vena cava, pulmonary artery, and left atrium for implantation

(For repair or resection procedures on the donor heart, see 33300, 33310, 33320, 33400, 33463, 33464, 33510, 33641, 35216, 35276 or 35685)

33945 Heart transplant, with or without recipient cardiectomy

Surgery: Cardiovascular System

Cardiac Assist

(For percutaneous implantation of extracorporeal ventricular assist device or for removal of percutaneously implanted extracorporeal ventricular assist device, see Category III codes 0048T-0050T)

33960 Prolonged extracorporeal circulation for cardiopulmonary insufficiency; initial 24 hours

+ 33961 each additional 24 hours (List separately in addition to code for primary procedure)

(Do not report modifier 63 in conjunction with 33960, 33961)

(Use 33961 in conjunction with 33960)

(For insertion of cannula for prolonged extracorporeal circulation, use 36822)

33967 Insertion of intra-aortic balloon assist device, percutaneous

33968 Removal of intra-aortic balloon assist device, percutaneous

33970 Insertion of intra-aortic balloon assist device through the femoral artery, open approach

33971 Removal of intra-aortic balloon assist device including repair of femoral artery, with or without graft

33973 Insertion of intra-aortic balloon assist device through the ascending aorta

33974 Removal of intra-aortic balloon assist device from the ascending aorta, including repair of the ascending aorta, with or without graft

33975 Insertion of ventricular assist device; extracorporeal, single ventricle

33976 extracorporeal, biventricular

33977 Removal of ventricular assist device; extracorporeal, single ventricle

33978 extracorporeal, biventricular

33979 Insertion of ventricular assist device, implantable intracorporeal, single ventricle

33980 Removal of ventricular assist device, implantable intracorporeal, single ventricle

Other Procedures

33999 Unlisted procedure, cardiac surgery

Arteries and Veins

Primary vascular procedure listings include establishing both inflow and outflow by whatever procedures necessary. Also included is that portion of the operative arteriogram performed by the surgeon, as indicated. Sympathectomy, when done, is included in the listed aortic procedures. For unlisted vascular procedure, use 37799.

Embolectomy/Thrombectomy

Arterial, With or Without Catheter

34001 Embolectomy or thrombectomy, with or without catheter; carotid, subclavian or innominate artery, by neck incision

34051 innominate, subclavian artery, by thoracic incision

34101 axillary, brachial, innominate, subclavian artery, by arm incision

34111 radial or ulnar artery, by arm incision

34151 renal, celiac, mesentery, aortoiliac artery, by abdominal incision

34201 femoropopliteal, aortoiliac artery, by leg incision

34203 popliteal-tibio-peroneal artery, by leg incision

Venous, Direct or With Catheter

34401 Thrombectomy, direct or with catheter; vena cava, iliac vein, by abdominal incision

34421 vena cava, iliac, femoropopliteal vein, by leg incision

34451 vena cava, iliac, femoropopliteal vein, by abdominal and leg incision

34471 subclavian vein, by neck incision

34490 axillary and subclavian vein, by arm incision

Venous Reconstruction

34501 Valvuloplasty, femoral vein

34502 Reconstruction of vena cava, any method

34510 Venous valve transposition, any vein donor

34520 Cross-over vein graft to venous system

34530 Saphenopopliteal vein anastomosis

Endovascular Repair of Abdominal Aortic Aneurysm

Codes 34800-34826 represent a family of component procedures to report placement of an endovascular graft for abdominal aortic aneurysm repair. These codes describe open femoral or iliac artery exposure, device manipulation and deployment, and closure of the arteriotomy sites. Balloon angioplasty and/or stent deployment within the target treatment zone for the endoprosthesis, either before or after endograft deployment, are not separately reportable. Introduction of guidewires and catheters should be reported separately (eg, 36200, 36245-36248, 36140). Extensive repair or replacement of an artery should be additionally reported (eg, 35226 or 35286).

For fluoroscopic guidance in conjunction with endovascular aneurysm repair, see code 75952 or 75953, as appropriate. Code 75952 includes angiography of the aorta and its branches for diagnostic imaging prior to deployment of the endovascular device (including all routine components of modular devices), fluoroscopic guidance in the delivery of the endovascular components, and intraprocedural arterial angiography (eg, confirm position, detect endoleak, evaluate runoff). Code 75953 includes the analogous services for placement of additional extension prostheses (not for routine components of modular devices).

Other interventional procedures performed at the time of endovascular abdominal aortic aneurysm repair should be additionally reported (eg, renal transluminal angioplasty, arterial embolization, intravascular ultrasound, balloon angioplasty or stenting of native artery(s) outside the endoprosthesis target zone, when done before or after deployment of graft).

34800 Endovascular repair of infrarenal abdominal aortic aneurysm or dissection; using aorto-aortic tube prosthesis

34802 using modular bifurcated prosthesis (one docking limb)

34803 using modular bifurcated prosthesis (two docking limbs)

(For endovascular repair of abdominal aortic aneurysm or dissection involving visceral vessels using a fenestrated modular bifurcated prosthesis (two docking limbs), use Category III codes 0078T, 0079T)

34804 using unibody bifurcated prosthesis

34805 using aorto-uniiliac or aorto-unifemoral prosthesis

+ 34808 Endovascular placement of iliac artery occlusion device (List separately in addition to code for primary procedure)

(Use 34808 in conjunction with 34800, 34805, 34813, 34825, 34826)

(For radiological supervision and interpretation, use 75952 in conjunction with 34800-34808)

(For open arterial exposure, report 34812, 34820, 34833, 34834 as appropriate, in addition to 34800-34808)

34812 Open femoral artery exposure for delivery of endovascular prosthesis, by groin incision, unilateral

(For bilateral procedure, use modifier 50)

+ 34813 Placement of femoral-femoral prosthetic graft during endovascular aortic aneurysm repair (List separately in addition to code for primary procedure)

(Use 34813 in conjunction with 34812)

▶(For femoral artery grafting, see 35521, 35533, 35539, 35540, 35551-35558, 35566, 35621, 35646, 35651-35661, 35666, 35700)◀

34820 Open iliac artery exposure for delivery of endovascular prosthesis or iliac occlusion during endovascular therapy, by abdominal or retroperitoneal incision, unilateral

(For bilateral procedure, use modifier 50)

34825 Placement of proximal or distal extension prosthesis for endovascular repair of infrarenal abdominal aortic or iliac aneurysm, false aneurysm, or dissection; initial vessel

+ 34826 each additional vessel (List separately in addition to code for primary procedure)

(Use 34826 in conjunction with 34825)

(Use 34825, 34826 in addition to 34800-34808, 34900 as appropriate)

(For staged procedure, use modifier 58)

(For radiological supervision and interpretation, use 75953)

34830 Open repair of infrarenal aortic aneurysm or dissection, plus repair of associated arterial trauma, following unsuccessful endovascular repair; tube prosthesis

34831 aorto-bi-iliac prosthesis

34832 aorto-bifemoral prosthesis

34833 Open iliac artery exposure with creation of conduit for delivery of aortic or iliac endovascular prosthesis, by abdominal or retroperitoneal incision, unilateral

(For bilateral procedure, use modifier 50)

(Do not report 34833 in addition to 34820)

34834 Open brachial artery exposure to assist in the deployment of aortic or iliac endovascular prosthesis by arm incision, unilateral

(For bilateral procedure, use modifier 50)

Endovascular Repair of Iliac Aneurysm

Code 34900 represents a procedure to report introduction, positioning, and deployment of an endovascular graft for treatment of aneurysm, pseudoaneurysm, or arteriovenous malformation or trauma of the iliac artery (common, hypogastric, external). All balloon angioplasty and/or stent deployments within the target treatment zone for the endoprosthesis, either before or after endograft deployment, are included in the work of 34900 and are not separately reportable. Open femoral or iliac artery exposure (eg, 34812, 34820), introduction of guidewires and catheters (eg, 36200, 36215-36218), and extensive repair or replacement of an artery (eg, 35206-35286) should be additionally reported.

Surgery: Cardiovascular System

For fluoroscopic guidance in conjunction with endovascular iliac aneurysm repair, see code 75954. Code 75954 includes angiography of the aorta and iliac arteries for diagnostic imaging prior to deployment of the endovascular device (including all routine components), fluoroscopic guidance in the delivery of the endovascular components, and intraprocedural arterial angiography to confirm appropriate position of the graft, detect endoleaks, and evaluate the status of the runoff vessels (eg, evaluation for dissection, stenosis, thrombosis, distal embolization, or iatrogenic injury).

Other interventional procedures performed at the time of endovascular iliac aneurysm repair should be additionally reported (eg, transluminal angioplasty outside the aneurysm target zone, arterial embolization, intravascular ultrasound).

34900 Endovascular graft placement for repair of iliac artery (eg, aneurysm, pseudoaneurysm, arteriovenous malformation, trauma)

(For radiological supervision and interpretation, use 75954)

(For placement of extension prosthesis during endovascular iliac artery repair, use 34825)

(For bilateral procedure, use modifier 50)

Direct Repair of Aneurysm or Excision (Partial or Total) and Graft Insertion for Aneurysm, Pseudoaneurysm, Ruptured Aneurysm, and Associated Occlusive Disease

Procedures 35001-35152 include preparation of artery for anastomosis including endarterectomy.

(For direct repairs associated with occlusive disease only, see 35201-35286)

(For intracranial aneurysm, see 61700 et seq)

(For endovascular repair of abdominal aortic aneurysm, see 34800-34826)

(For endovascular repair of iliac artery aneurysm, see 34900)

(For thoracic aortic aneurysm, see 33860-33875)

(For endovascular repair of descending thoracic aorta, involving coverage of left subclavian artery origin, use 33880)

35001 Direct repair of aneurysm, pseudoaneurysm, or excision (partial or total) and graft insertion, with or without patch graft; for aneurysm and associated occlusive disease, carotid, subclavian artery, by neck incision

35002 for ruptured aneurysm, carotid, subclavian artery, by neck incision

35005 for aneurysm, pseudoaneurysm, and associated occlusive disease, vertebral artery

35011 for aneurysm and associated occlusive disease, axillary-brachial artery, by arm incision

35013 for ruptured aneurysm, axillary-brachial artery, by arm incision

35021 for aneurysm, pseudoaneurysm, and associated occlusive disease, innominate, subclavian artery, by thoracic incision

35022 for ruptured aneurysm, innominate, subclavian artery, by thoracic incision

35045 for aneurysm, pseudoaneurysm, and associated occlusive disease, radial or ulnar artery

35081 for aneurysm, pseudoaneurysm, and associated occlusive disease, abdominal aorta

35082 for ruptured aneurysm, abdominal aorta

35091 for aneurysm, pseudoaneurysm, and associated occlusive disease, abdominal aorta involving visceral vessels (mesenteric, celiac, renal)

35092 for ruptured aneurysm, abdominal aorta involving visceral vessels (mesenteric, celiac, renal)

35102 for aneurysm, pseudoaneurysm, and associated occlusive disease, abdominal aorta involving iliac vessels (common, hypogastric, external)

35103 for ruptured aneurysm, abdominal aorta involving iliac vessels (common, hypogastric, external)

35111 for aneurysm, pseudoaneurysm, and associated occlusive disease, splenic artery

35112 for ruptured aneurysm, splenic artery

35121 for aneurysm, pseudoaneurysm, and associated occlusive disease, hepatic, celiac, renal, or mesenteric artery

35122 for ruptured aneurysm, hepatic, celiac, renal, or mesenteric artery

35131 for aneurysm, pseudoaneurysm, and associated occlusive disease, iliac artery (common, hypogastric, external)

35132 for ruptured aneurysm, iliac artery (common, hypogastric, external)

35141 for aneurysm, pseudoaneurysm, and associated occlusive disease, common femoral artery (profunda femoris, superficial femoral)

35142 for ruptured aneurysm, common femoral artery (profunda femoris, superficial femoral)

35151 for aneurysm, pseudoaneurysm, and associated occlusive disease, popliteal artery

35152 for ruptured aneurysm, popliteal artery

(35161, 35162 have been deleted. To report, use 37799)

Surgery: Cardiovascular System

Repair Arteriovenous Fistula

35180 Repair, congenital arteriovenous fistula; head and neck

35182 thorax and abdomen

35184 extremities

35188 Repair, acquired or traumatic arteriovenous fistula; head and neck

35189 thorax and abdomen

35190 extremities

Repair Blood Vessel Other Than for Fistula, With or Without Patch Angioplasty

(For AV fistula repair, see 35180-35190)

35201 Repair blood vessel, direct; neck

35206 upper extremity

35207 hand, finger

35211 intrathoracic, with bypass

35216 intrathoracic, without bypass

35221 intra-abdominal

35226 lower extremity

35231 Repair blood vessel with vein graft; neck

35236 upper extremity

35241 intrathoracic, with bypass

35246 intrathoracic, without bypass

35251 intra-abdominal

35256 lower extremity

35261 Repair blood vessel with graft other than vein; neck

35266 upper extremity

35271 intrathoracic, with bypass

35276 intrathoracic, without bypass

35281 intra-abdominal

35286 lower extremity

Thromboendarterectomy

(For coronary artery, see 33510-33536 and 33572)

▶(35301-35372 include harvest of saphenous or upper extremity vein when performed)◀

▲ 35301 Thromboendarterectomy, including patch graft, if performed; carotid, vertebral, subclavian, by neck incision

● 35302 superficial femoral artery

● 35303 popliteal artery

▶(Do not report 35302, 35303 in conjunction with 35483, 35500)◀

● 35304 tibioperoneal trunk artery

● 35305 tibial or peroneal artery, initial vessel

+● 35306 each additional tibial or peroneal artery (List separately in addition to code for primary procedure)

▶(Use 35306 in conjunction with 35305)◀

▶(Do not report 35304, 35305, 35306 in conjunction with 35485, 35500)◀

35311 subclavian, innominate, by thoracic incision

35321 axillary-brachial

35331 abdominal aorta

35341 mesenteric, celiac, or renal

35351 iliac

35355 iliofemoral

35361 combined aortoiliac

35363 combined aortoiliofemoral

35371 common femoral

35372 deep (profunda) femoral

▶(35381 has been deleted. For thromboendarterectomy of the superficial femoral artery, use 35302; of the popliteal artery, use 35303; of the tibioperoneal trunk, use 35304; of the tibial or peroneal artery, see 35305, 35306)◀

+ 35390 Reoperation, carotid, thromboendarterectomy, more than one month after original operation (List separately in addition to code for primary procedure)

(Use 35390 in conjunction with 35301)

Angioscopy

+ 35400 Angioscopy (non-coronary vessels or grafts) during therapeutic intervention (List separately in addition to code for primary procedure)

Transluminal Angioplasty

If done as part of another operation, use modifier 51 or use modifier 52.

(For radiological supervision and interpretation, see 75962-75968 and 75978)

Open

35450 Transluminal balloon angioplasty, open; renal or other visceral artery

35452 aortic

35454 iliac

35456 femoral-popliteal

35458 brachiocephalic trunk or branches, each vessel

35459 tibioperoneal trunk and branches

35460 venous

Percutaneous

Codes for catheter placement and the radiologic supervision and interpretation should also be reported, in addition to the code(s) for the therapeutic aspect of the procedure.

⊙ **35470** Transluminal balloon angioplasty, percutaneous; tibioperoneal trunk or branches, each vessel

⊙ **35471** renal or visceral artery

⊙ **35472** aortic

⊙ **35473** iliac

⊙ **35474** femoral-popliteal

⊙ **35475** brachiocephalic trunk or branches, each vessel

⊙ **35476** venous

(For radiological supervision and interpretation, use 75978)

Transluminal Atherectomy

If done as part of another operation, use modifier 51 or use modifier 52.

(For radiological supervision and interpretation, see 75992-75996)

Open

35480 Transluminal peripheral atherectomy, open; renal or other visceral artery

35481 aortic

35482 iliac

35483 femoral-popliteal

35484 brachiocephalic trunk or branches, each vessel

35485 tibioperoneal trunk and branches

Percutaneous

Codes for catheter placement and the radiologic supervision and interpretation should also be reported, in addition to the code(s) for the therapeutic aspect of the procedure.

35490 Transluminal peripheral atherectomy, percutaneous; renal or other visceral artery

35491 aortic

35492 iliac

35493 femoral-popliteal

35494 brachiocephalic trunk or branches, each vessel

35495 tibioperoneal trunk and branches

Bypass Graft

Vein

Procurement of the saphenous vein graft is included in the description of the work for 35501-35587 and should not be reported as a separate service or co-surgery. To report harvesting of an upper extremity vein, use 35500 in addition to the bypass procedure. To report harvesting of a femoropopliteal vein segment, use 35572 in addition to the bypass procedure. To report harvesting and construction of an autogenous composite graft of two segments from two distant locations, report 35682 in addition to the bypass procedure, for autogenous composite of three or more segments from distant sites, report 35683.

+ **35500** Harvest of upper extremity vein, one segment, for lower extremity or coronary artery bypass procedure (List separately in addition to code for primary procedure)

(Use 35500 in conjunction with 33510-33536, 35556, 35566, 35571, 35583-35587)

(For harvest of more than one vein segment, see 35682, 35683)

(For endoscopic procedure, use 33508)

▲ **35501** Bypass graft, with vein; common carotid-ipsilateral internal carotid

▲ **35506** carotid-subclavian or subclavian-carotid

▶(35507 has been deleted. For subclavian-carotid bypass with vein, use 35506)◀

35508 carotid-vertebral

▲ **35509** carotid-contralateral carotid

35510 carotid-brachial

35511 subclavian-subclavian

35512 subclavian-brachial

35515 subclavian-vertebral

35516 subclavian-axillary

35518 axillary-axillary

35521 axillary-femoral

(For bypass graft performed with synthetic graft, use 35621)

35522 axillary-brachial

35525 brachial-brachial

35526 aortosubclavian or carotid

(For bypass graft performed with synthetic graft, use 35626)

35531 aortoceliac or aortomesenteric

35533 axillary-femoral-femoral

(For bypass graft performed with synthetic graft, use 35654)

▲=Revised code ●=New code ▶ ◀=Contains new or revised text ⊘ =Modifier 51 exempt

Surgery: Cardiovascular System

35536 splenorenal

● 35537 aortoiliac

▶(For bypass graft performed with synthetic graft, use 35637)◀

▶(Do not report 35537 in conjunction with 35538)◀

● 35538 aortobi-iliac

▶(For bypass graft performed with synthetic graft, use 35638)◀

▶(Do not report 35538 in conjunction with 35537)◀

● 35539 aortofemoral

▶(For bypass graft performed with synthetic graft, use 35647)◀

▶(Do not report 35539 in conjunction with 35540)◀

● 35540 aortobifemoral

▶(For bypass graft performed with synthetic graft, use 35646)◀

▶(Do not report 35540 in conjunction with 35539)◀

▶(35541 has been deleted. For aortoiliac graft with vein, use 35537. For aortobi-iliac graft with vein, use 35538)◀

▶(35546 has been deleted. For aortofemoral graft with vein use 35539. For aortobifemoral graft with vein, use 35540)◀

35548 aortoiliofemoral, unilateral

(For bypass graft performed with synthetic graft, use 37799)

35549 aortoiliofemoral, bilateral

(For bypass graft performed with synthetic graft, use 37799)

35551 aortofemoral-popliteal

35556 femoral-popliteal

35558 femoral-femoral

35560 aortorenal

35563 ilioiliac

35565 iliofemoral

35566 femoral-anterior tibial, posterior tibial, peroneal artery or other distal vessels

35571 popliteal-tibial, -peroneal artery or other distal vessels

+ 35572 Harvest of femoropopliteal vein, one segment, for vascular reconstruction procedure (eg, aortic, vena caval, coronary, peripheral artery) (List separately in addition to code for primary procedure)

(Use 35572 in conjunction with 33510-33516, 33517-33523, 33533-33536, 34502, 34520, 35001, 35002, 35011-35022, 35102, 35103, 35121-35152, 35231-35256, 35501-35587, 35879-35907)

(For bilateral procedure, use modifier 50)

In-Situ Vein

(35582 has been deleted)

▶(To report aortobifemoral bypass using synthetic conduit, and femoral-popliteal bypass with vein conduit in-situ, use 35646 and 35583. To report aorto(uni)femoral bypass with synthetic conduit, and femoral-popliteal bypass with vein conduit in-situ, use 35647 and 35583. To report aortofemoral bypass using vein conduit, and femoral-popliteal bypass with vein conduit in-situ, use 35539 and 35583)◀

35583 In-situ vein bypass; femoral-popliteal

35585 femoral-anterior tibial, posterior tibial, or peroneal artery

35587 popliteal-tibial, peroneal

Other Than Vein

(For arterial transposition and/or reimplantation, see 35691-35695)

⊘ 35600 Harvest of upper extremity artery, one segment, for coronary artery bypass procedure

▲ 35601 Bypass graft, with other than vein; common carotid-ipsilateral internal carotid

35606 carotid-subclavian

(For open transcervical common carotid-common carotid bypass performed in conjunction with endovascular repair of descending thoracic aorta, use 33891)

(For open subclavian to carotid artery transposition performed in conjunction with endovascular thoracic aneurysm repair by neck incision, use 33889)

35612 subclavian-subclavian

35616 subclavian-axillary

35621 axillary-femoral

35623 axillary-popliteal or -tibial

35626 aortosubclavian or carotid

35631 aortoceliac, aortomesenteric, aortorenal

35636 splenorenal (splenic to renal arterial anastomosis)

● 35637 aortoiliac

▶(Do not report 35637 in conjunction with 35638, 35646)◀

● 35638 aortobi-iliac

▶(Do not report 35638 in conjunction with 35637, 35646)◀

▶(35641 has been deleted. For aortoiliac graft constructed with conduit other than vein, use 35637. For aortobi-iliac graft with other than vein, use 35638)◀

(For open placement of aorto-bi-iliac prosthesis following unsuccessful endovascular repair, use 34831)

35642	carotid-vertebral
35645	subclavian-vertebral
35646	aortobifemoral

►(For bypass graft performed with vein graft, use 35540)◄

(For open placement of aortobifemoral prosthesis following unsuccessful endovascular repair, use 34832)

35647	aortofemoral

►(For bypass graft performed with vein graft, use 35539)◄

35650	axillary-axillary
35651	aortofemoral-popliteal
35654	axillary-femoral-femoral
35656	femoral-popliteal
35661	femoral-femoral
35663	ilioiliac
35665	iliofemoral
35666	femoral-anterior tibial, posterior tibial, or peroneal artery
35671	popliteal-tibial or -peroneal artery

Composite Grafts

Codes 35682-35683 are used to report harvest and anastomosis of multiple vein segments from distant sites for use as arterial bypass graft conduits. These codes are intended for use when the two or more vein segments are harvested from a limb other than that undergoing bypass. Add-on codes 35682 and 35683 may be reported in addition to codes 35556, 35566, 35571, 35583-35587, as appropriate.

+ **35681** Bypass graft; composite, prosthetic and vein (List separately in addition to code for primary procedure)

(Do not report 35681 in addition to 35682, 35683)

+ **35682** autogenous composite, two segments of veins from two locations (List separately in addition to code for primary procedure)

(Do not report 35682 in addition to 35681, 35683)

+ **35683** autogenous composite, three or more segments of vein from two or more locations (List separately in addition to code for primary procedure)

(Do not report 35683 in addition to 35681, 35682)

Adjuvant Techniques

Adjuvant (additional) technique(s) may be required at the time a bypass graft is created to improve patency of the lower extremity autogenous or synthetic bypass graft (eg, femoral-popliteal, femoral-tibial, or popliteal-tibial arteries). Code 35685 should be reported in addition to

the primary synthetic bypass graft procedure, when an interposition of venous tissue (vein patch or cuff) is placed at the anastomosis between the synthetic bypass conduit and the involved artery (includes harvest).

Code 35686 should be reported in addition to the primary bypass graft procedure, when autogenous vein is used to create a fistula between the tibial or peroneal artery and vein at or beyond the distal bypass anastomosis site of the involved artery.

(For composite graft(s), see 35681-35683)

+ **35685** Placement of vein patch or cuff at distal anastomosis of bypass graft, synthetic conduit (List separately in addition to code for primary procedure)

(Use 35685 in conjunction with 35656, 35666, or 35671)

+ **35686** Creation of distal arteriovenous fistula during lower extremity bypass surgery (non-hemodialysis) (List separately in addition to code for primary procedure)

(Use 35686 in conjunction with 35556, 35566, 35571, 35583-35587, 35623, 35656, 35666, 35671)

Arterial Transposition

35691	Transposition and/or reimplantation; vertebral to carotid artery
35693	vertebral to subclavian artery
35694	subclavian to carotid artery

(For open subclavian to carotid artery transposition performed in conjunction with endovascular repair of descending thoracic aorta, use 33889)

35695	carotid to subclavian artery

+ **35697** Reimplantation, visceral artery to infrarenal aortic prosthesis, each artery (List separately in addition to code for primary procedure)

(Do not report 35697 in conjunction with 33877)

►Excision, Exploration, Repair, Revision◄

+ **35700** Reoperation, femoral-popliteal or femoral (popliteal)-anterior tibial, posterior tibial, peroneal artery, or other distal vessels, more than one month after original operation (List separately in addition to code for primary procedure)

(Use 35700 in conjunction with 35556, 35566, 35571, 35583, 35585, 35587, 35656, 35666, 35671)

35701	Exploration (not followed by surgical repair), with or without lysis of artery; carotid artery
35721	femoral artery
35741	popliteal artery
35761	other vessels

Surgery: Cardiovascular System

Surgery: Cardiovascular System

35800	Exploration for postoperative hemorrhage, thrombosis or infection; neck
35820	chest
35840	abdomen
35860	extremity
35870	Repair of graft-enteric fistula
35875	Thrombectomy of arterial or venous graft (other than hemodialysis graft or fistula);
35876	with revision of arterial or venous graft

(For thrombectomy of hemodialysis graft or fistula, see 36831, 36833)

Codes 35879 and 35881 describe open revision of graft-threatening stenoses of lower extremity arterial bypass graft(s) (previously constructed with autogenous vein conduit) using vein patch angioplasty or segmental vein interposition techniques. For thrombectomy with revision of any non-coronary arterial or venous graft, including those of the lower extremity, (other than hemodialysis graft or fistula), use 35876. For direct repair (other than for fistula) of a lower extremity blood vessel (with or without patch angioplasty), use 35226. For repair (other than for fistula) of a lower extremity blood vessel using a vein graft, use 35256.

35879	Revision, lower extremity arterial bypass, without thrombectomy, open; with vein patch angioplasty
35881	with segmental vein interposition

▶(For revision of femoral anastomosis of synthetic arterial bypass graft, see 35883, 35884)◀

(For excision of infected graft, see 35901-35907 and appropriate revascularization code)

● 35883	Revision, femoral anastomosis of synthetic arterial bypass graft in groin, open; with nonautogenous patch graft (eg, Dacron, ePTFE, bovine pericardium)

▶(For bilateral procedure, use modifier 50)◀

▶(Do not report 35883 in conjunction with 35700, 35875, 35876, 35884)◀

● 35884	with autogenous vein patch graft

▶(For bilateral procedure, use modifier 50)◀

▶(Do not report 35884 in conjunction with 35700, 35875, 35876, 35883)◀

35901	Excision of infected graft; neck
35903	extremity
35905	thorax
35907	abdomen

Vascular Injection Procedures

Listed services for injection procedures include necessary local anesthesia, introduction of needles or catheter, injection of contrast media with or without automatic power injection, and/or necessary pre- and postinjection care specifically related to the injection procedure.

Catheters, drugs, and contrast media are not included in the listed service for the injection procedures.

Selective vascular catheterization should be coded to include introduction and all lesser order selective catheterization used in the approach (eg, the description for a selective right middle cerebral artery catheterization includes the introduction and placement catheterization of the right common and internal carotid arteries).

Additional second and/or third order arterial catheterization within the same family of arteries or veins supplied by a single first order vessel should be expressed by 36012, 36218 or 36248.

Additional first order or higher catheterization in vascular families supplied by a first order vessel different from a previously selected and coded family should be separately coded using the conventions described above.

(For radiological supervision and interpretation, see **Radiology**)

(For injection procedures in conjunction with cardiac catheterization, see 93541-93545)

(For chemotherapy of malignant disease, see 96401-96549)

Intravenous

An intracatheter is a sheathed combination of needle and short catheter.

36000	Introduction of needle or intracatheter, vein
36002	Injection procedures (eg, thrombin) for percutaneous treatment of extremity pseudoaneurysm

▶(For imaging guidance, see 76942, 77002, 77012, 77021)◀

(For ultrasound guided compression repair of pseudoaneurysms, use 76936)

(Do not report 36002 for vascular sealant of an arteriotomy site)

36005	Injection procedure for extremity venography (including introduction of needle or intracatheter)

(For radiological supervision and interpretation, see 75820, 75822)

36010	Introduction of catheter, superior or inferior vena cava
36011	Selective catheter placement, venous system; first order branch (eg, renal vein, jugular vein)
36012	second order, or more selective, branch (eg, left adrenal vein, petrosal sinus)

36013 Introduction of catheter, right heart or main pulmonary artery

36014 Selective catheter placement, left or right pulmonary artery

36015 Selective catheter placement, segmental or subsegmental pulmonary artery

(For insertion of flow directed catheter (eg, Swan-Ganz), use 93503)

(For venous catheterization for selective organ blood sampling, use 36500)

Intra-Arterial—Intra-Aortic

(For radiological supervision and interpretation, see **Radiology**)

36100 Introduction of needle or intracatheter, carotid or vertebral artery

(For bilateral procedure, report 36100 with modifier 50)

36120 Introduction of needle or intracatheter; retrograde brachial artery

36140 extremity artery

36145 arteriovenous shunt created for dialysis (cannula, fistula, or graft)

(For insertion of arteriovenous cannula, see 36810-36821)

36160 Introduction of needle or intracatheter, aortic, translumbar

36200 Introduction of catheter, aorta

36215 Selective catheter placement, arterial system; each first order thoracic or brachiocephalic branch, within a vascular family

(For catheter placement for coronary angiography, use 93508)

36216 initial second order thoracic or brachiocephalic branch, within a vascular family

36217 initial third order or more selective thoracic or brachiocephalic branch, within a vascular family

+ 36218 additional second order, third order, and beyond, thoracic or brachiocephalic branch, within a vascular family (List in addition to code for initial second or third order vessel as appropriate)

(Use 36218 in conjunction with 36216, 36217)

(For angiography, see 75600-75790)

(For angioplasty, see 35470-35475)

(For transcatheter therapies, see 37200-37208, 61624, 61626)

(When coronary artery, arterial conduit (eg, internal mammary, inferior epigastric or free radical artery) or venous bypass graft angiography is performed in conjunction with cardiac catheterization, see the appropriate cardiac catheterization, injection procedure, and imaging supervision code(s) (93501-93556) in the **Medicine** section of the CPT codebook. When coronary artery, arterial coronary conduit or venous bypass graft angiography is performed without concomitant left heart cardiac catheterization, use 93508. When internal mammary artery angiography only is performed without a concomitant left heart cardiac catheterization, use 36216 or 36217 as appropriate.)

36245 Selective catheter placement, arterial system; each first order abdominal, pelvic, or lower extremity artery branch, within a vascular family

36246 initial second order abdominal, pelvic, or lower extremity artery branch, within a vascular family

36247 initial third order or more selective abdominal, pelvic, or lower extremity artery branch, within a vascular family

+ 36248 additional second order, third order, and beyond, abdominal, pelvic, or lower extremity artery branch, within a vascular family (List in addition to code for initial second or third order vessel as appropriate)

(Use 36248 in conjunction with 36246, 36247)

36260 Insertion of implantable intra-arterial infusion pump (eg, for chemotherapy of liver)

36261 Revision of implanted intra-arterial infusion pump

36262 Removal of implanted intra-arterial infusion pump

36299 Unlisted procedure, vascular injection

Venous

Venipuncture, needle or catheter for diagnostic study or intravenous therapy, percutaneous.

36400 Venipuncture, younger than age 3 years, necessitating physician's skill, not to be used for routine venipuncture; femoral or jugular vein

36405 scalp vein

36406 other vein

36410 Venipuncture, age 3 years or older, necessitating physician's skill (separate procedure), for diagnostic or therapeutic purposes (not to be used for routine venipuncture)

36415 Collection of venous blood by venipuncture

(Do not report modifier 63 in conjunction with 36415)

36416 Collection of capillary blood specimen (eg, finger, heel, ear stick)

Surgery: Cardiovascular System

36420 Venipuncture, cutdown; younger than age 1 year

(Do not report modifier 63 in conjunction with 36420)

36425 age 1 or over

36430 Transfusion, blood or blood components

36440 Push transfusion, blood, 2 years or younger

36450 Exchange transfusion, blood; newborn

(Do not report modifier 63 in conjunction with 36450)

36455 other than newborn

36460 Transfusion, intrauterine, fetal

(Do not report modifier 63 in conjunction with 36460)

(For radiological supervision and interpretation, use 76941)

36468 Single or multiple injections of sclerosing solutions, spider veins (telangiectasia); limb or trunk

36469 face

36470 Injection of sclerosing solution; single vein

36471 multiple veins, same leg

36475 Endovenous ablation therapy of incompetent vein, extremity, inclusive of all imaging guidance and monitoring, percutaneous, radiofrequency; first vein treated

+ 36476 second and subsequent veins treated in a single extremity, each through separate access sites (List separately in addition to code for primary procedure)

(Use 36476 in conjunction with 36475)

▶(Do not report 36475, 36476 in conjunction with 36000-36005, 36410, 36425, 36478, 36479, 37204, 75894, 76000, 76001, 76937, 76942, 77022, 93970, 93971)◀

36478 Endovenous ablation therapy of incompetent vein, extremity, inclusive of all imaging guidance and monitoring, percutaneous, laser; first vein treated

+ 36479 second and subsequent veins treated in a single extremity, each through separate access sites (List separately in addition to code for primary procedure)

(Use 36479 in conjunction with 36478)

▶(Do not report 36478, 36479 in conjunction with 36000-36005, 36410, 36425, 36475, 36476, 37204, 75894, 76000, 76001, 76937, 76942, 77022, 93970, 93971)◀

36481 Percutaneous portal vein catheterization by any method

(For radiological supervision and interpretation, see 75885, 75887)

36500 Venous catheterization for selective organ blood sampling

(For catheterization in superior or inferior vena cava, use 36010)

(For radiological supervision and interpretation, use 75893)

36510 Catheterization of umbilical vein for diagnosis or therapy, newborn

(Do not report modifier 63 in conjunction with 36510)

36511 Therapeutic apheresis; for white blood cells

36512 for red blood cells

36513 for platelets

36514 for plasma pheresis

36515 with extracorporeal immunoadsorption and plasma reinfusion

36516 with extracorporeal selective adsorption or selective filtration and plasma reinfusion

(For physician evaluation, use modifier 26)

36522 Photopheresis, extracorporeal

36540 Collection of blood specimen from a completely implantable venous access device

(Do not report 36540 in conjunction with 36415, 36416)

(For collection of venous blood specimen by venipuncture, use 36415)

(For collection of capillary blood specimen, use 36416)

36550 Declotting by thrombolytic agent of implanted vascular access device or catheter

Central Venous Access Procedures

To qualify as a central venous access catheter or device, the tip of the catheter/device must terminate in the subclavian, brachiocephalic (innominate) or iliac veins, the superior or inferior vena cava, or the right atrium. The venous access device may be either centrally inserted (jugular, subclavian, femoral vein or inferior vena cava catheter entry site) or peripherally inserted (eg, basilic or cephalic vein). The device may be accessed for use either via exposed catheter (external to the skin), via a subcutaneous port or via a subcutaneous pump.

The procedures involving these types of devices fall into five categories:

1) *Insertion* (placement of catheter through a newly established venous access)

2) *Repair* (fixing device without replacement of either catheter or port/pump, other than pharmacologic or mechanical correction of intracatheter or pericatheter occlusion (see 36595 or 36596))

3) *Partial replacement* of only the catheter component associated with a port/pump device, but not entire device

4) *Complete replacement* of entire device via same venous access site (complete exchange)

5) *Removal* of entire device.

There is no coding distinction between venous access achieved percutaneously versus by cutdown or based on catheter size.

For the repair, partial (catheter only) replacement, complete replacement, or removal of both catheters (placed from separate venous access sites) of a multi-catheter device, with or without subcutaneous ports/pumps, use the appropriate code describing the service with a frequency of two.

If an existing central venous access device is removed and a new one placed via a separate venous access site, appropriate codes for both procedures (removal of old, if code exists, and insertion of new device) should be reported.

►When imaging is used for these procedures, either for gaining access to the venous entry site or for manipulating the catheter into final central position, use 76937, 77001.◄

(For refilling and maintenance of an implantable pump or reservoir for intravenous or intra-arterial drug delivery, use 96522)

Insertion of Central Venous Access Device

⊙ **36555** Insertion of non-tunneled centrally inserted central venous catheter; younger than 5 years of age

(For peripherally inserted non-tunneled central venous catheter, younger than 5 years of age, use 36568)

36556 age 5 years or older

(For peripherally inserted non-tunneled central venous catheter, age 5 years or older, use 36569)

⊙ **36557** Insertion of tunneled centrally inserted central venous catheter, without subcutaneous port or pump; younger than 5 years of age

⊙ **36558** age 5 years or older

(For peripherally inserted central venous catheter with port, 5 years or older, use 36571)

⊙ **36560** Insertion of tunneled centrally inserted central venous access device, with subcutaneous port; younger than 5 years of age

(For peripherally inserted central venous access device with subcutaneous port, younger than 5 years of age, use 36570)

⊙ **36561** age 5 years or older

(For peripherally inserted central venous catheter with subcutaneous port, 5 years or older, use 36571)

⊙ **36563** Insertion of tunneled centrally inserted central venous access device with subcutaneous pump

⊙ **36565** Insertion of tunneled centrally inserted central venous access device, requiring two catheters via two separate venous access sites; without subcutaneous port or pump (eg, Tesio type catheter)

⊙ **36566** with subcutaneous port(s)

⊙ **36568** Insertion of peripherally inserted central venous catheter (PICC), without subcutaneous port or pump; younger than 5 years of age

(For placement of centrally inserted non-tunneled central venous catheter, without subcutaneous port or pump, younger than 5 years of age, use 36555)

36569 age 5 years or older

(For placement of centrally inserted non-tunneled central venous catheter, without subcutaneous port or pump, age 5 years or older, use 36556)

⊙ **36570** Insertion of peripherally inserted central venous access device, with subcutaneous port; younger than 5 years of age

(For insertion of tunneled centrally inserted central venous access device with subcutaneous port, younger than 5 years of age, use 36560)

⊙ **36571** age 5 years or older

(For insertion of tunneled centrally inserted central venous access device with subcutaneous port, age 5 years or older, use 36561)

Repair of Central Venous Access Device

(For mechanical removal of pericatheter obstructive material, use 36595)

(For mechanical removal of intracatheter obstructive material, use 36596)

36575 Repair of tunneled or non-tunneled central venous access catheter, without subcutaneous port or pump, central or peripheral insertion site

⊙ **36576** Repair of central venous access device, with subcutaneous port or pump, central or peripheral insertion site

Partial Replacement of Central Venous Access Device (Catheter Only)

⊙ **36578** Replacement, catheter only, of central venous access device, with subcutaneous port or pump, central or peripheral insertion site

(For complete replacement of entire device through same venous access, use 36582 or 36583)

Surgery: Cardiovascular System

Complete Replacement of Central Venous Access Device Through Same Venous Access Site

36580 Replacement, complete, of a non-tunneled centrally inserted central venous catheter, without subcutaneous port or pump, through same venous access

⊙ 36581 Replacement, complete, of a tunneled centrally inserted central venous catheter, without subcutaneous port or pump, through same venous access

⊙ 36582 Replacement, complete, of a tunneled centrally inserted central venous access device, with subcutaneous port, through same venous access

⊙ 36583 Replacement, complete, of a tunneled centrally inserted central venous access device, with subcutaneous pump, through same venous access

36584 Replacement, complete, of a peripherally inserted central venous catheter (PICC), without subcutaneous port or pump, through same venous access

⊙ 36585 Replacement, complete, of a peripherally inserted central venous access device, with subcutaneous port, through same venous access

Removal of Central Venous Access Device

36589 Removal of tunneled central venous catheter, without subcutaneous port or pump

⊙ 36590 Removal of tunneled central venous access device, with subcutaneous port or pump, central or peripheral insertion

(Do not report 36589 or 36590 for removal of non-tunneled central venous catheters)

Mechanical Removal of Obstructive Material

36595 Mechanical removal of pericatheter obstructive material (eg, fibrin sheath) from central venous device via separate venous access

(Do not report 36595 in conjunction with 36550)

(For venous catheterization, see 36010-36012)

(For radiological supervision and interpretation, use 75901)

36596 Mechanical removal of intraluminal (intracatheter) obstructive material from central venous device through device lumen

(Do not report 36596 in conjunction with 36550)

(For venous catheterization, see 36010-36012)

(For radiological supervision and interpretation, use 75902)

Other Central Venous Access Procedures

36597 Repositioning of previously placed central venous catheter under fluoroscopic guidance

(For fluoroscopic guidance, use 76000)

36598 Contrast injection(s) for radiologic evaluation of existing central venous access device, including fluoroscopy, image documentation and report

(Do not report 36598 in conjunction with 76000)

(Do not report 36598 in conjunction with 36595, 36596)

(For complete diagnostic studies, see 75820, 75825, 75827)

Arterial

36600 Arterial puncture, withdrawal of blood for diagnosis

⊘ 36620 Arterial catheterization or cannulation for sampling, monitoring or transfusion (separate procedure); percutaneous

36625 cutdown

36640 Arterial catheterization for prolonged infusion therapy (chemotherapy), cutdown

(See also 96420-96425)

(For arterial catheterization for occlusion therapy, see 75894)

⊘ 36660 Catheterization, umbilical artery, newborn, for diagnosis or therapy

(Do not report modifier 63 in conjunction with 36660)

Intraosseous

36680 Placement of needle for intraosseous infusion

Hemodialysis Access, Intervascular Cannulation for Extracorporeal Circulation, or Shunt Insertion

36800 Insertion of cannula for hemodialysis, other purpose (separate procedure); vein to vein

36810 arteriovenous, external (Scribner type)

36815 arteriovenous, external revision, or closure

36818 Arteriovenous anastomosis, open; by upper arm cephalic vein transposition

(Do not report 36818 in conjunction with 36819, 36820, 36821, 36830 during a unilateral upper extremity procedure. For bilateral upper extremity open arteriovenous anastomoses performed at the same operative session, use modifier 50 or 59 as appropriate)

36819 by upper arm basilic vein transposition

(Do not report 36819 in conjunction with 36818, 36820, 36821, 36830 during a unilateral upper extremity procedure. For bilateral upper extremity open arteriovenous anastomoses performed at the same operative session, use modifier 50 or 59 as appropriate)

36820 by forearm vein transposition

36821 direct, any site (eg, Cimino type) (separate procedure)

36822 Insertion of cannula(s) for prolonged extracorporeal circulation for cardiopulmonary insufficiency (ECMO) (separate procedure)

(For maintenance of prolonged extracorporeal circulation, see 33960, 33961)

36823 Insertion of arterial and venous cannula(s) for isolated extracorporeal circulation including regional chemotherapy perfusion to an extremity, with or without hyperthermia, with removal of cannula(s) and repair of arteriotomy and venotomy sites

(36823 includes chemotherapy perfusion supported by a membrane oxygenator/perfusion pump. Do not report 96409-96425 in conjunction with 36823)

36825 Creation of arteriovenous fistula by other than direct arteriovenous anastomosis (separate procedure); autogenous graft

(For direct arteriovenous anastomosis, use 36821)

36830 nonautogenous graft (eg, biological collagen, thermoplastic graft)

(For direct arteriovenous anastomosis, use 36821)

36831 Thrombectomy, open, arteriovenous fistula without revision, autogenous or nonautogenous dialysis graft (separate procedure)

36832 Revision, open, arteriovenous fistula; without thrombectomy, autogenous or nonautogenous dialysis graft (separate procedure)

36833 with thrombectomy, autogenous or nonautogenous dialysis graft (separate procedure)

36834 Plastic repair of arteriovenous aneurysm (separate procedure)

36835 Insertion of Thomas shunt (separate procedure)

36838 Distal revascularization and interval ligation (DRIL), upper extremity hemodialysis access (steal syndrome)

(Do not report 36838 in conjunction with 35512, 35522, 36832, 37607, 37618)

36860 External cannula declotting (separate procedure); without balloon catheter

36861 with balloon catheter

(If imaging guidance is performed, use 76000)

⊙ **36870** Thrombectomy, percutaneous, arteriovenous fistula, autogenous or nonautogenous graft (includes mechanical thrombus extraction and intra-graft thrombolysis)

(Do not report 36550 in conjunction with 36870)

(For catheterization, use 36145)

(For radiological supervision and interpretation, use 75790)

Portal Decompression Procedures

37140 Venous anastomosis, open; portocaval

(For peritoneal-venous shunt, use 49425)

37145 renoportal

37160 caval-mesenteric

37180 splenorenal, proximal

37181 splenorenal, distal (selective decompression of esophagogastric varices, any technique)

(For percutaneous procedure, use 37182)

37182 Insertion of transvenous intrahepatic portosystemic shunt(s) (TIPS) (includes venous access, hepatic and portal vein catheterization, portography with hemodynamic evaluation, intrahepatic tract formation/dilatation, stent placement and all associated imaging guidance and documentation)

(Do not report 75885 or 75887 in conjunction with 37182)

(For open procedure, use 37140)

37183 Revision of transvenous intrahepatic portosystemic shunt(s) (TIPS) (includes venous access, hepatic and portal vein catheterization, portography with hemodynamic evaluation, intrahepatic tract recanulization/dilatation, stent placement and all associated imaging guidance and documentation)

(Do not report 75885 or 75887 in conjunction with 37183)

(For repair of arteriovenous aneurysm, use 36834)

Transcatheter Procedures

Codes for catheter placement and the radiologic supervision and interpretation should also be reported, in addition to the code(s) for the therapeutic aspect of the procedure.

Mechanical Thrombectomy

Code(s) for catheter placement(s), diagnostic studies, and other percutaneous interventions (eg, transluminal balloon angioplasty, stent placement) provided are separately reportable.

Codes 37184-37188 specifically include intraprocedural fluoroscopic radiological supervision and interpretation services for guidance of the procedure.

Surgery: Cardiovascular System

Intraprocedural injection(s) of a thrombolytic agent is an included service and not separately reportable in conjunction with mechanical thrombectomy. However, subsequent or prior continuous infusion of a thrombolytic is not an included service and is separately reportable (see 37201, 75896, 75898).

For coronary mechanical thrombectomy, use 92973.

For mechanical thrombectomy for dialysis fistula, use 36870.

Arterial Mechanical Thrombectomy

Arterial mechanical thrombectomy may be performed as a "primary" transcatheter procedure with pretreatment planning, performance of the procedure, and postprocedure evaluation focused on providing this service. Primary mechanical thrombectomy is reported per vascular family using 37184 for the initial vessel treated and 37185 for second or all subsequent vessel(s) within the same vascular family. To report mechanical thrombectomy of an additional vascular family treated through a separate access site, use modifier 51 in conjunction with 37184-37185.

Do NOT report 37184-37185 for mechanical thrombectomy performed for treatment of thrombus or embolus complicating other percutaneous interventional procedures. See 37186 for these procedures.

Arterial mechanical thrombectomy is considered a "secondary" transcatheter procedure for removal or retrieval of short segments of thrombus or embolus when performed either before or after another percutaneous intervention (eg, percutaneous transluminal balloon angioplasty, stent placement). Secondary mechanical thrombectomy is reported using 37186. Do NOT report 37186 in conjunction with 37184-37185.

Venous Mechanical Thrombectomy

Use 37187 to report the initial application of venous mechanical thrombectomy. To report bilateral venous mechanical thrombectomy performed through a separate access site(s), use modifier 50 in conjunction with 37187. For repeat treatment on a subsequent day during a course of thrombolytic therapy, use 37188.

Arterial Mechanical Thrombectomy

⊙ **37184** Primary percutaneous transluminal mechanical thrombectomy, noncoronary, arterial or arterial bypass graft, including fluoroscopic guidance and intraprocedural pharmacological thrombolytic injection(s); initial vessel

(Do not report 37184 in conjunction with 76000, 76001, 90774, 99143-99150)

⊙+ **37185** second and all subsequent vessel(s) within the same vascular family (List separately in addition to code for primary mechanical thrombectomy procedure)

(Do not report 37185 in conjunction with 76000, 76001, 90775)

⊙+ **37186** Secondary percutaneous transluminal thrombectomy (eg, nonprimary mechanical, snare basket, suction technique), noncoronary, arterial or arterial bypass graft, including fluoroscopic guidance and intraprocedural pharmacological thrombolytic injections, provided in conjunction with another percutaneous intervention other than primary mechanical thrombectomy (List separately in addition to code for primary procedure)

(Do not report 37186 in conjunction with 76000, 76001, 90775)

Venous Mechanical Thrombectomy

⊙ **37187** Percutaneous transluminal mechanical thrombectomy, vein(s), including intraprocedural pharmacological thrombolytic injections and fluoroscopic guidance

(Do not report 37187 in conjunction with 76000, 76001, 90775)

⊙ **37188** Percutaneous transluminal mechanical thrombectomy, vein(s), including intraprocedural pharmacological thrombolytic injections and fluoroscopic guidance, repeat treatment on subsequent day during course of thrombolytic therapy

(Do not report 37188 in conjunction with 76000, 76001, 90775)

Other Procedures

37195 Thrombolysis, cerebral, by intravenous infusion

37200 Transcatheter biopsy

(For radiological supervision and interpretation, use 75970)

37201 Transcatheter therapy, infusion for thrombolysis other than coronary

(For radiological supervision and interpretation, use 75896)

37202 Transcatheter therapy, infusion other than for thrombolysis, any type (eg, spasmolytic, vasoconstrictive)

(For thrombolysis of coronary vessels, see 92975, 92977)

(For radiological supervision and interpretation, use 75896)

⊙ **37203** Transcatheter retrieval, percutaneous, of intravascular foreign body (eg, fractured venous or arterial catheter)

(For radiological supervision and interpretation, use 75961)

37204 Transcatheter occlusion or embolization (eg, for tumor destruction, to achieve hemostasis, to occlude a vascular malformation), percutaneous, any method, non-central nervous system, non-head or neck

(See also 61624, 61626)

(For radiological supervision and interpretation, use 75894)

Surgery: Cardiovascular System

►(For uterine fibroid embolization [uterine artery embolization performed to treat uterine fibroids], use 37210)◄

►(For obstetrical and gynecologic embolization procedures other than uterine fibroid embolization [eg, embolization to treat obstetrical or postpartum hemorrhage], use 37204)◄

37205 Transcatheter placement of an intravascular stent(s), (except coronary, carotid, and vertebral vessel), percutaneous; initial vessel

(For radiological supervision and interpretation, use 75960)

(For coronary stent placement, see 92980, 92981; intracranial, use 61635)

+ 37206 each additional vessel (List separately in addition to code for primary procedure)

(Use 37206 in conjunction with 37205)

(For transcatheter placement of intravascular cervical carotid artery stent(s), see 37215, 37216)

(For transcatheter placement of extracranial vertebral or intrathoracic carotid artery stent(s), see Category III codes 0075T, 0076T)

(For radiological supervision and interpretation, use 75960)

37207 Transcatheter placement of an intravascular stent(s), (non-coronary vessel), open; initial vessel

+ 37208 each additional vessel (List separately in addition to code for primary procedure)

(Use 37208 in conjunction with 37207)

(For radiological supervision and interpretation, use 75960)

(For catheterizations, see 36215-36248)

(For transcatheter placement of intracoronary stent(s), see 92980, 92981)

37209 Exchange of a previously placed intravascular catheter during thrombolytic therapy

(For radiological supervision and interpretation, use 75900)

⊙● 37210 Uterine fibroid embolization (UFE, embolization of the uterine arteries to treat uterine fibroids, leiomyomata), percutaneous approach inclusive of vascular access, vessel selection, embolization, and all radiological supervision and interpretation, intraprocedural roadmapping, and imaging guidance necessary to complete the procedure

►(37210 includes all catheterizations and intraprocedural imaging required for a UFE procedure to confirm the presence of previously known fibroids and to roadmap vascular anatomy to enable appropriate therapy)◄

►(Do not report 37210 in conjunction with 36200, 36245-36248, 37204, 75894, 75898)◄

►(For all other non-central nervous system (CNS) embolization procedures, use 37204)◄

⊙ 37215 Transcatheter placement of intravascular stent(s), cervical carotid artery, percutaneous; with distal embolic protection

⊙ 37216 without distal embolic protection

(37215 and 37216 include all ipsilateral selective carotid catheterization, all diagnostic imaging for ipsilateral, cervical and cerebral carotid arteriography, and all related radiological supervision and interpretation. When ipsilateral carotid arteriogram (including imaging and selective catheterization) confirms the need for carotid stenting, 37215 and 37216 are inclusive of these services. If carotid stenting is not indicated, then the appropriate codes for carotid catheterization and imaging should be reported in lieu of 37215 and 37216)

(Do not report 37215, 37216 in conjunction with 75671, 75680)

(For transcatheter placement of extracranial vertebral or intrathoracic carotid artery stent(s), see Category III codes 0075T, 0076T)

(For percutaneous transcatheter placement of intravascular stents other than coronary, carotid, or vertebral, see 37205, 37206)

Intravascular Ultrasound Services

Intravascular ultrasound services include all transducer manipulations and repositioning within the specific vessel being examined, both before and after therapeutic intervention (eg, stent placement).

Vascular access for intravascular ultrasound performed during a therapeutic intervention is not reported separately.

+ 37250 Intravascular ultrasound (non-coronary vessel) during diagnostic evaluation and/or therapeutic intervention; initial vessel (List separately in addition to code for primary procedure)

+ 37251 each additional vessel (List separately in addition to code for primary procedure)

(Use 37251 in conjunction with 37250)

(For catheterizations, see 36215-36248)

(For transcatheter therapies, see 37200-37208, 61624, 61626)

(For radiological supervision and interpretation see 75945, 75946)

Surgery: Cardiovascular System

Endoscopy

Surgical vascular endoscopy always includes diagnostic endoscopy.

37500 Vascular endoscopy, surgical, with ligation of perforator veins, subfascial (SEPS)

(For open procedure, use 37760)

37501 Unlisted vascular endoscopy procedure

Ligation

(For phleborraphy and arteriorraphy, see 35201-35286)

37565 Ligation, internal jugular vein

37600 Ligation; external carotid artery

37605 internal or common carotid artery

37606 internal or common carotid artery, with gradual occlusion, as with Selverstone or Crutchfield clamp

(For transcatheter permanent arterial occlusion or embolization, see 61624-61626)

(For endovascular temporary arterial balloon occlusion, use 61623)

(For ligation treatment of intracranial aneurysm, use 61703)

37607 Ligation or banding of angioaccess arteriovenous fistula

37609 Ligation or biopsy, temporal artery

37615 Ligation, major artery (eg, post-traumatic, rupture); neck

37616 chest

37617 abdomen

37618 extremity

37620 Interruption, partial or complete, of inferior vena cava by suture, ligation, plication, clip, extravascular, intravascular (umbrella device)

(For radiological supervision and interpretation, use 75940)

37650 Ligation of femoral vein

(For bilateral procedure, report 37650 with modifier 50)

37660 Ligation of common iliac vein

37700 Ligation and division of long saphenous vein at saphenofemoral junction, or distal interruptions

(Do not report 37700 in conjunction with 37718, 37722)

(For bilateral procedure, report 37700 with modifier 50)

37718 Ligation, division, and stripping, short saphenous vein

(For bilateral procedure, use modifier 50)

(Do not report 37718 in conjunction with 37735, 37780)

(37720 has been deleted)

37722 Ligation, division, and stripping, long (greater) saphenous veins from saphenofemoral junction to knee or below

(For ligation and stripping of the short saphenous vein, use 37718)

(For bilateral procedure, report 37722 with modifier 50)

(Do not report 37722 in conjunction with 37700, 37735)

(37730 has been deleted. For ligation, division, and stripping of the greater saphenous vein, use 37722. For ligation, division, and stripping of the short saphenous vein, use 37718)

37735 Ligation and division and complete stripping of long or short saphenous veins with radical excision of ulcer and skin graft and/or interruption of communicating veins of lower leg, with excision of deep fascia

(Do not report 37735 in conjunction with 37700, 37718, 37722, 37780)

(For bilateral procedure, report 37735 with modifier 50)

37760 Ligation of perforator veins, subfascial, radical (Linton type), with or without skin graft, open

(For endoscopic procedure, use 37500)

37765 Stab phlebectomy of varicose veins, one extremity; 10-20 stab incisions

(For less than 10 incisions, use 37799)

(For more than 20 incisions, use 37766)

37766 more than 20 incisions

37780 Ligation and division of short saphenous vein at saphenopopliteal junction (separate procedure)

(For bilateral procedure, report 37780 with modifier 50)

37785 Ligation, division, and/or excision of varicose vein cluster(s), one leg

(For bilateral procedure, report 37785 with modifier 50)

Other Procedures

37788 Penile revascularization, artery, with or without vein graft

37790 Penile venous occlusive procedure

37799 Unlisted procedure, vascular surgery

Hemic and Lymphatic Systems

Spleen

Excision

38100 Splenectomy; total (separate procedure)

38101 partial (separate procedure)

+ 38102 total, en bloc for extensive disease, in conjunction with other procedure (List in addition to code for primary procedure)

Surgery: Cardiovascular System

Repair

38115 Repair of ruptured spleen (splenorrhaphy) with or without partial splenectomy

Laparoscopy

Surgical laparoscopy always includes diagnostic laparoscopy. To report a diagnostic laparoscopy (peritoneoscopy) (separate procedure), use 49320.

38120 Laparoscopy, surgical, splenectomy

38129 Unlisted laparoscopy procedure, spleen

Introduction

38200 Injection procedure for splenoportography

(For radiological supervision and interpretation, use 75810)

General

Bone Marrow or Stem Cell Services/Procedures

Codes 38207-38215 describe various steps used to preserve, prepare and purify bone marrow/stem cells prior to transplantation or reinfusion. Each code may be reported only once per day regardless of the quantity of bone marrow/stem cells manipulated.

38204 Management of recipient hematopoietic progenitor cell donor search and cell acquisition

38205 Blood-derived hematopoietic progenitor cell harvesting for transplantation, per collection; allogenic

38206 autologous

38207 Transplant preparation of hematopoietic progenitor cells; cryopreservation and storage

(For diagnostic cryopreservation and storage, see 88240)

38208 thawing of previously frozen harvest, without washing

(For diagnostic thawing and expansion of frozen cells, see 88241)

38209 thawing of previously frozen harvest, with washing

38210 specific cell depletion within harvest, T-cell depletion

38211 tumor cell depletion

38212 red blood cell removal

38213 platelet depletion

38214 plasma (volume) depletion

38215 cell concentration in plasma, mononuclear, or buffy coat layer

(Do not report 38207-38215 in conjunction with 88182, 88184-88189)

38220 Bone marrow; aspiration only

38221 biopsy, needle or trocar

(For bone marrow biopsy interpretation, use 88305)

38230 Bone marrow harvesting for transplantation

(For autologous and allogenic blood-derived peripheral stem cell harvesting for transplantation, see 38205-38206)

38240 Bone marrow or blood-derived peripheral stem cell transplantation; allogenic

38241 autologous

38242 allogeneic donor lymphocyte infusions

(For bone marrow aspiration, use 38220)

(For modification, treatment, and processing of bone marrow or blood-derived stem cell specimens for transplantation, use 38210-38213)

(For cryopreservation, freezing and storage of blood-derived stem cells for transplantation, use 88240)

(For thawing and expansion of blood-derived stem cells for transplantation, use 88241)

(For compatibility studies, see 86812-86822)

Lymph Nodes and Lymphatic Channels

Incision

38300 Drainage of lymph node abscess or lymphadenitis; simple

38305 extensive

38308 Lymphangiotomy or other operations on lymphatic channels

38380 Suture and/or ligation of thoracic duct; cervical approach

38381 thoracic approach

38382 abdominal approach

Excision

(For injection for sentinel node identification, use 38792)

38500 Biopsy or excision of lymph node(s); open, superficial

(Do not report 38500 with 38700-38780)

38505 by needle, superficial (eg, cervical, inguinal, axillary)

►(If imaging guidance is performed, see 76942, 77012, 77021)◄

(For fine needle aspiration, use 10021 or 10022)

(For evaluation of fine needle aspirate, see 88172, 88173)

38510 open, deep cervical node(s)

38520 open, deep cervical node(s) with excision scalene fat pad

Surgery: Cardiovascular System

Surgery: Cardiovascular System

38525 open, deep axillary node(s)

38530 open, internal mammary node(s)

(Do not report 38530 with 38720-38746)

(For percutaneous needle biopsy, retroperitoneal lymph node or mass, use 49180. For fine needle aspiration, use 10022)

38542 Dissection, deep jugular node(s)

(For radical cervical neck dissection, use 38720)

38550 Excision of cystic hygroma, axillary or cervical; without deep neurovascular dissection

38555 with deep neurovascular dissection

Limited Lymphadenectomy for Staging

38562 Limited lymphadenectomy for staging (separate procedure); pelvic and para-aortic

(When combined with prostatectomy, use 55812 or 55842)

(When combined with insertion of radioactive substance into prostate, use 55862)

38564 retroperitoneal (aortic and/or splenic)

Laparoscopy

Surgical laparoscopy always includes diagnostic laparoscopy. To report a diagnostic laparoscopy (peritoneoscopy) (separate procedure), use 49320.

38570 Laparoscopy, surgical; with retroperitoneal lymph node sampling (biopsy), single or multiple

38571 with bilateral total pelvic lymphadenectomy

38572 with bilateral total pelvic lymphadenectomy and peri-aortic lymph node sampling (biopsy), single or multiple

(For drainage of lymphocele to peritoneal cavity, use 49323)

38589 Unlisted laparoscopy procedure, lymphatic system

Radical Lymphadenectomy (Radical Resection of Lymph Nodes)

(For limited pelvic and retroperitoneal lymphadenectomies, see 38562, 38564)

38700 Suprahyoid lymphadenectomy

(For bilateral procedure, report 38700 with modifier 50)

38720 Cervical lymphadenectomy (complete)

(For bilateral procedure, report 38720 with modifier 50)

38724 Cervical lymphadenectomy (modified radical neck dissection)

38740 Axillary lymphadenectomy; superficial

38745 complete

+ 38746 Thoracic lymphadenectomy, regional, including mediastinal and peritracheal nodes (List separately in addition to code for primary procedure)

+ 38747 Abdominal lymphadenectomy, regional, including celiac, gastric, portal, peripancreatic, with or without para-aortic and vena caval nodes (List separately in addition to code for primary procedure)

38760 Inguinofemoral lymphadenectomy, superficial, including Cloquets node (separate procedure)

(For bilateral procedure, report 38760 with modifier 50)

38765 Inguinofemoral lymphadenectomy, superficial, in continuity with pelvic lymphadenectomy, including external iliac, hypogastric, and obturator nodes (separate procedure)

(For bilateral procedure, report 38765 with modifier 50)

38770 Pelvic lymphadenectomy, including external iliac, hypogastric, and obturator nodes (separate procedure)

(For bilateral procedure, report 38770 with modifier 50)

38780 Retroperitoneal transabdominal lymphadenectomy, extensive, including pelvic, aortic, and renal nodes (separate procedure)

▶(For excision and repair of lymphedematous skin and subcutaneous tissue, see 15004-15005, 15570-15650)◀

Introduction

38790 Injection procedure; lymphangiography

(For bilateral procedure, report 38790 with modifier 50)

(For radiological supervision and interpretation, see 75801-75807)

⊘ **38792** for identification of sentinel node

(For excision of sentinel node, see 38500-38542)

(For nuclear medicine lymphatics and lymph gland imaging, use 78195)

38794 Cannulation, thoracic duct

Other Procedures

38999 Unlisted procedure, hemic or lymphatic system

Mediastinum and Diaphragm

Mediastinum

Incision

39000 Mediastinotomy with exploration, drainage, removal of foreign body, or biopsy; cervical approach

39010 transthoracic approach, including either transthoracic or median sternotomy

Excision

39200 Excision of mediastinal cyst

39220 Excision of mediastinal tumor

(For substernal thyroidectomy, use 60270)

(For thymectomy, use 60520)

Endoscopy

39400 Mediastinoscopy, with or without biopsy

Other Procedures

39499 Unlisted procedure, mediastinum

Diaphragm

Repair

(For transabdominal repair of diaphragmatic (esophageal hiatal) hernia, see 43324, 43325)

39501 Repair, laceration of diaphragm, any approach

39502 Repair, paraesophageal hiatus hernia, transabdominal, with or without fundoplasty, vagotomy, and/or pyloroplasty, except neonatal

39503 Repair, neonatal diaphragmatic hernia, with or without chest tube insertion and with or without creation of ventral hernia

(Do not report modifier 63 in conjunction with 39503)

39520 Repair, diaphragmatic hernia (esophageal hiatal); transthoracic

39530 combined, thoracoabdominal

39531 combined, thoracoabdominal, with dilation of stricture (with or without gastroplasty)

39540 Repair, diaphragmatic hernia (other than neonatal), traumatic; acute

39541 chronic

39545 Imbrication of diaphragm for eventration, transthoracic or transabdominal, paralytic or nonparalytic

39560 Resection, diaphragm; with simple repair (eg, primary suture)

39561 with complex repair (eg, prosthetic material, local muscle flap)

Other Procedures

39599 Unlisted procedure, diaphragm

Surgery: Cardiovascular System

Notes

Digestive System

Lips

(For procedures on skin of lips, see 10040 et seq)

Excision

40490 Biopsy of lip

40500 Vermilionectomy (lip shave), with mucosal advancement

40510 Excision of lip; transverse wedge excision with primary closure

40520 V-excision with primary direct linear closure

(For excision of mucous lesions, see 40810-40816)

40525 full thickness, reconstruction with local flap (eg, Estlander or fan)

40527 full thickness, reconstruction with cross lip flap (Abbe-Estlander)

40530 Resection of lip, more than one-fourth, without reconstruction

(For reconstruction, see 13131 et seq)

Repair (Cheiloplasty)

40650 Repair lip, full thickness; vermilion only

40652 up to half vertical height

40654 over one-half vertical height, or complex

40700 Plastic repair of cleft lip/nasal deformity; primary, partial or complete, unilateral

40701 primary bilateral, one stage procedure

40702 primary bilateral, one of two stages

40720 secondary, by recreation of defect and reclosure

(For bilateral procedure, report 40720 with modifier 50)

(To report rhinoplasty only for nasal deformity secondary to congenital cleft lip, see 30460, 30462)

(For repair of cleft lip, with cross lip pedicle flap (Abbe-Estlander type), use 40527)

40761 with cross lip pedicle flap (Abbe-Estlander type), including sectioning and inserting of pedicle

(For repair cleft palate, see 42200 et seq)

(For other reconstructive procedures, see 14060, 14061, 15120-15261, 15574, 15576, 15630)

Other Procedures

40799 Unlisted procedure, lips

Vestibule of Mouth

The vestibule is the part of the oral cavity outside the dentoalveolar structures; it includes the mucosal and submucosal tissue of lips and cheeks.

Incision

40800 Drainage of abscess, cyst, hematoma, vestibule of mouth; simple

40801 complicated

40804 Removal of embedded foreign body, vestibule of mouth; simple

40805 complicated

40806 Incision of labial frenum (frenotomy)

Excision, Destruction

40808 Biopsy, vestibule of mouth

40810 Excision of lesion of mucosa and submucosa, vestibule of mouth; without repair

40812 with simple repair

40814 with complex repair

40816 complex, with excision of underlying muscle

40818 Excision of mucosa of vestibule of mouth as donor graft

40819 Excision of frenum, labial or buccal (frenumectomy, frenulectomy, frenectomy)

40820 Destruction of lesion or scar of vestibule of mouth by physical methods (eg, laser, thermal, cryo, chemical)

Repair

40830 Closure of laceration, vestibule of mouth; 2.5 cm or less

40831 over 2.5 cm or complex

40840 Vestibuloplasty; anterior

40842 posterior, unilateral

40843 posterior, bilateral

40844 entire arch

40845 complex (including ridge extension, muscle repositioning)

►(For skin grafts, see 15002 et seq)◄

Other Procedures

40899 Unlisted procedure, vestibule of mouth

Tongue and Floor of Mouth

Incision

41000 Intraoral incision and drainage of abscess, cyst, or hematoma of tongue or floor of mouth; lingual

41005 sublingual, superficial

41006 sublingual, deep, supramylohyoid

41007 submental space

41008 submandibular space

41009 masticator space

41010 Incision of lingual frenum (frenotomy)

41015 Extraoral incision and drainage of abscess, cyst, or hematoma of floor of mouth; sublingual

41016 submental

41017 submandibular

41018 masticator space

(For frenoplasty, use 41520)

Excision

41100 Biopsy of tongue; anterior two-thirds

41105 posterior one-third

41108 Biopsy of floor of mouth

41110 Excision of lesion of tongue without closure

41112 Excision of lesion of tongue with closure; anterior two-thirds

41113 posterior one-third

41114 with local tongue flap

(List 41114 in addition to code 41112 or 41113)

41115 Excision of lingual frenum (frenectomy)

41116 Excision, lesion of floor of mouth

41120 Glossectomy; less than one-half tongue

41130 hemiglossectomy

41135 partial, with unilateral radical neck dissection

41140 complete or total, with or without tracheostomy, without radical neck dissection

41145 complete or total, with or without tracheostomy, with unilateral radical neck dissection

41150 composite procedure with resection floor of mouth and mandibular resection, without radical neck dissection

41153 composite procedure with resection floor of mouth, with suprahyoid neck dissection

41155 composite procedure with resection floor of mouth, mandibular resection, and radical neck dissection (Commando type)

Repair

41250 Repair of laceration 2.5 cm or less; floor of mouth and/or anterior two-thirds of tongue

41251 posterior one-third of tongue

41252 Repair of laceration of tongue, floor of mouth, over 2.6 cm or complex

Other Procedures

41500 Fixation of tongue, mechanical, other than suture (eg, K-wire)

41510 Suture of tongue to lip for micrognathia (Douglas type procedure)

41520 Frenoplasty (surgical revision of frenum, eg, with Z-plasty)

(For frenotomy, see 40806, 41010)

41599 Unlisted procedure, tongue, floor of mouth

Dentoalveolar Structures

Incision

41800 Drainage of abscess, cyst, hematoma from dentoalveolar structures

41805 Removal of embedded foreign body from dentoalveolar structures; soft tissues

41806 bone

Excision, Destruction

41820 Gingivectomy, excision gingiva, each quadrant

41821 Operculectomy, excision pericoronal tissues

41822 Excision of fibrous tuberosities, dentoalveolar structures

41823 Excision of osseous tuberosities, dentoalveolar structures

41825 Excision of lesion or tumor (except listed above), dentoalveolar structures; without repair

41826 with simple repair

41827 with complex repair

(For nonexcisional destruction, use 41850)

41828 Excision of hyperplastic alveolar mucosa, each quadrant (specify)

41830 Alveolectomy, including curettage of osteitis or sequestrectomy

41850 Destruction of lesion (except excision), dentoalveolar structures

Other Procedures

41870 Periodontal mucosal grafting

41872 Gingivoplasty, each quadrant (specify)

41874	Alveoloplasty, each quadrant (specify)
	(For closure of lacerations, see 40830, 40831)
	(For segmental osteotomy, use 21206)
	(For reduction of fractures, see 21421-21490)
41899	Unlisted procedure, dentoalveolar structures

Palate and Uvula

Incision

42000	Drainage of abscess of palate, uvula

Excision, Destruction

42100	Biopsy of palate, uvula
42104	Excision, lesion of palate, uvula; without closure
42106	with simple primary closure
42107	with local flap closure
	(For skin graft, see 14040-14300)
	(For mucosal graft, use 40818)
42120	Resection of palate or extensive resection of lesion
	(For reconstruction of palate with extraoral tissue, see 14040-14300, 15050, 15120, 15240, 15576)
42140	Uvulectomy, excision of uvula
42145	Palatopharyngoplasty (eg, uvulopalatopharyngoplasty, uvulopharyngoplasty)
	(For removal of exostosis of the bony palate, see 21031, 21032)
42160	Destruction of lesion, palate or uvula (thermal, cryo or chemical)

Repair

42180	Repair, laceration of palate; up to 2 cm
42182	over 2 cm or complex
42200	Palatoplasty for cleft palate, soft and/or hard palate only
42205	Palatoplasty for cleft palate, with closure of alveolar ridge; soft tissue only
42210	with bone graft to alveolar ridge (includes obtaining graft)
42215	Palatoplasty for cleft palate; major revision
42220	secondary lengthening procedure
42225	attachment pharyngeal flap
42226	Lengthening of palate, and pharyngeal flap
42227	Lengthening of palate, with island flap
42235	Repair of anterior palate, including vomer flap
	(For repair of oronasal fistula, use 30600)

42260	Repair of nasolabial fistula
	(For repair of cleft lip, see 40700 et seq)
42280	Maxillary impression for palatal prosthesis
42281	Insertion of pin-retained palatal prosthesis

Other Procedures

42299	Unlisted procedure, palate, uvula

Salivary Gland and Ducts

Incision

42300	Drainage of abscess; parotid, simple
42305	parotid, complicated
42310	Drainage of abscess; submaxillary or sublingual, intraoral
42320	submaxillary, external
	(42325, 42326 have been deleted)
42330	Sialolithotomy; submandibular (submaxillary), sublingual or parotid, uncomplicated, intraoral
42335	submandibular (submaxillary), complicated, intraoral
42340	parotid, extraoral or complicated intraoral

Excision

42400	Biopsy of salivary gland; needle
	(For fine needle aspiration, see 10021, 10022)
	(For evaluation of fine needle aspirate, see 88172, 88173)
	►(If imaging guidance is performed, see 76942, 77002, 77012, 77021)◄
42405	incisional
	►(If imaging guidance is performed, see 76942, 77002, 77012, 77021)◄
42408	Excision of sublingual salivary cyst (ranula)
42409	Marsupialization of sublingual salivary cyst (ranula)
42410	Excision of parotid tumor or parotid gland; lateral lobe, without nerve dissection
42415	lateral lobe, with dissection and preservation of facial nerve
42420	total, with dissection and preservation of facial nerve
42425	total, en bloc removal with sacrifice of facial nerve
42426	total, with unilateral radical neck dissection
	(For suture or grafting of facial nerve, see 64864, 64865, 69740, 69745)
42440	Excision of submandibular (submaxillary) gland
42450	Excision of sublingual gland

Surgery: Digestive System

Repair

42500 Plastic repair of salivary duct, sialodochoplasty; primary or simple

42505 secondary or complicated

42507 Parotid duct diversion, bilateral (Wilke type procedure);

42508 with excision of one submandibular gland

42509 with excision of both submandibular glands

42510 with ligation of both submandibular (Wharton's) ducts

Other Procedures

42550 Injection procedure for sialography

(For radiological supervision and interpretation, use 70390)

42600 Closure salivary fistula

42650 Dilation salivary duct

42660 Dilation and catheterization of salivary duct, with or without injection

42665 Ligation salivary duct, intraoral

42699 Unlisted procedure, salivary glands or ducts

Pharynx, Adenoids, and Tonsils

Incision

42700 Incision and drainage abscess; peritonsillar

42720 retropharyngeal or parapharyngeal, intraoral approach

42725 retropharyngeal or parapharyngeal, external approach

Excision, Destruction

42800 Biopsy; oropharynx

42802 hypopharynx

42804 nasopharynx, visible lesion, simple

42806 nasopharynx, survey for unknown primary lesion

(For laryngoscopic biopsy, see 31510, 31535, 31536)

42808 Excision or destruction of lesion of pharynx, any method

42809 Removal of foreign body from pharynx

42810 Excision branchial cleft cyst or vestige, confined to skin and subcutaneous tissues

42815 Excision branchial cleft cyst, vestige, or fistula, extending beneath subcutaneous tissues and/or into pharynx

42820 Tonsillectomy and adenoidectomy; younger than age 12

42821 age 12 or over

42825 Tonsillectomy, primary or secondary; younger than age 12

42826 age 12 or over

42830 Adenoidectomy, primary; younger than age 12

42831 age 12 or over

42835 Adenoidectomy, secondary; younger than age 12

42836 age 12 or over

42842 Radical resection of tonsil, tonsillar pillars, and/or retromolar trigone; without closure

42844 closure with local flap (eg, tongue, buccal)

42845 closure with other flap

(For closure with other flap(s), use appropriate number for flap(s))

(When combined with radical neck dissection, use also 38720)

42860 Excision of tonsil tags

42870 Excision or destruction lingual tonsil, any method (separate procedure)

(For resection of the nasopharynx (eg, juvenile angiofibroma) by bicoronal and/or transzygomatic approach, see 61586 and 61600)

42890 Limited pharyngectomy

42892 Resection of lateral pharyngeal wall or pyriform sinus, direct closure by advancement of lateral and posterior pharyngeal walls

(When combined with radical neck dissection, use also 38720)

42894 Resection of pharyngeal wall requiring closure with myocutaneous flap

(When combined with radical neck dissection, use also 38720)

(For limited pharyngectomy with radical neck dissection, use 38720 with 42890)

Repair

42900 Suture pharynx for wound or injury

42950 Pharyngoplasty (plastic or reconstructive operation on pharynx)

(For pharyngeal flap, use 42225)

42953 Pharyngoesophageal repair

(For closure with myocutaneous or other flap, use appropriate number in addition)

Other Procedures

42955 Pharyngostomy (fistulization of pharynx, external for feeding)

42960 Control oropharyngeal hemorrhage, primary or secondary (eg, post-tonsillectomy); simple

42961 complicated, requiring hospitalization

42962 with secondary surgical intervention

⊙ =Moderate sedation ✚ =Add-on code ✗ =FDA approval pending

Surgery: Digestive System

42970 Control of nasopharyngeal hemorrhage, primary or secondary (eg, postadenoidectomy); simple, with posterior nasal packs, with or without anterior packs and/or cautery

42971 complicated, requiring hospitalization

42972 with secondary surgical intervention

42999 Unlisted procedure, pharynx, adenoids, or tonsils

Esophagus

Incision

(For esophageal intubation with laparotomy, use 43510)

43020 Esophagotomy, cervical approach, with removal of foreign body

43030 Cricopharyngeal myotomy

43045 Esophagotomy, thoracic approach, with removal of foreign body

Excision

(For gastrointestinal reconstruction for previous esophagectomy, see 43360, 43361)

43100 Excision of lesion, esophagus, with primary repair; cervical approach

43101 thoracic or abdominal approach

(For wide excision of malignant lesion of cervical esophagus, with total laryngectomy without radical neck dissection, see 43107, 43116, 43124, and 31360)

(For wide excision of malignant lesion of cervical esophagus, with total laryngectomy with radical neck dissection, see 43107, 43116, 43124, and 31365)

43107 Total or near total esophagectomy, without thoracotomy; with pharyngogastrostomy or cervical esophagogastrostomy, with or without pyloroplasty (transhiatal)

43108 with colon interposition or small intestine reconstruction, including intestine mobilization, preparation and anastomosis(es)

43112 Total or near total esophagectomy, with thoracotomy; with pharyngogastrostomy or cervical esophagogastrostomy, with or without pyloroplasty

43113 with colon interposition or small intestine reconstruction, including intestine mobilization, preparation, and anastomosis(es)

43116 Partial esophagectomy, cervical, with free intestinal graft, including microvascular anastomosis, obtaining the graft and intestinal reconstruction

(Do not report 43116 in conjunction with 69990)

(Report 43116 with the modifier 52 appended if intestinal or free jejunal graft with microvascular anastomosis is performed by another physician)

(For free jejunal graft with microvascular anastomosis performed by another physician, use 43496)

43117 Partial esophagectomy, distal two-thirds, with thoracotomy and separate abdominal incision, with or without proximal gastrectomy; with thoracic esophagogastrostomy, with or without pyloroplasty (Ivor Lewis)

43118 with colon interposition or small intestine reconstruction, including intestine mobilization, preparation, and anastomosis(es)

(For total esophagectomy with gastropharyngostomy, see 43107, 43124)

(For esophagogastrectomy (lower third) and vagotomy, use 43122)

43121 Partial esophagectomy, distal two-thirds, with thoracotomy only, with or without proximal gastrectomy, with thoracic esophagogastrostomy, with or without pyloroplasty

43122 Partial esophagectomy, thoracoabdominal or abdominal approach, with or without proximal gastrectomy; with esophagogastrostomy, with or without pyloroplasty

43123 with colon interposition or small intestine reconstruction, including intestine mobilization, preparation, and anastomosis(es)

43124 Total or partial esophagectomy, without reconstruction (any approach), with cervical esophagostomy

43130 Diverticulectomy of hypopharynx or esophagus, with or without myotomy; cervical approach

43135 thoracic approach

Endoscopy

For endoscopic procedures, code appropriate endoscopy of each anatomic site examined.

Surgical endoscopy always includes diagnostic endoscopy.

⊙ **43200** Esophagoscopy, rigid or flexible; diagnostic, with or without collection of specimen(s) by brushing or washing (separate procedure)

⊙ **43201** with directed submucosal injection(s), any substance

(For injection sclerosis of esophageal varices, use 43204)

⊙ **43202** with biopsy, single or multiple

⊙ **43204** with injection sclerosis of esophageal varices

⊙ **43205** with band ligation of esophageal varices

⊙ **43215** with removal of foreign body

(For radiological supervision and interpretation, use 74235)

⊙ **43216** with removal of tumor(s), polyp(s), or other lesion(s) by hot biopsy forceps or bipolar cautery

⊙ **43217** with removal of tumor(s), polyp(s), or other lesion(s) by snare technique

⊙ **43219** with insertion of plastic tube or stent

⊙ **43220** with balloon dilation (less than 30 mm diameter)

(If imaging guidance is performed, use 74360)

(For endoscopic dilation with balloon 30 mm diameter or larger, use 43458)

(For dilation without visualization, use 43450-43453)

(For diagnostic fiberoptic esophagogastroscopy, use 43200, 43235)

(For fiberoptic esophagogastroscopy with biopsy or collection of specimen, use 43200, 43202, 43235, 43239)

(For fiberoptic esophagogastroscopy with removal of foreign body, use 43215, 43247)

(For fiberoptic esophagogastroscopy with removal of polyp(s), use 43217, 43251)

⊙ **43226** with insertion of guide wire followed by dilation over guide wire

(For radiological supervision and interpretation, use 74360)

⊙ **43227** with control of bleeding (eg, injection, bipolar cautery, unipolar cautery, laser, heater probe, stapler, plasma coagulator)

⊙ **43228** with ablation of tumor(s), polyp(s), or other lesion(s), not amenable to removal by hot biopsy forceps, bipolar cautery or snare technique

(For esophagoscopic photodynamic therapy, report 43228 in addition to 96570, 96571 as appropriate)

⊙ **43231** with endoscopic ultrasound examination

(Do not report 43231 in conjunction with 76975)

⊙ **43232** with transendoscopic ultrasound-guided intramural or transmural fine needle aspiration/biopsy(s)

(Do not report 43232 in conjunction with 76942, 76975)

(For interpretation of specimen, see 88172-88173)

⊙ **43234** Upper gastrointestinal endoscopy, simple primary examination (eg, with small diameter flexible endoscope) (separate procedure)

⊙ **43235** Upper gastrointestinal endoscopy including esophagus, stomach, and either the duodenum and/or jejunum as appropriate; diagnostic, with or without collection of specimen(s) by brushing or washing (separate procedure)

⊙ **43236** with directed submucosal injection(s), any substance

(For injection sclerosis of esophageal and/or gastric varices, use 43243)

⊙ **43237** with endoscopic ultrasound examination limited to the esophagus

(Do not report 43237 in conjunction with 76942, 76975)

⊙ **43238** with transendoscopic ultrasound-guided intramural or transmural fine needle aspiration/biopsy(s), esophagus (includes endoscopic ultrasound examination limited to the esophagus)

(Do not report 43238 in conjunction with 76942 or 76975)

⊙ **43239** with biopsy, single or multiple

(For upper gastrointestinal endoscopy with suturing of the esophagogastric junction, use Category III code 0008T)

(For upper gastrointestinal endoscopy with injection of implant material into and along the muscle of the lower esophageal sphincter, use Category III code 0133T)

⊙ **43240** with transmural drainage of pseudocyst

⊙ **43241** with transendoscopic intraluminal tube or catheter placement

⊙ **43242** with transendoscopic ultrasound-guided intramural or transmural fine needle aspiration/biopsy(s) (includes endoscopic ultrasound examination of the esophagus, stomach, and either the duodenum and/or jejunum as appropriate)

(Do not report 43242 in conjunction with 76942, 76975)

(For transendoscopic fine needle aspiration/biopsy limited to esophagus, use 43238)

(For interpretation of specimen, see 88172-88173)

⊙ **43243** with injection sclerosis of esophageal and/or gastric varices

⊙ **43244** with band ligation of esophageal and/or gastric varices

⊙ **43245** with dilation of gastric outlet for obstruction (eg, balloon, guide wire, bougie)

(Do not report 43245 in conjunction with 43256)

⊙ **43246** with directed placement of percutaneous gastrostomy tube

(For radiological supervision and interpretation, use 74350)

⊙ **43247** with removal of foreign body

(For radiological supervision and interpretation, use 74235)

⊙ **43248** with insertion of guide wire followed by dilation of esophagus over guide wire

⊙ **43249** with balloon dilation of esophagus (less than 30 mm diameter)

⊙ **43250** with removal of tumor(s), polyp(s), or other lesion(s) by hot biopsy forceps or bipolar cautery

⊙ **43251** with removal of tumor(s), polyp(s), or other lesion(s) by snare technique

⊙ **43255** with control of bleeding, any method

⊙ **43256** with transendoscopic stent placement (includes predilation)

⊙ **43257** with delivery of thermal energy to the muscle of lower esophageal sphincter and/or gastric cardia, for treatment of gastroesophageal reflux disease

⊙ **43258** with ablation of tumor(s), polyp(s), or other lesion(s) not amenable to removal by hot biopsy forceps, bipolar cautery or snare technique

(For injection sclerosis of esophageal varices, use 43204, 43243)

⊙ **43259** with endoscopic ultrasound examination, including the esophagus, stomach, and either the duodenum and/or jejunum as appropriate

(Do not report 43259 in conjunction with 76975)

⊙ **43260** Endoscopic retrograde cholangiopancreatography (ERCP); diagnostic, with or without collection of specimen(s) by brushing or washing (separate procedure)

(For radiological supervision and interpretation, see 74328, 74329, 74330)

⊙ **43261** with biopsy, single or multiple

(For radiological supervision and interpretation, see 74328, 74329, 74330)

⊙ **43262** with sphincterotomy/papillotomy

(For radiological supervision and interpretation, see 74328, 74329, 74330)

⊙ **43263** with pressure measurement of sphincter of Oddi (pancreatic duct or common bile duct)

(For radiological supervision and interpretation, see 74328, 74329, 74330)

⊙ **43264** with endoscopic retrograde removal of calculus/calculi from biliary and/or pancreatic ducts

(When done with sphincterotomy, also use 43262)

(For radiological supervision and interpretation, see 74328, 74329, 74330)

⊙ **43265** with endoscopic retrograde destruction, lithotripsy of calculus/calculi, any method

(When done with sphincterotomy, also use 43262)

(For radiological supervision and interpretation, see 74328, 74329, 74330)

⊙ **43267** with endoscopic retrograde insertion of nasobiliary or nasopancreatic drainage tube

(When done with sphincterotomy, also use 43262)

(For radiological supervision and interpretation, see 74328, 74329, 74330)

⊙ **43268** with endoscopic retrograde insertion of tube or stent into bile or pancreatic duct

(When done with sphincterotomy, also use 43262)

(For radiological supervision and interpretation, see 74328, 74329, 74330)

⊙ **43269** with endoscopic retrograde removal of foreign body and/or change of tube or stent

(When done with sphincterotomy, also use 43262)

(For radiological supervision and interpretation, see 74328, 74329, 74330)

⊙ **43271** with endoscopic retrograde balloon dilation of ampulla, biliary and/or pancreatic duct(s)

(When done with sphincterotomy, also use 43262)

(For radiological supervision and interpretation, see 74328, 74329, 74330)

⊙ **43272** with ablation of tumor(s), polyp(s), or other lesion(s) not amenable to removal by hot biopsy forceps, bipolar cautery or snare technique

(For radiological supervision and interpretation, see 74328, 74329, 74330)

Laparoscopy

Surgical laparoscopy always includes diagnostic laparoscopy. To report a diagnostic laparoscopy (peritoneoscopy) (separate procedure), use 49320.

43280 Laparoscopy, surgical, esophagogastric fundoplasty (eg, Nissen, Toupet procedures)

(For open approach, use 43324)

43289 Unlisted laparoscopy procedure, esophagus

Repair

43300 Esophagoplasty (plastic repair or reconstruction), cervical approach; without repair of tracheoesophageal fistula

43305 with repair of tracheoesophageal fistula

43310 Esophagoplasty (plastic repair or reconstruction), thoracic approach; without repair of tracheoesophageal fistula

43312 with repair of tracheoesophageal fistula

43313 Esophagoplasty for congenital defect (plastic repair or reconstruction), thoracic approach; without repair of congenital tracheoesophageal fistula

43314 with repair of congenital tracheoesophageal fistula

(Do not report modifier 63 in conjunction with 43313, 43314)

43320 Esophagogastrostomy (cardioplasty), with or without vagotomy and pyloroplasty, transabdominal or transthoracic approach

Surgery: Digestive System

43324 Esophagogastric fundoplasty (eg, Nissen, Belsey IV, Hill procedures)

(For laparoscopic procedure, use 43280)

43325 Esophagogastric fundoplasty; with fundic patch (Thal-Nissen procedure)

(For cricopharyngeal myotomy, use 43030)

43326 with gastroplasty (eg, Collis)

43330 Esophagomyotomy (Heller type); abdominal approach

43331 thoracic approach

(For thoracoscopic esophagomyotomy, use 32665)

43340 Esophagojejunostomy (without total gastrectomy); abdominal approach

43341 thoracic approach

43350 Esophagostomy, fistulization of esophagus, external; abdominal approach

43351 thoracic approach

43352 cervical approach

43360 Gastrointestinal reconstruction for previous esophagectomy, for obstructing esophageal lesion or fistula, or for previous esophageal exclusion; with stomach, with or without pyloroplasty

43361 with colon interposition or small intestine reconstruction, including intestine mobilization, preparation, and anastomosis(es)

43400 Ligation, direct, esophageal varices

43401 Transection of esophagus with repair, for esophageal varices

43405 Ligation or stapling at gastroesophageal junction for pre-existing esophageal perforation

43410 Suture of esophageal wound or injury; cervical approach

43415 transthoracic or transabdominal approach

43420 Closure of esophagostomy or fistula; cervical approach

43425 transthoracic or transabdominal approach

(For repair of esophageal hiatal hernia, see 39520 et seq)

Manipulation

(For associated esophagogram, use 74220)

43450 Dilation of esophagus, by unguided sound or bougie, single or multiple passes

(For radiological supervision and interpretation, use 74360)

⊙ **43453** Dilation of esophagus, over guide wire

(For dilation with direct visualization, use 43220)

(For dilation of esophagus, by balloon or dilator, see 43220, 43458, and 74360)

(For radiological supervision and interpretation, use 74360)

⊙ **43456** Dilation of esophagus, by balloon or dilator, retrograde

(For radiological supervision and interpretation, use 74360)

⊙ **43458** Dilation of esophagus with balloon (30 mm diameter or larger) for achalasia

(For dilation with balloon less than 30 mm diameter, use 43220)

(For radiological supervision and interpretation, use 74360)

43460 Esophagogastric tamponade, with balloon (Sengstaaken type)

(For removal of esophageal foreign body by balloon catheter, see 43215, 43247, 74235)

Other Procedures

43496 Free jejunum transfer with microvascular anastomosis

(Do not report code 69990 in addition to code 43496)

43499 Unlisted procedure, esophagus

Stomach

Incision

43500 Gastrotomy; with exploration or foreign body removal

43501 with suture repair of bleeding ulcer

43502 with suture repair of pre-existing esophagogastric laceration (eg, Mallory-Weiss)

43510 with esophageal dilation and insertion of permanent intraluminal tube (eg, Celestin or Mousseaux-Barbin)

43520 Pyloromyotomy, cutting of pyloric muscle (Fredet-Ramstedt type operation)

(Do not report modifier 63 in conjunction with 43520)

Excision

43600 Biopsy of stomach; by capsule, tube, peroral (one or more specimens)

43605 by laparotomy

43610 Excision, local; ulcer or benign tumor of stomach

43611 malignant tumor of stomach

43620 Gastrectomy, total; with esophagoenterostomy

43621 with Roux-en-Y reconstruction

43622 with formation of intestinal pouch, any type

43631 Gastrectomy, partial, distal; with gastroduodenostomy

43632 with gastrojejunostomy

43633 with Roux-en-Y reconstruction

43634 with formation of intestinal pouch

+ **43635** Vagotomy when performed with partial distal gastrectomy (List separately in addition to code(s) for primary procedure)

(Use 43635 in conjunction with 43631, 43632, 43633, 43634)

(43638, 43639 have been deleted)

43640 Vagotomy including pyloroplasty, with or without gastrostomy; truncal or selective

(For pyloroplasty, use 43800)

(For vagotomy, see 64752-64760)

43641 parietal cell (highly selective)

(For upper gastrointestinal endoscopy, see 43234-43259)

Laparoscopy

Surgical laparoscopy always includes diagnostic laparoscopy. To report a diagnostic laparoscopy (peritoneoscopy) (separate procedure), use 49320.

(For upper gastrointestinal endoscopy including esophagus, stomach, and either the duodenum and/or jejunum, see 43235-43259)

43644 Laparoscopy, surgical, gastric restrictive procedure; with gastric bypass and Roux-en-Y gastroenterostomy (roux limb 150 cm or less)

(Do not report 43644 in conjunction with 43846, 49320)

(Esophagogastroduodenoscopy (EGD) performed for a separate condition should be reported with modifier 59)

(For greater than 150 cm, use 43645)

(For open procedure, use 43846)

43645 with gastric bypass and small intestine reconstruction to limit absorption

(Do not report 43645 in conjunction with 49320, 43847)

● **43647** Laparoscopy, surgical; implantation or replacement of gastric neurostimulator electrodes, antrum

● **43648** revision or removal of gastric neurostimulator electrodes, antrum

▶(For open approach, see 43881, 43882)◀

▶(For insertion of gastric neurostimulator pulse generator, use 64590)◀

▶(For revision or removal of gastric neurostimulator pulse generator, use 64595)◀

▶(For electronic analysis and programming of gastric neurostimulator pulse generator, use 95999)◀

▶(For laparoscopic implantation, revision, or removal of gastric neurostimulator electrodes, lesser curvature [morbid obesity], see Category III codes 0155T, 0156T)◀

▶(For electronic analysis, programming, and reprogramming of gastric neurostimulator pulse generator, lesser curvature [morbid obesity], use Category III code 0162T)◀

43651 Laparoscopy, surgical; transection of vagus nerves, truncal

43652 transection of vagus nerves, selective or highly selective

43653 gastrostomy, without construction of gastric tube (eg, Stamm procedure) (separate procedure)

43659 Unlisted laparoscopy procedure, stomach

Introduction

⊙ **43750** Percutaneous placement of gastrostomy tube

(For radiological supervision and interpretation, use 74350)

43752 Naso- or oro-gastric tube placement, requiring physician's skill and fluoroscopic guidance (includes fluoroscopy, image documentation and report)

(For enteric tube placement, see 44500, 74340)

(Do not report 43752 in conjunction with critical care codes 99291-99292, neonatal critical care codes 99295-99296, pediatric critical care codes 99293-99294 or low birth weight intensive care service codes 99298-99299)

43760 Change of gastrostomy tube

(For endoscopic placement of gastrostomy tube, use 43246)

(For radiological supervision and interpretation, use 75984)

43761 Repositioning of the gastric feeding tube, any method, through the duodenum for enteric nutrition

(If imaging guidance is performed, use 75984)

Bariatric Surgery

Bariatric surgical procedures may involve the stomach, duodenum, jejunum, and/or the ileum.

Laparoscopy

Surgical laparoscopy always includes diagnostic laparoscopy. To report a diagnostic laparoscopy (separate procedure), use 49320.

Typical postoperative follow-up care (see Surgery Guidelines, CPT Surgical Package Definition) after gastric restriction using the adjustable gastric band technique includes subsequent band adjustment(s) through the postoperative period for the typical patient. Band adjustment refers to changing the gastric band component diameter by injection or aspiration of fluid through the subcutaneous port component.

Surgery: Digestive System

43770 Laparoscopy, surgical, gastric restrictive procedure; placement of adjustable gastric band (gastric band and subcutaneous port components)

(For individual component placement, report 43770 with modifier 52)

43771 revision of adjustable gastric band component only

43772 removal of adjustable gastric band component only

43773 removal and replacement of adjustable gastric band component only

(Do not report 43773 in conjunction with 43772)

43774 removal of adjustable gastric band and subcutaneous port components

(For removal and replacement of both gastric band and subcutaneous port components, use 43659)

Other Procedures

43800 Pyloroplasty

(For pyloroplasty and vagotomy, use 43640)

43810 Gastroduodenostomy

43820 Gastrojejunostomy; without vagotomy

43825 with vagotomy, any type

43830 Gastrostomy, open; without construction of gastric tube (eg, Stamm procedure) (separate procedure)

43831 neonatal, for feeding

(For change of gastrostomy tube, use 43760)

(Do not report modifier 63 in conjunction with 43831)

43832 with construction of gastric tube (eg, Janeway procedure)

(For percutaneous endoscopic gastrostomy, use 43246)

43840 Gastrorrhaphy, suture of perforated duodenal or gastric ulcer, wound, or injury

43842 Gastric restrictive procedure, without gastric bypass, for morbid obesity; vertical-banded gastroplasty

43843 other than vertical-banded gastroplasty

43845 Gastric restrictive procedure with partial gastrectomy, pylorus-preserving duodenoileostomy and ileoileostomy (50 to 100 cm common channel) to limit absorption (biliopancreatic diversion with duodenal switch)

(Do not report 43845 in conjunction with 43633, 43847, 44130, 49000)

43846 Gastric restrictive procedure, with gastric bypass for morbid obesity; with short limb (150 cm or less) Roux-en-Y gastroenterostomy

(For greater than 150 cm, use 43847)

(For laparoscopic procedure, use 43644)

43847 with small intestine reconstruction to limit absorption

43848 Revision, open, of gastric restrictive procedure for morbid obesity, other than adjustable gastric band (separate procedure)

(For adjustable gastric band procedures, see 43770-43774, 43886-43888)

43850 Revision of gastroduodenal anastomosis (gastroduodenostomy) with reconstruction; without vagotomy

43855 with vagotomy

43860 Revision of gastrojejunal anastomosis (gastrojejunostomy) with reconstruction, with or without partial gastrectomy or intestine resection; without vagotomy

43865 with vagotomy

43870 Closure of gastrostomy, surgical

43880 Closure of gastrocolic fistula

● **43881** Implantation or replacement of gastric neurostimulator electrodes, antrum, open

● **43882** Revision or removal of gastric neurostimulator electrodes, antrum, open

►(For laparoscopic approach, see 43647, 43648)◄

►(For insertion of gastric neurostimulator pulse generator, use 64590)◄

►(For revision or removal of gastric neurostimulator pulse generator, use 64595)◄

►(For electronic analysis and programming of gastric neurostimulator pulse generator, use 95999)◄

►(For open implantation, revision, or removal of gastric neurostimulator electrodes, lesser curvature [morbid obesity], see Category III codes 0157T, 0158T)◄

►(For electronic analysis, programming, and reprogramming of gastric neurostimulator pulse generator, lesser curvature [morbid obesity], use Category III code 0162T)◄

43886 Gastric restrictive procedure, open; revision of subcutaneous port component only

43887 removal of subcutaneous port component only

43888 removal and replacement of subcutaneous port component only

(Do not report 43888 in conjunction with 43774, 43887)

(For laparoscopic removal of both gastric band and subcutaneous port components, use 43774)

(For removal and replacement of both gastric band and subcutaneous port components, use 43659)

43999 Unlisted procedure, stomach

Intestines (Except Rectum)

Incision

44005 Enterolysis (freeing of intestinal adhesion) (separate procedure)

(Do not report 44005 in addition to 45136)

(For laparoscopic approach, use 44180)

44010 Duodenotomy, for exploration, biopsy(s), or foreign body removal

+ 44015 Tube or needle catheter jejunostomy for enteral alimentation, intraoperative, any method (List separately in addition to primary procedure)

44020 Enterotomy, small intestine, other than duodenum; for exploration, biopsy(s), or foreign body removal

44021 for decompression (eg, Baker tube)

44025 Colotomy, for exploration, biopsy(s), or foreign body removal

(For exteriorization of intestine (Mikulicz resection with crushing of spur), see 44602-44605)

44050 Reduction of volvulus, intussusception, internal hernia, by laparotomy

44055 Correction of malrotation by lysis of duodenal bands and/or reduction of midgut volvulus (eg, Ladd procedure)

(Do not report modifier 63 in conjunction with 44055)

Excision

Intestinal allotransplantation involves three distinct components of physician work:

1) ***Cadaver donor enterectomy***, which includes harvesting the intestine graft and cold preservation of the graft (perfusing with cold preservation solution and cold maintenance) (use 44132). ***Living donor enterectomy***, which includes harvesting the intestine graft, cold preservation of the graft (perfusing with cold preservation solution and cold maintenance), and care of the donor (use 44133).

2) ***Backbench work***:

Standard preparation of an intestine allograft prior to transplantation includes mobilization and fashioning of the superior mesenteric artery and vein (see 44715).

Additional reconstruction of an intestine allograft prior to transplantation may include venous and/or arterial anastomosis(es) (see 44720-44721).

3) ***Recipient intestinal allotransplantation with or without recipient enterectomy***, which includes transplantation of allograft and care of the recipient (see 44135, 44136).

44100 Biopsy of intestine by capsule, tube, peroral (one or more specimens)

44110 Excision of one or more lesions of small or large intestine not requiring anastomosis, exteriorization, or fistulization; single enterotomy

44111 multiple enterotomies

44120 Enterectomy, resection of small intestine; single resection and anastomosis

(Do not report 44120 in addition to 45136)

+ 44121 each additional resection and anastomosis (List separately in addition to code for primary procedure)

(Use 44121 in conjunction with 44120)

44125 with enterostomy

44126 Enterectomy, resection of small intestine for congenital atresia, single resection and anastomosis of proximal segment of intestine; without tapering

44127 with tapering

+ 44128 each additional resection and anastomosis (List separately in addition to code for primary procedure)

(Use 44128 in conjunction with 44126, 44127)

(Do not report modifier 63 in conjunction with 44126, 44127, 44128)

44130 Enteroenterostomy, anastomosis of intestine, with or without cutaneous enterostomy (separate procedure)

44132 Donor enterectomy (including cold preservation), open; from cadaver donor

44133 partial, from living donor

(For backbench intestinal graft preparation or reconstruction, see 44715, 44720, 44721)

44135 Intestinal allotransplantation; from cadaver donor

44136 from living donor

44137 Removal of transplanted intestinal allograft, complete

(For partial removal of transplant allograft, see 44120, 44121, 44140)

+ 44139 Mobilization (take-down) of splenic flexure performed in conjunction with partial colectomy (List separately in addition to primary procedure)

(Use 44139 in conjunction with 44140-44147)

44140 Colectomy, partial; with anastomosis

(For laparoscopic procedure, use 44204)

44141 with skin level cecostomy or colostomy

44143 with end colostomy and closure of distal segment (Hartmann type procedure)

(For laparoscopic procedure, use 44206)

44144 with resection, with colostomy or ileostomy and creation of mucofistula

44145 with coloproctostomy (low pelvic anastomosis)

(For laparoscopic procedure, use 44207)

Surgery: Digestive System

44146 with coloproctostomy (low pelvic anastomosis), with colostomy

(For laparoscopic procedure, use 44208)

44147 abdominal and transanal approach

44150 Colectomy, total, abdominal, without proctectomy; with ileostomy or ileoproctostomy

(For laparoscopic procedure, use 44210)

44151 with continent ileostomy

▶(44152 and 44153 have been deleted. To report, use 44799)◀

44155 Colectomy, total, abdominal, with proctectomy; with ileostomy

(For laparoscopic procedure, use 44212)

44156 with continent ileostomy

● **44157** with ileoanal anastomosis, includes loop ileostomy, and rectal mucosectomy, when performed

● **44158** with ileoanal anastomosis, creation of ileal reservoir (S or J), includes loop ileostomy, and rectal mucosectomy, when performed

▶(For laparoscopic procedure, use 44211)◀

44160 Colectomy, partial, with removal of terminal ileum with ileocolostomy

(For laparoscopic procedure, use 44205)

Laparoscopy

Surgical laparoscopy always includes diagnostic laparoscopy. To report a diagnostic laparoscopy (peritoneoscopy) (separate procedure), use 49320.

Incision

44180 Laparoscopy, surgical, enterolysis (freeing of intestinal adhesion) (separate procedure)

(For laparoscopy with salpingolysis, ovariolysis, use 58660)

Enterostomy—External Fistulization of Intestines

44186 Laparoscopy, surgical; jejunostomy (eg, for decompression or feeding)

44187 ileostomy or jejunostomy, non-tube

(For open procedure, use 44310)

44188 Laparoscopy, surgical, colostomy or skin level cecostomy

(For open procedure, use 44320)

(Do not report 44188 in conjunction with 44970)

(44200 has been deleted. To report, use 44180)

(44201 has been deleted. To report, use 44186)

Excision

44202 Laparoscopy, surgical; enterectomy, resection of small intestine, single resection and anastomosis

+ **44203** each additional small intestine resection and anastomosis (List separately in addition to code for primary procedure)

(Use 44203 in conjunction with 44202)

(For open procedure, see 44120, 44121)

44204 colectomy, partial, with anastomosis

(For open procedure, use 44140)

44205 colectomy, partial, with removal of terminal ileum with ileocolostomy

(For open procedure, use 44160)

44206 colectomy, partial, with end colostomy and closure of distal segment (Hartmann type procedure)

(For open procedure, use 44143)

44207 colectomy, partial, with anastomosis, with coloproctostomy (low pelvic anastomosis)

(For open procedure, use 44145)

44208 colectomy, partial, with anastomosis, with coloproctostomy (low pelvic anastomosis) with colostomy

(For open procedure, use 44146)

44210 colectomy, total, abdominal, without proctectomy, with ileostomy or ileoproctostomy

(For open procedure, use 44150)

▲ **44211** colectomy, total, abdominal, with proctectomy, with ileoanal anastomosis, creation of ileal reservoir (S or J), with loop ileostomy, includes rectal mucosectomy, when performed

▶(For open procedure, see 44157, 44158)◀

44212 colectomy, total, abdominal, with proctectomy, with ileostomy

(For open procedure, use 44155)

+ **44213** Laparoscopy, surgical, mobilization (take-down) of splenic flexure performed in conjunction with partial colectomy (List separately in addition to primary procedure)

(Use 44213 in conjunction with 44204-44208)

(For open procedure, use 44139)

Repair

44227 Laparoscopy, surgical, closure of enterostomy, large or small intestine, with resection and anastomosis

(For open procedure, see 44625, 44626)

Surgery: Digestive System

Other Procedures

44238 Unlisted laparoscopy procedure, intestine (except rectum)

(44239 has been deleted. To report, use 45499)

Enterostomy—External Fistulization of Intestines

44300 Enterostomy or cecostomy, tube (eg, for decompression or feeding) (separate procedure)

44310 Ileostomy or jejunostomy, non-tube

(For laparoscopic procedure, use 44187)

(Do not report 44310 in conjunction with 44144, 44150-44151, 44155, 44156, 45113, 45119, 45136)

44312 Revision of ileostomy; simple (release of superficial scar) (separate procedure)

44314 complicated (reconstruction in-depth) (separate procedure)

44316 Continent ileostomy (Kock procedure) (separate procedure)

(For fiberoptic evaluation, use 44385)

44320 Colostomy or skin level cecostomy;

(For laparoscopic procedure, use 44188)

(Do not report 44320 in conjunction with 44141, 44144, 44146, 44605, 45110, 45119, 45126, 45563, 45805, 45825, 50810, 51597, 57307, or 58240)

44322 with multiple biopsies (eg, for congenital megacolon) (separate procedure)

44340 Revision of colostomy; simple (release of superficial scar) (separate procedure)

44345 complicated (reconstruction in-depth) (separate procedure)

44346 with repair of paracolostomy hernia (separate procedure)

Endoscopy, Small Intestine and Stomal

Surgical endoscopy always includes diagnostic endoscopy.

(For upper gastrointestinal endoscopy, see 43234-43258)

⊙ **44360** Small intestinal endoscopy, enteroscopy beyond second portion of duodenum, not including ileum; diagnostic, with or without collection of specimen(s) by brushing or washing (separate procedure)

⊙ **44361** with biopsy, single or multiple

⊙ **44363** with removal of foreign body

⊙ **44364** with removal of tumor(s), polyp(s), or other lesion(s) by snare technique

⊙ **44365** with removal of tumor(s), polyp(s), or other lesion(s) by hot biopsy forceps or bipolar cautery

⊙ **44366** with control of bleeding (eg, injection, bipolar cautery, unipolar cautery, laser, heater probe, stapler, plasma coagulator)

⊙ **44369** with ablation of tumor(s), polyp(s), or other lesion(s) not amenable to removal by hot biopsy forceps, bipolar cautery or snare technique

⊙ **44370** with transendoscopic stent placement (includes predilation)

⊙ **44372** with placement of percutaneous jejunostomy tube

⊙ **44373** with conversion of percutaneous gastrostomy tube to percutaneous jejunostomy tube

(For fiberoptic jejunostomy through stoma, use 43235)

⊙ **44376** Small intestinal endoscopy, enteroscopy beyond second portion of duodenum, including ileum; diagnostic, with or without collection of specimen(s) by brushing or washing (separate procedure)

⊙ **44377** with biopsy, single or multiple

⊙ **44378** with control of bleeding (eg, injection, bipolar cautery, unipolar cautery, laser, heater probe, stapler, plasma coagulator)

⊙ **44379** with transendoscopic stent placement (includes predilation)

⊙ **44380** Ileoscopy, through stoma; diagnostic, with or without collection of specimen(s) by brushing or washing (separate procedure)

⊙ **44382** with biopsy, single or multiple

⊙ **44383** with transendoscopic stent placement (includes predilation)

⊙ **44385** Endoscopic evaluation of small intestinal (abdominal or pelvic) pouch; diagnostic, with or without collection of specimen(s) by brushing or washing (separate procedure)

⊙ **44386** with biopsy, single or multiple

⊙ **44388** Colonoscopy through stoma; diagnostic, with or without collection of specimen(s) by brushing or washing (separate procedure)

⊙ **44389** with biopsy, single or multiple

⊙ **44390** with removal of foreign body

⊙ **44391** with control of bleeding (eg, injection, bipolar cautery, unipolar cautery, laser, heater probe, stapler, plasma coagulator)

⊙ **44392** with removal of tumor(s), polyp(s), or other lesion(s) by hot biopsy forceps or bipolar cautery

⊙ **44393** with ablation of tumor(s), polyp(s), or other lesion(s) not amenable to removal by hot biopsy forceps, bipolar cautery or snare technique

⊙ **44394** with removal of tumor(s), polyp(s), or other lesion(s) by snare technique

(For colonoscopy per rectum, see 45330-45385)

⊙ **44397** with transendoscopic stent placement (includes predilation)

Introduction

⊙⊘ **44500** Introduction of long gastrointestinal tube (eg, Miller-Abbott) (separate procedure)

(For radiological supervision and interpretation, use 74340)

(For naso- or oro-gastric tube placement, use 43752)

Repair

44602 Suture of small intestine (enterorrhaphy) for perforated ulcer, diverticulum, wound, injury or rupture; single perforation

44603 multiple perforations

44604 Suture of large intestine (colorrhaphy) for perforated ulcer, diverticulum, wound, injury or rupture (single or multiple perforations); without colostomy

44605 with colostomy

44615 Intestinal stricturoplasty (enterotomy and enterorrhaphy) with or without dilation, for intestinal obstruction

44620 Closure of enterostomy, large or small intestine;

44625 with resection and anastomosis other than colorectal

44626 with resection and colorectal anastomosis (eg, closure of Hartmann type procedure)

►(For laparoscopic procedure, use 44227)◄

44640 Closure of intestinal cutaneous fistula

44650 Closure of enteroenteric or enterocolic fistula

44660 Closure of enterovesical fistula; without intestinal or bladder resection

44661 with intestine and/or bladder resection

(For closure of renocolic fistula, see 50525, 50526)

(For closure of gastrocolic fistula, use 43880)

(For closure of rectovesical fistula, see 45800, 45805)

44680 Intestinal plication (separate procedure)

Other Procedures

44700 Exclusion of small intestine from pelvis by mesh or other prosthesis, or native tissue (eg, bladder or omentum)

(For therapeutic radiation clinical treatment, see **Radiation Oncology** section)

✛ **44701** Intraoperative colonic lavage (List separately in addition to code for primary procedure)

(Use 44701 in conjunction with 44140, 44145, 44150, or 44604 as appropriate)

(Do not report 44701 in conjunction with 44300, 44950-44960)

44715 Backbench standard preparation of cadaver or living donor intestine allograft prior to transplantation, including mobilization and fashioning of the superior mesenteric artery and vein

44720 Backbench reconstruction of cadaver or living donor intestine allograft prior to transplantation; venous anastomosis, each

44721 arterial anastomosis, each

44799 Unlisted procedure, intestine

(For unlisted laparoscopic procedure, intestine except rectum, use 44238)

Meckel's Diverticulum and the Mesentery

Excision

44800 Excision of Meckel's diverticulum (diverticulectomy) or omphalomesenteric duct

44820 Excision of lesion of mesentery (separate procedure)

(With intestine resection, see 44120 or 44140 et seq)

Suture

44850 Suture of mesentery (separate procedure)

(For reduction and repair of internal hernia, use 44050)

Other Procedures

44899 Unlisted procedure, Meckel's diverticulum and the mesentery

Appendix

Incision

44900 Incision and drainage of appendiceal abscess; open

⊙ **44901** percutaneous

(For radiological supervision and interpretation, use 75989)

Excision

44950 Appendectomy;

(Incidental appendectomy during intra-abdominal surgery does not usually warrant a separate identification. If necessary to report, add modifier 52)

✛ **44955** when done for indicated purpose at time of other major procedure (not as separate procedure) (List separately in addition to code for primary procedure)

44960 for ruptured appendix with abscess or generalized peritonitis

Laparoscopy

Surgical laparoscopy always includes diagnostic laparoscopy. To report a diagnostic laparoscopy (peritoneoscopy) (separate procedure), use 49320.

44970 Laparoscopy, surgical, appendectomy

44979 Unlisted laparoscopy procedure, appendix

Rectum

Incision

45000 Transrectal drainage of pelvic abscess

45005 Incision and drainage of submucosal abscess, rectum

45020 Incision and drainage of deep supralevator, pelvirectal, or retrorectal abscess

(See also 46050, 46060)

Excision

45100 Biopsy of anorectal wall, anal approach (eg, congenital megacolon)

(For endoscopic biopsy, use 45305)

45108 Anorectal myomectomy

45110 Proctectomy; complete, combined abdominoperineal, with colostomy

(For laparoscopic procedure, use 45395)

45111 partial resection of rectum, transabdominal approach

45112 Proctectomy, combined abdominoperineal, pull-through procedure (eg, colo-anal anastomosis)

(For colo-anal anastomosis with colonic reservoir or pouch, use 45119)

45113 Proctectomy, partial, with rectal mucosectomy, ileoanal anastomosis, creation of ileal reservoir (S or J), with or without loop ileostomy

45114 Proctectomy, partial, with anastomosis; abdominal and transsacral approach

45116 transsacral approach only (Kraske type)

45119 Proctectomy, combined abdominoperineal pull-through procedure (eg, colo-anal anastomosis), with creation of colonic reservoir (eg, J-pouch), with diverting enterostomy when performed

(For laparoscopic procedure, use 45397)

45120 Proctectomy, complete (for congenital megacolon), abdominal and perineal approach; with pull-through procedure and anastomosis (eg, Swenson, Duhamel, or Soave type operation)

45121 with subtotal or total colectomy, with multiple biopsies

45123 Proctectomy, partial, without anastomosis, perineal approach

45126 Pelvic exenteration for colorectal malignancy, with proctectomy (with or without colostomy), with removal of bladder and ureteral transplantations, and/or hysterectomy, or cervicectomy, with or without removal of tube(s), with or without removal of ovary(s), or any combination thereof

45130 Excision of rectal procidentia, with anastomosis; perineal approach

45135 abdominal and perineal approach

45136 Excision of ileoanal reservoir with ileostomy

(Do not report 45136 in addition to 44005, 44120, 44310)

45150 Division of stricture of rectum

45160 Excision of rectal tumor by proctotomy, transsacral or transcoccygeal approach

45170 Excision of rectal tumor, transanal approach

Destruction

45190 Destruction of rectal tumor (eg, electrodessication, electrosurgery, laser ablation, laser resection, cryosurgery) transanal approach

Endoscopy

Definitions

Proctosigmoidoscopy is the examination of the rectum and sigmoid colon.

Sigmoidoscopy is the examination of the entire rectum, sigmoid colon and may include examination of a portion of the descending colon.

Colonoscopy is the examination of the entire colon, from the rectum to the cecum, and may include the examination of the terminal ileum.

For an incomplete colonoscopy, with full preparation for a colonoscopy, use a colonoscopy code with the modifier 52 and provide documentation.

Surgical endoscopy always includes diagnostic endoscopy.

45300 Proctosigmoidoscopy, rigid; diagnostic, with or without collection of specimen(s) by brushing or washing (separate procedure)

⊙ **45303** with dilation (eg, balloon, guide wire, bougie)

(For radiological supervision and interpretation, use 74360)

⊙ **45305** with biopsy, single or multiple

⊙ **45307** with removal of foreign body

⊙ **45308** with removal of single tumor, polyp, or other lesion by hot biopsy forceps or bipolar cautery

Surgery: Digestive System

⊙ **45309** with removal of single tumor, polyp, or other lesion by snare technique

⊙ **45315** with removal of multiple tumors, polyps, or other lesions by hot biopsy forceps, bipolar cautery or snare technique

⊙ **45317** with control of bleeding (eg, injection, bipolar cautery, unipolar cautery, laser, heater probe, stapler, plasma coagulator)

⊙ **45320** with ablation of tumor(s), polyp(s), or other lesion(s) not amenable to removal by hot biopsy forceps, bipolar cautery or snare technique (eg, laser)

⊙ **45321** with decompression of volvulus

⊙ **45327** with transendoscopic stent placement (includes predilation)

45330 Sigmoidoscopy, flexible; diagnostic, with or without collection of specimen(s) by brushing or washing (separate procedure)

45331 with biopsy, single or multiple

⊙ **45332** with removal of foreign body

⊙ **45333** with removal of tumor(s), polyp(s), or other lesion(s) by hot biopsy forceps or bipolar cautery

⊙ **45334** with control of bleeding (eg, injection, bipolar cautery, unipolar cautery, laser, heater probe, stapler, plasma coagulator)

⊙ **45335** with directed submucosal injection(s), any substance

⊙ **45337** with decompression of volvulus, any method

⊙ **45338** with removal of tumor(s), polyp(s), or other lesion(s) by snare technique

⊙ **45339** with ablation of tumor(s), polyp(s), or other lesion(s) not amenable to removal by hot biopsy forceps, bipolar cautery or snare technique

⊙ **45340** with dilation by balloon, 1 or more strictures

(Do not report 45340 in conjunction with 45345)

⊙ **45341** with endoscopic ultrasound examination

⊙ **45342** with transendoscopic ultrasound guided intramural or transmural fine needle aspiration/biopsy(s)

(Do not report 45341, 45342 in conjunction with 76942, 76975)

(For interpretation of specimen, see 88172-88173)

(For transrectal ultrasound utilizing rigid probe device, use 76872)

⊙ **45345** with transendoscopic stent placement (includes predilation)

⊙ **45355** Colonoscopy, rigid or flexible, transabdominal via colotomy, single or multiple

(For fiberoptic colonoscopy beyond 25cm to splenic flexure, see 45330-45345)

⊙ **45378** Colonoscopy, flexible, proximal to splenic flexure; diagnostic, with or without collection of specimen(s) by brushing or washing, with or without colon decompression (separate procedure)

⊙ **45379** with removal of foreign body

⊙ **45380** with biopsy, single or multiple

⊙ **45381** with directed submucosal injection(s), any substance

⊙ **45382** with control of bleeding (eg, injection, bipolar cautery, unipolar cautery, laser, heater probe, stapler, plasma coagulator)

⊙ **45383** with ablation of tumor(s), polyp(s), or other lesion(s) not amenable to removal by hot biopsy forceps, bipolar cautery or snare technique

⊙ **45384** with removal of tumor(s), polyp(s), or other lesion(s) by hot biopsy forceps or bipolar cautery

⊙ **45385** with removal of tumor(s), polyp(s), or other lesion(s) by snare technique

(For small intestine and stomal endoscopy, see 44360-44393)

⊙ **45386** with dilation by balloon, 1 or more strictures

(Do not report 45386 in conjunction with 45387)

⊙ **45387** with transendoscopic stent placement (includes predilation)

⊙ **45391** with endoscopic ultrasound examination

(Do not report 45391 in conjunction with 45330, 45341, 45342, 45378, 76872)

⊙ **45392** with transendoscopic ultrasound guided intramural or transmural fine needle aspiration/biopsy(s)

(Do not report 45392 in conjunction with 45330, 45341, 45342, 45378, 76872)

Laparoscopy

Surgical laparoscopy always includes diagnostic laparoscopy. To report a diagnostic laparoscopy (peritoneoscopy) (separate procedure), use 49320.

Excision

45395 Laparoscopy, surgical; proctectomy, complete, combined abdominoperineal, with colostomy

(For open procedure, use 45110)

45397 proctectomy, combined abdominoperineal pull-through procedure (eg, colo-anal anastomosis), with creation of colonic reservoir (eg, J-pouch), with diverting enterostomy, when performed

(For open procedure, use 45119)

Surgery: Digestive System

Repair

45400 Laparoscopy, surgical; proctopexy (for prolapse)

(For open procedure, use 45540, 45541)

45402 proctopexy (for prolapse), with sigmoid resection

(For open procedure, use 45550)

45499 Unlisted laparoscopy procedure, rectum

Repair

45500 Proctoplasty; for stenosis

45505 for prolapse of mucous membrane

45520 Perirectal injection of sclerosing solution for prolapse

45540 Proctopexy (eg, for prolapse); abdominal approach

(For laparoscopic procedure, use 45400)

45541 perineal approach

45550 with sigmoid resection, abdominal approach

(For laparoscopic procedure, use 45402)

45560 Repair of rectocele (separate procedure)

(For repair of rectocele with posterior colporrhaphy, use 57250)

45562 Exploration, repair, and presacral drainage for rectal injury;

45563 with colostomy

45800 Closure of rectovesical fistula;

45805 with colostomy

45820 Closure of rectourethral fistula;

45825 with colostomy

(For rectovaginal fistula closure, see 57300-57308)

Manipulation

45900 Reduction of procidentia (separate procedure) under anesthesia

45905 Dilation of anal sphincter (separate procedure) under anesthesia other than local

45910 Dilation of rectal stricture (separate procedure) under anesthesia other than local

45915 Removal of fecal impaction or foreign body (separate procedure) under anesthesia

Other Procedures

Surgical diagnostic anorectal exam (45990) includes the following elements: external perineal exam, digital rectal exam, pelvic exam (when performed), diagnostic anoscopy, and diagnostic rigid proctoscopy.

45990 Anorectal exam, surgical, requiring anesthesia (general, spinal, or epidural), diagnostic

(Do not report 45990 in conjunction with 45300- 45327, 46600, 57410, 99170)

45999 Unlisted procedure, rectum

(For unlisted laparoscopic procedure, rectum, use 45499)

Anus

Incision

(For subcutaneous fistulotomy, use 46270)

46020 Placement of seton

(Do not report 46020 in addition to 46060, 46280, 46600)

46030 Removal of anal seton, other marker

46040 Incision and drainage of ischiorectal and/or perirectal abscess (separate procedure)

46045 Incision and drainage of intramural, intramuscular, or submucosal abscess, transanal, under anesthesia

46050 Incision and drainage, perianal abscess, superficial

(See also 45020, 46060)

46060 Incision and drainage of ischiorectal or intramural abscess, with fistulectomy or fistulotomy, submuscular, with or without placement of seton

(Do not report 46060 in addition to 46020)

(See also 45020)

46070 Incision, anal septum (infant)

(For anoplasty, see 46700-46705)

(Do not report modifier 63 in conjunction with 46070)

46080 Sphincterotomy, anal, division of sphincter (separate procedure)

46083 Incision of thrombosed hemorrhoid, external

Excision

46200 Fissurectomy, with or without sphincterotomy

46210 Cryptectomy; single

46211 multiple (separate procedure)

46220 Papillectomy or excision of single tag, anus (separate procedure)

46221 Hemorrhoidectomy, by simple ligature (eg, rubber band)

46230	Excision of external hemorrhoid tags and/or multiple papillae
46250	Hemorrhoidectomy, external, complete
46255	Hemorrhoidectomy, internal and external, simple;
46257	with fissurectomy
46258	with fistulectomy, with or without fissurectomy
46260	Hemorrhoidectomy, internal and external, complex or extensive;
46261	with fissurectomy
46262	with fistulectomy, with or without fissurectomy

(For injection of hemorrhoids, use 46500; for destruction, see 46934-46936; for ligation, see 46945, 46946; for hemorrhoidopexy, use 46947)

46270	Surgical treatment of anal fistula (fistulectomy/fistulotomy); subcutaneous
46275	submuscular
46280	complex or multiple, with or without placement of seton

(Do not report 46280 in addition to 46020)

46285	second stage
46288	Closure of anal fistula with rectal advancement flap
46320	Enucleation or excision of external thrombotic hemorrhoid

Introduction

46500	Injection of sclerosing solution, hemorrhoids

(For excision of hemorrhoids, see 46250-46262; for destruction, see 46934-46936; for ligation, see 46945, 46946; for hemorrhoidopexy, use 46947)

46505	Chemodenervation of internal anal sphincter

(For chemodenervation of other muscles, see 64612-64614, 64640)

(Report the specific service in conjunction with the specific substance(s) or drug(s) provided)

Endoscopy

Surgical endoscopy always includes diagnostic endoscopy.

46600	Anoscopy; diagnostic, with or without collection of specimen(s) by brushing or washing (separate procedure)

(Do not report 46600 in addition to 46020)

46604	with dilation (eg, balloon, guide wire, bougie)
46606	with biopsy, single or multiple
46608	with removal of foreign body
46610	with removal of single tumor, polyp, or other lesion by hot biopsy forceps or bipolar cautery
46611	with removal of single tumor, polyp, or other lesion by snare technique
46612	with removal of multiple tumors, polyps, or other lesions by hot biopsy forceps, bipolar cautery or snare technique
46614	with control of bleeding (eg, injection, bipolar cautery, unipolar cautery, laser, heater probe, stapler, plasma coagulator)
46615	with ablation of tumor(s), polyp(s), or other lesion(s) not amenable to removal by hot biopsy forceps, bipolar cautery or snare technique

Repair

46700	Anoplasty, plastic operation for stricture; adult
46705	infant

(For simple incision of anal septum, use 46070)

(Do not report modifier 63 in conjunction with 46705)

46706	Repair of anal fistula with fibrin glue
46710	Repair of ileoanal pouch fistula/sinus (eg, perineal or vaginal), pouch advancement; transperineal approach
46712	combined transperineal and transabdominal approach
46715	Repair of low imperforate anus; with anoperineal fistula (cut-back procedure)
46716	with transposition of anoperineal or anovestibular fistula

(Do not report modifier 63 in conjunction with 46715, 46716)

46730	Repair of high imperforate anus without fistula; perineal or sacroperineal approach
46735	combined transabdominal and sacroperineal approaches

(Do not report modifier 63 in conjunction with 46730, 46735)

46740	Repair of high imperforate anus with rectourethral or rectovaginal fistula; perineal or sacroperineal approach
46742	combined transabdominal and sacroperineal approaches

(Do not report modifier 63 in conjunction with 46740, 46742)

46744	Repair of cloacal anomaly by anorectovaginoplasty and urethroplasty, sacroperineal approach

(Do not report modifier 63 in conjunction with 46744)

Surgery: Digestive System

46746 Repair of cloacal anomaly by anorectovaginoplasty and urethroplasty, combined abdominal and sacroperineal approach;

46748 with vaginal lengthening by intestinal graft or pedicle flaps

46750 Sphincteroplasty, anal, for incontinence or prolapse; adult

46751 child

46753 Graft (Thiersch operation) for rectal incontinence and/or prolapse

46754 Removal of Thiersch wire or suture, anal canal

46760 Sphincteroplasty, anal, for incontinence, adult; muscle transplant

46761 levator muscle imbrication (Park posterior anal repair)

46762 implantation artificial sphincter

Destruction

46900 Destruction of lesion(s), anus (eg, condyloma, papilloma, molluscum contagiosum, herpetic vesicle), simple; chemical

46910 electrodesiccation

46916 cryosurgery

46917 laser surgery

46922 surgical excision

46924 Destruction of lesion(s), anus (eg, condyloma, papilloma, molluscum contagiosum, herpetic vesicle), extensive (eg, laser surgery, electrosurgery, cryosurgery, chemosurgery)

46934 Destruction of hemorrhoids, any method; internal

46935 external

46936 internal and external

 (For excision of hemorrhoids, see 46250-46262; for injection, use 46500; for ligation, see 46945, 46946; for hemorrhoidopexy, use 46947)

46937 Cryosurgery of rectal tumor; benign

46938 malignant

46940 Curettage or cautery of anal fissure, including dilation of anal sphincter (separate procedure); initial

46942 subsequent

Suture

46945 Ligation of internal hemorrhoids; single procedure

46946 multiple procedures

46947 Hemorrhoidopexy (eg, for prolapsing internal hemorrhoids) by stapling

 (For excision of hemorrhoids, see 46250-46262; for injection, use 46500; for destruction, see 46934-46936)

Other Procedures

46999 Unlisted procedure, anus

Liver

Incision

47000 Biopsy of liver, needle; percutaneous

 ►(If imaging guidance is performed, see 76942, 77002, 77012, 77021)◄

+ 47001 when done for indicated purpose at time of other major procedure (List separately in addition to code for primary procedure)

 ►(If imaging guidance is performed, see 76942, 77002)◄

 (For fine needle aspiration in conjunction with 47000, 47001, see 10021, 10022)

 (For evaluation of fine needle aspirate in conjunction with 47000, 47001, see 88172, 88173)

47010 Hepatotomy; for open drainage of abscess or cyst, one or two stages

⊙ **47011** for percutaneous drainage of abscess or cyst, one or two stages

 (For radiological supervision and interpretation, use 75989)

47015 Laparotomy, with aspiration and/or injection of hepatic parasitic (eg, amoebic or echinococcal) cyst(s) or abscess(es)

Excision

47100 Biopsy of liver, wedge

47120 Hepatectomy, resection of liver; partial lobectomy

47122 trisegmentectomy

47125 total left lobectomy

47130 total right lobectomy

Liver Transplantation

Liver allotransplantation involves three distinct components of physician work:

1) *Cadaver donor hepatectomy*, which includes harvesting the graft and cold preservation of the graft (perfusing with cold preservation solution and cold maintenance) (use 47133). *Living donor hepatectomy*, which includes harvesting the graft, cold preservation of the graft (perfusing with cold preservation solution and cold maintenance), and care of the donor (see 47140-47142).

Surgery: Digestive System

2) *Backbench work*:

Standard preparation of the whole liver graft will include one of the following:

Preparation of whole liver graft (including cholecystectomy, if necessary, and dissection and removal of surrounding soft tissues to prepare vena cava, portal vein, hepatic artery, and common bile duct for implantation) (use 47143).

Preparation as described for whole liver graft, plus trisegment split into two partial grafts (use 47144).

Preparation as described for whole liver graft, plus lobe split into two partial grafts (use 47145).

Additional reconstruction of the liver graft may include venous and/or arterial anastomosis(es) (see 47146, 47147).

3) *Recipient liver allotransplantation*, which includes recipient hepatectomy (partial or whole), transplantation of the allograft (partial or whole), and care of the recipient (see 47135, 47136).

47133 Donor hepatectomy (including cold preservation), from cadaver donor

47135 Liver allotransplantation; orthotopic, partial or whole, from cadaver or living donor, any age

47136 heterotopic, partial or whole, from cadaver or living donor, any age

47140 Donor hepatectomy (including cold preservation), from living donor; left lateral segment only (segments II and III)

47141 total left lobectomy (segments II, III and IV)

47142 total right lobectomy (segments V, VI, VII and VIII)

47143 Backbench standard preparation of cadaver donor whole liver graft prior to allotransplantation, including cholecystectomy, if necessary, and dissection and removal of surrounding soft tissues to prepare the vena cava, portal vein, hepatic artery, and common bile duct for implantation; without trisegment or lobe split

47144 with trisegment split of whole liver graft into two partial liver grafts (ie, left lateral segment (segments II and III) and right trisegment (segments I and IV through VIII))

47145 with lobe split of whole liver graft into two partial liver grafts (ie, left lobe (segments II, III, and IV) and right lobe (segments I and V through VIII))

47146 Backbench reconstruction of cadaver or living donor liver graft prior to allotransplantation; venous anastomosis, each

47147 arterial anastomosis, each

(Do not report 47143-47147 in conjunction with 47120-47125, 47600, 47610)

Repair

47300 Marsupialization of cyst or abscess of liver

47350 Management of liver hemorrhage; simple suture of liver wound or injury

47360 complex suture of liver wound or injury, with or without hepatic artery ligation

47361 exploration of hepatic wound, extensive debridement, coagulation and/or suture, with or without packing of liver

47362 re-exploration of hepatic wound for removal of packing

Laparoscopy

Surgical laparoscopy always includes diagnostic laparoscopy. To report a diagnostic laparoscopy (peritoneoscopy) (separate procedure), use 49320.

47370 Laparoscopy, surgical, ablation of one or more liver tumor(s); radiofrequency

(For imaging guidance, use 76940)

47371 cryosurgical

(For imaging guidance, use 76940)

47379 Unlisted laparoscopic procedure, liver

Other Procedures

47380 Ablation, open, of one or more liver tumor(s); radiofrequency

(For imaging guidance, use 76940)

47381 cryosurgical

(For imaging guidance, use 76940)

47382 Ablation, one or more liver tumor(s), percutaneous, radiofrequency

▶(For imaging guidance and monitoring, see 76940, 77013, 77022)◀

47399 Unlisted procedure, liver

Biliary Tract

Incision

47400 Hepaticotomy or hepaticostomy with exploration, drainage, or removal of calculus

47420 Choledochotomy or choledochostomy with exploration, drainage, or removal of calculus, with or without cholecystotomy; without transduodenal sphincterotomy or sphincteroplasty

47425 with transduodenal sphincterotomy or sphincteroplasty

Surgery: Digestive System

47460 Transduodenal sphincterotomy or sphincteroplasty, with or without transduodenal extraction of calculus (separate procedure)

47480 Cholecystotomy or cholecystostomy with exploration, drainage, or removal of calculus (separate procedure)

47490 Percutaneous cholecystostomy

(For radiological supervision and interpretation, use 75989)

Introduction

47500 Injection procedure for percutaneous transhepatic cholangiography

(For radiological supervision and interpretation, use 74320)

47505 Injection procedure for cholangiography through an existing catheter (eg, percutaneous transhepatic or T-tube)

(For radiological supervision and interpretation, use 74305)

47510 Introduction of percutaneous transhepatic catheter for biliary drainage

(For radiological supervision and interpretation, use 75980)

47511 Introduction of percutaneous transhepatic stent for internal and external biliary drainage

(For radiological supervision and interpretation, use 75982)

47525 Change of percutaneous biliary drainage catheter

(For radiological supervision and interpretation, use 75984)

47530 Revision and/or reinsertion of transhepatic tube

(For radiological supervision and interpretation, use 75984)

Endoscopy

Surgical endoscopy always includes diagnostic endoscopy.

+ 47550 Biliary endoscopy, intraoperative (choledochoscopy) (List separately in addition to code for primary procedure)

47552 Biliary endoscopy, percutaneous via T-tube or other tract; diagnostic, with or without collection of specimen(s) by brushing and/or washing (separate procedure)

47553 with biopsy, single or multiple

47554 with removal of calculus/calculi

47555 with dilation of biliary duct stricture(s) without stent

47556 with dilation of biliary duct stricture(s) with stent

(For ERCP, see 43260-43272, 74363)

(If imaging guidance is performed, see 74363, 75982)

Laparoscopy

Surgical laparoscopy always includes diagnostic laparoscopy. To report a diagnostic laparoscopy (peritoneoscopy) (separate procedure), use 49320.

47560 Laparoscopy, surgical; with guided transhepatic cholangiography, without biopsy

47561 with guided transhepatic cholangiography with biopsy

47562 cholecystectomy

47563 cholecystectomy with cholangiography

47564 cholecystectomy with exploration of common duct

47570 cholecystoenterostomy

47579 Unlisted laparoscopy procedure, biliary tract

Excision

47600 Cholecystectomy;

47605 with cholangiography

(For laparoscopic approach, see 47562-47564)

47610 Cholecystectomy with exploration of common duct;

(For cholecystectomy with exploration of common duct with biliary endoscopy, use 47610 with 47550)

47612 with choledochoenterostomy

47620 with transduodenal sphincterotomy or sphincteroplasty, with or without cholangiography

47630 Biliary duct stone extraction, percutaneous via T-tube tract, basket, or snare (eg, Burhenne technique)

(For radiological supervision and interpretation, use 74327)

47700 Exploration for congenital atresia of bile ducts, without repair, with or without liver biopsy, with or without cholangiography

(Do not report modifier 63 in conjunction with 47700)

47701 Portoenterostomy (eg, Kasai procedure)

(Do not report modifier 63 in conjunction with 47701)

47711 Excision of bile duct tumor, with or without primary repair of bile duct; extrahepatic

47712 intrahepatic

(For anastomosis, see 47760-47800)

47715 Excision of choledochal cyst

►(47716 has been deleted. To report, use 47719)◄

Repair

● 47719 Anastomosis, choledochal cyst, without excision

47720 Cholecystoenterostomy; direct

(For laparoscopic approach, use 47570)

Surgery: Digestive System

47721 with gastroenterostomy

47740 Roux-en-Y

47741 Roux-en-Y with gastroenterostomy

47760 Anastomosis, of extrahepatic biliary ducts and gastrointestinal tract

47765 Anastomosis, of intrahepatic ducts and gastrointestinal tract

47780 Anastomosis, Roux-en-Y, of extrahepatic biliary ducts and gastrointestinal tract

47785 Anastomosis, Roux-en-Y, of intrahepatic biliary ducts and gastrointestinal tract

47800 Reconstruction, plastic, of extrahepatic biliary ducts with end-to-end anastomosis

47801 Placement of choledochal stent

47802 U-tube hepaticoenterostomy

47900 Suture of extrahepatic biliary duct for pre-existing injury (separate procedure)

Other Procedures

47999 Unlisted procedure, biliary tract

Pancreas

(For peroral pancreatic endoscopic procedures, see 43260-43272)

Incision

48000 Placement of drains, peripancreatic, for acute pancreatitis;

48001 with cholecystostomy, gastrostomy, and jejunostomy

▶(48005 has been deleted. To report, see 48105)◀

48020 Removal of pancreatic calculus

Excision

48100 Biopsy of pancreas, open (eg, fine needle aspiration, needle core biopsy, wedge biopsy)

48102 Biopsy of pancreas, percutaneous needle

▶(For radiological supervision and interpretation, see 76942, 77002, 77012, 77021)◀

(For fine needle aspiration, use 10022)

(For evaluation of fine needle aspirate, see 88172, 88173)

● **48105** Resection or debridement of pancreas and peripancreatic tissue for acute necrotizing pancreatitis

48120 Excision of lesion of pancreas (eg, cyst, adenoma)

48140 Pancreatectomy, distal subtotal, with or without splenectomy; without pancreaticojejunostomy

48145 with pancreaticojejunostomy

48146 Pancreatectomy, distal, near-total with preservation of duodenum (Child-type procedure)

48148 Excision of ampulla of Vater

48150 Pancreatectomy, proximal subtotal with total duodenectomy, partial gastrectomy, choledochoenterostomy and gastrojejunostomy (Whipple-type procedure); with pancreatojejunostomy

48152 without pancreatojejunostomy

48153 Pancreatectomy, proximal subtotal with near-total duodenectomy, choledochoenterostomy and duodenojejunostomy (pylorus-sparing, Whipple-type procedure); with pancreatojejunostomy

48154 without pancreatojejunostomy

48155 Pancreatectomy, total

48160 Pancreatectomy, total or subtotal, with autologous transplantation of pancreas or pancreatic islet cells

▶(48180 has been deleted. To report, see 48548)◀

Introduction

+ **48400** Injection procedure for intraoperative pancreatography (List separately in addition to code for primary procedure)

(For radiological supervision and interpretation, see 74300-74305)

Repair

48500 Marsupialization of pancreatic cyst

48510 External drainage, pseudocyst of pancreas; open

⊙ **48511** percutaneous

(For radiological supervision and interpretation, use 75989)

48520 Internal anastomosis of pancreatic cyst to gastrointestinal tract; direct

48540 Roux-en-Y

48545 Pancreatorrhaphy for injury

48547 Duodenal exclusion with gastrojejunostomy for pancreatic injury

● **48548** Pancreaticojejunostomy, side-to-side anastomosis (Puestow-type operation)

Pancreas Transplantation

Pancreas allotransplantation involves three distinct components of physician work:

1) *Cadaver donor pancreatectomy*, which includes harvesting the pancreas graft, with or without duodenal segment, and cold preservation of the graft (perfusing with cold preservation solution and cold maintenance) (use 48550).

2) *Backbench work*:

Standard preparation of a cadaver donor pancreas allograft prior to transplantation includes dissection of the allograft from surrounding soft tissues, splenectomy, duodenotomy, ligation of bile duct, ligation of mesenteric vessels, and Y-graft arterial anastomoses from the iliac artery to the superior mesenteric artery and to the splenic artery (use 48551).

Additional reconstruction of a cadaver donor pancreas allograft prior to transplantation may include venous anastomosis(es) (use 48552).

3) *Recipient pancreas allotransplantation*, which includes transplantation of allograft, and care of the recipient (use 48554).

48550 Donor pancreatectomy (including cold preservation), with or without duodenal segment for transplantation

48551 Backbench standard preparation of cadaver donor pancreas allograft prior to transplantation, including dissection of allograft from surrounding soft tissues, splenectomy, duodenotomy, ligation of bile duct, ligation of mesenteric vessels, and Y-graft arterial anastomoses from iliac artery to superior mesenteric artery and to splenic artery

48552 Backbench reconstruction of cadaver donor pancreas allograft prior to transplantation, venous anastomosis, each

(Do not report 48551 and 48552 in conjunction with 35531, 35563, 35685, 38100-38102, 44010, 44820, 44850, 47460, 47505-47525, 47550-47556, 48100-48120, 48545)

48554 Transplantation of pancreatic allograft

48556 Removal of transplanted pancreatic allograft

Other Procedures

48999 Unlisted procedure, pancreas

Abdomen, Peritoneum, and Omentum

Incision

49000 Exploratory laparotomy, exploratory celiotomy with or without biopsy(s) (separate procedure)

(To report wound exploration due to penetrating trauma without laparotomy, use 20102)

49002 Reopening of recent laparotomy

(To report re-exploration of hepatic wound for removal of packing, use 47362)

49010 Exploration, retroperitoneal area with or without biopsy(s) (separate procedure)

(To report wound exploration due to penetrating trauma without laparotomy, use 20102)

49020 Drainage of peritoneal abscess or localized peritonitis, exclusive of appendiceal abscess; open

(For appendiceal abscess, use 44900)

⊙ **49021** percutaneous

(For radiological supervision and interpretation, use 75989)

49040 Drainage of subdiaphragmatic or subphrenic abscess; open

⊙ **49041** percutaneous

(For radiological supervision and interpretation, use 75989)

49060 Drainage of retroperitoneal abscess; open

⊙ **49061** percutaneous

(For laparoscopic drainage, use 49323)

(For radiological supervision and interpretation, use 75989)

49062 Drainage of extraperitoneal lymphocele to peritoneal cavity, open

49080 Peritoneocentesis, abdominal paracentesis, or peritoneal lavage (diagnostic or therapeutic); initial

49081 subsequent

►(If imaging guidance is performed, see 76942, 77012)◄

►(49085 has been deleted. To report, see 49402)◄

Excision, Destruction

►(For lysis of intestinal adhesions, use 44005)◄

49180 Biopsy, abdominal or retroperitoneal mass, percutaneous needle

►(If imaging guidance is performed, see 76942, 77002, 77012, 77021)◄

(For fine needle aspiration, use 10021 or 10022)

(For evaluation of fine needle aspirate, see 88172, 88173)

49200 Excision or destruction, open, intra-abdominal or retroperitoneal tumors or cysts or endometriomas;

49201 extensive

►(For resection of recurrent ovarian, tubal, primary peritoneal, or uterine malignancy, see 58957, 58958)◄

(For open cryoablation of renal tumor, use 50250)

(For percutaneous cryotherapy ablation of renal tumors, use Category III code 0135T)

49215 Excision of presacral or sacrococcygeal tumor

(Do not report modifier 63 in conjunction with 49215)

49220 Staging laparotomy for Hodgkins disease or lymphoma (includes splenectomy, needle or open biopsies of both liver lobes, possibly also removal of abdominal nodes, abdominal node and/or bone marrow biopsies, ovarian repositioning)

49250 Umbilectomy, omphalectomy, excision of umbilicus (separate procedure)

49255 Omentectomy, epiploectomy, resection of omentum (separate procedure)

Laparoscopy

Surgical laparoscopy always includes diagnostic laparoscopy. To report a diagnostic laparoscopy (peritoneoscopy), (separate procedure), use 49320.

For laparoscopic fulguration or excision of lesions of the ovary, pelvic viscera, or peritoneal surface use 58662.

49320 Laparoscopy, abdomen, peritoneum, and omentum, diagnostic, with or without collection of specimen(s) by brushing or washing (separate procedure)

49321 Laparoscopy, surgical; with biopsy (single or multiple)

49322 with aspiration of cavity or cyst (eg, ovarian cyst) (single or multiple)

49323 with drainage of lymphocele to peritoneal cavity

 (For percutaneous or open drainage, see 49060, 49061)

● **49324** with insertion of intraperitoneal cannula or catheter, permanent

 ►(For subcutaneous extension of intraperitoneal catheter with remote chest exit site, use 49435 in conjunction with 49324)◄

 ►(For open insertion of permanent intraperitoneal cannula or catheter, use 49421)◄

● **49325** with revision of previously placed intraperitoneal cannula or catheter, with removal of intraluminal obstructive material if performed

+● **49326** with omentopexy (omental tacking procedure) (List separately in addition to code for primary procedure)

 ►(Use 49326 in conjunction with 49324, 49325)◄

49329 Unlisted laparoscopy procedure, abdomen, peritoneum and omentum

►Introduction, Revision, Removal◄

49400 Injection of air or contrast into peritoneal cavity (separate procedure)

 (For radiological supervision and interpretation, use 74190)

● **49402** Removal of peritoneal foreign body from peritoneal cavity

 ►(For lysis of intestinal adhesions, use 44005)◄

49419 Insertion of intraperitoneal cannula or catheter, with subcutaneous reservoir, permanent (ie, totally implantable)

 (For removal, use 49422)

49420 Insertion of intraperitoneal cannula or catheter for drainage or dialysis; temporary

49421 permanent

 ►(For laparoscopic insertion of permanent intraperitoneal cannula or catheter, use 49324)◄

 ►(For subcutaneous extension of intraperitoneal catheter with remote chest exit site, use 49435 in conjunction with 49421)◄

49422 Removal of permanent intraperitoneal cannula or catheter

 (For removal of a temporary catheter/cannula, use appropriate E/M code)

49423 Exchange of previously placed abscess or cyst drainage catheter under radiological guidance (separate procedure)

 (For radiological supervision and interpretation, use 75984)

49424 Contrast injection for assessment of abscess or cyst via previously placed drainage catheter or tube (separate procedure)

 (For radiological supervision and interpretation, use 76080)

49425 Insertion of peritoneal-venous shunt

49426 Revision of peritoneal-venous shunt

 (For shunt patency test, use 78291)

49427 Injection procedure (eg, contrast media) for evaluation of previously placed peritoneal-venous shunt

 (For radiological supervision and interpretation, see 75809, 78291)

49428 Ligation of peritoneal-venous shunt

49429 Removal of peritoneal-venous shunt

+● **49435** Insertion of subcutaneous extension to intraperitoneal cannula or catheter with remote chest exit site (List separately in addition to code for primary procedure)

 ►(Use 49435 in conjunction with 49324, 49421)◄

● **49436** Delayed creation of exit site from embedded subcutaneous segment of intraperitoneal cannula or catheter

Repair

Hernioplasty, Herniorrhaphy, Herniotomy

The hernia repair codes in this section are categorized primarily by the type of hernia (inguinal, femoral, incisional, etc).

Some types of hernias are further categorized as "initial" or "recurrent" based on whether or not the hernia has required previous repair(s).

Surgery: Digestive System

Additional variables accounted for by some of the codes include patient age and clinical presentation (reducible vs. incarcerated or strangulated).

With the exception of the incisional hernia repairs (see 49560-49566) the use of mesh or other prostheses is not separately reported.

The excision/repair of strangulated organs or structures such as testicle(s), intestine, ovaries are reported by using the appropriate code for the excision/repair (eg, 44120, 54520, and 58940) in addition to the appropriate code for the repair of the strangulated hernia.

(For reduction and repair of intra-abdominal hernia, use 44050)

(For debridement of abdominal wall, see 11042, 11043)

(Codes 49491-49651 are unilateral procedures. To report bilateral procedures, report modifier 50 with the appropriate procedure code)

49491 Repair, initial inguinal hernia, preterm infant (younger than 37 weeks gestation at birth), performed from birth up to 50 weeks postconception age, with or without hydrocelectomy; reducible

49492 incarcerated or strangulated

(Do not report modifier 63 in conjunction with 49491, 49492)

(Postconception age equals gestational age at birth plus age of infant in weeks at the time of the hernia repair. Initial inguinal hernia repairs that are performed on preterm infants who are older than 50 weeks postconception age and younger than age 6 months at the time of surgery, should be reported using codes 49495, 49496)

49495 Repair, initial inguinal hernia, full term infant younger than age 6 months, or preterm infant older than 50 weeks postconception age and younger than age 6 months at the time of surgery, with or without hydrocelectomy; reducible

49496 incarcerated or strangulated

(Do not report modifier 63 in conjunction with 49495, 49496)

(Postconception age equals gestational age at birth plus age in weeks at the time of the hernia repair. Initial inguinal hernia repairs that are performed on preterm infants who are younger than or up to 50 weeks postconception age but younger than 6 months of age since birth, should be reported using codes 49491, 49492. Inguinal hernia repairs on infants age 6 months to younger than 5 years should be reported using codes 49500-49501)

49500 Repair initial inguinal hernia, age 6 months to younger than 5 years, with or without hydrocelectomy; reducible

49501 incarcerated or strangulated

49505 Repair initial inguinal hernia, age 5 years or older; reducible

49507 incarcerated or strangulated

(For inguinal hernia repair, with simple orchiectomy, see 49505 or 49507 and 54520)

(For inguinal hernia repair, with excision of hydrocele or spermatocele, see 49505 or 49507 and 54840 or 55040)

49520 Repair recurrent inguinal hernia, any age; reducible

49521 incarcerated or strangulated

49525 Repair inguinal hernia, sliding, any age

(For incarcerated or strangulated inguinal hernia repair, see 49496, 49501, 49507, 49521)

49540 Repair lumbar hernia

49550 Repair initial femoral hernia, any age; reducible

49553 incarcerated or strangulated

49555 Repair recurrent femoral hernia; reducible

49557 incarcerated or strangulated

49560 Repair initial incisional or ventral hernia; reducible

49561 incarcerated or strangulated

49565 Repair recurrent incisional or ventral hernia; reducible

49566 incarcerated or strangulated

+ 49568 Implantation of mesh or other prosthesis for incisional or ventral hernia repair (List separately in addition to code for the incisional or ventral hernia repair)

49570 Repair epigastric hernia (eg, preperitoneal fat); reducible (separate procedure)

49572 incarcerated or strangulated

49580 Repair umbilical hernia, younger than age 5 years; reducible

49582 incarcerated or strangulated

49585 Repair umbilical hernia, age 5 years or older; reducible

49587 incarcerated or strangulated

49590 Repair spigelian hernia

49600 Repair of small omphalocele, with primary closure

(Do not report modifier 63 in conjunction with 49600)

49605 Repair of large omphalocele or gastroschisis; with or without prosthesis

49606 with removal of prosthesis, final reduction and closure, in operating room

(Do not report modifier 63 in conjunction with 49605, 49606)

49610 Repair of omphalocele (Gross type operation); first stage

49611 second stage

(Do not report modifier 63 in conjunction with 49610, 49611)

(For diaphragmatic or hiatal hernia repair, see 39502-39541)

(For surgical repair of omentum, use 49999)

Laparoscopy

Surgical laparoscopy always includes diagnostic laparoscopy. To report a diagnostic laparoscopy (peritoneoscopy) (separate procedure), use 49320.

49650 Laparoscopy, surgical; repair initial inguinal hernia

49651 repair recurrent inguinal hernia

49659 Unlisted laparoscopy procedure, hernioplasty, herniorrhaphy, herniotomy

Suture

49900 Suture, secondary, of abdominal wall for evisceration or dehiscence

(For suture of ruptured diaphragm, see 39540, 39541)

(For debridement of abdominal wall, see 11042, 11043)

Other Procedures

49904 Omental flap, extra-abdominal (eg, for reconstruction of sternal and chest wall defects)

(Code 49904 includes harvest and transfer. If a second surgeon harvests the omental flap, then the two surgeons should code 49904 as co-surgeons, using modifier 62)

+ **49905** Omental flap, intra-abdominal (List separately in addition to code for primary procedure)

(Do not report 49905 in conjunction with 44700)

49906 Free omental flap with microvascular anastomosis

(Do not report code 69990 in addition to 49906)

49999 Unlisted procedure, abdomen, peritoneum and omentum

Urinary System

▶(For provision of chemotherapeutic agents, report both the specific service in addition to code(s) for the specific substance(s) or drug(s) provided)◄

Kidney

Incision

(For retroperitoneal exploration, abscess, tumor, or cyst, see 49010, 49060, 49200, 49201)

50010 Renal exploration, not necessitating other specific procedures

(For laparoscopic ablation of renal mass lesion(s), use 50542)

50020 Drainage of perirenal or renal abscess; open

⊙ **50021** percutaneous

(For radiological supervision and interpretation, use 75989)

50040 Nephrostomy, nephrotomy with drainage

50045 Nephrotomy, with exploration

(For renal endoscopy performed in conjunction with this procedure, see 50570-50580)

50060 Nephrolithotomy; removal of calculus

50065 secondary surgical operation for calculus

50070 complicated by congenital kidney abnormality

50075 removal of large staghorn calculus filling renal pelvis and calyces (including anatrophic pyelolithotomy)

50080 Percutaneous nephrostolithotomy or pyelostolithotomy, with or without dilation, endoscopy, lithotripsy, stenting, or basket extraction; up to 2 cm

50081 over 2 cm

(For establishment of nephrostomy without nephrostolithotomy, see 50040, 50395, 52334)

(For fluoroscopic guidance, see 76000, 76001)

50100 Transection or repositioning of aberrant renal vessels (separate procedure)

50120 Pyelotomy; with exploration

(For renal endoscopy performed in conjunction with this procedure, see 50570-50580)

50125 with drainage, pyelostomy

50130 with removal of calculus (pyelolithotomy, pelviolithotomy, including coagulum pyelolithotomy)

50135 complicated (eg, secondary operation, congenital kidney abnormality)

(For supply of anticarcinogenic agents, use 99070 in addition to code for primary procedure)

Excision

(For excision of retroperitoneal tumor or cyst, see 49200, 49201)

(For laparoscopic ablation of renal mass lesion(s), use 50542)

50200 Renal biopsy; percutaneous, by trocar or needle

▶(For radiological supervision and interpretation, see 76942, 77002, 77012, 77021)◄

(For fine needle aspiration, use 10022)

(For evaluation of fine needle aspirate, see 88172, 88173)

50205 by surgical exposure of kidney

50220 Nephrectomy, including partial ureterectomy, any open approach including rib resection;

50225 complicated because of previous surgery on same kidney

50230 radical, with regional lymphadenectomy and/or vena caval thrombectomy

(When vena caval resection with reconstruction is necessary, use 37799)

50234 Nephrectomy with total ureterectomy and bladder cuff; through same incision

50236 through separate incision

50240 Nephrectomy, partial

(For laparoscopic partial nephrectomy, use 50543)

50250 Ablation, open, one or more renal mass lesion(s), cryosurgical, including intraoperative ultrasound, if performed

(For laparoscopic ablation of renal mass lesions, use 50542)

(For percutaneous cryotherapy ablation of renal tumors, use 0135T)

50280 Excision or unroofing of cyst(s) of kidney

(For laparoscopic ablation of renal cysts, use 50541)

50290 Excision of perinephric cyst

Renal Transplantation

Renal *auto*transplantation includes reimplantation of the autograft as the primary procedure, along with secondary extra-corporeal procedure(s) (eg, partial nephrectomy, nephrolithotomy) reported with modifier 51 (see 50380 and applicable secondary procedure(s)).

Renal *allo*transplantation involves three distinct components of physician work:

1) ***Cadaver donor nephrectomy, unilateral or bilateral***, which includes harvesting the graft(s) and cold preservation of the graft(s) (perfusing with cold preservation solution and cold maintenance)

Surgery: Urinary System

Surgery: Urinary System

(use 50300). *Living donor nephrectomy*, which includes harvesting the graft, cold preservation of the graft (perfusing with cold preservation solution and cold maintenance), and care of the donor (see 50320, 50547).

2) *Backbench work*:

Standard preparation of a cadaver donor renal allograft prior to transplantation including dissection and removal of perinephric fat, diaphragmatic and retroperitoneal attachments; excision of adrenal gland; and preparation of ureter(s), renal vein(s), and renal artery(s), ligating branches, as necessary (use 50323).

Standard preparation of a living donor renal allograft (open or laparoscopic) prior to transplantation including dissection and removal of perinephric fat and preparation of ureter(s), renal vein(s), and renal artery(s), ligating branches, as necessary (use 50325).

Additional reconstruction of a cadaver or living donor renal allograft prior to transplantation may include venous, arterial, and/or ureteral anastomosis(es) necessary for implantation (see 50327-50329).

3) *Recipient renal allotransplantation*, which includes transplantation of the allograft (with or without recipient nephrectomy) and care of the recipient (see 50360, 50365).

(For dialysis, see 90935-90999)

(For laparoscopic donor nephrectomy, use 50547)

(For laparoscopic drainage of lymphocele to peritoneal cavity, use 49323)

50300 Donor nephrectomy (including cold preservation); from cadaver donor, unilateral or bilateral

50320 open, from living donor

50323 Backbench standard preparation of cadaver donor renal allograft prior to transplantation, including dissection and removal of perinephric fat, diaphragmatic and retroperitoneal attachments, excision of adrenal gland, and preparation of ureter(s), renal vein(s), and renal artery(s), ligating branches, as necessary

(Do not report 50323 in conjunction with 60540, 60545)

50325 Backbench standard preparation of living donor renal allograft (open or laparoscopic) prior to transplantation, including dissection and removal of perinephric fat and preparation of ureter(s), renal vein(s), and renal artery(s), ligating branches, as necessary

50327 Backbench reconstruction of cadaver or living donor renal allograft prior to transplantation; venous anastomosis, each

50328 arterial anastomosis, each

50329 ureteral anastomosis, each

50340 Recipient nephrectomy (separate procedure)

(For bilateral procedure, report 50340 with modifier 50)

50360 Renal allotransplantation, implantation of graft; without recipient nephrectomy

50365 with recipient nephrectomy

(For bilateral procedure, report 50365 with modifier 50)

50370 Removal of transplanted renal allograft

50380 Renal autotransplantation, reimplantation of kidney

(For renal autotransplantation extra-corporeal (bench) surgery, use autotransplantation as the primary procedure and report secondary procedure(s) (eg, partial nephrectomy, nephrolithotomy) with modifier 51)

Introduction

Renal Pelvis Catheter Procedures

Internally Dwelling

⊙ 50382 Removal (via snare/capture) and replacement of internally dwelling ureteral stent via percutaneous approach, including radiological supervision and interpretation

(For bilateral procedure, use modifier 50)

⊙ 50384 Removal (via snare/capture) of internally dwelling ureteral stent via percutaneous approach, including radiological supervision and interpretation

(For bilateral procedure, use modifier 50)

(Do not report 50382, 50384 in conjunction with 50395)

Externally Accessible

⊙ 50387 Removal and replacement of externally accessible transnephric ureteral stent (eg, external/internal stent) requiring fluoroscopic guidance, including radiological supervision and interpretation

(For bilateral procedure, use modifier 50)

(For removal and replacement of externally accessible ureteral stent via ureterostomy or ilieal conduit, use 50688)

(For removal without replacement of an externally accessible ureteral stent not requiring fluoroscopic guidance, see **Evaluation and Management** services codes)

50389 Removal of nephrostomy tube, requiring fluoroscopic guidance (eg, with concurrent indwelling ureteral stent)

(Removal of nephrostomy tube not requiring fluoroscopic guidance is considered inherent to E/M services. Report the appropriate level of E/M service provided)

Other Introduction Procedures

50390 Aspiration and/or injection of renal cyst or pelvis by needle, percutaneous

▶(For radiological supervision and interpretation, see 74425, 74470, 76942, 77002, 77012, 77021)◀

(For evaluation of fine needle aspirate, see 88172, 88173)

50391 Instillation(s) of therapeutic agent into renal pelvis and/or ureter through established nephrostomy, pyelostomy or ureterostomy tube (eg, anticarcinogenic or antifungal agent)

50392 Introduction of intracatheter or catheter into renal pelvis for drainage and/or injection, percutaneous

▶(For radiological supervision and interpretation, see 74475, 76942, 77012)◀

50393 Introduction of ureteral catheter or stent into ureter through renal pelvis for drainage and/or injection, percutaneous

▶(For radiological supervision and interpretation, see 74480, 76942, 77002, 77012)◀

50394 Injection procedure for pyelography (as nephrostogram, pyelostogram, antegrade pyeloureterograms) through nephrostomy or pyelostomy tube, or indwelling ureteral catheter

(For radiological supervision and interpretation, use 74425)

50395 Introduction of guide into renal pelvis and/or ureter with dilation to establish nephrostomy tract, percutaneous

(For radiological supervision and interpretation, see 74475, 74480, 74485)

(For nephrostolithotomy, see 50080, 50081)

(For retrograde percutaneous nephrostomy, use 52334)

(For endoscopic surgery, see 50551-50561)

50396 Manometric studies through nephrostomy or pyelostomy tube, or indwelling ureteral catheter

(For radiological supervision and interpretation, see 74425, 74475, 74480)

50398 Change of nephrostomy or pyelostomy tube

(For radiological supervision and interpretation, use 75984)

Repair

50400 Pyeloplasty (Foley Y-pyeloplasty), plastic operation on renal pelvis, with or without plastic operation on ureter, nephropexy, nephrostomy, pyelostomy, or ureteral splinting; simple

50405 complicated (congenital kidney abnormality, secondary pyeloplasty, solitary kidney, calycoplasty)

(For laparoscopic approach, use 50544)

50500 Nephrorrhaphy, suture of kidney wound or injury

50520 Closure of nephrocutaneous or pyelocutaneous fistula

50525 Closure of nephrovisceral fistula (eg, renocolic), including visceral repair; abdominal approach

50526 thoracic approach

50540 Symphysiotomy for horseshoe kidney with or without pyeloplasty and/or other plastic procedure, unilateral or bilateral (one operation)

Laparoscopy

Surgical laparoscopy always includes diagnostic laparoscopy. To report a diagnostic laparoscopy (peritoneoscopy) (separate procedure), use 49320.

50541 Laparoscopy, surgical; ablation of renal cysts

50542 ablation of renal mass lesion(s)

(For open procedure, see 50220-50240)

(For open cryosurgical ablation, use 50250)

(For percutaneous cryotherapy ablation of renal tumors, use 0135T)

50543 partial nephrectomy

(For open procedure, use 50240)

50544 pyeloplasty

50545 radical nephrectomy (includes removal of Gerota's fascia and surrounding fatty tissue, removal of regional lymph nodes, and adrenalectomy)

(For open procedure, use 50230)

50546 nephrectomy, including partial ureterectomy

50547 donor nephrectomy (including cold preservation), from living donor

(For open procedure, use 50320)

(For backbench renal allograft standard preparation prior to transplantation, use 50325)

(For backbench renal allograft reconstruction prior to transplantation, see 50327-50329)

50548 nephrectomy with total ureterectomy

(For open procedure, see 50234, 50236)

50549 Unlisted laparoscopy procedure, renal

(For laparoscopic drainage of lymphocele to peritoneal cavity, use 49323)

Endoscopy

(For supplies and materials, use 99070)

50551 Renal endoscopy through established nephrostomy or pyelostomy, with or without irrigation, instillation, or ureteropyelography, exclusive of radiologic service;

50553 with ureteral catheterization, with or without dilation of ureter

50555 with biopsy

50557 with fulguration and/or incision, with or without biopsy

(50559 has been deleted)

50561 with removal of foreign body or calculus

50562 with resection of tumor

(When procedures 50570-50580 provide a significant identifiable service, they may be added to 50045 and 50120)

50570 Renal endoscopy through nephrotomy or pyelotomy, with or without irrigation, instillation, or ureteropyelography, exclusive of radiologic service;

(For nephrotomy, use 50045)

(For pyelotomy, use 50120)

50572 with ureteral catheterization, with or without dilation of ureter

50574 with biopsy

50575 with endopyelotomy (includes cystoscopy, ureteroscopy, dilation of ureter and ureteral pelvic junction, incision of ureteral pelvic junction and insertion of endopyelotomy stent)

50576 with fulguration and/or incision, with or without biopsy

(50578 has been deleted)

50580 with removal of foreign body or calculus

Other Procedures

50590 Lithotripsy, extracorporeal shock wave

⊙ 50592 Ablation, one or more renal tumor(s), percutaneous, unilateral, radiofrequency

(50592 is a unilateral procedure. For bilateral procedure, report 50592 with modifier 50)

▶(For imaging guidance and monitoring, see 76940, 77013, 77022)◀

(For percutaneous cryotherapy ablation of renal tumors, use 0135T)

Ureter

Incision

50600 Ureterotomy with exploration or drainage (separate procedure)

(For ureteral endoscopy performed in conjunction with this procedure, see 50970-50980)

50605 Ureterotomy for insertion of indwelling stent, all types

50610 Ureterolithotomy; upper one-third of ureter

50620 middle one-third of ureter

50630 lower one-third of ureter

(For laparoscopic approach, use 50945)

(For transvesical ureterolithotomy, use 51060)

(For cystotomy with stone basket extraction of ureteral calculus, use 51065)

(For endoscopic extraction or manipulation of ureteral calculus, see 50080, 50081, 50561, 50961, 50980, 52320-52330, 52352, 52353)

Excision

(For ureterocele, see 51535, 52300)

50650 Ureterectomy, with bladder cuff (separate procedure)

50660 Ureterectomy, total, ectopic ureter, combination abdominal, vaginal and/or perineal approach

Introduction

50684 Injection procedure for ureterography or ureteropyelography through ureterostomy or indwelling ureteral catheter

(For radiological supervision and interpretation, use 74425)

50686 Manometric studies through ureterostomy or indwelling ureteral catheter

50688 Change of ureterostomy tube or externally accessible ureteral stent via ileal conduit

(If imaging guidance is performed, use 75984)

50690 Injection procedure for visualization of ileal conduit and/or ureteropyelography, exclusive of radiologic service

(For radiological supervision and interpretation, use 74425)

Repair

50700 Ureteroplasty, plastic operation on ureter (eg, stricture)

50715 Ureterolysis, with or without repositioning of ureter for retroperitoneal fibrosis

(For bilateral procedure, report 50715 with modifier 50)

50722 Ureterolysis for ovarian vein syndrome

50725 Ureterolysis for retrocaval ureter, with reanastomosis of upper urinary tract or vena cava

50727 Revision of urinary-cutaneous anastomosis (any type urostomy);

50728 with repair of fascial defect and hernia

50740 Ureteropyelostomy, anastomosis of ureter and renal pelvis

50750 Ureterocalycostomy, anastomosis of ureter to renal calyx

50760 Ureteroureterostomy

50770 Transureteroureterostomy, anastomosis of ureter to contralateral ureter

(Codes 50780-50785 include minor procedures to prevent vesicoureteral reflux)

50780 Ureteroneocystostomy; anastomosis of single ureter to bladder

(For bilateral procedure, report 50780 with modifier 50)

(When combined with cystourethroplasty or vesical neck revision, use 51820)

50782 anastomosis of duplicated ureter to bladder

50783 with extensive ureteral tailoring

50785 with vesico-psoas hitch or bladder flap

(For bilateral procedure, report 50785 with modifier 50)

50800 Ureteroenterostomy, direct anastomosis of ureter to intestine

(For bilateral procedure, report 50800 with modifier 50)

50810 Ureterosigmoidostomy, with creation of sigmoid bladder and establishment of abdominal or perineal colostomy, including intestine anastomosis

50815 Ureterocolon conduit, including intestine anastomosis

(For bilateral procedure, report 50815 with modifier 50)

50820 Ureteroileal conduit (ileal bladder), including intestine anastomosis (Bricker operation)

(For bilateral procedure, report 50820 with modifier 50)

(For combination of 50800-50820 with cystectomy, see 51580-51595)

50825 Continent diversion, including intestine anastomosis using any segment of small and/or large intestine (Kock pouch or Camey enterocystoplasty)

50830 Urinary undiversion (eg, taking down of ureteroileal conduit, ureterosigmoidostomy or ureteroenterostomy with ureteroureterostomy or ureteroneocystostomy)

50840 Replacement of all or part of ureter by intestine segment, including intestine anastomosis

(For bilateral procedure, report 50840 with modifier 50)

50845 Cutaneous appendico-vesicostomy

50860 Ureterostomy, transplantation of ureter to skin

(For bilateral procedure, report 50860 with modifier 50)

50900 Ureterorrhaphy, suture of ureter (separate procedure)

50920 Closure of ureterocutaneous fistula

50930 Closure of ureterovisceral fistula (including visceral repair)

50940 Deligation of ureter

(For ureteroplasty, ureterolysis, see 50700-50860)

Laparoscopy

Surgical laparoscopy always includes diagnostic laparoscopy. To report a diagnostic laparoscopy (peritoneoscopy) (separate procedure), use 49320.

50945 Laparoscopy, surgical; ureterolithotomy

50947 ureteroneocystostomy with cystoscopy and ureteral stent placement

50948 ureteroneocystostomy without cystoscopy and ureteral stent placement

(For open ureteroneocystostomy, see 50780-50785)

50949 Unlisted laparoscopy procedure, ureter

Endoscopy

50951 Ureteral endoscopy through established ureterostomy, with or without irrigation, instillation, or ureteropyelography, exclusive of radiologic service;

50953 with ureteral catheterization, with or without dilation of ureter

50955 with biopsy

50957 with fulguration and/or incision, with or without biopsy

(50959 has been deleted)

50961 with removal of foreign body or calculus

(When procedures 50970-50980 provide a significant identifiable service, they may be added to 50600)

50970 Ureteral endoscopy through ureterotomy, with or without irrigation, instillation, or ureteropyelography, exclusive of radiologic service;

(For ureterotomy, use 50600)

50972 with ureteral catheterization, with or without dilation of ureter

50974 with biopsy

50976 with fulguration and/or incision, with or without biopsy

(50978 has been deleted)

50980 with removal of foreign body or calculus

Surgery: Urinary System

Bladder

Incision

51000 Aspiration of bladder by needle

51005 Aspiration of bladder; by trocar or intracatheter

51010 with insertion of suprapubic catheter

►(If imaging guidance is performed, see 76942, 77002, 77012)◄

51020 Cystotomy or cystostomy; with fulguration and/or insertion of radioactive material

51030 with cryosurgical destruction of intravesical lesion

51040 Cystostomy, cystotomy with drainage

51045 Cystotomy, with insertion of ureteral catheter or stent (separate procedure)

51050 Cystolithotomy, cystotomy with removal of calculus, without vesical neck resection

51060 Transvesical ureterolithotomy

51065 Cystotomy, with calculus basket extraction and/or ultrasonic or electrohydraulic fragmentation of ureteral calculus

51080 Drainage of perivesical or prevesical space abscess

Excision

51500 Excision of urachal cyst or sinus, with or without umbilical hernia repair

51520 Cystotomy; for simple excision of vesical neck (separate procedure)

51525 for excision of bladder diverticulum, single or multiple (separate procedure)

51530 for excision of bladder tumor

(For transurethral resection, see 52234-52240, 52305)

51535 Cystotomy for excision, incision, or repair of ureterocele

(For bilateral procedure, report 51535 with modifier 50)

(For transurethral excision, use 52300)

51550 Cystectomy, partial; simple

51555 complicated (eg, postradiation, previous surgery, difficult location)

51565 Cystectomy, partial, with reimplantation of ureter(s) into bladder (ureteroneocystostomy)

51570 Cystectomy, complete; (separate procedure)

51575 with bilateral pelvic lymphadenectomy, including external iliac, hypogastric, and obturator nodes

51580 Cystectomy, complete, with ureterosigmoidostomy or ureterocutaneous transplantations;

51585 with bilateral pelvic lymphadenectomy, including external iliac, hypogastric, and obturator nodes

51590 Cystectomy, complete, with ureteroileal conduit or sigmoid bladder, including intestine anastomosis;

51595 with bilateral pelvic lymphadenectomy, including external iliac, hypogastric, and obturator nodes

51596 Cystectomy, complete, with continent diversion, any open technique, using any segment of small and/or large intestine to construct neobladder

51597 Pelvic exenteration, complete, for vesical, prostatic or urethral malignancy, with removal of bladder and ureteral transplantations, with or without hysterectomy and/or abdominoperineal resection of rectum and colon and colostomy, or any combination thereof

(For pelvic exenteration for gynecologic malignancy, use 58240)

Introduction

51600 Injection procedure for cystography or voiding urethrocystography

(For radiological supervision and interpretation, see 74430, 74455)

51605 Injection procedure and placement of chain for contrast and/or chain urethrocystography

(For radiological supervision and interpretation, use 74430)

51610 Injection procedure for retrograde urethrocystography

(For radiological supervision and interpretation, use 74450)

51700 Bladder irrigation, simple, lavage and/or instillation

(Codes 51701-51702 are reported only when performed independently. Do not report 51701-51702 when catheter insertion is an inclusive component of another procedure.)

51701 Insertion of non-indwelling bladder catheter (eg, straight catheterization for residual urine)

51702 Insertion of temporary indwelling bladder catheter; simple (eg, Foley)

51703 complicated (eg, altered anatomy, fractured catheter/balloon)

51705 Change of cystostomy tube; simple

51710 complicated

(If imaging guidance is performed, use 75984)

51715 Endoscopic injection of implant material into the submucosal tissues of the urethra and/or bladder neck

▲ **51720** Bladder instillation of anticarcinogenic agent (including retention time)

Urodynamics

The following section (51725-51797) lists procedures that may be used separately or in many and varied combinations.

When multiple procedures are performed in the same investigative session, modifier 51 should be employed.

All procedures in this section imply that these services are performed by, or are under the direct supervision of, a physician and that all instruments, equipment, fluids, gases, probes, catheters, technician's fees, medications, gloves, trays, tubing and other sterile supplies be provided by the physician. When the physician only interprets the results and/or operates the equipment, a professional component, modifier 26, should be used to identify physicians' services.

51725	Simple cystometrogram (CMG) (eg, spinal manometer)
51726	Complex cystometrogram (eg, calibrated electronic equipment)
51736	Simple uroflowmetry (UFR) (eg, stop-watch flow rate, mechanical uroflowmeter)
51741	Complex uroflowmetry (eg, calibrated electronic equipment)
51772	Urethral pressure profile studies (UPP) (urethral closure pressure profile), any technique
51784	Electromyography studies (EMG) of anal or urethral sphincter, other than needle, any technique
51785	Needle electromyography studies (EMG) of anal or urethral sphincter, any technique
51792	Stimulus evoked response (eg, measurement of bulbocavernosus reflex latency time)
51795	Voiding pressure studies (VP); bladder voiding pressure, any technique
51797	intra-abdominal voiding pressure (AP) (rectal, gastric, intraperitoneal)
51798	Measurement of post-voiding residual urine and/or bladder capacity by ultrasound, non-imaging

Repair

51800	Cystoplasty or cystourethroplasty, plastic operation on bladder and/or vesical neck (anterior Y-plasty, vesical fundus resection), any procedure, with or without wedge resection of posterior vesical neck
51820	Cystourethroplasty with unilateral or bilateral ureteroneocystostomy
51840	Anterior vesicourethropexy, or urethropexy (eg, Marshall-Marchetti-Krantz, Burch); simple
51841	complicated (eg, secondary repair)
	(For urethropexy (Pereyra type), use 57289)

51845	Abdomino-vaginal vesical neck suspension, with or without endoscopic control (eg, Stamey, Raz, modified Pereyra)
51860	Cystorrhaphy, suture of bladder wound, injury or rupture; simple
51865	complicated
51880	Closure of cystostomy (separate procedure)
51900	Closure of vesicovaginal fistula, abdominal approach
	(For vaginal approach, see 57320-57330)
51920	Closure of vesicouterine fistula;
51925	with hysterectomy
	(For closure of vesicoenteric fistula, see 44660, 44661)
	(For closure of rectovesical fistula, see 45800-45805)
51940	Closure, exstrophy of bladder
	(See also 54390)
51960	Enterocystoplasty, including intestinal anastomosis
51980	Cutaneous vesicostomy

Laparoscopy

Surgical laparoscopy always includes diagnostic laparoscopy. To report a diagnostic laparoscopy (peritoneoscopy) (separate procedure), use 49320.

51990	Laparoscopy, surgical; urethral suspension for stress incontinence
51992	sling operation for stress incontinence (eg, fascia or synthetic)
	(For open sling operation for stress incontinence, use 57288)
	(For reversal or removal of sling operation for stress incontinence, use 57287)
51999	Unlisted laparoscopy procedure, bladder

Endoscopy—Cystoscopy, Urethroscopy, Cystourethroscopy

Endoscopic descriptions are listed so that the main procedure can be identified without having to list all the minor related functions performed at the same time. For example: meatotomy, urethral calibration and/or dilation, urethro-scopy, and cystoscopy prior to a transurethral resection of prostate; ureteral catheterization following extraction of ureteral calculus; internal urethrotomy and bladder neck fulguration when performing a cystourethroscopy for the female urethral syndrome. When the secondary procedure requires significant additional time and effort, it may be identified by the addition of modifier 22.

For example: urethrotomy performed for a documented pre-existing stricture or bladder neck contracture.

Surgery: Urinary System

52000 Cystourethroscopy (separate procedure)

52001 Cystourethroscopy with irrigation and evacuation of multiple obstructing clots

(Do not report 52001 in conjunction with 52000)

52005 Cystourethroscopy, with ureteral catheterization, with or without irrigation, instillation, or ureteropyelography, exclusive of radiologic service;

52007 with brush biopsy of ureter and/or renal pelvis

52010 Cystourethroscopy, with ejaculatory duct catheterization, with or without irrigation, instillation, or duct radiography, exclusive of radiologic service

(For radiological supervision and interpretation, use 74440)

Transurethral Surgery

Urethra and Bladder

▲ **52204** Cystourethroscopy, with biopsy(s)

52214 Cystourethroscopy, with fulguration (including cryosurgery or laser surgery) of trigone, bladder neck, prostatic fossa, urethra, or periurethral glands

52224 Cystourethroscopy, with fulguration (including cryosurgery or laser surgery) or treatment of MINOR (less than 0.5 cm) lesion(s) with or without biopsy

52234 Cystourethroscopy, with fulguration (including cryosurgery or laser surgery) and/or resection of; SMALL bladder tumor(s) (0.5 up to 2.0 cm)

52235 MEDIUM bladder tumor(s) (2.0 to 5.0 cm)

52240 LARGE bladder tumor(s)

52250 Cystourethroscopy with insertion of radioactive substance, with or without biopsy or fulguration

52260 Cystourethroscopy, with dilation of bladder for interstitial cystitis; general or conduction (spinal) anesthesia

52265 local anesthesia

52270 Cystourethroscopy, with internal urethrotomy; female

52275 male

52276 Cystourethroscopy with direct vision internal urethrotomy

52277 Cystourethroscopy, with resection of external sphincter (sphincterotomy)

52281 Cystourethroscopy, with calibration and/or dilation of urethral stricture or stenosis, with or without meatotomy, with or without injection procedure for cystography, male or female

52282 Cystourethroscopy, with insertion of urethral stent

52283 Cystourethroscopy, with steroid injection into stricture

52285 Cystourethroscopy for treatment of the female urethral syndrome with any or all of the following: urethral meatotomy, urethral dilation, internal urethrotomy, lysis of urethrovaginal septal fibrosis, lateral incisions of the bladder neck, and fulguration of polyp(s) of urethra, bladder neck, and/or trigone

52290 Cystourethroscopy; with ureteral meatotomy, unilateral or bilateral

52300 with resection or fulguration of orthotopic ureterocele(s), unilateral or bilateral

52301 with resection or fulguration of ectopic ureterocele(s), unilateral or bilateral

52305 with incision or resection of orifice of bladder diverticulum, single or multiple

52310 Cystourethroscopy, with removal of foreign body, calculus, or ureteral stent from urethra or bladder (separate procedure); simple

52315 complicated

52317 Litholapaxy: crushing or fragmentation of calculus by any means in bladder and removal of fragments; simple or small (less than 2.5 cm)

52318 complicated or large (over 2.5 cm)

Ureter and Pelvis

►Therapeutic cystourethroscopy always includes diagnostic cystourethroscopy. To report a diagnostic cystourethroscopy, use 52000. Therapeutic cystourethroscopy with ureteroscopy and/or pyeloscopy always includes diagnostic cystourethroscopy with ureteroscopy and/or pyeloscopy. To report a diagnostic cystourethroscopy with ureteroscopy and/or pyeloscopy, use 52351.

Do not report 52000 in conjunction with 52320-52343.

Do not report 52351 in conjunction with 52344-52346, 52352-52355.

The insertion and removal of a temporary ureteral catheter (52005) during diagnostic or therapeutic cystourethroscopic with ureteroscopy and/or pyeloscopy is included in 52320-52355 and should not be reported separately.

To report insertion of a self-retaining, indwelling stent performed during diagnostic or therapeutic cystourethroscopy with ureteroscopy and/or pyeloscopy, report 52332, in addition to primary procedure(s) performed (52320-52355), and append modifier 51. 52332 is used to report a unilateral procedure unless otherwise specified.◄

For bilateral insertion of self-retaining, indwelling ureteral stents, use code 52332, and append modifier 50.

▶To report cystourethroscopic removal of a self-retaining, indwelling ureteral stent, see 52310, 52315, and append modifier 58, if appropriate.◀

52320 Cystourethroscopy (including ureteral catheterization); with removal of ureteral calculus

52325 with fragmentation of ureteral calculus (eg, ultrasonic or electro-hydraulic technique)

52327 with subureteric injection of implant material

52330 with manipulation, without removal of ureteral calculus

52332 Cystourethroscopy, with insertion of indwelling ureteral stent (eg, Gibbons or double-J type)

52334 Cystourethroscopy with insertion of ureteral guide wire through kidney to establish a percutaneous nephrostomy, retrograde

(For percutaneous nephrostolithotomy, see 50080, 50081; for establishment of nephrostomy tract only, use 50395)

(For cystourethroscopy, with ureteroscopy and/or pyeloscopy, see 52351-52355)

(For cystourethroscopy with incision, fulguration, or resection of congenital posterior urethral valves or obstructive hypertrophic mucosal folds, use 52400)

52341 Cystourethroscopy; with treatment of ureteral stricture (eg, balloon dilation, laser, electrocautery, and incision)

52342 with treatment of ureteropelvic junction stricture (eg, balloon dilation, laser, electrocautery, and incision)

52343 with treatment of intra-renal stricture (eg, balloon dilation, laser, electrocautery, and incision)

52344 Cystourethroscopy with ureteroscopy; with treatment of ureteral stricture (eg, balloon dilation, laser, electrocautery, and incision)

52345 with treatment of ureteropelvic junction stricture (eg, balloon dilation, laser, electrocautery, and incision)

52346 with treatment of intra-renal stricture (eg, balloon dilation, laser, electrocautery, and incision)

(52347 has been deleted)

(For transurethral resection or incision of ejaculatory ducts, use 52402)

52351 Cystourethroscopy, with ureteroscopy and/or pyeloscopy; diagnostic

(For radiological supervision and interpretation, use 74485)

(Do not report 52351 in conjunction with 52341-52346, 52352-52355)

52352 with removal or manipulation of calculus (ureteral catheterization is included)

52353 with lithotripsy (ureteral catheterization is included)

52354 with biopsy and/or fulguration of ureteral or renal pelvic lesion

52355 with resection of ureteral or renal pelvic tumor

Vesical Neck and Prostate

52400 Cystourethroscopy with incision, fulguration, or resection of congenital posterior urethral valves, or congenital obstructive hypertrophic mucosal folds

52402 Cystourethroscopy with transurethral resection or incision of ejaculatory ducts

52450 Transurethral incision of prostate

52500 Transurethral resection of bladder neck (separate procedure)

52510 Transurethral balloon dilation of the prostatic urethra

52601 Transurethral electrosurgical resection of prostate, including control of postoperative bleeding, complete (vasectomy, meatotomy, cystourethroscopy, urethral calibration and/or dilation, and internal urethrotomy are included)

(For other approaches, see 55801-55845)

52606 Transurethral fulguration for postoperative bleeding occurring after the usual follow-up time

52612 Transurethral resection of prostate; first stage of two-stage resection (partial resection)

52614 second stage of two-stage resection (resection completed)

52620 Transurethral resection; of residual obstructive tissue after 90 days postoperative

52630 of regrowth of obstructive tissue longer than one year postoperative

52640 of postoperative bladder neck contracture

52647 Laser coagulation of prostate, including control of postoperative bleeding, complete (vasectomy, meatotomy, cystourethroscopy, urethral calibration and/or dilation, and internal urethrotomy are included if performed)

52648 Laser vaporization of prostate, including control of postoperative bleeding, complete (vasectomy, meatotomy, cystourethroscopy, urethral calibration and/or dilation, internal urethrotomy and transurethral resection of prostate are included if performed)

52700 Transurethral drainage of prostatic abscess

(For litholapaxy, use 52317, 52318)

Surgery: Urinary System

Urethra

(For endoscopy, see cystoscopy, urethroscopy, cystourethroscopy, 52000-52700)

(For injection procedure for urethrocystography, see 51600-51610)

Incision

53000 Urethrotomy or urethrostomy, external (separate procedure); pendulous urethra

53010 perineal urethra, external

53020 Meatotomy, cutting of meatus (separate procedure); except infant

53025 infant

(Do not report modifier 63 in conjunction with 53025)

53040 Drainage of deep periurethral abscess

(For subcutaneous abscess, see 10060, 10061)

53060 Drainage of Skene's gland abscess or cyst

53080 Drainage of perineal urinary extravasation; uncomplicated (separate procedure)

53085 complicated

Excision

53200 Biopsy of urethra

53210 Urethrectomy, total, including cystostomy; female

53215 male

53220 Excision or fulguration of carcinoma of urethra

53230 Excision of urethral diverticulum (separate procedure); female

53235 male

53240 Marsupialization of urethral diverticulum, male or female

53250 Excision of bulbourethral gland (Cowper's gland)

53260 Excision or fulguration; urethral polyp(s), distal urethra

(For endoscopic approach, see 52214, 52224)

53265 urethral caruncle

53270 Skene's glands

53275 urethral prolapse

Repair

(For hypospadias, see 54300-54352)

53400 Urethroplasty; first stage, for fistula, diverticulum, or stricture (eg, Johannsen type)

53405 second stage (formation of urethra), including urinary diversion

53410 Urethroplasty, one-stage reconstruction of male anterior urethra

53415 Urethroplasty, transpubic or perineal, one stage, for reconstruction or repair of prostatic or membranous urethra

53420 Urethroplasty, two-stage reconstruction or repair of prostatic or membranous urethra; first stage

53425 second stage

53430 Urethroplasty, reconstruction of female urethra

53431 Urethroplasty with tubularization of posterior urethra and/or lower bladder for incontinence (eg, Tenago, Leadbetter procedure)

53440 Sling operation for correction of male urinary incontinence (eg, fascia or synthetic)

53442 Removal or revision of sling for male urinary incontinence (eg, fascia or synthetic)

53444 Insertion of tandem cuff (dual cuff)

53445 Insertion of inflatable urethral/bladder neck sphincter, including placement of pump, reservoir, and cuff

53446 Removal of inflatable urethral/bladder neck sphincter, including pump, reservoir, and cuff

53447 Removal and replacement of inflatable urethral/bladder neck sphincter including pump, reservoir, and cuff at the same operative session

53448 Removal and replacement of inflatable urethral/bladder neck sphincter including pump, reservoir, and cuff through an infected field at the same operative session including irrigation and debridement of infected tissue

(Do not report 11040-11043 in addition to 53448)

53449 Repair of inflatable urethral/bladder neck sphincter, including pump, reservoir, and cuff

53450 Urethromeatoplasty, with mucosal advancement

(For meatotomy, see 53020, 53025)

53460 Urethromeatoplasty, with partial excision of distal urethral segment (Richardson type procedure)

53500 Urethrolysis, transvaginal, secondary, open, including cystourethroscopy (eg, postsurgical obstruction, scarring)

(For urethrolysis by retropubic approach, use 53899)

(Do not report 53500 in conjunction with 52000)

53502 Urethrorrhaphy, suture of urethral wound or injury, female

53505 Urethrorrhaphy, suture of urethral wound or injury; penile

53510 perineal

53515 prostatomembranous

53520 Closure of urethrostomy or urethrocutaneous fistula, male (separate procedure)

(For closure of urethrovaginal fistula, use 57310)

(For closure of urethrorectal fistula, see 45820, 45825)

Surgery: Urinary System

Manipulation

(For radiological supervision and interpretation, use 74485)

53600 Dilation of urethral stricture by passage of sound or urethral dilator, male; initial

53601 subsequent

53605 Dilation of urethral stricture or vesical neck by passage of sound or urethral dilator, male, general or conduction (spinal) anesthesia

53620 Dilation of urethral stricture by passage of filiform and follower, male; initial

53621 subsequent

53660 Dilation of female urethra including suppository and/or instillation; initial

53661 subsequent

53665 Dilation of female urethra, general or conduction (spinal) anesthesia

(For urethral catheterization, see 51701-51703)

Other Procedures

(For two or three glass urinalysis, use 81020)

53850 Transurethral destruction of prostate tissue; by microwave thermotherapy

53852 by radiofrequency thermotherapy

53853 by water-induced thermotherapy

53899 Unlisted procedure, urinary system

Notes

Male Genital System

Penis

Incision

(For abdominal perineal gangrene debridement, see 11004-11006)

54000 Slitting of prepuce, dorsal or lateral (separate procedure); newborn

(Do not report modifier 63 in conjunction with 54000)

54001 except newborn

54015 Incision and drainage of penis, deep

(For skin and subcutaneous abscess, see 10060-10160)

Destruction

54050 Destruction of lesion(s), penis (eg, condyloma, papilloma, molluscum contagiosum, herpetic vesicle), simple; chemical

54055 electrodesiccation

54056 cryosurgery

54057 laser surgery

54060 surgical excision

54065 Destruction of lesion(s), penis (eg, condyloma, papilloma, molluscum contagiosum, herpetic vesicle), extensive (eg, laser surgery, electrosurgery, cryosurgery, chemosurgery)

(For destruction or excision of other lesions, see **Integumentary System**)

Excision

54100 Biopsy of penis; (separate procedure)

54105 deep structures

54110 Excision of penile plaque (Peyronie disease);

54111 with graft to 5 cm in length

54112 with graft greater than 5 cm in length

54115 Removal foreign body from deep penile tissue (eg, plastic implant)

54120 Amputation of penis; partial

54125 complete

54130 Amputation of penis, radical; with bilateral inguinofemoral lymphadenectomy

54135 in continuity with bilateral pelvic lymphadenectomy, including external iliac, hypogastric and obturator nodes

(For lymphadenectomy (separate procedure), see 38760-38770)

▲ **54150** Circumcision, using clamp or other device with regional dorsal penile or ring block

(Do not report modifier 63 in conjunction with 54150)

►(Report 54150 with modifier 52 when performed without dorsal penile or ring block)◄

►(54152 has been deleted. To report, use 54150)◄

▲ **54160** Circumcision, surgical excision other than clamp, device, or dorsal slit; neonate (28 days of age or less)

(Do not report modifier 63 in conjunction with 54160)

▲ **54161** older than 28 days of age

54162 Lysis or excision of penile post-circumcision adhesions

54163 Repair incomplete circumcision

54164 Frenulotomy of penis

(Do not report 54164 with circumcision codes 54150-54161, 54162, 54163)

Introduction

54200 Injection procedure for Peyronie disease;

54205 with surgical exposure of plaque

54220 Irrigation of corpora cavernosa for priapism

54230 Injection procedure for corpora cavernosography

(For radiological supervision and interpretation, use 74445)

54231 Dynamic cavernosometry, including intracavernosal injection of vasoactive drugs (eg, papaverine, phentolamine)

54235 Injection of corpora cavernosa with pharmacologic agent(s) (eg, papaverine, phentolamine)

54240 Penile plethysmography

54250 Nocturnal penile tumescence and/or rigidity test

Repair

(For other urethroplasties, see 53400-53430)

(For penile revascularization, use 37788)

54300 Plastic operation of penis for straightening of chordee (eg, hypospadias), with or without mobilization of urethra

54304 Plastic operation on penis for correction of chordee or for first stage hypospadias repair with or without transplantation of prepuce and/or skin flaps

54308 Urethroplasty for second stage hypospadias repair (including urinary diversion); less than 3 cm

54312 greater than 3 cm

54316 Urethroplasty for second stage hypospadias repair (including urinary diversion) with free skin graft obtained from site other than genitalia

Surgery: Male/Female Genital System

54318 Urethroplasty for third stage hypospadias repair to release penis from scrotum (eg, third stage Cecil repair)

54322 One stage distal hypospadias repair (with or without chordee or circumcision); with simple meatal advancement (eg, Magpi, V-flap)

54324 with urethroplasty by local skin flaps (eg, flip-flap, prepucial flap)

54326 with urethroplasty by local skin flaps and mobilization of urethra

54328 with extensive dissection to correct chordee and urethroplasty with local skin flaps, skin graft patch, and/or island flap

(For urethroplasty and straightening of chordee, use 54308)

54332 One stage proximal penile or penoscrotal hypospadias repair requiring extensive dissection to correct chordee and urethroplasty by use of skin graft tube and/or island flap

54336 One stage perineal hypospadias repair requiring extensive dissection to correct chordee and urethroplasty by use of skin graft tube and/or island flap

54340 Repair of hypospadias complications (ie, fistula, stricture, diverticula); by closure, incision, or excision, simple

54344 requiring mobilization of skin flaps and urethroplasty with flap or patch graft

54348 requiring extensive dissection and urethroplasty with flap, patch or tubed graft (includes urinary diversion)

54352 Repair of hypospadias cripple requiring extensive dissection and excision of previously constructed structures including re-release of chordee and reconstruction of urethra and penis by use of local skin as grafts and island flaps and skin brought in as flaps or grafts

54360 Plastic operation on penis to correct angulation

54380 Plastic operation on penis for epispadias distal to external sphincter;

54385 with incontinence

54390 with exstrophy of bladder

54400 Insertion of penile prosthesis; non-inflatable (semi-rigid)

54401 inflatable (self-contained)

(For removal or replacement of penile prosthesis, see 54415, 54416)

54405 Insertion of multi-component, inflatable penile prosthesis, including placement of pump, cylinders, and reservoir

(For reduced services, report 54405 with modifier 52)

54406 Removal of all components of a multi-component, inflatable penile prosthesis without replacement of prosthesis

(For reduced services, report 54406 with modifier 52)

54408 Repair of component(s) of a multi-component, inflatable penile prosthesis

54410 Removal and replacement of all component(s) of a multi-component, inflatable penile prosthesis at the same operative session

54411 Removal and replacement of all components of a multi-component inflatable penile prosthesis through an infected field at the same operative session, including irrigation and debridement of infected tissue

(For reduced services, report 54411 with modifier 52)

(Do not report 11040-11043 in addition to 54411)

54415 Removal of non-inflatable (semi-rigid) or inflatable (self-contained) penile prosthesis, without replacement of prosthesis

54416 Removal and replacement of non-inflatable (semi-rigid) or inflatable (self-contained) penile prosthesis at the same operative session

54417 Removal and replacement of non-inflatable (semi-rigid) or inflatable (self-contained) penile prosthesis through an infected field at the same operative session, including irrigation and debridement of infected tissue

(Do not report 11040-11043 in addition to 54417)

54420 Corpora cavernosa-saphenous vein shunt (priapism operation), unilateral or bilateral

54430 Corpora cavernosa-corpus spongiosum shunt (priapism operation), unilateral or bilateral

54435 Corpora cavernosa-glans penis fistulization (eg, biopsy needle, Winter procedure, rongeur, or punch) for priapism

54440 Plastic operation of penis for injury

Manipulation

54450 Foreskin manipulation including lysis of preputial adhesions and stretching

Testis

Excision

(For abdominal perineal gangrene debridement, see 11004-11006)

54500 Biopsy of testis, needle (separate procedure)

(For fine needle aspiration, see 10021, 10022)

(For evaluation of fine needle aspirate, see 88172, 88173)

54505 Biopsy of testis, incisional (separate procedure)

(For bilateral procedure, report 54505 with modifier 50)

(When combined with vasogram, seminal vesiculogram, or epididymogram, use 55300)

54512 Excision of extraparenchymal lesion of testis

54520	Orchiectomy, simple (including subcapsular), with or without testicular prosthesis, scrotal or inguinal approach

(For bilateral procedure, report 54520 with modifier 50)

54522 Orchiectomy, partial

54530 Orchiectomy, radical, for tumor; inguinal approach

54535 with abdominal exploration

(For orchiectomy with repair of hernia, see 49505 or 49507 and 54520)

(For radical retroperitoneal lymphadenectomy, use 38780)

►Exploration◄

54550 Exploration for undescended testis (inguinal or scrotal area)

(For bilateral procedure, report 54550 with modifier 50)

54560 Exploration for undescended testis with abdominal exploration

(For bilateral procedure, report 54560 with modifier 50)

Repair

54600 Reduction of torsion of testis, surgical, with or without fixation of contralateral testis

54620 Fixation of contralateral testis (separate procedure)

54640 Orchiopexy, inguinal approach, with or without hernia repair

(For bilateral procedure, report 54640 with modifier 50)

(For inguinal hernia repair performed in conjunction with inguinal orchiopexy, see 49495-49525)

54650 Orchiopexy, abdominal approach, for intra-abdominal testis (eg, Fowler-Stephens)

(For laparoscopic approach, use 54692)

54660 Insertion of testicular prosthesis (separate procedure)

(For bilateral procedure, report 54660 with modifier 50)

54670 Suture or repair of testicular injury

54680 Transplantation of testis(es) to thigh (because of scrotal destruction)

Laparoscopy

Surgical laparoscopy always includes diagnostic laparoscopy. To report a diagnostic laparoscopy (peritoneoscopy) (separate procedure), use 49320.

54690 Laparoscopy, surgical; orchiectomy

54692 orchiopexy for intra-abdominal testis

54699 Unlisted laparoscopy procedure, testis

Epididymis

Incision

54700 Incision and drainage of epididymis, testis and/or scrotal space (eg, abscess or hematoma)

Excision

54800 Biopsy of epididymis, needle

(For fine needle aspiration, see 10021, 10022)

(For evaluation of fine needle aspirate, see 88172, 88173)

►(54820 has been deleted. To report, use 54865)◄

54830 Excision of local lesion of epididymis

54840 Excision of spermatocele, with or without epididymectomy

54860 Epididymectomy; unilateral

54861 bilateral

►Exploration◄

● **54865** Exploration of epididymis, with or without biopsy

Repair

54900 Epididymovasostomy, anastomosis of epididymis to vas deferens; unilateral

54901 bilateral

(For operating microscope, use 69990)

Tunica Vaginalis

Incision

55000 Puncture aspiration of hydrocele, tunica vaginalis, with or without injection of medication

Excision

55040 Excision of hydrocele; unilateral

55041 bilateral

(With hernia repair, see 49495-49501)

Repair

55060 Repair of tunica vaginalis hydrocele (Bottle type)

Surgery: Male/Female Genital System

Scrotum

Incision

55100 Drainage of scrotal wall abscess

(See also 54700)

55110 Scrotal exploration

55120 Removal of foreign body in scrotum

Excision

(For excision of local lesion of skin of scrotum, see **Integumentary System**)

55150 Resection of scrotum

Repair

55175 Scrotoplasty; simple

55180 complicated

Vas Deferens

Incision

55200 Vasotomy, cannulization with or without incision of vas, unilateral or bilateral (separate procedure)

Excision

55250 Vasectomy, unilateral or bilateral (separate procedure), including postoperative semen examination(s)

Introduction

55300 Vasotomy for vasograms, seminal vesiculograms, or epididymograms, unilateral or bilateral

(For radiological supervision and interpretation, use 74440)

(When combined with biopsy of testis, see 54505 and use modifier 51)

Repair

55400 Vasovasostomy, vasovasorrhaphy

(For bilateral procedure, report 55400 with modifier 50)

(For operating microscope, use 69990)

Suture

55450 Ligation (percutaneous) of vas deferens, unilateral or bilateral (separate procedure)

Spermatic Cord

Excision

55500 Excision of hydrocele of spermatic cord, unilateral (separate procedure)

55520 Excision of lesion of spermatic cord (separate procedure)

55530 Excision of varicocele or ligation of spermatic veins for varicocele; (separate procedure)

55535 abdominal approach

55540 with hernia repair

Laparoscopy

Surgical laparoscopy always includes diagnostic laparoscopy. To report a diagnostic laparoscopy (peritoneoscopy) (separate procedure), use 49320.

55550 Laparoscopy, surgical, with ligation of spermatic veins for varicocele

55559 Unlisted laparoscopy procedure, spermatic cord

Seminal Vesicles

Incision

55600 Vesiculotomy;

(For bilateral procedure, report 55600 with modifier 50)

55605 complicated

Excision

55650 Vesiculectomy, any approach

(For bilateral procedure, report 55650 with modifier 50)

55680 Excision of Mullerian duct cyst

(For injection procedure, see 52010, 55300)

Prostate

Incision

55700 Biopsy, prostate; needle or punch, single or multiple, any approach

(For prostate needle biopsy saturation sampling for prostate mapping, use Category III code 0137T)

(If imaging guidance is performed, use 76942)

(For fine needle aspiration, see 10021, 10022)

(For evaluation of fine needle aspirate, see 88172, 88173)

55705 incisional, any approach

55720 Prostatotomy, external drainage of prostatic abscess, any approach; simple

55725 complicated

(For transurethral drainage, use 52700)

Excision

(For transurethral removal of prostate, see 52601-52640)

(For transurethral destruction of prostate, see 53850-53852)

(For limited pelvic lymphadenectomy for staging (separate procedure), use 38562)

(For independent node dissection, see 38770-38780)

55801 Prostatectomy, perineal, subtotal (including control of postoperative bleeding, vasectomy, meatotomy, urethral calibration and/or dilation, and internal urethrotomy)

55810 Prostatectomy, perineal radical;

55812 with lymph node biopsy(s) (limited pelvic lymphadenectomy)

55815 with bilateral pelvic lymphadenectomy, including external iliac, hypogastric and obturator nodes

(If 55815 is carried out on separate days, use 38770 with modifier 50 and 55810)

55821 Prostatectomy (including control of postoperative bleeding, vasectomy, meatotomy, urethral calibration and/or dilation, and internal urethrotomy); suprapubic, subtotal, one or two stages

55831 retropubic, subtotal

55840 Prostatectomy, retropubic radical, with or without nerve sparing;

55842 with lymph node biopsy(s) (limited pelvic lymphadenectomy)

55845 with bilateral pelvic lymphadenectomy, including external iliac, hypogastric, and obturator nodes

(If 55845 is carried out on separate days, use 38770 with modifier 50 and 55840)

(For laparoscopic retropubic radical prostatectomy, use 55866)

▶(55859 has been deleted. To report, use 55875)◀

55860 Exposure of prostate, any approach, for insertion of radioactive substance;

(For application of interstitial radioelement, see 77776-77778)

55862 with lymph node biopsy(s) (limited pelvic lymphadenectomy)

55865 with bilateral pelvic lymphadenectomy, including external iliac, hypogastric and obturator nodes

Laparoscopy

Surgical laparoscopy always includes diagnostic laparoscopy. To report a diagnostic laparoscopy (peritoneoscopy) (separate procedure), use 49320.

55866 Laparoscopy, surgical prostatectomy, retropubic radical, including nerve sparing

(For open procedure, use 55840)

Other Procedures

(For artificial insemination, see 58321, 58322)

55870 Electroejaculation

55873 Cryosurgical ablation of the prostate (includes ultrasonic guidance for interstitial cryosurgical probe placement)

● **55875** Transperineal placement of needles or catheters into prostate for interstitial radioelement application, with or without cystoscopy

▶(For interstitial radioelement application, see 77776-77784)◀

▶(For ultrasonic guidance for interstitial radioelement application, use 76965)◀

● **55876** Placement of interstitial device(s) for radiation therapy guidance (eg, fiducial markers, dosimeter), prostate (via needle, any approach), single or multiple

▶(Report supply of device separately)◀

▶(For imaging guidance, see 76942, 77002, 77012, 77021)◀

55899 Unlisted procedure, male genital system

Intersex Surgery

55970 Intersex surgery; male to female

55980 female to male

Surgery: Male/Female Genital System

Notes

⊙=Moderate sedation ✚=Add-on code ⇗=FDA approval pending

Female Genital System

(For pelvic laparotomy, use 49000)

(For excision or destruction of endometriomas, open method, see 49200, 49201)

(For paracentesis, see 49080, 49081)

(For secondary closure of abdominal wall evisceration or disruption, use 49900)

(For fulguration or excision of lesions, laparoscopic approach, use 58662)

▶(For chemotherapy, see 96401-96549)◀

Vulva, Perineum, and Introitus

Definitions

The following definitions apply to the vulvectomy codes (56620-56640).

A *simple* procedure is the removal of skin and superficial subcutaneous tissues.

A *radical* procedure is the removal of skin and deep subcutaneous tissue.

A *partial* procedure is the removal of less than 80% of the vulvar area.

A *complete* procedure is the removal of greater than 80% of the vulvar area.

Incision

(For incision and drainage of sebaceous cyst, furuncle, or abscess, see 10040, 10060, 10061)

56405 Incision and drainage of vulva or perineal abscess

56420 Incision and drainage of Bartholin's gland abscess

(For incision and drainage of Skene's gland abscess or cyst, use 53060)

56440 Marsupialization of Bartholin's gland cyst

56441 Lysis of labial adhesions

● 56442 Hymenotomy, simple incision

Destruction

56501 Destruction of lesion(s), vulva; simple (eg, laser surgery, electrosurgery, cryosurgery, chemosurgery)

56515 extensive (eg, laser surgery, electrosurgery, cryosurgery, chemosurgery)

(For destruction of Skene's gland cyst or abscess, use 53270)

(For cautery destruction of urethral caruncle, use 53265)

Excision

56605 Biopsy of vulva or perineum (separate procedure); one lesion

+ 56606 each separate additional lesion (List separately in addition to code for primary procedure)

(Use 56606 in conjunction with 56605)

(For excision of local lesion, see 11420-11426, 11620-11626)

56620 Vulvectomy simple; partial

56625 complete

▶(For skin graft, see 15002 et seq)◀

56630 Vulvectomy, radical, partial;

▶(For skin graft, if used, see 15004-15005, 15120, 15121, 15240, 15241)◀

56631 with unilateral inguinofemoral lymphadenectomy

56632 with bilateral inguinofemoral lymphadenectomy

56633 Vulvectomy, radical, complete;

56634 with unilateral inguinofemoral lymphadenectomy

56637 with bilateral inguinofemoral lymphadenectomy

56640 Vulvectomy, radical, complete, with inguinofemoral, iliac, and pelvic lymphadenectomy

(For bilateral procedure, report 56640 with modifier 50)

(For lymphadenectomy, see 38760-38780)

56700 Partial hymenectomy or revision of hymenal ring

▶(56720 has been deleted. To report, use 56442)◀

56740 Excision of Bartholin's gland or cyst

(For excision of Skene's gland, use 53270)

(For excision of urethral caruncle, use 53265)

(For excision or fulguration of urethral carcinoma, use 53220)

(For excision or marsupialization of urethral diverticulum, see 53230, 53240)

Repair

(For repair of urethra for mucosal prolapse, use 53275)

56800 Plastic repair of introitus

56805 Clitoroplasty for intersex state

56810 Perineoplasty, repair of perineum, nonobstetrical (separate procedure)

(See also 56800)

(For repair of wounds to genitalia, see 12001-12007, 12041-12047, 13131-13133)

(For repair of recent injury of vagina and perineum, nonobstetrical, use 57210)

Surgery: Male/Female Genital System

(For anal sphincteroplasty, see 46750, 46751)

(For episiorrhaphy, episioperineorrhaphy for recent injury of vulva and/or perineum, nonobstetrical, use 57210)

Endoscopy

56820 Colposcopy of the vulva;

56821 with biopsy(s)

(For colposcopic examinations/procedures involving the vagina, see 57420, 57421; cervix, see 57452-57461)

Vagina

Incision

57000 Colpotomy; with exploration

57010 with drainage of pelvic abscess

57020 Colpocentesis (separate procedure)

57022 Incision and drainage of vaginal hematoma; obstetrical/postpartum

57023 non-obstetrical (eg, post-trauma, spontaneous bleeding)

Destruction

57061 Destruction of vaginal lesion(s); simple (eg, laser surgery, electrosurgery, cryosurgery, chemosurgery)

57065 extensive (eg, laser surgery, electrosurgery, cryosurgery, chemosurgery)

Excision

57100 Biopsy of vaginal mucosa; simple (separate procedure)

57105 extensive, requiring suture (including cysts)

57106 Vaginectomy, partial removal of vaginal wall;

57107 with removal of paravaginal tissue (radical vaginectomy)

57109 with removal of paravaginal tissue (radical vaginectomy) with bilateral total pelvic lymphadenectomy and para-aortic lymph node sampling (biopsy)

57110 Vaginectomy, complete removal of vaginal wall;

57111 with removal of paravaginal tissue (radical vaginectomy)

57112 with removal of paravaginal tissue (radical vaginectomy) with bilateral total pelvic lymphadenectomy and para-aortic lymph node sampling (biopsy)

57120 Colpocleisis (Le Fort type)

57130 Excision of vaginal septum

57135 Excision of vaginal cyst or tumor

Introduction

57150 Irrigation of vagina and/or application of medicament for treatment of bacterial, parasitic, or fungoid disease

57155 Insertion of uterine tandems and/or vaginal ovoids for clinical brachytherapy

(For insertion of radioelement sources or ribbons, see 77761-77763, 77781-77784)

57160 Fitting and insertion of pessary or other intravaginal support device

57170 Diaphragm or cervical cap fitting with instructions

57180 Introduction of any hemostatic agent or pack for spontaneous or traumatic nonobstetrical vaginal hemorrhage (separate procedure)

Repair

(For urethral suspension, Marshall-Marchetti-Krantz type, abdominal approach, see 51840, 51841)

(For laparoscopic suspension, use 51990)

57200 Colporrhaphy, suture of injury of vagina (nonobstetrical)

57210 Colpoperineorrhaphy, suture of injury of vagina and/or perineum (nonobstetrical)

57220 Plastic operation on urethral sphincter, vaginal approach (eg, Kelly urethral plication)

57230 Plastic repair of urethrocele

57240 Anterior colporrhaphy, repair of cystocele with or without repair of urethrocele

57250 Posterior colporrhaphy, repair of rectocele with or without perineorrhaphy

(For repair of rectocele (separate procedure) without posterior colporrhaphy, use 45560)

57260 Combined anteroposterior colporrhaphy;

57265 with enterocele repair

+ 57267 Insertion of mesh or other prosthesis for repair of pelvic floor defect, each site (anterior, posterior compartment), vaginal approach (List separately in addition to code for primary procedure)

(Use 57267 in addition to 45560, 57240-57265)

57268 Repair of enterocele, vaginal approach (separate procedure)

57270 Repair of enterocele, abdominal approach (separate procedure)

57280 Colpopexy, abdominal approach

57282 Colpopexy, vaginal; extra-peritoneal approach (sacrospinous, iliococcygeus)

57283 intra-peritoneal approach (uterosacral, levator myorrhaphy)

Surgery: Male/Female Genital System

57284 Paravaginal defect repair (including repair of cystocele, stress urinary incontinence, and/or incomplete vaginal prolapse)

57287 Removal or revision of sling for stress incontinence (eg, fascia or synthetic)

57288 Sling operation for stress incontinence (eg, fascia or synthetic)

(For laparoscopic approach, use 51992)

57289 Pereyra procedure, including anterior colporrhaphy

57291 Construction of artificial vagina; without graft

57292 with graft

57295 Revision (including removal) of prosthetic vaginal graft; vaginal approach

● **57296** open abdominal approach

57300 Closure of rectovaginal fistula; vaginal or transanal approach

57305 abdominal approach

57307 abdominal approach, with concomitant colostomy

57308 transperineal approach, with perineal body reconstruction, with or without levator plication

57310 Closure of urethrovaginal fistula;

57311 with bulbocavernosus transplant

57320 Closure of vesicovaginal fistula; vaginal approach

(For concomitant cystostomy, see 51005-51040)

57330 transvesical and vaginal approach

(For abdominal approach, use 51900)

57335 Vaginoplasty for intersex state

Manipulation

57400 Dilation of vagina under anesthesia

57410 Pelvic examination under anesthesia

57415 Removal of impacted vaginal foreign body (separate procedure) under anesthesia

(For removal without anesthesia of an impacted vaginal foreign body, use the appropriate E/M code)

Endoscopy

(For speculoscopy, see Category III codes 0031T, 0032T)

57420 Colposcopy of the entire vagina, with cervix if present;

57421 with biopsy(s) of vagina/cervix

(For colposcopic visualization of cervix and adjacent upper vagina, use 57452)

(When reporting colposcopies of multiple sites, use modifier 51 as appropriate. For colposcopic examinations/procedures involving the vulva, see 56820, 56821; cervix, see 57452-57461)

(For endometrial sampling (biopsy) performed in conjunction with colposcopy, use 58110)

57425 Laparoscopy, surgical, colpopexy (suspension of vaginal apex)

Cervix Uteri

(For cervicography, see Category III code 0003T)

Endoscopy

(For colposcopic examinations/procedures involving the vulva, see 56820, 56821; vagina, see 57420, 57421)

57452 Colposcopy of the cervix including upper/adjacent vagina;

(Do not report 57452 in addition to 57454-57461)

57454 with biopsy(s) of the cervix and endocervical curettage

57455 with biopsy(s) of the cervix

57456 with endocervical curettage

57460 with loop electrode biopsy(s) of the cervix

57461 with loop electrode conization of the cervix

(Do not report 57456 in addition to 57461)

(For endometrial sampling (biopsy) performed in conjunction with colposcopy, use 58110)

Excision

(For radical surgical procedures, see 58200-58240)

57500 Biopsy, single or multiple, or local excision of lesion, with or without fulguration (separate procedure)

57505 Endocervical curettage (not done as part of a dilation and curettage)

57510 Cautery of cervix; electro or thermal

57511 cryocautery, initial or repeat

57513 laser ablation

57520 Conization of cervix, with or without fulguration, with or without dilation and curettage, with or without repair; cold knife or laser

(See also 58120)

57522 loop electrode excision

57530 Trachelectomy (cervicectomy), amputation of cervix (separate procedure)

57531 Radical trachelectomy, with bilateral total pelvic lymphadenectomy and para-aortic lymph node sampling biopsy, with or without removal of tube(s), with or without removal of ovary(s)

(For radical abdominal hysterectomy, use 58210)

57540 Excision of cervical stump, abdominal approach;

57545 with pelvic floor repair

Surgery: Male/Female Genital System

57550 Excision of cervical stump, vaginal approach;

57555 with anterior and/or posterior repair

57556 with repair of enterocele

(For insertion of intrauterine device, use 58300)

(For insertion of any hemostatic agent or pack for control of spontaneous non-obstetrical hemorrhage, see 57180)

● **57558** Dilation and curettage of cervical stump

Repair

57700 Cerclage of uterine cervix, nonobstetrical

57720 Trachelorrhaphy, plastic repair of uterine cervix, vaginal approach

Manipulation

57800 Dilation of cervical canal, instrumental (separate procedure)

►(57820 has been deleted. To report, use 57558)◄

Corpus Uteri

Excision

58100 Endometrial sampling (biopsy) with or without endocervical sampling (biopsy), without cervical dilation, any method (separate procedure)

(For endocervical curettage only, use 57505)

(For endometrial sampling (biopsy) performed in conjunction with colposcopy (57420, 57421, 57452-57461), use 58110)

+ **58110** Endometrial sampling (biopsy) performed in conjunction with colposcopy (List separately in addition to code for primary procedure)

(Use 58110 in conjunction with 57420, 57421, 57452-57461)

58120 Dilation and curettage, diagnostic and/or therapeutic (nonobstetrical)

(For postpartum hemorrhage, use 59160)

58140 Myomectomy, excision of fibroid tumor(s) of uterus, 1 to 4 intramural myoma(s) with total weight of 250 g or less and/or removal of surface myomas; abdominal approach

58145 vaginal approach

58146 Myomectomy, excision of fibroid tumor(s) of uterus, 5 or more intramural myomas and/or intramural myomas with total weight greater than 250 g, abdominal approach

(Do not report 58146 in addition to 58140-58145, 58150-58240)

►Hysterectomy Procedures◄

58150 Total abdominal hysterectomy (corpus and cervix), with or without removal of tube(s), with or without removal of ovary(s);

58152 with colpo-urethrocystopexy (eg, Marshall-Marchetti-Krantz, Burch)

(For urethrocystopexy without hysterectomy, see 51840, 51841)

58180 Supracervical abdominal hysterectomy (subtotal hysterectomy), with or without removal of tube(s), with or without removal of ovary(s)

58200 Total abdominal hysterectomy, including partial vaginectomy, with para-aortic and pelvic lymph node sampling, with or without removal of tube(s), with or without removal of ovary(s)

58210 Radical abdominal hysterectomy, with bilateral total pelvic lymphadenectomy and para-aortic lymph node sampling (biopsy), with or without removal of tube(s), with or without removal of ovary(s)

(For radical hysterectomy with ovarian transposition, use also 58825)

58240 Pelvic exenteration for gynecologic malignancy, with total abdominal hysterectomy or cervicectomy, with or without removal of tube(s), with or without removal of ovary(s), with removal of bladder and ureteral transplantations, and/or abdominoperineal resection of rectum and colon and colostomy, or any combination thereof

(For pelvic exenteration for lower urinary tract or male genital malignancy, use 51597)

58260 Vaginal hysterectomy, for uterus 250 g or less;

58262 with removal of tube(s), and/or ovary(s)

58263 with removal of tube(s), and/or ovary(s), with repair of enterocele

(Do not report 58263 in addition to 57283)

58267 with colpo-urethrocystopexy (Marshall-Marchetti-Krantz type, Pereyra type) with or without endoscopic control

58270 with repair of enterocele

(For repair of enterocele with removal of tubes and/or ovaries, use 58263)

58275 Vaginal hysterectomy, with total or partial vaginectomy;

58280 with repair of enterocele

58285 Vaginal hysterectomy, radical (Schauta type operation)

58290 Vaginal hysterectomy, for uterus greater than 250 g;

58291 with removal of tube(s) and/or ovary(s)

58292 with removal of tube(s) and/or ovary(s), with repair of enterocele

⊙=Moderate sedation ✛=Add-on code ✗=FDA approval pending

58293 with colpo-urethrocystopexy (Marshall-Marchetti-Krantz type, Pereyra type) with or without endoscopic control

58294 with repair of enterocele

Introduction

(For insertion/removal of implantable contraceptive capsules, see 11975, 11976, 11977)

58300 Insertion of intrauterine device (IUD)

58301 Removal of intrauterine device (IUD)

58321 Artificial insemination; intra-cervical

58322 intra-uterine

58323 Sperm washing for artificial insemination

58340 Catheterization and introduction of saline or contrast material for saline infusion sonohysterography (SIS) or hysterosalpingography

(For radiological supervision and interpretation of saline infusion sonohysterography, use 76831)

(For radiological supervision and interpretation of hysterosalpingography, use 74740)

58345 Transcervical introduction of fallopian tube catheter for diagnosis and/or re-establishing patency (any method), with or without hysterosalpingography

(For radiological supervision and interpretation, use 74742)

58346 Insertion of Heyman capsules for clinical brachytherapy

(For insertion of radioelement sources or ribbons, see 77761-77763, 77781-77784)

58350 Chromotubation of oviduct, including materials

(For materials supplied by physician, use 99070)

58353 Endometrial ablation, thermal, without hysteroscopic guidance

(For hysteroscopic procedure, use 58563)

58356 Endometrial cryoablation with ultrasonic guidance, including endometrial curettage, when performed

(Do not report 58356 in conjunction with 58100, 58120, 58340, 76700, 76856)

Repair

58400 Uterine suspension, with or without shortening of round ligaments, with or without shortening of sacrouterine ligaments; (separate procedure)

58410 with presacral sympathectomy

(For anastomosis of tubes to uterus, use 58752)

58520 Hysterorrhaphy, repair of ruptured uterus (nonobstetrical)

58540 Hysteroplasty, repair of uterine anomaly (Strassman type)

(For closure of vesicouterine fistula, use 51920)

Laparoscopy/Hysteroscopy

Surgical laparoscopy always includes diagnostic laparoscopy. To report a diagnostic laparoscopy (peritoneoscopy) (separate procedure), use 49320. To report a diagnostic hysteroscopy (separate procedure), use 58555.

● **58541** Laparoscopy, surgical, supracervical hysterectomy, for uterus 250 g or less;

● **58542** with removal of tube(s) and/or ovary(s)

►(Do not report 58541, 58542 in conjunction with 49320, 57410, 58140, 58150, 58661, 58670, 58671)◄

● **58543** Laparoscopy, surgical, supracervical hysterectomy, for uterus greater than 250 g;

● **58544** with removal of tube(s) and/or ovary(s)

►(Do not report 58543, 58544 in conjunction with 49320, 57410, 58140, 58150, 58661, 58670, 58671)◄

58545 Laparoscopy, surgical, myomectomy, excision; 1 to 4 intramural myomas with total weight of 250 g or less and/or removal of surface myomas

58546 5 or more intramural myomas and/or intramural myomas with total weight greater than 250 g

● **58548** Laparoscopy, surgical, with radical hysterectomy, with bilateral total pelvic lymphadenectomy and para-aortic lymph node sampling (biopsy), with removal of tube(s) and ovary(s), if performed

►(Do not report 58548 in conjunction with 38570-38572, 58210, 58285, 58550-58554)◄

58550 Laparoscopy, surgical, with vaginal hysterectomy, for uterus 250 g or less;

58552 with removal of tube(s) and/or ovary(s)

58553 Laparoscopy, surgical, with vaginal hysterectomy, for uterus greater than 250 g;

58554 with removal of tube(s) and/or ovary(s)

58555 Hysteroscopy, diagnostic (separate procedure)

58558 Hysteroscopy, surgical; with sampling (biopsy) of endometrium and/or polypectomy, with or without D & C

58559 with lysis of intrauterine adhesions (any method)

58560 with division or resection of intrauterine septum (any method)

58561 with removal of leiomyomata

58562 with removal of impacted foreign body

58563 with endometrial ablation (eg, endometrial resection, electrosurgical ablation, thermoablation)

58565 with bilateral fallopian tube cannulation to induce occlusion by placement of permanent implants

(Do not report 58565 in conjunction with 58555 or 57800)

(For unilateral procedure, use modifier 52)

Surgery: Male/Female Genital System

58578 Unlisted laparoscopy procedure, uterus

58579 Unlisted hysteroscopy procedure, uterus

Oviduct/Ovary

Incision

58600 Ligation or transection of fallopian tube(s), abdominal or vaginal approach, unilateral or bilateral

58605 Ligation or transection of fallopian tube(s), abdominal or vaginal approach, postpartum, unilateral or bilateral, during same hospitalization (separate procedure)

(For laparoscopic procedures, use 58670, 58671)

+ 58611 Ligation or transection of fallopian tube(s) when done at the time of cesarean delivery or intra-abdominal surgery (not a separate procedure) (List separately in addition to code for primary procedure)

58615 Occlusion of fallopian tube(s) by device (eg, band, clip, Falope ring) vaginal or suprapubic approach

(For laparoscopic approach, use 58671)

(For lysis of adnexal adhesions, use 58740)

Laparoscopy

Surgical laparoscopy always includes diagnostic laparoscopy. To report a diagnostic laparoscopy (peritoneoscopy) (separate procedure), use 49320.

58660 Laparoscopy, surgical; with lysis of adhesions (salpingolysis, ovariolysis) (separate procedure)

58661 with removal of adnexal structures (partial or total oophorectomy and/or salpingectomy)

58662 with fulguration or excision of lesions of the ovary, pelvic viscera, or peritoneal surface by any method

58670 with fulguration of oviducts (with or without transection)

58671 with occlusion of oviducts by device (eg, band, clip, or Falope ring)

58672 with fimbrioplasty

58673 with salpingostomy (salpingoneostomy)

(Codes 58672 and 58673 are used to report unilateral procedures. For bilateral procedure, use modifier 50)

58679 Unlisted laparoscopy procedure, oviduct, ovary

►(For laparoscopic aspiration of ovarian cyst, use 49322)◄

►(For laparoscopic biopsy of the ovary or fallopian tube, use 49321)◄

Excision

58700 Salpingectomy, complete or partial, unilateral or bilateral (separate procedure)

58720 Salpingo-oophorectomy, complete or partial, unilateral or bilateral (separate procedure)

Repair

58740 Lysis of adhesions (salpingolysis, ovariolysis)

(For laparoscopic approach, use 58660)

(For excision or destruction of endometriomas, open method, see 49200, 49201)

(For fulguration or excision of lesions, laparoscopic approach, use 58662)

58750 Tubotubal anastomosis

58752 Tubouterine implantation

58760 Fimbrioplasty

(For laparoscopic approach, use 58672)

58770 Salpingostomy (salpingoneostomy)

(For laparoscopic approach, use 58673)

Ovary

Incision

58800 Drainage of ovarian cyst(s), unilateral or bilateral, (separate procedure); vaginal approach

58805 abdominal approach

58820 Drainage of ovarian abscess; vaginal approach, open

58822 abdominal approach

⊙ **58823** Drainage of pelvic abscess, transvaginal or transrectal approach, percutaneous (eg, ovarian, pericolic)

(For radiological supervision and interpretation, use 75989)

58825 Transposition, ovary(s)

Excision

58900 Biopsy of ovary, unilateral or bilateral (separate procedure)

(For laparoscopic biopsy of the ovary or fallopian tube, use 49321)

58920 Wedge resection or bisection of ovary, unilateral or bilateral

58925 Ovarian cystectomy, unilateral or bilateral

58940 Oophorectomy, partial or total, unilateral or bilateral;

(For oophorectomy with concomitant debulking for ovarian malignancy, use 58952)

58943 for ovarian, tubal or primary peritoneal malignancy, with para-aortic and pelvic lymph node biopsies, peritoneal washings, peritoneal biopsies, diaphragmatic assessments, with or without salpingectomy(s), with or without omentectomy

▲ **58950** Resection (initial) of ovarian, tubal or primary peritoneal malignancy with bilateral salpingo-oophorectomy and omentectomy;

58951 with total abdominal hysterectomy, pelvic and limited para-aortic lymphadenectomy

58952 with radical dissection for debulking (ie, radical excision or destruction, intra-abdominal or retroperitoneal tumors)

►(For resection of recurrent ovarian, tubal, primary peritoneal, or uterine malignancy, see 58957, 58958)◄

58953 Bilateral salpingo-oophorectomy with omentectomy, total abdominal hysterectomy and radical dissection for debulking;

58954 with pelvic lymphadenectomy and limited para-aortic lymphadenectomy

58956 Bilateral salpingo-oophorectomy with total omentectomy, total abdominal hysterectomy for malignancy

►(Do not report 58956 in conjunction with 49255, 58150, 58180, 58262, 58263, 58550, 58661, 58700, 58720, 58900, 58925, 58940, 58957, 58958)◄

● **58957** Resection (tumor debulking) of recurrent ovarian, tubal, primary peritoneal, uterine malignancy (intra-abdominal, retroperitoneal tumors), with omentectomy, if performed;

● **58958** with pelvic lymphadenectomy and limited para-aortic lymphadenectomy

►(Do not report 58957, 58958 in conjunction with 38770, 38780, 44005, 49000, 49200-49215, 49255, 58900-58960)◄

58960 Laparotomy, for staging or restaging of ovarian, tubal, or primary peritoneal malignancy (second look), with or without omentectomy, peritoneal washing, biopsy of abdominal and pelvic peritoneum, diaphragmatic assessment with pelvic and limited para-aortic lymphadenectomy

►(Do not report 58960 in conjunction with 58957, 58958)◄

In Vitro Fertilization

58970 Follicle puncture for oocyte retrieval, any method

(For radiological supervision and interpretation, use 76948)

58974 Embryo transfer, intrauterine

58976 Gamete, zygote, or embryo intrafallopian transfer, any method

(For laparoscopic adnexal procedures, see 58660-58673)

Other Procedures

58999 Unlisted procedure, female genital system (nonobstetrical)

Maternity Care and Delivery

The services normally provided in uncomplicated maternity cases include antepartum care, delivery, and postpartum care.

Antepartum care includes the initial and subsequent history, physical examinations, recording of weight, blood pressures, fetal heart tones, routine chemical urinalysis, and monthly visits up to 28 weeks gestation, biweekly visits to 36 weeks gestation, and weekly visits until delivery. Any other visits or services within this time period should be coded separately.

Delivery services include admission to the hospital, the admission history and physical examination, management of uncomplicated labor, vaginal delivery (with or without episiotomy, with or without forceps), or cesarean delivery. Medical problems complicating labor and delivery management may require additional resources and should be identified by utilizing the codes in the **Medicine** and **Evaluation and Management Services** section in addition to codes for maternity care.

Postpartum care includes hospital and office visits following vaginal or cesarean section delivery.

For medical complications of pregnancy (eg, cardiac problems, neurological problems, diabetes, hypertension, toxemia, hyperemesis, pre-term labor, premature rupture of membranes), see services in the **Medicine** and **Evaluation and Management Services** section.

For surgical complications of pregnancy (eg, appendectomy, hernia, ovarian cyst, Bartholin cyst), see services in the **Surgery** section.

If a physician provides all or part of the antepartum and/or postpartum patient care but does not perform delivery due to termination of pregnancy by abortion or referral to another physician for delivery, see the antepartum and postpartum care codes 59425-59426 and 59430.

(For circumcision of newborn, see 54150, 54160)

Antepartum Services

(For insertion of transcervical or transvaginal fetal oximetry sensor, use Category III code 0021T)

59000 Amniocentesis; diagnostic

(For radiological supervision and interpretation, use 76946)

59001 therapeutic amniotic fluid reduction (includes ultrasound guidance)

Surgery: Male/Female Genital System

59012 Cordocentesis (intrauterine), any method

(For radiological supervision and interpretation, use 76941)

59015 Chorionic villus sampling, any method

(For radiological supervision and interpretation, use 76945)

59020 Fetal contraction stress test

59025 Fetal non-stress test

59030 Fetal scalp blood sampling

(For repeat fetal scalp blood sampling, use 59030 and see modifiers 76 and 77)

59050 Fetal monitoring during labor by consulting physician (ie, non-attending physician) with written report; supervision and interpretation

59051 interpretation only

59070 Transabdominal amnioinfusion, including ultrasound guidance

59072 Fetal umbilical cord occlusion, including ultrasound guidance

59074 Fetal fluid drainage (eg, vesicocentesis, thoracocentesis, paracentesis), including ultrasound guidance

59076 Fetal shunt placement, including ultrasound guidance

(For unlisted fetal invasive procedure, use 59897)

Excision

59100 Hysterotomy, abdominal (eg, for hydatidiform mole, abortion)

(When tubal ligation is performed at the same time as hysterotomy, use 58611 in addition to 59100)

59120 Surgical treatment of ectopic pregnancy; tubal or ovarian, requiring salpingectomy and/or oophorectomy, abdominal or vaginal approach

59121 tubal or ovarian, without salpingectomy and/or oophorectomy

59130 abdominal pregnancy

59135 interstitial, uterine pregnancy requiring total hysterectomy

59136 interstitial, uterine pregnancy with partial resection of uterus

59140 cervical, with evacuation

59150 Laparoscopic treatment of ectopic pregnancy; without salpingectomy and/or oophorectomy

59151 with salpingectomy and/or oophorectomy

59160 Curettage, postpartum

Introduction

(For intrauterine fetal transfusion, use 36460)

(For introduction of hypertonic solution and/or prostaglandins to initiate labor, see 59850-59857)

59200 Insertion of cervical dilator (eg, laminaria, prostaglandin) (separate procedure)

Repair

(For tracheloplasty, use 57700)

59300 Episiotomy or vaginal repair, by other than attending physician

59320 Cerclage of cervix, during pregnancy; vaginal

59325 abdominal

59350 Hysterorrhaphy of ruptured uterus

Vaginal Delivery, Antepartum and Postpartum Care

(For insertion of transcervical or transvaginal fetal oximetry sensor, use Category III code 0021T)

59400 Routine obstetric care including antepartum care, vaginal delivery (with or without episiotomy, and/or forceps) and postpartum care

59409 Vaginal delivery only (with or without episiotomy and/or forceps);

59410 including postpartum care

59412 External cephalic version, with or without tocolysis

(Use 59412 in addition to code(s) for delivery)

59414 Delivery of placenta (separate procedure)

(For antepartum care only, see 59425, 59426 or appropriate E/M code(s))

(For 1-3 antepartum care visits, see appropriate E/M code(s))

59425 Antepartum care only; 4-6 visits

59426 7 or more visits

59430 Postpartum care only (separate procedure)

Cesarean Delivery

(For insertion of transcervical or transvaginal fetal oximetry sensor, use Category III code 0021T)

(For standby attendance for infant, use 99360)

(For low cervical cesarean section, see 59510, 59515, 59525)

59510 Routine obstetric care including antepartum care, cesarean delivery, and postpartum care

Surgery: Male/Female Genital System

59514 Cesarean delivery only;

59515 including postpartum care

 (For classic cesarean section, see 59510, 59515, 59525)

+ 59525 Subtotal or total hysterectomy after cesarean delivery
 (List separately in addition to code for primary procedure)

 (Use 59525 in conjunction with 59510, 59514, 59515, 59618, 59620, 59622)

 (For extraperitoneal cesarean section, or cesarean section with subtotal or total hysterectomy, see 59510, 59515, 59525)

Delivery After Previous Cesarean Delivery

Patients who have had a previous cesarean delivery and now present with the expectation of a vaginal delivery are coded using codes 59610-59622. If the patient has a successful vaginal delivery after a previous cesarean delivery (VBAC), use codes 59610-59614. If the attempt is unsuccessful and another cesarean delivery is carried out, use codes 59618-59622. To report elective cesarean deliveries use code 59510, 59514 or 59515.

 (For insertion of transcervical or transvaginal fetal oximetry sensor, use Category III code 0021T)

59610 Routine obstetric care including antepartum care, vaginal delivery (with or without episiotomy, and/or forceps) and postpartum care, after previous cesarean delivery

59612 Vaginal delivery only, after previous cesarean delivery (with or without episiotomy and/or forceps);

59614 including postpartum care

59618 Routine obstetric care including antepartum care, cesarean delivery, and postpartum care, following attempted vaginal delivery after previous cesarean delivery

59620 Cesarean delivery only, following attempted vaginal delivery after previous cesarean delivery;

59622 including postpartum care

Abortion

 (For medical treatment of spontaneous complete abortion, any trimester, use E/M codes 99201-99233)

 (For surgical treatment of spontaneous abortion, use 59812)

59812 Treatment of incomplete abortion, any trimester, completed surgically

59820 Treatment of missed abortion, completed surgically; first trimester

59821 second trimester

59830 Treatment of septic abortion, completed surgically

59840 Induced abortion, by dilation and curettage

59841 Induced abortion, by dilation and evacuation

59850 Induced abortion, by one or more intra-amniotic injections (amniocentesis-injections), including hospital admission and visits, delivery of fetus and secundines;

59851 with dilation and curettage and/or evacuation

59852 with hysterotomy (failed intra-amniotic injection)

 (For insertion of cervical dilator, use 59200)

59855 Induced abortion, by one or more vaginal suppositories (eg, prostaglandin) with or without cervical dilation (eg, laminaria), including hospital admission and visits, delivery of fetus and secundines;

59856 with dilation and curettage and/or evacuation

59857 with hysterotomy (failed medical evacuation)

Other Procedures

59866 Multifetal pregnancy reduction(s) (MPR)

59870 Uterine evacuation and curettage for hydatidiform mole

59871 Removal of cerclage suture under anesthesia (other than local)

59897 Unlisted fetal invasive procedure, including ultrasound guidance

59898 Unlisted laparoscopy procedure, maternity care and delivery

59899 Unlisted procedure, maternity care and delivery

Surgery: Male/Female Genital System

Notes

⊙=Moderate sedation ✚=Add-on code ✗=FDA approval pending

Endocrine System

(For pituitary and pineal surgery, see **Nervous System**)

Thyroid Gland

Incision

60000 Incision and drainage of thyroglossal duct cyst, infected

Excision

60001 Aspiration and/or injection, thyroid cyst

(For fine needle aspiration, see 10021, 10022)

►(If imaging guidance is performed, see 76942, 77012)◄

60100 Biopsy thyroid, percutaneous core needle

►(If imaging guidance is performed, see 76942, 77002, 77012, 77021)◄

(For fine needle aspiration, use 10021 or 10022)

(For evaluation of fine needle aspirate, see 88172, 88173)

60200 Excision of cyst or adenoma of thyroid, or transection of isthmus

60210 Partial thyroid lobectomy, unilateral; with or without isthmusectomy

60212 with contralateral subtotal lobectomy, including isthmusectomy

60220 Total thyroid lobectomy, unilateral; with or without isthmusectomy

60225 with contralateral subtotal lobectomy, including isthmusectomy

60240 Thyroidectomy, total or complete

(For thyroidectomy, subtotal or partial, use 60271)

60252 Thyroidectomy, total or subtotal for malignancy; with limited neck dissection

60254 with radical neck dissection

60260 Thyroidectomy, removal of all remaining thyroid tissue following previous removal of a portion of thyroid

(For bilateral procedure, report 60260 with modifier 50)

60270 Thyroidectomy, including substernal thyroid; sternal split or transthoracic approach

60271 cervical approach

60280 Excision of thyroglossal duct cyst or sinus;

60281 recurrent

(For thyroid ultrasonography, use 76536)

Parathyroid, Thymus, Adrenal Glands, Pancreas, and Carotid Body

Excision

(For pituitary and pineal surgery, see **Nervous System**)

60500 Parathyroidectomy or exploration of parathyroid(s);

60502 re-exploration

60505 with mediastinal exploration, sternal split or transthoracic approach

+ 60512 Parathyroid autotransplantation (List separately in addition to code for primary procedure)

(Use 60512 in conjunction with 60500, 60502, 60505, 60212, 60225, 60240, 60252, 60254, 60260, 60270, 60271)

60520 Thymectomy, partial or total; transcervical approach (separate procedure)

60521 sternal split or transthoracic approach, without radical mediastinal dissection (separate procedure)

60522 sternal split or transthoracic approach, with radical mediastinal dissection (separate procedure)

60540 Adrenalectomy, partial or complete, or exploration of adrenal gland with or without biopsy, transabdominal, lumbar or dorsal (separate procedure);

60545 with excision of adjacent retroperitoneal tumor

(Do not report 60540, 60545 in conjunction with 50323)

(For bilateral procedure, report 60540 with modifier 50)

(For excision of remote or disseminated pheochromocytoma, see 49200, 49201)

(For laparoscopic approach, use 60650)

60600 Excision of carotid body tumor; without excision of carotid artery

60605 with excision of carotid artery

Laparoscopy

Surgical laparoscopy always includes diagnostic laparoscopy. To report a diagnostic laparoscopy (peritoneoscopy) (separate procedure), use 49320.

60650 Laparoscopy, surgical, with adrenalectomy, partial or complete, or exploration of adrenal gland with or without biopsy, transabdominal, lumbar or dorsal

60659 Unlisted laparoscopy procedure, endocrine system

Other Procedures

60699 Unlisted procedure, endocrine system

Surgery: Nervous System

Notes

⊙=Moderate sedation ✛=Add-on code ✗=FDA approval pending

Surgery: Nervous System

Nervous System

Skull, Meninges, and Brain

(For injection procedure for cerebral angiography, see 36100-36218)

(For injection procedure for ventriculography, see 61026, 61120)

(For injection procedure for pneumoencephalography, use 61055)

Injection, Drainage, or Aspiration

61000 Subdural tap through fontanelle, or suture, infant, unilateral or bilateral; initial

61001 subsequent taps

61020 Ventricular puncture through previous burr hole, fontanelle, suture, or implanted ventricular catheter/reservoir; without injection

61026 with injection of medication or other substance for diagnosis or treatment

61050 Cisternal or lateral cervical (C1-C2) puncture; without injection (separate procedure)

61055 with injection of medication or other substance for diagnosis or treatment (eg, C1-C2)

(For radiological supervision and interpretation, see **Radiology**)

61070 Puncture of shunt tubing or reservoir for aspiration or injection procedure

(For radiological supervision and interpretation, use 75809)

Twist Drill, Burr Hole(s), or Trephine

61105 Twist drill hole for subdural or ventricular puncture

⊘▲ **61107** Twist drill hole(s) for subdural, intracerebral, or ventricular puncture; for implanting ventricular catheter, pressure recording device, or other intracerebral monitoring device

(For intracranial neuroendoscopic ventricular catheter placement, use 62160)

(For twist drill or burr hole performed to place thermal perfusion probe, use Category III code 0077T)

61108 for evacuation and/or drainage of subdural hematoma

61120 Burr hole(s) for ventricular puncture (including injection of gas, contrast media, dye, or radioactive material)

61140 Burr hole(s) or trephine; with biopsy of brain or intracranial lesion

61150 with drainage of brain abscess or cyst

61151 with subsequent tapping (aspiration) of intracranial abscess or cyst

61154 Burr hole(s) with evacuation and/or drainage of hematoma, extradural or subdural

(For bilateral procedure, report 61154 with modifier 50)

61156 Burr hole(s); with aspiration of hematoma or cyst, intracerebral

⊘▲ **61210** for implanting ventricular catheter, reservoir, EEG electrode(s), pressure recording device, or other cerebral monitoring device (separate procedure)

(For intracranial neuroendoscopic ventricular catheter placement, use 62160)

61215 Insertion of subcutaneous reservoir, pump or continuous infusion system for connection to ventricular catheter

(For refilling and maintenance of an implantable infusion pump for spinal or brain drug therapy, use 95990)

(For chemotherapy, use 96450)

61250 Burr hole(s) or trephine, supratentorial, exploratory, not followed by other surgery

(For bilateral procedure, report 61250 with modifier 50)

61253 Burr hole(s) or trephine, infratentorial, unilateral or bilateral

(If burr hole(s) or trephine are followed by craniotomy at same operative session, use 61304-61321; do not use 61250 or 61253)

Craniectomy or Craniotomy

61304 Craniectomy or craniotomy, exploratory; supratentorial

61305 infratentorial (posterior fossa)

61312 Craniectomy or craniotomy for evacuation of hematoma, supratentorial; extradural or subdural

61313 intracerebral

61314 Craniectomy or craniotomy for evacuation of hematoma, infratentorial; extradural or subdural

61315 intracerebellar

+ **61316** Incision and subcutaneous placement of cranial bone graft (List separately in addition to code for primary procedure)

(Use 61316 in conjunction with 61304, 61312, 61313, 61322, 61323, 61340, 61570, 61571, 61680-61705)

61320 Craniectomy or craniotomy, drainage of intracranial abscess; supratentorial

61321 infratentorial

61322 Craniectomy or craniotomy, decompressive, with or without duraplasty, for treatment of intracranial hypertension, without evacuation of associated intraparenchymal hematoma; without lobectomy

(Do not report 61313 in addition to 61322)

(For subtemporal decompression, use 61340)

61323 with lobectomy

(Do not report 61313 in addition to 61323)

(For subtemporal decompression, use 61340)

61330 Decompression of orbit only, transcranial approach

(For bilateral procedure, report 61330 with modifier 50)

61332 Exploration of orbit (transcranial approach); with biopsy

61333 with removal of lesion

61334 with removal of foreign body

61340 Subtemporal cranial decompression (pseudotumor cerebri, slit ventricle syndrome)

(For bilateral procedure, report 61340 with modifier 50)

(For decompressive craniotomy or craniectomy for intracranial hypertension, without hematoma evacuation, see 61322, 61323)

61343 Craniectomy, suboccipital with cervical laminectomy for decompression of medulla and spinal cord, with or without dural graft (eg, Arnold-Chiari malformation)

61345 Other cranial decompression, posterior fossa

(For orbital decompression by lateral wall approach, Kroenlein type, use 67445)

61440 Craniotomy for section of tentorium cerebelli (separate procedure)

61450 Craniectomy, subtemporal, for section, compression, or decompression of sensory root of gasserian ganglion

61458 Craniectomy, suboccipital; for exploration or decompression of cranial nerves

61460 for section of one or more cranial nerves

61470 for medullary tractotomy

61480 for mesencephalic tractotomy or pedunculotomy

61490 Craniotomy for lobotomy, including cingulotomy

(For bilateral procedure, report 61490 with modifier 50)

61500 Craniectomy; with excision of tumor or other bone lesion of skull

61501 for osteomyelitis

61510 Craniectomy, trephination, bone flap craniotomy; for excision of brain tumor, supratentorial, except meningioma

61512 for excision of meningioma, supratentorial

61514 for excision of brain abscess, supratentorial

61516 for excision or fenestration of cyst, supratentorial

(For excision of pituitary tumor or craniopharyngioma, see 61545, 61546, 61548)

+ 61517 Implantation of brain intracavitary chemotherapy agent (List separately in addition to code for primary procedure)

(Use 61517 only in conjunction with 61510 or 61518)

(Do not report 61517 for brachytherapy insertion. For intracavitary insertion of radioelement sources or ribbons, see 77781-77784)

61518 Craniectomy for excision of brain tumor, infratentorial or posterior fossa; except meningioma, cerebellopontine angle tumor, or midline tumor at base of skull

61519 meningioma

61520 cerebellopontine angle tumor

61521 midline tumor at base of skull

61522 Craniectomy, infratentorial or posterior fossa; for excision of brain abscess

61524 for excision or fenestration of cyst

61526 Craniectomy, bone flap craniotomy, transtemporal (mastoid) for excision of cerebellopontine angle tumor;

61530 combined with middle/posterior fossa craniotomy/craniectomy

61531 Subdural implantation of strip electrodes through one or more burr or trephine hole(s) for long term seizure monitoring

(For stereotactic implantation of electrodes, use 61760)

(For craniotomy for excision of intracranial arteriovenous malformation, see 61680-61692)

61533 Craniotomy with elevation of bone flap; for subdural implantation of an electrode array, for long term seizure monitoring

(For continuous EEG monitoring, see 95950-95954)

61534 for excision of epileptogenic focus without electrocorticography during surgery

61535 for removal of epidural or subdural electrode array, without excision of cerebral tissue (separate procedure)

61536 for excision of cerebral epileptogenic focus, with electrocorticography during surgery (includes removal of electrode array)

61537 for lobectomy, temporal lobe, without electrocorticography during surgery

61538 for lobectomy, temporal lobe, with electrocorticography during surgery

Surgery: Nervous System

61539 for lobectomy, other than temporal lobe, partial or total, with electrocorticography during surgery

61540 for lobectomy, other than temporal lobe, partial or total, without electrocorticography during surgery

61541 for transection of corpus callosum

61542 for total hemispherectomy

61543 for partial or subtotal (functional) hemispherectomy

61544 for excision or coagulation of choroid plexus

61545 for excision of craniopharyngioma

(For craniotomy for selective amygdalohippocampectomy, use 61566)

(For craniotomy for multiple subpial transections during surgery, use 61567)

61546 Craniotomy for hypophysectomy or excision of pituitary tumor, intracranial approach

61548 Hypophysectomy or excision of pituitary tumor, transnasal or transseptal approach, nonstereotactic

(Do not report code 69990 in addition to code 61548)

61550 Craniectomy for craniosynostosis; single cranial suture

61552 multiple cranial sutures

(For cranial reconstruction for orbital hypertelorism, see 21260-21263)

(For reconstruction, see 21172-21180)

61556 Craniotomy for craniosynostosis; frontal or parietal bone flap

61557 bifrontal bone flap

61558 Extensive craniectomy for multiple cranial suture craniosynostosis (eg, cloverleaf skull); not requiring bone grafts

61559 recontouring with multiple osteotomies and bone autografts (eg, barrel-stave procedure) (includes obtaining grafts)

(For reconstruction, see 21172-21180)

61563 Excision, intra and extracranial, benign tumor of cranial bone (eg, fibrous dysplasia); without optic nerve decompression

61564 with optic nerve decompression

(For reconstruction, see 21181-21183)

61566 Craniotomy with elevation of bone flap; for selective amygdalohippocampectomy

61567 for multiple subpial transections, with electrocorticography during surgery

61570 Craniectomy or craniotomy; with excision of foreign body from brain

61571 with treatment of penetrating wound of brain

(For sequestrectomy for osteomyelitis, use 61501)

61575 Transoral approach to skull base, brain stem or upper spinal cord for biopsy, decompression or excision of lesion;

61576 requiring splitting of tongue and/or mandible (including tracheostomy)

(For arthrodesis, use 22548)

Surgery of Skull Base

The surgical management of lesions involving the skull base (base of anterior, middle, and posterior cranial fossae) often requires the skills of several surgeons of different surgical specialties working together or in tandem during the operative session. These operations are usually not staged because of the need for definitive closure of dura, subcutaneous tissues, and skin to avoid serious infections such as osteomyelitis and/or meningitis.

The procedures are categorized according to: 1) *approach procedure* necessary to obtain adequate exposure to the lesion (pathologic entity), 2) *definitive procedure(s)* necessary to biopsy, excise or otherwise treat the lesion, and 3) *repair/reconstruction* of the defect present following the definitive procedure(s).

The *approach procedure* is described according to anatomical area involved, ie, anterior cranial fossa, middle cranial fossa, posterior cranial fossa, and brain stem or upper spinal cord.

The *definitive procedure(s)* describes the repair, biopsy, resection, or excision of various lesions of the skull base and, when appropriate, primary closure of the dura, mucous membranes, and skin.

The *repair/reconstruction procedure(s)* is reported separately if extensive dural grafting, cranioplasty, local or regional myocutaneous pedicle flaps, or extensive skin grafts are required.

For primary closure, see the appropriate codes, ie, 15732, 15756-15758.

When one surgeon performs the approach procedure, another surgeon performs the definitive procedure, and another surgeon performs the repair/reconstruction procedure, each surgeon reports only the code for the specific procedure performed.

If one surgeon performs more than one procedure (ie, approach procedure and definitive procedure), then both codes are reported, adding modifier 51 to the secondary, additional procedure(s).

Surgery: Nervous System

Approach Procedures

Anterior Cranial Fossa

61580 Craniofacial approach to anterior cranial fossa; extradural, including lateral rhinotomy, ethmoidectomy, sphenoidectomy, without maxillectomy or orbital exenteration

61581 extradural, including lateral rhinotomy, orbital exenteration, ethmoidectomy, sphenoidectomy and/or maxillectomy

61582 extradural, including unilateral or bifrontal craniotomy, elevation of frontal lobe(s), osteotomy of base of anterior cranial fossa

61583 intradural, including unilateral or bifrontal craniotomy, elevation or resection of frontal lobe, osteotomy of base of anterior cranial fossa

61584 Orbitocranial approach to anterior cranial fossa, extradural, including supraorbital ridge osteotomy and elevation of frontal and/or temporal lobe(s); without orbital exenteration

61585 with orbital exenteration

61586 Bicoronal, transzygomatic and/or LeFort I osteotomy approach to anterior cranial fossa with or without internal fixation, without bone graft

Middle Cranial Fossa

61590 Infratemporal pre-auricular approach to middle cranial fossa (parapharyngeal space, infratemporal and midline skull base, nasopharynx), with or without disarticulation of the mandible, including parotidectomy, craniotomy, decompression and/or mobilization of the facial nerve and/or petrous carotid artery

61591 Infratemporal post-auricular approach to middle cranial fossa (internal auditory meatus, petrous apex, tentorium, cavernous sinus, parasellar area, infratemporal fossa) including mastoidectomy, resection of sigmoid sinus, with or without decompression and/or mobilization of contents of auditory canal or petrous carotid artery

61592 Orbitocranial zygomatic approach to middle cranial fossa (cavernous sinus and carotid artery, clivus, basilar artery or petrous apex) including osteotomy of zygoma, craniotomy, extra- or intradural elevation of temporal lobe

Posterior Cranial Fossa

61595 Transtemporal approach to posterior cranial fossa, jugular foramen or midline skull base, including mastoidectomy, decompression of sigmoid sinus and/or facial nerve, with or without mobilization

61596 Transcochlear approach to posterior cranial fossa, jugular foramen or midline skull base, including labyrinthectomy, decompression, with or without mobilization of facial nerve and/or petrous carotid artery

61597 Transcondylar (far lateral) approach to posterior cranial fossa, jugular foramen or midline skull base, including occipital condylectomy, mastoidectomy, resection of C1-C3 vertebral body(s), decompression of vertebral artery, with or without mobilization

61598 Transpetrosal approach to posterior cranial fossa, clivus or foramen magnum, including ligation of superior petrosal sinus and/or sigmoid sinus

Definitive Procedures

Base of Anterior Cranial Fossa

61600 Resection or excision of neoplastic, vascular or infectious lesion of base of anterior cranial fossa; extradural

61601 intradural, including dural repair, with or without graft

Base of Middle Cranial Fossa

61605 Resection or excision of neoplastic, vascular or infectious lesion of infratemporal fossa, parapharyngeal space, petrous apex; extradural

61606 intradural, including dural repair, with or without graft

61607 Resection or excision of neoplastic, vascular or infectious lesion of parasellar area, cavernous sinus, clivus or midline skull base; extradural

61608 intradural, including dural repair, with or without graft

Codes 61609-61612 are reported in addition to code(s) for primary procedure(s) 61605-61608. Report only one transection or ligation of carotid artery code per operative session.

+ 61609 Transection or ligation, carotid artery in cavernous sinus; without repair (List separately in addition to code for primary procedure)

+ 61610 with repair by anastomosis or graft (List separately in addition to code for primary procedure)

+ 61611 Transection or ligation, carotid artery in petrous canal; without repair (List separately in addition to code for primary procedure)

+ 61612 with repair by anastomosis or graft (List separately in addition to code for primary procedure)

61613 Obliteration of carotid aneurysm, arteriovenous malformation, or carotid-cavernous fistula by dissection within cavernous sinus

Base of Posterior Cranial Fossa

61615 Resection or excision of neoplastic, vascular or infectious lesion of base of posterior cranial fossa, jugular foramen, foramen magnum, or C1-C3 vertebral bodies; extradural

61616 intradural, including dural repair, with or without graft

Repair and/or Reconstruction of Surgical Defects of Skull Base

61618 Secondary repair of dura for cerebrospinal fluid leak, anterior, middle or posterior cranial fossa following surgery of the skull base; by free tissue graft (eg, pericranium, fascia, tensor fascia lata, adipose tissue, homologous or synthetic grafts)

61619 by local or regionalized vascularized pedicle flap or myocutaneous flap (including galea, temporalis, frontalis or occipitalis muscle)

Endovascular Therapy

61623 Endovascular temporary balloon arterial occlusion, head or neck (extracranial/intracranial) including selective catheterization of vessel to be occluded, positioning and inflation of occlusion balloon, concomitant neurological monitoring, and radiologic supervision and interpretation of all angiography required for balloon occlusion and to exclude vascular injury post occlusion

(If selective catheterization and angiography of arteries other than artery to be occluded is performed, use appropriate catheterization and radiologic supervision and interpretation codes)

(If complete diagnostic angiography of the artery to be occluded is performed immediately prior to temporary occlusion, use appropriate radiologic supervision and interpretation codes only)

61624 Transcatheter permanent occlusion or embolization (eg, for tumor destruction, to achieve hemostasis, to occlude a vascular malformation), percutaneous, any method; central nervous system (intracranial, spinal cord)

(See also 37204)

(For radiological supervision and interpretation, use 75894)

61626 non-central nervous system, head or neck (extracranial, brachiocephalic branch)

(See also 37204)

(For radiological supervision and interpretation, use 75894)

61630 Balloon angioplasty, intracranial (eg, atherosclerotic stenosis), percutaneous

61635 Transcatheter placement of intravascular stent(s), intracranial (eg, atherosclerotic stenosis), including balloon angioplasty, if performed

(61630 and 61635 include all selective vascular catheterization of the target vascular family, all diagnostic imaging for arteriography of the target vascular family, and all related radiological supervision and interpretation. When diagnostic arteriogram (including imaging and selective catheterization) confirms the need for angioplasty or stent placement, 61630 and 61635 are inclusive of these services. If angioplasty or stenting are not indicated, then the appropriate codes for selective catheterization and imaging should be reported in lieu of 61630 and 61635)

61640 Balloon dilatation of intracranial vasospasm, percutaneous; initial vessel

+ 61641 each additional vessel in same vascular family (List separately in addition to code for primary procedure)

+ 61642 each additional vessel in different vascular family (List separately in addition to code for primary procedure)

(Use 61641 and 61642 in conjunction with 61640)

(61640, 61641, 61642 include all selective vascular catheterization of the target vessel, contrast injection(s), vessel measurement, roadmapping, postdilatation angiography, and fluoroscopic guidance for the balloon dilatation)

Surgery for Aneurysm, Arteriovenous Malformation or Vascular Disease

Includes craniotomy when appropriate for procedure.

61680 Surgery of intracranial arteriovenous malformation; supratentorial, simple

61682 supratentorial, complex

61684 infratentorial, simple

61686 infratentorial, complex

61690 dural, simple

61692 dural, complex

61697 Surgery of complex intracranial aneurysm, intracranial approach; carotid circulation

61698 vertebrobasilar circulation

(61697, 61698 involve aneurysms that are larger than 15 mm or with calcification of the aneurysm neck, or with incorporation of normal vessels into the aneurysm neck, or a procedure requiring temporary vessel occlusion, trapping or cardiopulmonary bypass to successfully treat the aneurysm)

61700 Surgery of simple intracranial aneurysm, intracranial approach; carotid circulation

61702 vertebrobasilar circulation

Surgery: Nervous System

61703 Surgery of intracranial aneurysm, cervical approach by application of occluding clamp to cervical carotid artery (Selverstone-Crutchfield type)

(For cervical approach for direct ligation of carotid artery, see 37600-37606)

61705 Surgery of aneurysm, vascular malformation or carotid-cavernous fistula; by intracranial and cervical occlusion of carotid artery

61708 by intracranial electrothrombosis

(For ligation or gradual occlusion of internal/common carotid artery, see 37605, 37606)

61710 by intra-arterial embolization, injection procedure, or balloon catheter

61711 Anastomosis, arterial, extracranial-intracranial (eg, middle cerebral/cortical) arteries

(For carotid or vertebral thromboendarterectomy, use 35301)

(Use 69990 when the surgical microscope is employed for the microsurgical procedure. Do not use 69990 for visualization with magnifying loupes or corrected vision)

Stereotaxis

61720 Creation of lesion by stereotactic method, including burr hole(s) and localizing and recording techniques, single or multiple stages; globus pallidus or thalamus

61735 subcortical structure(s) other than globus pallidus or thalamus

61750 Stereotactic biopsy, aspiration, or excision, including burr hole(s), for intracranial lesion;

61751 with computed tomography and/or magnetic resonance guidance

(For radiological supervision and interpretation of computerized tomography, see 70450, 70460, or 70470 as appropriate)

(For radiological supervision and interpretation of magnetic resonance imaging, see 70551, 70552, or 70553 as appropriate)

61760 Stereotactic implantation of depth electrodes into the cerebrum for long term seizure monitoring

61770 Stereotactic localization, including burr hole(s), with insertion of catheter(s) or probe(s) for placement of radiation source

61790 Creation of lesion by stereotactic method, percutaneous, by neurolytic agent (eg, alcohol, thermal, electrical, radiofrequency); gasserian ganglion

61791 trigeminal medullary tract

61793 Stereotactic radiosurgery (particle beam, gamma ray or linear accelerator), one or more sessions

(For intensity modulated beam delivery plan and treatment, see 77301, 77418)

+ 61795 Stereotactic computer-assisted volumetric (navigational) procedure, intracranial, extracranial, or spinal (List separately in addition to code for primary procedure)

Neurostimulators (Intracranial)

Codes 61850-61888 apply to both simple and complex neurostimulators. For initial or subsequent electronic analysis and programming of neurostimulator pulse generators, see codes 95970-95975.

Microelectrode recording, when performed by the operating surgeon in association with implantation of neurostimulator electrode arrays, is an inclusive service and should not be reported separately. If another physician participates in neurophysiological mapping during a deep brain stimulator implantation procedure, this service may be reported by the other physician with codes 95961-95962.

61850 Twist drill or burr hole(s) for implantation of neurostimulator electrodes, cortical

61860 Craniectomy or craniotomy for implantation of neurostimulator electrodes, cerebral, cortical

61863 Twist drill, burr hole, craniotomy, or craniectomy with stereotactic implantation of neurostimulator electrode array in subcortical site (eg, thalamus, globus pallidus, subthalamic nucleus, periventricular, periaqueductal gray), without use of intraoperative microelectrode recording; first array

+ 61864 each additional array (List separately in addition to primary procedure)

(Use 61864 in conjunction with 61863)

61867 Twist drill, burr hole, craniotomy, or craniectomy with stereotactic implantation of neurostimulator electrode array in subcortical site (eg, thalamus, globus pallidus, subthalamic nucleus, periventricular, periaqueductal gray), with use of intraoperative microelectrode recording; first array

+ 61868 each additional array (List separately in addition to primary procedure)

(Use 61868 in conjunction with 61867)

61870 Craniectomy for implantation of neurostimulator electrodes, cerebellar; cortical

61875 subcortical

61880 Revision or removal of intracranial neurostimulator electrodes

61885 Insertion or replacement of cranial neurostimulator pulse generator or receiver, direct or inductive coupling; with connection to a single electrode array

61886 with connection to two or more electrode arrays

(For open placement of cranial nerve (eg, vagal, trigeminal) neurostimulator electrode(s), use 64573)

Surgery: Nervous System

(For percutaneous placement of cranial nerve (eg, vagal, trigeminal) neurostimulator electrode(s), use 64553)

(For revision or removal of cranial nerve (eg, vagal, trigeminal) neurostimulator electrode(s), use 64585)

61888 Revision or removal of cranial neurostimulator pulse generator or receiver

(Do not report 61888 in conjunction with 61885 or 61886 for the same pulse generator)

Repair

62000 Elevation of depressed skull fracture; simple, extradural

62005 compound or comminuted, extradural

62010 with repair of dura and/or debridement of brain

62100 Craniotomy for repair of dural/cerebrospinal fluid leak, including surgery for rhinorrhea/otorrhea

(For repair of spinal dural/CSF leak, see 63707, 63709)

62115 Reduction of craniomegalic skull (eg, treated hydrocephalus); not requiring bone grafts or cranioplasty

62116 with simple cranioplasty

62117 requiring craniotomy and reconstruction with or without bone graft (includes obtaining grafts)

62120 Repair of encephalocele, skull vault, including cranioplasty

62121 Craniotomy for repair of encephalocele, skull base

62140 Cranioplasty for skull defect; up to 5 cm diameter

62141 larger than 5 cm diameter

62142 Removal of bone flap or prosthetic plate of skull

62143 Replacement of bone flap or prosthetic plate of skull

62145 Cranioplasty for skull defect with reparative brain surgery

62146 Cranioplasty with autograft (includes obtaining bone grafts); up to 5 cm diameter

62147 larger than 5 cm diameter

+ 62148 Incision and retrieval of subcutaneous cranial bone graft for cranioplasty (List separately in addition to code for primary procedure)

(Use 62148 in conjunction with 62140-62147)

Neuroendoscopy

Surgical endoscopy always includes diagnostic endoscopy.

+ 62160 Neuroendoscopy, intracranial, for placement or replacement of ventricular catheter and attachment to shunt system or external drainage (List separately in addition to code for primary procedure)

▶(Use 62160 only in conjunction with 61107, 61210, 62220-62230, 62258)◀

62161 Neuroendoscopy, intracranial; with dissection of adhesions, fenestration of septum pellucidum or intraventricular cysts (including placement, replacement, or removal of ventricular catheter)

62162 with fenestration or excision of colloid cyst, including placement of external ventricular catheter for drainage

62163 with retrieval of foreign body

62164 with excision of brain tumor, including placement of external ventricular catheter for drainage

62165 with excision of pituitary tumor, transnasal or transsphenoidal approach

Cerebrospinal Fluid (CSF) Shunt

62180 Ventriculocisternostomy (Torkildsen type operation)

62190 Creation of shunt; subarachnoid/subdural-atrial, -jugular, -auricular

62192 subarachnoid/subdural-peritoneal, -pleural, other terminus

62194 Replacement or irrigation, subarachnoid/subdural catheter

62200 Ventriculocisternostomy, third ventricle;

62201 stereotactic, neuroendoscopic method

(For intracranial neuroendoscopic procedures, see 62161-62165)

62220 Creation of shunt; ventriculo-atrial, -jugular, -auricular

(For intracranial neuroendoscopic ventricular catheter placement, use 62160)

62223 ventriculo-peritoneal, -pleural, other terminus

(For intracranial neuroendoscopic ventricular catheter placement, use 62160)

62225 Replacement or irrigation, ventricular catheter

(For intracranial neuroendoscopic ventricular catheter placement, use 62160)

62230 Replacement or revision of cerebrospinal fluid shunt, obstructed valve, or distal catheter in shunt system

(For intracranial neuroendoscopic ventricular catheter placement, use 62160)

62252 Reprogramming of programmable cerebrospinal shunt

62256 Removal of complete cerebrospinal fluid shunt system; without replacement

62258 with replacement by similar or other shunt at same operation

(For percutaneous irrigation or aspiration of shunt reservoir, use 61070)

(For reprogramming of programmable CSF shunt, use 62252)

▶(For intracranial neuroendoscopic ventricular catheter placement, use 62160)◀

Surgery: Nervous System

Spine and Spinal Cord

(For application of caliper or tongs, use 20660)

(For treatment of fracture or dislocation of spine, see 22305-22327)

Injection, Drainage, or Aspiration

▶Injection of contrast during fluoroscopic guidance and localization is an inclusive component of codes 62263-62264, 62270-62273, 62280-62282, 62310-62319, 0027T. Fluoroscopic guidance and localization is reported by code 77003, unless a formal contrast study (myelography, epidurography, or arthrography) is performed, in which case the use of fluoroscopy is included in the supervision and interpretation codes.◀

For radiologic supervision and interpretation of epidurography, use 72275. Code 72275 is only to be used when an epidurogram is performed, images documented, and a formal radiologic report is issued.

Code 62263 describes a catheter-based treatment involving targeted injection of various substances (eg, hypertonic saline, steroid, anesthetic) via an indwelling epidural catheter. Code 62263 includes percutaneous insertion and removal of an epidural catheter (remaining in place over a several-day period), for the administration of multiple injections of a neurolytic agent(s) performed during serial treatment sessions (ie, spanning two or more treatment days). If required, adhesions or scarring may also be lysed by mechanical means. Code 62263 is NOT reported for each adhesiolysis treatment, but should be reported ONCE to describe the entire series of injections/infusions spanning two or more treatment days. For endoscopic lysis of adhesions, use 0027T.

Code 62264 describes multiple adhesiolysis treatment sessions performed on the same day. Adhesions or scarring may be lysed by injections of neurolytic agent(s). If required, adhesions or scarring may also be lysed mechanically using a percutaneously-deployed catheter.

▶Codes 62263 and 62264 include the procedure of injections of contrast for epidurography (72275) and fluoroscopic guidance and localization (77003) during initial or subsequent sessions.◀

(Report 01996 for daily hospital management of continuous epidural or subarachnoid drug administration performed in conjunction with 62318-62319)

(For endoscopic lysis of epidural adhesions, use Category III code 0027T)

62263 Percutaneous lysis of epidural adhesions using solution injection (eg, hypertonic saline, enzyme) or mechanical means (eg, catheter) including radiologic localization (includes contrast when administered), multiple adhesiolysis sessions; 2 or more days

▶(62263 includes codes 72275 and 77003)◀

62264 1 day

(Do not report 62264 with 62263)

▶(62264 includes codes 72275 and 77003)◀

62268 Percutaneous aspiration, spinal cord cyst or syrinx

▶(For radiological supervision and interpretation, see 76942, 77002, 77012)◀

62269 Biopsy of spinal cord, percutaneous needle

▶(For radiological supervision and interpretation, see 76942, 77002, 77012)◀

(For fine needle aspiration, see 10021, 10022)

(For evaluation of fine needle aspirate, see 88172, 88173)

62270 Spinal puncture, lumbar, diagnostic

62272 Spinal puncture, therapeutic, for drainage of cerebrospinal fluid (by needle or catheter)

62273 Injection, epidural, of blood or clot patch

(For injection of diagnostic or therapeutic substance(s), see 62310, 62311, 62318, 62319)

62280 Injection/infusion of neurolytic substance (eg, alcohol, phenol, iced saline solutions), with or without other therapeutic substance; subarachnoid

62281 epidural, cervical or thoracic

62282 epidural, lumbar, sacral (caudal)

⊘ **62284** Injection procedure for myelography and/or computed tomography, spinal (other than C1-C2 and posterior fossa)

(For injection procedure at C1-C2, use 61055)

(For radiological supervision and interpretation, see **Radiology**)

62287 Aspiration or decompression procedure, percutaneous, of nucleus pulposus of intervertebral disc, any method, single or multiple levels, lumbar (eg, manual or automated percutaneous discectomy, percutaneous laser discectomy)

▶(For fluoroscopic guidance, use 77002)◀

(For injection of non-neurolytic diagnostic or therapeutic substance(s), see 62310, 62311)

62290 Injection procedure for discography, each level; lumbar

62291 cervical or thoracic

(For radiological supervision and interpretation, see 72285, 72295)

Surgery: Nervous System

62292 Injection procedure for chemonucleolysis, including discography, intervertebral disc, single or multiple levels, lumbar

62294 Injection procedure, arterial, for occlusion of arteriovenous malformation, spinal

62310 Injection, single (not via indwelling catheter), not including neurolytic substances, with or without contrast (for either localization or epidurography), of diagnostic or therapeutic substance(s) (including anesthetic, antispasmodic, opioid, steroid, other solution), epidural or subarachnoid; cervical or thoracic

62311 lumbar, sacral (caudal)

62318 Injection, including catheter placement, continuous infusion or intermittent bolus, not including neurolytic substances, with or without contrast (for either localization or epidurography), of diagnostic or therapeutic substance(s) (including anesthetic, antispasmodic, opioid, steroid, other solution), epidural or subarachnoid; cervical or thoracic

62319 lumbar, sacral (caudal)

(For transforaminal epidural injection, see 64479-64484)

(Report 01996 for daily hospital management of continuous epidural or subarachnoid drug administration performed in conjunction with 62318-62319)

Catheter Implantation

(For percutaneous placement of intrathecal or epidural catheter, see codes 62270-62273, 62280-62284, 62310-62319)

62350 Implantation, revision or repositioning of tunneled intrathecal or epidural catheter, for long-term medication administration via an external pump or implantable reservoir/infusion pump; without laminectomy

62351 with laminectomy

(For refilling and maintenance of an implantable infusion pump for spinal or brain drug therapy, see 95990, 95991)

62355 Removal of previously implanted intrathecal or epidural catheter

Reservoir/Pump Implantation

62360 Implantation or replacement of device for intrathecal or epidural drug infusion; subcutaneous reservoir

62361 non-programmable pump

62362 programmable pump, including preparation of pump, with or without programming

62365 Removal of subcutaneous reservoir or pump, previously implanted for intrathecal or epidural infusion

62367 Electronic analysis of programmable, implanted pump for intrathecal or epidural drug infusion (includes evaluation of reservoir status, alarm status, drug prescription status); without reprogramming

62368 with reprogramming

(For refilling and maintenance of an implantable infusion pump for spinal or brain drug therapy, use 95990-95991)

Posterior Extradural Laminotomy or Laminectomy for Exploration/ Decompression of Neural Elements or Excision of Herniated Intervertebral Discs

(When 63001-63048 are followed by arthrodesis, see 22590-22614)

63001 Laminectomy with exploration and/or decompression of spinal cord and/or cauda equina, without facetectomy, foraminotomy or discectomy, (eg, spinal stenosis), one or two vertebral segments; cervical

63003 thoracic

63005 lumbar, except for spondylolisthesis

63011 sacral

63012 Laminectomy with removal of abnormal facets and/or pars inter-articularis with decompression of cauda equina and nerve roots for spondylolisthesis, lumbar (Gill type procedure)

63015 Laminectomy with exploration and/or decompression of spinal cord and/or cauda equina, without facetectomy, foraminotomy or discectomy, (eg, spinal stenosis), more than 2 vertebral segments; cervical

63016 thoracic

63017 lumbar

63020 Laminotomy (hemilaminectomy), with decompression of nerve root(s), including partial facetectomy, foraminotomy and/or excision of herniated intervertebral disc; one interspace, cervical

(For bilateral procedure, report 63020 with modifier 50)

63030 one interspace, lumbar (including open or endoscopically-assisted approach)

(For bilateral procedure, report 63030 with modifier 50)

+ 63035 each additional interspace, cervical or lumbar (List separately in addition to code for primary procedure)

(Use 63035 in conjunction with 63020-63030)

(For bilateral procedure, report 63035 with modifier 50)

Surgery: Nervous System

63040 Laminotomy (hemilaminectomy), with decompression of nerve root(s), including partial facetectomy, foraminotomy and/or excision of herniated intervertebral disc, reexploration, single interspace; cervical

(For bilateral procedure, report 63040 with modifier 50)

63042 lumbar

(For bilateral procedure, report 63042 with modifier 50)

+ 63043 each additional cervical interspace (List separately in addition to code for primary procedure)

(Use 63043 in conjunction with 63040)

(For bilateral procedure, report 63043 with modifier 50)

+ 63044 each additional lumbar interspace (List separately in addition to code for primary procedure)

(Use 63044 in conjunction with 63042)

(For bilateral procedure, report 63044 with modifier 50)

63045 Laminectomy, facetectomy and foraminotomy (unilateral or bilateral with decompression of spinal cord, cauda equina and/or nerve root(s), (eg, spinal or lateral recess stenosis)), single vertebral segment; cervical

63046 thoracic

63047 lumbar

+ 63048 each additional segment, cervical, thoracic, or lumbar (List separately in addition to code for primary procedure)

(Use 63048 in conjunction with 63045-63047)

63050 Laminoplasty, cervical, with decompression of the spinal cord, two or more vertebral segments;

63051 with reconstruction of the posterior bony elements (including the application of bridging bone graft and non-segmental fixation devices (eg, wire, suture, mini-plates), when performed)

(Do not report 63050 or 63051 in conjunction with 22600, 22614, 22840-22842, 63001, 63015, 63045, 63048, 63295 for the same vertebral segment(s))

Transpedicular or Costovertebral Approach for Posterolateral Extradural Exploration/Decompression

63055 Transpedicular approach with decompression of spinal cord, equina and/or nerve root(s) (eg, herniated intervertebral disc), single segment; thoracic

63056 lumbar (including transfacet, or lateral extraforaminal approach) (eg, far lateral herniated intervertebral disc)

+ 63057 each additional segment, thoracic or lumbar (List separately in addition to code for primary procedure)

(Use 63057 in conjunction with 63055, 63056)

63064 Costovertebral approach with decompression of spinal cord or nerve root(s), (eg, herniated intervertebral disc), thoracic; single segment

+ 63066 each additional segment (List separately in addition to code for primary procedure)

(Use 63066 in conjunction with 63064)

(For excision of thoracic intraspinal lesions by laminectomy, see 63266, 63271, 63276, 63281, 63286)

Anterior or Anterolateral Approach for Extradural Exploration/Decompression

For the following codes, when two surgeons work together as primary surgeons performing distinct part(s) of spinal cord exploration/decompression operation, each surgeon should report his/her distinct operative work by appending modifier 62 to the procedure code (and any associated add-on codes for that procedure code as long as both surgeons continue to work together as primary surgeons). In this situation, modifier 62 may be appended to the definitive procedure code(s) 63075, 63077, 63081, 63085, 63087, 63090 and, as appropriate, to associated additional interspace add-on code(s) 63076, 63078 or additional segment add-on code(s) 63082, 63086, 63088, 63091 as long as both surgeons continue to work together as primary surgeons.

63075 Discectomy, anterior, with decompression of spinal cord and/or nerve root(s), including osteophytectomy; cervical, single interspace

+ 63076 cervical, each additional interspace (List separately in addition to code for primary procedure)

(Use 63076 in conjunction with 63075)

63077 thoracic, single interspace

+ 63078 thoracic, each additional interspace (List separately in addition to code for primary procedure)

(Use 63078 in conjunction with 63077)

(Do not report code 69990 in addition to codes 63075-63078)

63081 Vertebral corpectomy (vertebral body resection), partial or complete, anterior approach with decompression of spinal cord and/or nerve root(s); cervical, single segment

+ 63082 cervical, each additional segment (List separately in addition to code for primary procedure)

(Use 63082 in conjunction with 63081)

(For transoral approach, see 61575, 61576)

63085 Vertebral corpectomy (vertebral body resection), partial or complete, transthoracic approach with decompression of spinal cord and/or nerve root(s); thoracic, single segment

+ 63086 thoracic, each additional segment (List separately in addition to code for primary procedure)

(Use 63086 in conjunction with 63085)

Surgery: Nervous System

63087 Vertebral corpectomy (vertebral body resection), partial or complete, combined thoracolumbar approach with decompression of spinal cord, cauda equina or nerve root(s), lower thoracic or lumbar; single segment

+ 63088 each additional segment (List separately in addition to code for primary procedure)

(Use 63088 in conjunction with 63087)

63090 Vertebral corpectomy (vertebral body resection), partial or complete, transperitoneal or retroperitoneal approach with decompression of spinal cord, cauda equina or nerve root(s), lower thoracic, lumbar, or sacral; single segment

+ 63091 each additional segment (List separately in addition to code for primary procedure)

(Use 63091 in conjunction with 63090)

(Procedures 63081-63091 include discectomy above and/or below vertebral segment)

(If followed by arthrodesis, see 22548-22812)

(For reconstruction of spine, use appropriate vertebral corpectomy codes 63081-63091, bone graft codes 20930-20938, arthrodesis codes 22548-22812, and spinal instrumentation codes 22840-22855)

Lateral Extracavitary Approach for Extradural Exploration/Decompression

63101 Vertebral corpectomy (vertebral body resection), partial or complete, lateral extracavitary approach with decompression of spinal cord and/or nerve root(s) (eg, for tumor or retropulsed bone fragments); thoracic, single segment

63102 lumbar, single segment

+ 63103 thoracic or lumbar, each additional segment (List separately in addition to code for primary procedure)

(Use 63103 in conjunction with 63101 and 63102)

Incision

63170 Laminectomy with myelotomy (eg, Bischof or DREZ type), cervical, thoracic, or thoracolumbar

63172 Laminectomy with drainage of intramedullary cyst/syrinx; to subarachnoid space

63173 to peritoneal or pleural space

63180 Laminectomy and section of dentate ligaments, with or without dural graft, cervical; one or two segments

63182 more than two segments

63185 Laminectomy with rhizotomy; one or two segments

63190 more than two segments

63191 Laminectomy with section of spinal accessory nerve

(For bilateral procedure, report 63191 with modifier 50)

(For resection of sternocleidomastoid muscle, use 21720)

63194 Laminectomy with cordotomy, with section of one spinothalamic tract, one stage; cervical

63195 thoracic

63196 Laminectomy with cordotomy, with section of both spinothalamic tracts, one stage; cervical

63197 thoracic

63198 Laminectomy with cordotomy with section of both spinothalamic tracts, two stages within 14 days; cervical

63199 thoracic

63200 Laminectomy, with release of tethered spinal cord, lumbar

Excision by Laminectomy of Lesion Other Than Herniated Disc

63250 Laminectomy for excision or occlusion of arteriovenous malformation of spinal cord; cervical

63251 thoracic

63252 thoracolumbar

63265 Laminectomy for excision or evacuation of intraspinal lesion other than neoplasm, extradural; cervical

63266 thoracic

63267 lumbar

63268 sacral

63270 Laminectomy for excision of intraspinal lesion other than neoplasm, intradural; cervical

63271 thoracic

63272 lumbar

63273 sacral

63275 Laminectomy for biopsy/excision of intraspinal neoplasm; extradural, cervical

63276 extradural, thoracic

63277 extradural, lumbar

63278 extradural, sacral

63280 intradural, extramedullary, cervical

63281 intradural, extramedullary, thoracic

63282 intradural, extramedullary, lumbar

63283 intradural, sacral

63285 intradural, intramedullary, cervical

63286 intradural, intramedullary, thoracic

63287 intradural, intramedullary, thoracolumbar

63290 combined extradural-intradural lesion, any level

(For drainage of intramedullary cyst/syrinx, use 63172, 63173)

+ 63295 Osteoplastic reconstruction of dorsal spinal elements, following primary intraspinal procedure (List separately in addition to code for primary procedure)

(Use 63295 in conjunction with 63172, 63173, 63185, 63190, 63200-63290)

(Do not report 63295 in conjunction with 22590-22614, 22840-22844, 63050, 63051 for the same vertebral segment(s))

Excision, Anterior or Anterolateral Approach, Intraspinal Lesion

For the following codes, when two surgeons work together as primary surgeons performing distinct part(s) of an anterior approach for an intraspinal excision, each surgeon should report his/her distinct operative work by appending modifier 62 to the single definitive procedure code. In this situation, modifier 62 may be appended to the definitive procedure code(s) 63300-63307 and, as appropriate, to the associated additional segment add-on code 63308 as long as both surgeons continue to work together as primary surgeons.

(For arthrodesis, see 22548-22585)

(For reconstruction of spine, see 20930-20938)

63300 Vertebral corpectomy (vertebral body resection), partial or complete, for excision of intraspinal lesion, single segment; extradural, cervical

63301 extradural, thoracic by transthoracic approach

63302 extradural, thoracic by thoracolumbar approach

63303 extradural, lumbar or sacral by transperitoneal or retroperitoneal approach

63304 intradural, cervical

63305 intradural, thoracic by transthoracic approach

63306 intradural, thoracic by thoracolumbar approach

63307 intradural, lumbar or sacral by transperitoneal or retroperitoneal approach

+ 63308 each additional segment (List separately in addition to codes for single segment)

(Use 63308 in conjunction with 63300-63307)

Stereotaxis

63600 Creation of lesion of spinal cord by stereotactic method, percutaneous, any modality (including stimulation and/or recording)

63610 Stereotactic stimulation of spinal cord, percutaneous, separate procedure not followed by other surgery

63615 Stereotactic biopsy, aspiration, or excision of lesion, spinal cord

Neurostimulators (Spinal)

Codes 63650-63688 apply to both simple and complex neurostimulators. For initial or subsequent electronic analysis and programming of neurostimulator pulse generators, see codes 95970-95975.

Codes 63650, 63655, and 63660 describe the operative placement, revision, or removal of the spinal neurostimulator system components to provide spinal electrical stimulation. A neurostimulator system includes an implanted neurostimulator, external controller, extension, and collection of contacts. Multiple contacts or electrodes (4 or more) provide the actual electrical stimulation in the epidural space.

For percutaneously placed neurostimulator systems (63650, 63660), the contacts are on a catheter-like lead. An array defines the collection of contacts that are on one catheter.

For systems placed via an open surgical exposure (63655, 63660), the contacts are on a plate or paddle-shaped surface.

63650 Percutaneous implantation of neurostimulator electrode array, epidural

63655 Laminectomy for implantation of neurostimulator electrodes, plate/paddle, epidural

63660 Revision or removal of spinal neurostimulator electrode percutaneous array(s) or plate/paddle(s)

63685 Insertion or replacement of spinal neurostimulator pulse generator or receiver, direct or inductive coupling

(Do not report 63685 in conjunction with 63688 for the same pulse generator or receiver)

63688 Revision or removal of implanted spinal neurostimulator pulse generator or receiver

(For electronic analysis of implanted neurostimulator pulse generator system, see 95970-95975)

Repair

63700 Repair of meningocele; less than 5 cm diameter

63702 larger than 5 cm diameter

(Do not use modifier 63 in conjunction with 63700, 63702)

63704 Repair of myelomeningocele; less than 5 cm diameter

63706 larger than 5 cm diameter

(Do not use modifier 63 in conjunction with 63704, 63706)

(For complex skin closure, see **Integumentary System**)

63707 Repair of dural/cerebrospinal fluid leak, not requiring laminectomy

Surgery: Nervous System

63709 Repair of dural/cerebrospinal fluid leak or pseudomeningocele, with laminectomy

63710 Dural graft, spinal

(For laminectomy and section of dentate ligaments, with or without dural graft, cervical, see 63180, 63182)

Shunt, Spinal CSF

63740 Creation of shunt, lumbar, subarachnoid-peritoneal, -pleural, or other; including laminectomy

63741 percutaneous, not requiring laminectomy

63744 Replacement, irrigation or revision of lumbosubarachnoid shunt

63746 Removal of entire lumbosubarachnoid shunt system without replacement

(For insertion of subarachnoid catheter with reservoir and/or pump for intermittent or continuous infusion of drug including laminectomy, see 62351 and 62360, 62361 or 62362)

(For insertion or replacement of subarachnoid or epidural catheter, with reservoir and/or pump for drug infusion without laminectomy, see 62350 and 62360, 62361 or 62362)

Extracranial Nerves, Peripheral Nerves, and Autonomic Nervous System

(For intracranial surgery on cranial nerves, see 61450, 61460, 61790)

Introduction/Injection of Anesthetic Agent (Nerve Block), Diagnostic or Therapeutic

Somatic Nerves

64400 Injection, anesthetic agent; trigeminal nerve, any division or branch

64402 facial nerve

64405 greater occipital nerve

64408 vagus nerve

64410 phrenic nerve

64412 spinal accessory nerve

64413 cervical plexus

64415 brachial plexus, single

64416 brachial plexus, continuous infusion by catheter (including catheter placement) including daily management for anesthetic agent administration

(Do not report 64416 in conjunction with 01996)

64417 axillary nerve

64418 suprascapular nerve

64420 intercostal nerve, single

64421 intercostal nerves, multiple, regional block

64425 ilioinguinal, iliohypogastric nerves

64430 pudendal nerve

64435 paracervical (uterine) nerve

64445 sciatic nerve, single

64446 sciatic nerve, continuous infusion by catheter, (including catheter placement) including daily management for anesthetic agent administration

(Do not report 64446 in conjunction with 01996)

64447 femoral nerve, single

(Do not report 64447 in conjunction with 01996)

64448 femoral nerve, continuous infusion by catheter (including catheter placement) including daily management for anesthetic agent administration

(Do not report 64448 in conjunction with 01996)

64449 lumbar plexus, posterior approach, continuous infusion by catheter (including catheter placement) including daily management for anesthetic agent administration

(Do not report 64449 in conjunction with 01996)

64450 other peripheral nerve or branch

(For phenol destruction, see 64622-64627)

(For subarachnoid or subdural injection, see 62280, 62310-62319)

(For epidural or caudal injection, see 62273, 62281-62282, 62310-62319)

(Codes 64470-64484 are unilateral procedures. For bilateral procedures, use modifier 50)

▶(For fluoroscopic guidance and localization for needle placement and injection in conjunction with 64470-64484, use 77003)◀

64470 Injection, anesthetic agent and/or steroid, paravertebral facet joint or facet joint nerve; cervical or thoracic, single level

+ 64472 cervical or thoracic, each additional level (List separately in addition to code for primary procedure)

(Use 64472 in conjunction with 64470)

64475 lumbar or sacral, single level

+ 64476 lumbar or sacral, each additional level (List separately in addition to code for primary procedure)

(Use 64476 in conjunction with 64475)

64479 Injection, anesthetic agent and/or steroid, transforaminal epidural; cervical or thoracic, single level

+ 64480 cervical or thoracic, each additional level (List separately in addition to code for primary procedure)

(Use 64480 in conjunction with 64479)

64483 lumbar or sacral, single level

+ 64484 lumbar or sacral, each additional level (List separately in addition to code for primary procedure)

(Use 64484 in conjunction with 64483)

Sympathetic Nerves

64505 Injection, anesthetic agent; sphenopalatine ganglion

64508 carotid sinus (separate procedure)

64510 stellate ganglion (cervical sympathetic)

64517 superior hypogastric plexus

64520 lumbar or thoracic (paravertebral sympathetic)

64530 celiac plexus, with or without radiologic monitoring

Neurostimulators (Peripheral Nerve)

Codes 64553-64595 apply to both simple and complex neurostimulators. For initial or subsequent electronic analysis and programming of neurostimulator pulse generators, see codes 95970-95975.

64550 Application of surface (transcutaneous) neurostimulator

64553 Percutaneous implantation of neurostimulator electrodes; cranial nerve

(For open placement of cranial nerve (eg, vagal, trigeminal) neurostimulator pulse generator or receiver, see 61885, 61886, as appropriate)

64555 peripheral nerve (excludes sacral nerve)

64560 autonomic nerve

64561 sacral nerve (transforaminal placement)

64565 neuromuscular

64573 Incision for implantation of neurostimulator electrodes; cranial nerve

(For open placement of cranial nerve (eg, vagal, trigeminal) neurostimulator pulse generator or receiver, see 61885, 61886, as appropriate)

(For revision or removal of cranial nerve (eg, vagal, trigeminal) neurostimulator pulse generator or receiver, use 61888)

64575 peripheral nerve (excludes sacral nerve)

64577 autonomic nerve

64580 neuromuscular

64581 sacral nerve (transforaminal placement)

64585 Revision or removal of peripheral neurostimulator electrodes

▲ 64590 Insertion or replacement of peripheral or gastric neurostimulator pulse generator or receiver, direct or inductive coupling

(Do not report 64590 in conjunction with 64595)

▲ 64595 Revision or removal of peripheral or gastric neurostimulator pulse generator or receiver

Destruction by Neurolytic Agent (eg, Chemical, Thermal, Electrical or Radiofrequency)

Codes 64600-64681 include the injection of other therapeutic agents (eg, corticosteroids).

Somatic Nerves

64600 Destruction by neurolytic agent, trigeminal nerve; supraorbital, infraorbital, mental, or inferior alveolar branch

64605 second and third division branches at foramen ovale

64610 second and third division branches at foramen ovale under radiologic monitoring

64612 Chemodenervation of muscle(s); muscle(s) innervated by facial nerve (eg, for blepharospasm, hemifacial spasm)

64613 neck muscle(s) (eg, for spasmodic torticollis, spasmodic dysphonia)

64614 extremity(s) and/or trunk muscle(s) (eg, for dystonia, cerebral palsy, multiple sclerosis)

(For chemodenervation guided by needle electromyography or muscle electrical stimulation, see 95873, 95874)

(For chemodenervation for strabismus involving the extraocular muscles, use 67345)

(For chemodenervation of internal anal sphincter, use 46505)

64620 Destruction by neurolytic agent, intercostal nerve

►(For fluoroscopic guidance and localization for needle placement and neurolysis in conjunction with 64622-64627, use 77003)◄

64622 Destruction by neurolytic agent, paravertebral facet joint nerve; lumbar or sacral, single level

(For bilateral procedure, report 64622 with modifier 50)

+ 64623 lumbar or sacral, each additional level (List separately in addition to code for primary procedure)

(Use 64623 in conjunction with 64622)

(For bilateral procedure, report 64623 with modifier 50)

64626 cervical or thoracic, single level

(For bilateral procedure, report 64626 with modifier 50)

Surgery: Nervous System

+ 64627 cervical or thoracic, each additional level (List separately in addition to code for primary procedure)

(Use 64627 in conjunction with 64626)

(For bilateral procedure, report 64627 with modifier 50)

64630 Destruction by neurolytic agent; pudendal nerve

64640 other peripheral nerve or branch

Sympathetic Nerves

64650 Chemodenervation of eccrine glands; both axillae

64653 other area(s) (eg, scalp, face, neck), per day

(Report the specific service in conjunction with code(s) for the specific substance(s) or drug(s) provided)

(For chemodenervation of extremities (eg, hands or feet), use 64999)

64680 Destruction by neurolytic agent, with or without radiologic monitoring; celiac plexus

64681 superior hypogastric plexus

Neuroplasty (Exploration, Neurolysis or Nerve Decompression)

Neuroplasty is the decompression or freeing of intact nerve from scar tissue, including external neurolysis and/or transposition.

(For internal neurolysis requiring use of operating microscope, use 64727)

(For facial nerve decompression, use 69720)

64702 Neuroplasty; digital, one or both, same digit

64704 nerve of hand or foot

64708 Neuroplasty, major peripheral nerve, arm or leg; other than specified

64712 sciatic nerve

64713 brachial plexus

64714 lumbar plexus

64716 Neuroplasty and/or transposition; cranial nerve (specify)

64718 ulnar nerve at elbow

64719 ulnar nerve at wrist

64721 median nerve at carpal tunnel

(For arthroscopic procedure, use 29848)

64722 Decompression; unspecified nerve(s) (specify)

64726 plantar digital nerve

+ 64727 Internal neurolysis, requiring use of operating microscope (List separately in addition to code for neuroplasty) (Neuroplasty includes external neurolysis)

(Do not report code 69990 in addition to code 64727)

Transection or Avulsion

(For stereotactic lesion of gasserian ganglion, use 61790)

64732 Transection or avulsion of; supraorbital nerve

64734 infraorbital nerve

64736 mental nerve

64738 inferior alveolar nerve by osteotomy

64740 lingual nerve

64742 facial nerve, differential or complete

64744 greater occipital nerve

64746 phrenic nerve

(For section of recurrent laryngeal nerve, use 31595)

64752 vagus nerve (vagotomy), transthoracic

64755 vagus nerves limited to proximal stomach (selective proximal vagotomy, proximal gastric vagotomy, parietal cell vagotomy, supra- or highly selective vagotomy)

(For laparoscopic approach, use 43652)

64760 vagus nerve (vagotomy), abdominal

(For laparoscopic approach, use 43651)

64761 pudendal nerve

(For bilateral procedure, report 64761 with modifier 50)

64763 Transection or avulsion of obturator nerve, extrapelvic, with or without adductor tenotomy

(For bilateral procedure, report 64763 with modifier 50)

64766 Transection or avulsion of obturator nerve, intrapelvic, with or without adductor tenotomy

(For bilateral procedure, report 64766 with modifier 50)

64771 Transection or avulsion of other cranial nerve, extradural

64772 Transection or avulsion of other spinal nerve, extradural

(For excision of tender scar, skin and subcutaneous tissue, with or without tiny neuroma, see 11400-11446, 13100-13153)

Excision

Somatic Nerves

(For Morton neurectomy, use 28080)

64774 Excision of neuroma; cutaneous nerve, surgically identifiable

64776 digital nerve, one or both, same digit

+ 64778 digital nerve, each additional digit (List separately in addition to code for primary procedure)

(Use 64778 in conjunction with 64776)

Surgery: Nervous System

64782 hand or foot, except digital nerve

+ 64783 hand or foot, each additional nerve, except same digit (List separately in addition to code for primary procedure)

(Use 64783 in conjunction with 64782)

64784 major peripheral nerve, except sciatic

64786 sciatic nerve

+ 64787 Implantation of nerve end into bone or muscle (List separately in addition to neuroma excision)

(Use 64787 in conjunction with 64774-64786)

64788 Excision of neurofibroma or neurolemmoma; cutaneous nerve

64790 major peripheral nerve

64792 extensive (including malignant type)

64795 Biopsy of nerve

Sympathetic Nerves

64802 Sympathectomy, cervical

(For bilateral procedure, report 64802 with modifier 50)

64804 Sympathectomy, cervicothoracic

(For bilateral procedure, report 64804 with modifier 50)

64809 Sympathectomy, thoracolumbar

(For bilateral procedure, report 64809 with modifier 50)

64818 Sympathectomy, lumbar

(For bilateral procedure, report 64818 with modifier 50)

64820 Sympathectomy; digital arteries, each digit

(Do not report 69990 in addition to code 64820)

64821 radial artery

(Do not report 69990 in addition to code 64821)

64822 ulnar artery

(Do not report 69990 in addition to code 64822)

64823 superficial palmar arch

(Do not report 69990 in addition to code 64823)

Neurorrhaphy

64831 Suture of digital nerve, hand or foot; one nerve

+ 64832 each additional digital nerve (List separately in addition to code for primary procedure)

(Use 64832 in conjunction with 64831)

64834 Suture of one nerve, hand or foot; common sensory nerve

64835 median motor thenar

64836 ulnar motor

+ 64837 Suture of each additional nerve, hand or foot (List separately in addition to code for primary procedure)

(Use 64837 in conjunction with 64834-64836)

64840 Suture of posterior tibial nerve

64856 Suture of major peripheral nerve, arm or leg, except sciatic; including transposition

64857 without transposition

64858 Suture of sciatic nerve

+ 64859 Suture of each additional major peripheral nerve (List separately in addition to code for primary procedure)

(Use 64859 in conjunction with 64856, 64857)

64861 Suture of; brachial plexus

64862 lumbar plexus

64864 Suture of facial nerve; extracranial

64865 infratemporal, with or without grafting

64866 Anastomosis; facial-spinal accessory

64868 facial-hypoglossal

64870 facial-phrenic

+ 64872 Suture of nerve; requiring secondary or delayed suture (List separately in addition to code for primary neurorrhaphy)

(Use 64872 in conjunction with 64831-64865)

+ 64874 requiring extensive mobilization, or transposition of nerve (List separately in addition to code for nerve suture)

(Use 64874 in conjunction with 64831-64865)

+ 64876 requiring shortening of bone of extremity (List separately in addition to code for nerve suture)

(Use 64876 in conjunction with 64831-64865)

▶Neurorrhaphy With Nerve Graft, Vein Graft, or Conduit◀

64885 Nerve graft (includes obtaining graft), head or neck; up to 4 cm in length

64886 more than 4 cm length

64890 Nerve graft (includes obtaining graft), single strand, hand or foot; up to 4 cm length

64891 more than 4 cm length

64892 Nerve graft (includes obtaining graft), single strand, arm or leg; up to 4 cm length

64893 more than 4 cm length

64895 Nerve graft (includes obtaining graft), multiple strands (cable), hand or foot; up to 4 cm length

64896 more than 4 cm length

Surgery: Nervous System

64897 Nerve graft (includes obtaining graft), multiple strands (cable), arm or leg; up to 4 cm length

64898 more than 4 cm length

+ **64901** Nerve graft, each additional nerve; single strand (List separately in addition to code for primary procedure)

(Use 64901 in conjunction with 64885-64893)

+ **64902** multiple strands (cable) (List separately in addition to code for primary procedure)

(Use 64902 in conjunction with 64885, 64886, 64895-64898)

64905 Nerve pedicle transfer; first stage

64907 second stage

● **64910** Nerve repair; with synthetic conduit or vein allograft (eg, nerve tube), each nerve

● **64911** with autogenous vein graft (includes harvest of vein graft), each nerve

►(Do not report 69990 in addition to 64910, 64911)◄

Other Procedures

64999 Unlisted procedure, nervous system

Notes

⊙=Moderate sedation ✚=Add-on code ✗=FDA approval pending

Eye and Ocular Adnexa

(For diagnostic and treatment ophthalmological services, see **Medicine, Ophthalmology,** and 92002 et seq)

(Do not report code 69990 in addition to codes 65091-68850)

Eyeball

Removal of Eye

65091 Evisceration of ocular contents; without implant

65093 with implant

65101 Enucleation of eye; without implant

65103 with implant, muscles not attached to implant

65105 with implant, muscles attached to implant

(For conjunctivoplasty after enucleation, see 68320 et seq)

65110 Exenteration of orbit (does not include skin graft), removal of orbital contents; only

65112 with therapeutic removal of bone

65114 with muscle or myocutaneous flap

(For skin graft to orbit (split skin), see 15120, 15121; free, full thickness, see 15260, 15261)

(For eyelid repair involving more than skin, see 67930 et seq)

Secondary Implant(s) Procedures

An ocular implant is an implant inside muscular cone; an orbital implant is an implant outside muscular cone.

65125 Modification of ocular implant with placement or replacement of pegs (eg, drilling receptacle for prosthesis appendage) (separate procedure)

65130 Insertion of ocular implant secondary; after evisceration, in scleral shell

65135 after enucleation, muscles not attached to implant

65140 after enucleation, muscles attached to implant

65150 Reinsertion of ocular implant; with or without conjunctival graft

65155 with use of foreign material for reinforcement and/or attachment of muscles to implant

65175 Removal of ocular implant

(For orbital implant (implant outside muscle cone) insertion, use 67550; removal, use 67560)

Removal of Foreign Body

(For removal of implanted material: ocular implant, use 65175; anterior segment implant, use 65920; posterior segment implant, use 67120; orbital implant, use 67560)

(For diagnostic x-ray for foreign body, use 70030)

(For diagnostic echography for foreign body, use 76529)

(For removal of foreign body from orbit: frontal approach, use 67413; lateral approach, use 67430; transcranial approach, use 61334)

(For removal of foreign body from eyelid, embedded, use 67938)

(For removal of foreign body from lacrimal system, use 68530)

65205 Removal of foreign body, external eye; conjunctival superficial

65210 conjunctival embedded (includes concretions), subconjunctival, or scleral nonperforating

65220 corneal, without slit lamp

65222 corneal, with slit lamp

(For repair of corneal laceration with foreign body, use 65275)

65235 Removal of foreign body, intraocular; from anterior chamber of eye or lens

(For removal of implanted material from anterior segment, use 65920)

65260 from posterior segment, magnetic extraction, anterior or posterior route

65265 from posterior segment, nonmagnetic extraction

(For removal of implanted material from posterior segment, use 67120)

Repair of Laceration

(For fracture of orbit, see 21385 et seq)

(For repair of wound of eyelid, skin, linear, simple, see 12011-12018; intermediate, layered closure, see 12051-12057; linear, complex, see 13150-13160; other, see 67930, 67935)

(For repair of wound of lacrimal system, use 68700)

(For repair of operative wound, use 66250)

65270 Repair of laceration; conjunctiva, with or without nonperforating laceration sclera, direct closure

65272 conjunctiva, by mobilization and rearrangement, without hospitalization

65273 conjunctiva, by mobilization and rearrangement, with hospitalization

65275 cornea, nonperforating, with or without removal foreign body

65280 cornea and/or sclera, perforating, not involving uveal tissue

65285 cornea and/or sclera, perforating, with reposition or resection of uveal tissue

65286 application of tissue glue, wounds of cornea and/or sclera

(Repair of laceration includes use of conjunctival flap and restoration of anterior chamber, by air or saline injection when indicated)

(For repair of iris or ciliary body, use 66680)

65290 Repair of wound, extraocular muscle, tendon and/or Tenon's capsule

Anterior Segment

Cornea

Excision

65400 Excision of lesion, cornea (keratectomy, lamellar, partial), except pterygium

65410 Biopsy of cornea

65420 Excision or transposition of pterygium; without graft

65426 with graft

Removal or Destruction

65430 Scraping of cornea, diagnostic, for smear and/or culture

65435 Removal of corneal epithelium; with or without chemocauterization (abrasion, curettage)

65436 with application of chelating agent (eg, EDTA)

65450 Destruction of lesion of cornea by cryotherapy, photocoagulation or thermocauterization

65600 Multiple punctures of anterior cornea (eg, for corneal erosion, tattoo)

Keratoplasty

Corneal transplant includes use of fresh or preserved grafts, and preparation of donor material.

(Keratoplasty excludes refractive keratoplasty procedures, 65760, 65765, and 65767)

65710 Keratoplasty (corneal transplant); lamellar

65730 penetrating (except in aphakia)

65750 penetrating (in aphakia)

65755 penetrating (in pseudophakia)

Other Procedures

65760 Keratomileusis

65765 Keratophakia

65767 Epikeratoplasty

65770 Keratoprosthesis

65771 Radial keratotomy

65772 Corneal relaxing incision for correction of surgically induced astigmatism

65775 Corneal wedge resection for correction of surgically induced astigmatism

(For fitting of contact lens for treatment of disease, use 92070)

(For unlisted procedures on cornea, use 66999)

65780 Ocular surface reconstruction; amniotic membrane transplantation

65781 limbal stem cell allograft (eg, cadaveric or living donor)

65782 limbal conjunctival autograft (includes obtaining graft)

(For harvesting conjunctival allograft, living donor, use 68371)

Anterior Chamber

Incision

65800 Paracentesis of anterior chamber of eye (separate procedure); with diagnostic aspiration of aqueous

65805 with therapeutic release of aqueous

65810 with removal of vitreous and/or discission of anterior hyaloid membrane, with or without air injection

65815 with removal of blood, with or without irrigation and/or air injection

(For injection, see 66020-66030)

(For removal of blood clot, use 65930)

65820 Goniotomy

(Do not report modifier 63 in conjunction with 65820)

▶(For use of ophthalmic endoscope with 65820, use 66990)◀

65850 Trabeculotomy ab externo

65855 Trabeculoplasty by laser surgery, one or more sessions (defined treatment series)

(If re-treatment is necessary after several months because of disease progression, a new treatment or treatment series should be reported with a modifier, if necessary, to indicate lesser or greater complexity)

(For trabeculectomy, use 66170)

65860 Severing adhesions of anterior segment, laser technique (separate procedure)

Other Procedures

65865 Severing adhesions of anterior segment of eye, incisional technique (with or without injection of air or liquid) (separate procedure); goniosynechiae

(For trabeculoplasty by laser surgery, use 65855)

65870 anterior synechiae, except goniosynechiae

65875 posterior synechiae

▶(For use of ophthalmic endoscope with 65875, use 66990)◀

65880 corneovitreal adhesions

(For laser surgery, use 66821)

65900 Removal of epithelial downgrowth, anterior chamber of eye

65920 Removal of implanted material, anterior segment of eye

▶(For use of ophthalmic endoscope with 65920, use 66990)◀

65930 Removal of blood clot, anterior segment of eye

66020 Injection, anterior chamber of eye (separate procedure); air or liquid

66030 medication

(For unlisted procedures on anterior segment, use 66999)

Anterior Sclera

Excision

(For removal of intraocular foreign body, use 65235)

(For operations on posterior sclera, use 67250, 67255)

66130 Excision of lesion, sclera

66150 Fistulization of sclera for glaucoma; trephination with iridectomy

66155 thermocauterization with iridectomy

66160 sclerectomy with punch or scissors, with iridectomy

66165 iridencleisis or iridotasis

66170 trabeculectomy ab externo in absence of previous surgery

(For trabeculotomy ab externo, use 65850)

(For repair of operative wound, use 66250)

66172 trabeculectomy ab externo with scarring from previous ocular surgery or trauma (includes injection of antifibrotic agents)

(For transciliary body sclera fistulization, use Category III code 0123T)

▶**Aqueous Shunt**◀

66180 Aqueous shunt to extraocular reservoir (eg, Molteno, Schocket, Denver-Krupin)

66185 Revision of aqueous shunt to extraocular reservoir

(For removal of implanted shunt, use 67120)

Repair or Revision

(For scleral procedures in retinal surgery, see 67101 et seq)

66220 Repair of scleral staphyloma; without graft

66225 with graft

(For scleral reinforcement, see 67250, 67255)

66250 Revision or repair of operative wound of anterior segment, any type, early or late, major or minor procedure

(For unlisted procedures on anterior sclera, use 66999)

Iris, Ciliary Body

Incision

66500 Iridotomy by stab incision (separate procedure); except transfixion

66505 with transfixion as for iris bombe

(For iridotomy by photocoagulation, use 66761)

Excision

66600 Iridectomy, with corneoscleral or corneal section; for removal of lesion

66605 with cyclectomy

66625 peripheral for glaucoma (separate procedure)

66630 sector for glaucoma (separate procedure)

66635 optical (separate procedure)

(For coreoplasty by photocoagulation, use 66762)

Repair

66680 Repair of iris, ciliary body (as for iridodialysis)

(For reposition or resection of uveal tissue with perforating wound of cornea or sclera, use 65285)

66682 Suture of iris, ciliary body (separate procedure) with retrieval of suture through small incision (eg, McCannel suture)

Destruction

66700 Ciliary body destruction; diathermy

66710 cyclophotocoagulation, transscleral

66711 cyclophotocoagulation, endoscopic

(Do not report 66711 in conjunction with 66990)

⊙ 66720 cryotherapy

66740 cyclodialysis

66761 Iridotomy/iridectomy by laser surgery (eg, for glaucoma) (one or more sessions)

66762 Iridoplasty by photocoagulation (one or more sessions) (eg, for improvement of vision, for widening of anterior chamber angle)

66770 Destruction of cyst or lesion iris or ciliary body (nonexcisional procedure)

(For excision lesion iris, ciliary body, see 66600, 66605; for removal of epithelial downgrowth, use 65900)

(For unlisted procedures on iris, ciliary body, use 66999)

Lens

Incision

66820 Discission of secondary membranous cataract (opacified posterior lens capsule and/or anterior hyaloid); stab incision technique (Ziegler or Wheeler knife)

66821 laser surgery (eg, YAG laser) (one or more stages)

66825 Repositioning of intraocular lens prosthesis, requiring an incision (separate procedure)

Removal Cataract

Lateral canthotomy, iridectomy, iridotomy, anterior capsulotomy, posterior capsulotomy, the use of viscoelastic agents, enzymatic zonulysis, use of other pharmacologic agents, and subconjunctival or sub-tenon injections are included as part of the code for the extraction of lens.

66830 Removal of secondary membranous cataract (opacified posterior lens capsule and/or anterior hyaloid) with corneo-scleral section, with or without iridectomy (iridocapsulotomy, iridocapsulectomy)

66840 Removal of lens material; aspiration technique, one or more stages

66850 phacofragmentation technique (mechanical or ultrasonic) (eg, phacoemulsification), with aspiration

66852 pars plana approach, with or without vitrectomy

66920 intracapsular

66930 intracapsular, for dislocated lens

66940 extracapsular (other than 66840, 66850, 66852)

(For removal of intralenticular foreign body without lens extraction, use 65235)

(For repair of operative wound, use 66250)

66982 Extracapsular cataract removal with insertion of intraocular lens prosthesis (one stage procedure), manual or mechanical technique (eg, irrigation and aspiration or phacoemulsification), complex, requiring devices or techniques not generally used in routine cataract surgery (eg, iris expansion device, suture support for intraocular lens, or primary posterior capsulorrhexis) or performed on patients in the amblyogenic developmental stage

66983 Intracapsular cataract extraction with insertion of intraocular lens prosthesis (one stage procedure)

66984 Extracapsular cataract removal with insertion of intraocular lens prosthesis (one stage procedure), manual or mechanical technique (eg, irrigation and aspiration or phacoemulsification)

(For complex extracapsular cataract removal, use 66982)

66985 Insertion of intraocular lens prosthesis (secondary implant), not associated with concurrent cataract removal

(To code implant at time of concurrent cataract surgery, see 66982, 66983, 66984)

(For intraocular lens prosthesis supplied by physician, use 99070)

(For ultrasonic determination of intraocular lens power, use 76519)

(For removal of implanted material from anterior segment, use 65920)

(For secondary fixation (separate procedure), use 66682)

►(For use of ophthalmic endoscope with 66985, use 66990)◄

66986 Exchange of intraocular lens

►(For use of ophthalmic endoscope with 66986, use 66990)◄

+ 66990 Use of ophthalmic endoscope (List separately in addition to code for primary procedure)

►(66990 may be used only with codes 65820, 65875, 65920, 66985, 66986, 67036, 67038, 67039, 67040, 67112)◄

Other Procedures

66999 Unlisted procedure, anterior segment of eye

Surgery: Eye and Ocular Adnexa

Posterior Segment

Vitreous

67005　Removal of vitreous, anterior approach (open sky technique or limbal incision); partial removal

67010　　subtotal removal with mechanical vitrectomy

(For removal of vitreous by paracentesis of anterior chamber, use 65810)

(For removal of corneovitreal adhesions, use 65880)

67015　Aspiration or release of vitreous, subretinal or choroidal fluid, pars plana approach (posterior sclerotomy)

67025　Injection of vitreous substitute, pars plana or limbal approach, (fluid-gas exchange), with or without aspiration (separate procedure)

67027　Implantation of intravitreal drug delivery system (eg, ganciclovir implant), includes concomitant removal of vitreous

(For removal, use 67121)

67028　Intravitreal injection of a pharmacologic agent (separate procedure)

67030　Discission of vitreous strands (without removal), pars plana approach

67031　Severing of vitreous strands, vitreous face adhesions, sheets, membranes or opacities, laser surgery (one or more stages)

67036　Vitrectomy, mechanical, pars plana approach;

67038　　with epiretinal membrane stripping

67039　　with focal endolaser photocoagulation

67040　　with endolaser panretinal photocoagulation

▶(For use of ophthalmic endoscope with 67036, 67038, 67039, 67040, use 66990)◀

(For associated lensectomy, use 66850)

(For use of vitrectomy in retinal detachment surgery, use 67108)

(For associated removal of foreign body, see 65260, 65265)

(For unlisted procedures on vitreous, use 67299)

Retina or Choroid

Repair

(If diathermy, cryotherapy and/or photocoagulation are combined, report under principal modality used)

67101　Repair of retinal detachment, one or more sessions; cryotherapy or diathermy, with or without drainage of subretinal fluid

67105　　photocoagulation, with or without drainage of subretinal fluid

67107　Repair of retinal detachment; scleral buckling (such as lamellar scleral dissection, imbrication or encircling procedure), with or without implant, with or without cryotherapy, photocoagulation, and drainage of subretinal fluid

67108　　with vitrectomy, any method, with or without air or gas tamponade, focal endolaser photocoagulation, cryotherapy, drainage of subretinal fluid, scleral buckling, and/or removal of lens by same technique

67110　　by injection of air or other gas (eg, pneumatic retinopexy)

67112　　by scleral buckling or vitrectomy, on patient having previous ipsilateral retinal detachment repair(s) using scleral buckling or vitrectomy techniques

(For aspiration or drainage of subretinal or subchoroidal fluid, use 67015)

▶(For use of ophthalmic endoscope with 67112, use 66990)◀

67115　Release of encircling material (posterior segment)

67120　Removal of implanted material, posterior segment; extraocular

67121　　intraocular

(For removal from anterior segment, use 65920)

(For removal of foreign body, see 65260, 65265)

Prophylaxis

Repetitive services. The services listed below are often performed in multiple sessions or groups of sessions. The methods of reporting vary.

The following descriptors are intended to include all sessions in a defined treatment period.

67141　Prophylaxis of retinal detachment (eg, retinal break, lattice degeneration) without drainage, one or more sessions; cryotherapy, diathermy

67145　　photocoagulation (laser or xenon arc)

Destruction

67208　Destruction of localized lesion of retina (eg, macular edema, tumors), one or more sessions; cryotherapy, diathermy

67210　　photocoagulation

67218　　radiation by implantation of source (includes removal of source)

67220　Destruction of localized lesion of choroid (eg, choroidal neovascularization); photocoagulation (eg, laser), one or more sessions

(For destruction of macular drusen, photocoagulation, use Category III code 0017T)

(For destruction of localized lesion of choroid by transpupillary thermotherapy, use Category III code 0016T)

▲=Revised code　●=New code　▶ ◀=Contains new or revised text　⊘=Modifier 51 exempt

Surgery: Eye and Ocular Adnexa

67221 photodynamic therapy (includes intravenous infusion)

+ 67225 photodynamic therapy, second eye, at single session (List separately in addition to code for primary eye treatment)

 (Use 67225 in conjunction with 67221)

67227 Destruction of extensive or progressive retinopathy (eg, diabetic retinopathy), one or more sessions; cryotherapy, diathermy

67228 photocoagulation (laser or xenon arc)

 (For unlisted procedures on retina, use 67299)

▶Posterior Sclera◀

Repair

(For excision lesion sclera, use 66130)

67250 Scleral reinforcement (separate procedure); without graft

67255 with graft

 (For repair scleral staphyloma, see 66220, 66225)

Other Procedures

67299 Unlisted procedure, posterior segment

Ocular Adnexa

Extraocular Muscles

67311 Strabismus surgery, recession or resection procedure; one horizontal muscle

67312 two horizontal muscles

67314 one vertical muscle (excluding superior oblique)

67316 two or more vertical muscles (excluding superior oblique)

 (For adjustable sutures, use 67335 in addition to codes 67311-67334 for primary procedure reflecting number of muscles operated on)

67318 Strabismus surgery, any procedure, superior oblique muscle

+ 67320 Transposition procedure (eg, for paretic extraocular muscle), any extraocular muscle (specify) (List separately in addition to code for primary procedure)

 (Use 67320 in conjunction with 67311-67318)

+ 67331 Strabismus surgery on patient with previous eye surgery or injury that did not involve the extraocular muscles (List separately in addition to code for primary procedure)

 (Use 67331 in conjunction with 67311-67318)

+ 67332 Strabismus surgery on patient with scarring of extraocular muscles (eg, prior ocular injury, strabismus or retinal detachment surgery) or restrictive myopathy (eg, dysthyroid ophthalmopathy) (List separately in addition to code for primary procedure)

 (Use 67332 in conjunction with 67311-67318)

+ 67334 Strabismus surgery by posterior fixation suture technique, with or without muscle recession (List separately in addition to code for primary procedure)

 (Use 67334 in conjunction with 67311-67318)

+ 67335 Placement of adjustable suture(s) during strabismus surgery, including postoperative adjustment(s) of suture(s) (List separately in addition to code for specific strabismus surgery)

 (Use 67335 in conjunction with 67311-67334)

+ 67340 Strabismus surgery involving exploration and/or repair of detached extraocular muscle(s) (List separately in addition to code for primary procedure)

 (Use 67340 in conjunction with 67311-67334)

67343 Release of extensive scar tissue without detaching extraocular muscle (separate procedure)

 (Use 67343 in conjunction with 67311-67340, when such procedures are performed other than on the affected muscle)

67345 Chemodenervation of extraocular muscle

 (For chemodenervation for blepharospasm and other neurological disorders, see 64612 and 64613)

● 67346 Biopsy of extraocular muscle

 ▶(For repair of wound, extraocular muscle, tendon or Tenon's capsule, use 65290)◀

Other Procedures

 ▶(67350 has been deleted. To report, use 67346)◀

67399 Unlisted procedure, ocular muscle

Orbit

Exploration, Excision, Decompression

67400 Orbitotomy without bone flap (frontal or transconjunctival approach); for exploration, with or without biopsy

67405 with drainage only

67412 with removal of lesion

67413 with removal of foreign body

67414 with removal of bone for decompression

67415 Fine needle aspiration of orbital contents

 (For exenteration, enucleation, and repair, see 65101 et seq; for optic nerve decompression, use 67570)

67420 Orbitotomy with bone flap or window, lateral approach (eg, Kroenlein); with removal of lesion

67430 with removal of foreign body

67440 with drainage

67445 with removal of bone for decompression

(For optic nerve sheath decompression, use 67570)

67450 for exploration, with or without biopsy

(For orbitotomy, transcranial approach, see 61330-61334)

(For orbital implant, see 67550, 67560)

(For removal of eyeball or for repair after removal, see 65091-65175)

Other Procedures

67500 Retrobulbar injection; medication (separate procedure, does not include supply of medication)

67505 alcohol

67515 Injection of medication or other substance into Tenon's capsule

(For subconjunctival injection, use 68200)

67550 Orbital implant (implant outside muscle cone); insertion

67560 removal or revision

(For ocular implant (implant inside muscle cone), see 65093-65105, 65130-65175)

(For treatment of fractures of malar area, orbit, see 21355 et seq)

67570 Optic nerve decompression (eg, incision or fenestration of optic nerve sheath)

67599 Unlisted procedure, orbit

Eyelids

Incision

67700 Blepharotomy, drainage of abscess, eyelid

67710 Severing of tarsorrhaphy

67715 Canthotomy (separate procedure)

(For canthoplasty, use 67950)

(For division of symblepharon, use 68340)

►Excision, Destruction◄

Codes for removal of lesion include more than skin (ie, involving lid margin, tarsus, and/or palpebral conjunctiva).

(For removal of lesion, involving mainly skin of eyelid, see 11310-11313; 11440-11446; 11640-11646; 17000-17004)

(For repair of wounds, blepharoplasty, grafts, reconstructive surgery, see 67930-67975)

67800 Excision of chalazion; single

67801 multiple, same lid

67805 multiple, different lids

67808 under general anesthesia and/or requiring hospitalization, single or multiple

67810 Biopsy of eyelid

67820 Correction of trichiasis; epilation, by forceps only

67825 epilation by other than forceps (eg, by electrosurgery, cryotherapy, laser surgery)

67830 incision of lid margin

67835 incision of lid margin, with free mucous membrane graft

67840 Excision of lesion of eyelid (except chalazion) without closure or with simple direct closure

(For excision and repair of eyelid by reconstructive surgery, see 67961, 67966)

67850 Destruction of lesion of lid margin (up to 1 cm)

►(For Mohs micrographic surgery, see 17311-17315)◄

(For initiation or follow-up care of topical chemotherapy (eg, 5-FU or similar agents), see appropriate office visits)

Tarsorrhaphy

67875 Temporary closure of eyelids by suture (eg, Frost suture)

67880 Construction of intermarginal adhesions, median tarsorrhaphy, or canthorrhaphy;

67882 with transposition of tarsal plate

(For severing of tarsorrhaphy, use 67710)

(For canthoplasty, reconstruction canthus, use 67950)

(For canthotomy, use 67715)

Repair (Brow Ptosis, Blepharoptosis, Lid Retraction, Ectropion, Entropion)

67900 Repair of brow ptosis (supraciliary, mid-forehead or coronal approach)

(For forehead rhytidectomy, use 15824)

67901 Repair of blepharoptosis; frontalis muscle technique with suture or other material (eg, banked fascia)

67902 frontalis muscle technique with autologous fascial sling (includes obtaining fascia)

67903 (tarso) levator resection or advancement, internal approach

67904 (tarso) levator resection or advancement, external approach

67906 superior rectus technique with fascial sling (includes obtaining fascia)

67908 conjunctivo-tarso-Muller's muscle-levator resection (eg, Fasanella-Servat type)

▲=Revised code ●=New code ►◄=Contains new or revised text ⊘=Modifier 51 exempt

Surgery: Eye and Ocular Adnexa

67909 Reduction of overcorrection of ptosis

67911 Correction of lid retraction

(For obtaining autogenous graft materials, see 20920, 20922 or 20926)

(For correction of trichiasis by mucous membrane graft, use 67835)

67912 Correction of lagophthalmos, with implantation of upper eyelid lid load (eg, gold weight)

67914 Repair of ectropion; suture

67915 thermocauterization

67916 excision tarsal wedge

67917 extensive (eg, tarsal strip operations)

(For correction of everted punctum, use 68705)

67921 Repair of entropion; suture

67922 thermocauterization

67923 excision tarsal wedge

67924 extensive (eg, tarsal strip or capsulopalpebral fascia repairs operation)

(For repair of cicatricial ectropion or entropion requiring scar excision or skin graft, see also 67961 et seq)

Reconstruction

Codes for blepharoplasty involve more than skin (ie, involving lid margin, tarsus, and/or palpebral conjunctiva).

67930 Suture of recent wound, eyelid, involving lid margin, tarsus, and/or palpebral conjunctiva direct closure; partial thickness

67935 full thickness

67938 Removal of embedded foreign body, eyelid

(For repair of skin of eyelid, see 12011-12018; 12051-12057; 13150-13153)

(For tarsorrhaphy, canthorrhaphy, see 67880, 67882)

(For repair of blepharoptosis and lid retraction, see 67901-67911)

(For blepharoplasty for entropion, ectropion, see 67916, 67917, 67923, 67924)

(For correction of blepharochalasis (blepharorhytidectomy), see 15820-15823)

▶(For repair of skin of eyelid, adjacent tissue transfer, see 14060, 14061; preparation for graft, use 15004; free graft, see 15120, 15121, 15260, 15261)◀

(For excision of lesion of eyelid, use 67800 et seq)

(For repair of lacrimal canaliculi, use 68700)

67950 Canthoplasty (reconstruction of canthus)

67961 Excision and repair of eyelid, involving lid margin, tarsus, conjunctiva, canthus, or full thickness, may include preparation for skin graft or pedicle flap with adjacent tissue transfer or rearrangement; up to one-fourth of lid margin

67966 over one-fourth of lid margin

(For canthoplasty, use 67950)

(For free skin grafts, see 15120, 15121, 15260, 15261)

(For tubed pedicle flap preparation, use 15576; for delay, use 15630; for attachment, use 15650)

67971 Reconstruction of eyelid, full thickness by transfer of tarsoconjunctival flap from opposing eyelid; up to two-thirds of eyelid, one stage or first stage

67973 total eyelid, lower, one stage or first stage

67974 total eyelid, upper, one stage or first stage

67975 second stage

Other Procedures

67999 Unlisted procedure, eyelids

Conjunctiva

(For removal of foreign body, see 65205 et seq)

Incision and Drainage

68020 Incision of conjunctiva, drainage of cyst

68040 Expression of conjunctival follicles (eg, for trachoma)

Excision and/or Destruction

68100 Biopsy of conjunctiva

68110 Excision of lesion, conjunctiva; up to 1 cm

68115 over 1 cm

68130 with adjacent sclera

68135 Destruction of lesion, conjunctiva

Injection

(For injection into Tenon's capsule or retrobulbar injection, see 67500-67515)

68200 Subconjunctival injection

Conjunctivoplasty

(For wound repair, see 65270-65273)

68320 Conjunctivoplasty; with conjunctival graft or extensive rearrangement

68325 with buccal mucous membrane graft (includes obtaining graft)

68326 Conjunctivoplasty, reconstruction cul-de-sac; with conjunctival graft or extensive rearrangement

68328 with buccal mucous membrane graft (includes obtaining graft)

68330 Repair of symblepharon; conjunctivoplasty, without graft

68335 with free graft conjunctiva or buccal mucous membrane (includes obtaining graft)

68340 division of symblepharon, with or without insertion of conformer or contact lens

Other Procedures

68360 Conjunctival flap; bridge or partial (separate procedure)

68362 total (such as Gunderson thin flap or purse string flap)

(For conjunctival flap for perforating injury, see 65280, 65285)

(For repair of operative wound, use 66250)

(For removal of conjunctival foreign body, see 65205, 65210)

68371 Harvesting conjunctival allograft, living donor

68399 Unlisted procedure, conjunctiva

Lacrimal System

Incision

68400 Incision, drainage of lacrimal gland

68420 Incision, drainage of lacrimal sac (dacryocystotomy or dacryocystostomy)

68440 Snip incision of lacrimal punctum

Excision

68500 Excision of lacrimal gland (dacryoadenectomy), except for tumor; total

68505 partial

68510 Biopsy of lacrimal gland

68520 Excision of lacrimal sac (dacryocystectomy)

68525 Biopsy of lacrimal sac

68530 Removal of foreign body or dacryolith, lacrimal passages

68540 Excision of lacrimal gland tumor; frontal approach

68550 involving osteotomy

Repair

68700 Plastic repair of canaliculi

68705 Correction of everted punctum, cautery

68720 Dacryocystorhinostomy (fistulization of lacrimal sac to nasal cavity)

68745 Conjunctivorhinostomy (fistulization of conjunctiva to nasal cavity); without tube

68750 with insertion of tube or stent

68760 Closure of the lacrimal punctum; by thermocauterization, ligation, or laser surgery

68761 by plug, each

68770 Closure of lacrimal fistula (separate procedure)

Probing and/or Related Procedures

68801 Dilation of lacrimal punctum, with or without irrigation

(To report a bilateral procedure, use 68801 with modifier 50)

68810 Probing of nasolacrimal duct, with or without irrigation;

(For bilateral procedure, report 68810 with modifier 50)

68811 requiring general anesthesia

(For bilateral procedure, report 68811 with modifier 50)

68815 with insertion of tube or stent

(See also 92018)

(For bilateral procedure, report 68815 with modifier 50)

68840 Probing of lacrimal canaliculi, with or without irrigation

68850 Injection of contrast medium for dacryocystography

(For radiological supervision and interpretation, see 70170, 78660)

Other Procedures

68899 Unlisted procedure, lacrimal system

Notes

⊙=Moderate sedation **+**=Add-on code ✗=FDA approval pending

Surgery: Eye and Ocular Adnexa

Auditory System

(For diagnostic services (eg, audiometry, vestibular tests), see 92502 et seq)

External Ear

Incision

69000 Drainage external ear, abscess or hematoma; simple

69005 complicated

69020 Drainage external auditory canal, abscess

69090 Ear piercing

Excision

69100 Biopsy external ear

69105 Biopsy external auditory canal

69110 Excision external ear; partial, simple repair

69120 complete amputation

(For reconstruction of ear, see 15120 et seq)

69140 Excision exostosis(es), external auditory canal

69145 Excision soft tissue lesion, external auditory canal

69150 Radical excision external auditory canal lesion; without neck dissection

69155 with neck dissection

(For resection of temporal bone, use 69535)

►(For skin grafting, see 15004-15261)◄

►Removal◄

69200 Removal foreign body from external auditory canal; without general anesthesia

69205 with general anesthesia

69210 Removal impacted cerumen (separate procedure), one or both ears

69220 Debridement, mastoidectomy cavity, simple (eg, routine cleaning)

(For bilateral procedure, report 69220 with modifier 50)

69222 Debridement, mastoidectomy cavity, complex (eg, with anesthesia or more than routine cleaning)

(For bilateral procedure, report 69222 with modifier 50)

Repair

(For suture of wound or injury of external ear, see 12011-14300)

⊙ **69300** Otoplasty, protruding ear, with or without size reduction

(For bilateral procedure, report 69300 with modifier 50)

69310 Reconstruction of external auditory canal (meatoplasty) (eg, for stenosis due to injury, infection) (separate procedure)

69320 Reconstruction external auditory canal for congenital atresia, single stage

(For combination with middle ear reconstruction, see 69631, 69641)

(For other reconstructive procedures with grafts (eg, skin, cartilage, bone), see 13150-15760, 21230-21235)

Other Procedures

(For otoscopy under general anesthesia, use 92502)

69399 Unlisted procedure, external ear

Middle Ear

Introduction

69400 Eustachian tube inflation, transnasal; with catheterization

69401 without catheterization

69405 Eustachian tube catheterization, transtympanic

(69410 has been deleted)

Incision

69420 Myringotomy including aspiration and/or eustachian tube inflation

69421 Myringotomy including aspiration and/or eustachian tube inflation requiring general anesthesia

69424 Ventilating tube removal requiring general anesthesia

(For bilateral procedure, report 69424 with modifier 50)

(Do not report code 69424 in conjunction with 69205, 69210, 69420, 69421, 69433-69676, 69710-69745, 69801-69930)

69433 Tympanostomy (requiring insertion of ventilating tube), local or topical anesthesia

(For bilateral procedure, report 69433 with modifier 50)

69436 Tympanostomy (requiring insertion of ventilating tube), general anesthesia

(For bilateral procedure, report 69436 with modifier 50)

69440 Middle ear exploration through postauricular or ear canal incision

(For atticotomy, see 69601 et seq)

69450 Tympanolysis, transcanal

Surgery: Auditory System

Excision

69501 Transmastoid antrotomy (simple mastoidectomy)

69502 Mastoidectomy; complete

69505 modified radical

69511 radical

▶(For skin graft, see 15004 et seq)◀

(For mastoidectomy cavity debridement, see 69220, 69222)

69530 Petrous apicectomy including radical mastoidectomy

69535 Resection temporal bone, external approach

(For middle fossa approach, see 69950-69970)

69540 Excision aural polyp

69550 Excision aural glomus tumor; transcanal

69552 transmastoid

69554 extended (extratemporal)

Repair

69601 Revision mastoidectomy; resulting in complete mastoidectomy

69602 resulting in modified radical mastoidectomy

69603 resulting in radical mastoidectomy

69604 resulting in tympanoplasty

(For planned secondary tympanoplasty after mastoidectomy, see 69631, 69632)

69605 with apicectomy

(For skin graft, see 15120, 15121, 15260, 15261)

69610 Tympanic membrane repair, with or without site preparation of perforation for closure, with or without patch

69620 Myringoplasty (surgery confined to drumhead and donor area)

69631 Tympanoplasty without mastoidectomy (including canalplasty, atticotomy and/or middle ear surgery), initial or revision; without ossicular chain reconstruction

69632 with ossicular chain reconstruction (eg, postfenestration)

69633 with ossicular chain reconstruction and synthetic prosthesis (eg, partial ossicular replacement prosthesis (PORP), total ossicular replacement prosthesis (TORP))

69635 Tympanoplasty with antrotomy or mastoidotomy (including canalplasty, atticotomy, middle ear surgery, and/or tympanic membrane repair); without ossicular chain reconstruction

69636 with ossicular chain reconstruction

69637 with ossicular chain reconstruction and synthetic prosthesis (eg, partial ossicular replacement prosthesis (PORP), total ossicular replacement prosthesis (TORP))

69641 Tympanoplasty with mastoidectomy (including canalplasty, middle ear surgery, tympanic membrane repair); without ossicular chain reconstruction

69642 with ossicular chain reconstruction

69643 with intact or reconstructed wall, without ossicular chain reconstruction

69644 with intact or reconstructed canal wall, with ossicular chain reconstruction

69645 radical or complete, without ossicular chain reconstruction

69646 radical or complete, with ossicular chain reconstruction

69650 Stapes mobilization

69660 Stapedectomy or stapedotomy with reestablishment of ossicular continuity, with or without use of foreign material;

69661 with footplate drill out

69662 Revision of stapedectomy or stapedotomy

69666 Repair oval window fistula

69667 Repair round window fistula

69670 Mastoid obliteration (separate procedure)

69676 Tympanic neurectomy

(For bilateral procedure, report 69676 with modifier 50)

Other Procedures

69700 Closure postauricular fistula, mastoid (separate procedure)

69710 Implantation or replacement of electromagnetic bone conduction hearing device in temporal bone

(Replacement procedure includes removal of old device)

69711 Removal or repair of electromagnetic bone conduction hearing device in temporal bone

69714 Implantation, osseointegrated implant, temporal bone, with percutaneous attachment to external speech processor/cochlear stimulator; without mastoidectomy

69715 with mastoidectomy

69717 Replacement (including removal of existing device), osseointegrated implant, temporal bone, with percutaneous attachment to external speech processor/cochlear stimulator; without mastoidectomy

69718 with mastoidectomy

Surgery: Auditory System

69720	Decompression facial nerve, intratemporal; lateral to geniculate ganglion
69725	including medial to geniculate ganglion
69740	Suture facial nerve, intratemporal, with or without graft or decompression; lateral to geniculate ganglion
69745	including medial to geniculate ganglion

(For extracranial suture of facial nerve, use 64864)

69799	Unlisted procedure, middle ear

Inner Ear

Incision and/or Destruction

69801	Labyrinthotomy, with or without cryosurgery including other nonexcisional destructive procedures or perfusion of vestibuloactive drugs (single or multiple perfusions); transcanal

(69801 includes all required infusions performed on initial and subsequent days of treatment)

69802	with mastoidectomy
69805	Endolymphatic sac operation; without shunt
69806	with shunt
69820	Fenestration semicircular canal
69840	Revision fenestration operation

Excision

69905	Labyrinthectomy; transcanal
69910	with mastoidectomy
69915	Vestibular nerve section, translabyrinthine approach

(For transcranial approach, use 69950)

Introduction

69930	Cochlear device implantation, with or without mastoidectomy

Other Procedures

69949	Unlisted procedure, inner ear

Temporal Bone, Middle Fossa Approach

(For external approach, use 69535)

69950	Vestibular nerve section, transcranial approach
69955	Total facial nerve decompression and/or repair (may include graft)
69960	Decompression internal auditory canal
69970	Removal of tumor, temporal bone

Other Procedures

69979	Unlisted procedure, temporal bone, middle fossa approach

Operating Microscope

The surgical microscope is employed when the surgical services are performed using the techniques of microsurgery. Code 69990 should be reported (without modifier 51 appended) in addition to the code for the primary procedure performed. Do not use 69990 for visualization with magnifying loupes or corrected vision. Do not report code 69990 in addition to procedures where use of the operating microscope is an inclusive component (15756-15758, 15842, 19364, 19368, 20955-20962, 20969-20973, 26551-26554, 26556, 31526, 31531, 31536, 31541, 31545, 31546, 31561, 31571, 43116, 43496, 49906, 61548, 63075-63078, 64727, 64820-64823, 65091-68850).

+ 69990	Microsurgical techniques, requiring use of operating microscope (List separately in addition to code for primary procedure)

Surgery: Auditory System

Notes

⊙=Moderate sedation +=Add-on code ∕=FDA approval pending

Radiology Guidelines (Including Nuclear Medicine and Diagnostic Ultrasound)

Items used by all physicians in reporting their services are presented in the **Introduction.** Some of the commonalities are repeated here for the convenience of those physicians referring to this section on **Radiology (Including Nuclear Medicine and Diagnostic Ultrasound).** Other definitions and items unique to Radiology are also listed.

Subject Listings

Subject listings apply when radiological services are performed by or under the responsible supervision of a physician.

Separate Procedures

Some of the procedures or services listed in the CPT codebook that are commonly carried out as an integral component of a total service or procedure have been identified by the inclusion of the term "separate procedure." The codes designated as "separate procedure" should not be reported in addition to the code for the total procedure or service of which it is considered an integral component.

However, when a procedure or service that is designated as a "separate procedure" is carried out independently or considered to be unrelated or distinct from other procedures/services provided at that time, it may be reported by itself, or in addition to other procedures/services by appending modifier 59 to the specific "separate procedure" code to indicate that the procedure is not considered to be a component of another procedure, but is a distinct, independent procedure. This may represent a different session or patient encounter, different procedure or surgery, different site or organ system, separate incision/excision, separate lesion, or separate injury (or area of injury in extensive injuries).

Subsection Information

Several of the subheadings or subsections have special needs or instructions unique to that section. Where these are indicated (eg, "Radiation Oncology") special **"Notes"** will be presented preceding those procedural terminology listings, referring to that subsection specifically. If there is an "Unlisted Procedure" code number (see section below) for the individual subsection, it will be shown. Those subsections with **"Notes"** are as follows:

▶Functional MRI 70554-70555◀
Aorta and Arteries 75600-75790
Veins and Lymphatics 75801-75893
Transcatheter Procedures 75894-75989
Diagnostic Ultrasound 76506-76999
Abdomen and Retroperitoneum 76700-76776
Obstetrical . 76801-76828
Non-Obstetrical 76830-76857
Radiation Oncology 77261-77799
Clinical Treatment Planning 77261-77299
Radiation Treatment
Management . 77427-77499
Proton Beam Treatment
Delivery . 77520-77525
Hyperthermia 77600-77620
Clinical Brachytherapy 77750-77799
Nuclear Medicine 78000-78299
Musculoskeletal System 78300-78399
Cardiovascular System 78414-78499
Therapeutic . 79005-79999

Unlisted Service or Procedure

A service or procedure may be provided that is not listed in this edition of the CPT codebook. When reporting such a service, the appropriate "Unlisted Procedure" code may be used to indicate the service, identifying it by "Special Report" as discussed below. The "Unlisted Procedures" and accompanying codes for **Radiology (Including Nuclear Medicine and Diagnostic Ultrasound)** are as follows:

76496 Unlisted fluoroscopic procedure (eg, diagnostic, interventional)

76497 Unlisted computed tomography procedure (eg, diagnostic, interventional)

76498 Unlisted magnetic resonance procedure (eg, diagnostic, interventional)

76499	Unlisted diagnostic radiographic procedure
76999	Unlisted ultrasound procedure (eg, diagnostic, interventional)
77299	Unlisted procedure, therapeutic radiology clinical treatment planning
77399	Unlisted procedure, medical radiation physics, dosimetry and treatment devices, and special services
77499	Unlisted procedure, therapeutic radiology treatment management
77799	Unlisted procedure, clinical brachytherapy
78099	Unlisted endocrine procedure, diagnostic nuclear medicine
78199	Unlisted hematopoietic, reticuloendothelial and lymphatic procedure, diagnostic nuclear medicine
78299	Unlisted gastrointestinal procedure, diagnostic nuclear medicine
78399	Unlisted musculoskeletal procedure, diagnostic nuclear medicine
78499	Unlisted cardiovascular procedure, diagnostic nuclear medicine
78599	Unlisted respiratory procedure, diagnostic nuclear medicine
78699	Unlisted nervous system procedure, diagnostic nuclear medicine
78799	Unlisted genitourinary procedure, diagnostic nuclear medicine
78999	Unlisted miscellaneous procedure, diagnostic nuclear medicine
79999	Radiopharmaceutical therapy, unlisted procedure

▶Results/Testing/Reports◀

▶Results are the technical component of a service. Testing leads to results; results lead to interpretation. Reports are the work product of the interpretation of numerous test results.◀

Special Report

A service that is rarely provided, unusual, variable, or new may require a special report in determining medical appropriateness of the service. Pertinent information should include an adequate definition or description of the nature, extent, and need for the procedure; and the time, effort, and equipment necessary to provide the service. Additional items that may be included are:

- Complexity of symptoms
- Final diagnosis
- Pertinent physical findings
- Diagnostic and therapeutic procedures
- Concurrent problems
- Follow-up care

Supervision and Interpretation

When a procedure is performed by two physicians, the radiologic portion of the procedure is designated as "radiological supervision and interpretation." When a physician performs both the procedure and provides imaging supervision and interpretation, a combination of procedure codes outside the 70000 series and imaging supervision and interpretation codes are to be used.

(The Radiological Supervision and Interpretation codes are not applicable to the Radiation Oncology subsection.)

Administration of Contrast Material(s)

The phrase "with contrast" used in the codes for procedures performed using contrast for imaging enhancement represents contrast material administered intravascularly, intra-articularly or intrathecally.

For intra-articular injection, use the appropriate joint injection code. If radiographic arthrography is performed, also use the arthrography supervision and interpretation code for the appropriate joint (which includes fluoroscopy). If computed tomography (CT) or magnetic resonance (MR) arthrography are performed without radiographic arthrography, use the appropriate joint injection code, the appropriate CT or MR code ("with contrast" or "without followed by contrast"), and the appropriate imaging guidance code for needle placement for contrast injection.

For spine examinations using computed tomography, magnetic resonance imaging, magnetic resonance angiography, "with contrast" includes intrathecal or intravascular injection. For intrathecal injection, use also 61055 or 62284.

Injection of intravascular contrast material is part of the "with contrast" CT, computed tomographic angiography (CTA), magnetic resonance imaging (MRI), and magnetic resonance angiography (MRA) procedures.

Oral and/or rectal contrast administration alone does not qualify as a study "with contrast."

Written Report(s)

A written report, signed by the interpreting physician, should be considered an integral part of a radiologic procedure or interpretation.

Radiology

Diagnostic Radiology (Diagnostic Imaging)

Head and Neck

70010 Myelography, posterior fossa, radiological supervision and interpretation

70015 Cisternography, positive contrast, radiological supervision and interpretation

70030 Radiologic examination, eye, for detection of foreign body

70100 Radiologic examination, mandible; partial, less than four views

70110 complete, minimum of four views

70120 Radiologic examination, mastoids; less than three views per side

70130 complete, minimum of three views per side

70134 Radiologic examination, internal auditory meati, complete

70140 Radiologic examination, facial bones; less than three views

70150 complete, minimum of three views

70160 Radiologic examination, nasal bones, complete, minimum of three views

70170 Dacryocystography, nasolacrimal duct, radiological supervision and interpretation

70190 Radiologic examination; optic foramina

70200 orbits, complete, minimum of four views

70210 Radiologic examination, sinuses, paranasal, less than three views

70220 Radiologic examination, sinuses, paranasal, complete, minimum of three views

70240 Radiologic examination, sella turcica

70250 Radiologic examination, skull; less than four views

70260 complete, minimum of four views

70300 Radiologic examination, teeth; single view

70310 partial examination, less than full mouth

70320 complete, full mouth

70328 Radiologic examination, temporomandibular joint, open and closed mouth; unilateral

70330 bilateral

70332 Temporomandibular joint arthrography, radiological supervision and interpretation

►(Do not report 70332 in conjunction with 77002)◄

70336 Magnetic resonance (eg, proton) imaging, temporomandibular joint(s)

70350 Cephalogram, orthodontic

70355 Orthopantogram

70360 Radiologic examination; neck, soft tissue

70370 pharynx or larynx, including fluoroscopy and/or magnification technique

70371 Complex dynamic pharyngeal and speech evaluation by cine or video recording

70373 Laryngography, contrast, radiological supervision and interpretation

70380 Radiologic examination, salivary gland for calculus

70390 Sialography, radiological supervision and interpretation

70450 Computed tomography, head or brain; without contrast material

70460 with contrast material(s)

70470 without contrast material, followed by contrast material(s) and further sections

(To report 3D rendering, see 76376, 76377)

70480 Computed tomography, orbit, sella, or posterior fossa or outer, middle, or inner ear; without contrast material

70481 with contrast material(s)

70482 without contrast material, followed by contrast material(s) and further sections

(To report 3D rendering, see 76376, 76377)

70486 Computed tomography, maxillofacial area; without contrast material

70487 with contrast material(s)

70488 without contrast material, followed by contrast material(s) and further sections

(To report 3D rendering, see 76376, 76377)

70490 Computed tomography, soft tissue neck; without contrast material

70491 with contrast material(s)

70492 without contrast material followed by contrast material(s) and further sections

(To report 3D rendering, see 76376, 76377)

(For cervical spine, see 72125, 72126)

Radiology

70496 Computed tomographic angiography, head, without contrast material(s), followed by contrast material(s) and further sections, including image post-processing

70498 Computed tomographic angiography, neck, without contrast material(s), followed by contrast material(s) and further sections, including image post-processing

▲ **70540** Magnetic resonance (eg, proton) imaging, orbit, face, and/or neck; without contrast material(s)

(For head or neck magnetic resonance angiography studies, see 70544-70546, 70547-70549)

70542 with contrast material(s)

70543 without contrast material(s), followed by contrast material(s) and further sequences

▶(Report 70540-70543 once per imaging session)◀

70544 Magnetic resonance angiography, head; without contrast material(s)

70545 with contrast material(s)

70546 without contrast material(s), followed by contrast material(s) and further sequences

70547 Magnetic resonance angiography, neck; without contrast material(s)

70548 with contrast material(s)

70549 without contrast material(s), followed by contrast material(s) and further sequences

70551 Magnetic resonance (eg, proton) imaging, brain (including brain stem); without contrast material

70552 with contrast material(s)

70553 without contrast material, followed by contrast material(s) and further sequences

(For magnetic spectroscopy, use 76390)

▶Functional MRI involves identification and mapping of stimulation of brain function. When neurofunctional tests are administered by a technologist or other non-physician or non-psychologist, use 70554. When neurofunctional tests are entirely administered by a physician or psychologist, use 70555.◀

● **70554** Magnetic resonance imaging, brain, functional MRI; including test selection and administration of repetitive body part movement and/or visual stimulation, not requiring physician or psychologist administration

▶(Do not report 70554 in conjunction with 96020)◀

● **70555** requiring physician or psychologist administration of entire neurofunctional testing

▶(Do not report 70555 unless 96020 is performed)◀

▶(Do not report 70554, 70555 in conjunction with 70551-70553 unless a separate diagnostic MRI is performed)◀

70557 Magnetic resonance (eg, proton) imaging, brain (including brain stem and skull base), during open intracranial procedure (eg, to assess for residual tumor or residual vascular malformation); without contrast material

70558 with contrast material(s)

70559 without contrast material(s), followed by contrast material(s) and further sequences

▶(For stereotactic biopsy of intracranial lesion with magnetic resonance guidance, use 61751. 70557, 70558 or 70559 may be reported only if a separate report is generated. Report only one of the above codes once per operative session. Do not use these codes in conjunction with 61751, 77021, 77022)◀

Chest

▶(For fluoroscopic or ultrasonic guidance for needle placement procedures (eg, biopsy, aspiration, injection, localization device) of the thorax, see 76942, 77002)◀

71010 Radiologic examination, chest; single view, frontal

71015 stereo, frontal

71020 Radiologic examination, chest, two views, frontal and lateral;

71021 with apical lordotic procedure

71022 with oblique projections

71023 with fluoroscopy

71030 Radiologic examination, chest, complete, minimum of four views;

71034 with fluoroscopy

(For separate chest fluoroscopy, use 76000)

71035 Radiologic examination, chest, special views (eg, lateral decubitus, Bucky studies)

71040 Bronchography, unilateral, radiological supervision and interpretation

71060 Bronchography, bilateral, radiological supervision and interpretation

71090 Insertion pacemaker, fluoroscopy and radiography, radiological supervision and interpretation

(For procedure, see appropriate organ or site)

71100 Radiologic examination, ribs, unilateral; two views

71101 including posteroanterior chest, minimum of three views

71110 Radiologic examination, ribs, bilateral; three views

71111 including posteroanterior chest, minimum of four views

71120 Radiologic examination; sternum, minimum of two views

71130 sternoclavicular joint or joints, minimum of three views

Radiology

71250 Computed tomography, thorax; without contrast material

71260 with contrast material(s)

71270 without contrast material, followed by contrast material(s) and further sections

 ►(For cardiac computed tomography of the heart, see Category III codes 0144T-0151T)◄

 (To report 3D rendering, see 76376, 76377)

▲ **71275** Computed tomographic angiography, chest (noncoronary), without contrast material(s), followed by contrast material(s) and further sections, including image postprocessing

 ►(For coronary artery computed tomographic angiography including calcification score and/or cardiac morphology, see Category III codes 0146T-0149T)◄

71550 Magnetic resonance (eg, proton) imaging, chest (eg, for evaluation of hilar and mediastinal lymphadenopathy); without contrast material(s)

71551 with contrast material(s)

71552 without contrast material(s), followed by contrast material(s) and further sequences

 ►(For breast MRI, see 77058, 77059)◄

71555 Magnetic resonance angiography, chest (excluding myocardium), with or without contrast material(s)

Spine and Pelvis

72010 Radiologic examination, spine, entire, survey study, anteroposterior and lateral

72020 Radiologic examination, spine, single view, specify level

72040 Radiologic examination, spine, cervical; two or three views

72050 minimum of four views

72052 complete, including oblique and flexion and/or extension studies

72069 Radiologic examination, spine, thoracolumbar, standing (scoliosis)

72070 Radiologic examination, spine; thoracic, two views

72072 thoracic, three views

72074 thoracic, minimum of four views

72080 thoracolumbar, two views

72090 scoliosis study, including supine and erect studies

72100 Radiologic examination, spine, lumbosacral; two or three views

72110 minimum of four views

72114 complete, including bending views

72120 Radiologic examination, spine, lumbosacral, bending views only, minimum of four views

 (Contrast material in CT of spine is either by intrathecal or intravenous injection. For intrathecal injection, use also 61055 or 62284. IV injection of contrast material is part of the CT procedure)

72125 Computed tomography, cervical spine; without contrast material

72126 with contrast material

72127 without contrast material, followed by contrast material(s) and further sections

 (For intrathecal injection procedure, see 61055, 62284)

72128 Computed tomography, thoracic spine; without contrast material

72129 with contrast material

 (For intrathecal injection procedure, see 61055, 62284)

72130 without contrast material, followed by contrast material(s) and further sections

 (For intrathecal injection procedure, see 61055, 62284)

72131 Computed tomography, lumbar spine; without contrast material

72132 with contrast material

72133 without contrast material, followed by contrast material(s) and further sections

 (For intrathecal injection procedure, see 61055, 62284)

 (To report 3D rendering, see 76376, 76377)

72141 Magnetic resonance (eg, proton) imaging, spinal canal and contents, cervical; without contrast material

72142 with contrast material(s)

 (For cervical spinal canal imaging without contrast material followed by contrast material, use 72156)

72146 Magnetic resonance (eg, proton) imaging, spinal canal and contents, thoracic; without contrast material

72147 with contrast material(s)

 (For thoracic spinal canal imaging without contrast material followed by contrast material, use 72157)

72148 Magnetic resonance (eg, proton) imaging, spinal canal and contents, lumbar; without contrast material

72149 with contrast material(s)

 (For lumbar spinal canal imaging without contrast material followed by contrast material, use 72158)

72156 Magnetic resonance (eg, proton) imaging, spinal canal and contents, without contrast material, followed by contrast material(s) and further sequences; cervical

72157 thoracic

72158 lumbar

72159 Magnetic resonance angiography, spinal canal and contents, with or without contrast material(s)

72170 Radiologic examination, pelvis; one or two views

72190 complete, minimum of three views

(For pelvimetry, use 74710)

72191 Computed tomographic angiography, pelvis, without contrast material(s), followed by contrast material(s) and further sections, including image post-processing

(For CTA aorto-iliofemoral runoff, use 75635)

72192 Computed tomography, pelvis; without contrast material

72193 with contrast material(s)

72194 without contrast material, followed by contrast material(s) and further sections

(To report 3D rendering, see 76376, 76377)

(For computed tomographic colonography, see Category III codes 0066T, 0067T. Do not report 72192-72194 in conjunction with 0066T, 0067T)

72195 Magnetic resonance (eg, proton) imaging; pelvis; without contrast material(s)

72196 with contrast material(s)

72197 without contrast material(s), followed by contrast material(s) and further sequences

72198 Magnetic resonance angiography, pelvis, with or without contrast material(s)

72200 Radiologic examination, sacroiliac joints; less than three views

72202 three or more views

72220 Radiologic examination, sacrum and coccyx, minimum of two views

72240 Myelography, cervical, radiological supervision and interpretation

(For complete cervical myelography, see 61055, 62284, 72240)

72255 Myelography, thoracic, radiological supervision and interpretation

(For complete thoracic myelography, see 61055, 62284, 72255)

72265 Myelography, lumbosacral, radiological supervision and interpretation

(For complete lumbosacral myelography, see 61055, 62284, 72265)

72270 Myelography, two or more regions (eg, lumbar/thoracic, cervical/thoracic, lumbar/cervical, lumbar/thoracic/cervical), radiological supervision and interpretation

(For complete myelography of entire spinal canal, see 61055, 62284, 72270)

72275 Epidurography, radiological supervision and interpretation

▶(72275 includes 77003)◀

(For injection procedure, see 62280-62282, 62310-62319, 64479-64484, 0027T)

(Use 72275 only when an epidurogram is performed, images documented, and a formal radiologic report is issued)

72285 Discography, cervical or thoracic, radiological supervision and interpretation

● **72291** Radiological supervision and interpretation, percutaneous vertebroplasty or vertebral augmentation including cavity creation, per vertebral body; under fluoroscopic guidance

● **72292** under CT guidance

▶(For procedure, see 22520-22525)◀

72295 Discography, lumbar, radiological supervision and interpretation

Upper Extremities

▶(For stress views, any joint, use 77071)◀

73000 Radiologic examination; clavicle, complete

73010 scapula, complete

73020 Radiologic examination, shoulder; one view

73030 complete, minimum of two views

73040 Radiologic examination, shoulder, arthrography, radiological supervision and interpretation

▶(Do not report 77002 in conjunction with 73040)◀

73050 Radiologic examination; acromioclavicular joints, bilateral, with or without weighted distraction

73060 humerus, minimum of two views

73070 Radiologic examination, elbow; two views

73080 complete, minimum of three views

73085 Radiologic examination, elbow, arthrography, radiological supervision and interpretation

▶(Do not report 77002 in conjunction with 73085)◀

73090 Radiologic examination; forearm, two views

73092 upper extremity, infant, minimum of two views

73100 Radiologic examination, wrist; two views

73110 complete, minimum of three views

73115 Radiologic examination, wrist, arthrography, radiological supervision and interpretation

▶(Do not report 77002 in conjunction with 73115)◀

73120 Radiologic examination, hand; two views

73130 minimum of three views

73140 Radiologic examination, finger(s), minimum of two views

Radiology

73200 Computed tomography, upper extremity; without contrast material

73201 with contrast material(s)

73202 without contrast material, followed by contrast material(s) and further sections

(To report 3D rendering, see 76376, 76377)

73206 Computed tomographic angiography, upper extremity, without contrast material(s), followed by contrast material(s) and further sections, including image post-processing

73218 Magnetic resonance (eg, proton) imaging, upper extremity, other than joint; without contrast material(s)

73219 with contrast material(s)

73220 without contrast material(s), followed by contrast material(s) and further sequences

73221 Magnetic resonance (eg, proton) imaging, any joint of upper extremity; without contrast material(s)

73222 with contrast material(s)

73223 without contrast material(s), followed by contrast material(s) and further sequences

73225 Magnetic resonance angiography, upper extremity, with or without contrast material(s)

Lower Extremities

▶(For stress views, any joint, use 77071)◀

73500 Radiologic examination, hip, unilateral; one view

73510 complete, minimum of two views

73520 Radiologic examination, hips, bilateral, minimum of two views of each hip, including anteroposterior view of pelvis

73525 Radiologic examination, hip, arthrography, radiological supervision and interpretation

▶(Do not report 73525 in conjunction with 77002)◀

73530 Radiologic examination, hip, during operative procedure

73540 Radiologic examination, pelvis and hips, infant or child, minimum of two views

73542 Radiological examination, sacroiliac joint arthrography, radiological supervision and interpretation

▶(Do not report 73542 in conjunction with 77002)◀

▶(For procedure, use 27096. If formal arthrography is not performed, recorded, and a formal radiologic report is not issued, use 77003 for fluoroscopic guidance for sacroiliac joint injections)◀

73550 Radiologic examination, femur, two views

73560 Radiologic examination, knee; one or two views

73562 three views

73564 complete, four or more views

73565 both knees, standing, anteroposterior

73580 Radiologic examination, knee, arthrography, radiological supervision and interpretation

▶(Do not report 73580 in conjunction with 77002)◀

73590 Radiologic examination; tibia and fibula, two views

73592 lower extremity, infant, minimum of two views

73600 Radiologic examination, ankle; two views

73610 complete, minimum of three views

73615 Radiologic examination, ankle, arthrography, radiological supervision and interpretation

▶(Do not report 73615 in conjunction with 77002)◀

73620 Radiologic examination, foot; two views

73630 complete, minimum of three views

73650 Radiologic examination; calcaneus, minimum of two views

73660 toe(s), minimum of two views

73700 Computed tomography, lower extremity; without contrast material

73701 with contrast material(s)

73702 without contrast material, followed by contrast material(s) and further sections

(To report 3D rendering, see 76376, 76377)

73706 Computed tomographic angiography, lower extremity, without contrast material(s), followed by contrast material(s) and further sections, including image post-processing

(For CTA aorto-iliofemoral runoff, use 75635)

73718 Magnetic resonance (eg, proton) imaging, lower extremity other than joint; without contrast material(s)

73719 with contrast material(s)

73720 without contrast material(s), followed by contrast material(s) and further sequences

73721 Magnetic resonance (eg, proton) imaging, any joint of lower extremity; without contrast material

73722 with contrast material(s)

73723 without contrast material(s), followed by contrast material(s) and further sequences

73725 Magnetic resonance angiography, lower extremity, with or without contrast material(s)

Abdomen

74000 Radiologic examination, abdomen; single anteroposterior view

74010 anteroposterior and additional oblique and cone views

74020 complete, including decubitus and/or erect views

74022 complete acute abdomen series, including supine, erect, and/or decubitus views, single view chest

Radiology

74150 Computed tomography, abdomen; without contrast material

74160 with contrast material(s)

74170 without contrast material, followed by contrast material(s) and further sections

(To report 3D rendering, see 76376, 76377)

(For computed tomographic colonography, see Category III codes 0066T, 0067T. Do not report 74150-74170 in conjunction with 0066T, 0067T)

74175 Computed tomographic angiography, abdomen, without contrast material(s), followed by contrast material(s) and further sections, including image post-processing

(For CTA aorto-iliofemoral runoff, use 75635)

74181 Magnetic resonance (eg, proton) imaging, abdomen; without contrast material(s)

74182 with contrast material(s)

74183 without contrast material(s), followed by with contrast material(s) and further sequences

74185 Magnetic resonance angiography, abdomen, with or without contrast material(s)

74190 Peritoneogram (eg, after injection of air or contrast), radiological supervision and interpretation

(For procedure, use 49400)

(For computed tomography, see 72192 or 74150)

Gastrointestinal Tract

(For percutaneous placement of gastrostomy tube, use 43750)

74210 Radiologic examination; pharynx and/or cervical esophagus

74220 esophagus

74230 Swallowing function, with cineradiography/videoradiography

74235 Removal of foreign body(s), esophageal, with use of balloon catheter, radiological supervision and interpretation

(For procedure, see 43215, 43247)

74240 Radiologic examination, gastrointestinal tract, upper; with or without delayed films, without KUB

74241 with or without delayed films, with KUB

74245 with small intestine, includes multiple serial films

74246 Radiological examination, gastrointestinal tract, upper, air contrast, with specific high density barium, effervescent agent, with or without glucagon; with or without delayed films, without KUB

74247 with or without delayed films, with KUB

74249 with small intestine follow-through

74250 Radiologic examination, small intestine, includes multiple serial films;

74251 via enteroclysis tube

74260 Duodenography, hypotonic

74270 Radiologic examination, colon; barium enema, with or without KUB

74280 air contrast with specific high density barium, with or without glucagon

74283 Therapeutic enema, contrast or air, for reduction of intussusception or other intraluminal obstruction (eg, meconium ileus)

74290 Cholecystography, oral contrast;

74291 additional or repeat examination or multiple day examination

74300 Cholangiography and/or pancreatography; intraoperative, radiological supervision and interpretation

+ 74301 additional set intraoperative, radiological supervision and interpretation (List separately in addition to code for primary procedure)

(Use 74301 in conjunction with 74300)

74305 through existing catheter, radiological supervision and interpretation

(For procedure, see 47505, 48400, 47560-47561, 47563)

(For biliary duct stone extraction, percutaneous, see 47630, 74327)

74320 Cholangiography, percutaneous, transhepatic, radiological supervision and interpretation

74327 Postoperative biliary duct calculus removal, percutaneous via T-tube tract, basket, or snare (eg, Burhenne technique), radiological supervision and interpretation

(For procedure, use 47630)

74328 Endoscopic catheterization of the biliary ductal system, radiological supervision and interpretation

(For procedure, see 43260-43272 as appropriate)

74329 Endoscopic catheterization of the pancreatic ductal system, radiological supervision and interpretation

(For procedure, see 43260-43272 as appropriate)

74330 Combined endoscopic catheterization of the biliary and pancreatic ductal systems, radiological supervision and interpretation

(For procedure, see 43260-43272 as appropriate)

74340 Introduction of long gastrointestinal tube (eg, Miller-Abbott), including multiple fluoroscopies and films, radiological supervision and interpretation

(For tube placement, use 44500)

74350 Percutaneous placement of gastrostomy tube, radiological supervision and interpretation

Radiology

74355 Percutaneous placement of enteroclysis tube, radiological supervision and interpretation

74360 Intraluminal dilation of strictures and/or obstructions (eg, esophagus), radiological supervision and interpretation

74363 Percutaneous transhepatic dilation of biliary duct stricture with or without placement of stent, radiological supervision and interpretation

(For procedure, see 47510, 47511, 47555, 47556)

Urinary Tract

74400 Urography (pyelography), intravenous, with or without KUB, with or without tomography

74410 Urography, infusion, drip technique and/or bolus technique;

74415 with nephrotomography

74420 Urography, retrograde, with or without KUB

74425 Urography, antegrade, (pyelostogram, nephrostogram, loopogram), radiological supervision and interpretation

74430 Cystography, minimum of three views, radiological supervision and interpretation

74440 Vasography, vesiculography, or epididymography, radiological supervision and interpretation

74445 Corpora cavernosography, radiological supervision and interpretation

74450 Urethrocystography, retrograde, radiological supervision and interpretation

74455 Urethrocystography, voiding, radiological supervision and interpretation

74470 Radiologic examination, renal cyst study, translumbar, contrast visualization, radiological supervision and interpretation

74475 Introduction of intracatheter or catheter into renal pelvis for drainage and/or injection, percutaneous, radiological supervision and interpretation

74480 Introduction of ureteral catheter or stent into ureter through renal pelvis for drainage and/or injection, percutaneous, radiological supervision and interpretation

(For transurethral surgery (ureter and pelvis), see 52320-52355)

74485 Dilation of nephrostomy, ureters, or urethra, radiological supervision and interpretation

(For dilation of ureter without radiologic guidance, use 52341, 52344)

(For change of nephrostomy or pyelostomy tube, use 50398)

Gynecological and Obstetrical

(For abdomen and pelvis, see 72170-72190, 74000-74170)

74710 Pelvimetry, with or without placental localization

74740 Hysterosalpingography, radiological supervision and interpretation

(For introduction of saline or contrast for hysterosalpingography, see 58340)

74742 Transcervical catheterization of fallopian tube, radiological supervision and interpretation

(For procedure, use 58345)

74775 Perineogram (eg, vaginogram, for sex determination or extent of anomalies)

Heart

(For separate injection procedures for vascular radiology, see **Surgery** section, 36000-36299)

(For cardiac catheterization procedures, see 93501-93556)

75552 Cardiac magnetic resonance imaging for morphology; without contrast material

75553 with contrast material

75554 Cardiac magnetic resonance imaging for function, with or without morphology; complete study

75555 limited study

75556 Cardiac magnetic resonance imaging for velocity flow mapping

Vascular Procedures

Aorta and Arteries

Selective vascular catheterizations should be coded to include introduction and all lesser order selective catheterizations used in the approach (eg, the description for a selective right middle cerebral artery catheterization includes the introduction and placement catheterization of the right common and internal carotid arteries).

Additional second and/or third order arterial catheterizations within the same family of arteries supplied by a single first order artery should be expressed by 36218 or 36248. Additional first order or higher catheterizations in vascular families supplied by a first order vessel different from a previously selected and coded family should be separately coded using the conventions described above.

For angiography performed in conjunction with therapeutic transcatheter radiological supervision and interpretation services, see the Radiology Transcatheter Procedures guidelines.

Radiology

Diagnostic angiography (radiological supervision and interpretation) codes should NOT be used with interventional procedures for:

1. Contrast injections, angiography, roadmapping, and/or fluoroscopic guidance for the intervention,

2. Vessel measurement, and

3. Post-angioplasty/stent angiography,

as this work is captured in the radiological supervision and interpretation code(s).

Diagnostic angiography performed at the time of an interventional procedure is separately reportable if:

1. No prior catheter-based angiographic study is available and a full diagnostic study is performed, and the decision to intervene is based on the diagnostic study, OR

2. A prior study is available, but as documented in the medical record:

 a. The patient's condition with respect to the clinical indication has changed since the prior study, OR

 b. There is inadequate visualization of the anatomy and/or pathology, OR

 c. There is a clinical change during the procedure that requires new evaluation outside the target area of intervention.

Diagnostic angiography performed at a separate setting from an interventional procedure is separately reported.

Diagnostic angiography performed at the time of an interventional procedure is NOT separately reportable if it is specifically included in the interventional code descriptor.

> (For intravenous procedure, see 36000-36013, 36400-36425 and 36100-36248 for intra-arterial procedure)
>
> (For radiological supervision and interpretation, see 75600-75978)

75600 Aortography, thoracic, without serialography, radiological supervision and interpretation

> (For injection procedure, use 93544)

75605 Aortography, thoracic, by serialography, radiological supervision and interpretation

> (For injection procedure, use 93544)

75625 Aortography, abdominal, by serialography, radiological supervision and interpretation

> (For injection procedure, use 93544)

75630 Aortography, abdominal plus bilateral iliofemoral lower extremity, catheter, by serialography, radiological supervision and interpretation

75635 Computed tomographic angiography, abdominal aorta and bilateral iliofemoral lower extremity runoff, radiological supervision and interpretation, without contrast material(s), followed by contrast material(s) and further sections, including image post-processing

75650 Angiography, cervicocerebral, catheter, including vessel origin, radiological supervision and interpretation

75658 Angiography, brachial, retrograde, radiological supervision and interpretation

75660 Angiography, external carotid, unilateral, selective, radiological supervision and interpretation

75662 Angiography, external carotid, bilateral, selective, radiological supervision and interpretation

75665 Angiography, carotid, cerebral, unilateral, radiological supervision and interpretation

75671 Angiography, carotid, cerebral, bilateral, radiological supervision and interpretation

75676 Angiography, carotid, cervical, unilateral, radiological supervision and interpretation

75680 Angiography, carotid, cervical, bilateral, radiological supervision and interpretation

75685 Angiography, vertebral, cervical, and/or intracranial, radiological supervision and interpretation

75705 Angiography, spinal, selective, radiological supervision and interpretation

75710 Angiography, extremity, unilateral, radiological supervision and interpretation

75716 Angiography, extremity, bilateral, radiological supervision and interpretation

75722 Angiography, renal, unilateral, selective (including flush aortogram), radiological supervision and interpretation

75724 Angiography, renal, bilateral, selective (including flush aortogram), radiological supervision and interpretation

75726 Angiography, visceral, selective or supraselective, (with or without flush aortogram), radiological supervision and interpretation

> (For selective angiography, each additional visceral vessel studied after basic examination, use 75774)

75731 Angiography, adrenal, unilateral, selective, radiological supervision and interpretation

75733 Angiography, adrenal, bilateral, selective, radiological supervision and interpretation

75736 Angiography, pelvic, selective or supraselective, radiological supervision and interpretation

75741 Angiography, pulmonary, unilateral, selective, radiological supervision and interpretation

> (For injection procedure, use 93541)

75743 Angiography, pulmonary, bilateral, selective, radiological supervision and interpretation

> (For injection procedure, use 93541)

Radiology

75746 Angiography, pulmonary, by nonselective catheter or venous injection, radiological supervision and interpretation

(For injection procedure, use 93541)

(For introduction of catheter, injection procedure, see 93501-93533, 93539, 93540, 93545, 93556)

(For introduction of catheter, injection procedure, see 93501-93533, 93545, 93556)

(For introduction of catheter, injection procedure, see 93501-93533, 93539, 93540, 93545, 93556)

75756 Angiography, internal mammary, radiological supervision and interpretation

(For introduction of catheter, injection procedure, see 93501-93533, 93545, 93556)

+ 75774 Angiography, selective, each additional vessel studied after basic examination, radiological supervision and interpretation (List separately in addition to code for primary procedure)

(Use 75774 in addition to code for specific initial vessel studied)

(For angiography, see codes 75600-75790)

(For catheterizations, see codes 36215-36248)

(For introduction of catheter, injection procedure, see 93501-93533, 93545, 93555, 93556)

75790 Angiography, arteriovenous shunt (eg, dialysis patient), radiological supervision and interpretation

(For introduction of catheter, use 36140, 36145, 36215-36217, 36245-36247)

Veins and Lymphatics

For venography performed in conjunction with therapeutic transcatheter radiological supervision and interpretation services, see the Radiology Transcatheter Procedures guidelines.

Diagnostic venography (radiological supervision and interpretation) codes should NOT be used with interventional procedures for:

1. Contrast injections, venography, roadmapping, and/or fluoroscopic guidance for the intervention,

2. Vessel measurement, and

3. Post-angioplasty/stent venography,

as this work is captured in the radiological supervision and interpretation code(s).

Diagnostic venography performed at the time of an interventional procedure is separately reportable if:

1. No prior catheter-based venographic study is available and a full diagnostic study is performed, and decision to intervene is based on the diagnostic study, OR

2. A prior study is available, but as documented in the medical record:

a. The patient's condition with respect to the clinical indication has changed since the prior study, OR

b. There is inadequate visualization of the anatomy and/or pathology, OR

c. There is a clinical change during the procedure that requires new evaluation outside the target area of intervention.

Diagnostic venography performed at a separate setting from an interventional procedure is separately reported.

Diagnostic venography performed at the time of an interventional procedure is NOT separately reportable if it is specifically included in the interventional code descriptor.

(For injection procedure for venous system, see 36000-36015, 36400-36510)

(For injection procedure for lymphatic system, use 38790)

75801 Lymphangiography, extremity only, unilateral, radiological supervision and interpretation

75803 Lymphangiography, extremity only, bilateral, radiological supervision and interpretation

75805 Lymphangiography, pelvic/abdominal, unilateral, radiological supervision and interpretation

75807 Lymphangiography, pelvic/abdominal, bilateral, radiological supervision and interpretation

75809 Shuntogram for investigation of previously placed indwelling nonvascular shunt (eg, LeVeen shunt, ventriculoperitoneal shunt, indwelling infusion pump), radiological supervision and interpretation

(For procedure, see 49427 or 61070)

75810 Splenoportography, radiological supervision and interpretation

75820 Venography, extremity, unilateral, radiological supervision and interpretation

75822 Venography, extremity, bilateral, radiological supervision and interpretation

75825 Venography, caval, inferior, with serialography, radiological supervision and interpretation

75827 Venography, caval, superior, with serialography, radiological supervision and interpretation

75831 Venography, renal, unilateral, selective, radiological supervision and interpretation

75833 Venography, renal, bilateral, selective, radiological supervision and interpretation

75840 Venography, adrenal, unilateral, selective, radiological supervision and interpretation

75842 Venography, adrenal, bilateral, selective, radiological supervision and interpretation

Radiology

75860	Venography, venous sinus (eg, petrosal and inferior sagittal) or jugular, catheter, radiological supervision and interpretation
75870	Venography, superior sagittal sinus, radiological supervision and interpretation
75872	Venography, epidural, radiological supervision and interpretation
75880	Venography, orbital, radiological supervision and interpretation
75885	Percutaneous transhepatic portography with hemodynamic evaluation, radiological supervision and interpretation
75887	Percutaneous transhepatic portography without hemodynamic evaluation, radiological supervision and interpretation
75889	Hepatic venography, wedged or free, with hemodynamic evaluation, radiological supervision and interpretation
75891	Hepatic venography, wedged or free, without hemodynamic evaluation, radiological supervision and interpretation
75893	Venous sampling through catheter, with or without angiography (eg, for parathyroid hormone, renin), radiological supervision and interpretation

(For procedure, use 36500)

Transcatheter Procedures

Therapeutic transcatheter radiological supervision and interpretation code(s) include the following services associated with that intervention:

1. Contrast injections, angiography/venography, roadmapping, and fluoroscopic guidance for the intervention,

2. Vessel measurement, and

3. Completion angiography/venography (except for those uses permitted by 75898).

Unless specifically included in the code descriptor, diagnostic angiography/venography performed at the time of transcatheter therapeutic radiological and interpretation service(s) is separately reportable (eg, no prior catheter-based diagnostic angiography/venography study of the target vessel is available, prior diagnostic study is inadequate, patient's condition with respect to the clinical indication has changed since the prior study or during the intervention). See 75600-75893.

Codes 75956 and 75957 include all angiography of the thoracic aorta and its branches for diagnostic imaging prior to deployment of the primary endovascular devices (including all routine components of modular devices), fluoroscopic guidance in the delivery of the endovascular components, and intraprocedural arterial angiography (eg, confirm position, detect endoleak, evaluate runoff).

Code 75958 includes the analogous services for placement of each proximal thoracic endovascular extension. Code 75959 includes the analogous services for placement of a distal thoracic endovascular extension(s) placed during a procedure after the primary repair.

75894	Transcatheter therapy, embolization, any method, radiological supervision and interpretation

▶(For uterine fibroid embolization [uterine artery embolization performed to treat uterine fibroids], use 37210)◀

▶(For obstetrical and gynecologic embolization procedures other than uterine fibroid embolization [eg, embolization to treat obstetrical or postpartum hemorrhage], use 37204)◀

75896	Transcatheter therapy, infusion, any method (eg, thrombolysis other than coronary), radiological supervision and interpretation

(For infusion for coronary disease, see 92975, 92977)

75898	Angiography through existing catheter for follow-up study for transcatheter therapy, embolization or infusion
75900	Exchange of a previously placed intravascular catheter during thrombolytic therapy with contrast monitoring, radiological supervision and interpretation

(For procedure, use 37209)

75901	Mechanical removal of pericatheter obstructive material (eg, fibrin sheath) from central venous device via separate venous access, radiologic supervision and interpretation

(For procedure, use 36595)

(For venous catheterization, see 36010-36012)

75902	Mechanical removal of intraluminal (intracatheter) obstructive material from central venous device through device lumen, radiologic supervision and interpretation

(For procedure, use 36596)

(For venous catheterization, see 36010-36012)

75940	Percutaneous placement of IVC filter, radiological supervision and interpretation
75945	Intravascular ultrasound (non-coronary vessel), radiological supervision and interpretation; initial vessel
+ 75946	each additional non-coronary vessel (List separately in addition to code for primary procedure)

(Use 75946 in conjunction with 75945)

(For catheterizations, see codes 36215-36248)

(For transcatheter therapies, see codes 37200-37208, 61624, 61626)

(For procedure, see 37250, 37251)

Radiology

75952 Endovascular repair of infrarenal abdominal aortic aneurysm or dissection, radiological supervision and interpretation

(For implantation of endovascular grafts, see 34800-34808)

(For radiologic supervision and interpretation of endovascular repair of abdominal aortic aneurysm involving visceral vessels, see Category III codes 0078T-0081T)

75953 Placement of proximal or distal extension prosthesis for endovascular repair of infrarenal aortic or iliac artery aneurysm, pseudoaneurysm, or dissection, radiological supervision and interpretation

(For implantation of endovascular extension prostheses, see 34825, 34826)

75954 Endovascular repair of iliac artery aneurysm, pseudoaneurysm, arteriovenous malformation, or trauma, radiological supervision and interpretation

(For implantation of endovascular graft, see 34900)

75956 Endovascular repair of descending thoracic aorta (eg, aneurysm, pseudoaneurysm, dissection, penetrating ulcer, intramural hematoma, or traumatic disruption); involving coverage of left subclavian artery origin, initial endoprosthesis plus descending thoracic aortic extension(s), if required, to level of celiac artery origin, radiological supervision and interpretation

(For implantation of endovascular graft, use 33880)

75957 not involving coverage of left subclavian artery origin, initial endoprosthesis plus descending thoracic aortic extension(s), if required, to level of celiac artery origin, radiological supervision and interpretation

(For implantation of endovascular graft, use 33881)

75958 Placement of proximal extension prosthesis for endovascular repair of descending thoracic aorta (eg, aneurysm, pseudoaneurysm, dissection, penetrating ulcer, intramural hematoma, or traumatic disruption), radiological supervision and interpretation

(Report 75958 for each proximal extension)

(For implantation of proximal endovascular extension, see 33883, 33884)

75959 Placement of distal extension prosthesis(s) (delayed) after endovascular repair of descending thoracic aorta, as needed, to level of celiac origin, radiological supervision and interpretation

(Do not report 75959 in conjunction with 75956, 75957)

(Report 75959 once, regardless of number of modules deployed)

(For implantation of distal endovascular extension, use 33886)

75960 Transcatheter introduction of intravascular stent(s), (except coronary, carotid, and vertebral vessel), percutaneous and/or open, radiological supervision and interpretation, each vessel

(For procedure, see 37205-37208)

(For radiologic supervision and interpretation for transcatheter placement of extracranial vertebral or intrathoracic carotid artery stent(s), see Category III codes 0075T, 0076T)

75961 Transcatheter retrieval, percutaneous, of intravascular foreign body (eg, fractured venous or arterial catheter), radiological supervision and interpretation

(For procedure, use 37203)

75962 Transluminal balloon angioplasty, peripheral artery, radiological supervision and interpretation

+ 75964 Transluminal balloon angioplasty, each additional peripheral artery, radiological supervision and interpretation (List separately in addition to code for primary procedure)

(Use 75964 in conjunction with 75962)

75966 Transluminal balloon angioplasty, renal or other visceral artery, radiological supervision and interpretation

+ 75968 Transluminal balloon angioplasty, each additional visceral artery, radiological supervision and interpretation (List separately in addition to code for primary procedure)

(Use 75968 in conjunction with 75966)

(For percutaneous transluminal coronary angioplasty, see 92982-92984)

75970 Transcatheter biopsy, radiological supervision and interpretation

(For injection procedure only for transcatheter therapy or biopsy, see 36100-36299)

(For transcatheter renal and ureteral biopsy, use 52007)

(For percutaneous needle biopsy of pancreas, use 48102; of retroperitoneal lymph node or mass, use 49180)

75978 Transluminal balloon angioplasty, venous (eg, subclavian stenosis), radiological supervision and interpretation

75980 Percutaneous transhepatic biliary drainage with contrast monitoring, radiological supervision and interpretation

75982 Percutaneous placement of drainage catheter for combined internal and external biliary drainage or of a drainage stent for internal biliary drainage in patients with an inoperable mechanical biliary obstruction, radiological supervision and interpretation

75984 Change of percutaneous tube or drainage catheter with contrast monitoring (eg, gastrointestinal system, genitourinary system, abscess), radiological supervision and interpretation

(For change of nephrostomy or pyelostomy tube only, use 50398)

Radiology

(For introduction procedure only for percutaneous biliary drainage, see 47510, 47511)

(For percutaneous cholecystostomy, use 47490)

(For change of percutaneous biliary drainage catheter only, use 47525)

(For percutaneous nephrostolithotomy or pyelostolithotomy, see 50080, 50081)

75989 Radiological guidance (ie, fluoroscopy, ultrasound, or computed tomography), for percutaneous drainage (eg, abscess, specimen collection), with placement of catheter, radiological supervision and interpretation

Transluminal Atherectomy

75992 Transluminal atherectomy, peripheral artery, radiological supervision and interpretation

(For procedure, see 35481-35485, 35491-35495)

+ 75993 Transluminal atherectomy, each additional peripheral artery, radiological supervision and interpretation (List separately in addition to code for primary procedure)

(Use 75993 in conjunction with 75992)

(For procedure, see 35481-35485, 35491-35495)

75994 Transluminal atherectomy, renal, radiological supervision and interpretation

(For procedure, see 35480, 35490)

75995 Transluminal atherectomy, visceral, radiological supervision and interpretation

(For procedure, see 35480, 35490)

+ 75996 Transluminal atherectomy, each additional visceral artery, radiological supervision and interpretation (List separately in addition to code for primary procedure)

(Use 75996 in conjunction with 75995)

(For procedure, see 35480, 35490)

Other Procedures

(For computed tomography cerebral perfusion analysis, see Category III code 0042T)

(For arthrography of shoulder, use 73040; elbow, use 73085; wrist, use 73115; hip, use 73525; knee, use 73580; ankle, use 73615)

►(75998 has been deleted. To report, use 77001)◄

76000 Fluoroscopy (separate procedure), up to 1 hour physician time, other than 71023 or 71034 (eg, cardiac fluoroscopy)

76001 Fluoroscopy, physician time more than 1 hour, assisting a nonradiologic physician (eg, nephrostolithotomy, ERCP, bronchoscopy, transbronchial biopsy)

►(76003 has been deleted. To report, use 77002)◄

►(76005 has been deleted. To report, use 77003)◄

►(76006 has been deleted. To report, use 77071)◄

76010 Radiologic examination from nose to rectum for foreign body, single view, child

►(76012, 76013 have been deleted. To report, see 72291, 72292)◄

►(76020 has been deleted. To report, use 77072)◄

►(76040 has been deleted. To report, use 77073)◄

►(76061, 76062 have been deleted. To report, see 77074, 77075)◄

►(76065 has been deleted. To report, use 77076)◄

►(76066 has been deleted. To report, use 77077)◄

►(76070, 76071 have been deleted. To report, see 77078, 77079)◄

►(76075-76077 have been deleted. To report, see 77080-77082)◄

►(76078 has been deleted. To report, use 77083)◄

76080 Radiologic examination, abscess, fistula or sinus tract study, radiological supervision and interpretation

►(76082, 76083 have been deleted. To report, see 77051, 77052)◄

(76085 has been deleted. To report, see 77051, 77052)

►(76086 has been deleted. To report, use 77053)◄

►(76088 has been deleted. To report, use 77054)◄

►(76090, 76091 have been deleted. To report, see 77055, 77056)◄

►(76092 has been deleted. To report, use 77057)◄

►(76093, 76094 have been deleted. To report, see 77058, 77059)◄

►(76095 has been deleted. To report, use 77031)◄

►(76096 has been deleted. To report, use 77032)◄

76098 Radiological examination, surgical specimen

76100 Radiologic examination, single plane body section (eg, tomography), other than with urography

76101 Radiologic examination, complex motion (ie, hypercycloidal) body section (eg, mastoid polytomography), other than with urography; unilateral

76102 bilateral

(For nephrotomography, use 74415)

76120 Cineradiography/videoradiography, except where specifically included

+ 76125 Cineradiography/videoradiography to complement routine examination (List separately in addition to code for primary procedure)

76140 Consultation on X-ray examination made elsewhere, written report

76150 Xeroradiography

(76150 is to be used for non-mammographic studies only)

Radiology

76350 Subtraction in conjunction with contrast studies

▶(76355 has been deleted. To report, use 77011)◀

▶(76360 has been deleted. To report, use 77012)◀

▶(76362 has been deleted. To report, use 77013)◀

▶(76370 has been deleted. To report, use 77014)◀

(76375 has been deleted)

(2D reformatting is no longer separately reported. To report 3D rendering, see 76376, 76377)

(76376, 76377 require concurrent physician supervision of image postprocessing 3D manipulation of volumetric data set and image rendering)

76376 3D rendering with interpretation and reporting of computed tomography, magnetic resonance imaging, ultrasound, or other tomographic modality; not requiring image postprocessing on an independent workstation

(Use 76376 in conjunction with code[s] for base imaging procedure[s])

▶(Do not report 76376 in conjunction with 70496, 70498, 70544-70549, 71275, 71555, 72159, 72191, 72198, 73206, 73225, 73706, 73725, 74175, 74185, 75635, 76377, 78000-78999, 0066T, 0067T, 0144T-0151T)◀

76377 requiring image postprocessing on an independent workstation

(Use 76377 in conjunction with code[s] for base imaging procedure[s])

▶(Do not report 76377 in conjunction with 70496, 70498, 70544-70549, 71275, 71555, 72159, 72191, 72198, 73206, 73225, 73706, 73725, 74175, 74185, 75635, 76376, 78000-78999, 0066T, 0067T, 0144T-0151T)◀

76380 Computed tomography, limited or localized follow-up study

76390 Magnetic resonance spectroscopy

(For magnetic resonance imaging, use appropriate MRI body site code)

▶(76393 has been deleted. To report, use 77021)◀

▶(76394 has been deleted. To report, use 77022)◀

▶(76400 has been deleted. To report, use 77084)◀

76496 Unlisted fluoroscopic procedure (eg, diagnostic, interventional)

76497 Unlisted computed tomography procedure (eg, diagnostic, interventional)

76498 Unlisted magnetic resonance procedure (eg, diagnostic, interventional)

76499 Unlisted diagnostic radiographic procedure

Diagnostic Ultrasound

All diagnostic ultrasound examinations require permanently recorded images with measurements, when such measurements are clinically indicated. For those codes whose sole diagnostic goal is a biometric measure (ie, 76514, 76516, and 76519), permanently recorded images are not required. A final, written report should be issued for inclusion in the patient's medical record. The prescription form for the intraocular lens satisfies the written report requirement for 76519. For those anatomic regions that have "complete" and "limited" ultrasound codes, note the elements that comprise a "complete" exam. The report should contain a description of these elements or the reason that an element could not be visualized (eg, obscured by bowel gas, surgically absent).

If less than the required elements for a "complete" exam are reported (eg, limited number of organs or limited portion of region evaluated), the "limited" code for that anatomic region should be used once per patient exam session. A "limited" exam of an anatomic region should not be reported for the same exam session as a "complete" exam of that same region.

Doppler evaluation of vascular structures (other than color flow used only for anatomic structure identification) is separately reportable. To report, see Non-Invasive Vascular Diagnostic Studies (93875-93990).

Ultrasound guidance procedures also require permanently recorded images of the site to be localized, as well as a documented description of the localization process, either separately or within the report of the procedure for which the guidance is utilized.

Use of ultrasound, without thorough evaluation of organ(s) or anatomic region, image documentation, and final, written report, is not separately reportable.

Definitions

A-mode implies a one-dimensional ultrasonic measurement procedure.

M-mode implies a one-dimensional ultrasonic measurement procedure with movement of the trace to record amplitude and velocity of moving echo-producing structures.

B-scan implies a two-dimensional ultrasonic scanning procedure with a two-dimensional display.

Real-time scan implies a two-dimensional ultrasonic scanning procedure with display of both two-dimensional structure and motion with time.

(To report diagnostic vascular ultrasound studies, see 93875-93990)

(For focused ultrasound ablation treatment of uterine leiomyomata, see Category III codes 0071T, 0072T)

Head and Neck

▲ **76506** Echoencephalography, real time with image documentation (gray scale) (for determination of ventricular size, delineation of cerebral contents, and detection of fluid masses or other intracranial abnormalities), including A-mode encephalography as secondary component where indicated

76510 Ophthalmic ultrasound, diagnostic; B-scan and quantitative A-scan performed during the same patient encounter

76511 quantitative A-scan only

76512 B-scan (with or without superimposed non-quantitative A-scan)

76513 anterior segment ultrasound, immersion (water bath) B-scan or high resolution biomicroscopy

76514 corneal pachymetry, unilateral or bilateral (determination of corneal thickness)

76516 Ophthalmic biometry by ultrasound echography, A-scan;

76519 with intraocular lens power calculation

 (For partial coherence interferometry, use 92136)

76529 Ophthalmic ultrasonic foreign body localization

▲ **76536** Ultrasound, soft tissues of head and neck (eg, thyroid, parathyroid, parotid), real time with image documentation

Chest

▲ **76604** Ultrasound, chest (includes mediastinum), real time with image documentation

▲ **76645** Ultrasound, breast(s) (unilateral or bilateral), real time with image documentation

Abdomen and Retroperitoneum

►A complete ultrasound examination of the abdomen (76700) consists of real time scans of the liver, gall bladder, common bile duct, pancreas, spleen, kidneys, and the upper abdominal aorta and inferior vena cava including any demonstrated abdominal abnormality.

A complete ultrasound examination of the retroperitoneum (76770) consists of real time scans of the kidneys, abdominal aorta, common iliac artery origins, and inferior vena cava, including any demonstrated retroperitoneal abnormality. Alternatively, if clinical history suggests urinary tract pathology, complete evaluation of the kidneys and urinary bladder also comprises a complete retroperitoneal ultrasound.◄

Use of ultrasound, without thorough evaluation of organ(s) or anatomic region, image documentation and final, written report, is not separately reportable.

▲ **76700** Ultrasound, abdominal, real time with image documentation; complete

76705 limited (eg, single organ, quadrant, follow-up)

▲ **76770** Ultrasound, retroperitoneal (eg, renal, aorta, nodes), real time with image documentation; complete

76775 limited

● **76776** Ultrasound, transplanted kidney, real time and duplex Doppler with image documentation

 ►(For ultrasound of transplanted kidney without duplex Doppler, use 76775)◄

 ►(Do not report 76776 in conjunction with 93975, 93976)◄

 ►(76778 has been deleted. To report, see 76775, 76776)◄

Spinal Canal

76800 Ultrasound, spinal canal and contents

Pelvis

Obstetrical

Codes 76801 and 76802 include determination of the number of gestational sacs and fetuses, gestational sac/fetal measurements appropriate for gestation (younger than 14 weeks 0 days), survey of visible fetal and placental anatomic structure, qualitative assessment of amniotic fluid volume/gestational sac shape and examination of the maternal uterus and adnexa.

Codes 76805 and 76810 include determination of number of fetuses and amniotic/chorionic sacs, measurements appropriate for gestational age (older than or equal to 14 weeks 0 days), survey of intracranial/spinal/abdominal anatomy, 4 chambered heart, umbilical cord insertion site, placenta location and amniotic fluid assessment and, when visible, examination of maternal adnexa.

Codes 76811 and 76812 include all elements of codes 76805 and 76810 plus detailed anatomic evaluation of the fetal brain/ventricles, face, heart/outflow tracts and chest anatomy, abdominal organ specific anatomy, number/length/architecture of limbs and detailed evaluation of the umbilical cord and placenta and other fetal anatomy as clinically indicated.

Report should document the results of the evaluation of each element described above or the reason for non-visualization.

Code 76815 represents a focused "quick look" exam limited to the assessment of one or more of the elements listed in code 76815.

Code 76816 describes an examination designed to reassess fetal size and interval growth or reevaluate one or more anatomic abnormalities of a fetus previously demonstrated on ultrasound, and should be coded once for each fetus requiring reevaluation using modifier 59 for each fetus after the first.

Radiology

Code 76817 describes a transvaginal obstetric ultrasound performed separately or in addition to one of the transabdominal examinations described above. For transvaginal examinations performed for non-obstetrical purposes, use code 76830.

76801 Ultrasound, pregnant uterus, real time with image documentation, fetal and maternal evaluation, first trimester (< 14 weeks 0 days), transabdominal approach; single or first gestation

►(To report first trimester fetal nuchal translucency measurement, use 76813)◄

+ 76802 each additional gestation (List separately in addition to code for primary procedure)

(Use 76802 in conjunction with 76801)

►(To report first trimester fetal nuchal translucency measurement, use 76814)◄

76805 Ultrasound, pregnant uterus, real time with image documentation, fetal and maternal evaluation, after first trimester (> or = 14 weeks 0 days), transabdominal approach; single or first gestation

+ 76810 each additional gestation (List separately in addition to code for primary procedure)

(Use 76810 in conjunction with 76805)

76811 Ultrasound, pregnant uterus, real time with image documentation, fetal and maternal evaluation plus detailed fetal anatomic examination, transabdominal approach; single or first gestation

+ 76812 each additional gestation (List separately in addition to code for primary procedure)

(Use 76812 in conjunction with 76811)

● 76813 Ultrasound, pregnant uterus, real time with image documentation, first trimester fetal nuchal translucency measurement, transabdominal or transvaginal approach; single or first gestation

+● 76814 each additional gestation (List separately in addition to code for primary procedure)

►(Use 76814 in conjunction with 76813)◄

76815 Ultrasound, pregnant uterus, real time with image documentation, limited (eg, fetal heart beat, placental location, fetal position and/or qualitative amniotic fluid volume), one or more fetuses

(Use 76815 only once per exam and not per element)

►(To report first trimester fetal nuchal translucency measurement, see 76813, 76814)◄

76816 Ultrasound, pregnant uterus, real time with image documentation, follow-up (eg, re-evaluation of fetal size by measuring standard growth parameters and amniotic fluid volume, re-evaluation of organ system(s) suspected or confirmed to be abnormal on a previous scan), transabdominal approach, per fetus

(Report 76816 with modifier 59 for each additional fetus examined in a multiple pregnancy)

76817 Ultrasound, pregnant uterus, real time with image documentation, transvaginal

(For non-obstetrical transvaginal ultrasound, use 76830)

(If transvaginal examination is done in addition to transabdominal obstetrical ultrasound exam, use 76817 in addition to appropriate transabdominal exam code)

76818 Fetal biophysical profile; with non-stress testing

76819 without non-stress testing

(Fetal biophysical profile assessments for the second and any additional fetuses, should be reported separately by code 76818 or 76819 with the modifier 59 appended)

(For amniotic fluid index without non-stress test, use 76815)

76820 Doppler velocimetry, fetal; umbilical artery

76821 middle cerebral artery

76825 Echocardiography, fetal, cardiovascular system, real time with image documentation (2D), with or without M-mode recording;

76826 follow-up or repeat study

76827 Doppler echocardiography, fetal, pulsed wave and/or continuous wave with spectral display; complete

76828 follow-up or repeat study

(To report the use of color mapping, use 93325)

Nonobstetrical

Code 76856 includes the complete evaluation of the female pelvic anatomy. Elements of this examination include a description and measurements of the uterus and adnexal structures, measurement of the endometrium, measurement of the bladder (when applicable), and a description of any pelvic pathology (eg, ovarian cysts, uterine leiomyomata, free pelvic fluid).

Code 76856 is also applicable to a complete evaluation of the male pelvis. Elements of the examination include evaluation and measurement (when applicable) of the urinary bladder, evaluation of the prostate and seminal vesicles to the extent that they are visualized transabdominally, and any pelvic pathology (eg, bladder tumor, enlarged prostate, free pelvic fluid, pelvic abscess).

Code 76857 represents a focused examination limited to the assessment of one or more elements listed in code 76856 and/or the reevaluation of one or more pelvic abnormalities previously demonstrated on ultrasound. Code 76857, rather than 76770, should be utilized if the urinary bladder alone (ie, not including the kidneys) is imaged, whereas code 51798 should be utilized if a bladder volume or post-void residual measurement is obtained without imaging the bladder.

Radiology

Use of ultrasound, without thorough evaluation of organ(s) or anatomic region, image documentation, and final, written report, is not separately reportable.

76830 Ultrasound, transvaginal

(For obstetrical transvaginal ultrasound, use 76817)

(If transvaginal examination is done in addition to transabdominal non-obstetrical ultrasound exam, use 76830 in addition to appropriate transabdominal exam code)

76831 Saline infusion sonohysterography (SIS), including color flow Doppler, when performed

(For introduction of saline for saline infusion sonohysterography, use 58340)

▲ **76856** Ultrasound, pelvic (nonobstetric), real time with image documentation; complete

76857 limited or follow-up (eg, for follicles)

Genitalia

76870 Ultrasound, scrotum and contents

76872 Ultrasound, transrectal;

76873 prostate volume study for brachytherapy treatment planning (separate procedure)

Extremities

▲ **76880** Ultrasound, extremity, nonvascular, real time with image documentation

76885 Ultrasound, infant hips, real time with imaging documentation; dynamic (requiring physician manipulation)

76886 limited, static (not requiring physician manipulation)

Ultrasonic Guidance Procedures

76930 Ultrasonic guidance for pericardiocentesis, imaging supervision and interpretation

76932 Ultrasonic guidance for endomyocardial biopsy, imaging supervision and interpretation

76936 Ultrasound guided compression repair of arterial pseudoaneurysm or arteriovenous fistulae (includes diagnostic ultrasound evaluation, compression of lesion and imaging)

+ **76937** Ultrasound guidance for vascular access requiring ultrasound evaluation of potential access sites, documentation of selected vessel patency, concurrent realtime ultrasound visualization of vascular needle entry, with permanent recording and reporting (List separately in addition to code for primary procedure)

(Do not use 76937 in conjunction with 76942)

(If extremity venous non-invasive vascular diagnostic study is performed separate from venous access guidance, use 93965, 93970 or 93971)

▲ **76940** Ultrasound guidance for, and monitoring of, parenchymal tissue ablation

►(Do not report 76940 in conjunction with 76998)◄

►(For ablation, see 32998, 47370-47382, 50592)◄

(For percutaneous cryotherapy ablation of renal tumors, use 0135T)

76941 Ultrasonic guidance for intrauterine fetal transfusion or cordocentesis, imaging supervision and interpretation

(For procedure, see 36460, 59012)

76942 Ultrasonic guidance for needle placement (eg, biopsy, aspiration, injection, localization device), imaging supervision and interpretation

(Do not report 76942 in conjunction with 43232, 43237, 43242, 45341, 45342, or 76975)

(For microwave thermotherapy of the breast, use Category III code 0061T)

76945 Ultrasonic guidance for chorionic villus sampling, imaging supervision and interpretation

(For procedure, use 59015)

76946 Ultrasonic guidance for amniocentesis, imaging supervision and interpretation

76948 Ultrasonic guidance for aspiration of ova, imaging supervision and interpretation

76950 Ultrasonic guidance for placement of radiation therapy fields

76965 Ultrasonic guidance for interstitial radioelement application

Other Procedures

76970 Ultrasound study follow-up (specify)

76975 Gastrointestinal endoscopic ultrasound, supervision and interpretation

(Do not report 76975 in conjunction with 43231, 43232, 43237, 43238, 43242, 43259, 45341, 45342, or 76942)

76977 Ultrasound bone density measurement and interpretation, peripheral site(s), any method

►(76986 has been deleted. To report, use 76998)◄

● **76998** Ultrasonic guidance, intraoperative

►(Do not report 76998 in conjunction with 47370-47382)◄

►(For ultrasound guidance for open and laparoscopic radiofrequency tissue ablation, use 76940)◄

76999 Unlisted ultrasound procedure (eg, diagnostic, interventional)

Radiology

►Radiologic Guidance◄

►Fluoroscopic Guidance◄

+● 77001　Fluoroscopic guidance for central venous access device placement, replacement (catheter only or complete), or removal (includes fluoroscopic guidance for vascular access and catheter manipulation, any necessary contrast injections through access site or catheter with related venography radiologic supervision and interpretation, and radiographic documentation of final catheter position) (List separately in addition to code for primary procedure

►(Do not use 77001 in conjunction with 77002)◄

►(If formal extremity venography is performed from separate venous access and separately interpreted, use 36005 and 75820, 75822, 75825, or 75827)◄

● 77002　Fluoroscopic guidance for needle placement (eg, biopsy, aspiration, injection, localization device)

►(See appropriate surgical code for procedure and anatomic location)◄

►(77002 includes all radiographic arthrography with the exception of supervision and interpretation for CT and MR arthrography)◄

►(Do not report 77002 in addition to 70332, 73040, 73085, 73115, 73525, 73580, 73615)◄

►(77002 is included in the organ/anatomic specific radiological supervision and interpretation procedures 74320, 74350, 74355, 74445, 74470, 74475, 75809, 75810, 75885, 75887, 75980, 75982, 75989)◄

● 77003　Fluoroscopic guidance and localization of needle or catheter tip for spine or paraspinous diagnostic or therapeutic injection procedures (epidural, transforaminal epidural, subarachnoid, paravertebral facet joint, paravertebral facet joint nerve, or sacroiliac joint), including neurolytic agent destruction

►(Injection of contrast during fluoroscopic guidance and localization [77003] is included in 22526, 22527, 62263, 62264, 62270-62282, 62310-62319, 0027T)◄

►(Fluoroscopic guidance for subarachnoid puncture for diagnostic radiographic myelography is included in supervision and interpretation codes 72240-72270)◄

►(For epidural or subarachnoid needle or catheter placement and injection, see 62270-62282, 62310-62319)◄

►(For sacroiliac joint arthrography, see 27096, 73542. If formal arthrography is not performed and recorded, and a formal radiographic report is not issued, use 77003 for fluoroscopic guidance for sacroiliac joint injections)◄

►(For paravertebral facet joint injection, see 64470-64476. For transforaminal epidural needle placement and injection, see 64479-64484)◄

►(For destruction by neurolytic agent, see 64600-64680)◄

►(For percutaneous or endoscopic lysis of epidural adhesions, 62263, 62264, 0027T include fluoroscopic guidance and localization)◄

►Computed Tomography Guidance◄

● 77011　Computed tomography guidance for stereotactic localization

● 77012　Computed tomography guidance for needle placement (eg, biopsy, aspiration, injection, localization device), radiological supervision and interpretation

● 77013　Computerized tomography guidance for, and monitoring of, parenchymal tissue ablation

►(Do not report 77013 in conjunction with 20982)◄

►(For percutaneous cryotherapy ablation of renal tumors, use 0135T)◄

►(For percutaneous radiofrequency ablation, see 32998, 47382, 50592)◄

● 77014　Computed tomography guidance for placement of radiation therapy fields

►Magnetic Resonance Guidance◄

● 77021　Magnetic resonance guidance for needle placement (eg, for biopsy, needle aspiration, injection, or placement of localization device) radiological supervision and interpretation

►(For procedure, see appropriate organ or site)◄

● 77022　Magnetic resonance guidance for, and monitoring of, parenchymal tissue ablation

►(For percutaneous radiofrequency ablation, see 32998, 47382, 50592)◄

►(For focused ultrasound ablation treatment of uterine leiomyomata, see Category III codes 0071T, 0072T)◄

►(For percutaneous cryotherapy ablation of renal tumors, use 0135T)◄

►Other Radiologic Guidance◄

● 77031　Stereotactic localization guidance for breast biopsy or needle placement (eg, for wire localization or for injection), each lesion, radiological supervision and interpretation

►(For procedure, see 10022, 19000-19103, 19290, 19291)◄

►(For injection for sentinel node localization without lymphoscintigraphy, use 38792)◄

● 77032　Mammographic guidance for needle placement, breast (eg, for wire localization or for injection), each lesion, radiological supervision and interpretation

►(For procedure, see 10022, 19000, 19102, 19103, 19290, 19291)◄

►(For injection for sentinel node localization without lymphoscintigraphy, use 38792)◄

Radiology

▶Breast, Mammography◄

▶(For mammographic guidance for needle placement of breast lesion, use 77032)◄

+● 77051 Computer-aided detection (computer algorithm analysis of digital image data for lesion detection) with further physician review for interpretation, with or without digitization of film radiographic images; diagnostic mammography (List separately in addition to code for primary procedure)

▶(Use 77051 in conjunction with 77055, 77056)◄

+● 77052 screening mammography (List separately in addition to code for primary procedure)

▶(Use 77052 in conjunction with 77057)◄

● 77053 Mammary ductogram or galactogram, single duct, radiological supervision and interpretation

▶(For mammary ductogram or galactogram injection, use 19030)◄

● 77054 Mammary ductogram or galactogram, multiple ducts, radiological supervision and interpretation

● 77055 Mammography; unilateral

● 77056 bilateral

▶(Use 77055, 77056 in conjunction with 77051 for computer-aided detection applied to a diagnostic mammogram)◄

● 77057 Screening mammography, bilateral (2-view film study of each breast)

▶(Use 77057 in conjunction with 77052 for computer-aided detection applied to a screening mammogram)◄

▶(To report electrical impedance scan of the breast, bilateral, use Category III code 0060T)◄

● 77058 Magnetic resonance imaging, breast, without and/or with contrast material(s); unilateral

● 77059 bilateral

▶Bone/Joint Studies◄

● 77071 Manual application of stress performed by physician for joint radiography, including contralateral joint if indicated

▶(For radiographic interpretation of stressed images, see appropriate anatomic site and number of views)◄

● 77072 Bone age studies

● 77073 Bone length studies (orthoroentgenogram, scanogram)

● 77074 Radiologic examination, osseous survey; limited (eg, for metastases)

● 77075 complete (axial and appendicular skeleton)

● 77076 Radiologic examination, osseous survey, infant

● 77077 Joint survey, single view, 2 or more joints (specify)

● 77078 Computed tomography, bone mineral density study, 1 or more sites; axial skeleton (eg, hips, pelvis, spine)

● 77079 appendicular skeleton (peripheral) (eg, radius, wrist, heel)

● 77080 Dual-energy X-ray absorptiometry (DXA), bone density study, 1 or more sites; axial skeleton (eg, hips, pelvis, spine)

● 77081 appendicular skeleton (peripheral) (eg, radius, wrist, heel)

● 77082 vertebral fracture assessment

▶(To report dual-energy X-ray absorptiometry [DXA] body composition study, 1 or more sites, use Category III code 0028T)◄

● 77083 Radiographic absorptiometry (eg, photodensitometry, radiogrammetry), 1 or more sites

● 77084 Magnetic resonance (eg, proton) imaging, bone marrow blood supply

Radiation Oncology

Listings for Radiation Oncology provide for teletherapy and brachytherapy to include initial consultation, clinical treatment planning, simulation, medical radiation physics, dosimetry, treatment devices, special services, and clinical treatment management procedures. They include normal follow-up care during course of treatment and for three months following its completion.

When a service or procedure is provided that is not listed in this edition of the CPT codebook it should be identified by a Special Report (see page 234) and one of the following unlisted procedure codes:

77299 Unlisted procedure, therapeutic radiology clinical treatment planning

77399 Unlisted procedure, medical radiation physics, dosimetry and treatment devices, and special services

77499 Unlisted procedure, therapeutic radiology treatment management

77799 Unlisted procedure, clinical brachytherapy

For treatment by injectable or ingestible isotopes, see subsection **Nuclear Medicine.**

Consultation: Clinical Management

Preliminary consultation, evaluation of patient prior to decision to treat, or full medical care (in addition to treatment management) when provided by the therapeutic radiologist may be identified by the appropriate procedure codes from **Evaluation and Management, Medicine,** or **Surgery** sections.

Radiology

Clinical Treatment Planning (External and Internal Sources)

The clinical treatment planning process is a complex service including interpretation of special testing, tumor localization, treatment volume determination, treatment time/dosage determination, choice of treatment modality, determination of number and size of treatment ports, selection of appropriate treatment devices, and other procedures.

Definitions

Simple planning requires a single treatment area of interest encompassed in a single port or simple parallel opposed ports with simple or no blocking.

Intermediate planning requires three or more converging ports, two separate treatment areas, multiple blocks, or special time dose constraints.

Complex planning requires highly complex blocking, custom shielding blocks, tangential ports, special wedges or compensators, three or more separate treatment areas, rotational or special beam considerations, combination of therapeutic modalities.

77261 Therapeutic radiology treatment planning; simple

77262 intermediate

77263 complex

Definitions

Simple simulation of a single treatment area with either a single port or parallel opposed ports. Simple or no blocking.

Intermediate simulation of three or more converging ports, two separate treatment areas, multiple blocks.

Complex simulation of tangential portals, three or more treatment areas, rotation or arc therapy, complex blocking, custom shielding blocks, brachytherapy source verification, hyperthermia probe verification, any use of contrast materials.

Three-dimensional (3D) computer-generated 3D reconstruction of tumor volume and surrounding critical normal tissue structures from direct CT scans and/or MRI data in preparation for non-coplanar or coplanar therapy. The simulation uses documented 3D beam's eye view volume-dose displays of multiple or moving beams. Documentation with 3D volume reconstruction and dose distribution is required.

Simulation may be carried out on a dedicated simulator, a radiation therapy treatment unit, or diagnostic X-ray machine.

77280 Therapeutic radiology simulation-aided field setting; simple

77285 intermediate

77290 complex

77295 3-dimensional

77299 Unlisted procedure, therapeutic radiology clinical treatment planning

Medical Radiation Physics, Dosimetry, Treatment Devices, and Special Services

77300 Basic radiation dosimetry calculation, central axis depth dose calculation, TDF, NSD, gap calculation, off axis factor, tissue inhomogeneity factors, calculation of non-ionizing radiation surface and depth dose, as required during course of treatment, only when prescribed by the treating physician

77301 Intensity modulated radiotherapy plan, including dose-volume histograms for target and critical structure partial tolerance specifications

(Dose plan is optimized using inverse or forward planning technique for modulated beam delivery (eg, binary, dynamic MLC) to create highly conformal dose distribution. Computer plan distribution must be verified for positional accuracy based on dosimetric verification of the intensity map with verification of treatment set-up and interpretation of verification methodology)

77305 Teletherapy, isodose plan (whether hand or computer calculated); simple (one or two parallel opposed unmodified ports directed to a single area of interest)

77310 intermediate (three or more treatment ports directed to a single area of interest)

77315 complex (mantle or inverted Y, tangential ports, the use of wedges, compensators, complex blocking, rotational beam, or special beam considerations)

(Only one teletherapy isodose plan may be reported for a given course of therapy to a specific treatment area)

77321 Special teletherapy port plan, particles, hemibody, total body

77326 Brachytherapy isodose plan; simple (calculation made from single plane, one to four sources/ribbon application, remote afterloading brachytherapy, 1 to 8 sources)

(For definition of source/ribbon, see page 255)

77327 intermediate (multiplane dosage calculations, application involving 5 to 10 sources/ribbons, remote afterloading brachytherapy, 9 to 12 sources)

77328 complex (multiplane isodose plan, volume implant calculations, over 10 sources/ribbons used, special spatial reconstruction, remote afterloading brachytherapy, over 12 sources)

77331 Special dosimetry (eg, TLD, microdosimetry) (specify), only when prescribed by the treating physician

77332 Treatment devices, design and construction; simple (simple block, simple bolus)

77333 intermediate (multiple blocks, stents, bite blocks, special bolus)

77334 complex (irregular blocks, special shields, compensators, wedges, molds or casts)

Radiology

77336 Continuing medical physics consultation, including assessment of treatment parameters, quality assurance of dose delivery, and review of patient treatment documentation in support of the radiation oncologist, reported per week of therapy

77370 Special medical radiation physics consultation

►Stereotactic Radiation Treatment Delivery◄

● **77371** Radiation treatment delivery, stereotactic radiosurgery (SRS), complete course of treatment of cerebral lesion(s) consisting of 1 session; multi-source Cobalt 60 based

● **77372** linear accelerator based

►(For radiation treatment management, use 77432)◄

● **77373** Stereotactic body radiation therapy, treatment delivery, per fraction to 1 or more lesions, including image guidance, entire course not to exceed 5 fractions

►(Do not report 77373 in conjunction with 77401-77416, 77418)◄

►(For single fraction cranial lesion[s], see 77371, 77372)◄

►Other Procedures◄

77399 Unlisted procedure, medical radiation physics, dosimetry and treatment devices, and special services

Radiation Treatment Delivery

(Radiation treatment delivery [77401-77416] recognizes the technical component and the various energy levels)

77401 Radiation treatment delivery, superficial and/or ortho voltage

77402 Radiation treatment delivery, single treatment area, single port or parallel opposed ports, simple blocks or no blocks; up to 5 MeV

77403 6-10 MeV

77404 11-19 MeV

77406 20 MeV or greater

77407 Radiation treatment delivery, two separate treatment areas, three or more ports on a single treatment area, use of multiple blocks; up to 5 MeV

77408 6-10 MeV

77409 11-19 MeV

77411 20 MeV or greater

77412 Radiation treatment delivery, three or more separate treatment areas, custom blocking, tangential ports, wedges, rotational beam, compensators, electron beam; up to 5 MeV

77413 6-10 MeV

77414 11-19 MeV

77416 20 MeV or greater

77417 Therapeutic radiology port film(s)

77418 Intensity modulated treatment delivery, single or multiple fields/arcs, via narrow spatially and temporally modulated beams, binary, dynamic MLC, per treatment session

(For intensity modulated treatment planning, use 77301)

(For compensator-based beam modulation treatment delivery, use Category III code 0073T)

77421 Stereoscopic X-ray guidance for localization of target volume for the delivery of radiation therapy

►(Do not report 77421 in conjunction with 77432, 77435)◄

►(For placement of interstitial device[s] for radiation therapy guidance, prostate, use 55876)◄

Neutron Beam Treatment Delivery

77422 High energy neutron radiation treatment delivery; single treatment area using a single port or parallel-opposed ports with no blocks or simple blocking

77423 1 or more isocenter(s) with coplanar or non-coplanar geometry with blocking and/or wedge, and/or compensator(s)

Radiation Treatment Management

Radiation treatment management is reported in units of five fractions or treatment sessions, regardless of the actual time period in which the services are furnished. The services need not be furnished on consecutive days. Multiple fractions representing two or more treatment sessions furnished on the same day may be counted separately as long as there has been a distinct break in therapy sessions, and the fractions are of the character usually furnished on different days. Code 77427 is also reported if there are three or four fractions beyond a multiple of five at the end of a course of treatment; one or two fractions beyond a multiple of five at the end of a course of treatment are not reported separately. The professional services furnished during treatment management typically consist of:

- Review of port films;

- Review of dosimetry, dose delivery, and treatment parameters;

- Review of patient treatment set-up;

- Examination of patient for medical evaluation and management (eg, assessment of the patient's response to treatment, coordination of care and treatment, review of imaging and/or lab test results).

77427 Radiation treatment management, five treatments

77431 Radiation therapy management with complete course of therapy consisting of one or two fractions only

(77431 is not to be used to fill in the last week of a long course of therapy)

Radiology

77432 Stereotactic radiation treatment management of cerebral lesion(s) (complete course of treatment consisting of one session)

● **77435** Stereotactic body radiation therapy, treatment management, per treatment course, to one or more lesions, including image guidance, entire course not to exceed 5 fractions

▶(Do not report 77435 in conjunction with 77427-77432)◀

▶(When stereotactic radiation therapy is performed jointly by a surgeon and a radiation oncologist [eg, spinal or cranial], the surgeon reports radiosurgery with 61793)◀

77470 Special treatment procedure (eg, total body irradiation, hemibody radiation, per oral, endocavitary or intraoperative cone irradiation)

(77470 assumes that the procedure is performed one or more times during the course of therapy, in addition to daily or weekly patient management)

77499 Unlisted procedure, therapeutic radiology treatment management

Proton Beam Treatment Delivery

Definitions

Simple proton treatment delivery to a single treatment area utilizing a single non-tangential/oblique port, custom block with compensation (77522) and without compensation (77520).

Intermediate proton treatment delivery to one or more treatment areas utilizing two or more ports or one or more tangential/oblique ports, with custom blocks and compensators.

Complex proton treatment delivery to one or more treatment areas utilizing two or more ports per treatment area with matching or patching fields and/or multiple isocenters, with custom blocks and compensators.

77520 Proton treatment delivery; simple, without compensation

77522 simple, with compensation

77523 intermediate

77525 complex

Hyperthermia

Hyperthermia treatments as listed in this section include external (superficial and deep), interstitial, and intracavitary.

Radiation therapy when given concurrently is listed separately.

Hyperthermia is used only as an adjunct to radiation therapy or chemotherapy. It may be induced by a variety of sources (eg, microwave, ultrasound, low energy radio-frequency conduction, or by probes).

The listed treatments include management during the course of therapy and follow-up care for three months after completion.

Preliminary consultation is not included (see **Evaluation and Management** 99241-99255).

Physics planning and interstitial insertion of temperature sensors, and use of external or interstitial heat generating sources are included.

The following descriptors are included in the treatment schedule:

⊙ **77600** Hyperthermia, externally generated; superficial (ie, heating to a depth of 4 cm or less)

⊙ **77605** deep (ie, heating to depths greater than 4 cm)

⊙ **77610** Hyperthermia generated by interstitial probe(s); 5 or fewer interstitial applicators

⊙ **77615** more than 5 interstitial applicators

Clinical Intracavitary Hyperthermia

77620 Hyperthermia generated by intracavitary probe(s)

Clinical Brachytherapy

Clinical brachytherapy requires the use of either natural or man-made radioelements applied into or around a treatment field of interest. The supervision of radioelements and dose interpretation are performed solely by the therapeutic radiologist.

Services 77750-77799 include admission to the hospital and daily visits.

For insertion of ovoids and tandems, use 57155.

For insertion of Heyman capsules, use 58346.

Definitions

(Sources refer to intracavitary placement or permanent interstitial placement; ribbons refer to temporary interstitial placement)

A simple application has one to four sources/ribbons.

An intermediate application has five to 10 sources/ribbons.

A complex application has greater than 10 sources/ribbons.

77750 Infusion or instillation of radioelement solution (includes 3 months follow-up care)

(For administration of radiolabeled monoclonal antibodies, use 79403)

(For non-antibody radiopharmaceutical therapy by intravenous administration only, not including 3-month follow-up care, use 79101)

77761 Intracavitary radiation source application; simple

77762 intermediate

77763 complex

Radiology

77776	Interstitial radiation source application; simple
77777	intermediate
77778	complex
77781	Remote afterloading high intensity brachytherapy; 1-4 source positions or catheters
77782	5-8 source positions or catheters
77783	9-12 source positions or catheters
77784	over 12 source positions or catheters
77789	Surface application of radiation source
77790	Supervision, handling, loading of radiation source
77799	Unlisted procedure, clinical brachytherapy

Nuclear Medicine

Listed procedures may be performed independently or in the course of overall medical care. If the physician providing these services is also responsible for diagnostic work-up and/or follow-up care of patient, see appropriate sections also.

Radioimmunoassay tests are found in the **Clinical Pathology** section (codes 82000-84999). These codes can be appropriately used by any specialist performing such tests in a laboratory licensed and/or certified for radioimmunoassays. The reporting of these tests is not confined to clinical pathology laboratories alone.

The services listed do not include the radiopharmaceutical or drug. Diagnostic and therapeutic radiopharmaceuticals and drugs supplied by the physician should be reported separately using the appropriate supply code(s), in addition to the procedure code.

Diagnostic

Endocrine System

78000	Thyroid uptake; single determination
78001	multiple determinations
78003	stimulation, suppression or discharge (not including initial uptake studies)
78006	Thyroid imaging, with uptake; single determination
78007	multiple determinations
78010	Thyroid imaging; only
78011	with vascular flow
78015	Thyroid carcinoma metastases imaging; limited area (eg, neck and chest only)
78016	with additional studies (eg, urinary recovery)
78018	whole body

+ 78020	Thyroid carcinoma metastases uptake (List separately in addition to code for primary procedure)
	(Use 78020 in conjunction with 78018 only)
78070	Parathyroid imaging
78075	Adrenal imaging, cortex and/or medulla
78099	Unlisted endocrine procedure, diagnostic nuclear medicine
	(For chemical analysis, see **Chemistry** section)

Hematopoietic, Reticuloendothelial and Lymphatic System

78102	Bone marrow imaging; limited area
78103	multiple areas
78104	whole body
78110	Plasma volume, radiopharmaceutical volume-dilution technique (separate procedure); single sampling
78111	multiple samplings
78120	Red cell volume determination (separate procedure); single sampling
78121	multiple samplings
78122	Whole blood volume determination, including separate measurement of plasma volume and red cell volume (radiopharmaceutical volume-dilution technique)
78130	Red cell survival study;
78135	differential organ/tissue kinetics, (eg, splenic and/or hepatic sequestration)
78140	Labeled red cell sequestration, differential organ/tissue, (eg, splenic and/or hepatic)
	(78160, 78162, 78170, 78172 have been deleted)
78185	Spleen imaging only, with or without vascular flow
	(If combined with liver study, use procedures 78215 and 78216)
78190	Kinetics, study of platelet survival, with or without differential organ/tissue localization
78191	Platelet survival study
78195	Lymphatics and lymph nodes imaging
	(For sentinel node identification without scintigraphy imaging, use 38792)
	(For sentinal node excision, see 38500-38542)
78199	Unlisted hematopoietic, reticuloendothelial and lymphatic procedure, diagnostic nuclear medicine
	(For chemical analysis, see **Chemistry** section)

Radiology

Gastrointestinal System

78201 Liver imaging; static only

78202 with vascular flow

 (For spleen imaging only, use 78185)

78205 Liver imaging (SPECT);

78206 with vascular flow

78215 Liver and spleen imaging; static only

78216 with vascular flow

78220 Liver function study with hepatobiliary agents, with serial images

78223 Hepatobiliary ductal system imaging, including gallbladder, with or without pharmacologic intervention, with or without quantitative measurement of gallbladder function

78230 Salivary gland imaging;

78231 with serial images

78232 Salivary gland function study

78258 Esophageal motility

78261 Gastric mucosa imaging

78262 Gastroesophageal reflux study

78264 Gastric emptying study

78267 Urea breath test, C-14 (isotopic); acquisition for analysis

78268 analysis

78270 Vitamin B-12 absorption study (eg, Schilling test); without intrinsic factor

78271 with intrinsic factor

78272 Vitamin B-12 absorption studies combined, with and without intrinsic factor

78278 Acute gastrointestinal blood loss imaging

78282 Gastrointestinal protein loss

78290 Intestine imaging (eg, ectopic gastric mucosa, Meckel's localization, volvulus)

78291 Peritoneal-venous shunt patency test (eg, for LeVeen, Denver shunt)

 (For injection procedure, use 49427)

78299 Unlisted gastrointestinal procedure, diagnostic nuclear medicine

Musculoskeletal System

Bone and joint imaging can be used in the diagnosis of a variety of inflammatory processes (eg, osteomyelitis), as well as for localization of primary and/or metastatic neoplasms.

78300 Bone and/or joint imaging; limited area

78305 multiple areas

78306 whole body

78315 three phase study

78320 tomographic (SPECT)

78350 Bone density (bone mineral content) study, one or more sites; single photon absorptiometry

78351 dual photon absorptiometry, one or more sites

 ►(For radiographic bone density [photodensitometry], use 77083)◄

78399 Unlisted musculoskeletal procedure, diagnostic nuclear medicine

Cardiovascular System

Myocardial perfusion and cardiac blood pool imaging studies may be performed at rest and/or during stress. When performed during exercise and/or pharmacologic stress, the appropriate stress testing code from the 93015-93018 series should be reported in addition to 78460-78465, 78472-78492.

78414 Determination of central c-v hemodynamics (non-imaging) (eg, ejection fraction with probe technique) with or without pharmacologic intervention or exercise, single or multiple determinations

78428 Cardiac shunt detection

78445 Non-cardiac vascular flow imaging (ie, angiography, venography)

 (78455 has been deleted)

78456 Acute venous thrombosis imaging, peptide

78457 Venous thrombosis imaging, venogram; unilateral

78458 bilateral

78459 Myocardial imaging, positron emission tomography (PET), metabolic evaluation

 (For myocardial perfusion study, see 78491-78492)

78460 Myocardial perfusion imaging; (planar) single study, at rest or stress (exercise and/or pharmacologic), with or without quantification

78461 multiple studies, (planar) at rest and/or stress (exercise and/or pharmacologic), and redistribution and/or rest injection, with or without quantification

Radiology

▲=Revised code ●=New code ► ◄=Contains new or revised text ⊘=Modifier 51 exempt American Medical Association **257**

78464 tomographic (SPECT), single study (including attenuation correction when performed), at rest or stress (exercise and/or pharmacologic), with or without quantification

78465 tomographic (SPECT), multiple studies (including attenuation correction when performed), at rest and/or stress (exercise and/or pharmacologic) and redistribution and/or rest injection, with or without quantification

78466 Myocardial imaging, infarct avid, planar; qualitative or quantitative

78468 with ejection fraction by first pass technique

78469 tomographic SPECT with or without quantification

78472 Cardiac blood pool imaging, gated equilibrium; planar, single study at rest or stress (exercise and/or pharmacologic), wall motion study plus ejection fraction, with or without additional quantitative processing

(For assessment of right ventricular ejection fraction by first pass technique, use 78496)

78473 multiple studies, wall motion study plus ejection fraction, at rest and stress (exercise and/or pharmacologic), with or without additional quantification

+ 78478 Myocardial perfusion study with wall motion, qualitative or quantitative study (List separately in addition to code for primary procedure)

(Use 78478 in conjunction with 78460, 78461, 78464, 78465)

+ 78480 Myocardial perfusion study with ejection fraction (List separately in addition to code for primary procedure)

(Use 78480 in conjunction with 78460, 78461, 78464, 78465)

78481 Cardiac blood pool imaging, (planar), first pass technique; single study, at rest or with stress (exercise and/or pharmacologic), wall motion study plus ejection fraction, with or without quantification

78483 multiple studies, at rest and with stress (exercise and/ or pharmacologic), wall motion study plus ejection fraction, with or without quantification

(For cerebral blood flow study, use 78615)

78491 Myocardial imaging, positron emission tomography (PET), perfusion; single study at rest or stress

78492 multiple studies at rest and/or stress

78494 Cardiac blood pool imaging, gated equilibrium, SPECT, at rest, wall motion study plus ejection fraction, with or without quantitative processing

+ 78496 Cardiac blood pool imaging, gated equilibrium, single study, at rest, with right ventricular ejection fraction by first pass technique (List separately in addition to code for primary procedure)

(Use 78496 in conjunction with 78472)

78499 Unlisted cardiovascular procedure, diagnostic nuclear medicine

Respiratory System

78580 Pulmonary perfusion imaging, particulate

78584 Pulmonary perfusion imaging, particulate, with ventilation; single breath

78585 rebreathing and washout, with or without single breath

78586 Pulmonary ventilation imaging, aerosol; single projection

78587 multiple projections (eg, anterior, posterior, lateral views)

78588 Pulmonary perfusion imaging, particulate, with ventilation imaging, aerosol, one or multiple projections

78591 Pulmonary ventilation imaging, gaseous, single breath, single projection

78593 Pulmonary ventilation imaging, gaseous, with rebreathing and washout with or without single breath; single projection

78594 multiple projections (eg, anterior, posterior, lateral views)

78596 Pulmonary quantitative differential function (ventilation/perfusion) study

78599 Unlisted respiratory procedure, diagnostic nuclear medicine

Nervous System

78600 Brain imaging, limited procedure; static

78601 with vascular flow

78605 Brain imaging, complete study; static

78606 with vascular flow

78607 tomographic (SPECT)

78608 Brain imaging, positron emission tomography (PET); metabolic evaluation

78609 perfusion evaluation

78610 Brain imaging, vascular flow only

78615 Cerebral vascular flow

78630 Cerebrospinal fluid flow, imaging (not including introduction of material); cisternography

(For injection procedure, see 61000-61070, 62270-62319)

78635 ventriculography

(For injection procedure, see 61000-61070, 62270-62294)

78645 shunt evaluation

(For injection procedure, see 61000-61070, 62270-62294)

78647 tomographic (SPECT)

Radiology

78650 Cerebrospinal fluid leakage detection and localization

(For injection procedure, see 61000-61070, 62270-62294)

78660 Radiopharmaceutical dacryocystography

78699 Unlisted nervous system procedure, diagnostic nuclear medicine

Genitourinary System

▲ **78700** Kidney imaging morphology;

78701 with vascular flow

►(78704 has been deleted. To report, see 78707-78709)◄

▲ **78707** with vascular flow and function, single study without pharmacological intervention

▲ **78708** with vascular flow and function, single study, with pharmacological intervention (eg, angiotensin converting enzyme inhibitor and/or diuretic)

▲ **78709** with vascular flow and function, multiple studies, with and without pharmacological intervention (eg, angiotensin converting enzyme inhibitor and/or diuretic)

►(For introduction of radioactive substance in association with renal endoscopy, see 77776-77778)◄

▲ **78710** tomographic (SPECT)

►(78715 has been deleted. To report, see 78701-78709)◄

78725 Kidney function study, non-imaging radioisotopic study

+▲ **78730** Urinary bladder residual study (List separately in addition to code for primary procedure)

►(Use 78730 in conjunction with 78740)◄

►(For measurement of postvoid residual urine and/or bladder capacity by ultrasound, nonimaging, use 51798)◄

►(For ultrasound imaging of the bladder only, with measurement of postvoid residual urine when performed, use 76857)◄

78740 Ureteral reflux study (radiopharmaceutical voiding cystogram)

►(Use 78740 in conjunction with 78730 for urinary bladder residual study)◄

(For catheterization, see 51701, 51702, 51703)

►(78760 has been deleted. To report, use 78761)◄

▲ **78761** Testicular imaging with vascular flow

78799 Unlisted genitourinary procedure, diagnostic nuclear medicine

(For chemical analysis, see **Chemistry** section)

Other Procedures

(For specific organ, see appropriate heading)

(For radiophosphorus tumor identification, ocular, see 78800)

78800 Radiopharmaceutical localization of tumor or distribution of radiopharmaceutical agent(s); limited area

(For specific organ, see appropriate heading)

78801 multiple areas

78802 whole body, single day imaging

78803 tomographic (SPECT)

78804 whole body, requiring two or more days imaging

78805 Radiopharmaceutical localization of inflammatory process; limited area

78806 whole body

78807 tomographic (SPECT)

(For imaging bone infectious or inflammatory disease with a bone imaging radiopharmaceutical, see 78300, 78305, 78306)

(78810 has been deleted. To report, see 78811-78813)

(For PET of brain, see 78608, 78609)

(For PET myocardial imaging, see 78459, 78491, 78492)

78811 Tumor imaging, positron emission tomography (PET); limited area (eg, chest, head/neck)

78812 skull base to mid-thigh

78813 whole body

78814 Tumor imaging, positron emission tomography (PET) with concurrently acquired computed tomography (CT) for attenuation correction and anatomical localization; limited area (eg, chest, head/neck)

78815 skull base to mid-thigh

78816 whole body

(Report 78811-78816 only once per imaging session)

(Computed tomography (CT) performed for other than attenuation correction and anatomical localization is reported using the appropriate site specific CT code with modifier 59)

78890 Generation of automated data: interactive process involving nuclear physician and/or allied health professional personnel; simple manipulations and interpretation, not to exceed 30 minutes

78891 complex manipulations and interpretation, exceeding 30 minutes

(Use 78890 or 78891 in addition to primary procedure)

(78990 has been deleted)

78999 Unlisted miscellaneous procedure, diagnostic nuclear medicine

Radiology

Therapeutic

The oral and intravenous administration codes in this section are inclusive of the mode of administration. For intra-arterial, intra-cavitary, and intra-articular administration, also use the appropriate injection and/or procedure codes, as well as imaging guidance and radiological supervision and interpretation codes, when appropriate.

(79000, 79001 have been deleted. To report, use 79005)

79005 Radiopharmaceutical therapy, by oral administration

(79020, 79030, 79035 have been deleted. To report, use 79005)

(79100 has been deleted. To report, use 79101)

(For monoclonal antibody therapy, use 79403)

79101 Radiopharmaceutical therapy, by intravenous administration

(Do not report 79101 in conjunction with 36400, 36410, 79403, 90760, 90774 or 90775, 96409)

(For radiolabeled monoclonal antibody by intravenous infusion, use 79403)

(For infusion or instillation of non-antibody radioelement solution that includes 3 months follow-up care, use 77750)

79200 Radiopharmaceutical therapy, by intracavitary administration

79300 Radiopharmaceutical therapy, by interstitial radioactive colloid administration

(79400 has been deleted. To report, use 79101)

79403 Radiopharmaceutical therapy, radiolabeled monoclonal antibody by intravenous infusion

(For pre-treatment imaging, see 78802, 78804)

(Do not report 79403 in conjunction with 79101)

(79420 has been deleted. To report use 79445)

79440 Radiopharmaceutical therapy, by intra-articular administration

79445 Radiopharmaceutical therapy, by intra-arterial particulate administration

(Do not report 79445 in conjunction with 90773, 96420)

(Use appropriate procedural and radiological supervision and interpretation codes for the angiographic and interventional procedures provided prerequisite to intra-arterial radiopharmaceutical therapy)

(79900 has been deleted)

79999 Radiopharmaceutical therapy, unlisted procedure

Radiology

Pathology and Laboratory Guidelines

Items used by all physicians in reporting their services are presented in the **Introduction.** Some of the commonalities are repeated here for the convenience of those physicians referring to this section on **Pathology and Laboratory.** Other definitions and items unique to Pathology and Laboratory are also listed.

Services in Pathology and Laboratory

Services in Pathology and Laboratory are provided by a physician or by technologists under responsible supervision of a physician.

Separate or Multiple Procedures

It is appropriate to designate multiple procedures that are rendered on the same date by separate entries.

Subsection Information

Several of the subheadings or subsections have special needs or instructions unique to that section. Where these are indicated (eg, "Panel Tests"), special **"Notes"** will be presented preceding those procedural terminology listings referring to that subsection specifically. If there is an "Unlisted Procedure" code number (see the following section) for the individual subsection, it will be shown. Those subsections with **"Notes"** are as follows:

Organ or Disease Panels	80048-80076
Drug Testing	80100-80103
Therapeutic Drug Assays	80150-80299
Evocative/Suppression Testing	80400-80440
Consultations	
(Clinical Pathology)	80500-80502
Urinalysis.	81000-81099
Chemistry	82000-84999
Molecular Diagnostics	83890-83912
Infectious Agent: Detection	
of Antibodies	86602-86804
Microbiology	87001-87255
Infectious Agent Detection	87260-87999
Anatomic Pathology	88000-88099
Cytopathology	88104-88199
Cytogenetic Studies	88230-88299
Surgical Pathology	88300-88399

Unlisted Service or Procedure

A service or procedure may be provided that is not listed in this edition of the CPT codebook. When reporting such a service, the appropriate "Unlisted Procedure" code may be used to indicate the service, identifying it by "Special Report" as discussed below. The "Unlisted Procedures" and accompanying codes for **Pathology and Laboratory** are as follows:

81099	Unlisted urinalysis procedure
84999	Unlisted chemistry procedure
85999	Unlisted hematology and coagulation procedure
86586	Unlisted antigen, each
86849	Unlisted immunology procedure
86999	Unlisted transfusion medicine procedure
87999	Unlisted microbiology procedure
88099	Unlisted necropsy (autopsy) procedure
88199	Unlisted cytopathology procedure
88299	Unlisted cytogenetic study
88399	Unlisted surgical pathology procedure
89240	Unlisted miscellaneous pathology test

▶Results/Testing/Reports◀

▶Results are the technical component of a service. Testing leads to results; results lead to interpretation. Reports are the work product of the interpretation of numerous test results.◀

Special Report

A service that is rarely provided, unusual, variable, or new may require a special report in determining medical appropriateness of the service. Pertinent information should include an adequate definition or description of the nature, extent, and need for the procedure; and the time, effort, and equipment necessary to provide the service. Additional items that may be included are:

- Complexity of symptoms
- Final diagnosis
- Pertinent physical findings
- Diagnostic and therapeutic procedures
- Concurrent problems
- Follow-up care

Pathology and Laboratory Guidelines

Notes

Pathology and Laboratory

Organ or Disease-Oriented Panels

These panels were developed for coding purposes only and should not be interpreted as clinical parameters. The tests listed with each panel identify the defined components of that panel.

These panel components are not intended to limit the performance of other tests. If one performs tests in addition to those specifically indicated for a particular panel, those tests should be reported separately in addition to the panel code.

80048 Basic metabolic panel

This panel must include the following:

Calcium (82310)

Carbon dioxide (82374)

Chloride (82435)

Creatinine (82565)

Glucose (82947)

Potassium (84132)

Sodium (84295)

Urea nitrogen (BUN) (84520)

(Do not use 80048 in addition to 80053)

80050 General health panel

This panel must include the following:

Comprehensive metabolic panel (80053)

Blood count, complete (CBC), automated and automated differential WBC count (85025 or 85027 and 85004)

OR

Blood count, complete (CBC), automated (85027) and appropriate manual differential WBC count (85007 or 85009)

Thyroid stimulating hormone (TSH) (84443)

80051 Electrolyte panel

This panel must include the following:

Carbon dioxide (82374)

Chloride (82435)

Potassium (84132)

Sodium (84295)

80053 Comprehensive metabolic panel

This panel must include the following:

Albumin (82040)

Bilirubin, total (82247)

Calcium (82310)

Carbon dioxide (bicarbonate) (82374)

Chloride (82435)

Creatinine (82565)

Glucose (82947)

Phosphatase, alkaline (84075)

Potassium (84132)

Protein, total (84155)

Sodium (84295)

Transferase, alanine amino (ALT) (SGPT) (84460)

Transferase, aspartate amino (AST) (SGOT) (84450)

Urea nitrogen (BUN) (84520)

(Do not use 80053 in addition to 80048, 80076)

80055 Obstetric panel

This panel must include the following:

Blood count, complete (CBC), automated and automated differential WBC count (85025 or 85027 and 85004)

OR

Blood count, complete (CBC), automated (85027) and appropriate manual differential WBC count (85007 or 85009)

Hepatitis B surface antigen (HBsAg) (87340)

Antibody, rubella (86762)

Syphilis test, qualitative (eg, VDRL, RPR, ART) (86592)

Antibody screen, RBC, each serum technique (86850)

Blood typing, ABO (86900) AND

Blood typing, Rh (D) (86901)

80061 Lipid panel

This panel must include the following:

Cholesterol, serum, total (82465)

Lipoprotein, direct measurement, high density cholesterol (HDL cholesterol) (83718)

Triglycerides (84478)

80069 Renal function panel

This panel must include the following:

Albumin (82040)

Calcium (82310)

Carbon dioxide (bicarbonate) (82374)

Chloride (82435)

Pathology and Laboratory

Creatinine (82565)

Glucose (82947)

Phosphorus inorganic (phosphate) (84100)

Potassium (84132)

Sodium (84295)

Urea nitrogen (BUN) (84520)

80074 Acute hepatitis panel

This panel must include the following:

Hepatitis A antibody (HAAb), IgM antibody (86709)

Hepatitis B core antibody (HBcAb), IgM antibody (86705)

Hepatitis B surface antigen (HBsAg) (87340)

Hepatitis C antibody (86803)

80076 Hepatic function panel

This panel must include the following:

Albumin (82040)

Bilirubin, total (82247)

Bilirubin, direct (82248)

Phosphatase, alkaline (84075)

Protein, total (84155)

Transferase, alanine amino (ALT) (SGPT) (84460)

Transferase, aspartate amino (AST) (SGOT) (84450)

(Do not use 80076 in addition to 80053)

Drug Testing

The following list contains examples of drugs or classes of drugs that are commonly assayed by qualitative screen, followed by confirmation with a second method:

- Alcohols
- Amphetamines
- Barbiturates
- Benzodiazepines
- Cocaine and metabolites
- Methadones
- Methaqualones
- Opiates
- Phencyclidines
- Phenothiazines
- Propoxyphenes
- Tetrahydrocannabinoids
- Tricyclic antidepressants

Confirmed drugs may also be quantitated.

Use 80100 for each multiple drug class chromatographic procedure. Use 80102 for each procedure necessary for confirmation. For chromatography, each combination of stationary and mobile phase is to be counted as one procedure. For example, if detection of three drugs by chromatography requires one stationary phase with three mobile phases, use 80100 three (3) times. However, if multiple drugs can be detected using a single analysis (eg, one stationary phase with one mobile phase), use 80100 only once.

For quantitation of drugs screened, use appropriate code in **Chemistry** section (82000-84999) or **Therapeutic Drug Assay** section (80150-80299).

80100 Drug screen, qualitative; multiple drug classes chromatographic method, each procedure

80101 single drug class method (eg, immunoassay, enzyme assay), each drug class

80102 Drug confirmation, each procedure

80103 Tissue preparation for drug analysis

Therapeutic Drug Assays

The material for examination may be from any source. Examination is quantitative. For nonquantitative testing, see Drug Testing (80100-80103).

80150 Amikacin

80152 Amitriptyline

80154 Benzodiazepines

80156 Carbamazepine; total

80157 free

80158 Cyclosporine

80160 Desipramine

80162 Digoxin

80164 Dipropylacetic acid (valproic acid)

80166 Doxepin

80168 Ethosuximide

80170 Gentamicin

80172 Gold

80173 Haloperidol

80174 Imipramine

80176 Lidocaine

80178 Lithium

80182 Nortriptyline

80184 Phenobarbital

80185 Phenytoin; total

80186 free

80188 Primidone

80190 Procainamide;

80192 with metabolites (eg, n-acetyl procainamide)

80194 Quinidine

80195 Sirolimus

80196 Salicylate

80197 Tacrolimus

80198 Theophylline

80200 Tobramycin

80201 Topiramate

80202 Vancomycin

80299 Quantitation of drug, not elsewhere specified

Evocative/Suppression Testing

The following test panels involve the administration of evocative or suppressive agents, and the baseline and subsequent measurement of their effects on chemical constituents. These codes are to be used for the reporting of the laboratory component of the overall testing protocol. For the physician's administration of the evocative or suppressive agents, see 90760, 90761, 90772-90774, 90775; for the supplies and drugs, see 99070. To report physician attendance and monitoring during the testing, use the appropriate evaluation and management code, including the prolonged physician care codes if required. Prolonged physician care codes are not separately reported when evocative/suppression testing involves prolonged infusions reported with 90760-90761. In the code descriptors where reference is made to a particular analyte (eg, Cortisol (82533 x 2)) the "x 2" refers to the number of times the test for that particular analyte is performed.

80400 ACTH stimulation panel; for adrenal insufficiency

 This panel must include the following:

 Cortisol (82533 x 2)

80402 for 21 hydroxylase deficiency

 This panel must include the following:

 Cortisol (82533 x 2)

 17 hydroxyprogesterone (83498 x 2)

80406 for 3 beta-hydroxydehydrogenase deficiency

 This panel must include the following:

 Cortisol (82533 x 2)

 17 hydroxypregnenolone (84143 x 2)

80408 Aldosterone suppression evaluation panel (eg, saline infusion)

 This panel must include the following:

 Aldosterone (82088 x 2)

 Renin (84244 x 2)

80410 Calcitonin stimulation panel (eg, calcium, pentagastrin)

 This panel must include the following:

 Calcitonin (82308 x 3)

80412 Corticotropic releasing hormone (CRH) stimulation panel

 This panel must include the following:

 Cortisol (82533 x 6)

 Adrenocorticotropic hormone (ACTH) (82024 x 6)

80414 Chorionic gonadotropin stimulation panel; testosterone response

 This panel must include the following:

 Testosterone (84403 x 2 on three pooled blood samples)

80415 estradiol response

 This panel must include the following:

 Estradiol (82670 x 2 on three pooled blood samples)

80416 Renal vein renin stimulation panel (eg, captopril)

 This panel must include the following:

 Renin (84244 x 6)

80417 Peripheral vein renin stimulation panel (eg, captopril)

 This panel must include the following:

 Renin (84244 x 2)

80418 Combined rapid anterior pituitary evaluation panel

 This panel must include the following:

 Adrenocorticotropic hormone (ACTH) (82024 x 4)

 Luteinizing hormone (LH) (83002 x 4)

 Follicle stimulating hormone (FSH) (83001 x 4)

 Prolactin (84146 x 4)

 Human growth hormone (HGH) (83003 x 4)

 Cortisol (82533 x 4)

 Thyroid stimulating hormone (TSH) (84443 x 4)

80420 Dexamethasone suppression panel, 48 hour

 This panel must include the following:

 Free cortisol, urine (82530 x 2)

 Cortisol (82533 x 2)

 Volume measurement for timed collection (81050 x 2)

 (For single dose dexamethasone, use 82533)

Pathology and Laboratory

Pathology and Laboratory

80422 Glucagon tolerance panel; for insulinoma

This panel must include the following:

Glucose (82947 x 3)

Insulin (83525 x 3)

80424 for pheochromocytoma

This panel must include the following:

Catecholamines, fractionated (82384 x 2)

80426 Gonadotropin releasing hormone stimulation panel

This panel must include the following:

Follicle stimulating hormone (FSH) (83001 x 4)

Luteinizing hormone (LH) (83002 x 4)

80428 Growth hormone stimulation panel (eg, arginine infusion, l-dopa administration)

This panel must include the following:

Human growth hormone (HGH) (83003 x 4)

80430 Growth hormone suppression panel (glucose administration)

This panel must include the following:

Glucose (82947 x 3)

Human growth hormone (HGH) (83003 x 4)

80432 Insulin-induced C-peptide suppression panel

This panel must include the following:

Insulin (83525)

C-peptide (84681 x 5)

Glucose (82947 x 5)

80434 Insulin tolerance panel; for ACTH insufficiency

This panel must include the following:

Cortisol (82533 x 5)

Glucose (82947 x 5)

80435 for growth hormone deficiency

This panel must include the following:

Glucose (82947 x 5)

Human growth hormone (HGH) (83003 x 5)

80436 Metyrapone panel

This panel must include the following:

Cortisol (82533 x 2)

11 deoxycortisol (82634 x 2)

80438 Thyrotropin releasing hormone (TRH) stimulation panel; one hour

This panel must include the following:

Thyroid stimulating hormone (TSH) (84443 x 3)

80439 two hour

This panel must include the following:

Thyroid stimulating hormone (TSH) (84443 x 4)

80440 for hyperprolactinemia

This panel must include the following:

Prolactin (84146 x 3)

Consultations (Clinical Pathology)

A clinical pathology consultation is a service, including a written report, rendered by the pathologist in response to a request from an attending physician in relation to a test result(s) requiring additional medical interpretive judgment.

Reporting of a test result(s) without medical interpretive judgment is not considered a clinical pathology consultation.

80500 Clinical pathology consultation; limited, without review of patient's history and medical records

80502 comprehensive, for a complex diagnostic problem, with review of patient's history and medical records

(These codes may also be used for pharmacokinetic consultations)

(For consultations involving the examination and evaluation of the patient, see 99241-99255)

Urinalysis

For specific analyses, see appropriate section.

(For urinalysis, infectious agent detection, semi-quantitative analysis of volatile compounds, use Category III code 0041T)

81000 Urinalysis, by dip stick or tablet reagent for bilirubin, glucose, hemoglobin, ketones, leukocytes, nitrite, pH, protein, specific gravity, urobilinogen, any number of these constituents; non-automated, with microscopy

81001 automated, with microscopy

81002 non-automated, without microscopy

81003 automated, without microscopy

81005 Urinalysis; qualitative or semiquantitative, except immunoassays

(For non-immunoassay reagent strip urinalysis, see 81000, 81002)

(For immunoassay, qualitative or semiquantitative, use 83518)

(For microalbumin, see 82043, 82044)

81007	bacteriuria screen, except by culture or dipstick
	(For culture, see 87086-87088)
	(For dipstick, use 81000 or 81002)
81015	microscopic only
81020	two or three glass test
81025	Urine pregnancy test, by visual color comparison methods
81050	Volume measurement for timed collection, each
81099	Unlisted urinalysis procedure

Chemistry

The material for examination may be from any source unless otherwise specified in the code descriptor. When an analyte is measured in multiple specimens from different sources, or in specimens that are obtained at different times, the analyte is reported separately for each source and for each specimen. The examination is quantitative unless specified. To report an organ or disease oriented panel, see codes 80048-80076.

When a code describes a method where measurement of multiple analytes may require one or several procedures, each procedure is coded separately (eg, 82491-82492, 82541-82544). For example, if two (2) analytes are measured using column chromatography using a single stationary or mobile phase, use 82492. If the same two analytes are measured using different stationary or mobile phase conditions, 82491 would be used twice. If a total of four (4) analytes are measured where two (2) analytes are measured with a single stationary and mobile phase, and the other two (2) analytes are measured using a different stationary and mobile phase, use 82492 twice. If a total of three (3) analytes are measured where two (2) analytes are measured using a single stationary or mobile phase condition, and the third analyte is measured separately using a different stationary or mobile phase procedure, use 82492 once for the two (2) analytes measured under the same condition, and use 82491 once for the third analyte measured separately.

Clinical information derived from the results of laboratory data that is mathematically calculated (eg, free thyroxine index (T7)) is considered part of the test procedure and therefore is not a separately reportable service.

82000	Acetaldehyde, blood
82003	Acetaminophen
82009	Acetone or other ketone bodies, serum; qualitative
82010	quantitative
82013	Acetylcholinesterase
	(Acid, gastric, see gastric acid, 82926, 82928)
	(Acid phosphatase, see 84060-84066)

82016	Acylcarnitines; qualitative, each specimen
82017	quantitative, each specimen
	(For carnitine, use 82379)
82024	Adrenocorticotropic hormone (ACTH)
82030	Adenosine, 5-monophosphate, cyclic (cyclic AMP)
82040	Albumin; serum
82042	urine or other source, quantitative, each specimen
82043	urine, microalbumin, quantitative
82044	urine, microalbumin, semiquantitative (eg, reagent strip assay)
	(For prealbumin, use 84134)
82045	ischemia modified
82055	Alcohol (ethanol); any specimen except breath
	(For other volatiles, alcohol, use 84600)
82075	breath
82085	Aldolase
82088	Aldosterone
	(Alkaline phosphatase, see 84075, 84080)
82101	Alkaloids, urine, quantitative
	(Alphaketoglutarate, see 82009, 82010)
	(Alpha tocopherol (Vitamin E), use 84446)
82103	Alpha-1-antitrypsin; total
82104	phenotype
82105	Alpha-fetoprotein (AFP); serum
82106	amniotic fluid
● **82107**	AFP-L3 fraction isoform and total AFP (including ratio)
82108	Aluminum
82120	Amines, vaginal fluid, qualitative
	(For combined pH and amines test for vaginitis, use 82120 and 83986)
82127	Amino acids; single, qualitative, each specimen
82128	multiple, qualitative, each specimen
82131	single, quantitative, each specimen
82135	Aminolevulinic acid, delta (ALA)
82136	Amino acids, 2 to 5 amino acids, quantitative, each specimen
82139	Amino acids, 6 or more amino acids, quantitative, each specimen
82140	Ammonia
82143	Amniotic fluid scan (spectrophotometric)
	(For L/S ratio, use 83661)
	(Amobarbital, see 80100-80103 for qualitative analysis, 82205 for quantitative analysis)

Pathology and Laboratory

82145 Amphetamine or methamphetamine

(For qualitative analysis, see 80100-80103)

82150 Amylase

82154 Androstanediol glucuronide

82157 Androstenedione

82160 Androsterone

82163 Angiotensin II

82164 Angiotensin I - converting enzyme (ACE)

(Antidiuretic hormone (ADH), use 84588)

(Antimony, use 83015)

(Antitrypsin, alpha-1-, see 82103, 82104)

82172 Apolipoprotein, each

82175 Arsenic

(For heavy metal screening, use 83015)

82180 Ascorbic acid (Vitamin C), blood

(Aspirin, see acetylsalicylic acid, 80196)

(Atherogenic index, blood, ultracentrifugation, quantitative, use 83701)

82190 Atomic absorption spectroscopy, each analyte

82205 Barbiturates, not elsewhere specified

(For qualitative analysis, see 80100-80103)

(For B-Natriuretic peptide, use 83880)

82232 Beta-2 microglobulin

(Bicarbonate, use 82374)

82239 Bile acids; total

82240 cholylglycine

(For bile pigments, urine, see 81000-81005)

82247 Bilirubin; total

82248 direct

82252 feces, qualitative

82261 Biotinidase, each specimen

82270 Blood, occult, by peroxidase activity (eg, guaiac), qualitative; feces, consecutive collected specimens with single determination, for colorectal neoplasm screening (ie, patient was provided three cards or single triple card for consecutive collection)

82271 other sources

82272 Blood, occult, by peroxidase activity (eg, guaiac), qualitative, feces, single specimen (eg, from digital rectal exam)

(82273 has been deleted. To report, use 82271)

(Blood urea nitrogen (BUN), see 84520, 84525)

82274 Blood, occult, by fecal hemoglobin determination by immunoassay, qualitative, feces, 1-3 simultaneous determinations

82286 Bradykinin

82300 Cadmium

82306 Calcifediol (25-OH Vitamin D-3)

82307 Calciferol (Vitamin D)

(For 1,25-Dihydroxyvitamin D, use 82652)

82308 Calcitonin

82310 Calcium; total

82330 ionized

82331 after calcium infusion test

82340 urine quantitative, timed specimen

82355 Calculus; qualitative analysis

82360 quantitative analysis, chemical

82365 infrared spectroscopy

82370 x-ray diffraction

(Carbamates, see individual listings)

82373 Carbohydrate deficient transferrin

82374 Carbon dioxide (bicarbonate)

(See also 82803)

82375 Carbon monoxide, (carboxyhemoglobin); quantitative

82376 qualitative

(To report end-tidal carbon monoxide, use Category III code 0043T)

82378 Carcinoembryonic antigen (CEA)

82379 Carnitine (total and free), quantitative, each specimen

(For acylcarnitine, see 82016, 82017)

82380 Carotene

82382 Catecholamines; total urine

82383 blood

82384 fractionated

(For urine metabolites, see 83835, 84585)

82387 Cathepsin-D

82390 Ceruloplasmin

82397 Chemiluminescent assay

82415 Chloramphenicol

82435 Chloride; blood

82436 urine

82438 other source

(For sweat collection by iontophoresis, use 89230)

82441 Chlorinated hydrocarbons, screen

(Chlorpromazine, use 84022)

(Cholecalciferol (Vitamin D), use 82307)

82465 Cholesterol, serum or whole blood, total

(For high density lipoprotein (HDL), use 83718)

82480 Cholinesterase; serum

82482 RBC

82485 Chondroitin B sulfate, quantitative

(Chorionic gonadotropin, see gonadotropin, 84702, 84703)

82486 Chromatography, qualitative; column (eg, gas liquid or HPLC), analyte not elsewhere specified

82487 paper, 1-dimensional, analyte not elsewhere specified

82488 paper, 2-dimensional, analyte not elsewhere specified

82489 thin layer, analyte not elsewhere specified

82491 Chromatography, quantitative, column (eg, gas liquid or HPLC); single analyte not elsewhere specified, single stationary and mobile phase

82492 multiple analytes, single stationary and mobile phase

82495 Chromium

82507 Citrate

82520 Cocaine or metabolite

(Cocaine, qualitative analysis, see 80100-80103)

(Codeine, qualitative analysis, see 80100-80103)

(Codeine, quantitative analysis, see 82101)

(Complement, see 86160-86162)

82523 Collagen cross links, any method

82525 Copper

(Coproporphyrin, see 84119, 84120)

(Corticosteroids, use 83491)

82528 Corticosterone

82530 Cortisol; free

82533 total

(C-peptide, use 84681)

82540 Creatine

82541 Column chromatography/mass spectrometry (eg, GC/MS, or HPLC/MS), analyte not elsewhere specified; qualitative, single stationary and mobile phase

82542 quantitative, single stationary and mobile phase

82543 stable isotope dilution, single analyte, quantitative, single stationary and mobile phase

82544 stable isotope dilution, multiple analytes, quantitative, single stationary and mobile phase

82550 Creatine kinase (CK), (CPK); total

82552 isoenzymes

82553 MB fraction only

82554 isoforms

82565 Creatinine; blood

82570 other source

82575 clearance

82585 Cryofibrinogen

82595 Cryoglobulin, qualitative or semi-quantitative (eg, cryocrit)

(For quantitative, cryoglobulin, see 82784, 82785)

(Crystals, pyrophosphate vs. urate, use 89060)

82600 Cyanide

82607 Cyanocobalamin (Vitamin B-12);

82608 unsaturated binding capacity

(Cyclic AMP, use 82030)

(Cyclic GMP, use 83008)

(Cyclosporine, use 80158)

82615 Cystine and homocystine, urine, qualitative

82626 Dehydroepiandrosterone (DHEA)

82627 Dehydroepiandrosterone-sulfate (DHEA-S)

(Delta-aminolevulinic acid (ALA), use 82135)

82633 Desoxycorticosterone, 11-

82634 Deoxycortisol, 11-

(Dexamethasone suppression test, use 80420)

(Diastase, urine, use 82150)

82638 Dibucaine number

(Dichloroethane, use 84600)

(Dichloromethane, use 84600)

(Diethylether, use 84600)

82646 Dihydrocodeinone

(For qualitative analysis, see 80100-80103)

82649 Dihydromorphinone

(For qualitative analysis, see 80100-80103)

82651 Dihydrotestosterone (DHT)

82652 Dihydroxyvitamin D, 1,25-

82654 Dimethadione

(For qualitative analysis, see 80100-80103)

(Diphenylhydantoin, use 80185)

(Dipropylacetic acid, use 80164)

Pathology and Laboratory

(Dopamine, see 82382-82384)

(Duodenal contents, see individual enzymes; for intubation and collection, use 89100)

82656 Elastase, pancreatic (EL-1), fecal, qualitative or semi-quantitative

82657 Enzyme activity in blood cells, cultured cells, or tissue, not elsewhere specified; nonradioactive substrate, each specimen

82658 radioactive substrate, each specimen

82664 Electrophoretic technique, not elsewhere specified

(Endocrine receptor assays, see 84233-84235)

82666 Epiandrosterone

(Epinephrine, see 82382-82384)

82668 Erythropoietin

82670 Estradiol

82671 Estrogens; fractionated

82672 total

(Estrogen receptor assay, use 84233)

82677 Estriol

82679 Estrone

(Ethanol, see 82055 and 82075)

82690 Ethchlorvynol

(Ethyl alcohol, see 82055 and 82075)

82693 Ethylene glycol

82696 Etiocholanolone

(For fractionation of ketosteroids, use 83593)

82705 Fat or lipids, feces; qualitative

82710 quantitative

82715 Fat differential, feces, quantitative

82725 Fatty acids, nonesterified

82726 Very long chain fatty acids

(For long-chain (C20-22) omega-3 fatty acids in red blood cell (RBC) membranes, use Category III code 0111T)

82728 Ferritin

(Fetal hemoglobin, see hemoglobin 83030, 83033, and 85460)

(Fetoprotein, alpha-1, see 82105, 82106)

82731 Fetal fibronectin, cervicovaginal secretions, semi-quantitative

82735 Fluoride

82742 Flurazepam

(For qualitative analysis, see 80100-80103)

(Foam stability test, use 83662)

82746 Folic acid; serum

82747 RBC

(Follicle stimulating hormone (FSH), use 83001)

82757 Fructose, semen

(Fructosamine, use 82985)

(Fructose, TLC screen, use 84375)

82759 Galactokinase, RBC

82760 Galactose

82775 Galactose-1-phosphate uridyl transferase; quantitative

82776 screen

82784 Gammaglobulin; IgA, IgD, IgG, IgM, each

82785 IgE

(For allergen specific IgE, see 86003, 86005)

82787 immunoglobulin subclasses, (IgG1, 2, 3, or 4), each

(Gamma-glutamyltransferase (GGT), use 82977)

82800 Gases, blood, pH only

82803 Gases, blood, any combination of pH, pCO_2, pO_2, CO_2, HCO_3 (including calculated O_2 saturation);

(Use 82803 for two or more of the above listed analytes)

82805 with O_2 saturation, by direct measurement, except pulse oximetry

82810 Gases, blood, O_2 saturation only, by direct measurement, except pulse oximetry

(For pulse oximetry, use 94760)

82820 Hemoglobin-oxygen affinity (pO_2 for 50% hemoglobin saturation with oxygen)

82926 Gastric acid, free and total, each specimen

82928 Gastric acid, free or total, each specimen

82938 Gastrin after secretin stimulation

82941 Gastrin

(Gentamicin, use 80170)

(GGT, use 82977)

(GLC, gas liquid chromatography, use 82486)

82943 Glucagon

82945 Glucose, body fluid, other than blood

82946 Glucagon tolerance test

82947 Glucose; quantitative, blood (except reagent strip)

82948 blood, reagent strip

82950 post glucose dose (includes glucose)

82951 tolerance test (GTT), three specimens (includes glucose)

82952 tolerance test, each additional beyond three specimens

82953 tolbutamide tolerance test

(For insulin tolerance test, see 80434, 80435)

(For leucine tolerance test, use 80428)

(For semiquantitative urine glucose, see 81000, 81002, 81005, 81099)

82955 Glucose-6-phosphate dehydrogenase (G6PD); quantitative

82960 screen

▶(For glucose tolerance test with medication, use 90774 in addition)◀

82962 Glucose, blood by glucose monitoring device(s) cleared by the FDA specifically for home use

82963 Glucosidase, beta

82965 Glutamate dehydrogenase

82975 Glutamine (glutamic acid amide)

82977 Glutamyltransferase, gamma (GGT)

82978 Glutathione

82979 Glutathione reductase, RBC

82980 Glutethimide

(Glycohemoglobin, use 83036)

82985 Glycated protein

(Gonadotropin, chorionic, see 84702, 84703)

83001 Gonadotropin; follicle stimulating hormone (FSH)

83002 luteinizing hormone (LH)

(For luteinizing releasing factor (LRH), use 83727)

83003 Growth hormone, human (HGH) (somatotropin)

(For antibody to human growth hormone, use 86277)

83008 Guanosine monophosphate (GMP), cyclic

83009 Helicobacter pylori, blood test analysis for urease activity, non-radioactive isotope (eg, C-13)

(For H. pylori, breath test analysis for urease activity, see 83013, 83014)

83010 Haptoglobin; quantitative

83012 phenotypes

83013 Helicobacter pylori; breath test analysis for urease activity, non-radioactive isotope (eg, C-13)

83014 drug administration

(For H. pylori, stool, use 87338. For H. pylori, liquid scintillation counter, see 78267, 78268. For H. pylori, enzyme immunoassay, use 87339)

(For H. pylori, blood test analysis for urease activity, use 83009)

83015 Heavy metal (eg, arsenic, barium, beryllium, bismuth, antimony, mercury); screen

83018 quantitative, each

83020 Hemoglobin fractionation and quantitation; electrophoresis (eg, A2, S, C, and/or F)

83021 chromatography (eg, A2, S, C, and/or F)

83026 Hemoglobin; by copper sulfate method, non-automated

83030 F (fetal), chemical

83033 F (fetal), qualitative

83036 glycosylated (A1C)

(For fecal hemoglobin detection by immunoassay, use 82274)

83037 glycosylated (A1C) by device cleared by FDA for home use

83045 methemoglobin, qualitative

83050 methemoglobin, quantitative

83051 plasma

83055 sulfhemoglobin, qualitative

83060 sulfhemoglobin, quantitative

83065 thermolabile

83068 unstable, screen

83069 urine

83070 Hemosiderin; qualitative

83071 quantitative

(Heroin, see 80100-80103)

(HIAA, use 83497)

(High performance liquid chromatography (HPLC), use 82486)

83080 b-Hexosaminidase, each assay

83088 Histamine

(Hollander test, use 91052)

83090 Homocysteine

83150 Homovanillic acid (HVA)

(Hormones, see individual alphabetic listings in **Chemistry** section)

(Hydrogen breath test, use 91065)

83491 Hydroxycorticosteroids, 17- (17-OHCS)

(For cortisol, see 82530, 82533. For deoxycortisol, use 82634)

83497 Hydroxyindolacetic acid, 5-(HIAA)

(For urine qualitative test, use 81005)

(5-Hydroxytryptamine, use 84260)

83498 Hydroxyprogesterone, 17-d

Pathology and Laboratory

83499 Hydroxyprogesterone, 20-

83500 Hydroxyproline; free

83505 total

83516 Immunoassay for analyte other than infectious agent antibody or infectious agent antigen, qualitative or semiquantitative; multiple step method

83518 single step method (eg, reagent strip)

83519 Immunoassay, analyte, quantitative; by radiopharmaceutical technique (eg, RIA)

83520 not otherwise specified

(For immunoassays for antibodies to infectious agent antigens, see analyte and method specific codes in the **Immunology** section)

(For immunoassay of tumor antigen not elsewhere specified, use 86316)

(Immunoglobulins, see 82784, 82785)

83525 Insulin; total

(For proinsulin, use 84206)

83527 free

83528 Intrinsic factor

(For intrinsic factor antibodies, use 86340)

83540 Iron

83550 Iron binding capacity

83570 Isocitric dehydrogenase (IDH)

(Isonicotinic acid hydrazide, INH, see code for specific method)

(Isopropyl alcohol, use 84600)

83582 Ketogenic steroids, fractionation

(Ketone bodies, for serum, see 82009, 82010; for urine, see 81000-81003)

83586 Ketosteroids, 17- (17-KS); total

83593 fractionation

83605 Lactate (lactic acid)

83615 Lactate dehydrogenase (LD), (LDH);

83625 isoenzymes, separation and quantitation

83630 Lactoferrin, fecal; qualitative

83631 quantitative

83632 Lactogen, human placental (HPL) human chorionic somatomammotropin

83633 Lactose, urine; qualitative

83634 quantitative

(For tolerance, see 82951, 82952)

(For breath hydrogen test for lactase deficiency, use 91065)

83655 Lead

83661 Fetal lung maturity assessment; lecithin sphingomyelin (L/S) ratio

83662 foam stability test

83663 fluorescence polarization

83664 lamellar body density

(For phosphatidylglycerol, use 84081)

83670 Leucine aminopeptidase (LAP)

83690 Lipase

83695 Lipoprotein (a)

● 83698 Lipoprotein-associated phospholipase A_2, (Lp-PLA_2)

83700 Lipoprotein, blood; electrophoretic separation and quantitation

83701 high resolution fractionation and quantitation of lipoproteins including lipoprotein subclasses when performed (eg, electrophoresis, ultracentrifugation)

83704 quantitation of lipoprotein particle numbers and lipoprotein particle subclasses (eg, by nuclear magnetic resonance spectroscopy)

(83715, 83716 have been deleted. To report, use 83700, 83701)

83718 Lipoprotein, direct measurement; high density cholesterol (HDL cholesterol)

83719 VLDL cholesterol

83721 LDL cholesterol

(For fractionation by high resolution electrophoresis or ultracentrifugation, use 83701)

(For lipoprotein particle numbers and subclasses analysis by nuclear magnetic resonance spectroscopy, use 83704)

(To report direct measurement, intermediate density lipoproteins (remnant lipoproteins), use Category III code 0026T)

83727 Luteinizing releasing factor (LRH)

(Luteinizing hormone (LH), use 83002)

(For qualitative analysis, see 80100-80103)

(Macroglobulins, alpha-2, use 86329)

83735 Magnesium

83775 Malate dehydrogenase

(Maltose tolerance, see 82951, 82952)

(Mammotropin, use 84146)

83785 Manganese

(Marijuana, see 80100-80103)

83788 Mass spectrometry and tandem mass spectrometry (MS, MS/MS), analyte not elsewhere specified; qualitative, each specimen

83789 quantitative, each specimen

83805 Meprobamate

(For qualitative analysis, see 80100-80103)

83825 Mercury, quantitative

(Mercury screen, use 83015)

83835 Metanephrines

(For catecholamines, see 82382-82384)

83840 Methadone

(For methadone qualitative analysis, see 80100-80103)

(Methamphetamine, see 80100-80103, 82145)

(Methanol, use 84600)

83857 Methemalbumin

(Methemoglobin, see hemoglobin 83045, 83050)

83858 Methsuximide

(Methyl alcohol, use 84600)

(Microalbumin, see 82043 for quantitative, see 82044 for semiquantitative)

(Microglobulin, beta-2, use 82232)

83864 Mucopolysaccharides, acid; quantitative

83866 screen

83872 Mucin, synovial fluid (Ropes test)

83873 Myelin basic protein, cerebrospinal fluid

(For oligoclonal bands, use 83916)

83874 Myoglobin

(Nalorphine, use 83925)

83880 Natriuretic peptide

83883 Nephelometry, each analyte not elsewhere specified

83885 Nickel

83887 Nicotine

Codes 83890-83914 are intended for use with molecular diagnostic techniques for analysis of nucleic acids.

Codes 83890-83914 are coded by procedure rather than analyte.

Code separately for each procedure used in an analysis. For example, a procedure requiring isolation of DNA, restriction endonuclease digestion, electrophoresis, and nucleic acid probe amplification would be coded 83890, 83892, 83894, and 83898.

When molecular diagnostic procedures are performed to test for oncology, hematology, neurology or inherited disorder, use the appropriate modifier to specify probe type or condition tested. (See **Appendix I** for a listing of appropriate modifiers to report with molecular diagnostic and cytogenetic procedures.)

▶(For microbial identification, see 87470-87801)◀

(For array technology using more than 10 probes, see 88384-88386)

83890 Molecular diagnostics; molecular isolation or extraction

83891 isolation or extraction of highly purified nucleic acid

83892 enzymatic digestion

83893 dot/slot blot production

83894 separation by gel electrophoresis (eg, agarose, polyacrylamide)

83896 nucleic acid probe, each

83897 nucleic acid transfer (eg, Southern, Northern)

83898 amplification of patient nucleic acid, each nucleic acid sequence

83900 amplification of patient nucleic acid, multiplex, first two nucleic acid sequences

+ 83901 amplification of patient nucleic acid, multiplex, each additional nucleic acid sequence (List separately in addition to code for primary procedure)

(Use 83901 in conjunction with 83900)

83902 reverse transcription

83903 mutation scanning, by physical properties (eg, single strand conformational polymorphisms (SSCP), heteroduplex, denaturing gradient gel electrophoresis (DGGE), RNA'ase A), single segment, each

83904 mutation identification by sequencing, single segment, each segment

83905 mutation identification by allele specific transcription, single segment, each segment

83906 mutation identification by allele specific translation, single segment, each segment

83907 lysis of cells prior to nucleic acid extraction (eg, stool specimens, paraffin embedded tissue)

83908 signal amplification of patient nucleic acid, each nucleic acid sequence

(For multiplex amplification, see 83900, 83901)

83909 separation and identification by high resolution technique (eg, capillary electrophoresis)

83912 interpretation and report

● **83913** RNA stabilization

83914 Mutation identification by enzymatic ligation or primer extension, single segment, each segment (eg, oligonucleotide ligation assay (OLA), single base chain extension (SBCE), or allele-specific primer extension (ASPE))

83915 Nucleotidase 5'-

83916 Oligoclonal immune (oligoclonal bands)

Pathology and Laboratory

Pathology and Laboratory

83918	Organic acids; total, quantitative, each specimen
83919	qualitative, each specimen
83921	Organic acid, single, quantitative
83925	Opiates, (eg, morphine, meperidine)
83930	Osmolality; blood
83935	urine
83937	Osteocalcin (bone g1a protein)
83945	Oxalate
83950	Oncoprotein, HER-2/neu

(For tissue, see 88342, 88365)

83970	Parathormone (parathyroid hormone)

(Pesticide, quantitative, see code for specific method. For screen for chlorinated hydrocarbons, use 82441)

83986	pH, body fluid, except blood

(For blood pH, see 82800, 82803)

83992	Phencyclidine (PCP)

(For qualitative analysis, see 80100-80103)

(Phenobarbital, use 80184)

84022	Phenothiazine

(For qualitative analysis, see 80100, 80101)

84030	Phenylalanine (PKU), blood

(Phenylalanine-tyrosine ratio, see 84030, 84510)

84035	Phenylketones, qualitative
84060	Phosphatase, acid; total
84061	forensic examination
84066	prostatic
84075	Phosphatase, alkaline;
84078	heat stable (total not included)
84080	isoenzymes
84081	Phosphatidylglycerol

(Phosphates inorganic, use 84100)

(Phosphates, organic, see code for specific method. For cholinesterase, see 82480, 82482)

84085	Phosphogluconate, 6-, dehydrogenase, RBC
84087	Phosphohexose isomerase
84100	Phosphorus inorganic (phosphate);
84105	urine

(Pituitary gonadotropins, see 83001-83002)

(PKU, see 84030, 84035)

84106	Porphobilinogen, urine; qualitative
84110	quantitative
84119	Porphyrins, urine; qualitative
84120	quantitation and fractionation
84126	Porphyrins, feces; quantitative
84127	qualitative

(Porphyrin precursors, see 82135, 84106, 84110)

(For protoporphyrin, RBC, see 84202, 84203)

84132	Potassium; serum
84133	urine
84134	Prealbumin

(For microalbumin, see 82043, 82044)

84135	Pregnanediol
84138	Pregnanetriol
84140	Pregnenolone
84143	17-hydroxypregnenolone
84144	Progesterone

(Progesterone receptor assay, use 84234)

(For proinsulin, use 84206)

84146	Prolactin
84150	Prostaglandin, each
84152	Prostate specific antigen (PSA); complexed (direct measurement)
84153	total
84154	free
84155	Protein, total, except by refractometry; serum
84156	urine
84157	other source (eg, synovial fluid, cerebrospinal fluid)
84160	Protein, total, by refractometry, any source

(For urine total protein by dipstick method, use 81000-81003)

84163	Pregnancy-associated plasma protein-A (PAPP-A)
84165	Protein; electrophoretic fractionation and quantitation, serum
84166	electrophoretic fractionation and quantitation, other fluids with concentration (eg, urine, CSF)
84181	Western Blot, with interpretation and report, blood or other body fluid
84182	Western Blot, with interpretation and report, blood or other body fluid, immunological probe for band identification, each

(For Western Blot tissue analysis, use 88371)

84202	Protoporphyrin, RBC; quantitative
84203	screen
84206	Proinsulin

(Pseudocholinesterase, use 82480)

84207	Pyridoxal phosphate (Vitamin B-6)
84210	Pyruvate
84220	Pyruvate kinase
84228	Quinine
84233	Receptor assay; estrogen
84234	progesterone
84235	endocrine, other than estrogen or progesterone (specify hormone)
84238	non-endocrine (specify receptor)
84244	Renin
84252	Riboflavin (Vitamin B-2)
	(Salicylates, use 80196)
	(Secretin test, see 99070, 89100 and appropriate analyses)
84255	Selenium
84260	Serotonin
	(For urine metabolites (HIAA), use 83497)
84270	Sex hormone binding globulin (SHBG)
84275	Sialic acid
	(Sickle hemoglobin, use 85660)
84285	Silica
84295	Sodium; serum
84300	urine
84302	other source
	(Somatomammotropin, use 83632)
	(Somatotropin, use 83003)
84305	Somatomedin
84307	Somatostatin
84311	Spectrophotometry, analyte not elsewhere specified
84315	Specific gravity (except urine)
	(For specific gravity, urine, see 81000-81003)
	(Stone analysis, see 82355-82370)
84375	Sugars, chromatographic, TLC or paper chromatography
84376	Sugars (mono-, di-, and oligosaccharides); single qualitative, each specimen
84377	multiple qualitative, each specimen
84378	single quantitative, each specimen
84379	multiple quantitative, each specimen
84392	Sulfate, urine
	(Sulfhemoglobin, see hemoglobin, 83055, 83060)
	(T-3, see 84479-84481)
	(T-4, see 84436-84439)

84402	Testosterone; free
84403	total
84425	Thiamine (Vitamin B-1)
84430	Thiocyanate
84432	Thyroglobulin
	(Thyroglobulin, antibody, use 86800)
	(Thyrotropin releasing hormone (TRH) test, see 80438, 80439)
84436	Thyroxine; total
84437	requiring elution (eg, neonatal)
84439	free
84442	Thyroxine binding globulin (TBG)
84443	Thyroid stimulating hormone (TSH)
84445	Thyroid stimulating immune globulins (TSI)
	(Tobramycin, use 80200)
84446	Tocopherol alpha (Vitamin E)
	(Tolbutamide tolerance, use 82953)
84449	Transcortin (cortisol binding globulin)
84450	Transferase; aspartate amino (AST) (SGOT)
84460	alanine amino (ALT) (SGPT)
84466	Transferrin
	(Iron binding capacity, use 83550)
84478	Triglycerides
84479	Thyroid hormone (T3 or T4) uptake or thyroid hormone binding ratio (THBR)
84480	Triiodothyronine T3; total (TT-3)
84481	free
84482	reverse
84484	Troponin, quantitative
	(For troponin, qualitative assay, use 84512)
84485	Trypsin; duodenal fluid
84488	feces, qualitative
84490	feces, quantitative, 24-hour collection
84510	Tyrosine
	(Urate crystal identification, use 89060)
84512	Troponin, qualitative
	(For troponin, quantitative assay, use 84484)
84520	Urea nitrogen; quantitative
84525	semiquantitative (eg, reagent strip test)
84540	Urea nitrogen, urine
84545	Urea nitrogen, clearance

Pathology and Laboratory

Pathology and Laboratory

84550	Uric acid; blood
84560	other source
84577	Urobilinogen, feces, quantitative
84578	Urobilinogen, urine; qualitative
84580	quantitative, timed specimen
84583	semiquantitative

(Uroporphyrins, use 84120)

(Valproic acid (dipropylacetic acid), use 80164)

84585	Vanillylmandelic acid (VMA), urine
84586	Vasoactive intestinal peptide (VIP)
84588	Vasopressin (antidiuretic hormone, ADH)
84590	Vitamin A

(Vitamin B-1, use 84425)

(Vitamin B-2, use 84252)

(Vitamin B-6, use 84207)

(Vitamin B-12, use 82607)

(Vitamin B-12, absorption (Schilling), see 78270, 78271)

(Vitamin C, use 82180)

(Vitamin D, see 82306, 82307, 82652)

(Vitamin E, use 84446)

84591	Vitamin, not otherwise specified
84597	Vitamin K

(VMA, use 84585)

84600	Volatiles (eg, acetic anhydride, carbon tetrachloride, dichloroethane, dichloromethane, diethylether, isopropyl alcohol, methanol)

(For acetaldehyde, use 82000)

(Volume, blood, RISA or Cr-51, see 78110, 78111)

84620	Xylose absorption test, blood and/or urine

(For administration, use 99070)

84630	Zinc
84681	C-peptide
84702	Gonadotropin, chorionic (hCG); quantitative
84703	qualitative

(For urine pregnancy test by visual color comparison, use 81025)

84830	Ovulation tests, by visual color comparison methods for human luteinizing hormone
84999	Unlisted chemistry procedure

Hematology and Coagulation

(For blood banking procedures, see **Transfusion Medicine**)

(Agglutinins, see **Immunology**)

(Antiplasmin, use 85410)

(Antithrombin III, see 85300, 85301)

85002	Bleeding time
85004	Blood count; automated differential WBC count
85007	blood smear, microscopic examination with manual differential WBC count
85008	blood smear, microscopic examination without manual differential WBC count

(For other fluids (eg, CSF), see 89050, 89051)

85009	manual differential WBC count, buffy coat

(Eosinophils, nasal smear, use 89190)

85013	spun microhematocrit
85014	hematocrit (Hct)
85018	hemoglobin (Hgb)

(For other hemoglobin determination, see 83020-83069)

(For immunoassay, hemoglobin, fecal, use 82274)

85025	complete (CBC), automated (Hgb, Hct, RBC, WBC and platelet count) and automated differential WBC count
85027	complete (CBC), automated (Hgb, Hct, RBC, WBC and platelet count)
85032	manual cell count (erythrocyte, leukocyte, or platelet) each
85041	red blood cell (RBC), automated

(Do not report code 85041 in conjunction with 85025 or 85027)

85044	reticulocyte, manual
85045	reticulocyte, automated
85046	reticulocytes, automated, including one or more cellular parameters (eg, reticulocyte hemoglobin content (CHr), immature reticulocyte fraction (IRF), reticulocyte volume (MRV), RNA content), direct measurement
85048	leukocyte (WBC), automated
85049	platelet, automated
85055	Reticulated platelet assay
85060	Blood smear, peripheral, interpretation by physician with written report
85097	Bone marrow, smear interpretation

(For special stains, see 88312, 88313)

(For bone biopsy, see 20220, 20225, 20240, 20245, 20250, 20251)

85130	Chromogenic substrate assay
	(Circulating anti-coagulant screen (mixing studies), see 85611, 85732)
85170	Clot retraction
85175	Clot lysis time, whole blood dilution
	(Clotting factor I (fibrinogen), see 85384, 85385)
85210	Clotting; factor II, prothrombin, specific
	(See also 85610-85613)
85220	factor V (AcG or proaccelerin), labile factor
85230	factor VII (proconvertin, stable factor)
85240	factor VIII (AHG), one stage
85244	factor VIII related antigen
85245	factor VIII, VW factor, ristocetin cofactor
85246	factor VIII, VW factor antigen
85247	factor VIII, von Willebrand factor, multimetric analysis
85250	factor IX (PTC or Christmas)
85260	factor X (Stuart-Prower)
85270	factor XI (PTA)
85280	factor XII (Hageman)
85290	factor XIII (fibrin stabilizing)
85291	factor XIII (fibrin stabilizing), screen solubility
85292	prekallikrein assay (Fletcher factor assay)
85293	high molecular weight kininogen assay (Fitzgerald factor assay)
85300	Clotting inhibitors or anticoagulants; antithrombin III, activity
85301	antithrombin III, antigen assay
85302	protein C, antigen
85303	protein C, activity
85305	protein S, total
85306	protein S, free
85307	Activated Protein C (APC) resistance assay
85335	Factor inhibitor test
85337	Thrombomodulin
	(For mixing studies for inhibitors, use 85732)
85345	Coagulation time; Lee and White
85347	activated
85348	other methods
	(Differential count, see 85007 et seq)
	(Duke bleeding time, use 85002)
	(Eosinophils, nasal smear, use 89190)

85360	Euglobulin lysis
	(Fetal hemoglobin, see 83030, 83033, 85460)
85362	Fibrin(ogen) degradation (split) products (FDP)(FSP); agglutination slide, semiquantitative
	(Immunoelectrophoresis, use 86320)
85366	paracoagulation
85370	quantitative
85378	Fibrin degradation products, D-dimer; qualitative or semiquantitative
85379	quantitative
	(For ultrasensitive and standard sensitivity quantitative D-dimer, use 85379)
85380	ultrasensitive (eg, for evaluation for venous thromboembolism), qualitative or semiquantitative
85384	Fibrinogen; activity
85385	antigen
85390	Fibrinolysins or coagulopathy screen, interpretation and report
85396	Coagulation/fibrinolysis assay, whole blood (eg, viscoelastic clot assessment), including use of any pharmacologic additive(s), as indicated, including interpretation and written report, per day
85400	Fibrinolytic factors and inhibitors; plasmin
85410	alpha-2 antiplasmin
85415	plasminogen activator
85420	plasminogen, except antigenic assay
85421	plasminogen, antigenic assay
	(Fragility, red blood cell, see 85547, 85555-85557)
85441	Heinz bodies; direct
85445	induced, acetyl phenylhydrazine
	(Hematocrit (PCV), see 85014, 85025, 85027)
	(Hemoglobin, see 83020-83068, 85018, 85025, 85027)
85460	Hemoglobin or RBCs, fetal, for fetomaternal hemorrhage; differential lysis (Kleihauer-Betke)
	(See also 83030, 83033)
	(Hemolysins, see 86940, 86941)
85461	rosette
85475	Hemolysin, acid
	(See also 86940, 86941)
85520	Heparin assay
85525	Heparin neutralization
85530	Heparin-protamine tolerance test
85536	Iron stain, peripheral blood
	(For iron stains on bone marrow or other tissues with physician evaluation, use 88313)

85540 Leukocyte alkaline phosphatase with count

85547 Mechanical fragility, RBC

85549 Muramidase

(Nitroblue tetrazolium dye test, use 86384)

85555 Osmotic fragility, RBC; unincubated

85557 incubated

(Packed cell volume, use 85013)

(Partial thromboplastin time, see 85730, 85732)

(Parasites, blood (eg, malaria smears), use 87207)

(Plasmin, use 85400)

(Plasminogen, use 85420)

(Plasminogen activator, use 85415)

85576 Platelet, aggregation (in vitro), each agent

85597 Platelet neutralization

85610 Prothrombin time;

85611 substitution, plasma fractions, each

85612 Russell viper venom time (includes venom); undiluted

85613 diluted

(Red blood cell count, see 85025, 85027, 85041)

85635 Reptilase test

(Reticulocyte count, see 85044, 85045)

85651 Sedimentation rate, erythrocyte; non-automated

85652 automated

85660 Sickling of RBC, reduction

(Hemoglobin electrophoresis, use 83020)

(Smears (eg, for parasites, malaria), use 87207)

85670 Thrombin time; plasma

85675 titer

85705 Thromboplastin inhibition, tissue

(For individual clotting factors, see 85245-85247)

85730 Thromboplastin time, partial (PTT); plasma or whole blood

85732 substitution, plasma fractions, each

85810 Viscosity

(von Willebrand factor assay, see 85245-85247)

(WBC count, see 85025, 85027, 85048, 89050)

85999 Unlisted hematology and coagulation procedure

Immunology

(Acetylcholine receptor antibody, see 83519, 86255, 86256)

(Actinomyces, antibodies to, use 86602)

(Adrenal cortex antibodies, see 86255, 86256)

86000 Agglutinins, febrile (eg, Brucella, Francisella, Murine typhus, Q fever, Rocky Mountain spotted fever, scrub typhus), each antigen

(For antibodies to infectious agents, see 86602-86804)

86001 Allergen specific IgG quantitative or semiquantitative, each allergen

(Agglutinins and autohemolysins, see 86940, 86941)

86003 Allergen specific IgE; quantitative or semiquantitative, each allergen

(For total quantitative IgE, use 82785)

86005 qualitative, multiallergen screen (dipstick, paddle or disk)

(For total qualitative IgE, use 83518)

(Alpha-1 antitrypsin, see 82103, 82104)

(Alpha-1 feto-protein, see 82105, 82106)

(Anti-AChR (acetylcholine receptor) antibody titer, see 86255, 86256)

(Anticardiolipin antibody, use 86147)

(Anti-DNA, use 86225)

(Anti-deoxyribonuclease titer, use 86215)

86021 Antibody identification; leukocyte antibodies

86022 platelet antibodies

86023 platelet associated immunoglobulin assay

86038 Antinuclear antibodies (ANA);

86039 titer

(Antistreptococcal antibody, ie, anti-DNAse, use 86215)

(Antistreptokinase titer, use 86590)

86060 Antistreptolysin O; titer

(For antibodies to infectious agents, see 86602-86804)

86063 screen

(For antibodies to infectious agents, see 86602-86804)

(Blastomyces, antibodies to, use 86612)

(86064 has been deleted. For B cells, total count, use 86355)

Pathology and Laboratory

86077 Blood bank physician services; difficult cross match and/or evaluation of irregular antibody(s), interpretation and written report

86078 investigation of transfusion reaction including suspicion of transmissible disease, interpretation and written report

86079 authorization for deviation from standard blood banking procedures (eg, use of outdated blood, transfusion of Rh incompatible units), with written report

(Brucella, antibodies to, use 86622)

(Candida, antibodies to, use 86628. For skin testing, use 86485)

86140 C-reactive protein;

(Candidiasis, use 86628)

86141 high sensitivity (hsCRP)

86146 Beta 2 Glycoprotein I antibody, each

86147 Cardiolipin (phospholipid) antibody, each Ig class

86148 Anti-phosphatidylserine (phospholipid) antibody

(To report antiprothrombin (phospholipid cofactor) antibody, use Category III code 0030T)

86155 Chemotaxis assay, specify method

(Clostridium difficile toxin, use 87230)

(Coccidioides, antibodies to, see 86635. For skin testing, use 86490)

86156 Cold agglutinin; screen

86157 titer

86160 Complement; antigen, each component

86161 functional activity, each component

86162 total hemolytic (CH50)

86171 Complement fixation tests, each antigen

(Coombs test, see 86880-86886)

86185 Counterimmunoelectrophoresis, each antigen

(Cryptococcus, antibodies to, use 86641)

86200 Cyclic citrullinated peptide (CCP), antibody

86215 Deoxyribonuclease, antibody

86225 Deoxyribonucleic acid (DNA) antibody; native or double stranded

(Echinococcus, antibodies to, see code for specific method)

(For HIV antibody tests, see 86701-86703)

86226 single stranded

(Anti D.S., DNA, IFA, eg, using C.Lucilae, see 86255 and 86256)

86235 Extractable nuclear antigen, antibody to, any method (eg, nRNP, SS-A, SS-B, Sm, RNP, Sc170, J01), each antibody

86243 Fc receptor

(Filaria, antibodies to, see code for specific method)

86255 Fluorescent noninfectious agent antibody; screen, each antibody

86256 titer, each antibody

(Fluorescent technique for antigen identification in tissue, use 88346; for indirect fluorescence, use 88347)

(FTA, see 86781)

(Gel (agar) diffusion tests, use 86331)

86277 Growth hormone, human (HGH), antibody

86280 Hemagglutination inhibition test (HAI)

(For rubella, use 86762)

(For antibodies to infectious agents, see 86602-86804)

86294 Immunoassay for tumor antigen, qualitative or semiquantitative (eg, bladder tumor antigen)

86300 Immunoassay for tumor antigen, quantitative; CA 15-3 (27.29)

86301 CA 19-9

86304 CA 125

(For measurement of serum HER-2/neu oncoprotein, see 83950)

(For hepatitis delta agent, antibody, use 86692)

86308 Heterophile antibodies; screening

(For antibodies to infectious agents, see 86602-86804)

86309 titer

(For antibodies to infectious agents, see 86602-86804)

86310 titers after absorption with beef cells and guinea pig kidney

(Histoplasma, antibodies to, use 86698. For skin testing, use 86510)

(For antibodies to infectious agents, see 86602-86804)

(Human growth hormone antibody, use 86277)

86316 Immunoassay for tumor antigen, other antigen, quantitative (eg, CA 50, 72-4, 549), each

86317 Immunoassay for infectious agent antibody, quantitative, not otherwise specified

(For immunoassay techniques for antigens, see 83516, 83518, 83519, 83520, 87301-87450, 87810-87899)

(For particle agglutination procedures, use 86403)

86318 Immunoassay for infectious agent antibody, qualitative or semiquantitative, single step method (eg, reagent strip)

Pathology and Laboratory

Pathology and Laboratory

86320	Immunoelectrophoresis; serum
86325	other fluids (eg, urine, cerebrospinal fluid) with concentration
86327	crossed (2-dimensional assay)
86329	Immunodiffusion; not elsewhere specified
86331	gel diffusion, qualitative (Ouchterlony), each antigen or antibody
86332	Immune complex assay
86334	Immunofixation electrophoresis; serum
86335	other fluids with concentration (eg, urine, CSF)
86336	Inhibin A
86337	Insulin antibodies
86340	Intrinsic factor antibodies

(Leptospira, antibodies to, use 86720)

(Leukoagglutinins, use 86021)

86341	Islet cell antibody
86343	Leukocyte histamine release test (LHR)
86344	Leukocyte phagocytosis
86353	Lymphocyte transformation, mitogen (phytomitogen) or antigen induced blastogenesis

(Malaria antibodies, use 86750)

86355	B cells, total count
86357	Natural killer (NK) cells, total count
86359	T cells; total count
86360	absolute CD4 and CD8 count, including ratio
86361	absolute CD4 count
86367	Stem cells (ie, CD34), total count

(For flow cytometric immunophenotyping for the assessment of potential hematolymphoid neoplasia, see 88184-88189)

86376	Microsomal antibodies (eg, thyroid or liver-kidney), each
86378	Migration inhibitory factor test (MIF)

(Mitochondrial antibody, liver, see 86255, 86256)

(Mononucleosis, see 86308-86310)

(86379 has been deleted. For natural killer cells, total count, use 86357)

86382	Neutralization test, viral
86384	Nitroblue tetrazolium dye test (NTD)

(Ouchterlony diffusion, use 86331)

(Platelet antibodies, see 86022, 86023)

86403	Particle agglutination; screen, each antibody
86406	titer, each antibody

(Pregnancy test, see 84702, 84703)

(Rapid plasma reagin test (RPR), see 86592, 86593)

86430	Rheumatoid factor; qualitative
86431	quantitative

(Serologic test for syphilis, see 86592, 86593)

86480	Tuberculosis test, cell mediated immunity measurement of gamma interferon antigen response
86485	Skin test; candida

(For antibody, candida, use 86628)

86490	coccidioidomycosis
86510	histoplasmosis

(For histoplasma, antibody, use 86698)

86580	tuberculosis, intradermal

(For tuberculosis test, cell mediated immunity measurement of gamma interferon antigen response, use 86480)

(86585 has been deleted. To report tuberculosis testing by intradermal (Mantoux) test, use 86580)

(For skin tests for allergy, see 95010-95199)

(Smooth muscle antibody, see 86255, 86256)

(Sporothrix, antibodies to, see code for specific method)

86586	Unlisted antigen, each

(86587 has been deleted. For stem cells, total count, use 86367)

86590	Streptokinase, antibody

(For antibodies to infectious agents, see 86602-86804)

(Streptolysin O antibody, see antistreptolysin O, 86060, 86063)

86592	Syphilis test; qualitative (eg, VDRL, RPR, ART)

(For antibodies to infectious agents, see 86602-86804)

86593	quantitative

(For antibodies to infectious agents, see 86602-86804)

(Tetanus antibody, use 86774)

(Thyroglobulin antibody, use 86800)

(Thyroglobulin, use 84432)

(Thyroid microsomal antibody, use 86376)

(For toxoplasma antibody, see 86777-86778)

▶The following codes (86602-86804) are qualitative or semiquantitative immunoassays performed by multiple-step methods for the detection of antibodies to infectious agents. For immunoassays by single-step method (eg, reagent strips), use code 86318. Procedures for the identification of antibodies should be coded as precisely as possible. For example, an antibody to a virus could be coded with increasing specificity for virus, family, genus, species, or type. In some cases, further precision may be added to codes by specifying the class of immunoglobulin being detected. When multiple tests are done to detect antibodies to organisms classified more precisely than the

specificity allowed by available codes, it is appropriate to code each as a separate service. For example, a test for antibody to an enterovirus is coded as 86658. Coxsackie viruses are enteroviruses, but there are no codes for the individual species of enterovirus. If assays are performed for antibodies to coxsackie A and B species, each assay should be separately coded. Similarly, if multiple assays are performed for antibodies of different immunoglobulin classes, each assay should be coded separately. When a coding option exists for reporting IgM specific antibodies (eg, 86632), the corresponding nonspecific code (eg, 86631) may be reported for performance of either an antibody analysis not specific for a particular immunoglobulin class or for an IgG analysis.◄

(For the detection of antibodies other than those to infectious agents, see specific antibody [eg, 86021-86023, 86376, 86800, 86850-86870] or specific method [eg, 83516, 86255, 86256]).

(For infectious agent/antigen detection, see 87260-87899)

Code	Description
86602	Antibody; actinomyces
86603	adenovirus
86606	Aspergillus
86609	bacterium, not elsewhere specified
86611	Bartonella
86612	Blastomyces
86615	Bordetella
86617	Borrelia burgdorferi (Lyme disease) confirmatory test (eg, Western Blot or immunoblot)
86618	Borrelia burgdorferi (Lyme disease)
86619	Borrelia (relapsing fever)
86622	Brucella
86625	Campylobacter
86628	Candida

(For skin test, candida, use 86485)

Code	Description
86631	Chlamydia
86632	Chlamydia, IgM

(For chlamydia antigen, see 87270, 87320. For fluorescent antibody technique, see 86255, 86256)

Code	Description
86635	Coccidioides
86638	Coxiella burnetii (Q fever)
86641	Cryptococcus
86644	cytomegalovirus (CMV)
86645	cytomegalovirus (CMV), IgM
86648	Diphtheria
86651	encephalitis, California (La Crosse)

Code	Description
86652	encephalitis, Eastern equine
86653	encephalitis, St. Louis
86654	encephalitis, Western equine
86658	enterovirus (eg, coxsackie, echo, polio)

(Trichinella, antibodies to, use 86784)

(Trypanosoma, antibodies to, see code for specific method)

(Tuberculosis, use 86580 for skin testing)

(Viral antibodies, see code for specific method)

Code	Description
86663	Epstein-Barr (EB) virus, early antigen (EA)
86664	Epstein-Barr (EB) virus, nuclear antigen (EBNA)
86665	Epstein-Barr (EB) virus, viral capsid (VCA)
86666	Ehrlichia
86668	Francisella tularensis
86671	fungus, not elsewhere specified
86674	Giardia lamblia
86677	Helicobacter pylori
86682	helminth, not elsewhere specified
86684	Haemophilus influenza
86687	HTLV-I
86688	HTLV-II
86689	HTLV or HIV antibody, confirmatory test (eg, Western Blot)
86692	hepatitis, delta agent

(For hepatitis delta agent, antigen, use 87380)

Code	Description
86694	herpes simplex, non-specific type test
86695	herpes simplex, type 1
86696	herpes simplex, type 2
86698	histoplasma
86701	HIV-1
86702	HIV-2
86703	HIV-1 and HIV-2, single assay

(For HIV-1 antigen, use 87390)

(For HIV-2 antigen, use 87391)

(For confirmatory test for HIV antibody (eg, Western Blot), use 86689)

Code	Description
86704	Hepatitis B core antibody (HBcAb); total
86705	IgM antibody
86706	Hepatitis B surface antibody (HBsAb)
86707	Hepatitis Be antibody (HBeAb)
86708	Hepatitis A antibody (HAAb); total
86709	IgM antibody

Pathology and Laboratory

86710	Antibody; influenza virus
86713	Legionella
86717	Leishmania
86720	Leptospira
86723	Listeria monocytogenes
86727	lymphocytic choriomeningitis
86729	lymphogranuloma venereum
86732	mucormycosis
86735	mumps
86738	mycoplasma
86741	Neisseria meningitidis
86744	Nocardia
86747	parvovirus
86750	Plasmodium (malaria)
86753	protozoa, not elsewhere specified
86756	respiratory syncytial virus
86757	Rickettsia
86759	rotavirus
86762	rubella
86765	rubeola
86768	Salmonella
86771	Shigella
86774	tetanus
86777	Toxoplasma
86778	Toxoplasma, IgM
86781	Treponema pallidum, confirmatory test (eg, FTA-abs)
86784	Trichinella
86787	varicella-zoster
● 86788	West Nile virus, IgM
● 86789	West Nile virus
86790	virus, not elsewhere specified
86793	Yersinia
86800	Thyroglobulin antibody
	(For thyroglobulin, use 84432)
86803	Hepatitis C antibody;
86804	confirmatory test (eg, immunoblot)

Tissue Typing

(For pretransplant cross-match, see appropriate code or codes)

86805	Lymphocytotoxicity assay, visual crossmatch; with titration
86806	without titration

86807	Serum screening for cytotoxic percent reactive antibody (PRA); standard method
86808	quick method
86812	HLA typing; A, B, or C (eg, A10, B7, B27), single antigen
86813	A, B, or C, multiple antigens
86816	DR/DQ, single antigen
86817	DR/DQ, multiple antigens
86821	lymphocyte culture, mixed (MLC)
86822	lymphocyte culture, primed (PLC)
86849	Unlisted immunology procedure

Transfusion Medicine

(For apheresis, use 36511, 36512)

(For therapeutic phlebotomy, use 99195)

86850	Antibody screen, RBC, each serum technique
86860	Antibody elution (RBC), each elution
86870	Antibody identification, RBC antibodies, each panel for each serum technique
86880	Antihuman globulin test (Coombs test); direct, each antiserum
86885	indirect, qualitative, each antiserum
86886	indirect, titer, each antiserum
86890	Autologous blood or component, collection processing and storage; predeposited
86891	intra- or postoperative salvage
	(For physician services to autologous donors, see 99201-99204)
86900	Blood typing; ABO
86901	Rh (D)
86903	antigen screening for compatible blood unit using reagent serum, per unit screened
86904	antigen screening for compatible unit using patient serum, per unit screened
86905	RBC antigens, other than ABO or Rh (D), each
86906	Rh phenotyping, complete
86910	Blood typing, for paternity testing, per individual; ABO, Rh and MN
86911	each additional antigen system
86920	Compatibility test each unit; immediate spin technique
86921	incubation technique
86922	antiglobulin technique
86923	electronic
	(Do not use 86923 in conjunction with 86920-86922 for same unit crossmatch)

86927	Fresh frozen plasma, thawing, each unit
86930	Frozen blood, each unit; freezing (includes preparation)
86931	thawing
86932	freezing (includes preparation) and thawing
86940	Hemolysins and agglutinins; auto, screen, each
86941	incubated
86945	Irradiation of blood product, each unit
86950	Leukocyte transfusion

(For leukapheresis, use 36511)

86960	Volume reduction of blood or blood product (eg, red blood cells or platelets), each unit
86965	Pooling of platelets or other blood products
86970	Pretreatment of RBCs for use in RBC antibody detection, identification, and/or compatibility testing; incubation with chemical agents or drugs, each
86971	incubation with enzymes, each
86972	by density gradient separation
86975	Pretreatment of serum for use in RBC antibody identification; incubation with drugs, each
86976	by dilution
86977	incubation with inhibitors, each
86978	by differential red cell absorption using patient RBCs or RBCs of known phenotype, each absorption
86985	Splitting of blood or blood products, each unit
86999	Unlisted transfusion medicine procedure

Microbiology

Includes bacteriology, mycology, parasitology, and virology.

Presumptive identification of microorganisms is defined as identification by colony morphology, growth on selective media, Gram stains, or up to three tests (eg, catalase, oxidase, indole, urease). Definitive identification of microorganisms is defined as an identification to the genus or species level that requires additional tests (eg, biochemical panels, slide cultures). If additional studies involve molecular probes, chromatography, or immunologic techniques, these should be separately coded in addition to definitive identification codes (87140-87158). For multiple specimens/sites use modifier 59. For repeat laboratory tests performed on the same day, use modifier 91.

87001	Animal inoculation, small animal; with observation
87003	with observation and dissection
87015	Concentration (any type), for infectious agents

(Do not report 87015 in conjunction with 87177)

87040	Culture, bacterial; blood, aerobic, with isolation and presumptive identification of isolates (includes anaerobic culture, if appropriate)
87045	stool, aerobic, with isolation and preliminary examination (eg, KIA, LIA), Salmonella and Shigella species
87046	stool, aerobic, additional pathogens, isolation and presumptive identification of isolates, each plate
87070	any other source except urine, blood or stool, aerobic, with isolation and presumptive identification of isolates

(For urine, use 87088)

87071	quantitative, aerobic with isolation and presumptive identification of isolates, any source except urine, blood or stool

(For urine, use 87088)

87073	quantitative, anaerobic with isolation and presumptive identification of isolates, any source except urine, blood or stool

(For definitive identification of isolates, use 87076 or 87077. For typing of isolates see 87140-87158)

87075	any source, except blood, anaerobic with isolation and presumptive identification of isolates
87076	anaerobic isolate, additional methods required for definitive identification, each isolate

(For gas liquid chromatography (GLC) or high pressure liquid chromatography (HPLC), use 87143)

87077	aerobic isolate, additional methods required for definitive identification, each isolate

(For gas liquid chromatography (GLC) or high pressure liquid chromatography (HPLC), use 87143)

87081	Culture, presumptive, pathogenic organisms, screening only;
87084	with colony estimation from density chart
87086	Culture, bacterial; quantitative colony count, urine
▲ 87088	with isolation and presumptive identification of each isolate, urine
87101	Culture, fungi (mold or yeast) isolation, with presumptive identification of isolates; skin, hair, or nail
87102	other source (except blood)
87103	blood
87106	Culture, fungi, definitive identification, each organism; yeast

(Use 87106 in addition to codes 87101, 87102, or 87103 when appropriate)

87107	mold
87109	Culture, mycoplasma, any source

▲=Revised code ●=New code ▶ ◀=Contains new or revised text ⊘=Modifier 51 exempt

Pathology and Laboratory

87110 Culture, chlamydia, any source

(For immunofluorescence staining of shell vials, use 87140)

87116 Culture, tubercle or other acid-fast bacilli (eg, TB, AFB, mycobacteria) any source, with isolation and presumptive identification of isolates

(For concentration, use 87015)

87118 Culture, mycobacterial, definitive identification, each isolate

(For nucleic acid probe identification, use 87149)

(For GLC or HPLC identification, use 87143)

87140 Culture, typing; immunofluorescent method, each antiserum

87143 gas liquid chromatography (GLC) or high pressure liquid chromatography (HPLC) method

87147 immunologic method, other than immunofluoresence (eg, agglutination grouping), per antiserum

87149 identification by nucleic acid probe

87152 identification by pulse field gel typing

87158 other methods

87164 Dark field examination, any source (eg, penile, vaginal, oral, skin); includes specimen collection

87166 without collection

87168 Macroscopic examination; arthropod

87169 parasite

87172 Pinworm exam (eg, cellophane tape prep)

87176 Homogenization, tissue, for culture

87177 Ova and parasites, direct smears, concentration and identification

(Do not report 87177 in conjunction with 87015)

(For direct smears from a primary source, use 87207)

(For coccidia or microsporidia exam, use 87207)

(For complex special stain (trichrome, iron hematoxylin), use 87209)

(For nucleic acid probes in cytologic material, use 88365)

(For molecular diagnostics, see 83890-83898, 87470-87799)

87181 Susceptibility studies, antimicrobial agent; agar dilution method, per agent (eg, antibiotic gradient strip)

87184 disk method, per plate (12 or fewer agents)

87185 enzyme detection (eg, beta lactamase), per enzyme

87186 microdilution or agar dilution (minimum inhibitory concentration (MIC) or breakpoint), each multi-antimicrobial, per plate

+ 87187 microdilution or agar dilution, minimum lethal concentration (MLC), each plate (List separately in addition to code for primary procedure)

(Use 87187 in conjunction with 87186 or 87188)

87188 macrobroth dilution method, each agent

87190 mycobacteria, proportion method, each agent

(For other mycobacterial susceptibility studies, see 87181, 87184, 87186, or 87188)

87197 Serum bactericidal titer (Schlicter test)

87205 Smear, primary source with interpretation; Gram or Giemsa stain for bacteria, fungi, or cell types

87206 fluorescent and/or acid fast stain for bacteria, fungi, parasites, viruses or cell types

87207 special stain for inclusion bodies or parasites (eg, malaria, coccidia, microsporidia, trypanosomes, herpes viruses)

(For direct smears with concentration and identification, use 87177)

(For thick smear preparation, use 87015)

(For fat, meat, fibers, nasal eosinophils, and starch, see miscellaneous section)

87209 complex special stain (eg, trichrome, iron hemotoxylin) for ova and parasites

87210 wet mount for infectious agents (eg, saline, India ink, KOH preps)

(For KOH examination of skin, hair or nails, see 87220)

87220 Tissue examination by KOH slide of samples from skin, hair, or nails for fungi or ectoparasite ova or mites (eg, scabies)

87230 Toxin or antitoxin assay, tissue culture (eg, Clostridium difficile toxin)

87250 Virus isolation; inoculation of embryonated eggs, or small animal, includes observation and dissection

87252 tissue culture inoculation, observation, and presumptive identification by cytopathic effect

87253 tissue culture, additional studies or definitive identification (eg, hemabsorption, neutralization, immunofluoresence stain), each isolate

(Electron microscopy, use 88348)

(Inclusion bodies in tissue sections, see 88304-88309; in smears, see 87207-87210; in fluids, use 88106)

87254 centrifuge enhanced (shell vial) technique, includes identification with immunofluorescence stain, each virus

(Report 87254 in addition to 87252 as appropriate)

87255 including identification by non-immunologic method, other than by cytopathic effect (eg, virus specific enzymatic activity)

These codes are intended for primary source only. For similar studies on culture material, refer to codes 87140-87158. Infectious agents by antigen detection, immunofluorescence microscopy, or nucleic acid probe techniques should be reported as precisely as possible. The most specific code possible should be reported. If there is no specific agent code, the general methodology code (eg, 87299, 87449, 87450, 87797, 87798, 87799, 87899) should be used. For identification of antibodies to many of the listed infectious agents, see 86602-86804. When separate assays are performed for different species or strain(s) of organisms, each assay should be reported separately.

87260 Infectious agent antigen detection by immunofluorescent technique; adenovirus

87265 Bordetella pertussis/parapertussis

87267 Enterovirus, direct fluorescent antibody (DFA)

87269 giardia

87270 Chlamydia trachomatis

87271 Cytomegalovirus, direct fluorescent antibody (DFA)

87272 cryptosporidium

87273 Herpes simplex virus type 2

87274 Herpes simplex virus type 1

87275 influenza B virus

87276 influenza A virus

87277 Legionella micdadei

87278 Legionella pneumophila

87279 Parainfluenza virus, each type

87280 respiratory syncytial virus

87281 Pneumocystis carinii

87283 Rubeola

87285 Treponema pallidum

87290 Varicella zoster virus

87299 not otherwise specified, each organism

87300 Infectious agent antigen detection by immunofluorescent technique, polyvalent for multiple organisms, each polyvalent antiserum

(For physician evaluation of infectious disease agents by immunofluorescence, use 88346)

87301 Infectious agent antigen detection by enzyme immunoassay technique, qualitative or semiquantitative, multiple-step method; adenovirus enteric types 40/41

● **87305** Aspergillus

87320 Chlamydia trachomatis

87324 Clostridium difficile toxin(s)

87327 Cryptococcus neoformans

(For Cryptococcus latex agglutination, use 86403)

87328 cryptosporidium

87329 giardia

87332 cytomegalovirus

87335 Escherichia coli 0157

(For giardia antigen, use 87329)

87336 Entamoeba histolytica dispar group

87337 Entamoeba histolytica group

87338 Helicobacter pylori, stool

87339 Helicobacter pylori

(For H. pylori, stool, use 87338. For H. pylori, breath and blood by mass spectrometry, see 83013, 83014. For H. pylori, liquid scintillation counter, see 78267, 78268)

87340 hepatitis B surface antigen (HBsAg)

87341 hepatitis B surface antigen (HBsAg) neutralization

87350 hepatitis Be antigen (HBeAg)

87380 hepatitis, delta agent

87385 Histoplasma capsulatum

87390 HIV-1

87391 HIV-2

87400 Influenza, A or B, each

87420 respiratory syncytial virus

87425 rotavirus

87427 Shiga-like toxin

87430 Streptococcus, group A

87449 Infectious agent antigen detection by enzyme immunoassay technique qualitative or semiquantitative; multiple step method, not otherwise specified, each organism

87450 single step method, not otherwise specified, each organism

87451 multiple step method, polyvalent for multiple organisms, each polyvalent antiserum

87470 Infectious agent detection by nucleic acid (DNA or RNA); Bartonella henselae and Bartonella quintana, direct probe technique

87471 Bartonella henselae and Bartonella quintana, amplified probe technique

87472 Bartonella henselae and Bartonella quintana, quantification

87475 Borrelia burgdorferi, direct probe technique

87476 Borrelia burgdorferi, amplified probe technique

87477 Borrelia burgdorferi, quantification

87480 Candida species, direct probe technique

87481 Candida species, amplified probe technique

87482 Candida species, quantification

87485	Chlamydia pneumoniae, direct probe technique
87486	Chlamydia pneumoniae, amplified probe technique
87487	Chlamydia pneumoniae, quantification
87490	Chlamydia trachomatis, direct probe technique
87491	Chlamydia trachomatis, amplified probe technique
87492	Chlamydia trachomatis, quantification
87495	cytomegalovirus, direct probe technique
87496	cytomegalovirus, amplified probe technique
87497	cytomegalovirus, quantification
● 87498	enterovirus, amplified probe technique
87510	Gardnerella vaginalis, direct probe technique
87511	Gardnerella vaginalis, amplified probe technique
87512	Gardnerella vaginalis, quantification
87515	hepatitis B virus, direct probe technique
87516	hepatitis B virus, amplified probe technique
87517	hepatitis B virus, quantification
87520	hepatitis C, direct probe technique
87521	hepatitis C, amplified probe technique
87522	hepatitis C, quantification
87525	hepatitis G, direct probe technique
87526	hepatitis G, amplified probe technique
87527	hepatitis G, quantification
87528	Herpes simplex virus, direct probe technique
87529	Herpes simplex virus, amplified probe technique
87530	Herpes simplex virus, quantification
87531	Herpes virus-6, direct probe technique
87532	Herpes virus-6, amplified probe technique
87533	Herpes virus-6, quantification
87534	HIV-1, direct probe technique
87535	HIV-1, amplified probe technique
87536	HIV-1, quantification
87537	HIV-2, direct probe technique
87538	HIV-2, amplified probe technique
87539	HIV-2, quantification
87540	Legionella pneumophila, direct probe technique
87541	Legionella pneumophila, amplified probe technique
87542	Legionella pneumophila, quantification
87550	Mycobacteria species, direct probe technique
87551	Mycobacteria species, amplified probe technique
87552	Mycobacteria species, quantification
87555	Mycobacteria tuberculosis, direct probe technique

87556	Mycobacteria tuberculosis, amplified probe technique
87557	Mycobacteria tuberculosis, quantification
87560	Mycobacteria avium-intracellulare, direct probe technique
87561	Mycobacteria avium-intracellulare, amplified probe technique
87562	Mycobacteria avium-intracellulare, quantification
87580	Mycoplasma pneumoniae, direct probe technique
87581	Mycoplasma pneumoniae, amplified probe technique
87582	Mycoplasma pneumoniae, quantification
87590	Neisseria gonorrhoeae, direct probe technique
87591	Neisseria gonorrhoeae, amplified probe technique
87592	Neisseria gonorrhoeae, quantification
87620	papillomavirus, human, direct probe technique
87621	papillomavirus, human, amplified probe technique
87622	papillomavirus, human, quantification
● 87640	Staphylococcus aureus, amplified probe technique
● 87641	Staphylococcus aureus, methicillin resistant, amplified probe technique

▶(For assays that detect methicillin resistance and identify Staphylococcus aureus using a single nucleic acid sequence, use 87641)◀

87650	Streptococcus, group A, direct probe technique
87651	Streptococcus, group A, amplified probe technique
87652	Streptococcus, group A, quantification
● 87653	Streptococcus, group B, amplified probe technique
87660	Trichomonas vaginalis, direct probe technique
87797	Infectious agent detection by nucleic acid (DNA or RNA), not otherwise specified; direct probe technique, each organism
87798	amplified probe technique, each organism
87799	quantification, each organism
87800	Infectious agent detection by nucleic acid (DNA or RNA), multiple organisms; direct probe(s) technique
87801	amplified probe(s) technique

▶(For each specific organism nucleic acid detection from a primary source, see 87470-87660. For detection of specific infectious agents not otherwise specified, see 87797, 87798, or 87799 one time for each agent)◀

87802	Infectious agent antigen detection by immunoassay with direct optical observation; Streptococcus, group B
87803	Clostridium difficile toxin A
87804	Influenza
87807	respiratory syncytial virus
● 87808	Trichomonas vaginalis

87810 Infectious agent detection by immunoassay with direct optical observation; Chlamydia trachomatis

87850 Neisseria gonorrhoeae

87880 Streptococcus, group A

87899 not otherwise specified

87900 Infectious agent drug susceptibility phenotype prediction using regularly updated genotypic bioinformatics

87901 Infectious agent genotype analysis by nucleic acid (DNA or RNA); HIV 1, reverse transcriptase and protease

(For infectious agent drug susceptibility phenotype prediction for HIV-1, use 87900)

87902 Hepatitis C virus

87903 Infectious agent phenotype analysis by nucleic acid (DNA or RNA) with drug resistance tissue culture analysis, HIV 1; first through 10 drugs tested

+ 87904 each additional drug tested (List separately in addition to code for primary procedure)

(Use 87904 in conjunction with 87903)

87999 Unlisted microbiology procedure

Anatomic Pathology

Postmortem Examination

Procedures 88000 through 88099 represent physician services only. Use modifier 90 for outside laboratory services.

88000 Necropsy (autopsy), gross examination only; without CNS

88005 with brain

88007 with brain and spinal cord

88012 infant with brain

88014 stillborn or newborn with brain

88016 macerated stillborn

88020 Necropsy (autopsy), gross and microscopic; without CNS

88025 with brain

88027 with brain and spinal cord

88028 infant with brain

88029 stillborn or newborn with brain

88036 Necropsy (autopsy), limited, gross and/or microscopic; regional

88037 single organ

88040 Necropsy (autopsy); forensic examination

88045 coroner's call

88099 Unlisted necropsy (autopsy) procedure

Cytopathology

(For cervicography, see Category III code 0003T)

(For collection of cytology specimens via mammary duct catheter lavage, report 0046T-0047T)

88104 Cytopathology, fluids, washings or brushings, except cervical or vaginal; smears with interpretation

▲ **88106** simple filter method with interpretation

▲ **88107** smears and simple filter preparation with interpretation

▶(For nongynecological selective cellular enhancement including filter transfer techniques, use 88112)◀

88108 Cytopathology, concentration technique, smears and interpretation (eg, Saccomanno technique)

(For cervical or vaginal smears, see 88150-88155)

(For gastric intubation with lavage, see 89130-89141, 91055)

(For x-ray localization, use 74340)

88112 Cytopathology, selective cellular enhancement technique with interpretation (eg, liquid based slide preparation method), except cervical or vaginal

(Do not report 88112 with 88108)

88125 Cytopathology, forensic (eg, sperm)

88130 Sex chromatin identification; Barr bodies

88140 peripheral blood smear, polymorphonuclear drumsticks

(For Guard stain, use 88313)

Codes 88141-88155, 88164-88167, 88174-88175 are used to report cervical or vaginal screening by various methods and to report physician interpretation services. Use codes 88150-88154 to report conventional Pap smears that are examined using non-Bethesda reporting. Use codes 88164-88167 to report conventional Pap smears that are examined using the Bethesda System of reporting. Use codes 88142-88143 to report liquid-based specimens processed as thin-layer preparations that are examined using any system of reporting (Bethesda or non-Bethesda). Use codes 88174-88175 to report automated screening of liquid-based specimens that are examined using any system of reporting (Bethesda or non-Bethesda). Within each of these three code families choose the one code that describes the screening method(s) used. Codes 88141 and 88155 should be reported in addition to the screening code chosen when the additional services are provided. Manual rescreening requires a complete visual reassessment of the entire slide initially screened by either an automated or manual process. Manual review represents an assessment of selected cells or regions of a slide identified by initial automated review.

Pathology and Laboratory

88141 Cytopathology, cervical or vaginal (any reporting system), requiring interpretation by physician

(Use 88141 in conjunction with 88142-88154, 88164-88167, 88174-88175)

88142 Cytopathology, cervical or vaginal (any reporting system), collected in preservative fluid, automated thin layer preparation; manual screening under physician supervision

88143 with manual screening and rescreening under physician supervision

(For automated screening of automated thin layer preparation, see 88174, 88175)

88147 Cytopathology smears, cervical or vaginal; screening by automated system under physician supervision

88148 screening by automated system with manual rescreening under physician supervision

88150 Cytopathology, slides, cervical or vaginal; manual screening under physician supervision

88152 with manual screening and computer-assisted rescreening under physician supervision

88153 with manual screening and rescreening under physician supervision

88154 with manual screening and computer-assisted rescreening using cell selection and review under physician supervision

+ 88155 Cytopathology, slides, cervical or vaginal, definitive hormonal evaluation (eg, maturation index, karyopyknotic index, estrogenic index) (List separately in addition to code(s) for other technical and interpretation services)

(Use 88155 in conjunction with 88142-88154, 88164-88167, 88174-88175)

88160 Cytopathology, smears, any other source; screening and interpretation

88161 preparation, screening and interpretation

88162 extended study involving over 5 slides and/or multiple stains

(For aerosol collection of sputum, use 89220)

(For special stains, see 88312-88314)

88164 Cytopathology, slides, cervical or vaginal (the Bethesda System); manual screening under physician supervision

88165 with manual screening and rescreening under physician supervision

88166 with manual screening and computer-assisted rescreening under physician supervision

88167 with manual screening and computer-assisted rescreening using cell selection and review under physician supervision

(88170, 88171 have been deleted)

(To report collection of specimen via fine needle aspiration, see 10021, 10022)

88172 Cytopathology, evaluation of fine needle aspirate; immediate cytohistologic study to determine adequacy of specimen(s)

88173 interpretation and report

(For fine needle aspirate, see 10021, 10022)

(Do not report 88172, 88173 in conjunction with 88333 and 88334 for the same specimen)

88174 Cytopathology, cervical or vaginal (any reporting system), collected in preservative fluid, automated thin layer preparation; screening by automated system, under physician supervision

88175 with screening by automated system and manual rescreening or review, under physician supervision

(For manual screening, see 88142, 88143)

(88180 has been deleted. To report, see 88184-88189)

88182 Flow cytometry, cell cycle or DNA analysis

(For DNA ploidy analysis by morphometric technique, use 88358)

88184 Flow cytometry, cell surface, cytoplasmic, or nuclear marker, technical component only; first marker

+ 88185 each additional marker (List separately in addition to code for first marker)

(Report 88185 in conjunction with 88184)

88187 Flow cytometry, interpretation; 2 to 8 markers

88188 9 to 15 markers

88189 16 or more markers

88199 Unlisted cytopathology procedure

(For electron microscopy, see 88348, 88349)

Cytogenetic Studies

When molecular diagnostic procedures are performed to test for oncologic or inherited disorder, use the appropriate modifier to specify probe type or condition tested. (See **Appendix I** for a listing of appropriate modifiers to report with molecular diagnostic and cytogenetic procedures.)

(For acetylcholinesterase, use 82013)

(For alpha-fetoprotein, serum or amniotic fluid, see 82105, 82106)

(For laser microdissection of cells from tissue sample, see 88380)

88230 Tissue culture for non-neoplastic disorders; lymphocyte

88233 skin or other solid tissue biopsy

88235 amniotic fluid or chorionic villus cells

88237 Tissue culture for neoplastic disorders; bone marrow, blood cells

88239 solid tumor

88240　Cryopreservation, freezing and storage of cells, each cell line

(For therapeutic cryopreservation and storage, use 38207)

88241　Thawing and expansion of frozen cells, each aliquot

(For therapeutic thawing of previous harvest, use 38208)

88245　Chromosome analysis for breakage syndromes; baseline Sister Chromatid Exchange (SCE), 20-25 cells

88248　baseline breakage, score 50-100 cells, count 20 cells, 2 karyotypes (eg, for ataxia telangiectasia, Fanconi anemia, fragile X)

88249　score 100 cells, clastogen stress (eg, diepoxybutane, mitomycin C, ionizing radiation, UV radiation)

88261　Chromosome analysis; count 5 cells, 1 karyotype, with banding

88262　count 15-20 cells, 2 karyotypes, with banding

88263　count 45 cells for mosaicism, 2 karyotypes, with banding

88264　analyze 20-25 cells

88267　Chromosome analysis, amniotic fluid or chorionic villus, count 15 cells, 1 karyotype, with banding

88269　Chromosome analysis, in situ for amniotic fluid cells, count cells from 6-12 colonies, 1 karyotype, with banding

88271　Molecular cytogenetics; DNA probe, each (eg, FISH)

88272　chromosomal in situ hybridization, analyze 3-5 cells (eg, for derivatives and markers)

88273　chromosomal in situ hybridization, analyze 10-30 cells (eg, for microdeletions)

88274　interphase in situ hybridization, analyze 25-99 cells

88275　interphase in situ hybridization, analyze 100-300 cells

88280　Chromosome analysis; additional karyotypes, each study

88283　additional specialized banding technique (eg, NOR, C-banding)

88285　additional cells counted, each study

88289　additional high resolution study

88291　Cytogenetics and molecular cytogenetics, interpretation and report

88299　Unlisted cytogenetic study

Surgical Pathology

Services 88300 through 88309 include accession, examination, and reporting. They do not include the services designated in codes 88311 through 88365 and 88399, which are coded in addition when provided.

The unit of service for codes 88300 through 88309 is the specimen.

A specimen is defined as tissue or tissues that is (are) submitted for individual and separate attention, requiring individual examination and pathologic diagnosis. Two or more such specimens from the same patient (eg, separately identified endoscopic biopsies, skin lesions) are each appropriately assigned an individual code reflective of its proper level of service.

Service code 88300 is used for any specimen that in the opinion of the examining pathologist can be accurately diagnosed without microscopic examination. Service code 88302 is used when gross and microscopic examination is performed on a specimen to confirm identification and the absence of disease. Service codes 88304 through 88309 describe all other specimens requiring gross and microscopic examination, and represent additional ascending levels of physician work. Levels 88302 through 88309 are specifically defined by the assigned specimens.

Any unlisted specimen should be assigned to the code which most closely reflects the physician work involved when compared to other specimens assigned to that code.

►(Do not report 88302-88309 on the same specimen as part of Mohs surgery)◄

88300　**Level I** - Surgical pathology, gross examination only

88302　**Level II** - Surgical pathology, gross and microscopic examination

Appendix, incidental

Fallopian tube, sterilization

Fingers/toes, amputation, traumatic

Foreskin, newborn

Hernia sac, any location

Hydrocele sac

Nerve

Skin, plastic repair

Sympathetic ganglion

Testis, castration

Vaginal mucosa, incidental

Vas deferens, sterilization

88304　**Level III** - Surgical pathology, gross and microscopic examination

Abortion, induced

Abscess

Aneurysm - arterial/ventricular

Anus, tag

Appendix, other than incidental

Artery, atheromatous plaque

Bartholin's gland cyst

Bone fragment(s), other than pathologic fracture

Pathology and Laboratory

Bursa/synovial cyst

Carpal tunnel tissue

Cartilage, shavings

Cholesteatoma

Colon, colostomy stoma

Conjunctiva - biopsy/pterygium

Cornea

Diverticulum - esophagus/small intestine

Dupuytren's contracture tissue

Femoral head, other than fracture

Fissure/fistula

Foreskin, other than newborn

Gallbladder

Ganglion cyst

Hematoma

Hemorrhoids

Hydatid of Morgagni

Intervertebral disc

Joint, loose body

Meniscus

Mucocele, salivary

Neuroma - Morton's/traumatic

Pilonidal cyst/sinus

Polyps, inflammatory - nasal/sinusoidal

Skin - cyst/tag/debridement

Soft tissue, debridement

Soft tissue, lipoma

Spermatocele

Tendon/tendon sheath

Testicular appendage

Thrombus or embolus

Tonsil and/or adenoids

Varicocele

Vas deferens, other than sterilization

Vein, varicosity

88305 **Level IV** - Surgical pathology, gross and microscopic examination

Abortion - spontaneous/missed

Artery, biopsy

Bone marrow, biopsy

Bone exostosis

Brain/meninges, other than for tumor resection

Breast, biopsy, not requiring microscopic evaluation of surgical margins

Breast, reduction mammoplasty

Bronchus, biopsy

Cell block, any source

Cervix, biopsy

Colon, biopsy

Duodenum, biopsy

Endocervix, curettings/biopsy

Endometrium, curettings/biopsy

Esophagus, biopsy

Extremity, amputation, traumatic

Fallopian tube, biopsy

Fallopian tube, ectopic pregnancy

Femoral head, fracture

Fingers/toes, amputation, non-traumatic

Gingiva/oral mucosa, biopsy

Heart valve

Joint, resection

Kidney, biopsy

Larynx, biopsy

Leiomyoma(s), uterine myomectomy - without uterus

Lip, biopsy/wedge resection

Lung, transbronchial biopsy

Lymph node, biopsy

Muscle, biopsy

Nasal mucosa, biopsy

Nasopharynx/oropharynx, biopsy

Nerve, biopsy

Odontogenic/dental cyst

Omentum, biopsy

Ovary with or without tube, non-neoplastic

Ovary, biopsy/wedge resection

Parathyroid gland

Peritoneum, biopsy

Pituitary tumor

Placenta, other than third trimester

Pleura/pericardium - biopsy/tissue

Polyp, cervical/endometrial

Polyp, colorectal

Polyp, stomach/small intestine

Prostate, needle biopsy

Prostate, TUR

Salivary gland, biopsy

Sinus, paranasal biopsy

Skin, other than cyst/tag/debridement/plastic repair

Small intestine, biopsy

Soft tissue, other than tumor/mass/lipoma/debridement

Spleen

Stomach, biopsy

Synovium

Testis, other than tumor/biopsy/castration

Thyroglossal duct/brachial cleft cyst

Tongue, biopsy

Tonsil, biopsy

Trachea, biopsy

Ureter, biopsy

Urethra, biopsy

Urinary bladder, biopsy

Uterus, with or without tubes and ovaries, for prolapse

Vagina, biopsy

Vulva/labia, biopsy

88307 **Level V** - Surgical pathology, gross and microscopic examination

Adrenal, resection

Bone - biopsy/curettings

Bone fragment(s), pathologic fracture

Brain, biopsy

Brain/meninges, tumor resection

Breast, excision of lesion, requiring microscopic evaluation of surgical margins

Breast, mastectomy - partial/simple

Cervix, conization

Colon, segmental resection, other than for tumor

Extremity, amputation, non-traumatic

Eye, enucleation

Kidney, partial/total nephrectomy

Larynx, partial/total resection

Liver, biopsy - needle/wedge

Liver, partial resection

Lung, wedge biopsy

Lymph nodes, regional resection

Mediastinum, mass

Myocardium, biopsy

Odontogenic tumor

Ovary with or without tube, neoplastic

Pancreas, biopsy

Placenta, third trimester

Prostate, except radical resection

Salivary gland

Sentinel lymph node

Small intestine, resection, other than for tumor

Soft tissue mass (except lipoma) - biopsy/simple excision

Stomach - subtotal/total resection, other than for tumor

Testis, biopsy

Thymus, tumor

Thyroid, total/lobe

Ureter, resection

Urinary bladder, TUR

Uterus, with or without tubes and ovaries, other than neoplastic/prolapse

88309 **Level VI** - Surgical pathology, gross and microscopic examination

Bone resection

Breast, mastectomy - with regional lymph nodes

Colon, segmental resection for tumor

Colon, total resection

Esophagus, partial/total resection

Extremity, disarticulation

Fetus, with dissection

Larynx, partial/total resection - with regional lymph nodes

Lung - total/lobe/segment resection

Pancreas, total/subtotal resection

Prostate, radical resection

Small intestine, resection for tumor

Soft tissue tumor, extensive resection

Stomach - subtotal/total resection for tumor

Testis, tumor

Tongue/tonsil -resection for tumor

Urinary bladder, partial/total resection

Uterus, with or without tubes and ovaries, neoplastic

Vulva, total/subtotal resection

(For fine needle aspiration, see 10021, 10022)

(For evaluation of fine needle aspirate, see 88172-88173)

▶(Do not report 88302-88309 on the same specimen as part of Mohs surgery◀

+ **88311** Decalcification procedure (List separately in addition to code for surgical pathology examination)

+ **88312** Special stains (List separately in addition to code for primary service); Group I for microorganisms (eg, Gridley, acid fast, methenamine silver), each

+ **88313** Group II, all other, (eg, iron, trichrome), except immunocytochemistry and immunoperoxidase stains, each

(For immunocytochemistry and immunoperoxidase tissue studies, use 88342)

+ **88314** histochemical staining with frozen section(s)

►(Do not report 88314 with 17311-17315 for routine frozen section stain (eg, hematoxylin and eosin, toluidine blue), performed during Mohs surgery. When a nonroutine histochemical stain on frozen tissue is utilized, report 88314 with modifier 59)◄

88318 Determinative histochemistry to identify chemical components (eg, copper, zinc)

88319 Determinative histochemistry or cytochemistry to identify enzyme constituents, each

88321 Consultation and report on referred slides prepared elsewhere

88323 Consultation and report on referred material requiring preparation of slides

88325 Consultation, comprehensive, with review of records and specimens, with report on referred material

88329 Pathology consultation during surgery;

88331 first tissue block, with frozen section(s), single specimen

88332 each additional tissue block with frozen section(s)

88333 cytologic examination (eg, touch prep, squash prep), initial site

88334 cytologic examination (eg, touch prep, squash prep), each additional site

(For intraoperative consultation on a specimen requiring both frozen section and cytologic evaluation, use 88331 and 88334)

(For percutaneous needle biopsy requiring intraprocedural cytologic examination, use 88333)

(Do not report 88333 and 88334 for non-intraoperative cytologic examination, see 88160-88162)

(Do not report 88333 and 88334 for intraprocedural cytologic evaluation of fine needle aspirate, see 88172)

88342 Immunohistochemistry (including tissue immunoperoxidase), each antibody

(Do not report 88342 in conjunction with 88360 or 88361 for the same antibody)

(For quantitative or semiquantitative immunohistochemistry, see 88360, 88361)

88346 Immunofluorescent study, each antibody; direct method

88347 indirect method

88348 Electron microscopy; diagnostic

88349 scanning

88355 Morphometric analysis; skeletal muscle

88356 nerve

88358 tumor (eg, DNA ploidy)

(Do not report 88358 with 88313 unless each procedure is for a different special stain)

88360 Morphometric analysis, tumor immunohistochemistry (eg, Her-2/neu, estrogen receptor/progesterone receptor), quantitative or semiquantitative, each antibody; manual

88361 using computer-assisted technology

(Do not report 88360, 88361 with 88342 unless each procedure is for a different antibody)

(For morphometric analysis using in situ hybridization techniques, see 88367, 88368)

(When semi-thin plastic-embedded sections are performed in conjunction with morphometric analysis, only the morphometric analysis should be reported; if performed as an independent procedure, see codes 88300-88309 for surgical pathology.)

88362 Nerve teasing preparations

88365 In situ hybridization (eg, FISH), each probe

(Do not report 88365 in conjunction with 88367, 88368 for the same probe)

88367 Morphometric analysis, in situ hybridization, (quantitative or semi-quantitative) each probe; using computer-assisted technology

88368 manual

88371 Protein analysis of tissue by Western Blot, with interpretation and report;

88372 immunological probe for band identification, each

88380 Microdissection (eg, mechanical, laser capture)

88384 Array-based evaluation of multiple molecular probes; 11 through 50 probes

88385 51 through 250 probes

88386 251 through 500 probes

(For preparation of array-based evaluation, see 83890-83892, 83898-83901)

(For preparation and analyses of less than 11 probes, see 83890-83914)

88399 Unlisted surgical pathology procedure

Transcutaneous Procedures

88400 Bilirubin, total, transcutaneous

Other Procedures

89049 Caffeine halothane contracture test (CHCT) for malignant hyperthermia susceptibility, including interpretation and report

89050 Cell count, miscellaneous body fluids (eg, cerebrospinal fluid, joint fluid), except blood;

89051 with differential count

89055 Leukocyte assessment, fecal, qualitative or semiquantitative

▲ **89060** Crystal identification by light microscopy with or without polarizing lens analysis, tissue or any body fluid (except urine)

▶(Do not report 89060 for crystal identification on paraffin-embedded tissue)◀

89100 Duodenal intubation and aspiration; single specimen (eg, simple bile study or afferent loop culture) plus appropriate test procedure

89105 collection of multiple fractional specimens with pancreatic or gallbladder stimulation, single or double lumen tube

(For radiological localization, use 74340)

(For chemical analyses, see **Chemistry,** this section)

(Electrocardiogram, see 93000-93268)

(Esophagus acid perfusion test (Bernstein), see 91030)

89125 Fat stain, feces, urine, or respiratory secretions

89130 Gastric intubation and aspiration, diagnostic, each specimen, for chemical analyses or cytopathology;

89132 after stimulation

89135 Gastric intubation, aspiration, and fractional collections (eg, gastric secretory study); one hour

89136 two hours

89140 two hours including gastric stimulation (eg, histalog, pentagastrin)

89141 three hours, including gastric stimulation

(For gastric lavage, therapeutic, use 91105)

(For radiologic localization of gastric tube, use 74340)

(For chemical analyses, see 82926, 82928)

(Joint fluid chemistry, see **Chemistry,** this section)

89160 Meat fibers, feces

89190 Nasal smear for eosinophils

(Occult blood, feces, use 82270)

(Paternity tests, use 86910)

89220 Sputum, obtaining specimen, aerosol induced technique (separate procedure)

89225 Starch granules, feces

89230 Sweat collection by iontophoresis

89235 Water load test

89240 Unlisted miscellaneous pathology test

Reproductive Medicine Procedures

89250 Culture of oocyte(s)/embryo(s), less than 4 days;

89251 with co-culture of oocyte(s)/embryos

(For extended culture of oocyte(s)/embryo(s), see 89272)

89253 Assisted embryo hatching, microtechniques (any method)

89254 Oocyte identification from follicular fluid

89255 Preparation of embryo for transfer (any method)

89257 Sperm identification from aspiration (other than seminal fluid)

(For semen analysis, see 89300-89320)

(For sperm identification from testis tissue, use 89264)

89258 Cryopreservation; embryo(s)

89259 sperm

(For cryopreservation of reproductive tissue, testicular, use 89335)

(For cryopreservation of reproductive tissue, ovarian, use Category III code 0058T)

(For cryopreservation of oocyte(s), use Category III code 0059T)

89260 Sperm isolation; simple prep (eg, sperm wash and swim-up) for insemination or diagnosis with semen analysis

89261 complex prep (eg, Percoll gradient, albumin gradient) for insemination or diagnosis with semen analysis

(For semen analysis without sperm wash or swim-up, use 89320)

89264 Sperm identification from testis tissue, fresh or cryopreserved

(For biopsy of testis, see 54500, 54505)

(For sperm identification from aspiration, use 89257)

(For semen analysis, see 89300-89320)

89268 Insemination of oocytes

89272 Extended culture of oocyte(s)/embryo(s), 4-7 days

89280 Assisted oocyte fertilization, microtechnique; less than or equal to 10 oocytes

89281 greater than 10 oocytes

Pathology and Laboratory

89290 Biopsy, oocyte polar body or embryo blastomere, microtechnique (for pre-implantation genetic diagnosis); less than or equal to 5 embryos

89291 greater than 5 embryos

89300 Semen analysis; presence and/or motility of sperm including Huhner test (post coital)

89310 motility and count (not including Huhner test)

89320 complete (volume, count, motility, and differential)

(Skin tests, see 86485-86580 and 95010-95199)

89321 Semen analysis, presence and/or motility of sperm

(To report Hyaluronan binding assay (HBA), use Category III code 0087T)

89325 Sperm antibodies

(For medicolegal identification of sperm, use 88125)

89329 Sperm evaluation; hamster penetration test

89330 cervical mucus penetration test, with or without spinnbarkeit test

89335 Cryopreservation, reproductive tissue, testicular

(For cryopreservation of embryo(s), use 89258. For cryopreservation of sperm, use 89259)

(For cryopreservation of reproductive tissue, ovarian, use Category III code 0058T)

(For cryopreservation of oocyte, use Category III code 0059T)

89342 Storage, (per year); embryo(s)

89343 sperm/semen

89344 reproductive tissue, testicular/ovarian

89346 oocyte(s)

89352 Thawing of cryopreserved; embryo(s)

89353 sperm/semen, each aliquot

89354 reproductive tissue, testicular/ovarian

89356 oocytes, each aliquot

Medicine Guidelines

In addition to the definitions and commonly used terms presented in the **Introduction**, several other items unique to this section on **Medicine** are defined or identified here.

Multiple Procedures

It is appropriate to designate multiple procedures that are rendered on the same date by separate entries. For example: If individual medical psychotherapy (90829) is rendered in addition to subsequent hospital care (eg, 99231), the psychotherapy would be reported separately from the hospital visit. In this instance, both 99231 and 90829 would be reported.

Add-on Codes

Some of the listed procedures are commonly carried out in addition to the primary procedure performed. All add-on codes found in the CPT codebook are exempt from the multiple procedure concept. They are exempt from the use of modifier 51, as these procedures are not reported as stand-alone codes. These additional or supplemental procedures are designated as "add-on" codes. Add-on codes in the CPT codebook can be readily identified by specific descriptor nomenclature which includes phrases such as "each additional" or "(List separately in addition to primary procedure)."

Separate Procedures

Some of the procedures or services listed in the CPT codebook that are commonly carried out as an integral component of a total service or procedure have been identified by the inclusion of the term "separate procedure." The codes designated as "separate procedure" should not be reported in addition to the code for the total procedure or service of which it is considered an integral component.

However, when a procedure or service that is designated as a "separate procedure" is carried out independently or considered to be unrelated or distinct from other procedures/services provided at that time, it may be reported by itself, or in addition to other procedures/services by appending modifier 59 to the specific "separate procedure" code to indicate that the procedure is not considered to be a component of another procedure, but is a distinct, independent procedure. This may represent a different session or patient encounter, different procedure or surgery, different site or organ system, separate incision/excision, separate lesion, or separate injury (or area of injury in extensive injuries).

Subsection Information

Several of the subheadings or subsections have special instructions unique to that section. These special instructions will be presented preceding those procedural terminology listings, referring to that subsection specifically. If there is an "Unlisted Procedure" code number (see section below) for the individual subsection, it will also be shown. Those subsections within the **Medicine** section that have special instructions are as follows:

Immune Globulins 90281-90399
Immunization Administration for
 Vaccines/Toxoids 90465-90474
Vaccines, Toxoids 90476-90749
Hydration, Therapeutic, Prophylactic,
 and Diagnostic Injections and
 Infusions 90760-90779
 ▶**Hydration** 90760-90761
 Therapeutic, Prophylactic, and Diagnostic
 Injections and Infusions..... 90765-90779◀
Psychiatry 90801-90899
Dialysis 90918-90999
 ▶**Hemodialysis**............... 90935-90940
 Miscellaneous Dialysis Procedures 90945-90999◀
Ophthalmology 92002-92499
 ▶**General Ophthalmological**
 Services 92002-92014
 Ophthalmoscopy 92225-92260◀
 Contact Lens Services 92310-92326
 Spectacle Services............. 92340-92371
Special Otorhinolaryngologic
 Services 92502-92700
 Audiologic Function Tests 92551-92597
 Evaluative and Therapeutic
 Services 92601-92633
Echocardiography 93303-93350
Cardiac Catheterization........... 93501-93581
Intracardiac Electrophysiological
 Procedures/Studies............. 93600-93662
Peripheral Arterial Disease
 Rehabilitation....................... 93668
Noninvasive Vascular
 Diagnostic Studies............. 93875-93990
 ▶**Cerebrovascular Arterial Studies** ... 93875-93893◀
 ▶**Pulmonary** 94002-94799◀
Allergy and Clinical Immunology ... 95004-95199
Neurology and Neuromuscular 95805-95999
 ▶**Sleep Testing** 95805-95811
Routine Electroencephalography
 (EEG)........................ 95812-95830◀
Electromyography and Nerve Conduction
 Tests 95860-95904

Medicine Guidelines

Medicine Guidelines

Unlisted Service or Procedure

A service or procedure may be provided that is not listed in this edition of the CPT codebook. When reporting such a service, the appropriate "Unlisted Procedure" code may be used to indicate the service, identifying it by "Special Report" as discussed on this page. The "Unlisted Procedures" and accompanying codes for **Medicine** are as follows:

⊘ **90399** Unlisted immune globulin

⊘ **90749** Unlisted vaccine/toxoid

90779 Unlisted therapeutic, prophylactic or diagnostic intravenous or intra-arterial injection or infusion

90899 Unlisted psychiatric service or procedure

90999 Unlisted dialysis procedure, inpatient or outpatient

91299 Unlisted diagnostic gastroenterology procedure

92499 Unlisted ophthalmological service or procedure

92700 Unlisted otorhinolaryngological service or procedure

93799 Unlisted cardiovascular service or procedure

94799 Unlisted pulmonary service or procedure

95199 Unlisted allergy/clinical immunologic service or procedure

95999 Unlisted neurological or neuromuscular diagnostic procedure

96549 Unlisted chemotherapy procedure

96999 Unlisted special dermatological service or procedure

97039 Unlisted modality (specify type and time if constant attendance)

97139 Unlisted therapeutic procedure (specify)

97799 Unlisted physical medicine/rehabilitation service or procedure

99199 Unlisted special service, procedure or report

99600 Unlisted home visit service or procedure

►Results/Testing/Reports◄

►Results are the technical component of a service. Testing leads to results; results lead to interpretation. Reports are the work product of the interpretation of numerous test results.◄

Special Report

A service that is rarely provided, unusual, variable, or new may require a special report in determining medical appropriateness of the service. Pertinent information should include an adequate definition or description of the nature, extent, and need for the procedure; and the time, effort, and equipment necessary to provide the service. Additional items that may be included are:

- Complexity of symptoms
- Final diagnosis
- Pertinent physical findings
- Diagnostic and therapeutic procedures
- Concurrent problems
- Follow-up care

Materials Supplied by Physician

Supplies and materials provided by the physician (eg, sterile trays/drugs), over and above those usually included with the procedure(s) rendered are reported separately. List drugs, trays, supplies, and materials provided. Identify as 99070 or specific supply code.

Medicine

Immune Globulins

Codes 90281-90399 identify the immune globulin product only and must be reported in addition to the administration codes 90765-90768, 90772, 90774, 90775 as appropriate. Immune globulin products listed here include broad-spectrum and anti-infective immune globulins, antitoxins, and various isoantibodies.

⊘ **90281** Immune globulin (Ig), human, for intramuscular use

⊘ **90283** Immune globulin (IgIV), human, for intravenous use

⊘ **90287** Botulinum antitoxin, equine, any route

⊘ **90288** Botulism immune globulin, human, for intravenous use

⊘ **90291** Cytomegalovirus immune globulin (CMV-IgIV), human, for intravenous use

⊘ **90296** Diphtheria antitoxin, equine, any route

⊘ **90371** Hepatitis B immune globulin (HBIg), human, for intramuscular use

⊘ **90375** Rabies immune globulin (RIg), human, for intramuscular and/or subcutaneous use

⊘ **90376** Rabies immune globulin, heat-treated (RIg-HT), human, for intramuscular and/or subcutaneous use

⊘ **90378** Respiratory syncytial virus immune globulin (RSV-IgIM), for intramuscular use, 50 mg, each

⊘ **90379** Respiratory syncytial virus immune globulin (RSV-IgIV), human, for intravenous use

⊘ **90384** Rho(D) immune globulin (RhIg), human, full-dose, for intramuscular use

⊘ **90385** Rho(D) immune globulin (RhIg), human, mini-dose, for intramuscular use

⊘ **90386** Rho(D) immune globulin (RhIgIV), human, for intravenous use

⊘ **90389** Tetanus immune globulin (TIg), human, for intramuscular use

⊘ **90393** Vaccinia immune globulin, human, for intramuscular use

⊘ **90396** Varicella-zoster immune globulin, human, for intramuscular use

⊘ **90399** Unlisted immune globulin

Immunization Administration for Vaccines/Toxoids

Codes 90465-90474 must be reported in addition to the vaccine and toxoid code(s) 90476-90749.

Report codes 90465-90468 only when the physician provides face-to-face counseling of the patient and family

during the administration of a vaccine. For immunization administration of any vaccine that is not accompanied by face-to-face physician counseling to the patient/family, report codes 90471-90474.

If a significant separately identifiable Evaluation and Management service (eg, office or other outpatient services, preventive medicine services) is performed, the appropriate E/M service code should be reported in addition to the vaccine and toxoid administration codes.

(For allergy testing, see 95004 et seq)

(For skin testing of bacterial, viral, fungal extracts, see 86485-86586)

(For therapeutic or diagnostic injections, see 90772-90779)

90465 Immunization administration younger than 8 years of age (includes percutaneous, intradermal, subcutaneous, or intramuscular injections) when the physician counsels the patient/family; first injection (single or combination vaccine/toxoid), per day

(Do not report 90465 in conjunction with 90467)

+ **90466** each additional injection (single or combination vaccine/toxoid), per day (List separately in addition to code for primary procedure)

(Use 90466 in conjunction with 90465 or 90467)

90467 Immunization administration younger than age 8 years (includes intranasal or oral routes of administration) when the physician counsels the patient/family; first administration (single or combination vaccine/toxoid), per day

(Do not report 90467 in conjunction with 90465)

+ **90468** each additional administration (single or combination vaccine/toxoid), per day (List separately in addition to code for primary procedure)

(Use 90468 in conjunction with 90465 or 90467)

90471 Immunization administration (includes percutaneous, intradermal, subcutaneous, or intramuscular injections); one vaccine (single or combination vaccine/toxoid)

(Do not report 90471 in conjunction with 90473)

+ **90472** each additional vaccine (single or combination vaccine/toxoid) (List separately in addition to code for primary procedure)

(Use 90472 in conjunction with 90471 or 90473)

▶(For administration of immune globulins, see 90281-90399, 90760, 90761, 90765-90768, 90774)◀

(For intravesical administration of BCG vaccine, see 51720, 90586)

90473 Immunization administration by intranasal or oral route; one vaccine (single or combination vaccine/toxoid)

(Do not report 90473 in conjunction with 90471)

+ 90474 each additional vaccine (single or combination vaccine/toxoid) (List separately in addition to code for primary procedure)

(Use 90474 in conjunction with 90471 or 90473)

Vaccines, Toxoids

To assist users to report the most recent new or revised vaccine product codes, the American Medical Association currently uses the CPT Web-site, which features updates of CPT Editorial Panel actions regarding these products. Once approved by the CPT Editorial Panel, these codes will be made available for release on a semi-annual (twice a year—July 1 and January 1) basis. As part of the electronic distribution, there is a 6-month implementation period from the initial release date (ie, codes released on January 1 are eligible for use on July 1 and codes released on July 1 are eligible for use January 1).

The CPT Editorial Panel, in recognition of the public health interest in vaccine products, has chosen to publish new vaccine product codes prior to FDA approval. These codes are indicated with the ✓ symbol and will be tracked by the AMA to monitor FDA approval status. Once the FDA status changes to approval, the ✓ symbol will be removed. CPT users should refer to the AMA Internet site (www.ama-assn.org/ama/pub/category/10902.html) for the most up-to-date information on codes with the ✓ symbol.

Codes 90476-90748 identify the vaccine product **only.** To report the administration of a vaccine/toxoid, the vaccine/toxoid product codes 90476-90749 must be used in addition to an immunization administration code(s) 90465-90474. Do not append modifier 51 to the vaccine/toxoid product codes 90476-90749.

If a significantly separately identifiable Evaluation and Management (E/M) service (eg, office or other outpatient services, preventive medicine services) is performed, the appropriate E/M service code should be reported in addition to the vaccine and toxoid administration codes.

To meet the reporting requirements of immunization registries, vaccine distribution programs, and reporting systems (eg, Vaccine Adverse Event Reporting System) the exact vaccine product administered needs to be reported. Multiple codes for a particular vaccine are provided in the CPT codebook when the schedule (number of doses or timing) differs for two or more products of the same vaccine type (eg, hepatitis A, Hib) or the vaccine product is available in more than one chemical formulation, dosage, or route of administration.

Separate codes are available for combination vaccines (eg, DTP-Hib, DtaP-Hib, HepB-Hib). It is inappropriate to code each component of a combination vaccine separately. If a specific vaccine code is not available, the unlisted procedure code should be reported, until a new code becomes available.

(For immune globulins, see codes 90281-90399, 90765-90768, 90772-90775 for administration of immune globulins)

⊘ **90476** Adenovirus vaccine, type 4, live, for oral use

⊘ **90477** Adenovirus vaccine, type 7, live, for oral use

⊘ **90581** Anthrax vaccine, for subcutaneous use

⊘ **90585** Bacillus Calmette-Guerin vaccine (BCG) for tuberculosis, live, for percutaneous use

⊘ **90586** Bacillus Calmette-Guerin vaccine (BCG) for bladder cancer, live, for intravesical use

⊘ **90632** Hepatitis A vaccine, adult dosage, for intramuscular use

⊘ **90633** Hepatitis A vaccine, pediatric/adolescent dosage-2 dose schedule, for intramuscular use

⊘ **90634** Hepatitis A vaccine, pediatric/adolescent dosage-3 dose schedule, for intramuscular use

⊘ **90636** Hepatitis A and hepatitis B vaccine (HepA-HepB), adult dosage, for intramuscular use

⊘ **90645** Hemophilus influenza b vaccine (Hib), HbOC conjugate (4 dose schedule), for intramuscular use

⊘ **90646** Hemophilus influenza b vaccine (Hib), PRP-D conjugate, for booster use only, intramuscular use

⊘ **90647** Hemophilus influenza b vaccine (Hib), PRP-OMP conjugate (3 dose schedule), for intramuscular use

⊘ **90648** Hemophilus influenza b vaccine (Hib), PRP-T conjugate (4 dose schedule), for intramuscular use

⊘ **90649** Human Papilloma virus (HPV) vaccine, types 6, 11, 16, 18 (quadrivalent), 3 dose schedule, for intramuscular use

⊘▲ **90655** Influenza virus vaccine, split virus, preservative free, when administered to children 6-35 months of age, for intramuscular use

⊘▲ **90656** Influenza virus vaccine, split virus, preservative free, when administered to 3 years and older, for intramuscular use

⊘▲ **90657** Influenza virus vaccine, split virus, when administered to children 6-35 months of age, for intramuscular use

⊘▲ **90658** Influenza virus vaccine, split virus, when administered to 3 years of age and older, for intramuscular use

⊘ **90660** Influenza virus vaccine, live, for intranasal use

⊘ **90665** Lyme disease vaccine, adult dosage, for intramuscular use

⊘▲ **90669** Pneumococcal conjugate vaccine, polyvalent, when administered to children younger than 5 years, for intramuscular use

Medicine

⊘ **90675** Rabies vaccine, for intramuscular use

⊘ **90676** Rabies vaccine, for intradermal use

⊘ **90680** Rotavirus vaccine, pentavalent, 3 dose schedule, live, for oral use

⊘ **90690** Typhoid vaccine, live, oral

⊘ **90691** Typhoid vaccine, Vi capsular polysaccharide (ViCPs), for intramuscular use

⊘ **90692** Typhoid vaccine, heat- and phenol-inactivated (H-P), for subcutaneous or intradermal use

⊘ **90693** Typhoid vaccine, acetone-killed, dried (AKD), for subcutaneous use (U.S. military)

✎⊘ **90698** Diphtheria, tetanus toxoids, acellular pertussis vaccine, haemophilus influenza Type B, and poliovirus vaccine, inactivated (DTaP - Hib - IPV), for intramuscular use

⊘▲ **90700** Diphtheria, tetanus toxoids, and acellular pertussis vaccine (DTaP), when administered to younger than 7 years, for intramuscular use

⊘ **90701** Diphtheria, tetanus toxoids, and whole cell pertussis vaccine (DTP), for intramuscular use

⊘▲ **90702** Diphtheria and tetanus toxoids (DT) adsorbed when administered to younger than 7 years, for intramuscular use

⊘ **90703** Tetanus toxoid adsorbed, for intramuscular use

⊘ **90704** Mumps virus vaccine, live, for subcutaneous use

⊘ **90705** Measles virus vaccine, live, for subcutaneous use

⊘ **90706** Rubella virus vaccine, live, for subcutaneous use

⊘ **90707** Measles, mumps and rubella virus vaccine (MMR), live, for subcutaneous use

⊘ **90708** Measles and rubella virus vaccine, live, for subcutaneous use

⊘ **90710** Measles, mumps, rubella, and varicella vaccine (MMRV), live, for subcutaneous use

⊘ **90712** Poliovirus vaccine, (any type(s)) (OPV), live, for oral use

⊘ **90713** Poliovirus vaccine, inactivated, (IPV), for subcutaneous or intramuscular use

⊘▲ **90714** Tetanus and diphtheria toxoids (Td) adsorbed, preservative free, when administered to 7 years or older, for intramuscular use

⊘▲ **90715** Tetanus, diphtheria toxoids and acellular pertussis vaccine (Tdap), when administered to 7 years or older, for intramuscular use

⊘ **90716** Varicella virus vaccine, live, for subcutaneous use

⊘ **90717** Yellow fever vaccine, live, for subcutaneous use

⊘▲ **90718** Tetanus and diphtheria toxoids (Td) adsorbed when administered to 7 years or older, for intramuscular use

⊘ **90719** Diphtheria toxoid, for intramuscular use

⊘ **90720** Diphtheria, tetanus toxoids, and whole cell pertussis vaccine and Hemophilus influenza B vaccine (DTP-Hib), for intramuscular use

⊘ **90721** Diphtheria, tetanus toxoids, and acellular pertussis vaccine and Hemophilus influenza B vaccine (DtaP-Hib), for intramuscular use

⊘ **90723** Diphtheria, tetanus toxoids, acellular pertussis vaccine, Hepatitis B, and poliovirus vaccine, inactivated (DtaP-HepB-IPV), for intramuscular use

⊘ **90725** Cholera vaccine for injectable use

⊘ **90727** Plague vaccine, for intramuscular use

⊘▲ **90732** Pneumococcal polysaccharide vaccine, 23-valent, adult or immunosuppressed patient dosage, when administered to 2 years or older, for subcutaneous or intramuscular use

⊘ **90733** Meningococcal polysaccharide vaccine (any group(s)), for subcutaneous use

⊘ **90734** Meningococcal conjugate vaccine, serogroups A, C, Y and W-135 (tetravalent), for intramuscular use

⊘ **90735** Japanese encephalitis virus vaccine, for subcutaneous use

⊘ **90736** Zoster (shingles) vaccine, live, for subcutaneous injection

⊘ **90740** Hepatitis B vaccine, dialysis or immunosuppressed patient dosage (3 dose schedule), for intramuscular use

⊘ **90743** Hepatitis B vaccine, adolescent (2 dose schedule), for intramuscular use

⊘ **90744** Hepatitis B vaccine, pediatric/adolescent dosage (3 dose schedule), for intramuscular use

⊘ **90746** Hepatitis B vaccine, adult dosage, for intramuscular use

⊘ **90747** Hepatitis B vaccine, dialysis or immunosuppressed patient dosage (4 dose schedule), for intramuscular use

⊘ **90748** Hepatitis B and Hemophilus influenza b vaccine (HepB-Hib), for intramuscular use

⊘ **90749** Unlisted vaccine/toxoid

Hydration, Therapeutic, Prophylactic, and Diagnostic Injections and Infusions (Excludes Chemotherapy)

Physician work related to hydration, injection, and infusion services predominantly involves affirmation of treatment plan and direct supervision of staff.

If a significant separately identifiable Evaluation and Management service is performed, the appropriate E/M service code should be reported using modifier 25 in addition to 90760-90779. For same day E/M service a different diagnosis is not required.

If performed to facilitate the infusion or injection, the following services are included and are not reported separately:

Medicine

a. Use of local anesthesia

b. IV start

c. Access to indwelling IV, subcutaneous catheter or port

d. Flush at conclusion of infusion

e. Standard tubing, syringes, and supplies

(For declotting a catheter or port, see 36550)

When multiple drugs are administered, report the service(s) and the specific materials or drugs for each.

When administering multiple infusions, injections or combinations, only one "initial" service code should be reported, unless protocol requires that two separate IV sites must be used. The "initial" code that best describes the key or primary reason for the encounter should always be reported irrespective of the order in which the infusions or injections occur. If an injection or infusion is of a subsequent or concurrent nature, even if it is the first such service within that group of services, then a subsequent or concurrent code from the appropriate section should be reported (eg, the first IV push given subsequent to an initial one-hour infusion is reported using a subsequent IV push code).

When reporting codes for which infusion time is a factor, use the actual time over which the infusion is administered.

Hydration

Codes 90760-90761 are intended to report a hydration IV infusion to consist of a pre-packaged fluid and electrolytes (eg, normal saline, D5-Ω normal saline+30mEq KCl/liter), but are not used to report infusion of drugs or other substances. Hydration IV infusions typically require direct physician supervision for purposes of consent, safety oversight, or intraservice supervision of staff. Typically such infusions require little special handling to prepare or dispose of, and staff that administer these do not typically require advanced practice training. After initial set-up, infusion typically entails little patient risk and thus little monitoring.

90760 Intravenous infusion, hydration; initial, up to 1 hour

(Do not report 90760 if performed as a concurrent infusion service)

+▲ 90761 each additional hour (List separately in addition to code for primary procedure)

(Use 90761 in conjunction with 90760)

(Report 90761 for hydration infusion intervals of greater than 30 minutes beyond 1 hour increments)

(Report 90761 to identify hydration if provided as a secondary or subsequent service after a different initial service [90760, 90765, 90774, 96409, 96413] is provided)

Therapeutic, Prophylactic, and Diagnostic Injections and Infusions

►A therapeutic, prophylactic, or diagnostic IV infusion or injection (90765-90779) (other than hydration) is for the administration of substances/drugs. When fluids are used to administer the drug(s), the administration of the fluid is considered incidental hydration and is not separately reportable. These services typically require direct physician supervision for any or all purposes of patient assessment, provision of consent, safety oversight, and intra-service supervision of staff. Typically, such infusions require special consideration to prepare, dose or dispose of, require practice training and competency for staff who administer the infusions, and require periodic patient assessment with vital sign monitoring during the infusion.◄

Intravenous or intra-arterial push is defined as: a) an injection in which the health care professional who administers the substance/drug is continuously present to administer the injection and observe the patient, or b) an infusion of 15 minutes or less.

(Do not report 90765-90779 with codes for which IV push or infusion is an inherent part of the procedure (eg, administration of contrast material for a diagnostic imaging study))

90765 Intravenous infusion, for therapy, prophylaxis, or diagnosis (specify substance or drug); initial, up to 1 hour

+▲ 90766 each additional hour (List separately in addition to code for primary procedure)

(Report 90766 in conjunction with 90765, 90767)

(Report 90766 for additional hour(s) of sequential infusion)

(Report 90766 for infusion intervals of greater than 30 minutes beyond 1 hour increments)

+ 90767 additional sequential infusion, up to 1 hour (List separately in addition to code for primary procedure)

(Report 90767 in conjunction with 90765, 90774, 96409, 96413 if provided as a secondary or subsequent service after a different initial service. Report 90767 only once per sequential infusion of same infusate mix)

+ 90768 concurrent infusion (List separately in addition to code for primary procedure)

(Report 90768 only once per encounter)

►(Report 90768 in conjunction with 90765, 90766, 96413, 96415, 96416, 96422, 96423)◄

90772 Therapeutic, prophylactic or diagnostic injection (specify substance or drug); subcutaneous or intramuscular

(For administration of vaccines/toxoids, see 90465-90466, 90471-90472)

(Report 90772 for non-antineoplastic hormonal therapy injections)

*cannot be billed together, use only 1 phys add-on if necessary unless 2 IV sites

(Report 96401 for anti-neoplastic nonhormonal injection therapy)

(Report 96402 for anti-neoplastic hormonal injection therapy)

(Do not report 90772 for injections given without direct physician supervision. To report, use 99211)

(90772 does not include injections for allergen immunotherapy. For allergen immunotherapy injections, see 95115-95117)

90773 intra-arterial

90774 intravenous push, single or initial substance/drug

+ 90775 each additional sequential intravenous push of a new substance/drug (List separately in addition to code for primary procedure)

(Use 90775 in conjunction with 90765, 90774, 96409, 96413)

(Report 90775 to identify intravenous push of a new substance/drug if provided as a secondary or subsequent service after a different initial service is provided)

90779 Unlisted therapeutic, prophylactic or diagnostic intravenous or intra-arterial injection or infusion

(For allergy immunizations, see 95004 et seq)

(90780 and 90781 have been deleted. To report, see 90760, 90761, 90765-90768)

(90782 has been deleted. To report, use 90772)

(90783 has been deleted. To report, use 90773)

(90784 has been deleted. To report, use 90774)

(90788 has been deleted. To report, use 90772)

(90799 has been deleted. To report, use 90779)

Psychiatry

Hospital care by the attending physician in treating a psychiatric inpatient or partial hospitalization may be initial or subsequent in nature (see 99221-99233) and may include exchanges with nursing and ancillary personnel. Hospital care services involve a variety of responsibilities unique to the medical management of inpatients, such as physician hospital orders, interpretation of laboratory or other medical diagnostic studies and observations.

Some patients receive hospital evaluation and management services only and others receive evaluation and management services and other procedures. If other procedures such as electroconvulsive therapy or psychotherapy are rendered in addition to hospital evaluation and management services, these should be listed separately (ie, hospital care service plus electroconvulsive therapy or when psychotherapy is done, an appropriate code defining psychotherapy with medical evaluation and management services). Modifier 22 may

be used to indicate a more extensive service. Modifier 52 may be used to signify a service that is reduced or less extensive than the usual procedure.

Other evaluation and management services, such as office medical service or other patient encounters, may be described as listed in the section on **Evaluation and Management,** if appropriate.

The evaluation and management services should not be reported separately, when reporting codes 90805, 90807, 90809, 90811, 90813, 90815, 90817, 90819, 90822, 90824, 90827, 90829.

Consultation for psychiatric evaluation of a patient includes examination of a patient and exchange of information with the primary physician and other informants such as nurses or family members, and preparation of a report. These consultation services (99241-99255) are limited to initial or follow-up evaluation and do not involve psychiatric treatment.

Psychiatric Diagnostic or Evaluative Interview Procedures

Psychiatric diagnostic interview examination includes a history, mental status, and a disposition, and may include communication with family or other sources, ordering and medical interpretation of laboratory or other medical diagnostic studies. In certain circumstances other informants will be seen in lieu of the patient.

Interactive psychiatric diagnostic interview examination is typically furnished to children. It involves the use of physical aids and non-verbal communication to overcome barriers to therapeutic interaction between the clinician and a patient who has not yet developed, or has lost, either the expressive language communication skills to explain his/her symptoms and response to treatment, or the receptive communication skills to understand the clinician if he/she were to use ordinary adult language for communication.

90801 Psychiatric diagnostic interview examination

90802 Interactive psychiatric diagnostic interview examination using play equipment, physical devices, language interpreter, or other mechanisms of communication

Psychiatric Therapeutic Procedures

Psychotherapy is the treatment for mental illness and behavioral disturbances in which the clinician establishes a professional contract with the patient and, through definitive therapeutic communication, attempts to alleviate the emotional disturbances, reverse or change maladaptive patterns of behavior, and encourage personality growth and development. The codes for reporting psychotherapy are divided into two broad categories: Interactive Psychotherapy; and Insight Oriented, Behavior Modifying and/or Supportive Psychotherapy.

Medicine

Interactive psychotherapy is typically furnished to children. It involves the use of physical aids and non-verbal communication to overcome barriers to therapeutic interaction between the clinician and a patient who has not yet developed, or has lost, either the expressive language communication skills to explain his/her symptoms and response to treatment, or the receptive communication skills to understand the clinician if he/she were to use ordinary adult language for communication.

Insight oriented, behavior modifying and/or supportive psychotherapy refers to the development of insight or affective understanding, the use of behavior modification techniques, the use of supportive interactions, the use of cognitive discussion of reality, or any combination of the above to provide therapeutic change.

Some patients receive psychotherapy only and others receive psychotherapy and medical evaluation and management services. These evaluation and management services involve a variety of responsibilities unique to the medical management of psychiatric patients, such as medical diagnostic evaluation (eg, evaluation of comorbid medical conditions, drug interactions, and physical examinations), drug management when indicated, physician orders, interpretation of laboratory or other medical diagnostic studies and observations.

In reporting psychotherapy, the appropriate code is chosen on the basis of the type of psychotherapy (interactive using non-verbal techniques versus insight oriented, behavior modifying and/or supportive using verbal techniques), the place of service (office versus inpatient), the face-to-face time spent with the patient during psychotherapy, and whether evaluation and management services are furnished on the same date of service as psychotherapy.

To report medical evaluation and management services furnished on a day when psychotherapy is not provided, select the appropriate code from the **Evaluation and Management Services Guidelines.**

Office or Other Outpatient Facility

Insight Oriented, Behavior Modifying and/or Supportive Psychotherapy

90804 Individual psychotherapy, insight oriented, behavior modifying and/or supportive, in an office or outpatient facility, approximately 20 to 30 minutes face-to-face with the patient;

90805 with medical evaluation and management services

90806 Individual psychotherapy, insight oriented, behavior modifying and/or supportive, in an office or outpatient facility, approximately 45 to 50 minutes face-to-face with the patient;

90807 with medical evaluation and management services

90808 Individual psychotherapy, insight oriented, behavior modifying and/or supportive, in an office or outpatient facility, approximately 75 to 80 minutes face-to-face with the patient;

90809 with medical evaluation and management services

Interactive Psychotherapy

90810 Individual psychotherapy, interactive, using play equipment, physical devices, language interpreter, or other mechanisms of non-verbal communication, in an office or outpatient facility, approximately 20 to 30 minutes face-to-face with the patient;

90811 with medical evaluation and management services

90812 Individual psychotherapy, interactive, using play equipment, physical devices, language interpreter, or other mechanisms of non-verbal communication, in an office or outpatient facility, approximately 45 to 50 minutes face-to-face with the patient;

90813 with medical evaluation and management services

90814 Individual psychotherapy, interactive, using play equipment, physical devices, language interpreter, or other mechanisms of non-verbal communication, in an office or outpatient facility, approximately 75 to 80 minutes face-to-face with the patient;

90815 with medical evaluation and management services

Inpatient Hospital, Partial Hospital or Residential Care Facility

Insight Oriented, Behavior Modifying and/or Supportive Psychotherapy

90816 Individual psychotherapy, insight oriented, behavior modifying and/or supportive, in an inpatient hospital, partial hospital or residential care setting, approximately 20 to 30 minutes face-to-face with the patient;

90817 with medical evaluation and management services

90818 Individual psychotherapy, insight oriented, behavior modifying and/or supportive, in an inpatient hospital, partial hospital or residential care setting, approximately 45 to 50 minutes face-to-face with the patient;

90819 with medical evaluation and management services

90821 Individual psychotherapy, insight oriented, behavior modifying and/or supportive, in an inpatient hospital, partial hospital or residential care setting, approximately 75 to 80 minutes face-to-face with the patient;

90822 with medical evaluation and management services

Medicine

Interactive Psychotherapy

90823 Individual psychotherapy, interactive, using play equipment, physical devices, language interpreter, or other mechanisms of non-verbal communication, in an inpatient hospital, partial hospital or residential care setting, approximately 20 to 30 minutes face-to-face with the patient;

90824 with medical evaluation and management services

90826 Individual psychotherapy, interactive, using play equipment, physical devices, language interpreter, or other mechanisms of non-verbal communication, in an inpatient hospital, partial hospital or residential care setting, approximately 45 to 50 minutes face-to-face with the patient;

90827 with medical evaluation and management services

90828 Individual psychotherapy, interactive, using play equipment, physical devices, language interpreter, or other mechanisms of non-verbal communication, in an inpatient hospital, partial hospital or residential care setting, approximately 75 to 80 minutes face-to-face with the patient;

90829 with medical evaluation and management services

Other Psychotherapy

90845 Psychoanalysis

90846 Family psychotherapy (without the patient present)

90847 Family psychotherapy (conjoint psychotherapy) (with patient present)

90849 Multiple-family group psychotherapy

90853 Group psychotherapy (other than of a multiple-family group)

90857 Interactive group psychotherapy

Other Psychiatric Services or Procedures

►(For repetitive transcranial magnetic stimulation for treatment of clinical depression, see Category III codes 0160T, 0161T)◄

90862 Pharmacologic management, including prescription, use, and review of medication with no more than minimal medical psychotherapy

90865 Narcosynthesis for psychiatric diagnostic and therapeutic purposes (eg, sodium amobarbital (Amytal) interview)

90870 Electroconvulsive therapy (includes necessary monitoring)

(90871 has been deleted)

90875 Individual psychophysiological therapy incorporating biofeedback training by any modality (face-to-face with the patient), with psychotherapy (eg, insight oriented, behavior modifying or supportive psychotherapy); approximately 20-30 minutes

90876 approximately 45-50 minutes

90880 Hypnotherapy

90882 Environmental intervention for medical management purposes on a psychiatric patient's behalf with agencies, employers, or institutions

90885 Psychiatric evaluation of hospital records, other psychiatric reports, psychometric and/or projective tests, and other accumulated data for medical diagnostic purposes

90887 Interpretation or explanation of results of psychiatric, other medical examinations and procedures, or other accumulated data to family or other responsible persons, or advising them how to assist patient

90889 Preparation of report of patient's psychiatric status, history, treatment, or progress (other than for legal or consultative purposes) for other physicians, agencies, or insurance carriers

90899 Unlisted psychiatric service or procedure

Biofeedback

(For psychophysiological therapy incorporating biofeedback training, see 90875, 90876)

90901 Biofeedback training by any modality

90911 Biofeedback training, perineal muscles, anorectal or urethral sphincter, including EMG and/or manometry

(For incontinence treatment by pulsed magnetic neuromodulation, use Category III code 0029T)

(For testing of rectal sensation, tone and compliance, use 91120)

Dialysis

Codes 90918-90921 are reported ONCE per month to distinguish age-specific services related to the patient's end-stage renal disease (ESRD) performed in an outpatient setting. ESRD-related physician services include establishment of a dialyzing cycle, outpatient evaluation and management of the dialysis visits, telephone calls, and patient management during the dialysis, provided during a full month. These codes are not used if the physician also submits hospitalization codes during the month.

Codes 90918-90921 describe a full month of ESRD-related services provided in an outpatient setting. For ESRD and non-ESRD dialysis services performed in an inpatient setting, and for non-ESRD dialysis services performed in an outpatient setting, see 90935-90937 and 90945-90947.

Evaluation and management services unrelated to ESRD services that cannot be performed during the dialysis session may be reported separately.

Medicine

Codes 90922-90925 are reported when outpatient ESRD-related services are not performed consecutively during an entire full month (eg, when the patient spends part of the month as a hospital inpatient, or when the outpatient ESRD-related services are initiated after the first of the month). The appropriate age-related code from this series (90922-90925) is reported daily less the days of hospitalization. For reporting purposes, each month is considered 30 days.

Example:

Outpatient ESRD-related services are initiated on July 1 for a 57-year-old male. On July 11, he is admitted to the hospital as an inpatient and is discharged on July 27.

In this example, code 90925 should be reported for each day outside of the inpatient hospitalization (30 days/month less 17 days/hospitalization = 13 days). Report inpatient E/M services as appropriate. Dialysis procedures rendered during the hospitalization (July 11-27) should be reported as appropriate (90935-90937, 90945-90947).

End-Stage Renal Disease Services

90918 End-stage renal disease (ESRD) related services per full month; for patients younger than two years of age to include monitoring for the adequacy of nutrition, assessment of growth and development, and counseling of parents

90919 for patients between two and eleven years of age to include monitoring for the adequacy of nutrition, assessment of growth and development, and counseling of parents

90920 for patients between twelve and nineteen years of age to include monitoring for the adequacy of nutrition, assessment of growth and development, and counseling of parents

90921 for patients twenty years of age and older

90922 End-stage renal disease (ESRD) related services (less than full month), per day; for patients younger than two years of age

90923 for patients between two and eleven years of age

90924 for patients between twelve and nineteen years of age

90925 for patients twenty years of age and older

Hemodialysis

Codes 90935, 90937 are reported to describe the hemodialysis procedure with all evaluation and management services related to the patient's renal disease on the day of the hemodialysis procedure. These codes are used for inpatient ESRD and non-ESRD procedures or for outpatient non-ESRD dialysis services. Code 90935 is reported if only one evaluation of the patient is required related to that hemodialysis procedure. Code 90937 is

reported when patient re-evaluation(s) is required during a hemodialysis procedure. Use modifier 25 with Evaluation and Management codes for separately identifiable services unrelated to the dialysis procedure or renal failure which cannot be rendered during the dialysis session.

(For home visit hemodialysis services performed by a non-physician health care professional, use 99512)

(For cannula declotting, see 36831, 36833, 36860, 36861)

(For declotting of implanted vascular access device or catheter by thrombolytic agent, use 36550)

(For collection of blood specimen from a partially or completely implantable venous access device, use 36540)

(For prolonged physician attendance, see 99354-99360)

90935 Hemodialysis procedure with single physician evaluation

90937 Hemodialysis procedure requiring repeated evaluation(s) with or without substantial revision of dialysis prescription

(90939 has been deleted. To report, use 90940)

90940 Hemodialysis access flow study to determine blood flow in grafts and arteriovenous fistulae by an indicator method

(For duplex scan of hemodialysis access, use 93990)

Miscellaneous Dialysis Procedures

Codes 90945, 90947 describe dialysis procedures other than hemodialysis (eg, peritoneal dialysis, hemofiltration or continuous renal replacement therapies), and all evaluation and management services related to the patient's renal disease on the day of the procedure. Code 90945 is reported if only one evaluation of the patient is required related to that procedure. Code 90947 is reported when patient re-evaluation(s) is required during a procedure. Utilize modifier 25 with Evaluation and Management codes for separately identifiable services unrelated to the procedure or the renal failure which cannot be rendered during the dialysis session.

(For insertion of intraperitoneal cannula or catheter, see 49420, 49421)

(For prolonged physician attendance, see 99354-99360)

90945 Dialysis procedure other than hemodialysis (eg, peritoneal dialysis, hemofiltration, or other continuous renal replacement therapies), with single physician evaluation

(For home infusion of peritoneal dialysis, use 99601, 99602)

Medicine

90947 Dialysis procedure other than hemodialysis (eg, peritoneal dialysis, hemofiltration, or other continuous renal replacement therapies) requiring repeated physician evaluations, with or without substantial revision of dialysis prescription

90989 Dialysis training, patient, including helper where applicable, any mode, completed course

90993 Dialysis training, patient, including helper where applicable, any mode, course not completed, per training session

90997 Hemoperfusion (eg, with activated charcoal or resin)

90999 Unlisted dialysis procedure, inpatient or outpatient

Gastroenterology

(For duodenal intubation and aspiration, see 89100-89105)

(For gastrointestinal radiologic procedures, see 74210-74363)

(For esophagoscopy procedures, see 43200-43228; upper GI endoscopy 43234-43259; endoscopy, small intestine and stomal 44360-44393; proctosigmoidoscopy 45300-45321; sigmoidoscopy 45330-45339; colonoscopy 45355-45385; anoscopy 46600-46615)

91000 Esophageal intubation and collection of washings for cytology, including preparation of specimens (separate procedure)

91010 Esophageal motility (manometric study of the esophagus and/or gastroesophageal junction) study;

91011 with mecholyl or similar stimulant

91012 with acid perfusion studies

91020 Gastric motility (manometric) studies

91022 Duodenal motility (manometric) study

(If gastrointestinal endoscopy is performed, use 43235)

(If fluoroscopy is performed, use 76000)

(If gastric motility study is performed, use 91020)

91030 Esophagus, acid perfusion (Bernstein) test for esophagitis

(91032 and 91033 have been deleted. To report, see 91034, 91035)

91034 Esophagus, gastroesophageal reflux test; with nasal catheter pH electrode(s) placement, recording, analysis and interpretation

91035 with mucosal attached telemetry pH electrode placement, recording, analysis and interpretation

91037 Esophageal function test, gastroesophageal reflux test with nasal catheter intraluminal impedance electrode(s) placement, recording, analysis and interpretation;

91038 prolonged (greater than 1 hour, up to 24 hours)

91040 Esophageal balloon distension provocation study

(For balloon dilatation with endoscopy, see 43220, 43249, 43456, or 43458)

91052 Gastric analysis test with injection of stimulant of gastric secretion (eg, histamine, insulin, pentagastrin, calcium and secretin)

(For gastric biopsy by capsule, peroral, via tube, one or more specimens, use 43600)

(For gastric laboratory procedures, see also 89130-89141)

91055 Gastric intubation, washings, and preparing slides for cytology (separate procedure)

(For gastric lavage, therapeutic, use 91105)

►(91060 has been deleted)◄

(For biopsy by capsule, small intestine, per oral, via tube [one or more specimens], use 44100)

91065 Breath hydrogen test (eg, for detection of lactase deficiency, fructose intolerance, bacterial overgrowth, or oro-cecal gastrointestinal transit)

(For H. pylori breath test analysis, use 83013 for non-radioactive (C-13) isotope or 78268 for radioactive (C-14) isotope)

91100 Intestinal bleeding tube, passage, positioning and monitoring

91105 Gastric intubation, and aspiration or lavage for treatment (eg, for ingested poisons)

(For cholangiography, see 47500, 74320)

(For abdominal paracentesis, see 49080, 49081; with instillation of medication, see 96440, 96445)

(For peritoneoscopy, use 49320; with biopsy, use 49321)

(For peritoneoscopy and guided transhepatic cholangiography, use 47560; with biopsy, use 47561)

(For splenoportography, see 38200, 75810)

91110 Gastrointestinal tract imaging, intraluminal (eg, capsule endoscopy), esophagus through ileum, with physician interpretation and report

(Visualization of the colon is not reported separately)

(Append modifier 52 if the ileum is not visualized)

● **91111** Gastrointestinal tract imaging, intraluminal (eg, capsule endoscopy), esophagus with physician interpretation and report

►(Do not report 91111 in conjunction with 91110)◄

Medicine

91120 Rectal sensation, tone, and compliance test (ie, response to graded balloon distention)

(For biofeedback training, use 90911)

(For anorectal manometry, use 91122)

91122 Anorectal manometry

91123 Pulsed irrigation of fecal impaction

Gastric Physiology

91132 Electrogastrography, diagnostic, transcutaneous;

91133 with provocative testing

Other Procedures

91299 Unlisted diagnostic gastroenterology procedure

Ophthalmology

(For surgical procedures, see **Surgery,** Eye and Ocular Adnexa, 65091 et seq)

Definitions

Intermediate ophthalmological services describes an evaluation of a new or existing condition complicated with a new diagnostic or management problem not necessarily relating to the primary diagnosis, including history, general medical observation, external ocular and adnexal examination and other diagnostic procedures as indicated; may include the use of mydriasis for ophthalmoscopy.

For example:

a. Review of history, external examination, ophthalmoscopy, biomicroscopy for an acute complicated condition (eg, iritis) not requiring comprehensive ophthalmological services.

b. Review of interval history, external examination, ophthalmoscopy, biomicroscopy and tonometry in established patient with known cataract not requiring comprehensive ophthalmological services.

Comprehensive ophthalmological services describes a general evaluation of the complete visual system. The comprehensive services constitute a single service entity but need not be performed at one session. The service includes history, general medical observation, external and ophthalmoscopic examinations, gross visual fields and basic sensorimotor examination. It often includes, as indicated: biomicroscopy, examination with cycloplegia or mydriasis and tonometry. It always includes initiation of diagnostic and treatment programs.

Intermediate and comprehensive ophthalmological services constitute integrated services in which medical decision making cannot be separated from the examining techniques used. Itemization of service components, such

as slit lamp examination, keratometry, routine ophthalmoscopy, retinoscopy, tonometry, or motor evaluation is not applicable.

For example:

The comprehensive services required for diagnosis and treatment of a patient with symptoms indicating possible disease of the visual system, such as glaucoma, cataract or retinal disease, or to rule out disease of the visual system, new or established patient.

Initiation of diagnostic and treatment program includes the prescription of medication, and arranging for special ophthalmological diagnostic or treatment services, consultations, laboratory procedures and radiological services.

Special ophthalmological services describes services in which a special evaluation of part of the visual system is made, which goes beyond the services included under general ophthalmological services, or in which special treatment is given. Special ophthalmological services may be reported in addition to the general ophthalmological services or evaluation and management services.

For example:

Fluorescein angioscopy, quantitative visual field examination, refraction or extended color vision examination (such as Nagel's anomaloscope) should be separately reported.

Prescription of lenses, when required, is included in 92015. It includes specification of lens type (monofocal, bifocal, other), lens power, axis, prism, absorptive factor, impact resistance, and other factors.

Interpretation and report by the physician is an integral part of special ophthalmological services where indicated. Technical procedures (which may or may not be performed by the physician personally) are often part of the service, but should not be mistaken to constitute the service itself.

General Ophthalmological Services

New Patient

Solely for the purposes of distinguishing between new and established patients, **professional services** are those face-to-face services rendered by a physician and reported by a specific code(s). A new patient is one who has not received any professional services from the physician or another physician of the same specialty who belongs to the same group practice within the past three years.

92002 Ophthalmological services: medical examination and evaluation with initiation of diagnostic and treatment program; intermediate, new patient

92004 comprehensive, new patient, one or more visits

Medicine

Established Patient

Solely for the purposes of distinguishing between new and established patients, **professional services** are those face-to-face services rendered by a physician and reported by a specific code(s). An established patient is one who has received professional services from the physician or another physician of the same specialty who belongs to the same group practice within the past three years.

92012 Ophthalmological services: medical examination and evaluation, with initiation or continuation of diagnostic and treatment program; intermediate, established patient

92014 comprehensive, established patient, one or more visits

(For surgical procedures, see **Surgery,** Eye and Ocular Adnexa, 65091 et seq)

Special Ophthalmological Services

92015 Determination of refractive state

92018 Ophthalmological examination and evaluation, under general anesthesia, with or without manipulation of globe for passive range of motion or other manipulation to facilitate diagnostic examination; complete

92019 limited

92020 Gonioscopy (separate procedure)

(For gonioscopy under general anesthesia, use 92018)

● **92025** Computerized corneal topography, unilateral or bilateral, with interpretation and report

▶(Do not report 92025 in conjunction with 65710-65755)◀

▶(92025 is not used for manual keratoscopy, which is part of a single system Evaluation and Management or ophthalmological service)◀

92060 Sensorimotor examination with multiple measurements of ocular deviation (eg, restrictive or paretic muscle with diplopia) with interpretation and report (separate procedure)

92065 Orthoptic and/or pleoptic training, with continuing medical direction and evaluation

92070 Fitting of contact lens for treatment of disease, including supply of lens

92081 Visual field examination, unilateral or bilateral, with interpretation and report; limited examination (eg, tangent screen, Autoplot, arc perimeter, or single stimulus level automated test, such as Octopus 3 or 7 equivalent)

92082 intermediate examination (eg, at least 2 isopters on Goldmann perimeter, or semiquantitative, automated suprathreshold screening program, Humphrey suprathreshold automatic diagnostic test, Octopus program 33)

92083 extended examination (eg, Goldmann visual fields with at least 3 isopters plotted and static determination within the central 30°, or quantitative, automated threshold perimetry, Octopus program G-1, 32 or 42, Humphrey visual field analyzer full threshold programs 30-2, 24-2, or 30/60-2)

(Gross visual field testing (eg, confrontation testing) is a part of general ophthalmological services and is not reported separately)

92100 Serial tonometry (separate procedure) with multiple measurements of intraocular pressure over an extended time period with interpretation and report, same day (eg, diurnal curve or medical treatment of acute elevation of intraocular pressure)

92120 Tonography with interpretation and report, recording indentation tonometer method or perilimbal suction method

92130 Tonography with water provocation

92135 Scanning computerized ophthalmic diagnostic imaging (eg, scanning laser) with interpretation and report, unilateral

92136 Ophthalmic biometry by partial coherence interferometry with intraocular lens power calculation

92140 Provocative tests for glaucoma, with interpretation and report, without tonography

Ophthalmoscopy

Routine ophthalmoscopy is part of general and special ophthalmologic services whenever indicated. It is a non-itemized service and is not reported separately.

92225 Ophthalmoscopy, extended, with retinal drawing (eg, for retinal detachment, melanoma), with interpretation and report; initial

92226 subsequent

92230 Fluorescein angioscopy with interpretation and report

92235 Fluorescein angiography (includes multiframe imaging) with interpretation and report

92240 Indocyanine-green angiography (includes multiframe imaging) with interpretation and report

92250 Fundus photography with interpretation and report

92260 Ophthalmodynamometry

(For ophthalmoscopy under general anesthesia, use 92018)

Other Specialized Services

92265 Needle oculoelectromyography, one or more extraocular muscles, one or both eyes, with interpretation and report

92270 Electro-oculography with interpretation and report

Medicine

92275 Electroretinography with interpretation and report

(For electronystagmography for vestibular function studies, see 92541 et seq)

(For ophthalmic echography (diagnostic ultrasound), see 76511-76529)

92283 Color vision examination, extended, eg, anomaloscope or equivalent

(Color vision testing with pseudoisochromatic plates (such as HRR or Ishihara) is not reported separately. It is included in the appropriate general or ophthalmological service, or 99172)

92284 Dark adaptation examination with interpretation and report

92285 External ocular photography with interpretation and report for documentation of medical progress (eg, close-up photography, slit lamp photography, goniophotography, stereo-photography)

92286 Special anterior segment photography with interpretation and report; with specular endothelial microscopy and cell count

92287 with fluorescein angiography

Contact Lens Services

The prescription of contact lens includes specification of optical and physical characteristics (such as power, size, curvature, flexibility, gas-permeability). It is NOT a part of the general ophthalmological services.

The fitting of contact lens includes instruction and training of the wearer and incidental revision of the lens during the training period.

Follow-up of successfully fitted extended wear lenses is reported as part of a general ophthalmological service (92012 et seq).

The supply of contact lenses may be reported as part of the service of fitting. It may also be reported separately by using the appropriate supply codes.

(For therapeutic or surgical use of contact lens, see 68340, 92070)

92310 Prescription of optical and physical characteristics of and fitting of contact lens, with medical supervision of adaptation; corneal lens, both eyes, except for aphakia

(For prescription and fitting of one eye, add modifier 52)

92311 corneal lens for aphakia, one eye

92312 corneal lens for aphakia, both eyes

92313 corneoscleral lens

92314 Prescription of optical and physical characteristics of contact lens, with medical supervision of adaptation and direction of fitting by independent technician; corneal lens, both eyes except for aphakia

(For prescription and fitting of one eye, add modifier 52)

92315 corneal lens for aphakia, one eye

92316 corneal lens for aphakia, both eyes

92317 corneoscleral lens

92325 Modification of contact lens (separate procedure), with medical supervision of adaptation

92326 Replacement of contact lens

(92330, 92335 have been deleted)

(For prescription, fitting, and/or medical supervision of ocular prosthetic adaptation by a physician, see Evaluation and Management services or General Ophthalmological service codes 92002-92014)

Spectacle Services (Including Prosthesis for Aphakia)

Prescription of lenses, when required, is included in 92015 Determination of refractive state. It includes specification of lens type (monofocal, bifocal, other), lens power, axis, prism, absorptive factor, impact resistance, and other factors.

Fitting of spectacles is a separate service; when provided by the physician, it is reported as indicated by 92340-92371.

Fitting includes measurement of anatomical facial characteristics, the writing of laboratory specifications, and the final adjustment of the spectacles to the visual axes and anatomical topography. Presence of physician is not required.

Supply of materials is a separate service component; it is not part of the service of fitting spectacles.

92340 Fitting of spectacles, except for aphakia; monofocal

92341 bifocal

92342 multifocal, other than bifocal

92352 Fitting of spectacle prosthesis for aphakia; monofocal

92353 multifocal

92354 Fitting of spectacle mounted low vision aid; single element system

92355 telescopic or other compound lens system

92358 Prosthesis service for aphakia, temporary (disposable or loan, including materials)

92370 Repair and refitting spectacles; except for aphakia

92371 spectacle prosthesis for aphakia

(Codes 92390-92396 have been deleted. For supply of spectacles or contact lenses, use the appropriate supply codes)

Other Procedures

92499 Unlisted ophthalmological service or procedure

⊙=Moderate sedation ✚=Add-on code ⁄=FDA approval pending

Special Otorhinolaryngologic Services

Diagnostic or treatment procedures usually included in a comprehensive otorhinolaryngologic evaluation or office visit, are reported as an integrated medical service, using appropriate descriptors from the 99201 series. Itemization of component procedures (eg, otoscopy, rhinoscopy, tuning fork test) does not apply.

Special otorhinolaryngologic services are those diagnostic and treatment services not usually included in a comprehensive otorhinolaryngologic evaluation or office visit. These services are reported separately, using codes 92502-92700.

All services include medical diagnostic evaluation. Technical procedures (which may or may not be performed by the physician personally) are often part of the service, but should not be mistaken to constitute the service itself.

Code 92506 is used to report evaluation of speech production, receptive language, and expressive language abilities. Tests may examine speech sound production, articulatory movements of oral musculature, the patient's ability to understand the meaning and intent of written and verbal expressions, and the appropriate formulation and utterance of expressive thought. In contrast, 92626 and 92627 are reported for an evaluation of auditory rehabilitation status determining the patient's ability to use residual hearing in order to identify the acoustic characteristics of sounds associated with speech communication.

> (For laryngoscopy with stroboscopy, use 31579)

92502 Otolaryngologic examination under general anesthesia

92504 Binocular microscopy (separate diagnostic procedure)

92506 Evaluation of speech, language, voice, communication, and/or auditory processing

92507 Treatment of speech, language, voice, communication, and/or auditory processing disorder; individual

92508 group, 2 or more individuals

> (92510 has been deleted)

> (For auditory rehabilitation, prelingual hearing loss, use 92630)

> (For auditory rehabilitation, postlingual hearing loss, use 92633)

> (For cochlear implant programming, see 92601-92604)

92511 Nasopharyngoscopy with endoscope (separate procedure)

92512 Nasal function studies (eg, rhinomanometry)

92516 Facial nerve function studies (eg, electroneuronography)

92520 Laryngeal function studies (ie, aerodynamic testing and acoustic testing)

> (For performance of a single test, use modifier 52)

> (To report flexible fiberoptic laryngeal evaluation of swallowing and laryngeal sensory testing, see 92611-92617)

> (To report other testing of laryngeal function (eg, electroglottography), use 92700)

92526 Treatment of swallowing dysfunction and/or oral function for feeding

Vestibular Function Tests, With Observation and Evaluation by Physician, Without Electrical Recording

92531 Spontaneous nystagmus, including gaze

92532 Positional nystagmus test

92533 Caloric vestibular test, each irrigation (binaural, bithermal stimulation constitutes four tests)

92534 Optokinetic nystagmus test

Vestibular Function Tests, With Recording (eg, ENG, PENG), and Medical Diagnostic Evaluation

92541 Spontaneous nystagmus test, including gaze and fixation nystagmus, with recording

92542 Positional nystagmus test, minimum of 4 positions, with recording

92543 Caloric vestibular test, each irrigation (binaural, bithermal stimulation constitutes four tests), with recording

92544 Optokinetic nystagmus test, bidirectional, foveal or peripheral stimulation, with recording

92545 Oscillating tracking test, with recording

92546 Sinusoidal vertical axis rotational testing

+ 92547 Use of vertical electrodes (List separately in addition to code for primary procedure)

> (Use 92547 in conjunction with 92541-92546)

> (For unlisted vestibular tests, use 92700)

92548 Computerized dynamic posturography

Audiologic Function Tests With Medical Diagnostic Evaluation

The audiometric tests listed below imply the use of calibrated electronic equipment. Other hearing tests (such as whispered voice, tuning fork) are considered part of the general otorhinolaryngologic services and are not reported separately. All services include testing of both ears. Use modifier 52 if a test is applied to one ear instead

Medicine

of to two ears. All codes (except 92559) apply to testing of individuals; for testing of groups, use 92559 and specify test(s) used.

(For evaluation of speech, language and/or hearing problems through observation and assessment of performance, use 92506)

92551	Screening test, pure tone, air only
92552	Pure tone audiometry (threshold); air only
92553	air and bone
92555	Speech audiometry threshold;
92556	with speech recognition
92557	Comprehensive audiometry threshold evaluation and speech recognition (92553 and 92556 combined)

(For hearing aid evaluation and selection, see 92590-92595)

92559	Audiometric testing of groups
92560	Bekesy audiometry; screening
92561	diagnostic
92562	Loudness balance test, alternate binaural or monaural
92563	Tone decay test
92564	Short increment sensitivity index (SISI)
92565	Stenger test, pure tone
92567	Tympanometry (impedance testing)
92568	Acoustic reflex testing; threshold
92569	decay
92571	Filtered speech test
92572	Staggered spondaic word test

►(92573 has been deleted. To report the Lombard test, use 92700)◄

92575	Sensorineural acuity level test
92576	Synthetic sentence identification test
92577	Stenger test, speech
92579	Visual reinforcement audiometry (VRA)
92582	Conditioning play audiometry
92583	Select picture audiometry
92584	Electrocochleography
92585	Auditory evoked potentials for evoked response audiometry and/or testing of the central nervous system; comprehensive
92586	limited
92587	Evoked otoacoustic emissions; limited (single stimulus level, either transient or distortion products)
92588	comprehensive or diagnostic evaluation (comparison of transient and/or distortion product otoacoustic emissions at multiple levels and frequencies)

(92589 has been deleted)

(For central auditory function evaluation, see 92620, 92621)

92590	Hearing aid examination and selection; monaural
92591	binaural
92592	Hearing aid check; monaural
92593	binaural
92594	Electroacoustic evaluation for hearing aid; monaural
92595	binaural
92596	Ear protector attenuation measurements
92597	Evaluation for use and/or fitting of voice prosthetic device to supplement oral speech

(To report augmentative and alternative communication device services, see 92605, 92607, 92608)

Evaluative and Therapeutic Services

Codes 92601 and 92603 describe post-operative analysis and fitting of previously placed external devices, connection to the cochlear implant, and programming of the stimulator. Codes 92602 and 92604 describe subsequent sessions for measurements and adjustment of the external transmitter and re-programming of the internal stimulator.

(For placement of cochlear implant, use 69930)

92601	Diagnostic analysis of cochlear implant, patient younger than 7 years of age; with programming
92602	subsequent reprogramming

(Do not report 92602 in addition to 92601)

(For aural rehabilitation services following cochlear implant, including evaluation of rehabilitation status, see 92626-92627, 92630-92633)

92603	Diagnostic analysis of cochlear implant, age 7 years or older; with programming
92604	subsequent reprogramming

(Do not report 92604 in addition to 92603)

92605	Evaluation for prescription of non-speech-generating augmentative and alternative communication device
92606	Therapeutic service(s) for the use of non-speech-generating device, including programming and modification

Medicine

92607 Evaluation for prescription for speech-generating augmentative and alternative communication device, face-to-face with the patient; first hour

(For evaluation for prescription of a non-speech-generating device, use 92605)

+ 92608 each additional 30 minutes (List separately in addition to code for primary procedure)

(Use 92608 in conjunction with 92607)

92609 Therapeutic services for the use of speech-generating device, including programming and modification

(For therapeutic service(s) for the use of a non-speech-generating device, use 92606)

92610 Evaluation of oral and pharyngeal swallowing function

(For motion fluoroscopic evaluation of swallowing function, use 92611)

(For flexible endoscopic examination, use 92612-92617)

92611 Motion fluoroscopic evaluation of swallowing function by cine or video recording

(For radiological supervision and interpretation, use 74230)

(For evaluation of oral and pharyngeal swallowing function, use 92610)

(For flexible fiberoptic diagnostic laryngoscopy, use 31575. Do not report 31575 in conjunction with 92612-92617)

92612 Flexible fiberoptic endoscopic evaluation of swallowing by cine or video recording;

(If flexible fiberoptic or endoscopic evaluation of swallowing is performed without cine or video recording, use 92700)

92613 physician interpretation and report only

(To report an evaluation of oral and pharyngeal swallowing function, use 92610)

(To report motion fluoroscopic evaluation of swallowing function, use 92611)

92614 Flexible fiberoptic endoscopic evaluation, laryngeal sensory testing by cine or video recording;

(If flexible fiberoptic or endoscopic evaluation of swallowing is performed without cine or video recording, use 92700)

92615 physician interpretation and report only

92616 Flexible fiberoptic endoscopic evaluation of swallowing and laryngeal sensory testing by cine or video recording;

(If flexible fiberoptic or endoscopic evaluation of swallowing is performed without cine or video recording, use 92700)

92617 physician interpretation and report only

92620 Evaluation of central auditory function, with report; initial 60 minutes

92621 each additional 15 minutes

(Do not report 92620, 92621 in conjunction with 92506)

92625 Assessment of tinnitus (includes pitch, loudness matching, and masking)

(Do not report 92625 in conjunction with 92562)

(For unilateral assessment, use modifier 52)

92626 Evaluation of auditory rehabilitation status; first hour

+ 92627 each additional 15 minutes (List separately in addition to code for primary procedure)

(Use 92627 in conjunction with 92626)

(When reporting 92626, 92627, use the face-to-face time with the patient or family)

92630 Auditory rehabilitation; prelingual hearing loss

92633 postlingual hearing loss

►Special Diagnostic Procedures◄

● **92640** Diagnostic analysis with programming of auditory brainstem implant, per hour

►(Report nonprogramming services separately [eg, cardiac monitoring])◄

Other Procedures

92700 Unlisted otorhinolaryngological service or procedure

Cardiovascular

►Therapeutic Services and Procedures◄

(For nonsurgical septal reduction therapy [eg, alcohol ablation], use Category III code 0024T)

92950 Cardiopulmonary resuscitation (eg, in cardiac arrest)

(See also critical care services, 99291, 99292)

⊙ **92953** Temporary transcutaneous pacing

(For physician direction of ambulance or rescue personnel outside the hospital, use 99288)

⊙ **92960** Cardioversion, elective, electrical conversion of arrhythmia; external

⊙ **92961** internal (separate procedure)

(Do not report 92961 in addition to codes 93662, 93618-93624, 93631, 93640-93642, 93650-93652, 93741-93744)

92970 Cardioassist-method of circulatory assist; internal

92971 external

(For balloon atrial-septostomy, use 92992)

(For placement of catheters for use in circulatory assist devices such as intra-aortic balloon pump, use 33970)

⊙✛ **92973** Percutaneous transluminal coronary thrombectomy (List separately in addition to code for primary procedure)

(Use 92973 in conjunction with 92980, 92982)

⊙✛ **92974** Transcatheter placement of radiation delivery device for subsequent coronary intravascular brachytherapy (List separately in addition to code for primary procedure)

(Use 92974 in conjunction with 92980, 92982, 92995, 93508)

(For intravascular radioelement application, see 77781-77784)

⊙ **92975** Thrombolysis, coronary; by intracoronary infusion, including selective coronary angiography

92977 by intravenous infusion

(For thrombolysis of vessels other than coronary, see 37201, 75896)

(For cerebral thrombolysis, use 37195)

⊙✛ **92978** Intravascular ultrasound (coronary vessel or graft) during diagnostic evaluation and/or therapeutic intervention including imaging supervision, interpretation and report; initial vessel (List separately in addition to code for primary procedure)

⊙✛ **92979** each additional vessel (List separately in addition to code for primary procedure)

(Use 92979 in conjunction with 92978)

(Intravascular ultrasound services include all transducer manipulations and repositioning within the specific vessel being examined, both before and after therapeutic intervention (eg, stent placement))

⊙ **92980** Transcatheter placement of an intracoronary stent(s), percutaneous, with or without other therapeutic intervention, any method; single vessel

⊙✛ **92981** each additional vessel (List separately in addition to code for primary procedure)

(Use 92981 in conjunction with 92980)

(Codes 92980, 92981 are used to report coronary artery stenting. Coronary angioplasty (92982, 92984) or atherectomy (92995, 92996), in the same artery, is considered part of the stenting procedure and is not reported separately. Codes 92973 (percutaneous transluminal coronary thombectomy), 92974 (coronary brachytherapy) and 92978, 92979 (intravascular ultrasound) are add-on codes for reporting procedures performed in addition to coronary stenting, atherectomy, and angioplasty and are not included in the "therapeutic interventions" in 92980)

(To report additional vessels treated by angioplasty or atherectomy only during the same session, see 92984, 92996)

(To report transcatheter placement of radiation delivery device for coronary intravascular brachytherapy, use 92974)

(For intravascular radioelement application, see 77781-77784)

⊙ **92982** Percutaneous transluminal coronary balloon angioplasty; single vessel

⊙✛ **92984** each additional vessel (List separately in addition to code for primary procedure)

(Use 92984 in conjunction with 92980, 92982, 92995)

(For stent placement following completion of angioplasty or atherectomy, see 92980, 92981)

(To report transcatheter placement of radiation delivery device for coronary intravascular brachytherapy, use 92974)

(For intravascular radioelement application, see 77781-77784)

⊙ **92986** Percutaneous balloon valvuloplasty; aortic valve

⊙ **92987** mitral valve

92990 pulmonary valve

92992 Atrial septectomy or septostomy; transvenous method, balloon (eg, Rashkind type) (includes cardiac catheterization)

92993 blade method (Park septostomy) (includes cardiac catheterization)

⊙ **92995** Percutaneous transluminal coronary atherectomy, by mechanical or other method, with or without balloon angioplasty; single vessel

⊙✛ **92996** each additional vessel (List separately in addition to code for primary procedure)

(Use 92996 in conjunction with 92980, 92982, 92995)

(For stent placement following completion of angioplasty or atherectomy, see 92980, 92981)

(To report additional vessels treated by angioplasty only during the same session, use 92984)

92997 Percutaneous transluminal pulmonary artery balloon angioplasty; single vessel

✛ **92998** each additional vessel (List separately in addition to code for primary procedure)

(Use 92998 in conjunction with 92997)

Medicine

Cardiography

(For echocardiography, see 93303-93350)

93000 Electrocardiogram, routine ECG with at least 12 leads; with interpretation and report

93005 tracing only, without interpretation and report

93010 interpretation and report only

(For ECG monitoring, see 99354-99360)

93012 Telephonic transmission of post-symptom electrocardiogram rhythm strip(s), 24-hour attended monitoring, per 30 day period of time; tracing only

93014 physician review with interpretation and report only

93015 Cardiovascular stress test using maximal or submaximal treadmill or bicycle exercise, continuous electrocardiographic monitoring, and/or pharmacological stress; with physician supervision, with interpretation and report

93016 physician supervision only, without interpretation and report

93017 tracing only, without interpretation and report

93018 interpretation and report only

(For inert gas rebreathing measurement, see Category III codes 0104T, 0105T)

93024 Ergonovine provocation test

93025 Microvolt T-wave alternans for assessment of ventricular arrhythmias

93040 Rhythm ECG, one to three leads; with interpretation and report

93041 tracing only without interpretation and report

93042 interpretation and report only

93224 Electrocardiographic monitoring for 24 hours by continuous original ECG waveform recording and storage, with visual superimposition scanning; includes recording, scanning analysis with report, physician review and interpretation

93225 recording (includes hook-up, recording, and disconnection)

93226 scanning analysis with report

93227 physician review and interpretation

93230 Electrocardiographic monitoring for 24 hours by continuous original ECG waveform recording and storage without superimposition scanning utilizing a device capable of producing a full miniaturized printout; includes recording, microprocessor-based analysis with report, physician review and interpretation

93231 recording (includes hook-up, recording, and disconnection)

93232 microprocessor-based analysis with report

93233 physician review and interpretation

93235 Electrocardiographic monitoring for 24 hours by continuous computerized monitoring and non-continuous recording, and real-time data analysis utilizing a device capable of producing intermittent full-sized waveform tracings, possibly patient activated; includes monitoring and real-time data analysis with report, physician review and interpretation

93236 monitoring and real-time data analysis with report

93237 physician review and interpretation

93268 Patient demand single or multiple event recording with presymptom memory loop, 24-hour attended monitoring, per 30 day period of time; includes transmission, physician review and interpretation

93270 recording (includes hook-up, recording, and disconnection)

93271 monitoring, receipt of transmissions, and analysis

93272 physician review and interpretation only

(For postsymptom recording, see 93012, 93014)

(For implanted patient activated cardiac event recording, see 33282, 93727)

93278 Signal-averaged electrocardiography (SAECG), with or without ECG

(For interpretation and report only, use 93278 with modifier 26)

(For unlisted cardiographic procedure, use 93799)

Echocardiography

Echocardiography includes obtaining ultrasonic signals from the heart and great arteries, with two-dimensional image and/or Doppler ultrasonic signal documentation, and interpretation and report. When interpretation is performed separately use modifier 26.

Echocardiography is an ultrasound examination of the cardiac chambers and valves, the adjacent great vessels, and the pericardium. A complete transthoracic echocardiogram (93307) is a comprehensive procedure that includes 2-dimensional and selected M-mode examination of the left and right atria, left and right ventricles, the aortic, mitral, and tricuspid valves, the pericardium, and adjacent portions of the aorta. These structures are assessed using multiple views as required to obtain a complete functional and anatomic evaluation, and appropriate measurements are obtained and recorded. Despite significant effort, identification and measurement of some structures may not always be possible. In such instances, the reason that an element could not be visualized must be documented. Additional structures that may be visualized (eg, pulmonary veins, pulmonary artery, pulmonic valve, inferior vena cava) would be included as part of the service.

Medicine

A follow-up or limited echocardiographic study (93308) is an examination that does not evaluate or document the attempt to evaluate all the structures that comprise the complete echocardiographic exam. This is typically performed in follow-up of a complete echocardiographic examination when a repeat complete exam is unnecessary due to the more focused clinical concern. In some emergent clinical situations, a limited echocardiographic study may be performed primarily.

Report of an echocardiographic study, whether complete or limited, includes an interpretation of all obtained information, documentation of all clinically relevant findings including quantitative measurements obtained, plus a description of any recognized abnormalities. Pertinent images, videotape, and/or digital data are archived for permanent storage and are available for subsequent review. Use of echocardiography not meeting these criteria is not separately reportable.

Use of ultrasound, without thorough evaluation of organ(s) or anatomic region, image documentation and final, written report, is not separately reportable.

(For fetal echocardiography, see 76825-76828)

93303 Transthoracic echocardiography for congenital cardiac anomalies; complete

93304 follow-up or limited study

93307 Echocardiography, transthoracic, real-time with image documentation (2D) with or without M-mode recording; complete

93308 follow-up or limited study

⊙ **93312** Echocardiography, transesophageal, real time with image documentation (2D) (with or without M-mode recording); including probe placement, image acquisition, interpretation and report

⊙ **93313** placement of transesophageal probe only

⊙ **93314** image acquisition, interpretation and report only

⊙ **93315** Transesophageal echocardiography for congenital cardiac anomalies; including probe placement, image acquisition, interpretation and report

⊙ **93316** placement of transesophageal probe only

⊙ **93317** image acquisition, interpretation and report only

⊙ **93318** Echocardiography, transesophageal (TEE) for monitoring purposes, including probe placement, real time 2-dimensional image acquisition and interpretation leading to ongoing (continuous) assessment of (dynamically changing) cardiac pumping function and to therapeutic measures on an immediate time basis

+ **93320** Doppler echocardiography, pulsed wave and/or continuous wave with spectral display (List separately in addition to codes for echocardiographic imaging); complete

(Use 93320 in conjunction with 93303, 93304, 93307, 93308, 93312, 93314, 93315, 93317, 93350)

+ **93321** follow-up or limited study (List separately in addition to codes for echocardiographic imaging)

(Use 93321 in conjunction with 93303, 93304, 93307, 93308, 93312, 93314, 93315, 93317, 93350)

+ **93325** Doppler echocardiography color flow velocity mapping (List separately in addition to codes for echocardiography)

(Use 93325 in conjunction with 76825, 76826, 76827, 76828, 93303, 93304, 93307, 93308, 93312, 93314, 93315, 93317, 93320, 93321, 93350)

93350 Echocardiography, transthoracic, real-time with image documentation (2D), with or without M-mode recording, during rest and cardiovascular stress test using treadmill, bicycle exercise and/or pharmacologically induced stress, with interpretation and report

(The appropriate stress testing code from the 93015-93018 series should be reported in addition to 93350 to capture the exercise stress portion of the study)

Cardiac Catheterization

Cardiac catheterization is a diagnostic medical procedure which includes introduction, positioning and repositioning of catheter(s), when necessary, recording of intracardiac and intravascular pressure, obtaining blood samples for measurement of blood gases or dilution curves and cardiac output measurements (Fick or other method, with or without rest and exercise and/or studies) with or without electrode catheter placement, final evaluation and report of procedure. When selective injection procedures are performed without a preceding cardiac catheterization, these services should be reported using codes in the Vascular Injection Procedures section, 36011-36015 and 36215-36218.

When coronary artery, arterial coronary conduit or venous bypass graft angiography is performed without concomitant left heart cardiac catheterization, use 93508. Injection procedures 93539, 93540, 93544, and 93545 represent separate identifiable services and may be reported in conjunction with one another in addition to 93508, as appropriate. To report imaging supervision, interpretation and report in conjunction with 93508, use 93556.

Modifier 51 should not be appended to 93501-93533, 93539-93556.

⊙⊘ **93501** Right heart catheterization

(For bundle of His recording, use 93600)

⊘ **93503** Insertion and placement of flow directed catheter (eg, Swan-Ganz) for monitoring purposes

(For subsequent monitoring, see 99356-99357)

⊙⊘ **93505** Endomyocardial biopsy

⊙⊘ **93508** Catheter placement in coronary artery(s), arterial coronary conduit(s), and/or venous coronary bypass graft(s) for coronary angiography without concomitant left heart catheterization

(93508 is to be used only when left heart catheterization 93510, 93511, 93524, 93526 is not performed)

(93508 is to be used only once per procedure)

(To report transcatheter placement of radiation delivery device for coronary intravascular brachytherapy, use 92974)

(For intravascular radioelement application, see 77781-77784)

⊙⊘ **93510** Left heart catheterization, retrograde, from the brachial artery, axillary artery or femoral artery; percutaneous

⊙⊘ **93511** by cutdown

⊙⊘ **93514** Left heart catheterization by left ventricular puncture

⊙⊘ **93524** Combined transseptal and retrograde left heart catheterization

⊙⊘ **93526** Combined right heart catheterization and retrograde left heart catheterization

⊙⊘ **93527** Combined right heart catheterization and transseptal left heart catheterization through intact septum (with or without retrograde left heart catheterization)

⊙⊘ **93528** Combined right heart catheterization with left ventricular puncture (with or without retrograde left heart catheterization)

⊙⊘ **93529** Combined right heart catheterization and left heart catheterization through existing septal opening (with or without retrograde left heart catheterization)

⊙⊘ **93530** Right heart catheterization, for congenital cardiac anomalies

⊘ **93531** Combined right heart catheterization and retrograde left heart catheterization, for congenital cardiac anomalies

⊘ **93532** Combined right heart catheterization and transseptal left heart catheterization through intact septum with or without retrograde left heart catheterization, for congenital cardiac anomalies

⊘ **93533** Combined right heart catheterization and transseptal left heart catheterization through existing septal opening, with or without retrograde left heart catheterization, for congenital cardiac anomalies

(When injection procedures are performed in conjunction with cardiac catheterization, these services do not include introduction of catheters but do include repositioning of catheters when necessary and use of automatic power injectors. Injection procedures 93539-93545 represent separate identifiable services and may be coded in conjunction with one another when appropriate. The technical details of angiography, supervision of filming and processing, interpretation and report are not included. To report imaging supervision, interpretation and report, use 93555 and/or 93556. Modifier 51 should not be appended to 93539-93556.)

⊙⊘ **93539** Injection procedure during cardiac catheterization; for selective opacification of arterial conduits (eg, internal mammary), whether native or used for bypass

⊙⊘ **93540** for selective opacification of aortocoronary venous bypass grafts, one or more coronary arteries

⊙⊘ **93541** for pulmonary angiography

⊙⊘ **93542** for selective right ventricular or right atrial angiography

⊙⊘ **93543** for selective left ventricular or left atrial angiography

⊙⊘ **93544** for aortography

⊙⊘ **93545** for selective coronary angiography (injection of radiopaque material may be by hand)

(To report imaging supervision and interpretation, use 93555)

⊙⊘ **93555** Imaging supervision, interpretation and report for injection procedure(s) during cardiac catheterization; ventricular and/or atrial angiography

⊙⊘ **93556** pulmonary angiography, aortography, and/or selective coronary angiography including venous bypass grafts and arterial conduits (whether native or used in bypass)

(Codes 93561 and 93562 are not to be used with cardiac catheterization codes)

⊙ **93561** Indicator dilution studies such as dye or thermal dilution, including arterial and/or venous catheterization; with cardiac output measurement (separate procedure)

⊙ **93562** subsequent measurement of cardiac output

(For radioisotope method of cardiac output, see 78472, 78473, or 78481)

⊙+ **93571** Intravascular Doppler velocity and/or pressure derived coronary flow reserve measurement (coronary vessel or graft) during coronary angiography including pharmacologically induced stress; initial vessel (List separately in addition to code for primary procedure)

⊙+ **93572** each additional vessel (List separately in addition to code for primary procedure)

(Intravascular distal coronary blood flow velocity measurements include all Doppler transducer manipulations and repositioning within the specific vessel being examined, during coronary angiography or therapeutic intervention (eg, angioplasty))

(For unlisted cardiac catheterization procedure, use 93799)

Medicine

Repair of Septal Defect

93580 Percutaneous transcatheter closure of congenital interatrial communication (ie, Fontan fenestration, atrial septal defect) with implant

(Percutaneous transcatheter closure of atrial septal defect includes a right heart catheterization procedure. Code 93580 includes injection of contrast for atrial and ventricular angiograms. Codes 93501, 93529-93533, 93539, 93543, 93555 should not be reported separately in addition to code 93580)

93581 Percutaneous transcatheter closure of a congenital ventricular septal defect with implant

(Percutaneous transcatheter closure of ventricular septal defect includes a right heart catheterization procedure. Code 93581 includes injection of contrast for atrial and ventricular angiograms. Codes 93501, 93529-93533, 93539, 93543, 93555 should not be reported separately in addition to code 93581)

►(For ventricular septal defect closure via transmyocardial implant delivery, see 0166T, 0167T)◄

(For echocardiographic services performed in addition to 93580, 93581, see 93303-93317, 93662 as appropriate)

Intracardiac Electrophysiological Procedures/Studies

Intracardiac electrophysiologic studies (EPS) are an invasive diagnostic medical procedure which include the insertion and repositioning of electrode catheters, recording of electrograms before and during pacing or programmed stimulation of multiple locations in the heart, analysis of recorded information, and report of the procedure. Electrophysiologic studies are most often performed with two or more electrode catheters. In many circumstances, patients with arrhythmias are evaluated and treated at the same encounter. In this situation, a diagnostic *electrophysiologic study* is performed, induced tachycardia(s) are *mapped*, and on the basis of the diagnostic and mapping information, the tissue is *ablated*. Electrophysiologic study(ies), mapping, and ablation represent distinctly different procedures, requiring individual reporting whether performed on the same or subsequent dates.

Definitions

Arrhythmia Induction: In most electrophysiologic studies, an attempt is made to induce arrhythmia(s) from single or multiple sites within the heart. Arrhythmia induction is achieved by performing pacing at different rates, programmed stimulation (introduction of critically timed electrical impulses), and other techniques. Because arrhythmia induction occurs via the same catheter(s) inserted for the electrophysiologic study(ies), catheter insertion and temporary pacemaker codes are not additionally reported. Codes 93600-93603, 93610-93612 and 93618 are used to describe unusual situations where there may be recording, pacing or an attempt at

arrhythmia induction from only one site in the heart. Code 93619 describes only evaluation of the sinus node, atrioventricular node and His-Purkinje conduction system, without arrhythmia induction. Codes 93620-93624 and 93640-93642 all include recording, pacing and attempted arrhythmia induction from one or more site(s) in the heart.

Mapping: Mapping is a distinct procedure performed in addition to a diagnostic electrophysiologic procedure and should be separately reported using 93609 or 93613. Do not report standard mapping (93609) in addition to 3-D mapping (93613). When a tachycardia is induced, the site of tachycardia origination or its electrical path through the heart is often defined by mapping. Mapping creates a multidimensional depiction of a tachycardia by recording multiple electrograms obtained sequentially or simultaneously from multiple catheter sites in the heart. Depending upon the technique, certain types of mapping catheters may be repositioned from point-to-point within the heart, allowing sequential recording from the various sites to construct maps. Other types of mapping catheters allow mapping without a point-to-point technique by allowing simultaneous recording from many electrodes on the same catheter and computer-assisted three dimensional reconstruction of the tachycardia activation sequence.

Ablation: Once the part of the heart involved in the tachycardia is localized, the tachycardia may be treated by ablation (the delivery of a radiofrequency energy to the area to selectively destroy cardiac tissue). Ablation procedures (93651-93652) may be performed: independently on a date subsequent to a diagnostic electrophysiologic study and mapping; or, at the time a diagnostic electrophysiologic study, tachycardia(s) induction and mapping is performed. When an electrophysiologic study, mapping, and ablation are performed on the same date, each procedure should be separately reported. In reporting catheter ablation, 93651 and/or 93652 should be reported once to describe ablation of cardiac arrhythmias, regardless of the number of arrhythmias ablated.

Modifier 51 should not be appended to 93600-93660.

⊘ **93600** Bundle of His recording

⊘ **93602** Intra-atrial recording

⊘ **93603** Right ventricular recording

⊙+ **93609** Intraventricular and/or intra-atrial mapping of tachycardia site(s) with catheter manipulation to record from multiple sites to identify origin of tachycardia (List separately in addition to code for primary procedure)

(Use 93609 in conjunction with 93620, 93651, 93652)

(Do not report 93609 in addition to 93613)

⊘ **93610** Intra-atrial pacing

⊘ **93612** Intraventricular pacing

(Do not report 93612 in conjunction with 93620-93622)

⊙+ **93613** Intracardiac electrophysiologic 3-dimensional mapping (List separately in addition to code for primary procedure)

(Use 93613 in conjunction with 93620, 93651, 93652)

(Do not report 93613 in addition to 93609)

⊙⊘ **93615** Esophageal recording of atrial electrogram with or without ventricular electrogram(s);

⊙⊘ **93616** with pacing

⊙⊘ **93618** Induction of arrhythmia by electrical pacing

(For intracardiac phonocardiogram, use 93799)

⊙⊘ **93619** Comprehensive electrophysiologic evaluation with right atrial pacing and recording, right ventricular pacing and recording, His bundle recording, including insertion and repositioning of multiple electrode catheters, without induction or attempted induction of arrhythmia

(Do not report 93619 in conjunction with 93600, 93602, 93610, 93612, 93618, or 93620-93622)

⊙⊘ **93620** Comprehensive electrophysiologic evaluation including insertion and repositioning of multiple electrode catheters with induction or attempted induction of arrhythmia; with right atrial pacing and recording, right ventricular pacing and recording, His bundle recording

(Do not report 93620 in conjunction with 93600, 93602, 93610, 93612, 93618 or 93619)

⊙+ **93621** with left atrial pacing and recording from coronary sinus or left atrium (List separately in addition to code for primary procedure)

(Use 93621 in conjunction with 93620)

⊙+ **93622** with left ventricular pacing and recording (List separately in addition to code for primary procedure)

(Use 93622 in conjunction with 93620)

+ **93623** Programmed stimulation and pacing after intravenous drug infusion (List separately in addition to code for primary procedure)

(Use 93623 in conjunction with 93619, 93620)

⊙⊘ **93624** Electrophysiologic follow-up study with pacing and recording to test effectiveness of therapy, including induction or attempted induction of arrhythmia

⊘ **93631** Intra-operative epicardial and endocardial pacing and mapping to localize the site of tachycardia or zone of slow conduction for surgical correction

⊙⊘ **93640** Electrophysiologic evaluation of single or dual chamber pacing cardioverter-defibrillator leads including defibrillation threshold evaluation (induction of arrhythmia, evaluation of sensing and pacing for arrhythmia termination) at time of initial implantation or replacement;

⊙⊘ **93641** with testing of single or dual chamber pacing cardioverter-defibrillator pulse generator

(For subsequent or periodic electronic analysis and/or reprogramming of single or dual chamber pacing cardioverter-defibrillators, see 93642, 93741-93744)

⊙⊘ **93642** Electrophysiologic evaluation of single or dual chamber pacing cardioverter-defibrillator (includes defibrillation threshold evaluation, induction of arrhythmia, evaluation of sensing and pacing for arrhythmia termination, and programming or reprogramming of sensing or therapeutic parameters)

⊙⊘ **93650** Intracardiac catheter ablation of atrioventricular node function, atrioventricular conduction for creation of complete heart block, with or without temporary pacemaker placement

⊙⊘ **93651** Intracardiac catheter ablation of arrhythmogenic focus; for treatment of supraventricular tachycardia by ablation of fast or slow atrioventricular pathways, accessory atrioventricular connections or other atrial foci, singly or in combination

⊙⊘ **93652** for treatment of ventricular tachycardia

⊘ **93660** Evaluation of cardiovascular function with tilt table evaluation, with continuous ECG monitoring and intermittent blood pressure monitoring, with or without pharmacological intervention

(For testing of autonomic nervous system function, see 95921-95923)

+ **93662** Intracardiac echocardiography during therapeutic/diagnostic intervention, including imaging supervision and interpretation (List separately in addition to code for primary procedure)

(Use 93662 in conjunction with 92987, 93527, 93532, 93580, 93581, 93621, 93622, 93651, or 93652, as appropriate)

(Do not report 92961 in addition to 93662)

Peripheral Arterial Disease Rehabilitation

Peripheral arterial disease (PAD) rehabilitative physical exercise consists of a series of sessions, lasting 45-60 minutes per session, involving use of either a motorized treadmill or a track to permit each patient to achieve symptom-limited claudication. Each session is supervised by an exercise physiologist or nurse. The supervising provider monitors the individual patient's claudication threshold and other cardiovascular limitations for adjustment of workload. During this supervised rehabilitation program, the development of new arrhythmias, symptoms that might suggest angina or the continued inability of the patient to progress to an adequate level of exercise may require physician review and examination of the patient. These physician services would be separately reported with an appropriate level E/M service code.

93668 Peripheral arterial disease (PAD) rehabilitation, per session

Medicine

►Noninvasive Physiologic Studies and Procedures◄

(For arterial cannulation and recording of direct arterial pressure, use 36620)

(For radiographic injection procedures, see 36000-36299)

(For vascular cannulization for hemodialysis, see 36800-36821)

►(For chemotherapy for malignant disease, see 96409-96549)◄

(For penile plethysmography, use 54240)

93701 Bioimpedance, thoracic, electrical

93720 Plethysmography, total body; with interpretation and report

93721 tracing only, without interpretation and report

93722 interpretation and report only

(For regional plethysmography, see 93875-93931)

93724 Electronic analysis of antitachycardia pacemaker system (includes electrocardiographic recording, programming of device, induction and termination of tachycardia via implanted pacemaker, and interpretation of recordings)

93727 Electronic analysis of implantable loop recorder (ILR) system (includes retrieval of recorded and stored ECG data, physician review and interpretation of retrieved ECG data and reprogramming)

93731 Electronic analysis of dual-chamber pacemaker system (includes evaluation of programmable parameters at rest and during activity where applicable, using electrocardiographic recording and interpretation of recordings at rest and during exercise, analysis of event markers and device response); without reprogramming

93732 with reprogramming

93733 Electronic analysis of dual chamber internal pacemaker system (may include rate, pulse amplitude and duration, configuration of wave form, and/or testing of sensory function of pacemaker), telephonic analysis

93734 Electronic analysis of single chamber pacemaker system (includes evaluation of programmable parameters at rest and during activity where applicable, using electrocardiographic recording and interpretation of recordings at rest and during exercise, analysis of event markers and device response); without reprogramming

93735 with reprogramming

93736 Electronic analysis of single chamber internal pacemaker system (may include rate, pulse amplitude and duration, configuration of wave form, and/or testing of sensory function of pacemaker), telephonic analysis

93740 Temperature gradient studies

93741 Electronic analysis of pacing cardioverter-defibrillator (includes interrogation, evaluation of pulse generator status, evaluation of programmable parameters at rest and during activity where applicable, using electrocardiographic recording and interpretation of recordings at rest and during exercise, analysis of event markers and device response); single chamber or wearable cardioverter-defibrillator system, without reprogramming

(Do not report 93741 in conjunction with 93745)

93742 single chamber or wearable cardioverter-defibrillator system, with reprogramming

(Do not report 93742 in conjunction with 93745)

93743 dual chamber, without reprogramming

93744 dual chamber, with reprogramming

93745 Initial set-up and programming by a physician of wearable cardioverter-defibrillator includes initial programming of system, establishing baseline electronic ECG, transmission of data to data repository, patient instruction in wearing system and patient reporting of problems or events

(Do not report 93745 in conjunction with 93741, 93742)

93760 Thermogram; cephalic

93762 peripheral

93770 Determination of venous pressure

(For central venous cannulization see 36555-36556, 36500)

93784 Ambulatory blood pressure monitoring, utilizing a system such as magnetic tape and/or computer disk, for 24 hours or longer; including recording, scanning analysis, interpretation and report

93786 recording only

93788 scanning analysis with report

93790 physician review with interpretation and report

Other Procedures

93797 Physician services for outpatient cardiac rehabilitation; without continuous ECG monitoring (per session)

93798 with continuous ECG monitoring (per session)

93799 Unlisted cardiovascular service or procedure

Medicine

Noninvasive Vascular Diagnostic Studies

Vascular studies include patient care required to perform the studies, supervision of the studies and interpretation of study results with copies for patient records of hard copy output with analysis of all data, including bidirectional vascular flow or imaging when provided.

The use of a simple hand-held or other Doppler device that does not produce hard copy output, or that produces a record that does not permit analysis of bidirectional vascular flow, is considered to be part of the physical examination of the vascular system and is not separately reported.

Duplex scan (eg, 93880, 93882) describes an ultrasonic scanning procedure for characterizing the pattern and direction of blood flow in arteries or veins with the production of real time images integrating B-mode two-dimensional vascular structure with spectral and/or color flow Doppler mapping or imaging.

Noninvasive physiologic studies are performed using equipment separate and distinct from the duplex scanner. Codes 93875, 93965, 93922, 93923, and 93924 describe the evaluation of non-imaging physiologic recordings of pressures, Doppler analysis of bi-directional blood flow, plethysmography, and/or oxygen tension measurements appropriate for the anatomic area studied.

Cerebrovascular Arterial Studies

A complete transcranial Doppler (TCD) study (93886) includes ultrasound evaluation of the right and left anterior circulation territories and the posterior circulation territory (to include vertebral arteries and basilar artery). In a limited TCD study (93888) there is ultrasound evaluation of two or fewer of these territories. For TCD, ultrasound evaluation is a reasonable and concerted attempt to identify arterial signals through an acoustic window.

93875 Noninvasive physiologic studies of extracranial arteries, complete bilateral study (eg, periorbital flow direction with arterial compression, ocular pneumoplethysmography, Doppler ultrasound spectral analysis)

93880 Duplex scan of extracranial arteries; complete bilateral study

93882 unilateral or limited study

(To report common carotid intima-media thickness (IMT) study for evaluation of atherosclerotic burden or coronary heart disease risk factor assessment, use Category III code 0126T)

93886 Transcranial Doppler study of the intracranial arteries; complete study

93888 limited study

93890 vasoreactivity study

93892 emboli detection without intravenous microbubble injection

93893 emboli detection with intravenous microbubble injection

(Do not report 93890-93893 in conjunction with 93888)

Extremity Arterial Studies (Including Digits)

93922 Noninvasive physiologic studies of upper or lower extremity arteries, single level, bilateral (eg, ankle/brachial indices, Doppler waveform analysis, volume plethysmography, transcutaneous oxygen tension measurement)

93923 Noninvasive physiologic studies of upper or lower extremity arteries, multiple levels or with provocative functional maneuvers, complete bilateral study (eg, segmental blood pressure measurements, segmental Doppler waveform analysis, segmental volume plethysmography, segmental transcutaneous oxygen tension measurements, measurements with postural provocative tests, measurements with reactive hyperemia)

93924 Noninvasive physiologic studies of lower extremity arteries, at rest and following treadmill stress testing, complete bilateral study

93925 Duplex scan of lower extremity arteries or arterial bypass grafts; complete bilateral study

93926 unilateral or limited study

93930 Duplex scan of upper extremity arteries or arterial bypass grafts; complete bilateral study

93931 unilateral or limited study

Extremity Venous Studies (Including Digits)

93965 Noninvasive physiologic studies of extremity veins, complete bilateral study (eg, Doppler waveform analysis with responses to compression and other maneuvers, phleborheography, impedance plethysmography)

93970 Duplex scan of extremity veins including responses to compression and other maneuvers; complete bilateral study

93971 unilateral or limited study

Medicine

Visceral and Penile Vascular Studies

93975 Duplex scan of arterial inflow and venous outflow of abdominal, pelvic, scrotal contents and/or retroperitoneal organs; complete study

93976 limited study

93978 Duplex scan of aorta, inferior vena cava, iliac vasculature, or bypass grafts; complete study

93979 unilateral or limited study

93980 Duplex scan of arterial inflow and venous outflow of penile vessels; complete study

93981 follow-up or limited study

Extremity Arterial-Venous Studies

93990 Duplex scan of hemodialysis access (including arterial inflow, body of access and venous outflow)

(For measurement of hemodialysis access flow using indicator dilution methods, use 90940)

Pulmonary

▶Ventilator Management◀

● **94002** Ventilation assist and management, initiation of pressure or volume preset ventilators for assisted or controlled breathing; hospital inpatient/observation, initial day

● **94003** hospital inpatient/observation, each subsequent day

● **94004** nursing facility, per day

▶(Do not report 94002-94004 in conjunction with Evaluation and Management services 99201-99499)◀

● **94005** Home ventilator management care plan oversight of a patient (patient not present) in home, domiciliary or rest home (eg, assisted living) requiring review of status, review of laboratories and other studies and revision of orders and respiratory care plan (as appropriate), within a calendar month, 30 minutes or more

▶(Do not report 94005 in conjunction with 99339-99340, 99374-99378)◀

▶(Ventilator management care plan oversight is reported separately from home or domiciliary, rest home [eg, assisted living] services. A physician may report 94005, when performed, including when a different physician reports 99339-99340, 99374-99378 for the same 30 days)◀

▶Other Procedures◀

Codes 94010-94799 include laboratory procedure(s) and interpretation of test results. If a separate identifiable Evaluation and Management service is performed, the appropriate E/M service code should be reported in addition to 94010-94799.

94010 Spirometry, including graphic record, total and timed vital capacity, expiratory flow rate measurement(s), with or without maximal voluntary ventilation

94014 Patient-initiated spirometric recording per 30-day period of time; includes reinforced education, transmission of spirometric tracing, data capture, analysis of transmitted data, periodic recalibration and physician review and interpretation

94015 recording (includes hook-up, reinforced education, data transmission, data capture, trend analysis, and periodic recalibration)

94016 physician review and interpretation only

94060 Bronchodilation responsiveness, spirometry as in 94010, pre- and post-bronchodilator administration

(Report bronchodilator supply separately with 99070 or appropriate supply code)

(For prolonged exercise test for bronchospasm with pre- and post-spirometry, use 94620)

94070 Bronchospasm provocation evaluation, multiple spirometric determinations as in 94010, with administered agents (eg, antigen(s), cold air, methacholine)

(Report antigen(s) administration separately with 99070 or appropriate supply code)

94150 Vital capacity, total (separate procedure)

94200 Maximum breathing capacity, maximal voluntary ventilation

94240 Functional residual capacity or residual volume: helium method, nitrogen open circuit method, or other method

94250 Expired gas collection, quantitative, single procedure (separate procedure)

94260 Thoracic gas volume

(For plethysmography, see 93720-93722)

94350 Determination of maldistribution of inspired gas: multiple breath nitrogen washout curve including alveolar nitrogen or helium equilibration time

94360 Determination of resistance to airflow, oscillatory or plethysmographic methods

94370 Determination of airway closing volume, single breath tests

94375 Respiratory flow volume loop

94400 Breathing response to CO_2 (CO_2 response curve)

Medicine

94450 Breathing response to hypoxia (hypoxia response curve)

(For high altitude simulation test (HAST), see 94452, 94453)

94452 High altitude simulation test (HAST), with physician interpretation and report;

(For obtaining arterial blood gases, use 36600)

(Do not report 94452 in conjunction with 94453, 94760, 94761)

94453 with supplemental oxygen titration

(For obtaining arterial blood gases, use 36600)

(Do not report 94453 in conjunction with 94452, 94760, 94761)

⊘● **94610** Intrapulmonary surfactant administration by a physician through endotracheal tube

►(Do not report 94610 in conjunction with 99293-99296)◄

►(For endotracheal intubation, use 31500)◄

►(Report 94610 once per dosing episode)◄

▲ **94620** Pulmonary stress testing; simple (eg, 6-minute walk test, prolonged exercise test for bronchospasm with pre- and post-spirometry and oximetry)

94621 complex (including measurements of CO_2 production, O_2 uptake, and electrocardiographic recordings)

94640 Pressurized or nonpressurized inhalation treatment for acute airway obstruction or for sputum induction for diagnostic purposes (eg, with an aerosol generator, nebulizer, metered dose inhaler or intermittent positive pressure breathing [IPPB] device)

(For more than 1 inhalation treatment performed on the same date, append modifier 76)

►(For continuous inhalation treatment of 1 hour or more, see 94644, 94645)◄

94642 Aerosol inhalation of pentamidine for pneumocystis carinii pneumonia treatment or prophylaxis

● **94644** Continuous inhalation treatment with aerosol medication for acute airway obstruction; first hour

►(For services of less than 1 hour, use 94640)◄

+● **94645** each additional hour (List separately in addition to code for primary procedure)

►(Use 94645 in conjunction with 94644)◄

►(94656, 94657 have been deleted. To report, see 94002-94005)◄

94660 Continuous positive airway pressure ventilation (CPAP), initiation and management

94662 Continuous negative pressure ventilation (CNP), initiation and management

94664 Demonstration and/or evaluation of patient utilization of an aerosol generator, nebulizer, metered dose inhaler or IPPB device

(94664 can be reported one time only per day of service)

94667 Manipulation chest wall, such as cupping, percussing, and vibration to facilitate lung function; initial demonstration and/or evaluation

94668 subsequent

94680 Oxygen uptake, expired gas analysis; rest and exercise, direct, simple

94681 including CO_2 output, percentage oxygen extracted

94690 rest, indirect (separate procedure)

(For single arterial puncture, use 36600)

94720 Carbon monoxide diffusing capacity (eg, single breath, steady state)

94725 Membrane diffusion capacity

94750 Pulmonary compliance study (eg, plethysmography, volume and pressure measurements)

94760 Noninvasive ear or pulse oximetry for oxygen saturation; single determination

(For blood gases, see 82803-82810)

94761 multiple determinations (eg, during exercise)

94762 by continuous overnight monitoring (separate procedure)

94770 Carbon dioxide, expired gas determination by infrared analyzer

(For bronchoscopy, see 31622-31656)

(For placement of flow directed catheter, use 93503)

(For venipuncture, use 36410)

(For central venous catheter placement, see 36555-36556)

(For arterial puncture, use 36600)

(For arterial catheterization, use 36620)

(For thoracentesis, use 32000)

(For phlebotomy, therapeutic, use 99195)

(For lung biopsy, needle, use 32405)

(For intubation, orotracheal or nasotracheal, use 31500)

94772 Circadian respiratory pattern recording (pediatric pneumogram), 12-24 hour continuous recording, infant

(Separate procedure codes for electromyograms, EEG, ECG, and recordings of respiration are excluded when 94772 is reported)

Medicine

● **94774** Pediatric home apnea monitoring event recording including respiratory rate, pattern and heart rate per 30-day period of time; includes monitor attachment, download of data, physician review, interpretation, and preparation of a report

►(Do not report 94774 in conjunction with 94775-94777 during the same reporting period)◄

● **94775** monitor attachment only (includes hook-up, initiation of recording and disconnection)

● **94776** monitoring, download of information, receipt of transmission(s) and analyses by computer only

● **94777** physician review, interpretation and preparation of report only

►(When oxygen saturation monitoring is used in addition to heart rate and respiratory monitoring, it is not reported separately)◄

►(Do not report 94774-94777 in conjunction with 93224-93272)◄

►(Do not report apnea recording device separately)◄

►(For sleep study, see 95805-95811)◄

94799 Unlisted pulmonary service or procedure

Allergy and Clinical Immunology

Definitions

Immunotherapy (desensitization, hyposensitization) is the parenteral administration of allergenic extracts as antigens at periodic intervals, usually on an increasing dosage scale to a dosage which is maintained as maintenance therapy. Indications for immunotherapy are determined by appropriate diagnostic procedures coordinated with clinical judgment and knowledge of the natural history of allergic diseases.

Other therapy: for medical conferences on the use of mechanical and electronic devices (precipitators, air conditioners, air filters, humidifiers, dehumidifiers), climatotherapy, physical therapy, occupational and recreational therapy, see **Evaluation and Management** section.

Allergy Testing

►(For allergy laboratory tests, see 86000-86999)◄

►(For therapy for severe or intractable allergic disease, see 90765-90768, 90772, 90774, 90775)◄

95004 Percutaneous tests (scratch, puncture, prick) with allergenic extracts, immediate type reaction, specify number of tests

95010 Percutaneous tests (scratch, puncture, prick) sequential and incremental, with drugs, biologicals or venoms, immediate type reaction, specify number of tests

● **95012** Nitric oxide expired gas determination

►(For nitric oxide determination by spectroscopy, use Category III code 0064T)◄

95015 Intracutaneous (intradermal) tests, sequential and incremental, with drugs, biologicals, or venoms, immediate type reaction, specify number of tests

95024 Intracutaneous (intradermal) tests with allergenic extracts, immediate type reaction, specify number of tests

95027 Intracutaneous (intradermal) tests, sequential and incremental, with allergenic extracts for airborne allergens, immediate type reaction, specify number of tests

95028 Intracutaneous (intradermal) tests with allergenic extracts, delayed type reaction, including reading, specify number of tests

95044 Patch or application test(s) (specify number of tests)

95052 Photo patch test(s) (specify number of tests)

95056 Photo tests

95060 Ophthalmic mucous membrane tests

95065 Direct nasal mucous membrane test

95070 Inhalation bronchial challenge testing (not including necessary pulmonary function tests); with histamine, methacholine, or similar compounds

95071 with antigens or gases, specify

(For pulmonary function tests, see 94060, 94070)

95075 Ingestion challenge test (sequential and incremental ingestion of test items, eg, food, drug or other substance such as metabisulfite)

►(95078 has been deleted)◄

Allergen Immunotherapy

Codes 95115-95199 include the professional services necessary for allergen immunotherapy. Office visit codes may be used in addition to allergen immunotherapy if other identifiable services are provided at that time.

95115 Professional services for allergen immunotherapy not including provision of allergenic extracts; single injection

95117 two or more injections

95120 Professional services for allergen immunotherapy in prescribing physicians office or institution, including provision of allergenic extract; single injection

95125 two or more injections

95130 single stinging insect venom

95131 two stinging insect venoms

95132	three stinging insect venoms
95133	four stinging insect venoms
95134	five stinging insect venoms
95144	Professional services for the supervision of preparation and provision of antigens for allergen immunotherapy, single dose vial(s) (specify number of vials)

(A single dose vial contains a single dose of antigen administered in one injection)

95145	Professional services for the supervision of preparation and provision of antigens for allergen immunotherapy (specify number of doses); single stinging insect venom
95146	two single stinging insect venoms
95147	three single stinging insect venoms
95148	four single stinging insect venoms
95149	five single stinging insect venoms
95165	Professional services for the supervision of preparation and provision of antigens for allergen immunotherapy; single or multiple antigens (specify number of doses)
95170	whole body extract of biting insect or other arthropod (specify number of doses)

(For allergy immunotherapy reporting, a dose is the amount of antigen(s) administered in a single injection from a multiple dose vial)

95180	Rapid desensitization procedure, each hour (eg, insulin, penicillin, equine serum)
95199	Unlisted allergy/clinical immunologic service or procedure

(For skin testing of bacterial, viral, fungal extracts, see 95028, 86485-86586)

(For special reports on allergy patients, use 99080)

(For testing procedures such as radioallergosorbent testing (RAST), rat mast cell technique (RMCT), mast cell degranulation test (MCDT), lymphocytic transformation test (LTT), leukocyte histamine release (LHR), migration inhibitory factor test (MIF), transfer factor test (TFT), nitroblue tetrazolium dye test (NTD), see Immunology section in **Pathology** or use 95199)

Endocrinology

95250	Ambulatory continuous glucose monitoring of interstitial tissue fluid via a subcutaneous sensor for up to 72 hours; sensor placement, hook-up, calibration of monitor, patient training, removal of sensor, and printout of recording

(Do not report 95250 in conjunction with 99091)

95251	physician interpretation and report

(Do not report 95250, 95251 in conjunction with 99091)

Neurology and Neuromuscular Procedures

Neurologic services are typically consultative, and any of the levels of consultation (99241-99255) may be appropriate.

In addition, services and skills outlined under **Evaluation and Management** levels of service appropriate to neurologic illnesses should be reported similarly.

The EEG, autonomic function, evoked potential, reflex tests, EMG, NCV, and MEG services (95812-95829 and 95860-95967) include recording, interpretation by a physician, and report. For interpretation only, use modifier 26. For EMG guidance, see 95873, 95874.

▶(For repetitive transcranial magnetic stimulation for treatment of clinical depression, see Category III codes 0160T, 0161T)◀

(Do not report codes 95860-95875 in addition to 96000-96004)

Sleep Testing

Sleep studies and polysomnography refer to the continuous and simultaneous monitoring and recording of various physiological and pathophysiological parameters of sleep for 6 or more hours with physician review, interpretation and report. The studies are performed to diagnose a variety of sleep disorders and to evaluate a patient's response to therapies such as nasal continuous positive airway pressure (NCPAP). Polysomnography is distinguished from sleep studies by the inclusion of sleep staging which is defined to include a 1-4 lead electroencephalogram (EEG), an electro-oculogram (EOG), and a submental electromyogram (EMG). Additional parameters of sleep include: 1) ECG; 2) airflow; 3) ventilation and respiratory effort; 4) gas exchange by oximetry, transcutaneous monitoring, or end tidal gas analysis; 5) extremity muscle activity, motor activity-movement; 6) extended EEG monitoring; 7) penile tumescence; 8) gastroesophageal reflux; 9) continuous blood pressure monitoring; 10) snoring; 11) body positions; etc.

The sleep services (95805-95811) include recording, interpretation and report. For interpretation only, use modifier 26.

For a study to be reported as polysomnography, sleep must be recorded and staged.

(Report with modifier 52 if less than 6 hours of recording or in other cases of reduced services as appropriate)

(For unattended sleep study, use 95806)

95805	Multiple sleep latency or maintenance of wakefulness testing, recording, analysis and interpretation of physiological measurements of sleep during multiple trials to assess sleepiness

95806 Sleep study, simultaneous recording of ventilation, respiratory effort, ECG or heart rate, and oxygen saturation, unattended by a technologist

95807 Sleep study, simultaneous recording of ventilation, respiratory effort, ECG or heart rate, and oxygen saturation, attended by a technologist

95808 Polysomnography; sleep staging with 1-3 additional parameters of sleep, attended by a technologist

95810 sleep staging with 4 or more additional parameters of sleep, attended by a technologist

95811 sleep staging with 4 or more additional parameters of sleep, with initiation of continuous positive airway pressure therapy or bilevel ventilation, attended by a technologist

Routine Electroencephalography (EEG)

EEG codes 95812-95822 include hyperventilation and/or photic stimulation when appropriate. Routine EEG codes 95816-95822 include 20 to 40 minutes of recording. Extended EEG codes 95812-95813 include reporting times longer than 40 minutes.

95812 Electroencephalogram (EEG) extended monitoring; 41-60 minutes

95813 greater than one hour

95816 Electroencephalogram (EEG); including recording awake and drowsy

95819 including recording awake and asleep

95822 recording in coma or sleep only

95824 cerebral death evaluation only

95827 all night recording

(For 24-hour EEG monitoring, see 95950-95953 or 95956)

(For EEG during nonintracranial surgery, use 95955)

(For Wada test, use 95958)

(For digital analysis of EEG, use 95957)

95829 Electrocorticogram at surgery (separate procedure)

95830 Insertion by physician of sphenoidal electrodes for electroencephalographic (EEG) recording

Muscle and Range of Motion Testing

95831 Muscle testing, manual (separate procedure) with report; extremity (excluding hand) or trunk

95832 hand, with or without comparison with normal side

95833 total evaluation of body, excluding hands

95834 total evaluation of body, including hands

95851 Range of motion measurements and report (separate procedure); each extremity (excluding hand) or each trunk section (spine)

95852 hand, with or without comparison with normal side

95857 Tensilon test for myasthenia gravis

(95858 has been deleted)

Electromyography and Nerve Conduction Tests

Needle electromyographic procedures include the interpretation of electrical waveforms measured by equipment that produces both visible and audible components of electrical signals recorded from the muscle(s) studied by the needle electrode.

95860 Needle electromyography; one extremity with or without related paraspinal areas

95861 two extremities with or without related paraspinal areas

(For dynamic electromyography performed during motion analysis studies, see 96002-96003)

95863 three extremities with or without related paraspinal areas

95864 four extremities with or without related paraspinal areas

95865 larynx

(Do not report modifier 50 in conjunction with 95865)

(For unilateral procedure, report modifier 52 in conjunction with 95865)

95866 hemidiaphragm

95867 cranial nerve supplied muscle(s), unilateral

95868 cranial nerve supplied muscles, bilateral

95869 thoracic paraspinal muscles (excluding T1 or T12)

95870 limited study of muscles in one extremity or non-limb (axial) muscles (unilateral or bilateral), other than thoracic paraspinal, cranial nerve supplied muscles, or sphincters

(To report a complete study of the extremities, see 95860-95864)

(For anal or urethral sphincter, detrusor, urethra, perineum musculature, see 51785-51792)

(For eye muscles, use 92265)

95872 Needle electromyography using single fiber electrode, with quantitative measurement of jitter, blocking and/or fiber density, any/all sites of each muscle studied

+ 95873 Electrical stimulation for guidance in conjunction with chemodenervation (List separately in addition to code for primary procedure)

+ 95874 Needle electromyography for guidance in conjunction with chemodenervation (List separately in addition to code for primary procedure)

 (Use 95873, 95874 in conjunction with 64612-64614)

 (Do not report 95874 in conjunction with 95873)

 (Do not report 95873, 95874 in conjunction with 95860-95870)

95875 Ischemic limb exercise test with serial specimen(s) acquisition for muscle(s) metabolite(s)

 (For listing of nerves considered for separate study, see Appendix J)

⊘ **95900** Nerve conduction, amplitude and latency/velocity study, each nerve; motor, without F-wave study

⊘ **95903** motor, with F-wave study

⊘ **95904** sensory

 (Report 95900, 95903, and/or 95904 only once when multiple sites on the same nerve are stimulated or recorded)

Intraoperative Neurophysiology

+ 95920 Intraoperative neurophysiology testing, per hour (List separately in addition to code for primary procedure)

 (Use 95920 in conjunction with the study performed, 92585, 95822, 95860, 95861, 95867, 95868, 95870, 95900, 95904, 95925-95937)

 (Code 95920 describes ongoing electrophysiologic testing and monitoring performed during surgical procedures. Code 95920 is reported per hour of service, and includes only the ongoing electrophysiologic monitoring time distinct from performance of specific type(s) of baseline electrophysiologic study(s) (95860, 95861, 95867, 95868, 95870, 95900, 95904, 95928, 95929, 95933-95937) or interpretation of specific type(s) of baseline electrophysiologic study(s) (92585, 95822, 95870, 95925-95928, 95929, 95930). The time spent performing or interpreting the baseline electrophysiologic study(s) should not be counted as intraoperative monitoring, but represents separately reportable procedures. Code 95920 should be used once per hour even if multiple electrophysiologic studies are performed. The baseline electrophysiologic study(s) should be used once per operative session.)

 (For electrocorticography, use 95829)

 (For intraoperative EEG during nonintracranial surgery, use 95955)

 (For intraoperative functional cortical or subcortical mapping, see 95961-95962)

 (For intraoperative neurostimulator programming and analysis, see 95970-95975)

Autonomic Function Tests

95921 Testing of autonomic nervous system function; cardiovagal innervation (parasympathetic function), including two or more of the following: heart rate response to deep breathing with recorded R-R interval, Valsalva ratio, and 30:15 ratio

95922 vasomotor adrenergic innervation (sympathetic adrenergic function), including beat-to-beat blood pressure and R-R interval changes during Valsalva maneuver and at least five minutes of passive tilt

95923 sudomotor, including one or more of the following: quantitative sudomotor axon reflex test (QSART), silastic sweat imprint, thermoregulatory sweat test, and changes in sympathetic skin potential

Evoked Potentials and Reflex Tests

95925 Short-latency somatosensory evoked potential study, stimulation of any/all peripheral nerves or skin sites, recording from the central nervous system; in upper limbs

95926 in lower limbs

95927 in the trunk or head

 (To report a unilateral study, use modifier 52)

 (For auditory evoked potentials, use 92585)

95928 Central motor evoked potential study (transcranial motor stimulation); upper limbs

95929 lower limbs

95930 Visual evoked potential (VEP) testing central nervous system, checkerboard or flash

95933 Orbicularis oculi (blink) reflex, by electrodiagnostic testing

95934 H-reflex, amplitude and latency study; record gastrocnemius/soleus muscle

95936 record muscle other than gastrocnemius/soleus muscle

 (To report a bilateral study, use modifier 50)

95937 Neuromuscular junction testing (repetitive stimulation, paired stimuli), each nerve, any one method

Special EEG Tests

95950 Monitoring for identification and lateralization of cerebral seizure focus, electroencephalographic (eg, 8 channel EEG) recording and interpretation, each 24 hours

95951 Monitoring for localization of cerebral seizure focus by cable or radio, 16 or more channel telemetry, combined electroencephalographic (EEG) and video recording and interpretation (eg, for presurgical localization), each 24 hours

Medicine

95953 Monitoring for localization of cerebral seizure focus by computerized portable 16 or more channel EEG, electroencephalographic (EEG) recording and interpretation, each 24 hours

95954 Pharmacological or physical activation requiring physician attendance during EEG recording of activation phase (eg, thiopental activation test)

95955 Electroencephalogram (EEG) during nonintracranial surgery (eg, carotid surgery)

95956 Monitoring for localization of cerebral seizure focus by cable or radio, 16 or more channel telemetry, electroencephalographic (EEG) recording and interpretation, each 24 hours

95957 Digital analysis of electroencephalogram (EEG) (eg, for epileptic spike analysis)

95958 Wada activation test for hemispheric function, including electroencephalographic (EEG) monitoring

95961 Functional cortical and subcortical mapping by stimulation and/or recording of electrodes on brain surface, or of depth electrodes, to provoke seizures or identify vital brain structures; initial hour of physician attendance

+ 95962 each additional hour of physician attendance (List separately in addition to code for primary procedure)

(Use 95962 in conjunction with 95961)

95965 Magnetoencephalography (MEG), recording and analysis; for spontaneous brain magnetic activity (eg, epileptic cerebral cortex localization)

95966 for evoked magnetic fields, single modality (eg, sensory, motor, language, or visual cortex localization)

+ 95967 for evoked magnetic fields, each additional modality (eg, sensory, motor, language, or visual cortex localization) (List separately in addition to code for primary procedure)

(Use 95967 in conjunction with 95966)

(For electroencephalography performed in addition to magnetoencephalography, see 95812-95827)

(For somatosensory evoked potentials, auditory evoked potentials, and visual evoked potentials performed in addition to magnetic evoked field responses, see 92585, 95925, 95926, and/or 95930)

(For computerized tomography performed in addition to magnetoencephalography, see 70450-70470, 70496)

(For magnetic resonance imaging performed in addition to magnetoencephalography, see 70551-70553)

Neurostimulators, Analysis-Programming

A simple neurostimulator pulse generator/transmitter (95970, 95971) is one capable of affecting 3 or fewer of the following: pulse amplitude, pulse duration, pulse frequency, 8 or more electrode contacts, cycling, stimulation train duration, train spacing, number of programs, number of channels, alternating electrode polarities, dose time (stimulation parameters changing in time periods of minutes including dose lockout times), more than 1 clinical feature (eg, rigidity, dyskinesia, tremor). A complex neurostimulator pulse generator/transmitter (95970-95975) is one capable of affecting more than 3 of the above.

Code 95970 describes subsequent electronic analysis of a previously-implanted simple or complex brain, spinal cord, or peripheral neurostimulator pulse generator system, without reprogramming. Code 95971 describes intraoperative or subsequent electronic analysis of an implanted simple spinal cord, or peripheral (i.e., peripheral nerve, autonomic nerve, neuromuscular) neurostimulator pulse generator system, with programming. Codes 95972 and 95973 describe intraoperative (at initial insertion/revision) or subsequent electronic analysis of an implanted complex spinal cord or peripheral (except cranial nerve) neurostimulator pulse generator system, with programming. Codes 95974 and 95975 describe intraoperative (at initial insertion/revision) or subsequent electronic analysis of an implanted complex cranial nerve neurostimulator pulse generator system, with programming. Codes 95978 and 95979 describe initial or subsequent electronic analysis of an implanted brain neurostimulator pulse generator system, with programming.

▶(For insertion of neurostimulator pulse generator, see 61885, 63685, 64590)◀

(For revision or removal of neurostimulator pulse generator or receiver, see 61888, 63688, 64595)

▶(For implantation of neurostimulator electrodes, see 43647, 43881, 61850-61875, 63650-63655, 64553-64580, 0155T, 0157T. For revision or removal of neurostimulator electrodes, see 43648, 43882, 61880, 63660, 64585, 0156T, 0158T)◀

95970 Electronic analysis of implanted neurostimulator pulse generator system (eg, rate, pulse amplitude and duration, configuration of wave form, battery status, electrode selectability, output modulation, cycling, impedance and patient compliance measurements); simple or complex brain, spinal cord, or peripheral (ie, cranial nerve, peripheral nerve, autonomic nerve, neuromuscular) neurostimulator pulse generator/transmitter, without reprogramming

95971 simple spinal cord, or peripheral (ie, peripheral nerve, autonomic nerve, neuromuscular) neurostimulator pulse generator/transmitter, with intraoperative or subsequent programming

95972 complex spinal cord, or peripheral (except cranial nerve) neurostimulator pulse generator/transmitter, with intraoperative or subsequent programming, first hour

+ 95973 complex spinal cord, or peripheral (except cranial nerve) neurostimulator pulse generator/transmitter, with intraoperative or subsequent programming, each additional 30 minutes after first hour (List separately in addition to code for primary procedure)

(Use 95973 in conjunction with 95972)

95974 complex cranial nerve neurostimulator pulse generator/transmitter, with intraoperative or subsequent programming, with or without nerve interface testing, first hour

+ 95975 complex cranial nerve neurostimulator pulse generator/transmitter, with intraoperative or subsequent programming, each additional 30 minutes after first hour (List separately in addition to code for primary procedure)

(Use 95975 in conjunction with 95974)

►(For electronic analysis, programming, and reprogramming of gastric neurostimulator pulse generator, lesser curvature [morbid obesity], use Category III code 0162T)◄

95978 Electronic analysis of implanted neurostimulator pulse generator system (eg, rate, pulse amplitude and duration, battery status, electrode selectability and polarity, impedance and patient compliance measurements), complex deep brain neurostimulator pulse generator/transmitter, with initial or subsequent programming; first hour

+ 95979 each additional 30 minutes after first hour (List separately in addition to code for primary procedure)

(Use 95979 in conjunction with 95978)

Other Procedures

95990 Refilling and maintenance of implantable pump or reservoir for drug delivery, spinal (intrathecal, epidural) or brain (intraventricular);

(For analysis and/or reprogramming of implantable infusion pump, see 62367-62368)

►(For refill and maintenance of implanted infusion pump or reservoir for systemic drug therapy [eg, chemotherapy or insulin], use 96522)◄

95991 administered by physician

95999 Unlisted neurological or neuromuscular diagnostic procedure

Motion Analysis

Codes 96000-96004 describe services performed as part of a major therapeutic or diagnostic decision making process. Motion analysis is performed in a dedicated motion analysis laboratory (ie, a facility capable of performing videotaping from the front, back and both sides, computerized 3-D kinematics, 3-D kinetics, and dynamic electromyography). Code 96000 may include 3-D kinetics and stride characteristics. Codes 96002-96003 describe dynamic electromyography.

Code 96004 should only be reported once regardless of the number of study(ies) reviewed/interpreted.

(For performance of needle electromyography procedures, see 95860-95875)

(For gait training, use 97116)

96000 Comprehensive computer-based motion analysis by video-taping and 3-D kinematics;

96001 with dynamic plantar pressure measurements during walking

96002 Dynamic surface electromyography, during walking or other functional activities, 1-12 muscles

96003 Dynamic fine wire electromyography, during walking or other functional activities, 1 muscle

(Do not report 96002, 96003 in conjunction with 95860-95864, 95869-95872)

96004 Physician review and interpretation of comprehensive computer-based motion analysis, dynamic plantar pressure measurements, dynamic surface electromyography during walking or other functional activities, and dynamic fine wire electromyography, with written report

►Functional Brain Mapping◄

►Code 96020 includes selection and administration of testing of language, memory, cognition, movement, sensation, and other neurological functions when conducted in association with functional neuroimaging, monitoring of performance of this testing, and determination of validity of neurofunctional testing relative to separately interpreted functional magnetic resonance images.◄

● **96020** Neurofunctional testing selection and administration during noninvasive imaging functional brain mapping, with test administered entirely by a physician or psychologist, with review of test results and report

►(For functional magnetic resonance imaging [fMRI], brain, use 70555)◄

►(Do not report 96020 in conjunction with 96101-96103, 96116-96120)◄

►(Do not report 96020 in conjunction with 70554)◄

►(Evaluation and Management services codes should not be reported on the same day as 96020)◄

Medicine

▶Medical Genetics and Genetic Counseling Services◀

▶These services are provided by trained genetic counselors and may include obtaining a structured family genetic history, pedigree construction, analysis for genetic risk assessment, and counseling of the patient and family. These activities may be provided during one or more sessions and may include review of medical data and family information, face-to-face interviews, and counseling services.◀

● 96040 Medical genetics and genetic counseling services, each 30 minutes face-to-face with patient/family

 ▶(For genetic counseling and education provided by a physician to an individual, see the appropriate Evaluation and Management codes)◀

 ▶(For genetic counseling and education provided by a physician to a group, use 99078)◀

 ▶(For education regarding genetic risks by a nonphysician to a group, see 98961, 98962)◀

 ▶(For genetic counseling and/or risk factor reduction intervention provided by a physician to patient(s) without symptoms or established disease, see 99401-99412)◀

Central Nervous System Assessments/Tests (eg, Neuro-Cognitive, Mental Status, Speech Testing)

The following codes are used to report the services provided during testing of the cognitive function of the central nervous system. The testing of cognitive processes, visual motor responses, and abstractive abilities is accomplished by the combination of several types of testing procedures. It is expected that the administration of these tests will generate material that will be formulated into a report.

 (96100 has been deleted. To report, see 96101, 96102, 96103)

 (For development of cognitive skills, see 97532, 97533)

 (For mini-mental status examination performed by a physician, see **Evaluation and Management** services codes)

96101 Psychological testing (includes psychodiagnostic assessment of emotionality, intellectual abilities, personality and psychopathology, eg, MMPI, Rorschach, WAIS), per hour of the psychologist's or physician's time, both face-to-face time with the patient and time interpreting test results and preparing the report

96102 Psychological testing (includes psychodiagnostic assessment of emotionality, intellectual abilities, personality and psychopathology, eg, MMPI and WAIS), with qualified health care professional interpretation and report, administered by technician, per hour of technician time, face-to-face

96103 Psychological testing (includes psychodiagnostic assessment of emotionality, intellectual abilities, personality and psychopathology, eg, MMPI), administered by a computer, with qualified health care professional interpretation and report

96105 Assessment of aphasia (includes assessment of expressive and receptive speech and language function, language comprehension, speech production ability, reading, spelling, writing, eg, by Boston Diagnostic Aphasia Examination) with interpretation and report, per hour

96110 Developmental testing; limited (eg, Developmental Screening Test II, Early Language Milestone Screen), with interpretation and report

96111 extended (includes assessment of motor, language, social, adaptive and/or cognitive functioning by standardized developmental instruments) with interpretation and report

 (96115 has been deleted. To report, use 96116)

96116 Neurobehavioral status exam (clinical assessment of thinking, reasoning and judgment, eg, acquired knowledge, attention, language, memory, planning and problem solving, and visual spatial abilities), per hour of the psychologist's or physician's time, both face-to-face time with the patient and time interpreting test results and preparing the report

 (96117 has been deleted. To report, see 96118, 96119, 96120)

96118 Neuropsychological testing (eg, Halstead-Reitan Neuropsychological Battery, Wechsler Memory Scales and Wisconsin Card Sorting Test), per hour of the psychologist's or physician's time, both face-to-face time with the patient and time interpreting test results and preparing the report

96119 Neuropsychological testing (eg, Halstead-Reitan Neuropsychological Battery, Wechsler Memory Scales and Wisconsin Card Sorting Test), with qualified health care professional interpretation and report, administered by technician, per hour of technician time, face-to-face

96120 Neuropsychological testing (eg, Wisconsin Card Sorting Test), administered by a computer, with qualified health care professional interpretation and report

Medicine

Health and Behavior Assessment/Intervention

Health and behavior assessment procedures are used to identify the psychological, behavioral, emotional, cognitive, and social factors important to the prevention, treatment, or management of physical health problems.

The focus of the assessment is not on mental health but on the biopsychosocial factors important to physical health problems and treatments. The focus of the intervention is to improve the patient's health and well-being utilizing cognitive, behavioral, social, and/or psychophysiological procedures designed to ameliorate specific disease-related problems.

Codes 96150-96155 describe services offered to patients who present with primary physical illnesses, diagnoses, or symptoms and may benefit from assessments and interventions that focus on the biopsychosocial factors related to the patient's health status. These services do not represent preventive medicine counseling and risk factor reduction interventions.

For patients that require psychiatric services (90801-90899) as well as health and behavior assessment/intervention (96150-96155), report the predominant service performed. Do not report 96150-96155 in conjunction with 90801-90899 on the same date.

Evaluation and Management services codes (including **Preventive Medicine, Individual Counseling** codes 99401-99404, and **Preventive Medicine, Group Counseling** codes 99411-99412), should not be reported on the same day.

> (For health and behavior assessment and/or intervention performed by a physician, see **Evaluation and Management** or **Preventive Medicine** services codes)

96150 Health and behavior assessment (eg, health-focused clinical interview, behavioral observations, psychophysiological monitoring, health-oriented questionnaires), each 15 minutes face-to-face with the patient; initial assessment

96151 re-assessment

96152 Health and behavior intervention, each 15 minutes, face-to-face; individual

96153 group (2 or more patients)

96154 family (with the patient present)

96155 family (without the patient present)

Chemotherapy Administration

Chemotherapy administration codes 96401-96549 apply to parenteral administration of non-radionuclide anti-neoplastic drugs; and also to anti-neoplastic agents provided for treatment of noncancer diagnoses (eg, cyclophosphamide for auto-immune conditions) or to substances such as monoclonal antibody agents, and other biologic response modifiers. These services can be provided by any physician. Chemotherapy services are typically highly complex and require direct physician supervision for any or all purposes of patient assessment, provision of consent, safety oversight and intra-service supervision of staff. Typically, such chemotherapy services require advanced practice training and competency for staff who provide these services; special considerations for preparation, dosage or disposal; and commonly, these services entail significant patient risk and frequent monitoring. Examples are frequent changes in the infusion rate, prolonged presence of nurse administering the solution for patient monitoring and infusion adjustments, and frequent conferring with the physician about these issues.

If performed to facilitate the infusion or injection, the following services are included and are not reported separately:

a. Use of local anesthesia

b. IV start

c. Access to indwelling IV, subcutaneous catheter or port

d. Flush at conclusion of infusion

e. Standard tubing, syringes and supplies

f. Preparation of chemotherapy agent(s)

> (For declotting a catheter or port, use 36550)

Report separate codes for each parenteral method of administration employed when chemotherapy is administered by different techniques. The administration of medications (eg, antibiotics, steroidal agents, antiemetics, narcotics, analgesics) administered independently or sequentially as supportive management of chemotherapy administration, should be separately reported using 90760, 90761, 90765, 90779 as appropriate.

Report both the specific service as well as code(s) for the specific substance(s) or drug(s) provided. The fluid used to administer the drug(s) is considered incidental hydration and is not separately reportable.

When administering multiple infusions, injections or combinations, only one "initial" service code should be reported, unless protocol requires that two separate IV sites must be used. The "initial" code that best describes the key or primary reason for the encounter should always be reported irrespective of the order in which the infusions or injections occur. If an injection or infusion is

Medicine

of a subsequent or concurrent nature, even if it is the first such service within that group of services, then a subsequent or concurrent code from the appropriate section should be reported (eg, the first IV push given subsequent to an initial one-hour infusion is reported using a subsequent IV push code).

When reporting codes for which infusion time is a factor, use the actual time over which the infusion is administered.

If a significant separately identifiable Evaluation and Management service is performed, the appropriate E/M service code should be reported using modifier 25 in addition to 96401-96549. For same day E/M service, a different diagnosis is not required.

Regional (isolation) chemotherapy perfusion should be reported using the codes for arterial infusion (96420-96425). Placement of the intra-arterial catheter should be reported using the appropriate code from the **Cardiovascular Surgery** section. Placement of arterial and venous cannula(s) for extracorporeal circulation via a membrane oxygenator perfusion pump should be reported using 36823. Code 36823 includes dose calculation and administration of the chemotherapy agent by injection into the perfusate. Do not report 96409-96425 in conjunction with 36823.

(For home infusion services, see 99601-99602)

Injection and Intravenous Infusion Chemotherapy

Intravenous or intra-arterial push is defined as: a) an injection in which the healthcare professional who administers the substance/drug is continuously present to administer the injection and observe the patient, or b) an infusion of 15 minutes or less.

(96400 has been deleted. To report, see 96401, 96402)

96401 Chemotherapy administration, subcutaneous or intramuscular; non-hormonal anti-neoplastic

96402 hormonal anti-neoplastic

96405 Chemotherapy administration; intralesional, up to and including 7 lesions

96406 intralesional, more than 7 lesions

(96408 has been deleted. To report, use 96409)

96409 intravenous, push technique, single or initial substance/drug

(96410 has been deleted. To report, use 96413)

+ 96411 intravenous, push technique, each additional substance/drug (List separately in addition to code for primary procedure)

(Use 96411 in conjunction with 96409, 96413)

(96412 has been deleted. To report, use 96415)

96413 Chemotherapy administration, intravenous infusion technique; up to 1 hour, single or initial substance/drug

(96414 has been deleted. To report, use 96416)

+▲ 96415 each additional hour (List separately in addition to code for primary procedure)

(Use 96415 in conjunction with 96413)

(Report 96415 for infusion intervals of greater than 30 minutes beyond 1-hour increments)

(Report 90761 to identify hydration, or 90766, 90767, 90775 to identify therapeutic, prophylactic, or diagnostic drug infusion or injection, if provided as a secondary or subsequent service in association with 96413)

96416 initiation of prolonged chemotherapy infusion (more than 8 hours), requiring use of a portable or implantable pump

(For refilling and maintenance of a portable pump or an implantable infusion pump or reservoir for drug delivery, see 96521-96523)

+ 96417 each additional sequential infusion (different substance/drug), up to 1 hour (List separately in addition to code for primary procedure)

(Use 96417 in conjunction with 96413)

(Report only once per sequential infusion. Report 96415 for additional hour(s) of sequential infusion)

Intra-Arterial Chemotherapy

96420 Chemotherapy administration, intra-arterial; push technique

96422 infusion technique, up to one hour

+▲ 96423 infusion technique, each additional hour (List separately in addition to code for primary procedure)

(Use 96423 in conjunction with 96422)

(Report 96423 for infusion intervals of greater than 30 minutes beyond 1-hour increments)

(For regional chemotherapy perfusion via membrane oxygenator perfusion pump to an extremity, use 36823)

96425 infusion technique, initiation of prolonged infusion (more than 8 hours), requiring the use of a portable or implantable pump

(For refilling and maintenance of a portable pump or an implantable infusion pump or reservoir for drug delivery, see 96521-96523)

Other Chemotherapy

Code 96523 does not require direct physician supervision. Codes 96521-96523 may be reported when these devices are used for therapeutic drugs other than chemotherapy.

(For collection of blood specimen from a completely implantable venous access device, use 36540)

96440 Chemotherapy administration into pleural cavity, requiring and including thoracentesis

96445 Chemotherapy administration into peritoneal cavity, requiring and including peritoneocentesis

96450 Chemotherapy administration, into CNS (eg, intrathecal), requiring and including spinal puncture

(For intravesical (bladder) chemotherapy administration, use 51720)

(For insertion of subarachnoid catheter and reservoir for infusion of drug, see 62350, 62351, 62360-62362; for insertion of intraventricular catheter and reservoir, see 61210, 61215)

(96520 has been deleted. To report, use 96521)

96521 Refilling and maintenance of portable pump

96522 Refilling and maintenance of implantable pump or reservoir for drug delivery, systemic (eg, intravenous, intra-arterial)

(For refilling and maintenance of an implantable infusion pump for spinal or brain drug infusion, use 95990-95991)

96523 Irrigation of implanted venous access device for drug delivery systems

(Do not report 96523 if an injection or infusion is provided on the same day)

(96530 has been deleted. To report, use 96522)

96542 Chemotherapy injection, subarachnoid or intraventricular via subcutaneous reservoir, single or multiple agents

(96545 has been deleted)

(For radioactive isotope therapy, use 79005)

96549 Unlisted chemotherapy procedure

Photodynamic Therapy

(To report ocular photodynamic therapy, use 67221)

96567 Photodynamic therapy by external application of light to destroy premalignant and/or malignant lesions of the skin and adjacent mucosa (eg, lip) by activation of photosensitive drug(s), each phototherapy exposure session

+ 96570 Photodynamic therapy by endoscopic application of light to ablate abnormal tissue via activation of photosensitive drug(s); first 30 minutes (List separately in addition to code for endoscopy or bronchoscopy procedures of lung and esophagus)

+ 96571 each additional 15 minutes (List separately in addition to code for endoscopy or bronchoscopy procedures of lung and esophagus)

(96570, 96571 are to be used in addition to bronchoscopy, endoscopy codes)

(Use 96570, 96571 in conjunction with 31641, 43228 as appropriate)

Special Dermatological Procedures

Dermatologic services are typically consultative, and any of the five levels of consultation (99241-99255) may be appropriate.

In addition, services and skills outlined under **Evaluation and Management** levels of service appropriate to dermatologic illnesses should be coded similarly.

▶(For whole body photography, use 96904)◀

(For intralesional injections, see 11900, 11901)

▶(For Tzanck smear, see 88160-88161)◀

96900 Actinotherapy (ultraviolet light)

96902 Microscopic examination of hairs plucked or clipped by the examiner (excluding hair collected by the patient) to determine telogen and anagen counts, or structural hair shaft abnormality

● **96904** Whole body integumentary photography, for monitoring of high risk patients with dysplastic nevus syndrome or a history of dysplastic nevi, or patients with a personal or familial history of melanoma

96910 Photochemotherapy; tar and ultraviolet B (Goeckerman treatment) or petrolatum and ultraviolet B

96912 psoralens and ultraviolet A (PUVA)

96913 Photochemotherapy (Goeckerman and/or PUVA) for severe photoresponsive dermatoses requiring at least four to eight hours of care under direct supervision of the physician (includes application of medication and dressings)

96920 Laser treatment for inflammatory skin disease (psoriasis); total area less than 250 sq cm

96921 250 sq cm to 500 sq cm

96922 over 500 sq cm

96999 Unlisted special dermatological service or procedure

Physical Medicine and Rehabilitation

Codes 97001-97755 should be used to report each distinct procedure performed. Do not append modifier 51 to 97001-97755.

(For muscle testing, range of joint motion, electromyography, see 95831 et seq)

(For biofeedback training by EMG, use 90901)

(For transcutaneous nerve stimulation (TNS), use 64550)

97001 Physical therapy evaluation

97002 Physical therapy re-evaluation

97003 Occupational therapy evaluation

Medicine

97004 Occupational therapy re-evaluation

97005 Athletic training evaluation

97006 Athletic training re-evaluation

Modalities

Any physical agent applied to produce therapeutic changes to biologic tissue; includes but not limited to thermal, acoustic, light, mechanical, or electric energy.

Supervised

The application of a modality that does not require direct (one-on-one) patient contact by the provider.

97010 Application of a modality to one or more areas; hot or cold packs

97012 traction, mechanical

97014 electrical stimulation (unattended)

(For acupuncture with electrical stimulation, see 97813, 97814)

97016 vasopneumatic devices

97018 paraffin bath

(97020 has been deleted. To report, use 97024)

97022 whirlpool

97024 diathermy (eg, microwave)

97026 infrared

97028 ultraviolet

Constant Attendance

The application of a modality that requires direct (one-on-one) patient contact by the provider.

97032 Application of a modality to one or more areas; electrical stimulation (manual), each 15 minutes

97033 iontophoresis, each 15 minutes

97034 contrast baths, each 15 minutes

97035 ultrasound, each 15 minutes

97036 Hubbard tank, each 15 minutes

97039 Unlisted modality (specify type and time if constant attendance)

Therapeutic Procedures

A manner of effecting change through the application of clinical skills and/or services that attempt to improve function.

Physician or therapist required to have direct (one-on-one) patient contact.

97110 Therapeutic procedure, one or more areas, each 15 minutes; therapeutic exercises to develop strength and endurance, range of motion and flexibility

97112 neuromuscular reeducation of movement, balance, coordination, kinesthetic sense, posture, and/or proprioception for sitting and/or standing activities

97113 aquatic therapy with therapeutic exercises

97116 gait training (includes stair climbing)

(Use 96000-96003 to report comprehensive gait and motion analysis procedures)

97124 massage, including effleurage, petrissage and/or tapotement (stroking, compression, percussion)

(For myofascial release, use 97140)

97139 Unlisted therapeutic procedure (specify)

97140 Manual therapy techniques (eg, mobilization/manipulation, manual lymphatic drainage, manual traction), one or more regions, each 15 minutes

97150 Therapeutic procedure(s), group (2 or more individuals)

(Report 97150 for each member of group)

(Group therapy procedures involve constant attendance of the physician or therapist, but by definition do not require one-on-one patient contact by the physician or therapist)

(For manipulation under general anesthesia, see appropriate anatomic section in **Musculoskeletal System**)

(For osteopathic manipulative treatment (OMT), see 98925-98929)

(97504 has been deleted. To report, use 97760)

(97520 has been deleted. To report, use 97761)

97530 Therapeutic activities, direct (one-on-one) patient contact by the provider (use of dynamic activities to improve functional performance), each 15 minutes

97532 Development of cognitive skills to improve attention, memory, problem solving, (includes compensatory training), direct (one-on-one) patient contact by the provider, each 15 minutes

97533 Sensory integrative techniques to enhance sensory processing and promote adaptive responses to environmental demands, direct (one-on-one) patient contact by the provider, each 15 minutes

97535 Self-care/home management training (eg, activities of daily living (ADL) and compensatory training, meal preparation, safety procedures, and instructions in use of assistive technology devices/adaptive equipment) direct one-on-one contact by provider, each 15 minutes

97537 Community/work reintegration training (eg, shopping, transportation, money management, avocational activities and/or work environment/modification analysis, work task analysis, use of assistive technology device/adaptive equipment), direct one-on-one contact by provider, each 15 minutes

(For wheelchair management/propulsion training, use 97542)

97542 Wheelchair management (eg, assessment, fitting, training), each 15 minutes

97545 Work hardening/conditioning; initial 2 hours

+ **97546** each additional hour (List separately in addition to code for primary procedure)

(Use 97546 in conjunction with 97545)

Active Wound Care Management

Active wound care procedures are performed to remove devitalized and/or necrotic tissue and promote healing. Provider is required to have direct (one-on-one) patient contact.

(Do not report 97597-97602 in conjunction with 11040-11044)

97597 Removal of devitalized tissue from wound(s), selective debridement, without anesthesia (eg, high pressure waterjet with/without suction, sharp selective debridement with scissors, scalpel and forceps), with or without topical application(s), wound assessment, and instruction(s) for ongoing care, may include use of a whirlpool, per session; total wound(s) surface area less than or equal to 20 square centimeters

97598 total wound(s) surface area greater than 20 square centimeters

(97601 has been deleted. To report, use 97597, 97598)

97602 Removal of devitalized tissue from wound(s), non-selective debridement, without anesthesia (eg, wet-to-moist dressings, enzymatic, abrasion), including topical application(s), wound assessment, and instruction(s) for ongoing care, per session

97605 Negative pressure wound therapy (eg, vacuum assisted drainage collection), including topical application(s), wound assessment, and instruction(s) for ongoing care, per session; total wound(s) surface area less than or equal to 50 square centimeters

97606 total wound(s) surface area greater than 50 square centimeters

Tests and Measurements

Requires direct one-on-one patient contact.

(For muscle testing, manual or electrical, joint range of motion, electromyography or nerve velocity determination, see 95831-95904)

(97703 has been deleted. To report, use 97762)

97750 Physical performance test or measurement (eg, musculoskeletal, functional capacity), with written report, each 15 minutes

97755 Assistive technology assessment (eg, to restore, augment or compensate for existing function, optimize functional tasks and/or maximize environmental accessibility), direct one-on-one contact by provider, with written report, each 15 minutes

(To report augmentative and alternative communication devices, see 92605, 92607)

Orthotic Management and Prosthetic Management

97760 Orthotic(s) management and training (including assessment and fitting when not otherwise reported), upper extremity(s), lower extremity(s) and/or trunk, each 15 minutes

(Code 97760 should not be reported with 97116 for the same extremity)

97761 Prosthetic training, upper and/or lower extremity(s), each 15 minutes

97762 Checkout for orthotic/prosthetic use, established patient, each 15 minutes

Other Procedures

(For extracorporeal shock wave musculoskeletal therapy, see Category III codes 0019T, 0101T, 0102T)

(97780 has been deleted. To report, see 97810, 97811)

(97781 has been deleted. To report, see 97813, 97814)

97799 Unlisted physical medicine/rehabilitation service or procedure

Medical Nutrition Therapy

97802 Medical nutrition therapy; initial assessment and intervention, individual, face-to-face with the patient, each 15 minutes

97803 re-assessment and intervention, individual, face-to-face with the patient, each 15 minutes

97804 group (2 or more individual(s)), each 30 minutes

(For medical nutrition therapy assessment and/or intervention performed by a physician, see **Evaluation and Management** or **Preventive Medicine** service codes)

Medicine

Acupuncture

Acupuncture is reported based on 15-minute increments of personal (face-to-face) contact with the patient, not the duration of acupuncture needle(s) placement.

If no electrical stimulation is used during a 15-minute increment, use 97810, 97811. If electrical stimulation of any needle is used during a 15-minute increment, use 97813, 97814.

Only one code may be reported for each 15-minute increment. Use either 97810 or 97813 for the initial 15-minute increment. Only one initial code is reported per day.

Evaluation and Management services may be reported separately, using modifier 25, if the patient's condition requires a significant separately identifiable E/M service, above and beyond the usual preservice and postservice work associated with the acupuncture services. The time of the E/M service is not included in the time of the acupuncture service.

97810 Acupuncture, 1 or more needles; without electrical stimulation, initial 15 minutes of personal one-on-one contact with the patient

 (Do not report 97810 in conjunction with 97813)

+ 97811 without electrical stimulation, each additional 15 minutes of personal one-on-one contact with the patient, with re-insertion of needle(s) (List separately in addition to code for primary procedure)

 (Use 97811 in conjunction with 97810, 97813)

97813 with electrical stimulation, initial 15 minutes of personal one-on-one contact with the patient

 (Do not report 97813 in conjunction with 97810)

+ 97814 with electrical stimulation, each additional 15 minutes of personal one-on-one contact with the patient, with re-insertion of needle(s) (List separately in addition to code for primary procedure)

 (Use 97814 in conjunction with 97810, 97813)

Osteopathic Manipulative Treatment

Osteopathic manipulative treatment (OMT) is a form of manual treatment applied by a physician to eliminate or alleviate somatic dysfunction and related disorders. This treatment may be accomplished by a variety of techniques.

Evaluation and Management services may be reported separately if, using modifier 25, the patient's condition requires a significant separately identifiable E/M service, above and beyond the usual preservice and postservice work associated with the procedure. The E/M service may be caused or prompted by the same symptoms or condition for which the OMT service was provided. As such, different diagnoses are not required for the reporting of the OMT and E/M service on the same date.

Body regions referred to are: head region; cervical region; thoracic region; lumbar region; sacral region; pelvic region; lower extremities; upper extremities; rib cage region; abdomen and viscera region.

98925 Osteopathic manipulative treatment (OMT); one to two body regions involved

98926 three to four body regions involved

98927 five to six body regions involved

98928 seven to eight body regions involved

98929 nine to ten body regions involved

Chiropractic Manipulative Treatment

Chiropractic manipulative treatment (CMT) is a form of manual treatment to influence joint and neurophysiological function. This treatment may be accomplished using a variety of techniques.

The chiropractic manipulative treatment codes include a pre-manipulation patient assessment. Additional Evaluation and Management services may be reported separately using modifier 25, if the patient's condition requires a significant separately identifiable E/M service, above and beyond the usual preservice and postservice work associated with the procedure. The E/M service may be caused or prompted by the same symptoms or condition for which the CMT service was provided. As such, different diagnoses are not required for the reporting of the CMT and E/M service on the same date.

For purposes of CMT, the five spinal regions referred to are: cervical region (includes atlanto-occipital joint); thoracic region (includes costovertebral and costotransverse joints); lumbar region; sacral region; and pelvic (sacro-iliac joint) region. The five extraspinal regions referred to are: head (including temporomandibular joint, excluding atlanto-occipital) region; lower extremities; upper extremities; rib cage (excluding costotransverse and costovertebral joints) and abdomen.

98940 Chiropractic manipulative treatment (CMT); spinal, one to two regions

98941 spinal, three to four regions

98942 spinal, five regions

98943 extraspinal, one or more regions

Medicine

Education and Training for Patient Self-Management

The following codes are used to report educational and training services prescribed by a physician and provided by a qualified, nonphysician healthcare professional using a standardized curriculum to an individual or a group of patients for the treatment of established illness(s)/disease(s) or to delay comorbidity(s). Education and training for patient self-management may be reported with these codes only when using a standardized curriculum as described below. This curriculum may be modified as necessary for the clinical needs, cultural norms and health literacy of the individual patient(s).

The purpose of the educational and training services is to teach the patient (may include caregiver(s)) how to effectively self-manage the patient's illness(s)/disease(s) or delay disease comorbidity(s) in conjunction with the patient's professional healthcare team. Education and training related to subsequent reinforcement or due to changes in the patient's condition or treatment plan are reported in the same manner as the original education and training. The type of education and training provided for the patient's clinical condition will be identified by the appropriate diagnosis code(s) reported.

The qualifications of the nonphysician healthcare professionals and the content of the educational and training program must be consistent with guidelines or standards established or recognized by a physician society, nonphysician healthcare professional society/association, or other appropriate source.

> (For counseling and education provided by a physician to an individual, see the appropriate Evaluation and Management codes)
>
> (For counseling and education provided by a physician to a group, use 99078)
>
> (For counseling and/or risk factor reduction intervention provided by a physician to patient(s) without symptoms or established disease, see 99401-99412)
>
> (For medical nutrition therapy, see 97802-97804)
>
> (For health and behavior assessment/intervention that is not part of a standardized curriculum, see 96150-96155)
>
> ▶(For education provided as genetic counseling services, use 96040. For education to a group regarding genetic risks, see 98961, 98962)◀

98960 Education and training for patient self-management by a qualified, nonphysician health care professional using a standardized curriculum, face-to-face with the patient (could include caregiver/family) each 30 minutes; individual patient

98961 2-4 patients

98962 5-8 patients

Special Services, Procedures and Reports

The procedures with code numbers 99000 through 99091 provide the reporting physician or other qualified healthcare professional with the means of identifying the completion of special reports and services that are an adjunct to the basic services rendered. The specific number assigned indicates the special circumstances under which a basic procedure is performed.

Code 99091 should be reported no more than once in a 30-day period to include the physician or health care provider time involved with data accession, review and interpretation, modification of care plan as necessary (including communication to patient and/or caregiver), and associated documentation.

If the services described by 99091 are provided on the same day the patient presents for an E/M service, these services should be considered part of the E/M service and not separately reported.

Do not report 99091 if it occurs within 30 days of care plan oversight services 99374-99380. Do not report 99091 if other more specific CPT codes exist (eg, 93014, 93227, 93233, 93272 for cardiographic services; 95250 for continuous glucose monitoring). Do not report 99091 for transfer and interpretation of data from hospital or clinical laboratory computers.

Codes 99050-99060 are reported in addition to an associated basic service. Typically only a single adjunct code from among 99050-99060 would be reported per patient encounter. However, there may be circumstances in which reporting multiple adjunct codes per patient encounter may be appropriate.

Miscellaneous Services

99000 Handling and/or conveyance of specimen for transfer from the physician's office to a laboratory

99001 Handling and/or conveyance of specimen for transfer from the patient in other than a physician's office to a laboratory (distance may be indicated)

99002 Handling, conveyance, and/or any other service in connection with the implementation of an order involving devices (eg, designing, fitting, packaging, handling, delivery or mailing) when devices such as orthotics, protectives, prosthetics are fabricated by an outside laboratory or shop but which items have been designed, and are to be fitted and adjusted by the attending physician

> (For routine collection of venous blood, use 36415)

Medicine

99024 Postoperative follow-up visit, normally included in the surgical package, to indicate that an evaluation and management service was performed during a postoperative period for a reason(s) related to the original procedure

(As a component of a surgical "package," see **Surgery Guidelines**)

99026 Hospital mandated on call service; in-hospital, each hour

99027 out-of-hospital, each hour

(For physician standby services requiring prolonged physician attendance, use 99360, as appropriate. Time spent performing separately reportable procedure(s) or service(s) should not be included in the time reported as mandated on call service)

99050 Services provided in the office at times other than regularly scheduled office hours, or days when the office is normally closed (eg, holidays, Saturday or Sunday), in addition to basic service

99051 Service(s) provided in the office during regularly scheduled evening, weekend, or holiday office hours, in addition to basic service

(99052 has been deleted)

99053 Service(s) provided between 10:00 PM and 8:00 AM at 24-hour facility, in addition to basic service

(99054 has been deleted)

99056 Service(s) typically provided in the office, provided out of the office at request of patient, in addition to basic service

99058 Service(s) provided on an emergency basis in the office, which disrupts other scheduled office services, in addition to basic service

99060 Service(s) provided on an emergency basis, out of the office, which disrupts other scheduled office services, in addition to basic service

99070 Supplies and materials (except spectacles), provided by the physician over and above those usually included with the office visit or other services rendered (list drugs, trays, supplies, or materials provided)

(For supply of spectacles, use the appropriate supply codes)

99071 Educational supplies, such as books, tapes, and pamphlets, provided by the physician for the patient's education at cost to physician

99075 Medical testimony

99078 Physician educational services rendered to patients in a group setting (eg, prenatal, obesity, or diabetic instructions)

99080 Special reports such as insurance forms, more than the information conveyed in the usual medical communications or standard reporting form

(Do not report 99080 in conjunction with 99455, 99456 for the completion of Workmen's Compensation forms)

99082 Unusual travel (eg, transportation and escort of patient)

99090 Analysis of clinical data stored in computers (eg, ECGs, blood pressures, hematologic data)

(For physician/health care professional collection and interpretation of physiologic data stored/transmitted by patient/caregiver, see 99091)

(Do not report 99090 if other more specific CPT codes exist, eg, 93014, 93227, 93233, 93272 for cardiographic services; 95250 for continuous glucose monitoring, 97750 for musculoskeletal function testing)

99091 Collection and interpretation of physiologic data (eg, ECG, blood pressure, glucose monitoring) digitally stored and/or transmitted by the patient and/or caregiver to the physician or other qualified health care professional, requiring a minimum of 30 minutes of time

Qualifying Circumstances for Anesthesia

(For explanation of these services, see **Anesthesia Guidelines**)

+ 99100 Anesthesia for patient of extreme age, younger than 1 year and older than 70 (List separately in addition to code for primary anesthesia procedure)

(For procedure performed on infants younger than 1 year of age at time of surgery, see 00326, 00561, 00834, 00836)

+ 99116 Anesthesia complicated by utilization of total body hypothermia (List separately in addition to code for primary anesthesia procedure)

+ 99135 Anesthesia complicated by utilization of controlled hypotension (List separately in addition to code for primary anesthesia procedure)

+ 99140 Anesthesia complicated by emergency conditions (specify) (List separately in addition to code for primary anesthesia procedure)

(An emergency is defined as existing when delay in treatment of the patient would lead to a significant increase in the threat to life or body part.)

Moderate (Conscious) Sedation

Moderate (conscious) sedation is a drug induced depression of consciousness during which patients respond purposefully to verbal commands, either alone or accompanied by light tactile stimulation. No interventions are required to maintain a patent airway, and spontaneous ventilation is adequate. Cardiovascular function is usually maintained.

Medicine

Moderate sedation does not include minimal sedation (anxiolysis), deep sedation or monitored anesthesia care (00100-01999).

When providing moderate sedation, the following services are included and NOT reported separately:

- Assessment of the patient (not included in intraservice time);

- Establishment of IV access and fluids to maintain patency, when performed;

- Administration of agent(s);

- Maintenance of sedation;

- Monitoring of oxygen saturation, heart rate and blood pressure; and

- Recovery (not included in intraservice time).

Intraservice time starts with the administration of the sedation agent(s), requires continuous face-to-face attendance, and ends at the conclusion of personal contact by the physician providing the sedation.

Do not report 99143-99150 in conjunction with 94760-94762.

Do not report 99143-99145 in conjunction with codes listed in Appendix G. Do not report 99148-99150 in conjunction with codes listed in Appendix G when performed in the nonfacility setting.

When a second physician other than the healthcare professional performing the diagnostic or therapeutic services provides moderate sedation in the facility setting (eg, hospital, outpatient hospital/ambulatory surgery center, skilled nursing facility) for the procedures listed in Appendix G, the second physician reports 99148-99150. However, for the circumstance in which these services are performed by the second physician in the nonfacility setting (eg, physician office, freestanding imaging center), codes 99148-99150 are not reported.

(99141, 99142 have been deleted. To report, see 99143-99145)

⊘ **99143** Moderate sedation services (other than those services described by codes 00100-01999) provided by the same physician performing the diagnostic or therapeutic service that the sedation supports, requiring the presence of an independent trained observer to assist in the monitoring of the patient's level of consciousness and physiological status; younger than 5 years of age, first 30 minutes intra-service time

⊘ **99144** age 5 years or older, first 30 minutes intra-service time

✚ **99145** each additional 15 minutes intra-service time (List separately in addition to code for primary service)

(Use 99145 in conjunction with 99143, 99144)

⊘ **99148** Moderate sedation services (other than those services described by codes 00100-01999), provided by a physician other than the health care professional performing the diagnostic or therapeutic service that the sedation supports; younger than 5 years of age, first 30 minutes intra-service time

⊘ **99149** age 5 years or older, first 30 minutes intra-service time

✚ **99150** each additional 15 minutes intra-service time (List separately in addition to code for primary service)

(Use 99150 in conjunction with 99148, 99149)

Other Services and Procedures

99170 Anogenital examination with colposcopic magnification in childhood for suspected trauma

(For conscious sedation, use 99143-99150)

99172 Visual function screening, automated or semi-automated bilateral quantitative determination of visual acuity, ocular alignment, color vision by pseudoisochromatic plates, and field of vision (may include all or some screening of the determination(s) for contrast sensitivity, vision under glare)

(This service must employ graduated visual acuity stimuli that allow a quantitative determination of visual acuity (eg, Snellen chart). This service may not be used in addition to a general ophthalmological service or an E/M service)

(Do not report 99172 in conjunction with 99173)

99173 Screening test of visual acuity, quantitative, bilateral

(The screening test used must employ graduated visual acuity stimuli that allow a quantitative estimate of visual acuity (eg, Snellen chart). Other identifiable services unrelated to this screening test provided at the same time may be reported separately (eg, preventive medicine services). When acuity is measured as part of a general ophthalmological service or of an E/M service of the eye, it is a diagnostic examination and not a screening test.)

(Do not report 99173 in conjunction with 99172)

99175 Ipecac or similar administration for individual emesis and continued observation until stomach adequately emptied of poison

(For diagnostic intubation, see 82926-82928, 89130-89141)

(For gastric lavage for diagnostic purposes, see 91055)

99183 Physician attendance and supervision of hyperbaric oxygen therapy, per session

(Evaluation and Management services and/or procedures (eg, wound debridement) provided in a hyperbaric oxygen treatment facility in conjunction with a hyperbaric oxygen therapy session should be reported separately)

Medicine

99185 Hypothermia; regional

99186 total body

99190 Assembly and operation of pump with oxygenator or heat exchanger (with or without ECG and/or pressure monitoring); each hour

99191 45 minutes

99192 30 minutes

99195 Phlebotomy, therapeutic (separate procedure)

99199 Unlisted special service, procedure or report

Home Health Procedures/Services

These codes are used by non-physician health care professionals. Physicians should utilize the home visit codes 99341-99350, and utilize CPT codes other than 99500-99600 for any additional procedure/service provided to a patient living in a residence.

The following codes are used to report services provided in a patient's residence (including assisted living apartments, group homes, non-traditional private homes, custodial care facilities, or schools).

Health care professionals who are authorized to use Evaluation and Management Home Visit codes (99341-99350) may report 99500-99600 in addition to 99341-99350 if both services are performed. Evaluation and Management services may be reported separately, using modifier 25, if the patient's condition requires a significant separately identifiable E/M service, above and beyond the home health service(s)/procedure(s) codes 99500-99600.

99500 Home visit for prenatal monitoring and assessment to include fetal heart rate, non-stress test, uterine monitoring, and gestational diabetes monitoring

99501 Home visit for postnatal assessment and follow-up care

99502 Home visit for newborn care and assessment

99503 Home visit for respiratory therapy care (eg, bronchodilator, oxygen therapy, respiratory assessment, apnea evaluation)

99504 Home visit for mechanical ventilation care

99505 Home visit for stoma care and maintenance including colostomy and cystostomy

99506 Home visit for intramuscular injections

99507 Home visit for care and maintenance of catheter(s) (eg, urinary, drainage, and enteral)

99509 Home visit for assistance with activities of daily living and personal care

(To report self-care/home management training, see 97535)

(To report home medical nutrition assessment and intervention services, see 97802-97804)

(To report home speech therapy services, see 92507-92508)

99510 Home visit for individual, family, or marriage counseling

99511 Home visit for fecal impaction management and enema administration

99512 Home visit for hemodialysis

(For home infusion of peritoneal dialysis, use 99601, 99602)

99600 Unlisted home visit service or procedure

Home Infusion Procedures/Services

99601 Home infusion/specialty drug administration, per visit (up to 2 hours);

+ 99602 each additional hour (List separately in addition to code for primary procedure)

(Use 99602 in conjunction with 99601)

Medicine

Category II Codes

The following section of *Current Procedural Terminology (CPT)* contains a set of supplemental tracking codes that can be used for performance measurement. It is anticipated that the use of Category II codes for performance measurement will decrease the need for record abstraction and chart review, and thereby minimize administrative burden on physicians, other health care professionals, hospitals, and entities seeking to measure the quality of patient care. These codes are intended to facilitate data collection about the quality of care rendered by coding certain services and test results that support nationally established performance measures and that have an evidence base as contributing to quality patient care.

The use of these codes is optional. The codes are not required for correct coding and may not be used as a substitute for Category I codes.

These codes describe clinical components that may be typically included in evaluation and management services or clinical services and, therefore, do not have a relative value associated with them. Category II codes may also describe results from clinical laboratory or radiology tests and other procedures, identified processes intended to address patient safety practices, or services reflecting compliance with state or federal law.

Category II codes described in this section make use of alphabetical characters as the 5th character in the string (ie, 4 digits followed by the letter **F**). These digits are not intended to reflect the placement of the code in the regular (Category I) part of the CPT codebook. To promote understanding of these codes and their associated measures, users are referred to Appendix H, which contains information about performance measurement exclusion modifiers, measures, and their source.

CPT Category II codes are arranged according to the following categories derived from standard clinical documentation format:

Composite Measures 0001F

Patient Management . 0500F

Patient History . 1000F

Physical Examination. 2000F

Diagnostic/Screening Processes or Results. 3000F

Therapeutic, Preventive or Other Interventions . 4000F

Follow-up or Other Outcomes 5000F (no codes at this time)

►Patient Safety. 6005F◄

►Cross-references to the measures associated with each Category II code and their source are included for reference in Appendix H. In addition, acronyms for the related diseases or clinical condition(s) have been added at the end of each code descriptor to identify the topic or clinical category in which that code is included. A complete listing of the diseases/clinical conditions, and their acronyms are provided in alphabetical order in Appendix H. Users should review the complete measure(s) associated with each code prior to implementation.◄

Category II codes are reviewed by the Performance Measures Advisory Group (PMAG), an advisory body to the CPT Editorial Panel and the CPT/HCPAC Advisory Committee. The PMAG is comprised of performance measurement experts representing the Agency for Healthcare Research and Quality (AHRQ), the American Medical Association (AMA), the Centers for Medicare and Medicaid Services (CMS), the Joint Commission on Accreditation of Healthcare Organizations (JCAHO), the National Committee for Quality Assurance (NCQA), and the Physician Consortium for Performance Improvement (PCPI). The PMAG may seek additional expertise and/or input from other national health care organizations, as necessary, for the development of tracking codes. These may include national medical specialty societies, other national health care professional associations, accrediting bodies, and federal regulatory agencies.

►The most current listing of Category II codes, including guidelines, Code Change Proposal forms, and release and implementation dates for Category II codes may be accessed at www.ama-assn.org/go/cpt.◄

(For blood pressure measured, use 2000F)

(0002F has been deleted. To report, use 1000F)

►(0003F has been deleted. To report, see 1034F-1036F)◄

(0004F has been deleted. To report, use 4000F)

(For tobacco use cessation intervention, pharmacologic therapy, use 4001F)

(0006F has been deleted. To report, use 4002F)

(0007F has been deleted. To report, use 4006F)

(0008F has been deleted. To report, use 4009F)

(0009F has been deleted. To report, use 1002F)

(0010F has been deleted)

(0011F has been deleted. To report, use 4011F)

Modifiers

►The following performance measurement modifiers may be used for Category II codes to indicate that a service specified in the associated measure(s) was considered but, due to either medical, patient, or system circumstance(s) documented in the medical record, the service was not provided. These modifiers serve as denominator exclusions from the performance measure. The user should note that not all listed measures provide for exclusions (see Appendix H for more discussion regarding exclusion criteria).

Category II modifiers should only be reported with Category II codes—they should not be reported with Category I or Category III codes. In addition, the modifiers in the Category II section should only be used where specified in the guidelines, reporting instructions, parenthetic notes, or code descriptor language listed in the Category II section (code listing and Appendix H).◄

1P Performance Measure Exclusion Modifier due to Medical Reasons:

►Includes:

- Not indicated (absence of organ/limb, already received/performed, other)

- Contraindicated (patient allergic history, potential adverse drug interaction, other)

2P Performance Measure Exclusion Modifier due to Patient Reasons:

Includes:

- Patient declined

- Economic, social, or religious reasons

- Other patient reasons

3P Performance Measure Exclusion Modifier due to System Reasons:

Includes:

- Resources to perform the services not available

- Insurance coverage/payor-related limitations

- Other reasons attributable to health care delivery system◄

►Composite Codes◄

►Composite codes combine several measures grouped within a single code descriptor to facilitate reporting for a clinical condition when all components are met. If only some of the components are met or if services are provided in addition to those included in the composite code, they may be reported individually using the corresponding CPT Category II codes for those services.◄

▲ **0001F** Heart failure assessed (includes assessment of all the following components)(CAD, HF)[1]:

Blood pressure measured (2000F)[1]

Level of activity assessed (1003F)[1]

Clinical symptoms of volume overload (excess) assessed (1004F)[1]

Weight, recorded (2001F)[1]

Clinical signs of volume overload (excess) assessed (2002F)[1]

(To report blood pressure measured, use 2000F)

0005F Osteoarthritis assessed (OA)[1]

Includes assessment of all the following components:

Osteoarthritis symptoms and functional status assessed (1006F)[1]

Use of anti-inflammatory or over-the-counter (OTC) analgesic medications assessed (1007F)[1]

Initial examination of the involved joint(s) (includes visual inspection, palpation, range of motion) (2004F)[1]

(To report tobacco use cessation intervention, use 4001F)

● **0012F** Community-acquired bacterial pneumonia assessment (includes all of the following components) (CAP)[1]:

Co-morbid conditions assessed (1026F)[1]

Vital signs recorded (2010F)[1]

Mental status assessed (2014F)[1]

Hydration status assessed (2018F)[1]

Patient Management

Patient management codes describe utilization measures or measures of patient care provided for specific clinical purposes (eg, prenatal care, pre- and post-surgical care).

0500F Initial prenatal care visit (report at first prenatal encounter with health care professional providing obstetrical care. Report also date of visit and, in a separate field, the date of the last menstrual period - LMP) (Prenatal)[2]

Footnotes

[1] Physician Consortium for Performance Improvement, www.ama-assn.org/go/quality

[2] National Committee on Quality Assurance (NCQA), Health Employer Data Information Set (HEDIS®), www.ncqa.org

[3] Joint Commission on Accreditation of Healthcare Organizations (JCAHO), ORYX Initiative Performance Measures, www.jcaho.org/pms

[4] National Diabetes Quality Improvement Alliance (NDQIA), www.nationaldiabetesalliance.org

Category II Codes

0501F Prenatal flow sheet documented in medical record by first prenatal visit (documentation includes at minimum blood pressure, weight, urine protein, uterine size, fetal heart tones, and estimated date of delivery). Report also: date of visit and, in a separate field, the date of the last menstrual period - LMP (Note: If reporting 0501F Prenatal flow sheet, it is not necessary to report 0500F Initial prenatal care visit) (Prenatal)[1]

0502F Subsequent prenatal care visit (Prenatal)[2]

[Excludes: patients who are seen for a condition unrelated to pregnancy or prenatal care (eg, an upper respiratory infection; patients seen for consultation only, not for continuing care)]

0503F Postpartum care visit (Prenatal)[2]

Patient History

Patient history codes describe measures for select aspects of patient history or review of systems.

▲ **1000F** Tobacco use assessed (CAD, CAP, COPD, PV)[1] (DM)[4]

▶(1001F has been deleted. To report smoking use, tobacco use, or non-use of tobacco products, see 1034F-1036F)◀

1002F Anginal symptoms and level of activity assessed (CAD)[1]

1003F Level of activity assessed (HF)[1]

1004F Clinical symptoms of volume overload (excess) assessed (HF)[1]

1005F Asthma symptoms evaluated (includes physician documentation of numeric frequency of symptoms or patient completion of an asthma assessment tool/survey/questionnaire) (Asthma)[1]

1006F Osteoarthritis symptoms and functional status assessed (may include the use of a standardized scale or the completion of an assessment questionnaire, such as the SF-36, AAOS Hip & Knee Questionnaire) (OA)[1]

[Instructions: Report when osteoarthritis is addressed during the patient encounter]

1007F Use of anti-inflammatory or analgesic over-the-counter (OTC) medications for symptom relief assessed (OA)[1]

1008F Gastrointestinal and renal risk factors assessed for patients on prescribed or OTC non-steroidal anti-inflammatory drug (NSAID) (OA)[1]

● **1015F** Chronic obstructive pulmonary disease (COPD) symptoms assessed (Includes assessment of at least one of the following: dyspnea, cough/sputum, wheezing), or respiratory symptom assessment tool completed (COPD)[1]

● **1018F** Dyspnea assessed, not present (COPD)[1]

● **1019F** Dyspnea assessed, present (COPD)[1]

● **1022F** Pneumococcus immunization status assessed (CAP, COPD)[1]

● **1026F** Co-morbid conditions assessed (eg, includes assessment for presence or absence of: malignancy, liver disease, congestive heart failure, cerebrovascular disease, renal disease, chronic obstructive pulmonary disease, asthma, diabetes, other co-morbid conditions) (CAP)[1]

● **1030F** Influenza immunization status assessed (CAP)[1]

● **1034F** Current tobacco smoker (CAD, CAP, COPD, PV)[1] (DM)[4]

● **1035F** Current smokeless tobacco user (eg, chew, snuff) (PV)[1]

● **1036F** Current tobacco non-user (CAD, CAP, COPD, PV)[1] (DM)[4]

● **1038F** Persistent asthma (mild, moderate or severe) (Asthma)[1]

● **1039F** Intermittent asthma (Asthma)[1]

Physical Examination

Physical examination codes describe aspects of physical examination or clinical assessment.

2000F Blood pressure, measured (HF, CAD, HTN)[1]

2001F Weight recorded (HF)[1]

2002F Clinical signs of volume overload (excess) assessed (HF)[1]

▶(Code 2003F has been deleted. For performance measurement coding information regarding heart failure, see the Heart Failure Clinical Topic listing in Appendix H)◀

2004F Initial examination of the involved joint(s) (includes visual inspection, palpation, range of motion) (OA)[1]

[Instructions: Report only for initial osteoarthritis visit or for visits for new joint involvement]

● **2010F** Vital signs recorded (includes at minimum: temperature, pulse, respiration, and blood pressure)(CAP)[1]

● **2014F** Mental status assessed (normal/mildly impaired/severely impaired) (CAP)[1]

● **2018F** Hydration status assessed (normal/mildly dehydrated/severely dehydrated) (CAP)[1]

● **2022F** Dilated retinal eye exam with interpretation by an ophthalmologist or optometrist documented and reviewed (DM)[4]

● **2024F** Seven standard field stereoscopic photos with interpretation by an ophthalmologist or optometrist documented and reviewed (DM)[4]

Footnotes.

[1] Physician Consortium for Performance Improvement, www.ama-assn.org/go/quality

[2] National Committee on Quality Assurance (NCQA), Health Employer Data Information Set (HEDIS®), www.ncqa.org

[3] Joint Commission on Accreditation of Healthcare Organizations (JCAHO), ORYX Initiative Performance Measures, www.jcaho.org/pms

[4] National Diabetes Quality Improvement Alliance (NDQIA), www.nationaldiabetesalliance.org

● **2026F** Eye imaging validated to match diagnosis from seven standard field stereoscopic photos results documented and reviewed (DM)[4]

● **2028F** Foot examination performed (includes examination through visual inspection, sensory exam with monofilament, and pulse exam – report when any of the three components are completed) (DM)[4]

Diagnostic/Screening Processes or Results

Diagnostic/screening processes or results codes describe results of tests ordered (clinical laboratory tests, radiological or other procedural examinations).

▶(Code 3000F has been deleted. To report blood pressure use the corresponding systolic codes (3076F and 3077F) and diastolic codes (3078F, 3079F, 3080F)◀

▶(Code 3002F has been deleted. To report blood pressure use the corresponding systolic codes (3076F and 3077F) and diastolic codes (3078F, 3079F, 3080F)◀

● **3006F** Chest X-ray results documented and reviewed (CAP)[1]

● **3011F** Lipid panel results documented and reviewed (must include total cholesterol, HDL-C, triglycerides and calculated LDL-C) (CAD)[1]

● **3014F** Screening mammography results documented and reviewed (PV)[1]

● **3017F** Colorectal cancer screening results documented and reviewed (PV)[1]

(Includes: fecal occult blood testing annually, flexible sigmoidoscopy every 5 years, annual fecal occult blood testing plus flexible sigmoidoscopy every 5 years, double-contrast barium enema every 5 years, or colonoscopy every 10 years)

● **3020F** Left ventricular function (LVF) assessment (eg, echocardiography, nuclear test, or ventriculography) documented in the medical record (Includes quantitative or qualitative assessment results)(CHF)[1]

● **3021F** Left ventricular ejection fraction (LVEF) <40% or documentation of moderately or severely depressed left ventricular systolic function (CAD, HF)[1]

● **3022F** Left ventricular ejection fraction (LVEF) ≥40% or documentation as normal or mildly depressed left ventricular systolic function (CAD, HF)[1]

● **3023F** Spirometry results documented and reviewed (COPD)[1]

● **3025F** Spirometry test results demonstrate FEV_1/FVC<70% with COPD symptoms (eg, dyspnea, cough/sputum, wheezing) (CAP, COPD)[1]

● **3027F** Spirometry test results demonstrate FEV_1/FVC≥70% or patient does not have COPD symptoms (COPD)[1]

● **3028F** Oxygen saturation results documented and reviewed (Includes assessment through pulse oximetry or arterial blood gas measurement) (CAP, COPD)[1]

● **3035F** Oxygen saturation ≤ 88 % or a PaO2 ≤ 55 mm Hg (COPD)[1]

● **3037F** Oxygen saturation > 88% or PaO_2 > 55 mmHg (COPD)[1]

● **3040F** Functional expiratory volume (FEV_1) < 40% of predicted value (COPD)[1]

● **3042F** Functional expiratory volume (FEV_1) ≥ 40% of predicted value (COPD)[1]

● **3046F** Most recent hemoglobin A1c level > 9.0% (DM)[4]

● **3047F** Most recent hemoglobin A1c level ≤ 9.0% (DM)[4]

● **3048F** Most recent LDL-C <100 mg/dL (DM)[4]

● **3049F** Most recent LDL-C 100-129 mg/dL (DM)[4]

● **3050F** Most recent LDL-C ≥130 mg/dL (DM)[4]

● **3060F** Positive microalbuminuria test result documented and reviewed (DM)[4]

● **3061F** Negative microalbuminuria test result documented and reviewed (DM)[4]

● **3062F** Positive macroalbuminuria test result documented and reviewed (DM)[4]

● **3066F** Documentation of treatment for nephropathy (eg, patient receiving dialysis, patient being treated for ESRD, CRF, ARF, or renal insufficiency, any visit to a nephrologist) (DM)[4]

● **3072F** Low risk for retinopathy (no evidence of retinopathy in the prior year) (DM)[4]

● **3076F** Most recent systolic blood pressure < 140 mm Hg (HTN)[1] (DM)[4]

● **3077F** Most recent systolic blood pressure ≥ 140 mm Hg (HTN)[1] (DM)[4]

● **3078F** Most recent diastolic blood pressure < 80 mm Hg (HTN)[1] (DM)[4]

● **3079F** Most recent diastolic blood pressure 80-89 mm Hg (HTN)[1] (DM)[4]

● **3080F** Most recent diastolic blood pressure ≥ 90 mm Hg (HTN)[1] (DM)[4]

Footnotes

[1] Physician Consortium for Performance Improvement, www.ama-assn.org/go/quality

[2] National Committee on Quality Assurance (NCQA), Health Employer Data Information Set (HEDIS®), www.ncqa.org

[3] Joint Commission on Accreditation of Healthcare Organizations (JCAHO), ORYX Initiative Performance Measures, www.jcaho.org/pms

[4] National Diabetes Quality Improvement Alliance (NDQIA), www.nationaldiabetesalliance.org

Therapeutic, Preventive or Other Interventions

Therapeutic, preventive or other interventions codes describe pharmacologic, procedural, or behavioral therapies, including preventive services such as patient education and counseling.

4000F Tobacco use cessation intervention, counseling (COPD, CAP, CAD)[1]

4001F Tobacco use cessation intervention, pharmacologic therapy (COPD, CAD, CAP, PV)[1] (DM)[4]

4002F Statin therapy, prescribed (CAD)[1]

4003F Patient education, written/oral, appropriate for patients with heart failure, performed (HF)[1]

4006F Beta-blocker therapy, prescribed (CAD, HF)[1]

▲ **4009F** Angiotensin converting enzyme (ACE) inhibitor or Angiotensin Receptor Blocker (ARB) therapy, prescribed (HF, CAD)[1]

4011F Oral antiplatelet therapy prescribed (eg, aspirin, clopidogrel/Plavix, or combination of aspirin and dipyridamole/Aggrenox) (CAD)[1]

4012F Warfarin therapy prescribed (CHF)[1]

4014F Written discharge instructions provided to heart failure patients discharged home. (Instructions include all of the following components: activity level, diet, discharge medications, follow-up appointment, weight monitoring, what to do if symptoms worsen)[3]

(Excludes patients < 18 years of age)

▲ **4015F** Persistent asthma, preferred long term control medication or an acceptable alternative treatment, prescribed (Asthma)[1]

(Note: There are no medical exclusion criteria)

(Do not report modifier 1P with 4015F)

(To report patient reasons for not prescribing, use modifier 2P)

4016F Anti-inflammatory/analgesic agent prescribed (OA)[1]

(Use for prescribed or continued medication[s], including over-the-counter medication[s])

4017F Gastrointestinal prophylaxis for NSAID use prescribed (OA)[1]

4018F Therapeutic exercise for the involved joint(s) instructed or physical or occupational therapy prescribed (OA)[1]

● **4025F** Inhaled bronchodilator prescribed (COPD)[1]

● **4030F** Long term oxygen therapy prescribed (more than fifteen hours per day) (COPD)[1]

● **4033F** Pulmonary rehabilitation exercise training recommended (COPD)[1]

▶(Report 4033F with 1019F)◀

● **4035F** Influenza immunization recommended (COPD)[1]

● **4037F** Influenza immunization ordered or administered (COPD, PV)[1]

● **4040F** Pneumococcal immunization ordered or administered (COPD)[1]

● **4045F** Appropriate empiric antibiotic prescribed (See measure developer's Web site for definition of appropriate antibiotic) (CAP)[1]

● **4050F** Hypertension plan of care documented as appropriate (HTN)[1]

Follow-up or Other Outcomes

Follow-up or other outcomes codes describe review and communication of test results to patients, patient satisfaction or experience with care, patient functional status, and patient morbidity and mortality.

Patient Safety

Patient safety codes that describe patient safety practices.

● **6005F** Rationale (eg, severity of illness and safety) for level of care (eg, home, hospital) documented (CAP)[1]

Footnotes

[1] Physician Consortium for Performance Improvement, www.ama-assn.org/go/quality

[2] National Committee on Quality Assurance (NCQA), Health Employer Data Information Set (HEDIS®), www.ncqa.org

[3] Joint Commission on Accreditation of Healthcare Organizations (JCAHO), ORYX Initiative Performance Measures, www.jcaho.org/pms

[4] National Diabetes Quality Improvement Alliance (NDQIA), www.nationaldiabetesalliance.org

Category II Codes

Notes

⊙=Moderate sedation ✚=Add-on code ⚡=FDA approval pending

Category III Codes

The following section contains a set of temporary codes for emerging technology, services, and procedures. Category III codes allow data collection for these services/procedures. Use of unlisted codes does not offer the opportunity for the collection of specific data. If a Category III code is available, this code must be reported instead of a Category I unlisted code. This is an activity that is critically important in the evaluation of health care delivery and the formation of public and private policy. The use of the codes in this section allow physicians and other qualified health care professionals, insurers, health services researchers, and health policy experts to identify emerging technology, services, and procedures for clinical efficacy, utilization and outcomes.

The inclusion of a service or procedure in this section neither implies nor endorses clinical efficacy, safety or the applicability to clinical practice. The codes in this section may not conform to the usual requirements for CPT Category I codes established by the Editorial Panel. For Category I codes, the Panel requires that the service/procedure be performed by many health care professionals in clinical practice in multiple locations and that FDA approval, as appropriate, has already been received. The nature of emerging technology, services, and procedures is such that these requirements may not be met. For these reasons, temporary codes for emerging technology, services, and procedures have been placed in a separate section of the CPT codebook and the codes are differentiated from Category I CPT codes by the use of alphanumeric characters.

▶Services/procedures described in this section make use of alphanumeric characters. These codes have an alpha character as the 5th character in the string, preceded by four digits. The digits are not intended to reflect the placement of the code in the Category I section of CPT nomenclature. Codes in this section may or may not eventually receive a Category I CPT code. In either case, a given Category III code will be archived five years from its date of publication or revision in the CPT code book unless it is demonstrated that a temporary code is still needed. New codes in this section are released semi-annually via the AMA/CPT internet site, to expedite dissemination for reporting. The full set of temporary codes for emerging technology, services, and procedures are published annually in the CPT codebook. Go to www.ama-assn.org/go/cpt for the most current listing.◀

(0001T has been deleted. To report, use 34803)

▶(0003T has been deleted)◀

(0005T-0007T have been deleted. To report, see 0075T, 0076T)

▶(0008T has been deleted)◀

(0009T has been deleted. To report, use 58356)

(0010T has been deleted. To report, use 86480)

(0012T has been deleted. To report, use 29866)

(0013T has been deleted. To report, see 29867, 27415)

(0014T has been deleted. To report, use 29868)

0016T Destruction of localized lesion of choroid (eg, choroidal neovascularization), transpupillary thermotherapy

0017T Destruction of macular drusen, photocoagulation

▶(0018T has been deleted. To report, see 0160T, 0161T)◀

0019T Extracorporeal shock wave involving musculoskeletal system, not otherwise specified, low energy

(For application of high energy extracorporeal shock wave involving musculoskeletal system not otherwise specified, use 0101T)

(For application of high energy extracorporeal shock wave involving lateral humeral epicondyle, use 0102T)

(0020T has been deleted. To report, use 28890)

▶(0021T has been deleted)◀

(0023T has been deleted. To report, use 87900)

0024T Non-surgical septal reduction therapy (eg, alcohol ablation), for hypertrophic obstructive cardiomyopathy, with coronary arteriograms, with or without temporary pacemaker

0026T Lipoprotein, direct measurement, intermediate density lipoproteins (IDL) (remnant lipoproteins)

0027T Endoscopic lysis of epidural adhesions with direct visualization using mechanical means (eg, spinal endoscopic catheter system) or solution injection (eg, normal saline) including radiologic localization and epidurography

(For diagnostic epidurography, use 64999)

0028T Dual energy x-ray absorptiometry (DEXA) body composition study, one or more sites

0029T Treatment(s) for incontinence, pulsed magnetic neuromodulation, per day

0030T Antiprothrombin (phospholipid cofactor) antibody, each Ig class

Category III Codes

0031T Speculoscopy;

0032T with directed sampling

(0033T has been deleted. For endovascular repair of descending thoracic aorta, involving coverage of left subclavian artery origin, use 33880)

(0034T has been deleted. For endovascular repair of descending thoracic aorta, not involving coverage of left subclavian artery origin, use 33881)

(0035T has been deleted. For proximal extension during endovascular repair of descending thoracic aorta, use 33883. Distal extensions are included in 33880, 33881. Distal extensions performed after endovascular repair of descending thoracic aorta are reported with 33886)

(0036T has been deleted. For additional proximal extensions use 33884. Additional distal extensions during endovascular repair of descending thoracic aorta are included in 33880, 33881. Additional distal extensions placed after endovascular repair of thoracic aorta are included in 33886)

(0037T has been deleted. For open subclavian to carotid artery transposition performed in conjunction with endovascular thoracic aortic repair by neck incision, use 33889)

(0038T has been deleted. For endovascular repair of descending thoracic aorta, involving coverage of left subclavian artery origin, radiological supervision and interpretation, use 75956)

(0039T has been deleted. For endovascular repair of descending thoracic aorta, not involving coverage of left subclavian artery origin, radiological supervision and interpretation, use 75957)

(0040T has been deleted. For placement of proximal extension prosthesis for endovascular repair of descending thoracic aorta, radiological supervision and interpretation, use 75958. For placement of distal extension prosthesis after thoracic endovascular repair of descending thoracic aorta, radiological supervision and interpretation, use 75959)

0041T Urinalysis infectious agent detection, semi-quantitative analysis of volatile compounds

0042T Cerebral perfusion analysis using computed tomography with contrast administration, including post-processing of parametric maps with determination of cerebral blood flow, cerebral blood volume, and mean transit time

0043T Carbon monoxide, expired gas analysis (eg, $ETCO_2$/hemolysis breath test)

▶(0044T and 0045T have been deleted. To report, use 96904)◀

0046T Catheter lavage of a mammary duct(s) for collection of cytology specimen(s), in high risk individuals (GAIL risk scoring or prior personal history of breast cancer), each breast; single duct

0047T each additional duct

0048T Implantation of a ventricular assist device, extracorporeal, percutaneous transseptal access, single or dual cannulation

+ 0049T Prolonged extracorporeal percutaneous transseptal ventricular assist device, greater than 24 hours, each subsequent 24 hour period (List separately in addition to code for primary procedure)

(Use 0049T in conjunction with 0048T)

0050T Removal of a ventricular assist device, extracorporeal, percutaneous transseptal access, single or dual cannulation

0051T Implantation of a total replacement heart system (artificial heart) with recipient cardiectomy

(For implantation of heart assist or ventricular assist device, see 33975, 33976)

0052T Replacement or repair of thoracic unit of a total replacement heart system (artificial heart)

(For replacement or repair of other implantable components in a total replacement heart system (artificial heart), use 0053T)

0053T Replacement or repair of implantable component or components of total replacement heart system (artificial heart), excluding thoracic unit

(For replacement or repair of a thoracic unit of a total replacement heart system (artificial heart), use 0052T)

+ 0054T Computer-assisted musculoskeletal surgical navigational orthopedic procedure, with image-guidance based on fluoroscopic images (List separately in addition to code for primary procedure)

+ 0055T Computer-assisted musculoskeletal surgical navigational orthopedic procedure, with image-guidance based on CT/MRI images (List separately in addition to code for primary procedure)

(When CT and MRI are both performed, report 0055T only once)

+ 0056T Computer-assisted musculoskeletal surgical navigational orthopedic procedure, image-less (List separately in addition to code for primary procedure)

(0057T has been deleted. To report, use 43257)

0058T Cryopreservation; reproductive tissue, ovarian

0059T oocyte(s)

(For cryopreservation of embryo(s), sperm and testicular reproductive tissue, see 89258, 89259, 89335)

0060T Electrical impedance scan of the breast, bilateral (risk assessment device for breast cancer)

Category III Codes

0061T Destruction/reduction of malignant breast tumor including breast carcinoma cells in the margins, microwave phased array thermotherapy, disposable catheter with combined temperature monitoring probe and microwave sensor, externally applied microwave energy, including interstitial placement of sensor

►(For imaging guidance performed in conjunction with 0061T, see 76942, 76998)◄

▲ **0062T** Percutaneous intradiscal annuloplasty, any method except electrothermal, unilateral or bilateral including fluoroscopic guidance; single level

+ **0063T** 1 or more additional levels (List separately in addition to 0062T for primary procedure)

►(For CT or MRI guidance and localization for needle placement and annuloplasty in conjunction with 0062T, 0063T, see 77012, 77021)◄

►(For intradiscal electrothermal annuloplasty see 22526-22527)◄

0064T Spectroscopy, expired gas analysis (eg, nitric oxide/carbon dioxide test)

0065T Ocular photoscreening, with interpretation and report, bilateral

(Do not report 0065T in conjunction with 99172 or 99173)

0066T Computed tomographic (CT) colonography (ie, virtual colonoscopy); screening

0067T diagnostic

(Do not report 0066T or 0067T in conjunction with 72192-72194, 74150-74170)

+ **0068T** Acoustic heart sound recording and computer analysis; with interpretation and report (List separately in addition to codes for electrocardiography)

(Use 0068T in conjunction with 93000)

+ **0069T** acoustic heart sound recording and computer analysis only (List separately in addition to codes for electrocardiography)

(Use 0069T in conjunction with 93005)

+ **0070T** interpretation and report only (List separately in addition to codes for electrocardiography)

(Use 0070T in conjunction with 93010)

0071T Focused ultrasound ablation of uterine leiomyomata, including MR guidance; total leiomyomata volume less than 200 cc of tissue

0072T total leiomyomata volume greater or equal to 200 cc of tissue

►(Do not report 0071T, 0072T in conjunction with 51702 or 77022)◄

0073T Compensator-based beam modulation treatment delivery of inverse planned treatment using three or more high resolution (milled or cast) compensator convergent beam modulated fields, per treatment session

(For treatment planning, use 77301)

(Do not report 0073T in conjunction with 77401-77416, 77418)

Online Medical Evaluation

An online medical evaluation is a type of Evaluation and Management (E/M) service provided by a physician or qualified health care professional to a patient using internet resources in response to the patient's online inquiry. Reportable services involve the physician's personal timely response to the patient's inquiry and must involve permanent storage (electronic or hard copy) of the encounter. This service should not be reported for patient contacts (eg, telephone calls) considered to be pre-service or post-service work for other E/M or non E/M services. A reportable service would encompass the sum of communication (eg, related telephone calls, prescription provision, laboratory orders) pertaining to the online patient encounter or problem(s).

0074T Online evaluation and management service, per encounter, provided by a physician, using the Internet or similar electronic communications network, in response to a patient's request, established patient

0075T Transcatheter placement of extracranial vertebral or intrathoracic carotid artery stent(s), including radiologic supervision and interpretation, percutaneous; initial vessel

+ **0076T** each additional vessel (List separately in addition to code for primary procedure)

(Use 0076T in conjunction with 0075T)

(When the ipsilateral extracranial vertebral or intrathoracic carotid arteriogram (including imaging and selective catheterization) confirms the need for stenting, then 0075T and 0076T include all ipsilateral extracranial vertebral or intrathoracic selective carotid catheterization, all diagnostic imaging for ipsilateral extracranial vertebral or intrathoracic carotid artery stenting, and all related radiologic supervision and interpretation. If stenting is not indicated, then the appropriate codes for selective catheterization and imaging should be reported in lieu of code 0075T or 0076T.)

0077T Implanting and securing cerebral thermal perfusion probe, including twist drill or burr hole, to measure absolute cerebral tissue perfusion

(0078T-0081T should be reported in accordance with the Endovascular Abdominal Aneurysm Repair guidelines established for 34800-34826)

Category III Codes

0078T Endovascular repair using prosthesis of abdominal aortic aneurysm, pseudoaneurysm or dissection, abdominal aorta involving visceral branches (superior mesenteric, celiac and/or renal artery(s))

(Do not report 0078T in conjunction with 34800-34805, 35081, 35102, 35452, 35454, 35472, 37205-37208)

(Report 0078T in conjunction with 35454, 37205-37208 when these procedures are performed outside the target zone of the endoprosthesis)

+ 0079T Placement of visceral extension prosthesis for endovascular repair of abdominal aortic aneurysm involving visceral vessels, each visceral branch (List separately in addition to code for primary procedure)

(Use 0079T in conjunction with 0078T)

(Do not report 0079T in conjunction with 34800-34805, 35081, 35102, 35452, 35454, 35472, 37205-37208)

(Report 0079T in conjunction with 35454, 37205-37208 when these procedures are performed outside the target zone of the endoprosthesis)

0080T Endovascular repair of abdominal aortic aneurysm, pseudoaneurysm or dissection, abdominal aorta involving visceral vessels (superior mesenteric, celiac or renal), using fenestrated modular bifurcated prosthesis (two docking limbs), radiological supervision and interpretation

(Do not report 0080T in conjunction with 34800-34805, 35081, 35102, 35452, 35454, 35472, 37205-37208)

(Report 0080T in conjunction with 35454, 37205-37208 when these procedures are performed outside the target zone of the endoprosthesis)

+ 0081T Placement of visceral extension prosthesis for endovascular repair of abdominal aortic aneurysm involving visceral vessels, each visceral branch, radiological supervision and interpretation (List separately in addition to code for primary procedure)

(Use 0081T in conjunction with 0080T)

(Do not report 0081T in conjunction with 34800-34805, 35081, 35102, 35452, 35454, 35472, 37205-37208)

(Report 0081T in conjunction with 35454, 37205-37208 when these procedures are performed outside the target zone of the endoprosthesis)

►(0082T, 0083T have been deleted. To report, see 77373-77435)◄

0084T Insertion of a temporary prostatic urethral stent

0085T Breath test for heart transplant rejection

0086T Left ventricular filling pressure indirect measurement by computerized calibration of the arterial waveform response to Valsalva maneuver

0087T Sperm evaluation, Hyaluronan binding assay

0088T Submucosal radiofrequency tissue volume reduction of tongue base, one or more sites, per session (ie, for treatment of obstructive sleep apnea syndrome)

0089T Actigraphy testing, recording, analysis and interpretation (minimum of three-day recording)

▲ **0090T** Total disc arthroplasty (artificial disc), anterior approach, including discectomy to prepare interspace (other than for decompression) cervical; single interspace

►(0091T has been deleted)◄

►(To report total disc lumbar arthroplasty, use 22857)◄

+ 0092T each additional interspace (List separately in addition to code for primary procedure)

►(Use 0092T in conjunction with 0090T)◄

►(For total disc lumbar arthroplasty of additional interspaces, use 0163T)◄

►(Do not report 0092T in conjunction with 22857)◄

▲ **0093T** Removal of total disc arthroplasty, anterior approach cervical; single interspace

►(0094T has been deleted)◄

►(To report removal of total disc lumbar arthroplasty, use 22865)◄

+ 0095T each additional interspace (List separately in addition to code for primary procedure)

►(Use 0095T in conjunction with 0093T)◄

►(For removal of total disc lumbar arthroplasty additional interspaces, use 0164T)◄

►(Do not report 0095T in conjunction with 22865)◄

▲ **0096T** Revision of total disc arthroplasty, anterior approach cervical; single interspace

(Do not report 0096T in conjunction with 0093T)

►(0097T has been deleted)◄

►(To report revision of total disc lumbar arthroplasty, use 22862)◄

+ 0098T each additional interspace (List separately in addition to code for primary procedure)

►(Use 0098T in conjunction with 0096T)◄

►(0090T-0098T include fluoroscopy when performed)◄

(Do not report 0090T-0098T in conjunction with 22851, 49010, when performed at the same level)

►(Do not report 0098T in conjunction with 22862, 0095T)◄

►(For revision of total disc lumbar arthroplasty additional interspaces, use 0165T)◄

►(For decompression, see 63001-63048)◄

0099T Implantation of intrastromal corneal ring segments

0100T Placement of a subconjunctival retinal prosthesis receiver and pulse generator, and implantation of intra-ocular retinal electrode array, with vitrectomy

Category III Codes

0101T Extracorporeal shock wave involving musculoskeletal system, not otherwise specified, high energy

(For application of low energy musculoskeletal system extracorporeal shock wave, use 0019T)

0102T Extracorporeal shock wave, high energy, performed by a physician, requiring anesthesia other than local, involving lateral humeral epicondyle

(For application of low energy musculoskeletal system extracorporeal shock wave, use 0019T)

0103T Holotranscobalamin, quantitative

0104T Inert gas rebreathing for cardiac output measurement; during rest

0105T during exercise

0106T Quantitative sensory testing (QST), testing and interpretation per extremity; using touch pressure stimuli to assess large diameter sensation

0107T using vibration stimuli to assess large diameter fiber sensation

0108T using cooling stimuli to assess small nerve fiber sensation and hyperalgesia

0109T using heat-pain stimuli to assess small nerve fiber sensation and hyperalgesia

0110T using other stimuli to assess sensation

0111T Long-chain (C20-22) omega-3 fatty acids in red blood cell (RBC) membranes

(For very long chain fatty acids, use 82726)

Medication Therapy Management

Medication Therapy Management Service(s) (MTMS) describe face-to-face patient assessment and intervention as appropriate, by a pharmacist. MTMS is provided to optimize the response to medications or to manage treatment-related medication interactions or complications.

MTMS includes the following documented elements: review of the pertinent patient history, medication profile (prescription and non-prescription), and recommendations for improving health outcomes and treatment compliance. These codes are not to be used to describe the provision of product-specific information at the point of dispensing or any other routine dispensing-related activities.

0115T Medication therapy management service(s) provided by a pharmacist, individual, face-to-face with patient, initial 15 minutes, with assessment, and intervention if provided; initial encounter

0116T subsequent encounter

+ 0117T each additional 15 minutes (List separately in addition to code for primary service)

(Use 0117T in conjunction with 0115T, 0116T)

▶(0120T has been deleted. To report, use 19105)◀

0123T Fistulization of sclera for glaucoma, through ciliary body

0124T Conjunctival incision with posterior juxtascleral placement of pharmacological agent (does not include supply of medication)

0126T Common carotid intima-media thickness (IMT) study for evaluation of atherosclerotic burden or coronary heart disease risk factor assessment

0130T Validated, statistically reliable, randomized, controlled, single-patient clinical investigation of FDA approved chronic care drugs, provided by a pharmacist, interpretation and report to the prescribing health care professional

0133T Upper gastrointestinal endoscopy, including esophagus, stomach, and either the duodenum and/or jejunum as appropriate, with injection of implant material into and along the muscle of the lower esophageal sphincter (eg, for treatment of gastroesophageal reflux disease)

0135T Ablation, renal tumor(s), unilateral, percutaneous, cryotherapy

0137T Biopsy, prostate, needle, saturation sampling for prostate mapping

(Do not report 0137T in conjunction with 76942)

0140T Exhaled breath condensate pH

▶Pancreatic islet cells are transplanted by infusion into the portal vein. The portal vein may be cannulated percutaneously with imaging guidance, by laparoscopy, or by laparotomy. Codes 0141T-0143T include infusion of islet cells with monitoring and management of portal and systemic hemodynamics, monitoring and management of blood glucose and insulin therapy, immunotherapy infusion, antibiotic infusion, analgesic and sedative administration and monitoring, and all other therapeutic injections and infusions administered during the islet infusion. Codes 0141T-0143T also include typical postprocedural care. When reporting 0141T, percutaneous portal vein catheterization is reported separately (see codes 36481, 75887). Code 0142T includes diagnostic laparotomy (49000, 49002). Code 0143T includes diagnostic laparoscopy (49320).◀

● **0141T** Pancreatic islet cell transplantation through portal vein, percutaneous

▶(For open approach, use 0142T)◀

▶(For laparoscopic approach, use 0143T)◀

▶(For percutaneous portal vein catheterization, use 36481)◀

▶(For radiological supervision and interpretation, use 75887)◀

● **0142T** Pancreatic islet cell transplantation through portal vein, open

▶(For percutaneous approach, use 0141T)◀

▶(For laparoscopic approach, use 0143T)◀

▶(Do not report 0142T in conjunction with 49000, 49002)◀

● 0143T Laparoscopy, surgical, pancreatic islet cell transplantation through portal vein

►(For percutaneous approach, use 0141T)◄

►(For open approach, use 0142T)◄

►(Do not report 0143T in conjunction with 49320)◄

● 0144T Computed tomography, heart, without contrast material, including image postprocessing and quantitative evaluation of coronary calcium

►(Do not report 0144T in conjunction with 0145T-0151T)◄

● 0145T Computed tomography, heart, without contrast material followed by contrast material(s) and further sections, including cardiac gating and 3D image postprocessing; cardiac structure and morphology

►(For cardiac structure and morphology in congenital heart disease, use 0150T)◄

● 0146T computed tomographic angiography of coronary arteries (including native and anomalous coronary arteries, coronary bypass grafts), without quantitative evaluation of coronary calcium

● 0147T computed tomographic angiography of coronary arteries (including native and anomalous coronary arteries, coronary bypass grafts), with quantitative evaluation of coronary calcium

►(Do not report 0147T in conjunction with 0144T)◄

● 0148T cardiac structure and morphology and computed tomographic angiography of coronary arteries (including native and anomalous coronary arteries, coronary bypass grafts), without quantitative evaluation of coronary calcium

● 0149T cardiac structure and morphology and computed tomographic angiography of coronary arteries (including native and anomalous coronary arteries, coronary bypass grafts), with quantitative evaluation of coronary calcium

►(Do not report 0149T in conjunction with 0144T)◄

● 0150T cardiac structure and morphology in congenital heart disease

+● 0151T Computed tomography, heart, without contrast material followed by contrast material(s) and further sections, including cardiac gating and 3D image postprocessing, function evaluation (left and right ventricular function, ejection-fraction and segmental wall motion) (List separately in addition to code for primary procedure)

►(Use 0151T in conjunction with 0145T-0150T)◄

+● 0153T Transcatheter placement of wireless physiologic sensor in aneurysmal sac during endovascular repair, including radiological supervision and interpretation and instrument calibration (List separately in addition to code for primary procedure)

►(Use 0153T in conjunction with 34800, 34802, 34803, 34804, 34805, 34900)◄

►(0153T includes deployment of the sensor, repositioning if required, and intraoperative calibration)◄

● 0154T Noninvasive physiologic study of implanted wireless pressure sensor in aneurysmal sac following endovascular repair, complete study including recording, analysis of pressure and waveform tracings, interpretation and report

►(Do not report 0154T in conjunction with 0153T)◄

● 0155T Laparoscopy, surgical; implantation or replacement of gastric stimulation electrodes, lesser curvature (ie, morbid obesity)

● 0156T revision or removal of gastric stimulation electrodes, lesser curvature (ie, morbid obesity)

►(For open approach, see 0157T, 0158T)◄

►(For insertion of gastric neurostimulator pulse generator, use 64590)◄

►(For revision or removal of gastric neurostimulator pulse generator, use 64595)◄

►(For electronic analysis and programming of gastric neurostimulator pulse generator, see 95999)◄

● 0157T Laparotomy, implantation or replacement of gastric stimulation electrodes, lesser curvature (ie, morbid obesity)

● 0158T Laparotomy, revision or removal of gastric stimulation electrodes, lesser curvature (ie, morbid obesity)

►(For laparoscopic approach, see 0155T, 0156T)◄

►(For insertion of gastric neurostimulator pulse generator, use 64590)◄

►(For revision or removal of gastric neurostimulator pulse generator, use 64595)◄

►(For electronic analysis and programming of gastric neurostimulator pulse generator, see 95999)◄

►(For electronic analysis, programming and reprogramming of gastric neurostimulator, use 0162T)◄

+● 0159T Computer-aided detection, including computer algorithm analysis of MRI image data for lesion detection/characterization, pharmacokinetic analysis, with further physician review for interpretation, breast MRI (List separately in addition to code for primary procedure)

►(Use 0159T in conjunction with 77058, 77059)◄

Category III Codes

● **0160T** Therapeutic repetitive transcranial magnetic stimulation treatment planning

▶(Pre-treatment determination of optimal magnetic field strength via titration, treatment location determination and stimulation parameter and protocol programming in the therapeutic use of high power, focal magnetic pulses for the direct, noninvasive modulation of cortical neurons)◀

● **0161T** Therapeutic repetitive transcranial magnetic stimulation treatment delivery and management, per session

▶(Treatment session using high power, focal magnetic pulses for the direct, noninvasive modulation of cortical neurons. Clinical evaluation, safety monitoring and treatment parameter review in the therapeutic use of high power, focal magnetic pulses for the direct, noninvasive modulation of cortical neurons)◀

● **0162T** Electronic analysis and programming, reprogramming of gastric neurostimulator (ie, morbid obesity)

+● **0163T** Total disc arthroplasty (artificial disc), anterior approach, including discectomy to prepare interspace (other than for decompression), lumbar, each additional interspace

▶(Use 0163T in conjunction with 22857)◀

+● **0164T** Removal of total disc arthroplasty, anterior approach, lumbar, each additional interspace

▶(Use 0164T in conjunction with 22865)◀

+● **0165T** Revision of total disc arthroplasty, anterior approach, lumbar, each additional interspace

▶(Use 0165T in conjunction with 22862)◀

▶(0163T-0165T include fluoroscopy when performed)◀

▶(Do not report 0163T-0165T in conjunction with 22851, 49010, when performed at the same level)◀

▶(For cervical total disc arthroplasty procedures, see 0090T-0098T)◀

▶(For decompression, see 63001-63048)◀

● **0166T** Transmyocardial transcatheter closure of ventricular septal defect, with implant; without cardiopulmonary bypass

● **0167T** with cardiopulmonary bypass

▶(Do not report 0166T, 0167T in conjunction with 32020, 33210, 33211)◀

▶(For ventricular septal defect closure via percutaneous transcatheter implant delivery, use 93581)◀

● **0168T** Rhinophototherapy, intranasal application of ultraviolet and visible light, bilateral

● **0169T** Stereotactic placement of infusion catheter(s) in the brain for delivery of therapeutic agent(s), including computerized stereotactic planning and burr hole(s)

▶(Do not report code 0169T in conjunction with 20660, 61107, 61795)◀

● **0170T** Repair of anorectal fistula with plug (eg, porcine small intestine submucosa [SIS])

▶(For repair of anal fistula using fibrin glue, use 46706)◀

▶(Do not report 0170T in conjunction with 15430, 15431)◀

Category III Codes

Notes

⊙=Moderate sedation ✦=Add-on code ⨍=FDA approval pending

Appendix A

Modifiers

This list includes all of the modifiers applicable to *CPT 2007* codes.

21 **Prolonged Evaluation and Management Services:** When the face-to-face or floor/unit service(s) provided is prolonged or otherwise greater than that usually required for the highest level of evaluation and management service within a given category, it may be identified by adding modifier 21 to the evaluation and management code number. A report may also be appropriate.

22 **Unusual Procedural Services:** When the service(s) provided is greater than that usually required for the listed procedure, it may be identified by adding modifier 22 to the usual procedure number. A report may also be appropriate.

23 **Unusual Anesthesia:** Occasionally, a procedure, which usually requires either no anesthesia or local anesthesia, because of unusual circumstances must be done under general anesthesia. This circumstance may be reported by adding modifier 23 to the procedure code of the basic service.

24 **Unrelated Evaluation and Management Service by the Same Physician During a Postoperative Period:** The physician may need to indicate that an evaluation and management service was performed during a postoperative period for a reason(s) unrelated to the original procedure. This circumstance may be reported by adding modifier 24 to the appropriate level of E/M service.

25 **Significant, Separately Identifiable Evaluation and Management Service by the Same Physician on the Same Day of the Procedure or Other Service:** The physician may need to indicate that on the day a procedure or service identified by a CPT code was performed, the patient's condition required a significant, separately identifiable E/M service above and beyond the other service provided or beyond the usual preoperative and postoperative care associated with the procedure that was performed. A significant, separately identifiable E/M service is defined or substantiated by documentation that satisfies the relevant criteria for the respective E/M service to be reported (see **Evaluation and Management Services Guidelines** for instructions on determining level of E/M service). The E/M service may be prompted by the symptom or condition for which the procedure and/or service was provided. As such, different diagnoses are not required for reporting of the E/M services on the same date. This circumstance may be reported by adding modifier 25 to the appropriate level of E/M service. **Note:** This modifier is not used to report an E/M service that resulted in a decision to perform surgery. See modifier 57.

26 **Professional Component:** Certain procedures are a combination of a physician component and a technical component. When the physician component is reported separately, the service may be identified by adding modifier 26 to the usual procedure number.

32 **Mandated Services:** Services related to *mandated* consultation and/or related services (eg, PRO, third party payer, governmental, legislative or regulatory requirement) may be identified by adding modifier 32 to the basic procedure.

47 **Anesthesia by Surgeon:** Regional or general anesthesia provided by the surgeon may be reported by adding modifier 47 to the basic service. (This does not include local anesthesia.) **Note:** Modifier 47 would not be used as a modifier for the anesthesia procedures.

50 **Bilateral Procedure:** Unless otherwise identified in the listings, bilateral procedures that are performed at the same operative session should be identified by adding modifier 50 to the appropriate five digit code.

51 **Multiple Procedures:** When multiple procedures, other than E/M services, are performed at the same session by the same provider, the primary procedure or service may be reported as listed. The additional procedure(s) or service(s) may be identified by appending modifier 51 to the additional procedure or service code(s). **Note:** This modifier should not be appended to designated "add-on" codes (see Appendix D).

52 **Reduced Services:** Under certain circumstances a service or procedure is partially reduced or eliminated at the physician's discretion. Under these circumstances the service provided can be identified by its usual procedure number and the addition of modifier 52, signifying that the service is reduced. This provides a means of reporting reduced services without disturbing the identification of the basic service. **Note:** For hospital outpatient reporting of a previously scheduled procedure/service that is partially reduced or cancelled as a result of extenuating circumstances or those that threaten the well-being of the patient prior to or after administration of anesthesia, see modifiers 73 and 74 (see modifiers approved for ASC hospital outpatient use).

53 **Discontinued Procedure:** Under certain circumstances, the physician may elect to terminate a surgical or diagnostic procedure. Due to extenuating circumstances or those that threaten the well being of the patient, it may be necessary to indicate that a surgical or diagnostic procedure was started but discontinued. This circumstance may be reported by adding modifier 53 to the code reported by the physician for the discontinued procedure. **Note:** This modifier is not used to report the elective cancellation of a procedure prior to the patient's anesthesia induction and/or surgical preparation in the operating suite. For outpatient hospital/ambulatory surgery center (ASC) reporting of a previously scheduled procedure/service that is partially reduced or cancelled as a result of extenuating circumstances or those that threaten the well being of the

patient prior to or after administration of anesthesia, see modifiers 73 and 74 (see modifiers approved for ASC hospital outpatient use).

54 **Surgical Care Only:** When one physician performs a surgical procedure and another provides preoperative and/or postoperative management, surgical services may be identified by adding modifier 54 to the usual procedure number.

55 **Postoperative Management Only:** When one physician performed the postoperative management and another physician performed the surgical procedure, the postoperative component may be identified by adding modifier 55 to the usual procedure number.

56 **Preoperative Management Only:** When one physician performed the preoperative care and evaluation and another physician performed the surgical procedure, the preoperative component may be identified by adding modifier 56 to the usual procedure number.

57 **Decision for Surgery:** An evaluation and management service that resulted in the initial decision to perform the surgery may be identified by adding modifier 57 to the appropriate level of E/M service.

58 **Staged or Related Procedure or Service by the Same Physician During the Postoperative Period:** The physician may need to indicate that the performance of a procedure or service during the postoperative period was: a) planned prospectively at the time of the original procedure (staged); b) more extensive than the original procedure; or c) for therapy following a diagnostic surgical procedure. This circumstance may be reported by adding modifier 58 to the staged or related procedure. **Note:** This modifier is not used to report the treatment of a problem that requires a return to the operating room. See modifier 78.

59 **Distinct Procedural Service:** Under certain circumstances, the physician may need to indicate that a procedure or service was distinct or independent from other services performed on the same day. Modifier 59 is used to identify procedures/services that are not normally reported together, but are appropriate under the circumstances. This may represent a different session or patient encounter, different procedure or surgery, different site or organ system, separate incision/excision, separate lesion, or separate injury (or area of injury in extensive injuries) not ordinarily encountered or performed on the same day by the same physician. However, when another already established modifier is appropriate it should be used rather than modifier 59. Only if no more descriptive modifier is available, and the use of modifier 59 best explains the circumstances, should modifier 59 be used.

62 **Two Surgeons:** When two surgeons work together as primary surgeons performing distinct part(s) of a procedure, each surgeon should report his/her distinct operative work by adding modifier 62 to the procedure code and any associated add-on code(s) for that procedure as long as both surgeons continue to work together as primary surgeons. Each surgeon should report the co-surgery once using the same procedure code. If additional procedure(s) (including add-on procedure(s) are performed during the same surgical session, separate code(s) may also be reported with modifier 62 added. **Note:** If a co-surgeon acts as an assistant in the performance of additional procedure(s) during the same surgical session, those services may be reported using separate procedure code(s) with modifier 80 or modifier 82 added, as appropriate.

63 **Procedure Performed on Infants less than 4 kg:** Procedures performed on neonates and infants up to a present body weight of 4 kg may involve significantly increased complexity and physician work commonly associated with these patients. This circumstance may be reported by adding modifier 63 to the procedure number. **Note:** Unless otherwise designated, this modifier may only be appended to procedures/services listed in the 20000-69990 code series. Modifier 63 should not be appended to any CPT codes listed in the **Evaluation and Management Services, Anesthesia, Radiology, Pathology/Laboratory, or Medicine** sections.

66 **Surgical Team:** Under some circumstances, highly complex procedures (requiring the concomitant services of several physicians, often of different specialties, plus other highly skilled, specially trained personnel, various types of complex equipment) are carried out under the "surgical team" concept. Such circumstances may be identified by each participating physician with the addition of modifier 66 to the basic procedure number used for reporting services.

76 **Repeat Procedure by Same Physician:** The physician may need to indicate that a procedure or service was repeated subsequent to the original procedure or service. This circumstance may be reported by adding modifier 76 to the repeated procedure/service.

77 **Repeat Procedure by Another Physician:** The physician may need to indicate that a basic procedure or service performed by another physician had to be repeated. This situation may be reported by adding modifier 77 to the repeated procedure/service.

78 **Return to the Operating Room for a Related Procedure During the Postoperative Period:** The physician may need to indicate that another procedure was performed during the postoperative period of the initial procedure. When this subsequent procedure is related to the first, and requires the use of the operating room, it may be reported by adding modifier 78 to the related procedure. (For repeat procedures on the same day, see modifier 76.)

79 **Unrelated Procedure or Service by the Same Physician During the Postoperative Period:** The physician may need to indicate that the performance of a procedure or service during the postoperative period was unrelated to the original procedure. This circumstance may be reported by using modifier 79. (For repeat procedures on the same day, see modifier 76.)

80 **Assistant Surgeon:** Surgical assistant services may be identified by adding modifier 80 to the usual procedure number(s).

81 Minimum Assistant Surgeon: Minimum surgical assistant services are identified by adding modifier 81 to the usual procedure number.

82 Assistant Surgeon (when qualified resident surgeon not available): The unavailability of a qualified resident surgeon is a prerequisite for use of modifier 82 appended to the usual procedure code number(s).

90 Reference (Outside) Laboratory: When laboratory procedures are performed by a party other than the treating or reporting physician, the procedure may be identified by adding modifier 90 to the usual procedure number.

91 Repeat Clinical Diagnostic Laboratory Test: In the course of treatment of the patient, it may be necessary to repeat the same laboratory test on the same day to obtain subsequent (multiple) test results. Under these circumstances, the laboratory test performed can be identified by its usual procedure number and the addition of modifier 91. **Note:** This modifier may not be used when tests are rerun to confirm initial results; due to testing problems with specimens or equipment; or for any other reason when a normal, one-time, reportable result is all that is required. This modifier may not be used when other code(s) describe a series of test results (eg, glucose tolerance tests, evocative/suppression testing). This modifier may only be used for laboratory test(s) performed more than once on the same day on the same patient.

99 Multiple Modifiers: Under certain circumstances two or more modifiers may be necessary to completely delineate a service. In such situations modifier 99 should be added to the basic procedure, and other applicable modifiers may be listed as part of the description of the service.

Anesthesia Physical Status Modifiers

The Physical Status modifiers are consistent with the American Society of Anesthesiologists ranking of patient physical status, and distinguishing various levels of complexity of the anesthesia service provided. All anesthesia services are reported by use of the anesthesia five-digit procedure code (00100-01999) with the appropriate physical status modifier appended.

Example: 00100-P1

Under certain circumstances, when another established modifier(s) is appropriate, it should be used in addition to the physical status modifier.

Example: 00100-P4-53

Physical Status Modifier P1: A normal healthy patient

Physical Status Modifier P2: A patient with mild systemic disease

Physical Status Modifier P3: A patient with severe systemic disease

Physical Status Modifier P4: A patient with severe systemic disease that is a constant threat to life

Physical Status Modifier P5: A moribund patient who is not expected to survive without the operation

Physical Status Modifier P6: A declared brain-dead patient whose organs are being removed for donor purposes

Modifiers Approved for Ambulatory Surgery Center (ASC) Hospital Outpatient Use

CPT Level I Modifiers

25 Significant, Separately Identifiable Evaluation and Management Service by the Same Physician on the Same Day of the Procedure or Other Service: The physician may need to indicate that on the day a procedure or service identified by a CPT code was performed, the patient's condition required a significant, separately identifiable E/M service above and beyond the other service provided or beyond the usual preoperative and postoperative care associated with the procedure that was performed. A significant, separately identifiable E/M service is defined or substantiated by documentation that satisfies the relevant criteria for the respective E/M service to be reported (see **Evaluation and Management Services Guidelines** for instructions on determining level of E/M service). The E/M service may be prompted by the symptom or condition for which the procedure and/or service was provided. As such, different diagnoses are not required for reporting of the E/M services on the same date. This circumstance may be reported by adding modifier 25 to the appropriate level of E/M service. **Note:** This modifier is not used to report an E/M service that resulted in a decision to perform surgery (see modifier 57).

27 Multiple Outpatient Hospital E/M Encounters on the Same Date: For hospital outpatient reporting purposes, utilization of hospital resources related to separate and distinct E/M encounters performed in multiple outpatient hospital settings on the same date may be reported by adding modifier 27 to each appropriate level outpatient and/or emergency department E/M code(s). This modifier provides a means of reporting circumstances involving evaluation and management services provided by physician(s) in more than one (multiple) outpatient hospital setting(s) (eg, hospital emergency department, clinic). **Note:** This modifier is not to be used for physician reporting of multiple E/M services performed by the same physician on the same date. For physician reporting of all outpatient evaluation and management services provided by the same physician on the same date and performed in multiple outpatient setting(s) (eg, hospital emergency department, clinic), see **Evaluation and Management, Emergency Department, or Preventive Medicine Services** codes.

50 Bilateral Procedure: Unless otherwise identified in the listings, bilateral procedures that are performed at the same operative session should be identified by adding modifier 50 to the appropriate five digit code.

52 **Reduced Services:** Under certain circumstances a service or procedure is partially reduced or eliminated at the physician's discretion. Under these circumstances the service provided can be identified by its usual procedure number and the addition of modifier 52, signifying that the service is reduced. This provides a means of reporting reduced services without disturbing the identification of the basic service. **Note:** For hospital outpatient reporting of a previously scheduled procedure/service that is partially reduced or cancelled as a result of extenuating circumstances or those that threaten the well-being of the patient prior to or after administration of anesthesia, see modifiers 73 and 74.

58 **Staged or Related Procedure or Service by the Same Physician During the Postoperative Period:** The physician may need to indicate that the performance of a procedure or service during the postoperative period was: a) planned prospectively at the time of the original procedure (staged); b) more extensive than the original procedure; or c) for therapy following a diagnostic surgical procedure. This circumstance may be reported by adding modifier 58 to the staged or related procedure. **Note:** This modifier is not used to report the treatment of a problem that requires a return to the operating room (see modifier 78).

59 **Distinct Procedural Service:** Under certain circumstances, the physician may need to indicate that a procedure or service was distinct or independent from other services performed on the same day. Modifier 59 is used to identify procedures/services that are not normally reported together, but are appropriate under the circumstances. This may represent a different session or patient encounter, different procedure or surgery, different site or organ system, separate incision/excision, separate lesion, or separate injury (or area of injury in extensive injuries) not ordinarily encountered or performed on the same day by the same physician. However, when another already established modifier is appropriate it should be used rather than modifier 59. Only if no more descriptive modifier is available, and the use of modifier 59 best explains the circumstances, should modifier 59 be used.

73 **Discontinued Out-Patient Hospital/Ambulatory Surgery Center (ASC) Procedure Prior to the Administration of Anesthesia:** Due to extenuating circumstances or those that threaten the well being of the patient, the physician may cancel a surgical or diagnostic procedure subsequent to the patient's surgical preparation (including sedation when provided, and being taken to the room where the procedure is to be performed), but prior to the administration of anesthesia (local, regional block(s) or general). Under these circumstances, the intended service that is prepared for but cancelled can be reported by its usual procedure number and the addition of modifier 73. **Note:** The elective cancellation of a service prior to the administration of anesthesia and/or surgical preparation of the patient should not be reported. For physician reporting of a discontinued procedure, see modifier 53.

74 **Discontinued Out-Patient Hospital/Ambulatory Surgery Center (ASC) Procedure After Administration of Anesthesia:** Due to extenuating circumstances or those that threaten the well being of the patient, the physician may terminate a surgical or diagnostic procedure after the administration of anesthesia (local, regional block(s), general) or after the procedure was started (incision made, intubation started, scope inserted, etc). Under these circumstances, the procedure started but terminated can be reported by its usual procedure number and the addition of modifier 74. **Note:** The elective cancellation of a service prior to the administration of anesthesia and/or surgical preparation of the patient should not be reported. For physician reporting of a discontinued procedure, see modifier 53.

76 **Repeat Procedure by Same Physician:** The physician may need to indicate that a procedure or service was repeated subsequent to the original procedure or service. This circumstance may be reported by adding modifier 76 to the repeated procedure/service.

77 **Repeat Procedure by Another Physician:** The physician may need to indicate that a basic procedure or service performed by another physician had to be repeated. This situation may be reported by adding modifier 77 to the repeated procedure/service.

78 **Return to the Operating Room for a Related Procedure During the Postoperative Period:** The physician may need to indicate that another procedure was performed during the postoperative period of the initial procedure. When this subsequent procedure is related to the first, and requires the use of the operating room, it may be reported by adding modifier 78 to the related procedure. (For repeat procedures on the same day, see 76.)

79 **Unrelated Procedure or Service by the Same Physician During the Postoperative Period:** The physician may need to indicate that the performance of a procedure or service during the postoperative period was unrelated to the original procedure. This circumstance may be reported by using modifier 79. (For repeat procedures on the same day, see 76.)

91 **Repeat Clinical Diagnostic Laboratory Test:** In the course of treatment of the patient, it may be necessary to repeat the same laboratory test on the same day to obtain subsequent (multiple) test results. Under these circumstances, the laboratory test performed can be identified by its usual procedure number and the addition of modifier 91. **Note:** This modifier may not be used when tests are rerun to confirm initial results; due to testing problems with specimens or equipment; or for any other reason when a normal, one-time, reportable result is all that is required. This modifier may not be used when other code(s) describe a series of test results (eg, glucose tolerance tests, evocative/suppression testing). This modifier may only be used for laboratory test(s) performed more than once on the same day on the same patient.

Level II (HCPCS/National) Modifiers

E1 Upper left, eyelid

E2 Lower left, eyelid

E3 Upper right, eyelid

E4 Lower right, eyelid

F1 Left hand, second digit

F2 Left hand, third digit

F3 Left hand, fourth digit

F4 Left hand, fifth digit

F5 Right hand, thumb

F6 Right hand, second digit

F7 Right hand, third digit

F8 Right hand, fourth digit

F9 Right hand, fifth digit

FA Left hand, thumb

GG Performance and payment of a screening mammogram and diagnostic mammogram on the same patient, same day

GH Diagnostic mammogram converted from screening mammogram on same day

LC Left circumflex coronary artery (Hospitals use with codes 92980-92984, 92995, 92996)

LD Left anterior descending coronary artery (Hospitals use with codes 92980-92984, 92995, 92996)

LT Left side (used to identify procedures performed on the left side of the body)

QM Ambulance service provided under arrangement by a provider of services

QN Ambulance service furnished directly by a provider of services

RC Right coronary artery (Hospitals use with codes 92980-92984, 92995, 92996)

RT Right side (used to identify procedures performed on the right side of the body)

T1 Left foot, second digit

T2 Left foot, third digit

T3 Left foot, fourth digit

T4 Left foot, fifth digit

T5 Right foot, great toe

T6 Right foot, second digit

T7 Right foot, third digit

T8 Right foot, fourth digit

T9 Right foot, fifth digit

TA Left foot, great toe

Appendix B

Summary of Additions, Deletions, and Revisions

Appendix B shows the actual changes that were made to the code descriptors. New codes appear with a bullet (●) and are indicated as "Code Added." Revised codes are preceded with a triangle (▲). Within revised codes, the deleted language appears with a ~~strikethrough~~, while new text appears <u>underlined</u>. Codes with which conscious sedation would not be separately reported when performed at the same session by the same provider are denoted with the bullseye (⊙). The symbol ⁄ is used to identify codes for vaccines that are pending FDA approval (see **Appendix K**).

Revisions to the headings, notes, introductory paragraphs, and cross-references are not included in this Appendix, but are identified in the main text of the book with the "►◄" symbols and presented in green.

Evaluation and Management

▲ **99251** ~~Initial i~~<u>I</u>npatient consultation for a new or established patient, which requires these three key components:

- A problem focused history;
- A problem focused examination; and
- Straightforward medical decision making.

Counseling and/or coordination of care with other providers or agencies are provided consistent with the nature of the problem(s) and the patient's and/or family's needs.

Usually, the presenting problem(s) are self limited or minor. Physicians typically spend 20 minutes at the bedside and on the patient's hospital floor or unit.

▲ **99252** ~~Initial i~~<u>I</u>npatient consultation for a new or established patient, which requires these three key components:

- An expanded problem focused history;
- An expanded problem focused examination; and
- Straightforward medical decision making.

Counseling and/or coordination of care with other providers or agencies are provided consistent with the nature of the problem(s) and the patient's and/or family's needs.

Usually, the presenting problem(s) are of low severity. Physicians typically spend 40 minutes at the bedside and on the patient's hospital floor or unit.

▲ **99253** ~~Initial i~~<u>I</u>npatient consultation for a new or established patient, which requires these three key components:

- A detailed history;
- A detailed examination; and
- Medical decision making of low complexity.

Counseling and/or coordination of care with other providers or agencies are provided consistent with the nature of the problem(s) and the patient's and/or family's needs.

Usually, the presenting problem(s) are of moderate severity. Physicians typically spend 55 minutes at the bedside and on the patient's hospital floor or unit.

▲ **99254** ~~Initial i~~<u>I</u>npatient consultation for a new or established patient, which requires these three key components:

- A comprehensive history;
- A comprehensive examination; and
- Medical decision making of moderate complexity.

Counseling and/or coordination of care with other providers or agencies are provided consistent with the nature of the problem(s) and the patient's and/or family's needs.

Usually, the presenting problem(s) are of moderate to high severity. Physicians typically spend 80 minutes at the bedside and on the patient's hospital floor or unit.

▲ **99255** ~~Initial i~~<u>I</u>npatient consultation for a new or established patient, which requires these three key components:

- A comprehensive history;
- A comprehensive examination; and
- Medical decision making of high complexity.

Counseling and/or coordination of care with other providers or agencies are provided consistent with the nature of the problem(s) and the patient's and/or family's needs.

Usually, the presenting problem(s) are of moderate to high severity. Physicians typically spend 110 minutes at the bedside and on the patient's hospital floor or unit.

● **99363** Code added

● **99364** Code added

Anesthesia

● **00625** Code added

● **00626** Code added

~~01995~~ ~~Regional intravenous administration of local anesthetic agent or other medication (upper or lower extremity)~~

Surgery

~~15000~~ ~~Surgical preparation or creation of recipient site by excision of open wounds, burn eschar, or scar (including subcutaneous tissues), or incisional release of scar contracture; first 100 sq cm or one percent of body area of infants and children~~

+ ~~15001~~ ~~each additional 100 sq cm or each additional one percent of body area of infants and children (List separately in addition to code for primary procedure)~~

● **15002** Code added

+● **15003** Code added

● 15004 Code added

+● 15005 Code added

● 15731 Code added

● 15830 Code added

~~15831~~ ~~abdomen (eg, abdominoplasty) (includes umbilical transposition, fascial plication and undermining) (List separately in addition to code for primary procedure)~~

+● 15847 Code added

▲ 17000 Destruction (eg, laser surgery, electrosurgery, cryosurgery, chemosurgery, surgical curettement), ~~all benign or~~ premalignant lesions (eg, actinic keratoses) ~~other than skin tags or cutaneous vascular proliferative lesions~~; first lesion

⊘▲ 17004 Destruction (eg, laser surgery, electrosurgery, cryosurgery, chemosurgery, surgical curettement), ~~all benign or~~ premalignant lesions (eg, actinic keratoses), ~~other than skin tags or cutaneous vascular proliferative lesions,~~ 15 or more lesions

▲ 17110 Destruction (eg, laser surgery, electrosurgery, cryosurgery, chemosurgery, surgical curettement), <u>benign lesions other than skin tags or cutaneous vascular lesions</u>~~flat warts, molluscum contagiosum, or milia~~; up to 14 lesions

⊘ ~~17304~~ ~~Chemosurgery (Mohs micrographic technique), including removal of all gross tumor, surgical excision of tissue specimens, mapping, color coding of specimens, microscopic examination of specimens by the surgeon, and complete histopathologic preparation including the first routine stain (eg, hematoxylin and eosin, toluidine blue); first stage, fresh tissue technique, up to 5 specimens~~

~~17305~~ ~~second stage, fixed or fresh tissue, up to 5 specimens~~

~~17306~~ ~~third stage, fixed or fresh tissue, up to 5 specimens~~

~~17307~~ ~~additional stage(s), up to 5 specimens, each stage~~

+ ~~17310~~ ~~each additional specimen, after the first 5 specimens, fixed or fresh tissue, any stage (List separately in addition to code for primary procedure)~~

● 17311 Code added

+● 17312 Code added

● 17313 Code added

+● 17314 Code added

+● 17315 Code added

● 19105 Code added

▲ 19120 Excision of cyst, fibroadenoma, or other benign or malignant tumor, aberrant breast tissue, duct lesion, nipple or areolar lesion (except ~~19140~~ <u>19300</u>), open, male or female, one or more lesions

~~19140~~ ~~Mastectomy for gynecomastia~~

~~19160~~ ~~Mastectomy, partial (eg, lumpectomy, tylectomy, quadrantectomy, segmentectomy);~~

~~19162~~ ~~with axillary lymphadenectomy~~

~~19180~~ ~~Mastectomy, simple, complete~~

~~19182~~ ~~Mastectomy, subcutaneous~~

~~19200~~ ~~Mastectomy, radical, including pectoral muscles, axillary lymph nodes~~

~~19220~~ ~~Mastectomy, radical, including pectoral muscles, axillary and internal mammary lymph nodes (Urban type operation)~~

~~19240~~ ~~Mastectomy, modified radical, including axillary lymph nodes, with or without pectoralis minor muscle, but excluding pectoralis major muscle~~

● 19300 Code added

● 19301 Code added

● 19302 Code added

● 19303 Code added

● 19304 Code added

● 19305 Code added

● 19306 Code added

● 19307 Code added

▲ 19361 Breast reconstruction with latissimus dorsi flap, ~~with or~~ without prosthetic implant

~~21300~~ ~~Closed treatment of skull fracture without operation~~

⊙● 22526 Code added

+⊙● 22527 Code added

● 22857 Code added

● 22862 Code added

● 22865 Code added

● 25109 Code added

▲ 25600 Closed treatment of distal radial fracture (eg, Colles or Smith type) or epiphyseal separation, ~~with or without~~ <u>includes closed treatment of</u> fracture of ulnar styloid<u>, when performed</u>; without manipulation

● 25606 Code added

● 25607 Code added

● 25608 Code added

● 25609 Code added

~~25611~~ ~~Percutaneous skeletal fixation of distal radial fracture (eg, Colles or Smith type) or epiphyseal separation, with or without fracture of ulnar styloid, requiring manipulation, with or without external fixation~~

~~25620~~ ~~Open treatment of distal radial fracture (eg, Colles or Smith type) or epiphyseal separation, with or without fracture of ulnar styloid, with or without internal or external fixation~~

▲ 26170 Excision of tendon, palm, flexor <u>or extensor</u>, single ~~(separate procedure)~~, each <u>tendon</u>

▲ 26180 Excision of tendon, finger, flexor <u>or extensor</u> ~~(separate procedure)~~, each tendon

~~26504~~ ~~with tendon prosthesis (separate procedure)~~

~~27315~~ ~~Neurectomy, hamstring muscle~~

~~27320~~ ~~Neurectomy, popliteal (gastrocnemius)~~

● 27325 Code added

● 27326 Code added

~~28030~~	~~Neurectomy, intrinsic musculature of foot~~	
● 28055	Code added	
~~31700~~	~~Catheterization, transglottic (separate procedure)~~	
~~31708~~	~~Instillation of contrast material for laryngography or bronchography, without catheterization~~	
~~31710~~	~~Catheterization for bronchography, with or without instillation of contrast material~~	
● 32998	Code added	
~~33200~~	~~Insertion of permanent pacemaker with epicardial electrode(s); by thoracotomy~~	
~~33201~~	~~by xiphoid approach~~	
● 33202	Code added	
● 33203	Code added	
~~33245~~	~~Insertion of epicardial single or dual chamber pacing cardioverter defibrillator electrodes by thoracotomy;~~	
~~33246~~	~~with insertion of pulse generator~~	
~~33253~~	~~Operative incisions and reconstruction of atria for treatment of atrial fibrillation or atrial flutter (eg, maze procedure)~~	
● 33254	Code added	
● 33255	Code added	
● 33256	Code added	
● 33265	Code added	
● 33266	Code added	
● 33675	Code added	
● 33676	Code added	
● 33677	Code added	
▲ 33681	Closure of <u>single</u> ventricular septal defect, with or without patch;	
● 33724	Code added	
● 33726	Code added	
▲ 35301	Thromboendarterectomy, ~~with or without~~<u>including</u> patch graft<u>, if performed</u>; carotid, vertebral, subclavian, by neck incision	
● 35302	Code added	
● 35303	Code added	
● 35304	Code added	
● 35305	Code added	
+● 35306	Code added	
~~35381~~	~~femoral and/or popliteal, and/or tibioperoneal~~	
▲ 35501	Bypass graft, with vein; <u>common</u> carotid-<u>ipsilateral internal carotid</u>	
▲ 35506	carotid-subclavian <u>or subclavian-carotid</u>	
~~35507~~	~~subclavian-carotid~~	
▲ 35509	carotid-<u>contralateral</u> carotid	
● 35537	Code added	
● 35538	Code added	
● 35539	Code added	
● 35540	Code added	
~~35541~~	~~aortoiliac or bi-iliac~~	
~~35546~~	~~aortofemoral or bifemoral~~	
▲ 35601	Bypass graft, with other than vein; <u>common</u> carotid-<u>ipsilateral internal carotid</u>	
● 35637	Code added	
● 35638	Code added	
~~35641~~	~~aortoiliac or bi-iliac~~	
● 35883	Code added	
● 35884	Code added	
⊙● 37210	Code added	
● 43647	Code added	
● 43648	Code added	
● 43881	Code added	
● 43882	Code added	
~~44152~~	~~with rectal mucosectomy, ileoanal anastomosis, with or without loop ileostomy~~	
~~44153~~	~~with rectal mucosectomy, ileoanal anastomosis, creation of ileal reservoir (S or J), with or without loop ileostomy~~	
● 44157	Code added	
● 44158	Code added	
▲ 44211	colectomy, total, abdominal, with proctectomy, with ileoanal anastomosis, creation of ileal reservoir (S or J), with loop ileostomy, ~~with or without~~ <u>includes</u> rectal mucosectomy<u>, when performed</u>	
~~47716~~	~~Anastomosis, choledochal cyst, without excision~~	
● 47719	Code added	
~~48005~~	~~Resection or debridement of pancreas and peripancreatic tissue for acute necrotizing pancreatitis~~	
● 48105	Code added	
~~48180~~	~~Pancreaticojejunostomy, side-to-side anastomosis (Puestow-type operation)~~	
● 48548	Code added	
~~49085~~	~~Removal of peritoneal foreign body from peritoneal cavity~~	
● 49324	Code added	
● 49325	Code added	
+● 49326	Code added	
● 49402	Code added	
+● 49435	Code added	
● 49436	Code added	
▲ 51720	Bladder instillation of anticarcinogenic agent (including ~~detention~~<u>retention</u> time)	
▲ 52204	Cystourethroscopy, with biopsy<u>(s)</u>	
▲ 54150	Circumcision, using clamp or other device <u>with regional dorsal penile or ring block</u>,~~; newborn~~	
~~54152~~	~~older than 28 days of age~~	

▲ 54160 Circumcision, surgical excision other than clamp, device, or dorsal slit; ~~newborn~~neonate (28 days of age or less)

▲ 54161 ~~except newborn~~older than 28 days of age

~~54820~~ ~~Exploration of epididymis, with or without biopsy~~

● 54865 Code added

~~55859~~ ~~Transperineal placement of needles or catheters into prostate for interstitial radioelement application, with or without cystoscopy~~

● 55875 Code added

● 55876 Code added

● 56442 Code added

~~56720~~ ~~Hymenotomy, simple incision~~

● 57296 Code added

● 57558 Code added

~~57820~~ ~~Dilation and curettage of cervical stump~~

● 58541 Code added

● 58542 Code added

● 58543 Code added

● 58544 Code added

● 58548 Code added

▲ 58950 Resection (initial) of ovarian, tubal or primary peritoneal malignancy with bilateral salpingo-oophorectomy and omentectomy;

● 58957 Code added

● 58958 Code added

⊘▲ 61107 Twist drill hole(s) for subdural, intracerebral, or ventricular puncture; for implanting ventricular catheter, ~~or~~pressure recording device, or other intracerebral monitoring device

⊘▲ 61210 for implanting ventricular catheter, reservoir, EEG electrode(s), ~~or~~ pressure recording device, or other cerebral monitoring device (separate procedure)

▲ 64590 Insertion or replacement of peripheral or gastric neurostimulator pulse generator or receiver, direct or inductive coupling

▲ 64595 Revision or removal of peripheral or gastric neurostimulator pulse generator or receiver

● 64910 Code added

● 64911 Code added

● 67346 Code added

~~67350~~ ~~Biopsy of extraocular muscle~~

Radiology

▲ 70540 Magnetic resonance (eg, proton) imaging, orbit, face, and/or neck; without contrast material(s)

● 70554 Code added

● 70555 Code added

▲ 71275 Computed tomographic angiography, chest (noncoronary), without contrast material(s), followed by contrast material(s) and further sections, including image postprocessing

● 72291 Code added

● 72292 Code added

+ ~~75998~~ ~~Fluoroscopic guidance for central venous access device placement, replacement (catheter only or complete), or removal (includes fluoroscopic guidance for vascular access and catheter manipulation, any necessary contrast injections through access site or catheter with related venography radiologic supervision and interpretation, and radiographic documentation of final catheter position) (List separately in addition to code for primary procedure)~~

~~76003~~ ~~Fluoroscopic guidance for needle placement (eg, biopsy, aspiration, injection, localization device)~~

~~76005~~ ~~Fluoroscopic guidance and localization of needle or catheter tip for spine or paraspinous diagnostic or therapeutic injection procedures (epidural, transforaminal epidural, subarachnoid, paravertebral facet joint, paravertebral facet joint nerve or sacroiliac joint), including neurolytic agent destruction~~

~~76006~~ ~~Manual application of stress performed by physician for joint radiography, including contralateral joint if indicated~~

~~76012~~ ~~Radiological supervision and interpretation, percutaneous vertebroplasty or vertebral augmentation including cavity creation, per vertebral body; under fluoroscopic guidance~~

~~76013~~ ~~under CT guidance~~

~~76020~~ ~~Bone age studies~~

~~76040~~ ~~Bone length studies (orthoroentgenogram, scanogram)~~

~~76061~~ ~~Radiologic examination, osseous survey; limited (eg, for metastases)~~

~~76062~~ ~~complete (axial and appendicular skeleton)~~

~~76065~~ ~~Radiologic examination, osseous survey, infant~~

~~76066~~ ~~Joint survey, single view, two or more joints (specify)~~

~~76070~~ ~~Computed tomography, bone mineral density study, one or more sites; axial skeleton (eg, hips, pelvis, spine)~~

~~76071~~ ~~appendicular skeleton (peripheral) (eg, radius, wrist, heel)~~

~~76075~~ ~~Dual energy X-ray absorptiometry (DXA), bone density study, one or more sites; axial skeleton (eg, hips, pelvis, spine)~~

~~76076~~ ~~appendicular skeleton (peripheral) (eg, radius, wrist, heel)~~

~~76077~~ ~~vertebral fracture assessment~~

~~76078~~ ~~Radiographic absorptiometry (eg, photodensitometry, radiogrammetry), one or more sites~~

+ ~~76082~~ ~~Computer-aided detection (computer algorithm analysis of digital image data for lesion detection) with further physician review for interpretation, with or without digitization of film radiographic images; diagnostic mammography (List separately in addition to code for primary procedure)~~

+ ~~76083~~ ~~screening mammography (List separately in addition to code for primary procedure)~~

~~76086~~ ~~Mammary ductogram or galactogram, single duct, radiological supervision and interpretation~~

~~76088~~ ~~Mammary ductogram or galactogram, multiple ducts, radiological supervision and interpretation~~

~~76090~~ ~~Mammography; unilateral~~

~~76091~~ ~~bilateral~~

~~76092~~ ~~Screening mammography, bilateral (two-view film study of each breast)~~

76093 Magnetic resonance imaging, breast, without and/or with
 contrast material(s); unilateral

76094 bilateral

76095 Stereotactic localization guidance for breast biopsy or needle
 placement (eg, for wire localization or for injection), each lesion,
 radiological supervision and interpretation

76096 Mammographic guidance for needle placement, breast (eg, for
 wire localization or for injection), each lesion, radiological
 supervision and interpretation

76355 Computed tomography guidance for stereotactic localization

76360 Computed tomography guidance for needle placement (eg,
 biopsy, aspiration, injection, localization device), radiological
 supervision and interpretation

76362 Computed tomography guidance for, and monitoring of, visceral
 tissue ablation

76370 Computed tomography guidance for placement of radiation
 therapy fields

76393 Magnetic resonance guidance for needle placement (eg, for
 biopsy, needle aspiration, injection, or placement of localization
 device) radiological supervision and interpretation

76394 Magnetic resonance guidance for, and monitoring of, visceral
 tissue ablation

76400 Magnetic resonance (eg, proton) imaging, bone marrow blood
 supply

▲ 76536 Ultrasound, soft tissues of head and neck (eg, thyroid,
 parathyroid, parotid), B-scan and/or real time with image
 documentation

▲ 76604 Ultrasound, chest B-scan (includes mediastinum), and/or real
 time with image documentation

▲ 76645 Ultrasound, breast(s) (unilateral or bilateral), B-scan and/or real
 time with image documentation

▲ 76700 Ultrasound, abdominal, B-scan and/or real time with image
 documentation; complete

▲ 76770 Ultrasound, retroperitoneal (eg, renal, aorta, nodes), B-scan
 and/or real time with image documentation; complete

● 76776 Code added

76778 Ultrasound, transplanted kidney, B-scan and/or real time with
 image documentation, with or without duplex Doppler study

● 76813 Code added

+● 76814 Code added

▲ 76856 Ultrasound, pelvic (nonobstetric), B-scan and/or real time with
 image documentation; complete

▲ 76880 Ultrasound, extremity, nonvascular, B-scan and/or real time with
 image documentation

▲ 76940 Ultrasound guidance for, and monitoring of, visceral parenchymal
 tissue ablation

76986 Ultrasonic guidance, intraoperative

● 76998 Code added

+● 77001 Code added

● 77002 Code added

● 77003 Code added

● 77011 Code added

● 77012 Code added

● 77013 Code added

● 77014 Code added

● 77021 Code added

● 77022 Code added

● 77031 Code added

● 77032 Code added

+● 77051 Code added

+● 77052 Code added

● 77053 Code added

● 77054 Code added

● 77055 Code added

● 77056 Code added

● 77057 Code added

● 77058 Code added

● 77059 Code added

● 77071 Code added

● 77072 Code added

● 77073 Code added

● 77074 Code added

● 77075 Code added

● 77076 Code added

● 77077 Code added

● 77078 Code added

● 77079 Code added

● 77080 Code added

● 77081 Code added

● 77082 Code added

● 77083 Code added

● 77084 Code added

● 77371 Code added

● 77372 Code added

● 77373 Code added

● 77435 Code added

▲ 78700 Kidney imaging; static only morphology;

78704 with function study (ie, imaging renogram)

▲ 78707 Kidney imaging with vascular flow and function;, single study
 without pharmacological intervention

▲ 78708 with vascular flow and function, single study, with
 pharmacological intervention (eg, angiotensin converting enzyme
 inhibitor and/or diuretic)

▲ 78709 with vascular flow and function, multiple studies, with and
 without pharmacological intervention (eg, angiotensin converting
 enzyme inhibitor and/or diuretic)

▲ 78710 Kidney imaging, tomographic (SPECT)

~~78715~~ ~~Kidney vascular flow only~~

+▲ 78730 Urinary bladder residual study (List separately in addition to code for primary procedure)

~~78760~~ ~~Testicular imaging;~~

▲ 78761 Testicular imaging with vascular flow

Pathology and Laboratory

● 82107 Code added

● 83698 Code added

● 83913 Code added

● 86788 Code added

● 86789 Code added

▲ 87088 with isolation and presumptive identification of ~~isolates~~each isolate, urine

● 87305 Code added

● 87498 Code added

● 87640 Code added

● 87641 Code added

● 87653 Code added

● 87808 Code added

▲ 88106 simple filter method ~~only~~with interpretation

▲ 88107 smears and simple filter preparation with interpretation

▲ 89060 Crystal identification by light microscopy with or without polarizing lens analysis, tissue or any body fluid (except urine)

Medicine

⊘▲ 90655 Influenza virus vaccine, split virus, preservative free, ~~for~~when administered to children 6-35 months of age, for intramuscular use

⊘▲ 90656 Influenza virus vaccine, split virus, preservative free, ~~for use in individuals~~when administered to 3 years and older, for intramuscular use

⊘▲ 90657 Influenza virus vaccine, split virus, ~~for~~when administered to children 6-35 months of age, for intramuscular use

⊘▲ 90658 Influenza virus vaccine, split virus, ~~for use in individuals~~when administered to 3 years of age and older, for intramuscular use

⊘▲ 90669 Pneumococcal conjugate vaccine, polyvalent, ~~for~~when administered to children younger than 5 years, for intramuscular use

⊘▲ 90700 Diphtheria, tetanus toxoids, and acellular pertussis vaccine (DTaP), ~~for use in individuals~~when administered to younger than 7 years, for intramuscular use

⊘▲ 90702 Diphtheria and tetanus toxoids (DT) adsorbed ~~for use in individuals~~when administered to younger than 7 years, for intramuscular use

⊘▲ 90714 Tetanus and diphtheria toxoids (Td) adsorbed, preservative free, ~~for use in individuals~~when administered to 7 years or older, for intramuscular use

⊘▲ 90715 Tetanus, diphtheria toxoids and acellular pertussis vaccine (Tdap), ~~for use in individuals~~when administered to 7 years or older, for intramuscular use

⊘▲ 90718 Tetanus and diphtheria toxoids (Td) adsorbed ~~for use in individuals~~when administered to 7 years or older, for intramuscular use

⊘▲ 90732 Pneumococcal polysaccharide vaccine, 23-valent, adult or immunosuppressed patient dosage, ~~for use in individuals~~when administered to 2 years or older, for subcutaneous or intramuscular use

+▲ 90761 each additional hour~~, up to 8 hours~~ (List separately in addition to code for primary procedure)

+▲ 90766 each additional hour~~, up to 8 hours~~ (List separately in addition to code for primary procedure)

~~91060~~ ~~Gastric saline load test~~

● 91111 Code added

● 92025 Code added

~~92573~~ ~~Lombard test~~

● 92640 Code added

● 94002 Code added

● 94003 Code added

● 94004 Code added

● 94005 Code added

⊘● 94610 Code added

▲ 94620 Pulmonary stress testing; simple (eg, 6-minute walk test, prolonged exercise test for bronchospasm with pre- and post-spirometry and oximetry)

● 94644 Code added

+● 94645 Code added

~~94656~~ ~~Ventilation assist and management, initiation of pressure or volume preset ventilators for assisted or controlled breathing; first day~~

~~94657~~ ~~subsequent days~~

● 94774 Code added

● 94775 Code added

● 94776 Code added

● 94777 Code added

● 95012 Code added

~~95078~~ ~~Provocative testing (eg, Rinkel test)~~

● 96020 Code added

● 96040 Code added

+▲ 96415 each additional hour~~, 1 to 8 hours~~ (List separately in addition to code for primary procedure)

+▲ 96423 infusion technique, each additional hour ~~up to 8 hours~~ (List separately in addition to code for primary procedure)

● 96904 Code added

Category II Codes

▲ 0001F ~~Auscultation of heart performed (2003F)‡~~

● 0012F Code added

▲ 1000F Tobacco use~~, smoking,~~ assessed (CAD, CAP, COPD, PV)[1] (DM)[4]

~~1001F~~ ~~Tobacco use, non-smoking, assessed‡ (CAD)~~

- 1015F Code added
- 1018F Code added
- 1019F Code added
- 1022F Code added
- 1026F Code added
- 1030F Code added
- 1034F Code added
- 1035F Code added
- 1036F Code added
- 1038F Code added
- 1039F Code added
- ~~2003F~~ ~~Auscultation of the heart performed[1]~~
- 2010F Code added
- 2014F Code added
- 2018F Code added
- 2022F Code added
- 2024F Code added
- 2026F Code added
- 2028F Code added
- ~~3000F~~ ~~Blood pressure ≤ 140/90 mm Hg[2]~~
- ~~3002F~~ ~~Blood pressure > 140/90 mm Hg[2]~~
- 3006F Code added
- 3011F Code added
- 3014F Code added
- 3017F Code added
- 3020F Code added
- 3021F Code added
- 3022F Code added
- 3023F Code added
- 3025F Code added
- 3027F Code added
- 3028F Code added
- 3035F Code added
- 3037F Code added
- 3040F Code added
- 3042F Code added
- 3046F Code added
- 3047F Code added
- 3048F Code added
- 3049F Code added
- 3050F Code added
- 3060F Code added
- 3061F Code added
- 3062F Code added

- 3066F Code added
- 3072F Code added
- 3076F Code added
- 3077F Code added
- 3078F Code added
- 3079F Code added
- 3080F Code added
- ▲ 4009F Angiotensin converting enzyme (ACE) inhibitor <u>or angiotensin receptor blocker (ARB)</u> therapy, prescribed (HF[1], CAD[1])
- ▲ 4015F Persistent asthma, <u>preferred</u> long-term control medication [~~inhaled corticosteroids~~ or an acceptable alternative treatment, (~~cromolyn sodium, leukotriene modifier, nedocromil, OR sustained release theophylline)~~] prescribed (Asthma[1])
- 4025F Code added
- 4030F Code added
- 4033F Code added
- 4035F Code added
- 4037F Code added
- 4040F Code added
- 4045F Code added
- 4050F Code added
- 6005F Code added

Category III Codes

0003T Code added

0008T Code added

~~0018T~~ ~~Delivery of high power, focal magnetic pulses for direct stimulation to cortical neurons~~

0021T Code added

~~0044T~~ ~~Whole body integumentary photography, at request of a physician, for monitoring of high-risk patients; with dysplastic nevus syndrome or familial melanoma~~

~~0045T~~ ~~with history of dysplastic nevi or personal history of melanoma~~

▲ 0062T Percutaneous intradiscal annuloplasty, any method <u>except electrothermal</u>, unilateral or bilateral including fluoroscopic guidance; single level

~~0082T~~ ~~Stereotactic body radiation therapy, treatment delivery, one or more treatment areas, per day~~

~~0083T~~ ~~Stereotactic body radiation therapy, treatment management, per day~~

▲ 0090T Total disc arthroplasty (artificial disc), anterior approach, including discectomy to prepare interspace (other than for decompression)~~;~~ <u>cervical;</u> single interspace~~, cervical~~

~~0091T~~ ~~single interspace, lumbar~~

▲ 0093T Removal of total disc arthroplasty, anterior approach~~;~~ <u>cervical;</u> single interspace~~, cervical~~

~~0094T~~ ~~single interspace, lumbar~~

▲ 0096T Revision of total disc arthroplasty, anterior approach~~;~~ <u>cervical;</u> single interspace~~, cervical~~

	~~0097T~~	~~single interspace, lumbar~~
	~~0120T~~	~~Ablation, cryosurgical, of fibroadenoma, including ultrasound guidance, each fibroadenoma~~
●	0141T	Code added
●	0142T	Code added
●	0143T	Code added
●	0144T	Code added
●	0145T	Code added
●	0146T	Code added
●	0147T	Code added
●	0148T	Code added
●	0149T	Code added
●	0150T	Code added
+●	0151T	Code added
+●	0152T	Code added
+●	0153T	Code added
●	0154T	Code added
●	0155T	Code added
●	0156T	Code added
●	0157T	Code added
●	0158T	Code added
+●	0159T	Code added
●	0160T	Code added
●	0161T	Code added
●	0162T	Code added
+●	0163T	Code added
+●	0164T	Code added
+●	0165T	Code added
●	0166T	Code added
●	0167T	Code added
●	0168T	Code added
●	0169T	Code added
●	0170T	Code added

Appendix C

Clinical Examples

As described in *CPT 2007*, clinical examples of the CPT codes for Evaluation and Management (E/M) services are intended to be an important element of the coding system. The clinical examples, when used with the E/M descriptors contained in the full text of *CPT*, provide a comprehensive and powerful tool for physicians to report the services provided to their patients.

The American Medical Association is pleased to provide you with these clinical examples for *CPT 2007*. The clinical examples that are provided in this supplement are limited to Office or Other Outpatient Services, Hospital Inpatient Services, Consultations, Critical Care, Prolonged Services and Care Plan Oversight.

These clinical examples do not encompass the entire scope of medical practice. Inclusion or exclusion of any particular specialty group does not infer any judgment of importance or lack thereof; nor does it limit the applicability of the example to any particular specialty.

Of utmost importance is that these clinical examples are just that: examples. A particular patient encounter, depending on the specific circumstances, must be judged by the services provided by the physician for that particular patient. Simply because the patient's complaints, symptoms, or diagnoses match those of a particular clinical example, does not automatically assign that patient encounter to that particular level of service. The three components (history, examination, and medical decision making) must be met and documented in the medical record to report a particular level of service.

New Patient

Office or Other Outpatient Service

99201 Initial office visit for a 50-year-old male from out-of-town who needs a prescription refill for a nonsteroidal anti-inflammatory drug. (Anesthesiology)

Initial office visit for a 40-year-old female, new patient, requesting information about local pain clinics. (Anesthesiology/Pain Medicine)

Initial office visit for a 10-year-old girl for determination of visual acuity as part of a summer camp physical (does not include determination of refractive error). (Ophthalmology)

Initial office visit for an out-of-town patient requiring topical refill. (Dermatology)

Initial office visit for a 65-year-old male for reassurance about an isolated seborrheic keratosis on upper back. (Plastic Surgery)

Initial office visit for an out-of-state visitor who needs refill of topical steroid to treat lichen planus. (Dermatology)

Initial office visit for an 86-year-old male, out-of-town visitor, who needs prescription refilled for an anal skin preparation that he forgot. (General Surgery/Colon & Rectal Surgery)

Initial office visit for a patient with alveolar osteitis for repacking. (Oral & Maxillofacial Surgery)

Initial office visit for a patient with a pedunculated lesion of the neck which is unsightly. (Dermatology)

Initial office visit for a 10-year-old male for limited subungual hematoma not requiring drainage. (Internal Medicine)

Initial office visit with an out-of-town visitor who needs a prescription refilled because she forgot her hay fever medication. (Allergy & Immunology/Internal Medicine)

Initial office visit with a 9-month-old female with diaper rash. (Pediatrics)

Initial office visit with a 10-year-old male with severe rash and itching for the past 24 hours, positive history for contact with poison oak 48 hours prior to the visit. (Family Medicine)

Initial office visit with a 5-year-old female to remove sutures from simple wound placed by another physician. (Plastic Surgery)

Initial office visit for a 22-year-old male with a small area of sunburn requiring first aid. (Dermatology/Family Medicine/Internal Medicine)

Initial office visit for the evaluation and management of a contusion of a finger. (Orthopaedic Surgery)

99202 Initial office visit for a 13-year-old patient with comedopapular acne of the face unresponsive to over-the-counter medications. (Family Medicine)

Initial office visit for a patient with a clinically benign lesion or nodule of the lower leg which has been present for many years. (Dermatology)

Initial office visit for a patient with a circumscribed patch of dermatitis of the leg. (Dermatology)

Initial office visit for a patient with papulosquamous eruption of elbows. (Dermatology)

Initial office visit for a 9-year-old patient with erythematous grouped, vesicular eruption of the lip of three day's duration. (Pediatrics)

Initial office visit for an 18-year-old male referred by an orthodontist for advice regarding removal of four wisdom teeth. (Oral & Maxillofacial Surgery)

Initial office visit for a 14-year-old male, who was referred by his orthodontist, for advice on the exposure of impacted maxillary cuspids. (Oral & Maxillofacial Surgery)

Initial office visit for a patient presenting with itching patches on the wrists and ankles. (Dermatology)

Initial office visit for a 30-year-old male for evaluation and discussion of treatment of rhinophyma. (Plastic Surgery)

Initial office visit for a 16-year-old male with severe cystic acne, new patient. (Dermatology)

Initial office evaluation for gradual hearing loss, 58-year-old male, history and physical examination, with interpretation of complete audiogram, air bone, etc. (Otolaryngology)

Initial evaluation and management of recurrent urinary infection in female. (Internal Medicine)

Initial office visit with a 10-year-old girl with history of chronic otitis media and a draining ear. (Pediatrics)

Initial office visit for a 10-year-old female with acute maxillary sinusitis. (Family Medicine)

Initial office visit for a patient with recurring episodes of herpes simplex who has developed a clustering of vesicles on the upper lip. (Internal Medicine)

Initial office visit for a 25-year-old patient with a single season allergic rhinitis. (Allergy & Immunology)

99203 Initial office visit of a 76-year-old male with a stasis ulcer of three month's duration. (Dermatology)

Initial office visit for a 30-year-old female with pain in the lateral aspect of the forearm. (Physical Medicine & Rehabilitation)

Initial office visit for a 15-year-old patient with a four-year history of moderate comedopapular acne of the face, chest, and back with early scarring. Discussion of use of systemic medication. (Dermatology)

Initial office visit for a patient with papulosquamous eruption of the elbow with pitting of nails and itchy scalp. (Dermatology)

Initial office visit for a 57-year-old female who complains of painful parotid swelling for one week's duration. (Oral & Maxillofacial Surgery)

Initial office visit for a patient with an ulcerated non-healing lesion or nodule on the tip of the nose. (Dermatology)

Initial office visit for a patient with dermatitis of the antecubital and popliteal fossae. (Dermatology)

Initial office visit for a 22-year-old female with irregular menses. (Family Medicine)

Initial office visit for a 50-year-old female with dyspepsia and nausea. (Family Medicine)

Initial office visit for a 53-year-old laborer with degenerative joint disease of the knee with no prior treatment. (Orthopaedic Surgery)

Initial office visit for a 60-year-old male with Dupuytren's contracture of one hand with multiple digit involvement. (Orthopaedic Surgery)

Initial office visit for a 33-year-old male with painless gross hematuria without cystoscopy. (Internal Medicine)

Initial office visit for a 55-year-old female with chronic blepharitis. There is a history of use of many medications. (Ophthalmology)

Initial office visit for an 18-year-old female with a two-day history of acute conjunctivitis. Extensive history of possible exposures, prior normal ocular history, and medication use is obtained. (Ophthalmology)

Initial office visit for a 14-year-old male with unilateral anterior knee pain. (Physical Medicine & Rehabilitation)

Initial office visit of an adult who presents with symptoms of an upper-respiratory infection that has progressed to unilateral purulent nasal discharge and discomfort in the right maxillary teeth. (Otolaryngology, Head & Neck Surgery)

Initial office visit of a 40-year-old female with symptoms of atopic allergies including eye and sinus congestion, often associated with infections. She would like to be tested for allergies. (Otolaryngology, Head & Neck Surgery)

Initial office visit of a 65-year-old with nasal stuffiness. (Otolaryngology, Head & Neck Surgery)

Initial office visit for initial evaluation of a 48-year-old man with recurrent low back pain radiating to the leg. (General Surgery)

Initial office visit for evaluation, diagnosis, and management of painless gross hematuria in a new patient, without cystoscopy. (Internal Medicine)

Initial office visit with couple for counseling concerning voluntary vasectomy for sterility. Spent 30 minutes discussing procedure, risks and benefits, and answering questions. (Urology)

Initial office visit of a 49-year-old male with nasal obstruction. Detailed exam with topical anesthesia. (Plastic Surgery)

Initial office visit for evaluation of a 13-year-old female with progressive scoliosis. (Physical Medicine & Rehabilitation)

Initial office visit for a 21-year-old female desiring counseling and evaluation of initiation of contraception. (Family Practice/Internal Medicine/Obstetrics & Gynecology)

Initial office visit for a 49-year-old male presenting with painless blood per rectum associated with bowel movement. (Colon & Rectal Surgery)

Initial office visit for a 19-year-old football player with three-day-old acute knee injury; now with swelling and pain. (Orthopaedic Surgery)

99204 Initial office visit for a 13-year-old female with progressive scoliosis. (Orthopaedic Surgery)

Initial office visit for a 34-year-old female with primary infertility for evaluation and counseling. (Obstetrics & Gynecology)

Initial office visit for a 6-year-old male with multiple upper respiratory infections. (Allergy & Immunology)

Initial office visit for a patient with generalized dermatitis of 80 percent of the body surface area. (Dermatology)

Initial office visit for an adolescent who was referred by school counselor because of repeated skipping school. (Psychiatry)

Initial office visit for a 50-year-old machinist with a generalized eruption. (Dermatology)

Initial office visit for a 45-year-old female who has been abstinent from alcohol and benzodiazepines for three months but complains of headaches, insomnia, and anxiety. (Psychiatry)

Initial office visit for a 60-year-old male with recent change in bowel habits, weight loss, and abdominal pain. (Abdominal Surgery/General Surgery)

Initial office visit for a 50-year-old male with an aortic aneurysm who is considering surgery. (General Surgery)

Initial office visit for a 17-year-old female with depression. (Internal Medicine)

Initial office visit of a 40-year-old with chronic draining ear, imbalance, and probable cholesteatoma. (Otolaryngology, Head & Neck Surgery)

Initial office visit for initial evaluation of a 63-year-old male with chest pain on exertion. (Cardiology/Internal Medicine)

Initial office visit for evaluation of a 70-year-old patient with recent onset of episodic confusion. (Internal Medicine)

Initial office visit for a 7-year-old female with juvenile diabetes mellitus, new to area, past history of hospitalization times three. (Pediatrics)

Initial office visit of a 50-year-old female with progressive solid food dysphagia. (Gastroenterology)

Initial office visit for a 34-year-old patient with primary infertility, including counseling. (Obstetrics & Gynecology)

Initial office visit for evaluation of a 70-year-old female with polyarthralgia. (Rheumatology)

Initial office visit for a patient with papulosquamous eruption involving 60 percent of the cutaneous surface with joint pain. Combinations of topical and systemic treatments discussed. (Dermatology)

99205　Initial office visit for a patient with disseminated lupus erythematosus with kidney disease, edema, purpura, and scarring lesions on the extremities plus cardiac symptoms. (Dermatology/General Surgery/Internal Medicine)

Initial office visit for a 25-year-old female with systemic lupus erythematosus, fever, seizures, and profound thrombocytopenia. (Rheumatology/Allergy & Immunology)

Initial office visit for an adult with multiple cutaneous blisters, denuded secondarily infected ulcerations, oral lesions, weight loss, and increasing weakness refractory to high dose corticosteroid. Initiation of new immunosuppressive therapy. (Dermatology)

Initial office visit for a 28-year-old male with systemic vasculitis and compromised circulation to the limbs. (Rheumatology)

Initial office visit for a 41-year-old female new to the area requesting rheumatologic care, on disability due to scleroderma and recent hospitalization for malignant hypertension. (Rheumatology)

Initial office visit for a 52-year-old female with acute four extremity weakness and shortness of breath one week post-flu vaccination. (Physical Medicine & Rehabilitation)

Initial office visit for a 60-year-old male with previous back surgery; now presents with back and pelvic pain, two-month history of bilateral progressive calf and thigh tightness and weakness when walking, causing several falls. (Orthopaedic Surgery)

Initial office visit for an adolescent referred from ER after making suicide gesture. (Psychiatry)

Initial office visit for a 49-year-old female with a history of headaches and dependence on opioids. She reports weight loss, progressive headache, and depression. (Psychiatry)

Initial office visit for a 50-year-old female with symptoms of rash, swellings, recurrent arthritic complaints, and diarrhea and lymphadenopathy. Patient has had a 25 lb. weight loss and was recently camping in the Amazon. (Allergy & Immunology)

Initial office visit for a 34-year-old uremic Type I diabetic patient referred for ESRD modality assessment and planning. (Nephrology)

Initial office visit for a 75-year-old female with neck and bilateral shoulder pain, brisk deep tendon reflexes, and stress incontinence. (Physical Medicine & Rehabilitation)

Initial office visit for an 8-year-old male with cerebral palsy and spastic quadriparesis. (Physical Medicine & Rehabilitation)

Initial office visit for a 73-year-old male with known prostate malignancy, who presents with severe back pain and a recent onset of lower extremity weakness. (Physical Medicine & Rehabilitation)

Initial office visit for a 38-year-old male with paranoid delusions and a history of alcohol abuse. (Psychiatry)

Initial office visit for a 12-week-old with bilateral hip dislocations and bilateral club feet. (Orthopaedic Surgery)

Initial office visit for a 29-year-old female with acute orbital congestion, eyelid retraction, and bilateral visual loss from optic neuropathy. (Ophthalmology)

Initial office visit for a 70-year-old diabetic patient with progressive visual field loss, advanced optic disc cupping and neovascularization of retina. (Ophthalmology)

Initial office visit for a newly diagnosed Type I diabetic patient. (Endocrinology)

Initial office evaluation of a 65-year-old female with exertional chest pain, intermittent claudication, syncope and a murmur of aortic stenosis. (Cardiology)

Initial office visit for a 73-year-old male with an unexplained 20 lb. weight loss. (Hematology/Oncology)

Initial office evaluatin, patient with systemic lupus erythematosus, fever, seizures and profound thrombocytopenia. (Allergy & Immunology/Internal Medicine/Rheumatology)

Initial office evaluaton and management of patient with systemic vasculitis and compromised circulation to the limbs. (Rheumatology)

Initial office visit for a 24-year-old homosexual male who has a fever, a cough, and shortness of breath. (Infectious Disease)

Initial outpatient evaluation of a 69-year-old male with severe chronic obstructive pulmonary disease, congestive heart failure, and hypertension. (Family Medicine)

Initial office visit for a 17-year-old female who is having school problems and has told a friend that she is considering suicide. The patient and her family are consulted in regard to treatment options. (Psychiatry)

Initial office visit for a female with severe hirsutism, amenorrhea, weight loss and a desire to have children. (Endocrinology/Obstetrics & Gynecology)

Initial office visit for a 42-year-old male on hypertensive medication, newly arrived to the area, with diastolic blood pressure of 110, history of recurrent calculi, episodic headaches, intermittent chest pain and orthopnea. (Internal Medicine)

Established Patient

99211　Office visit for an 82-year-old female, established patient, for a monthly B12 injection with documented Vitamin B12 deficiency. (Geriatrics/Internal Medicine/Family Medicine)

Office visit for a 50-year-old male, established patient, for removal of uncomplicated facial sutures. (Plastic Surgery)

Office visit for an established patient who lost prescription for lichen planus. Returned for new copy. (Dermatology)

Office visit for an established patient undergoing orthodontics who complains of a wire which is irritating his/her cheek and asks you to check it. (Oral & Maxillofacial Surgery)

Office visit for a 50-year-old female, established patient, seen for her gold injection by the nurse. (Rheumatology)

Office visit for a 73-year-old female, established patient, with pernicious anemia for weekly B12 injection. (Gastroenterology)

Office visit for an established patient for dressing change on a skin biopsy. (Dermatology)

Office visit for a 19-year-old, established patient, for removal of sutures from a two cm. laceration of forehead, which you placed four days ago in ER. (Plastic Surgery)

Office visit of a 20-year-old female, established patient, who receives an allergy vaccine injection and is observed for a reaction by the nurse. (Otolaryngology, Head & Neck Surgery)

Office visit for a 45-year-old male, established patient, with chronic renal failure for the administration of erythropoietin. (Nephrology)

Office visit for an established patient, a Peace Corps enlistee, who requests documentation that third molars have been removed. (Oral & Maxillofacial Surgery)

Office visit for a 69-year-old female, established patient, for partial removal of antibiotic gauze from an infected wound site. (Plastic Surgery)

Office visit for a 9-year-old, established patient, successfully treated for impetigo, requiring release to return to school. (Dermatology/Pediatrics)

Office visit for an established patient requesting a return-to-work certificate for resolving contact dermatitis. (Dermatology)

Office visit for an established patient who is performing glucose monitoring and wants to check accuracy of machine with lab blood glucose by technician who checks accuracy and function of patient machine. (Endocrinology)

Follow-up office visit for a 65-year-old female with a chronic indwelling percutaneous nephrostomy catheter seen for routine pericatheter skin care and dressing change. (Interventional Radiology)

Outpatient visit with 19-year-old male, established patient, for supervised drug screen. (Addiction Medicine)

Office visit with 12-year-old male, established patient, for cursory check of hematoma one day after venipuncture. (Internal Medicine)

Office visit with 31-year-old female, established patient, for return to work certificate. (Anesthesiology)

Office visit for a 42-year-old, established patient, to read tuberculin test results. (Allergy & Immunology)

Office visit for 14-year-old, established patient, to re-dress an abrasion. (Orthopaedic Surgery)

Office visit for a 45-year-old female, established patient, for a blood pressure check. (Obstetrics & Gynecology)

Office visit for a 23-year-old, established patient, for instruction in use of peak flow meter. (Allergy & Immunology)

Office visit for prescription refill for a 35-year-old female, established patient, with schizophrenia who is stable but has run out of neuroleptic and is scheduled to be seen in a week. (Psychiatry)

99212 Office visit for an 11-year-old, established patient, seen in follow-up for mild comedonal acne of the cheeks on topical desquamating agents. (Dermatology/Family Medicine/Pediatrics)

Office visit for a 10-year-old female, established patient, who has been swimming in a lake, now presents with a one-day history of left ear pain with purulent drainage. (Family Medicine)

Office visit for a child, established patient, with chronic secretory otitis media. (Otolaryngology, Head & Neck Surgery)

Office visit for an established patient seen in follow-up of clearing patch of localized contact dermatitis. (Family Medicine/Dermatology)

Office visit for an established patient returning for evaluation of response to treatment of lichen planus on wrists and ankles. (Dermatology)

Office visit for an established patient with tinea pedis being treated with topical therapy. (Dermatology)

Office visit for an established patient with localized erythematous plaque of psoriasis with topical hydration. (Dermatology)

Office visit for a 50-year-old male, established patient, recently seen for acute neck pain, diagnosis of spondylosis, responding to physical therapy and intermittent cervical traction. Returns for evaluation for return to work. (Neurology)

Office visit for an established patient with recurring episodes of herpes simplex who has developed a clustering of vesicles on the upper lip. (Oral & Maxillofacial Surgery)

Evaluation of a 50-year-old male, established patient, who has experienced a recurrence of knee pain after he discontinued NSAID. (Anesthesiology/Pain Medicine)

Office visit for an established patient with an irritated skin tag for reassurance. (Dermatology)

Office visit for a 40-year-old, established patient, who has experienced a systemic allergic reaction following administration of immunotherapy. The dose must be readjusted. (Allergy & Immunology)

Office visit for a 33-year-old, established patient, for contusion and abrasion of lower extremity. (Orthopaedic Surgery)

Office visit for a 22-year-old male, established patient, one month after I & D of "wrestler's ear". (Plastic Surgery)

Office visit for a 21-year-old, established patient, who is seen in follow-up after antibiotic therapy for acute bacterial tonsilitis. (Otolaryngology, Head & Neck Surgery)

Office visit for a 4-year-old, established patient, with tympanostomy tubes, check-up. (Otolaryngology, Head & Neck Surgery)

Office visit for an established patient who has had needle aspiration of a peritonsillar abscess. (Otolaryngology, Head & Neck Surgery)

Follow-up office examination for evaluation and treatment of acute draining ear in a 5-year-old with tympanotomy tubes. (Otolaryngology, Head & Neck Surgery)

Office visit, established patient, 6-year-old with sore throat and headache. (Family Medicine/Pediatrics)

Office evaluation for possible purulent bacterial conjunctivitis with one- to two-day history of redness and discharge, 16-year-old female, established patient. (Pediatrics/Internal Medicine/Family Medicine)

Office visit for a 65-year-old female, established patient, returns for three-week follow-up for resolving severe ankle sprain. (Orthopaedic Surgery)

Office visit, sore throat, fever and fatigue in a 19-year-old college student, established patient. (Internal Medicine)

Office visit with a 33-year-old female, established patient, recently started on treatment for hemorrhoidal complaints, for re-evaluation. (Colon & Rectal Surgery)

Office visit with a 36-year-old male, established patient, for follow-up on effectiveness of medicine management of oral candidiasis. (Oral & Maxillofacial Surgery)

Office visit for a 27-year-old female, established patient, with complaints of vaginal itching. (Obstetrics & Gynecology)

Office visit for a 65-year-old, established patient, with eruptions on both arms from poison oak exposure. (Allergy & Immunology/Internal Medicine)

99213 Office visit for an established patient with new lesions of lichen planus in spite of topical therapies. (Dermatology)

Office visit for the quarterly follow-up of a 45-year-old male with stable chronic asthma requiring regular drug therapy. (Allergy & Immunology)

Office visit for a 13-year-old, established patient, with comedopapular acne of the face which has shown poor response to topical medication. Discussion of use of systemic medication. (Dermatology)

Office visit for a 62-year-old female, established patient, for follow-up for stable cirrhosis of the liver. (Internal Medicine/Family Medicine)

Office visit for a 3-year-old, established patient, with atopic dermatitis and food hypersensitivity for quarterly follow-up evaluation. The patient is on topical lotions and steroid creams as well as oral antihistamines. (Allergy & Immunology)

Office visit for an 80-year-old female, established patient, to evaluate medical management of osteoarthritis of the temporomandibular joint. (Rheumatology)

Office visit for a 70-year-old female, established patient, one year post excision of basal cell carcinoma of nose with nasolabial flap. Now presents with new suspicious recurrent lesion and suspicious lesion of the back. (Plastic Surgery)

Office visit for a 68-year-old female, established patient, with polymyalgia rheumatic, maintained on chronic low-dose corticosteroid, with no new complaints. (Rheumatology)

Office visit for a 3-year-old female, established patient, for earache and dyshidrosis of feet. (Pediatrics/Family Medicine)

Office visit for an established patient for 18-months post-operative follow-up of TMJ repair. (Oral & Maxillofacial Surgery)

Office visit for a 45-year-old male, established patient, being re-evaluated for recurrent acute prostatitis. (Urology)

Office visit for a 43-year-old male, established patient, with known reflex sympathetic dystrophy. (Anesthesiology)

Office visit for an established patient with an evenly pigmented superficial nodule of leg which is symptomatic. (Dermatology)

Office visit for an established patient with psoriasis involvement of the elbows, pitting of the nails, and itchy scalp. (Dermatology)

Office visit for a 27-year-old male, established patient, with deep follicular and perifollicular inflammation unable to tolerate systemic antibiotics due to GI upset, requires change of systemic medication. (Dermatology)

Office visit for a 16-year-old male, established patient, who is on medication for exercise-induced bronchospasm. (Allergy & Immunology)

Office visit for a 60-year-old, established patient, with chronic essential hypertension on multiple drug regimen, for blood pressure check. (Family Medicine)

Office visit for a 20-year-old male, established patient, for removal of sutures in hand. (Family Medicine)

Office visit for a 58-year-old female, established patient, with unilateral painful bunion. (Orthopaedic Surgery)

Office visit for a 45-year-old female, established patient, with known osteoarthritis and painful swollen knees. (Rheumatology)

Office visit for a 25-year-old female, established patient, complaining of bleeding and heavy menses. (Obstetrics & Gynecology)

Office visit for a 55-year-old male, established patient, with hypertension managed by a beta blocker/thiazide regime; now experiencing mild fatigue. (Nephrology)

Office visit for a 65-year-old female, established patient, with primary glaucoma for interval determination of intraocular pressure and possible adjustment of medication. (Ophthalmology)

Office visit for a 56-year-old man, established patient, with stable exertional angina who complains of new onset of calf pain while walking. (Cardiology)

Office visit for a 63-year-old female, established patient, with rheumatoid arthritis on auranofin and ibuprofen, seen for routine follow-up visit. (Rheumatology)

Office visit for an established patient with Graves' disease, three months post I-131 therapy, who presents with lassitude and malaise. (Endocrinology)

Office visit for the quarterly follow-up of a 63-year-old male, established patient, with chronic myofascial pain syndrome, effectively managed by doxepin, who presents with new onset urinary hesitancy. (Pain Medicine)

Office visit for the biannual follow-up of an established patient with migraine variant having infrequent, intermittent, moderate to severe headaches with nausea and vomiting, which are sometimes effectively managed by ergotamine tartrate and an antiemetic, but occasionally requiring visits to an emergency department. (Pain Medicine)

Office visit for an established patient after discharge from a pain rehabilitation program to review and adjust medication dosage. (Pain Medicine)

Office visit with 55-year-old male, established patient, for management of hypertension, mild fatigue, on beta blocker/thiazide regimen. (Family Medicine/Internal Medicine)

Outpatient visit with 37-year-old male, established patient, who is three years post total colectomy for chronic ulcerative colitis, presents for increased irritation at his stoma. (General Surgery)

Office visit for a 70-year-old diabetic hypertensive established patient with recent change in insulin requirement. (Internal Medicine/Nephrology)

Office visit with 80-year-old female, established patient, for follow-up osteoporosis, status-post compression fractures. (Rheumatology)

Office visit for an established patient with stable cirrhosis of the liver. (Gastroenterology)

Routine, follow-up office evaluation at a three-month interval for a 77-year-old female, established patient, with nodular small cleaved-cell lymphoma. (Hematology/Oncology)

Quarterly follow-up office visit for a 45-year-old male, established patient, with stable chronic asthma, on steroid and bronchodilator therapy. (Pulmonary Medicine)

Office visit for a 50-year-old female, established patient, with insulin-dependent diabetes mellitus and stable coronary artery disease, for monitoring. (Family Medicine/Internal Medicine)

99214 Office visit for an established patient now presenting with generalized dermatitis of 80 percent of the body surface area. (Dermatology)

Office visit for a 32-year-old female, established patient, with new onset right lower quadrant pain. (Family Medicine)

Office visit for reassessment and reassurance/counseling of a 40-year-old female, established patient, who is experiencing increased symptoms while on a pain management treatment program. (Pain Medicine)

Office visit for a 30-year-old, established patient, under management for intractable low back pain, who now presents with new onset right posterior thigh pain. (Pain Medicine)

Office visit for an established patient with frequent intermittent, moderate to severe headaches requiring beta blocker or tricyclic antidepressant prophylaxis, as well as four symptomatic treatments, but who is still experiencing headaches at a frequency of several times a month that are unresponsive to treatment. (Pain Medicine)

Office visit for an established patient with psoriasis with extensive involvement of scalp, trunk, palms, and soles with joint pain. Combinations of topical and systemic treatments discussed and instituted. (Dermatology)

Office visit for a 55-year-old male, established patient, with increasing night pain, limp, and progressive varus of both knees. (Orthopaedic Surgery)

Follow-up visit for a 15-year-old withdrawn patient with four-year history of papulocystic acne of the face, chest, and back with early scarring and poor response to past treatment. Discussion of use of systemic medication. (Dermatology)

Office visit for a 28-year-old male, established patient, with regional enteritis, diarrhea, and low-grade fever. (Internal Medicine)

Office visit for a 25-year-old female, established patient, following recent arthrogram and MR imaging for TMJ pain. (Oral & Maxillofacial Surgery)

Office visit for a 32-year-old female, established patient, with large obstructing stone in left mid-ureter, to discuss management options including urethroscopy with extraction or ESWL. (Urology)

Evaluation for a 28-year-old male, established patient, with new onset of low back pain. (Anesthesiology/Pain Medicine)

Office visit for a 28-year-old female, established patient, with right lower quadrant abdominal pain, fever, and anorexia. (Internal Medicine/Family Medicine)

Office visit for a 45-year-old male, established patient, four months follow-up of L4-5 diskectomy, with persistent incapacitating low back and leg pain. (Orthopaedic Surgery)

Outpatient visit for a 77-year-old male, established patient, with hypertension, presenting with a three-month history of episodic substernal chest pain on exertion. (Cardiology)

Office visit for a 25-year-old female, established patient, for evaluation of progressive saddle nose deformity of unknown etiology. (Plastic Surgery)

Office visit for a 65-year-old male, established patient, with BPH and severe bladder outlet obstruction, to discuss management options such as TURP. (Urology)

Office visit for an adult diabetic established patient with a past history of recurrent sinusitis who presents with a one-week history of double vision. (Otolaryngology, Head & Neck Surgery)

Office visit for an established patient with lichen planus and 60 percent of the cutaneous surface involved, not responsive to systemic steroids, as well as developing symptoms of progressive heartburn and paranoid ideation. (Dermatology)

Office visit for a 52-year-old male, established patient, with a 12-year history of bipolar disorder responding to lithium carbonate and brief psychotherapy. Psychotherapy and prescription provided. (Psychiatry)

Office visit for a 63-year-old female, established patient, with a history of familial polyposis, status post-colectomy with sphincter sparing procedure, who now presents with rectal bleeding and increase in stooling frequency. (General Surgery)

Office visit for a 68-year-old male, established patient, with the sudden onset of multiple flashes and floaters in the right eye due to a posterior vitreous detachment. (Ophthalmology)

Office visit for a 55-year-old female, established patient, on cyclosporin for treatment of resistant, small vessel vasculitis. (Rheumatology)

Follow-up office visit for a 55-year-old male, two months after iliac angioplasty with new onset of contralateral extremity claudication. (Interventional Radiology)

Office visit for a 68-year-old male, established patient, with stable angina, two months post myocardial infarction, who is not tolerating one of his medications. (Cardiology)

Weekly office visit for 5FU therapy for an ambulatory established patient with metastatic colon cancer and increasing shortness of breath. (Hematology/Oncology)

Follow-up office visit for a 60-year-old male, established patient, whose post-traumatic seizures have disappeared on medication and who now raises the question of stopping the medication. (Neurology)

Office evaluation on new onset RLQ pain in a 32-year-old woman, established patient. (Urology/General Surgery/Internal Medicine/Family Medicine)

Office evaluation of 28-year-old, established patient, with regional enteritis, diarrhea and low-grade fever. (Family Medicine/Internal Medicine)

Office visit with 50-year-old female, established patient, diabetic, blood sugar controlled by diet. She now complains of frequency of urination and weight loss, blood sugar of 320 and negative ketones on dipstick. (Internal Medicine)

Follow-up office visit for a 45-year-old, established patient, with rheumatoid arthritis on gold, methotrexate, or immunosuppressive therapy. (Rheumatology)

Office visit for a 60-year-old male, established patient, two years post-removal of intracranial meningioma, now with new headaches and visual disturbance. (Neurosurgery)

Office visit for a 68-year-old female, established patient, for routine review and follow-up of non-insulin dependent diabetes, obesity, hypertension and congestive heart failure. Complains of vision difficulties and admits dietary noncompliance. Patient is counseled concerning diet and current medications adjusted. (Family Medicine)

99215 Office visit for an established patient who developed persistent cough, rectal bleeding, weakness, and diarrhea plus pustular infection on skin. Patient on immunosuppressive therapy. (Dermatology)

Office visit for an established patient with disseminated lupus erythematosus, extensive edema of extremities, kidney disease, and weakness requiring monitored course on azathioprene, corticosteroid and complicated by acute depression. (Dermatology/Internal Medicine/Rheumatology)

Office visit for an established patient with progressive dermatomyositis and recent onset of fever, nasal speech, and regurgitation of fluids through the nose. (Dermatology)

Office visit for a 28-year-old female, established patient, who is abstinent from previous cocaine dependence, but reports progressive panic attacks and chest pains. (Psychiatry)

Office visit for an established adolescent patient with history of bipolar disorder treated with lithium; seen on urgent basis at family's request because of severe depressive symptoms. (Psychiatry)

Office visit for an established patient having acute migraine with new onset neurological symptoms and whose headaches are unresponsive to previous attempts at management with a combination of preventive and abortive medication. (Pain Medicine)

Office visit for an established patient with exfoliative lichen planus with daily fever spikes, disorientation, and shortness of breath. (Dermatology)

Office visit for a 25-year-old, established patient, two years post-burn with bilateral ectropion, hypertrophic facial burn scars, near absence of left breast, and burn syndactyly of both hands. Discussion of treatment options following examination. (Plastic Surgery)

Office visit for a 6-year-old, established patient, to review newly diagnosed immune deficiency with recommendations for therapy including IV immunoglobulin and chronic antibiotics. (Allergy & Immunology)

Office visit for a 36-year-old, established patient, three months status post-transplant, with new onset of peripheral edema, increased blood pressure, and progressive fatigue. (Nephrology)

Office visit for an established patient with Kaposi's sarcoma who presents with fever and widespread vesicles. (Dermatology)

Office visit for a 27-year-old female, established patient, with bipolar disorder who was stable on lithium carbonate and monthly supportive psychotherapy but now has developed symptoms of hypomania. (Psychiatry)

Office visit for a 25-year-old male, established patient with a history of schizophrenia who has been seen bi-monthly but is complaining of auditory hallucinations. (Psychiatry)

Office visit for a 62-year-old male, established patient, three years post-op abdominal perineal resection, now with a rising carcinoembryonic antigen, weight loss, and pelvic pain. (Abdominal Surgery)

Office visit for a 42-year-old male, established patient, nine months post-op emergency vena cava shunt for variceal bleeding, now presents with complaints of one episode of "dark" bowel movement, weight gain, tightness in abdomen, whites of eyes seem "yellow" and occasional drowsiness after eating hamburgers. (Abdominal Surgery)

Office visit for a 68-year-old male, established patient, with biopsy-proven rectal carcinoma, for evaluation and discussion of treatment options. (General Surgery)

Office visit for a 60-year-old, established patient, with diabetic nephropathy with increasing edema and dyspnea. (Endocrinology)

Office visit with 30-year-old male, established patient for three-month history of fatigue, weight loss, intermittent fever, and presenting with diffuse adenopathy and splenomegaly. (Family Medicine)

Office visit for restaging of an established patient with new lymphadenopathy one year post-therapy for lymphoma. (Hematology/Oncology)

Office visit for evaluation of recent onset syncopal attacks in a 70-year-old woman, established patient. (Internal Medicine)

Follow-up visit, 40-year-old mother of three, established patient, with acute rheumatoid arthritis, anatomical Stage 3, ARA function Class 3 rheumatoid arthritis, and deteriorating function. (Rheumatology)

Follow-up office visit for a 65-year-old male, established patient, with a fever of recent onset while on outpatient antibiotic therapy for endocarditis. (Infectious Disease)

Office visit for a 75-year-old, established patient, with ALS (amyotrophic lateral sclerosis), who is no longer able to swallow. (Neurology)

Office visit for a 70-year-old female, established patient, with diabetes mellitus and hypertension, presenting with a two-month history of increasing confusion, agitation and short-term memory loss. (Family Medicine/Internal Medicine)

Hospital Inpatient Services

Initial Hospital Care

New or Established Patient

99221 Initial hospital visit following admission for a 42-year-old male for observation following an uncomplicated mandible fracture. (Plastic Surgery/Oral & Maxillofacial Surgery)

Initial hospital visit for a 40-year-old patient with a thrombosed synthetic arteriovenous conduit. (Nephrology)

Initial hospital visit for a healthy 24-year-old male with an acute onset of low back pain following a lifting injury. (Internal Medicine/Anesthesiology/Pain Medicine)

Initial hospital visit for a 69-year-old female with controlled hypertension, scheduled for surgery. (Internal Medicine/Cardiology)

Initial hospital visit for a 24-year-old healthy female with benign tumor of palate. (Oral & Maxillofacial Surgery)

Initial hospital visit for a 14-year-old female with infectious mononucleosis and dehydration. (Internal Medicine)

Initial hospital visit for a 62-year-old female with stable rheumatoid arthritis, admitted for total joint replacement. (Rheumatology)

Initial hospital visit for a 12-year-old patient with a laceration of the upper eyelid, involving the lid margin and superior canaliculus, admitted prior to surgery for IV antibiotic therapy. (Plastic Surgery)

Initial hospital visit for a 69-year-old female with controlled hypertension, scheduled for surgery. (Cardiology)

Hospital admission, examination, and initiation of treatment program for a 67-year-old male with uncomplicated pneumonia who requires IV antibiotic therapy. (Internal Medicine)

Hospital admission for an 18-month-old with 10 percent dehydration. (Pediatrics)

Hospital admission for a 12-year-old with a laceration of the upper eyelid involving the lid margin and superior canaliculus, admitted prior to surgery for IV antibiotic therapy. (Ophthalmology)

Hospital admission for a 32-year-old female with severe flank pain, hematuria and presumed diagnosis of ureteral calculus as determined by Emergency Department physician. (Urology)

Initial hospital visit for a patient with several large venous stasis ulcers not responding to outpatient therapy. (Dermatology)

Initial hospital visit for 21-year-old pregnant patient (nine weeks gestation) with hyperemesis gravidarum. (Obstetrics & Gynecology)

Initial hospital visit for a 73-year-old female with acute pyelonephritis who is otherwise generally healthy. (Geriatrics)

Initial hospital visit for 62-year-old patient with cellulitis of the foot requiring bedrest and intravenous antibiotics. (Orthopaedic Surgery)

99222 Initial hospital visit for a 50-year-old patient with lower quadrant abdominal pain and increased temperature, but without septic picture. (General Surgery/Abdominal Surgery/Colon & Rectal Surgery)

Initial hospital visit for airway management, due to a benign laryngeal mass. (Otolaryngology, Head & Neck Surgery)

Initial hospital visit for a 66-year-old female with an L-2 vertebral compression fracture with acute onset of paralytic ileus; seen in the office two days previously. (Orthopaedic Surgery)

Initial hospital visit and evaluation of a 15-year-old male admitted with peritonsillar abscess or cellulitis requiring intravenous antibiotic therapy. (Otolaryngology, Head & Neck Surgery)

Initial hospital visit for a 42-year-old male with vertebral compression fracture following a motor vehicle accident. (Orthopaedic Surgery)

Initial hospital visit for a patient with generalized atopic dermatitis and secondary infection. (Dermatology)

Initial hospital visit for a 3-year-old patient with high temperature, limp, and painful hip motion of 18 hours' duration. (Pediatrics/Orthopaedic Surgery)

Initial hospital visit for a young adult, presenting with an acute asthma attack unresponsive to outpatient therapy. (Allergy & Immunology)

Initial hospital visit for an 18-year-old male who has suppurative sialoadenitis and dehydration. (Oral & Maxillofacial Surgery)

Initial hospital visit for a 65-year-old female for acute onset of thrombotic cerebrovascular accident with contralateral paralysis and aphasia. (Neurology)

Initial hospital visit for a 50-year-old male chronic paraplegic patient with pain and spasm below the lesion. (Anesthesiology)

Partial hospital admission for an adolescent patient from chaotic blended family, transferred from inpatient setting, for continued treatment to control symptomatic expressions of hostility and depression. (Psychiatry)

Initial hospital visit for a 15-year-old male with acute status asthmaticus, unresponsive to outpatient therapy. (Internal Medicine)

Initial hospital visit for a 61-year-old male with history of previous myocardial infarction, who now complains of chest pain. (Internal Medicine)

Initial hospital visit of a 15-year-old on medications for a sore throat over the last two weeks. The sore throat has worsened and patient now has dysphagia. The exam shows large necrotic tonsils with an adequate airway and small palpable nodes. The initial mono test was negative. (Otolaryngology, Head & Neck Surgery)

Initial hospital evaluation of a 23-year-old allergy patient admitted with eyelid edema and pain on fifth day of oral antibiotic therapy. (Otolaryngology, Head & Neck Surgery)

Hospital admission, young adult patient, failed previous therapy and now presents in acute asthmatic attack. (Family Medicine/Allergy & Immunology)

Hospital admission of a 62-year-old smoker, established patient, with bronchitis in acute respiratory distress. (Internal Medicine/Pulmonary Medicine)

Hospital admission, examination, and initiation of a treatment program for a 65-year-old female with new onset of right-sided paralysis and aphasia. (Neurology)

Hospital admission, examination, and initiation of treatment program for a 66-year-old chronic hemodialysis patient with fever and a new pulmonary infiltrate. (Nephrology)

Hospital admission for an 8-year-old febrile patient with chronic sinusitis and severe headache, unresponsive to oral antibiotics. (Allergy & Immunology)

Hospital admission for a 40-year-old male with submaxillary cellulitis and trismus from infected lower molar. (Oral & Maxillofacial Surgery)

99223 Initial hospital visit for a 45-year-old female, who has a history of rheumatic fever as a child and now has anemia, fever, and congestive heart failure. (Cardiology)

Initial hospital visit for a 50-year-old male with acute chest pain and diagnostic electrocardiographic changes of an acute anterior myocardial infarction. (Cardiology/Family Medicine/Internal Medicine)

Initial hospital visit of a 75-year-old with progressive stridor and dysphagia with history of cancer of the larynx treated by radiation therapy in the past. Exam shows a large recurrent tumor of the glottis with a mass in the neck. (Otolaryngology, Head & Neck Surgery)

Initial hospital visit for a 70-year-old male admitted with chest pain, complete heart block, and congestive heart failure. (Cardiology)

Initial hospital visit for an 82-year-old male who presents with syncope, chest pain, and ventricular arrhythmias. (Cardiology)

Initial hospital visit for a 75-year-old male with history of arteriosclerotic coronary vascular disease, who is severely dehydrated, disoriented, and experiencing auditory hallucinations. (Psychiatry)

Initial hospital visit for a 70-year-old male with alcohol and sedative-hypnotic dependence, admitted by family for severe withdrawal, hypertension, and diabetes mellitus. (Psychiatry)

Initial hospital visit for a persistently suicidal latency-aged child whose parents have requested admission to provide safety during evaluation, but are anxious about separation from her. (Psychiatry)

Initial psychiatric visit for an adolescent patient without previous psychiatric history, who was transferred from the medical ICU after a significant overdose. (Psychiatry)

Initial hospital visit for a 35-year-old female with severe systemic lupus erythematosus on corticosteroid and cyclophosphamide, with new onset of fever, chills, rash, and chest pain. (Rheumatology)

Initial hospital visit for a 52-year-old male with known rheumatic heart disease who presents with anasarca, hypertension, and history of alcohol abuse. (Cardiology)

Initial hospital visit for a 55-year-old female with a history of congenital heart disease; now presents with cyanosis. (Cardiology)

Initial hospital visit for a psychotic, hostile, violently combative adolescent, involuntarily committed, for seclusion and restraint in order to provide for safety on unit. (Psychiatry)

Initial hospital visit for a now subdued and sullen teenage male with six-month history of declining school performance, increasing self-endangerment, and resistance of parental expectations, including running away past weekend after physical fight with father. (Psychiatry)

Initial partial hospital admission for a 17-year-old female with history of borderline mental retardation who has developed auditory hallucinations. Parents are known to abuse alcohol, and Child Protective Services is investigating allegations of sexual abuse of a younger sibling. (Psychiatry)

Initial hospital visit of a 67-year-old male admitted with a large neck mass, dysphagia, and history of myocardial infarction three months before. (Otolaryngology, Head & Neck Surgery)

Initial hospital visit for a patient with suspected cerebrospinal fluid rhinorrhea which developed two weeks after head injury. (Otolaryngology, Head & Neck Surgery)

Initial hospital visit for a 25-year-old female with history of poly-substance abuse and psychiatric disorder. The patient appears to be psychotic with markedly elevated vital signs. (Psychiatry)

Initial hospital visit for a 70-year-old male with cutaneous T-cell lymphoma who has developed fever and lymphadenopathy. (Internal Medicine)

Initial hospital visit for a 62-year-old female with known coronary artery disease, for evaluation of increasing edema, dyspnea on exertion, confusion, and sudden onset of fever with productive cough. (Internal Medicine)

Initial hospital visit for a 3-year-old female with 36-hour history of sore throat and high fever; now with sudden onset of lethargy, irritability, photophobia, and nuchal rigidity. (Pediatrics)

Initial hospital visit for a 26-year-old female for evaluation of severe facial fractures (LeFort's II/III). (Plastic Surgery)

Initial hospital visit for a 55-year-old female for bilateral mandibular fractures resulting in flail mandible and airway obstruction. (Plastic Surgery)

Initial hospital visit for a 71-year-old patient with a red painful eye four days following uncomplicated cataract surgery due to endophthalmitis. (Ophthalmology)

Initial hospital visit for a 45-year-old patient involved in a motor vehicle accident who suffered a perforating corneoscleral laceration with loss of vision. (Ophthalmology)

Initial hospital visit for a 58-year-old male who has Ludwig's angina and progressive airway compromise. (Oral & Maxillofacial Surgery)

Initial hospital visit for a patient with generalized systemic sclerosis, receiving immunosuppressive therapy because of recent onset of cough, fever, and inability to swallow. (Dermatology)

Initial hospital visit for an 82-year-old male who presents with syncope, chest pain, and ventricular arrhythmias. (Cardiology)

Initial hospital visit for a 62-year-old male with history of previous myocardial infarction, comes in with recurrent, sustained ventricular tachycardia. (Cardiology)

Initial hospital visit for a chronic dialysis patient with infected PTFE fistula, septicemia, and shock. (Nephrology)

Initial hospital visit for a 1-year-old male, victim of child abuse, with central nervous system depression, skull fracture, and retinal hemorrhage. (Family Medicine/Neurology)

Initial hospital visit for a 25-year-old female with recent C4-5 quadriplegia, admitted for rehabilitation. (Physical Medicine & Rehabilitation)

Initial hospital visit for an 18-year-old male, post-traumatic brain injury with multiple impairment. (Physical Medicine & Rehabilitation)

Initial partial hospital admission for 16-year-old male, sullen and subdued, with six-month history of declining school performance, increasing self-endangerment, and resistance to parental expectations. (Psychiatry)

Initial hospital visit for a 16-year-old primigravida at 32 weeks gestation with severe hypertension (200/110), thrombocytopenia, and headache. (Obstetrics & Gynecology)

Initial hospital visit for a 49-year-old male with cirrhosis of liver with hematemesis, hepatic encephalopathy, and fever. (Gastroenterology)

Initial hospital visit for a 55-year-old female in chronic pain who has attempted suicide. (Psychiatry)

Initial hospital visit for a 70-year-old male with multiple organ system disease, admitted with history of being aneuric and septic for 24 hours prior to admission. (Urology)

Initial hospital visit for a 3-year-old female with 36-hour history of sore throat and high fever, now with sudden onset of lethargy, irritability, photophobia, and nuchal rigidity. (Internal Medicine)

Initial hospital visit for a 78-year-old male, transfers from nursing home with dysuria and pyuria, increasing confusion, and high fever. (Internal Medicine)

Initial hospital visit for a 1-day-old male with cyanosis, respiratory distress, and tachypnea. (Cardiology)

Initial hospital visit for a 3-year-old female with recurrent tachycardia and syncope. (Cardiology)

Initial hospital visit for a thyrotoxic patient who presents with fever, atrial fibrillation, and delirium. (Endocrinology)

Initial hospital visit for a 50-year-old Type I diabetic who presents with diabetic ketoacidosis with fever and obtundation. (Endocrinology)

Initial hospital visit for a 40-year-old female with anatomical stage 3, ARA functional class 3 rheumatoid arthritis on methotrexate, corticosteroid, and nonsteroidal anti-inflammatory drugs. Patient presents with severe arthritis flare, new oral ulcers, abdominal pain, and leukopenia. (Rheumatology)

Initial hospital exam of a pediatric patient with high fever and proptosis. (Otolaryngology, Head & Neck Surgery)

Initial hospital visit for a 25-year-old patient admitted for the first time to the rehab unit, with recent C-4-5 quadriplegia. (Physical Medicine & Rehabilitation)

Hospital admission, examination, and initiation of treatment program for a previously unknown 58-year-old male who presents with acute chest pain. (Cardiology)

Hospital admission, examination, and initiation of induction chemotherapy for a 42-year-old patient with newly diagnosed acute myelogenous leukemia. (Hematology/Oncology)

Hospital admission following a motor vehicle accident of a 24-year-old male with fracture dislocation of C5-6; neurologically intact. (Neurosurgery)

Hospital admission for a 78-year-old female with left lower lobe pneumonia and a history of coronary artery disease, congestive heart failure, osteoarthritis and gout. (Family Medicine)

Hospital admission, examination, and initiation of treatment program for a 65-year-old immunosuppressed male with confusion, fever, and a headache. (Infectious Disease)

Hospital admission for a 9-year-old with vomiting, dehydration, fever, tachypnea and an admitting diagnosis of diabetic ketoacidosis. (Pediatrics)

Initial hospital visit for a 65-year-old male who presents with acute myocardial infarction, oliguria, hypotension, and altered state of consciousness. (Cardiology)

Initial hospital visit for a hostile/resistant adolescent patient who is severely depressed and involved in poly-substance abuse. Patient is experiencing significant conflict in his chaotic family situation and was suspended from school following an attack on a teacher with a baseball bat. (Psychiatry)

Initial hospital visit for 89-year-old female with fulminant hepatic failure and encephalopathy. (Gastroenterology)

Initial hospital visit for a 42-year-old female with rapidly progressing scleroderma, malignant hypertension, digital infarcts, and oligurea. (Rheumatology)

Subsequent Hospital Care

99231 Subsequent hospital visit for a 65-year-old female, post-open reduction and internal fixation of a fracture. (Physical Medicine & Rehabilitation)

Subsequent hospital visit for a 33-year-old patient with pelvic pain who is responding to pain medication and observation. (Obstetrics & Gynecology)

Subsequent hospital visit for a 21-year-old female with hyperemesis who has responded well to intravenous fluids. (Obstetrics & Gynecology)

Subsequent hospital visit to re-evaluate post-op pain and titrate patient-controlled analgesia for a 27-year-old female. (Anesthesiology)

Follow-up hospital visit for a 35-year-old female, status post-epidural analgesia. (Anesthesiology/Pain Medicine)

Subsequent hospital visit for a 56-year-old male, post-gastrectomy, for maintenance of analgesia using an intravenous dilaudid infusion. (Anesthesiology)

Subsequent hospital visit for a 4-year-old on day three receiving medication for uncomplicated pneumonia. (Allergy & Immunology)

Subsequent hospital visit for a 30-year-old female with urticaria which has stabilized with medication. (Allergy & Immunology)

Subsequent hospital visit for a 76-year-old male with venous stasis ulcers. (Dermatology)

Subsequent hospital visit for a 24-year-old female with otitis externa, seen two days before in consultation, now to have otic wick removal. (Otolaryngology, Head & Neck Surgery)

Subsequent hospital visit for a 27-year-old with acute labyrinthitis. (Otolaryngology, Head & Neck Surgery)

Subsequent hospital visit for a 10-year-old male admitted for lobar pneumonia with vomiting and dehydration; is becoming afebrile and tolerating oral fluids. (Family Medicine/Pediatrics)

Subsequent hospital visit for a 62-year-old patient with resolving cellulitis of the foot. (Orthopaedic Surgery)

Subsequent hospital visit for a 25-year-old male admitted for supra-ventricular tachycardia and converted on medical therapy. (Cardiology)

Subsequent hospital visit for a 27-year-old male two days after open reduction and internal fixation for malar complex fracture. (Plastic Surgery)

Subsequent hospital visit for a 76-year-old male with venous stasis ulcers. (Geriatrics)

Subsequent hospital visit for a 67-year-old female admitted three days ago with bleeding gastric ulcer; now stable. (Gastroenterology)

Subsequent hospital visit for stable 33-year-old male, status post-lower gastrointestinal bleeding. (General Surgery/Gastroenterology)

Subsequent hospital visit for a 29-year-old auto mechanic with effort thrombosis of left upper extremity. (General Surgery)

Subsequent hospital visit for a 14-year-old female in middle phase of inpatient treatment, who is now behaviorally stable and making satisfactory progress in treatment. (Psychiatry)

Subsequent hospital visit for an 18-year-old male with uncomplicated asthma who is clinically stable. (Allergy & Immunology)

Subsequent hospital visit for a 55-year-old male with rheumatoid arthritis, two days following an uncomplicated total joint replacement. (Rheumatology)

Subsequent hospital visit for a 60-year-old dialysis patient with an access infection, now afebrile on antibiotic. (Nephrology)

Subsequent hospital visit for a 36-year-old female with stable post-rhinoplasty epistaxis. (Plastic Surgery)

Subsequent hospital visit for a 66-year-old female with L-2 vertebral compression fracture with resolving ileus. (Orthopaedic Surgery)

Subsequent hospital visit for a patient with peritonsillar abscess. (Otolaryngology, Head & Neck Surgery)

Subsequent hospital visit for an 18-year-old female responding to intravenous antibiotic therapy for ear or sinus infection. (Otolaryngology, Head & Neck Surgery)

Subsequent hospital visit for a 70-year-old male admitted with congestive heart failure who has responded to therapy. (Cardiology)

Follow-up hospital visit for a 32-year-old female with left ureteral calculus; being followed in anticipation of spontaneous passage. (Urology)

Subsequent hospital visit for a 50-year-old Type II diabetic who is clinically stable and without complications requiring regulation of a single dose of insulin daily. (Endocrinology)

Subsequent hospital visit to reassesses the status of a 65-year-old patient post-open reduction and internal fixation of hip fracture, on the rehab unit. (Physical Medicine & Rehabilitation)

Subsequent hospital visit for a 78-year-old male with cholangiocarcinoma managed by biliary drainage. (Interventional Radiology)

Subsequent hospital visit for a 50-year-old male with uncomplicated myocardial infarction who is clinically stable and without chest pain. (Family Medicine/Cardiology/Internal Medicine)

Subsequent hospital visit for a stable 72-year-old lung cancer patient undergoing a five-day course of infusion chemotherapy. (Hematology/Oncology)

Subsequent hospital visit, two days post admission for a 65-year-old male with a CVA (cerebral vascular accident) and left hemiparesis, who is clinically stable. (Neurology/Physical Medicine and Rehabilitation)

Subsequent hospital visit for now stable, 33-year-old male, status post lower gastrointestinal bleeding. (General Surgery)

Subsequent visit on third day of hospitalization for a 60-year-old female recovering from an uncomplicated pneumonia. (Infectious Disease/Internal Medicine/Pulmonary Medicine)

Subsequent hospital visit for a 3-year-old patient in traction for a congenital dislocation of the hip. (Orthopaedic Surgery)

Subsequent hospital visit for a 4-year-old female, admitted for acute gastroenteritis and dehydration, requiring IV hydration; now stable. (Family Medicine/Internal Medicine)

Subsequent hospital visit for 50-year-old female with resolving uncomplicated acute pancreatitis. (Gastroenterology)

99232 Subsequent hospital visit for a patient with venous stasis ulcers who developed fever and red streaks adjacent to the ulcer. (Dermatology/Internal Medicine/Family Medicine)

Subsequent hospital visit for a 66-year-old male for dressing changes and observation. Patient has had a myocutaneous flap to close a pharyngeal fistula and now has a low-grade fever. (Plastic Surgery)

Subsequent hospital visit for a 54-year-old female admitted for myocardial infarction, but who is now having frequent premature ventricular contractions. (Internal Medicine)

Subsequent hospital visit for an 80-year-old patient with a pelvic rim fracture, inability to walk, and severe pain; now 36 hours post-injury, experiencing urinary retention. (Orthopaedic Surgery)

Subsequent hospital visit for a 17-year-old female with fever, pharyngitis, and airway obstruction, who after 48 hours develops a maculopapular rash. (Pediatrics/Family Medicine)

Follow-up hospital visit for a 32-year-old patient admitted the previous day for corneal ulcer. (Dermatology)

Follow-up visit for a 67-year-old male with congestive heart failure who has responded to antibiotics and diuretics, and has now developed a monoarthropathy. (Internal Medicine)

Follow-up hospital visit for a 58-year-old male receiving continuous opioids who is experiencing severe nausea and vomiting. (Pain Medicine)

Subsequent hospital visit for a patient after an auto accident who is slow to respond to ambulation training. (Physical Medicine & Rehabilitation)

Subsequent hospital visit for a 14-year-old with unstable bronchial asthma complicated by pneumonia. (Allergy & Immunology)

Subsequent hospital visit for a 50-year-old diabetic, hypertensive male with back pain not responding to conservative inpatient management with continued radiation of pain to the lower left extremity. (Orthopaedic Surgery)

Subsequent hospital visit for a 37-year-old female on day five of antibiotics for bacterial endocarditis, who still has low-grade fever. (Cardiology)

Subsequent hospital visit for a 54-year-old patient, post MI (myocardial infarction), who is out of the CCU (coronary care unit) but is now having frequent premature ventricular contractions on telemetry. (Cardiology/Internal Medicine)

Subsequent hospital visit for a patient with neutropenia, a fever responding to antibiotics, and continued slow gastrointestinal bleeding on platelet support. (Hematology/Oncology)

Subsequent hospital visit for a 50-year-old male admitted two days ago for sub-acute renal allograft rejection. (Nephrology)

Subsequent hospital visit for a 35-year-old drug addict, not responding to initial antibiotic therapy for pyelonephritis. (Urology)

Subsequent hospital visit of an 81-year-old male with abdominal distention, nausea, and vomiting. (General Surgery)

Subsequent hospital care for a 62-year-old female with congestive heart failure, who remains dyspneic and febrile. (Internal Medicine)

Subsequent hospital visit for a 73-year-old female with recently diagnosed lung cancer, who complains of unsteady gait. (Pulmonary Medicine)

Subsequent hospital visit for a 20-month-old male with bacterial meningitis treated one week with antibiotic therapy; has now developed a temperature of 101.0. (Pediatrics)

Subsequent hospital visit for 13-year-old male admitted with left lower quadrant abdominal pain and fever, not responding to therapy. (General Surgery)

Subsequent hospital visit for a 65-year-old male with hemiplegia and painful paretic shoulder. (Physical Medicine & Rehabilitation)

99233 Subsequent hospital visit for a 38-year-old male, quadriplegic with acute autonomic hyperreflexia, who is not responsive to initial care. (Physical Medicine & Rehabilitation)

Follow-up hospital visit for a teenage female who continues to experience severely disruptive, violent and life-threatening symptoms in a complicated multi-system illness. Family/social circumstances also a contributing factor. (Psychiatry)

Subsequent hospital visit for a 42-year-old female with progressive systemic sclerosis (scleroderma), renal failure on dialysis, congestive heart failure, cardiac arrhythmias, and digital ulcers. (Allergy & Immunology)

Subsequent hospital visit for a 50-year-old diabetic, hypertensive male with nonresponding back pain and radiating pain to the lower left extremity, who develops chest pain, cough, and bloody sputum. (Orthopaedic Surgery)

Subsequent hospital visit for a 64-year-old female, status post-abdominal aortic aneurysm resection, with non-responsive coagulopathy, who has now developed lower GI bleeding. (Abdominal Surgery/Colon & Rectal Surgery/General Surgery) Follow-up hospital care of a patient with pansinusitis infection complicated by a brain abscess and asthma; no response to current treatment. (Otolaryngology, Head & Neck Surgery)

Subsequent hospital visit for a patient with a laryngeal neoplasm who develops airway compromise, suspected metastasis. (Otolaryngology, Head & Neck Surgery)

Subsequent hospital visit for a 49-year-old male with significant rectal bleeding, etiology undetermined, not responding to treatment. (Abdominal Surgery/General Surgery/Colon & Rectal Surgery)

Subsequent hospital visit for a 50-year-old male, post-aortocoronary bypass surgery; now develops hypotension and oliguria. (Cardiology)

Subsequent hospital visit for an adolescent patient who is violent, unsafe, and noncompliant, with multiple expectations for participation in treatment plan and behavior on the treatment unit. (Psychiatry)

Subsequent hospital visit for an 18-year-old male being treated for presumed PCP psychosis. Patient is still moderately symptomatic with auditory hallucinations and is insisting on signing out against medical advice. (Psychiatry)

Subsequent hospital visit for an 8-year-old female with caustic ingestion, who now has fever, dyspnea, and dropping hemoglobin. (Gastroenterology)

Follow-up hospital visit for a chronic renal failure patient on dialysis who develops chest pain and shortness of breath and a new onset pericardial friction rub. (Nephrology)

Subsequent hospital visit for a 44-year-old patient with electrical burns to the left arm with ascending infection. (Orthopaedic Surgery)

Subsequent hospital visit for a patient with systemic sclerosis who has aspirated and is short of breath. (Dermatology)

Subsequent hospital visit for a 65-year-old female, status post-op resection of abdominal aortic aneurysm, with suspected ischemic bowel. (General Surgery)

Subsequent hospital visit for a 50-year-old male, post-aortocoronary bypass surgery, now develops hypotension and oliguria. (Cardiology)

Subsequent hospital visit for a 65-year-old male, following an acute myocardial infarction, who complains of shortness of breath and new chest pain. (Cardiology)

Subsequent hospital visit for a 65-year-old female with rheumatoid arthritis (stage 3, class 3) admitted for urosepsis. On the third hospital day, chest pain, dyspnea and fever develop. (Rheumatology)

Follow-up hospital care of a pediatric case with stridor, laryngomalacia, established tracheostomy, complicated by multiple medical problems in PICU. (Otolaryngology, Head & Neck Surgery)

Subsequent hospital visit for a 60-year-old female, four days post uncomplicated inferior myocardial infarction who has developed severe chest pain, dyspnea, diaphoresis and nausea. (Family Medicine)

Subsequent hospital visit for a patient with AML (acute myelogenous leukemia), fever, elevated white count and uric acid undergoing induction chemotherapy. (Hematology/Oncology)

Subsequent hospital visit for a 38-year-old quadriplegic male with acute autonomic hyperreflexia, who is not responsive to initial care. (Physical Medicine & Rehabilitation)

Subsequent hospital visit for a 65-year-old female post-op resection of abdominal aortic aneurysm, with suspected ischemic bowel. (General Surgery)

Subsequent hospital visit for a 60-year-old female with persistent leukocytosis and a fever seven days after a sigmoid colon resection for carcinoma. (Infectious Disease)

Subsequent hospital visit for a chronic renal failure patient on dialysis, who develops chest pain, shortness of breath and new onset of pericardial friction rub. (Nephrology)

Subsequent hospital visit for a 65-year-old male with acute myocardial infarction who now demonstrates complete heart block and congestive heart failure. (Cardiology)

Subsequent hospital visit for a 25-year-old female with hypertension and systemic lupus erythematosus, admitted for fever and respiratory distress. On the third hospital day, the patient presented with purpuric skin lesions and acute renal failure. (Allergy & Immunology)

Subsequent hospital visit for a 55-year-old male with severe chronic obstructive pulmonary disease and bronchospasm; initially admitted for acute respiratory distress requiring ventilatory support in the ICU. The patient was stabilized, extubated and transferred to the floor, but has now developed acute fever, dyspnea, left lower lobe rhonchi and laboratory evidence of carbon dioxide retention and hypoxemia. (Family Medicine/Internal Medicine)

Subsequent hospital visit for 46-year-old female, known liver cirrhosis patient, with recent upper gastrointestinal hemorrhage from varices; now with worsening ascites and encephalopathy. (Gastroenterology)

Subsequent hospital visit for 62-year-old female admitted with acute subarachnoid hemorrhage, negative cerebral arteriogram, increased lethargy and hemiparesis with fever. (Neurosurgery)

Consultations

Office or Other Outpatient Consultations

New or Established Patient

99241 Initial office consultation for a 40-year-old female in pain from blister on lip following a cold. (Oral & Maxillofacial Surgery)

Initial office consultation for a 62-year-old construction worker with olecranon bursitis. (Orthopaedic Surgery)

Office consultation with 25-year-old postpartum female with severe symptomatic hemorrhoids. (Colon & Rectal Surgery)

Office consultation with 58-year-old male, referred for follow-up of creatinine level and evaluation of obstructive uropathy, relieved two months ago. (Nephrology)

Office consultation for 30-year-old female tennis player with sprain or contusion of the forearm. (Orthopaedic Surgery)

Office consultation for a 45-year-old male, requested by his internist, with asymptomatic torus palatinus requiring no further treatment. (Oral & Maxillofacial Surgery)

99242 Initial office consultation for a 20-year-old male with acute upper respiratory tract symptoms. (Allergy & Immunology)

Initial office consultation for a 29-year-old soccer player with painful proximal thigh/groin injury. (Orthopaedic Surgery)

Initial office consultation for a 66-year-old female with wrist and hand pain, numbness of finger tips, suspected median nerve compression by carpal tunnel syndrome. (Plastic Surgery)

Initial office consultation for a patient with a solitary lesion of discoid lupus erythematosus on left cheek to rule out malignancy or self-induced lesion. (Dermatology)

Office consultation for management of systolic hypertension in a 70-year-old male scheduled for elective prostate resection. (Geriatrics)

Office consultation with 27-year-old female, with old amputation, for evaluation of existing above-knee prosthesis. (Physical Medicine & Rehabilitation)

Office consultation with 66-year-old female with wrist and hand pain, and finger numbness, secondary to suspected carpal tunnel syndrome. (Orthopaedic Surgery)

Office consultation for 61-year-old female, recently on antibiotic therapy, now with diarrhea and leukocytosis. (Abdominal Surgery)

Office consultation for a patient with papulosquamous eruption of elbow with pitting of nails and itchy scalp. (Dermatology)

Office consultation for a 30-year-old female with single season allergic rhinitis. (Allergy & Immunology)

99243 Initial office consultation for a 60-year-old male with avascular necrosis of the left femoral head with increasing pain. (Orthopaedic Surgery)

Office consultation for a 31-year-old woman complaining of palpitations and chest pains. Her internist had described a mild systolic click. (Cardiology)

Office consultation for a 65-year-old female with persistent bronchitis. (Infectious Disease)

Office consultation for a 65-year-old man with chronic low-back pain radiating to the leg. (Neurosurgery)

Office consultation for 23-year-old female with Crohn's disease not responding to therapy. (Abdominal Surgery/Colon & Rectal Surgery)

Office consultation for 25-year-old patient with symptomatic knee pain and swelling, with torn anterior cruciate ligament and/or torn meniscus. (Orthopaedic Surgery)

Office consultation for a 67-year-old patient with osteoporosis and mandibular atrophy with regard to reconstructive alternatives. (Oral & Maxillofacial Surgery)

Office consultation for 39-year-old patient referred at a perimenopausal age for irregular menses and menopausal symptoms. (Obstetrics & Gynecology)

99244 Initial office consultation for a 28-year-old male, HIV+, with a recent change in visual acuity. (Ophthalmology)

Initial office consultation for a 15-year-old male with failing grades, suspected drug abuse. (Pediatrics)

Initial office consultation for a 36-year-old factory worker, status four months post-occupational low back injury and requires management of intractable low back pain. (Pain Medicine)

Initial office consultation for a 45-year-old female with a history of chronic arthralgia of TMJ and associated myalgia and sudden progressive symptomatology over last two to three months. (Oral & Maxillofacial Surgery)

Initial office consultation for evaluation of a 70-year-old male with appetite loss and diminished energy. (Psychiatry)

Initial office consultation for an elementary school-aged patient, referred by pediatrician, with multiple systematic complaints and recent onset of behavioral discontrol. (Psychiatry)

Initial office consultation for a 23-year-old female with developmental facial skeletal anomaly and subsequent abnormal relationship of jaw(s) to cranial base. (Oral & Maxillofacial Surgery)

Initial office consultation for a 45-year-old myopic patient with a one-week history of floaters and a partial retinal detachment. (Ophthalmology)

Initial office consultation for a 65-year-old female with moderate dementia, mild unsteadiness, back pain fatigue on ambulation, intermittent urinary incontinence. (Neurosurgery)

Initial office consultation for a 33-year-old female referred by endocrinologist with amenorrhea and galactorrhea, for evaluation of pituitary tumor. (Neurosurgery)

Initial office consultation for a 34-year-old male with new onset nephrotic syndrome. (Nephrology)

Initial office consultation for a 39-year-old female with intractable chest wall pain secondary to metastatic breast cancer. (Anesthesiology/Pain Medicine)

Initial office consultation for a patient with multiple giant tumors of jaws. (Oral & Maxillofacial Surgery)

Initial office consultation for a patient with a failed total hip replacement with loosening and pain upon walking. (Orthopaedic Surgery)

Initial office consultation for a 60-year-old female with three-year history of intermittent tic-like unilateral facial pain; now constant pain for six weeks without relief by adequate carbamazepine dosage. (Neurosurgery)

Initial office consultation for a 45-year-old male heavy construction worker with prior lumbar disk surgery two years earlier; now gradually recurring low back and unilateral leg pain for three months, unable to work for two weeks. (Neurosurgery)

Initial office consultation of a patient who presents with a 30-year history of smoking and right neck mass. (Otolaryngology, Head & Neck Surgery)

Office consultation with 38-year-old female, with inflammatory bowel disease, who now presents with right lower quadrant pain and suspected intra-abdominal abscess. (General Surgery/Colon & Rectal Surgery)

Office consultation with 72-year-old male with esophageal carcinoma, symptoms of dysphagia and reflux. (Thoracic Surgery)

Office consultation for discussion of treatment options for a 40-year-old female with a two-centimeter adenocarcinoma of the breast. (Radiation Oncology)

Office consultation for young patient referred by pediatrician because of patient's short attention span, easy distractibility and hyperactivity. (Psychiatry)

Office consultation for 66-year-old female, history of colon resection for adenocarcinoma six years earlier, now with severe mid-back pain; x-rays showing osteoporosis and multiple vertebral compression fractures. (Neurosurgery)

Office consultation for a patient with chronic pelvic inflammatory disease who now has left lower quadrant pain with a palpable pelvic mass. (Obstetrics & Gynecology)

Office consultation for a patient with long-standing psoriasis with acute onset of erythroderma, pustular lesions, chills and fever. Combinations of topical and systemic treatments discussed and instituted. (Dermatology)

99245 Initial office consultation for a 35-year-old multiple-trauma male patient with complex pelvic fractures, for evaluation and formulation of management plan. (Orthopaedic Surgery)

Initial emergency room consultation for 10-year-old male in status epilepticus, recent closed head injury, information about medication not available. (Neurosurgery)

Initial emergency room consultation for a 23-year-old patient with severe abdominal pain, guarding, febrile, and unstable vital signs. (Obstetrics & Gynecology)

Office consultation for a 67-year-old female longstanding uncontrolled diabetic who presents with retinopathy, nephropathy, and a foot ulcer. (Endocrinology)

Office consultation for a 37-year-old male for initial evaluation and management of Cushing's disease. (Endocrinology)

Office consultation for a 60-year-old male who presents with thyrotoxicosis, exophthalmos, frequent premature ventricular contractions and congestive heart failure. (Endocrinology)

Initial office consultation for a 36-year-old patient, one year status post occupational herniated cervical disk treated by laminectomy, requiring management of multiple sites of intractable pain, depression, and narcotic dependence. (Pain Medicine)

Office consultation for a 58-year-old man with a history of MI and CHF who complains of the recent onset of rest angina and shortness of breath. The patient has a systolic blood pressure of 90mmHG and is in Class IV heart failure. (Cardiology)

Emergency room consultation for a 1-year-old with a three-day history of fever with increasing respiratory distress who is thought to have cardiac tamponade by the ER physician. (Cardiology)

Office consultation in the emergency room for a 25-year-old male with severe, acute, closed head injury. (Neurosurgery)

Office consultation for a 23-year-old female with Stage II A Hodgkins disease with positive supraclavicular and mediastinal nodes. (Radiation Oncology)

Office consultation for a 27-year-old juvenile diabetic patient with severe diabetic retinopathy, gastric atony, nephrotic syndrome and progressive renal failure, now with a serum creatinine of 2.7, and a blood pressure of 170/114. (Nephrology)

Office consultation for independent medical evaluation of a patient with a history of complicated low back and neck problems with previous multiple failed back surgeries. (Orthopaedic Surgery)

Office consultation for an adolescent referred by pediatrician for recent onset of violent and self-injurious behavior. (Psychiatry)

Office consultation for a 6-year-old male for evaluation of severe muscle and joint pain and a diffuse rash. Patient well until 4-6 weeks earlier, when he developed arthralgia, myalgias, and a fever of 102 for one week. (Rheumatology)

Inpatient Consultations

New or Established Patient

99251 Initial hospital consultation for a 27-year-old female with fractured incisor post-intubation. (Oral & Maxillofacial Surgery)

Initial hospital consultation for an orthopaedic patient on IV antibiotics who has developed an apparent candida infection of the oral cavity. (Oral & Maxillofacial Surgery)

Initial inpatient consultation for a 30-year-old female complaining of vaginal itching, post orthopaedic surgery. (Obstetrics & Gynecology)

Initial inpatient consultation for a 36-year-old male on orthopaedic service with complaint of localized dental pain. (Oral & Maxillofacial Surgery)

99252 Initial hospital consultation for a 45-year-old male, previously abstinent alcoholic, who relapsed and was admitted for management of gastritis. The patient readily accepts the need for further treatment. (Addiction Medicine)

Initial hospital consultation for a 35-year-old dialysis patient with episodic oral ulcerations. (Oral & Maxillofacial Surgery)

Initial inpatient preoperative consultation for a 43-year-old woman with cholecystitis and well-controlled hypertension. (Cardiology)

Initial inpatient consultation for recommendation of antibiotic prophylaxis for a patient with a synthetic heart valve who will undergo urologic surgery. (Internal Medicine)

Initial inpatient consultation for possible drug induced skin eruption in 50-year-old male. (Dermatology)

Preoperative inpatient consultation for evaluation of hypertension in a 60-year-old male who will undergo a cholecystectomy. Patient had a normal annual check-up in your office four months ago. (Internal Medicine)

Initial inpatient consultation for 66-year-old patient with wrist and hand pain and finger numbness, secondary to carpal tunnel syndrome. (Orthopaedic Surgery/Plastic Surgery)

Initial inpatient consultation for a 66-year-old male smoker referred for pain management immediately status post-biliary tract surgery done via sub-costal incision. (Anesthesiology/Pain Medicine)

99253 Initial hospital consultation for a 50-year-old female with incapacitating knee pain due to generalized rheumatoid arthritis. (Orthopaedic Surgery)

Initial hospital consultation for a 60-year-old male with avascular necrosis of the left femoral heel with increasing pain. (Orthopaedic Surgery)

Initial hospital consultation for a 45-year-old female with compound mandibular fracture and concurrent head, abdominal and/or orthopaedic injuries. (Oral & Maxillofacial Surgery)

Initial hospital consultation for a 22-year-old female, paraplegic, to evaluate wrist and hand pain. (Orthopaedic Surgery)

Initial hospital consultation for a 40-year-old male with 10-day history of incapacitating unilateral sciatica, unable to walk now, not improved by bed rest. (Neurosurgery)

Initial hospital consultation, requested by pediatrician, for treatment recommendations for a patient admitted with persistent inability to walk following soft tissue injury to ankle. (Physiatry)

Initial hospital consultation for a 27-year-old previously healthy male who vomited during IV sedation and may have aspirated gastric contents. (Anesthesiology)

Initial hospital consultation for a 33-year-old female, post-abdominal surgery, who now has a fever. (Internal Medicine)

Initial inpatient consultation for a 57-year-old male, post lower endoscopy, for evaluation of abdominal pain and fever. (General Surgery)

Initial inpatient consultation for rehabilitation of a 73-year-old female one week after surgical management of a hip fracture. (Physical Medicine & Rehabilitation)

Initial inpatient consultation for diagnosis/management of fever following abdominal surgery. (Internal Medicine)

Initial inpatient consultation for a 35-year-old female with a fever and pulmonary infiltrate following cesarean section. (Pulmonary Medicine)

Initial inpatient consultation for a 42-year-old non-diabetic patient, post-op cholecystectomy, now with an acute urinary tract infection. (Nephrology)

Initial inpatient consultation for 53-year-old female with moderate uncomplicated pancreatitis. (Gastroenterology)

Initial inpatient consultation for 45-year-old patient with chronic neck pain with radicular pain of the left arm. (Orthopaedic Surgery)

Initial inpatient consultation for 8-year-old patient with new onset of seizures who has a normal examination and previous history. (Neurology)

99254 Initial hospital consultation for a 15-year-old patient with painless swelling of proximal humerus with lytic lesion by x-ray. (Orthopaedic Surgery)

Initial hospital consultation for evaluation of a 29-year-old female with a diffusely positive medical review of systems and history of multiple surgeries. (Psychiatry)

Initial hospital consultation for a 70-year-old diabetic female with gangrene of the foot. (Orthopaedic Surgery)

Initial inpatient consultation for a 47-year-old female with progressive pulmonary infiltrate, hypoxemia, and diminished urine output. (Anesthesiology)

Initial hospital consultation for a 13-month-old with spasmodic cough, respiratory distress, and fever. (Allergy & Immunology)

Initial hospital consultation for a patient with failed total hip replacement with loosening and pain upon walking. (Orthopaedic Surgery)

Initial hospital consultation for a 62-year-old female with metastatic breast cancer to the femoral neck and thoracic vertebra. (Orthopaedic Surgery)

Initial hospital consultation for a 39-year-old female with nephrolithiasis requiring extensive opioid analgesics, whose vital signs are now elevated. She initially denied any drug use, but today gives history of multiple substance abuse, including opioids and prior treatment for a personality disorder. (Psychiatry)

Initial hospital consultation for a 70-year-old female without previous psychiatric history, who is now experiencing nocturnal confusion and visual hallucinations following hip replacement surgery. (Psychiatry)

Initial inpatient consultation for evaluation of a 63-year-old in the ICU with diabetes and chronic renal failure who develops acute respiratory distress syndrome 36 hours after a mitral valve replacement. (Anesthesiology)

Initial inpatient consultation for a 66-year-old female with enlarged supraclavicular lymph nodes, found on biopsy to be malignant. (Hematology/Oncology)

Initial inpatient consultation for a 43-year-old female for evaluation of sudden painful visual loss, optic neuritis and episodic paresthesia. (Ophthalmology)

Initial inpatient consultation for evaluation of a 71-year-old male with hyponatremia (serum sodium 114) who was admitted to the hospital with pneumonia. (Nephrology)

Initial inpatient consultation for a 72-year-old male with emergency admission for possible bowel obstruction. (Internal Medicine/General Surgery)

Initial inpatient consultation for a 35-year-old female with fever, swollen joints, and rash of one-week duration. (Rheumatology)

99255 Initial inpatient consultation for a 76-year-old female with massive, life-threatening gastrointestinal hemorrhage and chest pain. (Gastroenterology)

Initial inpatient consultation for a 75-year-old female, admitted to intensive care with acute respiratory distress syndrome, who is hypersensitive, has a moderate metabolic acidosis, and a rising serum creatinine. (Nephrology)

Initial hospital consultation for patient with a history of complicated low back pain and neck problems with previous multiple failed back surgeries. (Orthopaedic Surgery/Neurosurgery)

Initial hospital consultation for a 66-year-old female, two days post-abdominal aneurysm repair, with oliguria and hypertension of one-day duration. (Nephrology/Internal Medicine)

Initial hospital consultation for a patient with shotgun wound to face with massive facial trauma and airway obstruction. (Oral & Maxillofacial Surgery)

Initial hospital consultation for patient with severe pancreatitis complicated by respiratory insufficiency, acute renal failure, and abscess formation. (General Surgery/Colon & Rectal Surgery)

Initial hospital consultation for a 35-year-old multiple-trauma male patient with complex pelvic fractures to evaluate and formulate management plan. (Orthopaedic Surgery)

Initial inpatient consultation for adolescent patient with fractured femur and pelvis who pulled out IVs and disconnected traction in attempt to elope from hospital. (Psychiatry)

Initial hospital consultation for a 16-year-old primigravida at 32 weeks gestation requested by a family practitioner for evaluation of severe hypertension, thrombocytopenia, and headache. (Obstetrics & Gynecology)

Initial hospital consultation for a 58-year-old insulin-dependent diabetic with multiple antibiotic allergies, now with multiple fascial plane abscesses and airway obstruction. (Oral & Maxillofacial Surgery)

Initial inpatient consultation for a 55-year-old male with known cirrhosis and ascites, now with jaundice, encephalopathy, and massive hematemesis. (Gastroenterology)

Initial hospital consultation for a 25-year-old male, seen in emergency room with severe, closed head injury. (Neurosurgery)

Initial hospital consultation for a 2-day-old male with single ventricle physiology and subaortic obstruction. Family counseling following evaluation for multiple, staged surgical procedures. (Thoracic Surgery)

Initial hospital consultation for a 45-year-old male admitted with subarachnoid hemorrhage and intracranial aneurysm on angiogram. (Neurosurgery)

Initial inpatient consultation for myxedematous patient who is hypoventilating and obtunded. (Endocrinology)

Initial hospital consultation for a 45-year-old patient with widely metastatic lung carcinoma, intractable back pain, and a history that includes substance dependence, NSAID allergy, and two prior laminectomies with fusion for low back pain. (Pain Medicine)

Initial hospital consultation for evaluation of treatment options in a 50-year-old patient with cirrhosis, known peptic ulcer disease, hypotension, encephalopathy, and massive acute upper gastrointestinal bleeding which cannot be localized by endoscopy. (Interventional Radiology)

Initial inpatient consultation in the ICU for a 70-year-old male who experienced a cardiac arrest during surgery and was resuscitated. (Cardiology)

Initial inpatient consultation for a patient with severe pancreatitis complicated by respiratory insufficiency, acute renal failure and abscess formation. (Gastroenterology)

Initial inpatient consultation for a 70-year-old cirrhotic male admitted with ascites, jaundice, encephalopathy, and massive hematemesis. (Gastroenterology)

Initial inpatient consultation in the ICU for a 51-year-old patient who is on a ventilator and has a fever two weeks after a renal transplantation. (Infectious Disease)

Initial inpatient consultation for evaluation and formulation of plan for management of multiple trauma patient with complex pelvic fracture, 35-year-old male. (General Surgery/Orthopaedic Surgery)

Initial inpatient consultation for a 50-year-old male with a history of previous myocardial infarction, now with acute pulmonary edema and hypotension. (Cardiology)

Initial inpatient consultation for 45-year-old male with recent, acute subarachnoid hemorrhage, hesitant speech, mildly confused, drowsy. High risk group for HIV+ status. (Neurosurgery)

Initial inpatient consultation for 36-year-old female referred by her internist to evaluate a patient being followed for abdominal pain and fever. The patient has developed diffuse abdominal pain, guarding, rigidity and increased fever. (Obstetrics & Gynecology)

Emergency Department Services

New or Established Patient

99281 Emergency department visit for a patient for removal of sutures from a well-healed, uncomplicated laceration. (Emergency Medicine)

Emergency department visit for a patient for tetanus toxoid immunization. (Emergency Medicine)

Emergency department visit for a patient with several uncomplicated insect bites. (Emergency Medicine)

99282 Emergency department visit for a 20-year-old student who presents with a painful sunburn with blister formation on the back. (Emergency Medicine)

Emergency department visit for a child presenting with impetigo localized to the face. (Emergency Medicine)

Emergency department visit for a patient with a minor traumatic injury of an extremity with localized pain, swelling, and bruising. (Emergency Medicine)

Emergency department visit for an otherwise healthy patient whose chief complaint is a red, swollen cystic lesion on his/her back. (Emergency Medicine)

Emergency department visit for a patient presenting with a rash on both legs after exposure to poison ivy. (Emergency Medicine)

Emergency department visit for a young adult patient with infected sclera and purulent discharge from both eyes without pain, visual disturbance or history of foreign body in either eye. (Emergency Medicine)

99283 Emergency department visit for a sexually active female complaining of vaginal discharge who is afebrile and denies experiencing abdominal or back pain. (Emergency Medicine)

Emergency department visit for a well-appearing 8-year-old who has a fever, diarrhea and abdominal cramps, is tolerating oral fluids and is not vomiting. (Emergency Medicine)

Emergency department visit for a patient with an inversion ankle injury, who is unable to bear weight on the injured foot and ankle. (Emergency Medicine)

Emergency department visit for a patient who has a complaint of acute pain associated with a suspected foreign body in the painful eye. (Emergency Medicine)

Emergency department visit for a healthy, young adult patient who sustained a blunt head injury with local swelling and bruising without subsequent confusion, loss of consciousness or memory deficit. (Emergency Medicine)

99284 Emergency department visit for a 4-year-old who fell off a bike sustaining a head injury with brief loss of consciousness. (Emergency Medicine)

Emergency department visit for an elderly female who has fallen and is now complaining of pain in her right hip and is unable to walk. (Emergency Medicine)

Emergency department visit for a patient with flank pain and hematuria. (Emergency Medicine)

Emergency department visit for a female presenting with lower abdominal pain and a vaginal discharge. (Emergency Medicine)

99285 Emergency department visit for a patient with a complicated overdose requiring aggressive management to prevent side effects from the ingested materials. (Emergency Medicine)

Emergency department visit for a patient with a new onset of rapid heart rate requiring IV drugs. (Emergency Medicine)

Emergency department visit for a patient exhibiting active, upper gastrointestinal bleeding. (Emergency Medicine)

Emergency department visit for a previously healthy young adult patient who is injured in an automobile accident and is brought to the emergency department immobilized and has symptoms compatible with intra-abdominal injuries or multiple extremity injuries. (Emergency Medicine)

Emergency department visit for a patient with an acute onset of chest pain compatible with symptoms of cardiac ischemia and/or pulmonary embolus. (Emergency Medicine)

Emergency department visit for a patient who presents with a sudden onset of "the worst headache of her life," and complains of a stiff neck, nausea, and inability to concentrate. (Emergency Medicine)

Emergency department visit for a patient with a new onset of a cerebral vascular accident. (Emergency Medicine)

Emergency department visit for acute febrile illness in an adult, associated with shortness of breath and an altered level of alertness. (Emergency Medicine)

Critical Care Services

99291 First hour of critical care of a 65-year-old man with septic shock following relief of ureteral obstruction caused by a stone.

First hour of critical care of a 15-year-old with acute respiratory failure from asthma.

First hour of critical care of a 45-year-old who sustained a liver laceration, cerebral hematoma, flailed chest, and pulmonary contusion after being struck by an automobile.

First hour of critical care of a 65-year-old woman who, following a hysterectomy, suffered a cardiac arrest associated with a pulmonary embolus.

First hour of critical care of a 6-month-old with hypovolemic shock secondary to diarrhea and dehydration.

First hour of critical care of a 3-year-old with respiratory failure secondary to pneumocystis carinii pneumonia.

Prolonged Services

Prolonged Physician Service With Direct (Face-to-Face) Patient Contact

Office or Other Outpatient

99354/ 99355 A 20-year-old female with history of asthma presents with acute bronchospasm and moderate respiratory distress. Initial evaluation shows respiratory rate 30, labored breathing and wheezing heard in all lung fields. Office treatment is initiated which includes intermittent bronchial dilation and subcutaneous epinephrine. Requires intermittent physician face-to-face time with patient over a period of 2-3 hours. (Family Medicine/Internal Medicine)

Inpatient

99356 A 34-year-old primigravida presents to hospital in early labor. Admission history and physical reveals severe preeclampsia. Physician supervises management of preeclampsia, IV magnesium initiation and maintenance, labor augmentation with pitocin, and close maternal-fetal monitoring. Physician face-to-face involvement includes 40 minutes of continuous bedside care until the patient is stable, then is intermittent over several hours until the delivery. (Family Medicine/Internal Medicine/Obstetrics & Gynecology)

Prolonged Physician Service Without Direct Patient (Face-to-Face) Contact

99358/ 99359 A 65-year-old new patient with multiple problems is seen and evaluated. After the visit, the physician requires extensive time to talk with the patient's daughter, to review complex, detailed medical records transferred from previous physicians and to complete a comprehensive treatment plan. This plan also requires the physician to personally initiate and coordinate the care plan with a local home health agency and a dietician. (Family Medicine/Internal Medicine)

Physician Standby Services

99360 A 24-year-old patient is admitted to OB unit attempting VBAC. Fetal monitoring shows increasing fetal distress. Patient's blood pressure is rising and labor progressing slowly. A primary care physician is requested by the OB/GYN to standby in the unit for possible cesarean delivery and neonatal resuscitation. (Family Medicine/Internal Medicine)

Care Plan Oversight Services

99375 First month of care plan oversight for terminal care of a 58-year-old woman with advanced intraabdominal ovarian cancer. Care plan includes home oxygen, diuretics IV for edema and ascites control and pain control management involving IV morphine infusion when progressive ileus occurred. Physician phone contacts with nurse, family, and MSW. Discussion with MSW concerning plans to withdraw supportive measures per patient wishes. Documentation includes review and modification of care plan and certifications from nursing, MSW, pharmacy, and DME. (Family Medicine/Internal Medicine)

Appendix D

Summary of CPT Add-on Codes

This listing is a summary of CPT add-on codes for *CPT 2007*. The codes listed below are identified in *CPT 2007* with a ✚ symbol.

				63035	75996	93572
				63043	76125	93609
				63044	76802	93613
				63048	76810	93621
				63057	76812	93622
				63066	76814	93623
				63076	76937	93662
				63078	77001	94645
				63082	77051	95873
				63086	77052	95874
				63088	78020	95920
01953	15366	31637	38746	63091	78478	95962
01968	15401	32501	38747	63103	78480	95967
01969	15421	33141	43635	63295	78496	95973
11001	15431	33225	44015	63308	78730	95975
11008	15787	33508	44121	64472	83901	95979
11101	15831	33530	44128	64476	87187	96411
11201	15847	33572	44139	64480	87904	96415
11732	16036	33768	44203	64484	88155	96417
11922	17003	33884	44213	64623	88185	96423
13102	17312	33924	44701	64627	88311	96570
13122	17314	33961	44955	64727	88312	96571
13133	17315	34808	47001	64778	88313	97546
13153	19001	34813	47550	64783	88314	97811
15003	19126	34826	48400	64787	90466	97814
15005	19291	35306	49326	64832	90468	99100
15101	19295	35390	49435	64837	90472	99116
15111	19297	35400	49568	64859	90474	99135
15116	22103	35500	49905	64872	90761	99140
15121	22116	35572	56606	64874	90766	99145
15131	22216	35681	57267	64876	90767	99150
15136	22226	35682	58110	64901	90768	99290
15151	22328	35683	58611	64902	90775	99292
15152	22522	35685	59525	66990	92547	99354
15156	22525	35686	60512	67225	92608	99355
15157	22527	35697	61316	67320	92627	99356
15171	22534	35700	61517	67331	92973	99357
15176	22585	36218	61609	67332	92974	99358
15201	22614	36248	61610	67334	92978	99359
15221	22632	36476	61611	67335	92979	99602
15241	26125	36479	61612	67340	92981	0049T
15261	26861	37185	61641	69990	92984	0054T
15301	26863	37186	61642	74301	92996	0055T
15321	27358	37206	61795	75774	92998	0056T
15331	27692	37208	61864	75946	93320	0063T
15336	31620	37250	61868	75964	93321	0068T
15341	31632	37251	62148	75968	93325	0069T
15361	31633	38102	62160	75993	93571	0070T

0076T

0079T

0081T

0092T

0095T

0098T

0117T

0151T

0153T

0159T

0163T

0164T

0165T

Appendix E

Summary of CPT Codes Exempt From Modifier 51

This listing is a summary of CPT codes that are exempt from the use of modifier 51 but have NOT been designated as CPT add-on procedures/services. The codes listed below are identified in *CPT 2007* with a ⊘ symbol.

17004	33521	90634	90716
20660	33522	90636	90717
20690	33523	90645	90718
20692	35600	90646	90719
20900	36620	90647	90720
20902	36660	90648	90721
20910	38792	90649	90723
20912	44500	90655	90725
20920	61107	90656	90727
20922	61210	90657	90732
20924	62284	90658	90733
20926	90281	90660	90734
20930	90283	90665	90735
20931	90287	90669	90736
20936	90288	90675	90740
20937	90291	90676	90743
20938	90296	90680	90744
20974	90371	90690	90746
20975	90375	90691	90747
22840	90376	90692	90748
22841	90378	90693	90749
22842	90379	90698	93501
22843	90384	90700	93503
22844	90385	90701	93505
22845	90386	90702	93508
22846	90389	90703	93510
22847	90393	90704	93511
22848	90396	90705	93514
22851	90399	90706	93524
31500	90476	90707	93526
32000	90477	90708	93527
32002	90581	90710	93528
32020	90585	90712	93529
33517	90586	90713	93530
33518	90632	90714	93531
33519	90633	90715	93532

93533
93539
93540
93541
93542
93543
93544
93545
93555
93556
93600
93602
93603
93610
93612
93615
93616
93618
93619
93620
93624
93631
93640
93641
93642
93650
93651
93652
93660
94610
95900
95903
95904
99143
99144
99148
99149

Appendix F

Summary of CPT Codes Exempt From Modifier 63

The listing is a summary of CPT codes that are exempt from the use of modifier 63. The codes listed below are additionally identified in *CPT 2007* with the parenthetical instruction "(Do not report modifier 63 in conjunction with…)"

30540	36660	63700
30545	39503	63702
31520	43313	63704
33401	43314	63706
33403	43520	65820
33470	43831	
33472	44055	
33502	44126	
33503	44127	
33505	44128	
33506	46070	
33610	46705	
33611	46715	
33619	46716	
33647	46730	
33670	46735	
33690	46740	
33694	46742	
33730	46744	
33732	47700	
33735	47701	
33736	49215	
33750	49491	
33755	49492	
33762	49495	
33778	49496	
33786	49600	
33922	49605	
33960	49606	
33961	49610	
36415	49611	
36420	53025	
36450	54000	
36460	54150	
36510	54160	

Appendix G

Summary of CPT Codes That Include Moderate (Conscious) Sedation

The following list of procedures includes conscious sedation as an inherent part of providing the procedure. These codes are identified in the CPT codebook with a ⊙ symbol.

Since these services include moderate sedation, it is not appropriate for the same physician to report both the service and the sedation codes 99143-99145. It is expected that if conscious sedation is provided to the patient as part of one of these services, it is provided by the same physician who is providing the service.

In the unusual event when a second physician other than the health care professional performing the diagnostic or therapeutic services provides moderate sedation in the facility setting (eg, hospital, outpatient hospital/ambulatory surgery center, skilled nursing facility) for the procedures listed in Appendix G, the second physician can report 99148-99150. However, for the circumstance in which these services are performed by the second physician in the nonfacility setting (eg, physician office, freestanding imaging center), codes 99148-99150 would not be reported. Moderate sedation does not include minimal sedation (anxiolysis), deep sedation, or monitored anesthesia care (00100-01999).

The inclusion of a procedure on this list does not prevent separate reporting of an associated anesthesia procedure/service (CPT codes 00100-01999) when performed by a physician other than the health care professional performing the diagnostic or therapeutic procedure. In such cases the person providing anesthesia services shall be present for the purpose of continuously monitoring the patient and shall not act as a surgical assistant. When clinical conditions of the patient require such anesthesia services, or in the circumstances when the patient does not require sedation, the operating physician is not required to report the procedure as a reduced service using modifier 52.

19298	31624	31725	33208	33218	43202	43456
20982	31625	32019	33210	33220	43204	43458
22526	31628	32020	33211	33222	43205	43750
22527	31629	32201	33212	33223	43215	44360
31615	31635	33010	33213	33233	43216	44361
31620	31645	33011	33214	33234	43217	44363
31622	31646	33206	33216	33235	43219	44364
31623	31656	33207	33217	33240	43220	44365
				33241	43226	44366
				33244	43227	44369
				33249	43228	44370
				35470	43231	44372
				35471	43232	44373
				35472	43234	44376
				35473	43235	44377
				35474	43236	44378
				35475	43237	44379
				35476	43238	44380
				36555	43239	44382
				36557	43240	44383
				36558	43241	44385
				36560	43242	44386
				36561	43243	44388
				36563	43244	44389
				36565	43245	44390
				36566	43246	44391
				36568	43247	44392
				36570	43248	44393
				36571	43249	44394
				36576	43250	44397
				36578	43251	44500
				36581	43255	44901
				36582	43256	45303
				36583	43257	45305
				36585	43258	45307
				36590	43259	45308
				36870	43260	45309
				37184	43261	45315
				37185	43262	45317
				37186	43263	45320
				37187	43264	45321
				37188	43265	45327
				37203	43267	45332
				37210	43268	45333
				37215	43269	45334
				37216	43271	45335
				43200	43272	45337
				43201	43453	45338

45339	92987	93650
45340	92995	93651
45341	92996	93652
45342	93312	
45345	93313	
45355	93314	
45378	93315	
45379	93316	
45380	93317	
45381	93318	
45382	93501	
45383	93505	
45384	93508	
45385	93510	
45386	93511	
45387	93514	
45391	93524	
45392	93526	
47011	93527	
48511	93528	
49021	93529	
49041	93530	
49061	93539	
50021	93540	
50382	93541	
50384	93542	
50387	93543	
50592	93544	
58823	93545	
66720	93555	
69300	93556	
77600	93561	
77605	93562	
77610	93571	
77615	93572	
92953	93609	
92960	93613	
92961	93615	
92973	93616	
92974	93618	
92975	93619	
92978	93620	
92979	93621	
92980	93622	
92981	93624	
92982	93640	
92984	93641	
92986	93642	

Appendix H

Alphabetic Index of Performance Measures by Clinical Condition or Topic

Appendix H is an alphabetical listing of the diseases with which the measures and codes are associated. It provides an overview of the performance measures, a listing of the CPT Category II codes that may be used with each measure, as well as any applicable reporting instructions. It is intended to be used as a crosswalk to the Category II codes section allowing users an overview of the measures and the Category II codes that should be used with each measure, linking the Category II codes to the specific measures and measure sets from which these codes were derived. The clinical conditions or topics are listed in alphabetic order within the appendix to allow rapid access to the conditions/topics currently included in the coding manual. For the latest Appendix H information, visit the website at www.ama-assn.org/go/cpt.

In order for a patient to be included in the numerator for a particular performance measure, a patient must meet the denominator inclusion criteria for that measure. Prior to coding, users must review (1) the complete description of the code in the Category II section of the CPT codebook and Web site and (2) the specification documents of its associated performance measure as found on the measure developer's Website. Symbols proceeding the specific performance measure direct users to footnotes at the bottom of each page of this appendix. The footnotes identify the measure developer and the developer's Web address.

In addition, the modifiers included within the Category II code section and Appendix H are only intended to be used when parenthetic notes, guidelines, or reporting language specifically allow use.

Performance measurement exclusion modifiers may be used to indicate that a service specified by a performance measure was considered but, due to either medical, patient, or sytems reason(s) documented in the medical record, the service was not provided. These modifiers serve as denominator exclusions from the performance measure. *Not all listed measures provide for exclusions.* The three modifiers currently in effect include the following:

Performance Measure Exclusion Modifiers

1P Performance measure exclusion modifier due to medical reasons

Reasons include:

- not indicated (absence of organ/limb, already received/performed, other)
- contraindicated (patient allergic history, potential adverse drug interaction, other)
- other medical reasons

2P Performance measure exclusion modifier due to patient reasons

Reasons include:

- Patient declined
- Economic, social, or religious reasons
- Other patient reasons

3P Performance measure exclusion modifier due to system reasons

Reasons include:

- Resources to perform the services not available (eg, equipment, supplies)
- Insurance coverage or payer-related limitations
- Other reasons attributable to health care delivery system

[1]Physician Consortium for Performance Improvement: www.physicianconsortium.org
[2]National Committee on Quality Assurance (NCQA): Health Employer Data Information Set (HEDIS®): www.ncqa.org
[3]Joint Commission on Accreditation of Healthcare Organizations (JCAHO), ORYX Initiative Performance Measures: www.jcaho.org/pms
[4]National Diabetes Quality Improvement Alliance (NDQIA): www.nationaldiabetesalliance.org

Brief Description of Performance Measure & Source and Reporting Instructions	CPT Code(s)	Short Code Descriptor
Asthma		
Asthma Assessment[1]—Whether or not patient was evaluated during at least one office visit during the reporting year for the frequency (numeric) of daytime and nocturnal asthma symptoms **Numerator:** Patients who were evaluated during at least one office visit during the reporting year for the frequency (numeric) of daytime and nocturnal asthma symptoms **Denominator:** All patients aged 5-40 years with asthma **Percentage** of patients aged 5-40 years with asthma who were evaluated during at least one office visit during the reporting year for the frequency (numeric) of daytime and nocturnal asthma symptoms **Reporting Instructions:** To be counted in calculations of this measure, symptom frequency must be numerically quantified. Measure may also be met by physician documentation or patient completion of an asthma assessment tool/survey/questionnaire. Assessment tool may include the Quality Metric Asthma Control Test™, National Asthma Education & Prevention Program (NAEPP) Asthma Symptoms and Peak Flow Diary	1005F	Asthma symptoms evaluated
Asthma Pharmacologic Therapy[1]—Whether or not patient with mild, moderate, or severe *persistent* asthma was prescribed *either* the preferred long-term control medication (inhaled corticosteroid) or an acceptable alternative treatment **Numerator:** Patients who were prescribed *either* the preferred[a] long-term control medication (inhaled corticosteroids) or an acceptable alternative treatment[b] (cromolyn sodium, leukotriene modifier, nedocromil, OR sustained release theophylline) **Denominator:** All patients aged 5-40 years with mild, moderate or severe persistent asthma **Exclusion(s):** Documentation of patient reason(s) (eg economic, social, religious) for not prescribing either the preferred long-term control medication (inhaled corticosteroids) or an acceptable alternative treatment. (There are no medical exclusion criteria.) **Percentage** of all patients with mild, moderate, or severe *persistent* asthma who were prescribed *either* the preferred long-term control medication (inhaled corticosteroids) or an acceptable alternative treatment **Reporting Instructions:** Report 1038F or 1039F for each asthma patient. If long-term control medication (or acceptable alternative treatment) prescribed, report 4015F. Report 4015F with 1038F. Report modifier 2P for patient who meets exclusion criteria. Modifier 1P may not be reported with 4015F. [a, b]Refer to complete description of measure developer's Web site for list of medications, treatment recommendations, dosages	4015F **Denominator Codes:** 1038F 1039F	Persist asthma medicine ctrl Persistent asthma Intermittent asthma
Chronic Obstructive Pulmonary Disease (COPD)		
Smoking Assessment[1]—Whether or not patient with COPD was queried about smoking **Numerator:** All patients who were queried about smoking during one or more office visits each year **Denominator:** All patients with the diagnosis of COPD **Percentage** of patients who were queried about smoking at least annually **Reporting Instructions:** When reporting 1000F, it is required to report 1034F, and/or 1035F, or 1036F	1000F 1034F 1035F 1036F	Tobacco use assessed Current tobacco smoker Smokeless tobacco user Tobacco non-user
Assessment of Symptoms[1]—Whether or not patient had COPD symptoms assessed at least annually **Numerator:** All patients with COPD symptoms assessed during one or more office visits each year **Denominator:** All patients with the diagnosis of COPD **Percentage** of patients who were assessed for COPD symptoms at least annually	1015F	COPD symptoms assess

[1]Physician Consortium for Performance Improvement: www.physicianconsortium.org
[2]National Committee on Quality Assurance (NCQA): Health Employer Data Information Set (HEDIS®): www.ncqa.org
[3]Joint Commission on Accreditation of Healthcare Organizations (JCAHO), ORYX Initiative Performance Measures: www.jcaho.org/pms
[4]National Diabetes Quality Improvement Alliance (NDQIA): www.nationaldiabetesalliance.org

Brief Description of Performance Measure & Source and Reporting Instructions	CPT Code(s)	Short Code Descriptor
Chronic Obstructive Pulmonary Disease (COPD), cont'd		
Spirometry Evaluation[1]—Whether or not patient spirometry results were documented **Numerator:** All patients with documented spirometry results on the medical record **Denominator:** All patients with the diagnosis of COPD **Exclusion Criteria:** Documentation of medical reason(s) for no spirometry evaluation OR Documentation of patient reason(s) for no spirometry evaluation Documentation of system reason(s) for no spirometry evaluation **Percentage** of patients with COPD who had a spirometry evaluation documented **Reporting Instructions:** For patients with appropriate exclusion criteria, report 3023F with modifier 1P, 2P, or 3P	**3023F**	Spirom doc rev
Smoking Cessation Intervention[1]—Whether or not the patient who is a smoker received a smoking cessation intervention **Numerator:** All smokers who received a smoking cessation intervention during one or more office visits each year **Denominator:** All patients with the diagnosis of COPD identified as smokers **Percentage** of smokers with COPD who received a smoking cessation intervention at least annually **Reporting Instructions:** Report 1034F for each cigarette smoker. Report either 1034F, 1035F, or 1036 for each patient. If patient is a smoker and received cessation intervention, report 4000F or 4001F, or both. Report 4000F or 4001F only if 1034F has been reported	**4000F** **4001F** **Denominator codes:** **1034F** **1035F** **1036F**	Tobacco use txmnt, counseling Tobacco use txmnt, pharmacol Current tobacco smoker Smokeless tobacco user Tobacco non-user
Inhaled Bronchodilator[1]—Whether or not the symptomatic patient was prescribed an inhaled bronchodilator **Numerator:** All symptomatic patients who were prescribed an inhaled bronchodilator **Denominator:** All patients with the diagnosis of COPD who have an $FEV_1/FVC < 70$ % and have symptoms **Denominator Inclusions:** Documentation of COPD symptoms; Documentation of $FEV_1/FVC < 70\%$ **Denominator Exclusions:** Documentation of medical reason(s) for not prescribing an inhaled bronchodilator or Documentation of patient reason(s) for not prescribing an inhaled bronchodilator or Documentation of system reason(s) for not prescribing an inhaled bronchodilator **Percentage** of symptomatic patients with COPD who were prescribed an inhaled bronchodilator **Reporting Instructions:** Report either 3025F or 3027F for all COPD patients. For patients with appropriate exclusion criteria, report 4025F with modifier 1P, 2P, or 3P	**4025F** **Denominator codes:** **3025F** **3027F**	Inhaled bronchodilator RX Spirom FEV/FVC<70% w COPD Spirom FEV/FVC≥70%/ w/o COPD
Assessment of Oxygen Saturation[1]—Whether or not oxygen saturation was assessed at least annually **Numerator:** All patients with oxygen saturation assessed and documented **Denominator:** All patients with the diagnosis of COPD and a FEV_1 40% of predicted value **Denominator Inclusion:** Documentation of $FEV_1 < 40\%$ of predicted value **Denominator Exclusions:** Documentation of medical reason(s) for not assessing oxygen saturation Documentation of patient reason(s) for not assessing oxygen saturation Documentation of systems reason(s) for not assessing oxygen saturation **Percentage** of COPD patients with oxygen saturation assessed at least annually **Reporting Instructions:** Report 3040F or 3042F for all COPD patients. If oxygen saturation assessed, also report 3028F. For patients with appropriate exclusion criteria, report 3028F with modifier 1P, 2P, or 3P	**3028F** **Denominator codes:** **3040F** **3042F**	O_2 saturation doc rev FEV<40% predicted value FEV≥ 40% predicted value

[1]Physician Consortium for Performance Improvement: www.physicianconsortium.org

[2]National Committee on Quality Assurance (NCQA): Health Employer Data Information Set (HEDIS®): www.ncqa.org

[3]Joint Commission on Accreditation of Healthcare Organizations (JCAHO), ORYX Initiative Performance Measures: www.jcaho.org/pms

[4]National Diabetes Quality Improvement Alliance (NDQIA): www.nationaldiabetesalliance.org

Brief Description of Performance Measure & Source and Reporting Instructions	CPT Code(s)	Short Code Descriptor
Chronic Obstructive Pulmonary Disease (COPD), cont'd		
Long-Term Oxygen Therapy[1]—Whether or not patient with COPD was prescribed long-term oxygen therapy **Numerator:** All patients who were prescribed long term oxygen therapy **Denominator:** All patients with a diagnosis of COPD and an oxygen saturation ≤ 88 % or a PaO_2 ≤ 55 mm Hg **Denominator Inclusion:** PaO_2 ≤ 55 mm Hg or oxygen saturation ≤ 88% **Denominator Exclusion:** Documentation of medical reason(s) for not prescribing long term oxygen therapy. Documentation of patient reason(s) for not prescribing long term oxygen therapy Documentation of system reason(s) for not prescribing long term oxygen therapy **Percentage** of patients with COPD that were prescribed long term oxygen therapy **Reporting Instructions:** Report 3035F or 3037F for all COPD patients. Report 4030F with 3035F if long term oxygen therapy prescribed For patients with appropriate exclusion criteria, report 4030F with modifier 1P, 2P, or 3P	4030F **Denominator codes:** 3035F 3037F	Oxygen therapy RX O_2 saturation ≤88% /PAO ≤55 O_2 saturation> 88% /PAO>55
Recommendation of Influenza Immunization[1]—Whether or not COPD patient received recommendation for influenza immunization annually **Numerator:** All patients who were recommended to receive an influenza immunization during one or more office visits every year **Denominator:** All patients with the diagnosis of COPD **Denominator Exclusion:** Documentation of immunization given during the current flu season; documentation of medical reason(s) for not recommending an influenza immunization; documentation of system reason(s) for not recommending an influenza immunization **Percentage** of patients with COPD who were recommended to receive an influenza immunization annually **Reporting Instructions:** Report only one code (4035F) for immunization recommended **or** immunization ordered or administrated (4037F) For patients with appropriate exclusion criteria, report 4035F with modifier 1P or 3P	4035F 4037F **Category I Codes:** 90656 90658 90660	Influenza imm rec Influenza imm order/admin Flu vaccine no preserv 3 & > Flu vaccine age 3 & over, im Flu vaccine, nasal
Influenza Immunization Administered[1]—Whether or not influenza immunization was received during a current flu season **Numerator:** All patients who are administered an influenza immunization during the visit or who have already received an influenza immunization during the current flu season **Denominator:** All patients with the diagnosis of COPD **Denominator Inclusion:** Documentation of visit during flu season **Denominator Exclusion:** Documentation that patient is planning to receive influenza immunization during current flu season; documentation of medical reason(s) for not administering the influenza immunization; documentation of patient reason(s) for not administering the influenza immunization; documentation of system reason(s) for not administering the influenza immunization **Percentage** of patients who received influenza immunization during the current flu season **Reporting Instructions:** Use 4037F with appropriate exclusion criteria (medical, patient, or system use 4037F with modifier 1P, 2P, or 3P) If patient planning to receive immunization use 1P modifier with order code (4037F) Report only one code	4037F **Category I Codes:** 90656 90658 90660	influenza imm order/admin Flu vaccine no preserv 3 & > Flu vaccine age 3 & over, im Flu vaccine, nasal
Assessment of Pneumococcus Immunization Status[1]—Whether or not pneumococcus immunization status was assessed **Numerator:** All patients who were assessed for pneumococcus immunization status **Denominator:** All patients with the diagnosis of COPD (continued)	1022F	Pneunmo imm status assess

[1]Physician Consortium for Performance Improvement: www.physicianconsortium.org
[2]National Committee on Quality Assurance (NCQA): Health Employer Data Information Set (HEDIS®): www.ncqa.org
[3]Joint Commission on Accreditation of Healthcare Organizations (JCAHO), ORYX Initiative Performance Measures: www.jcaho.org/pms
[4]National Diabetes Quality Improvement Alliance (NDQIA): www.nationaldiabetesalliance.org

Brief Description of Performance Measure & Source and Reporting Instructions	CPT Code(s)	Short Code Descriptor
Chronic Obstructive Pulmonary Disease (COPD), cont'd		
Denominator Exclusion: Documentation of medical reason(s) for not recommending pneumococcus immunization Documentation of patient reason(s) for not recommending pneumococcus immunization Documentation of system reason(s) for not recommending pneumococcus immunization **Percentage** of patients with COPD that were assessed for pneumococcus immunization status **Reporting Instructions:** For patients with appropriate exclusion criteria documented for not assessing pneumococcus immunization status, report 1022F with modifier 1P, 2P, or 3P		
Pneumococcus Immunization Administered[1]—Whether or not the patient was administered a pneumococcus immunization during a visit or had already received a pneumococcus immunization **Numerator:** All patients who are administered a pneumococcus immunization during a visit or who have already received a pneumococcus immunization status **Denominator:** All patients with the diagnosis of COPD **Denominator Exclusions:** Pneumococcus immunization recommended but not administered; documentation of medical reason(s) for not administering the pneumococcus immunization; documentation of patient reason(s) for not administering the pneumococcus immunization; documentation of system reason(s) for not administering the pneumococcus immunization **Percentage** of patients who were administered a pneumococcus immunization during a visit or who had already received a pneumococcus immunization **Reporting Instructions:** Report only one code for ordered or administered For patients with appropriate exclusion criteria, report 4040F with modifier 1P, 2P, or 3P If patient planning to receive immunization use 1P modifier with order code (4040F). Report only one code	**4040F** **Category I Codes:** **90669** **90732**	Pneumoc imm order/admin Pneumococcal vacc, ped <5 Pneumococcal vaccine
Pulmonary Rehabilitation: Exercise Training Recommended[1]—Whether or not patient exercise training was recommended **Numerator:** All patients for whom exercise training was recommended **Denominator:** All patients with the diagnosis of COPD and dyspnea **Denominator Inclusion:** Documentation of dyspnea (1019F) **Denominator Exclusion:** Documentation of medical reason(s) for not recommending exercise training Documentation of system reason(s) for not recommending exercise training **Percentage** of patients for whom exercise training was recommended **Reporting Instructions:** Report 1018F or 1019F for all COPD patients For patients with appropriate exclusion criteria, report 4033F with modifier 1P or 3P. Report 4033F with 1019F	**4033F** **Denominator Codes:** **1018F** **1019F**	Pulmonary rehab rec Assess dyspnea not present Assess dyspnea present
Community-Acquired Bacterial Pneumonia (CAP)		
Chest Radiograph[1]—Whether or not patient had a chest x-ray performed **Numerator:** All patients with a chest x-ray performed **Denominator:** All patients with the diagnosis of community-acquired bacterial pneumonia **Denominator Exclusion:** Documentation of medical reason(s) for not performing a chest x-ray; documentation of patient reason(s) for not performing a chest x-ray (eg, economic, social, religious, other patient reasons); documentation of system reason(s) for not performing a chest x-ray (eg, chest x-ray equipment not accessible) (continued)	**3006F**	Cxr doc rev

[1]Physician Consortium for Performance Improvement: www.physicianconsortium.org

[2]National Committee on Quality Assurance (NCQA): Health Employer Data Information Set (HEDIS®): www.ncqa.org

[3]Joint Commission on Accreditation of Healthcare Organizations (JCAHO), ORYX Initiative Performance Measures: www.jcaho.org/pms

[4]National Diabetes Quality Improvement Alliance (NDQIA): www.nationaldiabetesalliance.org

Brief Description of Performance Measure & Source and Reporting Instructions	CPT Code(s)	Short Code Descriptor
Community-Acquired Bacterial Pneumonia (CAP), cont'd		
Percentage of community-acquired bacterial pneumonia patients ≥ 18 years of age with a chest x-ray performed **Reporting Instructions:** For patients with appropriate exclusion criteria, report 3006F with modifier 1P, 2P, or 3P		
Composite Code: Community-Acquired Bacterial Pneumonia Assessment— See individual measures listed below for (includes all of the following components): Co-morbid conditions assessed (1026F) Vital signs recorded (2010F) Mental status assessed (2014F) Hydration status assessed (2018F)	0012F	Cap bacterial assess
Assessment of Comorbid Conditions[1]—Whether or not patient was assessed for comorbid conditions **Numerator:** All patients assessed for history of comorbid conditions **Denominator:** All patients with the diagnosis of community-acquired bacterial pneumonia **Percentage** of patients ≥ 18 years of age with community-acquired bacterial pneumonia who were assessed for comorbid conditions	1026F	Co-morbid condition assess
Vital Signs[1]—Whether or not patient had vital signs recorded **Numerator:** All patients with vital signs recorded **Denominator:** All patients with the diagnosis of community-acquired bacterial pneumonia **Percentage** of community-acquired bacterial pneumonia patients ≥ 18 years of age with vital signs recorded	2010F	Vital signs recorded
Assessment of Oxygen Saturation[1]—Whether or not patient had oxygen saturation assessed **Numerator:** All patients with oxygen saturation assessed **Denominator:** All patients with the diagnosis of community-acquired bacterial pneumonia **Exclusion Criteria:** Documentation of medical reason(s) for not assessing oxygen saturation; documentation of patient reason(s) for not assessing oxygen saturation (eg, economic, social, religious, other patient reasons); documentation of system reason(s) for not assessing oxygen saturation (eg, oxygen saturation equipment not available) **Percentage** of patients ≥ 18 years of age with community-acquired bacterial pneumonia with oxygen saturation assessed **Reporting Instructions:** For patients with appropriate exclusion criteria, report 3028F with modifier 1P, 2P, or 3P	3028F	O_2 saturation doc rev
Assessment of Mental Status[1]—Whether or not patient had mental status assessed **Numerator:** All patients with mental status assessed **Denominator:** All patients with the diagnosis of community-acquired bacterial pneumonia **Percentage** of community-acquired bacterial pneumonia patients age ≥ 18 years of age with mental status assessed	2014F	Mental status assess
Assessment of Hydration Status[1]—Whether or not the patient had hydration status assessed **Numerator:** All patients with hydration status assessed **Denominator:** All patients with the diagnosis of community-acquired bacterial pneumonia **Percentage** of community-acquired bacterial pneumonia patients age ≥ 18 years of age with hydration status assessed	2018F	Hydration status assessed

[1]Physician Consortium for Performance Improvement: www.physicianconsortium.org
[2]National Committee on Quality Assurance (NCQA): Health Employer Data Information Set (HEDIS®): www.ncqa.org
[3]Joint Commission on Accreditation of Healthcare Organizations (JCAHO), ORYX Initiative Performance Measures: www.jcaho.org/pms
[4]National Diabetes Quality Improvement Alliance (NDQIA): www.nationaldiabetesalliance.org

Brief Description of Performance Measure & Source and Reporting Instructions	CPT Code(s)	Short Code Descriptor
Community-Acquired Bacterial Pneumonia (CAP), cont'd		
Level of Care Rationale[1]—Whether or not an assessment was made to determine the level of care **Numerator:** All patients with documented rationale for level of care **Denominator:** All patients with the diagnosis of community-acquired bacterial pneumonia **Percentage** of community-acquired bacterial pneumonia patients ≥ 18 years of age who had a documented rationale for level of care based on severity of illness and safety of home care	**6005F**	Care level rationale doc
Empiric Antibiotic[1]—Whether or not patient was prescribed an appropriate empiric antibiotic **Numerator:** All patients with an appropriate empiric antibiotic prescribed **Denominator:** All patients with the diagnosis of community-acquired bacterial pneumonia **Denominator Exclusion:** Documentation of medical reason(s) for not prescribing an antibiotic (eg, allergy, drug interaction, contraindication, other medical reasons); documentation of patient reasons(s) for not prescribing an antibiotic (eg, economic, social, religious, other patient reasons); documentation of system reasons(s) for not prescribing an antibiotic **Percentage** of community-acquired bacterial pneumonia patients ≥ 18 years of age who were prescribed an appropriate empiric antibiotic **Reporting Instructions:** For patients with appropriate exclusion criteria, report 4045F with modifier 1P, 2P, or 3P	**4045F**	Empiric antibiotic RX (See measure developer's Web site for definition of appropriate antibiotic)
Smoking Assessment[1]—Whether or not patient was queried about smoking **Numerator:** All patients who were queried about smoking **Denominator:** All patients with the diagnosis of community-acquired bacterial pneumonia **Percentage** of patients with community-acquired bacterial pneumonia who were queried about smoking **Reporting Instructions:** When reporting 1000F, it is required to report 1034F, and/or 1035F, or 1036F	**1000F** **1034F** **1035F** **1036F**	Tobacco use assessed Current tobacco smoker Smokeless tobacco user Tobacco non-user
Smoking Cessation Intervention[1]—Whether or not patient received a smoking cessation intervention **Numerator:** All patients who received a smoking cessation intervention **Denominator:** All patients with the diagnosis with community-acquired bacterial pneumonia identified as smokers **Percentage** of patients ≥ 18 years of age with community-acquired bacterial pneumonia who received a smoking cessation intervention **Reporting Instructions:** Report 1034F for each cigarette smoker. Report either 1034F, 1035F, or 1036F for each patient. If patient is a smoker and received cessation intervention, report 4000F or 4001F, or both. Report 4000F or 4001F only if 1034F has been reported	**4000F** **4001F** **Denominator Codes:** **1034F** **1035F** **1036F**	Tobacco use txmnt counseling Tobacco use txmnt pharmacol Current tobacco smoker Smokeless tobacco user Tobacco non-user
Assessment of Influenza Immunization Status[1,2]—Whether or not patient was assessed for influenza immunization status **Numerator:** All patients who were assessed for influenza immunization status **Denominator:** All patients with the diagnosis of community-acquired bacterial pneumonia **Denominator Exclusion:** Documentation of medical, patient or system reason that immunization was not indicated **Percentage** of patients age ≥ 18 years of age with community-acquired bacterial pneumonia who were assessed for influenza immunization status **Reporting Instructions:** Use 1030F if documentation shows that influenza vaccine was administered. For patients with appropriate occlusion criteria, report 1030F with modifier 1P, 2P, or 3P	**1030F**	Influenza immunization status assessed

[1]Physician Consortium for Performance Improvement: www.physicianconsortium.org
[2]National Committee on Quality Assurance (NCQA): Health Employer Data Information Set (HEDIS®): www.ncqa.org
[3]Joint Commission on Accreditation of Healthcare Organizations (JCAHO), ORYX Initiative Performance Measures: www.jcaho.org/pms
[4]National Diabetes Quality Improvement Alliance (NDQIA): www.nationaldiabetesalliance.org

Brief Description of Performance Measure & Source and Reporting Instructions	CPT Code(s)	Short Code Descriptor
Community-Acquired Bacterial Pneumonia (CAP), cont'd		
Assessment of Pneumococcus Immunization Status[1,2]—Whether or not patient was assessed for pneumococcus immunization status **Numerator:** All patients who were assessed for pneumococcus immunization status **Denominator:** All patients with the diagnosis of community-acquired bacterial pneumonia **Denominator exclusion:** Documentation that immunization was not indicated; documentation of medical, patient, or system reason that immunization was not indicated **Percentage** of patients ≥ 18 years of age with community-acquired bacterial pneumonia who were assessed for pneumococcus immunization status **Reporting Instructions:** Use 1022F if documentation shows that pneumococcus vaccine was administered. For patient with appropriate exclusion criteria report 1022F with modifier 1P, 2P, or 3P	1022F	Pneumo imm status assess
Coronary Artery Disease (CAD)		
Smoking Cessation Evaluation[1]—Whether or not patient with CAD was queried one or more times about cigarette smoking **Numerator:** Patients who were queried one or more times about cigarette smoking **Denominator:** All patients with CAD **Percentage** of patients who were queried one or more times about cigarette smoking **Reporting Instructions:** When reporting 1000F, it is required to report 1034F, and/or 1035F, or 1036F	1000F 1034F 1035F 1036F	Tobacco use assessed Current tobacco smoker Smokeless tobacco user Tobacco non-user
Smoking Cessation Intervention[1]—Whether or not patient identified as a cigarette smoker received intervention for smoking cessation **Numerator:** Patients who were received smoking cessation intervention **Denominator:** All patients with CAD identified as cigarette smokers **Percentage** of patients identified as cigarette smokers who received intervention for smoking cessation **Reporting Instructions:** Report 1034F for each cigarette smoker. Report either 1034F, 1035F, or 1036F for each patient. If patient is a smoker and received cessation intervention, report 4000F or 4001F, or both. Report 4000F or 4001F only if 1034F has been reported	4000F 4001F **Denominator Codes:** 1034F 1035F 1036F	Tobacco use txmnt counseling Tobacco use txmnt pharmacol Current tobacco smoker Smokeless tobacco user Tobacco non-user
Symptom & Activity Assessment[1]—Whether or not patient's level of activity and anginal symptoms were evaluated during office visit **Numerator:** Patients evaluated for both level of activity and anginal symptoms during one or more office visits **Denominator:** All patients with CAD **Percentage** of patients who were evaluated for both level of activity and anginal symptoms during one or more office visits	1002F	Assess anginal symptom/level
Blood Pressure Measurement[1]—Most recent systolic and diastolic blood pressure measurement **Numerator:** Patients who had a blood pressure measurement during the last office visit **Denominator:** All patients with CAD **Percentage** of patients who had a blood pressure measurement during the last office visit	2000F	Blood pressure measured
Lipid Profile[1]—Whether or not a lipid profile was obtained **Numerator:** Patients who received at least one lipid profile (or ALL component tests) **Denominator:** All patients with CAD **Percentage** of patients who received at least one lipid profile (or ALL component tests)	3011F	Lipid panel doc rev

[1]Physician Consortium for Performance Improvement: www.physicianconsortium.org
[2]National Committee on Quality Assurance (NCQA): Health Employer Data Information Set (HEDIS®): www.ncqa.org
[3]Joint Commission on Accreditation of Healthcare Organizations (JCAHO), ORYX Initiative Performance Measures: www.jcaho.org/pms
[4]National Diabetes Quality Improvement Alliance (NDQIA): www.nationaldiabetesalliance.org

Brief Description of Performance Measure & Source and Reporting Instructions	CPT Code(s)	Short Code Descriptor
Coronary Artery Disease (CAD), cont'd		
Drug Therapy for Lowering LDL-Cholesterol[1]—Whether or not patient was prescribed lipid-lowering therapy **Numerator:** Patients who were prescribed lipid-lowering therapy **Denominator:** All patients with CAD **Denominator Exclusion(s):** Documentation of medical, patient, or system reason(s) for not prescribing lipid-lowering therapy **Percentage** of patients who were prescribed a lipid-lowering therapy (based on current ACC/AHA guidelines) **Reporting Instructions:** For patients with appropriate exclusion criteria, report code 4002F with modifier 1P, 2P, or 3P	**4002F**	Statin therapy RX
Beta-blocker Therapy—Prior Myocardial Infarction (MI)[1]—Whether or not CAD patient with prior MI at any time was prescribed beta-blocker therapy **Numerator:** Patients who were prescribed beta-blocker therapy **Denominator:** All patients with CAD who also have a prior MI at any time **Denominator Exclusion(s):** Documentation of medical, patient or system reason(s) for not prescribing beta-blocker therapy **Percentage** of CAD patients who also have prior MI at any time who were prescribed beta-blocker therapy **Reporting Instructions:** For patients with appropriate exclusion criteria, report code 4006F with modifier 1P, 2P, or 3P	**4006F**	Beta-blocker therapy RX
Angiotensin Converting Enzyme (ACE) Inhibitor or Angiotensin Receptor Blocker (ARB) Therapy[1]—Whether or not CAD patient with diabetes and/or left ventricular systolic dysfunction (LVSD) was prescribed ACE inhibitor or ARB therapy **Numerator:** Patients who were prescribed ACE inhibitor or ARB therapy **Denominator:** All CAD patients aged ≥ 18 years of age with diabetes and/or left ventricular ejection fraction (LVEF) < 40% or moderately or severely depressed left ventricular systolic function **Exclusion Criteria:** Documentation of medical reason for not prescribing ACE or ARB therapy (eg contraindication); documentation of patient reason(s) for not prescribing ACE or ARB therapy (eg economic, social or religious); documentation of system reason for not prescribing ACE or ARB therapy **Percentage** of CAD patients who also have diabetes and/or left ventricular systolic dysfunction (LVSD) who were prescribed ACE inhibitor or ARB therapy **Reporting Instructions:** Report either 3021F or 3022F or corresponding ICD-9 diagnosis code for diabetes for each CAD patient. For patient with appropriate exclusion criteria, report 4009F with modifier 1P, 2P, or 3P	**4009F** **Denominator Codes:** **3021F** **3022F**	ACE/ARB inhibitor therapy RX Lvef mod/sever deprs syst Lvef ≥40% systolic
Antiplatelet Therapy[1]—Whether or not patient was prescribed antiplatelet therapy **Numerator:** Patients who were prescribed antiplatelet therapy **Denominator:** All patients with CAD **Denominator Exclusion(s):** Documentation of medical reason(s) for not prescribing antiplatelet therapy; documentation of patient reason(s) for not prescribing antiplatelet therapy; documentation of system reason(s) for not prescribing antiplatelet therapy **Percentage** of patients who were prescribed antiplatelet therapy **Reporting Instructions:** For patients with appropriate exclusion criteria, report code 4011F with modifier 1P, 2P, or 3P	**4011F**	Oral antiplatelet therapy RX

[1]Physician Consortium for Performance Improvement: www.physicianconsortium.org

[2]National Committee on Quality Assurance (NCQA): Health Employer Data Information Set (HEDIS®): www.ncqa.org

[3]Joint Commission on Accreditation of Healthcare Organizations (JCAHO), ORYX Initiative Performance Measures: www.jcaho.org/pms

[4]National Diabetes Quality Improvement Alliance (NDQIA): www.nationaldiabetesalliance.org

Brief Description of Performance Measure & Source and Reporting Instructions	CPT Code(s)	Short Code Descriptor
Diabetes (DM)		
A1c Management[4]—Whether or not patient received one or more A1c test(s) **Numerator:** Patients who received one or more A1c test(s) **Denominator:** Patients with diagnosed diabetes 18-75 years of age **Percentage** of patients with diagnosed diabetes aged 18-75 years with one or more A1c test(s) **Reporting Instructions:** In order to meet this measure, the date of test when it was performed and the corresponding result are required. For this reason, report one of the two Category II codes listed and use the date of service as the date of the test, not the date of the reporting of the Category II code. The measure may also be met by reporting the Category I code, 83036 Hemoglobin; by copper sulfate method, non-automated, glycated, when performed	3046F 3047F **Category I Codes:** 83036	Hemoglobin A1C level > 9.0% Hemoglobin A1C level ≤ 9.0% Glycosylated hemoglobin test
A1c Management[4]—Whether or not patient's most recent A1c level > 9.0% (poor control) **Numerator:** Patients with most recent A1c level > 9.0% (poor control) **Denominator:** Patients diagnosed with diabetes 18-75 years of age **Percentage** of patients with most recent A1c level > 9.0% (poor control) **Reporting Instructions:** In order to meet this measure, the date of test when it was performed and the corresponding result are required. For this reason, report one of the two Category II codes listed and use the date of service as the date of the test, not the date of the reporting of the Category II code	3046F 3047F	Hemoglobin A1C level > 9.0% Hemoglobin A1C level ≤ 9.0%
Lipid Management[4]—Whether or not patient received at least one LDL-C test **Numerator:** Patients who received at least one LDL-C test **Denominator:** Patients diagnosed with diabetes 18-75 years of age **Percentage** of patients diagnosed with diabetes aged 18-75 years with at least one LDL-C test **Reporting Instructions:** In order to meet this measure, the date of test when it was performed and the corresponding result are required. For this reason, report one of the three Category II codes listed and use the date of service as the date of the test, not the date of the reporting of the Category II code. The measure may also be met by reporting the listed lipid test Category I codes, when performed	3048F 3049F 3050F **Category I Codes:** 80061 82465 83700 83701 83704 83721	LDL-C <100 MG/DL LDL-C 100-129 MG/DL LDL-C ≥ 130 MG/DL Lipid panel Assay, bld/serum cholesterol Lipopro bld, electrophoretic Lipoprotein bld, by hr fraction Lipoprotein bld, by nmr Assay of blood lipoprotein
Lipid Management[4]—Whether or not patient's most recent LDL-C < 130 mg/dL **Numerator:** Patients with most recent LDL-C < 130 mg/dL **Denominator:** Patients diagnosed with diabetes aged 18-75 years **Percentage** of patients diagnosed with diabetes aged 18-75 years with most recent LDL-C < 130 mg/dL **Reporting Instructions:** In order to meet this measure, the date of test when it was performed and the corresponding result are required. For this reason, report one of the three Category II codes listed and use the date of service as the date of the test, not the date of the reporting of the Category II code	3048F 3049F 3050F	LDL-C <100 MG/DL LDL-C 100-129 MG/DL LDL-C ≥ 130 MG/DL 130 mg/dL

[1]Physician Consortium for Performance Improvement: www.physicianconsortium.org
[2]National Committee on Quality Assurance (NCQA): Health Employer Data Information Set (HEDIS®): www.ncqa.org
[3]Joint Commission on Accreditation of Healthcare Organizations (JCAHO), ORYX Initiative Performance Measures: www.jcaho.org/pms
[4]National Diabetes Quality Improvement Alliance (NDQIA): www.nationaldiabetesalliance.org

Brief Description of Performance Measure & Source and Reporting Instructions	CPT Code(s)	Short Code Descriptor
Diabetes (DM), cont'd		
Lipid Management[4]—Whether or not patient's most recent LDL-C < 100 mg/dL **Numerator:** Patients whose most recent LDL-C is < 100 mg/dL **Denominator:** Patients diagnosed with diabetes 18-75 years of age **Percentage** of patients diagnosed with diabetes 18-75 years of age whose most recent LDL-C < 100 mg/dL **Reporting Instructions:** In order to meet this measure, the date of test when it was performed and the corresponding result are required. For this reason, report one of the three Category II codes listed and use the date of service as the date of the test, not the date of the reporting of the Category II code	3048F 3049F 3050F	LDL-C <100 MG/DL LDL-C 100-129 MG/DL LDL-C ≥ 130 MG/DL
Urine Protein Screening[4]—Whether or not a patient received at least one test for microalbumin during the measurement year **or** had evidence of medical attention for existing nephropathy **or** has documentation of microalbuminuria or albuminuria **or** is on an angiotensin converting enzyme (ACE) inhibitor or angiotensin receptor blocker (ARB) **Numerator:** Patients with at least one test for microalbumin during the measurement year; or who had evidence of medical attention for existing nephropathy or documentation of microalbuminuria or albuminuria or are on an ACE inhibitor or ARB therapy **Denominator:** Patients diagnosed with diabetes 18-75 years of age **Percentage** of patients diagnosed with diabetes 18-75 years of age with at least one test for microalbumin during the measurement year; or who had evidence of medical attention for existing nephropathy or documentation of microalbuminuria or albuminuria or are on an ACE inhibitor or ARB therapy **Reporting Instructions:** Report any one of the codes listed using the following: 1. Codes 3060F, 3061F, and 3062F may be used to indicate that a patient received at least one test for microalbuminuria 2. Code 3066F may be used if there is evidence of nephropathy **or** if there was a patient visit to a nephrologist 3. Code 3062F may be used to indicate that a patient had documentation of microalbuminuria or albuminuria 4. Code 4009F may be used if patient is on an ACE inhibitor or ARB therapy 5. Any CPT Category I code and corresponding result, when performed, and reported with any of the following ICD-9-CM diagnosis or procedure codes found in specifications: ICD-9-CM codes: 39.27, 39.42, 39.43, 39.53, 39.93-39.95, 54.98, 55.4-55.6, 250.4, 403, 404, 405.01, 405.11, 405.91, 581.81, 582.9, 583.81, 584-586, 588, 753.0, 753.1, 791.0; V codes: V42.0, V45.1, V56 6. CPT Category I codes for microalbumin measurement or quantitative timed urine albumin measurement and corresponding result as follows: 82042, 82043, 82044, 83518, 84156 or (84160, 84165, 84166) with code 81050	3060F 3061F 3062F 3066F 4009F **Category I Codes:** 82042, 82043, 82044, 83518, 84156, 84160, 84165, 84166, 81050, 90920, 90921, 90924, 90925, 90935, 90937, 90945, 90947, 90989, 90993, 90999	Pos microalbuminuria rev Neg microalbuminuria rev Pos macroalbuminuria rev Nephropathy doc tx ACE/ARB inhibitor therapy RX
Eye Examination[4]—Whether or not patient received a dilated eye exam or seven standard field stereoscopic photos with interpretation by an ophthalmologist or optometrist or imaging validated to match diagnosis from these photos during the reporting year or during the prior year if the patient is at low risk* for retinopathy **Numerator:** Patients who received a dilated eye exam or seven standard field stereoscopic photos with interpretation by an ophthalmologist or optometrist or imaging validated to match diagnosis from these photos during the reporting year, or during the prior year, if patient is at low risk* for retinopathy *A patient is considered low risk if the following criterion is met: has no evidence of retinopathy on one of the accepted examinations in the prior year (continued)	2022F 2024F 2026F 3072F **Category I Codes:** 99201	Dil retina exam interp rev 7 field photo interp doc rev Eye image valid to dx rev OR Low risk for retinopathy Office/outpatient visit, new

[1]Physician Consortium for Performance Improvement: www.physicianconsortium.org
[2]National Committee on Quality Assurance (NCQA): Health Employer Data Information Set (HEDIS®): www.ncqa.org
[3]Joint Commission on Accreditation of Healthcare Organizations (JCAHO), ORYX Initiative Performance Measures: www.jcaho.org/pms
[4]National Diabetes Quality Improvement Alliance (NDQIA): www.nationaldiabetesalliance.org

Brief Description of Performance Measure & Source and Reporting Instructions	CPT Code(s)	Short Code Descriptor
Diabetes (DM), cont'd		
Denominator: Patients with diagnosed diabetes 18-75 years of age; Low risk patient (defined as a patient who had no evidence of retinopathy in the prior year) must have had an evaluation in the prior year **Percentage** of patients who received a dilated eye exam or seven standard field stereoscopic photos with interpretation by an ophthalmologist or optometrist or imaging validated to match diagnosis from these photos during the reporting year **Reporting Instructions:** Only one of these codes should be reported	99212 99241 92002 92004 92012 92014 92225 92226	Office/outpatient visit Office consultation Eye exam, new patient Eye exam, new patient Eye exam, established pat Eye exam & treatment Special eye exam, initial Special eye exam, subsequent
Foot Examination[4]—Whether or not patient received at least one foot exam, defined in any manner **Numerator:** Patients who received at least one foot exam, defined in any manner **Denominator:** Patients diagnosed with diabetes 18-75 years of age **Denominator Exclusions:** Patients with bilateral foot/leg amputation **Percentage** of patients diagnosed with diabetes 18-75 years of age receiving at least one foot exam, defined in any manner **Reporting Instructions:** Report 2028F with modifier 1P for patients with bilateral foot/leg amputation	2028F	Foot exam performed
Blood Pressure Management[4]—Whether or not patient's most recent blood pressure is < 140/80 mm Hg **Numerator:** Patients in whose most recent blood pressure < 140/80 mm Hg **Denominator:** Patients diagnosed with diabetes 18-75 years of age **Percentage** of patients diagnosed with diabetes 18-75 years of age with most recent blood pressure < 140/80 mm Hg **Reporting Instructions:** Two codes must be reported here. For the systolic blood pressure value, report one of the two systolic codes; for the diastolic blood pressure value, report one of the three diastolic codes	**Systolic Codes:** 3076F 3077F **Diastolic Codes:** 3078F 3079F 3080F	 Syst BP < 140 MM HG Syst BP ≥ 140 MM HG6 it Diast BP < 80 MM HG Diast BP 80-89 MM HG Diast BP ≥ 90 MM HG
Smoking Cessation[4]—Whether or not patient's smoking status was ascertained and documented **Numerator:** Patients whose smoking status was ascertained and documented **Denominator:** Patients diagnosed with diabetes 18-75 years of age **Percentage** of patients diagnosed with diabetes 18-75 years of age whose smoking status was ascertained and documented **Reporting Instructions:** Report 1034F for each cigarette smoker. Report either 1034F, 1035F, or 1036F for each patient. If patient is a smoker and received cessation intervention, report 4000F or 4001F, or both. Report 4000F or 4001F only if 1034F has been reported	4000F 4001F **Denominator Codes:** 1034F 1035F 1036F	Tobacco use txmnt counseling Tobacco use txmnt pharmacol Current tobacco smoker Smokeless tobacco user Tobacco non-user
Heart Failure (HF)		
Composite Code: Heart Failure Assessment[1]—See individual measures listed below for the following: Level of activity assessed (1003F) Clinical symptoms of volume overload (excess) assessed (1004F) Blood pressure measured (2000F) Weight recorded (2001F) Clinical signs of volume overload (excess) assessed (2002F)	0001F	Heart failure composite

[1]Physician Consortium for Performance Improvement: www.physicianconsortium.org

[2]National Committee on Quality Assurance (NCQA): Health Employer Data Information Set (HEDIS®): www.ncqa.org

[3]Joint Commission on Accreditation of Healthcare Organizations (JCAHO), ORYX Initiative Performance Measures: www.jcaho.org/pms

[4]National Diabetes Quality Improvement Alliance (NDQIA): www.nationaldiabetesalliance.org

Brief Description of Performance Measure & Source and Reporting Instructions	CPT Code(s)	Short Code Descriptor
Heart Failure (HF), cont'd		
Assessment of Activity Level[1]—Number of visits with assessment of activity level per number of visits **Numerator:** Patient visits with assessment of current level of activity OR documentation of standardized scale OR completion of assessment tool (May include use of New York Heart Association Functional Classification of Congestive Heart Failure; Kansas City Cardiomyopathy Questionnaire; Minnesota™ Living with Heart Failure Questionnaire; or Guyatt's Chronic Heart Failure Questionnaire) **Denominator:** All patient visits for patients aged ≥ 18 years with heart failure **Percentage** of patient visits with assessment of activity level	1003F	Level of activity assessed
Assessment of Clinical Symptoms of Volume Overload (Excess)[1]—Number of patient visits with assessment of clinical symptoms of volume overload (excess) per number of visits **Numerator:** Patient visits with assessment of clinical *symptoms* of volume overload (excess) Assessment for absence or presence of symptoms of volume overload must include dyspnea, orthopnea, or documentation of standardized scale or completion of assessment tool (may include New York Heart Association Functional Classification of Congestive Heart Failure; Kansas City Cardiomyopathy Questionnaire; Minnesota™ Living with Heart Failure Questionnaire; or Guyatt's Chronic Heart Failure Questionnaire) **Denominator:** All patient visits for patients aged ≥ 18 years with heart failure **Percentage** of patient visits with assessment of clinical symptoms of volume overload (excess)	1004F	Clin symp vol ovrld assessed
Blood Pressure Measurement[1]—Number of visits with blood pressure measurement recorded per number of visits **Numerator:** Patient visits with blood pressure measurement recorded **Denominator:** All patient visits for patients aged ≥ 18 years with HF **Percentage** of patient visits with a blood pressure measurement recorded	2000F	Blood pressure measure
Weight Measurement[1]—Number of visits with weight measurement recorded per number of visits **Numerator:** Patient visits with weight measurement recorded **Denominator:** All patient visits for patients aged ≥ 18 years with heart failure **Percentage** of patient visits with weight measurement recorded	2001F	Weight record
Assessment of Clinical Signs of Volume Overload (Excess)[1]—Number of visits with assessment of clinical *signs* of volume overload (excess) per number of visits **Numerator:** Patient visits with assessment of clinical *signs* of volume overload (excess) Assessment for presence or absence of signs of volume overload must include: peripheral edema OR; Rales OR; Hepatomegaly OR; Ascites OR; Assessment of jugular venous pressure OR; S3 or S4 gallop **Denominator:** All patient visits for patients aged ≥ 18 years with heart failure **Percentage** of patient visits with assessment of clinical signs of volume overload (excess)	2002F	Clin sign vol ovrld assess
Left Ventricular Function (LVF) Assessment[1]—Whether or not patient has quantitative or qualitative results of LVF assessment recorded **Numerator:** Patients with quantitative or qualitative results of LVF assessment recorded **Denominator:** All patients aged ≥ 18 years with heart failure **Percentage** of patients with quantitative or qualitative results of LVF assessment recorded	3020F	Lvf assess
Patient Education[1]—Whether or not patient education was provided **Numerator:** Patients provided with patient education at at one or more visit(s) Patient education should include one or more of the following: weight monitoring; diet (sodium restriction); symptom management; physical activity; smoking cessation; (continued)	4003F	Pt ed write/oral, pts w/hf

[1]Physician Consortium for Performance Improvement: www.physicianconsortium.org
[2]National Committee on Quality Assurance (NCQA): Health Employer Data Information Set (HEDIS®): www.ncqa.org
[3]Joint Commission on Accreditation of Healthcare Organizations (JCAHO), ORYX Initiative Performance Measures: www.jcaho.org/pms
[4]National Diabetes Quality Improvement Alliance (NDQIA): www.nationaldiabetesalliance.org

Brief Description of Performance Measure & Source and Reporting Instructions	CPT Code(s)	Short Code Descriptor
Heart Failure (HF), cont'd		
medication instruction; minimizing or avoiding use of NSAIDs; referral for visiting nurse; referral for specific educational or management programs; or prognosis/end-of-life issues **Denominator:** All patients aged ≥ 18 years with heart failure and with one or more visit(s) **Denominator Inclusion(s):** Patients with one or more visit(s) **Percentage** of heart failure patients who were provided with patient education on disease management and health behavior changes during one or more visit(s)		
Beta-Blocker Therapy[1]—Whether or not HF patient with LVSD was prescribed beta-blocker therapy **Numerator:** Patients who were prescribed beta-blocker therapy **Denominator:** All heart failure patients ≥ 18 years of age with left ventricular ejection fraction (LVEF) <40% or with moderately or severely depressed left ventricular systolic function **Denominator Inclusion(s):** Patients with heart failure and left ventricular systolic dysfunction (LVSD) (LVEF <40% or with moderately or severely depressed left ventricular systolic function) **Denominator Exclusion(s):** Documentation of medical reason(s) for not prescribing beta-blocker therapy (eg, contraindication); documentation of patient reason(s) for not prescribing beta-blocker therapy (eg, economic, social and/or religious); documentation of system reason(s) for not prescribing beta-blocker therapy **Percentage** of heart failure patients with LVSD who were prescribed beta-blocker therapy **Reporting Instructions:** Report either 3021F or 3022F for each heart failure patient. For patient with appropriate exclusion criteria, report 4006F with modifier 1P, 2P, or 3P	4006F **Denominator Codes:** 3021F 3022F	Beta-blocker therapy RX LVEF mod/sever deprs syst LVEF ≥40% systolic
Angiotensin Converting Enzyme (ACE) Inhibitor or Angiotensin Receptor Blocker (ARB) Therapy for Left Ventricular Systolic Dysfunction (LVSD)[1]—Whether or not heart failure patients who also have LVSD were prescribed ACE inhibitor or ARB therapy **Numerator:** Patients who were prescribed ACE inhibitor or ARB therapy **Denominator Inclusion:** All heart failure patients aged ≥ 18 years with left ventricular ejection fraction (LVEF <40% or with moderately or severely depressed left ventricular systolic function) **Denominator Exclusion(s):** Documentation of medical reason(s) for not prescribing ACE inhibitor or ARB therapy; documentation of patient reasons for not prescribing ACE inhibitor or ARB therapy (economic, social or religious); documentation of system reasons for not prescribing ACE inhibitor or ARB therapy **Percentage** of heart failure patients who also have LVSD and who were prescribed ACE or ARB inhibitor **Reporting Instructions:** Report either 3021F or 3022F for each heart failure patient. For patients with appropriate exclusion criteria, report 4009F with modifier 1P, 2P, or 3P	4009F **Denominator Codes:** 3021F 3022F	ACE/ARB inhibitor therapy RX LVEF mod/sever deprs syst LVEF ≥40% systolic
Warfarin Therapy for Patients With Atrial Fibrillation[1]—Whether or not heart failure patient who also has paroxysmal or chronic atrial fibrillation was prescribed warfarin therapy **Numerator:** Patients who were prescribed warfarin therapy **Denominator:** All heart failure patients aged ≥ 18 years with paroxysmal or chronic atrial fibrillation **Denominator Inclusion:** Patients with heart failure and paroxysmal or chronic atrial fibrillation (continued)	4012F	Warfarin therapy RX

[1]Physician Consortium for Performance Improvement: www.physicianconsortium.org
[2]National Committee on Quality Assurance (NCQA): Health Employer Data Information Set (HEDIS®): www.ncqa.org
[3]Joint Commission on Accreditation of Healthcare Organizations (JCAHO), ORYX Initiative Performance Measures: www.jcaho.org/pms
[4]National Diabetes Quality Improvement Alliance (NDQIA): www.nationaldiabetesalliance.org

Brief Description of Performance Measure & Source and Reporting Instructions	CPT Code(s)	Short Code Descriptor
Heart Failure (HF), cont'd		
Denominator Exclusion(s): Documentation of medical reasons(s) for not prescribing warfarin therapy (eg, allergy to warfarin, risk of bleeding or bleeding disorder, compliance, etc); documentation of patient reason(s) (eg, economic, social, and/or religious) for not prescribing warfarin therapy, document of system reason **Percentage** of heart failure patients who also have paroxysmal or chronic atrial fibrillation who were prescribed warfarin therapy **Reporting Instructions:** For patients with appropriate exclusion criteria, report 4012F with modifier 1P, 2P, or 3P		
Heart Failure Discharge Instructions[3] **Numerator:** Heart failure patients in the denominator with documentation that they or their caregivers were given written discharge instructions or other educational material addressing all of the following: activity level, diet, discharge medications, follow-up appointment, weight monitoring, what to do if symptoms worsen **Denominator:** Heart failure patients discharged home **Exclusion(s):** Patients less than 18 years of age **Percentage** of hospitalized heart failure patients in the denominator who received written discharge instructions	4014F	Written discharge instr prvd
Hypertension (HTN)		
Blood Pressure Measurement[1]—Number of visits with blood pressure measurement recorded per number of visits **Numerator:** Patient visits with blood pressure measurement recorded **Denominator:** All patient visits for patients aged ≥ 18 years with hypertension **Percentage** of patient visits with blood pressure recorded for patients aged ≥ 18 years	2000F	Blood pressure measure
Plan of Care[1]—Number of visits with documented plan of care for hypertension per number of visits during which either systolic blood pressure ≥140 mm Hg or diastolic blood pressure ≥ 90 mm Hg **Numerator:** Patient visits with documented plan of care for hypertension Plan of care should include one or more of the following: Recheck blood pressure at specified future date, initiate or alter pharmacologic therapy, initiate or alter non-pharmacologic therapy **Denominator:** All patient visits during which patients ≥18 years of age diagnosed with hypertension have either systolic blood pressure ≥140 mm Hg or diastolic blood pressure ≥ 90 mm Hg **Percentage** of patient visits during which either systolic blood pressure ≥ 140 mm Hg or diastolic blood pressure ≥ 90 mm Hg, with documented plan of care for hypertension **Reporting Instructions:** For this measure to be met, three codes must be reported: one code for systolic blood pressure, one code for diastolic blood pressure, and the code for hypertension plan of care (4050F). If no documentation of plan of care, or patient does not have elevated blood pressure at the visit, report only two codes for corresponding systolic and diastolic blood pressure values	4050F **Denominator Codes:** **Systolic Codes:** 3076F 3077F **Diastolic Codes:** 3078F 3079F 3080F	Ht care plan doc Syst BP ≥ 140 MM HG Syst BP ≥ 140 MM HG Diast BP < 80 MM HG Diast BP 80-89 MM HG Diast BP ≥ 90 MM HG
Osteoarthritis (Adult) (OA)		
Composite Code: Osteoarthritis Assessment—See individual measures listed below for: Osteoarthritis symptoms and functional status assessed (1006F) Use of anti-inflammatory or over-the-counter (OTC) analgesic medications assessed (1007F) Initial examination of the involved joint(s) (includes visual inspection, palpation, range of motion) (2004F)	0005F	Osteoarthritis composite

[1]Physician Consortium for Performance Improvement: www.physicianconsortium.org
[2]National Committee on Quality Assurance (NCQA): Health Employer Data Information Set (HEDIS®): www.ncqa.org
[3]Joint Commission on Accreditation of Healthcare Organizations (JCAHO), ORYX Initiative Performance Measures: www.jcaho.org/pms
[4]National Diabetes Quality Improvement Alliance (NDQIA): www.nationaldiabetesalliance.org

Brief Description of Performance Measure & Source and Reporting Instructions	CPT Code(s)	Short Code Descriptor
Osteoarthritis (Adult) (OA), cont'd		
Symptom and Functional Assessment[1]—Patient visits with assessment for function and pain per number of visits during the reporting year **Numerator:** Patient visits with assessment for level of function and pain documented during the reporting year **Denominator:** All visits for patients aged ≥ 21 years of age with osteoarthritis **Percentage** of visits for patients ≥ 21 years of age with osteoarthritis who were assessed for function and pain during the reporting year **Reporting Instructions:** Use when osteoarthritis is addressed during the patient encounter	1006F	Osteoarthritis assess
Assessment for Use of Anti-inflammatory or Analgesic OTC Medications[1]—Patient visits with assessment for use of anti-inflammatory or analgesic OTC medications per number of visits during the reporting year **Numerator:** Patient visits with assessment for use of anti-inflammatory or analgesic OTC medications documented during the reporting year **Denominator:** All visits for patients aged ≥ 21 years of age with osteoarthritis **Percentage** of visits for patients ≥ 21 years of age with osteoarthritis with assessment for use of anti-inflammantory or analgesic over-the-counter (OTC) medications during the reporting year **Reporting Instructions:** Use when osteoarthritis is addressed during the patient encounter	1007F	Use of anti-inflam/anlgsc OTC assess
Non-steroidal Anti-inflammatory Drug (NSAID) Risk Assessment[1]—Whether or not patient on prescribed or OTC NSAIDs was assessed for GI/renal risk factors during the reporting year **Numerator:** Patients who were assessed for *all* of the following GI and Renal risk factors during the reporting year: • GI bleed • History of peptic ulcer disease (PUD) • Concomitant use of glucocorticoids or anticoagulants • Smoking • Significant alcohol use • Age > 65 years • Renal disease (Cr > 2.0 mg/dl) • Hypertension • Heart failure • Concomitant use of diuretic or angiotensin-converting enzyme (ACE) inhibitor **Denominator:** All patients ≥ 21 years of age with osteoarthritis on a prescribed or OTC NSAID **Percentage** of patients ≥ 21 years of age with osteoarthritis on prescribed or OTC NSAIDs who were assessed for gastrointestinal and renal risk factors during the reporting year	1008F	GI/renal risk assess
Physical Examination of the Involved Joint[1]—Whether or not a physical examination of the involved joint was performed during the initial visit during the reporting year **Numerator:** Patients for whom a physical examination of the involved joint was performed during the initial visit during the reporting year **Denominator:** All patients ≥ 21 years of age with osteoarthritis **Percentage** of patients ≥ 21 years of age with osteoarthritis for whom a physical examination of the involved joint was performed during the initial visit during the reporting year **Reporting Instructions:** Use only for initial osteoarthritis visit or for visits for new joint involvement	2004F	Initial exam involved joints

[1]Physician Consortium for Performance Improvement: www.physicianconsortium.org
[2]National Committee on Quality Assurance (NCQA): Health Employer Data Information Set (HEDIS®): www.ncqa.org
[3]Joint Commission on Accreditation of Healthcare Organizations (JCAHO), ORYX Initiative Performance Measures: www.jcaho.org/pms
[4]National Diabetes Quality Improvement Alliance (NDQIA): www.nationaldiabetesalliance.org

Brief Description of Performance Measure & Source and Reporting Instructions	CPT Code(s)	Short Code Descriptor
Osteoarthritis (Adult) (OA), cont'd		
Anti-inflammatory/Analgesic Therapy[1]—Patient visits during which an anti-inflammatory agent or analgesic was considered/Number of visits during the reporting year **Numerator:** Patient visits during which an anti-inflammatory agent or analgesic was considered during the reporting year **Denominator:** All patient visits for patients aged ≥ 21 years of age with osteoarthritis **Numerator Inclusion(s):** Documentation that an anti-inflammatory agent or analgesic was prescribed; Documentation of medical reason(s) for not prescribing an anti-inflammatory agent or analgesic (eg, allergy, drug interaction, contraindication); documentation of patient reasons(s) for not prescribing an anti-inflammatory agent or analgesic (eg, economic, social, religious) **Percentage** of visits for patients aged ≥ 21 years of age with osteoarthritis during which an anti-inflammatory agent or analgesic was considered during the reporting year **Reporting Instructions:** Report 4016F alone or with modifier (1P if medical reason for not prescribing an anti-inflammatory or analgesic was documented or 2P modifier if patient reason for not prescribing an anti-inflammatory or analgesic was documented.) For this measure, the modifiers do not act as denominator exclusions, but rather demonstate that therapy was considered and are included in the numerator when calculating the measure	4016F	Anti-inflm/anlgsc agent RX
Gastrointestinal Prophylaxis[1]—Patient visits during which GI prophylaxis was considered/Number of visits during the reporting year **Numerator:** Patient visits during which GI prophylaxis was considered during the reporting year **Denominator:** All visits for patients aged ≥ 21 years of age with osteoarthritis on a prescribed or OTC NSAID **Numerator Inclusion(s):** Documentation that GI prophylaxis was prescribed; documentation of medical reason(s) for not prescribing GI prophylaxis (eg, allergy, drug interaction, contraindication); documentation of patient reason(s) for not prescribing GI prophylaxis (eg, economic, social, or religious) **Percentage** of visits for patients ≥ 21 years of age with osteoarthritis during which GI prophylaxis was considered during the reporting year **Reporting Instructions:** Report 4017F alone or with modifier (1P if medical reason for not prescribing GI prophylaxis was documented or 2P modifier if patient reason for not prescribing GI prophylaxis was documented). For this measure, the modifiers do not act as denominator exclusions, but rather demonstrate that therapy was considered and are included in the numerator when calculating the measure	4017F	GI prophylaxis for NSAID RX
Therapeutic Exercise for the Involved Joint[1]—Patient visits during which therapeutic exercise for the hip or knee was considered/Number of visits during the reporting year **Numerator:** Patient visits during which therapeutic exercise for the knee or hip was considered during the reporting year **Denominator:** All patient visits for patients ≥ 21 years of age with osteoarthritis of the hip or knee **Numerator Inclusion(s):** Documentation of medical reason(s) for not instructing therapeutic exercise or prescribing physical therapy for the hip or knee; documentation of patient reason(s) for not instructing therapeutic exercise or prescribing physical therapy for the hip or knee (eg, economic, social, religious); documentation that therapeutic exercise for the hip or knee was instructed; documentation that physical therapy for the hip or knee was prescribed (continued)	4018F	Therapy exercise joint RX

[1]Physician Consortium for Performance Improvement: www.physicianconsortium.org
[2]National Committee on Quality Assurance (NCQA): Health Employer Data Information Set (HEDIS®): www.ncqa.org
[3]Joint Commission on Accreditation of Healthcare Organizations (JCAHO), ORYX Initiative Performance Measures: www.jcaho.org/pms
[4]National Diabetes Quality Improvement Alliance (NDQIA): www.nationaldiabetesalliance.org

Brief Description of Performance Measure & Source and Reporting Instructions	CPT Code(s)	Short Code Descriptor
Osteoarthritis (Adult) (OA), cont'd		
Percentage of visits for patients ≥ 21 years of age with osteoarthritis of the hip or knee during which therapeutic exercise for the hip or knee (therapeutic exercise instructed or physical therapy prescribed) was considered during the reporting year **Reporting Instructions:** Report 4018F alone or or with modifier (1P if medical reason for not instructing therapeutic exercise or prescribing physical therapy was documented; 2P if patient reason for not instructing therapeutic exercise or prescribing physical therapy was documented.) For this measure, the modifiers do not act as denominator exclusions, but rather demonstate that therapy was considered and are included in the numerator when calculating the measure.		
Prenatal-Postpartum Care (Prenatal)		
Timeliness of Prenatal Care[2] **Numerator:** Number of women who received a prenatal care visit as a member of the managed care organization (MCO) in the first trimester or within 42 days of enrollment in the MCO **Denominator:** Women who had live births between November 6th of the year prior to the measurement year and November 5th of the measurement year, who were continuously enrolled at least 43 days prior to delivery through 56 days after delivery **Percentage** of patients in the denominator who received prenatal care	0500F	Initial prenatal care visit
Prenatal Flow Sheet[1]—Whether or not patient has a prenatal flow sheet in use by the date of the first physician visit **Numerator:** Number of patients with a flow sheet in use by the date of the first physician visit, which contains at a minimum: blood pressure, weight, urine protein, uterine size, fetal heart tones, and estimated date of delivery **Denominator:** Pregnant women seen for prenatal care **Exclusion(s):** Patients seen for consultation only, not for continuing care **Percentage** of patients in the denominator with a prenatal flow sheet in use by the first physician visit	0501F	Prenatal flow sheet
Frequency of Ongoing Prenatal Care[2] **Numerator:** Number of women in the denominator who had an unduplicated count of less than 21%, 21%-40%, 41%-60%, 61%-80%, or greater than or equal to 81% of the expected number of prenatal care visits, adjusted for the month of pregnancy at time of enrollment and gestational age **Denominator:** Women who had live births during the measurement year **Exclusion(s):** MCOs must exclude members for whom a prenatal visit is not indicated **Percentage** of patients in the denominator with expected number of prenatal visits	0502F	Subsequent prenatal care
Postpartum Care[2] **Numerator:** Number of women in the denominator who had a postpartum visit on or between 21 days and 56 days after delivery **Denominator:** Women who had live births between November 6th of the year prior to the measurement year and November 5th of the measurement year, who were continuously enrolled at least 43 days prior to delivery through 56 days after delivery **Percentage** of patients in the denominator who had a postpartum visit between 21 and 56 days after delivery	0503F	Postpartum care visit
Preventive Care & Screening (PV)		
Adult Influenza Immunization[1]—Whether or not patient received an influenza immunization **Numerator:** Patients who received an influenza immunization (continued)	4037F 90656	Influenza imm order/admin Flu vaccine no preserv 3 & >

[1]Physician Consortium for Performance Improvement: www.physicianconsortium.org
[2]National Committee on Quality Assurance (NCQA): Health Employer Data Information Set (HEDIS®): www.ncqa.org
[3]Joint Commission on Accreditation of Healthcare Organizations (JCAHO), ORYX Initiative Performance Measures: www.jcaho.org/pms
[4]National Diabetes Quality Improvement Alliance (NDQIA): www.nationaldiabetesalliance.org

Brief Description of Performance Measure & Source and Reporting Instructions	CPT Code(s)	Short Code Descriptor
Preventive Care & Screening (PV), cont'd		
Denominator: All patients greater than or equal to 50 years of age **Exclusion Criteria:** Documentation of medical reason(s) for not providing immunization; documentation of patient reason(s) for declining immunization; documentation of system reason(s) for declining immunization **Percentage** of patients who received an influenza immunization **Reporting Instructions:** For patients with appropriate exclusion criteria use 4037F with modifier 1P, 2P, or 3P. Use 4037F with modifier 1P if previously immunized for current season	**90658** **90660**	Flu vaccine age 3 & over, im Flu vaccine, nasal
Adult Colorectal Cancer Screening[1]—Whether or not patient was screened for colorectal cancer during the one-year measurement period **Numerator:** Patients with any of the recommended colorectal cancer screening test(s) performed (fecal occult blood testing annually; flexible sigmoidoscopy every five years; annual fecal occult blood testing plus flexible sigmoidoscopy every five years; double contrast barium enema every five years; colonoscopy every ten years) **Denominator:** All patients aged greater than or equal to 50 years of age **Denominator Exclusion:** Documentation of medical reason(s) for not providing colorectal cancer screening; documentation of patient reason(s) for not providing colorectal cancer screening; documentation of system reason(s) for not providing colorectal cancer screening **Percentage** of patients screened for colorectal cancer **Reporting Instructions:** For patients with appropriate exclusion criteria, report 3017F with modifier 1P, 2P, or 3P	**3017F**	Colorectal ca screen doc rev
Screening Mammography[1]—Whether or not female patient had a mammogram performed during the two-year measurement period **Numerator:** Female patients who had a mammogram performed **Denominator:** All female patients aged 50-69 years **Exclusion criteria:** Documentation of medical reason(s) for not performing screening mammography; documentation of patient reason(s) for declining screening mammography; documentation of system reason(s) for declining screening mammography **Percentage** of female patients who had a mammogram performed during the two-year measurement period **Reporting Instructions:** For patients with appropriate exclusion criteria use 3014F with modifier 1P, 2P, or 3P	**3014F**	Screen mammo doc rev
Tobacco Use[1]—Whether or not patient was queried about tobacco use one or more times **Numerator:** Patients who were queried about tobacco use one or more times **Denominator:** All patients aged ≥ 18 years at the beginning of the two-year measurement period **Percentage** of patients queried about tobacco use one or more times during the two-year measurement period **Reporting Instructions:** When reporting 1000F, it is required to report 1034F, and/or 1035F, or 1036F	**1000F** **1034F** **1035F** **1036F**	Tobacco use assessed Current tobacco smoker Smokeless tobacco user Tobacco non-user
Tobacco Use Intervention[1]—Whether or not patient identified as a tobacco user received cessation intervention **Numerator:** Patients identified as tobacco users who received cessation intervention **Denominator:** All patients ≥ 18 years at the beginning of the two-year measurement period identified as tobacco users **Percentage** of patients identified as tobacco users who received cessation intervention during the two-year measurement period **Reporting Instructions:** Report 1034F, 1035F, or 1036F for each patient. If patient is a tobacco user (1034F or 1035F) and received cessation intervention, report 4000F or 4001F or both	**4000F** **4001F** **Denominator Codes:** **1034F** **1035F** **1036F**	Tobacco use txmnt counseling Tobacco use txmnt pharmacol Current tobacco smoker Smokeless tobacco user Tobacco non-user

[1]Physician Consortium for Performance Improvement: www.physicianconsortium.org
[2]National Committee on Quality Assurance (NCQA): Health Employer Data Information Set (HEDIS®): www.ncqa.org
[3]Joint Commission on Accreditation of Healthcare Organizations (JCAHO), ORYX Initiative Performance Measures: www.jcaho.org/pms
[4]National Diabetes Quality Improvement Alliance (NDQIA): www.nationaldiabetesalliance.org

Appendix I

Genetic Testing Code Modifiers

This listing of modifiers is intended for reporting with molecular laboratory procedures related to genetic testing. Genetic testing modifiers should be used in conjunction with CPT and HCPCS codes to provide diagnostic granularity of service to enable providers to submit complete and precise genetic testing information without altering test descriptors. These two-character modifiers are categorized by mutation. The first (numeric) character indicates the disease category and the second (alpha) character denotes gene type. Introductory guidelines in the molecular diagnostic and molecular cytogenetic code sections of the CPT codebook provide further guidance in interpretation and application of genetic testing modifiers.

Neoplasia (Solid Tumor, Excluding Sarcoma and Lymphoma)

0A	BRCA1 (hereditary breast/ovarian cancer)
0B	BRCA2 (hereditary breast cancer)
0C	Neurofibromin (neurofibromatosis, type 1)
0D	Merlin (neurofibromatosis, type 2)
0E	c-RET (multiple endocrine neoplasia, types 2A/B, familial medullary thyroid carcinoma)
0F	VHL (Von Hippel Lindau disease, renal carcinoma)
0G	SDHD (hereditary paraganglioma)
0H	SDHB (hereditary paraganglioma)
0I	ERRB2, commonly called Her-2/neu
0J	MLH1 (HNPCC, mismatch repair genes)
0K	MSH2, MSH6, or PMS2 (HNPCC, mismatch repair genes)
0L	APC (hereditary polyposis coli)
0M	Rb (retinoblastoma)
0N	TP53, commonly called p53
0O	PTEN (Cowden's syndrome)
0P	KIT, also called CD117 (gastrointestinal stromal tumor)
0Z	Solid tumor gene, not otherwise specified

Neoplasia (Sarcoma)

1A	WT1 or WT2 (Wilm's tumor)
1B	PAX3, PAX7, or FOXO1A (alveolar rhabdomyosarcoma)
1C	FLI1, ERG, ETV1, or EWSR1 (Ewing's sarcoma, desmoplastic round cell)
1D	DDIT3 or FUS (myxoid liposarcoma)
1E	NR4A3, RBF56, or TCF12 (myxoid chondrosarcoma)
1F	SSX1, SSX2, or SYT (synovial sarcoma)
1G	MYCN (neuroblastoma)
1H	COL1A1 or PDGFB (dermatofibrosarcoma protruberans)
1I	TFE3 or ASPSCR1 (alveolar soft parts sarcoma)
1J	JAZF1 or JJAZ1 (endometrial stromal sarcoma)
1Z	Sarcoma gene, not otherwise specified

Neoplasia (Lymphoid/Hematopoietic)

2A	RUNX1 or CBFA2T1, commonly called AML1 or ETO, genes associated with t(8;21) AML1—also ETO (acute myelogenous leukemia)
2B	BCR or ABL1, genes associated with t(9;22) (chronic myelogenous or acute leukemia) BCR—also ABL (chronic myeloid, acute lymphoid leukemia)
2C	PBX1 or TCF3, genes associated with t(1;19) (acute lymphoblastic leukemia) CGF1
2D	CBFB or MYH11, genes associated with inv 16 (acute myelogenous leukemia) CBF beta (leukemia)
2E	MLL (acute leukemia)
2F	PML or RARA, genes associated with t(15;17) (acute promyelocytic leukemia) PML/RAR alpha (promyelocytic leukemia)
2G	ETV6, commonly called TEL, gene associated with t(12;21) (acute leukemia) TEL (Leukemia)
2H	BCL2 (B cell lymphoma, follicle center cell origin) bcl-2 (Lymphoma)
2I	CCND1, commonly called BCL1, cyclin D1 (Mantle cell lymphoma, myeloma) bcl-1 (lymphoma)
2J	MYC (Burkitt lymphoma) c-myc (lymphoma)
2K	IgH (lymphoma/leukemia)
2L	IGK (lymphoma/leukemia)
2M	TRB, T cell receptor beta (lymphoma/leukemia)
2N	TRG, T cell receptor gamma (lymphoma/leukemia)

2O SIL or TAL1 (T cell leukemia)

2T BCL6 (B cell lymphoma)

2Q API1 or MALT1 (MALT lymphoma)

2R NPM or ALK, genes associated with t(2;5) (anaplastic large cell lymphoma)

2S FLT3 (Acute myelogenous leukemia)

2Z Lymphoid/hematopoietic neoplasia, not otherwise specified

Non-Neoplastic Hematology/Coagulation

3A F5, commonly called Factor V (Leiden, others) (hypercoagulable state)

3B FACC (Fanconi anemia)

3C FACD (Fanconi anemia)

3D HBB, beta globin (thalassemia, sickle cell anemia, other hemoglobinopathies)

3E HBA, commonly called alpha globin (thalassemia)

3F MTHFR (elevated homocystinemia)

3G F2, commonly called prothrombin (20210, others) (hypercoagulable state) prothrombin (factor II, 20210A) (hypercoagulable state)

3H F8, commonly called factor VIII (hemophilia A/VWF)

3I F9, commonly called factor IX (hemophilia B)

3K F13, commonly called factor XIII (bleeding or hypercoagulable state) beta globin

3Z Non-neoplastic hematology/coagulation, not otherwise specified

Histocompatiblity/Blood Typing/ Identity/Microsatellite

4A HLA-A

4B HLA-B

4C HLA-C

4D HLA-D

4E HLA-DR

4F HLA-DQ

4G HLA-DP

4H Kell

4I Fingerprint for engraftment (post allogeneic progenitor cell transplant)

4J Fingerprint for donor allelotype (allogeneic transplant)

4K Fingerprint for recipient allelotype (allogeneic transplant)

4L Fingerprint for leukocyte chimerism (allogeneic solid organ transplant)

4M Fingerprint for maternal versus fetal origin

4N Microsatellite instability

4O Microsatellite loss (loss of heterozygosity)

4Z Histocompatiblity/blood typing, not otherwise specified

Neurologic, Non-Neoplastic

5A ASPA, commonly called Aspartoacylase A (Canavan disease)

5B FMR-1 (fragile X, FRAXA, syndrome)

5C FRDA, commonly called Frataxin (Freidreich ataxia)

5D HD, commonly called Huntington (Huntington's disease)

5E GABRA5, NIPA1, UBE3A, or ANCR GABRA (Prader Willi-Angelman syndrome)

5F GJB2, commonly called Connexin-26 (hereditary hearing loss) Connexin-32 (GJB2) (hereditary deafness)

5G GJB1, commonly called Connexin-32 (X-linked Charcot-Marie-Tooth disease)

5H SNRPN (Prader Willi-Angelman syndrome)

5I SCA1, commonly called Ataxin-1 (spinocerebellar ataxia, type 1)

5J SCA2, commonly called Ataxin-2 (spinocerebellar ataxia, type 2)

5K MJD, commonly called Ataxin-3 (spinocerebellar ataxia, type 3, Machado-Joseph disease)

5L CACNA1A (spinocerebellar ataxia, type 6)

5M ATXN7 Ataxin-7 (spinocerebellar ataxia, type 7)

5N PMP-22 (Charcot-Marie-Tooth disease, type 1A)

5O MECP2 (Rett syndrome)

5Z Neurologic, non-neoplastic, not otherwise specified

Muscular, Non-Neoplastic

6A DMD, commonly called dystrophin (Duchenne/Becker muscular dystrophy)

6B DMPK (myotonic dystrophy, type 1)

6C ZNF-9 (myotonic dystrophy, type 2)

6D SMN1/SMN2 (autosomal recessive spinal muscular atrophy)

6E MTTK, commonly called tRNAlys (myotonic epilepsy, MERRF)

6F MTTL1, commonly called tRNAleu (mitochondrial encephalomyopathy, MELAS)

6Z Muscular, not otherwise specified

Metabolic, Other

7A APOE, commonly called apolipoprotein E (cardiovascular disease or Alzheimer's disease)

7B NPC1 or NPC2, commonly called sphingomyelin phosphodiesterase (Nieman-Pick disease)

7C GBA, commonly called acid beta glucosidase (Gaucher disease)

7D HFE (hemochromatosis)

7E HEXA, commonly called hexosaminidase A (Tay-Sachs disease)

7F ACADM (medium chain acyl CoA dehydrogenase deficiency)

7Z Metabolic, other, not otherwise specified

Metabolic, Transport

8A CFTR (cystic fibrosis)

8B PRSS1 (hereditary pancreatitis)

8C Long QT syndrome, KCN (Jervell and Lange-Nielsen syndromes, types 1, 2, 5, and 6) and SCN (Brugada syndrome, SIDS and type 3)

8Z Metabolic, transport, not otherwise specified

Metabolic-Pharmacogenetics

9A TPMT, commonly called (thiopurine methyltransferase) (patients on antimetabolite therapy)

9B CYP2 genes, commonly called cytochrome p450 (drug metabolism)

9C ABCB1, commonly called MDR1 or p-glycoprotein (drug transport)

9D NAT2 (drug metabolism)

9L Metabolic-pharmacogenetics, not otherwise specified

Dysmorphology

9M FGFR1 (Pfeiffer and Kallman syndromes)

9N FGFR2 (Crouzon, Jackson-Weiss, Apert, Saethre-Chotzen syndromes)

9O FGFR3 (achondroplasia, hypochondroplasia, thanatophoric dysplasia, types I and II, Crouzon syndrome with acanthosis nigricans, Muencke syndromes)

9P TWIST (Saethre-Chotzen syndrome)

9Q DGCR, commonly called CATCH-22 (DiGeorge and 22q11 deletion syndromes)

9Z Dysmorphology, not otherwise specified

Appendix J

Electrodiagnostic Medicine Listing of Sensory, Motor, and Mixed Nerves

This summary assigns each sensory, motor, and mixed nerve with its appropriate nerve conduction study code in order to enhance accurate reporting of codes 95900, 95903, and 95904. Each nerve constitutes one unit of service.

Motor Nerves Assigned to Codes 95900 and 95903

I. Upper extremity, cervical plexus, and brachial plexus motor nerves
 A. Axillary motor nerve to the deltoid
 B. Long thoracic motor nerve to the serratus anterior
 C. Median nerve
 1. Median motor nerve to the abductor pollicis brevis
 2. Median motor nerve, anterior interosseous branch, to the flexor pollicis longus
 3. Median motor nerve, anterior interosseous branch, to the pronator quadratus
 4. Median motor nerve to the first lumbrical
 5. Median motor nerve to the second lumbrical
 D. Musculocutaneous motor nerve to the biceps brachii
 E. Radial nerve
 1. Radial motor nerve to the extensor carpi ulnaris
 2. Radial motor nerve to the extensor digitorum communis
 3. Radial motor nerve to the extensor indicis proprius
 4. Radial motor nerve to the brachioradialis
 F. Suprascapular nerve
 1. Suprascapular motor nerve to the supraspinatus
 2. Suprascapular motor nerve to the infraspinatus
 G. Thoracodorsal motor nerve to the latissimus dorsi
 H. Ulnar nerve
 1. Ulnar motor nerve to the abductor digiti minimi
 2. Ulnar motor nerve to the palmar interosseous
 3. Ulnar motor nerve to the first dorsal interosseous
 4. Ulnar motor nerve to the flexor carpi ulnaris
 I. Other
II. Lower extremity motor nerves
 A. Femoral motor nerve to the quadriceps
 1. Femoral motor nerve to vastus medialis
 2. Femoral motor nerve to vastus lateralis
 3. Femoral motor nerve to vastus intermedialis
 4. Femoral motor nerve to rectus femoris
 B. Ilioinguinal motor nerve
 C. Peroneal (fibular) nerve
 1. Peroneal motor nerve to the extensor digitorum brevis
 2. Peroneal motor nerve to the peroneus brevis
 3. Peroneal motor nerve to the peroneus longus
 4. Peroneal motor nerve to the tibialis anterior
 D. Plantar motor nerve
 E. Sciatic nerve
 F. Tibial nerve
 1. Tibial motor nerve, inferior calcaneal branch, to the abductor digiti minimi
 2. Tibial motor nerve, medial plantar branch, to the abductor hallucis
 3. Tibial motor nerve, lateral plantar branch, to the flexor digiti minimi brevis
 G. Other

III. Cranial nerves and trunk
 A. Cranial nerve VII (facial motor nerve)
 1. Facial nerve to the frontalis
 2. Facial nerve to the nasalis
 3. Facial nerve to the orbicularis oculi
 4. Facial nerve to the orbicularis oris
 B. Cranial nerve XI (spinal accessory motor nerve)
 C. Cranial nerve XII (hypoglossal motor nerve)
 D. Intercostal motor nerve
 E. Phrenic motor nerve to the diaphragm
 F. Recurrent laryngeal nerve
 G. Other
IV. Nerve Roots
 A. Cervical nerve root stimulation
 1. Cervical level 5 (CT)
 2. Cervical level 6 (C6)
 3. Cervical level 7 (C7)
 4. Cervical level 8 (C8)
 B. Thoracic nerve root stimulation
 1. Thoracic level 1 (T1)
 2. Thoracic level 2 (T2)
 3. Thoracic level 3 (T3)
 4. Thoracic level 4 (T4)
 5. Thoracic level 5 (T5)
 6. Thoracic level 6 (T6)
 7. Thoracic level 7 (T7)
 8. Thoracic level 8 (T8)
 9. Thoracic level 9 (T9)
 10. Thoracic level 10 (T10)
 11. Thoracic level 11 (T11)
 12. Thoracic level 12 (T12)
 C. Lumbar nerve root stimulation
 1. Lumbar level 1 (L1)
 2. Lumbar level 2 (L2)
 3. Lumbar level 3 (L3)
 4. Lumbar level 4 (L4)
 5. Lumbar level 5 (L5)
 D. Sacral nerve root stimulation
 1. Sacral level 1 (S1)
 2. Sacral level 2 (S2)
 3. Sacral level 3 (S3)
 4. Sacral level 4 (S4)

Sensory and Mixed Nerves Assigned to Code 95904

I Upper extremity sensory and mixed nerves
 A. Lateral antebrachial cutaneous sensory nerve
 B. Medial antebrachial cutaneous sensory nerve
 C. Medial brachial cutaneous sensory nerve
 D. Median nerve
 1. Median sensory nerve to the first digit
 2. Median sensory nerve to the second digit
 3. Median sensory nerve to the third digit
 4. Median sensory nerve to the fourth digit
 5. Median palmar cutaneous sensory nerve
 6. Median palmar mixed nerve
 E. Posterior antebrachial cutaneous sensory nerve

 F. Radial sensory nerve
 1. Radial sensory nerve to the base of the thumb
 2. Radial sensory nerve to digit 1
 G. Ulnar nerve
 1. Ulnar dorsal cutaneous sensory nerve
 2. Ulnar sensory nerve to the fourth digit
 3. Ulnar sensory nerve to the fifth digit
 4. Ulnar palmar mixed nerve
 H. Intercostal sensory nerve
 I. Other
 II. Lower extremity sensory and mixed nerves
 A. Lateral femoral cutaneous sensory nerve
 B. Medial calcaneal sensory nerve
 C. Medial femoral cutaneous sensory nerve
 D. Peroneal nerve
 1. Deep peroneal sensory nerve
 2. Superficial peroneal sensory nerve, medial dorsal cutaneous branch
 3. Superficial peroneal sensory nerve, intermediate dorsal cutaneous branch
 E. Posterior femoral cutaneous sensory nerve
 F. Saphenous nerve
 1. Saphenous sensory nerve (distal technique)
 2. Saphenous sensory nerve (proximal technique)
 G. Sural nerve
 1. Sural sensory nerve, lateral dorsal cutaneous branch
 2. Sural sensory nerve
 H. Tibial sensory nerve (digital nerve to toe 1)
 I. Tibial sensory nerve (medial plantar nerve)
 J. Tibial sensory nerve (lateral plantar nerve)
 K. Other
 III. Head and trunk sensory nerves
 A. Dorsal nerve of the penis
 B. Greater auricular nerve
 C. Ophthalmic branch of the trigeminal nerve
 D. Pudendal sensory nerve
 E. Suprascapular sensory nerves
 F. Other

The following table provides a reasonable maximum number of studies performed per diagnostic category necessary for a physician to arrive at a diagnosis in 90% of patients with that final diagnosis. The numbers in each column represent the number of studies recommended. The appropriate number of studies to be performed is based upon the physician's discretion.

| Indication | Needle EMG (95860-95864 95867-95870) | Type of Study/Maximum Number of Studies | | | |
| | | Nerve Conduction Studies (95900, 95903, 95904) | | Other EMG Studies (95934, 95936, 95937) | |
		Motor NCS With and/or Without F wave	Sensory NCS	H-Reflex	Neuromuscular Junction Testing (Repetitive Stimulation)
Carpal Tunnel (Unilateral)	1	3	4	—	—
Carpal Tunnel (Bilateral)	2	4	6	—	—
Radiculopathy	2	3	2	2	—
Mononeuropathy	1	3	3	2	—
Polyneuropathy/ Mononeuropathy Multiplex	3	4	4	2	—
Myopathy	2	2	2	—	2
Motor Neuronopathy (eg, ALS)	4	4	2	—	2
Plexopathy	2	4	6	2	—
Neuromuscular Junction	2	2	2	—	3
Tarsal Tunnel Syndrome (Unilateral)	1	4	4	—	—
Tarsal Tunnel Syndrome (Bilateral)	2	5	6	—	—
Weakness, Fatigue, Cramps, or Twitching (Focal)	2	3	4	—	2
Weakness, Fatigue, Cramps, or Twitching (General)	4	4	4	—	2
Pain, Numbness, or Tingling (Unilateral)	1	3	4	2	—
Pain, Numbness, or Tingling (Bilateral)	2	4	6	2	—

Notes

⊙=Moderate sedation ✚=Add-on code ⚡=FDA approval pending

Appendix K

Product Pending FDA Approval

Some vaccine products have been assigned a CPT Category I code in anticipation of future approval from the Food and Drug Administration (FDA). Following is the vaccine product code pending FDA approval status that is identified in the CPT codebook with the (⋀) symbol. Upon revision of the approval status by the FDA, notation of this revision will be provided via the AMA CPT "Category I Vaccine Codes" Internet listing (www.ama-assn.org/ama/pub/category/10902.html) and in subsequent publications of the CPT codebook.

90698

Appendix L

Vascular Families

Assignment of branches to first, second, and third order in this table makes the assumption that the starting point is catheterization of the aorta. This categorization would not be accurate, for instance, if a femoral or carotid artery were catheterized directly in an antegrade direction. Arteries highlighted in bold are those more commonly reported during arteriographic procedures.

First Order	Second Order Branch	Third Order Branch	Beyond Third Order Branches

First Order: Innominate, L. common carotid

Innominate

- **R. common carotid**
 - **R. internal carotid**
 - R. ophthalmic
 - R. p. communicating
 - R. middle cerebral
 - R. a. cerebral
 - **R. external carotid**
 - R. superior thyroid
 - R. ascending pharyngeal
 - R. facial
 - R. lingual
 - R. occipital
 - R. p. auricular
 - R. superficial temporal
 - R. internal maxillary
 - R. middle meningeal
- **R. subclavian & axillary**
 - **R. vertebral** ——— Basilar
 - R. internal thoracic (internal mammary)
 - R. thyrocervical trunk
 - R. inferior thyroid
 - R. suprascapular
 - R. transverse cervical
 - R. costocervical trunk
 - R. highest intercostal
 - R. deep cervicall
 - R. lateral thoracic
 - R. thoracoacromial
 - R. humeral circumflex (A/P)
 - R. subscapular ——— R. circumflex scapular
 - **R. brachial**
 - R. deep brachial
 - R. ulnar
 - R. radial
 - R. interosseous
 - R. deep palmar arch
 - R. superficial palmar arch
 - R. metacarpals and digitals

L. common carotid

- **L. internal carotid**
 - L. ophthalmic
 - L. p. communicating
 - L. middle cerebral
 - L. a. cerebral
- **L. external carotid**
 - L. superior thyroid
 - L. ascending pharyngeal
 - L. facial
 - L. lingual
 - L. occipital
 - L. p. auricular
 - L. superficial temporal
 - L. internal maxillary ——— L. middle meningeal

R = right, L = left, A = anterior, P = posterior

First Order	Second Order Branch	Third Order Branch	Beyond Third Order Branches
	L. vertebral L. internal thoracic (internal mammary)		
	L. thyrocervical trunk	L. inferior thyroid L. suprascapular L. transverse cervical	
	L. costocervical trunk	L. highest intercostal L. deep cervical	
L. subclavian & axillary	L. lateral thoracic L. thoracoacromial L. humeral circumflex (A/P) L. subscapular **L. brachial**	L. circumflex scapular	
	L. deep brachial	L. ulnar L. radial L. interosseous	L. deep palmar arch L. superficial palmar arch L. metacarpals and digitals
Intercostals			
Bronchials			
Recurrent esophageal			
Inferior phrenic	Superior suprarenal		
	L. gastric	Esophageal branch	
	Splenic	Dorsal pancreatic Great pancreatic Caudal pancreatic Gastroepiploic Short gastrics	Inferior transverse pancreatic
Celiac trunk	Common hepatic	Gastroduodenal	P. superior pancreaticoduodenal A. superior pancreaticoduodenal
		Proper Hepatic	L. hepatic R. hepatic Cystic Gastroepiploic Supraduodenal Intermediate hepatic
Middle suprarenal			
Superior mesenteric	Middle colic Inferior pancreaticoduodenal	P. inferior pancreaticoduodenal A. inferior pancreaticoduodenal	
	Jejunal Ileocolic Appendicular P. cecal A. cecal Marginal R. colic		

R = right, L = left, A = anterior, P = posterior

First Order	Second Order Branch	Third Order Branch	Beyond Third Order Branches

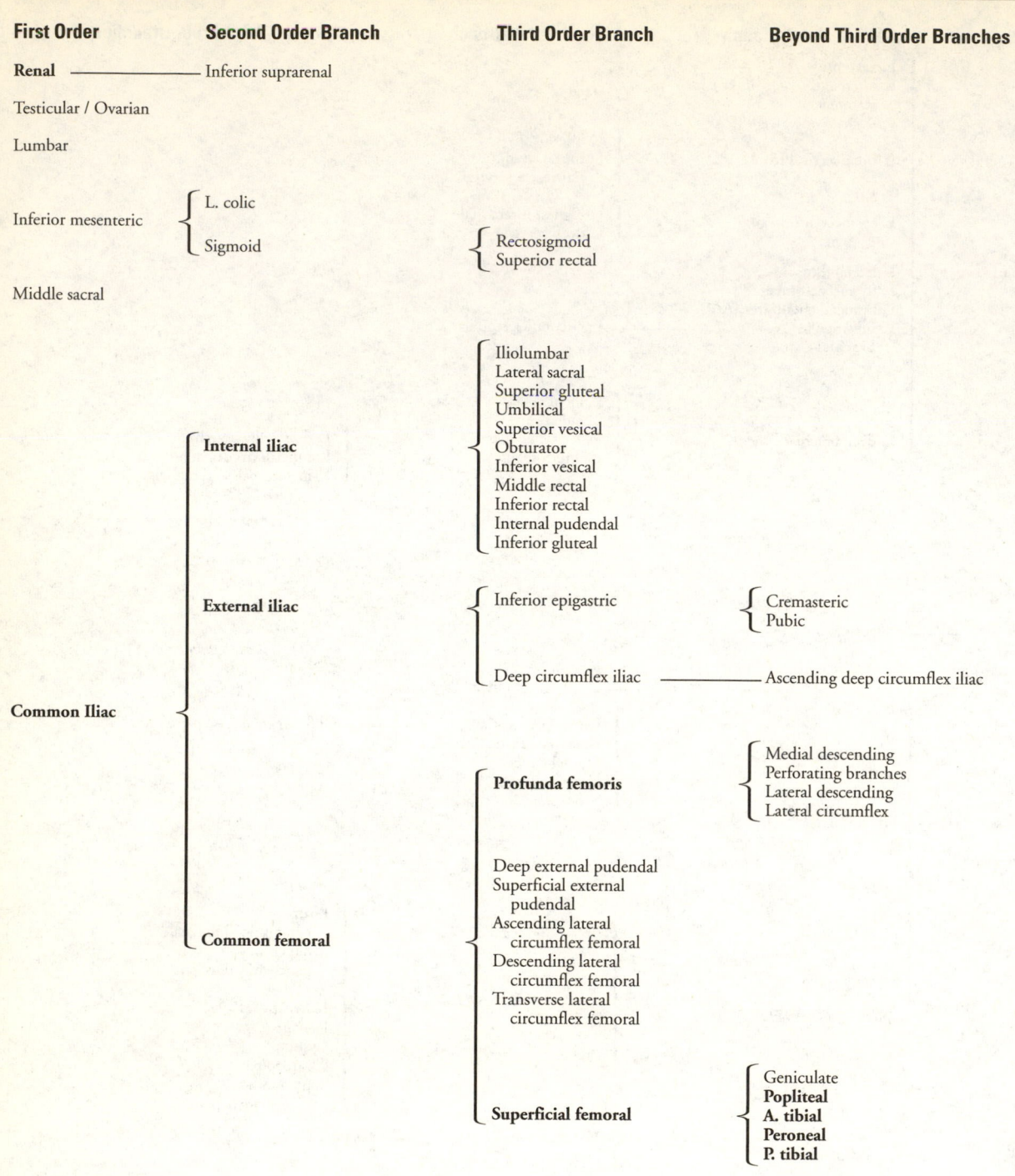

Renal ———————— Inferior suprarenal

Testicular / Ovarian

Lumbar

Inferior mesenteric
- L. colic
- Sigmoid
 - Rectosigmoid
 - Superior rectal

Middle sacral

Common Iliac

Internal iliac
- Iliolumbar
- Lateral sacral
- Superior gluteal
- Umbilical
- Superior vesical
- Obturator
- Inferior vesical
- Middle rectal
- Inferior rectal
- Internal pudendal
- Inferior gluteal

External iliac
- Inferior epigastric
 - Cremasteric
 - Pubic
- Deep circumflex iliac ——————— Ascending deep circumflex iliac

Common femoral
- **Profunda femoris**
 - Medial descending
 - Perforating branches
 - Lateral descending
 - Lateral circumflex
- Deep external pudendal
- Superficial external pudendal
- Ascending lateral circumflex femoral
- Descending lateral circumflex femoral
- Transverse lateral circumflex femoral
- **Superficial femoral**
 - Geniculate
 - **Popliteal**
 - **A. tibial**
 - **Peroneal**
 - **P. tibial**

R. & L. main pulmonary arteries (venous selective)

Reference: Kadir S. *Atlas of Normal and Variant Angiographic Anatomy.* Philadephia, Pa: WB Saunders Co; 1991.
R = right, L = left, A = anterior, P = posterior

Appendix M

Crosswalk to Deleted CPT Codes

This listing is a summary of the deleted *CPT 2006* codes and descriptors that have been crosswalked to *CPT 2007* codes.

Deleted CPT 2006 Code	CPT 2007 Code	CPT 2006 Code Descriptor
15000	15002, 15004	Surgical preparation or creation of recipient site by excision of open wounds, burn eschar, or scar (including subcutaneous tissues), or incisional release of scar contracture; first 100 sq cm or one percent of body area of infants and children
+15001	+15003, 15005	Surgical preparation or creation of recipient site by excision of open wounds, burn eschar, or scar (including subcutaneous tissues), or incisional release of scar contracture; each additional 100 sq cm or each additional one percent of body area of infants and children (List separately in addition to code for primary procedure)
15831	15830, 15847, 17999	Excision, excessive skin and subcutaneous tissue (includes lipectomy); abdomen (abdominoplasty)
17304	17311	Chemosurgery (Mohs micrographic technique), including removal of all gross tumor, surgical excision of tissue specimens, mapping, color coding of specimens, microscopic examination of specimens by the surgeon, and complete histopathologic preparation including the first routine stain (eg, hematoxylin and eosin, toluidine blue); first stage, fresh tissue technique, up to 5 specimens
17305	17312, 17314	Chemosurgery (Mohs micrographic technique), including removal of all gross tumor, surgical excision of tissue specimens, mapping, color coding of specimens, microscopic examination of specimens by the surgeon, and complete histopathologic preparation including the first routine stain (eg, hematoxylin and eosin, toluidine blue); second stage, fixed or fresh tissue, up to 5 specimens
17306	17312, 17314	Chemosurgery (Mohs micrographic technique), including removal of all gross tumor, surgical excision of tissue specimens, mapping, color coding of specimens, microscopic examination of specimens by the surgeon, and complete histopathologic preparation including the first routine stain (eg, hematoxylin and eosin, toluidine blue); third stage, fixed or fresh tissue, up to 5 specimens
17307	17312, 17314	Chemosurgery (Mohs micrographic technique), including removal of all gross tumor, surgical excision of tissue specimens, mapping, color coding of specimens, microscopic examination of specimens by the surgeon, and complete histopathologic preparation including the first routine stain (eg, hematoxylin and eosin, toluidine blue); additional stage(s), up to 5 specimens, each stage
+17310	+17315	Chemosurgery (Mohs micrographic technique), including removal of all gross tumor, surgical excision of tissue specimens, mapping, color coding of specimens, microscopic examination of specimens by the surgeon, and complete histopathologic preparation including the first routine stain (eg, hematoxylin and eosin, toluidine blue); each additional specimen, after the first 5 specimens, fixed or fresh tissue, any stage (List separately in addition to code for primary procedure)
19140	19300	Mastectomy for gynecomastia
19160	19301	Mastectomy, partial (eg, lumpectomy, tylectomy, quadrantectomy, segmentectomy);
19162	19302	Mastectomy, partial (eg, lumpectomy, tylectomy, quadrantectomy, segmentectomy); with axillary lymphadenectomy
19180	19303	Mastectomy, simple, complete
19182	19304	Mastectomy, subcutaneous
19200	19305	Mastectomy, radical, including pectoral muscles, axillary lymph nodes
19220	19306	Mastectomy, radical, including pectoral muscles, axillary and internal mammary lymph nodes (Urban type operation)

Deleted CPT 2006 Code	CPT 2007 Code	CPT 2006 Code Descriptor
19240	19307	Mastectomy, modified radical, including axillary lymph nodes, with or without pectoralis minor muscle, but excluding pectoralis major muscle
25611	25606	Percutaneous skeletal fixation of distal radial fracture (eg, Colles or Smith type) or epiphyseal separation, with or without fracture of ulnar styloid, requiring manipulation, with or without external fixation
25620	25607-25609	Open treatment of distal radial fracture (eg, Colles or Smith type) or epiphyseal separation, with or without fracture of ulnar styloid, with or without internal or external fixation
26504	26390	Reconstruction of tendon pulley, each tendon; with tendon prosthesis (separate procedure)
27315	27325	Neurectomy, hamstring muscle
27320	27326	Neurectomy, popliteal (gastrocnemius)
28030	28055	Neurectomy, intrinsic musculature of foot
33253	33254-33256	Operative incisions and reconstruction of atria for treatment of atrial fibrillation or atrial flutter (eg, maze procedure)
35381	35302-35306	Thromboendarterectomy, with or without patch graft; femoral and/or popliteal, and/or tibioperoneal
35507	35506	Bypass graft, with vein; subclavian-carotid
35541	35537, 35538	Bypass graft, with vein; aortoiliac or bi-iliac
35546	35539, 35540	Bypass graft, with vein; aortofemoral or bifemoral
35641	35637, 35638	Bypass graft, with other than vein; aortoiliac or bi-iliac
44152	44799	Colectomy, total, abdominal, without proctectomy; with rectal mucosectomy, ileoanal anastomosis, with or without loop ileostomy
44153	44799	Colectomy, total, abdominal, without proctectomy; with rectal mucosectomy, ileoanal anastomosis, creation of ileal reservoir (S or J), with or without loop ileostomy
47716	47719	Anastomosis, choledochal cyst, without excision
48005	48105	Resection or debridement of pancreas and peripancreatic tissue for acute necrotizing pancreatitis
48180	48548	Pancreaticojejunostomy, side-to-side anastomosis (Puestow-type operation)
49085	49402	Removal of peritoneal foreign body from peritoneal cavity
54152	54150	Circumcision, using clamp or other device; except newborn
54820	54865	Exploration of epididymis, with or without biopsy
55859	55875	Transperineal placement of needles or catheters into prostate for interstitial radioelement application, with or without cystoscopy
56720	56442	Hymenotomy, simple incision
57820	57558	Dilation and curettage of cervical stump
67350	67346	Biopsy of extraocular muscle
+75998	+77001	Fluoroscopic guidance for central venous access device placement, replacement (catheter only or complete), or removal (includes fluoroscopic guidance for vascular access and catheter manipulation, any necessary contrast injections through access site or catheter with related venography radiologic supervision and interpretation, and radiographic documentation of final catheter position) (List separately in addition to code for primary procedure)
76003	77002	Fluoroscopic guidance for needle placement (eg, biopsy, aspiration, injection, localization device)
76005	77003	Fluoroscopic guidance and localization of needle or catheter tip for spine or paraspinous diagnostic or therapeutic injection procedures (epidural, transforaminal epidural, subarachnoid, paravertebral facet joint, paravertebral facet joint nerve or sacroiliac joint), including neurolytic agent destruction
76006	77071	Manual application of stress performed by physician for joint radiography, including contralateral joint if indicated

Deleted CPT 2006 Code	CPT 2007 Code	CPT 2006 Code Descriptor
76012	72291	Radiological supervision and interpretation, percutaneous vertebroplasty or vertebral augmentation including cavity creation, per vertebral body; under fluoroscopic guidance
76013	72292	Radiological supervision and interpretation, percutaneous vertebroplasty or vertebral augmentation including cavity creation, per vertebral body; under CT guidance
76020	77072	Bone age studies
76040	77073	Bone length studies (orthoroentgenogram, scanogram)
76061	77074	Radiologic examination, osseous survey; limited (eg, for metastases)
76062	77075	Radiologic examination, osseous survey; complete (axial and appendicular skeleton)
76065	77076	Radiologic examination, osseous survey, infant
76066	77077	Joint survey, single view, two or more joints (specify)
76070	77078	Computed tomography, bone mineral density study, one or more sites; axial skeleton (eg, hips, pelvis, spine)
76071	77079	Computed tomography, bone mineral density study, one or more sites; appendicular skeleton (peripheral) (eg, radius, wrist, heel)
76075	77080	Dual energy X-ray absorptiometry (DXA), bone density study, one or more sites; axial skeleton (eg, hips, pelvis, spine)
76076	77081	Dual energy X-ray absorptiometry (DXA), bone density study, one or more sites; appendicular skeleton (peripheral) (eg, radius, wrist, heel)
76077	77082	Dual energy X-ray absorptiometry (DXA), bone density study, one or more sites; vertebral fracture assessment
76078	77083	Radiographic absorptiometry (eg, photodensitometry, radiogrammetry), one or more sites
+76082	+77051	Computer-aided detection (computer algorithm analysis of digital image data for lesion detection) with further physician review for interpretation, with or without digitization of film radiographic images; diagnostic mammography (List separately in addition to code for primary procedure)
+76083	+77052	Computer-aided detection (computer algorithm analysis of digital image data for lesion detection) with further physician review for interpretation, with or without digitization of film radiographic images; screening mammography (List separately in addition to code for primary procedure)
76086	77053	Mammary ductogram or galactogram, single duct, radiological supervision and interpretation
76088	77054	Mammary ductogram or galactogram, multiple ducts, radiological supervision and interpretation
76090	77055	Mammography; unilateral
76091	77056	Mammography; bilateral
76092	77057	Screening mammography, bilateral (two view film study of each breast)
76093	77058	Magnetic resonance imaging, breast, without and/or with contrast material(s); unilateral
76094	77059	Magnetic resonance imaging, breast, without and/or with contrast material(s); bilateral
76095	77031	Stereotactic localization guidance for breast biopsy or needle placement (eg, for wire localization or for injection), each lesion, radiological supervision and interpretation
76096	77032	Mammographic guidance for needle placement, breast (eg, for wire localization or for injection), each lesion, radiological supervision and interpretation
76355	77011	Computed tomography guidance for stereotactic localization
76360	77012	Computed tomography guidance for needle placement (eg, biopsy, aspiration, injection, localization device), radiological supervision and interpretation
76362	77013	Computed tomography guidance for, and monitoring of, parenchymal tissue ablation
76370	77014	Computed tomography guidance for placement of radiation therapy fields
76393	77021	Magnetic resonance guidance for needle placement (eg, for biopsy, needle aspiration, injection, or placement of localization device) radiological supervision and interpretation

Deleted CPT 2006 Code	CPT 2007 Code	CPT 2006 Code Descriptor
76394	77022	Magnetic resonance guidance for, and monitoring of, parenchymal tissue ablation
76400	77084	Magnetic resonance (eg, proton) imaging, bone marrow blood supply
76778	76775, 76776	Ultrasound, transplanted kidney, B-scan and/or real time with image documentation, with or without duplex Doppler study
76986	76998	Ultrasonic guidance, intraoperative
78704	78707-78709	Kidney imaging; with function study (ie, imaging renogram)
78715	78701-78709	Kidney vascular flow only
78760	78761	Testicular imaging
92573	92700	Lombard test
94656	94002, 94004	Ventilation assist and management, initiation of pressure or volume preset ventilators for assisted or controlled breathing; first day
94657	94003, 94004	Ventilation assist and management, initiation of pressure or volume preset ventilators for assisted or controlled breathing; subsequent days
0018T	0160T, 0161T	Delivery of high power, focal magnetic pulses for direct stimulation to cortical neurons
0044T	96904	Whole body integumentary photography, at request of a physician, for monitoring of high-risk patients; with dysplastic nevus syndrome or familial melanoma
0045T	96904	Whole body integumentary photography, at request of a physician, for monitoring of high-risk patients; with history of dysplastic nevi or personal history of melanoma
0082T	77371-77373	Stereotactic body radiation therapy, treatment delivery, one or more treatment areas, per day
0083T	77371-77373	Stereotactic body radiation therapy, treatment management, per day
0091T	22857	Total disc arthroplasty (artificial disc), anterior approach, including diskectomy to prepare interspace (other than for decompression); single interspace, lumbar
0094T	22865	Removal of total disc arthroplasty, anterior approach; single interspace, lumbar
0097T	22862	Removal of total disc arthroplasty, anterior approach; single interspace, lumbar
0120T	19105	Ablation, cryosurgical, of fibroadenoma, including ultrasound guidance, each fibroadenoma

Index

Instructions for the Use of the CPT Index

Main Terms

The index is organized by main terms. Each main term can stand alone, or be followed by up to three modifying terms. There are four primary classes of main entries:

1. Procedure or service.
 For example: Endoscopy; Anastomosis; Splint

2. Organ or other anatomic site.
 For example: Tibia; Colon; Salivary Gland

3. Condition.
 For example: Abscess; Entropion; Tetralogy of Fallot

4. Synonyms, Eponyms and Abbreviations.
 For example: EEG; Bricker Operation; Clagett Procedure

Modifying Terms

A main term may be followed by a series of up to three indented terms that modify the main term. When modifying terms appear, one should review the list, as these subterms do have an effect on the selection of the appropriate code for the procedure.

Code Ranges

Whenever more than one code applies to a given index entry, a code range is listed. If several non-sequential codes apply, they will be separated by a comma. For example:

Esophagus
 Reconstruction43300, 43310, 43313

If two or more sequential codes apply, they will be separated by a hyphen. For example:

Debridement
 Burns01951-01953, 16010-16030

Conventions

As a space saving convention, certain words infer some meaning. This convention is primarily used when a procedure or service is listed as a subterm. For example:

Knee
 Incision (of)

In this example, the word in parentheses (of) does not appear in the index, but it is inferred. As another example:

Pancreas
 Anesthesia (for procedures on)

In this example, as there is no such entity as pancreas anesthesia, the words in parentheses are inferred. That is, anesthesia for procedures on the pancreas.

The alphabetic index is NOT a substitute for the main text of *CPT*. Even if only one code appears, the user must refer to the main text to ensure that the code selection is accurate.

A

A Vitamin
See Vitamin, A

A-II
See Angiotensin II

Abbe-Estlander Procedure
See Reconstruction; Repair, Cleft Lip

Abdomen
Abdominal Wall
 Removal
 Mesh11008
 Prosthesis11008
 Repair
 Hernia49491-49496, 49501, 49507,
 49521, 49590
 Tumor
 Excision22900
 Unlisted Services and Procedures22999
Abscess
 Incision and Drainage49020, 49040
 Open49040
 Percutaneous49021
Angiography74175, 75635
Artery
 Ligation37617
Biopsy49000
Bypass Graft35907
Cannula/Catheter
 Removal49422
Celiotomy
 for Staging49220
CT Scan74150-74175, 75635
Cyst
 Destruction/Excision49200-49201
Drainage
 Fluid49080-49081
Ectopic Pregnancy59130
Endometrioma
 Destruction/Excision49200-49201
Exploration49000-49002
 Blood Vessel35840
 Staging58960
Incision49000
 Staging58960
Incision and Drainage
 Pancreatitis48000
Infraumbilical Panniculectomy15830
Injection
 Air49400
 Contrast Material49400
Insertion
 Catheter49419-49421, 49324
 Venous Shunt49425
Intraperitoneal
 Catheter Exit Site49436
 Catheter Insertion49324, 49435
 Catheter Removal49422
 Catheter Revision49325
 Shunt
 Ligation49428
 Removal49429

Laparotomy
 Staging49220
Magnetic Resonance Imaging
(MRI)74181-74183
Needle Biopsy
 Mass49180
Peritoneocentesis49080-49081
Radical Resection51597
Repair
 Blood Vessel35221
 with Other Graft35281
 with Vein Graft35251
 Hernia49491-49525, 49560-49587
 Suture49900
Revision
 Venous Shunt49426
Suture49900
Tumor
 Destruction/Excision49200-49201
Ultrasound76700-76705
Unlisted Services and Procedures49999
Wound Exploration
 Penetrating20102
X-Ray74000-74022

Abdominal Aorta
See Aorta, Abdominal

Abdominal Aortic Aneurysm
See Aorta, Abdominal, Aneurysm

Abdominal Deliveries
See Cesarean Delivery

Abdominal Hysterectomy
See Hysterectomy, Abdominal

Abdominal Lymphangiogram
See Lymphangiography, Abdomen

Abdominal Paracentesis
See Abdomen, Drainage

Abdominal Radiographies
See Abdomen, X-Ray

Abdominal Wall
Debridement
 Infected11005-11006
Reconstruction49905
Removal
 Mesh11008
 Prosthesis11008
Surgery22999
Tumor
 Excision22900

Abdominohysterectomy
See Hysterectomy, Abdominal

Abdominopelvic Amputation
See Amputation, Interpelviabdominal

Abdominoplasty
See Panniculectomy
Excision15847

Ablation
Anal
 Polyp46615
 Tumor46615

Bone
 Tumor20982
Colon
 Tumor45339
Cryosurgical
 Renal Mass50250
 Renal Tumor
 Percutaneous0135T
CT Scan Guidance77013
Endometrial58353-58356, 58563
Endometrium
 Ultrasound Guidance58356
Heart
 Arrhythmogenic Focus93650-93652
 See Cardiology; Diagnostic, Intracardiac
 Pacing and Mapping
Liver
 Tumor
 Laparoscopic47370-47371
 Open47380-47382
Lung
 Tumor
 Radiofrequency32998
Magnetic Resonance Guidance77022
Parenchymal Tissue
 CT Scan Guidance77013
Prostate55873
Pulmonary Tumor32998
Radiofrequency32998
Renal Cyst50541
Renal Mass50542
 Radiofrequency50592
Renal Tumor
 Cryotherapy
 Percutaneous0135T
Turbinate Mucosa30801-30802
Ultrasound
 Guidance76940
 Uterine Tumor0071T-0072T
Uterine Tumor
 Ultrasound, Focused0071T-0072T
Vein
 Endovenous36475-36479

Abortion
See Obstetrical Care
Incomplete59812
Induced
 by Dilation and Curettage59840
 by Dilation and Evacuation59841
 by Saline59850-59851
 by Vaginal Suppositories59855-59856
 with Hysterectomy59100, 59852, 59857
Missed
 First Trimester59820
 Second Trimester59821
Septic59830
Spontaneous59812
Therapeutic
 by Saline59850
 with Dilation and Curettage59851
 with Hysterectomy59852

Abrasion
Skin
 Chemical Peel15788-15793
 Dermabrasion15780-15783
 Lesion15786-15787

Abscess

Abdomen49040-49041
 Incision and Drainage
 Open49040
 Percutaneous49021
Anal
 Incision and Drainage46045-46050
Ankle27603
Appendix
 Incision and Drainage44900
 Open44900
 Percutaneous44901
Arm, Lower25028
 Excision25145
 Incision and Drainage25035
Arm, Upper
 Incision and Drainage23930-23935
Auditory Canal, External69020
Bartholin's Gland
 Incision and Drainage56420
Bladder
 Incision and Drainage51080
Brain
 Drainage61150-61151
 Excision61514, 61522
 Incision and Drainage61320-61321
Breast
 Incision and Drainage19020
Carpals
 Incision, Deep25035
Clavicle
 Sequestrectomy23170
Drainage
 with X-Ray75989
Ear, External
 Complicated69005
 Simple69000
Elbow
 Incision and Drainage23930-23935
Epididymis
 Incision and Drainage54700
Excision
 Olecranon Process24138
 Radius24136
 Ulna24138
Eyelid
 Incision and Drainage67700
Facial Bones
 Excision21026
Finger26010-26011
 Incision and Drainage26034
Foot
 Incision28005
Gums
 Incision and Drainage41800
Hand
 Incision and Drainage26034
Hematoma
 Incision and Drainage27603
Hip
 Incision and Drainage26990-26992
Humeral Head23174
Humerus
 Excision24134
 Incision and Drainage23935
Kidney
 Incision and Drainage50020

 Open50020
 Percutaneous50021
Leg, Lower
 Incision and Drainage27603
Liver47010
 Drainage
 Open47010
 Injection47015
 Repair47300
Localization
 Nuclear Medicine78806-78807
Lung
 Percutaneous Drainage32200-32201
Lymph Node
 Incision and Drainage38300-38305
Lymphocele Drainage49062
Mandible
 Excision21025
Mouth
 Incision and Drainage40800-40801,
 41005-41009, 41015-41018
Nasal Septum
 Incision and Drainage30020
Neck
 Incision and Drainage21501-21502
Ovarian
 Incision and Drainage58820-58822
 Abdominal Approach58822
 Vaginal Approach58820
Ovary
 Drainage
 Percutaneous58823
Palate
 Incision and Drainage42000
Paraurethral Gland
 Incision and Drainage53060
Parotid Gland Drainage42300-42305
Pelvic
 Drainage
 Percutaneous58823
Pelvis
 Incision and Drainage ..26990-26992, 45000
Pericolic
 Drainage
 Percutaneous58823
Perineum
 Incision and Drainage56405
Perirenal or Renal
 Drainage50020-50021
 Percutaneous50021
Peritoneum
 Incision and Drainage
 Open49020
 Percutaneous49021
Prostate
 Incision and Drainage55720-55725
 Transurethral Drainage52700
Radius
 Incision, Deep25035
Rectum
 Incision and Drainage45005-45020,
 46040, 46060
Retroperitoneal49060-49061
 Drainage
 Open49060
 Percutaneous49061

Salivary Gland
 Drainage42300-42320
Scapula
 Sequestrectomy23172
Scrotum
 Incision and Drainage54700, 55100
Shoulder
 Drainage23030
Skene's Gland
 Incision and Drainage53060
Skin
 Incision and Drainage10060-10061
 Puncture Aspiration10160
Soft Tissue
 Incision20000-20005
Spine
 Incision and Drainage22010-22015
Subdiaphragmatic49040-49041
Sublingual Gland
 Drainage42310-42320
Submaxillary Gland
 Drainage42310-42320
Subphrenic49040-49041
Testis
 Incision and Drainage54700
Thoracostomy32020
Thorax
 Incision and Drainage21501-21502
Throat
 Incision and Drainage42700-42725
Tongue
 Incision and Drainage41000-41006
Tonsil
 Incision and Drainage42700
Ulna
 Incision, Deep25035
Urethra
 Incision and Drainage53040
Uvula
 Incision and Drainage42000
Vagina
 Incision and Drainage57010
Vulva
 Incision and Drainage56405
Wrist
 Excision25145
 Incision and Drainage25028, 25035
X-Ray76080

Abscess, Nasal
See Nose, Abscess

Abscess, Parotid Gland
See Parotid Gland, Abscess

Absorptiometry
Dual Energy
 Body Composition0028T
 Bone
 Appendicular77081
 Axial Skeleton77080
 Vertebral77082
Dual Photon
 Bone78351
Radiographic
 Photodensity77083
Single Photon
 Bone78350

Adductor Tenotomy of Hip
See Tenotomy, Hip, Adductor

Adenoidectomy42820-42821,
42830-42836

Adenoids
Excision42830-42836
　　with Tonsils42820-42821
Unlisted Services and Procedures42999

Adenoma
Pancreas
　　Excision48120
Thyroid Gland Excision60200

Adenosine 3'5' Monophosphate
See Cyclic AMP

Adenosine Diphosphate
Blood82030

Adenosine Monophosphate (AMP)
Blood82030

Adenovirus
Antibody86603
Antigen Detection
　　Enzyme Immunoassay87301
　　Immunofluorescense87260

Adenovirus Vaccine
See Vaccines

Adenylic Acid
See Adenosine Monophosphate (AMP)

ADH
See Antidiuretic Hormone

Adhesions
Epidural0027T, 62263-62264
Eye
　　Corneovitreal65880
　　Incision
　　　　Anterior Segment65860-65870
　　　　Posterior Segment65875
Intermarginal
　　Construction67880
　　　　Transposition of Tarsal Plate67882
Intestinal
　　Enterolysis44005
　　Laparoscopic44180
Intracranial
　　Lysis62161
Intrauterine
　　Lysis58559
Labial
　　Lysis56441
Lungs
　　Lysis32124
Pelvic
　　Lysis58660, 58662, 58740
Penile
　　Lysis
　　　　Post-circumcision54162
Preputial
　　Lysis54450
Urethral
　　Lysis53500

Adipectomy
See Lipectomy

ADL
See Activities of Daily Living

Administration
Immunization
　　Each Additional Vaccine/Toxoid90472,
90474
　　　　with Counseling90466, 90468
　　One Vaccine/Toxoid90471, 90473
　　　　with Counseling90465, 90467

ADP
See Adenosine Diphosphate

ADP Phosphocreatine Phosphotransferase
See CPK

Adrenal Cortex Hormone
See Corticosteroids

Adrenal Gland
Biopsy60540-60545
Excision
　　Laparoscopy60650
　　Retroperitoneal Tumor60545
Exploration60540-60545
Nuclear Medicine
　　Imaging78075

Adrenal Medulla
See Medulla

Adrenalectomy60540
Anesthesia00866
Laparoscopic50545

Adrenalin
See Catecholamines
Blood82383
Urine82384

Adrenaline-Noradrenaline
Testing82382-82384

Adrenocorticotropic Hormone (ACTH) ...80400-80406, 80412, 80418, 82024
Blood or Urine82024
Stimulation Panel80400-80406

Adrenogenital Syndrome .56805, 57335

Adult T Cell Leukemia Lymphoma Virus I
See HTLV I

Advanced Life Support
See Emergency Department Services
Physician Direction99288

Advancement
Genioglossus21199
Tendon
　　Foot28238

Advancement Flap
See Skin, Adjacent Tissue Transfer

Aerosol Inhalation
See Pulmonology, Therapeutic
Pentamidine94642

AFB
See Acid Fast Bacilli (AFB)

Afferent Nerve
See Sensory Nerve

AFP
See Alpha-Fetoprotein

After Hours Medical Services99050

Agents, Anticoagulant
See Clotting Inhibitors

Agglutinin
Cold86156-86157
Febrile86000

Aggregation
Platelet85576

AHG
See Clotting Factor

AICD (Pacing Cardioverter-Defibrillator)
See Defibrillator, Heart; Pacemaker, Heart

Aid, Hearing
See Hearing Aid

AIDS Antibodies
See Antibody, HIV

AIDS Virus
See HIV-1

Akin Operation
See Bunion Repair

ALA
See Aminolevulinic Acid (ALA)

Alanine 2 Oxoglutarate Aminotransferase
See Transaminase, Glutamic Pyruvic

Alanine Amino (ALT)84460

Alanine Transaminase
See Transaminase, Glutamic Pyruvic

Albarran Test
See Water Load Test

Albumin
Ischemia modified82045
Serum82040
Urine82042-82044

Alcohol
Breath82075
Ethyl
　　Blood82055
　　Urine82055
Ethylene Glycol82693

Alcohol Dehydrogenase
See Antidiuretic Hormone

Heart	.00580
Kidney	.00868
Liver	.00796, 01990
Lungs	.00580
Organ Harvesting	.01990
Transurethral Procedures	.00910-00918
Tubal Ligation	.00851
Tuffier Vaginal Hysterectomy	.00944
TURP	.00914
Tympanostomy	.00120
Tympanotomy	.00126
Unlisted Services and Procedures	.01999
Urethra	.00910, 00918-00920, 00942
Urethrocystoscopy	.00910
Urinary Bladder	.00864, 00870, 00912
Urinary Tract	.00860
Uterus	.00952
Vagina	.00940-00942, 00950
Dilation	.57400
Removal	
Foreign Body	.57415
Vaginal Delivery	.01960
Vas Deferens	
Excision	.00921
Vascular Access	.00532
Vascular Shunt	.01844
Vascular Surgery	
Abdomen, Lower	.00880-00882
Abdomen, Upper	.00770
Arm, Lower	.01840-01852
Arm, Upper	.01770-01782
Brain	.00216
Elbow	.01770-01782
Hand	.01840-01852
Knee	.01430-01432, 01440-01444
Leg, Lower	.01500-01502, 01520-01522
Leg, Upper	.01260, 01270-01274
Neck	.00350-00352
Shoulder	.01650-01656, 01670
Wrist	.01840-01852
Vasectomy	.00921
Venography	.01916
Ventriculography	.00214, 01920
Vertebral Process	
Fracture/Dislocation	
Closed Treatment	.22315
Vertebroplasty	.01905
Vitrectomy	.00145
Vitreoretinal Surgery	.00145
Vitreous Body	.00145
Vulva	.00906
Vulvectomy	.00906
Wertheim Operation	.00846
Wrist	.00400, 01810-01860

Anesthesia Local
See Anesthesia, Local

Aneurysm Repair
See Aorta; Artery

Abdominal Aorta	.0078T, 0079T, 0080T, 0081T, 34800-34805, 34825-34832, 35081-35103, 75952-75953
Axillary Artery	.35011-35013
Basilar Artery	.61698, 61702
Brachial Artery	.35011-35013
Carotid Artery	.35001-35002, 61613, 61697, 61700, 61703

Celiac Artery	.35121-35122
Femoral Artery	.35141-35142
Hepatic Artery	.35121-35122
Iliac Artery	.34900, 35131-35132, 75953-75954
Innominate Artery	.35021-35022
Intracranial Artery	.61705-61708
Mesenteric Artery	.35121-35122
Popliteal Artery	.35151-35152
Radial Artery	.35045
Renal Artery	.35121-35122
Splenic Artery	.35111-35112
Subclavian Artery	.35001-35002, 35021-35022
Thoracoabdominal Aorta	.33877
Ulnar Artery	.35045
Vascular Malformation or Carotid-Cavernous Fistula	.61710
Vertebral Artery	.61698, 61702

Angel Dust
See Phencyclidine

Angina Assessment
See Performance Measure

Angiocardiographies
See Heart, Angiography

Angiography
See Aortography

Abdomen	.74175, 74185, 75635, 75726
Abdominal Aorta	.0080T, 0081T, 75635, 75952-75953
Adrenal	.75731-75733
Aorta	
Injection	.93544
Arm Artery	.73206, 75710-75716
Arteriovenous Shunt	.75790
Brachial Artery	.75658
Brain	.70496
Carotid Artery	.75660-75671
Cervical	
Bilateral	.75680
Unilateral	.75676
Chest	.71275, 71555
Coronary Artery	.93556
Coronary Calcium Evaluation	.0146T-0149T
Flow Velocity Measurement During Angiography	.93571-93572
Coronary Bypass	.93556
Endovascular Repair	.0080T, 0081T, 75952-75953
Extremity, Lower	.73725
Extremity, Upper	.73225
Fluorescein	.92235
Head	.70496, 70544-70546
Artery	.75650
Heart Vessels	
Injection	.93545
Indocyanine-green	.92240
Left Heart	
Injection	.93543
Leg Artery	.73706, 75635, 75710-75716
Lung	
Injection	.93541
	See Cardiac Catheterization, Injection
Mammary Artery	.75756
	See Aortography
Neck	.70498, 70547-70549
Artery	.75650

Nuclear Medicine	.78445
Other Artery	.75774
Pelvic Artery	.72198, 75736
Pelvis	.72191
Pulmonary	.75741-75746
Renal Artery	.75722-75724
Right Heart	
Injection	.93542
Spinal Artery	.75705
Spinal Canal	.72159
Thorax	.71275
Transcatheter Therapy	
Embolization	.75894, 75898
Infusion	.75894, 75898
Vertebral	.75685

Angioma
See Lesion, Skin

Angioplasties, Coronary Balloon
See Percutaneous Transluminal Angioplasty

Angioplasty
Aorta	
Intraoperative	.35452
Percutaneous	.35472
Axillary Artery	
Intraoperative	.35458
Brachiocephalic Artery	
Intraoperative	.35458
Percutaneous	.35475
Coronary Artery	
Percutaneous Transluminal	.92982-92984
Femoral Artery	
Intraoperative	.35456
Percutaneous	.35474
Iliac Artery	
Intraoperative	.35454
Percutaneous	.35473
Intracranial	
Percutaneous	.61630
Percutaneous Transluminal	
Angioplasty	.92982-92984
	See Angioplasty; Percutaneous, Transluminal
Popliteal Artery	
Intraoperative	.35456
Percutaneous	.35474
Pulmonary Artery	
Percutaneous Transluminal	.92997-92998
Renal Artery	
Intraoperative	.35450
Percutaneous	.35471
Subclavian Artery	
Intraoperative	.35458
Tibioperoneal Artery	
Intraoperative	.35459
Percutaneous	.35470
Transluminal	
Arterial	.75962-75968
Venous	.75978
Venous	
Intraoperative	.35460
Percutaneous	.35476
Visceral Artery	
Intraoperative	.35450
Percutaneous	.35471

Angioscopy
Non-Coronary Vessels	.35400

Angiotensin Converting Enzyme (ACE)82164
See Performance Measures

Angiotensin Forming Enzyme
See Renin

Angiotensin I84244
Riboflavin84252

Angiotensin II
Blood or Urine82163

Angle Deformity
Reconstruction
 Toe28313

Anhydride, Carbonic
See Carbon Dioxide

Anhydrides, Acetic
See Acetic Anhydrides

Animal Inoculation87001-87003, 87250

Ankle
See Fibula; Leg, Lower; Tibia; Tibiofibular Joint
Abscess
 Incision and Drainage27603
Amputation27888
Arthrocentesis20605
Arthrodesis27870
Arthrography73615
Arthroplasty27700-27703
Arthroscopy
 Surgical29891-29899
Arthrotomy27610-27612, 27620-27626
Biopsy27613-27614, 27620
Bursa
 Incision and Drainage27604
Disarticulation27889
Dislocation
 Closed Treatment27840-27842
 Open Treatment27846-27848
Exploration27610, 27620
Fracture
 Lateral27786-27814
 Medial27760-27766, 27808-27814
 Trimalleolar27816-27823
Fusion27870
Hematoma
 Incision and Drainage27603
Incision27607
Injection
 Radiologic27648
Lesion
 Excision27630
Magnetic Resonance Imaging
(MRI)73721-73723
Manipulation27860
Removal
 Foreign Body27610, 27620
 Implant27704
 Loose Body27620
Repair
 Achilles Tendon27650-27654
 Ligament27695-27698
 Tendon27612, 27680-27687
Strapping29540

Synovium
 Excision27625-27626
Tenotomy27605-27606
Tumor
 Excision27615-27619
Unlisted Services and Procedures27899
X-Ray73600-73610
 with Contrast73615

Ankylosis (Surgical)
See Arthrodesis

Annuloplasty
Percutaneous, Intradiscal0062T, 0063T, 22526-22527

Anogenital Region
See Perineum

Anoplasty
Stricture46700-46705

Anorectal
Biofeedback90911
Repair
 Fistula0170T, 46706

Anorectal Exam (Surgical)45990

Anorectal Myectomy
See Myomectomy, Anorectal

Anorectovaginoplasty46744-46746

Anoscopy
Ablation
 Polyp46615
 Tumor46615
Biopsy46606
Dilation46604
Exploration46600
Hemorrhage46614
Removal
 Foreign Body46608
 Polyp46610-46612
 Tumor46610-46612

Antebrachium
See Forearm

Antecedent, Plasma Thromboplastin
See Plasma Thromboplastin, Antecedent

Antepartum Care
Cesarean Delivery59510
 Previous59610, 59618
Vaginal Delivery59425-59426

Anterior Ramus of Thoracic Nerve
See Intercostal Nerve

Anthrax Vaccine
See Vaccines

Anthrogon
See Follicle Stimulating Hormone (FSH)

Anti Australia Antigens
See Antibody, Hepatitis B

Anti D Immunoglobulin
See Immune Globulins, Rho (D)

Anti-Human Globulin Consumption Test
See Coombs Test

Anti-Phospholipid Antibody
See Antibody, Phospholipid

Antiactivator, Plasmin
See Alpha-2 Antiplasmin

Antibiotic Administration
Injection90772

Antibiotic Sensitivity87181-87184, 87188
Enzyme Detection87185
Minimum Bactericidal Concentration87187
Minimum Inhibitory Concentration87186

Antibodies, Thyroid-Stimulating
See Immunoglobulin, Thyroid Stimulating

Antibodies, Viral
See Viral Antibodies

Antibody
See Antibody Identification; Microsomal Antibody
Actinomyces86602
Adenovirus86603
Antinuclear86038-86039
Antiphosphatidylserine (Phospholipid)86148
Antiprothrombin0030T
Antistreptolysin O86060-86063
Aspergillus86606
Bacterium86609
Bartonella86611
Beta 2 Glycoprotein I86146
Blastomyces86612
Blood Crossmatch86920-86923
Bordetella86615
Borrelia86618-86619
Brucella86622
Campylobacter86625
Candida86628
Cardiolipin86147
Chlamydia86631-86632
Coccidioides86635
Coxiella Burnetii86638
Cryptococcus86641
Cyclic Citrullinated Peptide (CCP)86200
Cytomegalovirus86644-86645
Cytotoxic Screen86807-86808
Deoxyribonuclease86215
Deoxyribonucleic Acid (DNA)86225-86226
Diphtheria86648
Ehrlichia86666
Encephalitis86651-86654
Enterovirus86658
Epstein-Barr Virus86663-86665
Fluorescent86255-86256
Francisella Tularensis86668
Fungus86671
Giardia Lamblia86674
Growth Hormone86277
Helicobacter Pylori86677
Helminth86682
Hemophilus Influenza86684
Hepatitis
 Delta Agent86692

Hepatitis A86708-86709
Hepatitis B
 Core86704
 IgM86705
 Surface86706
Hepatitis Be86707
Hepatitis C86803-86804
Herpes Simplex86694-86696
Heterophile86308-86310
Histoplasma86698
HIV86689, 86701-86703
HIV-186701, 86703
HIV-286702-86703
HTLV-I86687, 86689
HTLV-II86688
Influenza Virus86710
Insulin86337
Intrinsic Factor86340
Islet Cell86341
Legionella86713
Leishmania86717
Leptospira86720
Listeria Monocytogenes86723
Lyme Disease86617
Lymphocytic Choriomeningitis86727
Lymphogranuloma Venereum86729
Microsomal86376
Mucormycosis86732
Mumps86735
Mycoplasma86738
Neisseria Meningitidis86741
Nocardia86744
Nuclear Antigen86235
Other Virus86790
Parvovirus86747
Phospholipid86147
Phospholipid Cofactor0030T
Plasmodium86750
Platelet86022-86023
Protozoa86753
Red Blood Cell86850-86870
Respiratory Syncytial Virus86756
Rickettsia86757
Rotavirus86759
Rubella86762
Rubeola86765
Salmonella86768
Shigella86771
Sperm89325
Streptokinase86590
Tetanus86774
Thyroglobulin86800
Toxoplasma86777-86778
Treponema Pallidum86781
Trichinella86784
Varicella-Zoster86787
West Nile Virus86788-86789
White Blood Cell86021
Yersinia86793

Antibody Identification
Leukocyte Antibodies86021
Platelet86022-86023
Red Blood Cell
 Pretreatment86970-86972
Serum
 Pretreatment86975-86978

Antibody Neutralization Test
See Neutralization Test

Antibody Receptor
See FC Receptor

Anticoagulant
See Clotting Inhibitors

Anticoagulant Management99363-99364

Antidiabetic Hormone
See Glucagon

Antidiuretic Hormone Measurement
See Vasopressin

AntiDNA Autoantibody
See Antinuclear Antibodies (ANA)

Antigen
Allergen Immunotherapy95144
Carcinoembryonic82378
Prostate Specific84152-84153

Antigen Bronchial Provocation Tests
See Bronchial Challenge Test

Antigen Detection
Direct Fluorescence87265-87272, 87276,
 87278, 87280, 87285-87290
 Bordetella87265
 Chlamydia Trachomatis87270
 Cryptosporidium87272
 Cytomegalovirus87271
 Enterovirus87267
 Giardia87269
 Influenza A87276
 Legionella Pneumophila87278
 Not Otherwise Specified87299
 Respiratory Syncytial Virus87280
 Treponema Pallidum87285
 Varicella-Zoster87290
Enzyme Immunoassay87301-87451
 Adenovirus87301
 Aspergillus87305
 Chlamydia Trachomatis87320
 Clostridium Difficile87324
 Cryptococcus Neoformans87327
 Cryptosporidium87328
 Cytomegalovirus87332
 Entamoeba Histolytica Dispar Group ..87336
 Entamoeba Histolytica Group87337
 Escherichia coli O15787335
 Giardia87329
 Helicobacter Pylori87338-87339
 Hepatitis B Surface Antigen (HBsAg) ..87340
 Hepatitis B Surface Antigen (HBsAg) Neutralization ..87341
 Hepatitis Be Antigen (HBeAg)87350
 Hepatitis Delta Agent87380
 Histoplasma capsulatum87385
 HIV-187390
 HIV-287391
 Influenza A87400
 Influenza B87400

Multiple Step Method87301-87449
 Polyvalent87451
Not Otherwise Specified87449, 87451
Respiratory Syncytial Virus87420
Rotavirus87425
Shigella-like Toxin87427
Single Step Method87450
Streptococcus, Group A87430
Immunoassay
 Direct Optical
 Clostridium Difficile Toxin A87803
 Influenza87804
 Respiratory Syncytial Virus87807
 Streptococcus, Group B87802
 Trichomonas Vaginalis87808
Immunofluorescence87260-87300
 Adenovirus87260
 Herpes Simplex87273-87274
 Influenza B87275
 Legionella Micdadei87277
 Not Otherwise Specified87299
 Parainfluenza Virus87279
 Pneumocystis Carinii87281
 Polyvalent87300
 Rubeola87283

Antigen, Australia
See Hepatitis Antigen, B Surface

Antigen, CD4
See CD4

Antigen, CD8
See CD8

Antigens, CD142
See Thromboplastin

Antigens, CD143
See Angiotensin Converting Enzyme (ACE)

Antigens, E
See Hepatitis Antigen, Be

Antigens, Hepatitis
See Hepatitis Antigen

Antigens, Hepatitis B
See Hepatitis Antigen, B

Antihemophilic Factor B
See Christmas Factor

Antihemophilic Factor C
See Plasma Thromboplastin, Antecedent

Antihemophilic Globulin (AHG)85240

Antihuman Globulin86880-86886

Antimony83015

Antinuclear Antibodies (ANA)86038-86039

Antiplasmin, Alpha-285410

Antiplatelet Therapy
See Performance Measures

Antiprotease, Alpha 1
See Alpha-1 Antitrypsin

Antiprothrombin Antibody0030T

Antistreptococcal Antibody86215

Antistreptokinase Titer86590

Antistreptolysin O86060-86063

Antithrombin III85300-85301

Antithrombin VI
See Fibrin Degradation Products

Antitoxin Assay87230

Antiviral Antibody
See Viral Antibodies

Antrostomy
Sinus
 Maxillary31256-31267

Antrotomy
Sinus
 Maxillary31020-31032
Transmastoid69501

Antrum of Highmore
See Sinus, Maxillary

Antrum Puncture
Sinus
 Maxillary31000
 Sphenoid31002

Anus
See Hemorrhoids; Rectum
Ablation46615
Abscess
 Incision and Drainage46045-46050
Biofeedback90911
Biopsy
 Endoscopy46606
Crypt
 Excision46210-46211
Dilation
 Endoscopy46604
Endoscopy
 Biopsy46606
 Dilation46604
 Exploration46600
 Hemorrhage46614
 Removal
 Foreign Body46608
 Polyp46610, 46612
 Tumor46610, 46612
Excision
 Tag46220, 46230
Exploration
 Endoscopy46600
 Surgical45990
Fissure
 Destruction46940-46942
 Excision46200
Fistula
 Excision46270-46285
 Repair0170T, 46706
Hemorrhage
 Endoscopic Control46614
Hemorrhoids
 Clot Excision46320
 Destruction46934-46936

Excision46250-46262
Injection46500
Ligation46221, 46945-46946
Stapling46947
Suture46945-46946
Imperforated
 Repair46715-46742
Incision
 Septum46070
Lesion
 Destruction46900-46917, 46924
 Excision45108, 46922
Manometry91122
Placement
 Seton46020
Reconstruction46742
 Congenital Absence46730-46740
 Sphincter46750-46751, 46760-46762
 with Graft46753
 with Implant46762
Removal
 Foreign Body46608
 Seton46030
 Suture46754
 Wire46754
Repair
 Anovaginal Fistula46715-46716
 Cloacal Anomaly46748
 Fistula0170T, 46706
 Stricture46700-46705
Sphincter
 Chemodenervation46505
 Electromyography51784-51785
 Needle51785
Unlisted Services and Procedures46999

Aorta
Abdominal
 Aneurysm0078T, 0079T, 0080T, 0081T,
 34800-34805, 34825-34832,
 35081-35103, 75952-75953
 Thromboendarterectomy35331
Anastomosis
 to Pulmonary Artery33606
Angiogram
 Radiologic Injection93544
 See Cardiac Catheterization, Injection
Angioplasty35452
Aortography75600-75630
Balloon33967, 33970
Catheterization
 Catheter36200
 Intracatheter/Needle36160
Circulation Assist33967, 33970
Conduit to Heart33404
Excision
 Coarctation33840-33851
Insertion
 Balloon Device33967
 Graft33330-33335
 Intracatheter/Needle36160
Removal
 Balloon Assist Device33968, 33971
Repair33320-33322, 33802-33803
 Coarctation33840-33851
 Graft33860-33877
 Hypoplastic or Interrupted Aortic Arch
 with Cardiopulmonary Bypass33853
 without Cardiopulmonary Bypass ...33852

Sinus of Valsalva33702-33720
Suspension33800
Suture33320-33322
Thoracic
 Repair75956-75959
 Endovascular33880-33891
Valve
 Incision33415
 Repair33400-33403
 Left Ventricle33414
 Supravalvular Stenosis33417
 Replacement33405-33413
X-Ray with Contrast75600-75630

Aorta-Pulmonary ART Transposition
See Transposition, Great Arteries

Aortic Sinus
See Sinus of Valsalva

Aortic Stenosis
Repair33415
 Supravalvular33417

Aortic Valve
See Heart, Aortic Valve

Aortic Valve Replacement
See Replacement, Aortic Valve

Aortocoronary Bypass
See Coronary Artery Bypass Graft (CABG)

Aortocoronary Bypass for Heart Revascularization
See Artery, Coronary, Bypass

Aortography75600-75605,
 75630, 93544
See Angiography
Serial75625
with Iliofemoral Artery75630

Aortoiliac
Embolectomy34151-34201
Thrombectomy34151-34201

Aortopexy33800

Aortoplasty
Supravalvular Stenosis33417

AP
See Voiding Pressure Studies

Apert-Gallais Syndrome
See Adrenogenital Syndrome

Aphasia Testing96105
See Neurology, Diagnostic

Apheresis
Therapeutic36511-36516

Apical-Aortic Conduit33404

Apicectomy
with Mastoidectomy69605
 Petrous69530

Apoaminotransferase, Aspartate
See Transaminase, Glutamic Oxaloacetic

Artery Catheterization, Pulmonary
See Catheterization, Pulmonary Artery

Arthrectomy

Arthrocentesis

Arthrodeses
See Arthrodesis

Arthrodesis

Destruction
 Calculi (Stone)43265
Dilation
 Endoscopy43271, 47555-47556
Drainage
 Transhepatic75980
Endoscopy
 Biopsy .47553
 Destruction
 Calculi (Stone)43265
 Tumor .43272
 Dilation43271, 47555-47556
 Exploration .47552
 Intraoperative47550
 Removal
 Calculi (Stone)43264, 47554
 Foreign Body43269
 Stent .43269
 Specimen Collection43260
 Sphincter Pressure43263
 Sphincterotomy43262
 Tube Placement43267-43268
Exploration
 Atresia .47700
 Endoscopy .47552
Incision
 Sphincter43262, 47460
Incision and Drainage47420-47425
Insertion
 Catheter47510, 47525, 75982
 Revision .47530
 Stent47511, 47801
Nuclear Medicine
 Imaging .78223
Reconstruction
 Anastomosis47800
Removal
 Calculi (Stone)43264, 47420-47425
 Percutaneous47630
 Foreign Body43269
 Stent .43269
Repair .47701
 Cyst .47719
 Gastrointestinal Tract47785
 with Intestines47760, 47780
Tube Placement
 Nasobiliary .43267
 Stent .43268
Tumor
 Destruction43271
 Excision47711-47712
Unlisted Services and Procedures47999
X-Ray
 Guide Dilation74360
 with Contrast74300-74320
 Calculus Removal74327
 Guide Catheter74328, 74330

Bile Duct, Common, Cystic Dilatation
See Cyst, Choledochal

Bilirubin
Blood .82247-82248
Feces .82252
Total
 Direct82247-82248
 Transcutaneous88400

Billroth I or II
See Gastrectomy, Partial

Bilobectomy32482

Bimone
See Testosterone

Binding Globulin, Testosterone-Estradiol
See Globulin, Sex Hormone Binding

Binet Test96101-96103

Binet-Simon Test96101-96103

Binocular Microscopy92504

Biofeedback
See Training, Biofeedback
Anorectal .90911
Psychiatric Treatment90875-90876

Biofeedback Training
See Training, Biofeedback

Bioimpedance
Breast .0060T
Thorax .93701

Biological Skin Grafts
See Allograft, Skin

Biometry
Eye76516-76519, 92136

Biopsies, Needle
See Needle Biopsy

Biopsy
See Brush Biopsy; Needle Biopsy
Abdomen .49000
Adrenal Gland60540-60545
Anal
 Endoscopy46606
Ankle27613-27614, 27620
Arm, Lower25065-25066
Arm, Upper24065-24066
Artery
 Temporal .37609
Auditory Canal, External69105
Back/Flank21920-21925
Bile Duct
 Endoscopy47553
Bladder .52354
 Cystourethroscope52204
 Cystourethroscopy52224, 52250
Blood Vessel
 Transcatheter75970
Bone20220-20245
Bone Marrow38221
Brain .61140
 Stereotactic61750-61751
Brainstem61575-61576
Breast19100-19103
 Stereotactic Localization77031
Bronchi
 Catheterization31717
 Endoscopic31625-31629, 31632-31633
Brush
 Bronchi .31717
 Renal Pelvis52007

Ureter .52007
 with Cystourethroscopy52204
Carpometacarpal Joint
 Synovium .26100
Cervix57454-57455, 57460, 57500, 57520
Chorionic Villus59015
Colon44025, 44100
 Endoscopy44389, 45380, 45391-45392
 Multiple
 with Colostomy, Cecostomy44322
Colon-Sigmoid
 Endoscopy45305, 45331
Conjunctiva .68100
Cornea .65410
Duodenum .44010
Ear
 External .69100
Elbow24065-24066, 24101
 Synovium .24100
Embryo Blastomere89290-89291
Endometrium58100-58110, 58558
Epididymis54800, 54865
Esophagus
 Endoscopy43202
Eye Muscle .67346
Eyelid .67810
Forearm
 Soft Tissue25065-25066
Gallbladder
 Endoscopy43261
Gastrointestinal, Upper
 Endoscopy43239
Hand Joint
 Synovium .26100
Heart .93505
Hip .27040-27041
 Joint .27052
Hypopharynx42802
Ileum
 Endoscopy44382
Interphalangeal Joint
 Finger .26110
 Toe .28054
Intertarsal Joint
 Toe .28050
Intestines, Small44020, 44100
 Endoscopy44361, 44377
Kidney50200-50205
 Endoscopic50555-50557,
 50574-50576, 52354
Knee27323-27324
 Synovium .27330
Knee Joint
 Synovium .27330
Lacrimal Gland68510
Lacrimal Sac68525
Larynx
 Endoscopy31510, 31576
Leg
 Lower27613-27614
 Upper27323-27324
Lip .40490
Liver47000-47001, 47100
Lung
 Needle .32405
 Thoracotomy32095-32100

Biopsy, Skin
See Skin, Biopsy

Biopsy, Vein
See Vein, Biopsy

Biostatistics
See Biometry

Biosterol
See Vitamin, A

Birthing Room

Bischof Procedure
See Laminectomy, Surgical

Bizzozero's Corpuscle/Cell
See Blood, Platelet

Bladder

Urethrocystography74450-74455
Urethrotomy52270-52276
Urinary Incontinence Procedures
 Laparoscopy51990-51992
 Pulsed Magnetic Neuromodulation ...0029T
X-Ray74430
 with Contrast74450-74455

Bladder Voiding Pressure Studies51795

Blalock-Hanlon Procedure33735-33737
See Septostomy, Atrial

Blalock-Taussig Procedure
See Shunt, Great Vessel

Blast Cells
See Stem Cell

Blast Transformation
See Blastogenesis

Blastocyst Implantation
See Implantation

Blastocyst Transfer
See Embryo Transfer

Blastogenesis86353

Blastomyces
Antibody86612

Blastomycosis, European
See Cryptococcus

Bleeding
See Hemorrhage
Anal
 See Anus, Hemorrhage
Disorder
 See Coagulopathy
Time85002
Tube
 Passage and Placement91100
Uterine
 See Hemorrhage, Uterus
Vaginal
 See Hemorrhage, Vaginal

Blepharoplasty15820-15823
See Canthoplasty
Anesthesia00103

Blepharoptosis
Repair67901-67909
 Frontalis Muscle Technique67901
 with Fascial Sling67902
 Superior Rectus Technique with
 Fascial Sling67906
 Tarso Levator Resection/Advancement
 External Approach67904
 Internal Approach67903

Blepharorrhaphy
See Tarsorrhaphy

Blepharospasm
Chemodenervation64612

Blepharotomy67700

Blister
See Bulla

Blom-Singer Prosthesis31611

Blood
See Blood Cell Count, Complete Blood Count
Bleeding Time85002
Collection, for Autotransfusion
 Intraoperative86891
 Preoperative86890
Feces82270, 82272
 by Hemoglobin Immunoassay82274
Gastric Contents82273
Hemoglobin Concentration85046
Nuclear Medicine
 Flow Imaging78445
 Red Cell78140
 Red Cell Survival78130-78135
Osmolality83930
Other Source82273
Plasma
 Exchange36514-36516
Platelet
 Aggregation85576
 Automated Count85049
 Count85008
 Manual Count85032
Stem Cell
 Count86367
 Donor Search38204
 Harvesting38205-38206
 Transplantation38240-38242
 Cell Concentration38215
 Cryopreservation38207, 88240
 Plasma Depletion38214
 Platelet Depletion38213
 Red Blood Cell Depletion38212
 T-cell Depletion38210
 Thawing38208-38209, 88241
 Tumor Cell Depletion38211
 Washing38209
Transfusion36430
 Exchange36455
 Newborn36450
 Fetal36460
Push
 Infant36440
Unlisted Services and Procedures85999
Urine83491
Viscosity85810

Blood Banking
Frozen Blood Preparation86930-86932
Frozen Plasma Preparation86927
Physician Services86077-86079

Blood Cell
CD4 and CD8
 Including Ratio86360
Enzyme Activity82657
Exchange36511-36513
Sedimentation Rate
 Automated85652
 Manual85651

Blood Cell Count
Automated85049
B-Cells86355

Blood Smear85007-85008
Differential WBC Count85004-85007, 85009
Hematocrit85014
Hemoglobin85018
Hemogram
 Added Indices85025-85027
 Automated85025-85027
 Manual85032
Microhematocrit85013
Natural Killer (NK) Cells86357
Red Blood Cells85032-85041
Reticulocyte85044-85046
Stem Cells86367
T-Cells86359-86361
White Blood Cells85032, 85048, 89055

Blood Cell Count, Red
See Red Blood Cell (RBC), Count

Blood Cell Count, White
See White Blood Cell, Count

Blood Cell, Red
See Red Blood Cell (RBC)

Blood Cell, White
See Leukocyte

Blood Clot
Assay85396
Clot Lysis Time85175
Clot Retraction85170
Clotting Factor85250-85293
Clotting Factor Test85210-85244
Clotting Inhibitors ...85300-85302, 85305, 85307
Coagulation Time85345-85348

Blood Coagulation
Defect
 See Coagulopathy
Disorders
 See Clot
Factor
 See Clotting Factor
 Factor I
 See Fibrinogen
 Factor II
 See Prothrombin
 Factor III
 See Thromboplastin
 Factor IV
 See Calcium
 Factor VII
 See Proconvertin
 Factor VIII
 See Clotting Factor
 Factor IX
 See Christmas Factor
 Factor X
 See Stuart-Prower Factor
 Factor X, Activated
 See Thrombokinase
 Factor XI
 See Plasma Thromboplastin, Antecedent
 Factor XIII
 See Fibrin Stabilizing Factor
Test
 See Coagulation

Blood Component Removal
See Apheresis

Blood Count, Complete
See Complete Blood Count (CBC)

Blood Flow Check, Graft15860, 90940

Blood Gases
CO_282803
HCO_382803
O_2 Saturation82805-82810
pCO_282803
pH82800-82803
pO_282803

Blood Letting
See Phlebotomy

Blood Lipoprotein
See Lipoprotein

Blood Occult
See Occult, Blood

Blood Pool Imaging78472-78473,
78481-78483, 78494-78496

Blood Pressure
See Performance Measures
Left Ventricular Filling0086T
Monitoring, 24 Hour93784-93790
Venous93770

Blood Products
Irradiation86945
Pooling86965
Splitting86985
Volume Reduction86960

Blood Sample
Fetal59030

Blood Serum
See Serum

Blood Smear85060

Blood Syndrome
Chromosome Analysis88245-88248

Blood Tests
Nuclear Medicine
 Plasma Volume78110-78111
 Platelet Survival78190-78191
 Red Cell Volume78120-78121
 Whole Blood Volume78122
Panels
 Electrolyte80051
 General Health Panel80050
 Hepatic Function80076
 Hepatitis, Acute80074
 Lipid Panel80061
 Metabolic
 Basic80048
 Comprehensive80053
 Obstetric Panel80055
 Renal Function80069
Volume Determination78122

Blood Transfusion, Autologous
See Autotransfusion

Blood Typing
ABO Only86900
Antigen Screen86903-86904
Crossmatch86920-86923
Other RBC Antigens86905
Paternity Testing86910-86911
Rh (D)86901
Rh Phenotype86906

Blood Urea Nitrogen84520-84525

Blood Vessels
See Artery; Vein
Angioscopy
 Non-Coronary35400
Endoscopy
 Surgical37500
Excision
 Arteriovenous Malformation ...63250-63252
Exploration
 Abdomen35840
 Chest35820
 Extremity35860
 Neck35800
Great
 Suture33320-33322
Harvest
 Endoscopic33508
 Lower Extremity Vein35572
 Upper Extremity Artery35600
 Upper Extremity Vein35500
Kidney
 Repair50100
Repair
 Abdomen
 See Aneurysm Repair; Fistula, Repair
 with Composite Graft35681-35683
 with Other Graft35281
 with Vein Graft35251
 Aneurysm61705-61708
 Arteriovenous Malformation ..61680-61692,
 61705-61710, 63250-63252
 Chest
 with Composite Graft35681-35683
 with Other Graft35271-35276
 with Vein Graft35241-35246
 Direct35201-35226
 Finger35207
 Graft Defect35870
 Hand35207
 Lower Extremity35226
 with Composite Graft35681-35683
 with Other Graft35281
 with Vein Graft35251
 Neck
 with Composite Graft35681-35683
 with Other Graft35261
 with Vein Graft35231
 Upper Extremity35206
 with Composite Graft35681-35683
 with Other Graft35266
 with Vein Graft35236
Shunt Creation
 Direct36818, 36821
 Thomas Shunt36835

 with Bypass Graft35686
 with Graft36825-36830
Shunt Revision
 with Graft36832

Blood, Occult
See Occult Blood

Bloom Syndrome
Chromosome Analysis88245

Blot Test, Ink
See Inkblot Test

Blotting, Western
See Western Blot

Blow-Out Fracture
Orbital Floor21385-21395

Blue, Dome Cyst
See Breast, Cyst

BMT
See Bone Marrow, Transplantation

Boarding Home Care99324-99337

Bodies
Acetone
 See Acetone Body
Barr
 See Barr Bodies
Carotid
 See Carotid Body
Ciliary
 See Ciliary Body
Heinz
 See Heinz Bodies
Inclusion
 See Inclusion Bodies
Ketone
 See Ketone Body

Body Cast
Halo29000
Removal29700, 29710-29715
Repair29720
Risser Jacket29010-29015
Turnbuckle Jacket29020-29025
Upper Body and Head29040
Upper Body and Legs29046
Upper Body and One Leg29044
Upper Body Only29035

Body Composition
Dual Energy X-Ray Absorptiometry0028T

Body Fluid
Crystal Identification89060

Body of Vertebra
See Vertebral Body

Body Section
X-Ray76100
 Motion76101-76102

Body System, Neurologic
See Nervous System

Excision
Biopsy .19100-19103
Capsules .19371
Chest Wall Tumor19260-19272
Cyst .19120
Lactiferous Duct Fistula19112
Lesion19120-19126, 19301
by Needle Localization19125-19126
Mastectomy19300-19307
Nipple Exploration19110

Exploration .19020

Implants
Insertion19340-19342
Preparation of Moulage19396
Removal19328-19330
Supply .19396

Incision
Capsules .19370

Injection
Radiologic .19030

Magnetic Resonance Imaging
(MRI) .77058-77059
with Computer-aided Detection0159T

Mammoplasty
Augmentation19324-19325
Reduction .19318

Mastopexy .19316
Metallic Localization Clip Placement19295
Needle Biopsy .19100
Needle Wire Placement19290-19291
Periprosthetic Capsulectomy19371
Periprosthetic Capsulotomy19370

Reconstruction19357-19369
Augmentation19324-19325
Mammoplasty19318-19325
Nipple19350-19355
Areola .19350
Revision .19380
with Free Flap19364
with Latissimus Dorsi Flap19361
with Other Techniques19366
with Tissue Expander19357
with Transverse Rectus Abdominis
Myocutaneous Flap19367-19369

Reduction .19318

Removal
Capsules .19371
Modified Radical19307
Partial19300-19302
Radical19305-19306
Simple, Complete19303
Subcutaneous19304

Repair
Suspension .19316

Stereotactic Localization77031
Ultrasound .76645
Unlisted Services and Procedures19499
X-Ray .77055-77057
Localization Nodule77032
with Computer-aided Detection .77051-77052

Breath Odor Alcohol
See Alcohol, Breath

Breath Test
Alcohol, Ethyl .82075
Heart Transplant Rejection Detection0085T

Helicobacter Pylori . . .78267-78268, 83013-83014
Hydrogen .91065

Breathing, Inspiratory Positive-Pressure
See Intermittent Positive Pressure Breathing
(IPPB)

Bricker Procedure
Intestines Anastomosis50820

Bristow Procedure
See Capsulorrhaphy, Anterior

Brock Operation
See Valvotomy, Pulmonary Valve

Broken, Nose
See Fracture, Nasal Bone

Bronchi
Aspiration
Endoscopic31645-31646
Biopsy
Endoscopic31625-31629, 31632-31633
Catheterization
with Bronchial Brush Biopsy31717
Endoscopy
Aspiration31645-31646
Biopsy31625-31629, 31632-31633
Destruction
Tumor .31641
Dilation31630-31631, 31636-31638
Excision
Lesion .31640
Exploration .31622
Foreign Body Removal31635
Fracture .31630
Injection .31656
Lesion31640-31641
Stenosis .31641
Tumor31640-31641
Ultrasound .31620
Exploration
Endoscopic .31622
Fracture
Endoscopy .31630
Injection
X-Ray31656-31715
Needle Biopsy31629, 31633
Reconstruction .31770
Graft Repair .31770
Stenosis .31775
Removal
Foreign Body31635
Repair
Fistula .32815
Stenosis
Endoscopic Treatment31641
Stent
Placement31636-31637
Revision .31638
Tumor
Excision .31640
Ultrasound .31620
Unlisted Services and Procedures31899
X-Ray
with Contrast71040-71060

Bronchial Allergen Challenge
See Bronchial Challenge Test

Bronchial Alveolar Lavage31624

Bronchial Brush Biopsy
with Catheterization31717

Bronchial Brushings/Protected Brushing .31623

Bronchial Challenge Test
See Allergy Tests
with Antigens, Gases95070
with Chemicals .95071

Bronchial Provocation Tests
See Bronchial Challenge Test

Bronchioalveolar Lavage
See Lung, Lavage

Broncho-Bronchial Anastomosis .32486

Bronchoalveolar Lavage
See Lung, Lavage

Bronchography71040-71060
Injection
Transtracheal31715
Segmental
Injection .31656

Bronchoplasty32501
See Reconstruction, Bronchi
Excision Stenosis and Anastomosis31775
Graft Repair .31770

Bronchopneumonia, Hiberno-Vernal
See Q Fever

Bronchopulmonary Lavage
See Lung, Lavage

Bronchoscopy
Alveolar Lavage .31624
Aspiration31645-31646
Biopsy31625-31629, 31632-31633
Brushing/Protected Brushing31623
Catheter Placement
Intracavitary Radioelement31643
Dilation31630-31631, 31636-31638
Exploration .31622
Fracture .31630
Injection .31656
Needle Biopsy31629, 31633
Removal
Foreign Body31635
Tumor31640-31641
Stenosis .31641
Stent Placement31631, 31636-31637
Stent Revision .31638
Ultrasound .31620
X-Ray Contrast .31656

Bronchospasm Evaluation
See Pulmonology, Diagnostic, Spirometry

Bronkodyl
See Theophylline

Brow Ptosis
Repair67900

Brucella86000
Antibody86622

Bruise
See Hematoma

Brunschwig Operation58240
See Hip; Pelvis, Exenteration

Brush Biopsy
See Biopsy; Needle Biopsy
Bronchi31717

Brush Border ab
See Antibody, Heterophile

Bucca
See Cheek

Buccal Mucosa
See Mouth, Mucosa

Bulbourethral Gland
Excision53250

Bulla
Incision and Drainage
　　Puncture Aspiration10160
Lung
　　Excision-Plication32141
　　　Endoscopic32655

BUN
See Blood Urea Nitrogen; Urea Nitrogen

Bunion Repair28296-28299
Chevron Procedure28296
Concentric Procedure28296
Joplin Procedure28294
Keller Procedure28292
Lapidus Procedure28297
Mayo Procedure28292
McBride Procedure28292
Mitchell Procedure28296
Silver Procedure28290
with Implant28293

Burgess Amputation
See Disarticulation, Ankle

Burhenne Procedure
See Bile Duct, Removal, Calculi (Stone);
Gallbladder

Burkitt Herpesvirus
See Epstein-Barr Virus

Burns
Allograft15300-15336
Debridement01951-01953,
　　　　　15002-15005, 16020-16030
Dressings16020-16030
Escharotomy16035-16036
Excision01951-01953
Initial Treatment16000

Tissue Culture Skin Grafts15100-15157
Xenograft15400-15431

Burr Hole
Anesthesia00214
Skull
　　Biopsy Brain61140
　　Catheterization61210
　　Drainage
　　　Abscess61150-61151
　　　Cyst61150-61151
　　　Hematoma61154-61156
　　Exploration
　　　Infratentorial61253
　　　Supratentorial61250
　　for Implant of Neurostimulator
　　　Array61863-61868
　　Injection, Contrast Media61120
　　Insertion
　　　Catheter61210
　　　Reservoir61210

Burrow's Operation
See Skin, Adjacent Tissue Transfer

Bursa
Ankle27604
Arm, Lower25031
Elbow
　　Excision24105
　　Incision and Drainage23931
Femur
　　Excision27062
Foot
　　Incision and Drainage28001
Hip
　　Incision and Drainage26991
Injection20600-20610
Ischial
　　Excision27060
Joint
　　Aspiration20600-20610
　　Drainage20600-20610
　　Injection20600-20610
Knee
　　Excision27340
Leg, Lower27604
Palm
　　Incision and Drainage26025-26030
Pelvis
　　Incision and Drainage26991
Shoulder
　　Drainage23031
Wrist25031
　　Excision25115-25116

Bursectomy
See Excision, Bursa

Bursitis, Radiohumeral
See Tennis Elbow

Bursocentesis
See Aspiration, Bursa

Button
Nasal Septal Prosthesis
　　Insertion30220

Butyrylcholine Esterase
See Cholinesterase

Bypass Graft
Aortobi-iliac35538, 35638
Aortobifemoral35540
Aortofemoral35539
Aortoiliac35537, 35637
Axillary Artery35516-35522, 35533,
　　　　35616-35623, 35650, 35654
Brachial Artery35510, 35512, 35522-35525
Carotid Artery33891, 35501-35510, 35526,
　　　　35601-35606, 35626, 35642
Celiac Artery35531, 35631
Coronary Artery
　　Angiography93556
　　Arterial33533-33536
　　Venous Graft33510-33516
Excision
　　Abdomen35907
　　Extremity35903
　　Neck35901
　　Thorax35905
Femoral Artery35521, 35533, 35551-35558,
　　　　35566, 35621, 35646-35647,
　　　　35651-35661, 35666, 35700
Harvest
　　Endoscopic33508
　　Upper Extremity Vein35500
Iliac Artery35563, 35663
Iliofemoral Artery ..35548-35549, 35565, 35665
Mesenteric Artery35531, 35631
Peroneal Artery35566-35571, 35666-35671
Placement
　　Vein Patch35685
Popliteal Artery ...35551-35558, 35571, 35623,
　　　　35651, 35656, 35671, 35700
Renal Artery35536, 35560, 35631-35636
Reoperation35700
Repair
　　Abdomen35907
　　Extremity35903
　　Lower Extremity
　　　with Composite Graft35681-35683
　　Neck35901
　　Thorax35905
Revascularization
　　Extremity35903
　　Neck35901
　　Thorax35905
Revision
　　Lower Extremity
　　　Femoral Artery35883-35884
　　　with Angioplasty35879
　　　with Vein Interposition35881
Secondary Repair35870
Splenic Artery35536, 35636
Subclavian Artery35506, 35511-35516,
　　　　35526, 35606-35616, 35626, 35645
Thrombectomy37184-37186
　　Other than Hemodialysis Graft
　　or Fistula35875-35876
Tibial Artery ..35566-35571, 35623, 35666-35671
Vertebral Artery35508, 35515, 35642-35645
with Composite Graft35681

Bypass In-Situ
Femoral Artery35583-35585
Peroneal Artery35585-35587
Popliteal Artery35583, 35587
Tibial Artery35585-35587
Ventricular Restoration33548

Bypass, Cardiopulmonary
See Cardiopulmonary Bypass

C

C-13
Urea Breath Test83013-83014
Urease Activity83013-83014

C-14
Urea Breath Test78267-78268
Urease Activity83013-83014

C-Peptide80432, 84681

C-Reactive Protein86140-86141

C-Section
See Cesarean Delivery

C Vitamin
See Ascorbic Acid

CABG
See Coronary Artery Bypass Graft (CABG)

Cadmium
Urine82300

Caffeine Halothane Contracture Test (CHCT)89049

Calcaneal Spur
See Heel Spur

Calcaneus
Craterization28120
Cyst
 Excision28100-28103
Diaphysectomy28120
Excision28118-28120
Fracture
 Open Treatment28415-28420
 Percutaneous Fixation28406
 with Manipulation28405-28406
 without Manipulation28400
Repair
 Osteotomy28300
Saucerization28120
Tumor
 Excision27647, 28100-28103
X-Ray73650

Calcareous Deposits
Subdeltoid
 Removal23000

Calcifediol
Blood or Urine82306

Calcifediol Assay
See Calciferol

Calciferol
Blood or Urine82307

Calcification
See Calcium, Deposits

Calciol
See Vitamin, D-3

Calcitonin
Blood or Urine82308
Stimulation Panel80410

Calcium
Blood
 Infusion Test82331
Deposits
 See Removal, Calculi (Stone); Removal,
 Foreign Bodies
Ionized82330
Total82310
Urine82340

Calcium-Binding Protein, Vitamin K-Dependent
See Osteocalcin

Calcium-Pentagastrin Stimulation80410

Calculus
Analysis82355-82370
Destruction
 Bile Duct43265
 Pancreatic Duct43265
Removal
 Bile Duct43264, 47554, 74327
 Bladder51050, 52310-52318, 52352
 Kidney50060-50081, 50130, 50561,
 50580, 52352
 Pancreatic Duct43264
 Ureter50610-50630, 50961, 50980,
 51060-51065, 52320-52325, 52352
 Urethra52310-52315, 52352

Calculus of Kidney
See Calculus, Removal, Kidney

Caldwell-Luc Procedure
See Sinus/Sinuses, Maxillary; Sinusotomy;
Sternum, Fracture
Orbital Floor Blowout Fracture21385
Sinusotomy31030-31032

Caliper
Application/Removal20660

Callander Knee Disarticulation
See Disarticulation, Knee

Callosum, Corpus
See Corpus Callosum

Calmette Guerin Bacillus Vaccine
See BCG Vaccine

Caloric Vestibular Test92533

Calycoplasty50405

Camey Enterocystoplasty50825

CAMP
See Cyclic AMP

Campbell Procedure27422

Campylobacter
Antibody86625

Campylobacter Pylori
See Helicobacter Pylori

Canal, Ear
See Auditory Canal

Canal, Semicircular
See Semicircular Canal

Canaloplasty69631, 69635

Candida
Antibody86628
Skin Test86485

Cannulation36821
Arterial36620-36625
Sinus
 Maxillary31000
 Sphenoid31002
Thoracic Duct38794

Cannulation, Renoportal
See Anastomosis, Renoportal

Cannulization
See Catheterization
Arteriovenous36145, 36810-36815
Declotting36550, 36860-36861
ECMO36822
External
 Declotting36860-36861
Vas Deferens55200
Vein to Vein36800

Canthocystostomy
See Conjunctivorhinostomy

Canthopexy
Lateral21282
Medial21280

Canthoplasty67950

Canthorrhaphy67880-67882

Canthotomy67715

Canthus
Reconstruction67950

Cap, Cervical
See Cervical Cap

Capsule
See Capsulodesis
Elbow
 Arthrotomy24006
 Excision24006
Foot28264
Interphalangeal Joint
 Excision26525
 Incision26525

Cardiomyotomy
See Esophagomyotomy

Cardioplasty 43320

Cardiopulmonary Bypass 33926
See Heart; Lung, Transplantation

**Cardiopulmonary
Resuscitation** 92950

Cardiotomy 33310-33315

Cardiovascular Stress Test
See Exercise Stress Tests

Cardioversion 92960-92961

Care
Custodial
 See Nursing Facility Services
Intensive
 See Intensive Care
Neonatal Intensive
 See Intensive Care, Neonatal
Self
 See Self Care

Care Plan Oversight Services
See Physician Services

Carneous Mole
See Abortion

Carnitine 82379

Carotene 82380

Caroticum, Glomus
See Carotid Body

Carotid Artery
Aneurysm Repair
 Vascular Malformation or Carotid-Cavernous
 Fistula 61710
Excision 60605
Ligation 37600-37606
Stent, Transcatheter Placement 0075T-0076T
Transection
 with Skull Base Surgery 61609

Carotid Body
Lesion
 Carotid Artery 60605
 Excision 60600

Carpal Bone
See Wrist
Arthroplasty
 with Implant 25443
Cyst
 Excision 25130-25136
Dislocation
 Closed Treatment 25690
 Open Treatment 25695
Excision 25210-25215
 Partial 25145
Fracture
 Closed Treatment 25622, 25630
 Open Treatment 25628, 25645
 with Manipulation 25624, 25635
 without Manipulation 25630

Incision and Drainage 26034
Insertion
 Vascular Pedicle 25430
Osteoplasty 25394
Repair 25431-25440
Sequestrectomy 25145
Tumor
 Excision 25130-25136

Carpal Tunnel
Injection
 Therapeutic 20526

Carpal Tunnel Syndrome
Decompression 64721

Carpals
Incision and Drainage 25035

Carpectomy 25210-25215

Carpometacarpal Joint
Arthrodesis
 Hand 26843-26844
 Thumb 26841-26842
Arthrotomy 26070
Biopsy
 Synovium 26100
Dislocation
 Closed Treatment 26670
 with Manipulation 26675-26676
 Open Treatment 26685-26686
Exploration 26070
Fusion
 Hand 26843-26844
 Thumb 26841-26842
Removal
 Foreign Body 26070
Repair 25447
Synovectomy 26130

Cartilage Graft
Ear to Face 21235
Harvesting 20910-20912
Rib to Face 21230

Cartilage, Arytenoid
See Arytenoid

Cartilage, Ear
See Ear Cartilage

Cartilaginous Exostoses
See Exostosis

Case Management Services
Anticoagulant Management 99363-99364
Team Conferences 99361-99373
Telephone Calls 99361-99373

Cast
See Brace; Splint
Body
 Risser Jacket 29010-29015
Body Cast
 Halo 29000
 Turnbuckle Jacket 29020-29025
 Upper Body and Head 29040
 Upper Body and Legs 29046

 Upper Body and One Leg 29044
 Upper Body Only 29035
Clubfoot 29450
Cylinder 29365
Finger 29086
Hand 29085
Hip 29305-29325
Leg
 Rigid Total Contact 29445
Long Arm 29065
Long Leg 29345-29355, 29365, 29450
Long Leg Brace 29358
Patellar Tendon Bearing (PTB) 29435
Removal 29700-29715
Repair 29720
Short Arm 29075
Short Leg 29405-29435, 29450
Shoulder 29049-29058
Walking 29355, 29425
 Revision 29440
Wedging 29740-29750
Windowing 29730
Wrist 29085

Casting
Unlisted Services and Procedures 29799

Castration
See Orchiectomy

Castration, Female
See Oophorectomy

CAT Scan
See CT Scan

Cataract
Excision 66830
Incision 66820-66821
 Laser 66821
 Stab Incision 66820
Removal/Extraction
 Extracapsular 66982, 66984
 Intracapsular 66983

Catecholamines 80424, 82382-82384
Blood 82383
Urine 82382

Cathepsin-D 82387

Catheter
See Cannulization; Venipuncture
Aspiration
 Nasotracheal 31720
 Tracheobronchial 31725
Bladder 51701-51703
 Irrigation 51700
Breast Cytology 0046T, 0047T
Declotting 36550
Exchange
 Intravascular 37209, 75900
 Peritoneal 49423
Intracatheter
 Irrigation 99507
 Obstruction Clearance 36596
Pericatheter
 Obstruction
 Clearance 36595

Cell, Mother
See Stem Cell

Cell-Stimulating Hormone, Interstitial
See Luteinizing Hormone (LH)

Cellobiase
See Beta Glucosidase

Cellular Inclusion
See Inclusion Bodies

Central Shunt .33764

Central Venous Catheter Placement
Insertion
 Central36555-36558
 Peripheral36568-36569
Repair .36575
Replacement36580-36585
Repositioning .36597

Central Venous Catheter Removal .36589

Cephalic Version
of Fetus
 External .59412

Cephalocele
See Encephalocele

Cephalogram, Orthodontic
See Orthodontic Cephalogram

Cerclage
Cervix .57700
 Abdominal .59325
 Removal Under Anesthesia59871
 Vaginal .59320

Cerebellopontine Angle Tumor
See Brain, Tumor, Excision; Brainstem;
Mesencephalon; Skull Base Surgery

Cerebral Cortex Decortication
See Decortication

Cerebral Death
See Brain Death

Cerebral Hernia
See Encephalocele

Cerebral Perfusion Analysis . . .0042T

Cerebral Thermography
See Thermogram, Cephalic

Cerebral Ventriculographies
See Ventriculography

Cerebral Vessels
Angioplasty .61630
Dilation
 Intracranial Vasospasm61640-61642
Occlusion .61623
Placement
 Stent .61635

Cerebrose
See Galactose

Cerebrospinal Fluid86325
Nuclear Imaging78630-78650

Cerebrospinal Fluid Leak63744
Brain
 Repair61618-61619, 62100
Nasal/Sinus Endoscopy
 Repair31290-31291
Spinal Cord
 Repair63707-63709

Cerebrospinal Fluid Shunt63740, 63746
Creation62180-62192, 62200-62223
Irrigation .62194
Removal .62256-62258
Replacement62160, 62194, 62225-62230
Reprogramming .62252

Ceruloplasmin82390

Cerumen
Removal .69210

Cervical Cap .57170

Cervical Lymphadenectomy38720-38724

Cervical Mucus Penetration Test89330

Cervical Plexus
Injection
 Anesthetic .64413

Cervical Pregnancy59140

Cervical Puncture61050-61055

Cervical Smears88141, 88155,
 88164-88167, 88174-88175
See Cytopathology

Cervical Spine
See Vertebra, Cervical

Cervical Sympathectomy
See Sympathectomy, Cervical

Cervicectomy57530

Cervicography0003T

Cervicoplasty15819

Cervicothoracic Ganglia
See Stellate Ganglion

Cervix
See Cytopathology
Amputation
 Total .57530
Biopsy .57500, 57520
 Colposcopy57454-57455, 57460
Cauterization .57522
 Cryocautery .57511
 Electro or Thermal57510
 Laser Ablation57513
Cerclage .57700
 Abdominal .59325
 Removal Under Anesthesia59871
 Vaginal .59320

Cervicography .0003T
Colposcopy57452-57461
Conization57461, 57520-57522
Curettage
 Endocervical57454, 57456, 57505
Dilation
 Canal .57800
 Stump .57558
Dilation and Curettage57558
Ectopic Pregnancy59140
Excision
 Radical .57531
 Stump
 Abdominal Approach57540-57545
 Vaginal Approach57550-57556
 Total .57530
Exploration
 Endoscopy .57452
Insertion
 Dilation .59200
 Laminaria .59200
 Prostaglandin59200
 Sensor, Fetal Oximetry0021T
Repair
 Cerclage .57700
 Abdominal .59325
 Suture .57720
 Vaginal .59320
Unlisted Services and Procedures58999

Cesarean Delivery
Antepartum Care59610, 59618
Delivery
 after Attempted Vaginal Delivery59618
 Delivery Only59620
 Postpartum Care59622
 Routine Care59610, 59618
Delivery Only .59514
Postpartum Care59515
Routine Care .59510
Tubal Ligation at Time of58611
with Hysterectomy59525

CGMP
See Cyclic GMP

Chalazion
Excision .67805
 Multiple
 Different Lids67805
 Same Lid .67801
 Single .67800
 Under Anesthesia67808

Challenge Tests
Bronchial Ingestion95070-95075

Chambers Procedure28300

Change
Catheter
 Bile Duct .75984
Fetal Position
 by Manipulation59412
Tube or Stent
 Endoscopic
 Bile or Pancreatic Duct43269

Change of, Dressing
See Dressings, Change

Cholangiostomy
See Hepaticostomy

Cholangiotomy
See Hepaticostomy

Cholecalciferol
See Vitamin, D-3

Cholecystectomy47562-47564,
47600-47620
Any Method47562-47564
with Cholangiography . .47563, 47605, 47620
with Exploration Common
Duct .47564, 47610

Cholecystenterostomy47570,
47720-47741

Cholecystography74290-74291

Cholecystotomy47480, 48001
Percutaneous .47490

Choledochoplasty
See Bile Duct, Repair

Choledochoscopy47550

Choledochostomy47420-47425

Choledochotomy47420-47425

Choledochus, Cyst
See Cyst, Choledochal

Cholera Vaccine
Injectable .90725

Cholesterol
Measurement .83721
Serum .82465
Testing83718-83719

Choline Esterase I
See Acetylcholinesterase

Choline Esterase II
See Cholinesterase

Cholinesterase
Blood .82480-82482

Cholylglycine
Blood .82240

Chondroitin Sulfate82485

Chondromalacia Patella
Repair .27418

Chondropathia Patellae
See Chondromalacia Patella

Chondrosteoma
See Exostosis

Chopart Procedure28800-28805
See Amputation, Foot; Radical Resection;
Replantation

Chordotomies
See Cordotomy

Chorioangioma
See Lesion, Skin

Choriogonadotropin
See Chorionic Gonadotropin

Choriomeningitides, Lymphocytic
See Lymphocytic Choriomeningitis

Chorionic Gonadotropin80414,
84702-84703
Stimulation80414-80415

Chorionic Growth Hormone
See Lactogen, Human Placental

Chorionic Tumor
See Hydatidiform Mole

Chorionic Villi
See Biopsy, Chorionic Villus

Chorionic Villus
Biopsy .59015

Choroid
Destruction
Lesion0016T, 67220-67225

Choroid Plexus
Excision .61544

Christmas Factor85250

Chromaffinoma, Medullary
See Pheochromocytoma

Chromatin, Sex
See Barr Bodies

Chromatography
Column/Mass Spectrometry82541-82544
Gas Liquid or HPLC82486, 82491-82492
Paper .82487-82488
Thin-Layer .82489

Chromium .82495

Chromogenic Substrate Assay .85130

Chromosome Analysis
See Amniocentesis
Added Study88280-88289
Amniotic Fluid88267-88269
Culture .88235
Biopsy Culture
Tissue .88233
Bone Marrow Culture88237
Chorionic Villus88267
5 Cells .88261
15-20 Cells88262
20-25 Cells88264
45 Cells .88263
Culture .88235
for Breakage Syndromes88245-88249
Fragile-X .88248
Lymphocyte Culture88230
Pregnancy Associated Plasma Protein-A . . .84163
Skin Culture
Tissue .88233

Tissue Culture .88239
Unlisted Services and Procedures88299

Chromotubation58350
Oviduct .58350

Chronic Erection
See Priapism

Chronic Interstitial Cystitides
See Cystitis, Interstitial

Ciliary Body
Cyst
Destruction
Cryotherapy66720
Cyclodialysis66740
Cyclophotocoagulation66710-66711
Diathermy66700
Nonexcisional66770
Destruction
Cyclophotocoagulation66710-66711
Endoscopic66711
Lesion
Destruction66770
Repair .66680

Cimino Type Procedure36821

Cinefluorographies
See Cineradiography

Cineplasty
Arm, Lower or Upper24940

Cineradiography
Esophagus .74230
Pharynx70371, 74230
Speech Evaluation70371
Swallowing Evaluation74230
Unlisted Services and Procedures . .76120-76125

Circulation Assist
Aortic33967, 33970
Balloon33967, 33970
External33960-33961

Circulation, Extracorporeal
See Extracorporeal Circulation

Circulatory Assist
See Circulation Assist

Circumcision
Repair .54163
Surgical Excision54161
Newborn .54160
with Clamp or Other Device54152
Newborn .54150

Cisternal Puncture61050-61055

Cisternography70015
Nuclear .78630

Citrate
Blood or Urine .82507

Clagett Procedure
See Chest Wall, Repair, Closure

Factor XI
 See Plasma Thromboplastin, Antecedent
Factor XII
 See Hageman Factor
Factor XIII
 See Fibrin Stabilizing Factor

Coagulation Time85345-85348

Coagulation, Blood
See Blood Clot

Coagulation, Light
See Photocoagulation

Coagulin
See Thromboplastin

Coagulopathy85390
Assay85130

Cocaine
Blood or Urine82520
Screen82486

Coccidioides
Antibody86635

Coccidioidin Test
See Streptokinase, Antibody

Coccidioidomycosis
Skin Test86490

Coccygeal Spine Fracture
See Coccyx, Fracture

Coccygectomy15920-15922, 27080

Coccyx
Excision27080
Fracture
 Closed Treatment27200
 Open Treatment27202
Tumor
 Excision49215
X-Ray72220

Cochlear Device
Insertion69930
Programming92601-92604

Codeine
Alkaloid Screening82101

Codeine Screen82486

Cofactor Protein S
See Protein S

Coffey Operation
See Uterus, Repair, Suspension

Cognitive Function Tests96116
See Neurology, Diagnostic

**Cognitive Skills
Development**97532
See Physical Medicine/Therapy/Occupational
Therapy

Cold Agglutinin86156-86157

Cold Pack Treatment97010

Cold Preservation
See Cryopreservation

Cold Therapies
See Cryotherapy

Colectomy
Partial44140
 Laparoscopic44213
 with Anastomosis44140
 Laparoscopic44204, 44207-44208
 with Coloproctostomy44145-44146
 with Colostomy44141-44144
 Laparoscopic44206, 44208
 with Ileocolostomy
 Laparoscopic44205
 with Ileostomy44144
 with Ileum Removal44160
 with Transcanal Approach44147
Total
 Laparoscopic44210-44212
 with Proctectomy and
 Ileostomy44210-44212
 without Proctectomy44210
Open
 with Complete Proctectomy45121
 with Ileostomy44150-44151
 with Proctectomy44155-44158

Collagen Cross Links82523

Collagen Injection11950-11954

Collar Bone
See Clavicle

Collateral Ligament
Ankle
 Repair27695-27698
Interphalangeal Joint26545
Knee Joint
 Repair27409
Knee Repair27405
Metacarpophalangeal Joint26540-26542
Repair
 Ankle27695-27698

Collection and Processing
Allogenic Blood
 Harvesting of Stem Cells38205
Autologous Blood
 Harvesting of Stem Cells38206
 Intraoperative86891
 Preoperative86890
Specimen
 Capillary Blood36416
 Venous Blood36415, 36540
Washings
 Esophagus91000
 Stomach91055

Colles Fracture25600-25605

Colles Fracture Reversed
See Smith Fracture

Collins Syndrome, Treacher
See Treacher-Collins Syndrome

Collis Procedure
See Gastroplasty with Esophagogastric
Fundoplasty

Colon
See Colon-Sigmoid
Biopsy44025, 44100, 44322
 Endoscopic44389, 45380, 45391-45392
Colostomy
 Revision44340-44346
Colotomy44322
 Colostomy44320
CT Scan
 Colonography0066T, 0067T
 Virtual Colonoscopy0066T, 0067T
Destruction
 Lesion44393, 45383
 Tumor44393, 45383
Endoscopy
 Biopsy44389, 45380, 45391-45392
 Destruction
 Lesion44393
 Tumor44393, 45383
 Dilation45386
 Exploration44388, 45378, 45381, 45386
 Hemorrhage44391, 45382
 Injection, Submucosal45381
 Placement
 Stent45387
 Removal
 Foreign Body44390, 45379
 Polyp44392, 45384-45385
 Tumor45384-45385
 Specimen Collection45380
 Ultrasound45391-45392
 via Colotomy45355
 via Stoma44388-44397
 Virtual0066T, 0067T
Excision
 Partial44140-44147, 44160
 Laparoscopic44204-44208
 Total44150-44158
 Laparoscopic44210-44212
Exploration44025
 Endoscopy44388, 45378, 45381, 45386
Hemorrhage
 Endoscopic Control44391, 45382
Hernia44050
Incision
 Creation
 Stoma44320-44322
 Exploration44025
 Revision
 Stoma44340-44346
Lavage
 Intraoperative44701
Lesion
 Destruction45383
 Excision44110-44111
Lysis
 Adhesions44005
Obstruction44025-44050
Reconstruction
 Bladder from50810
Removal
 Foreign Body44025, 44390, 45379
 Polyp44392

Common Sensory Nerve
Repair/Suture .64834

Common Truncus
See Truncus Arteriosus

Communication Device
Non-Speech-Generating92605-92606
Speech-Generating92606-92609

Community/Work Reintegration
Training .97537
 See Physical Medicine/Therapy/Occupational
 Therapy

Compatibility Test
Blood .86920, 86923

Complement
Antigen .86160
Fixation Test .86171
Functional Activity86161
Hemolytic
 Total .86162
Total .86162

Complete Blood Count (CBC) .85025-85027
See Blood Cell Count

Complete Colectomy
See Colectomy, Total

Complete Pneumonectomy
See Pneumonectomy, Completion

Complete Transposition of Great Vessels
See Transposition, Great Arteries

Complex, Factor IX
See Christmas Factor

Complex, Vitamin B
See B Complex Vitamins

Component Removal, Blood
See Apheresis

Composite Graft15760-15770, 35681-35683

Compound B
See Corticosterone

Compound F
See Cortisol

Compression, Nerve, Median
See Carpal Tunnel Syndrome

Computed Tomographic Scintigraphy
See Emission Computerized Tomography

Computed Tomography (CT)
See CT Scan; Specific Anatomic Site

Computer Analysis
Acoustic Recording
 Heart Sounds
 with Computer Analysis0068T-0069T, 0070T

Computer Assisted Navigation
Orthopedic Surgery0054T, 0055T, 0056T

Computer Data Analysis99090

Computer-aided Detection
Chest X-Ray .0152T
Mammography77051-77052
 Magnetic Resonance Imaging (MRI) . . .0159T

Computer-Assisted Psychological Testing .96103

Computerized Emission Tomography
See Emission Computerized Tomography

Concentration of Specimen87015

Concentration, Hydrogen-Ion
See pH

Concentration, Minimum Inhibitory
See Minimum Inhibitory Concentration

Concentric Procedure28296

Concha Bullosa Resection
with Nasal/Sinus Endoscopy31240

Conchae Nasale
See Nasal Turbinate

Conduction, Nerve
See Nerve Conduction

Conduit, Ileal
See Ileal Conduit

Condyle
Humerus
 Fracture
 Closed Treatment24576-24577
 Open Treatment24579
 Percutaneous24582
Metatarsal
 Excision .28288
Phalanges
 Toe
 Excision .28126

Condyle, Mandibular
See Mandibular Condyle

Condylectomy
Temporomandibular Joint21050
with Skull Base Surgery61596-61597

Condyloma
Destruction54050-54065

Conference
Medical
 with Interdisciplinary Team99361-99373

Confirmation
Drug .80102

Congenital Arteriovenous Malformation
See Arteriovenous Malformation

Congenital Elevation of Scapula
See Sprengel's Deformity

Congenital Heart Septum Defect
See Septal Defect

Congenital Kidney Abnormality
Nephrolithotomy50070
Pyeloplasty .50405
Pyelotomy .50135

Congenital Laryngocele
See Laryngocele

Congenital Vascular Anomaly
See Vascular Malformation

Conisation
See Cervix, Conization

Conization
Cervix57461, 57520-57522

Conjoint Psychotherapy90847
See Psychiatric Treatment, Family

Conjunctiva
Biopsy .68100
Cyst
 Incision and Drainage68020
Fistulize for Drainage
 with Tube .68750
 without Tube68745
Graft .65782
 Harvesting .68371
Harvesting .68371
Incision .0124T
Insertion Stent .68750
Lesion
 Destruction .68135
 Excision68110-68130
 Over 1 cm68115
 with Adjacent Sclera68130
Reconstruction68320-68335
 Symblepharon
 with Graft68335
 with Flap
 Bridge or Partial68360
 Total .68362
Repair
 Symblepharon
 Division .68340
 with Graft68335
 without Graft68330
 Wound
 Direct Closure65270
 Mobilization and Rearrangement . . .65272-65273
Unlisted Services and Procedures68399

Conjunctivo-Tarso-Muller Resection .67908

Conjunctivocystorhinostomy
See Conjunctivorhinostomy

Conjunctivodacryocystostomy
See Conjunctivorhinostomy

Conjunctivoplasty68320-68330
Reconstruction Cul de Sac
 with Extensive Rearrangement68326
 with Graft68326
 Buccal Mucous Membrane68328
 with Extensive Rearrangement68320
 with Graft68320
 Buccal Mucous Membrane68325

Conjunctivorhinostomy
with Tube68750
without Tube68745

Conscious Sedation
See Sedation

Construction
Finger
 Toe to Hand Transfer26551-26556
Neobladder51596
Vagina
 with Graft57292
 without Graft57291

Consultation
Clinical Pathology80500-80502
Follow-up Inpatient
Inpatient99251-99255
 New or Established Patient ..99251-99255
Office and/or Other Outpatient99241-99245
 New or Established Patient ..99241-99245
Psychiatric, with Family90887
Radiation Therapy
 Radiation Physics77336-77370
Surgical Pathology88321-88325
 Intraoperation88329-88334
X-Ray76140

Consumption Test, Antiglobulin
See Coombs Test

Contact Lens Services
Fittings and Prescription92070, 92310-92313
Modification92325
Prescription92314-92317
Replacement92326

Continuous Negative Pressure Breathing (CNPB)94662

Continuous Positive Airway Pressure (CPAP)94660
See Pulmonology, Therapeutic

Contouring
Silicone Injections11950-11954
Tumor
 Facial Bone21029

Contraception
Cervical Cap
 Fitting57170
Diaphragm
 Fitting57170
Intrauterine Device (IUD)
 See Insertion, Intrauterine Device (IUD); Intrauterine Device (IUD); Removal, Intrauterine Device (IUD)
 Insertion58300
 Removal58301

Contraceptive Capsules, Implantable
Insertion11975
Removal11976
 with Reinsertion11977

Contraceptive Device, Intrauterine
See Intrauterine Device (IUD)

Contracture
Elbow
 Release
 with Radical Resection of Capsule ..24149
Palm
 Release26121-26125
Thumb
 Release26508

Contracture of Palmar Fascia
See Dupuytren's Contracture

Contralateral Ligament
Repair
 Knee27405

Contrast Aortogram
See Aortography

Contrast Bath Therapy97034
See Physical Medicine/Therapy/Occupational Therapy

Contrast Material
Injection
 via Peritoneal Catheter49424
Instillation

Contrast Phlebogram
See Venography

Contusion
See Hematoma

Converting Enzyme, Angiotensin
See Angiotensin Converting Enzyme (ACE)

Coombs Test86880

Copper82525

Coprobilinogen
Feces84577

Coproporphyrin84120

Coracoacromial Ligament Release23415

Coracoid Process Transfer23462

Cord, Spermatic
See Spermatic Cord

Cord, Spinal
See Spinal Cord

Cord, Vocal
See Vocal Cords

Cordectomy31300

Cordocenteses
See Cordocentesis

Cordocentesis59012

Cordotomy63194-63199

Corectomy
See Excision, Iris

Coreoplasty66762

Cornea
Biopsy65410
Curettage65435-65436
 with Chelating Agent65436
Epithelium
 Excision65435-65436
 with Chelating Agent65436
Lesion
 Destruction65450
 Excision65400
 with Graft65426
 without Graft65420
Pachymetry76514
Prosthesis65770
Pterygium
 Excision65420
Puncture65600
Relaxing Incisions65772-65775
Repair
 Astigmatism65772-65775
 Wedge Resection65775
 with Glue65286
 Wound
 Nonperforating65275
 Perforating65280-65285
 Tissue Glue65286
Reshape
 Epikeratoplasty65765
 Keratomileusis65760
 Keratoprosthesis65767
Scraping
 Smear65430
Tattoo65600
Thickness Measurement76514
Transplantation
 Autograft or Homograft
 Lamellar65710
 Penetrating65730-65755
 for Aphakia65750

Coronary
Atherectomy
 Percutaneous92995-92996
Thrombectomy
 Percutaneous92973

Coronary Angioplasty, Transluminal Balloon
See Percutaneous Transluminal Angioplasty

Coronary Artery
CT Scan0146T-0149T
Insertion
 Stent92980-92981
Ligation33502
Placement
 Radiation Delivery Device92974
Repair33500-33507

Coronary Artery Bypass Graft (CABG) 33503-33505, 33510-33516
Arterial 33533-33536
Arterial Graft 33548
Arterial-Venous 33517-33523
Harvest
 Upper Extremity Artery 35600
Reoperation 33530
Venous 33510-33516

Coronary Endarterectomy 33572

Coroner's Exam 88045

Coronoidectomy
Temporomandibular Joint 21070

Corpectomy 63101-63103

Corpora Cavernosa
Corpus Spongiosum Shunt 54430
Glans Penis Fistulization 54435
Injection 54235
Irrigation
 Priapism 54220
Saphenous Vein Shunt 54420
X-Ray with Contrast 74445

Corpora Cavernosa, Plastic Induration
See Peyronie Disease

Corpora Cavernosography 74445

Corpus Callosum
Transection 61541

Corpus Vertebrae (Vertebrale)
See Vertebral Body

Correction of Cleft Palate
See Cleft Palate, Repair

Correction of Lid Retraction
See Repair, Eyelid, Retraction

Correction of Malrotation of Duodenum
See Ladd Procedure

Correction of Syndactyly
See Syndactyly, Repair

Correction of Ureteropelvic Junction
See Pyeloplasty

Cortex Decortication, Cerebral
See Decortication

Cortical Mapping
Transection
 by Electric Stimulation 95961-95962

Corticoids
See Corticosteroids

Corticoliberin
See Corticotropic Releasing Hormone (CRH)

Corticosteroid Binding Globulin
See Transcortin

Corticosteroid Binding Protein
See Transcortin

Corticosteroids
Blood 83491
Urine 83491

Corticosterone
Blood or Urine 82528

Corticotropic Releasing Hormone (CRH) 80412

Cortisol 80400-80406, 80418-80420, 80436, 82530
Stimulation 80412
Total 82533

Cortisol Binding Globulin 84449

Costectomy
See Resection, Ribs

Costen Syndrome
See Temporomandibular Joint (TMJ)

Costotransversectomy 21610

Cothromboplastin
See Proconvertin

Cotte Operation 58400-58410
See Repair, Uterus, Suspension; Revision

Cotton Procedure
Bohler Procedure 28405

Counseling
See Preventive Medicine

Counseling and/or Risk Factor Reduction InterventionPreventive Medicine, Individual Counseling
See Preventive Medicine, Counseling and/or Risk Factor Reduction Intervention, Individual Counseling

Count
Blood Cell
 See Blood Cell Count
Blood Platelet
 See Blood, Platelet, Count
Cell
 See Cell Count
Complete Blood
 See Complete Blood Count (CBC)
Erythrocyte
 See Red Blood Cell (RBC), Count
Leukocyte
 See White Blood Cell, Count
Reticulocyte
 See Reticulocyte, Count

Counterimmuno-electrophoresis 86185

Counters, Cell
See Cell Count

Countershock, Electric
See Cardioversion

Coventry Tibial Wedge Osteotomy
See Osteotomy, Tibia

Cowper's Gland
Excision 53250

Coxa
See Hip

Coxiella Burnetii
Antibody 86638

Coxsackie
Antibody 86658

CPAP
See Continuous Positive Airway Pressure

CPK
Blood 82550-82552

CPR (Cardiopulmonary Resuscitation) 92950

Cranial Bone
Halo
 Thin Skull Osteology 20664
Reconstruction
 Extracranial 21181-21184
Tumor
 Excision 61563-61564

Cranial Halo 20661

Cranial Nerve
Avulsion 64732-64760, 64771
Cranial Nerve II
 See Optic Nerve
Cranial Nerve V
 See Trigeminal Nerve
Cranial Nerve VII
 See Facial Nerve
Cranial Nerve X
 See Vagus Nerve
Cranial Nerve XI
 See Accessory Nerve
Cranial Nerve XII
 See Hypoglossal Nerve
Decompression 61458, 64716
Implantation
 Electrode 64553, 64573
Incision 64732-64752, 64760, 65771
Injection
 Anesthetic 64400-64408, 64412
 Neurolytic 64600-64610
Insertion
 Electrode 64553, 64573
Neuroplasty 64716
Release 64716
Repair
 Suture, with or without Graft ... 64864-64865
Section 61460
Transection 64732-64760, 64771
Transposition 64716

Cranial Tongs
Application/Removal 20660
Removal 20665

D

D & C Yellow No. 7
See Fluorescein

D 2, Vitamin
See Calciferol

D and C
See Dilation and Curettage

D and E
See Dilation and Evacuation

D Galactose
See Galactose

D Glucose
See Glucose

D Vitamin
See Vitamin, D

D-Xylose Absorption Test84620

Dacryoadenectomy
Partial68505
Total68500

Dacryocystectomy68520

Dacryocystogram
See Dacryocystography

Dacryocystography68850, 70170
Nuclear Imaging78660

Dacryocystorhinostomy68720
Total
 with Nasal/Sinus Endoscopy31239

Dacryocystostomies
See Dacryocystotomy

Dacryocystotomy68420

Daily Living Activities
See Activities of Daily Living

Damus-Kaye-Stansel Procedure
See Anastomosis, Pulmonary

Dana Operation
See Rhizotomy

Dandy Operation
See Ventriculocisternostomy

Dark Adaptation Examination ..92284

Dark Field Examination ...87164-87166

Darkroom Test
See Glaucoma, Provocative Test

Darrach Procedure
See Excision, Ulna, Partial

Day Test
See Blood, Feces

de Quervain's Disease
Treatment25000

Death, Brain
See Brain Death

Debridement
Brain62010
Burns01951-01953, 16020-16030
Mastoid Cavity
 Complex69222
 Simple69220
Metatarsophalangeal Joint28289
Muscle
 Infected11004-11006
Nails11720-11721
Nose
 Endoscopic31237
Pancreatic Tissue48105
Skin
 Eczematous11000-11001
 Full Thickness11041
 Infected11000-11006
 Partial Thickness11040
 Subcutaneous Tissue11042-11044
 Infected11004-11006
 with Open Fracture and/or
 Dislocation11010-11012
Sternum21627
Wound
 Non-Selective97602
 Selective97597-97598

Debulking Procedure
Ovary/Pelvis58952-58958

Decompression
See Section
Arm, Lower24495, 25020-25025
Auditory Canal, Internal69960
Brainstem61575-61576
Cauda Equina63011, 63017, 63047-63048,
 63056-63057, 63087-63091
Cranial Nerve61458
Esophagogastric Varices37181
Facial Nerve61590
 Intratemporal
 Lateral to Geniculate Ganglion69720,
 69740
 Medial to Geniculate Ganglion69725,
 69745
 Total69955
Finger26035
Gasserian Ganglion
 Sensory Root61450
Hand26035-26037
Intestines
 Small44021
Jejunostomy
 Laparoscopic44186
Leg
 Fasciotomy27600-27602
Nerve64702-64727
 Root63020-63048, 63055-63103
Nucleus of Disk
 Lumbar62287
Optic Nerve67570
Orbit61330
 Removal of Bone67414, 67445

 Skull61322-61323, 61340-61345
Spinal Cord63001-63017, 63045-63103
 Cauda Equina63005
Tarsal Tunnel Release28035
Volvulus45321, 45337
with Nasal/Sinus Endoscopy
 Optic Nerve31294
 Orbit Wall31292-31293
Wrist25020-25025

Decortication
Lung
 Endoscopic32651-32652
 Partial32225
 Total32220
 with Parietal Pleurectomy32320

Decubiti
See Pressure Ulcer (Decubitus)

Decubitus Ulcers
See Debridement; Pressure Ulcer (Decubitus);
Skin Graft and Flap

Deetjeen's Body
See Blood, Platelet

Defect, Coagulation
See Coagulopathy

Defect, Heart Septal
See Septal Defect

Defect, Septal Closure, Atrial
See Heart, Repair, Atrial Septum

Deferens, Ductus
See Vas Deferens

Defibrillation
See Cardioversion

Defibrillator, Heart
See Pacemaker, Heart
Evaluation and Testing93640-93642,
 93741-93744
Insertion Single/Dual Chamber
 Electrodes33216-33217,
 33224-33225, 33249
 Pulse Generator33240
Removal Single/Dual Chamber
 Electrodes33243-33244
 Pulse Generator33241
Repair33218-33220
Repositioning Single/Dual Chamber
 Electrodes33215, 33226
Revise Pocket Chest33223
Wearable Device93741-93742, 93745

Deformity, Boutonniere
See Boutonniere Deformity

Deformity, Sprengel's
See Sprengel's Deformity

Degenerative, Articular Cartilage, Patella
See Chondromalacia Patella

Degradation Products, Fibrin
See Fibrin Degradation Products

Dehydroepiandrosterone82626

Dehydroepiandrosterone
Sulfate82627

Dehydrogenase,
6-Phosphogluconate
See Phosphogluconate-6, Dehydrogenase

Dehydrogenase, Alcohol
See Antidiuretic Hormone

Dehydrogenase,
Glucose-6-Phosphate
See Glucose-6-Phosphate, Dehydrogenase

Dehydrogenase, Glutamate
See Glutamate Dehydrogenase

Dehydrogenase, Isocitrate
See Isocitric Dehydrogenase

Dehydrogenase, Lactate
See Lactic Dehydrogenase

Dehydrogenase, Malate
See Malate Dehydrogenase

Dehydroisoandrosterone Sulfate
See Dehydroepiandrosterone Sulfate

Delay of Flap
Skin Graft15600-15630

Deligation
Ureter50940

Deliveries, Abdominal
See Cesarean Delivery

Delivery
See Cesarean Delivery; Vaginal Delivery

Delorme Operation
See Pericardiectomy

Denervation
Hip
 Femoral27035
 Obturator27035
 Sciatic27035

Denervation, Sympathetic
See Excision, Nerve, Sympathetic

Denis-Browne Splint29590

Dens Axis
See Odontoid Process

Denver Developmental
Screening Test96101-96103

Denver Krupic Procedure
See Aqueous Shunt, to Extraocular Reservoir

Denver Shunt
Patency Test78291

Denver-Krupin Procedure66180

Deoxycorticosterone
See Desoxycorticosterone

Deoxycortisol80436, 82634

Deoxyephedrine
See Methamphetamine

Deoxyribonuclease
Antibody86215

Deoxyribonuclease I
See DNAse

Deoxyribonucleic Acid
Antibody86225-86226

Depilation
See Removal, Hair

Depletion
Plasma38214
Platelet38213
T-Cell38210
Tumor Cell38211

Deposit Calcium
See Calcium, Deposits

Depth Electrode
Insertion61760

Derma-Fat-Fascia Graft15770

Dermabrasion15780-15783

Dermatology
Actinotherapy96900
Examination of Hair
 Microscopic96902
Ultraviolet A Treatment96912
Ultraviolet B Treatment96910-96913
Ultraviolet Light Treatment96900,
 96910-96913
Unlisted Services and Procedures96999

Dermatoplasty
Septal30620

Dermoid
See Cyst, Dermoid

Derrick-Burnet Disease
See Q Fever

Descending Abdominal Aorta
See Aorta, Abdominal

Desipramine
Assay80160

Desmotomy
See Ligament, Release

Desoxycorticosterone82633

Desoxycortone
See Desoxycorticosterone

Desoxyephedrine
See Methamphetamine

Desoxynorephedrin
See Amphetamine

Desoxyphenobarbital
See Primidone

Desquamation
See Exfoliation

Destruction
Acne17340-17360
 Cryotherapy17340
Arrhythmogenic Focus
 Heart33250-33251, 33261
Bladder51020, 52214-52224, 52354
Calculus
 Bile Duct43265
 Kidney50590
 Pancreatic Duct43265
Chemical Cauterization
 Granulation Tissue17250
Ciliary Body
 Cryotherapy66720
 Cyclodialysis66740
 Cyclophotocoagulation66710-66711
 Diathermy66700
 Endoscopic66711
Cyst
 Abdomen49200-49201
 Ciliary Body66770
 Iris66770
 Retroperitoneal49200-49201
Endometrial ablation58356
Endometriomas
 Abdomen49200-49201
 Retroperitoneal49200-49201
Fissure
 Anal46940-46942
Hemorrhoids46934-46936
Kidney52354
 Endoscopic50557, 50576
Lesion
 Anal46900-46917, 46924
 Bladder51030
 Breast0061T
 Choroid0016T, 67220-67225
 Ciliary Body66770
 Colon45383
 Conjunctiva68135
 Cornea65450
 Eyelid67850
 Facial17000-17004, 17280-17286
 Gastrointestinal, Upper43258
 Gums41850
 Intestines
 Large44393
 Small44369
 Iris66770
 Mouth40820
 Nose
 Intranasal30117-30118
 Palate42160
 Penis
 Cryosurgery54056
 Electrodesiccation54055
 Extensive54065
 Laser Surgery54057
 Simple54050-54060
 Surgical Excision54060
 Pharynx42808
 Prostate45320
 Thermotherapy53850-53853
 Microwave53850
 Radio Frequency53852
 Rectum45320

Dislocation, Radiocarpal Joint
See Radiocarpal Joint, Dislocation

Disorder
Blood Coagulation
 See Coagulopathy
Penis
 See Penis
Retinal
 See Retina

Displacement Therapy
Nose .30210

Dissection
Hygroma, Cystic
 Axillary/Cervical38550-38555
Lymph Nodes .38542

Dissection, Neck, Radical
See Radical Neck Dissection

Distention
See Dilation

Diverticula, Meckel's
See Diverticulum, Meckel's

Diverticulectomy44800
Esophagus .43130-43135

Diverticulectomy, Meckel's
See Meckel's Diverticulum, Excision

Diverticulum
Bladder
 See Bladder, Diverticulum
Meckel's
 Excision .44800
Repair
 Urethra .53400-53405

Division
Muscle
 Foot .28250
Plantar Fascia
 Foot .28250

Division, Isthmus, Horseshoe Kidney
See Symphysiotomy, Horseshoe Kidney

Division, Scalenus Anticus Muscle
See Muscle Division, Scalenus Anticus

DI-Amphetamine
See Amphetamine

DMO
See Dimethadione

DNA
Antibody .86225-86226

DNA Endonuclease
See DNAse

DNA Probe
See Cytogenetics Studies; Nucleic Acid Probe

DNAse
Antibody .86215

Domiciliary Services
See Nursing Facility Services
Assisted Living99339-99340
Discharge Services99315-99316
Established Patient99334-99337
New Patient99324-99328

Donor Procedures
Conjunctival Graft68371
Heart Excision33940
Heart/Lung Excision33930
Liver Segment47140-47142
Stem Cells
 Donor Search38204

Dopamine
See Catecholamines
Blood .82383-82384
Urine .82382, 82384

Doppler Echocardiography76827-
 76828, 93307-93308, 93320-93350
Extracranial .93875
Intracardiac .93662
Transesophageal93318
Transthoracic93303-93317

Doppler Scan
Arterial Studies
 Extremities93922-93924
 Fetal
 Middle Cerebral Artery76821
 Umbilical Artery76820
Extremities .93965
Intracranial Arteries93886-93893

Dorsal Vertebra
See Vertebra, Thoracic

Dose Plan
See Dosimetry

Dosimetry
Radiation Therapy77300, 77331
 Brachytherapy77326-77328
 Intensity Modulation77301
 Teletherapy77305-77321

Double-Stranded DNA
See Deoxyribonucleic Acid

Doxepin
Assay .80166

DPH
See Phenytoin

Drainage
See Excision; Incision; Incision and Drainage;
Paracentesis
Abdomen
 Abdomen Fluid49080-49081
Abscess
 Appendix44900-44901
 Percutaneous44901
 Brain61150-61151
 Eyelid .67700
 Liver47010-47011
Ovary
 Percutaneous58823

Pelvic
 Percutaneous58823
Pericolic
 Percutaneous58823
Perirenal or Renal50020-50021
 Percutaneous50021
Prostate .52700
Retroperitoneal49060-49061
 Percutaneous49061
Subdiaphragmatic or
Subphrenic49040-49041
 Percutaneous49040-49041
with X-Ray75989
Amniotic Fluid
 Diagnostic Aspiration59000
 Therapeutic Aspiration59001
Bile Duct
 Transhepatic75980
Brain Fluid .61070
Bursa .20600-20610
Cerebrospinal Fluid61000-61020, 61050,
 61070, 62272
Cervical Fluid61050
Cisternal Fluid61050
Cyst
 Bone .20615
 Brain61150-61151, 62161-62162
 Breast19000-19001
 Ganglion .20612
 Liver47010-47011
 Percutaneous47011
 Salivary Gland42409
 Sublingual Gland42409
Extraperitoneal Lymphocele
 Laparoscopic49323
 Open .49062
Eye
 Paracentesis
 with Aqueous Aspiration65800
 with Aqueous-Release65805
 with Removal
 Blood .65815
 Discission of Anterior Hyaloid
 Membrane65810
 Vitreous65810
Fetal Fluid .59074
Ganglion Cyst20612
Hematoma
 Brain61154-61156
 Vagina57022-57023
Hematoma, Subungual11740
Joint .20600-20610
Liver
 Abscess or Cyst47010-47011
 Percutaneous47011
Lymphocele
 Endoscopic49323
Onychia10060-10061
Orbit67405, 67440
Pancreas
 See Anastomosis, Pancreas to Intestines
 Pseudocyst48510-48511
 Percutaneous48511
Paronychia10060-10061
Pericardial Sac32659
Pericardium
 See Aspiration, Pericardium

DXA

See Dual X-Ray Absorptiometry (DXA)

Dynamometry

See Osteotomy, Calcaneus
Venous Studies
 See Osteotomy, Calcaneus
 with Ophthalmoscopy92260

E

E Antigens

See Hepatitis Antigen, Be

E B Virus

See Epstein-Barr Virus

E Vitamin

See Tocopherol

E1

See Estrone

E2

See Estradiol

E3

See Estriol

Ear

Collection of Blood36415-36416
Drum69420-69421, 69433-69436,
 69450, 69610-69620
 See Tympanic Membrane
External
 Abscess Incision and Drainage
 Complicated69005
 Simple .69000
 Biopsy .69100
 Excision
 Partial .69110
 Total .69120
 Hematoma
 Incision and Drainage69000-69005
 Reconstruction69300
 Unlisted Services and Procedures69399
Inner
 CT Scan70480-70482
 Excision
 Labyrinth69905-69910
 Exploration
 Endolymphatic Sac69805-69806
 Incision .69820
 Labyrinth69801-69802
 Semicircular Canal69840
 Insertion
 Cochlear Device69930
 Semicircular Canal69820
 Unlisted Services and Procedures69949
Middle
 Catheterization69405
 CT Scan70480-70482
 Exploration .69440

Inflation
 with Catheterization69400
 without Catheterization69401
Insertion
 Catheter .69405
Lesion
 Excision .69540
Reconstruction
 Tympanoplasty with Antrotomy
 or Mastoidotomy69635-69637
 Tympanoplasty with
 Mastoidectomy69641-69646
 Tympanoplasty without
 Mastoidectomy69631-69633
Removal
 Ventilating Tube69424
Repair
 Oval Window69666
 Round Window69667
Revision
 Stapes .69662
Tumor
 Excision69550-69554
Unlisted Services and Procedures69799
Outer
 CT Scan70480-70482

Ear Canal

See Auditory Canal

Ear Cartilage

Graft
 to Face .21235

Ear Lobes

Pierce .69090

Ear Protector Attenuation92596

See Hearing Aid Services

Ear Wax

See Cerumen

Ear, Nose, and Throat

See Hearing Aid Services; Otorhinolaryngology,
Diagnostic
Audiologic Function Tests
 Acoustic Reflex92568
 Acoustic Reflex Decay92569
 Audiometry
 Bekesy92560-92561
 Comprehensive92557
 Conditioning Play92582
 Evoked Response92585-92586
 Groups .92559
 Pure Tone92552-92553
 Select Picture92583
 Speech92555-92556
 Brainstem Evoked Response . . .92585-92586
 Central Auditory Function92620-92621
 Ear Protector Evaluation92596
 Electrocochleography92584
 Filtered Speech92571
 Hearing Aid Evaluation92590-92595
 Lombard Test92700
 Loudness Balance92562
 Screening Test92551
 Sensorineural Acuity92575
 Short Increment Sensitivity Index (SISI) 92564

Staggered Spondaic Word Test92572
Stenger Test92565, 92577
Synthetic Sentence Test92576
Tone Decay92563
Tympanometry92567
Audiometry
 Evoked Otoacoustic Emissions . .92587-92588
 Visual Reinforcement92579
Binocular Microscopy92504
Diagnostic Analysis
 Auditory Brainstem Implant92640
Facial Nerve Function Study92516
Hearing, Language and Speech Evaluation .92506
Laryngeal Function Study92520
Nasal Function Study92512
Nasopharyngoscopy92511
Vestibular Function Tests
 Additional Electrodes92547
 Caloric Tests92533, 92543
 Nystagmus
 Optokinetic92534, 92544
 Positional92532, 92542
 Spontaneous92531, 92541
 Posturography92548
 Torsion Swing Test92546
 Tracking Tests92545

Ebstein Anomaly Repair33468

Eccrine Glands

Chemodenervation
 Axillae .64650
 Feet .64999
 Hands .64999
 Other Area64653

ECG

See Electrocardiography

Echinococcosis86171, 86280

Echocardiography

Cardiac93320-93350
 Intracardiac93662
 Transesophageal93318
 Transthoracic93303-93317
Doppler93303-93317, 93320-93321, 93662
Fetal Heart76825-76826
 Doppler
 Complete76827
 Follow-up or Repeat Study76828
 for Congenital Anomalies
 Transesophageal93315-93317
 Transthoracic93303-93304
Intracardiac .93662
Transesophageal93318
 for Congenital Anomalies93315-93317
Transthoracic93303-93318, 93350
 for Congenital Anomalies93303-93304

Echoencephalography76506

Echography

Abdomen76700-76705
Arm .76880
Breast .76645
Cardiac93303-93317, 93320-93321,
 93350, 93662
 Guidance .76932
Chest .76604

Echotomography
See Echography

ECMO
See Extracorporeal Membrane Oxygenation

ECS
See Emission Computerized Tomography

ECSF (Erythrocyte Colony Stimulating Factor)
See Erythropoietin

ECT
See Emission Computerized Tomography

Ectasia
See Dilation

Ectopic Pregnancy
See Obstetrical Care

Ectropion

Education Services

Education Supplies99071

EEG
See Electroencephalography (EEG)

Egg
See Ova

Ehrlichia

EKG
See Electrocardiography

Elastase .82656

Elbow
See Humerus; Radius; Ulna

Elbow, Golfer
See Tennis Elbow

Elbows, Tennis
See Tennis Elbow

Electric Countershock
See Cardioversion

Electric Stimulation
See Electrical Stimulation

Electric Stimulation, Transcutaneous
See Application, Neurostimulation

Electrical Stimulation

Electro-Hydraulic Procedure .52325

Electro-Oculography92270

Electroanalgesia
See Application, Neurostimulation

Electrocardiography

Electrocautery17000-17286
See Destruction

Electrochemistry
See Electrolysis

Electroconvulsive Therapy90870

Electrocorticogram
Intraoperative95829

Electrode, Depth
See Depth Electrode
Electrode Array Intracranial61850-61868, 61885-61886
Peripheral Nerve64553-64581
Retinal0100T
Spinal63650-63655

Electrodesiccation17000-17286
Lesion
 Penis54055

Electroejaculation55870

Electroencephalography (EEG)95816
Brain Death95824
Coma95822
Digital Analysis95957
Electrode Placement95830
Intraoperative95955
Monitoring ...95812-95813, 95950-95953, 95956
 with Drug Activation95954
 with Physical Activation95954
 with WADA Activation95958
Sleep95822, 95827
Standard95819

Electrogastrography91132-91133

Electrogram, Atrial
Esophageal Recording93615-93616

Electrolysis17380

Electromyographs
See Electromyography, Needle

Electromyography
Anorectal with Biofeedback90911
Fine Wire
 Dynamic96004
Needle
 Extremities95861-95864
 Extremity95860
 Face and Neck Muscles95867-95868
 Guidance
 for Chemodenervation95874
 Hemidiaphragm95866
 Larynx95865
 Ocular92265
 Other than Thoracic Paraspinal95870
 Single Fiber Electrode95872
 Thoracic Paraspinal Muscles95869
Sphincter Muscles
 Anus51784-51785
 Needle51785
 Urethra51784-51785
 Needle51785
Surface
 Dynamic96002-96004

Electron Microscopy88348-88349

Electronic Analysis
Drug Infusion Pump62367-62368
Implantable Loop Recorder System93727
Neurostimulator Pulse Generator0162T, 95970-95979
Pacing Cardioverter-Defibrillator ...93741-93744

Electrophoresis
Counterimmuno-86185
Immuno-86320-86327
Immunofixation86334-86335
Protein84165-84166
Unlisted Services and Procedures82664

Electrophysiology Procedure93600-93660

Electroretinogram
See Electroretinography

Electroretinography92275

Electrostimulation, Analgesic Cutaneous
See Application, Neurostimulation

Electrosurgery
Trichiasis
 Correction67825

Electroversion, Cardiac
See Cardioversion

Elevation, Scapula, Congenital
See Sprengel's Deformity

Elliot Operation
See Excision, Lesion, Sclera

Eloesser Procedure
See Thoracostomy, Empyema

Eloesser Thoracoplasty
See Thoracoplasty

Embolectomy
Aortoiliac Artery34151-34201
Axillary Artery34101
Brachial Artery34101
Carotid Artery34001
Celiac Artery34151
Femoral34201
Iliac34151-34201
Innominate Artery34001-34101
Mesentery Artery34151
Peroneal Artery34203
Popliteal Artery34203
Pulmonary Artery33910-33916
Radial Artery34111
Renal Artery34151
Subclavian Artery34001-34101
Tibial Artery34203
Ulnar Artery34111

Embolization
Leiomyomata37210

Embryo
Biopsy89290-89291
Cryopreservation89258

Cryopreserved
Preparation
 Thawing89352
Culture89250
 with Co-Culture Oocyte89251
Hatching
 Assisted
 Microtechnique89253
Preparation
 for Transfer89255
Storage89342

Embryo Implantation
See Implantation

Embryo Transfer
In Vitro Fertilization58974-58976
 Intrafallopian Transfer58976
 Intrauterine Transfer58974

Embryo/Fetus Monitoring
See Monitoring, Fetal

Embryonated Eggs
Inoculation87250

Emergency Department Services99281-99288
See Critical Care; Emergency Department Services
Anesthesia99140
Physician Direction of Advanced
Life Support99288

Emesis Induction99175

EMG
See Electromyography, Needle

EMI Scan
See CT Scan

Emission Computerized Tomography78607

Emission-Computed Tomography, Single-Photon
See SPECT

Emmet Operation
See Vagina, Repair, Obstetric

Empyema
Closure
 Chest Wall32810
Thoracostomy32020-32036

Empyema, Lung
See Abscess, Thorax

Empyemectomy32540

Encephalitis
Antibody86651-86654

Encephalitis Virus Vaccine90735

Encephalocele
Repair62120
 Craniotomy62121

Encephalon
See Brain

End-Expiratory Pressure, Positive
See Pressure Breathing, Positive

End-Stage Renal Disease Services90918-90925

Endarterectomy
Coronary Artery33572
Pulmonary33916

Endemic Flea-Borne Typhus
See Murine Typhus

Endobronchial Challenge Tests
See Bronchial Challenge Test

Endocavitary Fulguration
See Electrocautery

Endocrine System
Unlisted Services and Procedures ..60699, 78099

Endocrine, Pancreas
See Islet Cell

Endolymphatic Sac
Exploration
 with Shunt69806
 without Shunt69805

Endometrial Ablation58353
Curettage58356
Exploration
 via Hysteroscopy58563

Endometrioma
Abdomen
 Destruction/Excision49200-49201
Retroperitoneal
 Destruction/Excision49200-49201

Endometriosis, Adhesive
See Adhesions, Intrauterine

Endometrium
Ablation58356
Biopsy58100-58110, 58558

Endonuclease, DNA
See DNAse

Endoscopic Retrograde Cannulation of Pancreatic Duct (ERCP)
See Cholangiopancreatography

Endoscopies, Pleural
See Thoracoscopy

Endoscopy
See Arthroscopy; Thoracoscopy
Adrenal Gland
 Biopsy60650
 Excision60650
Anus
 Biopsy46606
 Dilation46604
 Exploration46600
 Hemorrhage46614
 Removal
 Foreign Body46608
 Polyp46610, 46612
 Tumor46610, 46612

Atria
 Surgical33265-33266
Bile Duct
 Biopsy47553
 Destruction
 Calculi (Stone)43265
 Tumor43272
 Dilation43271, 47555-47556
 Exploration47552
 Intraoperative47550
 Percutaneous47552-47555
 Removal
 Calculi (Stone)43264, 47554
 Foreign Body43269
 Stent43269
 Specimen Collection43260
 Sphincter Pressure43263
 Sphincterotomy43262
 Tube Placement43267-43268
Bladder52000
 Biopsy52204, 52354
 Catheterization52005, 52010
 Destruction52354
 Lesion52400
 Evacuation
 Clot52001
 Excision
 Tumor52355
 Exploration52351
 Lithotripsy52353
 Removal
 Calculus52352
 Urethral Stent52282
Bladder Neck
 Injection of Implant Material51715
Brain
 Shunt
 Creation62201
Bronchi
 Aspiration31645-31646
 Biopsy31625-31629, 31632-31633
 Destruction
 Lesion31641
 Tumor31641
 Dilation31630-31631, 31636-31638
 Exploration31622
 Injection31656
 Lesion
 Destruction31641
 Needle Biopsy31629, 31633
 Placement
 Stent31631, 31636-31637
 Revision
 Stent31638
 Specimen Collection31623-31624
 Stenosis31641
 Tumor
 Destruction31641
 Ultrasound31620
Cervix
 Biopsy57454-57455, 57460
 Curettage57454, 57456
 Exploration57452
 Loop Electrode Biopsy57460
 Loop Electrode Conization57461
Chest Cavity
 Exploration32601-32606
 Surgical32650-32665

Colon
 Biopsy44389, 45380, 45392
 Destruction
 Lesion44393, 45383
 Tumor44393, 45383
 Exploration45378
 Hemorrhage44391, 45382
 Injection45381
 Placement
 Stent45387
 Removal
 Foreign Body44390, 45379
 Polyp44392, 45384-45385
 Tumor44392, 45384-45385
 Specimen Collection45380
 Ultrasound45391-45392
 via Colotomy45355
 via Stoma44388-44393, 44397
 Virtual0066T, 0067T
Colon-Sigmoid
 Ablation
 Polyp45339
 Tumor45339
 Biopsy45331
 Dilation45340
 Exploration45330, 45335
 Hemorrhage45334
 Needle Biopsy45342
 Placement
 Stent45327, 45345
 Removal
 Foreign Body45332
 Polyp45333, 45338
 Tumor45333, 45338
 Specimen Collection45331
 Ultrasound45341-45342
 Volvulus45337
Esophagus
 Biopsy43202
 Dilation43220-43226
 Exploration43200
 Hemorrhage43227
 Injection43201, 43204
 Insertion Stent43219
 Needle Biopsy43232
 Removal
 Foreign Body43215
 Polyp43216-43217, 43228
 Tumor43216, 43228
 Ultrasound43231-43232
 Vein Ligation43205
Eye66990
Foot
 Plantar Fasciotomy29893
Gastrointestinal
 Upper
 Biopsy43239
 Catheterization43241
 Destruction of Lesion43258
 Dilation43245, 43248-43249
 Drainage of Pseudocyst43240
 Exploration43234-43235
 Foreign Body43247
 Gastric Bypass43644-43645
 Gastroenterostomy43644-43645
 Hemorrhage43255
 Inject Varices43243
 Injection0133T, 43236

Needle Biopsy43238, 43242
Removal43247, 43250-43251
Roux-En-Y .43644
Stent Placement43256
Suturing .0008T
Thermal Radiation43257
Tube Placement43246
Ultrasound . .43237-43242, 43259, 76975
Vein Ligation43244
Heart
Atria33265-33266
Ileum
via Stoma .44383
Intestines, Small
Biopsy44361, 44377
Destruction
Lesion .44369
Tumor .44369
Diagnostic .44376
Exploration .44360
Hemorrhage44366, 44378
Insertion
Stent44370, 44379
Tube .44379
Pelvic Pouch44385-44386
Removal
Foreign Body44363
Lesion .44365
Polyp44364-44365
Tube Placement44372
Tube Revision44373
via Stoma44380-44383
Tumor44364-44365
Intracranial62160-62165
Kidney
Biopsy50555, 50574-50576, 52354
Catheterization50553, 50572
Destruction50557, 50576, 52354
Dilation of Ureter50553
Excision
Tumor .52355
Exploration .52351
Lithotripsy .52353
Removal
Calculus50561, 50580, 52352
Foreign Body50561, 50580
via Incision50562-50580
via Stoma50551-50561
Larynx
Biopsy31510, 31535-31536
Direct31515-31571
Exploration31505, 31520-31526, 31575
Fiberoptic31575-31579
Indirect31505-31513
Operative31530-31561
Removal
Foreign Body31530-31531
Lesion31511, 31545-31546
See Endoscopic
Lysis
Device .0027T
Mediastinoscopy
Biopsy .39400
Exploration .39400
Nose
Diagnostic31231-31235
Surgical31237-31294
Unlisted Services and Procedures31299

Pancreatic Duct
Destruction
Calculi (Stone)43265
Tumor .43272
Dilation .43271
Removal
Calculi (Stone)43264
Foreign Body43269
Stent .43269
Specimen Collection43260
Sphincter Pressure43263
Sphincterotomy43262
Tube Placement43267-43268
Pelvis
Aspiration .49322
Destruction of Lesion58662
Lysis of Adhesions58660
Oviduct Surgery58670-58671
Removal of Adnexal Structures58661
Peritoneum
Biopsy .47561
Drainage
Lymphocele49323, 54690
Radiologic .47560
Rectum
Biopsy .45305
Destruction
Tumor .45320
Dilation .45303
Exploration .45300
Hemorrhage45317
Removal
Foreign Body45307
Polyp45308-45315
Tumor45308-45315
Volvulus .45321
Spleen
Removal .38120
Testis
Removal .54690
Trachea
Dilation31630-31631, 31636-31638
via Tracheostomy31615
Ureter
Biopsy . . .50955-50957, 50974-50976, 52354
Catheterize50953, 50972
Destruction50957, 50976, 52354
Excision
Tumor .52355
Exploration .52351
Injection of Implant Material52327
Lithotripsy .52353
Manipulation of Ureteral Calculus52330
Placement
Stent .50947
Removal
Calculus50961, 50980, 52352
Foreign Body50961, 50980
Resection .52355
via Incision50970-50980
via Stoma50951-50961
Ureteral
Biopsy .52007
Catheterization52005
Urethra
Biopsy52204, 52354
Catheterization52010

Destruction .52354
Lesion .52400
Evacuation
Clot .52001
Excision
Tumor .52355
Exploration .52351
Incision
Ejaculatory Duct52402
Injection of Implant Material51715
Lithotripsy .52353
Removal
Calculus .52352
Resection
Ejaculatory Duct52402
Vasectomy .52402
Vasotomy .52402
Uterus
Anesthesia .00952
Hysteroscopy
Diagnostic58555
with Division/Resection Intrauterine
Septum .58560
with Lysis of Intrauterine
Adhesions58559
Placement
Fallopian Tube58565
Removal
Endometrial58563
Impacted Foreign Body58562
Leiomyomata58561
Surgical with Biopsy58558
Vagina
Anesthesia .00950
Biopsy .57454
Exploration .57452
Vascular
Surgical33508, 37500-37501
Virtual
Colon0066T, 0067T

Endosteal Implant
Reconstruction
Mandible21248-21249
Maxilla21248-21249

Endothelioma, Dural
See Meningioma

Endotracheal Intubation
See Insertion, Endotracheal Tube

Endotracheal Tube
Intubation .31500

Endovascular Repair0078T, 0079T,
0080T, 0081T, 33880-33891,
34800-34805, 34812-34826, 34833-34900
Angiography75952-75959

Endovascular Therapy
Ablation
Vein36475-36479
Occlusion .61623

Enema
Home Visit for Fecal Impaction99511
Intussusception74283
Therapeutic
for Intussusception74283

Energies, Electromagnetic
See Irradiation

ENT
See Ear, Nose, and Throat; Otorhinolaryngology,
Diagnostic
Therapeutic
 See Otorhinolaryngology

Entamoeba Histolytica
Antigen Detection
 Enzyme Immunoassay 87336-87337

Enterectomy 44120-44121,
 44126-44128, 44137, 44202
Donor 44132-44133
with Enterostomy 44125

Enterocele
Repair 57556
 Hysterectomy
 with Colpectomy 58280

Enterocystoplasty 51960
Camey 50825

Enteroenterostomy
See Anastomosis, Intestines

Enterolysis 44005
Laparoscopic 44180

Enteropancreatostomy
See Anastomosis, Pancreas to Intestines

Enterorrhaphy 44602-44603, 44615

Enterostomy 44300
Closure 44625-44626
with Enterectomy
 Intestine, Small 44125

Enterotomy 44615

Enterovirus
Antibody 86658

Entropion
Repair 67921-67924
 Excision Tarsal Wedge 67923
 Suture 67921
 Thermocauterization 67922

Enucleation
Eye
 with Implant 65103
 Muscles Attached 65105
 without Implant 65101
Pleural 32540

Enucleation, Cyst, Ovarian
See Cystectomy, Ovarian

Environmental Intervention
for Psychiatric Patients 90882

Enzyme Activity 82657
Radioactive Substrate 82658

Enzyme, Angiotensin Converting
See Angiotensin Converting Enzyme (ACE)

Enzyme, Angiotensin-Forming
See Renin

EOG
See Electro-oculography

Eosinocyte
See Eosinophils

Eosinophils
Nasal Smear 89190

Epiandrosterone 82666

Epicondylitides, Lateral Humeral
See Tennis Elbow

Epicondylitis, Radiohumeral
See Tennis Elbow

Epidemic Parotitis
See Mumps

Epididymectomy
Bilateral 54861
Unilateral 54860

Epididymis
Abscess
 Incision and Drainage 54700
Anastomosis
 to Vas Deferens
 Bilateral 54901
 Unilateral 54900
Biopsy 54800, 54865
Epididymography 74440
Excision
 Bilateral 54861
 Unilateral 54860
Exploration
 Biopsy 54865
Hematoma
 Incision and Drainage 54700
Lesion
 Excision
 Local 54830
 Spermatocele 54840
Needle Biopsy 54800
Spermatocele
 Excision 54840
Unlisted Services and Procedures ... 55899
X-Ray with Contrast 74440

Epididymograms 55300

Epididymography 74440

Epididymoplasty
See Repair, Epididymis

Epididymovasostomy
Bilateral 54901
Unilateral 54900

Epidural
Electrode
 Insertion : 61531
 Removal 61535
Injection 62281-62282, 62310-62319,
 64479-64484
Lysis 0027T, 62263-62264

Epidural Anesthesia
See Anesthesia, Epidural

Epidurography 72275

Epigastric
Hernia Repair 49572

Epiglottidectomy 31420

Epiglottis
Excision 31420

Epikeratoplasty 65767

Epilation
See Removal, Hair

Epinephrine
See Catecholamines
Blood 82383-82384
Urine 82384

Epiphyseal Arrest
Femur 20150, 27185, 27475, 27479-27485, 27742
Fibula 20150, 27477-27485, 27730-27742
Radius 20150, 25450-25455
Tibia ..20150, 27477-27485, 27730, 27734-27742
Ulna 20150, 25450-25455

Epiphyseal Separation
Radius
 Closed Treatment 25600
 Open Treatment 25607-25609

Epiphysiodesis
See Epiphyseal Arrest

Epiphysis
See Bone; Specific Bone

Epiploectomy 49255

Episiotomy 59300

Epispadias
Penis
 Reconstruction 54385
Repair 54380-54390
 with Exstrophy of Bladder 54390
 with Incontinence 54380-54390

Epistaxis 30901-30906
with Nasal/Sinus Endoscopy 31238

EPO
See Erythropoietin

Epstein-Barr Virus
Antibody 86663-86665

Equina, Cauda
See Cauda Equina

ERCP
See Bile Duct; Cholangiopancreatography;
Pancreatic Duct

ERG
See Electroretinography

Ergocalciferol
See Calciferol

Ergocalciferols
See Calciferol

Ergonovine Provocation Test . . .93024

Erythrocyte
See Red Blood Cell (RBC)

Erythrocyte ab
See Antibody, Red Blood Cell

Erythrocyte Count
See Red Blood Cell (RBC), Count

Erythropoietin82668

Escharotomy
Burns .16035-16036

Escherichia coli 0157
Antigen Detection
 Enzyme Immunoassay87335

ESD
See Endoscopy, Gastrointestinal, Upper

Esophageal Acid Infusion Test
See Acid Perfusion Test

Esophageal Polyp
See Polyp, Esophagus

Esophageal Tumor
See Tumor, Esophagus

Esophageal Varices
Ligation .43205, 43400
Transection/Repair43401

Esophagectomy
Partial .43116-43124
Total43107-43113, 43124

Esophagoenterostomy
with Total Gastrectomy43620

Esophagogastroduodenoscopies
See Endoscopy, Gastrointestinal, Upper

Esophagogastromyotomy
See Esophagomyotomy

Esophagogastrostomy43320

Esophagojejunostomy43340-43341

Esophagomyotomy . .32665, 43330-43331

Esophagorrhaphy
See Esophagus, Suture

Esophagoscopies
See Endoscopy, Esophagus

Esophagostomy43350-43352
Closure43420-43425

Esophagotomy43020, 43045

Esophagotracheal Fistula
See Fistula, Tracheoesophageal

Esophagus
Acid Perfusion Test91030
Acid Reflux Tests91034-91038
Balloon Distension
 Provocation Study91040

Biopsy
 Endoscopy43202
Cineradiography74230
Dilation43450-43458
 Endoscopic43220-43226, 43248-43249
 Surgical .43510
Endoscopy
 Biopsy .43202
 Dilation43220-43226
 Exploration43200
 Hemorrhage43227
 Injection43201, 43204
 Sphincter0133T
 Insertion Stent43219
 Needle Biopsy43232
 Removal
 Foreign Body43215
 Polyp43216-43217, 43228
 Tumor43216, 43228
 Ultrasound43231-43232
 Vein Ligation43205
Excision
 Diverticula43130-43135
 Partial43116-43124
 Total43107-43113, 43124
Exploration
 Endoscopy43200
Hemorrhage .43227
Incision43020, 43045
 Muscle .43030
Injection
 Sclerosing Agent43204
 Submucosal43201
Insertion
 Stent .43219
 Tamponade43460
 Tube .43510
Intubation with Specimen Collection91000
Lesion
 Excision43100-43101
Ligation .43405
Motility Study78258, 91010-91012
Needle Biopsy
 Endoscopy43232
Nuclear Medicine
 Imaging (Motility)78258
 Reflux Study78262
Reconstruction43300, 43310, 43313
 Creation
 Stoma43350-43352
 Esophagostomy43350
 Fistula43305, 43312, 43314
 Gastrointestinal43360-43361
Removal
 Foreign Bodies . .43020, 43045, 43215, 74235
 Lesion .43216
 Polyp43216-43217, 43228
Repair43300, 43310, 43313
 Esophagogastric Fundoplasty . .43324-43325
 Laparoscopic43280
 Esophagogastrostomy43320
 Esophagojejunostomy43340-43341
 Fistula . . .43305, 43312, 43314, 43420-43425
 Muscle43330-43331
 Pre-existing Perforation43405
 Varices .43401
 Wound43410-43415

Suture .43405
 Wound43410-43415
Ultrasound
 Endoscopy43231-43232
Unlisted Services and Procedures . .43289, 43499
Vein
 Ligation43205, 43400
Video .74230
X-Ray .74220

Esophagus Neoplasm
See Tumor, Esophagus

Esophagus, Varix
See Esophageal Varices

Established Patient
Domiciliary or Rest Home Visit99334-99337
Emergency Department Services . . .99281-99285
Home Services99347-99350
Hospital Inpatient Services99221-99239
Hospital Observation Services99217-99220
Inpatient Consultations99251-99255
Office and/or Other Outpatient
Consultations99241-99245
Office Visit99211-99215
Online Evaluation and Management
Services .0074T
Outpatient Visit99211-99215

Establishment
Colostomy
 Abdominal50810
 Perineal .50810

Estes Operation
See Ovary, Transposition

Estlander Procedure40525

Estradiol .82670
Response .80414

Estriol
Blood or Urine82677

Estrogen
Blood or Urine82671-82672
Receptor .84233

Estrone
Blood or Urine82679

Ethanediols
See Ethylene Glycol

Ethanol
Blood .82055
Breath .82075
Urine .82055

Ethchlorovynol
See Ethchlorvynol

Ethchlorvinol
See Ethchlorvynol

Ethchlorvynol
Blood .82690
Urine .82690

Ethmoid
Fracture
with Fixation .21340

Ethmoid, Sinus
See Sinus, Ethmoid

Ethmoidectomy31200-31205
Endoscopic31254-31255
Skull Base Surgery61580-61581
with Nasal/Sinus Endoscopy31254-31255

Ethosuccimid
See Ethosuximide

Ethosuximide80168
Assay .80168

Ethyl Alcohol
See Ethanol

Ethylene Dichlorides
See Dichloroethane

Ethylene Glycol82693

Ethylmethylsuccimide
See Ethosuximide

Etiocholanalone Measurement
See Etiocholanolone

Etiocholanolone82696

ETOH
See Alcohol, Ethyl

Euglobulin Lysis85360

European Blastomycosis
See Cryptococcus

Eustachian Tube
Catheterization .69405
Inflation
Myringotomy69420
Anesthesia69421
with Catheterization69400
without Catheterization69401
Insertion
Catheter .69405

Eutelegenesis
See Artificial Insemination

Evacuation
Cervical Pregnancy59140
Hematoma
Brain .61312-61315
Subungual .11740
Hydatidiform Mole59870

Evaluation
Aneurysm Pressure0154T
Cine .74230
Treatment .92526
Video .74230

Evaluation and Management
Assistive Technology
Assessment97755
Athletic Training
Evaluation .97005
Re-evaluation97006

Basic Life and/or Disability
Evaluation Services99450
Care Plan Oversight Services99339-99340,
99374-99380
Home Health Agency Care99374
Home or Rest Home Care99339-99340
Hospice99377-99378
Nursing Facility99379-99380
Case Management Services99361-99373
Consultation99241-99255
Critical Care99291-99292
Interfacility Pediatric Transport .99289-99290
Domiciliary or Rest Home
Established Patient99334-99337
New Patient99324-99328
Emergency Department99281-99288
Health Behavior
Assessment96150
Family Intervention96154-96155
Group Intervention96153
Individual Intervention96152
Re-assessment96151
Home Services99341-99350
Hospital99221-99233
Discharge99238-99239
Hospital Services
Observation Care99217-99220
Insurance Exam99455-99456
Internet Communication0074T
Low Birthweight Infant99298-99300
Medical
with Individual Psychotherapy
Hospital or Residential Care90817,
90819, 90822, 90824, 90827, 90829
Office or Outpatient . .90805, 90807, 90809
with Individual Psychotherapy, Interactive
Office or Outpatient . .90811, 90813, 90815
Neonatal Critical Care99295-99296
Newborn Care99431-99440
Nursing Facility
See Nursing Facility Services
Annual Assessment99318
Discharge99315-99316
Initial Care99304-99306
Other .99318
Subsequent Care99307-99310
Occupation Therapy Evaluation97003
Re-evaluation97004
Office and Other Outpatient99201-99215
Online .0074T
Pediatric Critical Care99293-99294
Pediatric Interfacility Transport99289-99290
Physical Therapy Evaluation97001
Re-evaluation97002
Physician Standby Services99360
Preventive Services99381-99429
Prolonged Services99356-99357
Psychiatric
Records or Reports90885
Unlisted Services and Procedures99499
Work-Related and/or Medical Disability
Evaluation .99450

Evaluation Studies, Drug, Pre-Clinical
See Drug Screen

Evisceration
Ocular Contents
with Implant65093
without Implant65091

Evisceration, Pelvic
See Exenteration, Pelvis

Evocative/Suppression Test80400-80440
Stimulation Panel80410

Evoked Potential
See Audiologic Function Tests
Auditory Brainstem92585-92586
Central Motor
Transcranial Motor Stimulation .95928-95929
Somatosensory Testing95925-95927
Visual, CNS .95930

Evoked Potential, Auditory
See Auditory Evoked Potentials

Ewart Procedure
See Palate, Reconstruction, Lengthening

Excavatum, Pectus
See Pectus Excavatum

Exchange
Drainage Catheter
Under Radiologic Guidance49423
Intraocular Lens66986
Intravascular Catheter37209, 75900

Exchange Transfusion
See Blood, Transfusion, Exchange

Excision
See Debridement; Destruction
Abscess
Brain61514, 61522
Olecranon Process24138
Radius .24136
Ulna .24138
Acromion
Shoulder .23130
Adenoids42830-42836
Adenoma
Thyroid Gland60200
Adrenal Gland60540
Laparoscopic60650
with Excision Retroperitoneal Tumor . .60545
Alveolus .41830
Anal Crypt46210-46211
Anal Fissure .46200
Anal Tag46220, 46230
Aorta
Coarctation33840-33851
Appendix44950-44960
Arteriovenous Malformation
Spinal63250-63252
Arytenoid Cartilage31400
Endoscopic31560-31561
Atrial Septum33735-33737
Bartholin's Gland56740
Bladder
Diverticulum51525
Neck .51520
Partial51550-51565

Total51570, 51580, 51590-51597
 with Nodes51575, 51585, 51595
Transurethral52640
Tumor51530
Bladder Neck Contracture
 Postoperative52640
Bone
 Facial21026
 Mandible21025
 Postoperative
 Femur20150
 Fibula20150
 Radius20150
 Tibia20150
 Ulna20150
Bone Abscess
 Facial21026
 Mandible21025
Brain
 Amygdala61566
 Epileptogenic Focus61536
 Hemisphere61542-61543
 Hippocampus61566
 Other Lobe61323, 61539-61540
 Temporal Lobe61537-61538
Brain Lobe
 See Lobectomy, Brain
Breast
 Biopsy19100-19103
 Chest Wall Tumor19260-19272
 Cyst19120-19126
 Lactiferous Duct Fistula19112
 Lesion19120-19126
 by Needle Localization19125-19126
 Mastectomy19300-19307
 Nipple Exploration19110
Bulbourethral Gland53250
Bullae
 Lung32141
 Endoscopic32655
Burns01951-01953, 15002-15005
Bursa
 Elbow24105
 Femur27062
 Ischial27060
 Knee27340
 Wrist25115-25116
Bypass Graft35901-35907
Calcaneus28118-28120
Calculi (Stone)
 Parotid Gland42330, 42340
 Salivary Gland42330-42340
 Sublingual Gland42330
 Submandibular Gland42330-42335
Carotid Artery60605
Carpal25145, 25210-25215
Cartilage
 Knee Joint27332-27333
 Shoulder Joint23101
 Temporomandibular Joint21060
 Wrist25107
Caruncle
 Urethra53265
Cataract
 Secondary66830

Cervix
 Radical57531
 Stump
 Abdominal Approach57540-57545
 Vaginal Approach57550-57556
 Total57530
Chalazion
 Multiple
 Different Lids67805
 Same Lid67801
 Single67800
 with Anesthesia67808
Chest Wall
 Tumor19260-19272
Choroid Plexus61544
Clavicle
 Partial23120, 23180
 Sequestrectomy23170
 Total23125
 Tumor
 Radical Resection23200
Coccyx27080
Colon
 Excision
 Partial44140-44147, 44160
 with Anastomosis44140
 Total44150-44158
 Laparoscopic
 with Anastomosis44204, 44207-44208
 with Colostomy44206, 44208
 with Ileocolostomy44205
Condyle
 Temporomandibular Joint21050
Constricting Ring
 Finger26596
Cornea
 Epithelium65435
 with Chelating Agent65436
 Scraping65430
Coronoidectomy21070
Cowper's Gland53250
Cranial Bone
 Tumor61563-61564
Cyst
 See Ganglion Cyst
 Bile Duct47715
 Bladder51500
 Brain61516, 61524, 62162
 Branchial42810-42815
 Calcaneus28100-28103
 Carpal25130-25136
 Cheekbone21030
 Clavicle23140
 with Allograft23146
 with Autograft23145
 Facial Bones21030
 Femur27065-27067, 27355-27358
 Fibula27635-27638
 Finger26160
 Foot28090
 Hand26160
 Hip27065-27067
 Humerus23150, 24110
 with Allograft23156, 24116
 with Autograft23155, 24115
 Ileum27065-27067
 Kidney50280-50290

Knee27345-27347
Lung32140
Mandible21040, 21046-21047
Maxilla21030, 21048-21049
Mediastinal39200
Mediastinum32662
Metacarpal26200-26205
Metatarsal28104-28107
Mullerian Duct55680
Nose30124-30125
Olecranon24120
Olecranon Process
 with Allograft24126
 with Autograft24125
Ovarian58925
 See Cystectomy, Ovarian
Pericardial33050
 Endoscopic32661
Phalanges26210-26215
 Toe28108
Pilonidal11770-11772
Pubis27066-27067
Radius24120, 25120-25126
 with Allograft24126
 with Autograft24125
Salivary Gland42408
Scapula23140
 with Allograft23146
 with Autograft23145
Seminal Vesicle55680
Sublingual Gland42408
Talus28100-28103
Tarsal28104-28107
Thyroglossal Duct60280-60281
Thyroid Gland60200
Tibia27635-27638
Toe28092
Ulna24120, 25120-25126
 with Allograft24126
 with Autograft24125
Urachal
 Bladder51500
 Vaginal57135
Destruction of the Vestibule of the Mouth
 See Mouth, Vestibule of, Excision, Destruction
Diverticulum, Meckel's
 See Meckel's Diverticulum, Excision
Ear, External
 Partial69110
 Total69120
Elbow Joint24155
Electrode57522
Embolectomy/Thrombectomy
 Aortoiliac Artery34151-34201
 Axillary Artery34101
 Brachial Artery34101
 Carotid Artery34001
 Celiac Artery34151
 Femoral Artery34201
 Heart33310-33315
 Iliac Artery34151-34201
 Innominate Artery34001-34101
 Mesentery Artery34151
 Peroneal Artery34203
 Popliteal Artery34203
 Radial Artery34111
 Renal Artery34151

Liver
- Extensive .47122
- Lobectomy47125-47130
- Partial . . .47120, 47125-47130, 47140-47142
- Total .47133

Lung
- Bronchus Resection32486
- Bullae
 - Endoscopic .32655
- Completion .32488
- Emphysematous32491
- Lobe32480-32482
- Segment .32484
- Total32440-32445
- Tumor, Apical Tumor
 - with Reconstruction32504
 - with Resection32503
- Wedge Resection32500
 - Endoscopic32657

Lung/Heart
- Donor .33930

Lymph Nodes38500, 38510-38530
- Abdominal .38747
- Inguinofemoral38760-38765
- Limited, for Staging
 - Para-Aortic38562
 - Pelvic .38562
 - Retroperitoneal38564
- Pelvic .38770
- Radical
 - Axillary38740-38745
 - Cervical38720-38724
 - Suprahyoid38700
 - Retroperitoneal Transabdominal38780
 - Thoracic .38746

Mandibular
- Exostosis .21031

Mastoid
- Complete .69502
- Radical .69511
 - Modified .69505
 - Petrous Apicectomy69530
- Simple .69501

Maxilla
- Exostosis .21032

Maxillary Torus Palatinus21032

Meningioma
- Brain61512, 61519

Meniscectomy
- Temporomandibular Joint21060

Metacarpal .26230

Metatarsal28110-28114, 28122, 28140
- Condyle .28288

Mouth
- Frenum .40819

Mucosa
- Gums .41828
- Mouth .40818

Nail Fold .11765

Nails .11750-11752

Nerve
- Foot .28055
- Leg, Lower .27326
- Leg, Upper .27325
- Sympathetic64802-64818

Neurofibroma64788-64790

Neurolemmoma64788-64792

Neuroma64774-64786

Nose
- Dermoid Cyst
 - Complex .30125
 - Simple .30124
- Polyp30110-30115
- Rhinectomy30150-30160
- Skin .30120
- Submucous Resection
 - Nasal Septum30520
 - Turbinate .30140
- Turbinate30130-30140

Odontoid Process22548

Olecranon Process24147

Omentum .49255

Ovary .58720
- Partial
 - Oophorectomy58940
 - Ovarian Malignancy58943
 - Peritoneal Malignancy58943
 - Tubal Malignancy58943
 - Wedge Resection58920
- Total58940-58943

Oviduct .58720

Palate42120, 42145

Pancreas
- Ampulla of Vater48148
- Duct .48148
- Partial48140-48146, 48150,
 48153-48154, 48160
- Peripancreatic Tissue48105
- Total48155-48160

Parathyroid Gland60500-60502

Parotid Gland .42340
- Partial42410-42415
- Total42420-42426

Patella .27350
- See Patellectomy

Penile Adhesions
- Post-circumcision54162

Penis
- Frenulum .54164
- Partial .54120
- Prepuce54150-54161, 54163
- Radical54130-54135
- Total .54125

Pericardium33030-33031
- Endoscopic .32659

Petrous Temporal
- Apex .69530

Phalanges
- Finger26235-26236
- Toe28124-28126, 28150-28160

Pharynx .42145
- Partial .42890
- Resection42892-42894
- with Larynx31390-31395

Pituitary Gland61546-61548

Pleura32310-32320
- Endoscopic .32656

Polyp
- Intestines .43250
- Nose
 - Extensive .30115
 - Simple .30110
- Sinus .31032
- Urethra .53260

Pressure Ulcers15920-15999
- See Skin Graft and Flap

Prostate
- Abdominoperineal45119
- Partial55801, 55821-55831
- Perineal55801-55815
- Radical55810-55815, 55840-55845
- Regrowth .52630
- Residual Obstructive Tissue52620
- Retropubic55831-55845
- Suprapubic .55821
- Transurethral52601, 52612-52614

Pterygium
- with Graft .65426

Pubis
- Partial27070-27071

Radical Synovium Wrist25115-25116

Radius24130, 24136, 24145,
24152-24153, 25145
- Styloid Process25230

Rectum
- Partial45111, 45113-45116, 45123
- Prolapse45130-45135
- Stricture .45150
- Total45119-45120
- with Colon .45121

Redundant Skin of Eyelid
- See Blepharoplasty

Ribs21600-21616, 32900

Scapula
- Ostectomy .23190
- Partial .23182
- Sequestrectomy23172
- Tumor
 - Radical Resection23210

Sclera .66160

Scrotum .55150

Semilunar Cartilage of Knee
- See Knee, Meniscectomy

Seminal Vesicle .55650

Sesamoid Bone
- Foot .28315

Sinus
- Ethmoid31200-31205
- Maxillary31225-31230

Skene's Gland .53270

Skin
- Excess15830-15839, 15847
- Lesion
 - Benign11400-11471
 - Malignant11600-11646
- Nose .30120

Skin Graft
- Preparation of Site15002-15005

Skull .61501

Spermatic Veins55530-55540
- Abdominal Approach55535
- Hernia Repair55540

Spleen .38100-38102
- Laparoscopic .38120

Stapes
- with Footplate Drill Out69661
- without Foreign Material69660

Sternum21620, 21630-21632

Stomach
- Partial43631-43635, 43845
- Total43620-43622

Sublingual Gland42450

Submandibular Gland42440, 42508

Vertebra, Lumbar22102
Vertebra, Thoracic22101
Wrist .25075-25077
Zygoma21030, 21034
Turbinate30130-30140
Tympanic Nerve69676
Ulcer
 Stomach .43610
Ulna .24147, 25145
 Complete .25240
 Partial25150-25151, 25240
Umbilicus .49250
Ureter
 See Ureterectomy
Ureterocele .51535
Urethra
 Diverticulum53230-53235
 Prolapse .53275
 Total
 Female .53210
 Male .53215
Uterus
 Laparoscopic58541-58544, 58550
 Leiomyomata58546
 Partial .58180
 Radical58210, 58285
 Laparoscopic58548
 Removal Tubes and/or
 Ovaries58262-58263, 58291,
 58552, 58554
 with Colpectomy58275-58280
 with Colpo-Urethrocystopexy58267,
 58293
 with Repair of Enterocele . . .58270, 58292,
 58294
 Total58150-58152, 58200
 Vaginal . .58260, 58290-58294, 58550, 58553
Uvula .42140-42145
Vagina
 Closure .57120
 Complete
 with Removal of Paravaginal Tissue .57111
 with Removal of Paravaginal Tissue
 with Lymphadenectomy57112
 with Removal of Vaginal Wall57110
 Partial
 with Removal of Paravaginal Tissue .57107
 with Removal of Paravaginal Tissue
 with Lymphadenectomy57109
 with Removal of Vaginal Wall57106
 Septum .57130
 Total .57110
 with Hysterectomy58275-58280
 Repair of Enterocele58280
Varicocele
 Spermatic Cord55530-55540
 Abdominal Approach55535
 Hernia Repair55540
Vas Deferens55250
Vascular Malformation
 Finger .26115
 Hand .26115
Vein
 Varicose37765-37766
Vertebra
 Additional Segment22103, 22116
 Cervical .22110
 for Tumor22100, 22110

Lumbar .22102
 for Tumor22114
Thoracic .22112
 for Tumor22101
Vertebral Body
 Decompression63081-63103
 Lesion63300-63308
Vitreous .67039
 Total
 Pars Plana Approach67036
 with Epiretinal Membrane
 Stripping67038
 with Retinal Surgery67038
Vulva
 Radical
 Complete56633-56640
 Partial56630-56632
 Simple
 Complete56625
 Partial .56620
Wrist Tendon25109

Exclusion

Duodenum .48547
Small Intestine44700

Exenteration

Eye
 Removal Orbital Contents65110
 Therapeutic Removal of Bone65112
 with Muscle or Myocutaneous Flap . . .65114
Pelvis45126, 58240

Exercise Stress Tests93015-93018

Exercise Test

See Electromyography, Needle
Ischemic Limb95875

Exercise Therapy97110-97113

See Physical Medicine/Therapy/Occupational
Therapy

Exfoliation

Chemical .17360

Exocrine, Pancreas

See Pancreas

Exomphalos

See Omphalocele

Exostectomy28288, 28290

Exostoses

See Exostosis

Exostoses, Cartilaginous

See Exostosis

Exostosis

Excision .69140

Expander, Skin, Inflatable

See Tissue, Expander

Expired Gas Analysis94680-94690,
 94770

See Pulmonology, Diagnostic
Carbon Monoxide
 Breath Test0043T

Nitric oxide .95012
Spectroscopic0064T

Exploration

Abdomen49000-49002
 Penetrating Wound20102
 Staging .58960
Adrenal Gland60540-60545
Anal
 Endoscopy46600
Ankle27610, 27620
Anus
 Surgical .45990
Arm, Lower .25248
Artery
 Brachial .24495
 Carotid .35701
 Femoral .35721
 Other .35761
 Popliteal .35741
Back
 Penetrating Wound20102
Bile Duct
 Atresia .47700
 Endoscopy47552-47553
Blood Vessel
 Abdomen .35840
 Chest .35820
 Extremity .35860
 Neck .35800
Brain
 Infratentorial61305
 Supratentorial61304
 via Burr Hole
 Infratentorial61253
 Supratentorial61250
Breast .19020
Bronchi
 Endoscopy31622
Bronchoscopy31622
Cauda Equina63005-63011, 63017
Chest
 Penetrating Wound20101
Colon
 Endoscopic44388, 45378
Colon-Sigmoid
 Endoscopic45330, 45335
Common Bile Duct
 with Cholecystectomy47610
Duodenum .44010
Ear, Inner
 Endolymphatic Sac
 with Shunt69806
 without Shunt69805
Ear, Middle .69440
Elbow24000, 24101
Epididymis .54865
Esophagus
 Endoscopy43200
Extremity
 Penetrating Wound20103
Finger Joint26075-26080
Flank
 Penetrating Wound20102
Gallbladder .47480
Gastrointestinal Tract, Upper
 Endoscopy43234-43236
Hand Joint .26070

Flurazepam
Blood or Urine82742

Flush Aortogram75722-75724

FNA
See Fine Needle Aspiration

Foam Stability Test83662

Fold, Vocal
See Vocal Cords

Foley Operation Pyeloplasty
See Pyeloplasty

Foley Y-Pyeloplasty50400-50405

Folic Acid82747
Blood82746

Follicle Stimulating Hormone (FSH)80418, 80426, 83001

Folliculin
See Estrone

Follitropin
See Follicle Stimulating Hormone (FSH)

Follow-up Inpatient Consultations
See Consultation, Follow-up Inpatient

Follow-up Services
See Hospital Services; Office and/or Other
Outpatient Services
Post-Op99024

Fontan Procedure
See Repair, Heart, Anomaly; Revision

Food Allergy Test95075
See Allergy Tests

Foot
See Metatarsal; Tarsal
Amputation28800-28805
Bursa
 Incision and Drainage28001
Capsulotomy28260-28264
Cast29450
Fasciectomy28060
 Radical28060-28062
Fasciotomy28008
 Endoscopic29893
Incision28002-28005
Joint
 See Talotarsal Joint; Tarsometatarsal Joint
 Magnetic Resonance Imaging
 (MRI)73721-73723
Lesion
 Excision28080, 28090
Magnetic Resonance Imaging
(MRI)73718-73720
Nerve
 Excision28055
 Incision28035
Neurectomy28055
Neuroma
 Excision28080
Reconstruction
 Cleft Foot28360

Removal
 Foreign Body28190-28193
Repair
 Muscle28250
 Tendon28200-28230, 28234-28238
Replantation20838
Sesamoid
 Excision28315
Splint29590
Strapping29540, 29590
Suture
 Tendon28200-28210
Tendon Sheath
 Excision28086-28088
Tenotomy28230, 28234
Tumor
 Excision28043-28046
Unlisted Services and Procedures28899
X-Ray73620-73630

Foot Abscess
See Abscess, Foot

Foot Navicular Bone
See Navicular

Forearm20805
See Arm, Lower

Forehead
Flap15731
Reconstruction21179-21180, 21182-21184
 Midface21159-21160
Reduction21137-21139

Forehead and Orbital Rim
Reconstruction21172-21180

Foreign Body Removal
Peritoneal Cavity49402
Pharynx42809
Shoulder23331

Forensic Exam88040
Cytopathology88125
Phosphatase, Acid84061

Foreskin of Penis
See Penis, Prepuce

Formycin Diphosphate
See Fibrin Degradation Products

Fournier's Gangrene
See Debridement, Skin, Subcutaneous Tissue,
Infected

Fowler-Stephens Orchiopexy
See Orchiopexy

Fowler-Stephens Procedure ...54650

Fox Operation
See Entropion, Repair

Fraction, Factor IX
See Christmas Factor

Fracture
Acetabulum
 Closed Treatment27220-27222
 Open Treatment27226-27228

 with Manipulation27222
 without Manipulation27220
Alveola
 Closed Treatment21421
 Open Treatment21422-21423
Alveolar Ridge
 Closed Treatment21440
 Open Treatment21445
Ankle
 Closed Treatment27816-27818
 Lateral27786-27814
 Medial27760-27766, 27808-27814
 Open Treatment27822-27823
 Trimalleolar27816-27823
 with Manipulation27818
 without Manipulation27816
Ankle Bone
 Medial27760-27762
Bennett's
 See Thumb, Fracture
Bronchi
 Endoscopy31630
Calcaneus
 Closed Treatment28400-28405
 Open Treatment28415-28420
 Percutaneous Fixation28436
 with Manipulation28405-28406
 without Manipulation28400
Carpal
 Closed Treatment
 with Manipulation25624, 25635
 without Manipulation25622, 25630
 Open Treatment25628, 25645
Carpal Scaphoid
 Closed Treatment25622
Cheekbone
 Open Treatment21360-21366
 with Manipulation21355
Clavicle
 Closed Treatment
 with Manipulation23505
 without Manipulation23500
 Open Treatment23515
Closed Treatment27520
Coccyx
 Closed Treatment27200
 Open Treatment27202
Colles
 See Colles Fracture
Colles-Reversed
 See Smith Fracture
Elbow
 Monteggia
 Closed Treatment24620
 Open Treatment24635
 Open Treatment24586-24587
Femur
 Closed Treatment27230, 27238-27240,
 27246, 27500-27503, 27508,
 27510, 27516-27517
 with Manipulation27232
 Distal27508, 27510, 27514
 Epiphysis27516-27519
 Intertrochanteric
 Closed Treatment27238
 Intramedullary Implant27245
 Plate/Screw Implant27244

Fruit Sugar
See Fructose

FSF85290-85291

FSH
See Follicle Stimulating Hormone (FSH)

FSP
See Fibrin Degradation Products

FT-484439

Fulguration
See Destruction
Bladder51020
Cystourethroscopy with52214
 Lesion52224
 Tumor52234-52240
Ureter50957, 50976
Ureterocele
 Ectopic52301
 Orthotopic52300

Fulguration, Endocavitary
See Electrocautery

Full Thickness Graft15200-15261

Function Test, Lung
See Pulmonology, Diagnostic

Function Test, Vestibular
See Vestibular Function Tests

Function, Study, Nasal
See Nasal Function Study

Functional Ability
See Activities of Daily Living

Fundoplasty
Esophagogastric43324-43325
 Laparoscopic43280
 with Gastroplasty43326

Fundoplication
See Fundoplasty, Esophagogastric

Fungus
Antibody86671
Culture
 Blood87103
 Hair87101
 Identification87106
 Nail87101
 Other87102
 Skin87101
Tissue Exam87220

Funnel Chest
See Pectus Excavatum

Furuncle
Incision and Drainage10060-10061

Furuncle, Vulva
See Abscess, Vulva

Fusion
See Arthrodesis
Pleural Cavity32005
Thumb
 in Opposition26820

Fusion, Epiphyseal-Diaphyseal
See Epiphyseal Arrest

Fusion, Joint
See Arthrodesis

Fusion, Joint, Ankle
See Ankle, Arthrodesis

Fusion, Joint, Interphalangeal, Finger
See Arthrodesis, Finger Joint, Interphalangeal

G

Gago Procedure
See Repair, Tricuspid Valve; Revision

Gait Training97116
See Physical Medicine/Therapy/Occupational Therapy

Galactogram77053-77054
Injection19030

Galactokinase
Blood82759

Galactose
Blood82760
Urine82760

Galactose-1-Phosphate
Uridyl Transferase82775-82776

Gall Bladder
See Gallbladder

Gallbladder
See Bile Duct
Anastomosis
 with Intestines47720-47741
Excision47562-47564, 47600-47620
Exploration47480
Incision47490
Incision and Drainage47480
Nuclear Medicine
 Imaging78223
Removal
 Calculi (Stone)47480
Repair
 with Gastroenterostomy47741
 with Intestines47720-47740
Unlisted Services and Procedures47999
X-Ray with Contrast74290-74291

Galvanocautery
See Electrocautery

Galvanoionization
See Iontophoresis

Gamete Intrafallopian Transfer (GIFT)58976

Gamete Transfer
In Vitro Fertilization58976

Gamma Camera Imaging
See Nuclear Medicine

Gamma Glutamyl Transferase82977

Gamma Seminoprotein
See Antigen, Prostate Specific

Gammacorten
See Dexamethasone

Gammaglobulin
Blood82784-82787

Gamulin Rh
See Immune Globulins, Rho (D)

Ganglia, Trigeminal
See Gasserian Ganglion

Ganglion
See Gasserian Ganglion
Cyst
 Aspiration/Injection20612
 Drainage20612
 Wrist
 Excision25111-25112
Injection
 Anesthetic64505, 64510

Ganglion Cervicothoracicum
See Stellate Ganglion

Ganglion Pterygopalatinum
See Sphenopalatine Ganglion

Ganglion, Gasser's
See Gasserian Ganglion

Gardner Operation
See Meningocele Repair

Gardnerella Vaginalis Detection87510-87512

Gasser Ganglion
See Gasserian Ganglion

Gasserian Ganglion
Sensory Root
 Decompression61450
 Section61450
Stereotactic61790

Gastrectomy
Partial43631-43635, 43845
 with Gastrojejunostomy43632
Total43621-43622
 with Esophagoenterostomy43620
with Gastroduodenostomy43631

Gastric Acid82926-82928

Gastric Analysis Test91052

Gastric Electrodes
Implantation
 Laparoscopic
 Neurostimulator43647
 Stimulation0155T
 Open
 Neurostimulator43881
 Stimulation0157T

Gentamicin80170
Assay80170

Gentamycin Level
See Gentamicin

Gentiobiase
See Beta Glucosidase

Genus: Human Cytomegalovirus Group
See Cytomegalovirus

GERD
See Gastroesophageal Reflux Test

German Measles
See Rubella

Gestational Trophoblastic Tumor
See Hydatidiform Mole

GGT
See Gamma Glutamyl Transferase

GI Tract
See Gastrointestinal Tract

Giardia
Antigen Detection
 Enzyme Immunoassay87329
 Immunofluorescence87269

Giardia Lamblia
Antibody86674

Gibbons Stent52332

GIF
See Somatostatin

GIFT
See Gamete Intrafallopian Transfer

Gill Operation63012

Gillies Approach
Fracture
 Zygomatic Arch21356

Gingiva
See Gums

Gingiva, Abcess
See Abscess
Fracture
 See Abscess, Gums; Gums
 Zygomatic Arch
 See Abscess, Gums; Gums, Abscess

Gingivectomy41820

Gingivoplasty41872

Girdlestone Laminectomy
See Laminectomy

Girdlestone Procedure
See Acetabulum, Reconstruction

Gla Protein (Bone)
See Osteocalcin

Gland
See Specific Gland

Gland, Adrenal
See Adrenal Gland

Gland, Bartholin's
See Bartholin's Gland

Gland, Bulbourethral
See Bulbourethral Gland

Gland, Lacrimal
See Lacrimal Gland

Gland, Mammary
See Breast

Gland, Parathyroid
See Parathyroid Gland

Gland, Parotid
See Parotid Gland

Gland, Pituitary
See Pituitary Gland

Gland, Salivary
See Salivary Glands

Gland, Sublingual
See Sublingual Gland

Gland, Sweat
See Sweat Glands

Gland, Thymus
See Thymus Gland

Gland, Thyroid
See Thyroid Gland

Glasses
See Spectacle Services

Glaucoma
Cryotherapy66720
Cyclophotocoagulation66710-66711
Diathermy66700
Fistulization of Sclera66150
Provocative Test92140

Glaucoma Drainage Implant
See Aqueous Shunt

Glenn Procedure33766-33767

Glenohumeral Joint
Arthrotomy23040
 with Biopsy23100
 with Synovectomy23105
Exploration23107
Removal
 Foreign or Loose Body23107

Glenoid Fossa
Reconstruction21255

GLN
See Glutamine

Globulin
Antihuman86880-86886
Immune90281-90399
Sex Hormone Binding84270

Globulin, Corticosteroid-Binding
See Transcortin

Globulin, Rh Immune
See Immune Globulins, Rho (D)

Globulin, Thyroxine-Binding
See Thyroxine Binding Globulin

Glomerular Procoagulant Activity
See Thromboplastin

Glomus Caroticum
See Carotid Body

Glossectomies
See Excision, Tongue

Glossopexy
See Tongue, Fixation

Glossorrhaphy
See Suture, Tongue

Glucagon82943
Tolerance Panel80422-80424
Tolerance Test82946

Glucose80422-80424, 80430-80435,
 95250-95251
Blood Test82947-82950, 82962
Body Fluid82945
Interstitial Fluid
 Continuous Monitoring95250-95251
Tolerance Test82951-82952
 with Tolbutamide82953

Glucose Phosphate Isomerase
See Phosphohexose Isomerase

Glucose Phosphate Isomerase Measurement
See Phosphohexose Isomerase

Glucose-6-Phosphate
Dehydrogenase82955-82960

Glucosidase82963

Glucuronide Androstanediol82154

Glue
Cornea Wound65286
Sclera Wound65286

Glukagon
See Glucagon

Glutamate Dehydrogenase
Blood82965

Glutamate Pyruvate Transaminase
See Transaminase, Glutamic Pyruvic

Glutamic Alanine Transaminase
See Transaminase, Glutamic Pyruvic

Glutamic Aspartic Transaminase
See Transaminase, Glutamic Oxaloacetic

Glutamic Dehydrogenase
See Glutamate Dehydrogenase

Glutamine82975

Glutamyltransferase, Gamma .. .82977

Glutathione82978

Groin Area
Repair
 Hernia49550-49557

Group Health Education . .98961-98962,
99078

Grouping, Blood
See Blood Typing

Growth Factors, Insulin-Like
See Somatomedin

Growth Hormone83003
Human80418, 80428-80430, 86277

Growth Hormone Release Inhibiting Factor
See Somatostatin

GTT
See Hydatidiform Mole

Guaiac Test
See Blood, Feces

Guanosine Monophosphate83008

Guanosine Monophosphate, Cyclic
See Cyclic GMP

Guanylic Acids
See Guanosine Monophosphate

Guard Stain .88313

Gullet
See Esophagus

Gums
Abscess
 Incision and Drainage41800
Alveolus
 Excision .41830
Cyst
 Incision and Drainage41800
Excision
 Gingiva .41820
 Operculum .41821
Graft
 Mucosa .41870
Hematoma
 Incision and Drainage41800
Lesion
 Destruction41850
 Excision41822-41828
Mucosa
 Excision .41828
Reconstruction
 Alveolus .41874
 Gingiva .41872
Removal
 Foreign Body41805
Tumor
 Excision41825-41827
Unlisted Services and Procedures41899

Gunning-Lieben Test
See Acetone, Blood or Urine

Guthrie Test .84030

H

H Flu
See Hemophilus Influenza

H-Reflex Study95934-95936

HAA (Hepatitis Associated Antigen)
See Hepatitis Antigen, B Surface

HAAb
See Antibody, Hepatitis

Haemoglobin F
See Fetal Hemoglobin

Haemorrhage
See Hemorrhage

Haemorrhage Rectum
See Hemorrhage, Rectum

Hageman Factor85280

HAI Test
See Hemagglutination Inhibition Test

Hair
Electrolysis .17380
KOH Examination87220
Microscopic Evaluation96902
Transplant
 Punch Graft15775-15776
 Strip Graft15220-15221

Hair Removal
See Removal, Hair

Hallux
See Great Toe

Halo
Body Cast .29000
Cranial .20661
 for Thin Skull Osteology20664
Femur .20663
Maxillofacial .21100
Pelvic .20662
Removal .20665

Haloperidol
Assay .80173

Halsted Mastectomy
See Mastectomy, Radical

Halsted Repair
See Hernia, Repair, Inguinal

Ham Test
See Hemolysins

Hammertoe Repair28285-28286

Hamster Penetration Test89329

Hand
See Carpometacarpal Joint; Intercarpal Joint

Amputation
 at Metacarpal25927
 at Wrist .25920
 Revision25922
 Revision25924, 25929-25931
Arthrodesis
 Carpometacarpal Joint26843-26844
 Intercarpal Joint25820-25825
Bone
 Incision and Drainage26034
Cast .29085
Decompression26035-26037
Fracture
 Metacarpal26600
Insertion
 Tendon Graft26392
Magnetic Resonance Imaging
(MRI) .73218-73223
Reconstruction
 Tendon Pulley26500-26502
Removal
 Implantation26320
 Tube/Rod26390-26392, 26416
Repair
 Blood Vessel35207
 Cleft Hand26580
 Muscle26591-26593
 Tendon
 Extensor26410-26416, 26426-26428,
26433-26437
 Flexor26350-26358, 26440
 Profundus26370-26373
Replantation .20808
Strapping .29280
Tendon
 Excision .26390
 Extensor26415
Tenotomy26450, 26460
Tumor
 Excision26115-26117
Unlisted Services and Procedures26989
X-Ray .73120-73130

Hand Abscess
See Abscess, Hand

Hand Phalange
See Finger, Bone

Hand(s) Dupuytrens Contracture(s)
See Dupuytren's Contracture

Handling
Device .99002
Radioelement .77790
Specimen99000-99001

Hanganutziu Deicher Antibodies
See Antibody, Heterophile

Haptoglobin83010-83012

Hard Palate
See Palate

Harelip Operation
See Cleft Lip, Repair

Harii Procedure25430

Human T Cell Leukemia Virus II Antibodies
See Antibody, HTLV II

Humeral Epicondylitides, Lateral
See Tennis Elbow

Humeral Fracture
See Fracture, Humerus

Humerus
See Arm, Upper; Shoulder
Abscess
 Incision and Drainage23935
Craterization23184, 24140
Cyst
 Excision23150, 24110
 with Allograft23156, 24116
 with Autograft23155, 24115
Diaphysectomy23184, 24140
Excision23174, 23184, 23195, 24134, 24140,
 24150-24151
Fracture
 Closed Treatment24500-24505
 with Manipulation23605
 without Manipulation23600
 Condyle
 Closed Treatment24576-24577
 Open Treatment24579
 Percutaneous Fixation24582
 Epicondyle
 Closed Treatment24560-24565
 Open Treatment24575
 Skeletal Fixation
 Percutaneous24566
 Greater Tuberosity Fracture
 Closed Treatment with
 Manipulation23625
 Closed Treatment without
 Manipulation23620
 Open Treatment23630
 Open Treatment23615-23616
 Shaft24500-24505, 24516
 Open Treatment24515
 Supracondylar
 Closed Treatment24530-24535
 Open Treatment24545-24546
 Percutaneous Fixation24538
 Transcondylar
 Closed Treatment24530-24535
 Open Treatment24545-24546
 Percutaneous Fixation24538
 with Dislocation23665-23670
Osteomyelitis24134
Pinning, Wiring23491, 24498
Prophylactic Treatment23491, 24498
Radical Resection23220-23222
Repair24430
 Nonunion, Malunion24430-24435
 Osteoplasty24420
 Osteotomy24400-24410
 with Graft24435
Resection Head23195
Saucerization23184, 24140
Sequestrectomy23174, 24134
Tumor
 Excision23150, 23220-23222, 24110
 with Allograft23156, 24116
 with Autograft23155, 24115

X-Ray73060

Hummelshein Operation
See Strabismus, Repair

Humor Shunt, Aqueous
See Aqueous Shunt

HVA
See Homovanillic Acid

Hyaluron Binding Assay0087T

Hybridization Probes, DNA
See Nucleic Acid Probe

Hydatid Disease
See Echinococcosis

Hydatid Mole
See Hydatidiform Mole

Hydatidiform Mole
Evacuation and Curettage59870
Excision59100

Hydration90760-90761

Hydrocarbons, Chlorinated
See Chlorinated Hydrocarbons

Hydrocele
Aspiration55000
Excision
 Bilateral
 Tunica Vaginalis55041
 Unilateral
 Spermatic Cord55500
 Tunica Vaginalis55040
Repair55060

Hydrochloric Acid, Gastric
See Acid, Gastric

Hydrochloride, Vancomycin
See Vancomycin

Hydrocodon
See Dihydrocodeinone

Hydrogen Ion Concentration
See pH

Hydrolase, Acetylcholine
See Acetylcholinesterase

Hydrolase, Triacylglycerol
See Lipase

Hydrolases, Phosphoric Monoester
See Phosphatase

Hydrotherapy (Hubbard Tank)97036
See Physical Medicine/Therapy/Occupational Therapy

Hydrotubation58350

Hydroxyacetanilide
See Acetaminophen

Hydroxycorticosteroid83491

Hydroxyindolacetic Acid83497
Urine83497

Hydroxypregnenolone80406, 84143

Hydroxyprogesterone80402-80406,
 83498-83499

Hydroxyproline83500-83505

Hydroxytyramine
See Dopamine

Hygroma
Cystic
 Axillary/Cervical
 Excision38550-38555

Hymen
Excision56700
Incision56442

Hymenal Ring
Revision56700

Hymenectomy56700

Hymenotomy56442

Hyoid
Bone
 Fracture
 Open Treatment21495
Muscle
 Incision and Suspension21685

Hyperbaric Oxygen Pressurization99183

Hypercycloidal X-Ray76101-76102

Hyperdactylies
See Supernumerary Digit

Hyperglycemic Glycogenolytic Factor
See Glucagon

Hyperhidrosis64650-64653

Hypertelorism of Orbit
See Orbital Hypertelorism

Hyperthermia Therapy
See Thermotherapy

Hyperthermia Treatment ..77600-77620

Hypnotherapy90880

Hypodermis
See Subcutaneous Tissue

Hypogastric Plexus
Destruction64681
Injection
 Anesthetic64517
 Neurolytic64681

Hypoglossal Nerve
Anastomosis
 to Facial Nerve64868

Hypoglossal-Facial Anastomosis
See Anastomosis, Nerve, Facial to Hypoglossal

Ventricular Assist Device33976
 Extracorporeal .0048T
 Intracorporeal .33979

Impression, Maxillofacial

Auricular Prosthesis21086
Definitive Obturator Prosthesis21080
Facial Prosthesis .21088
Interim Obturator .21079
Mandibular Resection Prosthesis21081
Nasal Prosthesis .21087
Oral Surgical Splint21085
Orbital Prosthesis21077
Palatal Augmentation Prosthesis21082
Palatal Lift Prosthesis21083
Speech Aid Prosthesis21084
Surgical Obturator21076

IMT

See Intima-Media Thickness Study

In Situ Hybridization

See Nucleic Acid Probe, Cytogenetic Studies,
Morphometric Analysis

In Vitro Fertilization58321-58322

In Vivo NMR Spectroscopy

See Magnetic Resonance Spectroscopy

Incision

See Incision and Drainage
Abdomen .49000
 Exploration .58960
Abscess
 Soft Tissue20000-20005
Accessory Nerve .63191
Anal
 Fistula46270, 46280
 Septum .46070
 Sphincter .46080
Ankle .27607
 Tendon27605-27606
Anus
 See Anus, Incision
Aortic Valve
 for Stenosis .33415
Artery
 Nose .30915-30920
Atrial Septum33735-33737
Bile Duct
 Sphincter43262, 47460
Bladder
 Catheterization51045
 with Destruction51020-51030
 with Radiotracer51020
Bladder Diverticulum52305
Brachial Artery
 Exposure .34834
Brain
 Amygdalohippocampectomy61566
 Subpial .61567
Breast
 Capsules .19370
Burn Scab16035-16036
Cataract
 Secondary
 Laser Surgery66821
 Stab Incision Technique66820

Chest
 Biopsy32095-32100
Colon
 Exploration .44025
 Stoma
 Creation44320-44322
 Revision44340-44346
Cornea
 for Astigmatism65772
Corpus Callosum61541
Cricothyroid Membrane31605
Dentate Ligament63180-63182
Duodenum .44010
Ear, Inner
 Labyrinth
 with Mastoidectomy69802
 with or without Cryosurgery69801
Elbow .24000
Esophagus43020, 43045
 Muscle .43030
Exploration
 Heart .33310-33315
 Kidney .50010
Eye
 Adhesions .65880
 Anterior Segment65860-65865
 Anterior Synechiae65870
 Corneovitreal65880
 Posterior65875
 Anterior Chamber65820
 Conjunctiva .0124T
 Trabeculae .65850
Eyelid
 Canthus .67715
 Sutures .67710
Femoral Artery
 Exposure34812-34813
Fibula .27607
Finger
 Decompression26035
 Tendon26060, 26455-26460
 Tendon Sheath26055
Foot .28005
 Capsule28260-28264
 Fasciotomy .28008
 for Infection28002-28003
 Tendon28230, 28234
Frontal Lobe .61490
Gallbladder .47490
Hand Decompression26035-26037
 Tendon26450, 26460
Heart
 Exploration33310-33315
Hemorrhoids
 External .46083
Hepatic Ducts
 See Hepaticostomy
Hip
 Denervation .27035
 Exploration .27033
 Fasciotomy .27025
 Joint Capsule
 for Flexor Release27036
 Tendon
 Abductor27006
 Adductor27000-27003
 Iliopsoas27005

Hymen
 See Hymen, Incision
Hymenotomy .56442
Hyoid
 Muscle .21685
Iliac Artery
 Exposure34820, 34833
Intercarpal Joint
 Dislocation .25670
Interphalangeal Joint
 Capsule .26525
Intestines (Except Rectum)
 See Enterotomy
Intestines, Small .44010
 Biopsy .44020
 Creation
 Pouch .44316
 Stoma44300-44310, 44314
 Decompression44021
 Exploration .44020
 Incision .44020
 Removal
 Foreign Body44020
 Revision
 Stoma .44312
Iris .66500-66505
Kidney .50010, 50045
Knee
 Capsule .27435
 Exploration .27310
 Fasciotomy .27305
 Removal of Foreign Body27310
Lacrimal Punctum68440
Lacrimal Sac
 See Dacryocystotomy
Larynx .31300-31320
Leg, Lower
 Fasciotomy27600-27602
Leg, Upper
 Fasciotomy .27305
 Tenotomy27306-27307, 27390-27392
Lip
 Frenum .40806
Liver
 See Hepatotomy
Lung
 Biopsy32095-32100
 Decortication
 Partial .32225
 Total .32220
Lymphatic Channels38308
Mastoid
 See Mastoidotomy
Medullary Tract .61470
Mesencephalic Tract61480
Metacarpophalangeal Joint
 Capsule .26520
Mitral Valve33420-33422
Muscle
 See Myotomy
Nerve .64573-64580,
 64585, 64595, 64702-64772
 Foot .28035
 Root .63185-63190
 Sacral .64581
 Vagus .43640-43641
Nose
 See Rhinotomy

Inhibitory Concentration, Minimum
See Minimum Inhibitory Concentration

Injection
See Allergen Immunotherapy; Infusion
Abdomen
 Air .49400
 Contrast Material49400
Angiography
 Pulmonary .75746
Ankle
 Radial .27648
Antibiotic
 See Antibiotic Administration
Antigen (Allergen)95115-95125
Aorta (Aortography)
 Radiologic .93544
Aponeurosis .20550
Bladder
 Radiologic51600-51610
Brain Canal .61070
Bronchography
 Segmental .31656
Bursa20600-20610
Cardiac Catheterization93539-93545
Carpal Tunnel
 Therapeutic20526
Chemotherapy96401-96542, 96545, 96549
Cistern
 Medication or Other61055
Contrast
 via Catheter36598, 49424
Corpora Cavernosa54235
Cyst
 Bone .20615
 Kidney .50390
 Pelvis .50390
 Thyroid .60001
Elbow
 Arthrography
 Radiologic24220
Epidural
 See Epidural, Injection
Esophageal Sphincter
 Endoscopy0133T
Esophageal Varices
 Endoscopy43243
Esophagus
 Sclerosing Agent43204
 Submucosal43201
Extremity
 Pseudoaneurysm36002
Eye
 Air .66020
 Medication66030
Eyelid
 Subconjunctional68200
Ganglion
 Anesthetic64505, 64510
Ganglion Cyst .20612
Gastric Secretion Stimulant91052
Gastric Varices
 Endoscopy43243
Heart Vessels
 Cardiac Catheterization93539-93545
 See Catheterization, Cardiac
 Radiologic93545

Hemorrhoids
 Sclerosing Solution46500
Hip
 Radiologic27093-27095
Insect Venom95130-95134
Intervertebral Disk
 Chemonucleolysis Agent62292
 Radiological62290-62291
Intra-Amniotic .59852
Intra-Arterial90773, 90779
 Thrombolytic37184-37186
Intradermal
 for Tattooing11920-11922
Intralesional
 Skin11900-11901
Intramuscular .90772
 Therapeutic90772, 99506
Intravenous .90779
 Diagnostic90779
 Thrombolytic37187-37188
 Unlisted .90779
 Vascular Flow Check, Graft15860
Intravenous Push90774-90775
Joint20600-20610
Kidney
 Drugs .50391
 Radiologic50394
Knee
 Radiologic27370
Lacrimal Gland
 Radiologic68850
Left Heart
 Radiologic93543
Lesion
 Skin11900-11901
Ligament .20550
Liver .47015
 Radiologic47500-47505
Mammary Ductogram/Galactogram19030
Muscle Endplate
 Extremity .64614
 Facial .64612
 Neck .64613
 Trunk .64614
Nerve
 Anesthetic01991-01992, 64400-64530
 Neurolytic Agent .64600-64640, 64680-64681
Orbit
 Retrobulbar
 Alcohol67505
 Medication67500
 Tenon's Capsule67515
Pancreatography48400
Paraveretebral Facet Joint/Nerve . .64470-64476
Penis
 for Erection54235
 Peyronie Disease54200
 with Surgical Exposure of Plaque . . .54205
 Radiology54230
 Vasoactive Drugs54231
Peritoneal Cavity Air
 See Pneumoperitoneum
Radiologic
 Breast .19030
Rectum
 Sclerosing Solution45520
Right Heart
 See Cardiac Catheterization, Injection
 Radiologic93542

Sacroiliac Joint
 for Arthrography27096
Salivary Duct .42660
Salivary Gland
 Radiologic42550
Sclerosing Agent
 Esophagus43204
 Intravenous36470-36471
Sentinel Node Identification38792
Shoulder
 Arthrography
 Radiologic23350
Shunt
 Peritoneal
 Venous49427
Sinus Tract .20500
 Diagnostic20501
Spider Veins
 Telangiectasia36468-36469
Spinal Artery .62294
Spinal Cord
 Anesthetic62310-62319
 Blood .62273
 Neurolytic Agent62280-62282
 Other62310-62311
 Radiological62284
Steroids
 Urethral Stricture52283
Subcutaneous .90772
 Silicone11950-11954
 Therapeutic90772, 90782
Temporomandibular Joint
 Arthrography21116
Tendon Origin, Insertion20551
Tendon Sheath20550
Therapeutic
 Extremity Pseudoaneurysm36002
 Lung .32960
 Thyroid .60001
 Turbinate .30200
Thoracic Cavity
 See Pleurodesis, Chemical
Trachea .31612
 Puncture .31612
Transtracheal
 Bronchography31715
Trigger Point(s)
 One or Two Muscles20552
 Three or More Muscles20553
Turbinate .30200
Ureter
 Drugs .50391
 Radiologic50684
Venography .36005
Ventricle
 Dye .61120
 Medication or Other61026
Vitreous .67028
 Fluid Substitute67025
Vocal Cords
 Therapeutic31513, 31570-31571
Wrist
 Carpal Tunnel
 Therapeutic20526
 Radiologic25246

Inner Ear
See Ear, Inner

Inspiratory Positive Pressure Breathing

See Intermittent Positive Pressure Breathing (IPPB)

Instillation

Instillation, Bladder

See Bladder, Instillation

Instrumentation

See Application; Bone, Fixation; Spinal Instrumentation

Insufflation, Eustachian Tube

See Eustachian Tube, Inflation

Insulin C-Peptide Measurement

See C-Peptide

Insulin Like Growth Factors

See Somatomedin

Insurance

Integumentary System

Integumentum Commune

See Integumentary System

Intensive Care

Ulcer44605
Wound44605
Transplantation
 Allograft Preparation44715-44721
 Donor Enterectomy44132-44133
 Removal of Allograft44137

Intestines, Large
See Anus; Cecum; Colon; Rectum

Intestines, Small
Anastomosis43845, 44130
Biopsy44020
 Endoscopy44361
Catheterization
 Jejunum44015
Decompression44021
Destruction
 Lesion44369
 Tumor44369
Endoscopy44364
 Biopsy44361, 44377
 Control of Bleeding44366, 44378
 via Stoma44382
 Destruction
 Lesion44369
 Tumor44369
 Diagnostic44376
 Exploration44360
 Hemorrhage44366
 Insertion
 Stent44370, 44379
 Tube44379
 Pelvic Pouch44385-44386
 Removal
 Foreign Body44363
 Lesion44365
 Polyp44364-44365
 Tumor44364-44365
 Tube Placement44372
 Tube Revision44373
 via Stoma44380
Enterostomy44300
Excision44120-44128
 Partial with Anastomosis44140
Exclusion44700
Exploration44020
Gastrostomy Tube44373
Hemorrhage44378
Hemorrhage Control44366
Ileostomy44310-44314, 45136
 Continent44316
Incision44020
 Creation
 Pouch44316
 Stoma44300-44310, 44314
 Decompression44021
 Exploration44020
 Revision
 Stoma44312
 Stoma Closure44620-44626
Insertion
 Catheter44015
 Jejunostomy Tube44372
Jejunostomy44310
Lysis
 Adhesions44005
Removal
 Foreign Body44020, 44363

Repair
 Diverticula44602-44603
 Enterocele
 Abdominal Approach57270
 Vaginal Approach57268
 Fistula44640-44661
 Hernia44050
 Malrotation44055
 Obstruction44050
 Ulcer44602-44603
 Volvulus44050
 Wound44602-44603
Revision
 Jejunostomy Tube44373
Specimen Collection89100-89105
Suture
 Diverticula44602-44603
 Fistula44640-44661
 Plication44680
 Ulcer44602-44603
 Wound44602-44603
X-Ray74245, 74249-74251
 Guide Intubation74355

Intestinovesical Fistula
See Fistula, Enterovesical

Intima-Media Thickness (IMT) Study
Artery
 Carotid, Common0126T

Intimectomy
See Endarterectomy

Intra Arterial Injections
See Injection, Intraarterial

Intra-Abdominal Voiding Pressure Studies51797

Intra-Osseous Infusion
See Infusion, Intraosseous

Intracapsular Extraction of Lens
See Extraction, Lens, Intracapsular

Intracardiac Echocardiography93662

Intracranial
Biopsy61140
Extracranial61623
Microdissection69990

Intracranial Arterial Perfusion
Thrombolysis61624

Intracranial Neoplasm, Acoustic Neuroma
See Brain, Tumor, Excision

Intracranial Neoplasm, Craniopharyngioma
See Craniopharyngioma

Intracranial Neoplasm, Meningioma
See Meningioma

Intrafallopian Transfer, Gamete
See GIFT

Intraluminal Angioplasty
See Angioplasty

Intramuscular Injection
See Injection, Intramuscular

Intraocular Lens
Exchange66986
Insertion66983
 Manual or Mechanical
 Technique66982, 66984
 Not Associated with Concurrent Cataract
 Removal66985

Intratracheal Intubation
See Insertion, Endotracheal Tube

Intrauterine Contraceptive Device
See Intrauterine Device (IUD)

Intrauterine Device (IUD)
Insertion58300
Removal58301

Intrauterine Synechiae
See Adhesions, Intrauterine

Intravascular Sensor
Pressure
 Complete Study0154T

Intravascular Stent
See Transcatheter, Placement, Intravascular Stents
X-Ray75960

Intravascular Ultrasound
Intraoperative37250-37251

Intravenous Infusion
Diagnosis90765-90768
Hydration90760-90761

Intravenous Injection
See Injection, Intravenous

Intravenous Pyelogram
See Urography, Intravenous

Intravenous Therapy
See Injection, Chemotherapy
Pain Management90773-90775

Intravesical Instillation
See Bladder, Instillation

Intravitreal Injection
Pharmacologic Agent67028

Intrinsic Factor83528
Antibody86340

Introduction
Breast
 Metallic Localization Clip Placement ..19295
 Preoperative Placement, Needle 19290-19291
Contraceptive Capsules
 Implantable11975-11977
Drug Delivery Implant11981, 11983
Gastrointestinal Tube44500
 with Fluoroscopic Guidance74340
Tissue Expanders
 Skin11960-11971

Jaboulay Operation Gastroduodenostomy
See Gastroduodenostomy

Jannetta Procedure
See Decompression, Cranial Nerve; Section

Japanese, River Fever
See Scrub Typhus

Jatene Type33770-33781

Jaw Joint
See Facial Bones; Mandible; Maxilla

Jaws
Muscle Reduction21295-21296
X-Ray
 for Orthodontics70355

Jejunostomy
Catheterization44015
Insertion
 Catheter44015
Laparoscopic44186-44187
Non-Tube44187, 44310
with Pancreatic Drain48001

Jejunum
Creation
 Stoma
Laparoscopic44186
Transfer
 with Microvascular Anastomosis
 Free43496

Johannsen Procedure53400

Johanson Operation
See Reconstruction, Urethra

Joint
See Specific Joint
Acromioclavicular
 See Acromioclavicular Joint
Arthrocentesis.................20600-20610
Aspiration20600-20610
Dislocation
 See Dislocation
Drainage20600-20610
Finger
 See Intercarpal Joint
Fixation (Surgical)
 See Arthrodesis
Foot
 See Foot, Joint
Hip
 See Hip Joint
Injection20600-20610
Intertarsal
 See Intertarsal Joint
Knee
 See Knee Joint
Ligament
 See Ligament
Metacarpophalangeal
 See Metacarpophalangeal Joint
Metatarsophalangeal
 See Metatarsophalangeal Joint
Nuclear Medicine
 Imaging78300, 78315

Radiology
 Stress Views77071
Sacroiliac
 See Sacroiliac Joint
Shoulder
 See Glenohumeral Joint
Sternoclavicular
 See Sternoclavicular Joint
Survey77077
Temporomandibular
 See Temporomandibular Joint (TMJ)
 Dislocation Temporomandibular
 See Dislocation, Temporomandibular Joint
 Implant
 See Prosthesis, Temporomandibular Joint
Wrist
 See Radiocarpal Joint

Joint Syndrome, Temporomandibular
See Temporomandibular Joint (TMJ)

Jones and Cantarow Test
See Blood Urea Nitrogen; Urea Nitrogen, Clearance

Jones Procedure28760

Joplin Procedure28294

Jugal Bone
See Cheekbone

Jugular Vein
See Vein, Jugular

K

K-Wire Fixation
Tongue41500

Kader Operation
See Incision, Stomach, Creation, Stoma; Incision and Drainage

Kala Azar Smear87207

Kallidin I /Kallidin 9
See Bradykinin

Kallikrein HK3
See Antigen, Prostate Specific

Kallikreinogen
See Fletcher Factor

Kasai Procedure47701

Kedani Fever
See Scrub Typhus

Keel
Insertion/Removal
 Laryngoplasty31580

Keen Operation
See Laminectomy

Kelikian Procedure28280

Keller Procedure28292

Kelly Urethral Plication57220

Keratectomy
Partial
 for Lesion65400

Keratomileusis65760

Keratophakia65765

Keratoplasty
Lamellar65710
Penetrating65730
 in Aphakia65750
 in Pseudophakia65755

Keratoprosthesis65770

Keratotomy
Radial65771

Ketogenic Steroids83582

Ketone Body
Acetone82009-82010

Ketosteroids83586-83593

Kidner Procedure28238

Kidney
Abscess
 Incision and Drainage50020
 Open50020
 Percutaneous50021
Anesthesia00862
Biopsy50200-50205
 Endoscopic50555-50557, 52354
Catheterization
 Endoscopic50572
Cyst
 Ablation50541
 Aspiration50390
 Excision50280-50290
 Injection50390
 X-Ray74470
Destruction
 Calculus50590
 Endoscopic50557, 50576, 52354
Dilation50395
Endoscopy
 Biopsy50555, 50574-50576, 52354
 Catheterization50553, 50572
 Destruction50557, 50576, 52354
 Dilation
 Intra-Renal Stricture52343, 52346
 Ureter50553
 Excision
 Tumor52355
 Exploration52351
 Lithotripsy52353
 Removal
 Calculus50561, 50580, 52352
 Foreign Body50561, 50580
 via Incision50562-50580
 via Stoma50551-50561
Excision
 Donor50300-50320, 50547

L

Kyphoplasty22523-22525

L Ascorbic Acid
See Ascorbic Acid

L Aspartate 2 Oxoglutarate Aminotransferase
See Transaminase, Glutamic Oxaloacetic

L Glutamine
See Glutamine

L-Alanine
See Aminolevulinic Acid (ALA)

L-Leucylnaphthylamidase
See Leucine Aminopeptidase

L/S Ratio
Amniotic Fluid .83661

Labial Adhesions
Lysis .56441

Labyrinth
See Ear, Inner

Labyrinthectomy69905
with Mastoidectomy69910
with Skull Base Surgery61596

Labyrinthotomy
with Mastoidectomy69802
with/without Cryosurgery69801

Laceration Repair
See Specific Site

Lacrimal Duct
Canaliculi
 Repair .68700
Exploration .68810
 Canaliculi .68840
 Stent .68815
 with Anesthesia68811
Insertion
 Stent .68815
Removal
 Dacryolith .68530
 Foreign Body68530
X-Ray with Contrast70170

Lacrimal Gland
Biopsy .68510
Close Fistula .68770
Excision
 Partial .68505
 Total .68500
Fistulization .68720
Incision and Drainage68400
Injection
 X-Ray .68850
Nuclear Medicine
 Tear Flow .78660

Removal
 Dacryolith .68530
 Foreign Body68530
Repair
 Fistula .68770
Tumor
 Excision
 Frontal Approach68540
 with Osteotomy68550
X-Ray .70170

Lacrimal Punctum
Closure
 by Plug .68761
 by Thermocauterization, Ligation or Laser
 Surgery .68760
Dilation .68801
Incision .68440
Repair .68705

Lacrimal Sac
Biopsy .68525
Excision .68520
Incision and Drainage68420

Lacrimal System
Unlisted Services and Procedures68899

Lactase Deficiency Breath Test .91065

Lactate .83605

Lactate Dehydrogenase . . .83615-83625

Lactic Acid .83605

Lactic Cytochrome Reductase
See Lactate Dehydrogenase

Lactic Dehydrogenase
See Lactate Dehydrogenase

Lactiferous Duct
See Mammary Duct; Mammary Ductogram
Excision .19112
Exploration .19110

Lactoferrin
Fecal .83630-83631

Lactogen, Human Placental83632

Lactogenic Hormone
See Prolactin

Lactose
Urine .83633-83634

Ladd Procedure44055

Lagophthalmos
Repair .67912

Laki Lorand Factor
See Fibrin Stabilizing Factor

Lamblia Intestinalis
See Giardia Lamblia

Lambrinudi Operation
See Arthrodesis, Foot Joint

Lamellar Keratoplasties
See Keratoplasty, Lamellar

Laminaria
Insertion .59200

Laminectomy . .62351, 63001, 63005-63011,
63015-63044, 63180-63200,
63265-63290, 63300-63655
Lumbar22630, 63012
Surgical63170-63172
with Facetectomy63045-63048

Laminoplasty
Cervical63050-63051

Langerhans Islands
See Islet Cell

Language Evaluation92506

Language Therapy92507-92508

LAP
See Leucine Aminopeptidase

Laparoscopic Appendectomy
See Appendectomy, Laparoscopic

Laparoscopic Biopsy of Ovary
See Biopsy, Ovary, Laparoscopic

Laparoscopy
Abdominal49320-49326, 49329
Adrenal Gland
 Biopsy .60650
 Excision .60650
Adrenalectomy .50545
Appendectomy .44970
Aspiration .49322
Biopsy .47561, 49321
 Lymph Nodes38570
Bladder
 Repair
 Sling Operation51992
 Urethral Suspension51990
 Unlisted .51999
Cecostomy .44188
 Laparoscopic44188
Cholangiography47560-47561
Cholecystectomy47562-47564
Cholecystenterostomy47570
Colectomy
 Laparoscopic44213
 Partial44204-44208, 44213
 Total44210-44212
Colostomy .44188
Destruction
 Lesion .58662
Diagnostic .49320
Drainage
 Extraperitoneal Lymphocele49323
Ectopic Pregnancy59150
 with Salpingectomy and/or
 Oophorectomy59151
Electrode Implantation
 Gastric43647, 0155T
Electrode Removal
 Gastric43648, 0156T
Electrode Replacement
 Gastric43647, 0155T

Stomach
 Excision43611
Testis
 Excision54512
Toe
 Excision28092
Tongue
 Excision41110-41114
Uvula
 Destruction42145
 Excision42104-42107
Vagina
 Destruction57061-57065
Vulva
 Destruction
 Extensive56515
 Simple56501
Wrist Tendon
 Excision25110

Leu 2 Antigens
See CD8

Leucine Aminopeptidase83670

Leukemia Lymphoma Virus I Antibodies, Human T Cell
See Antibody, HTLV-I

Leukemia Lymphoma Virus I, Adult T Cell
See HTLV I

Leukemia Lymphoma Virus II Antibodies, Human T Cell
See Antibody, HTLV-II

Leukemia Virus II, Hairy Cell Associated, Human T Cell
See HTLV II

Leukoagglutinins86021

Leukocyte
See White Blood Cell
Alkaline Phosphatase85540
Antibody86021
Count85032, 85048, 89055
Histamine Release Test86343
Phagocytosis86344
Transfusion86950

Levarterenol
See Noradrenalin

Levator Muscle Repair
See Blepharoptosis, Repair

LeVeen Shunt
Insertion49425
Patency Test78291
Revision49426

Levulose
See Fructose

LGV
See Lymphogranuloma Venereum

LH
See Luteinizing Hormone (LH)

LHR
See Leukocyte Histamine Release Test

Lid Suture
See Blepharoptosis, Repair

Lidocaine
Assay80176

Lift, Face
See Face Lift

Ligament
See Specific Site
Collateral
 Repair
 Knee
 with Cruciate Ligament27409
Dentate
 Section63180-63182
Injection20550
Release
 Coracoacromial23415
 Transverse Carpal29848
Repair
 Elbow24343-24346
 Knee Joint27405-27409

Ligation
Artery
 Abdomen37617
 Carotid37600-37606
 Chest37616
 Coronary33502
 Ethmoidal30915
 Extremity37618
 Fistula37607
 Maxillary30920
 Neck37615
 Temporal37609
Esophageal Varices43204, 43400
Fallopian Tube
 Oviduct58600-58611, 58670
Gastroesophageal43405
Hemorrhoids46945-46946
Oviducts59100
Salivary Duct42665
Shunt
 Aorta
 Pulmonary33924
 Peritoneal
 Venous49428
Thoracic Duct38380
 Abdominal Approach38382
 Thoracic Approach38381
Vas Deferens55450
Vein
 Clusters37785
 Esophagus43205, 43244, 43400
 Femoral37650
 Gastric43244
 Iliac37660
 Jugular, Internal37565
 Perforate37760
 Saphenous37700-37735, 37780
 Vena Cava37620

Ligature Strangulation
Skin Tags11200-11201

Light Coagulation
See Photocoagulation

Light Scattering Measurement
See Nephelometry

Light Therapy, UV
See Actinotherapy

Limb
See Extremity

Limited Lymphadenectomy for Staging
See Lymphadenectomy, Limited, for Staging

Limited Neck Dissection
with Thyroidectomy60252

Limited Resection Mastectomies
See Breast, Excision, Lesion

Lindholm Operation
See Tenoplasty

Lingual Bone
See Hyoid Bone

Lingual Frenectomy
See Excision, Tongue, Frenum

Lingual Nerve
Avulsion64740
Incision64740
Transection64740

Lingual Tonsil
See Tonsils, Lingual

Linton Procedure37760

Lip
Biopsy40490
Excision40500-40530
 Frenum40819
Incision
 Frenum40806
Reconstruction40525-40527
Repair40650-40654
 Cleft Lip40700-40761
 Fistula42260
Unlisted Services and Procedures40799

Lip, Cleft
See Cleft Lip

Lipase83690

Lipectomy
Excision15830-15839
Suction Assisted15876-15879

Lipectomy, Aspiration
See Liposuction

Lipids
Feces82705-82710

Lipo-Lutin
See Progesterone

Lipolysis, Aspiration
See Liposuction

Lipophosphodiesterase I
See Tissue Typing

Lipoprotein
(a) ...83695
Blood0026T, 83695, 83700-83721
LDL83700-83704, 83721
Phospholipase A283698

Lipoprotein, Alpha
See Lipoprotein

Lipoprotein, Pre-Beta
See Lipoprotein, Blood

Liposuction15876-15879

Lisfranc Operation
See Amputation, Foot; Radical Resection;
Replantation

Listeria Monocytogenes
Antibody86723

Lithium
Assay80178

Litholapaxy52317-52318

Lithotripsy
See Extracorporeal Shock Wave Therapy
Bile Duct Calculi (Stone)
 Endoscopy43265
Bladder52353
Kidney50590, 52353
Pancreatic Duct Calculi (Stone)
 Endoscopy43265
Ureter52353
Urethra52353
with Cystourethroscopy52353

Lithotrity
See Litholapaxy

Liver
See Hepatic Duct
Ablation
 Tumor47380-47382
 Laparoscopic47370-47371
Abscess
 Aspiration47015
 Incision and Drainage
 Open47010
 Percutaneous47011
 Injection47015
Aspiration47015
Biopsy47100
Cyst
 Aspiration47015
 Incision and Drainage
 Open47010
 Percutaneous47011
Excision
 Extensive47122
 Partial ...47120, 47125-47130, 47140-47142
 Total47133
Injection47015
 Radiologic47505
 X-Ray47500
Lobectomy47125-47130
 Partial47120

Needle Biopsy47000-47001
Nuclear Medicine
 Function Study78220
 Imaging78201-78216
 Vascular Flow78206
Repair
 Abscess47300
 Cyst47300
 Wound47350-47362
Suture
 Wound47350-47362
Transplantation47135-47136
 Allograft Preparation47143-47147
Trisegmentectomy47122
Unlisted Services and Procedures ..47379, 47399

Living Activities, Daily
See Activities of Daily Living

Lobectomy
Brain61323, 61537-61540
Contralateral Subtotal
 Thyroid Gland60212, 60225
Liver47120-47130
Lung32480-32482
 Sleeve32486
Parotid Gland42410-42415
Segmental32663
Sleeve32486
Temporal Lobe61537-61538
Thyroid Gland Partial60210-60212
 Total60220-60225
Total32663

Lobotomy
Frontal61490

Local Excision Mastectomies
See Breast, Excision, Lesion

Local Excision of Lesion or Tissue of Femur
See Excision, Lesion, Femur

Localization of Nodule
Radiographic
 Breast77032

Log Hydrogen Ion Concentration
See pH

Lombard Test
See Audiologic Function Test

Long Acting Thyroid Stimulator
See Thyrotropin Releasing Hormone (TRH)

Long-Term Care Facility Visits
See Nursing Facility Services

Longmire Operation
See Anastomosis, Hepatic Duct to Intestines

Loopogram
See Urography, Antegrade

Loose Body
Removal
 Ankle27620
 Carpometacarpal Joint26070
 Elbow24101

 Interphalangeal Joint28020
 Toe28024
 Knee Joint27331
 Metatarsophalangeal Joint28022
 Tarsometatarsal Joint28022
 Toe28022
 Wrist25101

Lord Procedure
See Anal Sphincter, Dilation

Louis Bar Syndrome
See Ataxia Telangiectasia

Low Birth Weight Intensive Care Services99298-99300

Low Density Lipoprotein
See Lipoprotein, LDL

Low Vision Aids
See Spectacle Services
Fitting92354-92355

Lower Extremities
See Extremity, Lower

Lower GI Series
See Barium Enema

LRH
See Luteinizing Releasing Factor

LSD
See Lysergic Acid Diethylamide

LTH
See Prolactin

Lumbar
See Spine
Aspiration, Disk
 Percutaneous62287

Lumbar Plexus
Decompression64714
Injection
 Anesthetic64449
Neuroplasty64714
Release64714
Repair/Suture64862

Lumbar Puncture
See Spinal Tap

Lumbar Spine Fracture
See Fracture, Vertebra, Lumbar

Lumbar Sympathectomy
See Sympathectomy, Lumbar

Lumbar Vertebra
See Vertebra, Lumbar

Lumen Dilation74360

Lumpectomy19301-19302

Lunate
Arthroplasty
 with Implant25444
Dislocation
 Closed Treatment25690
 Open Treatment25695

Lymphadenopathy Associated Antibodies/Virus
See Antibody, HIV

Lymphangiogram
See Lymphangiography

Lymphangiography
Abdomen75805-75807
Arm75801-75803
Injection38790
Leg75801-75803
Pelvis75805-75807

Lymphangioma, Cystic
See Hygroma; Lymph Nodes, Hygroma

Lymphangiotomy38308

Lymphatic Channels
Incision38308

Lymphatic Cyst
See Lymphocele

Lymphatic System
Unlisted Procedure38999

Lymphatics
See Specific Procedure

Lymphoblast Transformation
See Blastogenesis

Lymphocele
Drainage
 Laparoscopic49323
 Open49062

Lymphocoele
See Lymphocele

Lymphocyte
Culture86821-86822
Toxicity Assay86805-86806
Transformation86353

Lymphocyte, Thymus-Dependent
See T-Cells

Lymphocytes, CD4
See CD4

Lymphocytes, CD8
See CD8

Lymphocytic Choriomeningitis
Antibody86727

Lymphocytotoxicity86805-86806

Lymphogranuloma Venereum
Antibody86729

Lymphoma Virus, Burkitt
See Epstein-Barr Virus

Lynch Procedure31075

Lysergic Acid Diethylamide80102-80103, 80299

Lysergide
See Lysergic Acid Diethylamide

Lysis
Adhesions
 Epidural0027T, 62263-62264
 Fallopian Tube58740
 Foreskin54450
 Intestinal44005
 Labial56441
 Lung32124
 Nose30560
 Ovary58740
 Oviduct58740
 Penile
 Post-Circumcision54162
 Ureter50715-50725
 Urethra53500
 Uterus58559
Euglobulin85360
Labial
 Adhesions56441
Nose
 Intranasal Synechia30560

Lysozyme85549

M

MacEwen Operation
See Hernia, Repair, Inguinal

Machado Test
See Complement, Fixation Test

MacLean-De Wesselow Test
See Blood Urea Nitrogen; Urea Nitrogen, Clearance

Macrodactylia
Repair26590

Madlener Operation
See Tubal Ligation

Magnesium83735

Magnet Operation
See Ciliary Body; Cornea; Eye, Removal, Foreign Body; Iris; Lens; Retina; Sclera; Vitreous

Magnetic Resonance
Unlisted Services and Procedures76498

Magnetic Resonance Angiography (MRA)
Abdomen74185
Arm73225
Chest71555
Head70544-70546
Leg73725
Neck70547-70549
Pelvis72198
Spine72159

Magnetic Resonance Imaging (MRI)
3D Rendering76376-76377
Abdomen74181-74183

Ankle73721-73723
Arm73218-73220, 73223
Bone Marrow Study77084
Brain70551-70555
 Intraoperative70557-70559
Breast77058-77059
 with Computer-aided Detection0159T
Chest71550-71552
Elbow73221
Face70540-70543
Finger Joint73221
Foot73718-73719
Foot Joints73721-73723
Guidance
 Needle Placement77021
 Parenchymal Tissue Ablation77022
Hand73218-73220, 73223
Heart75552
 Complete Study75554
 Flow Mapping75556
 Limited Study75555
 Morphology75553
Joint
 Lower Extremity73721-73723
 Upper Extremity73221-73223
Knee73721-73723
Leg73718-73720
Neck70540-70543
Orbit70540-70543
Pelvis72195-72197
Spectroscopy76390
Spine
 Cervical72141-72142, 72156-72158
 Lumbar72148-72158
 Thoracic72146-72147, 72156-72158
Temporomandibular Joint (TMJ)70336
Toe73721-73723
Unlisted76498
Wrist73221

Magnetic Resonance Spectroscopy76390

Magnetic Stimulation
Transcranial0160T, 0161T

Magnetoencephalography (MEG)95965-95967

Magnuson Procedure23450

MAGPI Operation54322

MAGPI Procedure
See Hypospadias, Repair

Major Vestibular Gland
See Bartholin's Gland

Malar Area
Augmentation21270
Bone Graft21210
Fracture
 Open Treatment21360-21366
 with Bone Graft21366
 with Manipulation21355
Reconstruction21270

Malar Bone
See Cheekbone

Malaria Antibody86750

Malaria Smear87207

Malate Dehydrogenase83775

Maldescent, Testis
See Testis, Undescended

Male Circumcision
See Circumcision

Malformation, Arteriovenous
See Arteriovenous Malformation

Malic Dehydrogenase
See Malate Dehydrogenase

Malignant Hyperthermia Susceptibility
Caffeine Halothane Contracture
Test (CHCT)89049

Malleolus
See Ankle; Fibula; Leg, Lower; Tibia; Tibiofibular
Joint

Mallet Finger Repair26432

Maltose
Tolerance Test82951-82952

Malunion Repair
Femur
 with Graft27472
 without Graft27470
Metatarsal28322
Tarsal Joint28320

Mammalian Oviduct
See Fallopian Tube

Mammaplasty
See Breast, Reconstruction; Mammoplasty

Mammary Abscess
See Abscess, Breast

Mammary Arteries
See Artery, Mammary

Mammary Duct
Catheter Lavage for Cytology0046T, 0047T
X-Ray with Contrast77053-77054

Mammary Ductogram
Injection19030

Mammary Stimulating Hormone
See Prolactin

Mammillaplasty
See Nipples, Reconstruction

Mammogram
Breast
 Localization Nodule77032

Mammography77055-77057
Magnetic Resonance Imaging (MRI)
 with Computer-Aided Detection0159T
Screening77057
with Computer-Aided Detection77051-77052

Mammoplasty
Augmentation19324-19325
Reduction19318

Mammotomy
See Incision, Breast; Incision and Drainage,
Breast; Mastotomy

Mammotropic Hormone, Pituitary
See Prolactin

Mammotropic Hormone, Placental
See Lactogen, Human Placental

Mammotropin
See Prolactin

Mandated Services
On Call Services99027

Mandible
See Facial Bones; Maxilla; Temporomandibular
Joint (TMJ)
Abscess
 Excision21025
Bone Graft21215
Cyst
 Excision21040, 21046-21047
Fracture
 Closed Treatment
 with Interdental Fixation21453
 with Manipulation21451
 without Manipulation21450
 Open Treatment21454-21470
 External Fixation21454
 with Interdental Fixation21462
 without Interdental Fixation21461
 Percutaneous Treatment21452
Osteotomy21198-21199
Reconstruction
 with Implant21244-21246, 21248-21249
Removal
 Foreign Body41806
Torus Mandibularis
 Excision21031
Tumor
 Excision21040-21047
X-Ray70100-70110

Mandibular Body
Augmentation
 with Bone Graft21127
 with Prosthesis21125

Mandibular Condyle
Fracture
 Open Treatment21465
Reconstruction21247

Mandibular Condylectomy
See Condylectomy

Mandibular Fracture
See Fracture, Mandible

Mandibular Rami
Reconstruction
 with Bone Graft21194
 with Internal Rigid Fixation21196
 without Bone Graft21193
 without Internal Rigid Fixation21195

Mandibular Resection Prosthesis21081

Mandibular Staple Bone Plate
Reconstruction
 Mandible21244

Manganese83785

Manipulation
Chest Wall94667-94668
Chiropractic98940-98943
Dislocation and/or Fracture25535
 Acetabulum27222
 Acromioclavicular23545
 Ankle27810, 27818, 27860
 Carpometacarpal26670-26676
 Clavicular23505
 Elbow24300, 24640
 Femoral27232, 27502, 27510, 27517
 Pertrochanteric27240
 Fibula27781, 27788
 Finger26725-26727, 26742, 26755
 Greater Tuberosity
 Humeral23625
 Hand26670-26676
 Heel28405-28406
 Hip27257
 Hip Socket27222
 Humeral23605, 24505, 24535, 24577
 Epicondyle24565
 Intercarpal25660
 Interphalangeal Joint ...26340, 26770-26776
 Lunate25690
 Malar Area21355
 Mandibular21451
 Metacarpal26605-26607
 Metacarpophalangeal ..26700-26706, 26742
 Metacarpophalangeal Joint26340
 Metatarsal28475-28476
 Nasal Bone21315-21320
 Orbit21401
 Phalangeal Shaft26727
 Distal, Finger or Thumb26755
 Phalanges, Finger/Thumb26725
 Phalanges
 Finger26742, 26755, 26770-26776
 Finger/Thumb26727
 Great Toe28495-28496
 Toes28515
 Radial24655, 25565
 Radial Shaft25505
 Radiocarpal25660
 Radioulnar25675
 Scapular23575
 Shoulder23650-23655
 with Greater Tuberosity23665
 Shoulder Dislocation
 Sternoclavicular23525
 with Neck Fracture23675
 Talus28435-28436
 Tarsal28455-28456
 Thumb26641-26650
 Tibial27532, 27752
 Trans-Scaphoperilunar25680
 Ulnar24675, 25535, 25565
 Vertebral22315
 Wrist ...25259, 25624, 25635, 25660, 25675,
 25680, 25690

McIndoe Procedure
See Vagina, Construction

McKissock Surgery
See Breast, Reduction

McVay Operation
See Hernia, Repair, Inguinal

Measles Uncomplicated
See Rubeola

Measles Vaccine
See Vaccines

Measles, German
See Rubella

Meat Fibers
Feces89160

Meatoplasty69310

Meatotomy53020-53025
Cystourethroscopy52281
Infant53025
Prostate
 Laser Coagulation52647
 Laser Vaporization52648
Transurethral Electrosurgical Resection
 Prostate52601
Ureter52290
Ureteral
 Cystourethroscopy52290-52305

Meckel's Diverticulum
Excision44800
Unlisted Services and Procedures44899

Median Nerve
Decompression64721
Neuroplasty64721
Release64721
Repair/Suture
 Motor64835
Transposition64721

Median Nerve Compression
See Carpal Tunnel Syndrome

Mediastinal Cyst
See Cyst, Mediastinal; Mediastinum, Cyst

Mediastinoscopy39400

Mediastinotomy
Cervical Approach39000
Transthoracic Approach39010

Mediastinum
See Chest; Thorax
Cyst
 Excision32662, 39200
Endoscopy
 Biopsy39400
 Exploration39400
Exploration39000-39010
Incision and Drainage39000-39010
Needle Biopsy32405
Removal
 Foreign Body39000-39010

Tumor
 Excision32662, 39220
Unlisted Procedures39499

**Medical Disability Evaluation
Services**99455-99456

Medical Genetics96040
Genetic Counseling96040

Medical Testimony99075

Medicine, Preventive
See Preventive Medicine

Medicine, Pulmonary
See Pulmonology

Medulla
Tractotomy61470

Medullary Tract
Incision61470
Section61470

Meibomian Cyst
See Chalazion

**Membrane Oxygenation,
Extracorporeal**
See Extracorporeal Membrane Oxygenation

Membrane, Mucous
See Mucosa

Membrane, Tympanic
See Ear, Drum

Meninges
Tumor
 Excision61512, 61519

Meningioma
Excision61512, 61519
Tumor
 Excision61512, 61519

Meningitis, Lymphocytic Benign
See Lymphocytic Choriomeningitis

Meningocele Repair63700-63702

Meningococcal
See Vaccines

Meningococcal Vaccine
See Vaccines

Meningococcus
See Neisseria Meningitidis

Meningomyelocele
See Myelomeningocele

Meniscectomy
Knee Joint27332-27333
Temporomandibular Joint21060

Meniscus
Knee
 Excision27332-27333
 Repair27403
 Transplantation29868

Mental Nerve
Avulsion64736
Incision64736
Transection64736

Meprobamate83805

Mercury83015, 83825

Merskey Test
See Fibrin Degradation Products

Mesencephalic Tract
Incision61480
Section61480

Mesencephalon
Tractotomy61480

Mesenteric Arteries
See Artery, Mesenteric

Mesentery
Lesion
 Excision44820
Repair44850
Suture44850
Unlisted Services and Procedures44899

Mesh
Implantation
 Hernia49568
Insertion
 Pelvic Floor57267
Removal
 Abdominal Infected11008

Metabisulfite Test
See Red Blood Cell (RBC), Sickling

Metabolite82520

Metacarpal
Amputation26910
Craterization26230
Cyst
 Excision26200-26205
Diaphysectomy26230
Excision26230
 Radical
 for Tumor26250-26255
Fracture
 Closed Treatment26605
 with Fixation26607
 Open Treatment26615
 Percutaneous Fixation26608
 with Manipulation26605-26607
 without Manipulation26600
Ostectomy
 Radical
 for Tumor26250-26255
Repair
 Lengthening26568
 Nonunion26546
 Osteotomy26565
Saucerization26230
Tumor
 Excision26200-26205

Metacarpophalangeal Joint
Arthrodesis26850-26852
Arthroplasty26530-26531

Arthroscopy
 Diagnostic29900
 Surgical29901-29902
Arthrotomy26075
Biopsy
 Synovium26105
Capsule
 Excision26520
 Incision26520
Capsulodesis26516-26518
Dislocation
 Closed Treatment26700
 Open Treatment26715
 Percutaneous Fixation26705-26706
 with Manipulation26340
Exploration26075
Fracture
 Closed Treatment26740
 Open Treatment26746
 with Manipulation26742
Fusion26516-26518, 26850-26852
Removal of Foreign Body26075
Repair
 Collateral Ligament26540-26542
Synovectomy26135

Metadrenaline
See Metanephrines

Metals, Heavy
See Heavy Metal

Metamfetamine
See Methamphetamine

Metanephrines83835

Metatarsal
See Foot
Amputation28810
Condyle
 Excision28288
Craterization28122
Cyst
 Excision28104-28107
Diaphysectomy28122
Excision28110-28114, 28122, 28140
Fracture
 Closed Treatment
 with Manipulation28475-28476
 without Manipulation28470
 Open Treatment28485
 Percutaneous Fixation28476
Free Osteocutaneous Flap with Microvascular
Anastomosis20972
Repair28322
 Lengthening28306-28307
 Osteotomy28306-28309
Saucerization28122
Tumor
 Excision28104-28107, 28173

Metatarsectomy28140

Metatarsophalangeal Joint
Arthrotomy28022, 28052
Cheilectomy28289
Dislocation28630-28635, 28645
 Percutaneous Fixation28636
Exploration28022

Great Toe
 Arthrodesis28750
 Fusion28750
Removal
 of Foreign Body28022
 of Loose Body28022
Repair
 Hallux Rigidus28289
Synovial
 Biopsy28052
 Excision28072
Toe28270

Methadone83840

Methaemoglobin
See Methemoglobin

Methamphetamine
Blood or Urine82145

Methanol84600

Methbipyranone
See Metyrapone

Methemalbumin83857

Methemoglobin83045-83050

Methenamine Silver Stain88312

Methopyrapone
See Metyrapone

Methoxyhydroxymandelic Acid
See Vanillylmandelic Acid

Methsuximide83858

Methyl Alcohol
See Methanol

Methylamphetamine
See Methamphetamine

Methylene Bichloride
See Dichloromethane

Methylfluorprednisolone
See Dexamethasone

Methylmorphine
See Codeine

Metroplasty
See Hysteroplasty

Metyrapone80436

MIC
See Minimum Inhibitory Concentration

Micro-Ophthalmia
Orbit Reconstruction21256

Microalbumin
Urine82043-82044

Microbiology87001-87999

Microdissection88380

Microfluorometries, Flow
See Flow Cytometry

Microglobulin, Beta 2
Blood82232
Urine82232

Micrographic Surgery
Mohs Technique17311-17315

Micrographic Surgery, Mohs
See Mohs Micrographic Surgery

Micropigmentation
Correction11920-11922

Microscope, Surgical
See Operating Microscope

Microscopic Evaluation
Hair96902

Microscopies, Electron
See Electron Microscopy

Microscopy
Ear Exam92504

Microsomal Antibody86376

Microsomia, Hemifacial
See Hemifacial Microsomia

Microsurgery
Operating Microscope69990

Microvascular Anastomosis
Bone Graft
 Fibula20955
 Other20962
Fascial Flap, Free15758
Muscle Flap, Free15756
Osteocutaneous Flap with20969-20973
Skin Flap, Free15757

Microvite A
See Vitamin, A

Microwave Therapy97024
See Physical Medicine/Therapy/Occupational
Therapy

Midbrain
See Brain; Brainstem; Mesencephalon; Skull
Base Surgery

Midcarpal Medioccipital Joint
Arthrotomy25040

Middle Cerebral Artery Velocimetry76821

Middle Ear
See Ear, Middle

Midface
Reconstruction
 Forehead Advancement21159-21160
 with Bone Graft21145-21160, 21188
 without Bone Graft21141-21143

Migration Inhibitory Factor (MIF)86378

Mile Operation
See Colectomy, Total, with Proctectomy

Milia, Multiple
Removal .10040

Miller Procedure28737

Miller-Abbott
Intubation44500, 74340

Minerva Cast29035
Removal .29710

Minimum Inhibitory
Concentration87186

Minimum Lethal
Concentration87187

Minnesota Multiphasic Personality
Inventory
See MMPI

Miscarriage
Incomplete Abortion59812
Missed Abortion
　　First Trimester59820
　　Second Trimester59821
Septic Abortion .59830

Missed Abortion
See Abortion

Mitchell Procedure28296

Mitogen Blastogenesis86353

Mitral Valve
Incision .33420-33422
Repair .33420-33427
　　Incision33420-33422
Replacement .33430

Mitrofanoff Operation50845
See Appendico-Vesicostomy

Miyagawanella
See Chlamydia

MLC
See Lymphocyte, Culture

MMPI96101-96103
Computer-Assisted96103

MMR Shots90707
See Vaccines

Mobilization
Splenic Flexure .44139
　　Laparoscopic44213
Stapes .69650

Modified Radical Mastectomy
See Mastectomy, Modified Radical

Mohs Micrographic
Surgery17311-17315

Molar Pregnancy
See Hydatidiform Mole

Mold
Culture .87107

Mole, Carneous
See Abortion

Mole, Hydatid
See Hydatidiform Mole

Molecular Cytogenetics . .88271-88275
Interpretation and Report88291

Molecular Diagnostics . . .83890-83914
Amplification83898-83901
Cell Lysis .83907
Dot/Slot Production83893
Enzymatic Digestion83892
Extraction83890-83891
Interpretation .83912
Molecular Isolation (Extraction)83890
Mutation Identification83904-83906
　　Enzymatic Ligation83914
Mutation Scanning83903
Nucleic Acid Amplification . .83900-83901, 83908
Nucleic Acid Extraction83907
Nucleic Acid Probe83896
Nucleic Acid Transfer83897
Polymerase Reaction Chain83898
Reverse Transcription83902
RNA Stabilization .83913
Separation .83894
Separation and Identification
　　High Resolution Technique83909

Molecular Oxygen Saturation
See Oxygen Saturation

Molecular Probes88384-88386
Multiple
　　Array-Based Evaluation88384-88386

Molluscum Contagiosum
Destruction17110-17111, 54050-54065

Molteno Procedure66180

Monilia
See Candida

Monitoring
Blood Pressure, 24 Hour93784-93790
Electrocardiogram93224-93237
　　See Electrocardiography
Electroencephalogram95812-95813,
　　　　　　　　　　　　　95950-95953, 95956
　　with Drug Activation95954
　　with Physical Activation95954
　　with WADA Activation95958
Fetal
　　During Labor59050-59051, 99500
　　　　Interpretation Only59051
Glucose
　　Interstitial Fluid95250-95251
Interstitial Fluid Pressure20950
Pediatric Apnea94774-94777
Seizure .61531, 61760

Monitoring, Sleep
See Polysomnography

Monoethylene Glycol
See Ethylene Glycol

Mononucleosis Virus, Infectious
See Epstein-Barr Virus

Monophosphate, Adenosine
See Adenosine Monophosphate (AMP)

Monophosphate, Adenosine Cyclic
See Cyclic AMP

Monophosphate, Guanosine
See Guanosine Monophosphate

Monophosphate, Guanosine Cyclic
See Cyclic GMP

Monospot Test
See Rapid Test for Infection

Monoxide, Carbon
See Carbon Monoxide

Monteggia Fracture24620-24635

Monticelli Procedure
See Application, Bone Fixation Device

Morbilli
See Rubeola

Morphine Methyl Ether
See Codeine

Morphometric Analysis
Nerve .88356
Skeletal Muscle .88355
Tumor88358-88361, 88367-88368

Morton's Neuroma
See Neuroma, Foot, Excision
Excision .28080

Moschcowitz Operation
See Repair, Hernia, Femoral; Revision

Mosenthal Test
See Urinalysis, Routine

Mother Cell
See Stem Cell

Motility Study
Duodenal .91022
Esophagus91010-91012
　　Imaging .78258
Sperm .89300

Motion Analysis
by Video and 3D Kinematics96000, 96004
Computer-based96000, 96004

Mouth
Abscess
　　Incision and Drainage40800-40801,
　　　　　　　　　　41005-41009, 41015-41018
Biopsy .40808, 41108
Cyst
　　Incision and Drainage40800-40801,
　　　　　　　　　　41005-41009, 41015-41018
Excision
　　Frenum .40819
Hematoma
　　Incision and Drainage40800-40801,
　　　　　　　　　　41005-41009, 41015-41018
Lesion
　　Destruction .40820
　　Excision40810-40816, 41116

Sensitivity Studies87190

Mycoplasma
Antibody86738
Culture87109
Detection87580-87582

Mycota
See Fungus

Myectomy, Anorectal
See Myomectomy, Anorectal

Myelencephalon
See Medulla

Myelin Basic Protein
Cerebrospinal Fluid83873

Myelography
Brain70010
Spine
 Cervical72240
 Lumbosacral72265
 Thoracic72255
 Total72270

Myelomeningocele
Repair63704-63706

Myelotomy63170

Myocardial
Perfusion Imaging ...78460-78465, 78478-78480
 See Nuclear Medicine
Positron Emission Tomography (PET)78459

Myocardial Imaging78466-78469
Positron Emission Tomography
 Perfusion Study78491-78492
Repair
 Postinfarction33542

Myocutaneous Flaps 15731-15738, 15756

Myofascial Pain Dysfunction Syndrome
See Temporomandibular Joint (TMJ)

Myofibroma
See Leiomyomata

Myoglobin83874

Myomectomy
Anorectal45108
Uterus58140-58146, 58545-58546

Myoplasty
See Muscle, Repair

Myotomy
Esophagus43030
Hyoid21685

Myringoplasty69620

Myringostomy
See Myringotomy

Myringotomy69420-69421

Myxoid Cyst
See Ganglion

N

N. Meningitidis
See Neisseria Meningitidis

Naffziger Operation
See Decompression, Orbit; Section

Nagel Test
See Color Vision Examination

Nail Bed
Reconstruction11762
Repair11760

Nail Fold
Excision
 Wedge11765

Nail Plate Separation
See Nails, Avulsion

Nails
Avulsion11730-11732
Biopsy11755
Debridement11720-11721
Drainage10060-10061
Evacuation
 Hematoma, Subungual11740
Excision11750-11752
KOH Examination87220
Removal11730-11732, 11750-11752
Trimming11719

Narcosynthesis
Diagnostic and Therapeutic90865

Nasal Abscess
See Nose, Abscess

Nasal Area
Bone Graft21210

Nasal Bleeding
See Epistaxis

Nasal Bone
Fracture
 Closed Treatment21310-21320
 Open Treatment21325-21335
 with Manipulation21315-21320
 without Manipulation21310
X-Ray70160

Nasal Deformity
Repair40700-40761

Nasal Function Study92512

Nasal Polyp
See Nose, Polyp

Nasal Prosthesis
Impression21087

Nasal Septum
Abscess
 Incision and Drainage30020

Fracture
 Closed Treatment21337
 Open Treatment21336
Hematoma
 Incision and Drainage30020
Repair30630
Submucous Resection30520

Nasal Sinuses
See Sinus/Sinuses

Nasal Smear
Eosinophils89190

Nasal Turbinate
Fracture
 Therapeutic30930

Nasoethmoid Complex
Fracture
 Open Treatment21338-21339
 Percutaneous Treatment21340
Reconstruction21182-21184

Nasogastric Tube
Placement43752

Nasolacrimal Duct
Exploration68810
 with Anesthesia68811
Insertion
 Stent68815
X-Ray
 with Contrast70170

Nasomaxillary
Fracture
 Closed Treatment21345
 Open Treatment21346-21348
 with Bone Grafting21348

Nasopharynges
See Nasopharynx

Nasopharyngoscopy92511

Nasopharynx
See Pharynx
Biopsy42804-42806
Hemorrhage42970-42972
Unlisted Services and Procedures42999

Natriuretic Peptide83880

Natural Killer (NK) Cells
Count86357

Natural Ostium
Sinus
 Maxillary31000
 Sphenoid31002

Navicular
Arthroplasty
 with Implant25443
Fracture
 Closed Treatment25622
 Open Treatment25628
 with Manipulation25624
Repair25440

Navigation
Computer Assisted0054T-0056T

Neck
Angiography70498, 70547-70549
Artery
 Ligation .37615
Biopsy .21550
Bypass Graft .35901
CT Scan70490-70492, 70498
Dissection, Radical
 See Radical Neck Dissection
Exploration
 Blood Vessel35800
 Lymph Nodes38542
Incision and Drainage
 Abscess21501-21502
 Hematoma21501-21502
Lipectomy, Suction Assisted15876
Magnetic Resonance Angiography
(MRA) .70547-70549
Magnetic Resonance Imaging
(MRI) .70540-70543
Nerve
 Graft64885-64886
Repair
 Blood Vessel35201
 with Other Graft35261
 with Vein Graft35231
Skin
 Revision .15819
Tumor
 Excision21555-21556
 Excision/Resection21557
Ultrasound Exam76536
Unlisted Services and Procedures,
Surgery .21899
Urinary Bladder
 See Bladder, Neck
Wound Exploration
 Penetrating .20100
X-Ray .70360

Neck Muscle
Division
 Scalenus Anticus21700-21705
 Sternocleidomastoid21720-21725

Necropsy
Coroner's Exam .88045
Forensic Exam .88040
Gross and Micro Exam88020-88029
Gross Exam88000-88016
Organ .88037
Regional .88036
Unlisted Services and Procedures88099

Needle Biopsy
See Biopsy
Abdomen Mass .49180
Bone .20220-20225
Bone Marrow .38221
Breast .19100
Colon
 Endoscopy .45392
Colon-Sigmoid
 Endoscopy .45342
CT Scan Guidance77012
Epididymis .54800
Esophagus
 Endoscopy .43232
Fluoroscopic Guidance77002
Gastrointestinal, Upper
 Endoscopy43238, 43242
Kidney .50200
Liver .47000-47001
Lung .32405
Lymph Nodes .38505
Mediastinum .32405
Muscle .20206
Pancreas .48102
Pleura .32400
Prostate0137T, 55700
Retroperitoneal Mass49180
Salivary Gland .42400
Spinal Cord .62269
Testis .54500
Thyroid Gland .60100
Transbronchial31629, 31633

Needle Localization
Breast
 Placement19290-19291
 with Lesion Excision19125-19126
Magnetic Resonance Guidance77021

Needle Manometer
Technique .20950

Needle Wire
Introduction
 Trachea .31730
Placement
 Breast19290-19291

Neer Procedure23470

Neisseria Gonorrheae87590-87592,
87850

Neisseria Meningitidis
Antibody .86741

Neobladder
Construction .51596

Neonatal Critical Care
See Newborn Care
Initial .99295
Subsequent .99296

Neoplasm
Cancer Photoradiation Therapy
 See Photochemotherapy
Cardiac
 See Heart, Tumor
Colon
 See Colon, Tumor
Esophageal
 See Tumor, Esophagus
Spinal Cord
 See Spinal Cord, Neoplasm
Unspecified Nature of Brain
 See Brain, Tumor

Neoplastic Growth
See Tumor

Nephelometry83883

Nephrectomy
Donor50300-50320, 50547
Laparoscopic50545-50548
Partial .50240
 Laparoscopic50543
Recipient .50340
with Ureters50220-50236, 50546, 50548

Nephrolith
See Calculus, Removal, Kidney

Nephrolithotomy50060-50075

Nephropexy50400-50405

Nephroplasty
See Kidney, Repair

Nephropyeloplasty
See Pyeloplasty

Nephrorrhaphy50500

Nephroscopy
See Endoscopy, Kidney

Nephrostogram50394

Nephrostolithotomy
Percutaneous50080-50081

Nephrostomy50040
Change Tube .50398
Endoscopic50562-50570
Percutaneous .52334
with Drainage .50040
X-Ray with Contrast
 Guide Dilation74485

Nephrostomy Tract
Establishment .50395

Nephrotomogram
See Nephrotomography

Nephrotomography74415

Nephrotomy50040-50045
with Exploration50045

Nerve
Cranial
 See Cranial Nerve
Facial
 See Facial Nerve
Intercostal
 See Intercostal Nerve
Lingual
 See Lingual Nerve
Median
 See Median Nerve
Obturator
 See Obturator Nerve
Peripheral
 See Peripheral Nerve
Phrenic
 See Phrenic Nerve
Sciatic
 See Sciatic Nerve
Spinal
 See Spinal Nerve

Tibial
　　See Tibial Nerve
Ulnar
　　See Ulnar Nerve
Vestibular
　　See Vestibular Nerve

Nerve Conduction
Motor Nerve95900-95903
Sensory Nerve or Mixed95904

Nerve II, Cranial
See Optic Nerve

Nerve Root
See Cauda Equina; Spinal Cord
Decompression63020-63048, 63055-63103
Incision .63185-63190
Section .63185-63190

Nerve Stimulation, Transcutaneous
See Application, Neurostimulation

Nerve Teasing88362

Nerve V, Cranial
See Trigeminal Nerve

Nerve VII, Cranial
See Facial Nerve

Nerve X, Cranial
See Vagus Nerve

Nerve XI, Cranial
See Accessory Nerve

Nerve XII, Cranial
See Hypoglossal Nerve

Nerves
Anastomosis
　　Facial to Hypoglossal64868
　　Facial to Phrenic64870
　　Facial to Spinal Accessory64866
Avulsion .64732-64772
Biopsy .64795
Decompression64702-64727
Destruction64600-64681
　　Laryngeal, Recurrent31595
Foot
　　Incision .28035
Graft .64885-64907
Implantation
　　Electrode64553-64581
　　to Bone .64787
　　to Muscle .64787
Incision43640-43641, 64732-64772
Injection
　　Anesthetic01991-01992, 64400-64530
　　Neurolytic Agent64600-64681
Insertion
　　Electrode64553-64581
Lesion
　　Excision64774-64792
Neurofibroma
　　Excision64788-64792
Neurolemmoma
　　Excision64788-64792
Neurolytic
　　Internal .64727

Neuroma
　　Excision64774-64786
Neuroplasty64702-64721
Removal
　　Electrode .64585
Repair
　　Graft64885-64911
　　Microdissection69990
　　Suture64831-64876
Spinal Accessory
　　Incision .63191
　　Section .63191
Suture .64831-64876
Sympathectomy
　　Excision64802-64818
Transection43640-43641, 64732-64772
Transposition64718-64721
Unlisted Services and Procedures64999

Nervous System
Nuclear Medicine
　　Unlisted Services and Procedures78699

Nesidioblast
See Islet Cell

Neural Conduction
See Nerve Conduction

Neural Ganglion
See Ganglion

Neurectomy
Foot .28055
Gastrocnemius .27326
Hamstring Muscle27325
Leg, Lower .27326
Leg, Upper .27325
Popliteal .27326
Tympanic .69676

Neuroendoscopy
Intracranial62160-62165

Neurofibroma
Cutaneous Nerve
　　Excision .64788
Extensive
　　Excision .64792
Peripheral Nerve
　　Excision .64790

Neurolemmoma
Cutaneous Nerve
　　Excision .64788
Extensive
　　Excision .64792
Peripheral Nerve
　　Excision .64790

Neurologic System
See Nervous System

Neurology
Brain Cortex
Magnetic Stimulation0160T-0161T
Brain Mapping .96020
Brain Surface Electrode
Stimulation95961-95962

Central Motor
　　Transcranial Motor
　　Stimulation95928-95929
Diagnostic
　　Anal Sphincter51785
　　Autonomic Nervous Function
　　　　Heart Rate Response95921-95923
　　　　Pseudomotor Response95921-95923
　　　　Sympathetic Function95921-95923
Electrocorticogram
　　Intraoperative95829
Electroencephalogram (EEG)95812-95827,
　　　　　　　　　　　　　　　　　　　　　　95955
　　Brain Death .95824
　　Electrode Placement95830
　　Intraoperative95955
　　Monitoring95812-95813, 95950-95953,
　　　　　　　　　　　　　　　　　　　　　　95956
　　Physical or Drug Activation95954
　　Sleep95822, 95827
　　Standard .95819
　　WADA Activation95958
Electroencephalography (EEG)
　　Digital Analysis95957
Electromyography
　　Fine Wire
　　　　Dynamic96004
　　Ischemic Limb Exercise Test95875
　　Needle51785, 95860-95872
　　Surface
　　　　Dynamic96002-96004
Higher Cerebral Function
　　Aphasia Test96105
　　Cognitive Function Tests96116
　　Developmental Tests96110-96111
　　Neurobehavioral Status96116
　　Neuropsychological Testing96118-96120
　　Neuropsychological Testing, Computer-
　　　　Assisted96120
Magnetoencephalography
(MEG)95965-95967
Motion Analysis
　　by Video and 3D Kinematics . . .96000, 96004
　　Computer-based96000, 96004
Muscle Testing
　　Manual95831-95834
Nerve Conduction
　　Motor Nerve95900-95903
　　Sensory Nerve or Mixed95904
Neurofunctional Testing96020
Neuromuscular Junction Tests95937
Neurophysiological Testing
　　Intraoperative95920
Neuropsychological Testing96118-96120
　　Computer-Assisted96120
Plantar Pressure Measurements
　　Dynamic96001, 96004
Polysomnography95808-95811
Range of Motion95851-95852
Reflex
　　Blink Reflex95933
　　H-Reflex95933-95934
Sleep Study95807-95810
Somatosensory Testing95925-95927
Tensilon Test .95857

Therapeutic
 Magnetic Stimulation
 Transcranial0160T, 0161T
Unlisted Services and Procedures95999
Urethral Sphincter51785
Visual Evoked Potential, CNS95930

Neurolysis
Nerve64704-64708
 Internal64727

Neuroma
Acoustic
 See Brain, Tumor, Excision
Excision
 Cutaneous Nerve64774
 Digital Nerve64776-64778
 Foot28080
 Foot Nerve64782-64783
 Hand Nerve64782-64783
 Peripheral Nerve64784
 Sciatic Nerve64786
Interdigital
 See Mortons Neuroma; Neuroma, Foot,
 Excision

Neuromuscular Junction
Tests95937

Neuromuscular Pedicle
Reinnervation
 Larynx31590

Neuromuscular
Reeducation97112
See Physical Medicine/Therapy/Occupational
Therapy

Neurophysiologic Testing
Autonomic Nervous Function
 Heart Rate Response95921-95923
 Pseudomotor Response95921-95923
 Sympathetic Function95921-95923
Intraoperative, Per Hour95920

Neuroplasty64712
Cranial Nerve64716
Digital Nerve64702-64704
Peripheral Nerve ...64708-64714, 64718-64721

Neuropsychological
Testing96118-96120
Computer-Assisted96120

Neurorrhaphy64831-64876
Peripheral Nerve
 Conduit64910-64911
 with Graft64885-64907

Neurostimulators
Analysis0162T, 95970-95979
Application64550
Implantation64553-64565
 Electrodes43647, 43881
Insertion
 Pulse Generator61885-61886, 64590
 Receiver61885-61886, 64590
Removal
 Electrodes43648, 43882, 61880
 Pulse Generator61888, 64595
 Receiver61888, 64595

Replacement61885
 Electrodes43647, 43881

Neurotomy, Sympathetic
See Gasserian Ganglion, Sensory Root,
Decompression

Neurovascular Pedicle
Flaps15750

Neutralization Test
Virus86382

New Patient
Domiciliary or Rest Home Visit99324-99328
Emergency Department Services ..99281-99288
Home Services99341-99345
Hospital Inpatient Services99221-99239
Hospital Observation Services99217-99220
Initial Office Visit99201-99205
 See Evaluation and Management; Office and
 Other Outpatient
Inpatient Consultations99251-99255
Office and/or Other Outpatient
Consultations99241-99245

Newborn Care99431-99440, 99502
Attendance at Delivery99436
Birthing Room99431
Blood Transfusion36450
 See Neonatal Intensive Care
Circumcision
 Clamp or Other Device54150
 Surgical Excision54160
History and Examination99431, 99435
Laryngoscopy31520
Normal99431-99433
Prepuce Slitting54000
Preventive
 Office99432
Resuscitation99440
Standby for Cesarean Delivery99360
Subsequent Hospital Care99433
Umbilical Artery Catheterization36660

Nickel83885

Nicolas-Durand-Favre Disease
See Lymphogranuloma Venereum

Nicotine83887

Nidation
See Implantation

Nipples
See Breast
Inverted19355
Reconstruction19350

Nissen Operation
See Fundoplasty, Esophagogastric

Nissen Procedure43324
Laparoscopic43280

Nitrate Reduction Test
See Urinalysis

Nitric Oxide95012

Nitroblue Tetrazolium Dye
Test86384

Nitrogen, Blood Urea
See Blood Urea Nitrogen

NMR Imaging
See Magnetic Resonance Imaging (MRI)

NMR Spectroscopies
See Magnetic Resonance Spectroscopy

No Man's Land
Tendon Repair26356-26358

Noble Procedure
See Repair; Suture

Nocardia
Antibody86744

Nocturnal Penile Rigidity
Test54250

Nocturnal Penile Tumescence
Test54250

Node Dissection, Lymph
See Dissection, Lymph Nodes

Node, Lymph
See Lymph Nodes

Nodes
See Lymph Nodes

Non-Invasive Vascular Imaging
See Vascular Studies

Non-Office Medical Services ..99056
Emergency Care99060

Non-Stress Test, Fetal59025

Nonunion Repair
Femur
 with Graft27472
 without Graft27470
Metatarsal28322
Tarsal Joint28320

Noradrenalin
Blood82383-82384
Urine82384

Norchlorimipramine
See Imipramine

Norepinephrine
See Catecholamines
Blood82383-82384
Urine82384

Nortriptyline
Assay80182

Norwood Procedure33611-33612,
 33619
See Repair, Heart, Ventricle; Revision

Nose
Abscess
 Incision and Drainage30000-30020
Actinotherapy
 Intranasal0168T
Artery
 Incision30915-30920

Biopsy
 Intranasal .30100
Dermoid Cyst
 Excision
 Complex .30125
 Simple .30124
Displacement Therapy30210
Endoscopy
 Diagnostic31231-31235
 Surgical31237-31294
Excision
 Rhinectomy30150-30160
Fracture
 Closed Treatment21345
 Open Treatment21325-21336,
 21338-21339, 21346-21347
 Percutaneous Treatment21340
 with Fixation21330, 21340, 21345-21347
Hematoma
 Incision and Drainage30000-30020
Hemorrhage
 Cauterization30901-30906
Insertion
 Septal Prosthesis30220
Intranasal
 Actinotherapy0168T
 Lesion
 External Approach30118
 Internal Approach30117
 Phototherapy0168T
Lysis of Adhesions30560
Phototherapy
 Intranasal .0168T
Polyp
 Excision
 Extensive .30115
 Simple .30110
Reconstruction
 Cleft Lip/Cleft Palate30460-30462
 Dermatoplasty30620
 Primary30400, 30410-30420
 Secondary30430-30450
 Septum .30520
Removal
 Foreign Body30300
 Anesthesia30310
 Lateral Rhinotomy30320
Repair
 Adhesions .30560
 Cleft Lip40700-40761
 Fistula30580-30600, 42260
 Rhinophyma .30120
 Septum30540-30545, 30630
 Synechia .30560
 Vestibular Stenosis30465
Skin
 Excision .30120
 Surgical Planing30120
Submucous Resection Turbinate
 Excision .30140
Turbinate
 Excision30130-30140
 Fracture .30930
 Injection .30200
Turbinate Mucosa
 Cauterization30801-30802
Unlisted Services and Procedures30999

Nose Bleed30901-30906
See Hemorrhage, Nasal

NTD .86384
See Nitroblue Tetrazolium Dye Test

Nuclear Antigen
Antibody .86235

Nuclear Imaging
See Nuclear Medicine

Nuclear Magnetic Resonance Imaging
See Magnetic Resonance Imaging (MRI)

Nuclear Magnetic Resonance Spectroscopy
See Magnetic Resonance Spectroscopy

Nuclear Medicine
Adrenal Gland Imaging78075
Automated Data78890-78891
Bile Duct
 Imaging .78223
Bladder
 Residual Study78730
Blood
 Bone
 Density Study78350-78351
 Imaging78300-78320
 SPECT .78320
 Ultrasound76977
 Unlisted Services and Procedures . . .78399
 Flow Imaging78445
 Iron
 Red Cells78140
 Platelet Survival78190-78191
 Red Cell Survival78130-78135
 Red Cells78120-78121
 Unlisted Services and Procedures78199
 Whole Blood Volume78122
Bone Marrow
 Imaging78102-78104
Brain
 Blood Flow78610-78615
 Cerebrospinal Fluid78630-78650
 Imaging78600-78609
 Vascular Flow78610
Endocrine System
 Unlisted Services and Procedures78099
Esophagus
 Imaging (Motility)78258
 Reflux Study78262
Gallbladder
 Imaging .78223
Gastric Mucosa
 Imaging .78261
Gastrointestinal
 Blood Loss Study78278
 Protein Loss Study78282
 Shunt Testing78291
 Unlisted Services and Procedures78299
Genitourinary System
 Unlisted Services and Procedures78799
Heart
 Blood Flow .78414
 Blood Pool Imaging78472-78473,
 78481-78483, 78494-78496

Myocardial Imaging78459, 78466-78469
Myocardial Perfusion78460-78465,
 78478-78480
 Shunt Detection78428
 Unlisted Services and Procedures78499
Hepatic Duct
 Imaging .78223
Inflammatory Process78805-78807
Intestines
 Imaging .78290
Kidney
 Function Study78725
 Imaging78700-78707, 78710
Lacrimal Gland Tear Flow78660
Liver
 Function Study78220
 Imaging78201-78216
 Vascular Flow78206
Lung
 Imaging Perfusion78580-78585
 Imaging Ventilation78586-78594
 Unlisted Services and Procedures78599
Lymph Nodes .78195
Lymphatics .78195
 Unlisted Services and Procedures78199
Musculoskeletal System
 Unlisted Services and Procedures78399
Nervous System
 Unlisted Services and Procedures78699
Parathyroid Gland Imaging78070
Pulmonary Perfusion Imaging78588
Salivary Gland Function Study78232
 Imaging78230-78231
Spleen
 Imaging78185, 78215-78216
 Unlisted Services and Procedures78199
Stomach
 Blood Loss Study78278
 Emptying Study78264
 Protein Loss Study78282
 Reflux Study78262
 Vitamin B-12 Absorption78270-78272
Testes
 Imaging .78761
Therapeutic
 Interstitial .79300
 Intra-Arterial79445
 Intra-Articular79440
 Intracavitary79200
 Intravenous .79101
 Intravenous Infusion79403
 Oral .79005
 Thyroid79200-79300
 Unlisted Services and Procedures79999
Thyroid
 Imaging .78010
 Imaging for Metastases78015-78018
 Imaging with Flow78011
 Imaging with Uptake78006
 Metastases Uptake78020
 Uptake78000-78003
Tumor Imaging
 Positron Emission Tomography .78811-78816
 with Computed Tomography . .78814-78816
Tumor Localization78800-78804
Unlisted Services and Procedures78999
Urea Breath Test78267-78268

O

Obturator Nerve
Avulsion64763-64766
Incision64763-64766
Transection64763-64766

Obturator Prosthesis21076
Definitive21080
Insertion
　　Larynx31527
Interim21079

Occipital Nerve, Greater
Avulsion64744
Incision64744
Injection
　　Anesthetic64405
Transection64744

Occlusion
Extracranial
　　Intracranial61623
Fallopian Tube
　　Oviduct58565, 58615
Penis
　　Vein37790
Umbilical Cord59072

Occlusive Disease of Artery
See Repair, Artery; Revision

Occult Blood82270-82272
by Hemoglobin Immunoassay82274

Occupational Therapy
Evaluation97003-97004

Ocular Implant
See Orbital Implant
Insertion
　　in Scleral Shell65130
　　Muscles, Attached65140
　　Muscles, Not Attached65135
Modification65125
Reinsertion65150
　　with Foreign Material65155
Removal65175

Ocular Muscle
See Eye Muscles

Ocular Orbit
See Orbit

Ocular Photoscreening0065T

Ocular Prostheses
See Prosthesis, Ocular

Oculomotor Muscle
See Eye Muscles

Oddi Sphincter
See Sphincter of Oddi

Odontoid Dislocation
Open Treatment/Reduction22318
　　with Grafting22319

Odontoid Fracture
Open Treatment/Reduction22318
　　with Grafting22319

Odontoid Process
Excision22548

Oesophageal Neoplasm
See Tumor, Esophagus

Oesophageal Varices
See Esophageal Varices

Oesophagus
See Esophagus

Oestradiol
See Estradiol

Office and/or Other Outpatient Services
See History and Physical
Consultation
Established Patient99211-99215
New Patient99201-99205
Normal Newborn99432
Office Visit
　　Established Patient99211-99215
　　New Patient99201-99205
Outpatient Visit
　　Established Patient99211-99215
　　New Patient99201-99205
　　Prolonged Services99354-99355

Office Medical Services
After Hours99050
Emergency Care99058
Extended Hours99051

Office or Other Outpatient Consultations
See Consultation, Office and/or Other Outpatient

Olecranon
See Elbow; Humerus; Radius; Ulna
Bursa
　　Arthrocentesis20605
Cyst
　　Excision24125-24126
Tumor
　　Cyst24120
　　Excision24125-24126

Olecranon Process
Craterization24147
Diaphysectomy24147
Excision24147
　　Abscess24138
Fracture
　　See Elbow; Humerus; Radius
　　Closed Treatment24670-24675
　　Open Treatment24685
Osteomyelitis24138, 24147
Saucerization24147
Sequestrectomy24138

Oligoclonal Immunoglobulins ..83916

Omentectomy49255, 58950-58958
Laparotomy58960
Oophorectomy58943
Resection Ovarian Malignancy58950-58952
Resection Peritoneal Malignancy ..58950-58958
Resection Tubal Malignancy58950-58958

Omentum
Excision49255, 58950-58958
Flap49904-49905
　　Free
　　　with Microvascular Anastomosis ...49906
Omentopexy49326
Unlisted Services and Procedures49999

Omphalectomy49250

Omphalocele
Repair49600-49611

Omphalomesenteric Duct
Excision44800

Omphalomesenteric Duct, Persistent
See Diverticulum, Meckel's

Oncoprotein
HER-2/neu83950

One Stage Prothrombin Time85610-85611
See Prothrombin Time

Onychectomy
See Excision, Nails

Onychia
Drainage10060-10061

Oocyte
Assisted Fertilization
　　Microtechnique89280-89281
Biopsy89290-89291
Cryopreservation0059T
Culture
　　Extended89272
　　Less than 4 Days89250
　　with Co-Culture89251
Identification
　　Follicular Fluid89254
Insemination89268
Retrieval
　　for In Vitro Fertilization58970
Storage89346
Thawing89356

Oophorectomy .58262-58263, 58291-58292, 58552, 58554, 58661, 58940-58943
Ectopic Pregnancy
　　Laparoscopic Treatment59120
　　Surgical Treatment59120

Oophorectomy, Partial
See Excision, Ovary, Partial

Oophorocystectomy
See Cystectomy, Ovarian

Open Biopsy, Adrenal Gland
See Adrenal Gland, Biopsy

Operating Microscope69990

Operation

Blalock-Hanlon
 See Septostomy, Atrial
Blalock-Taussig Subclavian-Pulmonary
Anastomosis
 See Pulmonary Artery, Shunt, Subclavian
Borthen
 See Iridotasis
Dana
 See Rhizotomy
Dunn
 See Arthrodesis, Foot Joint
Duvries
 See Tenoplasty
Estes
 See Ovary, Transposition
Foley Pyeloplasty
 See Pyeloplasty
Fontan
 See Repair, Heart, Anomaly
Fox
 See Fox Operation
Gardner
 See Meningocele Repair
Green
 See Scapulopexy
Harelip
 See Cleft Lip, Repair
Heine
 See Cyclodialysis
Heller
 See Esophagomyotomy
Iris, Inclusion
 See Iridencleisis
Jaboulay Gastroduodenostomy
 See Gastroduodenostomy
Johanson
 See Reconstruction, Urethra
Keller
 See Keller Procedure
Krause
 See Gasserian Ganglion, Sensory Root,
 Decompression
Mumford
 See Claviculectomy, Partial
Nissen
 See Fundoplasty, Esophagogastric
Peet
 See Nerves, Sympathectomy, Excision
Ramstedt
 See Pyloromyotomy
Richardson Hysterectomy
 See Hysterectomy, Abdominal, Total
Schanz
 See Femur, Osteotomy
Schlatter Total Gastrectomy
 See Excision, Stomach, Total
Smithwick
 See Excision, Nerve, Sympathetic
Winiwarter Cholecystoenterostomy
 See Anastomosis, Gallbladder to Intestines

Operation Microscopes
See Operating Microscope

Operculectomy41821

Operculum
See Gums

Ophthalmic Mucous Membrane Test95060
See Allergy Tests

Ophthalmology
Unlisted Services and Procedures92499
 See Ophthalmology, Diagnostic

Ophthalmology, Diagnostic
Color Vision Exam92283
Computerized Scanning92135
Computerized Screening0065T, 99172
Dark Adaptation92284
Electro-oculography92270
Electromyography, Needle92265
Electroretinography92275
Endoscopy66990
Eye Exam
 Established Patient92012-92014
 New Patient92002-92004
 with Anesthesia92018-92019
Glaucoma Provocative Test92140
Gonioscopy92020
Ocular Photography
 External92285
 Internal92286-92287
Ophthalmoscopy92225-92226
 with Dynamometry92260
 with Fluorescein Angiography92235
 with Fluorescein Angioscopy92230
 with Fundus Photography92250
 with Indocyanine-Green Angiography ..92240
Photoscreening0065T
Refractive Determination92015
Sensorimotor Exam92060
Tonography92120
 with Provocation92130
Tonometry
 Serial92100
Ultrasound76511-76529
Visual Acuity Screen99172-99173
Visual Field Exam92081-92083
Visual Function Screen0065T, 99172

Ophthalmoscopy92225-92226
See Ophthalmology, Diagnostic

Opiates83925

Opinion, Second
See Confirmatory Consultations

Optic Nerve
Decompression67570
 with Nasal/Sinus Endoscopy31294

Optokinetic Nystagmus Test
See Nystagmus Tests, Optokinetic

Oral Lactose Tolerance Test82951-82953
See Glucose, Tolerance Test

Oral Mucosa
See Mouth, Mucosa

Oral Surgical Splint21085

Orbit
See Orbital Contents; Orbital Floor; Periorbital Region
Biopsy61332
 Exploration67450
 Fine Needle Aspiration or Orbital
 Contents67415
 Orbitotomy without Bone Flap67400
CT Scan70480-70482
Decompression61330
 Bone Removal67414, 67445
Exploration61332, 67400, 67450
 Lesion
 Excision61333
Fracture
 Closed Treatment
 with Manipulation21401
 without Manipulation21400
 Open Treatment21406-21408
 Blowout Fracture21385-21395
Incision and Drainage67405, 67440
Injection
 Retrobulbar67500-67505
 Tenon's Capsule67515
Insertion
 Implant67550
Lesion
 Excision67412, 67420
Magnetic Resonance Imaging
(MRI)70540-70543
Removal
 Decompression67445
 Exploration61334
 Foreign Body61334, 67413, 67430
 Implant67560
Sella Turcica70482
Unlisted Services and Procedures67599
X-Ray70190-70200

Orbit Area
Reconstruction
 Secondary21275

Orbit Wall
Decompression
 with Nasal/Sinus Endoscopy ...31292-31293

Orbital Contents
Aspiration67415

Orbital Floor
See Orbit; Periorbital Region
Fracture
 Blow Out21385-21395

Orbital Hypertelorism
Osteotomy
 Periorbital21260-21263

Orbital Implant
See Ocular Implant
Insertion67550
Removal67560

Orbital Prosthesis21077

Orbital Rim and Forehead
Reconstruction21172-21180

Orbital Rims
Reconstruction21182-21184

Orbital Transplant 67560

Orbital Walls
Reconstruction 21182-21184

Orbitocraniofacial Reconstruction
Secondary 21275

Orbitotomy
with Bone Flap
 for Exploration 67450
 Lateral Approach 67420
 with Drainage 67440
 with Removal Foreign Body 67430
 with Removal of Bone for
 Decompression 67445
with Removal Foreign Body 67413
with Removal of Bone for Decompression .67414
without Bone Flap
 for Exploration 67400
 with Drainage Only 67405
 with Removal Lesion 67412

Orchidectomies
See Excision, Testis

Orchidopexy
See Orchiopexy

Orchidoplasty
See Repair, Testis

Orchiectomy
Laparoscopic 54690
Partial 54522
Radical
 Abdominal Exploration 54535
 Inguinal Approach 54530
Simple 54520

Orchiopexy
Abdominal Approach 54650
Inguinal Approach 54640
Intra-Abdominal Testis 54692

Orchioplasty
See Repair, Testis

Organ Grafting
See Transplantation

Organ or Disease-Oriented Panel
Electrolyte 80051
General Health Panel 80050
Hepatic Function Panel 80076
Hepatitis Panel 80074
Lipid Panel 80061
Metabolic
 Basic 80048
 Comprehensive 80053
Obstetric Panel 80055
Renal Function 80069

Organ System, Neurologic
See Nervous System

Organic Acids 83918-83921

Ormond Disease
See Retroperitoneal Fibrosis

Orogastric Tube
Placement 43752

Oropharynx
Biopsy 42800

Orthodontic Cephalogram 70350

Orthomyxoviridae
See Influenza Virus

Orthomyxovirus
See Influenza Virus

Orthopantogram 70355

Orthopedic Cast
See Cast

Orthopedic Surgery
Computer Assisted Navigation 0054T-0056T
Stereotaxis
 Computer Assisted 0054T-0056T

Orthoptic Training 92065

Orthoroentgenogram 77073

Orthosis
See Orthotics

Orthotics
Check-Out 97762
Management and Training 97760

Os Calcis Fracture
See Calcaneus, Fracture

Osmolality
Blood 83930
Urine 83935

Osseous Survey 77074-77076

Osseous Tissue
See Bone

Ossicles
Excision
 Stapes
 with Footplate Drill Out 69661
 without Foreign Material 69660-69661
Reconstruction
 Ossicular Chain
 Tympanoplasty with
 Antrotomy or Mastoidotomy .69636-69637
 Tympanoplasty with
 Mastoidectomy 69642, 69644, 69646
 Tympanoplasty without
 Mastoidectomy 69632-69633
Release
 Stapes 69650
Replacement
 with Prosthesis 69633, 69637

Ostectomy
Metacarpal 26250-26255
Metatarsal 28288
Phalanges
 Finger 26260-26262

Pressure Ulcer
 Ischial 15941, 15945
 Sacral 15933, 15935, 15937
 Trochanteric 15951, 15953, 15958
Scapula 23190
Sternum 21620

Osteocalcin 83937

Osteocartilaginous Exostoses
See Exostosis

Osteochondroma
See Exostosis

Osteocutaneous Flap
with Microvascular Anastomosis ...20969-20973

Osteoma
Sinusotomy
 Frontal 31075

Osteomyelitis 20000-20005
Elbow
 Incision and Drainage 23935
Excision
 Clavicle 23180
 Facial 21026
 Humerus, Proximal 23184
 Mandible 21025
 Scapula 23182
Femur/Knee
 Incision and Drainage 27303
Finger
 Incision 26034
Hand Incision 26034
Hip
 Incision, Deep 26992
Humerus 24134
 Incision and Drainage 23935
Incision
 Foot 28005
 Shoulder 23035
 Thorax 21510
Olecranon Process 24138, 24147
Pelvis
 Incision, Deep 26992
Radius 24136, 24145
Sequestrectomy
 Clavicle 23170
 Humeral Head 23174
 Scapula 23172
 Skull 61501

Osteopathic Manipulation 98925-98929

Osteoplasty
Carpal Bone 25394
Facial Bones
 Augmentation 21208
 Reduction 21209
Femoral Neck 27179
Femur 27179
 Lengthening 27466-27468
 Shortening 27465, 27468
Fibula
 Lengthening 27715
Humerus 24420
Metacarpal 26568

P

P & P
See Proconvertin

P B Antibodies
See Antibody, Heterophile

P-Acetamidophenol
See Acetaminophen

Pacemaker, Heart
See Cardiology; Defibrillator, Heart;
Electrocardiography
Conversion .33214
Electronic Analysis
　　Antitachycardia System 93724
　　Dual Chamber . . .93731-93733, 93743-93744
　　Leads .93640-93641
　　Single Chamber . .93734-93735, 93741-93742
　　Single/Dual Chamber93641-93642
　　Wearable Device 93741-93742, 93745
Insertion .33206-33208
　　Electrode 33210-33211, 33216-33217,
　　　　　　　　　　　　　　　　　　33224-33225
　　Pulse Generator Only33212-33213
Removal .33233-33237
　　via Thoracotomy33236-33237
Repair
　　Electrode 33218-33220
Replacement
　　Catheter .33210
　　Electrode 33210-33211
　　Insertion 33206-33208
　　Pulse Generator33212-33213
Repositioning
　　Electrode 33215, 33226
Revise Pocket
　　Chest .33222
Telephonic Analysis 93733, 93736
Upgrade .33214

Pachymetry
Eye .76514

Packing
Nasal Hemorrhage 30901-30906

Pain Management
Epidural/Intrathecal 62350-62351,
　　　　　　　　　　　62360-62362, 99601-99602
Intravenous Therapy 90765-90768,
　　　　　　　　　　　　　　　　90774-90775

Palate
Abscess
　　Incision and Drainage 42000
Biopsy .42100
Excision .42120, 42145
Fracture
　　Closed Treatment 21421
　　Open Treatment 21422-21423
Lesion
　　Destruction .42160
　　Excision 42104-42120
Prosthesis
　　Augmentation 21082

Impression .42280
Insertion .42281
Lift .21083
Reconstruction
　　Lengthening 42226-42227
Repair
　　Cleft Palate42200-42225
　　Laceration42180-42182
　　Vomer Flap .42235
Unlisted Services and Procedures42299

Palate, Cleft
See Cleft Palate

Palatoplasty 42200-42225

Palatoschisis
See Cleft Palate

Palm
Bursa
　　Incision and Drainage 26025-26030
Fasciectomy 26121-26125
Fasciotomy 26040-26045
Tendon
　　Excision .26170
Tendon Sheath
　　Excision .26145
　　Incision and Drainage 26020

Palsy, Seventh Nerve
See Facial Nerve Paralysis

Pancreas
Anastomosis
　　with Intestines 48520-48540, 48548
Anesthesia .00794
Biopsy .48100
　　Needle Biopsy48102
Cyst
　　Anastomosis48520-48540
　　Repair .48500
Debridement
　　Peripancreatic Tissue 48105
Excision
　　Ampulla of Vater 48148
　　Duct .48148
　　Partial . . .48140-48146, 48150, 48154, 48160
　　Peripancreatic Tissue 48105
　　Total48155-48160
Lesion
　　Excision .48120
Needle Biopsy .48102
Placement
　　Drainage 48000-48001
Pseudocyst
　　Drainage
　　　Open .48510
　　　Percutaneous 48511
Removal
　　Calculi (Stone)48020
Removal Transplanted Allograft 48556
Repair
　　Cyst .48500
Resection .48105
Suture .48545
Transplantation48160, 48550, 48554-48556
　　Allograft Preparation 48550-48552
　　Islet Cell 0141T, 0142T, 0143T
Unlisted Services and Procedures 48999

X-Ray with Contrast 74300-74305
　　Injection Procedure 48400

Pancreas, Endocrine Only
See Islet Cell

Pancreatectomy
Donor .48550
Partial48140-48146, 48150-48154, 48160
Total .48155-48160
with Transplantation 48160

Pancreatic DNAse
See DNAse

Pancreatic Duct
Destruction
　　Calculi (Stone) 43265
Dilation
　　Endoscopy 43271
Endoscopy
　　Collection
　　　Specimen 43260
　　Destruction
　　　Calculi (Stone) 43265
　　　Tumor .43272
　　Dilation .43271
　　Removal (Endoscopic)
　　　Calculi (Stone) 43264
　　　Foreign Body 43269
　　　Stent .43269
　　Sphincter Pressure 43263
　　Sphincterotomy 43262
　　Tube Placement 43267-43268
Incision
　　Sphincter .43262
Removal
　　Calculi (Stone) 43264
　　Foreign Body 43269
　　Stent .43269
Tube Placement
　　Nasopancreatic 43267
　　Stent .43268
Tumor
　　Destruction 43272
X-Ray with Contrast
　　Guide Catheter74329-74330

Pancreatic Elastase 1 (PE1) 82656

Pancreatic Islet Cell AB
See Antibody, Islet Cell

Pancreaticojejunostomy 48548

Pancreatography
Injection Procedure 48400
Intraoperative 74300-74301
Postoperative .74305

Pancreatorrhaphy48545

Pancreatotomy
See Incision, Pancreas

Pancreozymin-Secretin Test . . .82938

Panel
See Blood Tests; Organ or Disease-Oriented Panel

Panniculectomy
See Lipectomy

Performance Test

See Physical Medicine/Therapy/Occupational Therapy

Perfusion

Perfusion Pump

See Infusion Pump

Perfusion, Intracranial Arterial

Pericardectomies

See Excision, Pericardium

Pericardial Cyst

See Cyst, Pericardial

Pericardial Sac

Pericardial Window

Pericardial Window Technic

See Pericardiostomy

Pericardiectomy

Pericardiocentesis

Pericardiostomy

Pericardiotomy

Pericardium

Peridural Anesthesia

See Anesthesia, Epidural

Peridural Injection

See Epidural, Injection

Perineal Prostatectomy

See Prostatectomy, Perineal

Perineoplasty

Perineorrhaphy

Perineum

Perionychia

See Paronychia

Periorbital Region

Peripheral Artery Disease (PAD) Rehabilitation

Peripheral Nerve

Platysmal Flap15825

PLC
See Lymphocyte, Culture; Tissue Typing

Pleoptic Training92065

Plethysmography
See Vascular Studies
Extremities93922-93923
 Veins93965
Penis54240
Total Body93720-93722

Pleura
Biopsy32095-32100, 32400-32402
Decortication32320
Empyema
 Excision32540
Excision32310-32320
 Endoscopic32656
Foreign Body
 Removal32150-32151
Needle Biopsy32400
Removal
 Foreign Body32653
Repair32215
Thoracotomy32095-32100
Unlisted Services and Procedures32999

Pleural Cavity
Aspiration32000-32002
Catheterization32019
Chemotherapy Administration96440
 See Chemotherapy
Fusion32005
Incision
 Empyema32035-32036
 Pneumothorax32020
Puncture and Drainage32000-32002
Thoracostomy32035-32036

Pleural Endoscopies
See Thoracoscopy

Pleural Scarification
for Repeat Pneumothorax32215

Pleural Tap
See Thoracentesis

Pleurectomy
Anesthesia00542
Parietal32310-32320
 Endoscopic32656

Pleuritis, Purulent
See Abscess, Thorax

Pleurocentesis
See Thoracentesis

Pleurodesis
Chemical32005
Endoscopic32650

Pleurosclerosis
See Pleurodesis

Pleurosclerosis, Chemical
See Pleurodesis, Chemical

Plexectomy, Choroid
See Choroid Plexus, Excision

Plexus
Brachialis
 See Brachial Plexus
Cervicalis
 See Cervical Plexus
Choroid
 See Choroid Plexus
Coeliacus
 See Celiac Plexus
Lumbalis
 See Lumbar Plexus

PLGN
See Plasminogen

Plication, Sphincter, Urinary Bladder
See Bladder, Repair, Neck

Pneumocentesis
Lung32420

Pneumocisternogram
See Cisternography

Pneumococcal Vaccine
See Vaccines

Pneumocystis Carinii
Antigen Detection
 Immunofluorescence87281

Pneumogastric Nerve
See Vagus Nerve

Pneumogram
Pediatric94772

Pneumolysis32940

Pneumonectomy32440-32500
Completion32488
Donor32850, 33930
Sleeve32442
Total32440-32445

Pneumonology
See Pulmonology

Pneumonolysis32940
Intrapleural32652
Open Intrapleural32124

Pneumonostomy32200-32201

Pneumonotomy
See Incision, Lung

Pneumoperitoneum49400

Pneumoplethysmography
Ocular93875

Pneumothorax
Chemical Pleurodesis32005
Pleural Scarification for Repeat32215
Therapeutic
 Injection Intrapleural Air32960
Thoracentesis with Tube Insertion32002

Polio
Antibody86658
Vaccine90712-90713

Poliovirus Vaccine
See Vaccines

Pollicization
Digit26550

Polya Gastrectomy
See Gastrectomy, Partial

Polydactylism
See Polydactyly; Supernumerary Digit

Polydactyly
Digit
 Reconstruction26587
 Repair26587
Toe28344

Polymerase Chain Reaction83898

Polyp
Antrochoanal
 Removal31032
Esophagus
 Ablation43228
Nose
 Excision
 Endoscopic31237-31240
 Extensive30115
 Simple30110
Sphenoid Sinus
 Removal31051
Urethra
 Excision53260

Polypectomy
Nose
 Endoscopic31237
Uterus58558

Polypeptide, Vasoactive Intestinal
See Vasoactive Intestinal Peptide

Polysomnography95808-95811

Polyuria Test
See Water Load Test

Pomeroy's Operation
See Tubal Ligation

Pooling
Blood Products86965

Popliteal Arteries
See Artery, Popliteal

Popliteal Synovial Cyst
See Baker's Cyst

Poradenitistras
See Lymphogranuloma Venereum

PORP (Partial Ossicular Replacement Prosthesis)69633, 69637

Porphobilinogen
Urine84106-84110

Positive
Continuous (CPAP)94660

Pressure
Blood
See Blood Pressure
Measurement of Sphincter of Oddi
See Sphincter of Oddi, Pressure
Measurement
Sensor, Aneurysm
Placement0153T
Study .0154T
Ulcer (Decubitus)
See Debridement; Skin Graft and Flap
Excision15920-15999
Venous
See Blood Pressure, Venous

Pretreatment
Red Blood Cell
Antibody Identification86970-86972
Serum
Antibody Identification86975-86978

Prevention & Control
See Prophylaxis

Preventive Medicine99381-99397
See Immunization; Newborn Care, Normal; Office
and/or Other Outpatient Services; Performance
Measures, Prophylactic Treatment
Administration/Interpretation of Health Risk
Assessment .99420
Counseling and/or Risk Factor Reduction
Intervention99401-99429
Group Counseling99411-99412
Individual Counseling99401-99404
Established Patient99382-99397
New Patient99381-99387
Newborn Care .99432
Respiratory Pattern Recording94772
Unlisted Services and Procedures99429

Priapism
Repair
Fistulization54435
with Shunt54420-54430

Primidone
Assay .80188

PRL
See Prolactin

Pro-Insulin C Peptide
See C-Peptide

Proalbumin
See Prealbumin

Probes, DNA
See Nucleic Acid Probe

Probes, Nucleic Acid
See Nucleic Acid Probe

Procainamide
Assay .80190-80192

Process
See Anatomic term (eg coracoid, odontoid)

Procidentia
Rectum
Excision45130-45135
Repair .45900

Procoagulant Activity, Glomerular
See Thromboplastin

Proconvertin85230

Proctectasis
See Dilation, Rectum

Proctectomy
Partial
Open45111, 45113-45116, 45123
Total45110, 45112, 45119-45120
Laparoscopic45395-45397
Open45110, 45112, 45119-45120
with Colon45121
with Colectomy44157-44158
with Colectomy/Ileostomy
Lapraroscopic44212
Open .44155

Proctocele
See Rectocele

Proctopexy
Laparoscopic45400-45402
with Sigmoid Resection45402
Open .45540-45541
with Sigmoid Excision45550

Proctoplasty45500-45505

Proctorrhaphy
See Rectum, Suture

Proctoscopies
See Anoscopy

Proctosigmoidoscopy
Ablation
Polyp or Lesion45320
Biopsy .45305
Destruction
Tumor .45320
Dilation .45303
Exploration .45300
Hemorrhage Control45317
Placement
Stent .45327
Removal
Foreign Body45307
Polyp45308-45315
Tumor .45315
Volvulus Repair45321

Products, Gene
See Protein

Proetz Therapy
Nose .30210

Profibrinolysin
See Plasminogen

Progenitor Cell
See Stem Cell

Progesterone84144

Progesterone Receptors84234

Progestin Receptors
See Progesterone Receptors

Proinsulin .84206

Projective Test96101-96103

Prokallikrein
See Fletcher Factor

Prokallikrein, Plasma
See Fletcher Factor

Prokinogenase
See Fletcher Factor

Prolactin80418, 80440, 84146

Prolapse
See Procidentia

Prolapse, Rectal
See Procidentia, Rectum

Prolastin
See Alpha-1 Antitrypsin

Prolonged Services99354-99357,
99360
without Direct Patient Contact99358-99359

Prophylactic Treatment
See Preventive Medicine
Femoral Neck and Proximal Femur
Nailing .27187
Pinning .27187
Wiring .27187
Femur .27495
Nailing .27495
Pinning .27495
Wiring .27495
Humerus
Pinning, Wiring24498
Radius25490, 25492
Nailing25490, 25492
Pinning25490, 25492
Plating25490, 25492
Wiring25490, 25492
Shoulder
Clavicle .23490
Humerus .23491
Tibia .27745
Ulna .25491-25492
Nailing25491-25492
Pinning25491-25492
Plating25491-25492
Wiring25491-25492

Prophylaxis
Retina
Detachment
Cryotherapy, Diathermy67141
Photocoagulation67145

Prostaglandin84150
Insertion .59200

Prostanoids
See Prostaglandin

Provitamin A
See Vitamin, A

Provocation Test
See Allergy Tests
for Glaucoma92140

Provocation Tonography92130

Prower Factor
See Stuart-Prower Factor

PSA
See Prostate Specific Antigen

Pseudocyst, Pancreas
See Pancreas, Pseudocyst

PSG
See Polysomnography

Psoriasis Treatment96910-96922
See Dermatology; Photochemotherapy

Psychiatric Diagnosis
Evaluation of Records or Reports90885
Interventional Evaluation
 Interactive90802
Interview and Evaluation90801-90802
Psychological Testing96101-96103
 Computer-Assisted96103
Unlisted Services and Procedures90899

Psychiatric Treatment
See Psychotherapy
Biofeedback Training90875-90876
Consultation with Family90887
Drug Management90862
Electroconvulsive Therapy90870
Environmental Intervention90882
Family90846-90849, 99510
Group.........................90853-90857
Hypnotherapy90880
Individual
 Insight-Oriented
 Home Visit99510
 Hospital or Residential Care ..90816-90822
 Office or Outpatient90804-90809
 Interactive
 Home Visit99510
 Hospital or Residential Care ..90823-90829
 Office or Outpatient90810-90815
Narcosynthesis Analysis90865
Psychoanalysis90845
Report Preparation90889
Residential
 Facility Care90816-90829
Unlisted Services and Procedures90899

Psychoanalysis90845

Psychophysiologic Feedback
See Biofeedback

Psychotherapy
Family90846-90849, 99510
Group.........................90853-90857
 Insight-Oriented
 Hospital or Residential Care ..90816-90822
 Office or Outpatient90804-90809

Interactive
 Hospital or Residential Care ..90823-90829
 Office or Outpatient90810-90815

PTA....................................85270

PTA (Factor XI)
See Clotting Factor

PTC Factor85250

PTCA
See Percutaneous Transluminal Angioplasty

Pteroylglutamic Acid
See Folic Acid

Pterygium
Excision65420
 with Graft65426

Pterygomaxillary Fossa
Incision31040

Pterygopalatine Ganglion
See Sphenopalatine Ganglion

PTH
See Parathormone

Ptosis
See Blepharoptosis; Procidentia

PTT
See Thromboplastin, Partial, Time

Ptyalectasis
See Dilation, Salivary Duct

Pubic Symphysis27282

Pubis
Craterization27070
Cyst
 Excision27065-27067
Excision27070
Saucerization27070
Tumor
 Excision27065-27067

Pudendal Nerve
Avulsion64761
Destruction64630
Incision64761
Injection
 Anesthetic64430
 Neurolytic64630
Transection64761

Puestow Procedure48548

Pulled Elbow
See Nursemaid Elbow

Pulmonary Artery
Banding33690
Catheterization36013-36015
Embolism33910-33916
 Excision33910-33916
Percutaneous Transluminal
Angioplasty92997-92998
Reimplantation33788
Repair33690, 33917-33920
 Reimplantation33788

Shunt
 from Aorta33755-33762, 33924
 from Vena Cava33766-33767
 Subclavian33750
Transection33922

Pulmonary Function Test
See Pulmonology, Diagnostic

Pulmonary Haemorrhage
See Hemorrhage, Lung

Pulmonary Perfusion Imaging
Nuclear Medicine78588

Pulmonary Valve
Incision33470-33474
Repair33470-33474
Replacement33475

Pulmonary Vein
Repair
 Complete33730
 Partial33724
 Stenosis33726
Stenosis
 Repair33726

Pulmonology
Diagnostic
 Airway Closing Volume94370
 Apnea Monitoring
 Pediatric94774-94777
 Bronchodilation94664
 Carbon Dioxide Response Curve94400
 Carbon Monoxide Diffusion Capacity ..94720
 Expired Gas Analysis
 CO0043T
 CO_294770
 NO95012
 O_2 and CO_294681
 O_2 Update, Direct94680
 O_2 Uptake, Indirect94690
 Quantitative94250
 Spectroscopy0064T
 Flow-Volume Loop94375
 Function Study78596
 Functional Residual Capacity94240
 Hemoglobin O_2 Affinity82820
 High Altitude Simulation
 Test (HAST)94452-94453
 Hypoxia Response Curve94450
 Inhalation Treatment94640
 Maldistribution of Inspired Air94350
 Maximum Breathing Capacity94200
 Maximum Voluntary Ventilation94200
 Membrane Compliance94750
 Membrane Diffusion Capacity94725
 Nitrogen Washout Curve94350
 Oximetry
 Ear or Pulse94760-94762
 Resistance to Airflow94360
 Spectroscopy0064T
 Spirometry94010-94070
 Evaluation94010-94070
 Patient Initiated with
 Bronchospasm94014-94016
 Sputum Mobilization with
 Inhalants94664
 Stress Test94621

Q

R

Radiation
See Irradiation

Radiation Physics
Consultation77336-77370
Unlisted Services and Procedures77399

Radiation Therapy77280-77295
Consultation
 Radiation Physics77336-77370
CT Guidance .77014
Dose Plan77300, 77305-77331
 Brachytherapy77326-77328
 Intensity Modulation77301
 Teletherapy77305-77321
Field Set-up77280-77295
Planning77261-77263, 77299
Special .77470
Stereotactic
 Body .77373
 Cerebral Lesions77371-77372
 Guidance77421
Treatment Delivery77371-77373
 2 Areas77407-77411
 3 or More Areas77412-77416
 Beam Modulation0073T
 High Energy Neutron Radiation .77422-77423
 Intensity Modulation77418
 Proton Beam77520-77525
 Single Area77402-77406, 77422
 Stereotactic77371-77373
 Body .77373
 Superficial77401
 Weekly .77427
Treatment Device77332-77334
Treatment Management
 1 or 2 Fractions Only77431
 Stereotactic
 Body .77435
 Cerebral77432
 Unlisted Services and Procedures77499
 Weekly .77427

Radiation, X
See X-Ray

Radical Excision of Lymph Nodes
See Excision, Lymph Nodes, Radical

Radical Mastectomies, Modified
See Mastectomy, Modified Radical

Radical Neck Dissection
Laryngectomy31365-31368
Pharyngolaryngectomy31390-31395
with Auditory Canal Surgery69155
with Thyroidectomy60254
with Tongue Excision 41135, 41145, 41153-41155

Radical Resection
See Resection, Radical
Abdomen .51597
Acetabulum .27076
Ankle .27615
Arm, Lower .25077
Calcaneus .27647
Elbow
 Capsule, Soft Tissue, Bone
 with Contracture Release24149
Face .21015

Fibula .27646
Finger .26117
Foot .28046
Forearm .25077
Hand .26115
Hip
 Soft Tissue27049
 Tumor or Infection27075-27076
Humerus23220-23222
Innominate .27077
Ischial27078-27079
Knee .27329
Leg
 Lower .27615
 Upper .27329
Metacarpal26250-26255
Metatarsal .28173
Mouth
 with Tongue Excision41150, 41155
Ovarian Tumor
 Bilateral Salpingo-Oophorectomy-
 Omentectomy58950-58956
 with Radical Dissection for
 Debulking58952-58954
 with Total Abdominal
 Hysterectomy58951, 58953-58956
Pelvis
 Soft Tissue27049
Peritoneal Tumor
 Bilateral Salpingo-Oophorectomy-
 Omentectomy58952-58956
 with Radical Dissection for
 Debulking58952-58954
Phalanges
 Finger26260-26262
 Toe .28175
Radius .25170
Scalp .21015
Scapula .23210
Shoulder .23077
Sternum21630-21632
Talus
 Tumor .27647
Tarsal .28171
Tibia .27645
Tonsil42842-42845
Tumor
 Back/Flank21935
 Femur .27365
 Knee27329, 27365
 Leg, Upper27329
 Neck .21557
 Thorax .21557
Ulna .25170
Wrist .25077

Radical Vaginal Hysterectomy
See Hysterectomy, Vaginal, Radical

Radical Vulvectomy
See Vulvectomy, Radical

Radio-Cobalt B12 Schilling Test
See Vitamin, B12, Absorption Study

Radioactive Colloid Therapy . . .79300

Radioactive Substance
Insertion

Prostate .55860

Radiocarpal Joint
Arthrotomy .25040
Dislocation
 Closed Treatment25660

Radiocinematographies
See Cineradiography

Radioelement
Application77761-77778
 Surface .77789
 with Ultrasound76965
Handling .77790
Infusion .77750

Radioelement Substance
Catheter Placement
 Breast19296-19298
 Bronchus31643
 Prostate .55875
Needle Placement
 Prostate55875-55876

Radiography
See Radiology, Diagnostic; X-Ray

Radioimmunosorbent Test
See Gammaglobulin, Blood

Radioisotope Brachytherapy
See Brachytherapy

Radioisotope Scan
See Nuclear Medicine

Radiological Marker
Preoperative Placement
 Excision of Breast Lesion19125-19126

Radiology
See Nuclear Medicine, Radiation Therapy, X-Ray,
Ultrasound
Diagnostic
 Unlisted Services and Procedures76499
Stress Views77071

Radionuclide CT Scan
See Emission Computerized Tomography

Radionuclide Imaging
See Nuclear Medicine

Radionuclide Therapy
See Radiopharmaceutical Therapy

Radionuclide Tomography, Single-Photon Emission-Computed
See SPECT

Radiopharmaceutical Therapy
Interstitial .79300
Intra-Arterial .79445
Intra-Articular79440
Intracavitary .79200
Intravenous79101, 79403
Oral .79005
Unlisted Services and Procedures79999

Radiotherapeutic
See Radiation Therapy

Artificial Intervertebral Disc
 Cervical Interspace0093T, 0095T
 Lumbar Interspace22865, 0164T
Balloon
 Intra-Aortic33974
Balloon Assist Device
 Intra-Aortic33968, 33971
Blood Clot
 Eye .65930
Blood Component
 Apheresis36511-36516
Breast
 Capsules19371
 Implants19328-19330
 Modified Radical19307
 Partial19300-19302
 Radical19305-19306
 Simple, Complete19303
 Subcutaneous19304
Calcareous Deposits
 Subdeltoid23000
Calculi (Stone)
 Bile Duct43264, 47420-47425
 Percutaneous47554, 47630
 Bladder51050, 52310-52318, 52352
 Gallbladder47480
 Hepatic Duct47400
 Kidney50060-50081, 50130, 50561,
 50580, 52352
 Pancreas48020
 Pancreatic Duct43264
 Salivary Gland42330-42340
 Ureter50610-50630, 50961, 50980,
 51060-51065, 52320-52330, 52352
 Urethra52310-52315, 52352
Cardiac Event Recorder33284
Cast .29700-29715
Cataract
 with Replacement
 Extracapsular66982, 66984
 Intracapsular66983
 Not Associated with Concurrent66983
Catheter
 Central Venous36589
 Fractured75961
 Peritoneum49422
 Spinal Cord62355
Cerclage
 Cervix .59871
Cerumen
 Auditory Canal, External69210
Clot
 Pericardium33020
 Endoscopic32658
Comedones .10040
Contraceptive Capsules11976-11977
Cranial Tongs20665
Cyst .10040
Dacryolith
 Lacrimal Duct68530
 Lacrimal Gland68530
Defibrillator
 Heart .33244
 Pulse Generator Only33241
 via Thoracotomy33243
Drug Delivery Implant11982-11983
Ear Wax
 Auditory Canal, External69210

Electrode
 Brain61535, 61880
 Heart .33238
 Nerve .64585
 Spinal Cord63660
 Stomach0156T, 0158T, 43648, 43882
Embolus
 See Embolectomy
External Fixation System20694
Eye
 Bone67414, 67445
 Ocular Contents
 with Implant65093
 without Implant65091
 Orbital Contents Only65110
 with Bone65112
 with Implant
 Muscles Attached65105
 Muscles, Not Attached65103
 with Muscle or Myocutaneous Flap . . .65114
 without Implant65101
Fallopian Tube
 Laparoscopy58661
 with Hysterectomy . . .58542, 58544, 58548
Fat
 Lipectomy15876-15879
Fecal Impaction
 Rectum45915
Fibrin Deposit32150
Fixation Device20670-20680
Foreign Body65205-65265
 Anal .46608
 Ankle Joint27610, 27620
 Arm
 Lower25248
 Upper24200-24201
 Auditory Canal, External69200
 with Anesthesia69205
 Bile Duct43269
 Bladder52310-52315
 Brain61570, 62163
 Bronchi31635
 Colon44025, 44390, 45379
 Colon-Sigmoid45332
 Conjunctival Embedded65210
 Cornea
 with Slit Lamp65222
 without Slit Lamp65220
 Duodenum44010
 Elbow24000, 24101, 24200-24201
 Esophagus43020, 43045, 43215, 74235
 External Eye65205
 Eyelid .67938
 Finger26075-26080
 Foot28190-28193
 Gastrointestinal, Upper43247
 Gum .41805
 Hand .26070
 Hip27033, 27086-27087
 Hysteroscopy58562
 Interphalangeal Joint
 Toe .28024
 Intertarsal Joint28020
 Intestines, Small44020, 44363
 Intraocular65235
 Kidney50561, 50580
 Knee Joint27310, 27331, 27372

Lacrimal Duct68530
Lacrimal Gland68530
Larynx31511, 31530-31531, 31577
Leg, Upper .27372
Lung .32151
Mandible .41806
Mediastinum39000-39010
Metatarsophalangeal Joint28022
Mouth40804-40805
Muscle20520-20525
Nose .30300
 Anesthesia30310
 Lateral Rhinotomy30320
Orbit61334, 67413, 67430
 with Bone Flap67430
 without Bone Flap67413
Pancreatic Duct43269
Patella
 See Patellectomy
Pelvis27086-27087
Penile Tissue54115
Penis .54115
Pericardium33020
 Endoscopic32658
Peritoneum49402
Pharynx .42809
Pleura32150-32151
 Endoscopic32653
Posterior Segment
 Magnetic Extraction65260
 Nonmagnetic Extraction65265
Rectum45307, 45915
Scrotum .55120
Shoulder23040-23044
 Complicated23332
 Deep .23331
 Subcutaneous23330
Skin
 with Debridement11010-11012
Stomach .43500
Subcutaneous Tissue10120-10121
 with Debridement11010-11012
Tarsometatarsal Joint28020
Tendon Sheath20520-20525
Toe .28022
Ureter50961, 50980
Urethra52310-52315
Uterus .58562
Vagina .57415
Wrist25040, 25101, 25248
Hair
 Electrolysis17380
Halo .20665
Hearing Aid
 Bone Conduction69711
Hematoma
 Brain61312-61315
Implantation20670-20680
 Ankle .27704
 Contraceptive Capsules11976-11977
 Disc .22865
 Elbow .24160
 Eye67120-67121
 Finger .26320
 Hand .26320
 Radius .24164
 Wrist .25449

Renal Abscess
See Abscess, Kidney

Renal Arteries
See Artery, Renal

Renal Autotransplantation
See Autotransplantation, Renal

Renal Calculus
See Calculus, Removal, Kidney

Renal Cyst
See Cyst, Kidney

Renal Dialyses
See Hemodialysis

Renal Disease Services
See Dialysis

Renal Transplantation
See Kidney, Transplantation

Renin80408, 80416, 84244
Peripheral Vein80417

Renin-Converting Enzyme82164

Reoperation
Carotid
 Thromboendarterectomy35390
Coronary Artery Bypass
 Valve Procedure33530
Distal Vessel Bypass35700

Repair

See Revision
Abdomen49900
 Hernia49491-49525, 49565, 49570,
 49582-49590
 Omphalocele49600-49611
 Suture49900
Abdominal Wall15830, 15847
Anal
 Anomaly46744-46748
 Fistula ...0170T, 46288, 46706, 46715-46716
 Stricture46700-46705
Anastomosis
 Cyst47719
Aneurysm
 Aorta
 Abdominal0078T-0081T
 Infrarenal34800-34805, 34825-34832
 Imaging75952-75953
 Thoracic33877-33886
 Arteriovenous36834
 Iliac Artery75954
 Intracranial Artery61697-61708
Ankle
 Ligament27695-27698
 Tendon ...27612, 27650-27654, 27680-27687
Aorta33320-33322, 33802-33803
 Coarctation33840-33851
 Graft33860-33877
 Sinus of Valsalva33702-33720
 Thoracic75956-75959
 Endovascular33880-33891
Aortic Arch
 with Cardiopulmonary Bypass33853
 without Cardiopulmonary Bypass33852
Aortic Valve33400-33403
 Obstruction
 Outflow Tract33414
 Septic Hypertrophy33416
 Stenosis33415
Arm
 Lower25260-25263, 25270
 Fasciotomy24495
 Secondary25265, 25272-25274
 Tendon25290
 Tendon Sheath25275
 Muscle24341
 Tendon24332, 24341, 25280, 25295,
 25310-25316
 Upper
 Muscle Revision24330-24331
 Muscle Transfer24301, 24320
 Tendon Lengthening24305
 Tendon Revision24320
 Tendon Transfer24301
 Tenotomy24310
Arteriovenous Aneurysm36834
Arteriovenous Fistula
 Abdomen35182
 Acquired or Traumatic35189
 Head35180
 Acquired or Traumatic35188
 Lower Extremity35184
 Acquired or Traumatic35190
 Neck35180
 Acquired or Traumatic35188
 Thorax35182
 Acquired or Traumatic35189

 Upper Extremity35184
 Acquired or Traumatic35190
Arteriovenous Malformation
 Intracranial61680-61692
 Intracranial Artery61705-61708
 Spinal Artery62294
 Spinal Cord63250-63252
Artery
 Angioplasty75962-75968
 Aorta35452, 35472
 Axillary35458
 Brachiocephalic35458, 35475
 Bypass Graft35501-35571, 35601-35683,
 35691-35695, 35700
 Bypass In-Situ35583-35587
 Bypass Venous Graft33510-33516,
 35510-35525
 Coronary33507
 Femoral35456, 35474
 Iliac34900, 35454, 35473
 Occlusive Disease35001, 35005-35021,
 35045-35081, 35091, 35102, 35111, 35121,
 35131, 35141, 35151
 Popliteal35456, 35474
 Pulmonary33690
 Renal35450
 Renal or Visceral35471
 Subclavian35458
 Thromboendarterectomy35301-35321,
 35341-35390
 Tibioperoneal35459, 35470
 Viscera35450, 35471
Arytenoid Cartilage31400
Atria
 Laparoscopic33265-33266
 Open33254-33256
Bile Duct47701
 Cyst47719
 with Intestines47760, 47780-47785
 Wound47900
Bladder
 Exstrophy51940
 Fistula44660-44661, 45800-45805,
 51880-51925
 Neck51845
 Resection52500
 Wound51860-51865
Blepharoptosis
 Frontalis Muscle Technique
 with Fascial Sling67902
Blood Vessel
 Abdomen35221
 with Other Graft35281
 with Vein Graft35251
 Chest35211-35216
 with Other Graft35271-35276
 with Vein Graft35241-35246
 Finger35207
 Graft Defect35870
 Hand35207
 Kidney50100
 Lower Extremity35226
 with Other Graft35286
 with Vein Graft35256
 Neck35201
 with Other Graft35261
 with Vein Graft35231

 Upper Extremity35206
 with Other Graft35266
 with Vein Graft35236
Body Cast29720
Brain
 Wound61571
Breast
 Suspension19316
Bronchi
 Fistula32815
Brow Pyrosis67900
Bunion28290-28299
Bypass Graft35901-35907
 Fistula35870
Calcaneus
 Osteotomy28300
Cannula36860-36861
Carpal25440
Carpal Bone25431
Cervix
 Cerclage57700
 Abdominal59320-59325
 Suture57720
Chest Wall32905
 Closure32810
 Fistula32906
Chin
 Augmentation21120, 21123
 Osteotomy21121-21123
Clavicle
 Osteotomy23480-23485
Cleft Hand26580
Cleft Lip40525-40527, 40700-40761
 Nasal Deformity .40700-40701, 40720-40761
Cleft Palate
 See Cleft Palate Repair
Colon
 Fistula44650-44661
 Hernia44050
 Malrotation44055
 Obstruction44050
Cornea
 See Cornea, Repair
Coronary Chamber Fistula33500-33501
Cyst
 Bartholin's Gland56440
 Choledochal47719
 Liver47300
Diaphragm
 for Eventration39545
 Hernia39502-39541
 Laceration39501
Ductus Arteriosus33820-33824
Ear, Middle
 Oval Window Fistula69666
 Round Window Fistula69667
Elbow
 Fasciotomy24350-24356
 Hemiepiphyseal Arrest24470
 Ligament24343-24346
 Muscle24341
 Muscle Transfer24301
 Tendon24340-24342
 Each24341
 Tendon Lengthening24305
 Tendon Transfer24301
 Tennis Elbow24350-24356

Wrist25260-25263, 25270, 25447
 Bone .25440
 Carpal Bone .25431
 Cartilage .25107
 Removal
 Implant .25449
 Secondary25265, 25272-25274
 Tendon .25280-25316
 Tendon Sheath25275
 Total Replacement25446

Repeat Surgeries
See Reoperation

Replacement
Adjustable Gastric Band43773
Aortic Valve33405-33413
Arthroplasties, Hip
 See Arthroplasty, Hip
Artificial Heart
 Intracorporeal0052T, 0053T
Cerebrospinal Fluid Shunt62160, 62194,
 62225-62230
Contact Lens
 See Contact Lens Services
Elbow
 Total .24363
Electrode
 Heart33210-33211, 33216-33217
 Stomach0155T, 0157T, 43647
Eye
 Drug Delivery System67121
Gastrostomy Tube43760
Hearing Aid
 Bone Conduction69710
Hip .27130-27132
 Revision27134-27138
Implant
 Bone
 for External Speech Processor/Cochlear
 Stimulator69717-69718
Intervertebral Disc
 Cervical Interspace0090T
 Lumbar Interspace0163T, 22862
Knee
 Total .27447
Mitral Valve .33430
Nephrostomy Tube
 See Nephrostomy, Change Tube
Nerve .64726
Neurostimulator
 Pulse Generator/Receiver
 Intracranial61885
 Peripheral Nerve64590
 Spinal .63685
Ossicles
 with Prosthesis69633, 69637
Ossicular Replacement
 See TORP (Total Ossicular Replacement
 Prosthesis)
Pacemaker33206-33208
 Catheter .33210
 Electrode33210-33211, 33216-33217
Pacing Cardioverter-Defibrillator
 Leads33243-33244
 Pulse Generator Only33241
Penile
 Prosthesis54410-54411, 54416-54417

Prosthesis
 Skull .62143
 Urethral Sphincter53448
Pulmonary Valve33475
Pulse Generator
 Brain .61885
 Peripheral Nerve64590
 Spinal Cord .63685
Receiver
 Brain .61885
 Peripheral Nerve64590
 Spinal Cord .63685
Skin
 Acellular Dermal Matrix15170-15176
Skull Plate .62143
Spinal Cord
 Reservoir .62360
Stent
 Ureteral50382, 50387
Subcutaneous Port
 for Gastric Restrictive Procedure43888
Tissue Expanders
 Skin .11970
Total Replacement
 See Hip, Total Replacement
Total Replacement Heart System
 Intracorporeal0052T, 0053T
Tricuspid Valve .33465
Ureter
 with Intestines50840
Venous Access Device36582-36583, 36585
 Catheter .36578
Venous Catheter
 Central36580-36581, 36584

Replantation
Arm, Upper .20802
Digit .20816-20822
Foot .20838
Forearm .20805
Hand .20808
Thumb .20824-20827

Report Preparation
Extended, Medical99080
Psychiatric .90889

Reposition
Toe to Hand26551-26556

Repositioning
Central Venous Catheter36597
Electrode
 Heart33215-33217, 33226
Gastrostomy Tube43761
Heart
 Defibrillator
 Leads33215-33216, 33226, 33249
Intraocular Lens66825
Tricuspid Valve .33468

Reproductive Tissue
Cryopreserved
 Preparation
 Thawing .89354
 Storage .89344

Reprogramming
Shunt
 Brain .62252

Reptilase Test85635

Reptilase Time
See Thrombin Time

Resection
Aortic Valve
 Stenosis .33415
Bladder Diverticulum52305
Bladder Neck
 Transurethral52500
Brain Lobe
 See Lobectomy, Brain
Chest Wall19260-19272
Diaphragm39560-39561
Endaural
 See Ear, Inner, Excision
Humeral Head .23195
Intestines, Small
 Laparoscopic44202-44203
Lung .32503-32504
Mouth
 with Tongue Excision41153
Myocardium
 Aneurysm .33542
 Septal Defect33545
Nasal Septum Submucous
 See Nasal Septum, Submucous Resection
Nose
 Septum .30520
Ovary, Wedge
 See Ovary, Wedge Resection
Palate .42120
Phalangeal Head
 Toe .28153
Prostate Transurethral
 See Prostatectomy, Transurethral
Radical
 Arm, Upper .24077
 Elbow .24077
 with Contracture Release24149
 Foot .28046
 Humerus24150-24151
 Radius24152-24153
 Tumor
 Ankle .27615
 Calcaneus or Talus27647
 Clavicle .23200
 Femur .27365
 Fibula .27646
 Humerus .23220
 Humerus with Autograft23221
 Humerus with Prosthetic
 Replacement23222
 Knee27329, 27365
 Leg, Lower27615
 Leg, Upper27329
 Metatarsal28173
 Phalanx, Toe28175
 Scapula .23210
 Tarsal .28171
 Tibia .27645
Ribs19260-19272, 32900
Synovial Membrane
 See Synovectomy
Temporal Bone .69535

Venous Access Device36576-36578,
36582-36583, 36585
Ventricle
Ventriculomyectomy33416
Ventriculomyotomy33416

Rh (D)
See Blood Typing

Rh Immune Globulin
See Immune Globulins, Rho (D)

Rheumatoid Factor86430-86431

Rhinectomy
Partial .30150
Total .30160

Rhinomanometry92512

Rhinopharynx
See Nasopharynx

Rhinophototherapy0168T

Rhinophyma
Repair .30120

Rhinoplasty
Cleft Lip/Cleft Palate30460-30462
Primary .30400-30420
Secondary30430-30450

Rhinoscopy
See Endoscopy, Nose

Rhinotomy
Lateral .30118, 30320

Rhizotomy63185-63190

Rho Variant Du86905

Rhytidectomy15824-15829

Rhytidoplasties
See Face Lift

Rib
Antibody .86756
Antigen Detection
by Immunoassay
with Direct Optical Observation
Direct Fluorescense87280
Enzyme Immunoassay87420
Excision21600-21616, 32900
Fracture
Closed Treatment21800
External Fixation21810
Open Treatment21805
Graft
to Face .21230
Resection19260-19272, 32900
X-Ray .71100-71111

Riboflavin .84252

**Richardson Operation
Hysterectomy**
See Hysterectomy, Abdominal, Total

Richardson Procedure53460

Rickettsia
Antibody .86757

Ridell Operation
See Sinusotomy, Frontal

Ridge, Alveolar
See Alveolar Ridge

Right Atrioventricular Valve
See Tricuspid Valve

Right Heart Cardiac Catheterization
See Cardiac Catheterization, Right Heart

Ripstein Operation
See Proctopexy

Risk Factor Reduction Intervention
See Performance Measures, Preventive Medicine

Risser Jacket29010-29015
Removal .29710

Rocky Mountain Spotted Fever 86000

Roentgen Rays
See X-Ray

Roentgenographic
See X-Ray

Roentgenography
See Radiology, Diagnostic

Ropes Test .83872

Rorschach Test96101

Ross Procedure33413

Rotation Flap
See Skin, Adjacent Tissue Transfer

Rotator Cuff
Repair .23410-23420

Rotavirus
Antibody .86759
Antigen Detection
Enzyme Immunoassay87425

Rotavirus Vaccine90680

Round Window
Repair Fistula .69667

Round Window Fistula
See Fistula, Round Window

Roux-En-Y Procedure43621,
43633-43634, 43644, 43846, 47740-47741,
47780-47785, 48540

RPR .86592-86593

RSV
See Immune Globulins; Respiratory Syncytial
Virus

RT3
See Triiodothyronine, Reverse

Rubbing Alcohol
See Isopropyl Alcohol

Rubella
Antibody .86762
Vaccine .90706

Rubella HI Test
See Hemagglutination Inhibition Test

Rubella/Mumps
See Vaccines

Rubeola
Antibody .86765
Antigen Detection
Immunofluorescence87283

Rubeolla
See Rubeola

**Russell Viper Venom
Time** .85612-85613

S

Sac, Endolymphatic
See Endolymphatic Sac

Saccomanno Technique88108

Sacral Nerve
Implantation
Electrode64561, 64581
Insertion
Electrode64561, 64581

Sacroiliac Joint
Arthrodesis .27280
Arthrotomy .27050
Biopsy .27050
Dislocation
Open Treatment27218
Fusion .27280
Injection for Arthrography27096
X-Ray72200-72202, 73542

Sacrum
Tumor
Excision .49215
X-Ray .72220

Sahli Test
See Gastroenterology, Diagnostic, Stomach

Salicylate
Assay .80196

Saline-Solution Abortion
See Abortion, Induced, by Saline

Salivary Duct
Catheterization .42660
Dilation .42650-42660
Ligation .42665
Repair .42500-42505
Fistula .42600

Salivary Gland Virus
See Cytomegalovirus

Dislocation
 Open Treatment23660
 with Greater Tuberosity Fracture
 Closed Treatment23665
 Open Treatment23670
 with Surgical or Anatomical Neck Fracture
 Closed Treatment with Manipulation 23675
 Open Treatment23680
Excision
 Torn Cartilage23101
Exploration23040-23044
Incision and Drainage23040-23044
Removal
 Foreign Body23040-23044
X-Ray .73050

Shunt(s)
Aqueous
 to Extraocular Reservoir66180
 Revision .66185
Arteriovenous
 See Arteriovenous Shunt
Brain
 Creation62180-62223
 Removal62256-62258
 Replacement62160, 62194,
 62225-62230, 62258
 Reprogramming62252
Cerebrospinal Fluid
 See Cerebrospinal Fluid Shunt
Creation
 Arteriovenous
 Direct .36821
 ECMO .36822
 Thomas Shunt36835
 Transposition36818-36820
 with Bypass Graft35686
 with Graft36825-36830
 Cerebrospinal Fluid62200
 Thomas Shunt36835
Fetal .59076
Great Vessel
 Aorta
 Pulmonary .33924
 Aorta to Pulmonary Artery
 Ascending .33755
 Descending33762
 Central .33764
 Subclavian Pulmonary Artery33750
 Vena Cava to Pulmonary Artery .33766-33768
Intra-Atrial33735-33737
LeVeen
 See LeVeen Shunt
Nonvascular
 X-Ray .75809
Peritoneal
 Venous
 Injection .49427
 Ligation .49428
 Removal .49429
 X-Ray .75809
Pulmonary Artery
 See Pulmonary Artery, Shunt
Revision
 Arteriovenous36832
Spinal Cord
 Creation63740-63741
 Irrigation .63744

 Removal .63746
 Replacement63744
Superior Mesenteric-Caval
 See Anastomosis, Caval to Mesenteric
Ureter to Colon .50815
Ventriculocisternal with Valve
 See Ventriculocisternostomy

Shuntogram75809

Sialic Acid .84275

Sialodochoplasty42500-42505

Sialogram
See Sialography

Sialography70390

Sickling
Electrophoresis .83020

Siderocytes .85536

Siderophilin
See Transferrin

Sigmoid
See Colon-Sigmoid

Sigmoid Bladder
Cystectomy .51590

Sigmoidoscopy
Ablation
 Polyp .45339
 Tumor .45339
Biopsy .45331
Collection
 Specimen .45331
Exploration45330, 45335
Hemorrhage Control45334
Injection
 Submucosal .45335
Needle Biopsy .45342
Placement
 Stent .45345
Removal
 Foreign Body45332
 Polyp45333, 45338
 Tumor45333, 45338
Repair
 Volvulus .45337
Ultrasound45341-45342

Signal-Averaged Electrocardiography
See Electrocardiogram

Silica .84285

Silicon Dioxide
See Silica

Silicone
Contouring Injections11950-11954

Silver Operation
See Keller Procedure

Silver Procedure28290

Simple Mastectomies
See Mastectomy

Single Photon Absorptiometry
See Absorptiometry, Single Photon

Single Photon Emission Computed Tomography
See SPECT

Sinu, Sphenoid
See Sinus/Sinuses, Sphenoid

Sinus/Sinuses
Ethmoid
 Excision31200-31205
 with Nasal/Sinus Endoscopy .31254-31255
 Repair of Cerebrospinal Leak31290
Ethmoidectomy
 Excision .31254
Frontal
 Destruction31080-31085
 Exploration31070-31075
 with Nasal/Sinus Endoscopy31276
 Fracture
 Open Treatment21343-21344
 Incision31070-31087
Injection .20500
 Diagnostic .20501
Maxillary
 Antrostomy31256-31267
 Excision31225-31230
 Exploration31020-31032
 with Nasal/Sinus Endoscopy31233
 Incision31020-31032, 31256-31267
 Irrigation .31000
 Skull Base .61581
 Surgery .61581
Multiple
 Incision .31090
 Paranasal
 Incision .31090
Pilonidal
 See Cyst, Pilonidal
Sinus of Valsalva
 Repair33702-33722
Sinus Venosus
 Repair .33645
Sphenoid
 Biopsy31050-31051
 Exploration31050-31051
 with Nasal/Sinus Endoscopy31235
 Incision31050-31051
 with Nasal/Sinus Endoscopy .31287-31288
 Irrigation .31002
 Repair of Cerebrospinal Leak31291
 Sinusotomy31050-31051
 Skull Base Surgery61580-61581
Unlisted Services and Procedures31299
X-Ray .70210-70220

Sinusectomy, Ethmoid
See Sinus/Sinuses; Ethmoidectomy

Sinusoidal Rotational Testing
See Ear, Nose and Throat

Drill Hole
Catheter61107
Drainage Hematoma61108
Exploration61105
Excision61501
Exploration
Drill Hole61105
Fracture62000-62010
Hematoma
Drainage61108
Incision
Suture61550-61552
Insertion
Catheter61107
Lesion
Excision ..61500, 61600-61608, 61615-61616
Orbit
Biopsy61332
Excision
Lesion61333
Exploration61332-61334
Removal Foreign Body61334
Puncture
Cervical61050
Cisternal61050
Drain Fluid61070
Injection61070
Subdural61000-61001
Ventricular Fluid61020
Reconstruction21172-21180
Defect62140-62141, 62145
Reduction
Craniomegalic62115-62117
Removal
Plate62142
Prosthesis62142
Repair
Cerebrospinal Fluid Leak62100
Encephalocele62120
Replacement
Plate62143
Prosthesis62143
Tumor
Excision61500
X-Ray70250-70260

Skull Base Surgery
Anterior Cranial Fossa
Bicoronal Approach61586
Craniofacial Approach61580-61583
Extradural61600-61601
LeFort I Osteotomy Approach61586
Orbitocranial Approach61584-61585
Transzygomatic Approach61586
Carotid Aneurysm61613
Carotid Artery61610
Transection/Ligation61609-61612
Craniotomy62121
Dura
Repair of Cerebrospinal Fluid
Leak61618-61619
Middle Cranial Fossa
Extradural61605, 61607
Infratemporal Approach61590-61591
Intradural61606, 61608
Orbitocranial Zygomatic Approach61592
Posterior Cranial Fossa
Extradural61615
Intradural61616

Transcondylar Approach61596-61597
Transpetrosal Approach61598
Transtemporal Approach61595

Sleep Study95806-95807
Actigraphy0089T

Sliding Inlay Graft, Tibia
See Ankle; Tibia, Repair

Sling Operation
Incontinence53440
Removal53442
Stress Incontinence51992, 57287
Vagina57287-57288

Small Bowel
See Intestines, Small
Neoplasm
See Tumor, Intestines, Small

SMAS Flap15829

Smear
Cervical
See Cervical Smears
Papanicolaou
See Pap Smears

Smear and Stain
See Cytopathology, Smears
Cornea65430
Fluorescent87206
Gram or Giesma87205
Ova/Parasites87177, 87209
Parasites87207-87209
Wet Mount87210

Smith Fracture25600-25605

Smith-Robinson Operation
See Arthrodesis, Vertebra

Smithwick Operation
See Excision, Nerve, Sympathetic

SO₄
See Sulfate

Soave Procedure45120

Sodium84295, 84302
Urine84300

Sodium Glycinate, Theophylline
See Theophylline

Sofield Procedure24410

Soft Tissue
See Tissue, Soft

Solar Plexus
See Celiac Plexus

Solitary Cyst
See Bone, Cyst

Somatomammotropin, Chorionic83632

Somatomedin84305

Somatosensory Testing
Lower Limbs95926

Trunk or Head95927
Upper Limbs95925

Somatostatin84307

Somatotropin83003

Somatotropin Release Inhibiting Hormone
See Somatostatin

Somatropin
See Growth Hormone, Human

Somnographies
See Polysomnography

Somophyllin T
See Theophylline

Sonography
See Echography

Sonohysterography76831
Saline Infusion
Injection Procedure58340

Sore, Bed
See Pressure Ulcer (Decubitus)

Spasm Eyelid
See Blepharospasm

Special Services
After Hours Medical Services99050
Analysis
Remote Physiologic Data99091
Computer Data Analysis99090
Device Handling99002
Emergency Care In Office99058
Emergency Care Out of Office99060
Extended Hours Medical Services ..99051-99053
Group Education99078
Self-Management98961-98962
Hyperbaric Oxygen99183
Hypothermia99185-99186
Individual Education
Self-management98960
Medical Testimony99075
Non-Office Medical Services99056
On Call Services99026-99027
Phlebotomy99199
Post-Op Visit99024
Pump Services99190-99192
Reports and Forms
Medical, Extended99080
Psychiatric90889
Specimen Handling99000-99001
Supply of Materials99070
Educational99071
Unlisted Services and Procedures99199
Unusual Travel99082

Specific Gravity
Body Fluid84315

Specimen Collection
Intestines89100-89105
Stomach89130-89141

Specimen Concentration87015

Specimen Handling99000-99001

Removal .63746
Replacement63744
Stereotaxis
 Aspiration63615
 Biopsy .63615
 Creation Lesion63600
 Excision Lesion63615
 Stimulation63610
Syrinx
 Aspiration62268
Tumor
 Excision63275-63290

Spinal Cord Neoplasms

See Spinal Cord
Tumor
 See Spinal Cord, Tumor; Tumor
 Excision
 See Spinal Cord, Tumor; Tumor, Spinal
 Cord

Spinal Fluid

See Cerebrospinal Fluid

Spinal Fracture

See Fracture, Vertebra

Spinal Instrumentation

Anterior22845-22847
 Removal .22855
Internal Fixation22841
Pelvic Fixation22848
Posterior Nonsegmental
 Harrington Rod Technique22840
 Removal .22850
Posterior Segmental22842-22844
 Removal .22852
Prosthetic Device22851
Reinsertion of Spinal Fixation Device22849

Spinal Manipulation

See Manipulation, Chiropractic

Spinal Nerve

Avulsion .64772
Transection .64772

Spinal Tap

See Cervical Puncture; Cisternal Puncture;
Subdural Tap; Ventricular Puncture
Drainage Fluid62272
Lumbar .62270

Spine

See Intervertebral Disc; Spinal Cord; Vertebra;
Vertebral Body; Vertebral Process
Allograft
 Morselized20930
 Structural20931
Arthroplasty
 Cervical0090T-0098T
 Lumbar0163T-0165T, 22857-22865
Augmentation
 Lumbar Vertebra22524-22525
 Thoracic Vertebra22523, 22525
Autograft
 Local .20936
 Morselized20937
 Structural20938
Biopsy20250-20251

CT Scan
 Cervical72125-72127
 Lumbar72131-72133
 Thoracic72128-72130
Fixation .22842
Fusion
 Anterior22808-22812
 Anterior Approach22548-22585, 22812
 Exploration22830
 Lateral Extracavitary22532-22534
 Posterior Approach22590-22802
Incision and Drainage
 Abscess22010-22015
Insertion
 Instrumentation22840-22848, 22851
 Kyphectomy22818-22819
Magnetic Resonance Angiography72159
Magnetic Resonance Imaging
 Cervical72141-72142, 72156-72158
 Lumbar72148-72158
 Thoracic72146-72147, 72156-72158
Manipulation
 with Anesthesia22505
Myelography
 Cervical72240
 Lumbosacral72265
 Thoracic72255
 Total .72270
Reconstruction
 Dorsal Spine Elements63295
Reinsertion
 Instrumentation22849
Removal
 Instrumentation22850, 22852-22855
Repair, Osteotomy
 Anterior22220-22226
 Posterior22210-22214
 Cervical Laminoplasty63050-63051
 Posterolateral22216
Ultrasound .76800
Unlisted Services and Procedures,
Surgery .22899
X-Ray72020, 72090
 Absorptiometry77080-77082
 Cervical72040-72052
 Lumbosacral72100-72120
 Standing72069
 Thoracic72070-72074
 Thoracolumbar72080
 Total .72010
 with Contrast
 Cervical72240
 Lumbosacral72265
 Thoracic72255
 Total .72270

Spine Chemotherapy

Administration96450
 See Chemotherapy

Spirometry94010-94070

See Pulmonology, Diagnostic
Patient Initiated94014-94016

Splanchnicectomy

See Nerves, Sympathectomy, Excision

Spleen

Excision38100-38102
 Laparoscopic38120
Injection
 Radiologic38200
Nuclear Medicine
 Imaging78185, 78215-78216
Repair .38115

Splenectomy

Laparoscopic38120
Partial .38101
Partial with Repair, Ruptured Spleen38115
Total .38100
 En bloc .38102

Splenoplasty

See Repair, Spleen

Splenoportography75810

Injection Procedures38200

Splenorrhaphy38115

Splint

See Casting; Strapping
Arm
 Long .29105
 Short29125-29126
Finger29130-29131
Foot .29590
Leg
 Long .29505
 Short .29515
Oral Surgical21085
Ureteral
 See Ureteral Splinting

Split Grafts15100-15101, 15120-15121

Split Renal Function Test

See Cystourethroscopy, Catheterization, Ureteral

Splitting

Blood Products86985

Spontaneous Abortion

See Abortion

Sprengel's Deformity23400

Spring Water Cyst

See Cyst, Pericardial

Spur, Bone

See Exostosis
Calcaneal
 See Heel Spur

Sputum Analysis89220

SRIH

See Somatostatin

Ssabanejew-Frank Operation

See Incision, Stomach, Creation, Stoma; Incision
and Drainage

Stabilizing Factor, Fibrin

See Fibrin Stabilizing Factor

Stable Factor85230

Stallard Procedure
See Conjunctivorhinostomy

Stamey Procedure51845
See Repair, Bladder, Neck

Standby Services
Physician99360

Stanford-Binet Test
See Psychiatric Diagnosis

Stanftan
See Binet Test

Stapedectomy
Revision69662
with Footplate Drill Out69661
without Foreign Material69660

Stapedotomy
Revision69662
with Footplate Drill Out69661
without Foreign Material69660

Stapes
Excision
 with Footplate Drill Out69661
 without Foreign Material69660
Mobilization
 See Mobilization, Stapes
Release69650
Revision69662

Staphyloma
Sclera
 Repair
 with Graft66225
 without Graft66220

Starch Granules
Feces89225

State Operation
See Proctectomy

Statin Therapy
See Performance Measures

Statistics/Biometry
See Biometry

Steindler Stripping28250

Stellate Ganglion
Injection
 Anesthetic64510

Stem Cell
Cell Concentration38215
Count86367
Cryopreservation38207, 88240
Donor Search38204
Harvesting38205-38206
Limbal
 Allograft65781
Plasma Depletion38214
Platelet Depletion38213
Red Blood Cell Depletion38212
T-Cell Depletion38210
Thawing38208-38209, 88241
Transplantation38240-38242

Tumor Cell Depletion38211
Washing38209

Stem, Brain
See Brainstem

Stenger Test92565, 92577
See Audiologic Function Test; Ear, Nose and Throat

Stenosis
Aortic
 See Aortic Stenosis
Bronchi31641
 Reconstruction31775
Excision
 Trachea31780-31781
Laryngoplasty31582
Reconstruction
 Auditory Canal, External69310
Repair
 Trachea31780-31781
Tracheal
 See Trachea Stenosis
Urethral
 See Urethral Stenosis

Stensen Duct
See Parotid Duct

Stent
Indwelling
 Insertion
 Ureter50605
Placement
 Bronchoscopy31631, 31636-31637
 Colonoscopy45387
 via Stoma44397
 Endoscopy
 Gastrointestinal, Upper43256
 Enteroscopy44370
 Proctosigmoidoscopy45327
 Sigmoidoscopy45345
 Transcatheter
 Intravascular ..37205-37208, 37215-37216
 Extracranial0075T-0076T
 Ureteroneocystomy50947-50948
Removal
 Ureteral50382-50387
Replacement
 Ureteral50382, 50387
Revision
 Bronchoscopy31638
Transcatheter
 Intravascular
 Intracranial61635
Urethra52282
 Prostatic0084T

Stent, Intravascular
See Transcatheter, Placement, Intravascular Stents

Stents, Tracheal
See Tracheal Stent

Stereotactic Frame
Application/Removal20660

Stereotaxis
Aspiration
 Brain Lesion61750
 with CT Scan and/or MRI61751
 Spinal Cord63615
Biopsy
 Aspiration
 Brain Lesion61750
 Brain61750
 with CT Scan and/or MRI61751
 Breast77031
 Spinal Cord63615
Catheter Placement
Brain
 Infusion0169T
 Radiation Source61770
Computer Assisted
 Brain Surgery61795
 Orthopedic Surgery0054T-0056T
Creation Lesion
 Brain
 Deep61720-61735
 Percutaneous61790
 Gasserian Ganglion61790
 Spinal Cord63600
 Trigeminal Tract61791
CT Scan
 Aspiration61751
 Biopsy61751
Excision Lesion
 Brain61750
 Spinal Cord63615
Focus Beam
 Radiosurgery61793, 77371-77373
Radiation Therapy77421, 77432-77435
Stimulation
 Spinal Cord63610
Target Volume Guidance77421

Sterile Coverings
See Dressings

Sternal Fracture
See Fracture, Sternum

Sternoclavicular Joint
Arthrotomy23044
 with Biopsy23101
 with Synovectomy23106
Dislocation
 Closed Treatment
 with Manipulation23525
 without Manipulation23520
 Open Treatment23530-23532
 with Fascial Graft23532

Sternocleidomastoid
Division21720-21725

Sternotomy
Closure21750

Sternum
Debridement21627
Excision21620, 21630-21632
Fracture
 Closed Treatment21820
 Open Treatment21825
Ostectomy21620

Radical Resection21630-21632
Reconstruction21740-21742, 21750
　　with Thoracoscopy21743
X-Ray .71120-71130

Steroid-Binding Protein, Sex
See Globulin, Sex Hormone Binding

Steroids
Anabolic
　See Androstenedione
Injection
　Urethral Stricture52283
Ketogenic
　Urine .83582

STH (Somatotropic Hormone)
See Growth Hormone

Stimulating Antibody, Thyroid
See Immunoglobulin, Thyroid Stimulating

Stimulation
Electric
　See Electrical Stimulation
Lymphocyte
　See Blastogenesis
Spinal Cord
　Stereotaxis .63610
Transcutaneous Electric
　See Application, Neurostimulation

Stimulator, Long-Acting Thyroid
See Thyrotropin Releasing Hormone (TRH)

Stimulators, Cardiac
See Heart, Pacemaker

Stimulus Evoked Response51792

Stoffel Operation
See Rhizotomy

Stoma
Creation
　Bladder .51980
　Kidney50551-50561
　Stomach
　　Neonatal .43831
　　Temporary43830-43831
　Ureter .50860
Ureter
　Endoscopy via50951-50961

Stomach
Anastomosis
　with Duodenum43810, 43850-43855
　with Jejunum . . .43820-43825, 43860-43865
Biopsy .43600-43605
Creation
　Stoma
　　Temporary43830-43831
　Temporary Stoma
　　Laparoscopic43653
Electrode
　Removal0156T, 0158T, 43882
Electrogastrography91132-91133
Excision
　Partial43631-43635, 43845
　Total43620-43622
Exploration .43500

Gastric Bypass43644-43645, 43846
　Revision .43848
Gastric Restrictive Procedures43770-43774,
　　　　　　　　　　　43848, 43886-43888
Implantation
　Electrodes0155T, 0157T, 43647, 43881
Incision43830-43832
　Exploration43500
　Pyloric Sphincter43520
　Removal
　　Foreign Body43500
Intubation with Specimen Prep91055
Laparoscopy0155T-0156T, 43647-43648
Nuclear Medicine
　Blood Loss Study78278
　Emptying Study78264
　Imaging .78261
　Protein Loss Study78282
　Reflux Study78262
　Vitamin B-12 Absorption78270-78272
Reconstruction
　for Obesity43644-43645, 43842-43847
　Roux-En-Y43644, 43846
Removal
　Foreign Body43500
Repair .48547
　Fistula .43880
　Fundoplasty43324-43325
　　Laparoscopic43280
　Laceration43501-43502
　Stoma .43870
　Ulcer .43501
Replacement
　Electrodes0155T, 0157T, 43647, 43881
Specimen Collection89130-89141
Stimulation of Secretion91052
Suture
　Fistula .43880
　for Obesity43842-43843
　Stoma .43870
　Ulcer .43840
　Wound .43840
Tumor
　Excision43610-43611
Ulcer
　Excision .43610
Unlisted Services and Procedures . .43659, 43999

Stomatoplasty
See Mouth, Repair

Stone, Kidney
See Calculus, Removal, Kidney

Stookey-Scarff Procedure
See Ventriculocisternostomy

Stool Blood
See Blood, Feces

Storage
Embryo .89342
Oocyte .89346
Reproductive Tissue89344
Sperm .89343

Strabismus
Chemodenervation67345
Repair
　Adjustable Sutures67335

Extraocular Muscles67340
One Horizontal Muscle67311
One Vertical Muscle67314
Posterior Fixation Suture
　Technique67334-67335
Previous Surgery, Not Involving Extraocular
　Muscles .67331
Release Extensive Scar Tissue67343
Superior Oblique Muscle67318
Transposition67320
Two Horizontal Muscles67312
Two or More Vertical Muscles67316

Strapping
See Cast; Splint
Ankle .29540
Back .29220
Chest .29200
Elbow .29260
Finger .29280
Foot29540, 29590
Hand .29280
Hip .29520
Knee .29530
Shoulder .29240
Thorax .29200
Toes .29550
Unlisted Services and Procedures29799
Unna Boot .29580
Wrist .29260

Strassman Procedure58540

Strayer Procedure
Leg, Lower .27687

Streptococcus pneumoniae Vaccine
See Vaccines

Streptococcus, Group A
Antigen Detection
　Enzyme Immunoassay87430
　Nucleic Acid87650-87652
Direct Optical Observation87880

Streptococcus, Group B
by Immunoassay
　with Direct Optical Observation87802

Streptokinase, Antibody86590

Stress Tests
Cardiovascular93015-93024
Multiple Gated Acquisition (MUGA) .78472-78473
Myocardial Perfusion Imaging78460-78465
Pulmonary94620-94621
　See Pulmonology, Diagnostic

Stricture
Repair
　Urethra53400-53405
Urethra
　See Urethral Stenosis

Stricturoplasty
Intestines .44615

Stroboscopy
Larynx .31579

Removal, Eye
 See Enucleation, Eye
Revision
 See Reoperation
Services
 Post-Op Visit99024

Surveillance
See Monitoring

Suspension
Aorta .33800
Kidney
 See Nephropexy
Muscle
 Hyoid .21685
Vagina
 See Colpopexy

Suture
See Repair
Abdomen .49900
Aorta .33320-33322
Bile Duct
 Wound .47900
Bladder
 Fistulization44660-44661,
 45800-45805, 51880-51925
 Vesicouterine51920-51925
 Vesicovaginal51900
 Wound51860-51865
Cervix .57720
Colon
 Diverticula44604-44605
 Fistula44650-44661
 Plication .44680
 Stoma44620-44625
 Ulcer44604-44605
 Wound44604-44605
Esophagus
 Wound43410-43415
Eyelid .67880
 Closure of67875
 with Transposition of Tarsal Plate67882
 Wound
 Full Thickness67935
 Partial Thickness67930
Facial Nerve
 Intratemporal
 Lateral to Geniculate Ganglion69740
 Medial to Geniculate Ganglion69745
Foot
 Tendon28200-28210
Gastroesophageal0008T, 43405
Great Vessel33320-33322
Hemorrhoids46945-46946
Hepatic Duct
 See Hepatic Duct, Repair
Intestine
 Large
 Diverticula44605
 Ulcer .44605
 Wound .44605
Intestines
 Large
 Diverticula44604
 Ulcer .44604
 Wound .44604

Small
 Diverticula44602-44603
 Fistula44640-44661
 Plication .44680
 Ulcer44602-44603
 Wound44602-44603
 Stoma44620-44625
Iris
 with Ciliary Body66682
Kidney
 Fistula50520-50526
 Horseshoe50540
 Wound .50500
Leg, Lower
 Tendon27658-27665
Leg, Upper
 Muscle27385-27386
Liver
 Wound47350-47361
Mesentery .44850
Nerve .64831-64876
Pancreas .48545
Pharynx
 Wound .42900
Rectum
 Fistula45800-45825
 Prolapse45540-45541
Removal
 Anesthesia15850-15851
Spleen
 See Splenorrhapy
Stomach
 Fistula .43880
 Laceration43501-43502
 Stoma .43870
 Ulcer43501, 43840
 Wound .43840
Tendon
 Foot28200-28210
 Knee27380-27381
Testis
 Injury .54670
 Suspension54620-54640
Thoracic Duct
 Abdominal Approach38382
 Cervical Approach38380
 Thoracic Approach38381
Throat
 Wound .42900
Tongue
 to Lip .41510
Trachea
 Fistula
 with Plastic Repair31825
 without Plastic Repair31820
 Stoma
 with Plastic Repair31825
 without Plastic Repair31820
 Wound
 Cervical31800
 Intrathoracic31805
Ulcer44604-44605
Ureter .50900
 Deligation50940
 Fistula50920-50930
Urethra
 Fistula45820-45825, 53520
 Stoma .53520

 to Bladder51840-51841
 Wound53502-53515
Uterus
 Fistula51920-51925
 Rupture58520, 59350
 Suspension58400-58410
Vagina
 Cystocele57240, 57260
 Enterocele57265
 Fistula
 Rectovaginal57300-57307
 Transvesical and Vaginal Approach . .57330
 Urethrovaginal57310-57311
 Vesicovaginal51900, 57320-57330
 Rectocele57250-57260
 Suspension57280, 57283
 Wound57200-57210
Vas Deferens55400
Vein
 Femoral .37650
 Iliac .37660
 Vena Cava37620
Wound44604-44605

Swallowing
 Evaluation92610-92613,
 92616-92617
 Imaging .74230
 Treatment92526

Swanson Procedure28309

Sweat Collection
Iontophoresis89230

Sweat Glands
Excision
 Axillary11450-11451
 Inguinal11462-11463
 Perianal11470-11471
 Perineal11470-11471
 Umbilical11470-11471

Sweat Test82435
See Chloride, Blood

Swenson Procedure45120

Syme Procedure27888

Sympathectomy
Artery
 Digital .64820
 Radial .64821
 Superficial Palmar Arch64823
 Ulnar .64822
Cervical .64802
Cervicothoracic64804
Digital Artery
 with Magnification64820
Lumbar .64818
Presacral .58410
Thoracic .32664
Thoracolumbar64809
with Rib Excision21616

Sympathetic Nerve
Excision64802-64818
Injection
 Anesthetic64508, 64520-64530

T

Transfer
 Arm, Lower 25310-25312, 25316
 Arm, Upper .24301
 Elbow .24301
 Finger26497-26498
 Hand26480-26489
 Leg, Lower27690-27692
 Leg, Upper27400
 Pelvis .27098
 Thumb26490-26492, 26510
 Wrist25310-25312, 25316
Transplant
 Leg, Upper27396-27397
Wrist
 Excision .25109
 Repair25260-25274

Tendon Origin
Insertion
 Injection .20551

Tendon Pulley Reconstruction of Hand
See Hand, Reconstruction, Tendon Pulley

Tendon Sheath
Arm
 Lower
 Repair .25275
Finger
 Incision .26055
 Incision and Drainage26020
 Lesion .26160
Foot
 Excision28086-28088
Hand Lesion26160
Injection .20550
Palm
 Incision and Drainage26020
Removal
 Foreign Body20520-20525
Wrist
 Excision, Radical25115-25116
 Incision25000-25001
 Repair .25275

Tenectomy, Tendon Sheath
See Excision, Lesion, Tendon Sheath

Tennis Elbow
Repair24350-24356

Tenodesis
Biceps Tendon
 at Elbow .24340
 Shoulder .23430
Finger26471-26474
Wrist25300-25301

Tenolysis
Ankle27680-27681
Arm, Lower25295
Arm, Upper24332
Finger
 Extensor26445-26449
 Flexor26440-26442
Foot28220-28226
Hand Extensor26445-26449
 Flexor26440-26442

Leg, Lower27680-27681
Wrist .25295

Tenomyotomy
Shoulder23405-23406

Tenon's Capsule
Injection .67515

Tenoplasty
Anesthesia01714

Tenorrhaphy
See Suture, Tendon

Tenosuspension
See Tenodesis

Tenosuture
See Suture, Tendon

Tenotomy
Achilles Tendon27605-27606
Ankle27605-27606
Arm, Lower25290
Arm, Upper24310
Finger26060, 26455-26460
Foot28230, 28234
Hand26450, 26460
Hip
 Iliopsoas Tendon27005
Hip, Abductor27006
Hip, Adductor27000-27003
Leg, Upper27306-27307, 27390-27392
Toe28010-28011, 28232-28234, 28240
Wrist .25290

TENS
See Application, Neurostimulation; Physical Medicine/Therapy/Occupational Therapy

Tensilon Test95857

Tension, Ocular
See Glaucoma

Tentorium Cerebelli
Section .61440

Terman-Merrill Test96101-96103

Termination, Pregnancy
See Abortion

Test
Antiglobulin
 See Coombs Test
Aphasia
 See Aphasia Testing
Bender Visual-Motor Gestalt
 See Bender-Gestalt Test
Binet
 See Binet Test
Blood
 See Blood Tests
Blood Coagulation
 See Coagulation
Breath
 See Breath Test
Cervical Mucus Penetration
 See Cervical Mucus Penetration Test

Clinical Chemistry
 See Chemistry Tests, Clinical
Complement Fixation
 See Complement, Fixation Test
Exercise
 See Exercise Stress Tests
Fern
 See Smear and Stain, Wet Mount
Fetal, Nonstress
 See Fetal Non-Stress Test
Function, Vestibular
 See Vestibular Function Tests
Gel Diffusion
 See Immunodiffusion
Glucose Tolerance
 See Glucose, Tolerance Test
Hearing
 See Audiologic Function Tests
Hemagglutination Inhibition
 See Hemagglutination Inhibition Test
Ink Blot
 See Inkblot Test
Intelligence
 See Intelligence Test
Lung Function
 See Pulmonology, Diagnostic
Neutralization
 See Neutralization Test
Papanicolaou
 See Pap Smears
Pregnancy
 See Pregnancy Test
Quick
 See Prothrombin Time
Radioimmunosorbent
 See Gammaglobulin, Blood
Rorschach
 See Rorschach Test
Schilling
 See Schilling Test
Skin
 See Skin, Tests
Stanford-Binet
 See Psychiatric Diagnosis
Tuberculin
 See Skin, Tests, Tuberculosis

Test Tube Fertilization
See In Vitro Fertilization

Tester, Color Vision
See Color Vision Examination

Testes
Cryopreservation89335
Nuclear Medicine
 Imaging .78761
Undescended
 See Testis, Undescended

Testicular Vein
See Spermatic Veins

Testimony, Medical99075

Testing, Histocompatibility
See Tissue Typing

Testing, Neurophysiologic
Intraoperative95920

Surgery
 Video-Assisted
 See Thoracoscopy
Vertebra
 See Vertebra, Thoracic
Wall
 See Chest Wall

Thoracocentesis
See Thoracentesis

Thoracoplasty32905
with Closure Bronchopleural Fistula32906

Thoracoscopy
Diagnostic32601-32606
 with Biopsy32602, 32604, 32606
 without Biopsy32601, 32603, 32605
Surgical32650-32665
 with Control Traumatic Hemorrhage ...32654
 with Creation Pericardial Window32659
 with Esophagomyotomy32665
 with Excision Mediastinal Cyst, Tumor
 and/or Mass32662
 with Excision Pericardial Cyst, Tumor
 and/or Mass32661
 with Excision-Plication of Bullae32655
 with Lobectomy32663
 with Parietal Pleurectomy32656
 with Partial Pulmonary Decortication ..32651
 with Pleurodesis32650
 with Removal Intrapleural Foreign
 Body32653
 with Removal of Clot/Foreign Body ...32658
 with Sternum Reconstruction21743
 with Thoracic Sympathectomy32664
 with Total Pericardiectomy32660
 with Total Pulmonary Decortication ..32652
 with Wedge Resection of Lung32657

Thoracostomy
Empyema32035-32036
Tube, with/without Water Seal32020

Thoracotomy
Cardiac Massage32160
for Post-Op Complications32120
Hemorrhage32110
Removal
 Bullae32141
 Cyst32140
 Defibrillator33243
 Electrodes33238
 Foreign Body
 Intrapleural32150
 Intrapulmonary32151
 Pacemaker33236-33237
 with Biopsy32095-32100
 with Excision-Plication of Bullae32141
 with Lung Repair32110
 with Open Intrapleural Pneumolysis .32124
Transmyocardial Laser Revascularization ..33140-
 33141

Thorax
See Chest; Chest Cavity; Mediastinum
Angiography71275
Bioimpedance93701
Biopsy21550
CT Scan71250-71275

Incision
 Empyema32035-32036
 Pneumothorax32020
Incision and Drainage
 Abscess21501-21502
 Deep21510
 Hematoma21501-21502
Strapping29200
Tumor
 Excision21555-21556
 Excision/Resection21557
Unlisted Services and Procedures, Surgery .21899

Three Glass Test
See Urinalysis, Glass Test

Three-Day Measles
See Rubella

Throat
See Pharynx
Abscess
 Incision and Drainage42700-42725
Biopsy42800-42806
Hemorrhage42960-42962
Reconstruction42950
Removal
 Foreign Body42809
Repair
 Pharyngoesophageal42953
 Wound42900
Suture
 Wound42900
Unlisted Services and Procedures42999

Thrombectomy
See Thromboendarterectomy
Aortoiliac Artery34151-34201
Arteriovenous Fistula
 Graft36870
Axillary Artery34101
Axillary Vein34490
Brachial Artery34101
Bypass Graft
 Other than Hemodialysis Graft or
 Fistula35875-35876
Carotid Artery34001
Celiac Artery34151
Dialysis Graft
 without Revision36831
Femoral34201
Femoropopliteal Vein34421-34451
Iliac34151-34201
Iliac Vein34401-34451
Innominate Artery34001-34101
Mesentery Artery34151
Percutaneous
 Coronary Artery92973
 Fluoroscopic Guidance37184-37188
 Mechanical Arterial37184-37186
 Mechanical Venous37187-37188
Peroneal Artery34203
Popliteal Artery34203
Radial Artery34111
Renal Artery34151
Subclavian Artery34001-34101
Subclavian Vein34471-34490
Tibial Artery34203
Ulnar Artery34111

Vena Cava34401-34451
Vena Caval50230

Thrombin Inhibitor I
See Antithrombin III

Thrombin Time85670-85675

Thrombocyte (Platelet)
See Blood, Platelet

Thrombocyte ab
See Antibody, Platelet

Thromboendarterectomy
See Thrombectomy
Aorta, Abdominal35331
Aortoiliofemoral Artery35363
Axillary Artery35321
Brachial Artery35321
Carotid Artery35301, 35390
Celiac Artery35341
Femoral Artery35371-35372
Iliac Artery35351, 35361-35363
Iliofemoral Artery35355, 35363
Innominate Artery35311
Mesenteric Artery35341
Peroneal Artery35305-35306
Popliteal Artery35303
Renal Artery35341
Subclavian Artery35301, 35311
Superficial Femoral Artery35302
Tibial Artery35305-35306
Tibioperoneal Trunk Artery35304
Vertebral Artery35301

Thrombokinase85260

Thrombolysin
See Plasmin

Thrombolysis
Catheter Exchange
 Intravascular37209, 75900
Cerebral
 Intravenous Infusion37195
Coronary Vessels92975-92977
Cranial Vessels37195

Thrombolysis Biopsy Intracranial
Arterial Perfusion61624

Thrombolysis Intracranial65205
See Ciliary Body; Cornea; Eye, Removal, Foreign
Body; Iris; Lens; Retina; Sclera; Vitreous

Thrombomodulin85337

Thromboplastin
Inhibition85705
Inhibition Test85347
Partial Time85730-85732

Thromboplastin Antecedent, Plasma
See Plasma Thromboplastin, Antecedent

Thromboplastinogen
See Clotting Factor

Thromboplastinogen B
See Christmas Factor

Thumb
See Phalanx
Amputation26910-26952
Arthrodesis
 Carpometacarpal Joint26841-26842
Dislocation
 with Fracture26645-26650
 Open Treatment26665
 with Manipulation26641
Fracture
 with Dislocation26645-26650
 Open Treatment26665
Fusion
 in Opposition26820
Reconstruction
 from Finger26550
 Opponensplasty26490-26496
Repair
 Muscle26508
 Muscle Transfer26494
 Tendon Transfer26510
Replantation20824-20827
Sesamoidectomy26185
Unlisted Services and Procedures26989

Thymectomy60520-60521
Sternal Split/Transthoracic
Approach60521-60522
Transcervical Approach60520

Thymotaxin
See Beta-2-Microglobulin

Thymus Gland60520
Excision60520-60521

Thyramine
See Amphetamine

Thyrocalcitonin
See Calcitonin

Thyroglobulin84432
Antibody86800

Thyroglossal Duct
Cyst
 Excision60280-60281

Thyroid Gland
Cyst
 Aspiration60001
 Excision60200
 Incision and Drainage60000
 Injection60001
Excision
 for Malignancy
 Limited Neck Dissection60252
 Radical Neck Dissection60254
 Partial60210-60225
 Secondary60260
 Total60240, 60271
 Cervical Approach60271
 Removal All Thyroid Tissue60260
 Sternal Split/Transthoracic
 Approach60270
 Transcervical Approach60520
Metastatic Cancer
 Nuclear Imaging78015-78018

Needle Biopsy60100
Nuclear Medicine
 Imaging78010
 Imaging for Metastases78015-78018
 Imaging with Flow78011
 Imaging with Uptake78006-78007
 Metastases Uptake78020
 Uptake78000-78003
Tumor
 Excision60200

Thyroid Hormone Binding Ratio84479

Thyroid Hormone Uptake84479

Thyroid Stimulating Hormone (TSH)80418, 80438-80440, 84443

Thyroid Stimulating Hormone Receptor ab
See Thyrotropin Releasing Hormone (TRH)

Thyroid Stimulating Immune Globulins84445

Thyroid Stimulator, Long Acting
See Thyrotropin Releasing Hormone (TRH)

Thyroid Suppression Test
See Nuclear Medicine, Thyroid, Uptake

Thyroidectomy
Partial60210-60225
Secondary60260
Total60240, 60271
 Cervical Approach60271
 for Malignancy
 Limited Neck Dissection60252
 Radical Neck Dissection60254
 Removal All Thyroid Tissue60260
 Sternal Split/Transthoracic Approach ..60270

Thyrolingual Cyst
See Cyst, Thyroglossal Duct

Thyrotomy31300

Thyrotropin Receptor Ab
See Thyrotropin Releasing Hormone (TRH)

Thyrotropin Releasing Hormone (TRH)80438-80439

Thyroxine
Free84439
Neonatal84437
Total84436
True84436

Thyroxine Binding Globulin84442

Tibia
See Ankle
Arthroscopy Surgical29891-29892
Craterization27360, 27640
Cyst
 Excision27635-27638
Diaphysectomy27360, 27640
Excision27360, 27640
 Epiphyseal Bar20150

Fracture
 Arthroscopic Treatment29855-29856
 Plafond29892
 Closed Treatment27824-27825
 Distal27824-27828
 Intercondylar27538-27540
 Malleolus27760-27766, 27808-27814
 Open Treatment27535-27536,
 27758-27759, 27826-27828
 Plateau29855-29856
 Closed Treatment27530-27536
 Shaft27752-27759
 with Manipulation27825
 without Manipulation27824
Incision27607
Osteoplasty
 Lengthening27715
Prophylactic Treatment27745
Reconstruction27418
 at Knee27440-27443, 27446
Repair27720-27725
 Epiphysis27477-27485, 27730-27742
 Osteochondritis Dissecans
 Arthroscopy29892
 Osteotomy27455-27457, 27705,
 27709-27712
 Pseudoarthrosis27727
Saucerization27360, 27640
Tumor
 Excision27635-27638, 27645
X-Ray73590

Tibial
Arteries
 See Artery, Tibial
Nerve
 Repair/Suture
 Posterior64840

Tibiofibular Joint
Arthrodesis27871
Dislocation27830-27832
Disruption
 Open Treatment27829
Fusion27871

TIG
See Immune Globulins, Tetanus

Time
Bleeding
 See Bleeding Time
Prothrombin
 See Prothrombin Time
Reptilase
 See Thrombin Time

Tinnitus
Assessment92625

Tissue
Crystal Identification89060
Culture
 Chromosome Analysis88230-88239
 Homogenization87176
 Non-neoplastic Disorder88230, 88237
 Skin Grafts15100-15101, 15120-15121
 Harvesting15040
 Solid Tumor88239

Toxin/Antitoxin87230
Virus87252-87253
Enzyme Activity82657
Examination for Ectoparasites87220
Examination for Fungi87220
Expander
 Breast Reconstruction with19357
 Insertion
 Skin11960
 Removal
 Skin11971
 Replacement
 Skin11970
Grafts
 Harvesting20926
Granulation
 See Granulation Tissue
Homogenization87176
Hybridization In Situ88365-88368
Mucosal
 See Mucosa
Preparation
 Drug Analysis80103
Skin Harvest for Culture15040
Soft
 Abscess20000-20005
Transfer
 Adjacent
 Eyelids67961
 Skin14000-14350
 Facial Muscles15845
 Finger Flap14350
 Toe Flap14350
Typing
 HLA Antibodies86812-86817
 Lymphocyte Culture86821-86822

Tissue Culture
from Skin Harvest15040
Skin Grafts15150-15157, 15340-15366

Tissue Factor
See Thromboplastin

TLC
See Chromatography, Thin-Layer
Screen84375

TMJ
See Temporomandibular Joint (TMJ)
Prostheses
 See Prosthesis, Temporomandibular Joint

Tobacco
See Performance Measures

Tobramycin
Assay80200

Tocolysis59412

Tocopherol84446

Toe
See Interphalangeal Joint, Toe;
Metatarsophalangeal Joint; Phalanx
Amputation28810-28825
Capsulotomy28270-28272
Fasciotomy28008
Fracture
 See Fracture, Phalanges, Toe

Lesion
 Excision28092
Reconstruction
 Angle Deformity28313
 Extra Toes28344
 Hammertoe28285-28286
 Macrodactyly28340-28341
 Syndactyly28345
 Webbed Toe28345
Repair
 Bunion28290-28299
 Muscle28240
 Tendon28232-28234, 28240
 Webbed28280
 Webbed Toe28345
Tenotomy28010-28011, 28232-28234
Unlisted Services and Procedures28899

Toe Flap
Tissue Transfer14350

Toes
Arthrocentesis20600
Dislocation
 See Specific Joint
Magnetic Resonance Imaging
(MRI)73721-73723
Reconstruction
 Extra Digit26587
Repair
 Extra Digit26587
 Macrodactylia26590
Reposition to Hand26551-26556
Strapping29550
X-Ray73660

Tolbutamide Tolerance Test82953

Tolerance Test
Glucagon82946
Glucose82951-82952
 with Tolbutamide82953
Heparin-Protamine85530
Insulin80434-80435
Maltose82951-82952
Tolbutamide82953

Tomodensitometries
See CT Scan

**Tomographic Scintigraphy,
Computed**
See Emission Computerized Tomography

Tomographic SPECT
Myocardial Imaging78469

Tomographies, Computed X-Ray
See CT Scan

Tomography, Computerized Axial
Abdomen
 See Abdomen, CT Scan
Head
 See Head, CT Scan

Tomography, Emission Computed
See Positron Emission Tomography
Single Photon
 See SPECT

Tompkins Metroplasty58540
See Uterus, Reconstruction

Tongue
Abscess
 Incision and Drainage ..41000-41006, 41015
Biopsy41100-41105
Cyst
 Incision and Drainage41000-41006,
 41015, 60000
Excision
 Complete41140-41155
 Frenum41115
 Partial41120-41135
 with Mouth Resection41150-41153
 with Radical Neck41135, 41145,
 41153-41155
Fixation41500
Hematoma
 Incision and Drainage ..41000-41006, 41015
Incision
 Frenum41010
Lesion
 Excision41110-41114
Reconstruction
 Frenum41520
Reduction for Sleep Apnea0088T
Repair
 See Repair, Tongue
 Laceration41250-41252
 Suture41510
Suture41510
Unlisted Services and Procedures41599

Tonography92120
with Provocation92130

Tonometry, Serial92100

Tonsil, Pharyngeal
See Adenoids

Tonsillectomy42820-42826

Tonsils
Abscess
 Incision and Drainage42700
Excision42825-42826
 Lingual42870
 Radical42842-42845
 Tag42860
 with Adenoids42820-42821
Lingual
 Destruction42870
Unlisted Services and Procedures42999

Topiramate
Assay80201

Torek Procedure
See Orchiopexy

Torkildsen Procedure62180

**TORP (Total Ossicular Replacement
Prosthesis)**69633, 69637

Torsion Swing Test92546

Torula
See Cryptococcus

Torus Mandibularis
Tumor Excision21031

Total
Abdominal Hysterectomy
 See Hysterectomy, Abdominal, Total
Bilirubin Level
 See Bilirubin, Total
Catecholamines
 See Catecholamines, Urine
Cystectomy
 See Bladder, Excision, Total
Dacryoadenectomy
 See Dacryoadenectomy, Total
Elbow Replacement
 See Replacement, Elbow, Total
Esophagectomy
 See Esophagectomy, Total
Gastrectomy
 See Excision, Stomach, Total
Hemolytic Complement
 See Complement, Hemolytic, Total
Hip Arthroplasty
 See Hip, Total Replacement
Knee Arthroplasty
 See Prosthesis, Knee
Mastectomies
 See Mastectomy
Ostectomy of Patella
 See Patellectomy
Splenectomy
 See Splenectomy, Total

Touroff Operation37615
See Ligation, Artery, Neck

Toxicology Screen80100-80103

Toxin Assay87230

Toxin, Botulinum
See Chemodenervation

Toxoplasma
Antibody86777-86778

Trabeculectomies
See Trabeculoplasty

Trabeculectomy ab Externo
in Absence of Previous Surgery66170
with Scarring Previous Surgery66172

Trabeculoplasty
by Laser Surgery65855

Trabeculotomy ab Externo
Eye65850

Trachea
Aspiration31720
 Catheter31720-31725
Dilation31630-31631, 31636-31638
Endoscopy
 via Tracheostomy31615
Excision
 Stenosis31780-31781
Fistula
 with Plastic Repair31825
 without Plastic Repair31820

Fracture
 Endoscopy31630
Incision
 Emergency31603-31605
 Planned31600-31601
 with Flaps31610
Introduction
 Needle Wire31730
Puncture
 Aspiration and/or Injection31612
Reconstruction
 Carina31766
 Cervical31750
 Fistula31755
 Intrathoracic31760
Repair
 Cervical31750
 Fistula31755
 Intrathoracic31760
 Stoma31613-31614
Revision
 Stoma
 Scars31830
Scar
 Revision31830
Stenosis
 Excision31780-31781
 Repair31780-31781
Stoma
 Repair
 with Plastic Repair31825
 without Plastic Repair31820
 Revision
 Scars31830
Tumor
 Excision
 Cervical31785
 Thoracic31786
Unlisted Services and Procedures
 Bronchi31899
Wound
 Suture
 Cervical31800
 Intrathoracic31805

Tracheal
Stent
 Placement31631
Tubes
 See Endotracheal Tube

Trachelectomy57530
Radical57531

Tracheloplasty
See Cervicoplasty

Trachelorrhaphy57720

Tracheo-Esophageal Fistula
See Fistula, Tracheoesophageal

Tracheobronchoscopy
through Tracheostomy31615

Tracheoplasty
Cervical31750
Intrathoracic31760
Tracheopharyngeal Fistulization31755

Tracheostoma
Revision31613-31614

Tracheostomy
Emergency31603-31605
Planned31600-31601
Revision
 Scar31830
Surgical Closure
 with Plastic Repair31825
 without Plastic Repair31820
Tracheobronchoscopy through31615
with Flaps31610

Tracheotomy
Tube Change31502

Tracking Tests (Ocular)92545
See Ear, Nose and Throat

Tract, Urinary
See Urinary Tract

Traction Therapy
See Physical Medicine/Therapy/Occupational
Therapy
Manual97140
Mechanical97012

Tractotomy
Medulla61470
Mesencephalon61480

Training
Activities of Daily Living97535, 99509
Biofeedback90901-90911
Cognitive Skills97532
Community/Work Reintegration97537
Home Management97535, 99509
Orthoptic/Pleoptic92065
Orthotics97760
Prosthetics97761
Self Care97535, 98960-98962, 99509
Sensory Integration97533
Walking (Physical Therapy)97116
Wheelchair Management97542

TRAM Flap
Breast Reconstruction19367-19369

Trans-Scaphoperilunar
Fracture/Dislocation
 Closed Treatment25680
 Open Treatment25685

Transaminase
Glutamic Oxaloacetic84450
Glutamic Pyruvic84460

Transcatheter
Biopsy37200
Closure
 Percutaneous
 Heart93580-93581
 Transmyocardial
 Heart0166T, 0167T
Embolization
 Percutaneous37204
 Cranial61624-61626

Peripheral Nerve
 Major .64856
Vein Valve .34510

Transthoracic Echocardiography
See Echocardiography

Transthyretin
See Prealbumin

Transureteroureterostomy50770

Transurethral Balloon Dilation
Prostatic Urethra52510

Transurethral Fulguration
Postoperative Bleeding52606

Transurethral Procedure
See Specific Procedure
Prostate
 Incision .52450
 Resection52612-52614
 Thermotherapy53850-53853
 Microwave53850
 Radiofrequency53852

Trapezium
Arthroplasty
 with Implant .25445

Travel, Unusual99082

Treacher-Collins Syndrome
Midface Reconstruction21150-21151

Treatment, Tocolytic
See Tocolysis

Trendelenburg Operation
See Varicose Vein, Removal, Secondary Varicosity

Trephine Procedure
Sinusotomy
 Frontal .31070

Treponema Pallidum
Antibody
 Confirmation Test86781
Antigen Detection
 Direct Fluorescence87285

TRH
See Thyrotropin Releasing Hormone (TRH)

Triacylglycerol
See Triglycerides

Triacylglycerol Hydrolase
See Lipase

Tributyrinase
See Lipase

Trichiasis
Repair .67825
 Epilation, by Forceps67820
 Epilation, by Other than Forceps67825
 Incision of Lid Margin67830
 with Free Mucous Membrane Graft .67835

Trichina
See Trichinella

Trichinella
Antibody .86784
Trichogram .96902

Trichomonas Vaginalis
Antigen Detection
 Nucleic Acid87660
 by Immunoassay with Direct
 Optical Observation87808

Trichrome Stain88313

Tricuspid Valve
Excision .33460
Repair33463-33465
Replacement .33465
Repositioning .33468

Tridymite
See Silica

Trigeminal Ganglia
See Gasserian Ganglion

Trigeminal Nerve
Destruction64600-64610
Injection
 Anesthetic64400
 Neurolytic64600-64610

Trigeminal Tract
Stereotactic
 Create Lesion61791

Trigger Finger Repair26055

Trigger Point
Injection
 One or Two Muscles20552
 Two or More Muscles20553

Triglyceridase
See Lipase

Triglyceride Lipase
See Lipase

Triglycerides84478

Trigonocephaly21175

Triiodothyronine
Free .84481
Reverse .84482
Total .84480
True .84480

Triolean Hydrolase
See Lipase

Trioxopurine
See Uric Acid

Tripcellim
See Trypsin

Trisegmentectomy47122

Trocar Biopsy
Bone Marrow .38221

Trochanteric Femur Fracture
See Femur, Fracture, Trochanteric

Trophoblastic Tumor GTT
See Hydatidiform Mole

Troponin .84484
Qualitative .84512
Quantitative .84484

Truncal Vagotomies
See Vagotomy, Truncal

Truncus Arteriosus
Repair .33786

Truncus Brachiocephalicus
See Artery, Brachiocephalic

Trunk, Brachiocephalic
See Artery, Brachiocephalic

Trypanosomiases
See Trypanosomiasis

Trypanosomiasis86171, 86280

Trypsin
Duodenum .84485
Feces84488-84490

Trypsin Inhibitor, Alpha 1-Antitrypsin
See Alpha-1 Antitrypsin

Trypure
See Trypsin

Tsalicylate Intoxication
See Salicylate

TSH
See Thyroid Stimulating Hormone

TSI
See Thyroid Stimulating Immunoglobulin

Tsutsugamushi Disease
See Scrub Typhus

TT
See Thrombin Time

TT-3
See Triiodothyronine, True

TT-4
See Thyroxine, True

Tuba Auditoria (Auditiva)
See Eustachian Tube

Tubal Embryo Stage Transfer
See Embryo Transfer

Tubal Ligation58600
Laparoscopic .58670
with Cesarean Delivery58611

Tubal Occlusion
See Fallopian Tube, Occlusion; Occlusion
Create Lesion

Phalanges
 Finger26210-26215, 26260-26262
 Toe .28108
 Excision .28175
Pituitary Gland
 Excision61546-61548, 62165
Positron Emission Tomography
(PET) .78811-78816
Pubis .27065-27067
Pulmonary
 Ablation .32998
Radiation Therapy77295
Radius25120-25126, 25170
 Excision .24120
 with Allograft
 Excision .24126
 with Autograft
 Excision .24125
Rectum
 Destruction45190, 45320, 46937-46938
 Excision45160-45170
Resection
 Face .21015
 Scalp .21015
 with Cystourethroscopy52355
Retroperitoneal
 Destruction/Excision . . .49200-49201
Sacrum .49215
Scapula
 Excision23140, 23210
 with Allograft23146
 with Autograft23145
Shoulder
 Excision23075-23077
Skull
 Excision .61500
Soft Tissue
 Elbow
 Excision .24075
 Finger
 Excision .26115
 Forearm
 Radical Resection25077
 Hand
 Excision .26115
 Wrist
 Excision .25075
 Radical Resection25077
Spinal Cord
 Excision63275-63290
Stomach
 Excision43610-43611
Talus .28100-28103
 Excision .27647
Tarsal .28104-28107
 Excision .28171
Temporal Bone
 Removal .69970
Testis
 Excision54530-54535
Thorax
 Excision21555-21556
 Radical Resection21557
Thyroid
 Excision .60200
Tibia27365, 27635-27638
 Excision .27645
Torus Mandibularis21031

Trachea
 Excision
 Cervical .31785
 Thoracic .31786
Ulna25120-25126, 25170
 Excision .24120
 with Allograft
 Excision .24126
 with Autograft
 Excision .24125
Ureter
 Excision .52355
Urethra52234-52240, 53220
 Excision .52355
Uterus
 Excision58140-58146
 Resection58950-58958
Vagina
 Excision .57135
Vertebra
 Additional Segment
 Excision .22116
 Cervical
 Excision .22100
 Lumbar
 Excision .22102
 Thoracic
 Excision .22101
Wrist25075-25077, 25135-25136
 Radical Resection25077

Tunica Vaginalis
Hydrocele
 Aspiration .55000
 Excision55040-55041
 Repair .55060

Turbinate
Excision .30130-30140
Fracture
 Therapeutic .30930
Injection .30200
Submucous Resection
 Nose Excision30140

Turbinate Mucosa
Cauterization30801-30802

Turcica, Sella
See Sella Turcica

Turnbuckle Jacket29020-29025
Removal .29715

TURP
See Prostatectomy, Transurethral

Tylectomy
See Breast, Excision, Lesion

Tylenol
Urine .82003

Tympanic Membrane
Create Stoma69433-69436
Incision .69420-69421
Reconstruction69620
Repair .69450, 69610

Tympanic Nerve
Excision .69676

Tympanolysis69450

Tympanomastoidectomy
See Tympanoplasty

Tympanometry92567
See Audiologic Function Tests

Tympanoplasty
See Myringoplasty
Radical or Complete69645
 with Ossicular Chain Reconstruction . .69646
with Antrotomy or Mastoidotomy69635
 with Ossicular Chain Reconstruction . .69636
 and Synthetic Prosthesis69637
with Mastoidectomy69641
 with Intact or Reconstructed Wall69643
 and Ossicular Chain Reconstruction .69644
 with Ossicular Chain Reconstruction . .69642
without Mastoidectomy69631
 with Ossicular Chain Reconstruction . .69632
 and Synthetic Prosthesis69633

Tympanostomy69433-69436

Tympanotomy
See Myringotomy

Typhoid Vaccine90690-90693
AKD .90693
Oral .90690
Polysaccharide90691

Typhus
Endemic
 See Murine Typhus
Mite-Borne
 See Scrub Typhus
Sao Paulo
 See Rocky Mountain Spotted Fever
Tropical
 See Scrub Typhus

Typing, Blood
See Blood Typing

Typing, HLA
See HLA Typing

Typing, Tissue
See Tissue Typing

Tyrosine .84510

Tzank Smear88160-88161

U

Uchida Procedure
See Tubal Ligation

UDP Galactose Pyrophosphorylase
See Galactose-1-Phosphate, Uridyl Transferase

UFR
See Uroflowmetry

Ulcer

Anal
　　See Anus, Fissure
Decubitus
　　See Debridement; Pressure Ulcer (Decubitus);
　　Skin Graft and Flap
Pinch Graft15050
Pressure15920-15999
Stomach
　　Excision43610

Ulcerative, Cystitis

See Cystitis, Interstitial

Ulna

See Arm, Lower; Elbow; Humerus; Radius
Arthrodesis
　　Radioulnar Joint
　　　　with Resection25830
Arthroplasty
　　with Implant25442
Centralization or Wrist25335
Craterization24147, 25150-25151
Cyst
　　Excision24125-24126, 25120-25126
Diaphysectomy24147, 25150-25151
Excision24147
　　Abscess24138
　　Complete25240
　　Epiphyseal Bar20150
　　Partial25145-25151, 25240
Fracture
　　Closed Treatment25530-25535
　　Olecranon24670-24675
　　　　Open Treatment24685
　　Open Treatment25545
　　Shaft25530-25545
　　　　Open Treatment25574
　　Styloid
　　　　Closed Treatment25650
　　　　Open Treatment25652
　　　　Percutaneous Fixation25651
　　with Dislocation
　　　　Closed Treatment24620
　　　　Open Treatment24635
　　with Manipulation25535
　　with Radius25560-25565
　　　　Open Treatment25575
　　without Manipulation25530
Incision and Drainage25035
Osteoplasty25390-25393
Prophylactic Treatment25491-25492
Reconstruction
　　Radioulnar25337
Repair
　　Epiphyseal Arrest25450-25455
　　Malunion or Nonunion25400, 25415
　　Osteotomy25360, 25370-25375
　　　　and Radius25365
　　with Graft25405, 25420-25426
Saucerization24147, 25150-25151
Sequestrectomy24138, 25145
Tumor
　　Cyst24120
　　Excision ..24125-24126, 25120-25126, 25170

Ulnar Arteries

See Artery, Ulnar

Ulnar Nerve

Decompression64718
Neuroplasty64718-64719
Reconstruction64718-64719
Release64718-64719
Repair/Suture
　　Motor64836
Transposition64718-64719

Ultrasonic

See Ultrasound

Ultrasonic Cardiography

See Echocardiography

Ultrasonic Procedure52325

Ultrasonography

See Echography

Ultrasound

See Echocardiography; Echography
3D Rendering76376-76377
Abdomen76700-76705
Arm76880
Artery
　　Intracranial93886-93893
　　Middle Cerebral76821
　　Umbilical76820
Bladder51798
Bone Density Study76977
Breast76645
Bronchi
　　Endoscopy31620
Chest76604
Colon
　　Endoscopic45391-45392
Colon-Sigmoid
　　Endoscopic45341-45342
Drainage
　　Abscess75989
Echoencephalography
　　See Echoencephalography
Esophagus
　　Endoscopy43231-43232
Eye76510-76513
　　Arteries93875
　　Biometry76516-76519
　　Foreign Body76529
　　Pachymetry76514
Fetus76818-76828
Follow-Up76970
for Physical Therapy97035
Gastrointestinal76975
Gastrointestinal, Upper
　　Endoscopic43237-43238, 43242, 43259
Guidance
　　Amniocentesis59001, 76946
　　Amnioinfusion59070
　　Arteriovenous Fistulae76936
　　Chorionic Villus Sampling76945
　　Cryosurgery55873
　　Drainage
　　　　Fetal Fluid59074
　　Endometrial Ablation58356
　　Fetal Cordocentesis76941
　　Fetal Transfusion76941
　　Heart Biopsy76932
　　Needle Biopsy43232, 43238, 43242,
　　　　　　　　　　　　　　45342, 45392, 76942

Occlusion
　　Umbilical Cord59072
Ova Retrieval76948
Pericardiocentesis76930
Pseudoaneurysm76936
Radiation Therapy76950
Radioelement76965
Shunt Placement
　　Fetal59076
Thoracentesis76942
Tissue Ablation76940
Vascular Access76937
Head76506, 76536
Heart
　　Fetal76825
Hips
　　Infant76885-76886
Hysterosonography76831
Intraoperative76998
Intravascular
　　Intraoperative37250-37251
Kidney76770-76776
Leg76880
Neck76536
Non-Coronary
　　Intravascular75945-75946
Pelvis76856-76857
Pregnant Uterus76801-76817
Prostate76873
Rectal76872-76873
Retroperitoneal76770-76775
Scrotum76870
Sonohysterography76831
Spine76800
Stimulation to Aid Bone Healing20979
Umbilical Artery76820
Unlisted Services and Procedures76999
Uterus
　　Tumor Ablation0071T-0072T
Vagina76830

Ultraviolet Light Therapy

Dermatology
　　Ultraviolet A96912
　　Ultraviolet B96910
for Dermatology96900
for Physical Medicine97028
for Respiratory Medicine0168T

Umbilectomy49250

Umbilical

Artery Ultrasound76820
Hernia
　　See Omphalocele
Vein Catheterization
　　See Catheterization, Umbilical Vein

Umbilical Cord

Occlusion59072

Umbilicus

Excision49250
Repair
　　Hernia49580-49587
　　Omphalocele49600-49611

Undescended Testicle

See Testis, Undescended

Unfertilized Egg
See Ova

Unguis
See Nails

Unilateral Simple Mastectomy
See Mastectomy

Unlisted Services and Procedures 99499, 99600
Abdomen 22999, 49329, 49999
Allergy/Immunology 95199
Anal 46999
Anesthesia 01999
Arm 25999
Arthroscopy 29999
Autopsy 88099
Bile Duct 47999
Bladder 51999
Brachytherapy 77799
Breast 19499
Bronchi 31899
Cardiac 33999
Cardiovascular Studies 93799
Casting 29799
Cervix 58999
Chemistry Procedure 84999
Chemotherapy 96549
Chest 32999
Coagulation 85999
Colon 44799
Conjunctiva Surgery 68399
Craniofacial 21299
CT Scan 76497
Cytogenetic Study 88299
Cytopathology 88199
Dermatology 96999
Dialysis 90999
Diaphragm 39599
Ear
 External 69399
 Inner 69949
 Middle 69799
Endocrine System 60699
Epididymis 55899
Esophagus 43289, 43499
Evaluation and Management Services 99499
Eye Muscle 67399
Eye Surgery
 Anterior Segment 66999
 Posterior Segment 67299
Eyelid 67999
Fluoroscopy 76496
Forearm 25999
Gallbladder 47999
Gastroenterology Test 91299
Gum 41899
Hand 26989
Hemic System 38999
Hepatic Duct 47999
Hip Joint 27299
Home Services 99600
Hysteroscopy 58579
Immunization 90749
Immunology 86849
Infusion 90779
Injection 90779
Injection of Medication 90779

Intestine 44238, 44799
Kidney 49659
Lacrimal System 68899
Laparoscopy 38129, 38589, 43289, 43659,
 44238, 44979, 47379, 47579, 49329,
 49659, 50549, 50949, 54699, 55559,
 58578, 58679, 59898, 60659
Larynx 31599
Lip 40799
Liver 47379, 47399
Lungs 32999
Lymphatic System 38999
Magnetic Resonance 76498
Maxillofacial 21299
Maxillofacial Prosthetics 21089
Meckel's Diverticulum 44899
Mediastinum 39499
Mesentery Surgery 44899
Microbiology 87999
Mouth 40899, 41599
Musculoskeletal 25999, 26989
Musculoskeletal Surgery
 Abdominal Wall 22999
 Neck 21899
 Spine 22899
 Thorax 21899
Musculoskeletal System 20999
 Ankle 27899
 Arm, Upper 24999
 Elbow 24999
 Head 21499
 Knee 27599
 Leg, Lower 27899
 Leg, Upper 27599
Necropsy 88099
Nervous System Surgery 64999
Neurology/Neuromuscular Testing 95999
Nose 30999
Nuclear Medicine 78999
 Blood 78199
 Bone 78399
 Endocrine System 78099
 Genitourinary System 78799
 Heart 78499
 Hematopoietic System 78199
 Lymphatic System 78199
 Musculoskeletal System 78399
 Nervous System 78699
 Therapeutic 79999
Obstetrical Care 59898-59899
Omentum 49329, 49999
Ophthalmology 92499
Orbit 67599
Otorhinolaryngology 92700
Ovary 58679, 58999
Oviduct 58679, 58999
Palate 42299
Pancreas Surgery 48999
Pathology 89240
Pelvis 27299
Penis 55899
Peritoneum 49329, 49999
Pharynx 42999
Physical Therapy 97039, 97139, 97799
Pleura 32999
Pressure Ulcer 15999
Preventive Medicine 99429
Prostate 55899

Psychiatric 90899
Pulmonology 94799
Radiation Physics 77399
Radiation Therapy 77499
 Planning 77299
Radiology, Diagnostic 76499
Radionuclide Therapy 79999
Radiopharmaceutical Therapy 79999
Rectum 45499, 45999
Salivary Gland 42699
Scrotum 55899
Seminal Vesicle 55899
Shoulder Surgery 23929
Sinuses 31299
Skin 17999
Special Services and Reports 99199
Spine 22899
Stomach 43659, 43999
Strapping 29799
Surgical Pathology 88399
Temporal Bone 69979
Testis 54699, 55899
Throat 42999
Tongue 41599
Tonsil/Adenoid 42999
Toxoid 90749
Trachea 31899
Transfusion 86999
Ultrasound 76999
Ureter 50949
Urinary System 53899
Uterus 58578-58579, 58999
Uvula 42299
Vaccine 90749
Vagina 58999
Vas Deferens 55899
Vascular 37799
Vascular Endoscopy 37501
Vascular Injection 36299
Vascular Studies 93799
Wrist 25999

Unna Paste Boot 29580
Removal 29700

UPP
See Urethra Pressure Profile

Upper
Digestive System Endoscopy
 See Endoscopy, Gastrointestinal, Upper
Extremity
 See Arm, Upper; Elbow; Humerus
Gastrointestinal Bleeding
 See Gastrointestinal, Upper, Hemorrhage
Gastrointestinal Endoscopy, Biopsy
 See Biopsy
 Planning
 See Biopsy, Gastrointestinal, Upper
 Endoscopy; Endoscopy, Gastrointestinal
GI Tract
 See Gastrointestinal Tract, Upper

Urachal Cyst
See Cyst, Urachal

Urea Breath Test 78267-78268, 83014

Urea Nitrogen
See Blood Urea Nitrogen

Dilation52260-52265, 53600-53621
 General .53665
 Suppository and/or Instillation .53660-53661
Diverticulum
 See Urethral Diverticulum
Drainage
 Extravasation53080-53085
Endoscopy .52000
 Biopsy52204, 52354
 Catheterization52010
 Destruction52354, 52400
 Evacuation
 Clot .52001
 Excision
 Tumor .52355
 Exploration .52351
 Incision
 Ejaculatory Duct52402
 Injection of Implant Material51715
 Lithotripsy .52353
 Removal
 Calculus .52352
 Resection
 Ejaculatory Duct52402
 Vasectomy .52402
 Vasotomy .52402
Excision
 Diverticulum53230-53235
 Total
 Female .53210
 Male .53215
Incision53000-53010
 Meatus53020-53025
Incision and Drainage53060
Insertion
 Stent0084T, 52282
Lesion
 Destruction .53265
 Excision .53260
Paraurethral Gland
 Incision and Drainage53060
Polyp
 Destruction .53260
 Excision .53260
Pressure Profile51772
Prolapse
 Destruction .53275
 Excision .53275
 Repair .53275
Prostate
 Transurethral Balloon Dilation52510
Radiotracer .52250
Reconstruction53410-53440, 53445
 and Bladder51800-51820
 Complications54340-54348
 Hypospadias
 One Stage54322-54328
 Second Stage54308-54316
 Third Stage54318
 Meatus53450-53460
Removal
 Calculus52310-52315
 Foreign Body52310-52315
 Sling .53442
 Urethral Stent52310-52315
Repair
 Diverticulum53240, 53400-53405
 Fistula . . .45820-45825, 53400-53405, 53520

Sphincter .57220
Stricture53400-53405
Urethrocele .57230
Wound53502-53515
Skene's Gland
 Incision and Drainage53060
Sphincter .52277
 Electromyography51784-51785
 Needle .51785
 Insertion
 Prosthesis53444
 Reconstruction53445
 Removal
 Prosthesis53446-53447
 Repair
 Prosthesis53449
 Replacement
 Prosthesis53448
Suture
 Fistula45820-45825, 53520
 to Bladder51840-51841
 Wound53502-53515
Tumor
 Destruction .53220
 Excision .53220
Unlisted Services and Procedures53899
Urethrocystography74450-74455
Urethrotomy52270-52276
X-Ray with Contrast74450-74455

Urethral

Diverticulum
 Marsupialization53240
Meatus, Dorsal
 See Epispadias
Sphincter
 Biofeedback Training90911
 Insertion
 Prosthesis53444
 Removal
 Prosthesis53446-53447
 Replacement
 Prosthesis53448
Stenosis
 Dilation .52281
Stent
 Insertion0084T, 52282
 Removal
 Bladder52310-52315
 Urethra52310-52315
Stricture
 Dilation52281, 53600-53621
 Injection
 Steroids .52283
Syndrome
 Cystourethroscopy52285

Urethrectomy

Total
 Female .53210
 Male .53215

Urethrocele

See Urethra, Prolapse

Urethrocystography74450-74455

Contrast and/or Chain51605
Retrograde .51610
Voiding .51600

Urethrocystopexy

See Vesicourethropexy

Urethromeatoplasty53450-53460

Urethropexy51840-51841

Urethroplasty46744-46746

First Stage .53400
One Stage
 Hypospadias54322-54328
Reconstruction
 Female Urethra53430
 Male Anterior Urethra53410
 Prostatic/Membranous Urethra
 First Stage53420
 One Stage53415
 Second Stage53425
Second Stage .53405
 Hypospadias54308-54316
Third Stage
 Hypospadias54318

Urethrorrhaphy53502-53515

Urethroscopy

See Endoscopy, Urethra

Urethrostomy53000-53010

Urethrotomy53000-53010

Direct Vision
 with Cystourethroscopy52276
Internal52601, 52647-52648
with Cystourethroscopy
 Female .52270
 Male .52275

Uric Acid

Blood .84550
Other Source .84560
Urine .84560

Uridyltransferase, Galactose-1-Phosphate

See Galactose-1-Phosphate, Uridyl Transferase

Uridylyltransferase, Galactosephosphate

See Galactose-1-Phosphate, Uridyl Transferase

Urinalysis0041T, 81000-81099

Automated81001, 81003
Glass Test .81020
Microalbumin82043-82044
Microscopic .81015
Pregnancy Test81025
Qualitative .81005
Routine .81002
Screen .81007
Semiquantitative0041T, 81005
Unlisted Services and Procedures81099
Volume Measurement81050
without Microscopy81002

Urinary Bladder

See Bladder

Urinary Catheter Irrigation

See Irrigation, Catheter

Vasoactive Intestinal Peptide84586

Vasogram
See Vasography

Vasography74440

Vasointestinal Peptide
See Vasoactive Intestinal Peptide

Vasopneumatic Device Therapy97016
See Physical Medicine/Therapy/Occupational Therapy

Vasopressin84588

Vasotomy55200, 55300
Transurethral
　Cystourethroscopic52402

Vasovasorrhaphy55400

Vasovasostomy55400

VATS
See Thoracoscopy

VDRL86592-86593

Vein
Ablation
　Endovenous36475-36479
Adrenal
　Venography75840-75842
Anastomosis
　Caval to Mesenteric37160
　Intrahepatic Portosystemic37182-37183
　Portocaval37140
　Reniportal37145
　Saphenopopliteal34530
　Splenorenal37180-37181
　to Vein37140-37160, 37182-37183
Angioplasty75978
　Transluminal35460
Arm
　Harvest of Vein for Bypass Graft35500
　Venography75820-75822
Axillary
　Thrombectomy34490
Biopsy
　Transcatheter75970
Cannulization
　to Artery36810-36815
　to Vein36800
Catheterization
　Central Insertion36555-36558
　Organ Blood36500
　Peripheral Insertion36568-36569
　Removal36589
　Repair36575
　Replacement36578-36581, 36584
　Umbilical36510
Division
　Saphenous37718-37722
Endoscopic Harvest
　for Bypass Graft33508
External Cannula
　Declotting36860-36861

Extremity
　Non-Invasive Studies93965-93971
Femoral
　Repair34501
Femoropopliteal
　Thrombectomy34421-34451
Guidance
　Fluoroscopic77001
　Ultrasound76937
Hepatic Portal
　Splenoportography75810
　Venography75885-75887
Iliac
　Thrombectomy34401-34451
Injection
　Sclerosing Agent36468-36471
Insertion
　IVC Filter75940
Interrupt
　Femoral37650
　Iliac37660
　Vena Cava37620
Jugular
　Venography75860
Leg
　Harvest for Vascular Reconstruction ...35572
　Venography75820-75822
Ligation
　Clusters37785
　Esophagus43205
　Jugular37565
　Perforation37760
　Saphenous37700-37735, 37780
　Secondary37785
Liver
　Venography75889-75891
Neck
　Venography75860
Nuclear Medicine
　Thrombosis Imaging78456-78458
Orbit
　Venography75880
Placement
　IVC Filter75940
Portal
　Catheterization36481
Pulmonary
　Repair33730
Removal
　Clusters37785
　Saphenous37735, 37780
　Varicose37765-37766
Renal
　Venography75831-75833
Repair
　Aneurysm36834
　Angioplasty75978
　Graft34520
Sampling
　Venography75893
Sinus
　Venography75870
Skull
　Venography75870-75872
Spermatic
　Excision55530-55540
　Ligation55550

Splenic
　Splenoportography75810
Stripping
　Saphenous37718-37735
Subclavian
　Thrombectomy34471-34490
Thrombectomy37187-37188
　Other than Hemodialysis Graft or
　Fistula35875-35876
Unlisted Services and Procedures37799
Valve Transposition34510
Varicose
　See Varicose Vein
Vena Cava
　Thrombectomy34401-34451
　Venography75825-75827

Velpeau Cast29058

Vena Cava
Catheterization36010
Reconstruction34502
Resection with Reconstruction37799

Vena Caval
Thrombectomy50230

Venereal Disease Research Laboratory
See VDRL

Venesection
See Phlebotomy

Venipuncture
See Cannulation; Catheterization
Child/Adult
　Cutdown36425
　Percutaneous36410
Infant
　Cutdown36420
　Percutaneous36400-36406
Routine36415

Venography
Adrenal75840-75842
Arm75820-75822
Epidural75872
Hepatic Portal75885-75887
Injection36005
Jugular75860
Leg75820-75822
Liver75889-75891
Neck75860
Nuclear Medicine78445, 78457-78458
Orbit75880
Renal75831-75833
Sagittal Sinus75870
Vena Cava75825-75827
Venous Sampling75893

Venorrhaphy
See Suture, Vein

Venotomy
See Phlebotomy

Venous Access Device
Fluoroscopic Guidance77001

VII, Cranial Nerve
See Facial Nerve

VIII, Coagulation Factor
See Clotting Factor

Villus, Chorionic
See Chorionic Villus

Villusectomy
See Synovectomy

VIP
See Vasoactive Intestinal Peptide

Viral Antibodies86280

Viral Warts
See Warts

Virtual Colonoscopy
Diagnostic0067T
Screening0066T

Virus
AIDS
 See HIV-1
Burkitt Lymphoma
 See Epstein-Barr Virus
Human Immunodeficiency
 See HIV
Influenza
 See Influenza Virus
Respiratory Syncytial
 See Respiratory Syncytial Virus
Salivary Gland
 See Cytomegalovirus

Virus Identification
Immunofluorescence87254

Virus Isolation87250-87255

Visceral Larval Migrans86280

Viscosities, Blood
See Blood, Viscosity

Visit, Home
See House Calls

Visual Acuity Screen99172-99173

Visual Field Exam92081-92083

Visual Function Screen ...0065T, 99172

Visual Reinforcement Audiometry92579
See Audiologic Function Tests

Visualization
Ileal Conduit50690

Vital Capacity Measurement ...94150

Vitamin84591
A84590
B Complex
 See B Complex Vitamins
B-184425
B-1282607-82608
 Absorption Study78270-78272
 Holotranscobalamin0103T

B-284252
B-684207
B-6 Measurement
 See Pyridoxal Phosphate
BC
 See Folic Acid
C82180
D82307, 82652
D, 25-Hydroxy Measurement
 See Calcifediol
D-2
 See Calciferol
D-382306
E84446
K84597
K Dependent Bone Protein
 See Osteocalcin
K-Dependent Protein S
 See Protein S

Vitelline Duct
See Omphalomesenteric Duct

Vitrectomy
Anterior Approach
 Partial67005
Pars Plana Approach67036
Subtotal67010
 with Endolaser Panretinal
 Photocoagulation67040
with Epiretinal Membrane Stripping67038
with Focal Endolaser Photocoagulation67039
with Implantation or Replacement
 Drug Delivery System67027

Vitreous
Aspiration67015
Excision
 Pars Planta Approach67036
 with Epiretinal Membrane Stripping ...67038
 with Focal Endolaser Photocoagulation 67039
Implantation
 Drug Delivery System67027
Incision
 Strands67030-67031
Injection
 Fluid Substitute67025
 Pharmacologic Agent67028
Removal
 Anterior Approach67005
 Subtotal67010
Replacement
 Drug Delivery System67027
Strands
 Discission67030
 Severing67031
Subtotal67010

VLDL
See Lipoprotein, Blood

VMA
See Vanillylmandelic Acid

Vocal Cords
Injection
 Endoscopy31513
 Therapeutic31570-31571

Voice Box
See Larynx

Voice Button31611

Voiding Pressure Studies
Abdominal51797
Bladder51795

Volatiles84600

Volhard's Test
See Water Load Test

Volkman Contracture25315-25316

Volume Reduction
Blood Products86960

Volume Reduction, Lung
See Lung Volume Reduction

Von Kraske Proctectomy
See Proctectomy, Partial

VP
See Voiding Pressure Studies

Vulva
Abscess
 Incision and Drainage56405
Colposcopy56820
 Biopsy56821
Excision
 Complete56625, 56633-56640
 Partial56620, 56630-56632
 Radical56630-56631, 56633-56640
 Complete56633-56640
 Partial56630-56632
 Simple
 Complete56625
 Partial56620
Lesion
 Destruction56501-56515
Perineum
 Biopsy56605-56606
 Incision and Drainage56405
Repair
 Obstetric59300

Vulvectomy
Complete56625, 56633-56640
Partial56620, 56630-56632
Radical56630-56631, 56633-56640
 Complete
 with Bilateral Inguinofemoral
 Lymphadenectomy56637
 with Inguinofemoral, Iliac, and Pelvic
 Lymphadenectomy56640
 with Unilateral Inguinofemoral
 Lymphadenectomy56634
 Partial
 with Bilateral Inguinofemoral
 Lymphadenectomy56632
 with Unilateral Inguinofemoral
 Lymphadenectomy56631
 Simple
 Complete56625
 Partial56620

VZIG
See Immune Globulins, Varicella-Zoster

W-Plasty
See Skin, Adjacent Tissue Transfer

WADA Activation Test95958
See Electroencephalography

WAIS96101-96102

Waldius Procedure27445

Wall, Abdominal
See Abdominal Wall

Walsh Modified Radical Prostatectomy
See Prostatectomy

Warts
Flat
 Destruction17111

Washing
Sperm58323

Wasserman Test
See Syphilis Test

Wassmund Procedure
Osteotomy
 Maxilla.........................21206

Water Load Test89235

Water Wart
See Molluscum Contagiosum

Waterston Procedure33755

**Watson-Jones
Procedure**.................27695-27698

Wave, Ultrasonic Shock
See Ultrasound

WBC
See White Blood Cell

Webbed
Toe
 Repair28280

Wedge Excision
Osteotomy21122

Wedge Resection
Ovary58920

Well-Baby Care99381, 99391, 99432

Wellness Behavior
See Evaluation and Management, Health
Behavior

Wernicke-Posadas Disease
See Coccidioidomycosis

West Nile Virus
Antibody86788-86789

Westergren Test
See Sedimentation Rate, Blood Cell

Western Blot
HIV86689
Protein84181-84182
Tissue Analysis88371-88372

Wheelchair Management
Training97542

Wheelchair Management/Propulsion
See Physical Medicine/Therapy/Occupational
Therapy

Wheeler Knife Procedure
See Discission, Cataract

Wheeler Procedure
See Blepharoplasty, Entropion
Discission Secondary Membranous
Cataract66820

Whipple Procedure48150

Whirlpool Therapy97022
See Physical Medicine/Therapy/Occupational
Therapy

White Blood Cell
Alkaline Phosphatase85540
Antibody86021
Count85032, 85048, 89055
Differential85004-85007, 85009
Histamine Release Test86343
Phagocytosis86344
Transfusion
 See Leukocyte, Transfusion

Whitemead Operation
See Hemorrhoidectomy, Complex

Whitman Astragalectomy
See Talus, Excision

Whitman Procedure27120

Wick Catheter Technique20950

Widal Serum Test
See Agglutinin, Febrile

Window
Oval
 See Oval Window
Round
 See Round Window

Window Technic, Pericardial
See Pericardiostomy

Windpipe
See Trachea

Winiwarter Operation
See Anastomosis, Gallbladder to Intestines

Winter Procedure54435

Wintrobe Test
See Sedimentation Rate, Blood Cell

Wire
See Pin
Insertion/Removal
 Skeletal Traction20650
Interdental
 without Fracture21497

Wiring
Prophylactic Treatment
 Humerus24498

Wirsung Duct
See Pancreatic Duct

Witzel Operation43500, 43520,
43830-43832
See Incision, Stomach, Creation, Stoma; Incision
and Drainage

Womb
See Uterus

Wood Alcohol
See Methanol

Work Hardening97545-97546
See Physical Medicine/Therapy/Occupational
Therapy

**Work Related Evaluation
Services**99455-99456

Worm
See Helminth

Wound
Closure
 Temporary
 Skin Allograft15300-15321
 Skin Xenograft15420-15421
Debridement
 Non-Selective97602
 Selective97597-97598
Dehiscence
 Repair12020-12021, 13160
Exploration
 Penetrating
 Abdomen/Flank/Back20102
 Chest20101
 Extremity20103
 Neck20100
 Penetrating Trauma20100-20103
Infection
 Incision and Drainage
 Postoperative10180
Negative Pressure Therapy97605-97606
Repair
 Complex13100-13160
 Intermediate12031-12057
 Simple12001-12021
 Urethra53502-53515
Suture
 Bladder51860-51865
 Kidney50500
 Trachea
 Cervical31800
 Intrathoracic31805
 Urethra53502-53515
Vagina
 Repair57200-57210

X

Sinuses70210-70220
Skull70250-70260
Specimen/Surgical76098
Spine72020, 72090
 Cervical72040-72052
 Lumbosacral72100-72120
 Thoracic72070-72074
 Thoracolumbar72080
 Total72010
Standing
 Spine72069
Sternum71120-71130
Teeth70300-70320
Tibia73590
Toe73660
Total Body
 Foreign Body76010
Unlisted Services and Procedures ..76120-76125
with Contrast
 Ankle73615
 Aorta0080T, 0081T, 75600-75630,
 75952-75953
 Artery
 Abdominal75726
 Additional Vessels75774
 Adrenal75731-75733
 Arm75710-75716
 Arteriovenous Shunt75790
 Brachial75658
 Carotid75660-75680
 Coronary93556
 Coronary Bypass93556
 Head and Neck75650
 Iliac75953
 Leg75710-75716
 Mammary75756
 Pelvic75736
 Pulmonary75741-75746
 Renal75722-75724
 Spine75705
 Transcatheter Therapy75894-75898
 Vertebral75685
 Bile Duct74300-74320
 Calculus Removal74327
 Catheterization75982-75984
 Drainage75980-75982
 Guide Catheter74328, 74330
 Bladder74430, 74450-74455
 Brain70010-70015
 Bronchi71040-71060
 Central Venous Access Device36598
 Colon
 Barium Enema74270-74280
 Corpora Cavernosa74445
 Elbow73085
 Epididymis74440
 Gallbladder74290-74291
 Gastrointestinal Tract74246-74249
 Hip73525
 Iliofemoral Artery75630
 Intervertebral Disk
 Cervical72285
 Lumbar72295
 Thoracic72285
 Joint
 Stress Views77071

Kidney
 Cyst74470
 Guide Catheter74475
Knee73560-73564, 73580
Lacrimal Duct70170
Larynx70373
Lymph Vessel
 Abdomen75805-75807
 Arm75801-75803
 Leg75801-75803
Mammary Duct77053-77054
Nasolacrimal Duct70170
 Guide Dilation74485
Oviduct74740
Pancreas74300-74305
Pancreatic Duct
 Guide Catheter74329-74330
Perineum74775
Peritoneum74190
Salivary Gland70390
Seminal Vesicles74440
Shoulder73040
Spine
 Cervical72240
 Lumbosacral72265
 Thoracic72255
 Total72270
Subtraction Method76350
Temporomandibular Joint
(TMJ)70328-70332
Ureter
 Guide Catheter74480
 Guide Dilation74485
Urethra74450-74455
Urinary Tract74400-74425
Uterus74740
Vas Deferens74440
Vein
 Adrenal75840-75842
 Arm75820-75822
 Hepatic Portal75810, 75885-75887
 Jugular75860
 Leg75820-75822
 Liver75889-75891
 Neck75860
 Orbit75880
 Renal75831-75833
 Sampling75893
 Sinus75870
 Skull75870-75872
 Splenic75810
 Vena Cava75825-75827
 Wrist73115
Wrist73100-73110

X-Ray Tomography, Computed
See CT Scan

Xa, Coagulation Factor
See Thrombokinase

Xenoantibodies
See Antibody, Heterophile

Xenograft15400-15401
Skin
 Acellular Implant15430-15431
 Dermal15420-15421

Xenografts, Skin
See Heterograft, Skin

Xenotransplantation
See Heterograft

Xerography
See Xeroradiography

Xeroradiography76150

XI, Coagulation Factor
See Plasma Thromboplastin, Antecedent

XI, Cranial Nerve
See Accessory Nerve

XII, Coagulation Factor
See Hageman Factor

XII, Cranial Nerve
See Hypoglossal Nerve

XIII, Coagulation Factor
See Fibrin Stabilizing Factor

Xylose Absorption Test
Blood84620
Urine84620

Y

Yeast
Culture87106

Yellow Fever Vaccine90717

Yersinia
Antibody86793

Z

Ziegler Procedure
Discission Secondary Membranous
Cataract66820

Zinc84630

Zinc Manganese Leucine Aminopeptidase
See Leucine Aminopeptidase

Zygoma
See Cheekbone

Zygomatic Arch
Fracture
 Open Treatment21356-21366
 with Manipulation21355

Notes

Notes

Time For a Practice Management Check-up?

The AMA offers a range of products to help your office run smooth and effectively

Maximizing Billing and Collections in the Medical Practice

Prevent undue financial losses in today's medical practice. Given the shrinking physician reimbursement environment, practices today need the tools and information necessary to maximize their billing and collections efforts; this book provides that and more. *Maximizing Billing and Collections in the Medical Practice* integrates the patient encounter with the billing and collections function to increase the likelihood of collecting every dollar the physician is entitled to receive.

Softbound with CD-ROM, 8-1/2"x11", 208 pages
Order #: OP318607CCW
ISBN: I-57947-867-0
Price: $75.95 AMA member price: $56.95

A Guide to Patient Safety in the Medical Practice

Discover a greater understanding of the risks, consequences of errors and adverse events in the medical practice. This book is designed to stimulate the evolution of a patient safety culture in today's physician practice. Readers are provided with an in-depth review of the practical patient safety process and available tools for providers and business cases for a safer physician practice is also discussed.

Softbound, 7"x10" 300 pages
Order #: OP401006CCW
ISBN: I-57947-674-0
Price: $59.95 AMA member price: $44.95

Other valuable practice management titles offered by the American Medical Association:

- Starting a Medical Practice
- Assessing the Value of the Medical Practice
- Managing the Medical Practice
- Buying, Selling and Owning a Medical Practice
- Financial Management of the Medical Practice
- Personnel Management in the Medical Practice

For more information on our practice success series or to review additional products and services visit *www.amabookstore.com* or call (800) 621-8335.